Tuttle

W9-BNR-569

Concise Chinese Dictionary

Chinese–English
English–Chinese

LI Dong 李冬

TUTTLE Publishing

Tokyo | Rutland, Vermont | Singapore

The Tuttle Story: "Books to Span the East and West"

Many people are surprised to learn that the world's leading publisher of books on Asia had humble beginnings in the tiny American state of Vermont. The company's founder, Charles E. Tuttle, belonged to a New England family steeped in publishing.

Immediately after WW II, Tuttle served in Tokyo under General Douglas MacArthur and was tasked with reviving the Japanese publishing industry. He later founded the Charles E. Tuttle Publishing Company, which thrives today as one of the world's leading independent publishers.

Though a westerner, Tuttle was hugely instrumental in bringing a knowledge of Japan and Asia to a world hungry for information about the East. By the time of his death in 1993, Tuttle had published over 6,000 books on Asian culture, history and art—a legacy honored by the Japanese emperor with the "Order of the Sacred Treasure," the highest tribute Japan can bestow upon a non-Japanese.

With a backlist of 1,500 titles, Tuttle Publishing is more active today than at any time in its past—inspired by Charles Tuttle's core mission to publish fine books to span the East and West and provide a greater understanding of each.

Published by Tuttle Publishing, an imprint of Periplus Editions (HK) Ltd.

www.tuttlepublishing.com

ISBN 978-0-8048-4199-3 (vinyl cover)
ISBN 978-0-8048-4567-0 (paperback)

Distributed by:

North America, Latin America and Europe
Tuttle Publishing
364 Innovation Drive, North Clarendon,
VT 05759-9436 USA.
Tel: 1(802) 773-8930 Fax: 1(802) 773-6993
info@tuttlepublishing.com
www.tuttlepublishing.com

Asia Pacific
Berkeley Books Pte. Ltd.
61 Tai Seng Avenue #02-12,
Singapore 534167
Tel: (65) 6280-1330 Fax: (65) 6280-62*
inquiries@periplus.com.sg
www.periplus.com

17 16 15 14   6 5 4 3 2 1   1412EP

Printed in Hong Kong

Contents

Introducing Chinese

1 PRONUNCIATION

1.1 Vowels

SINGLE VOWELS

There are seven basic single vowels:

a similar to *a* in *ah*

e similar to *a* in *ago*

ê similar to *e* in *ebb* (this sound never occurs alone and is transcribed as **e**, as in **ei**, **ie**, **ue**)

i similar to *ee* in *cheese* (spelled **y** when not preceded by a consonant)

o similar to *oe* in *toe*

u similar to *oo* in *boot* (spelled **w** when not preceded by a consonant)

ü similar to German *ü* in *über* or French *u* in *tu*; or you can also get *ü* by saying *i* and rounding your lips at the same time (spelled **u** after **j**, **q**, **x**; spelled **yu** when not preceded by a consonant)

VOWEL COMBINATIONS

These single vowels combine with each other or with the consonants of **n** or **ng** to form what are technically known as *diphthongs*. These combinations are pronounced as a single sound, with a little more emphasis on the first part of the sound.

You can learn these combinations in four groups:

Group 1: diphthongs starting with **a/e/ê**

   ai similar to *y* in *my*

   ao similar to *ow* in *how*

   an

   ang

   en

	eng	
	ei	similar to *ay* in *may*

Group 2: diphthongs starting with **i**

	ia	
	ie	similar to *ye* in *yes*
	iao	
	iou	similar to *you* (spelled **iu** when preceded by a consonant)
	ian	
	ien	similar to *in* (spelled **in** when preceded by a consonant)
	ieng	similar to *En* in *English* (spelled **ing** when preceded by a consonant)
	iang	similar to *young*
	iong	

Group 3: diphthongs starting with **u/o**

	ua	
	uo	
	uai	similar to *why* in British English
	uei	similar to *way* (spelled **ui** when preceded by a consonant)
	uan	
	uen	(spelled **un** when preceded by a consonant)
	ueng	
	uang	
	ong	

Group 4: diphthongs starting with **ü**

	üe	used only after **j**, **q**, **x**; spelled **ue**
	üen	used only after **j**, **q**, **x**; spelled **un**
	üan	used only after **j**, **q**, **x**; spelled **uan**

1.2 Consonants

Consonants may be grouped in the following ways.

Group 1:   These consonants are almost the same in Chinese and English.

Chinese	English
m	*m*
n	*n*
f	*f*
l	*l*
s	*s*
r	*r*
b	pronounced as hard *p* (as in *speak*)
p	*p* (as in *peak*)
g	pronounced as hard *k* (as in *ski*)
k	*k* (as in *key*)
d	pronounced as hard *t* (as in *star*)
t	*t* (as in *tar*)

Group 2:   Some modification is needed to get these Chinese sounds from English.

Chinese	English
j	as *j* in *jeep* (but unvoiced, not round-lipped)
q	as *ch* in *cheese* (but not round-lipped)
x	as *sh* in *sheep* (but not round-lipped)
c	as *ts* as in *cats* (make it long)
z	as *ds* as in *beds* (but unvoiced, and make it long)

Group 3:   No English counterparts

Chinese **zh**, **ch**, and **sh** have no English counterparts. You can learn to say **zh**, **ch** and **sh** starting from **z**, **c** and **s**. For example, say **s** (which is almost the same as the English *s* in *sesame*) and then roll up your tongue to touch the roof of your mouth. You get **sh**.

TONES

Chinese is a tonal language, i.e. a sound pronounced in different tones is understood as different words. So the tone is an indispensable component of the pronunciation of a word.

1.3 Basic tones

There are four basic tones. The following five-level pitch graph shows the values of the four tones:

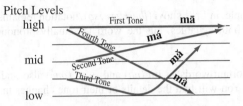

- The First Tone is a high, level tone and is represented as ˉ, e.g. 妈 **mā** (meaning *mother, mom*).

- The Second Tone is a high, rising tone and is represented by the tone mark ´, e.g. 麻 **má** (*hemp* or *sesame*).

- The Third Tone is a falling, then rising tone. As you can see from the pitch graph it falls from below the middle of the voice range to nearly the bottom and then rises to a point near the top. It is represented by the tone mark ˇ, e.g. 马 **mǎ** (*horse*).

- The Fourth Tone is a falling tone. It falls from high to low and is represented by the tone mark ` , e.g. 骂 **mà** (*curse*).

In Chinese speech, as in English speech, some sounds are unstressed, i.e. pronounced short and soft. They do not have any of the four tones. Such sounds are said to have Neutral Tone. Sounds with the neutral tone are not marked. For example in 爸爸 **bàba** (*daddy*) the first syllable is pronounced in the fourth tone and the second syllable in the neutral tone, i.e. unstressed.

TONE CHANGES

Tones may undergo changes in actual speech ("tone sandhi"). The third tone, when followed by a first, second, fourth or neutral tone sound, loses its final rise and stops at the low pitch. Followed by another third tone sound, it becomes the second tone. This is a general rule and the notation of third tone sounds remains unchanged.

For example, in 所以 **suǒyǐ** (*therefore, so*), notation remains the third tone for both syllables, but the word is actually pronounced like **suóyǐ**.

Two important words 不 **bù** (*no*) and 一 **yī** (*one*) also undergo tone changes. You will find the details of their tone changes under these entries.

1.4 Syllables: distinct units

Normally a consonant and a vowel, said in a particular tone, merge to form a syllable in Chinese. Every syllable is a distinct unit in speech. Learners should say each syllable clearly and give full value to most syllables in speech. The general impression of Chinese speech, described in musical terms, is staccato rather than legato (which could be used to describe English).

1.5 *Pinyin:* the romanization scheme to show pronunciation

As Chinese writing normally does not indicate pronunciation, a romanization scheme, known as *pinyin*, is used to represent the sounds and tones of Chinese, as in this dictionary. *Pinyin* is useful for learning the phonetics of Mandarin.

2   WRITING CHINESE: 汉字 **Hànzi**

Chinese is not phonetic like most European languages (in varying degrees). Chinese is written in logograms, known as 汉字 (**Hànzi**) and generally referred to as "Chinese characters", or "Sinograms."

2.1 Chinese characters as syllables

Each Chinese character is pronounced as a syllable. It is of course important to be able to read a character with the correct pronunciation.

2.2 The composition of Chinese characters: meaningful components

Chinese characters can be analyzed into components. It is acknowledged that there are three kinds of components. Of the three, the most interesting to learners of Chinese is a group of components that convey certain meanings. The presence of such a component in a character gives you some clue to its meaning of the character. Hence, learning the meaning of these component parts will deepen your understanding of characters you know, and help you guess the meaning of unfamiliar characters. See List 1 on page xv.

2.3 The writing of Chinese characters

STROKES

Each Chinese character is composed of strokes. The table below shows the basic strokes. Recognizing the strokes in a character is helpful for finding a character or radical in the Stroke Index, List of Radicals and Radical Index. Each of the strokes shown in the table is counted as one stroke.

Stroke	Writing the stroke	Examples
Héng	left to right 一	千 主 女
Shù	top to bottom ︳	千 山 北

Stroke	Writing the stroke	Examples
Piě	top (right) to bottom (left)	千 人 么
Nà	top (left) to bottom (right)	人 木 又
Diǎn	top to bottom	主 心 习
Tí	Bottom (left) to top (right)	习 打 北
Stroke with hook	left to right, top to bottom	买 打 以 心
Stroke with turn(s)		山 马 女 么 又
Stroke with turn(s) and hook		北 习 认 马

STROKE ORDER

For the character to look correct, its strokes should be written in the correct order. Knowing the order will also help you remember characters. The general rules of stroke order are as shown below.

Rule	Example	Stroke order
Top before bottom	三	一 二 三
Left before right	什	丿 亻 仁 什

Rule	Example	Stroke order
Horizontal before vertical/downward	天	一 二 于 天
"Enter the room, then close the door"	日	丨 冂 门 日
Vertical stroke before sides/bottom	小	丨 小 小

SIMPLIFIED AND TRADITIONAL CHARACTERS

The Chinese government simplified hundreds of Chinese characters in mid-1950 by reducing the numbers of their strokes. Such simplified characters are called 简体字 **jiǎntǐzì**. This dictionary uses **jiantizi**. Traditional versions (also known as complicated characters) are still used in Taiwan and Hong Kong, and they are shown after "Trad" where applicable, e.g.:

学 xué Trad 學

3 VOCABULARY: Word-formation

Chinese words are either of one syllable or more than one syllable (mostly two syllables). When they are made up of two or more syllables, their meanings are usually transparent; that is, the way a word is formed tells you a lot about its meaning. Therefore it is very helpful to know the meanings of the components in a word and the way the word is formed, and it also makes understanding the word easier and more interesting.

There are six basic word-formation methods:

- **Compounding:** the components of a word are complementary to each other in meaning and are of the same status. For example:

  重 *once again* + 复 *repeat* → 重复 *repeat*

- **Modification:** one component modifies the other. For example:

  外 *outside* + 国 *country* → 外国 *foreign country*

- **Verb+object:** the word has a verb-and-object relationship. For example:

  发 *develop* + 烧 *burning, fever* → 发烧 *to run a fever*

- **Verb+complementation:** the word has a verb-and-complement relationship, that is, the first component is a verb or an adjective and the second one modifies it. For example:

  提 *raise* + 高 *high* → 提高 *raise*

- **Suffixation:** the word contains a suffix. For example:

  本 *a book* + 子 *nominal suffix* → 本子 *notebook*

- **Idioms:** the word is an idiomatic expression. For example:

  马上 → at once, immediately

4 GRAMMAR

4.1 Main Features of Chinese Grammar

TOPIC+COMMENT STRUCTURE

The basic principle in making Chinese sentences is to follow the "topic+comment" structure. "Topic" means the subject matter you want to talk about, and "comment" is the information you give about the subject matter. To make a Chinese sentence, you simply first mention the subject matter you want to talk about, and then say what you have to say about it. For example, you can say 那本书 **nà běn shū** (that book) first as the "topic" and then add "comment":

那本书 **Nà běn shū** (that book) + 很有意思 **hěn yǒu yìsi** (very interesting) → *That book is very interesting*.

那本书 **Nà běn shū** (that book) + 卖完了 **mài wán le** (sold out) → *That book has been sold*.

那本书 **Nà běn shū** (that book) + 你有吗 **nǐ yǒu ma** (do you have) → *Do you have that book?*

那本书 **Nà běn shū** (that book) + 语言很优美 **yǔyán hěn yōuměi** (language is beautiful) → *The language of that book is beautiful*.

ELLIPSIS OF SENTENCE ELEMENTS

Chinese speakers may leave out words that are supposed to be understood, and therefore need not be spoken. Subjects and conjunctions are often omitted. For example, you may translate the English sentence *If you like it, you may buy it, but if you don't like it, you don't have to*, into the Chinese sentence 喜欢就买, 不喜欢就别买. **Xǐhuan jiùmǎi, bù xǐhuan jiù bié mǎi.** Literally, it means "Like it, and buy, don't like then don't buy." Compare the two sentences, and you will find that some English words, such as *if*, *you*, *it*, and *but* are not translated.

WORD CLASSES: FLEXIBILITY, NO INFLECTION

Chinese words do not have inflections, i.e. they do not change to indicate grammatical categories. For example, the verb 去 **qù** (*to go*) is invariably 去 **qù**; there is no past form or any other inflected form of this verb. Neither do Chinese words normally have formal markers of word class. Consequently it is rather easy for a word to be used in more than one word class. This relative flexibility in word classes, however, does not mean that Chinese does not have word classes (see Section 4.2).

MEASURE WORDS AND PARTICLES

Measure words (量词 **liàngcí**) and particles (助词 **zhùcí**) are two word classes found in Chinese but not in English and most other languages.

Measure words are usually required when a noun is modified by a numeral. For example, 两书 **liǎng shū** is unacceptable; you must use the measure word 本 **běn** between the numeral and the noun: 两本 书 **liǎng běn shū** (*two books*). Furthermore, Chinese nouns require specific measure words to go with them. For example, the noun 书 **shū** (*book*) must be used with the measure word 本 **běn**. See List 2 on pages xvii–xix for the common measure words.

In Chinese grammar, particles are words attached to other words or at the end of a sentence to indicate grammatical concepts or to express emotions. For example, the particles 了 **le**, 着 **zhe**, 过 **guo** are attached to verbs to indicate, respectively, whether the actions denoted are completed, in progress or past experiences.

4.2 Word Classes

Following are brief explanations of the basic terms in Chinese grammar used in this dictionary. (A word of warning: it is a rather complicated matter to define grammatical terms accurately. Here we will be content with some general but useful ideas.)

ADJECTIVE	a describing word, a word that describes people, things or actions, typically used before a noun
ADVERB	a word that modifies a verb, an adjective or another adverb
CONJUNCTION	a word used to link two words, phrases or sentences, indicating certain relationships between them
IDIOM	a set phrase, the meaning of which cannot be readily derived from its components
INTERJECTION	a word that expresses strong emotions
MEASURE WORD	a word that connects a numeral to a noun. Measure words are a special feature of Chinese; a list of measure words is given in List 2

MODAL VERB	a word used before a verb to indicate necessity, possibility, willingness, etc.
NOUN	a naming word, a word that names people, animals, plants, things, ideas, etc.
NUMERAL	a word that represents a number, typically used with a noun
ONOMATOPOEIA	a word that imitates the sounds of a thing or an action
PARTICLE	a word used with another word, phrase, or sentence to indicate certain grammatical meanings or to express strong emotions
PREPOSITION	a word used before a noun or pronoun to indicate time, place, direction, manner, reason of an action, etc.
PRONOUN	a word that is used in the place of a noun, a verb, an adjective, etc.
VERB	an action word, a word that indicates what somebody does or feels

List 1
Meaningful Character Components

冫 = freezing, ice (e.g. 冰 **bīng**, 冷 **lěng**, 寒 **hán**)

讠, 言 = word (e.g. 语 **yǔ**, 词 **cí**)

八 = dividing (e.g. 分 **fēn**, 半 **bàn**)

亻, 人 = man, person (e.g. 他 **tā**, 信 **xìn**)

刂, 刀 = knife (e.g. 利 **lì**, 剩 **shèng**)

力 = muscle, strength (e.g. 男 **nán**, 办 **bàn**)

阝 (on the left) = mound, steps (e.g. 院 **yuàn**, 附 **fù**)

阝 (on the right) = city, region (e.g. 部 **bù**, 邮 **yóu**)

氵, 水 = water (e.g. 河 **hé**, 海 **hǎi**)

忄, 心 = the heart, emotions (e.g. 情 **qíng**, 怕 **pà**, 感 **gǎn**)

宀 = roof, house (e.g. 家 **jiā**, 室 **shì**)

广 = roof, hut (e.g. 庭 **tíng**, 店 **diàn**)

门 = door, gate (e.g. 闻 **wén**, 间 **jiān**)

土 = earth (e.g. 场 **chǎng**, 城 **chéng**)

女 = woman (e.g. 妇 **fù**, 妈 **mā**)

饣, 食 = food (e.g. 饭 **fàn**, 饱 **bǎo**)

口 = the mouth, speech, eating (e.g. 问 **wèn**, 吃 **chī**)

囗 = boundary (e.g. 围 **wéi**, 园 **yuán**)

孑, 子 = child (e.g. 孩 **hái**, 学 **xué**)

艹 = plant, vegetation (e.g. 草 **cǎo**, 菜 **cài**)

纟 = silk, texture (e.g. 组 **zǔ**, 纸 **zhǐ**)

辶 = walking (e.g. 道 **dào**, 过 **guò**)

彳 = path, walking (e.g. 行 **xíng**, 往 **wǎng**)

巾 = cloth (e.g. 布 **bù**, 带 **dài**)

马 = horse (e.g. 骑 **qí**)

扌, 手, 攵 = the hand, action (e.g. 拿 **ná**, 擦 **cā**)

灬, 火 = fire, heat (e.g. 烧 **shāo**, 热 **rè**)

礻, 示 = spirit (e.g. 神 **shén**, 祖 **zǔ**)

户 = door, window (e.g. 房 **fáng**)

父 = father (e.g. 爸 **bà**)

日 = the sun (e.g. 晴 **qíng**, 暖 **nuǎn**)

月 = the moon (e.g. 阴 **yīn**, 明 **míng**)

月, 肉 = flesh, human organ (e.g. 脸 **liǎn**, 脚 **jiǎo**)

贝 = shell, treasure (e.g. 贵 **guì**)

止 = toe (e.g. 步 **bù**)

木 = tree, timber (e.g. 树 **shù**, 板 **bǎn**)

王, 玉 = jade (e.g. 理 **lǐ**, 球 **qiú**)

见 = seeing (e.g. 视 **shì**, 现 **xiàn**)

气 = vapor (e.g. 汽 **qì**)

车 = vehicle (e.g. 辆 **liàng**)

疒 = disease, ailment (e.g. 病 **bìng**, 疼 **téng**)

立 = standing (e.g. 站 **zhàn**, 位 **wèi**)

穴 = cave, hole (e.g. 空 **kōng**, 窗 **chuāng**)

衤, 衣 = clothing (e.g. 裤 **kù**, 袜 **wà**)

钅, 金 = metal (e.g. 银 **yín**, 钱 **qián**)

石 = stone, rock (e.g. 碗 **wǎn**, 磁 **cí**)

目 = the eye (e.g. 眼 **yǎn**, 睡 **shuì**)

田 = farm, field (e.g. 界 **jiè**, 里 **lǐ**)

瓜 = melon, gourd (e.g. 瓢 **piáo**, 瓣 **bàn**)

禾 = seedling, crop (e.g. 种 **zhǒng**, 秋 **qiū**)

鸟 = bird (e.g. 鸡 **jī**)

米 = rice (e.g. 糖 **táng**, 精 **jīng**)

竹 = bamboo (e.g. 筷 **kuài**, 笔 **bǐ**)

舌 = the tongue (e.g. 话 **huà**, 活 **huó**)

舟 = boat (e.g. 船 **chuán**)

酉 = fermentation (e.g. 酒 **jiǔ**)

走 = walking (e.g. 起 **qǐ**)

足 = the foot (e.g. 跳 **tiào**, 踢 **tì**)

List 2
Measure Words

Measure words are a special feature of Chinese. A particular measure word, or set of measure words, occurs with each noun whenever one is speaking of numbers. The measure word may function like a collective noun (like a *pride* [of lions] or a *school* [of fish]) or may be related to the shape of the object. Noun phrases using measure words often have the structure "number + measure word + noun," e.g.

- 一把刀 **yì bǎ dāo** = *a knife*
- 两道难题 **liǎng dào nántí** = *two difficult questions*

Some measure words occur with verbs, and may be related to the frequency or duration of the action. For verbs, the expression may have the structure "verb + number + measure word," e.g.

- 看了三遍 **kànle sān biàn** = *read three times*
- 去过两次 **qùguo liǎng cì** = *have been ... twice*

bǎ 把 for objects with handles; a handful

bān 班 class (in school)

bèi 倍 fold, time

běn 本 for books

bǐ 笔 for a sum of money

biàn 遍 times, indicating the frequency of an action done in its complete duration from the beginning to the end

cè 册 volume (books)

céng 层 story, floor

chǎng 场 for movies, sport events

chǐ 尺 a traditional Chinese unit of length (equal to ⅓ meter)

cì 次 time, expressing frequency of an act

cùn 寸 a traditional Chinese unit of length (equal to ⅓₀ meter)

dào 道 for questions in a school exercise, examination, etc.; for things in the shape of a line

dī 滴 drop (of liquid)

diǎn 点 o'clock

dù 度 degree (of temperature, longitude, latitude, etc.)

duàn 段 section of something long

dùn 顿 for meals

duǒ 朵 for flowers

fēn 分 Chinese currency (1 分 **fēn** = 0.1 角 **jiǎo** = 0.01 元 **yuán**), cent

fèn 份 for a set of things or newspapers, documents, etc.

fēng 封 for letters

fú 幅 for pictures, poster, maps, etc.

gè 个 the most commonly used measure word for nouns that do not take special measure words, or in default of any other measure word

gēn 根 for long, thin things

gōngchǐ 公尺 meter (formal)

gōngjīn 公斤 kilogram

gōnglǐ 公里 kilometer

háng 行 used with nouns that are formed in lines; line, row, queue

hù 户 used with nouns denoting households and families

huí 回 number of times

jiā 家 for families or businesses

jiān 间 for rooms

jiàn 件 for things, affairs, clothes or furniture

jiǎo 角 Chinese currency (0.1 **yuan** or 10 **fen**), ten cents, a dime

jié 节 a period of time

jīn 斤 a Chinese unit of weight equivalent to half a kilogram

jù 句 for sentences

kē 棵 for trees

kè 克 gram

kè 刻 quarter of an hour

kǒu 口 for members of a family

kuài 块 for things that can be broken into lumps or chunks; for money; yuan, dollar

lǐ 里 a Chinese unit of length, equivalent to 0.5 kilometers

lì 粒 for rice, pearls

liǎng 两 a traditional Chinese unit of weight, equivalent to 50 grams; ounce

liàng 辆 for vehicles

liè 列 for trains

máo 毛 a Chinese money unit, colloquialism for 角 **jiǎo** (= 0.1 元 **yuán** or 10 分 **fēn**)

mén 门 for school subjects, languages, etc.

mǐ 米 meter (colloquial)

miàn 面 for flat objects

miǎo 秒 second (of time)

míng 名 for people, especially for those with a specific position or occupation

mǔ 亩 a traditional Chinese unit of area, especially in farming (equal to ⅟₁₅ hectare or 667 square meters)

pái 排 for things arranged in a row

pī 批 for a batch of goods, and for things/people arriving at the same time

pǐ 匹 for horses

piān 篇 for a piece of writing

piàn 片 for a thin and flat piece, slice

píng 瓶 a bottle of

qún 群 a crowd/group of

shēn 身 for clothes

shǒu 首 for songs and poems

shuāng 双 a pair of (shoes, chopsticks, etc.)

suì 岁 year (of age)

suǒ 所 for houses, or institutions housed in a building

tái 台 for machines, big instruments, etc.

tàng 趟 for trips

tào 套 a set of

tiáo 条 for things with a long, narrow shape

tóu 头 for cattle or sheep

wèi 位 a polite measure word for people

xià 下 used with certain verbs to indicate the number of times the action is done

xiàng 项 item, component

yè 页 for pages (of a book)

yīngchǐ 英尺 foot (as a measurement of length)

yīngcùn 英寸 inch

yuán 元 the basic unit of Chinese currency (1 元 **yuán** = 10 角 **jiǎo**/毛 **máo** = 100 分 **fēn**), dollar

zhāng 张 for paper, beds, tables, desks

zhèn 阵 for an action or event that lasts for some time

zhī 支 for stick-like things

zhī 只 for animals, utensils, or objects

zhǒng 种 kind, sort

zuò 座 for large and solid objects, such as a large building

Using the Dictionary

Note: You are recommended to read *Introducing Chinese* (pp.v-xvii) before using the dictionary.

1 Pronunciation

The pronunciation of Chinese words as transcribed in this dictionary uses the *pinyin* scheme, which is the official, internationally recognized Chinese romanization system. Every Chinese character in this dictionary is accompanied by its *pinyin* spelling so that you will know how to pronounce every word and say every sentence.

2 Word class

The word class of each headword is indicated after the word-formation or immediately after the head word, e.g.

> 爱护 àihù v care for and protect, cherish
> 阿姨 āyí N mother's sister

When a headword may be used in different word classes, they are shown by I, II, and so on, e.g.

> 爱好 àihào **I** v like, be interested in, have as a hobby
> **II** N hobby, interest

3 Traditional characters

If a character has a traditional version (传统字 **chuántǒng zì**, also known as 繁体字 **fántǐzì** "complicated character"), it is shown as part of the headword, preceded by TRAD, e.g. 爱 ài TRAD 愛.

4 Definitions

For Chinese headwords English equivalents or near equivalents are given, in most cases, as definitions, e.g.

> 高兴 gāoxìng ADJ joyful, delighted, willing

For grammatical words that have no English equivalents, concise explanations are given in brackets, e.g.

> 的 de PARTICLE (attached to a word, phrase or clause to indicate that it is an attribute; 的 de is normally followed by a noun)

When a headword has more than one meaning under the same word class, the different meanings are indicated by **1**, **2**, etc. For example:

> 月 yuè N **1** month **2** the moon

Homonyms (words pronounced and written the same but with different, unrelated meanings) are treated as separate words, e.g.

> 代¹ dài v take the place of, perform on behalf of
> 代² dài N **1** generation

For English headwords, Chinese equivalents or near equivalents are given, e.g.

> **ability** N 能力 nénglì, 才能 cáinéng

5 Measure Words

After the definition of a Chinese noun, the specific measure word used with the noun is shown, if it is one of the headwords in the dictionary, e.g.

> 书 shū book (本 běn)

When the specific measure word is not within the scope of this dictionary and therefore is not shown, you can often use the default measure word 个 **ge**.

6 Common Collocations

Collocations are words habitually juxtaposed with each other. This dictionary shows common collocations related to the headwords, with clear definitions and necessary sample sentences. For example:

包 bāo N parcel, bag
钱包 qiánbāo wallet, purse
书包 shūbāo schoolbag
邮包 yóubāo mailbag, parcel for posting

7 How to find Chinese words

BY PINYIN SPELLING

Headwords are arranged alphabetically according to their *pinyin* spelling. So if you know how a word is pronounced, you can find it easily, just like the way you will look up an English word in an English dictionary.

If you do not know the pronunciation of a word you can find it either by its radical or the number of its strokes.

BY RADICALS

Radicals (部首 **bùshǒu**) are certain component parts of characters that have been used in Chinese dictionary-making for nearly 2,000 years. Characters sharing a radical are grouped together under the heading of that radical. To find a character in a dictionary, follow these steps:

(i)   In the List of Radicals, look up the character's radical according to the number of strokes in the radical. This gives a Radical Index number.

(ii) Turn to the number in the Radical Index.

(iii) Locate the character according to the number of remaining strokes needed to write the character (i.e. number of total strokes minus radical strokes = remaining strokes). You will find the *pinyin* by the character.

For example, to find 活 by Radical Index:

(i)   The radical group of 活 is 氵, which has three strokes. In the List of Radicals, look up 氵 in the section marked "3 strokes":

3 strokes

氵   33

(ii) Turn to number 33 in the Radical Index.

(iii) As there are nine strokes in 活, and the radical has three strokes, six strokes remain to complete the character 活 $(9 - 3 = 6)$. Look in the section "6 strokes" and locate 活:

6 strokes

活　**huó**

(iv) Turn to **huó** in the section:

huó 活 …

BY STROKE NUMBERS

Unfortunately, looking for a character by its radical is not an entirely satisfactory method as learners may not always know which part of the character is the radical. Therefore, this section includes a Stroke Index to aid the learner further. Simply look for the character according to the number of its strokes, and then locate the character by its first stroke.

For example, to find 活 by Stroke Index:

(i) There are nine strokes in 活. Go to the section of nine strokes.
　　9 strokes

(ii) As the first stroke of 活 is " 、", locate 活 under " 、".

丶

活　**huó**

(iii) Turn to **huó** in the dictionary.
　　huó 活 …

List of Radicals

1 stroke

丶	1
一	2
乙	3
亅	4
丿	5

2 strokes

亠	6
丷	7
冫	8
讠	9
二	10
十	11
厂	12
匚	13
匕	14
卜	15
刂	16
冂	17
勹	18
刀	19
力	20
夕	21
八	22
人	23
儿	24
几	25
又	26
凵	27
厶	28
卩	30
阝(on left)	31
阝(on right)	32

3 strokes

氵	33
忄	34
小	35
宀	36
丬	37
广	38
门	39
辶	40
工	41
干	42
土	43
士	44
屮	45
艹	46
廾	47
大	48
寸	49
扌	50
口	51
囗	52
巾	53
山	54
彳	55
彡	56
夕	57
夂	58
犭	59
饣	60
彐	61
尸	62
已	63
己	64
巳	65
弓	66
女	67
子	68
纟	69
马	70

4 strokes

灬	71
文	72
方	73
心	74
户	75
斗	76
王, 玉	77
木	78
犬	79
歹	80
瓦	81
车	82
比	83
日	84
曰	85
贝	86
见	87
父	88
攵	89
牛	90
手	91
毛	92
气	93
片	94
斤	95
爪	96
月	97
欠	98
天	99
风	100
殳	101
火	102
礻	103
戈	104
水	105
聿	106
止	107

5 strokes

龙	108
石	109
业	110
目	111
田	112
四	113
皿	114
钅	115
矢	116
禾	117
白	118
用	119
鸟	120
疒	121
立	122
穴	123
衤	124
示	125
主	126
母	127
去	128
疋	129
皮	130

6 strokes

老	131
耳	132
西	133
页	134
虍	135
虫	136
缶	137
舌	138
竹	139
自	140
舟	141
衣	142
羊	143
米	144
艮	145
羽	146
纟	147

7 strokes

麦	148
走	149
里	150
足	151
采	152
豸	153
身	154
角	155
言	156
辛	157
系	158
束	159
非	160
酉	161
豆	162

8 strokes

隹	163
青	164
鱼	165
雨	166
齿	167

9 strokes

革	168
是	169
食	170
鬼	171
音	172

11 strokes

麻	173

12 strokes

黑	174

Radical Index

All characters are listed here under their radical plus the number of additional strokes needed to write them.

1 、		专	zhuān	夏	xià	艳	yàn	乔	qiáo
举	jǔ	**4 strokes**		严	yán	中	zhōng	丘	qiū
为	wèi	丙	bǐng	昼	zhòu	**5 丿**		凸	tū
永	yǒng	册	cè	**3 乙**		**1–2 strokes**		向	xiàng
之	zhī	丛	cóng	巴	bā	川	chuān	**6-13 strokes**	
州	zhōu	东	dōng	承	chéng	乏	fá	秉	bǐng
主	zhǔ	甘	gān	丑	chǒu	九	jiǔ	重	chóng,
2 一		可	kě	刁	diāo	久	jiǔ		zhòng
一	yī, yí, yì	平	píng	飞	fēi	么	me	囱	cōng
1–2 strokes		正	zhèng	了	le, liǎo	千	qiān	垂	chuí
才	cái	**5 strokes**		隶	lì	义	yì	复	fù
丁	dīng	而	ér	买	mǎi	**3–4 strokes**		够	gòu
亏	kuī	亚	yà	矛	máo	长	cháng,	乖	guāi
七	qī	再	zài	民	mín		zhǎng	卵	luǎn
三	sān	**6 strokes**		乞	qǐ	丹	dān	甥	shēng
万	wàn	辰	chén	司	sī	瓜	guā	鼠	shǔ
下	xià	更	gēng,	疏	shū	乎	hū	舞	
于	yú, yù		gèng	乡	xiāng	及	jí	**6 亠**	
与	yǔ	来	lái	也	yě	乐	lè, yuè	**2–3 strokes**	
丈	zhàng	丽	lì	乙	yǐ	升	shēng	亢	kàng
3 strokes		两	liǎng	予	yǔ	生	shēng	六	liù
不	bú, bù	求	qiú	**4 丨**		失	shī	市	shì
丰	fēng	**7-13 strokes**		凹	āo	氏	shì	亡	wáng
互	hù	甫	béng	卜	bó, bǔ	丸	wán	**4-5 strokes**	
世	shì	哥	gē	串	chuàn	乌	wū	充	chōng
屯	tún	赫	hè	鉴	jiàn	爪	zhuǎ	交	jiāo
无	wú	柬	jiǎn	临	lín	**5 strokes**		亩	mǔ
五	wǔ	面	miàn	且	qiě	丢	diū	齐	qí
牙	yá	甚	shèn	师	shī	年	nián	弃	qì
尤	yóu	事	shì	书	shū	乒	pīng	亦	yì

医	yī

13 匕

北	běi
疑	yí
旨	zhǐ

14 卜

卡	kǎ
卧	wò
占	zhàn
贞	zhēn

15 刂

4–5 strokes

别	bié, biè
创	chuàng
刚	gāng
划	huá, huà
利	lì
列	liè
判	pàn
刨	páo
删	shān
则	zé

6–8 strokes

剥	bāo, bō
刺	cì
到	dào
刮	guā
剂	jì
剑	jiàn
剧	jù
刻	kè
剖	pōu
刹	shā
刷	shuā
剃	tì

削	xiāo, xuē
制	zhì

9–10 strokes

副	fù
割	gē
剩	shèng

16 冖

冠	guàn
罕	hǎn
军	jūn
农	nóng
写	xiě
冤	yuān

17 冂

内	nèi
肉	ròu
甩	shuǎi
同	tóng
网	wǎng
用	yòng
周	zhōu

18 勹

包	bāo
匆	cōng
勾	gōu
句	jù
勺	sháo
勿	wù
旬	xún
匀	yún

19 刀

刀	dāo
刃	rèn

2–5 strokes

负	fù

龟	guī
切	qiē, qiè
韧	rèn
色	sè
危	wēi
召	zhào
争	zhēng

6–13 strokes

剪	jiǎn
免	miǎn
劈	pī
券	quàn
兔	tù
象	xiàng
豫	yù

20 力

力	lì

2–4 strokes

办	bàn
动	dòng
加	jiā
劳	láo
劣	liè
另	lìng
劝	quàn
幼	yòu

5–11 strokes

勃	bó
劫	jié
劲	jìn
舅	jiù
勘	kān
励	lì
勉	miǎn
努	nǔ

勤	qín
势	shì
勇	yǒng
助	zhù

21 八

八	bā

2–4 strokes

半	bàn
并	bìng
分	fēn, fèn
公	gōng
共	gòng
关	guān
兰	lán
兴	xīng, xìng

5–6 strokes

兵	bīng
单	dān
弟	dì
典	diǎn
兑	duì
具	jù
其	qí

7–8 strokes

兼	jiān
前	qián
首	shǒu
兽	shòu
养	yǎng
益	yì

22 亻

1–2 strokes

仇	chóu
化	huà
仅	jǐn

仁	rén
仆	pú
仍	réng
什	shén
亿	yì
仔	zǐ

3 strokes

传	chuán
代	dài
付	fù
们	men
他	tā
仙	xiān
仪	yí

4 strokes

伐	fá
仿	fǎng
份	fèn
伏	fú
伙	huǒ
价	jià
件	jiàn
任	rèn
伤	shāng
似	sì
伪	wěi
伟	wěi
伍	wǔ
休	xiū
仰	yǎng
伊	yī
优	yōu
传	zhuàn

5 strokes

伴	bàn

伯	bó	俄	é	做	zuò	余	yú	**27 凵**
伺	cì, sì	俭	jiǎn	**11–15 strokes**		**24 儿**		出	chū
但	dàn	俱	jù	催	cuī	儿	ér	函	hán
低	dī	俊	jùn	僵	jiāng	兄	xiōng	画	huà
佛	fó, fú	俏	qiào	僚	liáo	先	xiān	击	jī
估	gū	侵	qīn	僻	pì	兆	zhào	凶	xiōng
何	hé	俗	sú	傻	shǎ	**25 几**		凿	záo
你	nǐ	侮	wǔ	像	xiàng	凳	dèng	**28 厶**
伸	shēn	信	xìn	**23 入**		兜	dōu	参	cān
体	tǐ	**8 strokes**		个	gè, ge	凡	fán	能	néng
位	wèi	倍	bèi	人	rén	凰	huáng	叁	sān
佣	yōng	倡	chàng	入	rù	几	jī, jǐ	台	tái
住	zhù	倒	dǎo, dào	**2 strokes**		凯	kǎi	县	xiàn
作	zuò	俯	fǔ	仓	cāng	凭	píng	允	yǔn
6 strokes		候	hòu	从	cóng	秃	tū	**29 廴**
侧	cè	健	jiàn	介	jiè	**26 又**		建	jiàn
侈	chǐ	借	jiè	今	jīn	又	yòu	延	yán
俘	fú	俱	jù	以	yǐ	**1–2 strokes**		**30 卩**
供	gōng, gòng	倦	juàn	**3–4 strokes**		叉	chā	即	jí
佳	jiā	偶	ǒu	合	hé	反	fǎn	卷	juǎn
例	lì	倾	qīng	会	huì, kuài	双	shuāng	却	què
俩	liǎ	倘	tǎng	令	lìng	友	yǒu	危	wēi
侣	lǚ	倚	yǐ	企	qǐ	**3–8 strokes**		卫	wèi
佩	pèi	值	zhí	全	quán	变	biàn	卸	xiè
侨	qiáo	**9–10 strokes**		伞	sǎn	叠	dié	印	yìn
使	shǐ	傲	ào	众	zhòng	对	duì	**31 阝 (on left)**
侍	shì	傍	bàng	**5–10 strokes**		发	fā	**2–3 strokes**
修	xiū	偿	cháng	含	hán	观	guān	队	duì
依	yī	储	chǔ	盒	hé	欢	huān	防	fáng
侦	zhēn	傅	fù	金	jīn	艰	jiān	**4–5 strokes**
侄	zhí	假	jiǎ, jià	命	mìng	难	nán, nàn	阿	ā
7 strokes		偏	piān	拿	ná	叛	pàn	陈	Chén
保	bǎo	停	tíng	禽	qín	叔	shū	附	fù
便	biàn, pián	偷	tōu	舍	shě, shè	叙	xù	际	jì
促	cù	债	zhài	舒	shū			阶	jiē

陆	lù	邮	yóu	泌	mì	洒	sǎ	淆	xiáo
阳	yáng	郁	yù	沫	mò	洗	xǐ	淹	yān
阴	yīn	郑	zhèng	泥	ní	洋	yáng	液	yè

33 氵

2–4 strokes

阵	zhèn			泞	nìng	洲	zhōu	淫	yín
阻	zǔ			泡	pào	浊	zhuó	渔	yú
6–12 strokes		沉	chén	泼	pō	**7 strokes**		渣	zhā
隘	ài	池	chí	泣	qì	海	hǎi	**9 strokes**	
除	chú	泛	fàn	浅	qiǎn	浸	jìn	溉	gài
陡	dǒu	沟	gōu	泻	xiè	酒	jiǔ	湖	hú
隔	gé	汗	hàn	泄	xiè	浩	hào	滑	huá
降	jiàng	汉	hàn	沿	yán	涝	lào	溅	jiàn
隆	lóng	沪	hù	泳	yǒng	流	liú	渴	kě
陋	lòu	汇	huì	油	yóu	润	rùn	溜	liù
陌	mò	江	jiāng	沾	zhān	涉	shè	湿	shī
陪	péi	沥	lì	泽	zé	涛	tāo	滩	tān
随	suí	没	méi	沼	zhǎo	涕	tì	湾	wān
隧	suì	沛	pèi	治	zhì	消	xiāo	温	wēn
陶	táo	沏	qī	注	zhù	涌	yǒng	游	yóu
隙	xì	汽	qì	**6 strokes**		浴	yù	滞	zhì
险	xiǎn	沙	shā	测	cè	涨	zhǎng	滋	zī
陷	xiàn	汰	tài	涤	dí	**8 strokes**		**10–18 strokes**	
限	xiàn	潭	tán	洞	dòng	淡	dàn	澳	ào
隐	yǐn	汤	tāng	浮	fú	淀	diàn	滨	bīn
院	yuàn	汪	wāng	洪	hóng	渡	dù	潮	cháo
障	zhàng	沃	wò	浑	hún	港	gǎng	澄	dēng
32 阝 (on right)		污	wū	活	huó	混	hùn	滴	dī
邦	bāng	汹	xiōng	济	jì	渐	jiàn	灌	guàn
鄙	bǐ	汁	zhī	浇	jiāo	淋	lín	滚	gǔn
部	bù	**5 strokes**		洁	jié	漠	mò	激	jí
都	dōu, dū	波	bō	津	jīn	清	qīng	滥	làn
郊	jiāo	泊	bó	浪	làng	深	shēn	潦	liáo
郎	láng	法	fǎ	浏	liú	渗	shèn	漏	lòu
邻	lín	沸	fèi	浓	nóng	淘	táo	滤	lù
那	nà, nèi	河	hé	派	pài	添	tiān	满	mǎn
邪	xié	泪	lèi	洽	qià	涂	tú	漫	màn

漂	piāo, piào	恼	nǎo	党	dǎng	宾	bīn	序	xù
瀑	pù	恰	qià	辉	huī	害	hài	应	yīng, yìng
漆	qī	悄	qiāo	尚	shàng	寂	jì	庄	zhuāng
潜	qiǎn	情	qíng	省	shěng	寄	jì	**5–8 strokes**	
溶	róng	惕	tì	**36 宀**		家	jiā	底	dǐ
滔	tāo	惋	wǎn	**2–4 strokes**		寇	kòu	度	dù
潭	tán	悟	wù	安	ān	宽	kuān	废	fèi
溪	xī	惜	xī	宏	hóng	密	mì	庙	miào
演	yǎn	悦	yuè	牢	láo	容	róng	庞	páng
源	yuán	**9–13 strokes**		宁	níng, nìng	宿	sù	**6-11 strokes**	
澡	zǎo	懂	dǒng	守	shǒu	宵	xiāo	腐	fǔ
34 忄		惰	duò	它	tā	宴	yàn	康	kāng
3–5 strokes		愤	fèn	完	wán	寓	yù	廊	láng
怖	bù	惯	guàn	宇	yǔ	**9-11 strokes**		廉	lián
怪	guài	憾	hàn	灾	zāi	察	chá	唐	táng
恒	héng	慌	huāng	宅	zhái	富	fù	庭	tíng
怀	huái	慨	kǎi	字	zì	寡	guǎ	席	xí
快	kuài	慷	kāng	**5–6 strokes**		寒	hán	庸	yōng
怜	lián	愧	kuì	宝	bǎo	蜜	mì	座	zuò
忙	máng	懒	lǎn	宠	chǒng	寞	mò	**39 门**	
怕	pà	愣	lèng	定	dìng	塞	sāi	门	mén
怯	qiè	慢	màn	宫	gōng	寨	zhài	**2–4 strokes**	
性	xìng	慎	shèn	官	guān	**37 爿**		闭	bì
忆	yì	愉	yú	客	kè	将	jiāng	闯	chuǎng
忧	yōu	**35 小**		审	shěn	妆	zhuāng	间	jiān, jiàn
6–8 strokes		小	xiǎo	实	shí	壮	zhuàng	闷	mēn, mèn
惭	cán	**2–3 strokes**		室	shì	状	zhuàng	闪	shǎn
惨	cǎn	尘	chén	宪	xiàn	**38 广**		问	wèn
悼	dào	当	dāng, dàng	宣	xuān	广	guǎng	闲	xián
惦	diàn	光	guāng	宜	yí	**3–4 strokes**		**5–9 strokes**	
恨	hèn	尖	jiān	窄	zhǎi	床	chuáng	阐	chǎn
恢	huī	少	shǎo, shào	宙	zhòu	店	diàn	阀	fá
悔	huǐ	肖	xiào	宗	zōng	府	fǔ	闺	guī
惊	jīng	**4–9 strokes**		**7–8 strokes**		库	kù	阁	hé
惧	jù	尝	cháng	案	àn	庆	qìng	阔	kuò

闹	nào	退	tuì	巧	qiǎo	坦	tǎn	壳	ké
闻	wén	选	xuǎn	式	shì	型	xíng	吉	jí
阅	yuè	追	zhuī	项	xiàng	幸	xìng	嘉	jiā
闸	zhá	**7-8 strokes**		巫	wū	址	zhǐ	声	shēng
40 辶		逮	dài	左	zuǒ	坐	zuò	士	shì
2–3 strokes		递	dì	**42 干**		**7–8 strokes**		喜	xǐ
边	biān	逗	dòu	干	gān, gàn	埠	bù	壹	yī
达	dá	逢	féng	刊	kān	堵	dù	志	zhì
过	guò, guo	逛	guàng	**43 土**		堆	duī	**45 上**	
辽	liáo	逻	luó	土	tǔ	堕	duò	上	shàng
迈	mài	逝	shì	**2–3 strokes**		基	jī	**46 艹**	
迁	qiān	速	sù	场	chǎng	埋	mái, mán	**1–4 strokes**	
巡	xún	通	tōng	地	de, dì	培	péi	艾	ài
迅	xùn	透	tòu	均	jūn	塔	tǎ	芭	bā
4 strokes		途	tú	圣	shèng	堂	táng	苍	cāng
迟	chí	造	zào	在	zài	域	yù	芳	fāng
还	hái, huán	逐	zhú	至	zhì	**9-17 strokes**		芬	fēn
进	jìn	**9–13 strokes**		**4–6 strokes**		堡	bǎo	花	huā
近	jìn	逼	bī	坝	bà	壁	bì	节	jié
连	lián	避	bì	城	chéng	堤	dī	芹	qín
迫	pò	遍	biàn	赤	chì	鼓	gǔ	苏	sū
违	wéi	道	dào	坊	fāng	境	jìng	芽	yá
迎	yíng	谴	qiǎn	坟	fén	堪	kān	艺	yì
远	yuǎn	邀	yāo	坏	huài	墙	qiáng	芝	zhī
运	yùn	遥	yáo	圾	jī	壤	rǎng	**5–6 strokes**	
这	zhè, zhèi	遗	yí	坚	jiān	塞	sāi	草	cǎo
5–6 strokes		遇	yù	垦	kěn	塑	sù	茶	chá
迪	dí	遭	zāo	坑	kēng	塌	tā	范	fàn
迹	jì	遵	zūn	垮	kuǎ	塘	táng	荒	huāng
迷	mí	**41 工**		块	kuài	填	tián	茧	jiǎn
逆	nì	工	gōng	垃	lā	墟	xū	荐	jiàn
适	shì	功	gōng	垒	lěi	增	zēng	茎	jīng
述	shù	攻	gōng	垄	lǒng	遮	zhē	苦	kǔ
送	sòng	巩	gǒng	坡	pō	**44 士**		荔	lì
逃	táo	贡	gòng	坛	tán	壶	hú	茫	máng

拼	pīn	掉	diào	摄	shè	右	yòu	咙	lóng
拾	shí	接	jiē	摊	tān	只	zhī, zhǐ	呢	ne
拴	shuān	捷	jié	摇	yáo	**3 strokes**		呻	shēn
挑	tiāo, tiǎo	掘	jué	**11–16 strokes**		吃	chī	味	wèi
挺	tǐng	控	kòng	播	bō	吗	ma	呜	wū
挖	wā	掠	lüè	擦	cā	舌	shé	咏	yǒng
挣	zhēng,	描	miáo	操	cāo	吐	tǔ, tù	咋	zǎ
	zhèng	捻	niǎn	撤	chè	吸	xī	**6 strokes**	
拽	zhuài	排	pái	撑	chēng	吓	xià	哆	duō
指	zhǐ	捧	pěng	摧	cuī	右	yòu	哈	hā
7 strokes		掐	qiā	撵	niǎn	只	zhī, zhǐ	哄	hǒng,
挨	āi	探	tàn	撇	piē	**4 strokes**			hòng
捌	bā	掏	tāo	撒	sā	吧	bā, ba	哗	huá
捕	bǔ	推	tuī	擅	shàn	吵	chǎo	咳	ké
挫	cuò	挽	wǎn	摔	shuāi	呈	chéng	骂	mà
捍	hàn	掩	yǎn	撕	sī	吹	chuī	鸣	míng
换	huàn	掷	zhì	搜	sōu	呆	dāi	哪	nǎ
捡	jiǎn	**9 strokes**		掀	xiān	吨	dūn	品	pǐn
据	jù	搏	bó	携	xié	吩	fēn	虽	suī
捐	juān	插	chā	攒	zǎn	否	fǒu	哇	wā
挎	kuà	搁	gē	摘	zhāi	告	gào	响	xiǎng
捆	kǔn	搅	jiǎo	撞	zhuàng	谷	gǔ	哑	yǎ
捞	lāo	揭	jiē	**51 口**		叽	hǒu	咽	yàn
捏	niē	揪	jiū	口	kǒu	呕	ǒu	咬	yǎo
揉	róu	揽	lǎn	**2 strokes**		听	tīng	咱	zán
捎	shāo	搜	sōu	叭	bā	吞	tūn	咨	zī
授	shòu	提	tí	叼	diào	吻	wěn	**7–9 strokes**	
损	sǔn	握	wò	叮	dīng	呀	yā, ya	啊	ā
哲	zhé	援	yuán	号	hào	员	yuán	唉	āi
振	zhèn	揍	zòu	叫	jiào	**5 strokes**		啡	fēi
捉	zhuō	**10 strokes**		另	lìng	哎	āi	唱	chàng
8 strokes		摆	bǎi	史	shǐ	咐	fù	喘	chuǎn
措	cuò	搬	bān	叹	tàn	呵	hē	唇	chún
捣	dǎo	搞	gǎo	兄	xiōng	呼	hū	喊	hǎn
掂	diàn	摸	mō	叶	yè	咖	kā	喝	hē

饶	ráo	**65 巳**		妻	qī	纺	fǎng	绒	róng
蚀	shí	导	dǎo	始	shǐ	纷	fēn	统	tǒng
饰	shì	巷	xiàng	姓	xìng	纲	gāng	**7–13 strokes**
馅	xiàn	**66 弓**		**6–11 strokes**		红	hóng	绷	bēng
61 彐		弓	gōng	婚	hūn	幻	huàn	编	biān
归	guī	疆	jiāng	嫁	jià	级	jí	缠	chán
录	lù	弥	mí	娇	jiāo	纪	jì	绸	chóu
寻	xún	强	qiáng,	姥	lǎo	纠	jiū	缝	féng, fèng
62 尸			qiǎng	媒	méi	纳	nà	缚	fù
层	céng	弱	ruò	嫩	nèn	纽	niǔ	缓	huǎn
尺	chǐ	弦	xián	娘	niáng	纱	shā	继	jì
届	jiè	引	yǐn	娶	qǔ	丝	sī	绩	jì
尽	jǐn, jìn	张	zhāng	嫂	sǎo	纤	xiān	缴	jiǎo
居	jū	**67 女**		耍	shuǎ	约	yuē	绢	juàn
局	jú	女	nǚ	娃	wá	纸	zhǐ	绿	lù
履	lǚ	**2–4 strokes**		媳	xí	纵	zòng	绵	mián
屡	lǚ	妒	dù	嫌	xián	**5 strokes**		缈	miǎo
尼	ní	妨	fáng	姨	yí	练	liàn	婶	shěn
屁	pì	妇	fù	姻	yīn	绍	shào	绳	shéng
屏	píng	好	hǎo, hào	婴	yīng	绅	shēn	缩	suō
屈	qū	奸	jiān	娱	yú	细	xì	维	wéi
尸	shī	妈	mā	姿	zī	线	xiàn	纹	wén
屎	shǐ	妙	miào	**68 子**		织	zhī	绣	xiù
属	shǔ	奶	nǎi	存	cún	终	zhōng	续	xù
屉	tì	奴	nú	孤	gū	组	zǔ	绪	xù
屠	tú	如	rú	嫉	jí	**6 strokes**		缘	yuán
尾	wěi	她	tā	孩	hái	绑	bǎng	缀	zhuì
屋	wū	妥	tuǒ	孔	kǒng	给	gěi, jǐ	综	zōng
屑	xiè	妄	wàng	孙	sūn	绘	huì	**70 马**	
展	zhǎn	妖	yāo	学	xué	绞	jiǎo	驳	bó
63 己		**5 strokes**		孕	yùn	结	jiē, jié	驰	chí
已	yǐ	姑	gū	子	zǐ, zi	经	jīng	驾	jià
64 巳		姐	jiě	**69 纟**		绝	jué	骄	jiāo
己	jǐ	妹	mèi	**2–4 strokes**		络	luò	驴	lú
		姆	mǔ	纯	chún	绕	rǎo	骆	luò

马	mǎ	施	shī	惑	huò	瑰	guī	朱	zhū
骂	mà	旋	xuán	您	nín	瑚	hú	**3 strokes**	
骗	piàn	族	zú	烹	pēng	环	huán	材	cái
骑	qí	**74 心**		惹	rě	玖	jiǔ	村	cūn
驱	qū	心	xīn	悉	xī	璃	lí	杆	gǎn
骚	sāo	**1–4 strokes**		悬	xuán	理	lǐ	杠	gàng
驶	shǐ	必	bì	悠	yōu	玲	líng	极	jí
驼	tuó	忌	jì	愚	yú	珑	lóng	李	Lǐ
验	yàn	忽	hū	**9–11 strokes**		玫	méi	条	tiáo
骤	zhòu	念	niàn	憋	biē	琴	qín	**4 strokes**	
驻	zhù	忍	rěn	愁	chóu	球	qiú	板	bǎn
71 灬		态	tài	慈	cí	瑞	ruì	杯	bēi
杰	jié	忘	wàng	感	gǎn	珊	shān	构	gòu
5–6 strokes		忠	zhōng	慧	huì	玩	wán	柜	guì
点	diǎn	**5–6 strokes**		慕	mù	王	Wáng	果	guǒ
烈	liè	恶	ě, è, wù	慰	wèi	现	xiàn	枚	méi
热	rè	恩	ēn	想	xiǎng	玉	yù	枪	qiāng
8–12 strokes		恭	gōng	熏	xūn	珍	zhēn	松	sōng
熬	áo	急	jí	意	yì	珠	zhū	枉	wǎng
煎	jiān	悬	kěn	愈	yù	琢	zuó	杨	yáng
焦	jiāo	恐	kǒng	愿	yuàn	**78 木**		枣	zǎo
然	rán	恋	liàn	**75 户**		木	mù	枕	zhěn
熟	shú	虑	lǜ	扁	biǎn	**1–2 strokes**		柱	zhù
熊	xióng	怒	nù	房	fáng	本	běn	枝	zhī
燕	yàn	思	sī	雇	gù	朵	duǒ	**5 strokes**	
照	zhào	息	xī	户	hù	机	jī	柄	bǐng
煮	zhǔ	怨	yuàn	启	qǐ	林	lín	标	biāo
72 文		怎	zěn	扇	shàn	末	mò	查	chá
文	wén	总	zǒng	**76 斗**		朴	pǔ	架	jià
73 方		**7–8 strokes**		斗	dòu	权	quán	枯	kū
方	fāng	悲	bēi	斜	xié	杀	shā	栏	lán
放	fàng	惫	bèi	**77 王, 玉**		术	shù	柳	liǔ
旅	lǚ	惩	chéng	斑	bān	朽	xiǔ	某	mǒu
旁	páng	患	huàn	班	bān	未	wèi	柠	níng
旗	qí	惠	huì	玻	bō	杂	zá	柒	qī

染	rǎn	械	xiè	**80 歹**		**84 日**		昨	zuó

染 rǎn
柔 róu
柿 shì
树 shù
相 xiāng,
　 xiàng

6 strokes

柴 chái
档 dàng
栋 dòng
格 gé
根 gēn
梗 gěng
桂 guì
核 hé
桨 jiǎng
栗 lì
桥 qiáo
桑 sāng
桃 táo
校 xiào
桅 wéi
样 yàng
株 zhū
桌 zhuō

7 strokes

检 jiǎn
梨 lí
梁 liáng
梅 méi
渠 qú
梢 shāo
梳 shū
梯 tī
桶 tǒng

械 xiè
棕 zōng

8 strokes

棒 bàng
概 gài
棺 guān
棍 gùn
椒 jiāo
棵 kē
棱 léng
棉 mián
棚 péng
棋 qí
森 sēn
椭 tuǒ
椅 yǐ
植 zhí

9–13 strokes

榜 bǎng
槽 cáo
槐 huái
横 héng
橘 jú
榴 liú
楼 lóu
檬 méng
模 mó
榷 què
橡 xiàng
樱 yīng
榨 zhà

79 犬

犬 quǎn
哭 kū
献 xiàn

80 歹

残 cán
歹 dǎi
歼 jiān
殊 shū
死 sǐ
映 yāng
殖 zhí

81 瓦

瓷 cí
瓶 píng
瓦 wǎ

82 车

辈 bèi
车 chē
辅 fú
轨 guǐ
轰 hōng
辑 jí
较 jiào
较 jiào
辆 liàng
轮 lún
轻 qīng
输 shū
舆 yú
辖 xiá
斩 zhǎn
转 zhuǎn

83 比

比 bǐ
毙 bì
毕 bì

84 日

量 liáng,
　 liàng
曲 qū, qǔ
替 tì
显 xiǎn
暂 zàn
最 zuì

85 日

日 rì

1–4 strokes

昂 áng
昌 chāng
旦 dàn
旱 hàn
昏 hūn
旧 jiù
旷 kuàng
昆 kūn
明 míng
时 shí
旺 wàng
易 yì
早 zǎo
者 zhě

5–6 strokes

春 chūn
晃 huǎng
晋 jìn
晒 shài
是 shì
晓 xiǎo
星 xīng
映 yìng
晕 yùn

昨 zuó

7–11 strokes

暗 àn
暴 bào
曾 céng
晨 chén
晶 jīng
景 jǐng
晾 liàng
昧 mèi
暮 mù
暖 nuǎn
普 pǔ
晴 qíng
暑 shǔ
晚 wǎn
晰 xī
晤 wù

86 贝

贝 bèi

2–3 strokes

财 cái
员 yuán
则 zé

4 strokes

败 bài
贬 biǎn
贩 fàn
购 gòu
货 huò
贫 pín
贪 tān
贤 xián
质 zhì

5 strokes		爷	yé	拳	quán	**2–3 strokes**		脊	jǐ
贷	dài	**89 攵**		手	shǒu	肠	cháng	胶	jiāo
费	fèi	**2–5 strokes**		摩	mó	肚	dù	朗	lǎng
贯	guàn	改	gǎi	掌	zhǎng	肝	gān	脑	nǎo
贵	guì	故	gù	**92 毛**		肌	jī	胸	xiōng
贺	hè	收	shōu	耗	hào	有	yǒu	脏	zāng, zàng
贱	jiàn	政	zhèng	毫	háo	**4 strokes**		脂	zhī
贸	mào	**6–7 strokes**		毛	máo	肮	āng	**7–8 strokes**	
贴	tiē	敌	dí	髦	máo	肪	fáng	脖	bó
6–12 strokes		复	fù	毯	tǎn	肥	féi	朝	cháo, zhāo
赌	dǔ	敢	gǎn	**93 气**		肤	fū	脚	jiǎo
贿	huì	教	jiāo, jiào	氛	fēn	服	fú	腊	là
赖	lài	救	jiù	气	qì	股	gǔ	脸	liǎn
赂	lù	敏	mǐn	氢	qīng	肩	jiān	脾	pí
赔	péi	效	xiào	**94 片**		朋	péng	期	qī
赛	sài	致	zhì	版	bǎn	肾	shèn	腔	qiāng
赏	shǎng	**8-11 strokes**		牌	pái	胁	xié	脱	tuō
赞	zàn	敞	chǎng	片	piàn	育	yù	望	wàng
责	zé	敷	fū	**95 斤**		胀	zhàng	**9–12 strokes**	
贼	zéi	敬	jìng	斥	chì	肢	zhī	膀	bǎng
赠	zèng	散	sǎn, sàn	断	duàn	肿	zhǒng	臂	bì
智	zhì	数	shǔ, shù	斧	fǔ	**5 strokes**		膊	bó
赚	zhuàn	**90 牛**		斤	jīn	胞	bāo	腹	fù
资	zī	辐	fú	斯	sī	背	bēi, bèi	膏	gāo
87 见		牧	mù	所	suǒ	胆	dǎn	膜	mó
观	guān	牛	niú	欣	xīn	肺	fèi	膛	táng
规	guī	牵	qiān	新	xīn	骨	gǔ	腾	téng
见	jiàn	牲	shēng	**96 爪**		胡	hú	腿	tuǐ
觉	jiào, jué	特	tè	爱	ài	脉	mài	膝	xī
览	lǎn	物	wù	采	cǎi	胖	pàng	腥	xīng
88 父		牺	xī	爬	pá	胜	shèng	腰	yāo
爸	bà	**91 手**		受	shòu	胃	wèi	**98 欠**	
爹	diē	掰	bāi	爪	zhuǎ	**6 strokes**		歌	gē
斧	fǔ	拜	bài	**97 月**		脆	cuì	款	kuǎn
父	fù	攀	pān	月	yuè	胳	gē	欧	ōu

穿	chuān	**126 主**		**134 页**		蚊	wén	竿	gǎn
窗	chuāng	责	zé	颁	bān	虾	xiā	笼	lóng
窜	cuàn	主	zhǔ	颤	chàn	蚁	yǐ	笋	sǔn
窖	jiào	**127 母**		颠	diān	蛀	zhù	笑	xiào
究	jiū	毒	dú	顶	dǐng	**7–11 strokes**		**6–7 strokes**	
空	kōng, kòng	每	měi	顿	dùn	蝉	chán	策	cè
窟	kū	母	mǔ	额	é	蠢	chǔn	筹	chóu
窟	kū	**128 去**		顾	gù	蝶	dié	答	dā, dá
帘	lián	去	qù	颈	jǐng	蛾	é	等	děng
隆	lóng	**129 疋**		颗	kē	蜂	fēng	简	jiǎn
窃	qiè	楚	chǔ	领	lǐng	蝴	hú	筋	jīn
穷	qióng	**130 皮**		频	pín	蝗	huáng	筷	kuài
突	tū	皮	pí	颇	pō	蜡	là	签	qiān
窝	wō	皱	zhòu	顷	qǐng	螺	luó	筛	shāi
窑	yáo	**131 老**		颂	sòng	蜜	mì	筒	tǒng
窄	zhǎi	考	kǎo	顺	shùn	蜻	qīng	筑	zhù
124 衤		老	lǎo	顽	wán	融	róng	**8–14 strokes**	
2–3 strokes		**132 耳**		颜	yán	蝇	yíng	簸	bǒ
袄	ǎo	耻	chǐ	页	yè	蜘	zhī	管	guǎn
补	bǔ	聪	cōng	颖	yǐng	**137 缶**		籍	jí
衬	chèn	耽	dān	预	yù	缸	gāng	箭	jiàn
初	chū	耳	ěr	**135 虍**		罐	guàn	篮	lán
衫	shān	聚	jù	虎	hǔ	缺	quē	篱	lí
4–8 strokes		联	lián	虏	lǔ	**138 舌**		箩	luó
被	bèi	聊	liáo	虚	xū	辞	cí	篇	piān
袱	fú	聋	lóng	**136 虫**		乱	luàn	算	suàn
裤	kù	聘	pìn	虫	chóng	**139 竹**		箱	xiāng
袍	páo	取	qǔ	**1–6 strokes**		竹	zhú	**140 自**	
裙	qún	耸	sǒng	蚕	cán	**3–5 strokes**		鼻	bí
袜	wà	职	zhí	蛋	dàn	笆	bā	臭	chòu
袖	xiù	**133 西**		虹	hóng	笨	bèn	自	zì
裕	yù	覆	fù	蚂	mǎ	笔	bǐ	**141 舟**	
125 示		票	piào	蛮	mán	笛	dí	般	bān
禁	jìn	西	xī	蛇	shé	第	dì	舶	bó
示	shì	要	yāo, yào	蛙	wā	符	fú	舱	cāng

船 chuán	**7–11 strokes**	趁 chèn	躁 zào	**160 非**
航 háng	粹 cuì	赴 fù	踪 zōng	非 fēi
舰 jiàn	糕 gāo	赶 gǎn	**152 采**	靠 kào
艇 tǐng	糊 hú	趴 pā	番 fān	**161 酉**
舟 zhōu	精 jīng	起 qǐ	释 shì	酬 chóu
142 衣	糠 kāng	趣 qù	**153 豸**	醋 cù
表 biǎo	粮 liáng	趟 tàng	貌 mào	酱 jiàng
袋 dài	糖 táng	越 yuè	**154 身**	酷 kù
裂 liè	粤 yuè	走 zǒu	躲 duǒ	酶 méi
裳 shang	糟 zāo	**150 里**	身 shēn	酿 niàng
袭 xí	粥 zhōu	里 lǐ	躺 tǎng	配 pèi
衣 yī	籽 zǐ	野 yě	**155 角**	酸 suān
装 zhuāng	**145 艮**	**151 足**	触 chù	醒 xǐng
143 羊	既 jì	足 zú	角 jiǎo	酗 xù
差 chà	良 liáng	**3–5 strokes**	解 jiě	酝 yùn
盖 gài	**146 羽**	踩 cǎi	**156 言**	酌 zhuó
美 měi	翅 chì	跌 diē	警 jǐng	醉 zuì
群 qún	翻 fān	践 jiàn	譬 pì	**162 豆**
善 shàn	翘 qiào	距 jù	言 yán	登 dēng
羡 xiàn	翁 wēng	跨 kuà	誉 yù	豆 dòu
羞 xiū	翔 xiáng	跑 pǎo	**157 辛**	豌 wān
羊 yáng	耀 yào	跃 yuè	辫 biàn	**163 隹**
氧 yǎng	翼 yì	**6–12 strokes**	辩 biàn	雌 cí
着 zháo, zhe,	羽 yǔ	蹦 bèng	辨 biàn	雕 diāo
zhuó	**147 系**	蹈 dǎo	辜 gū	集 jí
144 米	繁 fán	跺 duò	辣 là	雀 què
米 mǐ	紧 jǐn	蹲 dūn	辟 pì	售 shòu
3–5 strokes	素 sù	跟 gēn	辛 xīn	雄 xióng
粗 cū	索 suǒ	跪 guì	**158 系**	雅 yǎ
粉 fěn	絮 xù	路 lù	系 xì	**164 青**
粪 fèn	紫 zǐ	踏 tā, tà	**159 束**	静 jìng
类 lèi	**148 麦**	踢 tī	束 shù	青 qīng
粒 lì	麦 mài	蹄 tí	整 zhěng	**165 鱼**
料 liào	**149 走**	跳 tiào		鲸 jīng
	超 chāo			鲁 lǔ

鲜	xiān	霜	shuāng	**168 革**		题	tí	韵	yùn

鲜	xiān	霜	shuāng	**168 革**		题	tí	韵	yùn
鱼	yú	雾	wù	鞭	biān	**170 食**		**173 麻**	
166 雨		需	xū	革	gé	餐	cān	麻	má
霸	bà	霞	xiá	鞠	jū	食	shí	摩	mó
雹	báo	雪	xuě	勒	lè	**171 鬼**		**174 黑**	
霍	huò	雨	yǔ	鞋	xié	鬼	guǐ	黑	hēi
雷	léi	震	zhèn	靴	xuē	魂	hún	墨	mò
零	líng	**167 齿**		**169 是**		魔	mó	默	mò
露	lù	齿	chǐ	匙	chí, shì	**172 音**			
霉	méi					音	yīn		

Stroke Index

This index lists all characters in this dictionary according to the number of strokes used to write them. Characters with the same number of strokes are grouped together according to the first stroke used. These groups are listed in the following order:

1. 一 (including ㇀ ㇏)
2. 丨 (including 丿 ㇂)
3. 丿 (including 丿 一 丿)
4. 丶 (including 丶 ㇏)
5. ㇆ (including 乛 ㇇ ㇉ ㇌ ㇟ 乙 ㇊)
6. ㇊ (including ㇆ ㇈ ㇉ ㇇)

Within each group, characters are arranged alphabetically according to *pinyin*.

1–2 strokes				**丨**				
一		卜	bó, bǔ			寸	cùn	于	yú, yù
厂	chǎng					大	dà, dài	丈	zhàng
丁	dīng	**丿**		刀	dāo	干	gān, gàn	**丨**	
二	èr	八	bā	刁	diāo	工	gōng	巾	jīn
弓	gōng	儿	ér	了	le, liǎo	亏	kuī	口	kǒu
七	qī	几	jī, jǐ	力	lì	三	sān	山	shān
十	shí	九	jiǔ	乙	yǐ	尸	shī	上	shàng
一	yī, yí, yì	人	rén	又	yòu	士	shì	小	xiǎo
		入	rù	**3 strokes**		土	tǔ		
				一		万	wàn	**丿**	
				才	cái	下	xià	川	chuān

凡 fán	丰 fēng	中 zhōng	勾 yún	本 běn
个 gè	夫 fū	ノ	爪 zhuǎ	丙 bǐng
及 jí	戈 gē	、	、	布 bù
久 jiǔ	互 hù	币 bì	订 dìng	打 dǎ
么 me	井 jǐng	仓 cāng	斗 dòu	东 dōng
乞 qǐ	巨 jù	长 cháng,	方 fāng	甘 gān
千 qiān	开 kāi	zhǎng	户 hù	功 gōng
勺 sháo	历 lì	仇 chóu	火 huǒ	古 gǔ
丸 wán	木 mù	从 cóng	讥 jī	击 jī
夕 xī	匹 pǐ	丹 dān	计 jì	节 jié
义 yì	区 qū	乏 fá	亢 kàng	刊 kān
亿 yì	犬 quǎn	反 fǎn	六 liù	可 kě
、	市 shì	分 fēn, fèn	认 rèn	厉 lì
广 guǎng	世 shì	风 fēng	为 wéi, wèi	龙 lóng
门 mén	太 tài	凤 fèng	文 wén	灭 miè
亡 wáng	天 tiān	父 fù	心 xīn	末 mò
之 zhī	厅 tīng	公 gōng	忆 yì	平 píng
丁	屯 tún	勾 gōu		扑 pū
叉 chā	瓦 wǎ	化 huà	丁	巧 qiǎo
飞 fēi	王 wáng	介 jiè	巴 bā	切 qiè
己 jǐ	无 wú	斤 jīn	办 bàn	去 qù
马 mǎ	五 wǔ	今 jīn	尺 chǐ	扔 rēng
刃 rèn	牙 yá	仅 jǐn	丑 chǒu	石 shí
卫 wèi	艺 yì	毛 máo	队 duì	示 shì
习 xí	尤 yóu	牛 niú	孔 kǒng	术 shù
也 yě	友 yǒu	片 piàn	劝 quàn	未 wèi
已 yǐ	元 yuán	仆 pú	书 shū	轧 yà
子 zǐ, zi	云 yún	气 qì	双 shuāng	右 yòu
ㄣ	扎 zhā	欠 qiàn	引 yǐn	玉 yù
女 nǚ	支 zhī	仁 rén	予 yú	扎 zhā
乡 xiāng	专 zhuān	仍 réng	丁	正 zhēng,
与 yǔ	丨	什 shén	比 bǐ	zhèng
4 strokes	贝 bèi	升 shēng	幻 huàn	左 zuǒ
一	见 jiàn	氏 shì	以 yǐ	丨
不 bú, bù	内 nèi	手 shǒu	允 yǔn	凹 āo
车 chē	日 rì	乌 wū	**5 strokes**	叭 bā
歹 dǎi	少 shǎo, shào	午 wǔ	一	北 běi
	水 shuǐ	勿 wù	艾 ài	出 chū
	止 zhǐ	凶 xiōng	扒 bá, pá	旦 dàn
		月 yuè		

来 lái	运 yùn	园 yuán	你 nǐ	宏 hóng
劳 láo	找 zhǎo	帐 zhàng	刨 páo	沪 hù
李 lǐ	折 zhē, zhé	助 zhù	伸 shēn	怀 huái
丽 lì	址 zhǐ	状 zhuàng	身 shēn	间 jiān, jiàn
励 lì	志 zhì	足 zú	私 sī	究 jiū
连 lián	抓 zhuā		体 tǐ	库 kù
两 liǎng	走 zǒu	**丿**	条 tiáo	快 kuài
抡 lūn		伴 bàn	秃 tū	况 kuàng
麦 mài	**丨**	狈 bèi	妥 tuǒ	牢 láo
拟 nǐ	吧 ba	兵 bīng	位 wèi	冷 lěng
尿 niào	别 bié	伯 bó	我 wǒ	沥 lì
扭 niǔ	步 bù	岔 chà	希 xī	疗 liáo
弄 nòng	财 cái	肠 cháng	系 xì	没 méi
抛 pāo	吵 chǎo	彻 chè	仙 xiān	闷 mēn, mèn
批 pī	呈 chéng	伺 cì, sì	秀 xiù	亩 mǔ
抢 qiǎng	串 chuàn	囱 cōng	役 yì	判 pàn
芹 qín	吹 chuī	但 dàn	饮 yǐn	沛 pèi
求 qiú	呆 dāi	岛 dǎo	迎 yíng	评 píng
却 què	盯 dīng, dìng	低 dī	佣 yōng	沏 qī
扰 rǎo	吨 dūn	钉 dìng	犹 yóu	柴 qī
韧 rèn	吩 fēn	肚 dù	余 yú	启 qǐ
声 shēng	岗 gāng	返 fǎn	皂 zào	弃 qì
寿 shòu	旱 hàn	饭 fàn	针 zhēn	汽 qì
束 shù	吼 hǒu	佛 fó, fú	住 zhù	穷 qióng
苏 sū	坚 jiān	肝 gān	作 zuò	任 rèn
坛 tán	旷 kuàng	告 gào	坐 zuò	沙 shā
投 tóu	困 kùn	估 gū		社 shè
吞 tūn	里 lǐ	龟 guī	**、**	识 shí
违 wéi	男 nán	含 hán	补 bǔ	诉 sù
巫 wū	呕 ǒu	何 hé	灿 càn	汰 tài
孝 xiào	时 shí	角 jiǎo	沉 chén	完 wán
形 xíng	听 tīng	近 jìn	初 chū	汪 wāng
杏 xìng	围 wéi	灸 jiǔ	床 chuáng	忘 wàng
芽 yá	吻 wěn	狂 kuáng	词 cí	沃 wò
严 yán	呜 wū	利 lì	弟 dì	闲 xián
杨 yáng	县 xiàn	邻 lín	冻 dòng	辛 xīn
医 yī	肖 xiào	卵 luǎn	兑 duì	汹 xiōng
抑 yì	呀 yā, ya	乱 luàn	泛 fàn	序 xù
远 yuǎn	邮 yóu	每 měi	沟 gōu	言 yán
	员 yuán	免 miǎn	罕 hǎn	

咏	yǒng	佳	jiā	侄	zhí	炕	kàng	沿	yán
咋	ză	金	jīn	制	zhì	刻	kè	炎	yán
帜	zhì	径	jìng	质	zhì	空	kōng,	夜	yè
忠	zhōng	例	lì	肿	zhǒng		kòng	宜	yí
卓	zhuó	侣	lǚ	周	zhōu	郎	láng	泳	yǒng
		命	mìng			帘	lián	油	yóu
	丿	牧	mù		丶	怜	lián	育	yù
爸	bà	念	niàn	宝	bǎo	泪	lèi	泽	zé
版	bǎn	爬	pá	变	biàn	炉	lú	闸	zhá
饱	bǎo	佩	pèi	波	bō	庙	miào	沾	zhān
卑	bēi	朋	péng	泊	bó	盲	máng	沼	zhǎo
备	bèi	贫	pín	怖	bù	氓	máng	郑	zhèng
彼	bǐ	凭	píng	诧	chà	泌	mì	治	zhì
秉	bǐng	迫	pò	炒	chǎo	沫	mò	宙	zhòu
采	cǎi	侨	qiáo	衬	chèn	闹	nào	注	zhù
侧	cè	侵	qīn	诚	chéng	泥	ní	宗	zōng
侈	chǐ	乳	rǔ	宠	chǒng	泞	níng		
垂	chuí	刹	shā	炊	chuī	顷	qǐng		乛
的	de, dí	舍	shě, shè	单	dān	怕	pà	承	chéng
钓	diào	使	shǐ	诞	dàn	庞	páng	孤	gū
肪	fáng	侍	shì	底	dǐ	泡	pào	函	hán
肥	féi	饰	shì	店	diàn	泣	qì	驾	jià
肺	fèi	受	shòu	定	dìng	浅	qiǎn	艰	jiān
氛	fēn	饲	sì	法	fǎ	怯	qiè	建	jiàn
肤	fū	所	suǒ	房	fáng	券	quàn	降	jiàng
服	fú	贪	tān	放	fàng	衫	shān	届	jiè
斧	fǔ	兔	tù	废	fèi	审	shěn	居	jū
供	gōng,	往	wǎng	沸	fèi	诗	shī	隶	lì
	gòng	委	wěi	府	fǔ	实	shí	陋	lòu
		物	wù	该	gāi	试	shì	录	lù
狗	gǒu	胁	xié	怪	guài	视	shì	弥	mí
谷	gǔ	欣	xīn	官	guān	祥	xiáng	陌	mò
股	gǔ	依	yī	河	hé	享	xiǎng	屈	qū
刮	guā	鱼	yú	话	huà	泄	xiè	刷	shuā
乖	guāi	胀	zhàng	剂	jì	泻	xiè	肃	sù
和	hé	侦	zhēn	肩	jiān	性	xìng	弦	xián
忽	hū	征	zhēng	郊	jiāo	学	xué	限	xiàn
狐	hú	知	zhī	京	jīng	询	xún	驻	zhù
昏	hūn	肢	zhī	净	jìng				
货	huò			卷	juǎn				
季	jì								

皇	huáng	须	xū	姜	jiāng	诵	sòng	眉	méi
急	jí	叙	xù	将	jiāng	剃	tì	屏	píng
剑	jiàn	选	xuǎn	奖	jiǎng	庭	tíng	柔	róu
饺	jiǎo	衍	yǎn	浇	jiāo	亭	tíng	屎	shǐ
狡	jiǎo	钥	yào	觉	jiào, jué	突	tū	退	tuì
矩	jǔ	盈	yíng	洁	jié	弯	wān	屋	wū
俊	jùn	狱	yù	诫	jiè	闻	wén	险	xiǎn
看	kān, kàn	怨	yuàn	津	jīn	诬	wū	逊	xùn
科	kē	怎	zěn	举	jǔ	误	wù	勇	yǒng
俩	liǎ	钟	zhōng	烤	kǎo	洗	xǐ	院	yuàn
铃	líng	种	zhǒng,	客	kè	宪	xiàn	昼	zhòu
律	lǜ		zhòng	烂	làn	宣	xuān		
脉	mài	追	zhuī	类	lèi	洋	yáng	绑	bǎng
贸	mào			炼	liàn	养	yǎng	怠	dài
勉	miǎn	、		亮	liàng	疫	yì	给	gěi, jǐ
秒	miǎo	哀	āi	浏	liú	音	yīn	绘	huì
胖	pàng	袄	ǎo	美	měi	诱	yòu	娇	jiāo
盆	pén	疤	bā	迷	mí	语	yǔ	绞	jiǎo
俏	qiào	扁	biǎn	恼	nǎo	炸	zhá	结	jiē, jié
钦	qīn	测	cè	逆	nì	洲	zhōu	皆	jiē
氢	qīng	差	chā, chà	浓	nóng	祝	zhù	经	jīng
秋	qiū	穿	chuān	派	pài	浊	zhuó	绝	jué
泉	quán	疮	chuāng	叛	pàn	咨	zī	姥	lǎo
饶	ráo	帝	dì	炮	pào	姿	zī	垒	lěi
牲	shēng	洞	dòng	柒	qī	籽	zǐ	络	luò
胜	shèng	度	dù	恰	qià	总	zǒng	怒	nù
狮	shī	阀	fá	洽	qià	祖	zǔ	绕	rào
食	shí	疯	fēng	前	qián			绒	róng
蚀	shí	宫	gōng	窃	qiè	除	chú	统	tǒng
适	shì	冠	guàn	亲	qīn	陡	dǒu	娃	wá
顺	shùn	闺	guī	染	rǎn	盾	dùn	姨	yí
俗	sú	阁	hé	洒	sǎ	费	fèi	姻	yīn
逃	táo	恨	hèn	神	shén	孩	hái		
侮	wǔ	恒	héng	施	shī	贺	hè	**10 strokes**	
狭	xiá	洪	hóng	室	shì	既	jì		
香	xiāng	恢	huī	首	shǒu	架	jià	挨	ái
卸	xiè	浑	hún	说	shuō	骄	jiāo	捌	bā
信	xìn	活	huó	烁	shuò	垦	kěn	班	bān
修	xiū	迹	jì	送	sòng	骆	luò	捕	bǔ
		济	jì						

宾 bīn
病 bìng
部 bù
瓷 cí
递 dì
涤 dí
调 diào, tiáo
读 dú
饿 è
烦 fán
诽 fěi
粉 fěn
浮 fú
高 gāo
海 hǎi
害 hài
浩 hào
烘 hōng
悔 huǐ
疾 jí
家 jiā
兼 jiān
浸 jìn
竞 jìng
酒 jiǔ
课 kè
宽 kuān
朗 lǎng
浪 làng
涝 lào
离 lí
恋 liàn
凉 liáng
谅 liàng
料 liào
凌 líng
流 liú
旅 lǚ
旁 páng

袍 páo
疲 pí
瓶 píng
剖 pōu
凄 qī
悄 qiāo
请 qǐng
拳 quán
容 róng
润 rùn
扇 shàn
烧 shāo
涉 shè
谁 shéi, shuí
衰 shuāi
谈 tán
唐 táng
烫 tàng
涛 tāo
疼 téng
涕 tì
涂 tú
袜 wà
悟 wù
席 xí
消 xiāo
宵 xiāo
效 xiào
羞 xiū
袖 xiù
畜 xù
烟 yān
宴 yàn
谊 yì
益 yì
涌 yǒng
浴 yù
冤 yuān
悦 yuè

阅 yuè
宰 zǎi
窄 zhǎi
站 zhàn
涨 zhǎng
症 zhèng
衷 zhōng
诸 zhū
烛 zhú
准 zhǔn
资 zī
座 zuò

┐

剥 bāo, bō
剧 jù
恳 kěn
陪 péi
弱 ruò
桑 sāng
陶 táo
通 tōng
陷 xiàn
屑 xiè
验 yàn
预 yù
展 zhǎn

└

继 jì
绢 juàn
能 néng
娘 niáng
射 shè
绣 xiù
娱 yú

11 strokes

一

菠 bō
埠 bù

菜 cài
捶 chuí
措 cuò
掂 diān
掉 diào
堵 dǔ
堆 duī
辅 fú
副 fù
梗 gěng
菇 gū
硅 guī
黄 huáng
基 jī
检 jiǎn
教 jiāo, jiào
接 jiē
捷 jié
救 jiù
菊 jú
据 jú
掘 jué
菌 jūn
勘 kān
控 kòng
勒 lè
理 lǐ
辆 liàng
聊 liáo
聋 lóng
掠 lüè
啰 luō
萝 luó
梅 méi
萌 méng
梦 mèng
描 miáo
捻 niǎn
排 pái

培 péi
捧 pěng
票 piào
萍 píng
戚 qī
掐 qiā
球 qiú
娶 qǔ
啥 shà
梢 shāo
奢 shē
盛 shèng
授 shòu
爽 shuǎng
硕 shuò
探 tàn
掏 tāo
萄 tao
梯 tī
桶 tǒng
推 tuī
袭 xí
掀 xiān
厢 xiāng
械 xiè
酗 xù
雪 xuě
掩 yǎn
营 yíng
域 yù
酝 yùn
职 zhí
掷 zhì
著 zhù

丨

崩 bēng
蝉 chán
常 cháng
唱 chàng

棒	bàng	棉	mián	琢	zuó	装	zhuāng	锐	ruì
逼	bī	棚	péng			紫	zǐ	筛	shāi
博	bó	葡	pú	丨		最	zuì	稍	shāo
裁	cái	期	qī	悲	bēi			甥	shēng
插	chā	欺	qī	辈	bèi	丿		剩	shèng
搀	chān	棋	qí	敞	chǎng	傲	ào	释	shì
超	chāo	翘	qiáo	喘	chuǎn	奥	ào	舒	shū
朝	cháo	琴	qín	跌	diē	掰	bāi	税	shuì
趁	chèn	趋	qū	赌	dǔ	傍	bàng	锁	suǒ
厨	chú	确	què	幅	fú	惫	bèi	毯	tǎn
葱	cōng	惹	rě	喊	hǎn	策	cè	艇	tǐng
搓	cuō	揉	róu	喝	hē	馋	chán	筒	tǒng
搭	dā	萨	sà	黑	hēi	程	chéng	稀	xī
堤	dī	散	sǎn, sàn	喉	hóu	惩	chěng	销	xiāo
董	dǒng	森	sēn	辉	huī	锄	chú	锌	xīn
搁	gē	斯	sī	践	jiàn	储	chǔ	锈	xiù
辜	gū	搜	sōu	晶	jīng	答	dā, dá	循	xún
棺	guān	塔	tǎ	景	jǐng	氮	dàn	粤	yuè
棍	gùn	提	tí	喇	lǎ	等	děng	智	zhì
葫	hú	替	tì	量	liáng,	短	duǎn	筑	zhù
惠	huì	椭	tuǒ		liàng	鹅	é	铸	zhù
惑	huò	握	wò	晾	liàng	番	fān		
颊	jiá	喜	xǐ	帽	mào	锋	fēng	丶	
椒	jiāo	雄	xióng	跑	pǎo	傅	fù	谤	bàng
搅	jiǎo	雅	yǎ	赔	péi	猴	hóu	遍	biàn
揭	jiē	雁	yàn	喷	pēn	猾	huá	曾	céng
敬	jìng	壹	yī	嵌	qiàn	集	jí	窗	chuāng
揪	jiū	椅	yǐ	晴	qíng	焦	jiāo	窜	cuàn
堪	kān	硬	yìng	啥	shá	街	jiē	道	dào
棵	kē	援	yuán	赏	shǎng	筋	jīn	渡	dù
款	kuǎn	越	yuè	暑	shǔ	腊	là	惰	duò
葵	kuí	暂	zàn	蛙	wā	链	liàn	愤	fèn
落	là, luò	葬	zàng	喂	wèi	猎	liè	粪	fèn
揽	lǎn	朝	zhāo	晰	xī	鲁	lǔ	富	fù
棱	léng	植	zhí	啸	xiào	牌	pái	溉	gài
联	lián	殖	zhí	喧	xuān	脾	pí	港	gǎng
裂	liè	煮	zhǔ	遗	yí	铺	pū	割	gē
硫	liú	棕	zōng	喻	yù	腔	qiāng	雇	gù
搂	lǒu	揍	zòu	遇	yù	禽	qín	寒	hán
				凿	záo	然	rán	湖	hú

Chinese–English

A

阿 **ā** PREFIX (used to address certain relatives or friends to convey sentiment of intimacy)
阿爸 **ā bà** daddy
阿婆 **ā pó** (maternal) granny
阿拉伯文 **Ālābówén** N the Arabic language (especially the writing)
阿拉伯语 **Ālābóyǔ** N the Arabic language
阿姨 **āyí** N mother's sister

NOTES: (1) 阿姨 **āyí** is a form of address used by a child for a woman about his/her mother's age.(2) 阿姨 **āyí** is also used by adults and children for domestic helpers and female nursery staff.

啊 **ā** I INTERJ (used to express strong emotions such as surprise, admiration, regret etc.) oh, ah II PARTICLE (attached to a sentence to express strong emotions such as surprise, admiration, regret etc.)

哎 **āi** INTERJ (used to attract attention or express surprise)
哎呀 **āiyā** INTERJ (used to express surprise or annoyance)
哎哟 **āiyō** INTERJ (used to express surprise or pain)

唉 **āi** INTERJ 1 (as a sigh) alas 2 (as a response) yes, right

哀 **āi** I V mourn II ADJ grieved

哀悼 **āidào** V mourn
哀求 **āiqiú** V entreat, implore

挨 **ái** V undergo (some painful or unpleasant experience)

癌 **ái** N cancer
肺癌 **fèi'ái** lung cancer
胃癌 **wèi'ái** stomach cancer

蔼 **ǎi** TRAD 藹 ADJ amiable, friendly (See 和蔼 **hé'ǎi**)

矮 **ǎi** ADJ (of a person or plant) of short stature, short

爱 **ài** TRAD 愛 V 1 love 2 like, be fond of
爱戴 **àidài** V love and esteem
爱好 **àihào** I V like, be interested in, have as a hobby II N hobby, interest
爱护 **àihù** V care for and protect, cherish
爱面子 **ài miànzi** V be overly concerned about one's image
爱情 **àiqíng** N romantic love
爱情小说 **àiqíng xiǎoshuō** love story, romance fiction
爱人 **àirén** N husband or wife

NOTE: 爱人 **àirén** as husband or wife is only used in Mainland China as a colloquialism. On formal occasions 丈夫 **zhàngfu** (husband) and 妻子 **qīzi** (wife) are used instead. Now there is a decreasing tendency to use 爱人 **àirén** in China. In its place 先生 **xiānsheng** and 太太 **tàitai** are used to refer to husband and wife, a long established practice in Taiwan, Hong Kong and overseas Chinese communities.

爱惜 **àixī** V cherish, value highly
爱惜自己的名誉 **àixī zìjǐ de míngyù** treasure one's reputation

碍 **ài** TRAD 礙 V hinder
碍事 **àishì** V be in one's way

艾 **ài** N mugwort

艾滋病 àizībìng N AIDS

NOTE: 艾滋病 is a transliteration, i.e. reproducing the sounds of the English word AIDS.

隘
隘 ài ADJ narrow (See 狭隘 xiá'ài)

安
安 ān ADJ peaceful, safe

安定 āndìng ADJ peaceful and stable
安静 ānjìng ADJ quiet, peaceful, serene
安乐死 ānlèsǐ N euthanasia
安宁 ānníng ADJ calm, composed
安排 ānpái V arrange, make arrangements, plan
安全 ānquán I N security, safety
　安全带 ānquándài safety belt
　安全帽 ānquánmào safety helmet
　II ADJ safe, secure
安慰 ānwèi V comfort, console
安稳 ānwěn ADJ safe and secure
安详 ānxiáng ADJ (of facial expression) serene, composed
安心 ānxīn ADJ be relaxed and content
安置 ānzhì V find an appropriate place (for people)
安装 ānzhuāng V install, fix
　安装空调设备 ānzhuāng kōngtiáo shèbèi install an air-conditioner

岸
岸 àn N bank or shore (of a river, lake, or sea)
　海岸 hǎi àn coast
　河岸 hé'àn river bank
　上岸 shàng àn go ashore

按
按 àn PREP according to, in accordance with
按揭 ànjiē N mortgage
按期 ànqī ADV on schedule
按时 ànshí ADV according to a fixed time, on time
按照 ànzhào PREP according to, in accordance with (same as 按 àn)

案
案 àn N case, plan
案件 ànjiàn N case, legal case
　民事案件 mínshì ànjiàn civil case
　刑事案件 xíngshì ànjiàn criminal case

调查案件 diàochá ànjiàn investigate a (police) case

暗
暗 àn ADJ dark, dim

暗暗 àn'àn ADV secretly
暗暗得意 àn'àn déyì secretly very pleased with oneself
暗淡 àndàn ADJ dim, gloomy
　光线暗淡的房间 guāngxiàn àndàn de fángjiān a dimly-lit room
暗杀 ànshā V assassinate
暗示 ànshì I V drop a hint II N hint
暗室 ànshì N darkroom (for developing films)
暗中 ànzhōng ADV in the dark, in secret
暗中帮忙 ànzhōng bāngmáng secretly help

肮
肮 āng TRAD 骯 as in 肮脏
肮脏 āngzāng ADJ dirty, unclean

昂
昂 áng V hold (the head) high

昂起头 ángqǐ tóu hold the head high
昂贵 ángguì ADJ very expensive, costly
昂扬 ángyáng ADJ in high spirits

凹
凹 āo ADJ concave, sunken, dented

凹凸不平 āotū bùpíng rugged, full of bumps and holes

熬
熬 áo V stew, boil

熬汤 áo tāng prepare soup by simmering

袄
袄 ǎo TRAD 襖 N a Chinese-style coat/jacket
棉袄 mián'ǎo padded coat

傲
傲 ào ADJ arrogant (See 骄傲 jiāo'ào)

奥
奥 ào ADJ deep, profound

奥林匹克运动会 Àolínpǐkè Yùndònghuì N Olympic Games
奥秘 àomì N deep secret, profound mystery
探索奥秘 tànsuǒ àomì explore a mystery

澳
澳 ào N deep waters

澳大利亚 Àodàlìyà N Australia

B

八 **bā** NUM eight

捌 **bā** NUM Same as 八 bā

扒 **bā** v **1** strip off, take off (clothes, etc.) **2** hold on to, cling to

叭 **bā** ONOMATOPEIA crack

巴 **bā** N cheek

巴结 bājie v flatter, fawn on

芭 **bā** N flower

芭蕾舞 bālěiwǔ N ballet

笆 **bā** N bamboo fence (See 篱笆 líbā)

疤 **bā** N scar (See 伤疤 shāngbā)

吧 **bā** N bar

酒吧 jiǔbā wine bar, bar, pub
网吧 wǎngbā Internet café

拔 **bá** v pull out, pull up

拔苗助长 bá miáo zhù zhǎng pull up a young plant to help it grow (→ spoil things by excessive enthusiasm)

把 **1** **bǎ** PREP (used before a noun or pronoun to indicate it is the object of the sentence)

把 **2** **bǎ** **I** N handle **II** M. WD **1** (for objects with handles) **2** a handful of
一把刀 yì bǎ dāo a knife
一把米 yì bǎ mǐ a handful of rice

把柄 bǎbǐng N **1** handle **2** something that may be used against someone
抓住了他的把柄 zhuāzhùle tāde bǎbǐng have got evidence that may be used against him

把关 bǎguān v check on

把手 bǎshǒu N handle, handrail

把握 bǎwò **I** N being certain and assured, confidence **II** v seize (an opportunity)
把握时机 bǎwò shíjī seize an opportunity

把戏 bǎxì N trick
玩把戏 wán bǎxì play a trick

爸 **bà** N dad, daddy, papa

爸爸 bàba N daddy, papa

坝 **bà** TRAD 壩 N dam, embankment
大坝 dàbà big dam

霸 **bà** **I** N tyrant **II** v dominate, rule by might
恶霸 èbà local tyrant

霸道 bàdào ADJ overbearing, high-handed

霸权 bàquán N hegemony
霸权主义 bàquán zhǔyì hegemonism

霸占 bàzhàn v occupy or possess by force
霸占民房 bàzhàn mínfáng seize possession of private property by force

罢 **bà** TRAD 罷 v stop

罢工 bàgōng v stage a strike, down tools

吧 **ba** PARTICLE **1** (used to make a suggestion) **2** (used to indicate supposition)

掰 **bāi** v break off with hands

白 **bái** **I** ADJ white **II** ADV in vain, without any result **III** ADV for free

> **NOTE:** In Chinese tradition, white symbolizes death and is the color for funerals.

白白 báibái ADV in vain, for nothing

白菜 báicài N cabbage (棵 kē)

白酒 báijiǔ N spirits usually distilled from sorghum or rice, white spirits

白开水 báikāishuǐ N plain boiled water

白领 báilǐng N white-collar worker

白人 báirén N Caucasian person, Caucasian people

白天 báitiān N daytime

百 **bǎi** NUM hundred
三百元 sānbǎi yuán three hundred yuan/dollars

> **NOTE:** 百 bǎi may have the abstract sense of *a great deal of* and *a multitude of*. This sense can be found in many expressions, e.g. 百闻不如一见 Bǎi wén bùrú yí jiàn,

which literally means *A hundred sounds are not as good as one sight* and may be translated as *Seeing is believing*.

百货 **bǎihuò** N general merchandise
百货商店 **bǎihuò shāngdiàn** department store
百日咳 **bǎirìké** N whooping cough
百姓 **bǎixìng** N common people

NOTE: 老百姓 **lǎobǎixìng** is also used to mean "common people".

柏 **bǎi** N cypress

柏树 **bǎishù** cypress tree, cypress

摆 **bǎi** TRAD 擺 V put, place, arrange

摆动 **bǎidòng** V sway, swing
摆脱 **bǎituō** V break away from, shake off

败 **bài** TRAD 敗 V be defeated

败坏 **bàihuài** V ruin, corrupt
道德败坏 **dàodé bàihuài** rotten morals

拜 **bài** V do obeisance, pay respect to

拜访 **bàifǎng** V pay a visit (to a senior person), make a courtesy call
拜会 **bàihuì** V make an official call
拜年 **bài nián** V pay a New Year's call, wish someone a Happy New Year

班 **bān** N 1 class (in school) 2 shift (in a workplace)

加班 **jiābān** work overtime
上班 **shàngbān** go to work
下班 **xiàbān** finish work
班机 **bānjī** N airliner, flight
班长 **bānzhǎng** N leader (of a class in school, a squad in the army, etc.)

斑 **bān** N spot, speck

斑点 **bāndiǎn** spot, stain
斑马 **bānmǎ** N zebra

般 **bān** N kind, sort (See 一般 **yìbān**)

搬 **bān** V move (heavy objects)

搬不动 **bān bu dòng** cannot move/cannot be moved
搬得动 **bān de dòng** can move/can be moved
搬家 **bānjiā** V move (house)
搬运 **bānyùn** V transport, move
搬运工人 **bānyùn gōngrén** mover

颁 **bān** V issue, confer on

颁布 **bānbù** V promulgate, proclaim
颁发 **bānfā** V issue, distribute
颁发奖状 **bānfā jiǎngzhuàng** issue a certificate of merit

扳 **bān** V pull, turn

扳手 **bānshǒu** N spanner, wrench

板 **bǎn** N board

木板 **mùbǎn** wooden plank

版 **bǎn** N printing plate

第一版 **dìyī bǎn** the first edition

办 **bàn** TRAD 辦 V handle, manage

办法 **bànfǎ** N 1 way of doing things 2 method
想办法 **xiǎng bànfǎ** think up a plan, find a way of doing things
有办法 **yǒu bànfǎ** have a way with ..., be resourceful
没有办法 **méiyǒu bànfǎ** there's nothing we can do
办公 **bàngōng** V work (as a white-collar worker, usually in an office)
办公大楼 **bàngōng dàlóu** office building
办公时间 **bàngōng shíjiān** office hours, working hours
办公室 **bàngōngshì** office (间 jiān)
办理 **bànlǐ** V deal with, go through
办事 **bànshì** V conduct affairs, manage affairs
办学 **bànxué** V run a school

半 **bàn** M. WD half

半岛 **bàndǎo** N peninsula
九龙半岛 **Jiǔlóng bàndǎo** Kowloon Peninsula (in Hong Kong)
半径 **bànjìng** N radius

半路 bànlù N halfway, midway

半数 bànshù N half the number, half

半天 bàntiān N **1** half a day **2** a period of time felt to be very long; a very long time

半途而废 bàntú ér fèi IDIOM give up halfway

半夜 bànyè N midnight, at midnight

拌
伴 bàn V mix

伴 bàn N companion

同伴 tóngbàn companion

伴侣 bànlǚ N companion (especially husband or wife)

终身伴侣 zhōngshēn bànlǚ life-long companion, husband and wife

伴随 bànsuí V go along with, keep company

伴奏 bànzòu V accompany with musical instrument

扮 bàn V disguise as

扮演 bànyǎn V play the role of (a character in a play, movie, etc.)

瓣 bàn N petal, segment

花瓣 huābàn petal, flower petal

帮 bāng TRAD 幫 V help, assist

NOTE: 帮 bāng, 帮忙 bāngmáng and 帮助 bāngzhù are synonyms. Their differences are: (1) 帮忙 bāngmáng is a verb that takes no object, while 帮 bāng and 帮助 bāngzhù are usually followed by an object. (2) As verbs, 帮 bāng and 帮助 bāngzhù are interchangeable, but 帮 bāng is more colloquial than 帮助 bāngzhù. (3) 帮助 bāngzhù can also be used as a noun.

帮忙 bāngmáng V help, help out

NOTE: See note on 帮 bāng.

帮助 bāngzhù I V help, assist II N help, assistance

NOTE: See note on 帮 bāng.

邦 bāng N country

绑 bǎng TRAD 綁 V tie, bind (with a rope)

绑架 bǎngjià V kidnap

榜 bǎng N list of names, honor roll

榜样 bǎngyàng N (positive) example, role model

膀 bǎng N upper arm

翅膀 chìbǎng wing

傍 bàng V be close to

傍晚 bàngwǎn N dusk, at dusk

磅 bàng N (measurement for weight) pound

两磅牛肉 liǎng bàng niúròu two pounds of beef

谤 bàng TRAD 謗 V slander

诽谤 fěibàng slander

棒 bàng I N stick, club (根 gēn)

铁棒 tiěbàng iron bar

II ADJ strong, very good

棒球 bàngqiú N baseball

棒球场 bàngqiúchǎng baseball court

棒球运动员 bàngqiú yùndòngyuán baseball player

包 bāo I N parcel, bag

钱包 qiánbāo wallet, purse

书包 shūbāo schoolbag

邮包 yóubāo mailbag, parcel for posting

II V wrap up

包办 bāobàn V assume full responsibility for, do entirely by oneself

包办宴席 bāobàn yànxí (of a restaurant) take care of everything for banquets

包袱 bāofu N a bundle wrapped in a cloth-wrapper

包裹 bāoguǒ N parcel, package

包含 bāohán V contain, have as ingredients

包括 bāokuò V include, embrace

包围 bāowéi V surround, encircle, lay siege

包装 bāozhuāng N package, packaging
　包装材料 bāozhuāng cáiliào packaging material
包子 bāozi N steamed bun with filling

胞 **bāo** N the placenta
　细胞 xìbāo cell

剥 **bāo** V peel, peel off

薄 **báo** ADJ thin, flimsy

NOTE: See note on 薄 bó.

雹 **báo** N hail
　雹子 báozi hail

宝 **bǎo** TRAD 寶 N treasure
　宝岛 bǎodǎo treasure island
宝库 bǎokù treasure house
宝贝 bǎobèi N treasured object, treasure
　小宝贝 xiǎo bǎobèi (endearment for children) darling, dear
宝贵 bǎoguì ADJ valuable, precious
宝剑 bǎojiàn N double-edged sword (把 bǎ)
宝石 bǎoshí N precious stone

保 **bǎo** V conserve, protect

保安 bǎo'ān N security guard
保持 bǎochí V keep, maintain
保存 bǎocún V keep, save
保管 bǎoguǎn V take charge of
　保管员 bǎoguǎnyuán storekeeper
保护 bǎohù V protect, safeguard, conserve
保健 bǎojiàn N health care, health protection
　保健食品 bǎojiàn shípǐn health food
　妇幼保健 fùyòu bǎojiàn maternity and child care
保龄球 bǎolíngqiú N bowling
保留 bǎoliú V retain, reserve
保密 bǎomì V keep ... secret
　保密文件 bǎomì wénjiàn classified document
保姆 bǎomǔ N (children's) nurse, nanny
　当保姆 dāng bǎomǔ work as a nanny

保守 bǎoshǒu I V guard, keep II ADJ conservative
保卫 bǎowèi V defend
保温 bǎowēn V preserve heat
保险 bǎoxiǎn I ADJ safe, risk-free II V insure III N insurance
保险单 bǎoxiǎndān insurance policy
保险费 bǎoxiǎnfèi insurance premium
保险公司 bǎoxiǎn gōngsī insurance company
保养 bǎoyǎng V 1 take good care of one's health
　(人)保养得很好 (rén) bǎoyǎng de hěn hǎo (of people) well preserved
　2 maintain (automobiles, machines, etc.), keep in good state
　车辆保养 chēliàng bǎoyǎng vehicle maintenance
保障 bǎozhàng V secure, insure, guarantee
　社会保障 shèhuì bǎozhàng social security
保证 bǎozhèng I V guarantee, pledge II N guarantee
　产品保证书 chǎnpǐn bǎozhèngshū (product) quality guarantee
保重 bǎozhòng V take good care of oneself

堡 **bǎo** N fortress, castle
　堡垒 bǎolěi N fort, fortress

饱 **bǎo** TRAD 飽 ADJ having eaten one's fill, full
　饱吃一顿 bǎo chī yídùn have a square meal, eat to one's fill
吃得饱 chī de bǎo have enough to eat
吃不饱 chī bu bǎo not have enough to eat (→ not have enough food)

NOTE: It is customary for a Chinese host to ask a guest who seems to have finished the meal: 您吃饱了吗? Nín chī bǎo le ma? *Have you had (eaten) enough?* The guest is expected to reply: 吃饱了。多谢。您慢慢吃。 Chī bǎo le. Duō xiè. Nín mànman chī. *Yes, I have. Thank you. Please take your time to eat.*

饱和 bǎohé ADJ saturated

饱满 bǎomǎn ADJ full, plump

报 bào TRAD 報 I N newspaper (same as 报纸 bàozhǐ)

看报 kànbào read a newspaper

II v respond, reciprocate

报仇 bàochóu v avenge, revenge

报酬 bàochou N renumeration, reward

报酬很高 bàochou hěn gāo well-paid

报到 bàodào v report for duty, register

报道 bàodào (or 报导 bàodǎo) I v report (news), cover II N news story

独家报道 dújiā bàodào exclusive report

深入报道 shēnrù bàodào in-depth report

现场报道 xiànchǎng bàodào on-the-spot ("alive") report

报恩 bào'ēn v pay a debt of gratitude

报复 bàofù v retaliate, revenge

报告 bàogào I v report, make known II N report, talk (at a large-scale meeting) (份 fèn)

财务报告 cáiwù bàogào financial report

秘密报告 mìmì bàogào confidential report

报刊 bàokān N newspapers and periodicals, the press

报考 bàokǎo v enter oneself for an examination

报名 bàomíng v enter one's name, sign up, apply for (a place in school)

报社 bàoshè N newspaper office

报销 bàoxiāo v submit an expense account, get reimbursement

报纸 bàozhǐ N newspaper (张 zhāng, 份 fèn)

NOTE: In colloquial Chinese, 报 bào is often used instead of 报纸 bàozhǐ, e.g.: 你看得懂中文报吗? Nǐ kàndedǒng Zhōngwén bào ma? *Can you understand Chinese newspapers?*

抱 bào v hold ... in arms, embrace, hug

抱负 bàofù N aspiration, ambition

抱歉 bàoqiàn ADJ apologetic, be sorry, regretful

抱怨 bàoyuàn v complain, grumble

暴 bào ADJ fierce and brutal

暴动 bàodòng N rebellion, insurrection

暴力 bàolì N violence, brutal force

暴力电影 bàolì diànyǐng violent movie

有暴力倾向 yǒu bàolì qīngxiàng have a tendency to violence

暴露 bàolù v expose, lay bare

暴雨 bàoyǔ N rainstorm, torrential rain

爆 bào v explode

爆发 bàofā v break out, burst out

爆破 bàopò v demolish with dynamite

爆炸 bàozhà I v explode II N explosion

自杀炸弹爆炸 zìshā zhàdàn bàozhà the explosion of a suicide bomb

杯 bēi N cup, mug, glass (只 zhī)

杯子 bēizi cup, mug, glass

茶杯 chábēi teacup

酒杯 jiǔbēi wine glass

一杯茶/酒 yì bēi chá/jiǔ a cup of tea, a glass of wine

NOTE: 杯 bēi may denote either *cup*, *mug*, or *glass*. 杯 bēi is seldom used alone. It is usually suffixed with 子 zi: 杯子 bēizi, or combined with 茶 chá or 酒 jiǔ: 茶杯 chábēi, 酒杯 jiǔbēi.

背 bēi v carry ... on the back

背包 bēibāo N backpack, knapsack

卑 bēi ADJ 1 low and humble 2 mean, contemptible

卑鄙 bēibǐ ADJ contemptible, despicable

卑鄙小人 bēibǐ xiǎorén contemptible person/people

碑 bēi N stone tablet

纪念碑 jìniànbēi monument

悲 bēi N grieved

悲哀 bēi'āi ADJ deeply grieved

悲惨 bēicǎn ADJ miserable, tragic

悲愤 bēifèn ADJ very sad and angry, filled with grief and indignation

悲观 bēiguān ADJ pessimistic

悲观主义 bēiguānzhǔyì pessimism
悲观者 bēiguānzhě pessimist
悲剧 bēijù N tragedy
悲伤 bēishāng ADJ deeply sorrowful
悲痛 bēitòng ADJ deeply grieved, agonized, with deep sorrow

北 **běi** N north, northern

北边 běibian N north side, to the north, in the north
北方 běifāng N northern region
北极 běijí the North Pole (← the north extreme)
北极星 běijíxīng the North Star, Polaris
北京 Běijīng N Beijing (Peking) (the capital of the People's Republic of China)
北面 běimiàn N Same as 北边 běibian

辈 **bèi** TRAD 輩 N generation, lifetime

贝 **bèi** TRAD 貝 N shellfish

贝壳 bèiké N shell

狈 **bèi** TRAD 狽 N a legendary beast, similar to the wolf

备 **bèi** TRAD 備 V prepare

备忘录 bèiwànglù N memorandum, memo
备用 bèiyòng V reserve, spare
  备用轮胎 bèiyòng lúntāi spare tire

惫 **bèi** TRAD 憊 ADJ fatigued

背 **bèi** I V 1 turn away, leave, go away
2 learn by heart II N back

背面 bèimiàn N reverse side, the back of an object
背叛 bèipàn V betray
  背叛…的信任 bèipàn…de xìnrèn betray the trust of …
背诵 bèisòng V repeat from memory
背心 bèixīn N vest, waistcoat

被 **bèi** PREP by (introducing the doer of an action)

被动 bèidòng ADJ passive
  被动式 bèidòngshì (in grammar) the passive voice
  被动吸烟 bèidòng xīyān passive smoking
被告(人) bèigào(rén) N defendant

被迫 bèipò V be forced to, be compelled to
被子 bèizi N quilt, blanket (条 tiáo)

倍 **bèi** M. WORD (-fold, times)

倍数 bèishù N (in math) multiple

奔 **bēn** V run fast

奔驰 bēnchí V (of animals and vehicles) run fast, speed
奔跑 bēnpǎo V run fast, whizz
奔腾 bēnténg V gallop

本 **běn** I N principal, capital

赔本 péi běn lose one's capital in investments or other business dealings
II M. WD (for books, magazines, etc.)
一本书 yì běn shū a book
III ADJ this one, one's own

NOTE: 本 běn in the sense of *this one* is only used on formal occasions.

本地 běndì N this locality
本来 běnlái ADV originally, at first
本领 běnlǐng N skill, ability, capability
本能 běnnéng N instinct, intuition
  求生的本能 qiúshēng de běnnéng the instinct to survive
本钱 běnqián N the money with which one makes investments or conducts other business dealings, capital
本事 běnshì N ability, capability

NOTE: 本领 běnlǐng and 本事 běnshì are synonyms, but 本领 běnlǐng emphasizes skills while 本事 běnshì has a more general sense of "the ability to get things done" and may be used with negative connotations.

本性 běnxìng N natural character, inherent quality
本质 běnzhì N innate character, true nature
本子 běnzi N notebook (本 běn)

笨 **bèn** ADJ dumb, stupid

笨蛋 bèndàn N fool, idiot
笨重 bènzhòng ADJ heavy and cumbersome
笨拙 bènzhuō ADJ clumsy

崩 **bēng** v collapse

崩溃 **bēngkuì** v collapse, crumble

绷 **bēng** TRAD 繃 v stretch tight

绷带 **bēngdài** N bandage

甭 **béng** ADV (contraction of 不用 **búyòng**) don't

蹦 **bèng** v jump

蹦床 **bèngchuáng** trampoline

蹦极跳 **bèngjítiào** bungee jump

逼 **bī** v 1 force, compel 2 get close to, press on towards

逼近 **bījìn** v close in on, gain on

逼迫 **bīpò** v force, coerce

鼻 **bí** N nose

鼻子 **bízi** the nose

鼻涕 **bítì** N nasal mucus

比 **bǐ** I PREP (introducing the object that is compared with the subject of a sentence), than II v compete, compare, contrast

比方 **bǐfang** N example, analogy

打比方 **dǎ bǐfang** make an analogy

比分 **bǐfēn** N score (of a game or sporting competition)

比价 **bǐjià** N 1 price ratio 2 exchange rate

比较 **bǐjiào** I v compare

和…比较 **hé…bǐjiào** compare ... with

II ADV relatively, quite, to some degree

比例 **bǐlì** N percentage

比如 **bǐrú** CONJ for example

NOTE: In spoken Chinese you can also use 比如说 **bǐrúshuō**.

比赛 **bǐsài** I v compete, have a match II N competition, match, game

比赛项目 **bǐsài xiàngmù** event (of a sports meet)

参加比赛 **cānjiā bǐsài** participate in a game (or sports event)

和跟…比赛 **hé/gēn…bǐsài** have a match/race with

看比赛 **kàn bǐsài** watch a game/sports event

比喻 **bǐyù** N metaphor

比重 **bǐzhòng** N 1 specific gravity 2 proportion

鄙 **bǐ** ADJ low, base (See 卑鄙 **bēibǐ**)

笔 **bǐ** TRAD 筆 N writing instrument, pen, pencil (支 **zhī**)

钢笔 **gāngbǐ** fountain pen

画笔 **huàbǐ** paintbrush (for art)

毛笔 **máobǐ** Chinese writing brush

圆珠笔 **yuánzhūbǐ** ballpen

笔记 **bǐjì** N notes (taken in class or while reading)

记笔记 **jì bǐjì** take notes (in class, at a lecture, etc.)

做笔记 **zuò bǐjì** make notes (while reading).

笔记本 **bǐjìběn** N notebook

笔记本电脑 **bǐjìběn diànnǎo** notebook computer

笔迹 **bǐjì** N handwriting

辨认笔迹 **biànrèn bǐjì** decipher someone's handwriting

笔试 **bǐshì** N written test, written examination

笔直 **bǐzhí** ADJ perfectly straight

彼 **bǐ** PRON that, the other

彼此 **bǐcǐ** PRON each other

碧 **bì** ADJ green

碧绿 **bìlǜ** ADJ green, dark green

蔽 **bì** v cover, conceal (See 隐蔽 **yǐnbì**)

毙 **bì** TRAD 斃 v die (See 枪毙 **qiāngbì**)

币 **bì** TRAD 幣 N currency (See 人民币 **Rénmínbì**)

痹 **bì** N paralysis (See 麻痹 **mábì**)

必 **bì** I ADV certainly, inevitably II MODAL v must

必定 **bìdìng** ADV certainly, definitely

必将 **bìjiāng** ADV will surely

必然 **bìrán** ADJ inevitable, be bound to

必胜客 **Bìshèngkè** N Pizza Hut (Restaurant)

必修 **bìxiū** ADJ compulsory (courses, subjects of study)
  必修课 **bìxiūkè** compulsory subject, required course
必须 **bìxū** MODAL V must
必需 **bìxū** V must have
  必需品 **bìxūpǐn** daily necessities
必要 **bìyào** ADJ necessary
  必要条件 **bìyào tiáojiàn** necessary condition

毕 bì TRAD 畢 V finish

毕竟 **bìjìng** ADV after all, anyway
毕业 **bìyè** V graduate from school

闭 bì TRAD 閉 V close, shut up

NOTE: 闭嘴! **Bìzuǐ!** *Shut your mouth!* is a very impolite expression to tell people to stop talking. You can also say 闭上你的嘴! **Bì shang nǐ de zuǐ!** *Shut your mouth!*

闭幕 **bìmù** V the curtain falls (of a theatrical performance, an event, etc.), close
闭幕式 **bìmùshì** N closing ceremony
闭塞 **bìsè** ADJ cut off from the outside world, secluded

弊 bì N fraud, corrupt practice

  作弊 **zuòbì** cheat (especially in examinations)
  舞弊 **wǔbì** be engaged in fraud, misconduct or malpractice
弊病 **bìbìng** N malpractice, disadvantage

避 bì V evade, avoid

避免 **bìmiǎn** V avoid, avert
避孕 **bìyùn** N contraception, birth control
  避孕套 **bìyùntào** condom
  避孕药 **bìyùnyào** contraceptive pill

壁 bì N wall (See 隔壁 **gébì**)

臂 bì N arm

  一臂之力 **yí bì zhī lì** a helping hand

鞭 biān N whip

  鞭子 **biānzi** whip (条 tiáo)

鞭策 **biāncè** V spur on, urge on
鞭炮 **biānpào** N firecracker
  放鞭炮 **fàng biānpào** set off firecrackers

边 biān TRAD 邊 N side, border

NOTE: The most frequent use of 边 **biān** is to form "compound location nouns": 东边 **dōngbian** *east side*, 南边 **nánbian** *south side*, 西边 **xībian** *west side*, 北边 **běibian** *north side*, 里边 **lǐbian** *inside*, 外边 **wàibian** *outside*. 边 **biān** in such cases is often pronounced in the neutral tone.

边…边 **biān…biān** CONJ (used with verbs to indicate simultaneous actions)
边防 **biānfáng** N frontier defense
  边防部队 **biānfáng bùduì** frontier guards
  边防检查站 **biānfáng jiǎncházhàn** frontier checkpoint
边疆 **biānjiāng** N border area
  边疆地区 **biānjiāng dìqū** border area
边界 **biānjiè** N border (between two countries)
  边界线 **biānjiè xiàn** boundary (between two countries)
边境 **biānjìng** N frontier, border
边缘 **biānyuán** N edge, periphery
  边缘状态 **biānyuán zhuàngtài** borderline case

编 biān TRAD 編 V compile, compose

编号 **biānhào** N serial number
  护照编号 **hùzhào biānhào** passport's serial number
编辑 **biānjí** I V edit, compile II N editor
  财经编辑 **cáijīng biānjí** finance editor
  特约编辑 **tèyuē biānjí** contributing editor
  总编辑 **zǒngbiānjí** chief editor
编制 **biānzhì** V **1** weave, braid **2** draw up (a plan, a computer programme, etc.)

贬 biǎn V reduce, derogate

贬低 **biǎndī** V belittle, play down
  贬低别人的成绩 **biǎndī biéren de chéngjì** belittle someone's achievements
贬值 **biǎnzhí** V devalue, depreciate

货币贬值 huòbì biǎnzhí currency devaluation

扁 **biǎn** ADJ flat

变 **biàn** TRAD 變 V transform, change

变成 biànchéng V change into

变动 biàndòng V 1 alter, change 2 (of organizations) reshuffle, reorganize
人事变动 rénshì biàndòng reshuffle of personnel

变革 biàngé V transform, change

变更 biàngēng V alter, modify
变更旅行路线 biàngēng lǚxíng lùxiàn change one's itinerary

变化 biànhuà I V transform, change
千变万化 qiānbiàn wànhuà always in a state of flux, everchanging
II N transfomation, change
巨大变化 jùdà biànhuà tremendous changes

NOTE: As a verb 变化 biànhuà is interchangeable with 变 biàn, 变化 biànhuà being a little more formal than 变 biàn.

变换 biànhuàn V vary, alternate

变迁 biànqiān V change, evolve

变形 biànxíng V deform, transfigure
变形金刚 biànxíng jīn'gāng transformer (a toy)

变质 biànzhì V change the nature of, deteriorate

便 **biàn** ADV Same as 就 jiù 3 ADV. Used only in written Chinese.

便道 biàndào N shortcut

便利 biànlì ADJ convenient, easy

便条 biàntiáo N informal written message
留便条 liú biàntiáo leave a note

便于 biànyú V be easy to, be convenient for

辩 **biàn** TRAD 辯 V argue, debate

辩个明白 biàn ge míngbai debate until the truth is out

辩护 biànhù V speak in defense of
辩护律师 biànhù lǜshī defense lawyer, defense counselor

辩解 biànjiě V try to defend oneself

无力的辩解 wúlì de biànjiě feeble excuses

辩论 biànlùn I V debate II N debate (场 chǎng)
举行一场辩论 jǔxíng yì chǎng biànlùn hold a debate

辨 **biàn** V distinguish, discriminate

辨别 biànbié V distinguish, tell ... from ...
辨别是非 biànbié shìfēi distinguish what is right from what is wrong

辨认 biànrèn V identify, recognize
辨认罪犯 biànrèn zuìfàn identify a criminal

辫 **biàn** TRAD 辮 N pigtail, braid
辫子 biànzi pigtail, braid (条 tiáo)

遍 **biàn** M. WD (for frequency of an action done in its complete duration from start to end)

遍地 biàndì N everywhere

标 **biāo** TRAD 標 V mark

标本 biāoběn N sample, specimen
采集标本 cǎijí biāoběn collect samples or specimen

标点 biāodiǎn N punctuation mark
标点符号 biāodiǎn fúhào punctuation marks

标题 biāotí N title, heading
大标题 dà biāotí banner headline

标语 biāoyǔ N slogan

标志 biāozhì N sign, mark
社会地位的标志 shèhuì dìwèi de biāozhì status symbol

标准 biāozhǔn I N standard, criterion
符合标准 fúhé biāozhǔn conform to the standard
达到标准 dádào biāozhǔn reach the standard
II ADJ standard, perfect

表 1 **biǎo** TRAD 錶 N watch (块 kuài, 只 zhī)
男表 nán biǎo men's watch
女表 nǚ biǎo ladies' watch

表 2 **biǎo** N form (张 zhāng, 份 fèn)

表³ biǎo v express, show
表表心意 biǎobiǎo xīnyì show one's goodwill (or gratitude)
表达 biǎodá v express (thoughts or emotions)
表面 biǎomiàn n surface
表面文章 biǎomiàn wénzhāng something done just for the show, pay lip service
表明 biǎomíng v make clear, demonstrate
表情 biǎoqíng n facial expression
一付严肃的表情 yífù yánsù de biǎoqíng with a serious expression
表示 biǎoshì v express, show
表现 biǎoxiàn v 1 display, show 2 perform
表演 biǎoyǎn I v put on (a show), perform, demonstrate II n performance, show (场 cháng)
参加表演 cānjiā biǎoyǎn participate in a performance/demonstration
看表演 kàn biǎoyǎn watch a performance
表扬 biǎoyáng v praise, commend
表彰 biǎozhāng v commend, honor

憋 biē v suppress resentment with effort, contain oneself
憋不住 biē bu zhù cannot contain oneself, unable to hold oneself back

别¹ bié adv don't

NOTE: 别 bié is a contraction of 不要 búyào in an imperative sentence. It is only used colloquially.

别² bié pron other, the other
别处 biéchù n other place(s), elsewhere
别的 biéde pron other
别人 biérén pron other people, others
别字 biézì n a character which is not written or pronounced correctly

别³ bié n farewell
告别 gàobié bid farewell

别 biè See 别扭 bièniu

别扭 bièniu adj awkward, uncomfortable
闹别扭 nào bièniu to be at odds with someone, to be difficult with someone; make difficulties for someone

宾 bīn trad 賓 n guest
嘉宾 jiābīn distinguished guest, guest speaker
宾馆 bīnguǎn n guesthouse

滨 bīn trad 濱 n shore, bank
海滨 hǎibīn seashore

冰 bīng n ice
冰棍儿 bīnggùnr n flavored popsicle
冰淇淋 bīngqílín n ice cream
冰箱 bīngxiāng n refrigerator
电冰箱 diàn bīngxiāng refrigerator

兵 bīng n soldier
当兵 dāng bīng be a soldier, serve in the armed forces

饼 bǐng trad 餅 n cake (只 zhī)
大饼 dàbǐng sesame cake (a breakfast food)
烙饼 làobǐng pancake
月饼 yuèbǐng mooncake (for the Mid-Autumn Festival)
饼干 bǐnggān n cookie(s), biscuit(s) (片 piàn, 包 bāo)
一包饼干 yì bāo bǐnggān a package of cookies
一片饼干 yí piàn bǐnggān a cookie

丙 bǐng n the third of the "Celestial Stems," the third

柄 bǐng n handle, stem

秉 bǐng v hold in hand

并 bìng trad 並 I adv (used before a negative word for emphasis) II conj Same as 并且 bìngqiě. Used only in written Chinese. III v combine, incorporate

NOTE: 并 bìng is used to emphasize negation. It is not grammatically essential;

without 并 bìng the sentences still stand. The following is perfectly acceptable:
事情（并）不象你想象的那么简单。
Shìqing (bìng) bú xiàng nǐ xiǎngxiàng de nàme jiǎndān. *Things are not as simple as you imagine.*

并存 bìngcún V co-exist
并非 bìngfēi ADV not, not at all
　并非如此 bìngfēi rúcǐ not like that
并排 bìngpái V be side by side, be abreast with
并且 bìngqiě CONJ moreover, what's more, and

病 bìng I V fall ill, be ill II N illness, disease
　肺病 fèibìng lung disease, tuberculosis
　急性病 jíxìngbìng acute disease
　慢性病 mànxìngbìng chronic disease
　生病 shēng bìng to fall ill
病床 bìngchuáng N hospital bed
病虫害 bìngchónghài N plant diseases and insect pests
病毒 bìngdú N virus
　电脑病毒 diànnǎo bìngdú computer virus
病房 bìngfáng N (hospital) ward
　小儿科病房 xiǎo'érkē bìngfáng pediatrics ward
　重病房 zhòngbìngfáng intensive care ward
病假 bìng jià N sick leave
　请病假 qǐng bìngjià ask for/apply for sick leave
病菌 bìngjūn N pathogenic bacteria
病情 bìngqíng N patient's conditions
病人 bìngrén N patient
　门诊病人 ménzhěn bìngrén outpatient
　住院病人 zhùyuàn bìngrén inpatient (warded patient)
病史 bìngshǐ N medical record

剥 bō V peel, strip

波 bō N ripple, wave
波动 bōdòng V fluctuate (like a wave)

情绪波动 qíngxù bōdòng constantly changing moods
波浪 bōlàng N wave
波涛 bōtāo N high wave
　汹涌波涛 xiōngyǒng bōtāo roaring waves

玻 bō N glass
玻璃 bōli N glass
　玻璃杯 bōlibēi glass
　玻璃窗 bōlichuāng glass window, glass pane

菠 bō N spinach
　菠菜 bōcài spinach

播 bō V 1 sow 2 broadcast
播放 bōfàng V broadcast (radio or TV programs)
播送 bōsòng V broadcast (radio programs)
播音 bōyīn V broadcast (radio programs)
　播音员 bōyīnyuán newsreader
播种 bōzhòng V sow seeds

拨 bō Trad 撥 V 1 stir with a finger or stick 2 allocate
拨款 bōkuǎn V allocate funds, appropriate (money)

伯 bó N Same as 伯父 bófù
伯父 bófù N father's elder brother

NOTE: 伯父 bófù is also a form of address for men older than your father but not old enough to be your grandfather. The colloquialism for 伯父 bófù is 伯伯 bóbo.

伯母 bómǔ N father's elder brother's wife

NOTE: 伯母 bómǔ is also a form of address for women older than your mother but not old enough to be your grandmother. It is generally used by well-educated urban Chinese.

勃 bó ADJ vigorous

舶 bó N ship

泊 bó V (of ships) anchor, moor

驳 bó TRAD 駁 V refute

驳斥 bóchì V refute, rebut

脖 bó N neck

脖子 bózi neck

博 bó ADJ 1 plentiful, abundant 2 wide, extensive

博客 bókè N blogger

博论坛 bókè lùntán blog

NOTE: 博客 bókè is a transliteration of *blogger*. To blog, i.e. write as a blogger, is 写博 xiě bó.

博览会 bólǎnhuì N exposition, exhibition, fair

世界博览会 shìjiè bólǎnhuì World Exposition, World Expo

博士 bóshì N doctor, Ph.D.

博士生 bóshìshēng Ph.D. candidate

博士生导师 bóshìshēng dǎoshī Ph.D. supervisor

博士后 bóshìhòu post-doctorate

博士学位 bóshì xuéwèi Ph.D. degree

博物馆 bówùguǎn N museum

历史博物馆 lìshǐ bówùguǎn museum of history

胳 bó N arm (See 胳膊 gēbo)

搏 bó V be engaged in a hand-to-hand combat, fight

搏斗 bódòu V battle, wrestle

薄 bó ADJ meager, small

一份薄礼 yí fèn bó lǐ an insignificant gift

NOTE: The character 薄 has two pronunciations: báo and bó. While 薄 báo is used to describe material "thin-ness" (eg. 一条薄被子 yì tiáo báo bèizi *a thin blanket*), 薄 bó is used in a figurative sense. See 薄 báo for examples.

薄膜 bómó N membrane, film

薄弱 bóruò ADJ frail, weak

簸 bǒ V jerk (See 颠簸 diānbǒ)

卜 bo TRAD 蔔 (See 萝卜 luóbo)

捕 bǔ V catch, arrest

捕捞 bǔlāo V catch (fish)

卜 bǔ V divine, predict

未卜先知 wèi bǔ xiān zhī have foresight, foresee

补 bǔ TRAD 補 V mend, patch

补偿 bǔcháng V compensate, make up

补充 bǔchōng V make up, supplement

补救 bǔjiù V remedy

补救办法 bǔjiù bànfǎ corrective measure, remedial measure

补课 bǔkè V make up for missed lessons

补贴 bǔtiē I N subsidy II V subsidize

补习 bǔxí V take or give supplementary lessons

补习班 bǔxíbān (after school) class

补助 bǔzhù N subsidy, grant-in-aid

不 bù ADV no, not

NOTE: When followed by a syllable in the fourth (falling) tone, 不 undergoes tone change (tone sandhi) from the normal fourth tone to the second (rising) tone, e.g. 不对 búduì, 不是 búshì.

不必 búbì ADV need not, not have to, unnecessarily

不比 bùbǐ V unlike

不辞而别 bù cí ér bié IDIOM leave without saying good-bye, take French leave

不错 búcuò ADJ 1 not wrong 2 quite right, not bad, quite good

NOTE: …得不错 …de búcuò is ambiguous. It may mean either … *correctly* or … *rather well*. For example, the sentence: 你说得不错。Nǐ shuō de búcuò. may mean either *You spoke correctly.* (→ *You're right.*) or *You spoke quite well.* (→ *Well said.*)

不大 búdà ADV not very, not much

不但 búdàn CONJ not only … (but also)

···不但···，而且···**búdàn ..., érqiě** CONJ not only ..., but also ...

不当 **búdàng** ADJ improper, unsuitable

不得不 **bùdébù** ADV have to, have no choice but

不得了 **bùdéliǎo** I ADJ horrible, extremely serious II ADV extremely (used after an adjective and introduced by 得 de)

不得已 **bùdéyǐ** ADJ having no alternative but to ..., acting against one's will

不等 **bùděng** V vary, differ

不定 **búdìng** ADJ indefinite, not sure

不断 **búduàn** ADV without interruption, continuously, incessantly

不法 **bùfǎ** ADJ illegal, lawless
  不法分子 **bùfǎ fènzi** criminal
  不法行为 **bùfǎ xíngwéi** illegal act, illegal practice

不妨 **bùfáng** ADV might as well

不敢当 **bùgǎndāng** IDIOM Thank you, I don't dare to accept (a polite/modest reply to a compliment)

不公 **bùgōng** ADJ unfair, unjust

不够 **búgòu** ADJ not enough, insufficient

不顾 **búgù** I V disregard II PREP in spite of

不管 **bùguǎn** CONJ no matter (what, who, how, etc.)

NOTE: 不管 bùguǎn may be replaced by 不论 búlùn or 无论 wúlùn, but 不管 bùguǎn is more colloquial.

不过 **búguò** CONJ Same as 但是 dànshì. Used colloquially.

不好意思 **bù hǎoyìsi** IDIOM I'm embarrassed (a polite phrase used when you are offering an apology, giving a gift, or receiving a gift or other acts of kindness)

NOTE: 不好意思 bù hǎoyìsi literally means *I'm embarrassed*. It is easy to understand why you say it when you are apologizing or receiving a gift. When you are giving a gift, however, you also say it to imply that the gift is so insignificant that you feel embarrassed about it.

不见 **bújiàn** V disappear, be lost

不见得 **bú jiànde** ADV not necessarily, unlikely

不禁 **bùjīn** ADV cannot help oneself from, cannot refrain from

不仅 **bùjǐn** CONJ Same as 不但 búdàn. Tends to be used in writing.

不久 **bùjiǔ** ADV not long afterwards, in the near future, soon

不堪 **bùkān** I V cannot bear, cannot stand
  不堪设想 **bùkān shèxiǎng** (of consequences) too serious to face, very bad
  II ADV (used after an adjective) utterly
  混乱不堪 **hùnluàn bùkān** in utter chaos

不愧 **búkuì** V be worthy of, deserve to be called

不利 **búlì** ADJ unfavorable, disadvantageous

不料 **búliào** ADV unexpectedly

不论 **búlùn** CONJ Same as 不管 bùguǎn. Used more in writing.

不满 **bùmǎn** ADJ Same as 不满意 bùmǎnyì dissatisfied

不免 **bùmiǎn** ADV unavoidable, inevitable, would only be natural

不平 **bùpíng** N injustice, resentment

不然 **bùrán** CONJ otherwise, or

NOTE: To be more emphatic, you can use 不然的话 bùrán de huà instead of 不然 bùrán, as in this sentence: 你别说了，不然（的话）我真要生气了。Nǐ bié shuō le, bùrán (de huà) wǒ zhēn yào shēngqì le. *Don't say any more, or I'll really be angry.*

不容 **bùróng** V not tolerate, not allow

不如 **bùrú** V be not as good as, not as ... as

不少 **bùshǎo** ADJ quite a few

不是 **búshi** N fault, blame

不是···而是··· **bú shì...ér shì...** CONJ not ... but ...

不是···就是··· **bú shì...jiùshì...** CONJ either ... or ...

不时 **bùshí** ADV now and then, from time to time

不停 **bùtíng** ADV without letup, incessantly

不同 **bùtóng** ADJ not the same, different
···和跟···不同 **...hé/gēn...bùtóng** ... is/are different from ...

不惜 **bù xī** v not hesitate, not spare
  不惜工本 **bù xī gōngběn** spare neither labor or money, spare no expense

不像话 **búxiànghuà** ADJ totally unreasonable, outrageous

不相上下 **bù xiāng shàng xià** IDIOM equally matched, be as good as

不幸 **búxìng** ADJ unfortunate

NOTE: 不幸 **búxìng** is used to describe serious events or matters, often involving death. Do not use 不幸 **búxìng** for trivial matters. For example, even though in English it is acceptable to say, "Unfortunately, I haven't seen the film," in Chinese it would be wrong to say 我不幸没有看过那个电影。 Wǒ búxìng méiyǒu kànguo nàge diànyǐng.

不行 **bùxíng** ADJ **1** will not do, not allowed **2** not (be) good (at ...)

不朽 **bùxiǔ** ADJ immortal

不许 **bùxǔ** v not permitted, not allowed

不言而喻 **bú yán ér yù** IDIOM it goes without saying, it is self-evident

不要 **búyào** ADV (used in an imperative sentence or as advice) do not

NOTE: See note on 别 **bié**.

不宜 **bùyí** ADV unsuitable

不用 **búyòng** ADV no need, there's no need, don't have to

不由得 **bù yóude** ADV cannot but, cannot help

不在乎 **búzàihu** v not mind, not care
  满不在乎 **mǎn búzàihu** not care at all, couldn't care less

不怎么样 **bù zěnmeyàng** ADV not up to too much, not very

不止 **bùzhǐ** ADV more than, not limited to

不只 **bùzhǐ** ADV not only

不至于 **búzhìyú** ADV not as far as, not so bad as

不足 **bùzú** ADJ inadequate, insufficient
  资金不足 **zījīn bùzú** insufficient funds

布 1 **bù** N cotton or linen cloth (块 kuài, 片 piàn)

棉布 **miánbù** cotton cloth, cotton material

布 2 **bù** TRAD 佈 v arrange, deploy

布告 **bùgào** I v announce publicly II N public announcement, bulletin
布局 **bùjú** N layout, overall arrangement
布置 **bùzhì** v decorate, furnish

埠 **bù** N dock, port

步 **bù** N step, pace

步子 **bùzi** step, pace
下一步 **xià yí bù** the next step, the next stage
步兵 **bùbīng** N infantry, infantryman
步伐 **bùfá** N step, pace
步骤 **bùzhòu** N procedure, steps

怖 **bù** v fear (See 恐怖 kǒngbù)

部 **bù** N part, unit

部队 **bùduì** N troops, the army
部分 **bùfen** N portion, part
  大部分 **dà bùfen** most of ..., the majority of ...
部件 **bùjiàn** N component, part
部门 **bùmén** N department
部署 **bùshǔ** I v map out, deploy II N plan
部位 **bùwèi** N in position, location
部长 **bùzhǎng** N (government) minister
  教育部长 **jiàoyù bùzhǎng** minister of education
  外交部长 **wàijiāo bùzhǎng** minister of foreign affairs, foreign minister

C

擦 **cā** v clean or erase by wiping or rubbing

猜 **cāi** v guess

猜测 **cāicè** v guess, conjecture
猜想 **cāixiǎng** v suppose, conjecture

才 1 **cái** TRAD 纔 ADV **1** (before a verb) a short time ago, just **2** (used before a word of time or quantity to indicate that the speaker feels the time is too early, too short or the quantity is too little), only, as early as, as few/little as **3** (used after a word of time to indicate that the speaker feels the time is too late or there is too much delay) as late as

才 **2 cái** N talent, remarkable ability

才干 cáigàn N talent, competence
有才干 yǒu cáigàn capable and talented
才能 cáinéng N talent, ability
才智 cáizhì N talent and high intelligence, ability and wisdom

财 **cái** TRAD 財 N wealth, property

财产 cáichǎn N property, belongings
个人财产 gèrén cáichǎn private property, personal belongings
财富 cáifù N wealth, fortune
财经 cáijīng N finance and economy
财会 cáikuài N finance and accounting
财会专业 cáikuài zhuānyè the profession (or department) of finance and accounting

NOTE: 会 is pronounced kuài here, not huì.

财力 cáilì N financial capacity
财务 cáiwù N financial affairs, finance
财务部门 cáiwù bùmén department(s) of finance (in a company or an institution)
财务主任 cáiwù zhǔrèn director of finance (in a company or an institution)
财政 cáizhèng N public finance
财政部 cáizhèngbù the Ministry of Finance
财政年度 cáizhèng niándù fiscal year

材 **cái** N material

材料 cáiliào N **1** materials, e.g. steel, timber, plastic **2** data (for a thesis, a report, etc.)

裁 **cái** V **1** cut into parts, cut down **2** judge, decide

裁缝 cáifeng N tailor, dressmaker
裁减 cáijiǎn V cut down, reduce
裁决 cáijué V judge, rule
裁判 cáipàn I V **1** (in law) judge **2** (in sports) act as referee or umpire

II N referee, umpire (位 wèi, 名 míng)
当裁判 dāng cáipàn act as a referee
裁判员 cáipànyuán N Same as 裁判 cáipàn II
裁员 cáiyuán V reduce staff

采 **cǎi** TRAD 採 V pick, gather

采访 cǎifǎng V (of mass media) interview
采购 cǎigòu V (corporate) purchase
采购员 cǎigòuyuán purchasing agent
采集 cǎijí V gather, collect
采集标本 cǎijí biāoběn collect (plant, insect, etc.) specimen
采纳 cǎinà V accept, adopt
采纳建议 cǎinà jiànyì accept a proposal
采取 cǎiqǔ V adopt (a policy, a measure, an attitude, etc.)
采用 cǎiyòng V use, employ
采用新技术 cǎiyòng xīn jìshù adopt a new technique

彩 **cǎi** ADJ colorful, multi-colored

彩票 cǎipiào N lottery, lottery ticket
彩色 cǎisè ADJ multi-colored

踩 **cǎi** V step on, tread on

睬 **cǎi** V pay attention to

菜 **cài** N **1** vegetables

种菜 zhòng cài grow vegetables
2 any non-staple food such as vegetables, meat, fish, eggs etc
买菜 mǎi cài buy non-staple food, do grocery shopping
3 cooked dish
点菜 diǎn cài order a dish (in a restaurant)
中国菜 Zhōngguócài Chinese dishes, Chinese food
菜单 càidān N menu

参 **cān** TRAD 參 V call, enter

参观 cānguān V visit (a place)
参加 cānjiā V **1** join **2** participate, attend
参考 cānkǎo V consult, refer to
参考书 cānkǎo shū reference book(s)

仅供参考 jǐn gōng cānkǎo for reference only

参谋 cānmóu **I** v offer advice **II** n **1** staff officer
参谋长 cānmóuzhǎng chief of staff
2 advice
给我当参谋 gěi wǒ dāng cānmóu give me advice

参议员 cānyìyuán n senator

参议院 cānyìyuàn n senate, the Senate

参与 cānyù v participate, involve

参阅 cānyuè v consult (a book, a periodical, etc.)

参照 cānzhào v use as reference, refer to

餐 **cān** n meal

一日三餐 yīrì sāncān three meals a day
餐车 cānchē n dining car (on a train)
餐厅 cāntīng n restaurant

残 **cán** TRAD 殘 ADJ damaged, savage

残暴 cánbào ADJ ferocious, brutal
残暴的独裁统治 cánbào de dúcái tǒngzhì tyrannical dictatorship
残疾 cánjí ADJ disabled
残疾人 cánjírén disabled person(s)
残酷 cánkù ADJ cruel, brutal
残忍 cánrěn ADJ cruel, merciless
使用残忍的手段 shǐyòng cánrěnde shǒuduàn with most cruel means
残余 cányú ADJ remnants, survivors
残障 cánzhàng Same as 残疾 cánjí

惭 **cán** TRAD 慚 n shame

惭愧 cánkuì ADJ be ashamed

蚕 **cán** TRAD 蠶 n silkworm (条 tiáo)

惨 **cǎn** TRAD 慘 ADJ miserable, tragic

灿 **càn** TRAD 燦 ADJ brilliant

灿烂 cànlàn ADJ magnificent, splendid

仓 **cāng** TRAD 倉 n storage

仓促 cāngcù ADJ hasty, hurried
仓促离去 cāngcù líqù leave in a hurry
仓库 cāngkù n warehouse

苍 **cāng** TRAD 蒼 n dark green

苍白 cāngbái ADJ pallid, pale
苍蝇 cāngying n housefly
苍蝇拍 cāngying pāi flyswatter

舱 **cāng** TRAD 艙 n cabin (in a ship or an airplane)

经济舱 jīngjìcāng economy class (on a plane)
商务舱 shāngwùcāng business class (on a plane)
头等舱 tóuděngcāng first class (on a plane)

藏 **cáng** v hide, conceal

捉迷藏 zhuō mícáng hide-and-seek

操 **cāo** n drill, exercise

操场 cāochǎng n sports ground, playground
(在)操场上 (zài) cāochǎng shang on the sports ground
操劳 cāoláo v toil, work very hard
操练 cāoliàn v drill, practice, train
操心 cāoxīn v deeply concern, be at pains
操纵 cāozòng v control, operate
操作 cāozuò v operate
操作手册 cāozuò shǒucè operating manual
操作系统 cāozuò xìtǒng operating system

槽 **cáo** n trough

跳槽 tiàocáo abandon one's job in favor of another, get a new job

草 **cǎo** n grass, weed (棵 kē)

野草 yěcǎo weed
草案 cǎo'àn n draft (of a plan, proposal, a document, etc.)
草地 cǎodì n **1** lawn **2** meadow
草率 cǎoshuài ADJ careless, sloppy
草原 cǎoyuán n grassland, steppe, pasture

册 **cè** m. wd (used for books) volume

两千册图书 liǎngqiān cè túshū two thousand [volumes of] books

厕 **cè** TRAD 廁 n toilet

厕所 cèsuǒ N toilet

公共厕所 gōnggòng cèsuǒ public toilet

男厕所 náncèsuǒ men's toilet

女厕所 nǚcèsuǒ women's toilet

NOTE: See note on 洗手间 xǐshǒujiān (in 洗 xǐ).

测 cè TRAD 測 V measure, gauge

测定 cèdìng V determine (the position, speed, etc.) by measuring

测量 cèliáng V survey, measure

测试 cèshì V test

测算 cèsuàn V measure and calculate

测算有害气体排放量 cèsuàn yǒuhài qìtǐ páifàngliáng calculate the emission of harmful gases

测验 cèyàn I V test (in a school) II N test, examination

测验题目 cèyàn tímù test questions.

侧 cè I N side

大楼的右侧 dàlóu de yòucè the right side of the building

II V incline, lean

侧面 cèmiàn N side, flank

策 cè N plan (See 政策 zhèngcè)

策划 cèhuà V plan (an event, a theatrical performance, etc.)

策划人 cèhuàrén planner

策略 cèlüè N tactics

有策略的 yǒu cèlüè de tactful

层 céng TRAD 層 M. WD story (storey), level, floor

NOTE: See note on 楼 lóu.

层次 céngcì N 1 administrative or educational level 2 arrangement of ideas in writing or colors in painting

曾 céng ADV Same as 曾经 céngjīng. Used more in writing.

曾经 céngjīng ADV once, formerly

NOTE: 曾经 céngjīng is used to emphasize that an action or situation took place in the past.

叉 chā N fork (把 bǎ)

叉子 chāzi fork (把 bǎ)

差 chā N 1 difference, discrepancy

时差 shíchā time difference (between time zones)

2 mistake, error

差别 chābié N disparity, gap

城乡差别 chéngxiāng chābié the urban-rural gap

差错 chācuò N error, fault

没有差错 méiyǒu chācuò error-free

差距 chājù N gap, disparity

贫富差距 pín-fù chājù the gap between rich and poor

差异 chāyì N diversity, difference

插 chā V insert, stick in

插花艺术 chāhuā yìshù the art of flower arrangement

插秧 chāyāng V transplant rice seedlings

插嘴 chāzuǐ V interrupt by saying something

茶 chá N tea

茶杯 chá bēi teacup

茶袋 chá dài teabag

茶壶 chá hú teapot

茶叶 cháyè tea leaf

红茶 hóngchá black tea

绿茶 lǜchá green tea

喝茶 hē chá drink tea

茶馆 cháguǎn N teahouse

茶话会 cháhuà huì N tea party

查 chá V check, investigate, look up

查词典 chá cídiǎn look up words in a dictionary

查办 chábàn V investigate and punish

查获 cháhuò V hunt down and seize (stolen goods, criminals, etc.)

查明 chámíng V investigate and clarify, prove after an investigation

查询 cháxún V inquire about

电话号码查询服务 diànhuà hàomǎ cháxún fúwù telephone directory service

查阅 **cháyuè** v search (reference books, documents, etc.)

  查阅五年前的统计数字 **cháyuè wǔ nián qián de tǒngjì shùzì** search the statistics from five years ago

察 chá v examine, look over closely (See 观察 **guānchá**, 警察 **jǐngchá**)

岔 chà I N branching off

  岔路 **chàlù** fork (in a road)

  II v change the subject

  打岔 **dǎchà** interrupt and change the subject (of a talk)

差 chà I v be short of, lack in II ADJ poor, not up to standard

差不多 **chàbùduō** ADV 1 more or less the same 2 almost

差点儿 **chàdiǎnr** ADV almost, nearly

诧 chà TRAD 詫 v be surprised

诧异 **chàyì** v be surprised, be amazed

拆 chāi v take apart, demolish

拆除 **chāichú** v demolish and remove

拆穿 **chāichuān** v expose (a lie, a plot, etc.)

拆迁 **chāiqiān** v demolish (a dwelling) and relocate (inhabitants)

柴 chái N firewood (See 火柴 **huǒchái**)

  柴油 **cháiyóu** N diesel oil

搀 chān TRAD 攙 v 1 help by the arm 2 mix, mingle

蝉 chán TRAD 蟬 N cicada

馋 chán TRAD 饞 ADJ too fond of eating, gluttonous

  嘴馋 **zuǐchán** too fond of eating

缠 chán TRAD 纏 v 1 wind, twine 2 pester

产 chǎn TRAD 產 v produce

产地 **chǎndì** N origin of manufacturing

产量 **chǎnliàng** N (production) output, yield

产品 **chǎnpǐn** N product

产生 **chǎnshēng** v produce, give rise to, lead to

产物 **chǎnwù** N outcome, result

产业 **chǎnyè** N property, estate

产值 **chǎnzhí** N output value

铲 chǎn TRAD 鏟 N spade

  铲子 **chǎnzi** spade

阐 chǎn TRAD 闡 v explain

阐明 **chǎnmíng** v explain clearly, clarify

阐述 **chǎnshù** v elaborate, explain

颤 chàn TRAD 顫 v quiver, vibrate

颤动 **chàndòng** v quiver, shake

颤抖 **chàndǒu** v (of people) tremble, shake

昌 chāng v prosper

昌盛 **chāngshèng** ADJ prosperous, flourishing

猖 chāng ADJ ferocious

猖狂 **chāngkuáng** ADJ ferocious, savage

长 cháng TRAD 長 ADJ long

长城 **Chángchéng** N the Great Wall (a historic landmark in Northern China)

长处 **chángchu** N strong point, merit, strength

长度 **chángdù** N length

长短 **chángduǎn** N 1 length 2 right and wrong 3 mishap, accident

NOTE: See note on 大小 **dàxiǎo**.

长江 **Chángjiāng** N the Yangtze River (China's longest river)

长跑 **chángpǎo** N long-distance running

长跑运动员 **chángpǎo yùndòngyuán** long-distance runner

长期 **chángqī** N a long period of time

长寿 **chángshòu** ADJ enjoying longevity

长途 **chángtú** N long distance

长途电话 **chángtú diànhuà** long-distance telephone call

国际长途电话 **guójì chángtú diànhuà** international telephone call

长途汽车 **chángtú qìchē** long-distance bus, coach

长远 **chángyuǎn** ADJ long-term, long-range

长远打算 **chángyuǎn dǎsuàn** long-term plan

尝 **cháng** TRAD 嘗 V taste

尝试 **chángshì** V try

偿 **cháng** TRAD 償 V make up, compensate

偿还 **chánghuán** V pay back (a debt)

常 **cháng** I ADV often

常常 **chángcháng** ADV often

NOTE: Colloquially, 常常 **chángcháng** is often used instead of 常 **cháng**.

不常 **bù cháng** not often, seldom
II ADJ 1 common, regular 2 normal

常规 **chángguī** ADJ regular, conventional

常规武器 **chángguī wǔqì** conventional weapon

常年 **chángnián** ADV all year round

常识 **chángshí** N 1 common sense 2 basic knowledge

常务 **chángwù** ADJ day-to-day

常务委员 **chángwù wěiyuán** member of a standing committee

常务委员会 **chángwù wěiyuánhuì** standing committee

肠 **cháng** TRAD 腸 N intestine

大肠 **dàcháng** large intestine

小肠 **xiǎocháng** small intestine

肠胃病 **chángwèibìng** N gastrointestinal disease

肠炎 **chángyán** N enteritis

厂 **chǎng** TRAD 廠 N factory, works, mill

钢铁厂 **gāngtiěchǎng** iron and steel-works

造纸厂 **zàozhǐchǎng** paper mill

厂房 **chǎngfáng** N factory building

厂商 **chǎngshāng** N 1 factory, firm 2 factory owner

厂长 **chǎngzhǎng** N factory manager

敞 **chǎng** V open

敞开 **chǎngkāi** V open wide

场 **chǎng** TRAD 場 I N ground, field

体育场 **tǐyùchǎng** stadium

飞机场 **fēijīchǎng** airport

市场 **shìchǎng** market

II M. WD (for movies, sport events, etc.)

一场电影 **yì chǎng diànyǐng** a show of film

一场球赛 **yì chǎng qiúsài** a ball game, a ball match

场地 **chǎngdì** N venue (especially for sports)

场合 **chǎnghé** N occasion, situation

场面 **chǎngmiàn** N scene (in a play, movie, etc.)

场所 **chǎngsuǒ** N place (for public activity)

公共场所 **gōnggòng chǎngsuǒ** public place(s)

倡 **chàng** V initiate

倡议 **chàngyì** I V propose II N proposal, suggestion (项 **xiàng**)

唱 **chàng** V sing

唱歌 **chànggē** sing songs, sing

畅 **chàng** TRAD 暢 ADJ uninhibited, unimpeded

畅快 **chàngkuài** ADJ carefree

畅谈 **chàngtán** V talk freely and openly

畅通 **chàngtōng** ADJ unimpeded, flowing freely and smoothly

畅销 **chàngxiāo** V sell well

畅销书 **chàngxiāoshū** bestseller

抄 **chāo** V copy by hand

抄写 **chāoxiě** V Same as 抄 **chāo**

超 **chāo** V go beyond, exceed

超产 **chāochǎn** V exceed production quota

超出 **chāochū** V go beyond, exceed

超额 **chāo'é** V exceed quotas

超过 **chāoguò** V 1 overtake 2 exceed

超级 **chāojí** ADJ super

超级大国 **chāojí dàguó** superpower

超级公路 **chāojí gōnglù** super-highway, motorway

超级市场 chāojí shìchǎng supermarket

超声波 chāoshēngbō N ultrasonic wave, supersonic wave

超越 chāoyuè v transcend, surpass

钞 chāo TRAD 鈔 N paper money

现钞 xiànchāo cash, ready money

钞票 chāopiào N paper money, banknotes (张 zhāng)

朝 cháo I v face II PREP towards, to III N dynasty

朝代 cháodài N dynasty

潮 cháo ADJ wet

潮湿 cháoshī ADJ damp, humid

潮水 cháoshuǐ N tidewater

嘲 cháo v jeer, mock

嘲笑 cháoxiào v ridicule, sneer at

吵 chǎo I v (Same as 吵架 chǎojià) quarrel II ADJ (Same as 吵闹 chǎonào II) noisy

吵架 chǎojià v quarrel

NOTE: For "quarrel," 吵架 chǎojià is more commonly used than 吵 chǎo, for example: 他们夫妻俩又吵架了。Tāmen fūqī liǎ yòu chǎojià le. *The couple quarreled again.*

吵闹 chǎonào I v wrangle, raise hell II ADJ noisy, hustle and bustle

吵嘴 chǎozuǐ v bicker, quarrel

炒 chǎo v 1 stir-fry, roast 2 sensationalize, create a commotion

炒股票 chǎo gǔpiào speculate on the stock exchange

炒鱿鱼 chǎo yóuyú fire (an employee), send ... packing

车 chē TRAD 車 N vehicle, traffic (辆 liàng)

车牌 chē pái (vehicle) license plate

车牌号 chē pái hào (vehicle) license plate number

开车 kāi chē drive an automobile

骑车 qí chē ride a bicycle

停车场 tíngchēchǎng parking lot, car-park

修车 xiū chē repair a car/bicycle

修车行 xiūchēháng motor vehicle repair and servicing shop

学车 xué chē learn to drive (or to ride a bicycle)

车床 chēchuáng N machine tool

车间 chējiān N workshop (in a factory)

车辆 chēliàng N vehicles, traffic

车辆管理 chēliàng guǎnlǐ vehicle administration

车厢 chēxiāng N carriage (in a train)

车站 chēzhàn N bus stop, coach station, railway station

长途汽车站 chángtú qìchēzhàn coach station

出租汽车站 chūzū qìchēzhàn taxi stand

火车站 huǒchēzhàn railway station

扯 chě v 1 pull 2 tear 3 chat

撤 chè v 1 remove 2 withdraw, retreat

撤退 chètuì v retreat

撤销 chèxiāo v cancel, revoke

彻 chè TRAD 徹 ADJ thorough

彻底 chèdǐ ADJ thorough, complete

臣 chén N (in ancient times) minister, official

辰 chén N 1 celestial body 2 time

沉 chén I v sink II ADJ 1 deep, profound 2 heavy

沉淀 chéndiàn I v (of a substance) precipitate, settle II N sediment

沉静 chénjìng ADJ serene, placid

沉闷 chénmèn ADJ 1 (of weather) depressing, oppressive 2 (of moods) in low spirit 3 (of ambiance, atmosphere) dull, boring

沉默 chénmò ADJ silent, reticent

沉思 chénsī v ponder, be lost in thought

沉痛 chéntòng ADJ deeply grieved, in deep sorrow

沉重 chénzhòng ADJ heavy, serious

沉着 chénzhuó ADJ cool-headed, composed

陈 chén TRAD 陳 I ADJ old, stale II v display

陈酒 chénjiǔ N vintage wine

陈旧 chénjiù ADJ old-fashioned, outdated

陈列 chénliè V display, exhibit

陈列橱窗 chénliè chúchuāng showcase

陈列厅 chénlièutīng exhibition hall, showroom

陈述 chenshù V state (one's views, reasons, etc.)

晨 chén N early morning (See 早晨 zǎochén)

尘 chén TRAD 塵 N dust (See 灰尘 huīchén)

尘土 chéntǔ dust, dirt

衬 chèn TRAD 襯 N (clothes) lining, underwear

衬衫 chènshān N shirt (件 jiàn)

衬衣 chènyī N shirt or similar underwear (件 jiàn)

趁 chèn PREP taking advantage of, while, when

称 chèn TRAD 稱 V suit, fit well

称心 chènxīn ADJ very much to one's liking, find ... satisfactory

称 chēng TRAD 稱 V 1 call, be known as, address ... as 2 weigh

称号 chēnghào N honorific title

称呼 chēnghu I V call, address II N form of address

称赞 chēngzàn V compliment, praise

撑 chēng V prop up, support

成 chéng V become, turn into

成本 chéngběn N (in business) cost

生产成本 shēngchǎn chéngběn production cost

成分 chéngfèn N component part, ingredient (种 zhǒng)

成功 chénggōng I V succeed II ADJ successful

成果 chéngguǒ N positive result, achievement (项 xiàng)

成绩 chéngjì N achievement, examination result

考试成绩 kǎoshì chéngjì examination result

取得成绩 qǔdé chéngjì make an achievement, get (positive, good) results

成见 chéngjiàn N prejudice

成交 chéng jiāo V complete a business deal

成就 chéngjiù N great achievement (项 xiàng)

成立 chénglì V establish, set up

成名 chéng míng V become famous

成品 chéngpǐn N end product, finished product

成千上万 chéng qiān shàng wàn IDIOM thousands of, a large number of

成人 chéngrén N adult

成人教育 chéngrén jiàoyù adult education

成人电影 chéngrén diànyǐng adult movie

成熟 chéngshú I V mature II ADJ ripe, mature

成套 chéngtào ADJ in a complete set

成套设备 chéngtào shèbèi complete set of equipment (or machinery)

成天 chéngtiān ADV all day long, all the time

成为 chéngwéi V become

成效 chéngxiào N desired effect, beneficial effect

成心 chéngxīn ADV intentionally, purposely

成语 chéngyǔ N idiom, set phrase

成员 chéngyuán N member

成长 chéngzhǎng V grow up

城 chéng N city, town (座 zuò)

城里 chéngli in town, downtown

城外 chéngwài out of town, suburban area

进城 jìn chéng go to town, go to the city center

城市 chéngshì N city, urban area (as opposed to rural area) (座 zuò)

城市生活 chéngshì shēnghuó city life

城市规划 chéngshì guīhuà city planning

大城市 dà chéngshì big city, metropolis

国际城市 guójì chéngshì cosmopolis

城镇 chéngzhèn N cities and towns, urban area

城镇人口 chéngzhèn rénkǒu urban population

诚 chéng TRAD 誠 ADJ sincere

以诚待人 yǐ chéng dài rén treat people with sincerity

诚恳 chéngkěn ADJ sincere
诚实 chéngshí ADJ honest, simple
诚心诚意 chéngxīn chéngyì ADJ very sincerely
诚信 chéngxìn N sincerity and trust, trust
诚意 chéngyì N good faith, sincerity
诚挚 chéngzhì ADJ sincere, cordial

承 chéng V bear, undertake

承办 chéngbàn V undertake
承包 chéngbāo V contract
　承包商 chéngbāoshāng contractor
承认 chéngrèn V **1** acknowledge, recognize **2** admit (mistake, error, etc.)
承受 chéngshòu V endure, bear
　承受力 chéngshòulì endurance

乘 1 chéng V **1** use (a means of transport), travel (by car, train, plane, etc.) **2** take advantage of

乘人之危 chéng rén zhì wēi take advantage of the misfortune (or weakness) of others

乘 2 chéng V multiply

乘客 chéngkè N passenger
乘机 chéngjī V seize an opportunity
乘务员 chéngwùyuán N attendant (on a train, coach, etc.)

呈 chéng V **1** appear, assume **2** present

呈现 chéngxiàn V appear, show

程 chéng N regulation, procedure

程度 chéngdù N level, degree
程序 chéngxù N procedure
　计算机程序 jìsuànjī chéngxù computer program

惩 chéng TRAD 懲 V punish

惩办 chéngbàn V (of the authorities) punish

惩罚 chéngfá V punish, penalize

澄 chéng ADJ (of water) clear, clean

澄清 chéngqīng V clarify
　澄清事实 chéngqīng shìshí clarify a matter

秤 chèng N scale(s)

吃 chī V eat

吃惊 chījīng V be shocked, be startled, be alarmed
　大吃一惊 dà chī yì jīng greatly shocked, have the fright of one's life
吃苦 chīkǔ V endure hardships, suffer
　吃了很多苦 chī le hěn duō kǔ have suffered a lot
吃亏 chīkuī V suffer losses, be at a disadvantage
吃力 chīlì ADJ making or requiring great efforts

痴 chī ADJ foolish, stupid

白痴 báichī idiot

池 chí N pool, pond

游泳池 yóuyǒngchí swimming pool
池塘 chítáng N pond

迟 chí TRAD 遲 ADJ late

迟到 chídào V come late, be late (for work, school, etc.)
迟缓 chíhuǎn ADJ (of movement) slow, sluggish
迟疑 chíyí V hesitate, waver

持 chí V persevere

持久 chíjiǔ ADJ enduring, lasting
持续 chíxù V continue, sustain, persist
　可持续发展 kě chíxù fāzhǎn sustainable development

匙 chí N spoon

汤匙 tāngchí soup spoon

驰 chí TRAD 馳 V move quickly, gallop

尺 **chǐ I** N ruler (把 bǎ)
尺子 chǐzi ruler
II M. WD a traditional Chinese unit of length (equal to ⅓ meter)
公尺 gōngchǐ meter
英尺 yīngchǐ foot (as a measurement of length)
尺寸 chǐcun N size, measurements
尺码 chǐmǎ N size (of shoes, shirts, ready-made clothing, etc.)

侈 **chǐ** ADJ wasteful (See 奢侈 shēchǐ)

齿 **chǐ** TRAD 齒 N tooth, teeth
齿轮 chǐlún N gear wheel, gear

耻 **chǐ** TRAD 恥 N shame
可耻 kěchǐ shameful, disgraceful
耻辱 chǐrǔ N deep shame, humiliation

赤 **chì** ADJ red
赤道 chìdào N the equator
赤字 chìzì N the number in red, deficit

翅 **chì** N wing
翅膀 chìbǎng N wing (of a bird)

斥 **chì** v scold, shout at

冲 **chōng** TRAD 衝 v **1** clash **2** charge, rush, dash
冲锋 chōngfēng v (of troops) charge, assault
冲浪 chōnglàng v surf
冲破 chōngpò v break through, breach
冲突 chōngtū **I** v clash **II** N conflict, clash
利益冲突 lìyì chōngtū conflict of interest

充 **chōng** ADJ sufficient, full
充分 chōngfèn ADJ abundant, ample, adequate
充满 chōngmǎn ADJ full of, be filled with
充沛 chōngpèi ADJ abundant, plentiful
精力充沛 jīnglì chōngpèi full of vigor and vitality, very energetic
充实 chōngshí **I** ADJ substantial **II** v strengthen, enrich

充足 chōngzú ADJ sufficient, adequate, enough

虫 **chóng** TRAD 蟲 N insect, worm
虫子 chóngzi N insect, worm (只 zhī)

重 **chóng** ADV again, once again
重叠 chóngdié v overlap
重复 chóngfù v repeat
重新 chóngxīn ADV Same as 重 chóng

崇 **chóng** ADJ high, lofty
崇拜 chóngbài v worship, adore
崇高 chónggāo ADJ lofty, sublime
崇敬 chóngjìng v hold in high esteem, revere

宠 **chǒng** TRAD 寵 v pamper, indulge
宠物 chǒngwù N pet

冲 **chòng** ADJ strong, forceful

抽 **chōu** v take out (from in-between)
抽空 chōukòng v manage to find time
抽水机 chōushuǐjī N water pump
抽屉 chōuti N drawer
抽象 chōuxiàng ADJ abstract
抽烟 chōuyān v smoke a cigarette (cigar), smoke

绸 **chóu** TRAD 綢 N silk (See 丝绸 sīchóu)

愁 **chóu** v worry

酬 **chóu** v reward

稠 **chóu** ADJ thick, dense
稠密 chóumì ADJ dense
人口稠密 rénkǒu chóumì densely populated

筹 **chóu** TRAD 籌 v prepare
筹备 chóubèi v prepare (a conference, an event, etc.)
筹建 chóujiàn v prepare to construct (a factory, a school, etc.)

仇 **chóu** N deep hatred

25

仇恨 chóuhèn intense hatred

丑 chǒu TRAD 醜 ADJ ugly

丑恶 chǒu'è ADJ ugly, hideous

丑闻 chǒuwén N scandal

臭 chòu ADJ smelly, stinking

出 chū v emerge from, go out, exit

出版 chūbǎn v publish

出差 chūchāi v be on a business trip, leave town on business

出产 chūchǎn v produce, manufacture

出动 chūdòng v set out, go into action

出发 chūfā v set off (on a journey), start (a journey)

出发点 chūfādiǎn starting point, point of departure

出国 chūguó v go abroad, go overseas

出境 chūjìng v leave the country, exit

办理出境手续 bànlǐ chūjìng shǒuxù go through exit formalities

出口 chūkǒu I v 1 export

出口公司 chūkǒu gōngsī export company

出口贸易 chūkǒu màoyì export business in foreign trade

2 speak, utter II N exit

出来 chūlai v come out

出路 chūlù N outlet, way out

出卖 chūmài v 1 sell, be for sale 2 betray, sell out

出门 chūmén v leave home, go out

出面 chūmiàn v act in the name of

出名 chūmíng ADJ famous, well-known

出纳 chūnà N Same as 出纳员 chūnà yuán

出纳员 chūnàyuán N cashier

出品 chūpǐn N product

出去 chūqu v go out

出入 chūrù I v go in and come out II N inconsistency, discrepancy

出色 chūsè ADJ outstanding, remarkable

出身 chūshēn N family background, (a person's) social origin

出神 chūshén v be lost in thought, spellbound

出生 chūshēng v be born

出生地 chūshēng dì place of birth

出生日期 chūshēng rìqī date of birth

出生证 chūshēng zhèng birth certificate

出事 chūshì v (an accident) take place

出事地点 chūshìdìdiǎn the scene of an accident

出席 chūxí v attend (a meeting, a court trial, etc.)

出息 chūxi N (a person's) future

有出息 yǒu chūxi (especially of a young person) have a bright future, promising

出现 chūxiàn v come into view, appear, emerge

出洋相 chūyángxiàng v make a fool of oneself, cut a ridiculous figure

出院 chūyuàn v be discharged from hospital

出租 chūzū v have ... for hire, rent

房屋出租 fángwū chūzū house for rent, house to let

出租汽车 chūzū qìchē N taxi

NOTE: The slang expression 打的 dǎdī, which means *to call a taxi* or *to travel by taxi*, is very popular in everyday Chinese.

初 chū I N beginning

月初 yuèchū at the beginning of a month

年初 niánchū at the beginning of a year

II ADJ at the beginning, for the first time

III PREFIX (used for the first ten days of a lunar month), the first

初一 chū yī the first day (of a lunar month)

五月初八 Wǔyuè chū bā the eighth day of the fifth lunar month

年初一/大年初一 nián chū yī/dà nián chū yī the first day of the first lunar month (Chinese New Year's Day)

初步 chūbù ADJ initial, tentative

初级 chūjí ADJ elementary, initial

初级小学/初小 chūjí xiǎoxué/chūxiǎo elementary school (from Grade 1 to Grade 4 of a primary school)

初级中学/初中 chūjí zhōngxué/chūzhōng junior high school

初期 chūqī N initial stage

除 chú I v get rid of II PREP except, apart from

26

除草 chú cǎo v to weed
除草剂 chúcǎojì weed killer, herbicide

除虫 chú chóng I v to kill insects II N insecticide

除此以外 chúcǐ yǐwài PREP apart from this, besides

除非 chúfēi CONJ unless, only if

除了…(以外) chúle ... (yǐwài) PREP except, besides

NOTE: (1) While except and besides are two distinct words in English, 除了…以外, chúle...yǐwài may mean either except or besides, as is shown in the examples: 这个动物园除了圣诞节每天开放。 Zhège dòngwùyuán chúle shèngdànjié měi tiān kāifàng. This zoo is open to the public all year round except on Christmas Day.; 我除了英文以外，还会说一点儿中文。 Wǒ chúle Yīngwén yǐwài, hái huì shuō yìdiǎnr Zhōngwén. Besides English I speak a little Chinese. (2) 以外 yǐwài may be omitted, i.e. 除了…以外 chúle...(yǐwài) and 除了… chúle are the same.

除夕 chúxī N New Year's eve

NOTE: In colloquial Chinese, the Chinese New Year's eve is called 大年夜 dàniányè. The dinner on the Chinese New Year's eve is 年夜饭 niányèfàn, or 团圆饭 tuányuánfàn, a family reunion dinner.

厨 chú TRAD 廚 N kitchen

厨房 chúfáng N kitchen
厨房设备 chúfáng shèbèi kitchen equipment
厨房用具 chúfáng yòngjù kitchen utensils

厨师 chúshī N chef
大厨师 dàchúshī master chef

锄 chú TRAD 鋤 I N hoe

锄头 chútou hoe (把 bǎ)
II v do hoeing

处 chǔ TRAD 處 v handle, deal with

处罚 chǔfá v penalize, discipline

处方 chǔfāng N (doctor's) prescription
处方药 chǔfāng yào prescribed medicine
非处方药 fēi chǔfāng yào over-the-counter medicine
开处方 kāi chǔfāng write out a prescription

处分 chǔfèn I N disciplinary action
警告处分 jǐnggào chǔfèn disciplinary warning
II v take disciplinary action
处分服用兴奋剂的运动员 chǔfèn fúyòng xīngfènjì de yùndòngyuán take disciplinary action against athletes who have taken stimulants

处境 chǔjìng N (usually) bad situation, plight
处境危险 chǔjìng wēixiǎn in a dangerous situation

处决 chǔjué v put to death, execute

处理 chǔlǐ v 1 handle, deal with 2 sell at reduced prices
处理品 chǔlǐpǐn goods sold at reduced prices
3 take disciplinary action
处理违反校纪的学生 chǔlǐ wéifǎn xiào jì de xuésheng take disciplinary action against students who have violated school regulations

处于 chǔyú v be in state of, be situated at

处置 chǔzhì v dispose of, handle, deal with

础 chǔ TRAD 礎 N plinth (See 基础 jīchǔ)

楚 chǔ ADJ clear, neat (See 清楚 qīngchu)

储 chǔ TRAD 儲 v store

储备 chǔbèi v store away

储存 chǔcún v 1 store away, keep in reserve 2 (in computing) save a file

储蓄 chǔxù v save (money), deposit (money)
定期储蓄 dìngqī chǔxù fixed deposits, term deposit
活期储蓄 huóqī chǔxù checking account

处 chù TRAD 處 N place, location

处处 chùchù ADV everywhere

触 chù TRAD 觸 V touch, contact
触电 chùdiàn V get an electric shock
触犯 chùfàn V violate (law), offend (a person)

穿 chuān V 1 wear (clothes, shoes), be dressed in
穿着 chuānzhe be dressed in
2 put on (clothes, shoes)

川 chuān N river

船 chuán N boat, ship
划船 huá chuán row a boat
坐船 zuò chuán travel by boat/ship
船舶 chuánbó N boats and ships
船舶公司 chuánbó gōngsī shipping company

传 chuán TRAD 傳 V 1 pass (something) on, transmit 2 spread (news, rumor)
传播 chuánbō V propagate, disseminate
传达 chuándá V pass on, relay, transmit
传达室 chuándá shì reception office
传达总公司的指令 chuándá zǒnggōngsī de zhǐlìng pass on instructions from the company's HQ
传递 chuándì V transmit, deliver
传媒 chuánméi N media, mass media
大众传媒 dàzhòng chuánméi mass media
传染 chuánrǎn V infect
传染病 chuánrǎnbìng infectious (contagious) disease
传授 chuánshòu V teach, pass on (knowledge, skill, etc.)
传说 chuánshuō I N legend, folklore
民间传说 mínjiān chuánshuō folktale
II V it is said, they say
传送 chuánsòng V convey, deliver
传送带 chuánsòngdài conveyor belt
传统 chuántǒng N tradition, heritage
传统服装 chuántǒng fúzhuāng traditional costume
传销 chuánxiāo N pyramid selling
传真 chuánzhēn N fax

喘 chuǎn V breathe with difficulty, pant

串 chuàn V string together

疮 chuāng N sore, open sore
冻疮 dòngchuāng chilblain
疮疤 chuāngbā N scar

窗 chuāng N window (扇 shàn)
玻璃窗 bōlichuāng glass window
窗户 chuānghu N window (扇 shàn)
打开窗户 dǎkāi chuānghu open a window
关上窗户 guānshang chuānghu close a window
窗口 chuāngkǒu N window
窗帘 chuānglián N (window) curtain (块 kuài)
窗台 chuangtái N window sill

床 chuáng N bed (张 zhāng)
单人床 dānrénchuáng single bed
双人床 shuāngrénchuáng double bed
床单 chuángdān N bedsheet (条 tiáo)
床铺 chuángpù N bed (in school dormitories, army barracks, etc.) (张 zhāng)
床位 chuángwèi N bed (in a hospital, ship, train, etc.) (张 zhāng)

闯 chuǎng TRAD 闖 V charge, rush
闯祸 chuǎnghuò V cause disasters, get into trouble

创 chuàng TRAD 創 V create
创建 chuàngjiàn V found (a company, an institution, etc.)
创立 chuànglì V set up, found
创业 chuàngyè V start an undertaking
创业精神 chuàngyè jīngshen pioneering spirit
创造 chuàngzào V create
创造性 chuàngzàoxing N creativity
创作 chuàngzuò I V create (works of art and literature) II N work of art or literature

吹 chuī V blow, puff

28

吹牛 **chuīniú** V brag, boast
吹牛大王 **chuīniú dàwáng** braggart
吹捧 **chuīpěng** V lavish praise on, flatter
相互吹捧 **xiānghù chuīpěng** flatter each
other

炊 **chuī** V cook
炊事员 **chuīshìyuán** N cook, kitchen staff
(in a school, a factory, etc.)

垂 **chuí** V hang down
垂直 **chuízhí** ADJ vertical
垂直线 **chuízhíxiàn** vertical line

锤 **chuí** V hammer
锤子 **chuízi** hammer (把 **bǎ**)

捶 **chuí** V beat with a fist or stick

春 **chūn** N spring
春季 **chūnjì** spring (season)
春节 **Chūnjié** N Spring Festival (the Chinese New Year)
春天 **chūntiān** N spring

纯 **chún** TRAD 純 ADJ pure
纯粹 **chúncuì** ADJ unadulterated, pure and
simple
纯洁 **chúnjié** ADJ pure, ingenuous

唇 **chún** TRAD 脣 N lip
嘴唇 **zuǐchún** (mouth) lip
嘴唇皮儿 **zuǐchúnpír** (mouth) lip

蠢 **chún** ADJ stupid, foolish
蠢事 **chǔnshì** an act of folly
干蠢事 **gān chǔnshì** do a stupid thing,
commit a folly

雌 **cí** ADJ (of animals) female

词 **cí** TRAD 詞 N word
词典 **cídiǎn** N dictionary (本 **běn**)
查词典 **chá cídiǎn** consult a dictionary

瓷 **cí** N porcelain
瓷器 **cíqì** N porcelain

磁 **cí** N magnetism
磁带 **cídài** N magnetic tape, audio tape
(盘 **pán**)
磁卡 **cíkǎ** N magnetic card (for making
telephone calls, etc.)
磁盘 **cípán** N magnetic disc

慈 **cí** ADJ kind and loving
慈爱 **cí'ài** N love and affection (from an
elderly person, e.g. a grandmother)
慈祥 **cíxiáng** ADJ (of an elderly person's
countenance) kindly

辞 **cí** TRAD 辭 V take leave
辞职 **cízhí** V resign (from job, position)

此 **cǐ** PRON **1** this
此时此地 **cǐshícǐdì** here and now
2 here
此后 **cǐhòu** CONJ after this, ever after
此刻 **cǐkè** N this moment
此时 **cǐshí** ADV right now
此外 **cǐwài** CONJ besides, apart from (that),
as well

次 **1 cì** M. WD time (expressing frequency of an act)
下次 **xiàcì** next time
次数 **cìshù** N number of times

次 **2 cì** ADJ inferior
次品 **cìpǐn** N substandard product, seconds
(used goods)
次要 **cìyào** ADJ next in importance, of
secondary importance

次 **3 cì** N order, sequence
次序 **cìxù** N order, sequence

伺 **cì** V wait on
伺候 **cìhou** V wait on, serve

刺 **cì** I V prick II N thorn
刺激 **cìjī** V **1** irritate **2** stimulate, give
incentive to

囱 **cōng** N chimney (See 烟囱
yāncōng)

聪 cōng TRAD 聰 N acute hearing

聪明 cōngmíng ADJ clever, bright, intelligent

匆 cōng TRAD 忽 ADJ hurriedly

匆匆 cōngcōng ADV hurriedly, in a rush

匆忙 cōngmáng ADJ in a hurry, in haste

葱 cōng N onion, scallion

大葱 dàcōng green Chinese onion

洋葱 yángcōng onion

小葱 xiǎocōng spring onion

从 cóng TRAD 從 PREP following, from

从…出发 cóng...chūfā set out from ...

从不 cóngbù ADV never

从此 cóngcǐ CONJ since then, from then on

从…到… cóng...dào... PREP from ... to ..., from ... till ...

从早到晚 cóng-zǎo-dào-wǎn from morning till night, many hours in a day.

从古到今 cóng-gǔ-dào-jīn from the remote past till now

从而 cóng'ér CONJ thus, thereby

从来 cónglái ADV always, ever

从来不 cónglái bù never

从…起 cóng...qǐ PREP starting from ...

从前 cóngqián N **1** past, in the past **2** once upon a time (used in story-telling)

从容 cóngróng ADJ unhurried, leisurely

从事 cóngshì V be engaged in (business, education, law, etc.)

从未 cóngwèi ADV never in the past

丛 cóng TRAD 叢 N shrub, thicket

丛书 cóngshū N a series of books on a specific topic

凑 còu V put together, pool

凑钱 còu qián pool money

凑合 còuhe V make do, make do with

凑巧 còuqiǎo ADV luckily, as luck would have it

粗 cū ADJ thick, crude

粗暴 cūbào ADJ rough, brutal

粗鲁 cūlǔ ADJ rude, boorish

粗细 cūxì N degree of thickness

NOTE: See note on 大小 dàxiǎo.

粗心 cūxīn ADJ careless

促 cù V urge

促进 cùjìn V promote, advance

促使 cùshǐ V impel, urge

醋 cù N vinegar

窜 cuàn TRAD 竄 V **1** rush about **2** falsify, fabricate

催 cuī V urge, hurry

摧 cuī V break, destroy

摧残 cuīcán V devastate, wreck

摧毁 cuīhuǐ V destroy completely

脆 cuì ADJ crisp

脆弱 cuìruò ADJ fragile, frail

粹 cuì ADJ pure

翠 cuì N green, bluish green

村 cūn N village

村庄 cūnzhuāng N village

村子 cūnzi N village (座 zuò)

存 cún V store, keep

存储 cúnchǔ V **1** save a file (in computing) **2** store

存放 cúnfàng V leave in someone's care

存款 cúnkuǎn N savings

存盘 cún pán V save (a computer file)

存在 cúnzài V exist

寸 cùn M. WD a traditional Chinese unit of length (equal to ⅟₃₀ meter)

英寸 yīngcùn inch

磋 cuō V consult

磋商 cuōshāng V consult, discuss

搓 cuō V rub with the hands

错 cuò TRAD 錯 ADJ wrong

错字 cuòzì wrong character
错误 cuòwù I N mistake, error
犯错误 fàn cuòwù make a mistake
纠正错误 jiūzhèng cuòwù correct a
mistake
II ADJ wrong, erroneous

措 cuò V arrange, handle

措施 cuòshī N measure, step

挫 cuò V frustrate, defeat

受挫 shòucuò be frustrated, be defeated
挫折 cuòzhé N setback, frustration

D

答 dā V answer

答应 dāying V 1 answer, reply 2 promise

搭 dā V put up, build

搭配 dāpèi I V arrange in pairs or groups
II N (word) collocation

达 dá TRAD 達 V reach, attain

达成 dáchéng V reach (an agreement, an
understanding, a business deal, etc.)
达到 dádào V reach, achieve

答 dá V answer, reply

答案 dá'àn N answer (to a list of questions)
答辩 dábiàn V speak in self-defense
论文答辩 lùnwén dábiàn (postgraduate
students') oral examination in defense of
a thesis
答复 dáfù I V (formally) reply II N (formal)
reply
答卷 dájuàn N answer sheet

打 dǎ V 1 strike, hit 2 play (certain
games)
打高尔夫球 dǎ gāo'ěrfūqiú play golf
打篮球 dǎ lánqiú play basketball
打台球 dǎ táiqiú play pool

打败 dǎbài V defeat, beat
打扮 dǎbàn V dress up, make up
打车 dǎ chē V call a taxi
打倒 dǎdǎo V strike down, overthrow,
down with ...
打的 dǎ dī V Same as 打车 dǎ chē
打电话 dǎ diànhuà V make a telephone
call
打发 dǎfa V dispatch, send away
打工 dǎgōng V work (especially as a
manual laborer)
打击 dǎjí V strike a blow against (a crime,
a bad tendency, etc.), deal with and punish severely
打击盗版 dǎjí dàobǎn attack the crime
of piracy (of intellectual products)
打架 dǎjià V fight (between people), come
to blows
打交道 dǎ jiāodao V to have dealings
with, negotiate with
和各式各样的人打交道 hé gèshìgèyàng
de rén dǎ jiāodao deal with all kinds of
people
打瞌睡 dǎ kēshuì V doze, doze off
打一会儿瞌睡 dǎ yíhuìr kēshuì have a
doze-off
打量 dǎliang V measure with the eye,
size up
打猎 dǎliè V hunt
打破 dǎpò V break
打破花瓶 dǎpò huāpíng break a vase
打破世界纪录 dǎpò shìjiè jìlù break a
world record
打球 dǎ qiú V play baseball/basketball/
volleyball, etc.
打扰 dǎrǎo V disturb, interrupt

NOTE: You can use 打搅 dǎjiǎo instead of
打扰 dǎrǎo, with the same meaning.
When you call on someone, especially at
their home, you can say 打扰你们了
Dǎrǎo nǐmen le as a polite expression.

打扫 dǎsǎo V clean up
打算 dǎsuàn V plan, contemplate

打听 dǎtīng v inquire, ask

打压 dǎyā v press hard, oppress

打仗 dǎzhàng v go to war, fight in a war

打招呼 dǎ zhāohu v **1** greet, say hello to **2** let know, notify

打针 dǎzhēn v give (or get) an injection

打字 dǎzì v type

大 dà ADJ big, large

大半 dàbàn ADV more than half

大便 dàbiàn **I** N solid waste from the body, stool **II** v move the bowels

大臣 dàchén N official (in a royal court), minister

大大 dàdà ADV greatly, enormously

大胆 dàdǎn ADJ bold, courageous

NOTE: See note on 胆 dǎn.

大道 dàdào N main road, thoroughfare

大地 dàdì N land, the earth

大都 dàdōu Same as 大多 dàduō

大多 dàduō ADV mostly

大多数 dàduōshù N great majority, over-whelming majority

大方 dàfang ADJ **1** generous, liberal 出手大方 chūshǒu dàfang spend money freely, very generous **2** elegant and natural 式样大方 shìyàng dàfang elegant style

大概 dàgài **I** ADJ general, more or less **II** ADV probably

大锅饭 dàguōfàn N food prepared in a big pot 吃大锅饭 chī dàguōfàn IDIOM everyone getting the same reward regardless of different functions and contributions

大后天 dàhòutiān N three days from now

大会 dàhuì N assembly, congress, rally

大伙儿 dàhuǒr PRON everybody, all the people

NOTE: 大伙儿 dàhuǒr is a very colloquial word. For general use, 大家 dàjiā is preferred.

大家 dàjiā PRON all, everybody 我们大家 wǒmen dàjiā all of us 你们大家 nǐmen dàjiā all of you

他们大家 tāmen dàjiā all of them

大街 dàjiē N main street 逛大街 guàng dàjiē take a stroll in the streets, do window-shopping

大局 dàjú N overall public interest

大理石 dàlǐshí N marble

大力 dàlì ADJ vigorous, energetic

大量 dàliàng ADJ a large amount of, a large number of

大陆 dàlù N continent, mainland 中国大陆 Zhōngguó dàlù mainland China

大米 dàmǐ N rice

大拇指 dàmǔzhǐ N the thumb

NOTE: 拇指 mǔzhǐ can also be used to denote *the thumb*. In Chinese the thumb is considered one of the fingers—手指 shǒuzhǐ.

大脑 dànǎo N cerebrum, brain

大牌 dàpái N celebrity, hotshot 大牌明星 dàpái míngxīng celebrity movie star

大炮 dàpào N cannon

大批 dàpī ADJ a large quantity of, lots of

大片 dàpiān N blockbuster 好莱坞大片 Hǎoláiwù dàpiān Hollywood blockbuster

大气 dàqì N atmosphere

大人 dàren N adult, grown-up

NOTE: 大人 dàren is a colloquialism. The general word for *adult* is 成年人 chéngnián rén.

大人物 dà rénwù great personage, big shot, very important person (VIP)

大厦 dàshà N super-big, imposing build-ing (座 zuò)

大声 dàshēng ADJ in a loud voice

大师 dàshī N master (of art or scholarship) 国画大师 guóhuà dàshī master of tradi-tional Chinese art

大使 dàshǐ N ambassador 中国驻美国大使 Zhōngguó zhù Měiguó dàshǐ Chinese ambassador in the U.S.

大使馆 dàshǐguǎn N embassy

大事 dàshì N matter of importance

大肆 dàsì ADV wantonly, without restraint

大体 dàtǐ N on the whole, in the main

大体来说 dàtǐ láishuō on the whole

大小 dàxiǎo N size

NOTE: 大 dà and 小 xiǎo are opposites. Put together, 大小 dàxiǎo means *size*. There are other Chinese nouns made up of antonyms: 长短 chángduǎn *length*, 粗细 cūxì *thickness*, 好坏 hǎohuài *quality*, 高低 gāodī *height*.

大型 dàxíng ADJ large-scale, large-sized

大学 dàxué N university (座 zuò, 所 suǒ)

考大学 kǎo dàxué sit for the university entrance examination

考上大学 kǎo shàng dàxué pass the university entrance examination

上大学 shàng dàxué go to university, study in a university

大洋洲 Dàyángzhōu N Oceania

大衣 dàyī N overcoat

大意 dàyì N rough idea

大约 dàyuē ADJ, ADV approximate, approximately, about, nearly

大致 dàzhì ADJ rough, general

大众 dàzhòng N the masses

大众媒体 dàzhòng méitǐ mass media

大自然 dàzìrán N Nature, Mother Nature

呆 **dāi** I ADJ foolish, stupid

呆子 dāizi idiot

II V Same as 待 dāi

待 **dāi** V stay

NOTE: 待 dāi in the sense of *stay* may be replaced by 呆 dāi.

歹 **dǎi** ADJ bad, evil

歹徒 dǎitú N bad guy, criminal

大 **dài** as in 丈夫 dàifu.

大夫 dàifu N doctor (位 wèi). Same as 医生 yīshēng, used more as a colloquialism.

代 1 **dài** N 1 generation 2 dynasty

NOTE: The major Chinese dynasties are 秦 Qín, 汉 Hàn, 唐 Táng, 宋 Sòng, 元 Yuán, 明 Míng, 清 Qīng.

代 2 **dài** V take the place of, perform on behalf of

代课老师 dàikè lǎoshī relief teacher

代部长 dài bùzhǎng acting minister

代孕妈妈 dàiyùn māma surrogate mother

代校长 dài xiàozhǎng acting principal

代办 dàibàn I V do or act for another II N charge d'affaires

代表 dàibiǎo I N representative, delegate II V represent, indicate

代表团 dàibiǎotuán N delegation, mission

美国商业代表团 Měiguó shāngyè dàibiǎotuán U.S. trade mission

代词 dàicí N pronoun

人称代词 rénchēng dàicí personal pronoun

代号 dàihào N code name

代价 dàijià N price (for achieving something), cost

代理 dàilǐ V act on behalf of, act as agent

代理人 dàilǐrén agent

代数 dàishù N algebra

代数方程式 dàishù fāngchéngshì algebraic formula

代替 dàitì V substitute for, replace

贷 **dài** TRAD 貸 V loan

贷款 dàikuǎn I N loan

无息贷款 wúxī dàikuǎn interest-free loan

II V loan money to, borrow money from

贷款给一家小企业 dàikuǎn gěi yì jiā xiǎo qǐyè loan money to a small business

向银行贷款 xiàng yínháng dàikuǎn ask the bank for a loan

带 1 **dài** TRAD 帶 V bring, take

带动 dàidòng V spur on

带劲 dàijìn ADJ 1 interesting, exciting 2 energetic, forceful

带来/带…来 dàilai/dài...lái v bring ...

带领 dàilǐng V lead, guide

带去/带…去 dàiqu/dài...qù V take

带头 dàitóu V take the lead, be the first
带头发言 dàitóu fāyán be the first to
speak (at a meeting), set the ball rolling

带 2 dài TRAD 帶 N belt, ribbon, band

安全带 ānquándài safety belt
皮带 pídài leather belt
丝带 sīdài silk ribbon

带 3 dài TRAD 帶 N zone, area

寒带 hándài frigid zone
热带 rèdài tropical zone, tropics
温带 wēndài temperate zone

待 dài V 1 treat, deal with 2 wait for

待业 dài yè wait for a job opportunity
待遇 dàiyù N 1 treatment 2 remuneration

逮 dài V catch

逮捕 dàibǔ V arrest, take into custody

袋 dài N sack, bag (只 zhī)

口袋 kǒudài pocket

NOTE: 袋 dài is seldom used alone. It is
either used with the nominal suffix 子 zi to
form 袋子 dài zi, or with another noun to
form a compound word, e.g. 口袋 kǒudài
(pocket).

戴 dài V wear, put on

戴手套儿 dài shǒutàor wear gloves
戴眼镜 dài yǎnjìng wear spectacles

怠 dài ADJ idle, slack

怠工 dàigōng N slowdown (as workers'
protest)
怠慢 dàimàn V slight, give the cold
shoulder to

单 dān TRAD 單 ADJ single, separate

单人床 dānrénchuáng single bed
单人房间 dānrén fángjiān (hotel) room
for a single person
单数 dānshù odd number

单纯 dānchún ADJ simple-minded,
ingenuous
单词 dāncí N word
单调 dāndiào ADJ monotonous
单独 dāndú ADJ alone, on one's own
单亲家庭 dānqīn jiātíng N single-parent
family
单身贵族 dānshēn guìzú N a single person
with lots of money to spend, yuppy
单位 dānwèi N work unit, e.g. a factory, a
school, a government department
单元 dānyuán N unit (in an apartment
house), apartment, flat

丹 dān N red color

担 dān TRAD 擔 V carry on the shoulder,
take on (responsibility, burden etc)

担保 dānbǎo V guarantee, vouch for
担保人 dānbǎorén guarantor
担负 dānfù V take on (responsibility),
meet (expenditure), hold (a position)
担负使命 dānfù shǐmìng undertake a
mission
担负子女的教育费 dānfù zǐnǚ de jiàoyù-
fèi meet children's educational costs
担任 dānrèn V assume the office of, act in
the capacity of
担心 dānxīn V worry, fret
担忧 dānyōu V worry

耽 dān V delay

耽误 dānwù V delay
耽误时间 dānwù shíjiān waste time

胆 dǎn TRAD 膽 N 1 gallbladder
2 courage

胆子 dǎnzi courage
胆子大 dǎnzi dà be brave, be bold
胆子小 dǎnzi xiǎo be timid, be cowardly

NOTE: The ancient Chinese believed that
the gallbladder was the organ of courage;
hence the expressions: 他胆子很大 Tā
dǎnzi hěn dà and 他很大胆 Tā hěn dàdǎn
to mean He is bold; 他胆子很小 Tā dǎnzi
hěn xiǎo and 他很胆小 Tā hěn dǎnxiǎo to
mean He is timid.

胆量 dǎnliàng N courage, guts

试试他的胆量 shìshì tāde dǎnliàng test his courage, see how brave he is

胆怯 **dǎnqiè** ADJ timid, cowardly

旦 **dàn** N dawn (See 元旦 yuándàn)

但 **dàn** CONJ Same as 但是 dànshì. Used in writing.

但是 **dànshì** CONJ but, yet

担 **dàn** TRAD 擔 N load, burden

担子 **dànzi** load, burden
担子重 **dànzi zhòng** great burden, heavy responsibility

淡 **dàn** ADJ 1 not salty, tasteless, bland 2 (of tea, coffee) weak

氮 **dàn** nitrogen

氮肥 **dànféi** nitrogenous fertilizer

蛋 **dàn** N egg (especially chicken egg)

蛋白质 **dànbáizhì** N protein
蛋糕 **dàngāo** N (western-style) cake

诞 **dàn** TRAD 誕 V be born

诞辰 **dànchén** birthday
诞生 **dànshēng** V be born

弹 **dàn** TRAD 彈 N bullet

弹药 **dànyào** N ammunition
弹药库 **dànyàokù** arms depot

当 1 **dāng** TRAD 當 PREP at the time of, when

当…的时候 **dāng...de shíhou** CONJ when ...

NOTE: 当 dāng may be omitted, especially colloquially, e.g. （当）我在工作的时候，不希望别人来打扰我。(Dāng) Wǒ zài gōngzuò de shíhou, bù xīwàng biérén lái dárǎo wǒ. *(When) I am working, I don't want to be disturbed.*

当 2 **dāng** TRAD 當 V work as, serve as

当场 **dāngchǎng** N on the spot
当场抓获 **dāngchǎng zhuāhuò** catch red-handed
当初 **dāngchū** N originally, at the outset

当代 **dāngdài** ADJ contemporary, present-day

当地 **dāngdì** N at the place in question, local

当地人 **dāngdì rén** a local
当地时间 **dāngdì shíjiān** local time

当局 **dāngjú** N the authorities

当面 **dāngmiàn** ADV to someone's face, in the very presence of

当面撒谎 **dāngmiàn sāhuǎng** tell a barefaced lie

当年 **dāngnián** N in those years, then

当前 **dāngqián** N at present, now

当然 **dāngrán** ADV of course

当时 **dāngshí** N at that time, then

当事人 **dāngshìrén** N person/people concerned, party (to a lawsuit)

当心 **dāngxīn** V be cautious, take care

当选 **dāngxuǎn** V be elected

当选为代表 **dāngxuǎn wéi dàibiǎo** be elected a delegate

当中 **dāngzhōng** N right in the middle, in the center

挡 **dǎng** TRAD 擋 V block, keep off

党 **dǎng** TRAD 黨 N political party

NOTE: As China is under a one-party rule, when people mention 党 dǎng in China, they usually refer to 中国共产党 Zhōngguó Gòngchǎn Dǎng *the Chinese Communist Party.*

党派 **dǎngpài** N political party/group

党委 **dǎngwěi** N (Chinese Communist) Party committee

党委书记 **dǎngwěi shūjì** (Chinese Communist) Party committee secretary, (Chinese Communist) Party chief

NOTE: The Chinese Communist Party Committee in a province is called 省委 shěngwěi, and that in a city 市委 shìwěi. These are the most powerful organs in a Chinese province or city (not the local governments—政府 zhèngfǔ).

党员 **dǎngyuán** N party member

荡 **dàng** TRAD 蕩 V swing, sway

荡秋千 dàng qiūqiān play on the swings

当 **dàng** TRAD 當 V **1** treat as, regard as **2** think

当天 dàngtiān N the same day

当做 dàngzuò V treat as, regard as

档 **dàng** TRAD 檔 N **1** shelf, cabinet **2** grade, class

档案 dàng'àn N (份 fèn) file, archive

档次 dàngcì N standard or level of quality, grade, class

刀 **dāo** N knife (把 bǎ)

刀子 dāozi a small knife

铅笔刀 qiānbǐ dāo pencil sharpener

水果刀 shuǐguǒ dāo penknife

刀刃 dāorèn N edge of a knife

岛 **dǎo** TRAD 島 N island

岛屿 dǎoyǔ N island, islet

捣 **dǎo** TRAD 搗 V beat, smash

捣蛋 dǎodàn V make trouble (in a mischievous way)

故意捣蛋 gùyì dǎodàn be deliberately mischievous

捣乱 dǎoluàn V make trouble, sabotage

捣乱公共秩序 dǎoluàn gōnggòng zhìxù disrupt public order

蹈 **dǎo** V dance (See 舞蹈 wúdǎo)

导 **dǎo** TRAD 導 V lead, guide (See 辅导 fǔdǎo, 领导 lǐngdǎo, 指导 zhǐdǎo)

导弹 dǎodàn N guided missile (枚 méi)

导航 dǎoháng N navigation (by electronic devices)

导师 dǎoshī N supervisor (for postgraduate students)

导演 dǎoyǎn I N director (for films or play)

名导演 míng dǎoyǎn famous director

II V direct (a film or play)

导游 dǎoyóu N tourist guide

导致 dǎozhì V lead to, cause

倒 **dǎo** V fall, topple

倒闭 dǎobì go bust, cease operations

倒卖 dǎomài V resell at a profit

倒霉 dǎoméi V have bad luck, be out of luck

到 **dào** V arrive, come to, up to

到处 dàochù ADV everywhere

NOTE: 到处 dàochù is always placed before a verbal phrase, and is often followed by 都 dōu.

到达 dàodá V arrive, reach

到底 dàodǐ ADV **1** in the end, finally **2** after all (used in a question)

到来 dàolái V arrive

到期 dàoqī V become due, expire

到…为止 dào...wéizhǐ PREP until, by, up to

倒 **dào** I V **1** put upside down **2** pour (water), make (tea) II ADV contrary to what may be expected (used before a verb or an adjective to indicate an unexpected action or state)

倒计时 dàojìshí N countdown

倒退 dàotuì V go backward, regress

悼 **dào** V mourn

悼念 dàoniàn V mourn, grieve over

盗 **dào** N robber, bandit (See 强盗 qiángdào, 盗版 dàobǎn)

盗版 dàobǎn I N pirated edition, pirated copy

盗版书 dàobǎn shū pirated edition of a book

盗版电影 dàobǎn diànyǐng pirated movie

II V make pirated copies

盗窃 dàoqiè V steal, embezzle, commit larceny

盗窃犯 dàoqièfàn thief, one who commits larceny

道 I **dào** N way, path

道德 dàodé N morals, ethics

不道德 bú dàodé immoral

道理 dàolǐ N principle, reason, hows and whys

讲道理 jiǎng dàolǐ (of a person) be reasonable

有道理 yǒu dàoli reasonable, true

NOTE: 道 dào and 理 lǐ are two important concepts in Chinese thought. The original meaning of 道 dào is *path*, *way*. By extension it denotes "the fundamental principle of the universe." 理 lǐ originally meant *the grain of a piece of jade* and came to mean "the underlying logic of things."

道路 dàolù N road, path

道 2 dào M. WD 1 (for things in the shape of a line)
一道光线 yí dào guāngxiàn a ray of sunshine
2 (for questions in a school exercise, examinations, etc.)
两道难题 liǎng dào nántí two difficult questions

道 3 dào V Same as 说 shuō, used only in old-fashioned writing
能说会道 néng shuō huì dào eloquent, glib
道歉 dàoqiàn V apologize, say sorry

稻 dào N rice, paddy
稻子 dàozi rice, paddy rice

得 dé V get, obtain
得到 dédào succeed in getting/obtaining

NOTE: The verb 得 dé is seldom used alone. It is often followed by 到 dào, grammatically a complement, to mean *get* or *obtain*.

得病 débìng V fall ill, contract a disease
得力 délì ADJ competent and efficient, very capable
得力助手 délìzhùshǒu very capable assistant, indispensable right-hand assistant
得失 déshī N gain and loss, success and failure
得以 déyǐ MODAL V so that, can
得意 déyì ADJ complacent, deeply pleased with oneself
得意忘形 déyì wàng xíng be dizzy with success

得意洋洋 déyì yángyáng show extreme self-complacency, be elated
得罪 dézuì V offend, incur displeasure of ...
得罪不起 dézuì bùqǐ can't afford to offend

德 dé N virtue

德国 Déguó N Germany
德文 Déwén N the German language (especially the writing)
德语 Déyǔ N the German language

地 de PARTICLE (attached to a word or phrase to indicate that it is an adverb. 地 de is normally followed by a verb or an adjective.)
慢慢地说 mànman de shuō speak slowly
愉快地旅行 yúkuài de lǚxíng travel pleasantly

NOTE: See note on 的 de.

得 de PARTICLE (introducing a word, phrase or clause to indicate that it is a complement. 得 de is normally preceded by a verb or an adjective.)
说得大家都笑了起来 shuō de dàjiā dōu xiàole qǐlái talk in such a way that everybody starts laughing
贵得很 guì de hěn very expensive
来得很早 lái de hěn zǎo come early

NOTE: See note on 的 de.

的 de PARTICLE (attached to a word or phrase to indicate that it is an attribute. 的 de is normally followed by a noun.)
我的电脑 wǒ de diànnǎo my computer
最新型的电脑 zuì xīnxíng de diànnǎo the latest computer model
学校刚买来的电脑 xuéxiào gāng mǎilai de diànnǎo the computer that the school just bought

NOTE: 的, 得, 地 have different functions and are three distinct words. However, as they are pronounced the same (de) in everyday speech, some Chinese speakers do not distinguish them.

···的话 ...de huà CONJ if

NOTE: See note on 要是 yàoshì.

得 **děi** MODAL V have to

灯 **dēng** TRAD 燈 N lamp, lighting

电灯 diàndēng light, electric light
关灯 guān dēng turn off the light
开灯 kāi dēng turn on the light
日光灯 rìguāngdēng fluorescent lamp
台灯 táidēng desk lamp

灯火 dēnghuǒ N lights
灯火通明 dēnghuǒ tōngmíng (of a building) brightly lit
灯笼 dēnglóng N lantern
灯泡 dēngpào N light bulb (只 zhī)

登 **dēng** V 1 publish (in a newspaper, a journal, etc.)
登广告 dēng guǎnggào place an advertisement, advertise
2 go up, ascend
登机 dēngjī V board a plane
登机卡 dēngjīkǎ boarding card
登记 dēngjì V register, check in
登陆 dēnglù V land (from waters, especially by troops)
登山 dēngshān V climb a mountain or hill
登山运动 dēngshān yùndòng mountaineering
登山运动员 dēngshān yùndòngyuán mountaineer

等 1 **děng** V wait, wait for
等一下 děng yíxià wait a minute
等待 děngdài V wait (usually used in writing)
等到 děngdào CONJ by the time, as late as
等候 děnghòu V Same as 等待 děngdài

等 2 **děng** N grade, rank, class
等级 děngjí N grade, rank
确定(商品的)等级 quèdìng (shāngpǐn de) děngjí determine the grades (of a commodity)
等于 děngyú V be equal to, equal, amount to

等 3 **děng** PARTICLE 1 and so on and so forth, et cetera 2 (used at the end of a list)

瞪 **dèng** V open one's eyes wide, stare, glare

凳 **dèng** N stool (low chair)
凳子 dèngzi stool (个 gè)

低 **dī** I ADJ low II V lower
低调 dīdiào ADJ low key
低估 dīgū V underestimate
低级 dījí ADJ 1 elementary 2 vulgar
低级趣味 dījí qùwèi vulgar interests, base taste
低劣 dīliè ADJ inferior

堤 **dī** N dike, embankment

滴 **dī** M. WORD drop (used for liquids)

敌 **dí** TRAD 敵 N enemy
敌对 díduì ADJ hostile, antagonistic
敌对的态度 díduì de tàidu hostile attitude
敌人 dírén N enemy
敌视 díshì V be hostile to

笛 **dí** N flute
笛子 dízi flute
吹笛子 chuī dízi play the flute

涤 **dí** TRAD 滌 V wash, wash away

的 **dí** as in 的确 díquè
的确 díquè ADV really, truly
的士 díshì N taxi

迪 **dí** V enlighten
迪斯科 dísīkē N disco

底 **dǐ** N base, bottom
底片 dǐpiàn N (film) negative
底下 dǐxia N underneath, under
底线 dǐxiàn N bottom line

抵 **dǐ** V 1 arrive 2 resist

抵偿 dǐcháng v compensate for

抵达 dǐdá v arrive at

抵抗 dǐkàng v resist

抵押 dǐyā v pledge ... as security for a loan, mortgage

抵押品 dǐyāpǐn security (for a loan)

抵制 dǐzhì v boycott, reject

地 dì N earth, ground

地板 dìbǎn N floor, timber floor

地步 dìbù N 1 extent 2 (poor) condition

地带 dìdài N region, zone

地道 dìdào N tunnel, underpass (条 tiáo)

地道 dìdao ADJ genuine, authentic

地道的中国菜 dìdao de Zhōngguócài authentic Chinese cuisine

地点 dìdiǎn N the place for an event or activity, venue

地方 dìfang N 1 place, location, area (个 gè) 2 part of, aspect

NOTE: 地方 dìfang is a word of wide application. It has both concrete, specific senses and abstract, general senses, as in the following examples: 医生: 你什么地方不舒服? Yīshēng: Nǐ shénme dìfang bù shūfu? *Doctor: What spot ails you?* (→ *What's wrong with you?*); 照顾不到的地方, 请多多原谅。Zhàogù búdào de dìfang, qǐng duōduō yuánliàng. *If there's anything not well attended to, please accept my sincere apology.*

地理 dìlǐ N geography

地理学家 dìlǐxuéjiā geographer

国家地理学会 Guójiā Dìlǐ Xuéhuì National Geographic Society

地面 dìmiàn N the earth's surface, ground

地球 dìqiú N the earth

地球科学 dìqiú kēxué earth science

地区 dìqū N region, area

地势 dìshì N physical features of a place, terrain

地毯 dìtǎn N carpet (张 zhāng)

地铁 dìtiě N underground railway, subway

地图 dìtú N map (张 zhāng)

地图册 dìtúcè atlas

地位 dìwèi N status, position

地下 dìxià N underground

地下商场 dìxià shāngchǎng underground shopping center

地下铁路 (地铁) dìxià tiělù (dìtiě) underground railway, subway

地下停车场 dìxià tíngchēchǎng parking garage, underground carpark

地形 dìxíng N topography, terrain

地震 dìzhèn N earthquake, seism (场 cháng)

地址 dìzhǐ N address

地质 dìzhì N geology

地质调查 dìzhì diàochá geological survey

地质学家 dìzhìxuéjiā geologist

帝 dì N the Supreme Being

帝国 dìguó N empire

帝国主义 dìguózhǔyì imperialism

弟 dì N younger brother

弟弟 dìdi younger brother

弟妹 dìmèi N 1 younger brother and younger sister 2 younger brother's wife

弟兄 dìxiōng N brothers

递 dì TRAD 遞 v hand over, pass on

快递 kuàidì fast delivery (of mail)

快递服务 kuài dì fúwù fast delivery service

递交 dìjiāo v hand over, present

递增 dìzēng v increase progressively

第 dì PREFIX (used before a number to form an ordinal number)

第一 dì-yī the first

第一天 dì-yī tiān the first day

第十 dì-shí the tenth

第十课 dì-shí kè the tenth lesson, Lesson 10

第三者 dì-sānzhě N third party, one who has an affair with a married person

颠 diān TRAD 顛 v bump, jolt

颠簸 diānbǒ v bump, bump along

颠倒 diāndǎo v turn upside down, reverse

颠倒黑白 diāndǎo hēibái confound black and white, confuse right and wrong

颠覆 **diānfù** v subvert or overturn in an illegal way

掂 diān TRAD 战 v weigh in the hand

点 diān TRAD 點 I N 1 drop, point, dot
墨点 mò diǎn ink stain
水点 shuǐ diǎn water stain
2 (indicating decimal)
三点四 sān diǎn sì 3.4 (three point four)
十二点三五 shí'èr diǎn sān wǔ 12.35 (twelve point three five)
II M. WD 1 a little, a bit
有(一)点儿… yǒu (yì) diǎnr... a bit ..., a little ... (used before nouns and adjectives)
2 o'clock III v drip, put a dot, touch
点火 diǎnhuǒ v light a fire
点名 diǎnmíng v call the roll, do roll-call
点燃 diǎnrán v kindle, ignite
点心 diǎnxīn N snack, light refreshments

NOTE: The Cantonese pronunciation of 点心 is "dim sum." Many Chinese restaurants overseas sell Cantonese-style refreshments or snack known as "dim sum." To have such refreshments for a meal is "yum cha," the Cantonese pronunciation of 饮茶 yǐnchá, which literally means *drink tea*.

点钟 **diǎnzhōng** N o'clock

NOTE: In colloquial Chinese 点钟 diǎnzhōng can be shortened to 点 diǎn, e.g. "现在几点?" "三点。" "Xiànzài jǐ diǎn?" "Sān diǎn." *"What time is it?" "Three o'clock."*

点缀 **diǎnzhuì** v embellish, decorate
点子 **diǎnzi** N idea
鬼点子 guǐdiǎnzi wicked idea, trick
出点子 chū diǎnzi come up with ideas

典 diǎn N standard, law

典礼 **diǎnlǐ** N ceremony
结婚典礼 jiéhūn diǎnlǐ wedding ceremony
典型 **diǎnxíng** ADJ typical, representative
典型事例 diǎnxíng shìlì typical case

电 diàn TRAD 電 N electricity, power, electronics

电报 **diànbào** N telegram, cable (份 fèn)
电车 **diànchē** N trolley bus, streetcar (辆 liàng)
电池 **diànchí** N battery, electrical cell (节 jié)
可充电电池 kě chōngdiàn diànchí rechargeable battery
电灯 **diàndēng** N electric light (个 gè)
关电灯 guān diàndēng turn off the light
开电灯 kāi diàndēng turn on the light
电动机 **diàndòngjī** N (electric) motor (台 tái)
电风扇 **diànfēngshàn** N Same as 电扇 diàn shàn
电话 **diànhuà** N telephone, telephone call (个 gè)
无绳电话 wú shéng diànhuà cordless telephone
移动电话 yídòng diànhuà mobile phone
打电话 dǎ diànhuà use the telephone, be on the phone.
给…打电话 gěi...dǎ diànhuà call ... on the telephone, ring ...
听电话 tīng diànhuà answer a telephone call
电缆 **diànlǎn** N (electric) cable (条 tiáo)
电力 **diànlì** N electric power, power
电铃 **diànlíng** N electric bell
电炉 **diànlú** N electric stove, hot plate
电路 **diànlù** N electric circuit
电脑 **diànnǎo** N computer (台 tái)
笔记本电脑 bǐjìběn diànnǎo notebook computer
电钮 **diànniǔ** N switch (on an electrical appliance)
电器 **diànqì** N electrical appliance
电器商店 diànqì shāngdiàn electrical appliances store
电扇 **diànshàn** N electric fan (台 tái)
电视 **diànshì** N television
电视机 diànshìjī TV set (台 tái)
电视剧 diànshìjù TV show, soap opera
电视台 diànshìtái TV station
有线电视 yǒuxiàn diànshì cable TV
看电视 kàn diànshì watch TV
电台 **diàntái** N radio station
电梯 **diàntī** N elevator, lift (部 bù)

乘电梯 **chéng diàntī** go up/down by elevator

电影 **diànyǐng** N movie, film (场 chǎng, 部 bù, 个 gè)

电影票 **diànyǐngpiào** film ticket

电影院 **diànyǐngyuàn** cinema, cinema complex, movie theater (座 zuò)

看电影 **kàn diànyǐng** watch a film, go to the movies.

电源 **diànyuán** N power supply, mains

电子 **diànzǐ** N electron

电子工业 **diànzǐ gōngyè** electronics industry

电子贺卡 **diànzǐ hèkǎ** e-card

电子邮件 **diànzǐ yóujiàn** e-mail

电子游戏 **diànzǐ yóuxì** electronic game

垫 **diàn** TRAD 墊 I V put something under something else to raise it or make it level II N mat, pad, cushion

垫子 **diànzi** mat, pad, cushion

店 **diàn** N Same as 商店 shāngdiàn

店员 **diànyuán** N sales clerk, shop assistant

惦 **diàn** V keep thinking about, remember with concern

惦记 **diànji** V keep thinking about, remember with concern

淀 **diàn** as in 淀粉 diànfěn

淀粉 **diànfěn** N starch, amylum

殿 **diàn** N hall (in a palace, temple, etc.)

雕 **diāo** V carve

浮雕 **fúdiāo** relief (sculpture)

石雕 **shídiāo** stone carving

雕刻 **diāokè** V carve, engrave (a work of art)

雕塑 **diàosù** N sculpture

雕像 **diàoxiàng** N statue

刁 **diāo** ADJ sly, tricky

刁难 **diāonàn** make things unnecessarily difficult in order to harrass

叼 **diāo** V hold in the mouth

掉 **diào** V fall, drop

NOTE: 掉 diào is often used after a verb, as a complement to mean *finish (doing ...)*, e.g.

吃掉 **chīdiào** eat up: 水果都吃掉了。 Shuǐguǒ dōu chīdiao le. *The fruit is all eaten up.*

卖掉 **màidiào** sell out: 那些书还没有卖掉。Nà xiē shū hái méiyǒu màidiao. *Those books aren't sold out yet.*

扔掉 **rēngdiào** throw away, discard: 这件衣服太小了，不能穿了，你扔掉吧! Zhè jiàn yīfu tài xiǎo le, bù néng chuān le, nǐ rēngdiào ba! *This dress is too small for you. You'd better throw it away.*

忘掉 **wàngdiào** forget: 这件事我怎么也忘不掉。Zhè jiàn shì wǒ zěnme yě wàng bu diao. *I can't forget this incident, no matter how hard I try.*

钓 **diào** TRAD 釣 V to fish with hook and line, angle

调 **diào** TRAD 調 V **1** exchange, swap **2** transfer

调查 **diàochá** I V investigate II N investigation

调查团 **diàochátuán** investigation team

调查人员 **diàochá rényuán** investigator

调动 **diàodòng** V transfer to another post

申请调动工作 **shēnqǐng diàodòng gōngzuò** apply for a job transfer

调度 **diàodù** V dispatch (vehicles or workers)

调换 **diàohuàn** V exchange (a purchase, a seat, etc.)

吊 **diào** TRAD 弔 V hang, suspend

上吊 **shàngdiào** hang oneself (to commit suicide)

吊车 **diàochē** N crane (a heavy machine)

吊环 **diàohuán** N rings (in gymnastics)

吊销 **diàoxiāo** V revoke (a license, a permit, a certificate, etc.)

吊销营业执照 **diàoxiāo yíngyè zhízhào** revoke a business permit

跌 **diē** V **1** fall, tumble **2** (prices) fall, drop

爹 **diē** N dad, daddy

爹爹 diēdie dad, daddy

碟 dié N small dish, small plate

碟子 diézi small dish
茶碟 chádié saucer

蝶 dié N butterfly (See 蝴蝶 húdié)

叠 dié TRAD 疊 V pile up

丁 dīng N small cube

肉丁 ròudīng diced meat

钉 dīng TRAD 釘 N (metal) nail

叮 dīng V 1 (of mosquitos) bite 2 remind repeatedly

叮嘱 dīngzhǔ V urge repeatedly, exhort

盯 dīng V gaze, stare

顶 dǐng TRAD 頂 I N top (of the head), peak, summit

山顶 shāndǐng peak
头顶 tóudǐng crown of the head
屋顶 wūdǐng roof

II V carry on the head, hit with the head

顶点 dǐngdiǎn N zenith, apex
顶端 dǐngduān N top, peak

订 dìng TRAD 訂 V book

订房间 dìng fángjiān reserve a hotel/ motel room
订票 dìng piào book tickets
订座 dìng zuò book a table (at a restaurant), book a seat (in a theater)

NOTE: 定 dìng can also be used in this sense, e.g. 定房间 = 订房间.

订购 dìnggòu V place an order
订户 dìnghù N subscriber (to a newspaper or magazine)
订婚 dìnghūn V be engaged (for marriage)

订婚戒指 dìnghūn jièzhǐ engagement ring (枚 méi, 只 zhī)
和…订婚 hé…dìnghūn be engaged to ...

订货 dìnghuò V order goods (in bulk), order

订货单 dìnghuòdān (written) order (份 fèn)

订阅 dìngyuè V subscribe (a newspaper or magazine)

钉 dìng TRAD 釘 V drive a nail into

定 dìng I V fix, set, determine II ADJ fixed, set, decided

定额 dìng'é N quota (for sales, production, etc.)
完成销售定额 wánchéng xiāoshòu dìng'é fill a sales quota
定价 dìngjià N fixed price, price
定居 dìngjū V start living in a place, settle down
定理 dìnglǐ N theorem (条 tiáo)
定量 dìngliàng V determine the quantity of
定量分析 dìngliàng fēnxī quantitative analysis
定律 dìnglǜ N (scientific) law
定期 dìngqī ADV at regular intervals
定期维修车辆 dìngqī wéixiū chēliàng regular maintenance of vehicles
定位 dìngwèi V determine the position of
定位仪 dìngwèiyí GPS navigation system, GPS
定性 dìngxìng V determine the quality of
定性分析 dìngxìng fēnxī qualitative analysis
定义 dìngyì N definition
下定义 xià dìngyì give a definition

丢 diū V lose, throw away

丢脸 diūliǎn lose face, be disgraced
丢三落四 diū-sān-là-sì V be forgetful, be scatter-brained

NOTE: 落 here is pronounced as là, not its usual luò.

丢失 diūshī V lose

东 dōng TRAD 東 N east, eastern

东北 dōngběi N northeast, the Northeast

NOTE: 东北 dōngběi as a specific geographical term refers to the northeastern part of China, which used to be known in the West as Manchuria.

东边 **dōngbian** N the east side, to the east, in the east

东道 **dōngdào** N host

东道国 **dōngdàoguó** host country

东道主 **dōngdàozhǔ** host (usually for an official function)

东方 **dōngfāng** N the East, the Orient

东面 **dōngmiàn** N Same as 东边 dōngbian

东南 **dōngnán** N southeast

东西 **dōngxi** N **1** thing, things (个 gè, 件 jiàn, 种 zhǒng) **2** a person or animal (used affectionately or disapprovingly in colloquial Chinese)

NOTE: 东西 dōngxi, which literally means *east and west*, is an extremely common "all-purpose" noun that can denote any object or objects in Chinese. More examples: 妈妈出去买东西了。 *Māma chūqu mǎi dōngxi le.* Mother's gone shopping.; 图书馆里不能吃东西。 *Túshūguǎn lǐ bù néng chī dōngxi.* No food in the library.

冬 **dōng** N winter

冬季 **dōngjì** winter season

冬天 **dōngtiān** N winter

董 **dǒng** as in 董事 dǒngshì

董事 **dǒngshì** N director (of a company), trustee

董事长 **dǒngshìzhǎng** chairman of the board of directors

懂 **dǒng** V comprehend, understand

NOTE: 懂 is often used after another verb as a complement, e.g.

读懂 **dúdǒng** read and understand: 这本书我读了两遍才读懂。 *Zhè běn shū wǒ dúle liǎng biàn cái dúdǒng.* I understood this book only after reading it twice.

看懂 **kàndǒng** see (or read) and understand: 这个电影我没有看懂。 *Zhège diànyǐng wǒ méiyǒu kàndǒng.* I didn't understand that movie.

听懂 **tīngdǒng** listen and understand: 我听得懂一些简单的中文。 *Wǒ tīng de dǒng*

yìxiē jiǎndān de Zhōngwén. *I can understand a little simple spoken Chinese.*

懂事 **dǒngshì** ADJ be sensible

动 **dòng** TRAD 動 V move, act

动工 **dònggōng** V begin construction

动机 **dòngjī** N motive, intention

动机不纯 **dòngjī bùchún** with hidden motives

动静 **dòngjing** N signs of activity

动力 **dònglì** N **1** source of power, power **2** driving force (to do something), motivation

动乱 **dòngluàn** N (social) turmoil, upheaval

动脉 **dòngmài** N artery

主动脉 **zhǔ dòngmài** main artery

动人 **dòngrén** ADJ moving, touching

动身 **dòngshēn** V start (a journey), set off (on a journey)

动手 **dòngshǒu** V start work

动态 **dòngtài** N general tendency of affairs, developments

科技动态 **kējì dòngtài** developments in science and technology, what's new in science and technology

动物 **dòngwù** N animal (只 zhī)

动物学 **dòngwùxué** zoology

动物园 **dòngwùyuán** zoo

动摇 **dòngyáo** V waver, vacillate

决不动摇 **jué bú dòngyáo** will not waver, be very firm and determined

动用 **dòngyòng** V put to use, draw on

动用预备金 **dòngyòng yùbèi jīn** draw on reserve fund

动员 **dòngyuán** V mobilize

动作 **dòngzuò** N movement (of the body)

冻 **dòng** TRAD 凍 V freeze

冻肉 **dòngròu** frozen meat

肉冻 **ròudòng** jellied meat

水果冻 **shuǐguǒdòng** fruit jelly

冻结 **dòngjié** V freeze

工资冻结 **gōngzī dòngjié** wage freeze

栋 **dòng** TRAD 棟 M. WD (for buildings)

43

一栋古典风格的小楼 yí dòng gǔdiǎn fēnggé de xiǎo lóu a nice house in classical style

洞 **dòng** N hole, cave, cavity

都 **dōu** ADV all, both, without exception

NOTE: When words like 每天 měitiān (every day), 每个 měi ge (every one), 大家 dàjiā (everybody) or 所有的 suǒyǒu de (all) are used, they usually occur with the adverb 都 dōu.

兜 **dōu** I N pocket, bag II v 1 wrap up 2 move around 3 canvass, solicit

抖 **dǒu** v shake, tremble

陡 **dǒu** ADJ steep, precipitous

斗 **dòu** TRAD 鬥 v fight

斗争 dòuzhēng I v struggle, fight II N struggle, fight

斗志 dòuzhì N will to fight, militancy

豆 **dòu** N bean, pea

豆子 dòuzi bean, pea

豆腐 dòufu N bean curd, tofu

豆浆 dòujiāng N soybean milk

逗 **dòu** v play with, tease

逗留 dòuliú v stay briefly

都 **dū** N big city, metropolis

首都 shǒudū capital city, capital

都市 dūshì N big city, metropolis

督 **dū** v supervise

督促 dūcù v supervise and urge

毒 **dú** N 1 poison, toxin

毒蛇 dúshé poisonous snake

蛇毒 shédú snake's venom

有毒 yǒudú poisonous, venomous 2 narcotic drug (e.g. heroin, cocaine, etc.)

贩毒 fàndú drug trafficking

吸毒 xīdú drug taking

毒害 dúhài v poison

毒害青少年 dúhài qīng shàonián poison the minds of young people

毒品 dúpǐn Same as 毒 dú 1.

毒药 dúyào N poison, toxicant

独 **dú** TRAD 獨 ADJ solitary, alone

独裁 dúcái v establish a dictatorship, rule arbitrarily

独裁者 dúcáizhě dictator

独裁政权 dúcái zhèngquán dictatorial regime

独唱 dúchàng N (singing) solo

男高音独唱 nángāoyīn dúchàng tenor solo

独立 dúlì v be independent

独特 dútè ADJ unique, distinctive

独特的风格 dútè de fēnggé unique style

独自 dúzì ADV all by oneself, alone

独自旅游 dúzì lǚyóu have a holiday all by oneself

独奏 dúzòu N solo performance on an musical instrument

萨克斯管独奏 sà kè sī guǎn dúzòu saxophone solo

读 **dú** TRAD 讀 v 1 read, read aloud 2 attend (a school), study (in a school)

读小学/中学/大学 dú xiǎoxué/ zhōngxué/ dàxué attend a primary school/high school/university

NOTE: (1) In colloquial Chinese, 读 dú may be replaced by 看 kàn when used in the sense of read, e.g. 看书 kàn shū, 看报 kàn bào. (2) When used in the sense of attend (school) or study (in a school) 读 dú may be replaced by 念 niàn to become 念小学/中学/大学 niàn xiǎoxué/zhōngxué/ dàxué, which is more colloquial.

读书 dúshū v 1 read 2 be a student, study (in a school)

读物 dúwù N reading material

儿童读物 értóng dúwù children's books

读者 dúzhě N reader

堵 **dǔ** v block

堵塞 dǔsè v block

交通堵塞 jiāotōng dǔsè traffic jam

赌 **dǔ** v gamble

赌博 **dǔbó** v gamble

赌场 **dǔchǎng** N gambling house, casino

肚 **dù** N stomach

肚子 **dùzi** abdomen, stomach, belly

度 **dù** I N limit, extent

难度 **nándù** degree of difficult

II M. WD degree (of temperature, longitude, latitude, etc.)

度过 **dùguò** v spend (a period of time)

渡 **dù** v cross (a body of water, e.g. a river, a strait, etc.)

渡船 **dùchuán** N ferry boat, ferry (条 tiáo)

渡口 **dùkǒu** N a place where people or things are carried across, ferry landing

渡轮 **dùlún** N ferry boat, ferry (艘 sōu)

镀 **dù** TRAD 鍍 v plate

镀金 **dùjīn** v get gilded

妒 **dù** v be jealous

妒嫉 **dùjì** v be jealous of

妒嫉别人的财富/成就 **dùjì biéren de cáifù/chéngjiù** be jealous of someone's wealth/achievements

妒忌心 **dùjìxīn** N jealousy

端 **duān** v carry ... level with one or both hands

端正 **duānzhèng** ADJ upright, proper

短 **duǎn** ADJ (of length, time) short

短处 **duǎnchù** N shortcoming, defect

短促 **duǎncù** ADJ very brief

短期 **duǎnqī** N short-term

短信 **duǎnxìn** N text message (by cell phone), text

短信息服务 **duǎnxìnxī fúwù** short message service (SMS)

短暂 **duǎnzàn** ADJ short and temporary, momentary

段 **duàn** M. WD section (for something long)

一段经历 **yí duàn jīnglì** an experience in life

一段路 **yí duàn lù** a section of a road/street, part of a journey

断 **duàn** TRAD 斷 v 1 break, snap 2 break off, cut off

断电 **duàn diàn** cut off electricity

断奶 **duàn nǎi** wean (a child)

断水 **duàn shuǐ** cut off water supply

断定 **duàndìng** v conclude

断断续续 **duàn-duàn-xù-xù** ADV off and on, intermittently

断绝 **duànjué** v break off, sever

断绝贸易关系 **duànjué màoyì guānxì** break off trade relations

锻 **duàn** TRAD 鍛 v forge, shape metal

锻炼 **duànliàn** v undergo physical training, do physical exercises

缎 **duàn** TRAD 緞 See 绸缎 chóuduàn satin, 缎子 duànzi satin

堆 **duī** v heap up, pile up

堆积 **duījī** v pile up

对 **duì** 1 TRAD 對 v treat, deal with

对 **duì** 2 TRAD 對 PREP 1 opposite 2 Same as 对于 duìyú

对岸 **duì'àn** N the other side of the river, lake or sea

对比 **duìbǐ** v compare and contrast

对不起 **duìbuqǐ** IDIOM I'm sorry, I beg your pardon

NOTE: 对不起 **duìbuqǐ** is a very useful idiomatic expression in colloquial Chinese. It is used when you've done something wrong or caused some inconvenience to others. For more formal occasions, use 请原谅 **qǐng yuánliàng** *please forgive me*.

对策 **duìcè** N countermeasure

对称 **duìchèn** ADJ symmetrical

不对称 **búduìchèn** asymmetrical

对待 **duìdài** v treat (people), approach (matters)

对得起 **duìdeqǐ** v be worthy of, not let down

对得起良心 duìdeqǐ liángxīn be at peace with one's conscience

对方 duìfāng N the other side, the other party

对付 duìfu V cope with, deal with

对话 duìhuà I V have a dialogue II N dialogue

对抗 duìkàng V antagonize, oppose vigorously

对立 duìlì V oppose, be hostile

对联 duìlián N antithetical couplet written on scrolls

对面 duìmiàn N opposite, the opposite side

对手 duìshǒu N opponent

竞争对手 jìngzhēng duìshǒu opponent in a competition, rival

对象 duìxiàng N 1 person or thing to which action or feeling is directed, object 2 marriage partner, fiancé(e)

找对象 zhǎo duìxiàng look for a marriage partner

对应 duìyìng ADJ corresponding

对应词 duìyìng cí corresponding word

对照 duìzhào V contrast and compare, refer to

对于 duìyú PREP 1 (introducing the object of an action) regarding 2 (indicating a certain relationship) to, towards

对³ duì TRAD 對 ADJ correct, true

NOTE: 对不对 duì bu duì is used at the end of a sentence to form a question, e.g. 中华文明是世界上最古老的文明，对不对? Zhōnghuá wénmíng shì shìjiè shang zuì gǔlǎo de wénmíng, duì bu duì? Chinese civilization is the oldest in the world, isn't it?

对头 duìtóu ADJ correct, on the right track

不对头 búduìtóu wrong, not right

对⁴ duì TRAD 對 M. WD pair, two (matching people or things)

一对花瓶 yí duì huāpíng two matching vases

一对夫妻 yí duì fūqī a couple (husband and wife)

队 duì TRAD 隊 N team

篮球队 lánqiúduì basketball team

足球队 zúqiúduì soccer team

队伍 duìwu N troops

队员 duìyuán N member of a team

队长 duìzhǎng N team leader

兑 duì V exchange, convert

兑换 duìhuàn V (of currency) exchange, convert

兑换率 duìhuànlǜ exchange rate

兑现 duìxiàn V cash (a check)

吨 dūn TRAD 噸 M. WD ton

蹲 dūn V squat

盾 dùn N shield (See 矛盾 máodùn)

顿 dùn TRAD 頓 M. WD (for meals)

顿时 dùnshí ADV immediately, at once

多 duō I ADJ many, much

比…得多 bǐ…de duō much more … than II NUM more, over III ADV how …!

多半 duōbàn ADV probably, most likely

多亏 duōkuī ADV luckily, fortunately

多么 duōme ADV Same as 多 III ADV. Used in colloquial Chinese.

多媒体 duōméitǐ N multimedia

多少 duōshǎo PRON how many, how much

…多少钱…duōshǎo qián How much is …?

没有多少 méiyǒu duōshǎo not many, not much

NOTE: See note on 几 jǐ.

多数 duōshù N majority

多余 duōyú ADJ surplus

哆 duō as in 哆嗦 duōsuo

哆嗦 duōsuo V tremble, shiver

夺 duó TRAD 奪 V take by force, win

夺取 duóqǔ V capture, seize

朵 **duǒ** M. WD (for flowers)

躲 **duǒ** V hide (oneself)

躲避 **duǒbì** V hide, avoid, keep away from
躲债主 **duǒbì zhàizhǔ** hide from the creditor

躲藏 **duǒcáng** V go into hiding

跺 **duò** V stamp (one's foot)

舵 **duò** N rudder, helm

惰 **duò** ADJ be lazy (See 懒惰 **lǎnduò**)

堕 **duò** TRAD 墮 V fall

堕落 **duòluò** V (of one's morals or behavior) become worse, degenerate

E

俄 **é** N (a shortened form of 俄国 Russia or 俄语 Russian)

俄国 **Éguó** N Russia

俄文 **Éwén** N the Russian language (especially the writing)

俄语 **Éyǔ** N the Russian language

鹅 **é** TRAD 鵝 N goose (只 zhī)
天鹅 **tiān'é** swan

蛾 **é** N moth
蛾子 **ézi** moth (个 gè)

额 **é** TRAD 額 N forehead

额外 **éwài** ADJ additional, extra
额外的开支 **éwài de kāizhī** extra expenditure

讹 **é** TRAD 訛 V extort, blackmail

讹诈 **ézhà** V extort, blackmail

恶 **ě** TRAD 惡 V vomit

恶心 **ěxīn** V **1** feel sick, be sickened **2** feel disgusted, be nauseated

恶 **è** TRAD 惡 ADJ bad, wicked

恶毒 **èdú** ADJ vicious, malicious

恶化 **èhuà** V get worse, aggravate

恶劣 **èliè** ADJ very bad, abominable

恶性 **èxìng** ADJ malicious
恶性肿瘤 **èxìng zhǒngliú** malignant tumor, cancer
恶性事件 **èxìng shìjiàn** vicious crime

饿 **è** TRAD 餓 ADJ hungry

恩 **ēn** N kindness, grace

恩爱 **ēn'ài** ADJ (between husband and wife) deep, caring love

恩惠 **ēnhuì** N kindness that brings about great benefits

恩情 **ēnqíng** N lovingkindness

恩人 **ēnrén** N benefactor

儿 **ér** TRAD 兒 N child, son

儿女 **érnǚ** N son(s) and daughter(s), children

儿童 **értóng** N child(ren)
儿童时代 **értóng shídài** childhood

儿子 **érzi** N son (个 gè)

而 **ér** CONJ (indicating a contrast) but, yet, on the other hand

而且 **érqiě** CONJ moreover, what's more

耳 **ěr** N ear

耳朵 **ěrduo** N the ear (只 zhī)

耳环 **ěrhuán** N earring (只 zhī)

一 **èr** NUM second, two

二千二百二十二 **èrqiān èrbǎi èrshí'èr** two thousand, two hundred and twenty-two (2,222)

NOTE: See note on 两 **liǎng**.

二奶 **èr-nǎi** N mistress, concubine, kept woman
包二奶 **bāo èr-nǎi** keep a woman as mistress

二手 **èrshǒu** ADJ second-hand, used
二手车 **èrshǒu chē** used car
二手房 **èrshǒu fáng** second-hand housing

二氧化碳 **èryǎnghuàtàn** N carbon dioxide

F

发 fā TRAD 發 v 1 send out, release
发传真 fā chuánzhēn send a fax
发电子邮件 fā diànzǐ yóujiàn send an e-mail message
发(手机)短信 fā (shǒujī) duǎnxìn send a text message (by cell phone)
2 develop (into a state)
发表 fābiǎo v publicize, make known, publish
发布 fābù v release, issue
发布通告 fābù tōnggào release an announcement
发布新闻 fābù xīnwén release news
发财 fācái v make a fortune, become prosperous
发出 fāchū v 1 produce, emit, give off
2 send out
发达 fādá ADJ developed, well-developed
发电 fādiàn v generate electricity
发电厂 fādiànchǎng power plant
发电机 fādiànjī generator
火力发电 huǒlì fādiàn thermal power
水力发电 shuǐlì fādiàn hydro power
发动 fādòng v launch (a massive campaign)
发抖 fādǒu v tremble
发挥 fāhuī v allow display, give free rein to
发火 fāhuǒ v lose temper, get angry
发觉 fājué v find, find out, become aware of
发明 fāmíng I v invent II N invention (项 xiàng)
发脾气 fā píqi v lose one's temper, flare up
发票 fāpiào N receipt (张 zhāng)
发起 fāqǐ v launch, initiate
发热 fārè v Same as 发烧 fāshāo
发烧 fāshāo v run a fever
发高烧 fā gāoshāo run a high fever
发射 fāshè v shoot, launch
发射嫦娥一号探月卫星 fāshè Cháng'é yíhào tànyuè wèixīng launch Chang'e No. 1 Lunar Orbiting Spacecraft

发生 fāshēng v take place, happen
发誓 fāshì v pledge, vow
发誓不再抽烟 fāshì búzài chōuyān vow not to smoke again
发现 fāxiàn v discover, find, find out
发行 fāxíng v issue (books, stamps, etc.), publish
发言 fāyán I v speak (at a meeting), make a speech II N speech
发言人 fāyánrén spokesperson
发炎 fāyán v become inflamed
发扬 fāyáng v develop, carry forward
发音 fāyīn N pronunciation
发育 fāyù v (of humans) develop physically
发展 fāzhǎn v develop
发展中国家 fāzhǎnzhōng guójiā developing country

乏 fá v lack (See 缺乏 quēfá.)

罚 fá TRAD 罰 v punish, penalize
罚款 fákuǎn I v fine II N fine
罚款单 fákuǎndān fine notice
缴罚款 jiǎo fákuǎn pay a fine

伐 fá v fell, cut down
伐木 fámù fell trees, do logging
伐木工人 fámù gōngrén lumberjack

阀 fá TRAD 閥 N valve
阀门 fámén valve

法 fǎ N method, law
法定 fǎdìng ADJ required by law, legal
法定年龄 fǎdìng niánlíng legal age (for certain rights)
法定人数 fǎdìng rénshù quorum
法官 fǎguān N judge
法规 fǎguī N laws and regulations
法律 fǎlǜ N law
违反法律 wéifǎn fǎlǜ violate the law
修改法律 xiūgǎi fǎlǜ amend a law
法人 fǎrén N legal person
法庭 fǎtíng N law court, court
法文 Fǎwén N the French language (especially the writing)

法西斯 **Fǎxīsī** N Fascism

法语 **Fǎyǔ** N the French language

法院 **fǎyuàn** N law court, court
高级人民法院 **gāojí rénmín fǎyuàn** supreme people's court
中级人民法院 **zhōngjí rénmín fǎyuàn** intermediate people's court

法则 **fǎzé** N rule, law
自然法则 **zìrán fǎzé** law of nature

法治 **fǎzhì** N rule of law

法制 **fǎzhì** N legal system, rule by law

法子 **fǎzi** N way of doing things, method
没有法子 **méifǎzi** no way, there's nothing I can do

翻 **fān** V 1 turn, turn over 2 translate, interpret

翻译 **fānyì** I V translate, interpret
把...翻译成... **bǎ...fānyì chéng...** translate ... into ...
II N translator, interpreter
当翻译 **dāng fānyì** to work as a translator (or interpreter)

帆 **fān** N sail

帆船 **fānchuán** N sailboat (艘 **sōu**)

番 **fān** ADJ foreign, outlandish

番茄 **fānqié** N tomato (只 **zhī**)

凡 **fán** ADV every

凡是 **fánshì** ADV every, all

NOTE: 凡是 **fánshì** is used before a noun phrase to emphasize that what is referred to is all-embracing, without a single exception. The phrase introduced by 凡是 **fánshì** usually occurs at the beginning of a sentence, and 都 **dōu** is used in the second half of the sentence.

烦 **fán** TRAD 煩 ADJ annoyed

烦闷 **fánmèn** ADJ worried and unhappy

烦恼 **fánnǎo** ADJ annoyed and angry, vexed

烦躁 **fánzào** ADJ annoyed and impatient, fidgety

繁 **fán** ADJ numerous, abundant, complicated

繁多 **fánduō** ADJ numerous, various
品种繁多 **pǐnzhǒng fánduō** a great variety of

繁华 **fánhuá** ADJ flourishing, booming, bustling

繁忙 **fánmáng** ADJ busy, fully occupied

繁荣 **fánróng** ADJ prosperous, thriving

繁体字 **fántǐzì** N old-styled, unsimplified Chinese character, e.g. 門 for 门.

NOTE: As 繁体字 literally means *complicated style character*, some people don't like the negative implication, and prefer to use the term 传统字 *traditional character*. 繁体字 or 传统字 are used in Taiwan, Hong Kong and overseas Chinese communities. Also see 简体字 **jiǎntǐzì**.

繁殖 **fánzhí** V reproduce, breed

繁重 **fánzhòng** ADJ strenuous, onerous

反 **fǎn** I ADJ reverse, opposite II V oppose

反驳 **fǎnbó** V argue against, refute, retort

反常 **fǎncháng** ADJ abnormal, unusual

反倒 **fǎndào** ADV Same as 反而 **fǎn'ér**

反动 **fǎndòng** ADJ reactionary
反动派 **fǎndòngpài** reactionaries

反对 **fǎnduì** V oppose, object to
反对意见 **fǎnduì yìjiàn** opposing opinion
反对党 **fǎnduìdǎng** the Opposition [party]

反而 **fǎn'ér** ADV on the contrary (to expectations), instead

反复 **fǎnfù** ADV repeatedly, over and over again

反感 **fǎngǎn** ADJ feel disgusted, be averse to
对他的行为很反感 **duì tāde xíngwéi hěn fǎngǎn** feel disgusted with his behavior

反攻 **fǎngōng** I N counterattack, counter-offensive II V launch a counterattack

反抗 **fǎnkàng** V resist, fight back, rebel

反馈 **fǎnkuì** N feedback

反射 **fǎnshè** V reflect
条件反射 **tiáojiàn fǎnshè** conditional reflection

反思 **fǎnsī** v think from a new angle, reflect on

反问 **fǎnwèn** v ask a question as a reply

反问句 **fǎnwènjù** N rhetorical question (e.g. 你难道不知道吗? Nǐ nándào bùzhīdào ma? *Don't you know?*)

反应 **fǎnyìng** N response, reaction

反映 **fǎnyìng** v **1** reflect, mirror **2** report, make known, convey

反正 **fǎnzhèng** ADV anyway, at any rate

返 fǎn v return

返回 **fǎnhuí** return to, come back to

返回主页 **fǎnhuí zhǔyè** return to the homepage

犯 fàn v violate, offend

犯错误 **fàn cuòwù** make a mistake, commit an offense

犯法 **fàn fǎ** v break the law

犯规 **fàn guī** v foul (in sports), break a rule

犯人 **fànrén** N convict

犯罪 **fànzuì** v commit a crime, be engaged in criminal activities

犯罪分子 **fànzuì fènzǐ** criminal

犯罪现场 **fànzuì xiànchǎng** crime scene

范 1 **fàn** TRAD 範 N model (See 模范 mófàn)

范 2 **fàn** TRAD 範 N border, mould

范围 **fànwéi** N scope, range, limits

饭 fàn TRAD 飯 N **1** cooked rice **2** meal (顿 dùn)

饭店 **fàndiàn** N **1** restaurant (家 jiā) **2** hotel (家 jiā)

NOTE: The original meaning of 饭店 **fàndiàn** is *restaurant*, but 饭店 is also used to denote *a hotel*. For example, 北京饭店 Běijīng fàndiàn may mean *Beijing Restaurant* or *Beijing Hotel*.

饭碗 **fànwǎn** N rice bowl, way of making a living, job

贩 fàn v buy to resell

贩卖 **fànmài** v buy and sell for a profit (usually in an illegal way)

贩卖毒品 **fànmài dúpǐn** drug trafficking

贩卖人口 **fànmài rénkǒu** human trafficking

泛 fàn I v **1** float **2** flood II ADJ general, extensive

泛滥 **fànlàn** v overflow, flood, go rampant

方 fāng ADJ square

长方 **chángfāng** oblong, rectangular

正方 **zhèngfāng** square

方案 **fāng'àn** N plan, program (for a major project)

方便 **fāngbiàn** ADJ convenient, handy

方便面 **fāngbiàn miàn** instant noodles

NOTE: A euphemism for "going to the toilet" is 方便一下 fāngbiàn yíxià, e.g. 我要方便一下。Wǒ yào fāngbiàn yíxià. *I'm going to use the restroom.*

方程 **fāngchéng** N equation

方程式 **fāngchéngshì** N Same as 方程 fāngchéng

方程式赛车 **fāngchéngshì sàichē** formula racing car

方法 **fāngfǎ** N method

方面 **fāngmiàn** N side, aspect

方式 **fāngshì** N manner, way

生活方式 **shēnghuó fāngshì** way of life, lifestyle

方向 **fāngxiàng** N direction, orientation

方针 **fāngzhēn** N guiding principle, policy

坊 fāng N side street, lane

芳 fāng ADJ fragrant (See 芬芳 fēnfāng)

芳香 **fāngxiāng** sweet-smelling, fragrant

芳香的玫瑰 **fāngxiāng de méigui** fragrant roses

肪 fáng N fat (See 脂肪 zhīfáng)

防 fáng v prevent, guard against

防火 **fánghuǒ** fire prevention

防火墙 **fánghuǒqiáng** firewall

防病 **fángbìng** disease prevention

防盗 **fángdào** anti-burglary measures

防护 **fánghù** v protect, shelter

防护林 fánghùlín shelter forest
防守 fángshǒu v defend, guard
防线 fángxiàn N defense line
防汛 fángxùn N flood prevention
防疫 fángyì N epidemic prevention
防疫针 fángyìzhēn inoculation
打防疫针 dǎ fángyìzhēn be inoculated (against)
防御 fángyù v defend (usually in wars)
防止 fángzhǐ v prevent, guard against
防治 fángzhì v prevent and treat (diseases)
防治病虫害 fángzhì bìngchónghài prevention and treatment of plant diseases and elimination of pests

妨 **fáng** v hinder, impede
妨碍 fáng'ài v hinder, hamper, disturb

房 **fáng** N 1 house (幢 zhuàng)
草房 cǎofáng thatched cottage
楼房 lóufáng house of two or more levels
平房 píngfáng single-story house, bungalow
2 room (间 jiān)
病房 bìngfáng sickroom, hospital ward
客房 kèfáng guestroom, spare room
房产 fángchǎn N real estate, property
房产商 fángchǎnshāng real estate agent, housing developer
房贷 fàngdài N home loan, mortgage
房东 fángdōng N landlord, landlady
房间 fángjiān N room (间 jiān)
房屋 fángwū N houses, buildings
房子 fángzi N house, housing
房租 fángzū N rent (for housing)

仿 **fǎng** v imitate
仿佛 fǎngfú v be like, be alike

纺 **fǎng** TRAD 紡 v spin (into thread/yarn)
纺车 fǎngchē spinning wheel
纺织 fǎngzhī v spin and weave
纺织工业 fǎngzhī gōngyè textile industry
纺织品 fǎngzhīpǐn textile goods

访 **fǎng** TRAD 訪 v visit

访问 fǎngwèn v visit, interview

放 **fàng** v put, put in
放大 fàngdà v enlarge, magnify
放大镜 fàngdàjìng magnifying glass
放假 fàngjià v be on holiday, have the day off
放弃 fàngqì v abandon, give up
放射 fàngshè v radiate
放射科 fàngshèkē department of radiology (in a hospital)
放射科治疗 fàngshèkē zhìliáo radiotherapy (= 放射疗法 fàngshè liáofǎ)
放松 fàngsōng v relax, rest and relax
放心 fàngxīn v set one's mind at ease, be at ease
放学 fàngxué v 1 (of schools) be over 2 (of pupils) return home after school
放映 fàngyìng v show (a movie)

飞 **fēi** TRAD 飛 v fly
飞机 fēijī N airplane (架 jià)
飞机票 fēijīpiào air ticket
飞机场 fēijīchǎng airport
开飞机 kāi fēijī pilot a plane
坐/乘飞机 zuò/chéng fēijī travel by plane
飞快 fēikuài ADJ with the speed of a flying object, very fast
飞翔 fēixiáng v circle in the air (like an eagle), hover
飞行 fēixíng v (of aircraft) fly
飞行员 fēixíngyuán N aircraft pilot
飞跃 fēiyuè **I** v go forward in leaps and bounds **II** N sudden and rapid development

非 **fēi** ADV not, do not
非…不可 fēi...bùkě ADV have no choice but to ..., simply must ...

NOTE: 非…不可… fēi...bùkě is used to emphasize the verb after 非 fēi. 不可 bùkě may be omitted, e.g. 我今天非写完这个报告。Wǒ jīntiān fēi xiěwán zhège bàogào. *I simply must finish writing this report today.* Instead of 非, we can also use 非得 fēiděi

非得…不可…, e.g. 我今天非得写完这个报告(不可)。Wǒ jīntiān fēiděi xiěwán zhège bàogào (bùkě).

非常 fēicháng I ADV unusually, very **II** ADJ unusual, out of the ordinary
非常事件 fēicháng shìjiàn unusual incident
非常措施 fēicháng cuòshī emergency measures

非但 fēidàn Same as 不但 búdàn

非法 fēifǎ ADJ illegal, unlawful
非法同居 fēifǎ tóngjū illegal cohabitation

非洲 Fēizhōu N Africa

啡
fēi as in 咖啡 kāfēi

肥
féi ADJ fat, fattened

NOTE: 肥 féi is normally used to describe animals. It is insulting to use it to describe humans.

肥料 féiliào N fertilizer
有机肥料 yǒujī féiliào organic fertilizer
肥沃 féiwò ADJ (of soil) fertile
肥皂 féizào N soap (块 kuài)
肥皂粉 féizàofěn detergent powder

匪
fěi N bandit
匪帮 fěibāng gang of bandits, criminal gang
匪徒 fěitú bandit, criminal gangster

诽
fěi TRAD 誹 V slander
诽谤 fěibàng V slander, libel

肺
fèi N the lungs
肺气肿 fèiqìzhǒng pulmonary emphysema
肺炎 fèiyán pneumonia

费
fèi TRAD 費 **I** N fee, charge
管理费 guǎnlǐfèi administration charge
机场费 jīchǎngfèi airport tax
水电费 shuǐdiànfèi water and electricity bill
学费 xuéfèi tuition fee

交费 jiāofèi pay fees, a charge, etc
II V cost, spend
费了九牛二虎之力 fèile jiǔ-niú-èr-hǔ zhī lì IDIOM spend the strength of nine bulls and two tigers, make tremendous efforts
费力 fèilì ADJ requiring great effort, painstaking
费力不讨好 fèilì bù tǎohǎo a thankless job
费用 fèiyòng N expense, costs
生活费用 shēnghuó fèiyòng living expenses, cost of living
办公费用 bàngōng fèiyòng administration cost, overheads

废
fèi TRAD 廢 ADJ useless
废除 fèichú V abolish, abrogate
废话 fèihuà N nonsense, rubbish
废品 fèipǐn N **1** reject, useless product **2** junk
废品回收 fèipǐnhuíshōu collecting junk, recycling
废气 fèiqì N waste gas
减少废气排放 jiǎnshǎo fèiqì páifàng reduce waste gas emission
废物 fèiwù N **1** waste material **2** good-for-nothing
废墟 fèixū N ruins, debris

沸
fèi V boil
沸腾 fèiténg V **1** boil **2** seethe with excitement

分
fēn I V **1** divide **2** distribute **3** distinguish **II** N **1** point, mark (obtained in an exam) **2** minute **III** M. WD (Chinese currency: 1 分 fēn = 0.1 角 jiǎo = 0.01 元 yuán), cent
…分之……fēnzhī… NUM (indicating fraction)
三分之二 sān fēnzhī èr two thirds
八分之一 bā fēnzhī yī one eighth
…百分之…bǎi fēnzhī … percent
百分之七十 bǎi fēnzhī qīshí seventy percent
百分之四十五 bǎi fēnzhī sìshíwǔ forty-five percent
分辨 fēnbiàn V distinguish, differentiate

分辨不同的声调 fēnbiàn bùtóng de shēngdiào differentiate different tones (of Chinese syllables)

分辩 fēnbiàn v defend oneself (against a charge), make excuses

分别 fēnbié v **1** part with, be separated from **2** distinguish

分布 fēnbù v be distributed (over an area)

分寸 fēncùn N proper limits for speech or action, sense of propriety

分割 fēngē v carve up, cut into pieces

分工 fēngōng v have a division of labor

分红 fēnhóng v pay or receive dividends

分化 fēnhuà v split up, break up

分解 fēnjiě v resolve, decompose

分类 fēnlèi v classify

分类账 fēnlèizhàng ledger

把文件分类存档 bǎ wénjiàn fēnlèi cúndàng classify and file documents

分离 fēnlí v separate, sever

分裂 fēnliè v split, break up

分泌 fēnmì v secrete

分泌胃液 fēnmì wèiyè secrete gastric juice

分明 fēnmíng ADJ **1** sharply contoured **2** distinct

分母 fēnmǔ N denominator (in a fraction, e.g. "3" in ²/₃)

分配 fēnpèi v distribute, allocate

分批 fēnpī ADV in batches, in groups

分批送货 fēnpī sònghuò deliver goods in batches

分期 fēnqī ADV by stages, in instalments

分期付款 fēnqī fùkuǎn pay (a bill) in instalments

分歧 fēnqí N difference (in opinions), divergence

消除分歧 xiāochú fēnqí settle differences

分清 fēnqīng v distinguish

分清主次 fēnqīng zhǔcì distinguish what is important from what is less so, prioritize

分散 fēnsàn I v disperse, scatter

分散投资 fēnsàn tóuzī diversify one's investments

II ADJ scattered

分数 fēnshù N **1** grade, point **2** fraction

分析 fēnxī I v analyze II N analysis

分享 fēnxiǎng v share (joy, benefits, etc.)

分钟 fēnzhōng N minute (of an hour)

分子 fēnzǐ N numerator (in a fraction, e.g. "2" in ²/₃)

芬 fēn N fragrance, sweet smell

芬芳 fēnfāng ADJ fragrant, sweet-smelling

吩 fēn v instruct

吩咐 fēnfù v instruct, tell (what to do)

纷 fēn TRAD 紛 ADJ **1** numerous, varied **2** disorderly, confused

纷纷 fēnfēn ADV numerous and disorderly

氛 fēn N fog, atmosphere

坟 fén N tomb

坟墓 fénmù N grave, tomb (座 zuò)

粉 fěn N powder

面粉 miànfěn wheat flour

奶粉 nǎifěn milk powder

药粉 yàofěn (medicinal) powder

粉笔 fěnbǐ N chalk (支 zhī)

粉末 fěnmò N powder, dust

粉碎 fěnsuì v smash, crush

分 fèn N **1** component **2** limit

糖分 tángfèn sugar content

分量 fènliàng N weight

分外 fènwài ADV especially, unusually

分子 fènzǐ N member or element (of a social group)

犯罪分子 fànzuìfènzǐ criminal element, criminal

份 fèn M. WD (for a set of things or newspapers, documents, etc.)

一份礼物 yí fèn lǐwù a present

一份晚报 yí fèn wǎnbào a copy of the evening paper

一份报告 yí fèn bàogào a report

奋 fèn TRAD 奮 v exert oneself

奋斗 fèndòu v fight, struggle, strive

奋勇 fènyǒng ADJ courageous, brave, fearless

粪 fèn

粪 fèn TRAD 糞 N excrement, feces

愤 fèn TRAD 憤 N anger

愤恨 fènhèn V be angry and bitter, be very resentful

愤怒 fènnù ADJ enraged, angry

丰 fēng TRAD 豐 ADJ abundant, plentiful

丰富 fēngfù ADJ abundant, rich, plenty

丰满 fēngmǎn ADJ 1 plump 2 plentiful
身材丰满 shēncái fēngmǎn with a full (and attractive) figure
羽毛丰满 yǔmáo fēngmǎn full-fledged, developed well enough to be independent

丰收 fēngshōu N bumper harvest

封 fēng I M. WD (for letters) II V seal, block

封闭 fēngbì V close, seal

封建 fēngjiàn ADJ 1 feudal 2 traditional (in a bad sense)

封锁 fēngsuǒ V block, seal off
封锁消息 fēngsuǒ xiāoxī news blackout

风 fēng TRAD 風 N wind

风向 fēngxiàng wind direction

风暴 fēngbào N windstorm (场 chǎng)

风度 fēngdù N bearing, (elegant) demeanor
很有风度 hěn yǒu fēngdù with elegant demeanor

风格 fēnggé N style (of doing things)
管理风格 guǎnlǐ fēnggé managerial style
建筑风格 jiànzhù fēnggé architectural style

风光 fēngguāng N scenery, sight

风景 fēngjǐng N landscape, scenery

风浪 fēnglàng I N high winds and big waves II ADJ stormy

风力 fēnglì N wind force, wind power

风气 fēngqì N general mood and common practice (of a society, a locality or an organization)

风趣 fēngqù N humor, wit
有风趣 yǒu fēngqù witty, humorous

风沙 fēngshā N sand blown up by winds

风尚 fēngshàng N prevailing norm or practice (in a positive sense)

风俗 fēngsú N custom, social customs

风味 fēngwèi N special flavor, local color

风险 fēngxiǎn N risk
冒风险 mào fēngxiǎn run a risk

风筝 fēngzheng N kite (只 zhī)
放风筝 fàngfēngzheng fly a kite

疯 fēng TRAD 瘋 ADJ insane, crazy

疯狂 fēngkuáng ADJ insane, frenzied

疯子 fēngzi N lunatic, a crazy guy

蜂 fēng N wasp, bee

蜂蜜 fēngmì N honey

峰 fēng N mountain peak, peak (See 山峰 shānfēng)

锋 fēng TRAD 鋒 N sharp point of a knife

锋利 fēnglì ADJ sharp

逢 féng V come upon, meet

逢年过节 féng-nián-guò-jié ADV on festival days and the New Year's Day, on festive occasions

缝 féng TRAD 縫 N sew

讽 fěng TRAD 諷 V satirize

讽刺 fěngcì I N satire II V use satire, satirize

奉 fèng V offer, obey, believe in

奉献 fèngxiàn V offer as a tribute, present with respect

奉行 fèngxíng V believe in and act upon, pursue (a policy, principle, etc.)

凤 fèng TRAD 鳳 N as in 凤凰 fènghuáng

凤凰 fènghuáng N a mythical bird symbolic of peace and prosperity, phoenix

缝 fèng TRAD 縫 N seam

见缝插针 jiànfèng chāzhēn IDIOM stick a needle in a seam (→ make full use of every minute available)

佛 Fó N Buddha

佛教 Fójiào N Buddhism

否 fǒu V negate

否定 fǒudìng V negate, deny

否决 fǒujué V vote down, veto, overrule

否认 fǒurèn V deny, repudiate

否则 fǒuzé CONJ otherwise, or

夫 fū N man, husband (See 丈夫 zhàngfu)

夫妇 fūfù Same as 夫妻 fūqī

夫妻 fūqī N husband and wife

夫妻关系 fūqī guānxi marital relationship

夫人 fūrén N (formal term for another person's) wife

肤 fū TRAD 膚 N skin (See 皮肤 pífū)

敷 fū V apply

敷药 fū yào apply medicine (to a wound)

敷衍 fūyǎn V go through the motions, be perfunctory

扶 fú V support with the hand

扶着老人过马路 fúzhe lǎorén guò mǎlù help an old person walk across the street

佛 fú (only used in 仿佛 fǎngfú)

服 fú I V obey II N clothing

服从 fúcóng V obey, submit to

服气 fúqì V be convinced

服务 fúwù V serve, work for

为…服务 wèi...fúwù serve, work for ....

服务器 fúwùqì N (of computer) server

服务业 fúwùyè N service industry

服务员 fúwùyuán N attendant, waiter/waitress

NOTE: Though 服务员 fúwùyuán is used to refer to or address an attendant, a waiter or waitress, in everyday usage 小姐 xiǎojiě is more common (if the attendant is a woman).

服装 fúzhuāng N garments, apparel

服装工业 fúzhuāng gōngyè garment industry

服装商店 fúzhuāng shāngdiàn clothes store

浮 fú V float

浮雕 fúdiāo N relief sculpture

浮动 fúdòng V float, fluctuate

浮动汇率 fúdòng huìlǜ floating exchange rate

俘 fú V capture

战俘 zhànfú prisoner of war

俘虏 fúlǔ N captive, prisoner of war

幅 fú M. WD (for pictures, posters, maps, etc.)

一幅中国画 yì fú Zhōngguó huà a Chinese painting

幅度 fúdù N range, extent

福 fú N blessing, happiness

福利 fúlì N welfare, well-being

为职工谋福利 wéi zhígōng móu fúlì work for the welfare of the staff

福气 fúqì N good fortune

有福气 yǒu fúqi have good fortune, be very lucky

辐 fú TRAD 輻 N (of a wheel) spoke

辐射 fúshè V radiate, spread out N radiation

核辐射 héfúshè nuclear radiation

符 fú V be in accord

符号 fúhào N symbol, mark

符合 fúhé V conform to, accord with

伏 fú V bend over

袱 fú TRAD 襆 N cloth-wrapper (See 包袱 bāofu)

抚 fǔ TRAD 撫 V **1** touch softly **2** foster (a child)

抚养 fǔyǎng V bring up (a child), provide for (a child)

抚育 fǔyù V bring up (a child), educate (a child)

府 fǔ N government office (See 政府 zhèngfǔ)

俯 fǔ V bow one's head, bend down

斧 fǔ N hatchet, ax

斧子 fǔzi hatchet, ax

辅 fǔ TRAD 輔 V assist, supplement

辅导 fǔdǎo V coach, tutor

辅导课 fǔdǎokè tutorial class, tutorial

辅导老师 fǔdǎo lǎoshī tutor, teaching assistant

辅助 fǔzhù V assist, play an auxiliary role

腐 fǔ ADJ rotten, decayed

腐败 fǔbài I ADJ 1 badly decayed

腐败食品 fǔbài shípǐn food that has gone bad

2 corrupt II N corruption

腐化 fǔhuà ADJ degenerate, corrupt

腐烂 fǔlàn ADJ decomposed, putrid

腐蚀 fǔshí V 1 corrode, etch 2 make (people) corrupt

腐朽 fǔxiǔ ADJ decayed, rotten

父 fù N father

父亲 fùqin N father

NOTE: 爸爸 bàba and 父亲 fùqin denote the same person. While 爸爸 bàba is colloquial, like *daddy*, 父亲 fùqin is formal, equivalent to *father*. When referring to another person's father, 父亲 fùqin is preferred. As a form of address to your own father, only 爸爸 bàba is normally used.

赴 fù V go to, attend

负 fù TRAD 負 V 1 carry on the back 2 shoulder, bear

负担 fùdān I V bear (costs)

负担旅费 fùdān lǚfèi bear travel expenses

II N burden, load

负伤 fùshāng V get wounded, get injured

负责 fùzé I V be responsible, be in charge

负责人 fùzérén the person-in-charge

II ADJ responsible

妇 fù TRAD 婦 N woman

妇女 fùnǔ N woman, womankind

付 fù V pay

付出 fùchū V pay out, contribute

付款 fùkuǎn V pay a sum of money

附 fù V 1 be close to 2 attach, add

附带 fùdài ADJ additional

附带条件 fùdài tiáojiàn additional condition

附和 fùhé V chime in with, echo

附加 fùjiā ADJ extra

增值附加税 zēngzhí fùjiāshuì value-added tax

附近 fùjìn N the area nearby

附属 fùshǔ V attach, affiliate

北京师范大学附属中学 Běijīng Shīfàn Dàxué Fùshǔ Zhōngxué a middle school affiliated to Beijing Normal University

咐 fù V instruct (See 吩咐 fēnfù, 嘱咐 zhǔfu)

复 fù TRAD 復 ADJ repeat, complex, compound

复合 fùhé V compound

复活节 Fùhuójié N Easter

复述 fùshù V retell, repeat

复习 fùxí V review (one's lesson)

复兴 fùxīng V revive, rejuvenate

复印 fùyìn V photocopy

复印机 fùyìnjī photocopier

复杂 fùzá ADJ complicated, complex

复制 fùzhì V copy, clone

覆 fù V cover

覆盖 fùgài V cover, cover up

腹 fù N abdomen, belly

副 1 fù M. WD (for objects in pairs or sets) pair, set

一副手套儿 yí fù shǒutàor a pair of gloves

一副眼镜 yí fù yǎnjìng a pair of spectacles

副 2 fù ADJ 1 deputy, vice-... 2 secondary

副食 fùshí N non-staple foodstuffs

副业 fùyè N side occupation, sideline

副作用 fùzuòyòng N side effect

富 **fù** ADJ rich, wealthy

富人 fùrén rich person, rich people

NOTE: In everyday Chinese, 富 fù is not used as much as 有钱 yǒuqián to mean *rich*.

富强 fùqiáng ADJ (of a country) rich and powerful

富有 fùyǒu ADJ rich, affluent

富裕 fùyù ADJ rich, well-to-do

富余 fùyu V have more and to spare

傅 **fù** N teacher, advisor (See 师傅 shīfu)

缚 **fù** TRAD 縛 V bind, tie up

G

该 1 **gāi** TRAD 該 MODAL V should, ought to

该 2 **gāi** TRAD 該 V **1** be somebody's turn to do something **2** deserve

该 3 **gāi** Trad 該 PRON that, the said, the above-mentioned

NOTE: 该 gāi in this sense is used only in formal writing.

改 **gǎi** V alter, change, correct

改行 gǎiháng change one's profession/trade

改期 gǎiqī change a scheduled time, change the date (of an event)

改变 gǎibiàn V transform, change **II** N change, transformation

改革 gǎigé **I** V reform **II** N reform

改建 gǎijiàn V rebuild

改进 gǎijìn **I** V improve, make ... more advanced/sophisticated **II** N improvement (项 xiàng)

改良 gǎiliáng V improve, reform

改善 gǎishàn **I** V ameliorate, make ...

better/more favorable **II** N improvement, amelioration

改邪归正 gǎi-xié-guī-zhèng IDIOM give up evil and return to good, turn over a new leaf

改造 gǎizào **I** V remold, rebuild, reform **II** N remolding, rebuilding

改正 gǎizhèng V put ... right, rectify

改组 gǎizǔ V re-organize

盖 1 **gài** TRAD 蓋 V build

盖 2 **gài** TRAD 蓋 N cover, lid

盖子 gàizi cover, lid

掩盖 yǎngài conceal, cover up

概 **gài** ADJ broadly, general

概况 gàikuàng N general situation, basic facts

中国概况 Zhōngguó gàikuàng basic facts about China, a profile of China

概括 gàikuò V summarize

概念 gàiniàn N concept, notion

概念车 gàiniànchē concept car

溉 **gài** V irrigate (See 灌溉 guàngài)

钙 **gài** N calcium

钙片 gàipiàn calcium tablet

甘 **gān** I V be willing, be convinced

甘拜下风 gānbài xiàfēng IDIOM accept willingly defeat or inferiority

不甘失败 bùgān shībài not be reconciled to defeat, not accept defeat

II ADJ sweet, pleasant

甘心 gānxīn V be willing to, be ready to

甘蔗 gānzhe N sugar cane

干 **gān** TRAD 乾 ADJ dry

干杯 gānbēi V drink a toast, "Bottoms up!"

干脆 gāncuì **I** ADJ decisive, not hesitant, straight to the point **II** ADV just, simply

干旱 gānhàn N drought, dry spell

干红 gānhóng N dry red wine

干红葡萄酒 gān hóng pútaojiǔ dry red wine

干净 gānjìng ADJ clean

干涉 gānshè V intervene, interfere
干涉内政 gānshè nèizhèng interfere with the internal affairs (of a country)

干预 gānyù V intervene, meddle with
干预子女的婚姻 gānyù zǐnǚ de hūnyīn meddle in the marriage of (one's adult child)

干燥 gānzào ADJ dry, arid

杆 gān N pole
电线杆 diànxiàn gān electric pole, telephone/utility pole

肝 gān N the liver

竿 gān N pole, rod
钓鱼竿 diàoyúgán fishing rod

杆 gān N stick
枪杆 qiānggǎn the barrel of a rifle

赶 gǎn TRAD 趕 V **1** catch up with **2** hurry up, rush for, try to catch
赶上 gǎnshang catch up, catch up with
赶得上 gǎn de shàng can catch up
赶不上 gǎn bu shàng cannot catch up
没赶上 méi gǎn shàng fail to catch up

赶紧 gǎnjǐn ADV hasten (to do something)

赶快 gǎnkuài ADV Same as 赶紧 gǎnjǐn

赶忙 gǎnmáng ADV hurriedly, hastily

敢 gǎn MODAL V dare
敢于 gǎnyú V dare to, have the courage to

感 gǎn V feel

感到 gǎndào V feel

感动 gǎndòng V move, touch emotionally

感化 gǎnhuà V reform … through gentle persuasion and/or by setting a good example

感激 gǎnjī V feel deeply grateful

感觉 gǎnjué I V feel II N feeling, impression

感慨 gǎnkǎi V sigh with deep inner feelings (over a revelation, an experience, etc.)

感冒 gǎnmào V catch a cold

感情 gǎnqíng N **1** feelings, emotion **2** affection, love

感染 gǎnrǎn V **1** (of a wound) become infected **2** (of a movie, a story, music, etc.) affect

感受 gǎnshòu N impression or lesson learned from personal experiences

感想 gǎnxiǎng N impressions, reflections

感谢 gǎnxiè V be grateful, thank

感兴趣 gǎn xìngqù V be interested (in)

干 gàn TRAD 幹 V do, work

干部 gànbù N cadre, official (位 wèi)

NOTE: 干部 gànbù is a communist party term, denoting party (or government) officials. It is not commonly used today. In its stead, 官员 guānyuán is the word for government officials.

干劲 gànjìn N drive and enthusiasm (for a job)
干劲不足 gànjìn bùzú lack of enthusiasm
干劲十足 gànjìn shízú with enormous enthusiasm

干吗 gànmá ADV **1** why **2** Same as 做什么 zuò shénme

NOTE: 干吗 gànmá is a highly colloquial expression, used in casual conversational style.

缸 gāng N vat, jar (只 zhī)

刚 gāng TRAD 剛 ADV just, barely

刚才 gāngcái N a short while ago, just

刚刚 gānggāng ADV Same as 刚 gāng, but more emphatic

钢 gāng TRAD 鋼 N steel

钢笔 gāngbǐ N fountain pen (支 zhī)

钢材 gāngcái N steel products, rolled steel

钢琴 gāngqín N piano (架 jià)
弹钢琴 tán gāngqín play the piano

钢铁 gāngtiě N iron and steel, steel

纲 gāng TRAD 綱 N guiding principle, outline

纲领 gānglǐng N fundamental principle, guideline

纲要 gāngyào N outline, essentials

岗 gǎng TRAD 崗 N sentry post

岗位 gǎngwèi N post (as a job)
脱离工作岗位 tuōlí gōngzuò gǎngwèi leave one's job

港 gǎng N port, harbor

海港 hǎigǎng seaport
港口 gǎngkǒu port, harbor

杠 gàng N big, thick stick, bar

杠杆 gànggǎn N lever

高 gāo ADJ 1 tall, high 2 above average, superior

高超 gāochāo ADJ (of skills) superior, consummate

高潮 gāocháo N high tide, high water

高大 gāodà ADJ tall and big

高档 gāodàng ADJ top grade, high quality
高档家具 gāodàng jiājù fine furniture

高等 gāoděng ADJ advanced, higher
高等教育 gāoděng jiàoyù higher education
高等学校 gāoděng xuéxiào institution of higher education, colleges and universities

高低 gāodī N 1 height 2 difference in quality, skills, etc.

NOTE: See note on 大小 dàxiǎo.

高度 gāodù I N altitude, height II ADJ a high degree

高峰 gāofēng N peak, summit
高峰会议 gāofēng huìyì summit meeting

高贵 gāoguì ADJ 1 (of moral) noble, admirable 2 (of people) aristocratic, elitist
出身高贵 chūshēn gāoguì of an aristocratic or elitist family background

高级 gāojí ADJ advanced, high-level
高级小学 (高小) gāojí xiǎoxué (gāoxiǎo) higher primary school (Grades 5 and 6)
高级中学 (高中) gāojí zhōngxué (gāozhōng) senior high school

高级旅馆 gāojí lǚguǎn exclusive hotel

高考 gāokǎo N university entrance examinations

NOTE: 高考 gāokǎo is the shortened form of 高等学校入学考试 gāoděng xuéxiào rùxué kǎoshì. In everyday use of the language the Chinese have a tendency to shorten a long-winding term into a two-character word, e.g. 股市 gǔshì from 股票市场 gǔpiào shìchǎng share market; 人大 Réndà from 人民代表大会 Rénmín Dàibiǎo Dàhuì the people's Congress.

高空 gāokōng N high altitude

高粱 gāoliang N sorghum

高明 gāomíng ADJ (of ideas or skills) brilliant, consummate

高尚 gāoshàng ADJ (of moral, behavior, etc.) noble, lofty

高烧 gāoshāo N high fever
发高烧 fā gāoshāo run a high fever

高深 gāoshēn ADJ (of learning) profound, recondite, obscure

高速 gāosù ADJ high-speed
高速公路 gāosù gōnglù superhighway, motorway

高兴 gāoxìng ADJ joyful, delighted, willing

高血压 gāoxuèyā N high blood pressure

高压 gāoyā N high pressure
高压手段 gāoyā shǒuduàn high-handed measure

高雅 gāoyǎ ADJ elegant, refined

高原 gāoyuán N highland, plateau

高涨 gāozhàng V upsurge, rise

高中 gāozhōng N See 高级 gāojí.

膏 gāo N paste, ointment (See 牙膏 yágāo.)

糕 gāo N cake (See 蛋糕 dàngāo, 糟糕 zāogāo.)

搞 gǎo V do, be engaged in (a trade, profession, etc.)

搞鬼 gǎoguǐ V play dirty tricks on the sly

搞活 gǎohuó V vitalize, invigorate

稿 gǎo V draft (of an essay, a painting, etc.)

稿子 gǎozi draft

打稿子 dǎgǎozi draw up a draft
初稿 chūgǎo initial draft
稿件 gǎojiàn N manuscript, contribution (to a magazine, a publisher, etc.)

告 gào v **1** tell, inform **2** sue, bring a legal action against
告别 gàobié v bid farewell to, part with
告辞 gàocí v bid farewell formally
告诫 gàojiè v warn sternly, exhort, admonish
告诉 gàosu v tell, inform
告状 gàozhuàng v **1** file a lawsuit **2** bring a complaint (with someone's superior), report someone's wrongdoing

哥 gē N elder brother
哥哥 gēge N elder brother

歌 gē N song (首 shǒu)
唱歌 chànggē sing a song
歌词 gēcí N words of a song
歌剧 gējù N opera
歌剧院 gējù yuàn opera house
歌曲 gēqǔ N song
流行歌曲 liúxíng gēqǔ pop song
歌手 gēshǒu N singer
歌颂 gēsòng v sing the praise of, eulogize
歌星 gēxīng N pop star
歌咏 gēyǒng N singing
歌咏队 gēyǒngduì singing group, chorus

胳 gē N arm
胳膊 gēbo N arm (只 zhī)

搁 gē v put, place

割 gē v cut

鸽 gē N dove (只 zhī)
鸽子 gēzi dove

革 gé v **1** expel, remove **2** transform, change
革命 gémìng N revolution (场 chǎng)
革新 géxīn v innovate, reform
技术革新 jìshù géxīn technological innovation

格 gé N pattern, standard

格格不入 gé-gé-bú-rù IDIOM like a square peg in a round hole, incompatible
格局 géjú N arrangement pattern, layout
格式 géshi N format, form
格外 géwài ADV exceptionally, unusually

隔 gé v separate, partition
隔壁 gébì N next door
隔阂 géhé N feelings of alienation or estrangement, often caused by misunderstanding
消除隔阂 xiāochú géhé banish feelings of estrangement by clearing up a misunderstanding
隔绝 géjué v be completely cut off, be isolated
与世隔绝 yǔ shì géjué be isolated from the outside world
隔离 gélí v isolate (a patient, a criminal), quarantine
隔离病房 gélí bìngfáng isolation ward

个 gè TRAD 個 M. WD (the most common measure word)
一个人 yí ge rén a person
两个苹果 liǎng ge píngguǒ two apples
三个工厂 sān ge gōngchǎng three factories

NOTE: 个 gè can be used as a "default" measure word, i.e. if you do not know the correct measure word to go with a noun, you can use this one. It is normally pronounced in the neutral tone.

个别 gèbié ADJ **1** very few, exceptional **2** individual, one-to-one
个儿 gèr N size (of a person)
高个儿 gāogèr tall guy

NOTE: 个儿 gèr is only used in an informal situation.

个人 gèrén N **1** individual **2** personal
个人所得税 gèrénsuǒdé shuì personal income tax
个人隐私 gèrén yǐnsī personal and confidential matter, privacy
个体 gètǐ N individual
个性 gèxìng N personality

个性开朗 gèxìng kāilǎng an outgoing personality

个子 gèzi N height and size (of a person), build

各 gè PRON each, every

各别 gèbié ADV individually

各别会见 gèbié huìjiàn meet individually

各别情况 gèbié qíngkuàng isolated case

各行各业 gè-háng-gè-yè N every trade and profession

各式各样 gè-shì-gè-yàng ADJ all kinds of, of every description

各式各样的电子产品 gèshì gèyàng de diànzǐ chǎnpǐn all kinds of electronic products

各种 gè zhǒng ADJ all kinds of

各自 gèzì PRON each

各自为政 gè zì wéi zhèng each doing things in his/her/their own way, administer autonomously

给 gěi TRAD 給 I V give, provide II PREP for, to

给以 gěiyǐ V be given

给以支持 gěiyǐ zhīchí be given support

根 gēn I N root II M. WD (for long, thin things)

一根筷子 yì gēn kuàizi a chopstick

根本 gēnběn I N essence, what is fundamental II ADJ essential, fundamental, basic

根据 gēnjù I V do according to, on the basis of II N grounds, basis

根深蒂固 gēnshēn dìgù IDIOM deep-rooted, ingrained

根深蒂固的种族偏见 gēnshēn dìgùde zhǒngzú piānjiàn deep-rooted racial prejudice

根源 gēnyuán N root cause, origin

宗教的根源 zōngjiào de gēnyuán the root cause of religion

跟 gēn I V follow II PREP with

跟上 gēnshàng V catch up with, keep abreast with

跟前 gēnqián N near, nearby

跟随 gēnsuí V Same as 跟 gēn (= follow)

跟头 gēntou N 1 fall

跌跟头 diēgēntou have a fall, fall down 2 somersault

翻跟头 fāngēntou do a somersault

跟…一起 gēn...yìqǐ PREP together with ...

跟踪 gēnzōng V follow the tracks of, trail, shadow, stalk

发现被人跟踪 fāxiàn bèi rén gēnzōng find oneself be followed

耕 gēng V plough

耕地 gēngdì I V plough the field II N farmland

可耕地 kěgēngdì arable land

耕种 gēngzhòng V farm, raise crops

更 gēng V change

更改 gēnggǎi V change, alter

更换 gēnghuàn V replace

更换旧电脑 gēnghuàn jiù diànnǎo replace old computer(s)

更新 gēngxīn V renew, replace

设备更新 shèbèi gēngxīn renewal of equipment

更正 gēngzhèng V make corrections

更正错误的数据 gēngzhèng cuòwù de shùjù correct wrong data

梗 gěng N stem, stalk

更 gèng ADV still more, even more

更加 gèngjiā ADV Same as 更 gèng

工 gōng N 1 work 2 worker

汽车修理工 qìchē xiūlǐ gōng automobile repairman (→ mechanic)

工厂 gōngchǎng N factory, works (座 zuò, 家 jiā)

办工厂 bàn gōngchǎng run a factory

建工厂 jiàn gōngchǎng build a factory

开工厂 kāi gōngchǎng set up a factory

工程 gōngchéng N 1 project, construction work (项 xiàng) 2 engineering

土木工程 tǔmù gōngchéng civil engineering

水利工程 shuǐlì gōngchéng water conservancy project

工程师 gōngchéngshī

ertion **1** time **2** efforts

工会 gōnghuì N labor union, trade union

工具 gōngjù N tool (件 jiàn)
工具箱 gōngjùxiāng tool box

工龄 gōnglíng N length of service

工钱 gōngqián N Same as 工资 gōngzī

工人 gōngrén N workman, worker
当工人 dāng gōngrén be a worker

工伤 gōngshāng N industrial injury
工伤事故 gōngshāng shìgù industrial injury, industrial accident

工事 gōngshì N defense works

工薪阶层 gōngxīn jiēcéng N wage or salary earners

工序 gōngxù N industrial procedure

工业 gōngyè N (manufacturing) industry
轻工业 qīnggōngyè light industry
新兴工业 xīnxīng gōngyè sunrise industry
重工业 zhònggōngyè heavy industry

工艺品 gōngyìpǐn N handicraft (件 jiàn)

工资 gōngzī N wages, salary

工作 gōngzuò I V work II N work, job (件 jiàn)

工作餐 gōngzuò cān N staff meal

功 gōng N **1** skill **2** achievement, merit

功夫 gōngfu N **1** Same as 工夫 gōngfu (= efforts) **2** martial arts
功夫片 gōngfu piàn martial arts film
练功夫 liàn gōngfu practice martial arts

功绩 gōngjì N merits and achievements

功课 gōngkè N **1** schoolwork **2** homework
做功课 zuò gōngkè do homework.

功劳 gōngláo N contribution, credit

功能 gōngnéng N function
功能键 gōngnéngjiàn function key(s)

功效 gōngxiào N effect, efficacy

攻 gōng V attack

攻读 gōngdú V study hard, specialize
攻读博士学位 gōngdúbóshì xuéwèi work hard to gain a Ph.D. degree

tack and capture (a city, a fortress, etc.)

攻心 gōngxīn V win the hearts and minds of
攻心战 gōngxīnzhàn psychological warfare

公 gōng ADJ male (of certain animals)

公 gōng ADJ **1** public **2** open, public **3** fair

公安 gōng'ān N public security
公安局 gōng'ān jú public security bureau (police bureau)
公安人员 gōng'ān rényuán public security personnel, policeman

NOTE: See note on 警察 jǐngchá.

公报 gōngbào N communiqué, bulletin

公布 gōngbù V make a public announcement, publish

公尺 gōngchǐ M. WD (unit of measurement) meter

公道 gōngdào ADJ fair, just, impartial

公费 gōngfèi N (at) public expense
公费医疗 gōngfèi yīliáo medical care paid for by the government (→ free medical care for government officials and others)

公分 gōngfēn M. WD centimeter

公告 gōnggào N announcement (by a government agency)

公共 gōnggòng ADJ public, communal

公共关系 gōnggòng guānxi N public relations

公共汽车 gōnggòng qìchē bus

NOTE: The word for *bus* in Taiwan is 公车 gōngchē. In Hong Kong, *bus* is 巴士 bāshì, obviously a transliteration of the English word *bus*.

公斤 gōngjīn M. WD kilogram

公关 gōngguān N (shortening of 公共关系 gōnggòng guānxi) public relations

公开 gōngkāi I ADJ open, public II V make public, reveal

公里 gōnglǐ N kilometer

公路 gōnglù N public road, highway (条 tiáo)

高速公路 gāosù gōnglù motorway, expressway

公民 gōngmín N citizen

公平 gōngpíng ADJ fair, impartial
买卖公平 mǎimai gōngpíng fair trade

公顷 gōngqīng N hectare (= 10,000 square meters)

公然 gōngrán ADV brazenly, openly
公然撒谎 gōngrán sāhuǎng tell a bare-faced lie

公认 gōngrèn V generally acknowledge, universally accept

公社 gōngshè N commune

公式 gōngshì N formula
数学公式 shùxué gōngshì mathematics formula

公司 gōngsī N commercial firm, company, corporation (家 jiā)
分公司 fēn gōngsī branch of a company
总公司 zǒng gōngsī company headquarters

公务 gōngwù N public affairs, official duty

公务员 gōngwùyuán N civil servant, government office holders

公用 gōngyòng ADJ for public use

公用电话 gōngyòng diànhuà N public telephone, payphone

公元 gōngyuán N of the Christian/common era, AD (Anno Domini)
公元前 gōngyuán qián BC (before Christ), BCE (before the Christian/common era)

公园 gōngyuán N public garden, park (座 zuò)

公约 gōngyuē N 1 agreement, convention, pact 2 pledge
服务公约 fúwù gōngyuē service pledge

公债 gōng zhài N government bonds
公债券 gōngzhài quàn bond

公证 gōngzhèng V notarize
公证处 gōngzhèngchù notary office
公证人 gōngzhèngrén notary public, notary

恭 **gōng** ADJ deferential, reverent

恭敬 gōngjìng ADJ very respectful, deferential

供 **gōng** V supply

供给 gōngjǐ V supply, provide

NOTE: 给 in 供给 is pronounced as jǐ, not its usual gěi.

宫 **gōng** N palace

宫殿 gōngdiàn palace
王宫 wánggōng royal palace

弓 **gōng** I N bow II V bend, arch

弓箭 gōngjiàn bow and arrows

汞 **gǒng** N mercury

巩 **gǒng** TRAD 鞏 V consolidate

巩固 gǒnggù I V consolidate, strengthen II ADJ solid, firm

拱 **gǒng** N arch

拱门 gǒngmén arched gate, arched door

共 **gòng** ADV 1 altogether, in total 2 jointly, together (used only in writing)

共产党 gòngchǎndǎng N communist party

共和国 gònghéguó N republic

共计 gòngjì V total, add up to

共鸣 gòngmíng N 1 resonance 2 sympathetic response
引起共鸣 yǐnqǐ gòngmíng find a ready echo

共青团 Gòngqīngtuán N (shortening from 中国共产主义青年团 Zhōngguó gòngchǎnzhǔyì qīngniántuán) the Chinese Communist Youth League

共识 gòngshí N common understanding
达成共识 dáchéng gòngshí achieve common understanding

共同 gòngtóng I ADJ common, shared II ADV together, jointly

共性 gòngxìng N generality, common characteristics

供 **gòng** V 1 confess, own up
口供 kǒugòng (criminal) confession
2 lay (offerings)

贡 gòng TRAD 貢 N tribute

贡献 gòngxiàn I v contribute, dedicate II N contribution, devotion, dedication
为…作出贡献 wèi...zuòchu gòngxiàn make a contribution to ....

勾 gōu v 1 strike out with a pen 2 delineate (the outline of a drawing) 3 induce, evoke

勾结 gōujié v collaborate secretly with (on criminal matters)

沟 gōu TRAD 溝 N ditch, trench (条 tiáo)

沟通 gōutōng v link up, connect
沟通意见 gōutōng yìjiàn exchange ideas

钩 gōu TRAD 鈎 N hook (只 zhī)

钩子 gōuzi hook

狗 gǒu N dog (只 zhī, 条 tiáo)

母狗 mǔ gǒu bitch
小狗 xiǎo gǒu puppy

构 gòu TRAD 構 v construct, form

构成 gòuchéng v make up, form
构件 gòujiàn N component, part
构思 gòusī v (of writers or artists) work out the plot of a story or composition of a picture
构造 gòuzào N structure

购 gòu v purchase

购买 gòumǎi v purchase
购买采矿设备 gòumǎi cǎi kuàng shèbèi purchase mining equipment
购买力 gòumǎilì purchasing power

够 gòu ADJ enough, sufficient

足够 zúgòu enough, sufficient

孤 gū ADJ lonely

孤儿 gū'ér N orphan
孤儿院 gū'éryuàn orphanage
孤立 gūlì ADJ isolated, without support or sympathy

辜 gū v (as in 辜负 gūfù)

辜负 gūfù v fail to live up to, let down
辜负父母的期望 gūfù fùmǔ de qīwàng fail to live up to parents' expectations

估 gū v estimate

估计 gūjì I v estimate, reckon, size up II N estimate, approximate calculation, appraisal

姑 gū N aunt, woman

姑姑 gūgu N Same as 姑妈 gūmā, especially as a colloquialism
姑妈 gūmā N father's sister, aunt
姑母 gūmǔ N Same as 姑妈 gūmā, especially used in writing.
姑娘 gūniang N unmarried young woman, girl, lass
大姑娘 dàgūniang young woman (usually unmarried), lass
小姑娘 xiǎo gūniang little girl

NOTE: 姑娘 gūniang is a colloquial word. When used to mean *unmarried young lady*, 姑娘 gūniang is used together with the word 小伙子 xiǎohuǒzi (young man), e.g. 姑娘小伙子都爱热闹。Gūniang xiǎohuǒzi dōu ài rènao. *Young people all like having fun.*

姑且 gūqiě ADV tentatively, for the time being

菇 gū N mushroom

香菇 xiānggū dried mushroom

古 gǔ ADJ ancient

古代 gǔdài N ancient times
古典 gǔdiǎn ADJ classical
古典音乐 gǔdiǎn yīnyuè classical music
古董 gǔdǒng N antique, old curio (件 jiàn)
老古董 lǎogǔdǒng old fogey (个 gè)
古怪 gǔguài ADJ weird, queer
行为古怪 xíngwéi gǔguài behave strangely
古迹 gǔjì N historic site, place of historic interest
古老 gǔlǎo ADJ ancient, time-honored

鼓 gǔ N drum

鼓吹 gǔchuī v advocate, preach (usually wrong and harmful ideas)

鼓励 gǔlì v encourage

物质鼓励 wùzhì gǔlì material incentive

精神鼓励 jīngshén gǔlì moral incentive, moral encouragement

鼓舞 gǔwǔ v inspire, fire up … with enthusiasm, hearten

鼓掌 gǔzhǎng v applaud

骨 gǔ N bone

骨头 gǔtou N bone (根 gēn)

骨干 gǔgàn N backbone (denoting people)

公司的骨干 gōngsī de gǔgàn the backbone (most important staff) of a company

骨肉 gǔròu N one's flesh and blood

骨折 gǔzhé v fracture a bone

股 gǔ N share, stock (in a company)

股东 gǔdōng N shareholder, stockholder

股份 gǔfèn N share, stock

股票 gǔpiào N share, stock (份 fèn)

股市 gǔshì N share market

谷 gǔ TRAD 穀 N grain, cereal

谷子 gǔzi grain (粒 lì)

谷物 gǔwù N grain, cereal (collectively)

谷物价格 gǔwù jiàgé grain prices

雇 gù TRAD 僱 v employ, hire

雇佣 gùyōng v hire, employ

NOTE: 雇佣 gùyōng is used when hiring low-rank employees, e.g. unskilled workers. To employ a professional, the verb to use is 聘用 pìnyòng.

雇员 gùyuán N employee, staff member

故 gù I ADJ old, former II ADV on purpose, deliberately

故事 gùshi N story, tale

讲故事 jiǎng gùshi tell a story

听故事 tīng gùshi listen to a story

故乡 gùxiāng N native place, hometown

故意 gùyì ADV deliberately, intentionally, on purpose

故障 gùzhàng N breakdown (of a machine)

排除故障 páichú gùzhàng troubleshooting

顾 gù TRAD 顧 v attend to, care for

顾此失彼 gùcǐ shībǐ IDIOM pay too much attention to one thing at the expense of another

顾客 gùkè N customer, client (位 wèi)

顾虑 gùlù v have misgivings, worry

顾虑重重 gùlù chóngchóng be filled with misgivings

顾问 gùwèn N advisor, consultant (位 wèi)

固 gù I ADJ secure, solid II v secure, consolidate, strengthen

固定 gùdìng v fix, make immovable

固定资产 gùdìng zīchǎn fixed assets

固然 gùrán CONJ granted (that), although

固体 gùtǐ N solid matter, solid

固有 gùyǒu ADJ inherent, innate

固执 gùzhí ADJ obstinate, stubborn

固执己见 gùzhí jǐjiàn stubbornly stick to one's opinions, pigheaded

瓜 guā N melon, gourd (只 zhī)

瓜子 guāzǐ N melon seeds (颗 kē)

刮 guā v (of a wind) blow

寡 guǎ ADJ 1 few, insufficient 2 widowed

孤儿寡母 gū'ér guǎmǔ orphan and widow

寡妇 guǎfù N widow

挂 guà TRAD 掛 v hang

挂钩 guàgōu v hook up, couple together

挂号 guàhào v register (at a hospital)

挂号费 guàhào fèi N registration fee, doctor's consultation fee

挂号处 guàhào chù registration office

NOTE: In China if you are sick you go to a hospital where doctors work in their specialist departments, e.g. internal medicine, gynecology and dermatology. 挂号 **guàhào** means *to tell a receptionist which department you want to go to and pay the consultation fee*. Dentistry is usually one of the departments and a dentist is generally considered just another doctor.

挂念 **guàniàn** v miss and worry about (a person)

乖 **guāi** ADJ (of children) be good, be well-behaved
乖孩子 **guāi háizi** a well-behaved child

拐 **guǎi** v turn, make a turn
拐弯 **guǎiwān** v turn a corner
拐弯抹角 **guǎiwān mòjiǎo** IDIOM talk in a roundabout way, beat around the bush

怪 **guài** I ADJ strange, odd, queer (See 奇怪 **qíguài**) II v blame
怪不得 **guàibudé** ADV no wonder, so that's why

关 **guān** TRAD 關 v 1 close 2 turn off, switch off
把电灯/电视机/录音机/机器关掉 bǎ diàndēng/diànshì jī/ lùyīnjī/jīqì guāndiào turn off the lights/TV/recorder/machine
3 v concern, involve
关闭 **guānbì** v close down, shut down
关闭机场 **guānbì jīchǎng** shut down the airport
关怀 **guānhuái** v be kindly concerned about, show loving care to
关键 **guānjiàn** N what is crucial or critical
关键词 **guānjiàncí** keyword
关节炎 **guānjiéyán** N arthritis
风湿性关节炎 **fēngshīxìng guānjiéyán** rheumatic arthritis
关切 **guānqiè** v be deeply concerned
关头 **guāntóu** N juncture, moment
在紧要关头 zài jǐnyào guāntóu at a critical juncture, at a crucial moment
关系 **guānxi** I N connection, relation
和…有关系 hé…yǒu guānxi have something to do with

没(有)关系 méi(yǒu)guānxi it doesn't matter, it's OK
II v have bearing on
关心 **guānxīn** v be concerned about, care for
关于 **guānyú** PREP about, on
关照 **guānzhào** v 1 look after, take care of 2 notify, inform

NOTE: "请你多关照。" "Qǐng nǐ duō guānzhào." is often said by someone who has just arrived or started working in a place, to someone who has been working there longer. It is a polite expression meaning something to the effect of "I'd appreciate your guidance."

观 **guān** TRAD 觀 I v look at, observe
II N view, outlook
观测 **guāncè** v observe
观测市场动向 **guāncè shìchǎng dòngxiàng** pay close attention to the market trend
观察 **guānchá** v observe, watch
观察员 **guāncháyuán** observer (at a conference, especially an international conference)
观点 **guāndiǎn** N viewpoint, view
观光 **guānguāng** v go sightseeing, visit and observe
观看 **guānkàn** v watch (a theatrical performance, sports event)
观念 **guānniàn** N concept, sense
是非观念 **shìfēi guānniàn** the sense of what is right and what is wrong
观赏 **guānshǎng** v view and admire (beautiful flowers, rare animals, etc.)
观赏野生动物 **guānshǎng yěshēng dòngwù** observe wild animals
观众 **guānzhòng** N audience (in a theater, on TV, etc.), spectator

官 **guān** N (government) official

NOTE: 官 **guān** is a colloquial word. For more formal occasions, use 官员 guānyuán.

官方 **guānfāng** ADJ official

官方消息 guānfāng xiāoxi official news, news released by the authorities
官僚 guānliáo N bureaucrat
　官僚主义 guānliáozhǔyì bureaucracy
官员 guānyuán N official (位 wèi)

NOTE: See note on 干部 gànbù.

棺 guān N coffin
棺材 guāncái coffin (口 kǒu)

管 1 guǎn V be in charge, take care
管理 guǎnlǐ V manage, administer
　商业管理 shāngyè guǎnlǐ business administration
管辖 guǎnxiá V have jurisdiction over

管 2 guǎn N tube, pipe
管子 guǎnzi tube, pipe (根 gēn)
管道 guǎndào N pipeline, conduit

馆 guǎn TRAD 館 N building (for a specific purpose)
饭馆 fànguǎn restaurant
体育馆 tǐyùguǎn gymnasium
图书馆 túshūguǎn library
馆子 guǎnzi N restaurant (colloquial) (家 jiā)

冠 guàn N the best
冠军 guànjūn N champion, championship

贯 guàn V pass through
贯彻 guànchè V implement, carry out

惯 guàn I ADJ accustomed to II N custom, convention
惯例 guànlì N usual practice, convention
　打破惯例 dǎpò guànlì break with convention
惯用语 guànyòngyǔ N idiomatic expression
惯于 guànyú V be used to, habitually
　惯于撒谎 guànyú sāhuǎng be a habitual liar

灌 guàn V fill (water, air), pour
灌溉 guàngài V irrigate
灌木 guànmù N bush

罐 guàn N tin, jar
罐头 guàntou N can, tin
　罐头食品 guàntou shípǐn canned food

光 1 guāng I N light
灯光 dēngguāng lamplight
阳光 yángguāng sunlight
月光 yuèguāng moonlight
II ADJ smooth, shiny
光彩 guāngcǎi I N luster, splendor II ADJ honorable
　觉得光彩 juéde guāngcǎi feel proud
光碟 guāngdié N compact disk (CD) (盘 pán)
光滑 guānghuá ADJ smooth, glossy
光辉 guānghuī I N brilliance, radiance II ADJ brilliant, splendid
光亮 guāngliàng ADJ bright, shiny
光临 guānglín V (a polite expression) be present, come
　欢迎光临！Huānyíng guānglín! You're cordially welcome! We welcome you.
光明 guāngmíng ADJ bright, promising
光荣 guāngróng ADJ glorious, honorable
光线 guāngxiàn N light, ray (道 dào)

光 2 guāng ADV only, sole
光棍儿 guānggùnr N unmarried man, bachelor
　打光棍儿 dǎ guānggùnr remain unmarried, be a bachelor

广 guǎng TRAD 廣 ADJ extensive, wide
广播 guǎngbō I V broadcast II N broadcasting
广播电台 guǎngbō diàntái radio station
广播公司 guǎngbō gōngsī broadcasting company
　英国广播公司 Yīngguó Guǎngbō Gōngsī the British Broadcasting Company (BBC)
广播员 guǎngbōyuán newsreader
广场 guǎngchǎng N square
广大 guǎngdà ADJ vast, extensive
广泛 guǎngfàn ADJ widespread, wide-ranging, extensive
广告 guǎnggào N advertisement

广阔 **guǎngkuò** ADJ vast, wide

逛 **guàng** V stroll, take a random walk
逛公园 **guàng gōngyuán** stroll in the park
逛街 **guàng jiē** stroll around the streets, do window shopping

瑰 **guī** as in 玫瑰 **méigui**

规 **guī** TRAD 規 N compass, regulation, rule
规定 **guīdìng** I V stipulate, prescribe II N regulation
规范 **guīfàn** N standard, norm
符合规范 **fúhé guīfàn** meet the standard
规格 **guīgé** N specifications (of a product), norm
规划 **guīhuà** V 1 long-term program
五年发展规划 **wǔ nián fāzhǎn guīhuà** five-year development plan
2 draw up a long-term program
规矩 **guīju** I N 1 custom, established practice
老规矩 **lǎoguīju** well-established practice II ADJ well behaved, behave within the norm
规律 **guīlǜ** N law, regular pattern
规模 **guīmó** N scale
规则 **guīzé** N rule, regulation
交通规则 **jiāotōng guīzé** traffic regulations
游戏规则 **yóuxì guīzé** game rules
规章 **guīzhāng** N rules, regulations
规章制度 **guīzhāng zhìdù** rules and regulations (of an organization, an institution, etc.)

归 **guī** TRAD 歸 V return, go back to
归根结底 **guī-gēn-jié-dǐ** in the final analysis
归还 **guīhuán** V return, revert
归还原主 **guīhuán yuánzhǔ** be returned to the original owner
归结 **guījié** V sum up, put in a nutshell
归纳 **guīnà** V sum up, induce
归纳法 **guīnàfǎ** inductive method

硅 **guī** N silicon
硅谷 **guīgǔ** silicon valley

龟 **guī** TRAD 龜 N turtle
海龟 **hǎiguī** sea turtle

闺 **guī** N boudoir, a lady's chamber
闺女 **guīnǚ** N 1 girl, maiden 2 daughter

鬼 **guǐ** N ghost
鬼故事 **guǐ gùshi** ghost story
鬼屋 **guǐ wū** haunted house
鬼话 **guǐhuà** N wild and ridiculous talk, nonsense (aimed to deceive)
鬼话连篇 **guǐhuà liánpiān** a pack of lies

轨 **guǐ** N rail
出轨 **chūguǐ** (of a train) derail
轨道 **guǐdào** N track, orbit
上了轨道 **shàng le guǐdào** settle into normal routine

桂 **guì** N cassia, bay tree, sweet-scented asmanthus
桂冠 **guìguān** N laurel (emblem of victory or success)

柜 **guì** TRAD 櫃 N cupboard, cabinet
柜台 **guìtái** N counter, bar

贵 **guì** TRAD 貴 ADJ 1 expensive, of great value 2 extremely valuable, precious
贵金属 **guìjīnshǔ** rare metal, precious metal
3 of noble birth, high-ranking
贵宾 **guìbīn** N distinguished guest (位 **wèi**)
贵姓 **guìxìng** IDIOM your family name

NOTE: (1) While 贵姓 guìxìng is the polite form when asking about somebody's family name, the polite way to ask somebody's given name is "请问, 您大名是…?" "Qingwèn, nín dàmíng shì…?" 大名 literally means *big name*. The answer to this question is "我叫XX。" "Wǒ jiào XX." (2) The word 贵 guì in the sense of *valuable* is added to certain nouns to mean *your ...*, e.g. 贵姓 guìxìng *your family name*, 贵国 guìguó *your country*, 贵校 guìxiào *your school*. They are only used in formal and polite contexts.

贵重 guìzhòng ADJ valuable, precious

贵族 guìzú N aristocrat, aristocracy

跪 guì V kneel

跪下去 guìxià qù kneel down

滚 gǔn V roll

NOTE: 滚 gǔn is used to tell somebody "get out of here" or "beat it," e.g. 滚! 滚出去! Gǔn! Gǔn chūqu! *Get lost! Get out of here!*; 滚开! Gǔn kāi! *Beat it!* These are highly offensive.

滚动 gǔndòng V roll

棍 gùn N stick, rod

棍子 gùnzi stick, rod (根 gēn)

锅 guō TRAD 鍋 N pot, pan, wok

锅炉 guōlú N boiler

国 guó TRAD 國 N country, nation

德国 Déguó Germany
俄国 Éguó Russia
法国 Fǎguó France
美国 Měiguó the United States of America
英国 Yīngguó England, the United Kingdom
中国 Zhōngguó China

国法 guófǎ N the law of a country

国防 guófáng N national defense
国防部 guófángbù Ministry of National Defense

国会 guóhuì N (the U.S.) Congress, Parliament
国会议员 guóhuì yìyuán Congressman, member of Parliament (MP)

国籍 guójí N nationality
加入美国国籍 jiārù Měiguó guójí be naturalized as a U.S. citizen

国际 guójì ADJ international

国家 guójiā N country, state

NOTE: It is significant that the Chinese word meaning *country*—国家 guójiā—is composed of the word 国 guó (country)

and the word 家 jiā (family). In traditional Chinese thought, China was one big family and the country was ruled as such, with the emperor as the patriarch.

国库 guókù N national treasury

国民 guómín N national (of a country)

国民党 Guómíndǎng N the Kuomintang (KMT, the political party which ruled China before 1949 and is now a major party in Taiwan.)

国旗 guóqí N national flag (面 miàn)

国情 guóqíng N the conditions of a country

国庆节 guóqìngjié N National Day (October 1st in the People's Republic of China)

国王 guówáng N king, monarch

国务卿 guówùqīng N (the U.S.) Secretary of State

国务院 guówùyuàn N (Chinese) State Council, (the U.S.) State Department

国务院总理 Guówùyuàn Zǒnglǐ N (Chinese) Premier

国营 guóyíng ADJ state-operated

国有 guóyǒu ADJ state-owned

果 guǒ N fruit

果断 guǒduàn ADJ resolute
采取果断措施 cǎiqǔ guǒduàn cuòshī take decisive measures

果然 guǒrán ADV sure enough, as expected

果实 guǒshí N fruit

果树 guǒshù N fruit tree (棵 kē)

果园 guǒyuán N orchard (座 zuò)

过 guò TRAD 過 V 1 pass, cross

过来 guòlai come over, come across (towards the speaker)

过去 guòqu go over, go across (away from the speaker)

2 spend (time), live (a life), observe (a festival)

过日子 guò rìzi live a life

过年 guò nián observe New Year's Day

过节 guò jié observe a festival

过程 guòchéng N process, course

过度 guòdù ADJ excessive, over-
饮酒过度 yǐnjiǔ guò dù drink excessively
过渡 guòdù N transition
过分 guòfèn ADJ excessive, going overboard
过分的要求 guòfèn de yāoqiú excessive demands
过后 guòhòu ADV afterwards, later
过劳死 guòláosǐ N death from overwork
过滤 guòlǜ V filter
过去 guòqù N (something) in the past
过失 guòshī N fault, error
过问 guòwèn V take an interest in, concern oneself with
过于 guòyú ADV too, excessively
过 guo TRAD 過 PARTICLE (used after a verb or an adjective to emphasize a past experience)

H

哈 hā ONOMATOPOEIA (sound of loud laughter)
哈哈 hāha ONOMATOPOEIA (representing loud laughter)
哈欠 hāqian V yawn
打哈欠 dǎhāqian give a yawn
还 hái TRAD 還 ADV still, as before
还是 háishi I ADV still, as before II CONJ or
孩 hái N child, children
孩子 háizi child, children
海 hǎi N sea
海岸 hǎi'àn N seashore, sea coast
海岸线 hǎi'ànxiàn coastline
海拔 hǎibá N height above sea level, elevation
海拔一百米 hǎibá yìbǎi mǐ 100 meters from sea level
海报 hǎibào N playbill, poster
贴海报 tiē hǎibào put up a poster
海滨 hǎibīn N seaside
海带 hǎidài N seaweed, kelp

海港 hǎigǎng N seaport (座 zuò)
海关 hǎiguān N customs, customs house
海关检查 hǎiguān jiǎnchá customs inspection, customs examination
海关手续 hǎiguān shǒuxù customs formalities
海关人员 hǎiguān rényuán customs officer
海军 hǎijūn N navy
海面 hǎimiàn N sea/ocean surface
海鸥 hǎi'ōu N seagull (只 zhī)
海外 hǎiwài ADJ overseas
海外华侨 hǎiwài Huáqiáo overseas Chinese
海峡 hǎixiá N straits, channel
台湾海峡 Táiwān hǎixiá Taiwan Straits
海鲜 hǎixiān N seafood
海鲜馆 hǎixiān guǎn seafood restaurant
海啸 hǎixiào N tsunami
海洋 hǎiyáng N seas, ocean
海洋生物 hǎiyáng shēngwù marine creatures
海员 hǎiyuán N seaman, sailor
海运 hǎiyùn N sea transportation, ocean shipping
海蜇 hǎizhé N jellyfish
害 hài I V harm, cause harm to II N harm
有害 yǒuhài harmful
害虫 hàichóng N pest (insect)
害处 hàichu N harm
害怕 hàipà V fear, be fearful
害羞 hàixiū ADJ be bashful, be shy
含 hán V 1 hold in the mouth 2 contain, have ... as ingredient
含糊 hánhu ADJ vague, ambiguous
含量 hánliàng N amount of ingredient, content
含义 hányì N implied meaning, meaning
寒 hán ADJ cold
寒带 hándài N frigid zone
寒假 hánjià N winter vacation
寒冷 hánlěng ADJ freezing cold, frigid
寒流 hánliú N cold current
寒暄 hánxuān V exchange greetings (at the beginning of a meeting)

函 hán N letter
公函 gōnghán official letter
函授 hánshòu V teach by correspondence
函授学校 hánshòu xuéxiào correspondence school

喊 hǎn V shout
喊叫 hǎnjiào V cry out, shout

罕 hǎn ADV rarely, seldom
罕见 hǎnjiàn ADJ rare

汗 hàn N sweat, perspiration
出汗 chūhàn to sweat, to perspire

汉 Hàn TRAD 漢 N the Han people (the main ethnic group among the Chinese)
汉奸 hànjiān N traitor (to China), Chinese collaborator (with a foreign country)
汉人 Hànrén N a Han Chinese, Han Chinese people
汉学 Hànxué N Sinology
汉学家 Hànxuéjiā sinologist
汉语 Hànyǔ N the language of the Han people, the Chinese language

NOTE: In Chinese there are a number of words denoting "the Chinese language." 汉语 Hànyǔ literally means *the language of the Han Chinese people*, in contrast with the languages of the non-Han peoples in China. 汉语 Hànyǔ is therefore the accurate, scientific term for the language. However, the most popular term for the Chinese language is 中文 Zhōngwén. In Singapore and other Southeast Asian countries, the standard Chinese language is often referred to as 华语 Huáyǔ in contrast to the various Chinese dialects spoken there. Also see note on 普通话 Pǔtōnghuà.

汉字 Hànzì N Chinese character, sinogram
常用汉字 chángyòng Hànzì frequently used Chinese characters, common Chinese characters
汉族 Hànzú N the Han nationality, Han Chinese people

旱 hàn ADJ (of climate) dry
旱冰场 hànbīngchǎng N roller-skating rink
旱灾 hànzāi N drought

焊 hàn V weld
电焊工 diànhàngōng welder

捍 hàn V defend, guard
捍卫 hànwèi V defend, protect
捍卫公司的利益 hànwèi gōngsī de lìyì defend the interests of a company

憾 hàn N regret (See 遗憾 yíhàn)

行 háng I M. WD line, row, queue (used with nouns that are formed in lines)
第四页第二行 dì-sì yè dì-èr háng line two on page 4
十四行诗 shísì háng shī sonnet
II N profession, trade
行情 hángqíng N price quotations
行业 hángyè N trade and profession, industry
各行各业 gè-háng-gè-yè every trade and profession

航 háng V navigate
航班 hángbān N flight, flight number
105班 yāo-líng-wǔ hángbān Flight No 105
飞往广州的航班 fēiwǎng Guǎngzhōu de hángbān the flight to Guangzhou
航道 hángdào N waterway, channel
航海 hánghǎi N (ocean) navigation
航海家 hánghǎijiā (great) navigator
航空 hángkōng N aviation
航空公司 hángkōng gōngsī aviation company, airline
航空信 hángkōngxìn airmail letter
航空学校 hángkōng xuéxiào aviation school
航天 hángtiān N spaceflight
航天飞机 hángtiān fēijī space shuttle, spaceship
航线 hángxiàn N ocean or air route

航行 hángxíng V (of a ship) sail, (of an aircraft) fly

航运 hángyùn N shipping

航运公司 hángyùn gōngsī shipping company

豪 **háo** ADJ bold and unrestrained

豪华 háohuá ADJ luxurious, sumptuous

毫 **háo** N fine long hair

毫不 háo bù ADV not in the least, not at all

NOTE: 毫不 háo bù is an adverb used before an adjective of two or more syllables. For example, you can say 毫不奇怪 háo bù qíguài *not at all strange*, but you cannot say 毫不怪 háo bú guài.

毫米 háomǐ N millimeter

毫无 háo wú V have no ... at all, be in total absence of

NOTE: The object of 毫无 háo wú usually takes a word of two or more syllables, and usually refers to something abstract, like 毫无同情心 háowú tóngqíngxīn *totally without sympathy*.

好 1 **hǎo** ADJ good, all right

好比 hǎobǐ V may be compared as, be like, same as

好吃 hǎochī ADJ delicious

好处 hǎochu N benefit, advantage

对⋯有好处 duì...yǒu hǎochu be beneficial to

好感 hǎogǎn N favorable impression, fondness (for somebody)

对他有好感 duì tā yǒu hǎogǎn be fond of him, have a soft spot for him

好汉 hǎohàn N brave man, hero

好好儿 hǎohāor ADJ normal, nothing wrong

好坏 hǎohuài N what is good and what is bad (for somebody)

不知好坏 bùzhī hǎohuài don't know what is good and what is bad for oneself, be insensible

好久 hǎojiǔ ADV a long time

好看 hǎokàn ADJ 1 pleasant to the eye, good-looking, pretty) 2 interesting, absorbing

好容易 hǎo róngyì ADV with great difficulty

NOTE: 好容易 hǎo róngyì is an idiomatic expression. You can also say 好不容易 hǎo bù róngyì, with exactly the same meaning, e.g. 我好不容易找到他家, 他偏不在。Wǒ hǎo bù róngyì zhǎodào tā jiā, tā piān bú zài. *I found his home with great difficulty, and he had to be out.*

好听 hǎotīng ADJ pleasant to the ear, melodious

好玩儿 hǎowánr ADJ great fun

好像 hǎoxiàng V be like, similar to

好心 hǎoxīn ADJ kindhearted

好在 hǎozài ADV fortunately, luckily

好转 hǎozhuǎn V take a turn for the better, improve

好 2 **hǎo** ADV 1 very, very much 2 How...!

好多 hǎo duō ADJ a good many, many, much

好些 hǎoxiē ADJ a good many, a large number of, lots of

NOTE: 好些 hǎoxiē is a colloquial word, only used in casual, familiar styles.

好 **hào** V be fond of

好吃 hào chī ADJ fond of eating, gluttonous

好动 hào dòng ADJ hyperactive

好客 hàokè ADJ hospitable

热情好客 rèqíng hàokè warm and hospitable

好奇 hào qí ADJ be curious, inquisitive

好色 hào sè ADJ oversexed, lewd

好学 hào xué ADJ fond of learning, thirsty for knowledge

耗 **hào** V consume

耗费 hàofèi V consume (especially in a wasteful way), cost (a large amount of money, time, etc.)

号 hào TRAD 號 N 1 order of sequence 2 date of month

NOTE: See note on 日 rì.

号称 hàochēng V be known as (something great), claim to be
号码 hàomǎ N serial number, size
号召 hàozhào V call upon, appeal

浩 hào ADJ vast, numerous

浩大 hàodà ADJ huge, gigantic
浩大的工程 hàodà de gōngchéng a huge engineering project

呵 hē V blow a puff of breath, exhale through the mouth

喝 hē V drink

NOTE: 喝 hē (drink) and 渴 kě (thirsty) look similar. Be careful not to confuse the two characters.

合 hé V 1 close 2 co-operate, do in partnership
合办企业 hébàn qǐyè run an enterprise in partnership
3 conform with
不合我的口味 bùhé wǒde kǒuwèi not to my taste
4 be equal to
合法 héfǎ ADJ legal, legitimate
合格 hégé ADJ qualified, up to standard
合乎 héhū V conform with, correspond to
合乎惯例 héhū guànlì conform with normal practice
合伙 héhuǒ V form a partnership, work in a partnership
和老同学合伙开公司 hé lǎo tóngxué héhuǒ kāi gōngsī set up a company in partnership with an old classmate
合金 héjīn N alloy
合理 hélǐ ADJ conforming to reason, reasonable, logical
合适 héshì ADJ suitable, appropriate
合算 hésuàn ADJ worthwhile paying
合同 hétóng N contract, agreement (份 fèn)
合资 hézī V pool capital to run a business

合资企业 hézī qǐyè joint venture
合作 hézuò I V cooperate, work together II N cooperation

盒 hé N box
盒子 hézi box (只 zhī)

何 hé PRON which, what

何等 héděng I ADJ what kind II ADV how, what
何况 hékuàng CONJ 1 what's more, moreover 2 let alone

荷 hé N lotus
荷花 héhuā lotus flower

河 hé N river (条 tiáo)

NOTE: In modern Chinese, 江 jiāng and 河 hé both mean river. Usually (not always) rivers in the south are known as 江 jiāng and rivers in the north are 河 hé.

河道 hédào N river course
河流 héliú N rivers

阂 hé V hinder, obstruct

禾 hé N seedling, (especially) rice seedling
禾苗 hémiáo N seedling (of cereal crops)

和 hé I CONJ and II PREP with
和…一起 hé...yìqǐ together with …

核 hé N kernel, core, pit
核电站 hédiànzhàn N nuclear power plant
核辐射 héfúshè N nuclear radiation
核桃 hétáo N walnut (颗 kē)
核武器 héwǔqì N nuclear weapon
核心 héxīn N core, kernel

贺 hè TRAD 賀 V congratulate
贺词 hècí N speech of congratulations
贺卡 hèkǎ N greeting card (张 zhāng)

赫 hè ADJ conspicuous, grand
显赫 xiǎnhè distinguished and influential, illustrious

赫赫 **hèhè** ADJ illustrious, impressive
赫赫有名 **hèhè yǒumíng** very famous, illustrious

黑 **hēi** ADJ black, dark
黑暗 **hēi'àn** ADJ dark
黑板 **hēibǎn** N blackboard
黑夜 **hēiyè** N night
白天黑夜 **báitiān hēiyè** day and night

嘿 **hēi** INTERJ 1 (used to attract someone's attention in a casual or impolite manner) 2 (used to indicate admiration)

痕 **hén** N trace
伤痕 **shānghén** scar
痕迹 **hénjì** N trace, mark, stain

狠 **hěn** ADJ 1 cruel, relentless
心毒手狠 **xīndú shǒuhěn** with a vicious mind and cruel means
2 severe, stern
狠狠地批评 **hěnhěnde pīpíng** criticize severely
狠毒 **hěndú** ADJ cruel and vicious
狠心 **hěnxīn** I ADJ ruthless II V make a painful decision
下狠心 **xià hěnxīn** make a tough decision resolutely

很 **hěn** ADV very, quite

NOTE: When used as predicates, Chinese adjectives normally require an adverb. For example, 我高兴 Wǒ gāoxìng sounds unnatural, while 我很高兴 Wǒ hěn gāoxìng (I'm [very] happy), 我不高兴 Wǒ bù gāoxìng (I'm not happy) or 我非常高兴 Wǒ fēicháng gāoxìng (I'm very happy) are normal sentences. The adverb 很 hěn is often used as a default adverb before an adjective. In such cases the meaning of 很 hěn is very weak.

恨 **hèn** V 1 hate, be angry with 2 regret deeply
恨不得 **hènbude** ADV how … wish to

NOTE: We use 恨不得 to express a wish that is very strong but cannot be fulfilled. If we say 他恨不得马上回家过年。Hā hènbude mǎshàng huíjiā guònián, it means *it is quite impossible for him to go back home right now*.

哼 **hēng** V 1 snort 2 hum

衡 **héng** I N weighing instrument II V weigh, consider
衡量 **héngliáng** V judge, consider
衡量利弊 **héngliáng lìbì** consider the pros and cons

恒 **héng** I ADJ permanent, forever II N perseverance
恒心 **héngxīn** N perseverance
恒星 **héngxīng** N star (颗 kē)

横 **héng** ADJ 1 horizontal 2 violent, fierce
横路 **hénglù** N side street
横行 **héngxíng** V play the tyrant, run amok

轰 **hōng** TRAD 轟 V rumble, explode
轰动 **hōngdòng** V cause a sensation
轰炸 **hōngzhà** V bomb
轰炸机 **hōngzhàjī** bomber

烘 **hōng** V dry or warm by the fire, roast
烘干机 **hōnggānjī** (clothes) dryer

红 **hóng** TRAD 紅 ADJ 1 red 2 popular, favored
红包 **hóngbāo** N a red envelope (containing money), bribe
收红包 **shōu hóngbāo** take bribes
红茶 **hóngchá** N black tea
红绿灯 **hónglǜdēng** N traffic lights, stoplights
红人 **hóngrén** N a trusted and favored employee or member of an organization
红外线 **hóngwàixiàn** N infrared ray
红血球 **hóngxuèqiú** N red blood cell, erythrocyte
红眼病 **hóngyǎnbìng** N 1 conjunctivitis (eye disease) 2 envy, jealousy

虹 **hóng** N rainbow

彩虹 cǎihóng rainbow (道 dào)

宏 hóng ADJ grand, magnificent

宏大 hóngdà ADJ great, grand

宏观 hóngguān ADJ macroscopic

宏观经济学 hóngguān jīngjìxué macroeconomics

宏伟 hóngwěi ADJ magnificent, grand

洪 hóng N big

洪水 hóngshuǐ flood

哄 hǒng v 1 coax 2 cheat, hoodwink

哄骗 hǒngpiàn v lie in order to cheat

哄 hòng N horseplay

起哄 qǐhòng start a horseplay

喉 hóu N throat

喉咙 hóulóng N throat, larynx

喉咙疼 hóulóng téng have a sore throat

猴 hóu N monkey

猴子 hóuzi monkey (只 zhī)

吼 hǒu v roar, howl

吼叫 hǒujiào v howl, roar

后 hòu TRAD 後 N back, rear)

后边 hòubian N back, rear

后代 hòudài N succeeding generations, posterity

后方 hòufāng N rear, behind

后果 hòuguǒ N consequences

后悔 hòuhuǐ v regret, feel sorry (for having done something)

后来 hòulái N afterwards, later on

后面 hòumian N Same as 后边 hòubian

后年 hòunián N the year after next

后期 hòuqī N later stage, later periods

后勤 hòuqín N logistics, support services

后台 hòutái N 1 backstage 2 behind-the-scenes supporter

后天 hòutiān N the day after tomorrow

后头 hòutou N Same as 后面 hòumian or 后边 hòubian, used colloquially.

后退 hòutuì v retreat, draw back

厚 hòu ADJ thick

厚度 hòudù N thickness

候 hòu v wait

候补 hòubǔ v be a candidate (for a position)

候补委员 hòubǔ wěiyuán alternative member of a committee

候选人 hòuxuǎnrén N candidate (for an election or selection)

乎 hū PARTICLE (added to another word to express strong emotions) (See 几乎 jīhū, 似乎 sìhū.)

呼 hū v 1 exhale 2 shout, cry out

呼声 hūshēng N 1 call, crying 2 public voice, expression of public opinion

呼吸 hūxī v breathe

呼吁 hūyù v appeal, call on

忽 hū ADV suddenly

忽略 hūlüè v neglect, overlook

忽然 hūrán ADV suddenly

忽视 hūshì v overlook, neglect

胡 1 hú TRAD 鬍 N beard, mustache

胡子 húzi beard, whiskers

刮胡子 guā húzi shave (beard, whiskers)

胡 2 hú ADJ foreign, outlandish

NOTE: In ancient China, 胡 hú was used to refer to foreigners, especially the nomadic tribesmen from Central Asia. A number of words with 胡 hú were created to denote objects introduced to China by or through these people. Words with 胡 hú may also have derogatory meanings.

胡来 húlái v fool with, mess up

胡乱 húluàn ADV rashly, carelessly

胡萝卜 húluóbo N carrot

胡闹 húnào v act noisily and willfully, create a scene

胡琴 húqin N a traditional musical instrument with two strings, also called 二胡 èrhú (把 bǎ)

拉胡琴(二胡)lā húqin (èrhú) play the *erhu*

胡说 húshuō I v talk nonsense II N nonsense

胡说八道 húshuō bādào pure nonsense

胡同 hútòng N narrow lane in Beijing

瑚 hú as in 珊瑚 shānhú

葫 hú as in 葫芦 húlu

葫芦 húlu N bottle gourd, calabash

糊 hú I v paste II N mush, gruel

糊涂 hútú ADJ muddle-headed, muddled, confused

糊涂虫 hútú chóng N muddle-headed person, bungler

湖 hú N lake

湖泊 húpō N lakes

蝴 hú as in 蝴蝶 húdié

蝴蝶 húdié N butterfly

壶 hú TRAD 壺 N kettle (把 bǎ)

水壶 shuǐhú kettle

狐 hú N fox

狐狸 húli fox

虎 hǔ N tiger (See 老虎 lǎohǔ, 马虎 mǎhu)

互 hù I ADJ reciprocal II ADV mutually, each other

互利 hùlì ADJ of mutual benefit

互联网 hùliánwǎng N the Internet, the World Wide Web

互相 hùxiāng ADV each other, one another

互助 hùzhù v help each other

户 hù M. WD (used with nouns denoting households and families)

户口 hùkǒu N registered permanent residence

城镇户口 chéngzhèn hùkǒu urban residence

农村户口 nóngcūn hùkǒu rural residence

护 hù TRAD 護 V protect

护士 hùshi N nurse

NOTE: In China nurses are almost exclusively women. To address a nurse politely, use 护士小姐 hùshi xiǎojiě, e.g. 护士小姐，我还需要吃这个药吗? Hùshi xiǎojiě, wǒ hái xūyào chī zhè ge yào ma? *Nurse, do I still need to take this medicine?* or you can put her family name before 护士 hùshì, e.g. 张护士 Zhāng hùshì.

护照 hùzhào N passport (份 fèn)

申请护照 shēnqǐng hùzhào apply for a passport

沪 hù TRAD 滬 N a shortened form for the metropolis of Shanghai

沪东 Hù-Dōng East Shanghai

花 1 huā N flower (朵 duǒ)

种花 zhòng huā plant flowers, do gardening

NOTE: In colloquial Chinese 花儿 huār may be used instead of 花 huā, e.g. 去医院看病人，可以带一些花儿。Qù yīyuàn kàn bìngrén, kěyǐ dài yìxiē huār. *You can take some flowers with you when you visit a patient in the hospital.*

花朵 huāduǒ N flowers

花瓶 huāpíng N vase (只 zhī)

瓷器花瓶 cíqì huāpíng porcelain vase

花儿 huār I N Same as 花 huā II ADJ full of colors, mottled, loud

花色 huāsè N 1 (of fabric) design and color 2 (of a commodity) variety of designs, colors, sizes, etc.

花生 huāshēng N peanut

花生酱 huāshēngjiàng peanut butter

花纹 huāwén N decorative pattern, pattern

花样 huāyàng N 1 pattern, variety

花样溜冰 huāyàngliūbīng figure skate 2 trick

和我玩花样 hé wǒ wán huāyang play tricks on me

花园 huāyuán N garden (座 zuò)

花 2 huā v 1 spend 2 cost (money) 3 take (time)

NOTE: In writing, the character 化 huā can be used instead of 花 huā as a verb meaning *spend*, *cost*, etc.

花费 huāfèi **I** v consume, spend
花费大量心血 huāfèi dàliàng xīnxuè put in a great deal of effort
II N money spent, expenses

划 huá TRAD 劃 v **1** row, paddle
划船 huáchuán row a boat
2 scratch or scrape with a sharp object
3 be worth the money spent
划算 huásuàn ADJ worth it, getting money's worth

滑 huá ADJ slippery
滑冰 huábīng v skate (on ice), ice-skating
滑头 huátóu **I** ADJ crafty, shifty **II** N a crafty, shifty person
滑雪 huáxuě **I** v ski **II** N skiing

猾 huá as in 狡猾 jiǎohuá

华 huá TRAD 華 **I** N China **II** ADJ magnificent, gorgeous
华丽 huálì ADJ gorgeous, magnificent
华侨 huáqiáo N overseas Chinese
华人 huárén N ethnic Chinese
华氏 huáshì N Fahrenheit scale
华氏温度计 huáshì wēndùjì Fahrenheit thermometer

哗 huá TRAD 嘩 N noise

化 huà **I** v **1** melt **2** transform **II** N chemistry
化肥 huàféi N chemical fertilizer
化工 huàgōng N chemical industry
化工厂 huàgōngchǎng chemical plant
化合 huàhé N chemical combination
化石 huàshí N fossil
化纤 huàxiān N chemical fiber
化学 huàxué N chemistry
化学家 huàxuéjiā N chemist
化学工业(化工) huàxué gōngyè (huàgōng) chemical industry
化验 huàyàn N chemical test, laboratory test

化验报告 huàyàn bàogào laboratory test report
化验单 huàyàn dān laboratory test application (a form signed by a doctor for the patient to have a test done in a laboratory)
化验室 huàyàn shì laboratory
化验员 huàyàn yuán laboratory assistant, laboratory technician
化妆 huàzhuāng v put on make-up
化妆品 huàzhuāngpǐn cosmetics

划 huà TRAD 劃 v **1** plan **2** delimit
划分 huàfēn v divide, differentiate

画 huà TRAD 畫 v draw, paint
国画 guóhuà traditional Chinese painting
铅笔画 qiānbǐ huà pencil drawing
水彩画 shuǐcǎi huà watercolor (painting)
油画 yóuhuà oil painting
中国画 Zhōngguóhuà Same as 国画 guóhuà
画儿 huàr N picture, drawing (张 zhāng, 幅 fú)

NOTE: You can use 画 huà instead of 画儿 huàr, e.g. 这张画画得真好! Zhè zhāng huà huà de zhēn hǎo! *This picture is so well done!*

画报 huàbào N illustrated magazine, pictorial (份 fèn, 本 běn)
画家 huàjiā N painter, artist (位 wèi)
画面 huàmiàn N image on the screen or the canvas
画蛇添足 huà shé tiān zú IDIOM add legs to a snake (→ do superfluous things, thus causing damage or attracting ridicule)

话 huà TRAD 話 N speech, what is said, words (句 jù)
话剧 huàjù N stage play (as opposed to opera)
话题 huàtí N topic of conversation, subject of a talk, theme

槐 huái N Chinese scholar tree
槐树 huáishù Chinese scholar tree (棵 kē)

徊 **huái** v walk to and fro (See 徘徊 páihuái)

怀 **huái** TRAD 懷 I N bosom II v 1 keep in mind 2 miss, think of

怀念 **huáiniàn** v think of tenderly

怀疑 **huáiyí** v 1 disbelieve, doubt 2 think something is unlikely, suspect

NOTE: 怀疑 huáiyí has two seemingly contradictory meanings – *disbelieve* and *think something is unlikely*, but the context will make the meaning clear.

怀孕 **huáiyùn** v be pregnant

坏 **huài** TRAD 壞 I ADJ bad II v break down, be out of order

坏处 **huàichu** N negative effect, disadvantage

NOTE: 坏处 huàichu and 害处 hàichu both refer to the undesirable effects of an action or actions. 坏处 huàichu connotes general negativity while 害处 hàichu emphasizes the harm that results.

坏蛋 **huàidàn** N bad person, villain, rascal

欢 **huān** TRAD 歡 ADJ joyful

欢呼 **huānhū** v cheer, hail

欢乐 **huānlè** ADJ joyful, happy

欢送 **huānsòng** v send off (a guest)
　欢送会 **huānsònghuì** a send-off party (e.g. a farewell tea party)

欢喜 **huānxǐ** ADJ joyful, happy, delighted

欢笑 **huānxiào** v laugh heartily

欢迎 **huānyíng** v welcome

欢迎光临 **huānyíng guānglín** INTERJ Welcome!

还 **huán** TRAD 還 v return, pay back

还原 **huányuán** v return to the original, restore

环 **huán** TRAD 環 N circle, ring

环节 **huánjié** N link
　重要环节 **zhòngyào huánjié** important link

环境 **huánjìng** N environment
　环境保护（环保）**huánjìng bǎohù (huánbǎo)** environmental protection

缓 **huǎn** TRAD 緩 ADV leisurely

缓和 **huǎnhé** I v ease up, alleviate II ADJ relaxed, gentle
　口气缓和 **kǒuqì huǎnhé** with a gentle, mild tone

缓慢 **huǎnmàn** ADJ slow, unhurried

换 **huàn** TRAD 換 v change, replace

换取 **huànqǔ** v exchange for, get in return

唤 **huàn** v call out

痪 **huàn** N paralysis (See 瘫痪 tānhuàn)

幻 **huàn** ADJ illusory

幻灯 **huàndēng** N slide show

幻灯机 **huàndēngjī** slide projector

幻灯片 **huàndēngpiàn** slide, lantern slide (张 zhāng)

幻想 **huànxiǎng** v fantasize, have illusions

患 **huàn** v suffer (from a disease)

患者 **huànzhě** N patient
　精神病患者 **jīngshénbìng huànzhě** one who suffers from a mental disorder

荒 **huāng** I ADJ 1 barren, desolate 2 absurd II N crop falure, famine

荒地 **huāngdì** N uncultivated land, wasteland

荒凉 **huāngliáng** ADJ bleak, desolate

荒谬 **huāngmiù** ADJ absurd, preposterous
　荒谬至极 **huāngmiù zhìjí** absolutely absurd

荒唐 **huāngtáng** ADJ preposterous, way off the mark
　荒唐透顶 **huāngtáng tòudǐng** incredibly silly, totally unreasonable

慌 **huāng** ADJ flustered, panic-stricken
　慌了手脚 **huāngle shǒu jiǎo** be so flustered as to not know what to do, be at a loss as to what to do

慌乱 **huāngluàn** ADJ panic-stricken, flustered

慌张 **huāngzhāng** ADJ in frantic haste, flustered

皇 **huáng** N emperor

皇帝 huángdì N emperor
皇后 huánghòu N wife of an emperor, empress [NB the traditional form 後 hòu doesn't apply here for 皇后]

蝗 **huáng** N locust

蝗虫 huángchóng locust
蝗灾 huángzāi locust disaster

凰 **huáng** N female phoenix (See 凤凰 fènghuáng)

煌 **huáng** ADJ intensely bright (See 辉煌 huīhuáng)

黄 **huáng** ADJ yellow

黄瓜 huángguā N cucumber (根 gēn)
黄色 huángsè I N the yellow color II ADJ pornographic
  黄色电影 huángsè diànyǐng pornographic movie
  黄色网站 huángsè wǎngzhàn pornographic website
黄油 huángyóu N butter

晃 **huǎng** V sway, shake

谎 **huǎng** N lie

谎话 huǎnghuà lie (especially used in speech)
谎言 huǎngyán lie (especially used in writing)

徽 **huī** N emblem, sign

国徽 guóhuī national emblem
校徽 xiàohuī school badge

灰 **huī** I ADJ gray II N ash, dust

灰尘 huīchén N dust
灰心 huīxīn ADJ disheartened, discouraged

恢 **huī** ADJ extensive, vast

恢复 huīfù V recover, restore

挥 **huī** TRAD 揮 V **1** wave (See 发挥 fāhuī.) **2** scatter, disperse

挥霍 huīhuò V spend money carelessly, be a spendthrift, squander

辉 **huī** TRAD 輝 N splendor

辉煌 huīhuáng ADJ brilliant, splendid

回 1 **huí** **1** V return (to a place), go back **2** reply, answer

回电话 huí diànhuà call back
回避 huíbì V evade, dodge
  回避问题 huíbì wèntí evade a question
回答 huídá V reply, answer
回顾 huígù V look back, review
回国 huíguó V return to one's home country
回击 huíjī V counterattack
回来 huílai V return to a place (coming towards the speaker)
回去 huíqù V return to a place (away from the speaker)
回收 huíshōu V reclaim, recover
  废品回收 fèipǐn huíshōu collect junk for recycling
回头 huítóu ADV later

NOTE: 回头 huítóu is a colloquialism, used only in very informal styles.

回想 huíxiǎng V recall, recollect
回信 huíxìn N reply (either spoken or written)
回忆 huíyì I V recall, recollect II N recollection, memory

回 2 **huí** M. WD number of times (of doing something)

读了两回 dúle liǎnghuí read ... twice

毁 **huǐ** V destroy

毁坏 huǐhuài V do irreparable damage
  毁坏名誉 huǐhuài míngyù destroy one's reputation
毁灭 huǐmiè V exterminate
  毁灭罪证 huǐmiè zuìzhèng destroy incriminating evidence

悔 **huǐ** V repent, regret (See 后悔 hòuhuǐ)

悔改 huǐgǎi V repent and mend one's way
悔恨 huǐhèn V repent bitterly

惠 **huì** N benefits, kindness (See 恩惠 ēnhuì)

慧 **huì** ADJ wise, intelligent (See 智慧 zhìhuì)

贿 **huì** TRAD 賄 V bribe

贿赂 huìlù I V bribe II N bribery

汇 **huì** TRAD 匯 V 1 converge, gather 2 remit

汇报 huìbào V report (to one's superior)

汇集 huìjí V compile, collect, gather
汇集有关的文件 huìjí yǒuguān de wénjiàn compile relevant documents

汇款 huìkuǎn V remit money, send remittance

汇率 huìlǜ N (currency) exchange rate

会 **1 huì** TRAD 會 I MODAL V 1 know how to, can 2 probably, will II V have the ability or knowledge

NOTE: 会 huì as a full verb meaning *have the ability* or *knowledge* is used with a limited range of nouns, such as nouns denoting languages. Using 会 huì in this way is colloquial.

会 **2 huì** TRAD 會 N 1 meeting, conference
大会 dàhuì an assembly, a rally
开会 kāi huì have a meeting
2 association
读书会 dúshū huì book club
工会 gōnghuì labor union
学生会 xuéshenghuì students union

会场 huìchǎng N venue for a meeting, conference, assembly or rally

会话 huìhuà I V talk, hold a conversation II N conversation

会见 huìjiàn V (formal) meet

会客 huìkè V receive visitors

会谈 huìtán V hold (formal) talks

会晤 huìwù V meet (formally)

会议 huìyì N meeting, conference
参加会议 cānjiā huìyì participate in a meeting or conference
出席会议 chūxí huìyì attend a meeting or conference
举行会议 jǔxíng huìyì hold a meeting or conference
取消会议 qǔxiāo huìyì cancel a meeting or conference

召开会议 zhàokāi huìyì convene a meeting or conference

会员 huìyuán N member of an association
会员证 huìyuánzhèng membership card
工会会员 gōnghuì huìyuán labor union member
俱乐部会员 jùlèbù huìyuán club member

绘 **huì** V paint, draw

绘画 huìhuà N painting, drawing

昏 **hūn** V faint

昏迷 hūnmí V fall into a coma

婚 **hūn** N marriage

婚姻 hūnyīn N marriage

魂 **hún** N soul (See 灵魂 línghún)

浑 **hún** ADJ 1 muddy 2 whole, all over

浑身 húnshēn ADJ from head to foot, all over the body
浑身疼痛 húnshēn téngtòng ache all over

混 **hùn** V 1 mix up

混为一谈 hùn wéi yì tán lump different things together, fail to make a distinction between different things
2 pass for, pass off as **3** get along, get along with

混合 hùnhé V mix, blend, mingle

混乱 hùnluàn ADJ chaotic, confused

混凝土 hùnníngtǔ N cement, concrete

混淆 hùnxiáo V eliminate differences in order to confuse, mix up
混淆是非 hùnxiáo shìfēi confuse right and wrong

混浊 hùnzhuó ADJ murky, turbid

活 **huó** I V 1 be alive 2 work II ADJ alive, living

活动 huódòng I V do physical exercise II N activity
参加活动 cānjiā huódòng participate in an activity

活该 huógāi V serve one right, deserve

活力 huólì N vitality, vigor

活泼 huópo ADJ lively, vivacious

活儿 huór N work, job
干活儿 gàn huór work, do a job

NOTE: 活儿 huór and 干活儿 gàn huór are very colloquial, and usually refer to manual work.

活跃 huóyuè ADJ active, brisk

火 **huǒ** N fire
着火 zháo huǒ catch fire, be caught on fire
火柴 huǒchái N match (根 gēn, 盒 hé)
火柴盒 huǒchái hé a matchbox
划火柴 huá huǒchái strike a match
火车 huǒchē N train (辆 liàng, 列 liè)
火车站 huǒchē zhàn railway station
火车票 huǒchē piào train ticket
火车时刻表 huǒchē shíkè biǎo railway timetable
火箭 huǒjiàn N rocket (枚 méi)
发射火箭 fāshè huǒjiàn launch a rocket
火力 huǒlì N 1 fire power 2 thermal energy
火力发电 huǒlì fādiàn thermal power
火山 huǒshān N volcano (座 zuò)
火山爆发 huǒshān bàofā the eruption of a volcano
活火山 huó huǒshān active volcano
死火山 sǐ huǒshān dormant volcano
火焰 huǒyàn N flame
熊熊火焰 xióngxióng huǒyàn raging flames
火药 huǒyào N gunpowder
火灾 huǒzāi N fire disaster, fire (场 cháng)

伙 **huǒ** TRAD 夥 N partner
伙伴 huǒbàn N partner, mate
伙食 huǒshí N meals (provided by a school, a factory, etc.)

霍 **huò** as in 霍乱 huòluàn
霍乱 huòluàn N cholera

祸 **huò** TRAD 禍 N disaster, calamity
车祸 chēhuò traffic accident
嫁祸 jiàhuò shift the blame onto some other person

祸害 huòhài I N disaster, scourge II V bring disaster to, ruin

或 **huò** CONJ Same as 或者 huòzhě. Used more in writing.
或多或少 huòduō huòshǎo ADV more or less, somehow
或许 huòxǔ ADV perhaps, maybe
或者 huòzhě CONJ or, either ... or

惑 **huò** V confuse (See 迷惑 míhuo)

货 **huò** TRAD 貨 N goods
货币 huòbì N currency
货币贬值 huòbì biǎnzhí currency devaluation
货币升值 huòbì shēngzhí currency appreciation
次货 cìhuò inferior/substandard goods
货物 huòwù N goods, commodities, merchandise

获 **huò** TRAD 獲 V gain, win
获得 huòdé V win, obtain, get
获取 huòqǔ V gain, obtain

J

击 **jī** TRAD 擊 V strike (See 打击 dǎjī)

几 **jī** TRAD 幾 ADV nearly
几乎 jīhū ADV almost, nearly

饥 **jī** TRAD 飢 ADJ starved
饥饿 jī'è ADJ starved, hungry

机 **jī** TRAD 機 N 1 machine 2 opportunity
机场 jīchǎng N airport
机车 jīchē N locomotive (辆 liàng)
机床 jīchuáng N machine tool (台 tái)
机动 jīdòng ADJ 1 flexible
机动资金 jīdòng zījīn emergency fund, reserve fund
2 motorized, machine-powdered
机动车 jīdòngchē motorized vehicle (e.g. automobiles, motorcycles)

机构 jīgòu N government agency, organization

机关 jīguān N government office, state organ

机会 jīhuì N opportunity, chance
放弃机会 fàngqì jīhuì give up an opportunity
抓住机会 zhuāzhù jīhuì grasp an opportunity
错过机会 cuòguò jīhuì miss an opportunity

机灵 jīling ADJ quick-witted

机密 jīmì ADJ secret, classified, confidential
机密文件 jīmì wénjiàn classified document

机器 jīqì N machine (台 tái)
使用机器 shǐyòng jīqì operate a machine
修理机器 xiūlǐ jīqì repair a machine

机器人 jīqì rén N robot

机体 jītǐ N organism

机械 jīxiè N machine, machinery

机遇 jīyù N rare opportunity, favorable situation

机智 jīzhì I N wit II ADJ sharp-witted

肌 Jī N muscle, flesh

肌肉 jīròu N muscle

讥 Jī TRAD 譏 V sneer, mock

讥笑 jīxiào V sneer at, laugh at, ridicule

鸡 Jī TRAD 雞 N chicken (只 zhī)

公鸡 gōngjī rooster
母鸡 mǔjī hen
小鸡 xiǎojī chick
肯德基烤鸡 Kěn dé jī kǎojī Kentucky Fried Chicken (KFC)

NOTE: 鸡 jī, as a general term, may denote either a *hen*, a *rooster* or *chick*, though they may be specified by 公鸡 gōngjī *cock*, 母鸡 mǔjī *hen* and 小鸡 xiǎojī *chicken*. As food, it is always 鸡 jī.

鸡蛋 jīdàn N hen's egg (只 zhī, 个 gè)

积 Jī TRAD 積 V accumulate, amass

积极 jījí ADJ 1 enthusiastic, active 2 positive

积极性 jījíxìng N initiative, enthusiasm, zeal

积累 jīlěi V accumulate, build up

积压 jīyā V keep too long in store, overstock
积压物资 jīyā wùzī overstocked supplies

基 Jī N (earthen) foundation

基本 jīběn ADJ fundamental, basic
基本上 jīběn shang basically, on the whole

基层 jīcéng N primary level, grass-roots

基础 jīchǔ N foundation, basis

基地 jīdì N base

基金 jījīn N fund
教育基金 jiàoyù jījīn educational fund

基金会 jījīnhuì N foundation
儿童福利基金会 értóng fúlì jījīnhuì Foundation for Children's Welfare

基因 jīyīn N gene

激 Jī I V arouse, excite II ADJ violent, fervent

激动 jīdòng I V arouse, excite II ADJ excited, very emotional

激发 jīfā V arouse, stir up
激发爱国主义 jīfā àiguózhǔyì arouse patriotism

激光 jīguāng N laser
激光打印机 jīguāng dǎyìnjī laser printer

激励 jīlì V excite and urge, strongly encourage

激烈 jīliè ADJ fierce, intense

激情 jīqíng N intense emotion, passion

激素 jīsù N hormone

圾 Jī N garbage (See 垃圾 lājī.)

及 Jí I CONJ and, with II V reach, come up to III ADV in time for

及格 jígé V pass (a test, an examination etc.)

及时 jíshí I ADJ timely, at the proper time II ADV immediately, promptly, without delay

及早 jízǎo ADV as soon as possible, promptly

籍 **jí** N **1** registration **2** membership

会籍 huìjí N membership of an association

籍贯 jíguàn N place of one's birth or origin

级 **jí** TRAD 級 N grade, rank

级别 jíbié N grade, scale

工资级别 gōngzījíbié wage/salary scale

极 **jí** TRAD 極 ADV extremely, highly

极端 jíduān ADV extremely

走极端 zǒu jíduān go to extremes

极了 jíle ADV extremely, very

> NOTE: 极了 jíle is used after adjectives or some verbs to mean *extremely ...* or *very ...* For example: 忙极了 máng jíle *extremely busy*; 高兴极了 gāoxìng jíle *very happy, delighted*

极力 jílì ADV to one's utmost

极力劝他戒烟 jílì quàn tā jiè yān try all one can to persuade him to give up smoking

极其 jíqí ADV extremely, highly

极限 jíxiàn N the ultimate, the limit

吉 **jí** ADJ lucky, fortunate, auspicious

吉普车 jípǔchē N jeep (辆 liàng)

吉祥 jíxiáng ADJ lucky, auspicious

吉祥物 jíxiángwù N mascot

辑 **jí** V compile, edit (See 编辑 biānjí)

疾 **jí** N disease

疾病 jíbìng N disease, illness

嫉 **jí** V be jealous

嫉妒 jídù V be jealous

嫉妒她妹妹的美貌 jídù tā mèimei de měimào be jealous of her younger sister's beauty

己 **jí** V be, mean

非此即彼 fēicǐ jíbǐ if it is not this one, it must be that one

即便 jíbiàn CONJ even if, even though

即将 jíjiāng ADV soon

即使 jíshǐ CONJ even if, even though

急 **jí** ADJ **1** anxious **2** urgent

急剧 jíjù ADJ sudden and intense, abrupt

急忙 jímáng ADJ hurried, hasty

急切 jíqiè ADJ eager and impatient, urgent

急性子 jíxìngzi N an impatient or impetuous person

急于 jíyú V be eager to, be anxious to

急于求成 jí yú qiú chéng eager to have immediate success

急躁 jízào ADJ impetuous, impatient

集 **jí** V gather

集合 jíhé V gather together, assemble

集会 jíhuì N meeting, assembly

集市 jíshì N country fair, market

集体 jítǐ ADJ collective

集团 jítuán N group, grouping

集邮 jíyóu N stamp collecting, philately

集中 jízhōng I V concentrate, focus II ADJ concentrated, focused

集资 jízī V raise funds

几 **jǐ** TRAD 幾 PRON **1** several, some **2** how many

> NOTE: When 几 jǐ is used in a question to mean *how many*, it is presumed that the answer will be a number less than ten. Otherwise 多少 duōshǎo should be used instead. Compare: 你有几个哥哥? Nǐ yǒu jǐ ge gēge? *How many elder brothers do you have?*; 你们学校有多少学生? Nǐmen xuéxiào yǒu duōshǎo xuéshēng? *How many students are there in your school?*

几何 jǐhé N geometry

脊 **jǐ** N spine, backbone

脊梁 jǐliang N spine, backbone

脊椎 jǐzhuī N vertebra

己 **jǐ** PRON self (See 自己 zìjǐ.)

挤 **jǐ** TRAD 擠 I V squeeze, crowd II ADJ crowded (See 拥挤 yōngjǐ)

给 **jǐ** TRAD 給 V provide (See 供给 gōngjǐ)

计 jì TRAD 計 v **1** plan **2** calculate

计划 jìhuà N, v plan
制定计划 zhìdìng jìhuà draw up a plan
执行计划 zhíxíng jìhuà implement a plan

计较 jìjiào v **1** be fussy, haggle over **2** argue, dispute
斤斤计较 jīnjīn jìjiào haggle over insignificant things, quibble over trivia

计算 jìsuàn v calculate

计算机 jìsuànjī Same as 电脑 diànnǎo. Used as a more formal term.

记 jì TRAD 記 v **1** remember, recall **2** record (usually by writing down), bear in mind

记得 jìde v can remember, can recall
记不得 jìbude cannot remember, cannot recall

记笔记 jì bǐjì v take notes

记号 jìhao N mark, sign
做记号 zuò jìhao put a mark
留下记号 liúxia jìhao leave a mark

记录 jìlù v, N record
会议记录 huìyì jìlù minutes (of a meeting)

记性 jìxing N ability to memorize things, memory

记忆 jìyì I v remember, memorize II N memory

记载 jìzài v written record

记者 jìzhě N correspondent, reporter
记者招待会 jìzhě zhāodàihuì press conference, news conference
新闻记者 xīnwén jìzhě news reporter, journalist

记住 jìzhù v learn by heart, bear in mind

纪 jì TRAD 紀 N **1** discipline **2** record

纪律 jìlù N discipline (条 tiáo)

纪念 jìniàn v commemorate

纪要 jìyào N major points, summary, digest

技 jì N skill, ability

技能 jìnéng N skill, technical skill

技巧 jìqiǎo N skill, craftsmanship
写作技巧 xiězuòjìqiǎo writing skills

技术 jìshù N technique, technology, skill

技术工人 jìshù gōngrén skilled worker

技术员 jìshùyuán N technician (位 wèi)

际 jì N boundary, border (See 国际 guójì, 实际 shíjì.)

季 jì N season

季度 jìdù N quarter (of a year)

季节 jìjié N season

济 jì TRAD 濟 v aid (See 经济 jīngjì.)

剂 jì TRAD 劑 N medicine

灭虫剂 mièchóngjì insecticide

剂量 jìliàng N dose, dosage

迹 jì N remains, trace (See 古迹 gǔjì.)

迹象 jìxiàng N sign, indication
地震的迹象 dìzhèn de jìxiàng signs of a (forthcoming) earthquake

既 jì CONJ **1** same as 既然 jìrán. Used more in writing. **2** both ... and ...
既…又… jì...yòu... both ... and ....
既…也… jì...yě... both ... and ....

既然 jìrán CONJ now that, since, as

忌 jì v **1** avoid, shun **2** be jealous

忌酒 jìjiǔ avoid wine, refrain from drinking wines

忌妒 jìdu Same as 嫉妒 jídù.

绩 jì TRAD 績 N accomplishment (See 成绩 chéngjì.)

继 jì TRAD 繼 v continue

继承 jìchéng v inherit, carry on
继承人 jìchéngrén N heir, successor

继续 jìxù v continue

寂 jì ADJ lonely

寂静 jìjìng ADJ peaceful and quiet, still

寂寞 jìmò ADJ lonely

寄 jì v **1** send by mail, post

寄快件 jì kuàijiàn send by express mail **2** entrust

寄托 jìtuō v entrust
寄托希望 jìtuō xīwàng place one's hope on

加 **jiā** v **1** add, plus **2** increase

加班 **jiābān** v work overtime

加班费 **jiābān fèi** overtime pay

加工 **jiāgōng** v process (unfinished products)

来料加工 **láiliào jiāgōng** processing of supplied materials

食品加工 **shípǐn jiāgōng** food processing

加紧 **jiājǐn** v intensify, speed up

加紧准备 **jiājǐn zhǔnbèi** speed up preparations

加剧 **jiājù** v aggravate, exacerbate

加拿大 **Jiānádà** N Canada

加强 **jiāqiáng** v strengthen, reinforce

加热 **jiārè** v heat, heat up

加入 **jiārù** v **1** become a member of **2** add in, mix into

加入网球俱乐部 **jiārù wǎngqiú jùlèbù** join a tennis club

加深 **jiāshēn** v deepen

加深两国之间的相互理解 **jiāshēn liǎngguó zhījiān de xiānghù lǐjiě** deepen mutual understanding between the two countries

加速 **jiāsù** v accelerate, quicken

加速器 **jiāsù qì** accelerator

加以 **jiāyǐ** **I** v (used before a verb to indicate what should be done) **II** CONJ in addition, moreover

NOTE: 加以 jiāyǐ as a verb smacks of officialese and is chiefly used in writing. The sentence still stands when 加以 jiāyǐ is omitted, e.g. 这个问题应及时（加以）解决。Zhège wèntí yīng jíshí (jiāyǐ) jiějué. *This problem should be solved promptly.*

加油 **jiāyóu** v **1** add fuel, fuel up

加油站 **jiāyóuzhàn** gas station, service station

2 make extra efforts

加油干 **jiāyóugàn** double one's efforts, put more effort into one's work

NOTE: 加油 jiāyóu is the colloquial expression used to cheer on a sportsperson or a sporting team in a competition, equivalent to *Come on!*, or *Go! Go!*

加重 **jiāzhòng** v increase the amount, aggravate

加重负担 **jiāzhòng fùdān** increase the burden

嘉 **jiā** ADJ good, fine

嘉宾 **jiābīn** honored guest

嘉奖 **jiājiǎng** v commend, cite

佳 **jiā** ADJ good, fine, beautiful

佳节 **jiājié** joyous festival

夹 **jiā** v pinch, squeeze, wedge between, sandwich

夹杂 **jiāzá** v be mixed up with

夹子 **jiāzi** N tong, clip

衣服夹子 **yīfu jiāzi** clothes pin

家 **jiā** **I** N **1** family, household **2** home **II** M. WD (for families or businesses)

四家人家 **sì jiā rénjiā** four families

一家商店 **yì jiā shāngdiàn** a store

两家工厂 **liǎng jiā gōngchǎng** two factories

III SUFFIX (denoting an accomplished expert)

画家 **huàjiā** painter, artist

教育家 **jiàoyùjiā** educator

科学家 **kēxuéjiā** scientist

家常 **jiācháng** ADJ everyday life, commonplace

谈家常 **tán jiācháng** have a chitchat

家常便饭 **jiācháng biànfàn** simple meal, usually home-cooked

家畜 **jiāchù** N domesticated animal (头 tóu)

家教 **jiājiào** N **1** private tutor **2** family upbringing

家具 **jiājù** N furniture (套 tào, 件 jiàn)

家属 **jiāshǔ** N family member, one's dependent (名 míng)

家庭 **jiātíng** N family (个 gè)

NOTE: 家 jiā has more meanings than 家庭 jiātíng. While 家庭 jiātíng means only *family*, 家 jiā may mean *family*, *household* or *home*.

家务 **jiāwù** N household chores, housework (件 jiàn)

家乡 **jiāxiāng** N hometown, home village

家喻户晓 jiā yù hù xiǎo IDIOM be a household name, widely known

家长 jiāzhǎng N **1** head of a family **2** parent

颊 jiá N cheek

甲 **1** jiǎ N first

甲 **2** jiǎ N shell, nail
指甲 zhījiǎ fingernail
甲板 jiǎbǎn N deck (of a ship)

假 jiǎ ADJ **1** false, untrue **2** artificial
假定 jiǎdìng V Same as 假设 jiǎshè
假话 jiǎhuà N falsehood, lie
假货 jiǎhuò N fake (goods), forgery, counterfeit
假冒 jiǎmào V pass off as genuine
假如 jiǎrú CONJ supposing, if
假若 jiǎruò CONJ Same as 假如 jiǎrú
假设 jiǎshè V suppose, assume
假腿 jiǎtuǐ N artificial leg
假牙 jiǎyá N dentures
假装 jiǎzhuāng V pretend, feign

稼 jià N crops (See 庄稼 zhuāngjià.)

价 jià TRAD 價 N price, value
价格 jiàgé N price
价钱 jiàqian N price
价值 jiàzhí N value
价值观 jiàzhíguān N values

驾 jià TRAD 駕 V drive, pilot
驾驶 jiàshǐ V drive, pilot
驾驶轮船 jiàshǐ lúnchuan pilot a ship
驾驶飞机 jiàshǐ fēijī pilot a plane
驾驶汽车 jiàshǐ qìchē drive an automobile
驾驶员 jiàshǐyuán N driver, pilot

架 **1** jià M. WD (used for machines, aircraft etc.)
一架客机 yí jià kèjī a passenger plane

架 **2** jià N shelf, stand
书架 shūjià bookshelf

嫁 jià V (of a woman) marry

NOTE: 嫁 jià means specifically (for a woman) *to marry*, while (for a man) *to marry* is 娶 qǔ. However more and more people simply use the verb 和…结婚 hé…jiéhūn to mean *marry*, e.g. 他们的女儿和一个美国人结婚。Tāmen de nǚ'ér he yí ge Měiguórén jiéhūn. *Their daughter married an American.*

假 jià N holiday, leave
假期 jiàqī N holiday period, leave
假条 jiàtiáo N an application for leave, a leave form
病假条 bìngjiàtiáo an application for sick leave, a doctor's certificate of illness, a medical certificate

尖 jiān ADJ sharp, pointed
尖端 jiānduān I N pointed end II ADJ sophisticated
尖端产品 jiānduān chǎnpǐn technologically advanced product
尖端科学 jiānduān kēxué sophisticated science
尖端技术 jiānduān jìshù most advanced technology
尖锐 jiānruì ADJ **1** very sharp, penetrating **2** fierce, uncompromising
尖子 jiānzi N the pick (of a group), top student

坚 jiān TRAD 堅 ADJ hard, firm
坚持 jiānchí V uphold, persist (in)
坚定 jiāndìng ADJ firm
坚固 jiāngù ADJ solid, sturdy
坚决 jiānjué ADJ resolute, determined
坚强 jiānqiáng ADJ strong, staunch
性格坚强 xìnggé jiānqiáng strong character
坚实 jiānshí ADJ solid, substantial
打下坚实的基础 dǎxià jiānshí de jīchǔ lay a solid foundation
坚硬 jiānyìng ADJ solid and hard

间 jiān TRAD 間 I N room (for a special purpose)

洗澡间 xǐzǎo jiān bathroom

手术间 shǒushù jiān operating theater, surgical room

II M. WD (for rooms)

一间教室 yì jiān jiàoshì a classroom

两间办公室 liǎng jiān bàngōngshì two offices

肩 jiān N the shoulder

艰 jiān TRAD 艱 ADJ difficult

艰巨 jiānjù ADJ (of a big and important task) very difficult, strenuous

艰苦 jiānkǔ ADJ difficult, hard, tough

艰难 jiānnán ADJ arduous, hard

艰难的任务 jiānnán de rènwu arduous task

艰险 jiānxiǎn ADJ hard and difficult, perilous

兼 jiān ADV concurrently

监 jiān TRAD 監 I V supervise, inspect II N prison, jail

监察 jiānchá V supervise, monitor

监督 jiāndū V 1 supervise, superintend 2 have under surveillance, watch over

监视 jiānshì V keep under surveillance, monitor

监狱 jiānyù N jail, prison (座 zuò)

歼 jiān V wipe out

歼击机 jiānjījī N fighter plane

歼灭 jiānmiè V annihilate, wipe out

奸 jiān I ADJ wicked and treacherous II N traitor

汉奸 hànjiān traitor to the Han people, traitor to the Chinese people

煎 jiān V fry, shallow-fry

剪 jiǎn V cut (with scissors), shear

剪彩 jiǎncǎi V cut the ribbon at an opening ceremony

剪刀 jiǎndāo N scissors, shears (把 bǎ)

茧 jiǎn TRAD 繭 N 1 callus 2 cocoon

老茧 lǎojiǎn callus

柬 jiǎn N letter

请柬 qǐngjiǎn letter of invitation, invitation

检 jiǎn TRAD 檢 V examine

检测 jiǎncè V check and measure, verify

检查 jiǎnchá V examine, inspect, check

检察 jiǎnchá N procuratorial work

检察员 jiǎncháyuán procurator

检察院 jiǎncháyuàn procuratorate

最高人民检察院 Zuìgāo Rénmín Jiǎncháyuàn the Supreme People's Procuratorate

检讨 jiǎntǎo I V 1 examine 2 review II N self-criticism

书面检讨 shūmiàn jiǎntǎo written self-criticism

做检讨 zuò jiǎntǎo make a self-criticism

检修 jiǎnxiū V examine and repair (a machine), maintain

大检修 dàjiǎnxiū overhaul

汽车检修工 qìchē jiǎnxiū gōng car mechanic

检验 jiǎnyàn I V examine, test II N examination, testing

捡 jiǎn TRAD 撿 V pick up

俭 jiǎn TRAD 儉 ADJ thrifty (See 勤俭 qínjiǎn)

拣 jiǎn TRAD 揀 V 1 choose, select 2 Same as 捡 jiǎn

减 jiǎn V 1 subtract, deduct

减数 jiǎnshù subtrahend (e.g. 268 in the example: 367–268—the number that's to be subtracted from the minuend)

被减数 bèi jiǎnshù minuend (e.g. 367 in the example in 减数 jiǎnshù)

2 reduce, lighten

减轻 jiǎnqīng V lighten, alleviate

减弱 jiǎnruò V weaken, reduce in force

减少 jiǎnshǎo V make fewer, make less, reduce

简 jiǎn TRAD 簡 ADJ simple

简便 jiǎnbiàn ADJ simple and convenient, handy

简称 jiǎnchēng I v be called ... for short, be abbreviated as II N shortened form, shortening

简单 jiǎndān ADJ simple, uncomplicated

简短 jiǎnduǎn ADJ simple and short, brief
简短的发言 jiǎnduǎn de fāyán a brief speech, a short talk

简化 jiǎnhuà v simplify
简化手续 jiǎnhuà shǒuxù simplify formalities

简陋 jiǎnlòu ADJ simple and crude

简明 jiǎnmíng ADJ simple and clear, concise

简体字 jiǎntǐzì N simplified Chinese character

NOTE: See note on 繁体字 fántǐzì.

简讯 jiǎnxùn N news in brief, bulletin

简要 jiǎnyào ADJ brief and to the point
简要提纲 jiǎnyào tígāng brief outline

简易 jiǎnyì ADJ simple and easy

简直 jiǎnzhí ADV simply, virtually
简直叫人不敢相信 jiǎnzhí jiào rén bùgǎn xiāngxìn simply unbelievable

碱 jiǎn N alkali, soda

件 jiàn M. WD (for things, clothes or furniture)
一件东西 yí jiàn dōngxi a thing, something
一件事情 yí jiàn shìqing a matter
一件衣服 yí jiàn yīfu a piece of clothing (e.g. a jacket, dress)

见 jiàn TRAD 見 v see, perceive

见解 jiànjiě N opinion, view
提出见解 tíchū jiànjiě voice one's opinion

见面 jiànmiàn v meet, see (a person)

见识 jiànshi N knowledge, experience

见效 jiànxiào v produce the desired result, be effective

舰 jiàn TRAD 艦 N warship (艘 sōu)

航空母舰 hángkōng mǔjiàn aircraft carrier

驱逐舰 qūzhújiàn destroyer

巡洋舰 xúnyángjiàn cruiser

舰队 jiànduì N fleet of warships

剑 jiàn TRAD 劍 N sword (把 bǎ) (See 宝剑 bǎojiàn)

建 jiàn v 1 build, construct 2 found, set up

建交 jiànjiāo v establish diplomatic relations

建立 jiànlì v 1 establish, set up 2 Same as 建 jiàn (= build, construct)

建设 jiànshè v build, construct

建议 jiànyì v suggest, propose

建造 jiànzào v construct, build
建造一座大水库 jiànzào yízuò dà shuǐkù build a big reservoir

建筑 jiànzhù N 1 building, edifice (座 zuò) 2 architecture

建筑师 jiànzhùshī N architect

建筑物 jiànzhùwù N architectural structure, building

建筑学 jiànzhùxué N (the discipline of) architecture

健 jiàn ADJ strong

健儿 jiàn'ér N athlete (as a term of approbation) (位 wèi)

健康 jiànkāng I N health II ADJ healthy, in good health

健美 jiànměi ADJ vigorous and graceful, of athletic beauty

健美操 jiànměicāo N calisthenics

健全 jiànquán I ADJ sound, perfect
身心健全 shēn-xīn jiànquán a healthy body and a sound mind
健全的税收制度 jiànquán de shuìshōu zhìdù a sound tax system
II v make perfect, improve

健身 jiànshēn v do physical exercises, have a work-out

健身房 jiànshēnfáng N gymnasium, health club

健壮 jiànzhuàng ADJ healthy and strong, robust

键 **jiàn** N key (See 关键 guānjiàn.)

键盘 **jiànpán** N keyboard

荐 **jiàn** TRAD 薦 V recommend (See 推荐 tuījiàn.)

鉴 **jiàn** TRAD 鑒 I N mirror

以史为鉴 **yǐ shǐ wéi jiàn** take history as a mirror (→ learn from history)

II V inspect, examine

鉴别 **jiànbié** V distinguish, discern

鉴别古画 **jiànbié gǔhuà** appraise an ancient painting, study an ancient painting to determine its authenticity and/or value

鉴于 **jiànyú** PREP in view of, considering

贱 **jiàn** TRAD 賤 ADJ cheap

溅 **jiàn** TRAD 濺 V splash, spatter

践 **jiàn** TRAD 踐 V trample

践踏 **jiàntà** V trample underfoot

践踏公民权利 **jiàntà gōngmín quánlì** trample on civil rights

渐 **jiàn** TRAD 漸 ADV Same as 渐渐 jiànjiàn

渐渐 **jiànjiàn** ADV gradually, by and by

箭 **jiàn** N arrow

箭头 **jiàntóu** N 1 arrow head 2 sign of an arrow to show direction

间 **jiàn** TRAD 間 V separate

间隔 **jiàngé** I N interval, space between II V have intervals

间接 **jiànjiē** ADJ indirect

江 **jiāng** N river (条 tiáo)

NOTE: The most famous 江 jiāng in China is 长江 Cháng jiāng, the longest river in China. 长江 Cháng jiāng, which literally means *long river*, is also known as the Yangtze River. See note on 河 hé.

疆 **jiāng** N border, boundary

僵 **jiāng** ADJ stiff and numb, dead-locked

冻僵 **dòngjiāng** frozen stiff

姜 **jiāng** TRAD 薑 N ginger

将 1 **jiāng** TRAD 將 PREP Same as 把 bǎ, but only used in writing.

将 2 **jiāng** TRAD 將 ADV will, shall, going to, be about to

将近 **jiāngjìn** ADV be close to, near

将军 **jiāngjūn** N (armed forces) general

将来 **jiānglái** N future

将要 **jiāngyào** ADV Same as 将 jiāng 2 ADV

浆 **jiāng** TRAD 漿 N thick liquid

豆浆 **dòujiāng** soybean milk, soy milk

讲 **jiǎng** TRAD 講 V 1 talk 2 tell

讲故事 **jiǎng gùshi** tell a story

3 pay attention to, attach importance to

讲卫生 **jiǎng wèishēng** pay attention to personal hygiene

讲话 **jiǎnghuà** N speech, talk

讲解 **jiǎngjiě** V explain orally

讲究 **jiǎngjiu** I V be particular about, pay much attention to II ADJ exquisite, of very high standard

讲课 **jiǎngkè** V lecture, teach

讲理 **jiǎnglǐ** V Same as 讲道理 jiǎng dàoli

讲述 **jiǎngshù** V give an account of, narrate, tell about

讲演 **jiǎngyǎn** V deliver a speech

讲义 **jiǎngyì** N lecture notes, teaching materials

讲座 **jiǎngzuò** N lecture, course of lectures

奖 **jiǎng** TRAD 獎 I N prize, award II V award

奖杯 **jiǎngbēi** N trophy, cup (given as a prize)

奖金 **jiǎngjīn** N 1 prize money (笔 bǐ) 2 bonus (笔 bǐ)

奖励 **jiǎnglì** V reward in order to encourage

奖励助人为乐者 **jiǎnglì zhù-rén-wéi-lè zhě** reward and encourage a good Samaritan

奖品 **jiǎngpǐn** N prize, award (份 fèn, 件 jiàn)

颁发奖品 **bānfā jiǎngpǐn** present a prize/
an award

领取奖品 **lǐngqǔ jiǎngpǐn** receive a
prize/an award

奖学金 **jiǎngxuéjīn** N scholarship

奖状 **jiǎngzhuàng** N certificate of award,
certificate of merit (张 zhāng)

桨 **jiǎng** TRAD 槳 N oar

降 **jiàng** V fall, lower

降低 **jiàngdī** V lower, cut down, reduce

降价 **jiàngjià** V reduce prices

降临 **jiànglín** V befall, arrive

酱 **jiàng** TRAD 醬 N soy paste

酱油 **jiàngyóu** N soy sauce

匠 **jiàng** N craftsman

交 **jiāo** V 1 hand over, pay (bills, fees)
2 cross, intersect

交叉 **jiāochā** V intersect, cross

交叉点 **jiāochādiǎn** Same as 交点 jiāodiǎn

交错 **jiāocuò** V crisscross, interlock

交代 **jiāodài** V 1 leave word, hand over
交代任务 **jiāodài rènwu** give information about a job, brief on a task
2 confess (a wrongdoing)

交待 **jiāodài** Same as 交代 jiāodài

交点 **jiāodiǎn** N point of intersection

交付 **jiāofù** V pay, hand over

交换 **jiāohuàn** V exchange

交际 **jiāojì** I N social contact, social
intercourse, communication II V make
social contacts

交际费 **jiāojìfèi** N entertainment expense

交际花 **jiāojìhuā** N social butterfly

交际舞 **jiāojìwǔ** N ballroom dancing

交流 **jiāoliú** V exchange, communicate

交涉 **jiāoshè** V negotiate

交手 **jiāoshǒu** V fight hand to hand, cross
swords with

交谈 **jiāotán** V have a conversation, talk
with
用中文交谈 **yòng Zhōngwén jiāotán**
have a conversation in Chinese

交替 **jiāotì** V 1 replace 2 alternate

交通 **jiāotōng** N transport, transportation,
traffic

交通事故 **jiāotōng shìgù** traffic accident,
road accident

交通警察 **jiāotōng jǐngchá** traffic policeman, traffic police

交往 **jiāowǎng** V associate with, be in
contact with

交易 **jiāoyì** N business transaction, business deal (笔 bǐ)
做一笔交易 **zuò yìbǐ jiāoyì** do a business
deal

胶 **jiāo** TRAD 膠 N rubber

胶卷 **jiāojuǎn** N roll of film

胶片 **jiāopiàn** N film (for a camera)

郊 **jiāo** N outskirts, suburbs

郊区 **jiāoqū** N suburbs, outskirts (of a city)

浇 **jiāo** TRAD 澆 V water

浇花 **jiāohuā** water flowers

浇水 **jiāoshuǐ** supply water to plants or
crops

浇灌 **jiāoguàn** V irrigate, water

教 **jiāo** V teach

骄 **jiāo** TRAD 驕 ADJ conceited

骄傲 **jiāo'ào** ADJ proud, conceited, arrogant

娇 **jiāo** ADJ 1 tender and beautiful
2 Same as 娇气 jiāoqi

娇惯 **jiāoguàn** V pamper, spoil

娇气 **jiāoqi** ADJ 1 finicky, squeamish
2 fragile, delicate

焦 **jiāo** ADJ 1 scorched, burnt 2 anxious, worried

焦点 **jiāodiǎn** N focus

焦急 **jiāojí** ADJ anxious, very worried
焦急地等待 **jiāojí de děngdài** wait
anxiously

蕉 **jiāo** N banana (See 香蕉 xiāngjiāo)

椒 **jiāo** N hot spice plant (See 辣椒
làjiāo)

嚼 jiáo v chew, munch

角 1 jiǎo N corner

角度 jiǎodù N angle, point of view
角落 jiǎoluò N corner, nook

角 2 jiǎo M. WD (Chinese currency: 1 角 jiǎo = 0.1 元 yuán = 10 分 fēn) ten cents, a dime
两角钱 liǎng jiǎo qián two *jiao*, twenty cents
八块九角五分 bā kuài jiǔ jiǎo wǔ fēn eight *yuan* nine *jiao* and five *fen* = eight dollars and ninety-five cents

NOTE: In colloquial Chinese 毛 máo is often used instead of 角 jiǎo, e.g. 两毛钱 liǎng máo qián is equivalent to two *jiao* twenty cents

饺 jiǎo TRAD 餃 N Same as 饺子 jiǎozi
饺子 jiǎozi N stuffed dumpling, jiaozi
包饺子 bāo jiǎozi make jiaozi

狡 jiǎo ADJ sly, cunning
狡猾 jiǎohuá ADJ cunning, crafty

脚 jiǎo N foot (只 zhī)
脚步 jiǎobù N footstep, step

搅 jiǎo TRAD 攪 v 1 mix 2 confuse, disturb
搅拌 jiǎobàn v stir, mix

缴 jiǎo v 1 pay, hand in 2 capture
缴纳 jiǎonà v pay, hand in
缴纳罚款 jiǎonà fákuǎn pay a fine

绞 jiǎo v wring, twist
把毛巾绞干 bǎ máojīn jiǎo gān wring a towel dry

轿 jiào TRAD 轎 N sedan chair
轿车 jiàochē N sedan car, car

叫 1 jiào v call, address, shout, cry out
叫喊 jiàohǎn v shout, call out
叫唤 jiàohuan v cry out, call out

叫嚷 jiàorǎng v yell, howl
叫做 jiàozuò v be called, be known as, be referred to as

叫 2 jiào PREP Same as 被 bèi. Used more in colloquialisms.

教 jiào N teaching

教材 jiàocái N teaching material, textbook, coursebook (份 fèn, 本 běn)
教导 jiàodǎo v instruct, give moral guidance
教会 jiàohuì N organized religious group, church
天主教会 Tiānzhǔ jiàohuì the Catholic Church
教练 jiàoliàn N (sports) coach
教师 jiàoshī N teacher (位 wèi, 名 míng)
教室 jiàoshì N classroom (间 jiān)
教室大楼 jiàoshì dàlóu classroom block
教授 jiàoshòu N university professor
副教授 fùjiàoshòu associate professor
教唆 jiàosuō v instigate and abet
教堂 jiàotáng N church building, church
大教堂 dàjiàotáng cathedral
上教堂 shàng jiàotáng go to church (for worship)
教条 jiàotiáo N dogma
教学 jiàoxué N teaching, education
教训 jiàoxun I v lecture, talk down to II N lesson (learnt from mistakes or experience), moral
教养 jiàoyǎng N upbringing, education
有教养 yǒu jiàoyǎng well brought up, well-bred
教育 jiàoyù I v educate, teach II N education
教员 jiàoyuán N teacher (in a particular school)

觉 jiào TRAD 覺 See 睡觉 shuìjiào

较 jiào TRAD 較 I PREP Same as 比 bǐ 1 PREP. Used only in writing. II ADV 1 Same as 比较 bǐjiào 2 Used only in writing.
较量 jiàoliàng v test the strength of, compete

窖 jiào N cellar

地窖 dìjiào cellar, pit

阶 jiē TRAD 階 N steps, grade

阶段 jiēduàn N period, stage

阶级 jiējí N social class

揭 jiē V take off, reveal

揭发 jiēfā V expose, uncover

揭发一起逃税案 jiēfā yìqǐ táoshuì àn expose a case of tax evasion

揭露 jiēlù V uncover, reveal

揭露阴谋 jiēlù yīnmóu uncover a conspiracy

揭示 jiēshì V bring to light, reveal

揭示真相 jiēshì zhēnxiàng reveal the truth

皆 jiē PRON all, both

结 jiē TRAD 結 V bear (fruit)

结实 jiēshi ADJ sturdy, strong, robust

接 jiē V 1 receive (a letter, a telephone call) 2 meet and greet (a visitor)

接班 jiēbān V take over from, carry on

接触 jiēchù V get in touch (with)

接待 jiēdài V receive (a visitor)

接到 jiēdao V have received

接见 jiējiàn V receive (somebody), meet (somebody), give an audience

NOTE: 接见 jiējiàn meaning *receive* or *meet* is only used for formal or official occasions. It implies that the receiving party is superior in status to the one being received.

接近 jiējìn V be close to, be near

接连 jiēlián ADV successively, one after another

接洽 jiēqià V arrange with

接受 jiēshòu V accept

接受批评 jiēshòu pīpíng accept criticism, take criticism

接着 jiēzhe CONJ and immediately, then, at the heels of (a previous action or event)

街 jiē N street (条 tiáo)

街上 jiē shang on the street

步行街 bùxíng jiē pedestrian street

逛大街 guàng dàjiē stroll the streets, do window shopping

街道 jiēdào N street (条 tiáo)

街道委员会 jiēdào wěiyuánhuì neighborhood committee

街坊 jiēfang N neighbor

街头 jiētóu N street

街头流浪汉 jiētóu liúlànghàn a homeless being in the street

节 jié TRAD 節 I N 1 festival

过节 guò jié observe a festival, celebrate a festival

中秋节 zhōngqiūjié Mid-Autumn Festival (on the fifteenth day of the eighth lunar month)

2 section, division II M. WD a period of time

一节课 yì jié kè a period of class

III V save, economize

节目 jiémù N program

儿童节目 értóng jiémù children's program

体育节目 tǐyù jiémù sports program

文艺节目 wényì jiémù theatrical program

新闻节目 xīnwén jiémù news program (on TV or radio)

节日 jiérì N festival day

节省 jiéshěng V save, be frugal with

节约 jiéyuē V economize, save, practice thrift

节约能源 (节能) jiéyuē néngyuán (jiénéng) conserve energy

节制 jiézhì V control, be moderate in

节制生育 (节育) jiézhì shēngyù (jiéyù) birth control, family planning

节奏 jiézòu N rhythm, tempo

结 jié TRAD 結 V 1 tie, end 2 form, congeal

结构 jiégòu N structure, construction

结果 jiéguǒ I N result, consequence II ADV as a result, consequently, finally

结合 jiéhé V combine, integrate

结婚 jiéhūn v marry

结晶 jiéjīng N 1 crystallization 2 fruit, result
多年努力的结晶 duōnián nǔlì de jiéjīng
the fruit of many years' painstaking efforts

结局 jiéjú N outcome, final result

结论 jiélùn N verdict, conclusion

结束 jiéshù v end, terminate

结算 jiésuàn v settle an account, close an account

结业 jiéyè v complete a course of study, graduate

洁 jié TRAD 潔 ADJ clean (See 清洁 qīngjié)

洁白 jiébái ADJ pure white, spotless

截 jié v intercept, stop

截止 jiézhǐ v end, up to

劫 jié v rob, raid

劫持 jiéchí v kidnap, hijack

杰 jié TRAD 傑 ADJ outstanding, excellent

杰出 jiéchū ADJ outstanding, distinguished

杰作 jiézuò N outstanding work (of art, music or literature)

捷 jié ADJ quick (See 敏捷 mǐnjié)

竭 jié v exhaust

竭力 jiélì v do one's utmost, do everything within one's power
竭力满足顾客 jiélì mǎnzú gùkè do all one can to satisfy customers

姐 jiě N Same as 姐姐 jiějie

姐姐 jiějie N elder sister

解 jiě v untie, undo

解答 jiědá v provide an answer, give an explanation

解放 jiěfàng I v set free, liberate, emancipate II N liberation, emancipation

解雇 jiěgù v dismiss (an employee), discharge

解决 jiějué v solve (a problem), settle (an issue)

解剖 jiěpōu v 1 dissect 2 analyse, probe

解散 jiěsàn v dismiss, disband

解释 jiěshì I v explain, account for II N explanation, interpretation

介 jiè v lie between, interpose

介绍 jièshào v 1 introduce 2 provide information, brief
介绍人 jièshào rén matchmaker, sponsor (for membership in a club, a political party, an association etc.)
介绍信 jièshào xìn letter of recommendation

届 jiè M. WD (used for a conference or congress held at regular intervals, for graduating classes)

界 jiè N 1 border, boundary 2 realm, circle
商业界 shāngyè jiè business circle
体育界 tǐyù jiè sporting circle

界限 jièxiàn N dividing line, limits

界线 jièxiàn N boundary line, demarcation line
把球打出界线 bǎ qiú dǎchū jièxiàn send the ball outside (the court)

借 jiè v borrow, lend

NOTE: This verb may mean either *borrow* or *lend*, depending on the patterns in which it occurs: A借给B… A jiègei B… *A lends B …*; A向B借… A xiàng B jiè… *A borrows … from B*

借鉴 jièjiàn v use for reference, learn (lessons) from

借口 jièkǒu I v use as an excuse
借口身体不好不上班 jièkǒu shēntǐ bùhǎo bú shàngbān use poor health as an excuse for not going to work II excuse, pretext
找借口 zhǎo jièkǒu make up an excuse

借助 jièzhù v have the aid of, make use of

戒 jiè v guard against

戒严 jièyán I N curfew, martial law II v enforce martial law, impose a curfew

诚 jiè TRAD 誡 v admonish, warn (See 告诫 gàojiè)

巾 jīn N towel (See 毛巾 máojīn.)

今 jīn N now, the present

今后 jīnhòu N from today, from now on

今年 jīnnián N this year

今天 jīntiān N today

筋 jīn N tendon, vein

津 jīn v ferry

津贴 jīntiē N subsidy, stipend

斤 jīn N jin (a traditional Chinese unit of weight equal to half a kilogram)

金 jīn N 1 gold (两 liǎng *ounce*)

金子 jīnzi gold
2 money

金额 jīn'é N sum of money (笔 bǐ)
一大笔金额 yí dàbǐ jīn'é a large sum of money

金黄 jīnhuáng ADJ golden (color)

金牌 jīnpái N gold medal
金牌获得者/金牌得主 jīnpái huòdézhě/jīnpái dezhǔ gold medalist

金钱 jīnqián N money

金融 jīnróng N finance, banking

金属 jīnshǔ N metal

金鱼 jīnyú N goldfish (条 tiáo)
金鱼缸 jīnyúgāng goldfish bowl
养金鱼 yǎng jīnyú keep goldfish

金字塔 jīnzìtǎ N the pyramid

仅 jīn TRAD 僅 ADV only, merely

仅仅 jīnjǐn ADV Same as 仅 jǐn, but more emphatic.

尽 jǐn TRAD 儘 v to the greatest extent

尽管 jǐnguǎn I ADV feel free to, not hesitate II CONJ even though

尽量 jǐnliàng ADV to the best of one's capacity, to the greatest extent
尽量…一点 jǐnliàng…yìdiǎn as ... as possible, as soon as possible

锦 jǐn N brocade

锦绣 jǐnxiù ADJ splendid, beautiful

谨 jǐn ADJ cautious

谨慎 jǐnshèn ADJ cautious, careful
谨慎驾驶 jǐnshèn jiàshǐ drive carefully

紧 jǐn TRAD 緊 ADJ 1 tight, taut
2 urgent, tense
握紧方向盘 wòjǐn fāngxiàngpán grip the steering wheel firmly
3 be close to
紧靠着地铁站 jǐn kàozhe dìtiězhàn very close to a subway station
4 in short supply **5** pressing, urgent

紧急 jǐnjí ADJ urgent, pressing
紧急任务 jǐnjírènwu urgent task
紧急状况 jǐnjí zhuàngkuàng emergency situation, contingency

紧密 jǐnmì ADJ very close, intimate
紧密配合 jǐnmì pèihé in close coordination

紧缩 jǐnsuō v tighten, reduce
紧缩开支 jǐnsuō kāizhī cut back expenditure

紧张 jǐnzhāng ADJ tense, nervous

晋 jìn v go forward, advance

晋升 jìnshēng v promote (to a higher position)
晋升为教授 jìnshēng wéi jiàoshòu be promoted to professorship level

尽 jìn TRAD 盡 v exhaust, use up

尽力 jìnlì v do all one can

进 jìn TRAD 進 v move forward, enter

进步 jìnbù I ADJ progressive II N progress

进程 jìnchéng N course (of progress), process

进而 jìn'ér ADV and then, subsequently

进攻 jìngōng v advance and attack, attack

进化 jìnhuà v evolve, develop

进化论 jìnhuàlùn N (Charles Darwin's) theory of evolution

进军 jìnjūn v march, advance

进口 jìnkǒu I v import II N entry, entrance

进来 jìnlái v come in, come into
进取 jìnqǔ v be enterprising, be aggressive and ambitious
进取心 jìnqǔxīn enterprising spirit
进去 jìnqù v go in, go into
进入 jìnrù v enter, enter into
进行 jìnxíng v conduct, carry out

NOTE: The object that 进行 jìnxíng takes must be a noun of two or more syllables, e.g. 进行教育 jìnxíng jiàoyù *be educated*. 进行 jìnxíng is used only in formal Chinese.

进修 jìnxiū v do advanced studies, undergo in-service advanced training
进一步 jìnyíbù ADV advancing a step further, further, more deeply

近 jìn ADJ close to, close by

离…近 lí…jìn be close to
近代 jìndài N modern times (usually from the year 1840)
近来 jìnlái ADV recently, nowadays, these days
近年 jìnnián N recent years
近期 jìnqī N in the near future
近视 jìnshi N nearsightedness, shortsightedness
近视眼镜 jìnshi yǎnjìng spectacles for nearsightedness
近似 jìnsì ADJ similar, approximate
近似值 jìnsì zhí approximate value, approximation

劲 jìn TRAD 勁 N physical strength

没劲 méijìn dull, boring, bored
劲头 jìntóu N 1 strength, energy 2 zeal, vigor
劲头十足 jìntóu shízú full of vigor, in high spirits

浸 jìn v soak, steep

禁 jìn v forbid

禁区 jìnqū N forbidden zone
军事禁区 jūnshì jìnqū military zone
禁止 jìnzhǐ v forbid, prohibit

京 jīng N 1 capital city 2 (shortened for) Beijing
京剧 jīngjù N Beijing (Peking) opera

鲸 jīng N whale

鲸鱼 jīngyú whale (条 tiáo)

晶 jīng N crystal (See 结晶 jiéjīng)

茎 jīng N stem or stalk (of a plant)

经 jīng TRAD 經 v pass through, experience
经常 jīngcháng ADV often
经典 jīngdiǎn N classic
经费 jīngfèi N outlay, fund (for a specific purpose or the regular running of an organization)
经过 jīngguò I v go through, pass II PREP through, after
经济 jīngjì N economy
经济学 jīngjìxué economics
经济学家 jīngjìxuéjiā economist
市场经济 shìchǎng jīngjì market economy
经纪人 jīngjìrén N agent, manager
经理 jīnglǐ N manager (位 wèi)
副经理 fùjīnglǐ deputy manager
市场经理 shìchǎng jīnglǐ marketing manager
总经理 zǒngjīnglǐ general manager, chief executive officer (CEO)
经历 jīnglì I v experience, undergo II N personal experience
经商 jīngshāng v engage in business, be a businessman
经受 jīngshòu v undergo, withstand
经受考验 jīngshòu kǎoyàn face a test, undergo a test
经销 jīngxiāo v sell, deal with
经销豪华汽车 jīngxiāo háohuá qìchē deal with luxury cars
经验 jīngyàn N experience, lesson (learnt from experiences)
取得经验 qǔdé jīngyàn acquire experience
有经验 yǒu jīngyàn experienced
经营 jīngyíng v operate (a business)

惊 jīng

惊 jīng TRAD 驚 V startle, surprise

惊动 jīngdòng V disturb, alarm
惊慌 jīnghuāng ADJ panic-stricken, alarmed
惊慌失措 jīnghuāng shīcuò be panic-stricken
惊奇 jīngqí V be surprised and incredulous, be amazed
惊讶 jīngyà V be astonished, be surprised
惊异 jīngyì V be astounded and puzzled

睛 jīng N the pupil of the eye (See 眼睛 yǎnjing.)

精 jīng ADJ choice, refined

精彩 jīngcǎi ADJ (of a theatrical performance or sports event) brilliant, thrilling, wonderful
精打细算 jīngdǎ xìsuàn IDIOM be very careful in budgeting to save every cent
精华 jīnghuá N the cream of the crop, the very best
精简 jīngjiǎn V trim and prune (an organization), reduce staffing
精力 jīnglì N energy, vigor
精美 jīngměi ADJ exquisite and beautiful
精密 jīngmì ADJ precise
　精密仪器 jīngmì yíqì precision instrument
精确 jīngquè ADJ accurate, precise
精神 jīngshén N 1 vigor, vitality 2 spirit, the mind
精神病 jīngshénbìng N mental illness
　精神病院 jīngshénbìngyuàn mental institution
　精神病医生 jīngshénbìng yīshēng psychiatrist
精通 jīngtōng ADJ having great proficiency in, be master of
精细 jīngxì ADJ paying attention to details, meticulous
精益求精 jīng yì qiú jīng V seek perfection
精致 jīngzhì ADJ exquisite, fine

景 jīng N view, scenery

景色 jīngsè N view, scenery
景象 jīngxiàng N sight, scene

警 jǐng I V alert II N 1 police 2 alarm

警车 jǐngchē police car
火警 huǒjǐng fire alarm
警察 jǐngchá N policeman, police

NOTE: In China the police bureau is called 公安局 gōng'ānjú *Public Security Bureau*, which should be distinguished from 国安局 guó'ānjú *Bureau of National Security*.

警告 jǐnggào I V warn, caution II N warning
警戒 jǐngjiè V guard against, be on alert
警惕 jǐngtì V be vigilant
警卫 jǐngwèi V guard and defend (a military installation, a VIP, etc.)

井 jǐng N well, (water) well

水井 shuǐjǐng water well
油井 yóujǐng oil well

颈 jǐng TRAD 頸 N neck

头颈 tóujǐng the neck
长颈鹿 chángjǐnglù (long-neck-deer) giraffe

竞 jìng TRAD 競 V compete

竞赛 jìngsài V contest, compete
竞选 jìngxuǎn V run for office
竞争 jìngzhēng I V compete II N competition

竟 jìng ADV unexpectedly

竟然 jìngrán ADV unexpectedly, contrary to expectation

境 jìng N boundary, place

国境 guójìng territory (of a country), border
国境线 guójìngxiàn national boundary line
境地 jìngdì N situation, plight
　危险的境地 wēixiǎn de jìngdì dangerous position

镜 jìng TRAD 鏡 N mirror

镜子 jìngzi mirror (面 miàn)

照镜子 zhào jìngzi look at oneself in a mirror

镜头 jìngtóu N 1 camera lens 2 shot, scene

径 jìng TRAD 徑 N track (See 田径 tiánjìng)

敬 jìng V respect

敬爱 jìng'ài V respect and love

敬而远之 jìng-ér-yuǎn-zhī IDIOM keep a respectful distance from, give a wide berth to

敬酒 jìngjiǔ V propose a toast

敬礼 jìnglǐ V salute

静 jìng ADJ quiet, peaceful, silent

静悄悄 jìngqiāoqiāo ADJ perfectly quiet and hushed

静坐 jìngzuò V 1 meditate
静坐养生 jìngzuò yǎngshēng meditate to keep in good health
2 stage a sit-in

净 jìng ADJ clean (See 干净 gānjing.)

净化 jìnghuà V purify
净化废水 jìnghuà fèishuǐ purify waste water

究 jiū V investigate, probe

究竟 jiūjìng ADV Same as 到底 dàodǐ

纠 jiū TRAD 糾 V rectify

纠纷 jiūfēn N dispute

纠正 jiūzhèng V rectify, correct

揪 jiū TRAD 揫 V hold tight, seize

九 jiǔ NUM nine

九一一 jiǔ-yāo-yāo 9/11 September 11

九千九百九十九 jiǔqiān jiǔbǎi jiǔshíjiǔ 9,999

NOTE: See note on 一 yī regarding pronunciation of 一 as yāo.

玖 jiǔ NUM nine

久 jiǔ ADV for a long time

灸 jiǔ N moxibustion (See 针灸 zhēnjiǔ.)

酒 jiǔ N alcoholic beverage (种 zhǒng, 瓶 píng)

白酒 bái jiǔ colorless spirit distilled from grains
葡萄酒 pútaojiǔ (grape) wine
黄酒 huáng jiǔ yellow rice wine

酒吧 jiǔ bā N (wine) bar, pub

酒店 jiǔ diàn N 1 wine shop 2 restaurant 3 hotel

NOTE: Although 酒店 jiǔ diàn literally means *wine shop*, it is sometimes used to mean *a hotel*, usually a luxury one. This usage is especially common in Hong Kong, e.g. 香港半岛酒店 Xiānggǎng bàndǎo jiǔdiàn *The Peninsula Hong Kong Hotel*. Also see note on 饭店 fàndiàn.

酒会 jiǔhuì N cocktail party, reception

酒精 jiǔjīng N alcohol

旧 jiù TRAD 舊 ADJ (of things) old, second-hand

舅 jiù N mother's brother, uncle

舅父 jiùfù mother's brother, uncle
舅舅 jiùjiù Same as 舅父 jiùfù, used as a form of address
舅妈 jiùmā Same as 舅母 jiùmǔ, used as a form of address
舅母 jiùmǔ mother's brother's wife, aunt

救 jiù V save, rescue

救火 jiùhuǒ put out a fire, fire fighting
救火车 jiùhuǒchē fire engine
救护车 jiùhùchē ambulance

救济 jiùjì V provide relief

就 1 jiù PREP 1 with regard to, concerning 2 as far as ... is concerned, in terms of

就 2 jiù ADV as early as ..., as soon as ... (used before a verb to emphasize that the action takes place very early, very quickly or only for a very short period of time)

一···就··· yī...jiù... as soon as ...

就餐 jiùcān V take a meal

就地 jiùdì ADV on the spot
就近 jiùjìn ADV nearby
就是 jiùshì CONJ even if
就算 jiùsuàn CONJ even if, even though
就业 jiùyè V obtain employment
就职 jiuzhí V take office

居 jū V 1 occupy (See 邻居 línjū, 居民 jūmín, 居住 jūzhù.) 2 inhabit, dwell
居留 jūliú V reside, live
　居留权 jūliúquán right of residency, residency
　居留证 jūliúzhèng residency permit
居民 jūmín N resident, inhabitant
　居民委员会 jūmín wěiyuánhuì neighborhood committee

NOTE: 居民委员会 jūmín wěiyuánhuì is the grassroot organization in Chinese cities, under government supervision. In colloquial Chinese it is shortened to 居委会 jūwěihuì.

居然 jūrán ADV unexpectedly
居室 jūshì N bedroom
　一套三居室的公寓 yítào sān jūshì de gōngyù a three-bedroom apartment
居住 jūzhù V reside, inhabit, live

拘 jū V 1 detain, arrest 2 limit
拘留 jūliú V detain by the police
　拘留所 jūliúsuǒ detention center/camp
拘束 jūshù ADJ restrained, ill at ease

鞠 jū V as in 鞠躬 jūgōng
鞠躬 jūgōng V bow, take a bow

菊 jú N chrysanthemum
菊花 júhuā chrysanthemum
　菊花展览 júhuā zhǎnlǎn chrysanthemum show
　秋菊 qiū jú chrysanthemum

局 jú N office
局部 júbù ADJ part (not whole), local
局面 júmiàn N situation, phase
　打开局面 dǎkāi júmiàn usher in a new phase, make a breakthrough
局势 júshì N situation

局限 júxiàn V limit, confine
局长 júzhǎng N director/chief of a bureau

橘 jú N tangerine
橘树 jú shù tangerine tree
橘子 júzi tangerine

NOTE: 橘子 júzi can also be written as 桔子 júzi.

矩 jǔ N carpenter's square (See 规矩 guīju)

举 jǔ TRAD 舉 V hold high, raise, lift
举办 jǔbàn V conduct (a meeting, an event)
举动 jǔdòng N (body) movement, act
　一举一动 yìjǔ yídòng every movement (of a person)
举世闻名 jǔshì wénmíng IDIOM world-renowned
举行 jǔxíng V hold (a meeting, a ceremony)

聚 jù V assemble, get together
聚会 jùhuì N social gathering, (social) party
　举行生日聚会 jǔxíng shēngri jùhuì throw a birthday party

NOTE: See note on 派对 pàiduì.

聚集 jùjí V gather, collect
　聚集资金(集资) jùjí zījīn (jízī) collect funds, raise funds
聚精会神 jùjīng huìshén IDIOM give undivided attention to

句 jù M. WD (for sentences)
　一句话 yí jù huà one sentence
　这句话 zhè jù huà this sentence
句子 jùzi N sentence (句 jù, 个 gè)

具 jù V own, possess
具备 jùbèi V possess, be provided with
具体 jùtǐ ADJ specific, concrete
具有 jùyǒu V have, possess, be provided with

俱 **jù** ADV together

俱乐部 jùlèbù N club

惧 **jù** TRAD 懼 V fear

惧内 jùnèi fear one's wife, be henpecked

剧 **jù** TRAD 劇 I N drama, play II ADJ severe, intense

剧本 jùběn N script of a play
电影剧本 diànyǐng jùběn script of a film, scenario

剧场 jùchǎng N theater (座 zuò)

剧烈 jùliè ADJ fierce, severe
剧烈的疼痛 jùliè de téngtòng acute pain

剧团 jùtuán N theatrical company

剧院 jùyuàn N playhouse, theater (座 zuò)

据 **jù** TRAD 據 PREP according to

据说 jùshuō IDIOM it is said, they say, rumor has it

锯 **jù** N saw

锯子 jùzi hand saw (把 bǎ)
电锯 diànjù chainsaw

巨 **jù** ADJ gigantic

巨大 jùdà ADJ huge, gigantic, tremendous

拒 **jù** V repel, resist

拒不认错 jù bú rèncuò refuse to admit to a mistake

拒绝 jùjué V refuse, reject

距 **jù** N a stretch of distance

距离 jùlí N distance

捐 **juān** V donate, contribute

捐款 juānkuǎn I V contribute money, make a cash donation II N cash donation, financial donation

捐献 juānxiàn V donate (something of considerable value)

捐赠 juānzèng V contribute as a gift, donate

卷 **juǎn** V roll up

绢 **juàn** TRAD 絹 N silk (See 手绢 shǒujuàn.)

倦 **juàn** ADJ tired (See 疲倦 píjuàn.)

掘 **jué** V dig

掘土机 juétǔjī excavation machine, earth mover

决 1 **jué** ADV definitely, under any circumstance used before a negative word, e.g. 不 bù)

决 2 **jué** V decide, determine

决策 juécè I V decide on a policy, formulate strategy II N policy decision, strategic decision (项 xiàng)

决定 juédìng I V decide, determine, make up one's mind II N decision
做决定 zuò juédìng make a decision

决赛 juésài N final game, final round, finals

决心 juéxīn I N determination
下决心 xià juéxīn make up one's mind, be determined
II V be determined, make up one's mind

决议 juéyì N resolution
提出决议 tíchū juéyì put forward a resolution
作出决议 zuòchū juéyì adopt a resolution

决战 juézhàn I V wage a decisive battle II N decisive battle

觉 **jué** TRAD 覺 V feel, sense

觉察 juéchá V detect, perceive

觉得 juéde V feel, find, think

觉悟 juéwù V gain understanding, become aware of

觉醒 juéxǐng V be awakened (to truth, reality, etc.)

绝 **jué** TRAD 絕 I ADJ absolute II V cut off, sever

绝对 juéduì ADV absolutely
绝对多数 juéduì duōshù absolute majority

绝望 juéwàng V despair, give up all hope

绝缘 juéyuán V (of electricity) insulate

绝症 juézhèng N terminal illness

军 jūn TRAD 軍 N army, armed forces

海军 hǎijūn navy
空军 kōngjūn air force
陆军 lùjūn army

军备 jūnbèi N weapons and equipment, armaments
军队 jūnduì N armed forces, troops (支 zhī)
军官 jūnguān N military officer, officer (名 míng, 位 wèi)
军火 jūnhuǒ N arms and ammunition
军舰 jūnjiàn N warship (艘 sōu)
军人 jūnrén N serviceman, soldier (名 míng)
军事 jūnshì N military affairs
军需 jūnxū N military supplies
军用 jūnyòng ADJ for military use
军装 jūnzhuāng N army uniform

君 jūn N 1 monarch 2 gentleman

君主 jūnzhǔ N monarch
君主立宪 jūnzhǔ lìxiàn constitutional monarchy
君子 jūnzǐ N cultured and honorable man, gentleman

NOTE: In Confucianism 君子 jūnzǐ refers to *a cultured gentleman* and *a man of virtue*. 君子 jūnzǐ is in contrast with 小人 xiǎorén, *a mean person* or *an inferior being*.

均 jūn ADJ equal

均匀 jūnyún ADJ well distributed, evenly applied
菌 jūn N fungus, bacterium (See 细菌 xìjūn.)
峻 jūn ADJ harsh, stern (See 严峻 yánjùn.)
俊 jùn ADJ handsome (See 英俊 yīngjùn.)
美女俊男 měinǚ jùnnán beautiful women and handsome men

K

咖 kā used in 咖啡 kāfēi only

咖啡 kāfēi N coffee (杯 bēi)
浓咖啡 nóng kāfēi espresso
速溶咖啡 sùróng kāfēi instant coffee
冲咖啡 chōng kāfēi make (instant) coffee
煮咖啡 zhǔ kāfēi brew coffee

NOTE: 咖啡 kāfēi is one of the few transliterations (音译词 yīnyìcí) in Chinese vocabulary, as it represents more or less the sound of "coffee."

卡 kǎ N card (张 zhāng)

贺卡 hèkǎ greeting card
借书卡 jièshū kǎ library card
信用卡 xìnyòng kǎ credit card
银行卡 yínháng kǎ banking card
卡车 kǎchē N lorry, truck (辆 liàng)

NOTE: The composition of 卡车 kǎchē is a semi-transliteration (半音译词 bàn yīnyìcí): 卡 kǎ represents the sound of the English word "car" and 车 chē means *vehicle*. See 咖啡 kāfēi for an example of transliteration.

卡片 kǎpiàn N card (张 zhāng)
开 kāi TRAD 開 V 1 open, open up 2 turn on, switch on 3 drive (a vehicle), pilot (a plane) 4 start

开采 kāicǎi V mine, excavate
开除 kāichú V expel
被学校开除 bèi xuéxiào kāichú be expelled from the school
开刀 kāidāo V perform a medical operation
开发 kāifā V develop (land, resources, products, etc.)
开发商 kāifāshāng (real estate, land) developer
开放 kāifàng V open, open up
开工 kāigōng V (of a factory) start production, (of a construction project) start building
开关 kāiguān N switch

开会 kāihuì v attend a meeting, hold a meeting

开课 kāikè v introduce a course, teach a subject

开垦 kāikěn v reclaim (wasteland)

开口 kāikǒu v start to talk
难以开口 nányǐ kāikǒu find it difficult to bring up a matter

开阔 kāikuò ADJ open and wide, expansive, spacious

开朗 kāilǎng ADJ broad-minded and outspoken, always cheerful
性格开朗 xìnggé kāilǎng of a cheerful disposition

开门 kāimén v open for business

开明 kāimíng ADJ civilized, enlightened

开幕 kāimù v (of a play, a ceremony, conference, etc.) open, start
开幕式 kāimùshì opening ceremony

开辟 kāipì v open up, start

开设 kāishè v 1 offer (a course in a college) 2 open (an office, a factory, etc.)

开始 kāishǐ I v begin, commence II N beginning, start

开头 kāitóu N Same as 开始 kāishǐ, used colloquially.

开拓 kāituò v open up

开玩笑 kāi wánxiào v joke
跟和···开玩笑 gēn/hé...kāi wánxiào joke with ..., make fun of ....

开心 kāixīn ADJ feeling happy, delighted

开学 kāixué v start (school)

开演 kāiyǎn v start (a performance, a film, etc.)

开夜车 kāi yèchē v burn the midnight oil

开展 kāizhǎn v launch, develop, expand

开支 kāizhī I v pay (expenses) II N expenditure, expenses
日常家用开支 rìcháng jiāyòng kāizhī daily household expenses

凯 kǎi ADJ triumphant

凯旋 kǎixuán v return in triumph

慨 kǎi ADJ deeply touched (See 感慨 gǎnkǎi)

刊 kān v publish

刊登 kāndēng v publish (in a newspaper, magazine, etc.)

刊物 kānwù N periodical, journal, magazine

勘 kān v survey, investigate

勘探 kāntàn N prospecting, exploration
石油勘探队 shíyóukāntàn duì oil prospecting team

堪 kān MODAL v may, can

看 kān v look after, take care of
看孩子 kān háizi look after children, baby-sit

NOTE: This verb 看 is pronounced in the first tone when used in this sense.

砍 kǎn v chop, hack

看 kàn v 1 look, watch 2 read
看电视 kàn diànshì watch TV
看电影 kàn diànyǐng watch a film
看体育比赛 kàn tǐyù bǐsài watch a sport event

NOTE: See note on 看见 kànjiàn.

看病 kànbìng v see a doctor

看不起 kànbuqǐ v look down upon, despise
看得起 kàndeqǐ respect, hold in esteem

NOTE: In colloquial Chinese, 瞧不起 qiáobuqǐ can be used instead of 看不起 kànbuqǐ. Likewise 看得起 kàndeqǐ may be replaced by 瞧得起 qiáodeqǐ.

看待 kàndài v look upon, regard, treat

看法 kànfǎ N 1 way of looking at things, view 2 negative opinion

看见 kànjiàn v see, get sight of
看不见 kànbujiàn cannot see
看得见 kàndejiàn can see
没(有)看见 méi (yǒu) kànjiàn fail to see

NOTE: While 看 kàn is *to look* or *to look at*, 看见 kànjiàn is *to see* or *to catch sight of*. For example: 我朝窗外看，没有看见什么。Wǒ cháo chuāng wài kàn, méiyǒu kànjiàn shénme. *I looked out of the window and did not see anything.*

看来 kànlái ADV it looks as if, it seems as if
看望 kànwàng V call on, pay a visit to
看样子 kànyàngzi ADV Same as 看来 kànlái
看做 kànzuò V regard as, look upon as
把你我看做我的好朋友 bǎ nǐ kàn zuò wǒde hǎo péngyou (I) regard you as my good friend, take you for my good friend

康 **kāng** N good health (See 健康 jiànkāng.)

慷 **kāng** as in 慷慨 kāngkài

慷慨 kāngkài ADJ generous, liberal

糠 **kāng** N husk, bran, chaff

抗 **kàng** V resist (See 反抗 fǎnkàng, 抗议 kàngyì.)
抗击 kàngjī V beat back, resist by fighting
抗议 kàngyì V, N protest

亢 **kàng** ADJ high, haughty

炕 **kàng** N a heatable brick bed, *kang*

考 **kǎo** V examine, test
考察 kǎochá V 1 inspect, make an on-the-spot investigation 2 test and judge (a person)
考古 kǎogǔ V do archaeological studies
考古学 kǎogǔxué archaeology
考核 kǎohé V examine and check
年终考核 niánzhōng kǎohé annual (staff) performance review
考虑 kǎolù V think over carefully, consider, contemplate
考取 kǎoqǔ V pass an examination for admission to employment or study
考取名牌大学 kǎoqǔ míngpái dàxué gain admission to a famous university by passing an examination
考试 kǎoshì I V examine, test

考得好 kǎo de hǎo do well in an examination
考得不好 kǎo de bù hǎo do poorly in an examination
II N examination, test (次 cì, 场 cháng)
高等学校入学考试 (高考) gāoděng xuéxiào rùxué kǎoshì (gāokǎo) university entrance examination
汉语水平考试 Hànyǔ Shuǐpíng Kǎoshì (HSK) Chinese Proficiency Test
考验 kǎoyàn I V test, put through rigorous testing II N rigorous test, trial

烤 **kǎo** V bake, roast

靠 **kào** V rely on, depend on
靠得住 kàodezhù trustworthy, reliable
靠不住 kàobuzhù untrustworthy, unreliable
靠近 kàojìn V close to, near

科 **kē** N 1 section (of an administration office)
财务科 cáiwùkē finance section
2 branch (of academic study)
工科 gōngkē faculty of engineering
理科 lǐkē faculty of (natural) sciences
文科 wénkē faculty of arts
3 shortening for 科学 kēxué
科技 kējì science and technology
科目 kēmù N (school) subject, course
科学 kēxué N science
科学研究 (科研) kēxué yánjiū (kēyán) scientific research
科学家 kēxuéjiā N scientist (位 wèi)
科学院 kēxuéyuàn N academy of science
科长 kēzhǎng N section head

棵 **kē** M. WD (for plants)
三棵树 sān kē shù three trees
一棵草 yì kē cǎo a blade of grass

颗 **kē** M. WD (for beans, pearl, etc.)
一颗黄豆 yìkē huángdòu a soybean

磕 **kē** V knock
磕头 kētóu V kowtow

咳 **ké** V cough

咳嗽 késou V cough

咳嗽药水 késou yàoshuǐ cough syrup

咳嗽糖 késou táng cough lozenge/drop

壳 ké N shell

鸡蛋壳 jīdànké egg shell

可 kě I ADV 1 indeed (used before an adjective for emphasis) 2 after all (used before a verb for emphasis) 3 be sure to (used in an imperative sentence for emphasis) II MODAL V can be, may be III CONJ Same as 可是 kěshì

NOTE: 可 kě is only used colloquially. When using 可 kě to emphasize an adjective or a verb, 啦 la, 呢 ne or 了 le is often used at the end of the sentence, e.g. 当父母可不容易呢! Dāng fùmǔ kě bù róngyì ne! *Being a parent is indeed no easy job!*

可爱 kě'ài ADJ lovable, lovely

NOTE: 可 in the sense of *can be, may be* plus a verb forms an adjective, similar to English adjectives of *v+-able/ible*. For example, 可爱 kě'ài is similar to *lovable*. Quite a number of Chinese adjectives are formed in the same way as 可爱 kě'ài.

可耻 kěchǐ ADJ shameful, disgraceful

可观 kěguān ADJ considerable, sizeable

一笔可观的现金 yìbǐ kěguān de xiànjīn a considerable sum of cash

可贵 kěguì ADJ valuable, recommendable

可见 kějiàn CONJ it can be seen, it is thus clear

可靠 kěkào ADJ reliable, trustworthy

可口 kěkǒu ADJ palatable, tasty

可口可乐 kěkǒukělè N Coca-Cola (瓶 píng)

百事可乐 bǎishìkělè Pepsi[-Cola]

NOTE: 可口可乐 kěkǒukělè is a transliteration of "Coca-Cola." It can be shortened into 可乐 kělè.

可怜 kělián ADJ pitiful, pitiable

可能 kěnéng I MODAL V may, possible, possibly II N possibility

(没)有可能 (méi) yǒu kěnéng (im)possible, (im)possibly

可怕 kěpà ADJ fearsome, frightening

可是 kěshì CONJ Same as 但是 dànshì, used colloquially

可恶 kěwù ADJ detestable, hateful

可惜 kěxī ADJ be a pity, be a shame

可喜 kěxǐ ADJ gratifying, heartening

可笑 kěxiào ADJ laughable, ridiculous

可行 kěxíng ADJ can be done, feasible

可行性 kěxíngxìng feasibility

可行性报告 kěxíngxìng bàogào feasibility report

可疑 kěyí ADJ suspicious

可疑分子 kěyífènzǐ a suspect

行为可疑 xíngwéi kěyí suspicious behavior

可以 kěyǐ MODAL V giving permission, may, can, be allowed

渴 kě ADJ thirsty

口渴 kǒukě thirsty

NOTE: See note on 喝 hē.

渴望 kěwàng V thirst for, long for

克 kè M. WD gram

五百克 wǔbǎi kè 500 grams

克服 kèfú V overcome, conquer

刻¹ kè V carve

刻² kè M. WD quarter of an hour

一刻钟 yí kè zhōng a quarter of an hour, 15 minutes

三点一刻 sān diǎn yí kè a quarter past three

刻苦 kèkǔ ADJ hardworking, assiduous, painstaking

客 kè N guest

客车 kèchē N 1 passenger train 2 coach

客观 kèguān ADJ objective

客观的报道 kèguān de bàodào objective report

客户 kèhù N client, buyer

客气 kèqi ADJ 1 polite, standing on ceremony 2 modest

客人 kèrén N guest, visitor

客厅 **kètīng** N living room, sitting room

课 **kè** TRAD 課 N lesson, class, lecture

上课 shàng kè go to class

下课 xià kè finish class

课本 **kèběn** N textbook, course book (本 běn)

课程 **kèchéng** N course, a program of study

课时 **kèshí** N class hour

课堂 **kètáng** N classroom

课题 **kètí** N research topic

课文 **kèwén** N text (篇 piān)

肯 **kěn** MODAL V be willing to

肯定 **kěndìng** I V confirm, acknowledge
 II ADJ affirmative, positive, definite

啃 **kěn** V gnaw, nibble

恳 **kěn** TRAD 懇 ADJ sincere

恳切 **kěnqiè** ADJ earnest, sincere

恳求 **kěnqiú** V implore, entreat

垦 **kěn** TRAD 墾 V cultivate (land)

垦荒 **kěnhuāng** V reclaim wasteland

坑 **kēng** N pit, hollow

空 **kōng** I ADJ empty II N sky

空洞 **kōngdòng** ADJ hollow, devoid of content

空洞的承诺 kōngdòng de chéngnuò hollow promise

空话 **kōnghuà** N empty talk, hollow words

空间 **kōngjiān** N space, room

空军 **kōngjūn** N air force

空气 **kōngqì** N air

空前 **kōngqián** ADJ unprecedented

空调 **kōngtiáo** N air conditioning

空调机 **kōngtiáojī** air conditioner

有空调的房间 yǒu kòngtiáo de fángjiān air-conditioned room

空想 **kōngxiǎng** N pipe-dream, fantasy

空心 **kōngxīn** ADJ hollow

空虚 **kōngxū** ADJ void, empty

生活空虚 shēnghuó kōngxū live a life devoid of any meaning, a meaningless existence

空中 **kōngzhōng** N in the sky, in the air

恐 **kǒng** V fear

恐怖 **kǒngbù** ADJ horrible, terrifying

恐怖电影 kǒngbù diànyǐng horror movie

恐怖分子 kǒngbù fènzi terrorist

恐怖活动 kǒngbù huódòng terrorist activity

恐怖主义 kǒngbù zhǔyì terrorism

恐惧 **kǒngjù** V be in great fear of, dread

恐怕 **kǒngpà** ADV I'm afraid, perhaps

NOTE: 恐怕 kǒngpà and 也许 yěxǔ may both mean *perhaps*, but 恐怕 kǒngpà implies that what might perhaps happen is undesirable.

孔 **kǒng** N aperture, hole

孔夫子 **Kǒngfūzǐ** N Confucius

NOTE: 孔夫子 Kǒngfūzǐ—also called 孔子 Kǒngzǐ in Chinese—is the most influential Chinese philosopher. His Europeanized name is *Confucius*. His teachings are referred to as 孔子学说 Kǒngzǐ xuéshuō or 儒家学说 Rújiā xuéshuō.

孔雀 **kǒngquè** N peacock (只 zhī)

空 **kòng** I ADJ unoccupied, vacant

空房 kòngfáng vacant room
 II N free time

空白 **kòngbái** ADJ blank space

空白支票 kòngbái zhīpiào blank check

空缺 **kòngquē** N vacant position

空隙 **kòngxì** N narrow gap, brief interval

空闲 **kòngxián** I ADJ be free II N free time, leisure

空子 **kòngzi** N loophole

钻空子 zuān kòngzi take advantage of a loophole

控 **kòng** V 1 control 2 accuse

控告 **kònggào** V accuse, sue

控股公司 **kònggǔ gōngsī** N holding company

控制 **kòngzhì** V control, dominate

抠 **kōu** v dig with a finger

口 **kǒu** I N mouth II M. wD (for members of a family)

口岸 **kǒu' àn** N port

口才 **kǒucái** I N the ability to speak well, gift of gab II ADJ eloquent

有口才 **yǒu kǒucái** be eloquent

口吃 **kǒuchī** v stammer, stutter

口齿 **kǒuchǐ** N the ability to pronounce sounds and words clearly

口齿清楚 **kǒuchǐ qīngchǔ** with clear enunciation

口袋 **kǒudài** N pocket (只 zhī)

口号 **kǒuhào** N slogan (条 tiáo)

口气 **kǒuqì** N 1 tone (of speech)

温和的口气 **wēnhé de kǒuqì** gentle tone 2 manner of speaking

听他的口气 **tīng tāde kǒuqì** judging by the way he spoke

口腔 **kǒuqiāng** N oral cavity

口试 **kǒushì** N oral examination

口头 **kǒutóu** ADJ oral, spoken

口头协议 **kǒutóu xiéyì** oral agreement

口语 **kǒuyǔ** N spoken language, speech

扣 **kòu** I N 1 button

扣子 **kòuzi** button 2 knot

系个扣儿 **xì gè kòur** make a knot II v 1 button up

扣扣子 **kòu kòuzi** do up the buttons 2 detain, arrest 3 deduct

扣除 **kòuchú** v deduct

扣留 **kòuliú** v detain, hold in custody

扣留驾驶执照 **kòuliú jiàshǐ zhízhào** suspend a driving license

扣押 **kòuyā** v distrain, detain

扣压 **kòuyā** v withhold, pigeonhole

寇 **kòu** N bandit

哭 **kū** v cry, weep, sob

枯 **kū** ADJ withered

枯燥 **kūzào** ADJ dull and dry

枯燥乏味 **kūzào fáwèi** dull and insipid

窟 **kū** N cave, hole

窟窿 **kūlong** N hole, cavity

苦 **kǔ** ADJ 1 bitter 2 (of life) hard, miserable

吃苦 **chīkǔ** suffer hardships, endure hardships

苦闷 **kǔmèn** ADJ depressed, dejected

苦难 **kǔnàn** N great suffering, misery

苦恼 **kǔnǎo** ADJ vexed, troubled

库 **kù** TRAD 庫 N warehouse (See 仓库 cāngkù)

库存 **kùcún** N stock, reserve

裤 **kù** TRAD 褲 N trousers

裤子 **kùzi** N trousers (条 tiáo)

酷 **kù** ADJ 1 cruel

酷刑 **kùxíng** cruel torture, torture 2 cool (loanword for "very good")

夸 **kuā** v 1 exaggerate, boast 2 praise

夸大 **kuādà** v exaggerate

夸奖 **kuājiǎng** v praise, commend

垮 **kuǎ** v collapse, break down

打垮 **dǎkuǎ** defeat, rout, smash

跨 **kuà** v take big strides

跨国公司 **kuàguó gōngsī** multinational company

挎 **kuà** v carry on the arm

快 **kuài** ADJ quick, fast

快餐 **kuàicān** N fast food

快车 **kuài chē** N express train

快递 **kuàidì** N express delivery

快乐 **kuàilè** ADJ joyful, happy

快速 **kuàisù** ADJ highspeed

会 **kuài** as in 会计 **kuàijì**

会计 **kuàijì** N 1 accounting

会计年度 **kuàijì niándù** fiscal year 2 accountant

会计主任 **kuàijì zhǔrèn** chief accountant

块 kuài TRAD 塊 M. WD **1** (for things that can be broken into lumps or chunks)

一块蛋糕 yí kuài dàngāo a piece/slice of cake

两块面包 liǎng kuài miànbāo two pieces of bread

2 (for money) yuan, dollar (only in spoken Chinese)

三块钱 sǎn kuài qián three yuan (or dollars)

NOTE: See note on 元 yuán.

筷 kuài N chopstick

筷子 kuàizi N chopstick, chopsticks

一双筷子 yì shuāng kuàizi a pair of chopsticks

宽 kuān TRAD 寬 ADJ **1** wide, broad **2** lenient, generous **3** well-off

宽敞 kuānchang ADJ spacious

宽大 kuāndà ADJ **1** roomy, spacious **2** lenient

宽带 kuāndài N broadband

宽广 kuānguǎng ADJ extensive, expansive

宽阔 kuānkuò ADJ broad, wide

款 kuǎn N sum of money (笔 bǐ)

款待 kuǎndài V entertain hospitably

狂 kuáng ADJ mad, wild

狂风 kuángfēng N terrible wind, strong fast wind

狂人 kuángrén N madman, maniac

狂妄 kuángwàng ADJ outrageously conceited

况 kuàng N situation (See 情况 qíngkuàng, 状况 zhuàngkuàng.)

况且 kuàngqiě CONJ moreover, besides

矿 kuàng TRAD 礦 N (coal, gold, etc.) mine (座 zuò), mineral

金矿 jīnkuàng gold mine

煤矿 méikuàng coal mine

油矿 yóukuàng oilfield

矿藏 kuàngcáng N mineral resources

矿产 kuàngchǎn N mineral products

矿工 kuànggōng N miner

矿区 kuàngqū N mining area

矿山 kuàngshān N mine

矿石 kuàngshí N mineral ore

矿物 kuàngwù N mineral

旷 kuàng ADJ free from worries

旷工 kuànggōng V absent from work without leave

旷课 kuàngkè V absent from school without leave

亏 kuī I N loss

转亏为盈 zhuǎn kuī wéi yíng turn loss into gain

II V **1** lose, be deficient **2** thank to

亏待 kuīdài V treat shabbily

亏损 kuīsǔn N loss, deficiency

葵 kuí as in 葵花 kuíhuā

葵花 kuíhuā N sunflower

愧 kuì ADJ ashamed (See 惭愧 cánkuì.)

昆 kūn as in 昆虫 kūnchóng

昆虫 kūnchóng N insect (只 zhī)

捆 kǔn I V bundle up, tie II M. WD bundle

困 kùn I V be stranded, be in a tough spot II ADJ sleepy

困苦 kùnkǔ ADJ poverty-stricken, destitute

困难 kùnnan I N difficulty

克服困难 kèfú kùnnan overcome difficulty

II ADJ difficult

扩 kuò TRAD 擴 V spread out

扩充 kuòchōng V strengthen, reinforce

扩大 kuòdà V expand, enlarge

扩散 kuòsàn V spread, proliferate

扩张 kuòzhāng V expand, extend

括 kuò V include, embrace (See 概括 gàikuò.)

阔 kuò ADJ wide (See 广阔 guǎngkuò.)

L

拉 **lā** v pull

垃 **lā** as in 垃圾 lājī

垃圾 **lājī** n rubbish, garbage
　垃圾处理 lājī chǔlǐ rubbish disposal
　垃圾袋 lājī dài rubbish bag
　垃圾箱 lājī xiāng rubbish bin
垃圾邮件 **lājī yóujiàn** n junk mail
　阻止垃圾邮件 zǔzhǐ lājī yóujiàn prevent
　junk mail

喇 **lā** as in 喇叭 lǎba

喇叭 **lǎba** n 1 horn, trumpet 2 loudspeaker
　吹喇叭 chuī lǎba blow the horn, play the
　trumpet

蜡 **là** trad 蠟 n wax
蜡烛 **làzhú** n candle (支 chi)
　点蜡烛 diǎn làzhú light a candle

腊 **là** trad 臘 adj 1 of the twelfth
month of the lunar year 2 (of meat)
salted and dried, cured
腊肉 **làròu** n cured meat, ham
腊月 **làyuè** n the twelfth (and last) month
of the lunar year

落 **là** v 1 leave out 2 lag behind

NOTE: When used in these senses, 落 is
pronounced as là, not as luò, which it usually is. 见 丢三落四 diū-sān-là-sì.

辣 **là** adj spicy hot, peppery
辣椒 **làjiāo** n red pepper, chilli

啦 **la** particle (an exclamation indicating completion of an action and/
or emergence of a new situation; 了 le
+ 啊 a)

NOTE: 啦 la is the combination of 了 le
and 啊 a. It is only used at the end of a sentence. You can replace 啦 la with 了 le but
then the strong emotive coloring of 啊

a is lost. Compare: 我赢啦! Wǒ yíng la! *I
won!* and 我赢了。Wǒ yíng le. *I won.*

来 1 **lái** trad 來 v come, come to,
move towards to the speaker
来宾 **láibīn** n guest, visitor
来不及 **láibují** v not have enough time (to
do something), there isn't enough time (to
do something)

NOTE: The opposite to 来不及 láibují is 来
得及 láidejí, e.g.: 还来得及吃早饭。Hái
láidejí chī zǎofàn. *There is still enough time
to have breakfast.*

来访 **láifǎng** v come to visit, come to call
来回 **láihuí** v make a round trip, make a
return journey
来客 **láikè** n guest, customer (to a restaurant, hotel, etc.)
来历 **láilì** n origin, background
　来历不明 láilì bùmíng of uncertain
　origin, of dubious background
来临 **láilín** v arrive, approach
来年 **láinián** n the coming year
来往 **láiwǎng** n dealings, connection
　和他们没有来往 hé tāmen méiyǒu
　láiwang have had no dealings with them
来信 **láixìn** n letter received, incoming
letter
来源 **láiyuán** n source, origin
　消息来源 xiāoxi láiyuán source of the
　news
来自 **láizì** v come from

来 2 **lái** trad 來 num approximately,
more or less, close to (used after
the number 10 or a multiple of 10 to
indicate approximation)
十来辆车 shí lái liàng chē about ten cars
五十来个学生 wǔshí lái ge xuésheng
approximately fifty students
三百四十来块钱 sānbǎi sìshí lái kuài
qián about 340 yuan

赖 **lài** trad 賴 v rely (See 依赖 yīlài.)

兰 **lán** trad 蘭 n orchid

兰花 **lánhuā** orchid

栏 **lán** TRAD 欄 N railing, fence

栏杆 lángān N railing, banister, balustrade

拦 **lán** TRAD 攔 V stop, block, hold back

蓝 **lán** TRAD 藍 ADJ blue

篮 **lán** TRAD 籃 N basket

篮球 lánqiú N basketball
　篮球比赛 lánqiú bǐsài basketball match
　篮球队 lánqiú duì basketball team
　打篮球 dǎ lánqiú play basketball
篮子 lánzi N basket

览 **lǎn** TRAD 覽 V view (See 游览 yóulǎn, 阅览室 yuèlǎnshì, 展览 zhǎnlǎn.)

揽 **lǎn** TRAD 攬 V **1** pull into one's arms, take into one's arms **2** take on
　揽生意 lǎn shēngyì canvass for business

懒 **lǎn** TRAD 懶 ADJ lazy, indolent

懒惰 lǎnduò ADJ lazy
懒骨头 lǎn gútou N lazybones

烂 **làn** TRAD 爛 I V rot, go bad II ADJ rotten (See 腐烂 fǔlàn.)

滥 **làn** TRAD 濫 I V overflow, flood (See 泛滥 fànlàn.) II ADJ excessive, indiscriminate

滥用 lànyòng V abuse, misuse
　滥用职权 lànyòng zhíquán abuse one's power

狼 **láng** N wolf (只 zhī)
　披着羊皮的狼 pīzhe yángpí de láng a wolf in sheep's clothing
　一群狼 yì qún láng a pack of wolves
狼狈 lángbèi ADJ in an awkward position
狼狈为奸 lángbèi wéijiān V act in collusion with each other

廊 **láng** N corridor

郎 **láng** SUFFIX (for certain nouns of people)
　放羊郎 fàng yángláng shepherd

朗 **lǎng** ADJ loud and clear

朗读 lǎngdú V read in a loud and clear voice
朗诵 lǎngsòng V recite (a poem) theatrically

浪 **làng** I N wave II ADJ uncontrolled, dissolute

浪潮 làngcháo N tide, tidal wave
浪费 làngfèi V waste
浪漫 làngmàn ADJ romantic

捞 **lāo** TRAD 撈 V pull or drag out of water

打捞 dǎlāo salvage (a sunken ship, etc.)

劳 **láo** TRAD 勞 V toil

劳动 láodòng V do manual labor
　脑力劳动 nǎolì láodòng mental work
　体力劳动 tǐlì láodòng physical (manual) labor
劳动节 láodòng jié N Labor Day (on May 1)
劳动力 láodònglì N work force, manpower
　劳动力不足 láodònglì bùzú short of manpower
劳驾 láojià IDIOM Excuse me, Would you mind (doing ... for me)

NOTE: 劳驾 láojià is a northern dialect expression. To say *Excuse me*, 对不起 duìbuqǐ is more widely used.

唠 **láo** as in 唠叨 láodao

唠叨 láodao ADJ be garrulous
　唠唠叨叨说个没完 láoláo dāodāo shuō ge méiwán chatter on and on

牢 **láo** I ADJ firm, fast II N shortening for 牢房 láofáng
　坐牢 zuòláo serve jail term
牢房 láofáng N Same as 监狱 jiānyù, used only informally.
牢固 láogù ADJ firm, solid
牢骚 láosāo N discontent, grumbling
　发牢骚 fālāosāo grumble

老 **lǎo** I ADJ **1** old, elderly
　老太太 lǎo tàitai old lady, old woman
　老先生 lǎo xiānsheng old gentleman, old man

2 long-standing

老朋友 lǎopéngyou long-standing friend

II PREFIX (added to numbers to indicate seniority among siblings)

老大 lǎo dà the eldest child

老二 lǎo èr the second child

NOTE: Chinese tradition values and respects old age. Today, people still attach 老 lǎo to a family name as a form of address to show respect and friendliness to an older person, e.g. 老李 Lǎo Lǐ, 老王 Lǎo Wáng. See note on 小 xiǎo.

老百姓 lǎobǎixìng N common people, ordinary folk

老板 lǎobǎn N **1** boss **2** owner of a store, a business, etc.

老成 lǎochéng ADJ (of a youngster) mature and experienced

老大娘 lǎodàniáng N (a respectful form of address or reference to an old woman) (位 wèi)

NOTE: See note on 老大爷 lǎodàye.

老大爷 lǎodàye N (a respectful form of address or reference to an old man) (位 wèi)

NOTE: 老大娘 lǎodàniáng and 老大爷 lǎodàye both have a rustic flavor. They are normally not used in cities or among better-educated people. 老太太 lǎotàitai/老先生 lǎoxiānsheng is a more appropriate name.

老汉 lǎohàn N old man, old fellow

老虎 lǎohǔ N tiger (头 tóu, 只 zhī)

小老虎 xiǎo lǎohǔ tiger cub

老化 lǎohuà V **1** becoming old

人口老化 rénkǒulǎohuà ageing of the population

2 becoming outdated

知识老化 zhīshi lǎohuà outdated knowledge

老家 lǎojiā N native place

老龄 lǎolíng N old age, people of old age

老年 lǎonián N old age

老年人 lǎoniánrén N old person

老婆 lǎopó N (vulgarism) wife, old girl

老人 lǎorén N old person, elderly person (位 wèi)

老人家 lǎorenjiā N (respectful form of address for an old person)

老师 lǎoshī N teacher (位 wèi)

NOTE: 老师 lǎoshī, usually prefixed by a family name, is the standard form of address to a teacher in Mainland China or other Chinese-speaking regions, e.g. 王老师 Wáng Lǎoshī. There is no equivalent of 王老师 Wáng Lǎoshī in English.

老是 lǎoshi ADV always, constantly

老实 lǎoshi ADJ honest

老实话 lǎoshi huà plain truth

老实人 lǎoshi rén honest person

老实说 lǎoshi shuō to tell the truth

老鼠 lǎoshǔ N mouse/mice, rat(s) (只 zhī)

老太婆 lǎotàipó N old woman

NOTE: See note on 老头儿 lǎotóur.

老太太 lǎotàitai N (a respectful form of address or reference to an old woman) (位 wèi)

老天爷 lǎotiānyé N the Old Lord of Heaven, Heaven, God

老头儿 lǎotóur N old man (个 gè)

NOTE: (1) 老头儿 lǎotóur is an impolite way of referring to an *old man*. As a form of address, 老头儿 lǎotóur is very rude. Instead, use the neutral term 老人 lǎorén or the polite terms 老先生 lǎoxiānsheng or 老大爷 lǎodàye. (2) The corresponding impolite word for an *old woman* is 老太婆 lǎotàipó. Use 老太太 lǎotàitai or 老大娘 lǎodàniáng instead.

老外 lǎowài N foreigner

NOTE: 老外 lǎowài is a familiar term for *foreigner* in China. It is quite informal, but not really impolite. The formal term is 外国人 wàiguórén.

老先生 lǎoxiānsheng N (a respectful form of address or reference to an old man) (位 wèi)

老爷 lǎoye N (old fashioned) lord, sir

老字号 lǎozìhào N established brand or shop

姥 lǎo as in 姥姥 lǎolao

姥姥 lǎolao N (maternal) granny

涝 lào N waterlogging, flooding

旱涝保收 hànlào bǎoshōu (of crops) sure to reap a good harvest even if there is drought or flooding

乐 lè TRAD 樂 ADJ happy, delighted, joyful

乐观 lèguān ADJ optimistic

乐观主义 lèguān zhǔyì optimism

乐观主义者 lèguānzhǔyìzhě optimist

乐趣 lèqù N pleasure, joy

乐事 lèshì N pleasure, delight

乐意 lèyì ADJ be happy to, be willing to

勒 lè V rein in

勒索 lèsuǒ V extort, blackmail

了 le PARTICLE **1** (used after a verb to indicate the completion of an action) **2** (used at the end of a sentence to indicate the emergence of a new situation)

雷 léi N thunder

打雷 dǎléi thunder

雷达 léidá N radar

雷雨 léiyǔ N thunderstorm

蕾 lěi N (flower) bud

垒 lěi TRAD 壘 N as in 垒球 lěiqiú

垒球 lěiqiú N softball

垒球棒 lěiqiúbàng softball bat (根 gēn)

泪 lèi TRAD 淚 N teardrop, tear (See 眼泪 yǎnlèi.)

类 lèi TRAD 類 N kind, category, class

类似 lèisì ADJ similar

类型 lèixíng N type (种 zhǒng)

累 lèi ADJ exhausted, tired

棱 léng N edge

冷 lěng ADJ cold

冷淡 lěngdàn ADJ cold, indifferent, apathetic

冷静 lěngjìng ADJ calm, sober

冷却 lěngquè **I** V to make cool **II** N cooling

冷却剂 lěngquèjì coolant, cooler

冷饮 lěngyǐn N cold drink, ice-cream

愣 lèng ADJ stupefied, blank

发愣 fālèng look stupefied, stare blankly

厘 lí M. WD one thousandth of a foot

厘米 límǐ M. WD centimeter

离 lí TRAD 離 **I** V depart, leave **II** PREP (indicating distance in space or time) away from, from

离…近 lí…jìn close to

离…远 lí…yuǎn far away from

离别 líbié V leave, bid farewell

离婚 líhūn V divorce

离婚协议 líhūn xiéyì divorce settlement

申请离婚 shēnqǐng líhūn file a divorce, sue for a divorce

离开 líkāi V **1** depart, leave **2** do without

离不开 líbukāi cannot do without

离休 líxiū V (of officials) retire

篱 lí TRAD 籬 N hedge, fence

篱笆 líba N bamboo fence, twig fence

黎 lí as in 黎明 límíng

黎明 límíng N dawn, daybreak

狸 lí N racoon dog

梨 lí N pear (只 zhī)

犁 lí N plough

璃 lí N glass (See 玻璃 bōli.)

李 Lǐ N (a family name)

NOTE: 李 Lǐ is the most common family name in China.

110

礼 lǐ TRAD 禮 N 1 rite, ceremony 2 gift

礼拜天 Lǐbàitiān N Same as 星期天
Xīngqītiān. A rather old-fashioned word.

礼节 lǐjié N etiquette, protocol

礼貌 lǐmào ADJ polite, courteous

礼品 lǐpǐn N gift (件 jiàn)

礼堂 lǐtáng N auditorium, assembly hall
(座 zuò)

礼物 lǐwù N gift, present (件 jiàn)

结婚礼物 jiéhūn lǐwù wedding present
生日礼物 shēngrì lǐwù birthday present
新年礼物 xīnnián lǐwù New Year present

NOTE: Chinese modesty requires that you
belittle your present, describing it as 一件
小礼物 yí jiàn xiǎo lǐwù a small/insignifi-
cant gift. Upon receiving a present, it is
bad manners to open it immediately. The
recipient is first supposed to say 不用
不用 búyòng búyòng You didn't have to and
then express thanks for the gift, describing
it as 这么好的礼物 Zhème hǎo de lǐwù
such a nice gift, e.g. 谢谢你送给我这么
好的礼物。Xièxie nǐ sònggei wǒ zhème
hǎo de lǐwù. Thank you for giving me such
a nice gift.

里 1 lǐ TRAD 裏 N inside

里边 lǐbian N inside

里面 lǐmiàn N Same as 里边 lǐbian

里 2 lǐ M.WD (a traditional Chinese
unit of distance, equivalent to half a
kilometer)

理 lǐ N pattern, reason II v manage,
handle

理睬 lǐcǎi v (usu. negative sense) show
interest in, pay attention to

理发 lǐfà v have a haircut and shampoo,
have one's hair done

理发店 lǐfàdiàn barbershop, hair salon

理发师 lǐfàshī barber, hairdresser, hairstylist

NOTE: Instead of the plain word 理发店
lǐfàdiàn, many hair salons now give
themselves fanciful names such as 美发厅
měifàtīng.

理会 lǐhuì v 1 comprehend, understand
2 take notice of

不理会 bùlǐhuì take no notice of, ignore

理解 lǐjiě v understand, comprehend

理亏 lǐkuī ADJ be in the wrong

自知理亏 zìzhī lǐkuī know oneself to be
in the wrong, realize that justice is not
on one's side

理论 lǐlùn N theory

理念 lǐniàn N notion, ideal

理事 lǐshì N member of a council

理所当然 lǐsuǒdāngrán ADJ naturally, as
should be expected

理想 lǐxiǎng N ideal, aspiration

理想主义 lǐxiǎng zhǔyì idealism
实现理想 shíxiàn lǐxiǎng realize an ideal

理由 lǐyóu N reason, justification, ground,
argument

理直气壮 lǐzhíqìzhuàng ADJ bold and assured that justice is on one's side

力 lì N strength, force, might

力量 lìliàng N 1 strength 2 efforts, ability

力气 lìqi N physical strength

力求 lìqiú v strive for, do one's best for

力求完美 lìqiú wánměi strive for perfection

力图 lìtú v try hard, try one's best to

力图改善处境 lìtú gǎishàn chǔjìng try
hard to improve one's situation

力争 lìzhēng v work hard for, do all one
can to

历 lì TRAD 歷 N past experience

历代 lìdài N successive dynasties

历来 lìlái ADV all through the ages, always,
ever since

历史 lìshǐ N history

历史学家 lìshǐxuéjiā historian

沥 lì TRAD 瀝 v drip, trickle

沥青 lìqīng N asphalt

荔 lì as in 荔枝 lìzhī

荔枝 lìzhī N litchi, lichee

隶 lì N slave (See 奴隶 núlì)

栗 **lì** chestnut

栗子 lìzi chestnut (颗 kē)

立 **lì** v stand

坐立不安 zuò-lì-bù-ān on pins and needles, on tenterhooks, anxious **II** ADV immediately, at once

立场 lìchǎng N position, standpoint

立方 lìfāng M. WD (mathematics) cube

三立方米/公尺 sān lìfāng mǐ/gōngchǐ 3 cubic meters

立即 lìjí ADV immediately, without delay

立交桥 lìjiāoqiáo N overpass, flyover (座 zuò)

立刻 lìkè ADV at once, immediately

立体 lìtǐ ADJ three-dimensional

厉 **lì** TRAD 厲 ADJ severe, strict

厉害 lìhai ADJ severe, fierce, formidable

NOTE: (1) 厉害 lìhai is often used with 得 de to indicate a very high degree, e.g.: 这两天热得厉害。Zhèliǎngtiān rède lìhai. *These days are terribly hot.* / 情人节花儿贵得厉害。Qíngrénjié huār guìde lìhai. *Flowers are terribly expensive on Valentine's Day.* (2) 厉害 lìhai may be written as 利害 lìhai.

丽 **lì** TRAD 麗 ADJ beautiful (See 美丽 měilì.)

励 **lì** TRAD 勵 v encourage (See 鼓励 gǔlì.)

利 **lì** N **1** benefit, advantage **2** profit, interest

利弊 lìbì N pros and cons

利害 lìhai Same as 厉害 lìhai

利率 lìlǜ N interest rate

利润 lìrùn N interest

利息 lìxī N interest (on a loan)

利益 lìyì N benefit, interest

利用 lìyòng v make use of, benefit from

例 **lì** N example

例子 lìzi N example (个 gè)

举例子 jǔ lìzi give an example

例如 lìrú CONJ for example, such as

例外 lìwài N exception

粒 **lì** M. WD (for rice, pearls, etc)

一粒米 yí lì mǐ a grain of rice

俩 **liǎ** TRAD 倆 NUM two people

连 **lián** TRAD 連 **I** v connect, join **II** ADV in succession, repeatedly **III** PREP even

连…都… lián…dōu… IDIOM even

NOTE: (1) 连…都… lián…dōu… is an emphatic expression, stressing the word after 连 lián. (2) 都 dōu may be replaced by 也 yě, i.e. 连…也… lián…yě… is the same as 连…都… lián…dōu…, e.g.: 连三岁小孩也［都］知道。Lián sān suì xiǎohái yě [dōu] zhīdào. *Even a toddler knows this.*

连队 liánduì N company (in the army)

连连 liánlián ADV repeatedly, again and again

连忙 liánmáng v make haste, hasten without the slightest delay

连绵 liánmián v continue, be continuous, be uninterrrupted

连同 liántóng CONJ together with

连续 liánxù v be continuous, in succession, in a row

连续剧 liánxùjù N TV series

连夜 liányè ADV that very night

莲 **lián** N lotus

莲子 liánzǐ lotus seed

廉 **lián** ADJ **1** inexpensive, cheap **2** morally clean

廉价 liánjià ADJ low-priced, inexpensive

廉价出售 liánjià chūshòu sell at low prices

廉洁 liánjié ADJ (of officials) honest and clean, not corrupt

镰 **lián** N sickle

镰刀 liándāo sickle (把 bǎ)

帘 **lián** N curtain (See 窗帘 chuānglián)

怜 **lián** TRAD 憐 v pity (See 可怜 kělián.)

联 lián TRAD 聯 v connect

联邦 liánbāng N federation, union

联合 liánhé v unite, get together (to do something)

联合国 Liánhé Guó the United Nations

联合国部队 Liánhé Guó bùduì United Nations troops

联欢 liánhuān v have a get-together, have a gala/party

联络 liánluò v liaise, get in touch with

联络员 liánluòyuán liaison officer

联盟 liánméng N alliance, coalition

联系 liánxì I v get in touch, contact II N connection, relationship

联想 liánxiǎng v make a connection in the mind, associate with

脸 liǎn TRAD 臉 N face (张 zhāng)

丢脸 diūliǎn be disgraced, lose face

脸盆 liǎnpén N wash basin (只 zhī)

脸色 liǎnsè N 1 complexion

脸色苍白 liǎnsè cāngbái pale complexion

2 facial expression

链 liàn N chain

练 liàn TRAD 練 v practice, drill

练习 liànxí I v exercise, train, drill II N exercise, drill

炼 liàn TRAD 煉 v smelt (See 锻炼 duànliàn, 训练 xùnliàn.)

恋 liàn TRAD 戀 N infatuation, love

恋爱 liàn'ài I v be in romantic love, be courting II N romantic love

谈恋爱 tán liàn'ài be in courtship, in love

良 liáng ADJ good

良好 liánghǎo ADJ good, fine, commendable

良种 liángzhǒng N fine breed, improved variety

凉 liáng ADJ cool, chilly

凉菜 liángcài N cold dish, salad

凉快 liángkuai ADJ pleasantly cool

量 liáng v measure, take measurements

粮 liáng TRAD 糧 N grain

粮食 liángshi N grain, cereal, staple food

梁 liáng TRAD 樑 N beam (in structure) (See 桥梁 qiáoliáng.)

两 1 **liǎng** TRAD 兩 M. WD (a traditional Chinese unit of weight equivalent to 50 grams), ounce

两 2 **liǎng** TRAD 兩 NUM **1** two

两个人 liǎng ge rén two people

两本书 liǎng běn shū two books

2 (as an approximation) a couple of, a few

NOTE: Both 两 liǎng and 二 èr may mean *two*, but are used differently. 二 èr must be used in mathematics or when saying the number 2 in isolation, e.g.: 一、二、三、四…yī, èr, sān, sì… *1, 2, 3, 4 …*; 二加三是五. Èr jiā sān shì wǔ. *2 plus 3 is 5.* Use 两 liǎng when referring to "two something," e.g.: 两张桌子 liǎng zhāng zhuōzi *two tables.*

亮 liàng ADJ bright

亮丽 liànglì ADJ spectacularly beautiful

谅 liàng TRAD 諒 v forgive (See 原谅 yuánliàng.)

晾 liàng v dry in the sun, dry in the air

辆 liàng M. WD (for vehicles)

一辆汽车 yí liàng qìchē a car

两辆自行车 liǎng liàng zìxíngchē two bicycles

量 liàng N quantity, capacity

酒量 jiǔliàng capacity for liquor, how much wine one can hold

保质保量 bǎozhì bǎoliàng ensure both the quality and quantity (of products)

聊 liáo v chat

聊天 liáotiān v chat

聊天室 liáotiānshì N (Internet) chatroom

僚 liáo N official (See 官僚 guānliáo)

潦 liáo ADJ slovenly

潦草 liáocǎo ADJ (of handwriting) illegible, done hastily and carelessly

辽 TRAD 遼 ADJ vast

辽阔 liáokuò ADJ vast, extensive

疗 TRAD 療 V treat, cure

疗养 liáoyǎng V recuperate, convalesce
疗养院 liáoyǎngyuàn sanitorium

了 liǎo V finish, be done with

NOTE: 了 liǎo, together with 得 de or 不 bu, is often used after a verb as a complement to mean can ... or cannot ... e.g.: 这件事我干得了，那件事我干不了。Zhè jiàn shì wǒ gàn de liǎo, nà jiàn shì wǒ gàn bu liǎo. *I can do this job, but I can't do that job.*

了不起 liǎobuqǐ ADJ wonderful, terrific
了解 liǎojiě V know, understand, find out

料 1 liào N material (See 材料 cáiliào, 燃料 ránliào, 染料 rǎnliào, 塑料 sùliào, 饮料 yǐnliào, 原料 yuánliào, 资料 zīliào.)

料 2 liào V anticipate, expect

料事如神 liàoshìrúshén predict accurately as if one were a god

列 liè M. WD (for trains)

一列火车 yí liè huǒchē a train

烈 liè ADJ intense

烈火 lièhuǒ N raging flame
烈士 lièshì N martyr (位 wèi)

裂 liè V crack, splint

猎 TRAD 獵 V hunt

猎人 lièrén hunter
打猎 dǎliè go hunting, hunt

劣 liè ADJ inferior, bad (quality) (See 恶劣 èliè)

磷 lín N phosphorus (P)

邻 lín TRAD 鄰 N neighbor

邻居 línjū N neighbor

林 lín N forest, woods

林场 línchǎng N forestry center
林区 línqū N forest, forest land
林业 línyè N forestry/timber industry

淋 lín V drench/pour

淋浴 línyù N shower (bath)
洗淋浴 xǐ línyù take a shower

临 lín TRAD 臨 V arrive

临时 línshí ADJ tentative, provisional

灵 líng TRAD 靈 I N fairy II ADJ agile, quick

灵魂 línghún N soul, spirit
灵活 línghuó ADJ flexible, agile

零 líng I NUM zero

一百零二 yìbǎi líng èr 102
四千零五 sìqiān líng wǔ 4,005
II ADJ fractional, fragmentary

NOTE: (1) No matter how many zeros there are between digits, only one 零 líng is used. For example, 4005 is 四千零五 sìqiān líng wǔ, not 四千零零五 sìqiān líng líng wǔ. (2) 零 líng can also be written as O, e.g 四千O五 sìqiān líng wǔ *4005*.

零件 língjiàn N part, spare part
零钱 língqián N allowance, pocket money, small change

铃 líng TRAD 鈴 N bell

玲 líng as in 玲珑 línglóng

玲珑 línglóng ADJ 1 (of things) exquisite 2 (of people) clever and nimble

龄 líng TRAD 齡 N age (See 年龄 niánlíng.)

凌 líng v approach

凌晨 língchén N the time before dawn

岭 líng N mountain range, ridge

领 líng TRAD 領 v lead, take

领导 lǐngdǎo **I** v **1** lead, provide leadership **2** have jurisdiction over **II** N leader, the person in charge

NOTE: (1) 领导 lǐngdǎo as a verb is somewhat pompous, appropriate only for grand occasions. (2) As a noun 领导 lǐngdǎo is no longer very popular in China and has never been very popular in other Chinese-speaking communities. To refer to "the person in charge," many Chinese use 老板 lǎobǎn (boss) or specific terms such as 厂长 chǎngzhǎng (factory manager) or 校长 xiàozhǎng (headmaster, school principal, university president).

领土 lǐngtǔ N territory

领袖 lǐngxiù N leader (位 wèi)

令 lìng v command, cause to (See 命令 mìnglìng.)

另 lìng ADJ Same as 另外 lìngwài. Used before a monosyllabic verb.

另外 lìngwài ADJ other, another

溜 liū v **1** slide, glide **2** sneak off, slip away

留 liú v remain (in the same place), stay behind

留学 liúxué v study abroad

留学生 liúxuéshēng international students (especially in a university)

瘤 liú N tumor

榴 liú N pomegranate

石榴 shíliú pomegranate

硫 liú N sulfur

硫酸 liúsuān sulfuric acid

流 liú v flow

流动 liúdòng v flow, move from place to place

流动人口 liúdòng rénkǒu floating population, migrant population

流利 liúlì ADJ fluent

流氓 liúmáng N hooligan, gangster

流行 liúxíng v be fashionable, be popular

流行歌手 liúxíng gēshǒu pop singer

流行音乐 liúxíng yīnyuè pop music

流行病 liúxíngbìng N epidemic

流行性感冒(流感) liúxíngxìng gǎnmào (liúgǎn) N influenza, flu

浏 liú as in 浏览 liúlǎn

浏览 liúlǎn v browse

浏览器 liúlǎnqì N (computer) browser

柳 liǔ N willow

杨柳 yángliǔ willow

柳树 liǔshù willow, willow tree (棵 kē)

六 liù NUM six

六十六 liùshí liù sixty-six, 66

六十五岁 liùshí wǔ suì sixty-five years of age

龙 lóng TRAD 龍 N dragon (条 tiáo)

聋 lóng TRAD 聾 ADJ deaf, hard of hearing

聋子 lóngzi deaf person

聋哑人 lóngyǎrén N deaf and dumb person, deaf mute

笼 lóng TRAD 籠 N cage

笼子 lóngzi cage

鸟笼 niǎolóng bird cage

窿 lóng N pit, hole (See 窟窿 kūlong)

隆 lóng ADJ grand

隆重 lóngzhòng ADJ grand, ceremonious

咙 lóng TRAD 嚨 N as in 喉咙 hóulóng

珑 lóng TRAD 瓏 ADJ as in 玲珑 línglóng

垄 lǒng TRAD 壟 N ridge

115

垄断 lǒngduàn v monopolize

拢 lǒng TRAD 攏 v hold together

楼 lóu TRAD 樓 N **1** building with two or more stories (座 zuò) **2** floor (层 céng)
楼上 lóushàng upstairs
楼下 lóuxià downstairs
大楼 dàlóu a big building (especially a high-rise building)
高楼 gāolóu high-rise

NOTE: In naming floors, the Chinese system is the same as the American system but different from the British one, i.e. 一楼 yī-lóu is the American first floor, and the British ground floor.

楼房 lóufáng N multi-storied building (cf. 平房 píngfáng one-story building, bungalow)
楼梯 lóutī N stairs, stairway, staircase

搂 lǒu TRAD 摟 v embrace, hold in arms

漏 lòu v **1** leak **2** leave out by mistake
漏洞 lòudòng N loophole, inconsistency (in argument)
漏税 lòushuì I v evade tax II N tax evasion

陋 lòu ADJ ugly (See 简陋 jiǎnlòu)

炉 lú TRAD 爐 N stove, furnace
炉子 lúzi stove, furnace

虏 lǔ TRAD 虜 N captive (See 俘虏 fúlǔ)

鲁 lǔ ADJ rash (See 粗鲁 cūlǔ)

陆 lù TRAD 陸 N land
陆军 lùjūn N army
陆续 lùxù ADV one after another, in succession

录 lù TRAD 錄 v record
录取 lùqǔ v enroll (students), appoint (job applicants)
录像 lùxiàng v record with a video camera or video recorder
录像机 lùxiàngjī video recorder

录音 lùyīn v make a recording of sounds (e.g. music, reading)
录音机 lùyīnjī audio/sound recorder
录用 lùyòng v employ (staff)

禄 lù ADJ busy (See 忙碌 mánglù)

路 lù N road (条 tiáo)
马路 mǎlù road (in a city)
路程 lùchéng N distance traveled, journey
路过 lùguò v pass, pass by, pass through
路口 lùkǒu N intersection, crossing
路面 lùmiàn N road surface
路上 lùshang N **1** on one's way (to) **2** on the road
路线 lùxiàn N route, itinerary
路子 lùzi N way and means of doing things
很有路子 hěn yǒu lùzi very resourceful

露 lù v show, reveal

赂 lù TRAD 賂 v bribe (See 贿赂 huìlù)

鹿 lù N deer

驴 lǘ N donkey
驴子 lǘzi donkey

铝 lǚ N aluminum (Al)

侣 lǚ N companion (See 伴侣 bànlǚ)

旅 lǚ v travel
旅馆 lǚguǎn N hotel (座 zuò, 家 jiā)
汽车旅馆 qìchē lǚguǎn motel
五星旅馆 wǔxīng lǚguǎn five-star hotel
旅客 lǚkè N hotel guest, passenger (of coach, train, plane, etc.)
旅途 lǚtú N journey, travels
旅行 lǚxíng v travel
旅行社 lǚxíngshè travel agency
旅游 lǚyóu v travel for pleasure
旅游车 lǚyóuchē tour bus
旅游公司 lǚyóu gōngsī travel company
旅游路线 lǚyóu lùxiàn tour itinerary
旅游团 lǚyóutuán tour group

旅游业 lǚyóuyè the tourism industry, tourism

旅游者 lǚyóuzhě tourist, holiday-maker

履 **lǚ** I N shoe II v carry out, fulfill

履历 lǚlì N résumé

履行 lǚxíng v fulfill (one's promise), perform (one's obligation)

屡 **lǚ** TRAD 屢 ADV repeatedly

屡次 lǚcì ADV repeatedly

率 **lǜ** N rate (See 效率 xiàolǜ.)

绿 **lǜ** TRAD 綠 ADJ green

绿党 lǜdǎng the Green Party

绿化 lǜhuà v make green by planting trees, afforest

绿卡 lǜkǎ N green card (permanent residency permit in the U.S.A. and some other countries)

律 **lǜ** N law

律师 lǜshī N lawyer

律师事务所 lǜshī shìwùsuǒ law firm

虑 **lǜ** TRAD 慮 v ponder (See 考虑 kǎolǜ.)

滤 **lǜ** TRAD 濾 v filter

卵 **luǎn** N egg (a cell)

卵子 luǎnzǐ egg

乱 **luàn** TRAD 亂 ADJ 1 disorderly, chaotic 2 at will, random

乱码 luànmǎ N crazy code, confusion code

乱七八糟 luàn-qī-bā-zāo IDIOM in an aw-ful mess, very messy

略 **lüè** v capture (See 侵略 qīnlüè.)

略微 lüèwēi ADJ slight

掠 **lüè** v plunder

掠夺 lüèduó v plunder, rob

抡 **lūn** TRAD 掄 v brandish, swing

轮 **lún** TRAD 輪 I N wheel II v take turns

轮船 lúnchuán N steamship, ship

轮廓 lúnkuò N outline, contour

轮流 lúnliú v take turns

轮流值班 lúnliú zhíbān be on duty by turns

轮子 lúnzi N wheel

论 **lùn** TRAD 論 v discuss

论点 lùndiǎn N argument, point of contest (个 gè)

提出两个论点 tíchū liǎng gè lùndiǎn put forward two arguments

论述 lùnshù v explain (an argument), discuss

论文 lùnwén N dissertation, thesis, essay (篇 piān)

论证 lùnzhèng v prove (an argument), demonstrate, discuss

啰 **luō** as in 啰唆 luō suō

啰唆 luōsuō ADJ long-winded, wordy, verbose

螺 **luó** N snail

螺丝 luósī screw

螺丝刀 luósīdāo screwdriver (把 bǎ)

螺丝钉 luósīdīng screw (颗 kē)

骡 **luó** N mule

骡子 luózi mule (头 tóu)

锣 **luó** N gong (面 miàn)

箩 **luó** N bamboo basket

箩筐 luókuāng N large bamboo or wicker basket (只 zhī)

萝 **luó** TRAD 蘿 N trailing plant

萝卜 luóbo N turnip, radish, carrot (根 gēn, 个 gè)

白萝卜 bái luóbo turnip

红萝卜 hóng luóbo radish

胡萝卜 hú luóbo carrot

逻 **luó** v petrol

逻辑 luóji

逻辑 luóji N logic

骆 luò as in 骆驼 luòtuo

骆驼 luòtuo N camel (头 tóu)

络 luò TRAD 絡 N net

络绎不绝 luòyì bùjué ADV, ADJ in an endless stream, endless

落 luò V fall, drop

落成 luòchéng V (of a building or engineering project) be completed

落后 luòhòu ADJ backward, outdated

落实 luòshí V (of a policy or idea) be implemented, be fulfilled

落选 luòxuǎn V lose an election, fail to be chosen

M

妈 mā TRAD 媽 N ma, mom

妈妈 māma N mom, mommy

抹 mā V wipe, wipe off

抹桌子 mā zhuōzi wipe the table

抹布 mābù N rag (块 kuài)

麻 má I N hemp

麻袋 mádài sack (只 zhī)
II ADJ numb

麻痹 mábì I V benumb, lull II N paralysis

小儿麻痹症 xiǎoér mábìzhèng infantile paralysis

麻烦 máfan I V bother II ADJ troublesome, complicated

NOTE: 麻烦您 máfan nín is a polite expression to request somebody's service or to ask a favor: 麻烦您把盐递给我。 Máfan nín bǎ yán dì gei wǒ. *Please pass the salt [to me].*

麻将 májiàng N (the game) mahjong

打麻将 dǎ májiàng play mahjong

麻木 mámù ADJ unable to feel anything, numb

麻雀 máquè N sparrow (只 zhī)

麻醉 mázuì I V anesthetize II N anesthesia

麻醉师 mázuìshī anesthetist, anesthesiologist

局部麻醉 júbù mázuì localized anesthesia

全身麻醉 quánshēnmázuì general anesthesia

马 mǎ TRAD 馬 N horse (匹 pǐ)

马达 mǎdá N motor

马虎 mǎhu ADJ sloppy, careless

NOTE: 马马虎虎 mǎ-mǎ-hū-hū is a common idiomatic expression meaning *so-so, not too bad* or *just managing*. For example: "去年你考试成绩怎么样?" "马马虎虎。" "Qùnián nǐ kǎoshì chéngjì zénmeyàng?" "Mǎ-mǎ-hū-hū." *"How did you do in the exams last year?" "So-so."*

马力 mǎlì N horse power

马铃薯 mǎlíngshǔ N potato

马路 mǎlù N street, avenue (条 tiáo)

马路上 mǎlù shang in the street, on the road

过马路 guò mǎlù walk across a street

马上 mǎshàng IDIOM ADV at once, immediately

马戏 mǎxì N circus performance (场 cháng)

马戏团 mǎxìtuán circus

码 mǎ TRAD 碼 V stack up

码头 mǎtóu N dock, wharf

码头工人 mǎtóu gōngrén docker, longshoreman

蚂 mǎ TRAD 螞 as in 蚂蚁 mǎyǐ

蚂蚁 mǎyǐ ant (只 zhī)

骂 mà TRAD 罵 V curse, swear

嘛 ma PARTICLE surely, that goes without saying (used at the end of a sentence to indicate that the truth of the statement is obvious)

吗 ma TRAD 嗎 PARTICLE (used at the end of a sentence to turn it into a yes-or-no question)

118

埋 **mái** v bury

埋没 **máimò** v stifle (talent)

埋头 **máitóu** v devote wholeheartedly to, be engrossed in

埋头苦干 **máitóu kǔgàn** devote oneself to hard work without complaint and for a long time

买 **mǎi** TRAD 買 v buy

买卖 **mǎimai** N trade, business

做买卖 **zuò mǎimai** do business, be engaged in business

迈 **mài** TRAD 邁 v step forward

麦 **mài** TRAD 麥 N wheat (See 小麦 xiǎomài.)

卖 **mài** TRAD 賣 v sell

脉 **mài** TRAD 脈 N blood vessel

脉搏 **màibó** N pulse

埋 **mán** as in 埋怨 mányuàn

埋怨 **mányuàn** v blame, complain

瞒 **mán** TRAD 瞞 v conceal truth from

馒 **mán** as in 馒头 mántou

馒头 **mántou** N steamed bun (只 zhī)

蛮 **mán** TRAD 蠻 ADJ unrestrained and wild

蛮不讲理 **mán bù jiǎnglǐ** totally unreasonable and behaving atrociously

满 **mǎn** TRAD 滿 I ADJ 1 full, full to the brim 2 satisfied II v reach the limit

满额 **mǎn'é** ADJ reaching full quota

满意 **mǎnyì** ADJ satisfied, pleased

对…满意 **duì…mǎnyì** be satisfied with

满月 **mǎnyuè** I v (of a newborn baby) be one month old

满月酒 **mǎnyuè jiǔ** dinner party in celebration of a baby's first month II N full moon

满足 **mǎnzú** v meet the needs of, satisfy

慢 **màn** ADJ slow

慢性 **mànxìng** ADJ 1 (of diseases) chronic

慢性肝炎 **mànxìng gānyán** chronic hepatitis

2 Same as 慢性子 mànxìngzi

慢性子 **mànxìngzi** ADJ (of a person) slow or indolent

漫 **màn** v overflow (See 浪漫 làngmàn)

漫长 **màncháng** ADJ long, endless

蔓 **màn** as in 蔓延 mànyán

蔓延 **mànyán** v spread, extend

忙 **máng** ADJ busy

NOTE: When friends meet in China, a common conversation opener is: 你最近忙吗? Nǐ zuìjìn máng ma? *Have you been busy lately?*

忙碌 **mánglù** ADJ busy

忙忙碌碌 **mángmáng lùlù** very busy, always engaged in doing something

茫 **máng** ADJ boundless and indistinct

茫茫 **mángmáng** boundless and blurred, vast

茫然 **mángrán** ADJ knowing nothing about, ignorant, in the dark

盲 **máng** ADJ blind

盲从 **mángcóng** v follow blindly

盲人 **mángrén** N blind person

盲人学校 **mángrén xuéxiào** school for the blind

盲文 **mángwén** N braille

氓 **máng** N man (See 流氓 liúmáng)

猫 **māo** TRAD 貓 N cat (只 zhī)

猫头鹰 **māotóuyīng** N owl (只 zhī)

毛 1 **máo** N hair

羊毛 **yángmáo** wool

毛笔 **máobǐ** N traditional Chinese writing brush (支 zhī, 管 guǎn)

毛病 máobìng N **1** illness **2** trouble, breakdown

毛巾 máojīn N towel (条 tiáo)

毛衣 máoyī N woolen sweater, woolen pullover (件 jiàn)

毛 **2** máo **1** M. WD Same as 角 jiǎo **2** M WD. Used colloquially.

髦 máo N long hair (See 时髦 shímáo)

矛 máo N spear, lance

矛盾 máodùn **I** N contradiction, conflict **II** ADJ contradictory, inconsistent
自相矛盾 zìxiāng máodùn self-contradictory, inconsistent

NOTE: 矛盾 máodùn is a colorful word derived from an ancient Chinese fable. A man who sold spears (矛 máo) and shields (盾 dùn) boasted that his spears were so sharp that they could penetrate any shield, and that his shields were so strong that no spear could ever penetrate them. As there seemed to be a contradiction there, 矛盾 máodùn came to mean *inconsistency* or *contradiction*.

茅 máo N cogongrass

茅屋 máowū N thatched cottage (间 jiān)

茂 mào ADJ luxuriant

茂密 màomì ADJ (of vegetation) luxuriant, thick, dense

茂盛 màoshèng ADJ (of vegetation) luxuriant, lush

冒 mào V **1** emit, send forth, give off **2** risk **3** make false claims

冒牌 màopái V counterfeit, forge
冒牌货 màopáihuò (goods) counterfeit, fake, forgery

冒险 màoxiǎn V risk, take a risk

帽 mào N hat, cap

帽子 màozi N hat, cap (顶 dǐng)
戴帽子 dài màozi put on/wear a hat/cap
脱帽子 tuō màozi take off a hat/cap

贸 mào TRAD 貿 N trade

贸易 màoyì N trade, exchange
贸易公司 màoyì gōngsī trading company
对外贸易 duìwài màoyì foreign trade
国际贸易 guójì màoyì international trade

貌 mào N appearance (See 礼貌 lǐmào, 面貌 miànmào.)

么 me TRAD 麼 PARTICLE (used to form certain words) (See 多么 duōme, 那么 nàme, 什么 shénme, 为什么 wèishénme, 怎么 zěnme, 怎么样 zěnmeyàng, 这么 zhème.)

眉 méi N eyebrow

眉毛 méimao eyebrow

没 méi ADJ Same as 没有 méiyǒu, used colloquially.

没错 méicuò ADJ quite right

没关系 méi guānxi See 关系 guānxi.

没什么 méishénme IDIOM nothing serious, it doesn't matter

没说的 méishuōde ADJ above reproach, perfect

没意思 méi yìsi See 意思 yìsi.

没用 méiyòng ADJ useless

没有 méiyǒu **I** V **1** do not have **2** there is/are no **II** ADV did not, have not (indicating negation of past experiences, usually used before a verb or at the end of a question)

还没有 hái méiyǒu not yet

NOTE: In spoken Chinese, 没有 méiyǒu is often shortened to 没 méi, but it cannot be replaced by 没 méi if it is used at the end of a sentence. For example, you can say: 你去过中国没有? Nǐ qùguo Zhōngguó méiyǒu? but not 你去过中国没? Nǐ qùguo Zhōngguó méi?

枚 méi M. WD (for small objects, such as a coin)
一枚硬币 yìméi yìngbì a coin

玫 méi as in 玫瑰 méigui

玫瑰 méigui N rose (朵 duǒ)

两朵玫瑰花 liǎng duǒ méiguihuā two roses

一束玫瑰花 yí shù méiguihuā a bouquet of roses

煤 **méi** N coal

煤矿 méikuàng coal mine

煤矿工 méikuànggōng coal miner, collier

煤气 méiqì coal gas

煤田 méitián coalfield

媒 **méi** N **1** matchmaking

媒人 méirén matchmaker

2 go-between, intermediary

媒介 méijiè N medium

媒体 méitǐ N medium

大众媒体 dàzhòng méitǐ mass media

梅 **méi** N plum tree

梅花 méihuā plum blossom

NOTE: 梅花 méihuā is unique to China, as you cannot find this flower in other parts of the world. Therefore, though conventionally translated as *plum*, it is actually not the same thing.

酶 **méi** N enzyme

霉 **méi** N mold, mildew

发霉 fā méi go moldy

每 **méi** I ADV every, each II PRON every, each

NOTE: Usage in Chinese requires that 每 měi is followed by 都 dōu *all*, without exception: 你每天都看电视吗? Nǐ měitiān dōu kàn diànshì ma? *Do you watch TV every day?*

美 **měi** ADJ beautiful

美德 měidé N virtue, moral excellence

美观 měiguān ADJ pleasing to the eye

美国 Měiguó N the U.S.A., America

美好 měihǎo ADJ (of abstract things) fine, beautiful

美丽 měilì ADJ beautiful

美满 měimǎn ADJ (of marriage, family, etc.) totally satisfactory, happy

美妙 měimiào ADJ wonderful, splendid

美容 měiróng I V make one's skin and face more beautiful II N comestics

美容师 měiróngshī beautician

美容院 měiróngyuàn beauty salon, beauty parlor

美术 měishù N fine arts

美术馆 měishùguǎn gallery, art museum

美术家 měishùjiā artist

美元 Měiyuán N U.S. dollar, greenback

美中不足 měi-zhōng-bù-zú IDIOM a blemish in something otherwise perfect

美洲 Měizhōu N continent of America, America

镁 **měi** TRAD 鎂 N magnesium (Mg)

妹 **mèi** N younger sister

妹妹 mèimei younger sister

昧 **mèi** ADJ ignorant (See 愚昧 yúmèi)

闷 **mēn** TRAD 悶 ADJ stuffy, close

门 **1 mén** TRAD 門 N door, gate (道 dào)

大门 dàmén gate

门口 ménkǒu N doorway, by the door, by the gate

门市部 ménshìbù N sales department

门诊 ménzhěn N outpatient service

门诊部 ménzhěnbù outpatient department (of a hospital)

门 **2 mén** TRAD 門 M. WD (for school subjects, languages, etc.)

闷 **mén** TRAD 悶 ADJ in low spirits, lonely, depressed

们 **men** TRAD 們 SUFFIX (indicating plural number)

NOTE: As a plural number marker, 们 men is only used with nouns denoting people. It is not used when there are words indicating plurality, such as numbers or words like 一些 yìxiē, 很多 hěn duō. In many cases, the plural number of a personal noun is implicit without the use of 们 men. In the example sentence, 们 men is not obligatory, i.e. 学生都 很喜欢这位新老师。Xuéshēng dōu hěn xǐhuan zhè wèi xīn lǎoshī. *All the students like this new teacher.* is correct and idiomatic.

蒙 **méng** V cover

檬 **méng** as in 柠檬 níngméng

萌 **méng** V sprout

萌芽 méngyá V sprout, bud, shoot forth

盟 **méng** N alliance

结盟 jiéméng forge an alliance, form an alliance
盟国 méngguó N ally (country)

猛 **měng** ADJ fierce, violent

猛烈 měngliè ADJ fierce, furious

梦 **mèng** TRAD 夢 **I** N dream

做梦 zuòmèng have a dream
II V dream, have a dream
梦想 mèngxiǎng V dream of, have a pipe dream

眯 **mī** V narrow one's eyes

迷 **mí** V be lost, be deluded

迷糊 míhu ADJ **1** (of vision) blurred **2** muddle-headed
迷惑 míhuò V **1** puzzle, be puzzled **2** delude, be deluded
迷失 míshī V lose one's bearings
迷失方向 míshī fāngxiàng lose one's bearings
迷信 míxìn N superstition

谜 **mí** TRAD 謎 N riddle

谜语 míyǔ N riddle
猜谜语 (猜谜) cāi míyǔ (cāi mí) guess a riddle

弥 **mí** TRAD 彌 ADJ full, overflowing

弥补 míbǔ V make up, remedy
弥漫 mímàn ADJ fill (the air)

米¹ **mǐ** M. WD meter (colloquial)

一米 yì mǐ one meter
三米半 sān mǐ bàn three and half meters

NOTE: The formal word for meter is 公尺 gōngchǐ.

米² **mǐ** N rice, paddy rice (粒 lì)

米饭 mǐfàn N cooked rice (碗 wǎn)

NOTE: The staple food for southern Chinese (Chinese living south of the Yangtze River) is 米饭 mǐfàn and northern Chinese mainly eat 面食 miànshí (food made of wheat flour), such as 面条儿 miàntiáor (noodles), 馒头 mántou (steamed buns).

米酒 mǐjiǔ N rice wine

秘 **mì** ADJ secret

秘密 mìmì **I** N secret **II** ADJ secret, confidential
秘密警察 mìmì jǐngchá secret police
秘密文件 mìmì wénjiàn classified document
秘书 mìshū N secretary
私人秘书 sīrén mìshū private secretary

泌 **mì** V secrete (See 分泌 fēnmì)

密 **mì** ADJ close, dense

密度 mìdù N density, thickness
密封 mìfēng V seal, seal up
密切 mìqiè ADJ close, intimate

蜜 **mì** N honey

蜜蜂 mìfēng N bee (只 zhī)

棉 **mián** N cotton

棉花 miánhua N cotton
棉衣 miányī N cotton-padded jacket (件 jiàn)
棉大衣 miándàyī cotton-padded overcoat

绵 **mián** TRAD 綿 N silk floss

绵羊 **miányáng** sheep (只 zhī)

眠 **mián** V sleep (See 睡眠 shuìmián)

免 **miǎn** V avoid, do without

免除 **miǎnchú** V be free from, be exempt from

免得 **miǎnde** CONJ so as not to, lest

免费 **miǎnfèi** ADJ free of charge, free

勉 **miǎn** V 1 strive 2 encourage, exhort 3 force

勉励 **miǎnlì** V encourage, urge

勉强 **miǎnqiǎng** I ADV grudgingly, barely II V force to do

面 1 **miàn** N 1 face 2 (maths) surface

面对 **miànduì** V be faced with

面对一个复杂的问题 **miànduì yí ge fùzá de wèntí** be faced with a complicated problem

面簿 **miànbù** N (social networking tool) Facebook

面积 **miànjī** N (mathematics) area

面孔 **miànkǒng** N (human) face, facial features

面临 **miànlín** V be faced with, be up against

面临新的挑战 **miànlín xīn de tiǎozhàn** be up against a new challenge

面貌 **miànmào** N appearance, state (of things)

面面俱到 **miànmiàn jùdào** IDIOM cover every aspect (of a matter)

面目 **miànmù** N appearance, look

面前 **miànqián** N in the face of, in front of, before

面容 **miànróng** N facial features

面子 **miànzi** N face, honor

爱面子 **ài miànzi** be keen on face-saving

丢面子 **diū miànzi** lose face (=丢脸 diūliǎn)

给…留面子 **gěi...liú miànzi** save face (for somebody)

面 2 **miàn** TRAD 麵 N 1 (面条儿 miàntiáor) noodle

方便面 **fāngbiàn miàn** instant noodles 2 wheat flour

和面 **huómiàn** knead dough

面包 **miànbāo** N bread (片 piàn, 只 zhī, 条 tiáo)

一片面包 **yípiàn miànbāo** a slice of bread

面包车 **miànbāochē** N minibus, van (辆 liàng)

面包房 **miànbāo fáng** bakery

面粉 **miànfěn** N flour

面条儿 **miàntiáor** N noodles (碗 wǎn)

面 3 **miàn** M. WD (for flat objects)

一面镜子 **yí miàn jìngzi** a mirror

两面旗子 **liǎng miàn qízi** two flags

苗 **miáo** N seedling

描 **miáo** V trace, copy

描绘 **miáohuì** V depict, describe

描述 **miáoshù** V describe, give an account of

描写 **miáoxiě** V describe (in writing)

秒 **miǎo** M. WD (of time) second

缈 **miǎo** ADJ distant and indistinct

渺小 **miáoxiǎo** ADJ tiny, insignificant

妙 **miào** ADJ wonderful, ingenious

不妙 **búmiào** not good, unpromising

妙不可言 **miào bùkěyán** IDIOM so wonderful as to beg description

庙 **miào** TRAD 廟 N temple (座 zuò)

灭 **miè** TRAD 滅 V extinguish, put out, go out

灭火器 **mièhuǒqì** N fire extinguisher

灭亡 **mièwáng** V exterminate, be exterminated, become extinct

蔑 **miè** V disdain, smear

蔑视 **mièshì** V look upon with contempt

民 **mín** N 1 people 2 civilian

民兵 **mínbīng** N militia

民航 mínháng N civil aviation
民间 mínjiān ADJ 1 among common folks
民间故事 mínjiān gùshì folk tale
2 people-to-people
民间往来 mínjiān wǎnglái people-to-people exchange
民生 mínshēng N the people's (economic) life, economy
民事 mínshì ADJ (of law) civil
民事案件 mínshì ànjiàn civil case
民意 mínyì N the will of the masses
民意调查 mínyì diàochá opinion poll
民用 mínyòng ADJ for civilian use
民众 mínzhòng N the masses of the people
民主 mínzhǔ I N democracy II ADJ democratic
民族 mínzú N ethnic group, nationality (个 gè)
少数民族 shǎoshù mínzú minority ethnic group
多民族文化 duō mínzú wénhuà multi-culturalism

敏 mǐn ADJ quick, agile

敏感 mǐngǎn ADJ sensitive
敏捷 mǐnjié ADJ agile, nimble
敏锐 mǐnruì ADJ alert, sharp-witted

名 1 míng N 1 name 2 (personal) given name 3 reputation
出名 chūmíng become famous
国名 guómíng name of a country

名 2 míng M. WD (used for people, esp. those with a specific position or occupation)
一名军人 yì míng jūnrén a soldier
两名学生 liǎng míng xuésheng two students
名称 míngchēng N (non-personal) name
公司的名称 gōngsī de míngchēng company name
名单 míngdān N name list, roll (张 zhāng, 份 fèn)
学生名单 xuésheng míngdān class roll
名额 míng'é N the number of people assigned or allowed for a particular purpose, quota of people

大学招生名额 dàxué zhāoshēng míng'é university enrolment quota
名副其实 míngfùqíshí IDIOM be worthy of the name
名副其实的好老师 míngfùqíshí de hǎo lǎoshī a good teacher in every sense of the word
名贵 míngguì ADJ precious, of great value
名牌 míngpái N famous brand, branded name
名人 míngrén N famous person, well-known personality
名声 míngshēng N reputation
破坏我们的名声 pòhuài wǒmende míngshēng smear our reputation
名胜 míngshèng N famous scenic spot
名义 míngyì N name, capacity
以我个人的名义 yǐ wǒ gèrén de míngyì in my own name
以总经理代表的名义 yǐ zǒngjīnglǐ dàibiǎo de míngyì in the capacity of the representative of the CEO
名誉 míngyù N reputation, honor
名誉博士 míngyù bóshì honorary doctorate
恢复名誉 huīfù míngyù restore one's honor
名字 míngzi N name, given name

NOTE: To be exact, 名字 míngzi only means *given name*, but informally 名字 míngzi may also mean *full name* (family name + given name). The formal word for *full name* is 姓名 xìngmíng. See 姓 xìng.

明 míng ADJ bright

明白 míngbai I ADJ clear, obvious II V understand, see the point
明亮 míngliàng ADJ bright, well-lit
明明 míngmíng ADV clearly, obviously, as clear as day
明年 míngnián N next year

NOTE: 明年 míngnián is next year relative only to this year 今年 jīnnián. For the year after another year, we use 第二年 dì-èr nián or 下一年 xià yì nián. For

example: 他们在2007年结婚，第二年生了一个儿子。Tāmen zài èr-líng-líng-qī nián jiéhūn, dì-èr nián shēngle yí ge érzi.
They married in 2007 and had a son the following year. It would be wrong to use 明年 míngnián in this example.

明确 míngquè **I** ADJ definite and explicit **II** V make definite and explicit

明天 míngtiān N tomorrow

明显 míngxiǎn ADJ obvious, apparent, evident

明信片 míngxìnpiàn N postcard (张 zhāng)

明星 míngxīng N movie star, star
体育明星 tǐyù míngxīng sports star

鸣 míng TRAD 鳴 V (of bird) chirp, crow
耳鸣 ěrmíng ringing in the ears

命 mìng N 1 life 2 fate, destiny
命令 mìnglìng N, V order
命名 mìngmíng V give a name to, name
命题 mìngtí V set a question for an examination, assign a subject or topic for writing
命运 mìngyùn N fate, destiny

谬 miù ADJ mistaken, absurd
谬论 miùlùn N fallacy, spurious argument
谬误 miùwù N mistake, error

摸 mō V 1 touch 2 grope
摸索 mōsuǒ V grope, search for, explore

模 mó **I** N model, copy **II** V imitate
模特儿(模特) mótèr (mótè) N (fashion) model
模范 mófàn N good example, model
模仿 mófǎng V imitate, ape, be a copycat
模型 móxíng N copy, model

膜 mó N membrane
塑料薄膜 sùliào bómó plastic film

磨 mó V 1 grind
磨刀 módāo sharpen a knife
2 rub, wear 3 waste time

磨时间 móshíjiān stall, kill time

磨洋工 móyánggōng IDIOM loaf during working hours, stage a slow-down

蘑 mó N mushroom
蘑菇 mógu mushroom

摩 mó V rub, scrape
摩擦 mócā **I** V rub **II** N friction, clash
和同事发生摩擦 hé tóngshì fāshēng mócā generate friction among colleagues
摩托车 mótuōchē N motorcycle (辆 liàng)

魔 mó **I** N demon, monster **II** ADJ magic
魔鬼 móguǐ N monster, demon (个 gè)
魔术 móshù N magic
魔术师 móshùshī magician
变魔术 biàn móshù do magic (as entertainment)

抹 mǒ V 1 apply by smearing 2 strike out, erase
抹杀 mǒshā V totally ignore (one's merit, achievement, etc.)

莫 mò V don't
莫名其妙 mòmíng qímiào IDIOM be utterly baffled

漠 mò N desert (See 沙漠 shāmò.)

寞 mò ADJ silent, desolate (See 寂寞 jìmò)

末 mò N end (See 周末 zhōumò)

沫 mò N foam, froth
啤酒沫 píjiǔmò beer froth
肥皂沫 féizàomò soap suds, lather

墨 mò N ink
墨水 mòshuǐ N ink

默 mò ADJ silent
默默 mòmò ADV quietly, silently

陌 mò N path
陌生 mòshēng ADJ unfamiliar

陌生人 mòshēngrén stranger

谋 móu TRAD 謀 v plot, plan

谋害 móuhài v plot to murder

谋求 móuqiú v seek, be in quest of

谋求最大利润 móuqiú zuìdà lìrùn seek the maximum profits

某 mǒu PRON certain (used to denote an indefinite person or thing, usually in writing)

某人 mǒurén N certain person, certain people, somebody

某事 mǒushì N certain thing or event, something

某些 mǒuxiē PRON some, certain ones

模 mú N mould, matrix

模样 múyàng I N appearance, look II ADV approximately, about

母 mǔ I ADJ 1 maternal, of a mother 2 female (of certain animals) II N mother

母亲 mǔqīn N mother

母亲节 Mǔqīnjié Mother's Day

母性 mǔxìng N maternal instinct

母语 mǔyǔ N mother tongue

姆 mǔ N woman tutor (See 保姆 bǎomǔ)

拇 mǔ N thumb

拇指 mǔzhǐ thumb

亩 mǔ TRAD 畝 M. WD (a traditional Chinese unit of area, especially in farming: 1 mu is equivalent to 1/15 hectare, about 667 square meters)

十亩地(田) shí mǔ dì (tián) 10 mu of ground (paddy fields/farmland)

木 mù N 1 Same as 木头 mùtou 2 tree

木材 mùcái N timber, wood

木匠 mùjiang N carpenter

木头 mùtou N wood, timber

目 mù N eye

双目失明 shuāngmù shīmíng having lost sight in both eyes, be blind

目标 mùbiāo N target, objective, goal

目的 mùdì N aim, purpose

目睹 mùdǔ V see with one's own eyes, witness

目光 mùguāng N sight, vision

目光远大 mùguāng yuǎndà farseeing, farsighted and ambitious

目录 mùlù N catalog

产品目录 chǎnpǐn mùlù product catalog

图书目录 túshū mùlù library catalog

目前 mùqián N at present

目中无人 mùzhōng wúrén IDIOM believe no one is better than oneself; overweening, conceited and arrogant

暮 mù I N dusk, evening twilight II ADJ late

暮年 mùnián old age

慕 mù V admire (See 羡慕 xiànmù)

慕名 mùmíng V be attacted by somebody's reputation

慕名而来 mùmíng érlái come out of admiration

墓 mù N tomb

公墓 gōngmù cemetery

墓地 mùdì N graveyard

幕 mù N curtain, screen

谢幕 xièmù answer a curtain call

穆 mù ADJ solemn

穆斯林 Mùsīlín N Muslim

牧 mù I V herd (cattle, horses, etc.)

牧羊 mùyáng herd sheep

II N animal husbandry

牧场 mùchǎng N grazing land, pastureland

牧民 mùmín N herdsmen

牧区 mùqū N pastoral area

牧业 mùyè N animal husbandry

睦 mù ADJ peaceful, harmonious

睦邻 mùlín N good neighborhood

N

拿 ná I v hold, carry in hand II PREP regarding, as to
拿…来说 ná...láishuō v take ... for example
拿手 náshǒu ADJ very good at, adept at
拿手好戏 náshǒu hǎoxì something that one is adept at, one's favorite game
拿主意 ná zhǔyi v make a decision
拿走 ná zǒu v take away, remove

哪 nǎ PRON 1 which 2 whatever, whichever
哪里 nǎli ADV where

NOTE: 哪里哪里 nǎli nǎli is an idiomatic expression used as a modest reply to a compliment, e.g.: "你汉字写得真漂亮。" "哪里哪里。" "Nǐ Hànzì xiě de zhēn piàoliang." "Nǎli, nǎli." "You write beautiful Chinese characters." "Thank you."

哪怕 nǎpà CONJ even if, even though

NOTE: 哪怕 nǎpà introduces an exaggerated, rather unlikely situation to emphasize the statement of a sentence.

哪儿 nǎr ADV Same as 哪里 nǎli. Used colloquially.
哪些 nǎxiē PRON the plural form of 哪 nǎ

那 nà I PRON that II Same as 那么 nàme
那个 nàge PRON that one
那里 nàli ADV there, over there

NOTES: (1) 那里 nàli is used after a personal noun or pronoun to make it a place word, as a personal noun or pronoun cannot be used immediately after a preposition, e.g.: 我从张小姐听到这个消息。Wǒ cóng Zhāng xiǎojiě tīngdao zhège xiāoxi. is incorrect. 那里 nàli must be added after 张小姐 Zhāng xiǎojiě (Miss Zhang): 我从张小姐那里听到这个消息。Wǒ cóng Zhāng xiǎojiě nàli tīngdao zhège xiāoxi. I learned the news from Miss Zhang. In this case 张小姐那里 Zhāng xiǎojiě nàli becomes a place word which can occur after

the preposition 从 cóng. (2) Colloquially, 那儿 nàr may replace 那里 nàli.

那么 nàme I ADV like that II CONJ in that case, then

NOTE: Although 那么 nàme as a conjunction is glossed as in that case, then, Chinese speakers tend to use it much more than English speakers use "in that case" or "then." In colloquial Chinese 那么 nàme is often shortened to 那 nà, e.g.: 你不喜欢吃米饭，那吃面包吧。Nǐ bù xǐhuan chī mǐfàn, nà chī miànbāo ba. You don't like rice; in that case eat bread.

那儿 nàr PRON Same as 那里 nàli, used colloquially.
那些 nàxiē PRON those
那样 nàyàng ADV Same as 那么 nàme I ADV

纳 nà v pay, offer
纳闷儿 nàmènr v be wondering (why, what, who, how, etc.), be perplexed
纳税 nàshuì v pay taxes
纳税人 nàshuìrén tax-payer

奶 nǎi N milk
奶粉 nǎifěn N milk powder
奶奶 nǎinai N paternal grandmother, granny

NOTE: The formal word for paternal grandmother is 祖母 zǔmǔ and that for maternal grandmother is 外祖母 wàizǔmǔ. While 奶奶 nǎinai is the colloquialism for 祖母 zǔmǔ, that for 外祖母 wàizǔmǔ is 姥姥 lǎolao, or 外婆 wàipó.

奶油 nǎiyóu N cream

耐 nài v able to endure
耐烦 nàifán ADJ patient

NOTE: 耐烦 nàifán is only used in its negative form, 不耐烦 bú nàifán.

耐力 nàilì N endurance, staying power
耐心 nàixīn I ADJ patient II N patience
耐用 nàiyòng ADJ durable

男 nán

男 nán ADJ (of humans) male

男孩子 nán háizi boy
男青年 nán qīngnián young man
男人 nánrén man, men
男生 nánshēng N male student/pupil
男性 nánxìng N the male gender, male
男子 nánzǐ N male adult
　大男子主义 dànánzǐzhǔyì male chauvinisim
男子汉 nánzǐhàn N **1** man, men **2** hero

南 nán

南 nán N south, southern

南边 nánbian N south side, to the south, in the south
南部 nánbù N southern region (of a country)
南方 nánfāng N the southern part, the south of a country
南方人 nánfāngrén southerner
南面 nánmiàn N Same as 南边 nánbian

难 nán

难 nán TRAD 難 ADJ difficult

难产 nánchǎn N difficult childbirth, difficult labor
难道 nándào ADV (used at the beginning of a sentence or before a verb to make it a rhetorical question)
难得 nándé ADJ hard to come by, rare
难度 nándù N degree of difficulty
难怪 nánguài ADV no wonder
难关 nánguān N critical moment, crisis
　度过难关 dùguò nánguān go through a crisis
难过 nánguò ADJ sad, grieved

NOTE: 难过 nánguò is usually used as a predicate, and seldom as an attribute.

难堪 nánkān ADJ embarrassed, embarrassing
　难堪的局面 nánkān de júmiàn embarrassing situation, awkward plight
难看 nánkàn ADJ ugly
难免 nánmiǎn ADJ hardly avoidable
难受 nánshòu ADJ **1** feeling ill, uncomfortable **2** feeling sorry, feeling bad/sad

难题 nántí N difficult issue, insoluble problem
难以 nányǐ ADV difficult to
　难以理解 nányǐ lǐjiě difficult to understand, incomprehensible

难 nàn

难 nàn TRAD 難 N disaster, adversity

逃难 táonàn flee from war or natural disaster
难民 nànmín N refugee
难民营 nànmínyíng refugee camp

囊 náng

囊 náng N bag, pocket

挠 náo

挠 náo V scratch

挠痒痒 náoyǎngyang scratch at an itch

脑 nǎo

脑 nǎo TRAD 腦 N brain

脑外科 nǎo wàikē brain surgery
脑袋 nǎodai N Same as 头 tóu. Used only colloquially and in a derogatory sense.
脑筋 nǎojīn N brains, mental capacity
　动脑筋 dòng nǎojīn rack one's brains
脑力 nǎolì N brain power
　脑力劳动 nǎolì láodòng mental work
脑子 nǎozi N brain, mind
　动脑子 dòng nǎozi use brains

恼 nǎo

恼 nǎo ADJ irritated, vexed (See 烦恼 fánnǎo)

恼火 nǎohuǒ ADJ annoyed, angry

闹 nào

闹 nào TRAD 鬧 V make trouble, cause a disturbance

闹脾气 nào píqi V throw a tantrum
闹事 nào shì V make trouble, provoke a disturbance
闹笑话 nào xiàohua V make a fool of oneself, cut a ridiculous figure

呢 ne

呢 ne PARTICLE **1** (used at the end of a question to soften the tone of an enquiry) **2** How about ...? Where is (are) ...?

那 nèi

那 nèi Same as 那 nà. Used colloquially.

内 nèi

内 nèi N inside, within

内部 nèibù N interior, inside
内部资料 nèibù zīliào document for

internal circulation (e.g. within a government department)

内地 **nèidì** N the interior part (of a country), inland

内阁 **nèigé** N (government) cabinet

内行 **nèiháng** N expert, professional

内科 **nèikē** N department of internal medicine (in a hospital)

内幕 **nèimù** N inside story

内容 **nèiróng** N content, substance

内心 **nèixīn** N one's heart of hearts, one's inner world

内在 **nèizài** ADJ inherent, intrinsic

内脏 **nèizàng** N internal organs

内战 **nèizhàn** N civil war

内政 **nèizhèng** N internal affairs, domestic affairs

干涉内政 gānshè nèizhèng interfere in the internal affairs (of another country)

嫩 **nèn** ADJ young and tender, tender

能 **néng** I MODAL V can, be able to II N energy

NOTE: See note on 会 huì *modal verb*.

能干 **nénggàn** ADJ (of people) able, capable, efficient

能歌善舞 **nénggēshànwǔ** IDIOM be good at singing and dancing

能够 **nénggòu** MODAL V Same as 能 néng MODAL V

能力 **nénglì** N ability

能量 **néngliàng** N energy, capabilities

能手 **néngshǒu** N expert, dab hand

能源 **néngyuán** N energy resources

嗯 **ng** INTERJ (used after a question to reinforce questioning)

尼 **ní** N Buddhist nun

尼庵 **ní'ān** Buddhist nunnery

尼姑 **nígū** Buddhist nun

尼龙 **nílóng** N nylon

泥 **ní** N mud

泥泞 **nínìng** ADJ muddy, miry

泥土 **nítǔ** N soil, earth, clay

拟 **nǐ** TRAD 擬 V draw up, draft

拟订 **nǐdìng** V draw up, work out

拟订计划 **nǐdìng jìhuà** draw up a plan

你 **nǐ** PRON you (singular)

你们 **nǐmen** PRON you (plural)

你们好! Nǐmen hǎo! Hello!

逆 **nì** ADJ contrary, counter

逆流 **nìliú** N adverse current (of water)

年 **nián** N year (no measure word required)

今年 jīnnián this year

明年 míngnián next year

去年 qùnián last year

NOTE: No measure word is used with 年 nián, e.g. 一年 yì nián (one year), 两年 liǎng nián (two years).

年代 **niándài** N a decade of a century

年度 **niándù** I N year

财务年度 cáiwù niándù fiscal year

II ADJ annual

年度报表 niándù bàobiǎo annual report

年级 **niánjí** N grade (in school)

年纪 **niánjì** N age

NOTE: 您多大年纪了? Nín duōdà niánjì le? is an appropriate way to ask the age of an elderly person. To ask a young child his/her age, the question should be: 你几岁了? Nǐ jǐ suì le? For people who are neither children nor elderly, the question to use is: 你多大岁数? Nǐ duō dà suìshù?

年龄 **niánlíng** N age (of a person or other living things)

年轻 **niánqīng** ADJ young

年轻人 **niánqīngrén** young person, youth

撵 **niǎn** TRAD 攆 V drive away, oust

捻 **niǎn** V twist with the fingers

念 **niàn** I V 1 read, read aloud 2 study (in a school) II N idea, thought

NOTE: See note on 读 dú.

念头 niàntou N idea, thought

娘 niáng N 1 mom, ma (used in the northern dialect) 2 girl (See 姑娘 gūniang.)

酿 niàng TRAD 釀 V brew, make (wine)

酿酒 niàngjiǔ make wine

鸟 niǎo TRAD 鳥 N bird (只 zhī)

尿 niào N urine

撒尿 sāniào piss, pee, go pee

NOTE: 撒尿 sāniào is a vulgar or childish word for *urinate*. The formal word for *urinate* is 小便 xiǎopiàn.

捏 niē V 1 mold, knead 2 make up, fabricate

捏造 niēzào V fabricate, make up

您 nín PRON you (honorific)

NOTE: 您 nín is the honorific form of 你 nǐ. Use 您 nín when respect or deference is called for. Normally, 您 nín does not have a plural form. 您们 nínmen is absolutely unacceptable in spoken Chinese, and only marginally so in written Chinese. To address more than one person politely, you can say 您两位 nín liǎng wèi (two people), 您三位 nín sān wèi (three people), or 您几位 nín jǐ wèi (several people).

凝 níng V curdle, coagulate

凝结 níngjié V (of gas or hot air) condense
凝视 níngshì V look at steadily and for a long time, gaze fixedly, stare

宁 níng TRAD 寧 ADJ peaceful, tranquil

宁静 níngjìng ADJ tranquil and peaceful, serene

柠 níng TRAD 檸 as in 柠檬 níngméng

柠檬 níngméng N lemon (只 zhī)

拧 níng TRAD 擰 V wring, twist

拧毛巾 níng máojīn wring a towel

拧 nǐng TRAD 擰 V screw, wrench

拧螺丝 nǐng luósī turn a screw (to tighten or loosen it)

泞 nìng TRAD 濘 as in 泥泞 nínìng

宁 nìng TRAD 寧 MODAL V would rather

宁死不屈 nìng sǐ bù qū would rather die than succumb

宁可 nìngkě MODAL V Same as 宁肯 nìngkěn
宁肯 nìngkěn MODAL V would rather

NOTE: As is shown in the example sentence, 宁肯 nìngkěn is often used alongside with 也 yě: 她宁肯走去，也不搭他的车。 Tā nìngkěn zǒuqù, yě bù dā tāde chē. *She would rather walk there than go in his car.*

宁愿 nìngyuàn MODAL V Same as 宁肯 nìngkěn

牛 niú V ox, cow (头 tóu)

牛奶 niúnǎi cow's milk, milk
牛肉 niúròu beef
公牛 gōng niú bull
黄牛 huángniú ox
奶牛 nǎiniú cow
水牛 shuǐniú water buffalo
小牛 xiǎo niú calf

NOTE: In the Chinese context, the ox (黄牛 huángniú) and the water buffalo (水牛 shuǐniú) are more important than the milk cow (奶牛 nǎiniú).

扭 niǔ V turn (one's head, back, etc.)

扭转 niǔzhuǎn V turn around, reverse

纽 niǔ TRAD 紐 N knob, button

纽扣 niǔkòu N button (颗 kē, 个 gè)

农 nóng TRAD 農 N farming

农产品 nóngchǎnpǐn N farm produce
农场 nóngchǎng N farm
农场主 nóngchǎngzhǔ farmer

农村 nóngcūn N farming area, rural area, countryside

农户 nónghù N rural household

农具 nóngjù N farm implements

农贸市场 nóngmào shìchǎng N farm produce market

农民 nóngmín N peasant, farmer

农田 nóngtián N farm land

农药 nóngyào N agricultural chemical, pesticide

农业 nóngyè N agriculture

农作物 nóngzuòwù N agricultural crop

浓 nóng TRAD 濃 ADJ (of gas/liquid) thick, dense, concentrated

浓厚 nónghòu ADJ **1** (of smoke, cloud, etc.) thick **2** (of atmosphere, interest, etc.) strong, heavy

弄 nòng V **1** do, manage, get … done **2** fool with

弄虚作假 nòngxū zuòjiǎ IDIOM use deception, practice fraud

奴 nú N slave

奴隶 núlì N slave

奴役 núyì V enslave

努 nǔ V work hard

努力 nǔlì ADJ making great efforts

怒 nù ADJ angry, outraged

怒吼 nùhǒu N angry roar

怒火 nùhuǒ N fury

女 nǚ ADJ (of humans) female

女孩子 nǚ háizi girl

女青年 nǚ qīngnián young woman

女生 nǚshēng female student

女儿 nǚ'ér N daughter (个 gè)

女人 nǚrén N woman, adult woman

女士 nǚshì N (respectful form of address or reference to a woman) Madam, Ms, lady

女子 nǚzǐ N female adult

暖 nuǎn ADJ warm

暖和 nuǎnhuo ADJ pleasantly warm

暖瓶 nuǎnpíng N thermos bottle (只 zhī)

暖气 nuǎnqì N central heating

暖水瓶 nuǎnshuǐpíng N Same as 暖瓶 nuǎnpíng

挪 nuó V move, shift

挪用 nuóyòng V divert (funds)

挪用公款 nuóyòng gōngkuǎn misappropriate public funds

O

噢 ō INTERJ (used to indicate understanding or a promise)

哦 ó INTERJ (used to indicate doubt)

欧 ōu TRAD 歐 N Europe

欧元 Ōuyuán N Euro

欧洲 Ōuzhōu N Europe

殴 ōu TRAD 毆 V beat up (people)

殴打 ōudǎ V beat up (people)

呕 ǒu TRAD 嘔 V vomit

呕吐 ǒutù V vomit, be sick

偶 ¹ ǒu ADV **1** occasionally

偶尔 ǒu'ěr occasionally, once in a while **2** accidentally

偶然 ǒurán accidentally, by chance

偶 ² ǒu N even number

偶数 ǒushù even number

P

趴 pā V lie on one's stomach

爬 pá V crawl, climb

爬行 páxíng V crawl, creep

爬行动物 páxíng dòngwù reptile

扒 pá V rake up

扒手 páshǒu N pickpocket

怕 pà I v fear, be afraid II ADV Same as 恐怕 kǒngpà, but with less force.

拍 pāi v pat, clap

拍马屁 pāi mǎpì v flatter sickeningly, lick the boots of

拍卖 pāimài v auction, sell at a reduced price

拍摄 pāishè v take a photo, shoot (a movie)

拍手 pāishǒu v clap, applaud

拍照 pāizhào v take photos, have one's photo taken

拍子 pāizi N **1** bat, racket

乒乓球拍子 pīngpāngqiú pāizi table tennis racket

羽毛球拍子 yǔmáoqiúpāi zi tennis racket **2** measurement of musical time, beat, time

打拍子 dǎpāizi beat time

排 pái I v **1** arrange in a definite order **2** reject, expel II N **1** row, rank **2** (army) platoon

排长 páizhǎng platoon leader

III M. WD (for things arranged in a row)

一排椅子 yì pái yǐzi a row of chairs

排斥 páichì v expel, reject

排除 páichú v rule out, eliminate

排除这种可能性 páichú zhè zhǒng kěnéngxìng rule out this possibility

排除障碍 páichú zhàng'ài surmount an obstacle

排队 páiduì v form a line, line up, queue up

排挤 páijǐ v elbow out, push aside, squeeze out

排列 páiliè v arrange, put in order

按字母顺序排列 àn zìmǔ shùnxù páiliè arrange in alphabetical order

排球 páiqiú N volleyball (只 zhī)

徘 pái v as in 徘徊 páihuái

徘徊 páihuái v pace up and down, move hesitantly

牌 1 pái N playing cards (张 zhāng, 副 fù)

打牌 dǎpái play cards

发牌 fāpái deal cards

洗牌 xǐpái shuffle cards

牌 2 pái N brand name, brand

名牌 míngpái famous brand, branded name

牌子 páizi N **1** signboard (块 kuài) **2** brand, brand name

派 1 pài I v **1** dispatch **2** assign (a job)

派 2 pài N faction, school (of thought)

保守派 bǎoshǒupài the conservative faction, conservatives

派别 pàibié N faction, group, school (of thought)

派出所 pàichūsuǒ N police station

派对 pàiduì N (social) party

NOTE: 派对 pàiduì is a transliteration of (social) party, used among urban fashionable people. 聚会 jùhuì is a more formal word.

派遣 pàiqiǎn v send, dispatch (troops, formal delegate, etc.)

攀 pān v climb

攀登 pāndēng v climb, scale

盘 pán TRAD 盤 N dish, plate

盘子 pánzi plate, dish, tray (只 zhī)

盘旋 pánxuán v (of a bird or airplane) spiral, circle

判 pàn v judge, distinguish

判处 pànchǔ v (in a law court) sentence

判处无期徒刑 pànchǔ wúqí túxíng sentenced to life imprisonment

判定 pàndìng v decide, come to a conclusion

判断 pànduàn I v judge, decide II N judgment, verdict

判决 pànjué N court decision, judgment

盼 pàn v expect, hope for

盼望 pànwàng v look forward to, long for

畔 pàn N (river, lake, etc.) side, bank

叛 **pàn** v betray, revolt

叛变 **pànbiàn** v turn traitor, become a turncoat

叛徒 **pàntú** N traitor, turncoat

旁 **páng** N side

旁边 **pángbiān** N side

旁观 **pángguān** v look on, observe

庞 **páng** TRAD 龐 ADJ huge

庞大 **pángdà** ADJ huge, enormous

胖 **pàng** ADJ fat, plump

胖子 **pàngzi** N fat person, "fatty"

抛 **pāo** v throw, hurl

抛弃 **pāoqì** v abandon, forsake

刨 **páo** v dig, unearth, excavate

袍 **páo** N gown, robe

袍子 **páozi** gown, robe

跑 **pǎo** v run

跑步 **pǎobù** v jog

跑道 **pǎodào** N runway, track (in a sports ground)

炮 **pào** N cannon, gun (门 mén, 座 zuò)

炮兵 **pàobīng** N artillery man

炮弹 **pàodàn** N artillery shell (发 fā, 颗 kē)

炮火 **pàohuǒ** N artillery fire

泡 **pào** I N 1 bubble

肥皂泡 féizàopào soap bubble
2 blister II v soak, steep

泡沫 **pàomò** N foam, froth

泡沫塑料 **pàomò sùliào** N styrofoam

陪 **péi** v accompany

陪同 **péitóng** v accompany

培 **péi** v cultivate

培训 **péixùn** I N training

培训班 **péixùnbān** training class, training course

培训生 **péixùn shēng** trainee
II v train

培训新职工 **péixùn xīn zhígōng** train new staff

培养 **péiyǎng** v 1 train, develop 2 cultivate, breed

培育 **péiyù** v bring up, nurture and educate

培育下一代 **péiyù xià yídài** bring up the next generation, bring up one's children

赔 **péi** TRAD 賠 v compensate, pay for (damage, loss, etc.)

赔偿 **péicháng** v compensate

赔款 **péikuǎn** N reparation, indemnity

佩 **pèi** v 1 wear 2 admire

佩服 **pèifu** v admire

NOTE: You can utter 佩服 Pèifu or 佩服! 佩服! Pèifu! Pèifu! to express great admiration for a feat or a remarkable achievement, e.g.: "你五门功课都是一百分？佩服！佩服！" "Nǐ wǔ mén gōngkè dōu shì yìbǎi fēn? Pèifu! Pèifu!" "You got full marks for all the five subjects? Wow!"

配 **pèi** v 1 match, blend 2 be worthy of, deserve

配得上 **pèi de shàng** be worthy of, good enough to be

配不上 **pèi bushàng** not good enough to be, unworthy of

配备 **pèibèi** v allocate, provide with, be equipped with

配方 **pèifāng** N medical prescription, formula

配合 **pèihé** v cooperate, coordinate

配偶 **pèi'ǒu** N spouse

配套 **pèitào** v make up a complete set

沛 **pèi** ADJ abundant (See 充沛 chōngpèi)

喷 **pēn** TRAD 噴 v sprinkle, spray

喷射 **pēnshè** v spurt, spray

喷水池 **pēnshuǐchí** N fountain

盆 **pén** N basin, pot (个 gè)

花盆 huāpén flower pot

洗脸盆 xǐliǎnpén washbasin

盆地 péndì N (in geography) basin

烹 pēng V boil, cook

烹饪 pēngrèn N cuisine, cooking
烹调 pēngtiáo V cook
　烹调技术 pēngtiáo jìshù cooking skill
　中华烹调 Zhōnghuá pēngtiáo Chinese cuisine

朋 péng N companion, friend

朋友 péngyou N friend
　跟/和…交朋友 gēn/hé…jiāo péngyou make friends with …
　男朋友 nánpéngyou boyfriend
　女朋友 nǚpéngyou girlfriend

棚 péng N shed

棚子 péngzi shed

膨 péng V expand, inflate

膨胀 péngzhàng V expand, dilate
　通货膨胀 tōnghuò péngzhàng inflation

捧 pěng V 1 hold in both hands (with care, pride, etc.) 2 sing somebody's praise (especially insincerely), flatter

碰 pèng V bump into, touch

碰到 pèngdao meet unexpectedly, run into
碰钉子 pèng dīngzi IDIOM meet with a sharp rebuff, be given the cold shoulder

批 pī I M. WD (for a batch of goods, and for things/people arriving at the same time)
　一批新书 yì pī xīn shū a batch of new books (published at about the same time)
　两批旅游者 liǎng pī lǚyóuzhě two groups of tourists
II V criticize, comment on, give instructions
批发 pīfā V sell wholesale
批改 pīgǎi V correct and grade (students' exercises, essays, etc.)
批判 pīpàn V criticize
批评 pīpíng I V criticize, scold II N criticism
批示 pīshì I V write comments on a document (e.g. report, request) submitted by subordinates II N comments on a document (e.g. report, request) submitted by subordinates
批准 pīzhǔn V approve, ratify

劈 pī V chop to split

披 pī V drape over the shoulder

皮 pí N 1 skin 2 leather, hide

牛皮 niúpí ox hide
皮带 pídài N leather belt
　系上皮带 xìshang pídài buckle up one's belt
皮肤 pífū N skin (human)
皮革 pígé N leather, hide
　皮革制品 pígé zhìpǐn leather product, leatherware
皮鞋 píxié N leather shoes
皮衣 píyī N fur coat, leather jacket

疲 pí ADJ fatigued

疲惫 píbèi ADJ physically and mentally exhausted
疲乏 pífá ADJ tired, weary
疲倦 píjuàn ADJ weary, tired
疲劳 píláo ADJ fatigued, tired

啤 pí N beer

啤酒 píjiǔ N beer (瓶 píng, 杯 bēi)

NOTE: 啤酒 píjiǔ is an example of a semi-transliteration: 啤 pí represents the sound of English word *beer* and 酒 jiǔ means *alcoholic drink*.

脾 pí N spleen

脾气 píqi N disposition, temper
　脾气坏 píqi huài have an irritable temper
　发脾气 fā píqi throw a tantrum, lose one's temper

匹 pǐ M. WD (for horses)

一匹快马 yì pǐ kuài mǎ a fast horse

屁 pì N flatulence, fart

屁股 pìgu N bottom, buttocks

辟 pì TRAD 闢 V open up (See 开辟 kāipì.)

僻 pì ADJ unusual, out-of-the-way (See 偏僻 piānpì)

譬 pì N example

譬如 pìrú CONJ Same as 比如 bǐrú

偏 1 piān I ADJ not straight, slanting II V be prejudiced, show favoritism

偏爱 piān'ài V be partial, favor
偏爱他的小女儿 piān'ài tā de xiǎonǚ'ér favor one's youngest daughter

偏差 piānchā N deviation, error

偏见 piānjiàn N prejudice, bias
对同性恋者有偏见 duì tóngxìngliànzhě yǒu piānjiàn hold prejudice against homosexuals

偏僻 piānpì ADJ remote, out-of-the-way

偏向 piānxiàng I V show favoritism II N erroneous tendency

偏 2 piān ADV must (used to indicate that the action in question is contrary to one's expectation or wishes)

NOTE: You can use 偏偏 piānpian instead of 偏 piān.

篇 piān M. WD (for a piece of writing)
一篇文章 yì piān wénzhāng an article/ essay

便 pián as in 便宜 piányi

便宜 piányi ADJ inexpensive, cheap
便宜货 piányi huò cheap goods, bargain

片 piàn I N thin and flat piece II M. WD (for thin, flat pieces)
一片面包 yí piàn miànbāo a slice of bread

片面 piànmiàn ADJ one-sided, unilateral

骗 piàn V deceive, fool (See 欺骗 qīpiàn)

骗局 piànjú N hoax, fraud
揭穿一个骗局 jiēchuān yí ge piànjú expose a fraud

骗子 piànzi N swindler, con-man

漂 piāo V float, drift

飘 piāo TRAD 飄 V flutter

飘扬 piāoyáng V (of banners, flags, etc.) flutter, wave

票 piāo N ticket (张 zhāng)
电影票 diànyǐng piào movie ticket
飞机票 fēijī piào air ticket
火车票 huǒchē piào train ticket
门票 ménpiào admission ticket (to a show, sporting event, etc.)
汽车票 qìchē piào bus/coach ticket

漂 piào as in 漂亮 piàoliang

漂亮 piàoliang ADJ pretty, good-looking

撇 piē V 1 discard, abandon 2 skim off from the surface of a liquid

瞥 piē I V take a glance at, shoot a glance at II N glimpse

拼 pīn V 1 fight bitterly, risk one's life 2 put together

拼搏 pīnbó V fight hard against a formidable adversary (often figuratively)

拼搏精神 pīnbó jīngshen fierce fighting spirit

拼命 pīnmìng V do all one can, risk one's life

拼音 pīnyīn I V spell, phonetize II N Romanized Chinese writing, pinyin
拼音文字 pīnyīn wénzì phonetic writing
汉语拼音方案 Hànyǔ pīnyīn fāng'àn Scheme for the Chinese Phonetic Alphabet

频 pín TRAD 頻 ADV frequently

频道 píndào N frequency channel, (TV) channel

频繁 pínfán ADJ frequent

频率 pínlǜ N frequency

贫 pín TRAD 貧 ADJ poor, lacking

贫乏 pínfá ADJ lacking in, deficient
资源贫乏 zīyuán pínfá poor in natural resources

贫苦 pínkǔ ADJ poor and miserable, poverty-stricken

贫困 pínkùn ADJ poor, destitute

贫民 pínmín N poor people, people living below the poverty line

贫穷 pínqióng ADJ poor, poverty-stricken

品 pǐn I N 1 article, product 2 quality, grade

上品 shàngpǐn superior quality, product of superior quality

II V savor

品尝 pǐncháng V savor, taste

品德 pǐndé N moral character

品德高尚 pǐndé gāoshàng of lofty (excellent) moral character

品行 pǐnxíng N moral character and conduct, behavior

品行不良 pǐnxíng bùliáng of poor moral standard and behave badly

品质 pǐnzhì N 1 (of people) moral character, intrinsic quality 2 (of products) quality

品种 pǐnzhǒng N variety, breed

聘 pìn V invite for service/employment

聘请 pìnqǐng V invite for service, employ

聘任 pìnrèn V appoint (for a professional or managerial position)

聘书 pìnshū N letter of appointment (份 fèn)

乒 pīng N bang (sound)

乒乓球 pīngpāngqiú N table tennis, table tennis ball (只 zhī)

平 píng ADJ 1 flat, level, smooth 2 be on the same level, equal 3 average, common

平安 píng'ān ADJ safe and sound

平常 píngcháng I ADJ ordinary, common II ADV ordinarily, usually, normally

平等 píngděng I ADJ equal (in status) II N equality

平凡 píngfán ADJ ordinary, common

平方 píngfāng N (in maths) square

三平方公尺 sān píngfāng gōngchǐ 3 square meters

平衡 pínghéng I N balance, equilibrium II V to keep in balance

平静 píngjìng ADJ calm, quiet, uneventful

平均 píngjūn ADJ average

平面 píngmiàn N (in mathematics) plane

平面几何 píngmiàn jǐhé plane geometry

平民 píngmín N the common people, civilian (个 gè, 名 míng)

平日 píngrì ADV on an ordinary day (not a holiday or festival)

平时 píngshí ADV usually, under normal circumstances

平坦 píngtǎn ADJ level and broad

平稳 píngwěn ADJ smooth and stable

平行 píngxíng ADJ parallel

平行线 píngxíngxiàn parallel lines

平庸 píngyōng ADJ mediocre, ordinary

平原 píngyuán N flatland, plain

评 píng TRAD 評 V 1 comment 2 appraise

评比 píngbǐ V appraise through comparison

年终评比 niánzhōng píngbǐ end-of-the-year appraisal (of performance of a number of people or groups)

评定 píngdìng V evaluate, assess

评估 pínggū V assess, appraise

资产评估 zīchǎn pínggū assets appraisal

评价 píngjià I V appraise, evaluate II N evaluation

高度评价 gāodù píngjià place a high value on, speak highly of

评论 pínglùn I V comment II N comment, commentary

评选 píngxuǎn V appraise and select, select by public appraisal

苹 píng TRAD 蘋 N apple

苹果 píngguǒ N apple (个 gè)

苹果园 píngguǒ yuán apple orchard

萍 píng N duckweed

萍水相逢 píngshuǐ xiāngféng IDIOM (of strangers) meet by chance like drifting duckweed

凭 píng TRAD 憑 I N evidence, proof

真凭实据 zhēnpíng shíjù hard evidence II V go by, base on

凭票入场 píngpiào rùchǎng admission by tickets

屏 **píng** N screen

屏风 **píngfēng** N partition
屏幕 **píngmù** N (movie, TV, computer) screen

瓶 **píng** I N bottle (个 gè)

瓶子 **píngzi** bottle
II M. WD a bottle of
一瓶啤酒 yì píng píjiǔ a bottle of beer
两瓶可口可乐 liǎng píng kěkǒukělè two bottles of Coca-Cola.

坡 **pō** N slope

泼 **pō** TRAD 潑 I V sprinkle II ADJ vigorous, bold (See 活泼 huópo.)

颇 **pō** ADV quite, rather

迫 **pò** V compel, oppress

迫害 **pòhài** V persecute
迫切 **pòqiè** ADJ urgent, pressing
迫使 **pòshǐ** V compel, force

破 **pò** I V 1 break, damage 2 break, split II ADJ torn, damaged
破产 **pòchǎn** I V go bankrupt II N bankruptcy
破除 **pòchú** V do away with, eradicate
破坏 **pòhuài** V sabotage, damage
破获 **pòhuò** V solve (a criminal case), catch (criminals)
破旧 **pòjiù** ADJ old and worn-out, shabby
破旧的厂房 pòjiù de chǎngfáng run-down factory building
破烂 **pòlàn** ADJ worn-out, tattered
捡破烂 jiǎn pòlàn pick up what is valuable from among garbage, make a living by doing this
破裂 **pòliè** V split, break down
破碎 **pòsuì** I V break into pieces, smash II ADJ broken into pieces, smashed, crushed

魄 **pò** N 1 soul, spirit 2 vigor

魄力 **pòlì** N daring, resolution

剖 **pōu** V cut open

剖析 **pōuxī** V dissect
剖析一个典型事例 pōuxī yí ge diǎnxíng shìlì study a typical case in great detail

扑 **pū** V 1 pounce on 2 flap

扑克 **pūkè** N playing cards
扑克牌 **pūkèpái** (张 zhāng, 副 fù)

NOTE: 扑克 pūkè is a transliteration of *poker*, to mean *playing cards*, not the card game. 扑克牌 pūkèpái, however, is more commonly used in everyday Chinese. We say 打扑克牌 dǎ pūkè pái, or 打牌 dǎ pái for the verb *to play cards*.

扑灭 **pūmiè** V extinguish, put out

铺 **pū** V spread, unfold

葡 **pú** N as in 葡萄 pútao

葡萄 **pútao** N grape (颗 kē)
葡萄酒 **pútaojiǔ** grape wine
葡萄园 **pútaoyuán** vineyard

仆 **pú** TRAD 僕 N servant

仆人 **púrén** (domestic) servant (个 gè, 名 míng)

NOTE: 仆人 púrén is an old-fashioned word for *servant*. Use 用人 yòngrén or 保姆 bǎomǔ.

菩 **pú** as in 菩萨 Púsà

菩萨 **Púsà** N Buddha, Bodhisattva

朴 **pǔ** TRAD 樸 ADJ plain, simple

朴实 **pǔshí** ADJ 1 (of style) simple and plain, down-to-earth 2 (of people) sincere and honest
朴素 **pǔsù** ADJ simple and plain

普 **pǔ** ADJ common, universal

普遍 **pǔbiàn** ADJ widespread, commonplace
普查 **pǔchá** N survey
人口普查 rénkǒu pǔchá census
普及 **pǔjí** V popularize, make commonplace

普通 pǔtōng ADJ common, commonplace, ordinary

普通话 Pǔtōnghuà N Standard Modern Chinese, Mandarin, Putonghua

NOTE: Modern Standard Chinese is known as 普通话 Pǔtōnghuà in China, 国语 Guóyǔ in Taiwan and 华语 Huáyǔ in Singapore and other Southeast Asian countries. They refer to the same language, though slight differences do exist among them.

谱 pǔ I v set to music II N musical score

乐谱 yuèpǔ musical score
钢琴谱 gāngqín pǔ piano score
谱曲 pǔqǔ v set music to words

瀑 pù N waterfall

瀑布 pùbù N waterfall

Q

七 qī NUM seven, 7

七个小矮人 qī ge xiǎo ǎirén the seven dwarves
七百七十七 qībǎi qīshíqī seven hundred and seventy-seven, 777

柒 qī NUM seven

沏 qī v infuse

沏茶 qīchá make tea

妻 qī N wife

妻子 qīzi wife

凄 qī ADJ chilly, cold

凄惨 qīcǎn ADJ miserable, wretched
凄凉 qīliáng ADJ desolate, dreary, miserable

漆 qī N lacquer, paint

漆黑 qīhēi ADJ pitch dark, pitch black
漆黑一团 qīhēiyìtuán pitch dark

期 qī I N fixed time

按期 àn qī according to the schedule, on time
到期 dàoqī expire, due
过期 guòqī overdue, expired
II v expect
期待 qīdài v expect, look forward to
期间 qījiān N period, time
期刊 qīkān N periodical, journal (本 běn)
期望 qīwàng I v expect, hope II N expectations, hope
期望过高 qīwàng guògāo expect too much
期限 qīxiàn N deadline, time limit
超过期限 chāoguò qīxiàn exceed the time limit, become overdue
定一个期限 dìng yí ge qīxiàn set a deadline

戚 qī N relative (See 亲戚 qīnqi)

欺 qī v cheat, bully

欺负 qīfu v bully, take advantage of (someone)
欺骗 qīpiàn v deceive

歧 qí ADJ different, divergent

歧视 qíshì I v discriminate against
歧视残疾人士 qíshì cánjírénshì discriminate against the disabled
II N discrimination
种族歧视 zhǒngzú qíshì racial discrimination

齐 qí TRAD 齊 I ADJ neat, in a straight line II v reaching to the same height
III ADV together, all ready
齐全 qíquán ADJ complete, all in readiness
品种齐全 pǐnzhǒng qíquán have a complete range of products (goods)

其 qí PRON this, that

其次 qícì ADV next, secondary, secondly
其实 qíshí ADV actually, as a matter of fact
其他 qítā PRON other, else
其余 qíyú PRON the rest, the remainder
其中 qízhōng N among them, in it

棋 qí N chess

下棋 xiàqí play chess
下一盘棋 xià yì pán qí play a game of chess
棋盘 qípán N chess board
棋子 qízǐ N chess piece

旗 qí N flag, banner (面 miàn)

旗杆 qígān flagstaff, flag pole
国旗 guóqí national flag
升旗 shēngqí hoist a flag
旗袍 qípáo N a woman's dress with high neck and slit skirt, cheongsam
旗帜 qízhì N banner (面 miàn)
旗子 qízi N flag, banner (面 miàn)

奇 qí ADJ strange

奇怪 qíguài ADJ strange, unusual, odd
奇花异草 qíhuāyìcǎo N rare, exotic flora
奇迹 qíjì N miracle, wonder
    创造奇迹 chuàngzào qíjì perform a miracle, work wonders
奇妙 qímiào ADJ marvelous, intriguing
奇特 qítè ADJ peculiar, unique

骑 qí TRAD 騎 V ride (a horse, bicycle etc.)

骑马 qí mǎ ride a horse
骑自行车 qí zìxíngchē ride a bicycle

岂 qí TRAD 豈 ADV (forming a rhetorical question)

岂不 qǐbù ADV wouldn't it, doesn't it
岂有此理 qǐyǒucǐlǐ IDIOM preposterous, outrageous

企 qǐ V hope, eagerly look forward to

企图 qǐtú I V attempt, try II N attempt

NOTE: 企图 qǐtú is usually used for negative situations. For example, we usually do not say 他企图帮助我。 Tā qǐtú bāngzhù wǒ. *He tried to help me.* but 他企图欺骗我。 Tā qǐtú qīpiàn wǒ. *He tried to deceive me.*

企业 qǐyè N enterprise (家 jiā)
企业家 qǐyèjiā entrepreneur
国有企业 guóyǒu qǐyè state-owned enterprise

私有企业 sīyǒu qǐyè private enterprise

启 qǐ TRAD 啟 V 1 open 2 start, initiate

启程 qǐchéng V start a journey, set out
启发 qǐfā I V enlighten, arouse II N enlightenment, inspiration
启示 qǐshì N revelation, inspiration, enlightenment
启事 qǐshì N public announcement

乞 qǐ V beg

乞丐 qǐgài N beggar
乞求 qǐqiú V implore, beg for
乞求宽恕 qǐqiú kuānshù beg for mercy

起 qǐ V rise, get up

从…起 cóng...qǐ starting from ...

NOTE: 起 qǐ is seldom used alone. To express *to get up (out of bed)*, 起床 qǐchuáng is more common than 起 qǐ. One can very well say: 快十点钟了，他还没起床呢! Kuài shí diǎnzhōng le, tā hái méi qǐchuáng ne! *It's almost ten o'clock and he still isn't up!*

起草 qǐcǎo V make a draft of (a plan, a document, etc.)
起初 qǐchū ADV at first, at the onset
起床 qǐchuáng V get up (out of bed)
起点 qǐdiǎn N starting point
起飞 qǐfēi V (of a plane) take off
起伏 qǐfú I V undulate, fluctuate II N fluctuation, setback
起哄 qǐhòng V set up a commotion in a light-hearted or mocking manner
起劲 qǐjìn ADV enthusiastically, in high spirits
起来 qǐlái V get up (out of bed), stand up

NOTE: 起来 qǐlái is often used after a verb as a complement to express various meanings. Among other meanings, 起来 qǐlái may be used after a verb to mean *begin to ...*, e.g.: 我们不等爸爸了，吃起来吧。Wǒmen bù děng bàba le, chī qǐlái ba. *We're not going to wait for daddy any longer. Let's start eating.*

起码 qǐmǎ ADJ the very least, minimum
起身 qǐshén V 1 get up 2 set out, set off
起诉 qǐsù V sue, file a lawsuit against
　起诉书 qǐsùshū indictment
起义 qǐyì I V stage an uprising, revolt II N uprising
　农民起义 nóngmín qǐyì peasants' uprising
起源 qǐyuán I N origin II V originate

砌 qì V lay (bricks), build by laying bricks
　砌一堵墙 qì yì dǔ qiáng build a brick wall

泣 qì V sob, cry
　哭泣 kūqì cry, weep and sob

气 1 qì TRAD 氣 N 1 air, gas 2 breath 3 spirit, morale

NOTE: Apart from its concrete meaning of *air, gas,* 气 qì is an important concept in traditional Chinese thought, meaning something like *vital force of life.*

气喘 qìchuǎn I V gasp for air II N asthma
　气喘病 qìchuǎn bìng asthma
气氛 qìfēn N atmosphere, ambiance
气概 qìgài N lofty spirit, (heroic) mettle
气功 qìgōng N a form of exercises involving deep breath, *qigong*
　练气功 liàn qìgōng practice exercises of deep breath, practice *qigong*
气候 qìhòu N climate
气力 qìlì N strength, energy
　花很大气力 huā hěn dà qìlì make great efforts
气流 qìliú N air current
气魄 qìpò N daring, boldness
气球 qìqiú N balloon
　热气球 rèqìqiú hot-air balloon
气势 qìshì N momentum
气体 qìtǐ N gas
气味 qìwèi N smell, odor
气温 qìwēn N atmospheric temperature

NOTE: See note on 温度 wēndù.

气息 qìxī N 1 breath, breathing 2 flavor
气象 qìxiàng N meteorological phenomena, weather

气象台 qìxiàngtái meteorological observatory
气象学 qìxiàngxué meteorology
气象预报 qìxiàng yùbào weather forecast
气压 qìyā N atmospheric pressure, air pressure

气 2 qì TRAD 氣 V be angry, make angry

气愤 qìfèn ADJ very angry, fumingly mad

汽 qì N vapor, steam

汽车 qìchē N automobile, car (辆 liàng)
　开汽车 kāi qìchē drive a car

NOTE: In everyday Chinese, 车 chē is often used instead of 汽车 qìchē to refer to a car, e.g.: 我可以把车停在这里吗? Wǒ kěyǐ bǎ chē tíng zài zhèlǐ ma? *May I park my car here?*

汽船 qìchuán N steamboat (艘 sōu)
汽水 qìshuǐ N soda water, soft drink, soda, pop (瓶 píng, 杯 bēi)
汽油 qìyóu N gasoline, petroleum

弃 qì TRAD 棄 V abandon (See 放弃 fàngqì, 抛弃 pāoqì)

器 qì N utensil

器材 qìcái N equipment, material
器官 qìguān N (human and animal) organ
器械 qìxiè N apparatus, instrument
　医疗器械 yīliáo qìxiè medical equipment

掐 qiā V pinch, nip

恰 qià ADV just, exactly

恰当 qiàdàng ADJ appropriate, suitable, proper
恰到好处 qiàdào hǎochù IDIOM just right, hitting the spot
恰好 qiàhǎo ADV just right, in the nick of time
恰恰 qiàqià ADV exactly, precisely
恰巧 qiàqiǎo ADV as luck would have it, fortunately
恰如其分 qiàrúqífèn IDIOM no more no less, apt

洽 **qià** v consult, discuss

洽谈 **qiàtán** v hold a talk
和他们公司洽谈合作项目 hé tāmen gōngsī qiàtán hézuò xiàngmù hold talks with their company over co-operation

牵 **qiān** v lead along by hand

牵扯 **qiānchě** v involve, implicate
牵引 **qiānyǐn** v tow, draw
牵制 **qiānzhì** v restrain, be bogged down

千 **qiān** NUM thousand, 1,000

一千零一夜 yìqiān líng yí yè a thousand and one nights
四千五百八十 sìqiān wǔbǎi bāshí four thousand, five hundred and eighty, 4,580
千方百计 qiānfāng bǎijì IDIOM in a thousand and one ways, by every possible means
千克 qiānkè N kilogram (kg)
千瓦 qiānwǎ N kilowatt (kW)
千万 qiānwàn ADV be sure to, must never (used in an imperative sentence for emphasis)

迁 **qiān** TRAD 遷 v move

迁就 qiānjiù v accommodate oneself to, yield to

签 **qiān** TRAD 簽 v sign, autograph

签订 qiāndìng v sign (a treaty, an agreement, etc.)
签发 qiānfā v (of an official) sign and issue (an document, certificate, etc.)
签名 qiānmíng I v autograph, sign one's name II N autograph, signature
请歌星签名 qǐng gēxīng qiānmíng ask a singer for his/her autograph
签署 qiānshǔ v sign (a treaty, a contract, etc.)
签证 qiānzhèng N visa
签证处 qiānzhèngchù visa section (of a consulate or embassy)
入境签证 rùjìng qiānzhèng entry visa
申请签证 shēnqǐng qiānzhèng apply for a visa

签字 qiānzì I v sign (a document)
在支票上签字 zài zhīpiào shang qiānzì sign a check
II N signature

铅 **qiān** TRAD 鉛 N lead (Pb)

铅笔 qiānbǐ N pencil (支 zhī)
铅笔盒 qiānbǐ hé pencil box
铅笔刀 qiānbǐ dāo pencil sharpener

谦 **qiān** TRAD 謙 ADJ modest

谦虚 qiānxū ADJ modest, self-effacing
谦逊 qiānxùn ADJ modest, unassuming

前 **qián** I N 1 front, in front of 2 Same as 以前 yǐqián II ADV forward

NOTE: In everyday Chinese, 前 qián is seldom used alone to mean *front* or *in front of*. Often it is better to use 前边 qiánbian.

前辈 qiánbèi N the older generation, elders, trailblazer
前边 qiánbian N front
前程 qiánchéng N future, prospects
远大前程 yuǎndà qiánchéng bright future
前方 qiánfāng N (in war) front, frontline
前后 qiánhòu ADV (of time) around, about
在2000年前后 zài èr-líng-líng-líng nián qiánhòu around the year 2000
前进 qiánjìn v go forward, advance
前景 qiánjǐng N prospect, vista
前列 qiánliè N front rank, forefront
前面 qiánmian N Same as 前边 qiánbian
前年 qiánnián N the year before last
前期 qiánqī N early stage, early days
工程的前期 gōngchéng de qiánqī the early stage of an engineering project
前人 qiánrén N predecessor, forefather
前所未有 qián suǒ wèi yǒu IDIOM unprecedented, hitherto unheard of
前提 qiántí N 1 prerequisite, the prime consideration 2 (in logic) premise
前天 qiántiān N the day before yesterday
前头 qiántou Same as 前面 qiánmian, used colloquially
前途 qiántú N future, prospects, future prospects

前往 qiánwǎng V go to, proceed

前线 qiánxiàn N (in war) front, frontline
上前线 shàng qiánxiàn go to the front, go to war

钳 qián TRAD 鉗 N pincer, plier, forceps

钳子 qiánzi pincer, plier, forceps (把 bǎ)
老虎钳 lǎohǔqián plier, pincer

潜 qián TRAD 潛 ADJ hidden, latent

潜伏 qiánfú V hide, lie low
潜伏期 qiánfúqī (in medicine) incubation period
潜力 qiánlì N latent capacity, potential, potentiality
潜水 qiánshuǐ V go under water, dive
潜水员 qiánshuǐyuán diver
潜水艇 qiánshuǐtǐng N submarine (艘 sōu)

钱 qián TRAD 錢 N money (笔 bǐ)

钱包 qiánbāo wallet, purse

浅 qián TRAD 淺 ADJ 1 shallow (See 深浅 shēnqiǎn) 2 easy, of low standard

遣 qiǎn V send, dispatch (See 派遣 pàiqiǎn)

谴 qiǎn TRAD 譴 V as in 谴责 qiǎnzé

谴责 qiǎnzé V condemn, denounce

嵌 qiàn V inlay, imbed

欠 qiàn V owe, be in debt to

欠人情 qiàn rénqíng V owe a debt of gratitude

歉 qiàn N 1 apology (See 道歉 dàoqiàn) 2 crop failure

歉意 qiànyì N apology, regret
深表歉意 shēn biǎo qiànyì offer one's profound apology

腔 qiāng N cavity

口腔 kǒuqiāng oral cavity

枪 qiāng TRAD 槍 N small arms, gun, pistol (支 zhī, 把 bǎ)

手枪 shǒuqiāng handgun (revolver, pistol)
枪毙 qiāngbì V execute by shooting

强 qiáng I ADJ strong II ADV by force

强大 qiángdà ADJ powerful
强盗 qiángdào N bandit, robber
强调 qiángdiào V emphasize, lay stress on
强度 qiángdù N intensity, strength
强化 qiánghuà V strengthen, intensify
强奸 qiángjiān V rape
强奸幼女 qiángjiān yòunǚ rape an underage girl
强烈 qiángliè ADJ strong, intense, violent
强盛 qiángshèng ADJ (of a country) strong and prosperous, powerful and wealthy
强制 qiángzhì V coerce, force

墙 qiáng TRAD 牆 N wall (道 dào)

墙壁 qiángbì N wall

强 qiǎng V make an effort

强迫 qiǎngpò V force, coerce

抢 qiǎng TRAD 搶 V 1 seize, grab 2 rob, loot

抢劫 qiǎngjié V rob
抢劫银行 qiǎngjié yínháng rob a bank
抢救 qiǎngjiù V rescue, salvage
抢救病人 qiǎngjiù bìngrén rescue a patient, give emergency treatment to a patient

悄 qiāo ADJ quiet

悄悄 qiāoqiāo ADV quietly, on the quiet

敲 qiāo V knock, rap

锹 qiāo TRAD 鍬 N spade

铁锹 tiěqiāo spade (把 bǎ)

桥 qiáo TRAD 橋 N bridge (座 zuò)

过桥 guò qiáo cross a bridge
桥梁 qiáoliáng N big bridge (座 zuò)

乔 qiáo TRAD 喬 disguise

乔装 qiáozhuāng V disguise
乔装成一个海盗 qiáozhuāng chéng yí ge hǎidào disguise oneself as a pirate

侨 qiáo TRAD 僑 v sojourn, live abroad (See 华侨 huáqiáo)

侨胞 qiáobāo N countrymen residing overseas

瞧 qiáo v Same as 看 kàn v 1. Used only as a colloquialism.

巧 qiǎo I ADV coincidentally II ADJ skilled, clever

巧妙 qiǎomiào ADJ ingenious, very clever

翘 qiào TRAD 翹 v stick up, bend upward

俏 qiào ADJ pretty and cute

切 qiē v cut, slice

茄 qié N eggplant

茄子 qiézi eggplant (只 zhī)

且 qiě CONJ moreover (See 而且 érqiě)

怯 qiè ADJ timid (See 胆怯 dǎnqiè)

切 qiè v be close to, tally with (See 亲切 qīnqiè)

切实 qièshí ADJ 1 feasible, practical 2 earnest

切实可行的办法 qièshí kěxíng de bànfǎ practical measure

窃 qiè TRAD 竊 v steal, pilfer

窃取 qièqǔ v steal, grab

窃听 qiètīng v eavesdrop, bug

窃听器 qiètīngqì listening-in device, bug

钦 qīn v admire

钦佩 qīnpèi v admire, esteem

令人钦佩 lìngrén qīnpèi admirable

亲 qīn TRAD 親 I N blood relation II ADJ close, intimate

亲爱 qīn'ài ADJ dear, beloved, darling

NOTE: Although 亲爱 qīn'ài is glossed as *dear*, the Chinese reserve 亲爱(的) qīn'ài (de) for the very few people who are really dear and close to their hearts.

亲笔 qīnbǐ ADV (written) in one's own handwriting

亲密 qīnmì ADJ intimate, close

亲戚 qīnqi N relative, relation

亲戚朋友 qīnqi péngyou relatives and friends

走亲戚 zǒu qīnqi visit a relative

亲切 qīnqiè ADJ cordial

亲热 qīnrè ADJ affectionate, warm-hearted

亲人 qīnrén N family member

亲身 qīnshēn ADJ personal, firsthand

亲身经历 qīnshēn jīnglì personal experience

亲生 qīnshēng ADJ one's biological (parents or children)

她的亲生父亲 tāde qīnshēng fùqin her biological father

亲手 qīnshǒu ADV with one's own hands, by oneself, personally

亲眼 qīnyǎn ADV with one's own eyes

亲友 qīnyǒu N relatives and friends

走亲访友 zǒu qīn fǎng yǒu visit relatives and friends

亲自 qīnzì ADV by oneself, personally

侵 qīn v invade, intrude, encroach

侵略 qīnlüè v invade (by force)

侵入 qīnrù v intrude into, make incursions into

侵蚀 qīnshí v corrode, erode

侵占 qīnzhàn v invade and occupy

琴 qín N (stringed) musical instrument

钢琴 gāngqín piano (架 jià)

提琴 tíqín violin (把 bǎ)

勤 qín ADJ diligent, hard-working

勤奋 qínfèn ADJ diligent, applying oneself to

勤俭 qínjiǎn ADJ diligent and frugal

勤恳 qínkěn ADJ diligent and conscientious

勤劳 qínláo ADJ hard-working, industrious

芹 qín celery

芹菜 qíncài celery

禽 qín N bird, fowl

青 qīng ADJ green

青菜 qīngcài N Chinese cabbage (棵 kē)
青春 qīngchūn N the quality of being young, youth
青春期 qīngchūnqī puberty
永葆青春 yǒngbǎo qīngchūn have eternal youth
青年 qīngnián N young person, young people, youth (especially male) (位 wèi, 个 gè)
青蛙 qīngwā N frog (只 zhī)

清 **qīng I** ADJ **1** clear (water), clean **2** (of matters) clear, easy to understand **II** V make clear
清查 qīngchá V check thoroughly
清晨 qīngchén N early morning
清除 qīngchú V remove, clear away
清除垃圾邮件 qīngchú lājī yóujiàn delete junk mail
清楚 qīngchu ADJ clear (of speech or image)
清洁 qīngjié V clean, clear up
清洁工 qīngjiégōng cleaner
清理 qīnglǐ V sort out, clear out
清理办公桌 qīnglǐ bàngōngzhuō clear out a desk
清晰 qīngxī ADJ very clear, distinct
清新 qīngxīn ADJ pure and fresh, refreshing
清新的空气 qīngxīn de kōngqì fresh air
清醒 qīngxǐng ADJ clear-headed, sober

轻 **qīng** TRAD 輕 ADJ **1** light (of weight) **2** low, soft (of voice) **3** of a low degree
轻便 qīngbiàn ADJ lightweight and handy, portable
轻工业 qīnggōngyè N light industry
轻快 qīngkuài ADJ **1** light-hearted, lively **2** light-footed, brisk
轻视 qīngshì V think ... unimportant, underestimate, belittle
轻松 qīngsōng ADJ (of a job) easy, not requiring much effort, relaxed
轻微 qīngwēi ADJ slight, trifling
只有轻微的损失 zhǐyǒu qīngwēi de sǔnshī only slightly damaged
轻易 qīngyì ADV **1** easily, demanding little effort **2** without much consideration, rashly

轻易下结论 qīngyì xià jiélùn reach a hasty conclusion
轻音乐 qīng yīnyuè N light music

氢 **qīng** N hydrogen (H)
氢气 qīngqì hydrogen

倾 **qīng** V incline, lean
倾听 qīngtīng V listen attentively
倾向 qīngxiàng N tendency, inclination
倾销 qīngxiāo V dump (goods)
反倾销法 fǎn qīngxiāo fǎ anti-dumping regulation
倾斜 qīngxié V tilt, incline

蜻 **qīng** as in 蜻蜓 qīngtíng
蜻蜓 qīngtíng N dragonfly (只 zhī)

情 **qíng** N **1** circumstance **2** feeling, sentiment
情报 qíngbào N intelligence, information
情感 qínggǎn N emotion, feeling
情节 qíngjié N plot (of a story, movie, etc.)
情景 qíngjǐng N scene, occasion
情况 qíngkuàng N situation, circumstance
情理 qínglǐ N accepted code of conduct, reason
不近情理 bú jìn qínglǐ violate the accepted code of conduct, unreasonable
情形 qíngxíng N circumstances, situation
情绪 qíngxù N mood, feelings
情愿 qíngyuàn V would rather, prefer

> NOTE: 情愿 qíngyuàn is usually used together with 也 yě, as shown in the example sentence, e.g.: 我情愿多花些钱，也要买到称心的东西。Wǒ qíngyuàn duō huā xiē qián, yě yāomǎi dào chènxīn de dōngxi. *I'd rather spend more money in order to get things that satisfy me.* 也 yě may be replaced by 都 dōu.

晴 **qíng** ADJ (of weather) fine, clear
晴朗 qínglǎng ADJ fine, sunny
晴天 qíngtiān N fine day

请 **qǐng** TRAD 請 V **1** invite **2** ask, request

NOTE: 请 qǐng is used to start a polite request, equivalent to *Please ...*, e.g.: 请您别在这里吸烟。Qǐng nín bié zài zhèlǐ xīyān. *Please don't smoke here.*; 请坐! Qǐng zuò! *Sit down, please!*

请假 qǐngjià v ask for leave
请病假 qǐng bìngjià ask for sick leave
请事假 qǐng shìjià ask for leave of absence
请柬 qǐngjiǎn N letter of invitation, invitation card (份 fèn)
请教 qǐngjiào v ask for advice, consult

NOTE: 请教 qǐngjiào is a polite word, used when you want to ask for advice or information, e.g.: 请教，这个汉字是什么意思？Qǐngjiào, zhège Hànzì shì shénme yìsi? *Would you please tell me the meaning of this Chinese character?*

请客 qǐngkè v 1 invite to dinner 2 treat (someone to something)
请客送礼 qǐngkè sònglǐ invite to dinner and give gift to, bribe by gifts and dinner parties
请求 qǐngqiú I v request, ask for II N request
请示 qǐngshì v ask (a person of superior position) for instruction
请帖 qǐngtiě N letter of invitation, invitation card (份 fèn)
请问… qǐng wèn… Excuse me, …

NOTE: When you want some information from someone, start your query with 请问… qǐng wèn…, e.g.: 请问，去火车站怎么走？Qǐng wèn, qù huǒchēzhàn zěnme zǒu? *Excuse me, could you show me the way to the railway station?*

顷 qǐng TRAD 頃 N a unit of area (= 6.6667 hectares)
庆 qìng TRAD 慶 v celebrate
庆贺 qìnghè v congratulate, celebrate
庆祝 qìngzhù v celebrate
穷 qióng TRAD 窮 ADJ poor, poverty-stricken

穷苦 qióngkǔ ADJ poor, poverty-stricken
穷人 qióngrén poor person, the poor
秋 qiū N fall, autumn
秋收 qiūshōu N autumn harvest
秋天 qiūtiān N fall, autumn
丘 qiū N mound, low and small hill
丘陵 qiūlíng N hills, hilly land
求 qiú v beseech, beg, humbly ask for
求婚 qiúhūn v propose marriage, make a marriage offer
球 qiú N 1 ball (只 zhī) 2 ball game (场 chǎng)
比球 bǐ qiú have a (ball game) match
棒球 bàngqiú baseball
打球 dǎ qiú play basketball or volleyball
看球 kàn qiú watch a ball game
篮球 lánqiú basketball
排球 páiqiú volleyball
踢球 tī qiú play soccer
足球 zúqiú soccer
球场 qiúchǎng N sports ground (especially where ball games are played)
球队 qiúduì N (ball game) team
球迷 qiúmí N (ball game) fan
足球迷 zúqiúmí soccer fan
球员 qiúyuán N (ball game) player
曲 qū ADJ crooked, bent
曲线 qūxiàn N curve
曲线图 qūxiàntú line graph, graph
曲折 qūzhé ADJ tortuous, winding
区 qū TRAD 區 N district
商业区 shāngyèqū commercial area, business district
工业区 gōngyèqū industrial zone, industrial district
区别 qūbié I v set apart, differentiate II N difference
区分 qūfēn I v put in different categories, differentiate II N differentiation
区域 qūyù N region, area
驱 qū TRAD 驅 v drive

驱逐 qūzhú

驱车前往 qūchē qiánwǎng drive (in a car) to

驱逐 qūzhú v drive out, banish

驱逐出境 qūzhú chūjìng deport, deportation

驱逐舰 qūzhújiàn n destroyer

趋 qū TRAD 趨 v tend (to become)

趋势 qūshì n tendency

令人担忧的趋势 lìngrén dānyōu de qūshì a worrying tendency

趋向 qūxiàng v tend to, incline to

屈 qū I v bend, bow II ADJ wrong (See 委屈 wěiqū)

屈服 qūfú v yield (to), knuckle under

渠 qú n 1 ditch, canal 2 medium, channel

灌溉渠 guàngàiqú irrigation channel

渠道 qúdào n 1 irrigation ditch 2 medium of communication, channel

曲 qǔ n melody, tune

曲调 qǔdiào n tune, melody

曲子 qǔzi n song, melody

熟悉的曲子 shúxī de qǔzi familiar tune

取 qǔ v fetch, collect

取款 qǔkuǎn withdraw money

取代 qǔdài v replace, substitute for

取得 qǔdé v obtain, achieve

取消 qǔxiāo v cancel, call off

娶 qǔ v (of a man) marry

娶媳妇 qǔ xífù (of a man) marry, take a wife

NOTE: See note on 嫁 jià.

去 qù v leave for, go to

去年 qùnián last year

去世 qùshì v die, pass away

NOTE: 去世 qùshì must be used when you want to show respect and/or love to the deceased. For instance, the normal word for *die*, 死 sǐ, would be totally inappropriate in the example sentence: 他的祖父在上个月去世了。Tā de zǔfù zài shàngge

yuè qùshìle. *His grandfather passed away last month.*

趣 qù n interest

趣味 qùwèi n 1 interest, delight 2 taste, preference

低级趣味 dījí qùwèi vulgar taste

圈 quān n circle, ring

圈套 quāntào n snare, trap

设下圈套 shèxià quāntào set a trap, lay a snare

落入圈套 luòrù quāntào be caught in a trap, be snared

圈子 quānzi n circle, ring

权 quán TRAD 權 n 1 authority, power 2 right, privilege

权利 quánlì n right

权力 quánlì n authority, power

权威 quánwēi n authority, authoritativeness

国际法权威 guójìfǎ quánwēi an authority in international law

权限 quánxiàn n limits of one's authority, extent of one's authority

超出他的权限 chāochū tā de quánxiàn exceed the limit of his authority

权益 quányì n rights, rights and interests

全 quán ADJ whole, complete

全国 quánguó the whole country

全世界 quánshìjiè the entire world

全部 quánbù n all, without exception

全都 quándōu ADV all, without exception

全会 quánhuì n plenary session, plenary meeting

中共中央十六届二中全会 Zhōnggòng Zhōngyāng shíliù jiè èr-zhōng quánhuì the second plenary meeting of the 16th Central Committee of the Chinese Communist Party

全集 quánjí n completed works (of an author)

全局 quánjú n overall situation

全力 quánlì ADV with all of one's strength, making every effort

全力以赴 quánlì yǐfù spare no efforts, go all out

全面 quánmiàn ADJ all-round, comprehensive

全民 quánmín N the entire people (of a country)

全体 quántǐ N all, each and every one (of a group of people)

全心全意 quánxīn quányì IDIOM whole-heartedly

拳 quán N fist

拳头 quántou N fist

泉 quán N spring (a small brook)

矿泉 kuàngquán mineral water

温泉 wēnquán hot spring

犬 quǎn N dog

警犬 jǐngquǎn police dog

劝 quàn TRAD 勸 V 1 try to talk … into (or out of) doing something, advise 2 encourage

劝告 quàngào I V exhort, advise II N advice

劝说 quànshuō V persuade, advise

劝阻 quànzǔ V dissuade from, advise … not to

劝阻无效 quànzǔ wúxiào try in vain to dissuade someone from doing something

券 quàn N ticket, certificate

入场券 rùchǎngquàn admission ticket

缺 quē V 1 lack, be short of

缺人手 quē rénshǒu shorthanded 2 be incomplete, be absent

缺点 quēdiǎn N shortcoming, defect

缺乏 quēfá V be deficient in, lack

缺口 quēkǒu N breach, indenture

缺少 quēshǎo V be short of, lack

NOTE: 缺乏 quēfá and 缺少 quēshǎo are synonyms, but 缺乏 quēfá has abstract nouns as objects, while 缺少 quēshǎo takes as objects nouns denoting concrete persons or things.

缺席 quēxí V be absent from (a meeting, a class, etc.)

缺陷 quēxiàn N defect, shortcoming

瘸 qué V be lame

瘸子 quézi lame person, cripple

却 què TRAD 卻 ADV unexpectedly, contrary to what may be normally expected, but, yet

鹊 què TRAD 鵲 N magpie

喜鹊 xǐquè magpie (只 zhī)

榷 què V discuss

商榷 shāngquè discuss

雀 què N finch

麻雀 máquè sparrow (只 zhī)

确 què TRAD 確 I ADJ true, authentic II ADV firmly

确保 quèbǎo V ensure, guarantee

确定 quèdìng V confirm, fix, determine

确立 quèlì V establish

确切 quèqiè ADJ precise, specific

确认 quèrèn V affirm, confirm

确实 quèshí ADJ verified to be true, indeed

确信 quèxìn V firmly believe, be convinced

确凿 quèzáo ADJ conclusive, irrefutable

裙 qún N skirt

裙子 qúnzi N skirt (条 tiáo)

群 qún M. WD a crowd of, a group of (for people or animals)

一群狗 yì qún gǒu a pack of dogs

一群鸟 yì qún niǎo a flock of birds

一群牛 yì qún niú a herd of cattle

一群小学生 yì qún xiǎoxuéshēng a group of primary schoolchildren

群岛 qúndǎo N archipelago

群体 qúntǐ N (social) group

弱势群体 ruòshì qúntǐ weak social group

群众 qúnzhòng N the masses (people), the general public

R

然 rán CONJ however

然

然而 rán'ér CONJ Same as 但是 dànshì. Usually used in written Chinese.

然后 ránhòu IDIOM CONJ afterwards, ... and then
先…然后… xiān...ránhòu... first ... and then...

燃 rán V burn

燃料 ránliào N fuel

燃烧 ránshāo V burn

染 rǎn V dye

染料 rǎnliào N dyestuff

壤 rǎng N soil (See 土壤 tǔrǎng)

嚷 rǎng V yell, shout

让 ràng TRAD 讓 V 1 let, give way 2 allow, make

饶 ráo TRAD 饒 V have mercy on, forgive

扰 rǎo TRAD 擾 V harass (See 打扰 dǎrǎo.)

绕 rào TRAD 繞 V make a detour, bypass

惹 rě V cause (something undesirable), invite (trouble etc.)

热 rè TRAD 熱 ADJ 1 hot 2 ardent, passionate

热爱 rè'ài V ardently love, be in deep love with

热潮 rècháo N upsurge, craze

热带 rèdài N the tropics, the tropical zone

热量 rèliàng N quantity of heat

热烈 rèliè ADJ warm, ardent

热闹 rènao ADJ noisy and exciting in a pleasant way, boisterous, bustling, lively (of a scene or occasion)

热情 rèqíng ADJ enthusiastic, warmhearted

热水瓶 rèshuǐpíng N thermos, thermos flask

热心 rèxīn ADJ warmhearted, enthusiastic

对… 热心 duì...rèxīn be warmhearted towards, be enthusiastic about

人 rén N human being, person

人才 réncái N talented person, person of ability

人才市场 réncái shìchǎng personnel market, job fair

人才外流 réncái wàiliú brain drain

人道主义 réndàozhǔyì N humanitarianism

人道主义援助 réndàozhǔyì yuánzhù humanitarian aid

人格 réngé N personality, moral quality
以我的人格担保 yǐ wǒ de réngé dānbǎo give (you) my personal guarantee

人工 réngōng I ADJ artificial, man-made
人工智能 réngōng zhìnéng artificial intelligence
II N manpower, man-day

人家 rénjia PRON 1 other people 2 he, she, they (used to refer to another person or other people) 3 I, me (used to refer to oneself, used only among intimate friends or family members)

人间 rénjiān N the earth, the human world
人间天堂 rénjiān tiāntáng paradise on earth

人均 rénjūn N average, per capita

人口 rénkǒu N population (human)

> NOTE: It is interesting that the Chinese word for *population* is made up of 人 rén (human) and 口 kǒu (the mouth). It suggests that feeding people (mouths) has been the primary concern in China.

人类 rénlèi N humankind, mankind

人类学 rénlèixué N anthropology

人力 rénlì N manpower
人力资源 rénlì zīyuán human resource

人们 rénmen N people, the public

人民 rénmín N the people (of a state)

人民币 Rénmínbì N the Chinese currency, Renminbi (RMB)

人情 rénqíng N 1 common sense, reason
不近人情 bú jìn rénqíng unreasonable (in dealing with interpersonal matters)
2 human feelings

讲人情 jiǎng rénqíng resort to feeings (instead of regulations, law, etc.)

3 gift, favor

送人情 sòng rénqíng give a gift (in order to gain favors)

人权 rénquán N human rights

人蛇 rénshé N illegal (especially smuggled) immigrant

人参 rénshēn N ginseng

人生 rénshēng N (one's entire) life

人事 rénshì N human resources matters

人事部门 rénshì bùmén human resources department, personnel department

人寿 rénshòu N human lifespan

人寿保险 rénshòu bǎoxiǎn life insurance

人体 réntǐ N human body

人体解剖学 réntǐ jiěpōuxué human anatomy, anatomy

人为 rénwéi ADJ man-made, artificial

人物 rénwù N well-known and important person, figure, personage (位 wèi)

人心 rénxīn N popular feelings, the will of the people

人性 rénxìng N human nature

人员 rényuán N personnel, staff

人造 rénzào ADJ man-made, artificial

人质 rénzhì N hostage

扣留人质 kòuliú rénzhì hold a hostage

仁 rén I N benevolence, humanity

II ADJ benevolent, humane

仁慈 réncí ADJ benevolent, merciful

忍 rěn V endure, tolerate, put up with

忍耐 rěnnài V bear, put up with, exercise patience

忍受 rěnshòu V tolerate, stand

忍心 rěnxīn V have the heart to (do), be hard-hearted

NOTE: 忍心 rěnxīn is usually used in its negative form of 不忍心 bùrěn xīn, which means *not have the heart to (do)*, e.g.: 我不忍心把这个可怕的消息告诉她。Wǒ bù rěnxīn bǎ zhè ge kěpà de xiāoxi gàosu tā. *I don't have the heart to tell her this terrible news.*

忍住 rěnzhù V endure, bear

忍不住 rěnbuzhù unable to bear, cannot help

忍得住 rěndezhù can endure, can bear

韧 rèn TRAD 韌 ADJ strong and pliable, tenacious

认 rèn TRAD 認 V **1** recognize **2** identify

认得 rènde V Same as 认识 rènshi

认定 rèndìng V be firmly convinced, maintain, decide on

认可 rènkě V approve

质量认可书 zhìliàng rènkě shū certificate of quality approval

认识 rènshi V know, understand

认为 rènwéi V think, consider (normally followed by a clause)

认真 rènzhēn ADJ earnest, conscientious, serious

任 rèn I CONJ no matter II V **1** appoint, take up **2** give free rein to

任何 rènhé PRON any, whatever

任何人 rènhé rén anyone

任何事 rènhé shì any matter, anything, everything

任命 rènmìng V appoint (to a position of importance)

任命他为副总裁 rènmìng tā wéi fùzǒngcái appoint him Vice-CEO

任务 rènwù N assignment, mission

任性 rènxìng ADJ willful, headstrong

任意 rènyì ADV randomly, at random

饪 rèn TRAD 飪 V cook (See 烹饪 pēngrèn)

刃 rèn N the edge of a knife, blade

扔 rēng V throw, toss

仍 réng ADV Same as 仍然 réngrán

仍旧 réngjiù ADV Same as 仍然 réngrán

仍然 réngrán ADV still, as before

日 rì N date, day

三月二十四日 Sānyuè èrshí sì rì the twenty-fourth of March

日报 rìbào

九月一日 Jiǔyuè yí rì the first of September

NOTE: In writing, 日 rì is used for dates as shown above. However, in speech it is more common to say 号 hào. For example, to say *the twenty-fourth of March* 三月二十四号 Sānyuè èrshí sì hào is more natural than 三月二十四日 Sānyuè èrshí sì rì.

日报 rìbào N daily newspaper, daily
日本 Rìběn N Japan
日常 rìcháng ADJ daily, routine
日程 rìchéng N daily schedule, schedule
  议事日程 yìshì rìchéng agenda
日程表 rìchéngbiǎo N timetable (for a schedule)
日光 rìguāng N sunlight
日记 rìjì N diary (本 běn, 篇 piān)
  日记本 rìjìběn diary
  记日记 jì rìjì keep a diary
日期 rìqī N date (especially of an event)
日文 Rìwén N the Japanese language (especially the writing)
日夜 rìyè ADV day and night, round the clock
  日夜服务 rìyè fúwù round-the-clock service
日益 rìyì ADV day by day, increasingly
日用品 rìyòngpǐn N daily necessities
日语 Rìyǔ N the Japanese language
日元 Rìyuán N Japanese currency, yen
日子 rìzi N 1 day, date 2 life

融 **róng** V 1 melt, thaw 2 be in harmony, blend, fuse
融化 rónghuà V melt, thaw
融洽 róngqià ADJ harmonious, very friendly

荣 **róng** TRAD 荣 I ADJ glorious, flourishing II N glory, honor
荣誉 róngyù N honor, great credit
荣誉称号 róngyù chēnghào title of honor

容 **róng** V 1 tolerate 2 hold, accommodate
容积 róngjī N amount of space, volume
容量 róngliàng N the amount that something can hold, capacity

容纳 róngnà V have a capacity of, hold, contain
容器 róngqì N container, vessel
容忍 róngrěn V tolerate
容许 róngxǔ V permit, allow
容易 róngyì ADJ 1 easy, not difficult 2 having a tendency to, likely

溶 **róng** V dissolve, melt
溶化 rónghuà V dissolve
溶解 róngjiě V dissolve, melt
溶液 róngyè N solution

熔 **róng** V melt, smelt

绒 **róng** TRAD 絨 N fine hair, down
鸭绒被 yāróngbèi duckdown quilt

柔 **róu** ADJ soft, gentle
柔和 róuhé ADJ soft and mild, gentle
  柔和的口气 róuhé de kǒuqì a gentle and soothing voice
柔软 róuruǎn ADJ soft, lithe

揉 **róu** V rub, knead
揉面 róumiàn knead dough

肉 **ròu** N flesh, meat
鸡肉 jīròu chicken meat
牛肉 niúròu beef
羊肉 yángròu mutton
鱼肉 yúròu fish meat
猪肉 zhūròu pork

NOTE: The most popular meat in China is pork. Unspecified, 肉 ròu often refers to *pork*.

如 **rú** I V 1 be like, be similar to 2 according to 3 for example, such as II CONJ Same as 如果 rúguǒ. Used only in writing.
如此 rúcǐ CONJ so, such as
  如此说来 rúcǐ shuōlái in that case, then, so

NOTE: See note on 如何 rúhé.

如果 rúguǒ CONJ if, in the event that

NOTE: 如果 rúguǒ is usually used with 就 jiù.

如何 rúhé PRON how, what

NOTE: 如何 rúhé is one of the few remnants of Classical Chinese still used in Modern Chinese, but it is usually used in writing only. The same is true with 如此 rúcǐ, 如今 rújīn and 如同 rútóng.

如今 rújīn PRON today, now

NOTE: See note on 如何 rúhé.

如同 rútóng V be like, as

NOTE: See note on 如何 rúhé.

如意 rúyì ADJ as one wishes
称心如意 chènxīn rúyì to one's heart's content
万事如意 wànshì rúyì best of luck for everything

辱 rǔ V insult (See 侮辱 wǔrǔ)

乳 rǔ N 1 breast 2 milk
乳房 rǔfáng N female breast, udder
乳牛 rǔniú N dairy cattle, cow (头 tóu)
乳制品 rǔzhìpǐn N dairy product

入 rù V 1 enter, go in 2 join, become a member of
入境 rùjìng V enter a country
入口 rùkǒu N entry, entrance
入侵 rùqīn V invade, make inroads
入手 rùshǒu V start with, proceed
入学 rùxué V start school

软 ruǎn TRAD 軟 ADJ 1 soft, supple 2 weak, feeble
软件 ruǎnjiàn N computer software, software
软盘 ruǎnpán N floppy disk
软驱 ruǎnqū N floppy drive
软弱 ruǎn ruò ADJ weak, feeble

锐 ruì TRAD 銳 ADJ sharp
锐利 ruìlì ADJ sharp, pointed

瑞 ruì ADJ auspicious

瑞雪 ruìxuě N timely snow

润 rùn TRAD 潤 V moisten, enrich (See 利润 lìrùn, 湿润 shīrùn)

弱 ruò ADJ weak, feeble
弱势群体 ruòshì qúntǐ N weak social group, the disadvantaged

若 ruò CONJ if
若干 ruògān NUM a certain number

S

撒 sā V cast, spread out
撒渔网 sā yúwǎng spread out a fishing net

洒 sǎ TRAD 灑 V sprinkle, spray

萨 sà TRAD 薩 as in 菩萨 Púsà

腮 sāi N cheek

塞 sāi V plug, stuff
把很多衣服塞进旅行袋 bǎ hěn duō yīfu sāijìn lǚxíngdài stuff lots of clothes in the duffel bag

赛 sài TRAD 賽 V compete (See 比赛 bǐsài, 竞赛 jìngsài.)

三 sān NUM three, 3
十三 shísān thirteen, 13
三十 sānshí thirty, 30

叁 sān NUM three, 3

伞 sǎn TRAD 傘 N umbrella (把 bǎ)

散 sǎn ADJ loose
散文 sǎnwén N prose, essay (篇 piān)

散 sàn V 1 disperse, scatter 2 disseminate, distribute
散步 sànbù V take a short leisurely walk, stroll

散布 **sànbù** v disseminate, spread
散布谣言 **sànbù yáoyán** spread rumors
散发 **sànfā** v distribute, give out
散发广告纸 **sànfā guǎnggào zhǐ** pass out fliers

丧 sāng TRAD 喪 N funeral
奔丧 **bēnsāng** travel to attend a funeral
丧事 **sāngshì** N funeral arrangements
办丧事 **bàn sāngshì** make funeral arrangements

桑 sāng N mulberry
桑树 **sāngshù** mulberry tree (棵 **kē**)
桑叶 **sāngyè** mulberry leaf (张 **zhāng**)
桑拿浴 **sāngnàyù** N sauna

NOTE: This is a case of a semi-transliteration. 桑拿 represents the sound of *sauna* and 浴 means *bath*.

嗓 sǎng N throat
嗓子 **sǎngzi** N 1 throat 2 voice

丧 sàng TRAD 喪 v lose
丧失 **sàngshī** v lose, forfeit

骚 sāo TRAD 騷 v disturb, upset
骚动 **sāodòng** I v disturb, cause a commotion II N social disturbance, commotion
骚乱 **sāoluàn** I v riot II N riot, disturbance
平息骚乱 **píngxī sāoluàn** put down a riot

嫂 sǎo N elder brother's wife
嫂子 **sǎozi** N elder brother's wife, sister-in-law

NOTE: One's younger brother's wife is 弟妹 **dìmèi**.

扫 sǎo TRAD 掃 v sweep
扫地 **sǎo dì** sweep the floor
扫除 **sǎochú** v clean (a room, a courtyard, etc.)

扫 sào as in 扫帚 **sàozhou**
扫帚 **sàozhou** N broom (把 **bǎ**)

色 sè N 1 color 2 sex
色彩 **sècǎi** N color, hue
色彩丰富 **sècǎi fēngfù** a riot of colors
色狼 **sèláng** N a lascivious man, sexual molester
色盲 **sèmáng** N color blindness, achromatopsia
色情 **sèqíng** N pornography
色欲 **sèyù** N lust, sexual lust

森 sēn N forest
森林 **sēnlín** N forest

杀 shā TRAD 殺 v kill
谋杀 **móuhài** murder
杀害 **shāhài** v kill, murder

刹 shā as in 刹车 **shāchē**
刹车 **shāchē** I N brake II v apply brakes, brake
急刹车 **jíshāchē** brake suddenly

沙 shā N sand, grit
沙发 **shāfā** N upholstered chair, sofa, couch
沙漠 **shāmò** N desert
沙滩 **shātān** N sandy beach
沙土 **shātǔ** N sandy soil
沙眼 **shāyǎn** N trachoma
沙子 **shāzi** N sand, grit (粒 **lì**)

砂 shā N grit, sand

纱 shā TRAD 紗 N yarn
棉纱 **miánshā** cotton yarn

傻 shǎ ADJ foolish, stupid
傻子 **shǎzi** N fool, idiot

厦 shà N a tall building, mansion
高楼大厦 **gāolóu dàshà** tall buildings and great mansions

啥 shà PRON what
有啥吃啥 **yǒu shà chī shà** eat whatever you've got

NOTE: 啥 shà is a dialectal word, used on very casual occasions.

筛 **shāi** V sieve, sift
筛子 **shāizi** sieve

晒 **shài** TRAD 曬 V dry in the sun, bask
晒太阳 **shài tàiyang** sunbathe

山 **shān** N mountain, hill (座 zuò)
爬山 **páshān** mountain climbing, mountaineering
山地 **shāndì** N hilly area, mountainous region
山地车 **shāndìchē** mountain bike (辆 liàng)
山峰 **shānfēng** N mountain peak (座 zuò)
山冈 **shāngāng** N low hill (座 zuò)
山沟 **shāngōu** N gully, ravine (条 tiáo)
山谷 **shāngǔ** N valley (条 tiáo)
山河 **shānhé** N mountains and rivers, land (of a country)
大好山河 **dàhǎo shānhé** the beautiful land (of a country)
山脚 **shānjiǎo** N the foot of a hill (mountain)
在山脚下 **zài shānjiǎo xià** at the foot of the hill (mountain)
山岭 **shānlǐng** N mountain ridge
山脉 **shānmài** N mountain range (条 tiáo)
山水 **shānshuǐ** N landscape
游山玩水 **yóu-shān-wán-shuǐ** enjoy the landscape, go sightseeing
山头 **shāntóu** N hilltop (座 zuò)
山腰 **shānyāo** N halfway up the mountain, mountainside

衫 **shān** N shirt (See 衬衫 chènshān.)

珊 **shān** N as in 珊瑚 shānhú
珊瑚 **shānhú** N coral

删 **shān** V delete (words)

闪 **shǎn** TRAD 閃 V 1 flash, sparkle 2 glitter, twinkle
闪电 **shǎndiàn** N lightning

闪盘 **shǎnpán** N (computing) flash memory disk
闪烁 **shǎnshuò** V twinkle, glitter
闪耀 **shǎnyào** V shine

扇 **shàn** N fan (See 电扇 diànshàn.)

善 **shàn** ADJ good, kind, friendly
善良 **shànliáng** ADJ kind-hearted, good-hearted
善于 **shànyú** V be good at

擅 **shàn** I V be good at II ADV (doing things) without authorization
擅长 **shàncháng** ADJ expert in, having a special skill
擅长谈判 **shàncháng tánpàn** be especially good at negotiation, be an expert negotiator
擅自 **shànzì** ADV without permission, without authorization

伤 **shāng** TRAD 傷 I V wound, injure, hurt II N wound, injury
受伤 **shòushāng** be wounded, be injured
伤疤 **shāngbā** N scar
伤风 **shāngfēng** V catch a cold
伤害 **shānghài** V harm, hurt
伤痕 **shānghén** N bruise, scar
伤口 **shāngkǒu** N wound, cut
伤脑筋 **shāng nǎojīn** I V be vexed, be frustrated II ADJ troublesome, vexing
伤脑筋的问题 **shāng nǎojīn de wèntí** a very difficult problem, a thorny problem
伤心 **shāngxīn** ADJ heartbreaking, heart-broken
伤员 **shāngyuán** N wounded soldier (名 míng)

商 **shāng** I V discuss, consult II N commerce, business
商标 **shāngbiāo** N trademark
商场 **shāngchǎng** N 1 shopping center, mall (家 jiā, 座 zuò) 2 department store
商店 **shāngdiàn** N shop, store (家 jiā)
开商店 **kāi shāngdiàn** open or keep a shop
商量 **shāngliang** V discuss, consult
商品 **shāngpǐn** N commodity (件 jiàn, 种 zhǒng)

商榷 shāngquè v discuss politely, deliberate

商人 shāngrén n merchant, business person

商讨 shāngtǎo v exchange views in order to reach a consensus

商业 shāngyè n commerce, business
　商业管理 shāngyè guǎnlǐ business administration
　商业管理硕士 shāngyè guǎnlǐ shuòshì Master of Business Administration (MBA)
　商业区 shāngyèqū n business district
　商业中心区 shāngyè zhōngxīnqū central business district (CBD)

商议 shāngyì v discuss, confer

赏 **shǎng** TRAD 賞 v 1 admire, enjoy
2 reward, grant

赏罚分明 shǎngfá fēnmíng IDIOM rewarding merit and punishing mistake fairly, exercise discipline judiciously

赏识 shǎngshí v recognize and admire the talent of (people), appreciate the worth of (people)

上 **shàng** I N on top of, on, above
II ADJ previous, last

上星期 shàng xīngqī last week

上一课 shàng yí kè the previous class (lesson)

NOTE: 上 shàng is often used after a noun to form words of location. While its basic meaning is *on top*, 上 shàng may have various, often semi-idiomatic meanings, e.g.

报纸上 bàozhǐ shang in the newspaper
地上 dì shang on the ground
工作上 gōngzuò shang in work
会上 huì shang at the meeting
世界上 shìjiè shang in the world
手上 shǒu shang in hand, in the hands of

上边 shàngbian n above, high up

上层 shàngcéng n upper stratum (of a society)
　上层社会 shàngcéng shèhuì upper social class

上等 shàngděng ADJ (of products) superior, first-rate

上帝 Shàngdì N God

上级 shàngjí n higher authorities, superior

上空 shàngkōng n overhead, in the sky

上面 shàngmian n Same as 上边 shàngbian

上升 shàngshēng v rise

上述 shàngshù n above-mentioned

上诉 shàngsù v appeal (to a higher court)

上午 shàngwǔ n morning (usually from 8 a.m. to noon)

NOTE: 上午 shàngwǔ does not mean the whole morning. It denotes the part of morning from about eight or nine o'clock to noon. The period before eight or nine o'clock is 早晨 zǎochén or 早上 zǎoshang.

上下 shàngxià n from top to bottom, up and down

上旬 shàngxún n the first 10 days of a month

上衣 shàngyī n upper garment, jacket (件 jiàn)

上游 shàngyóu n upper reaches (of a river)

上载 shàng zài v upload

上涨 shàngzhǎng v (of rivers, prices) rise, go up

上 **2 shàng** v 1 go upwards, ascend

上楼 shàng lóu go upstairs

上来 shànglai come up

上去 shàngqu go up

2 get on (a vehicle), go aboard (a plane, ship)

上车 shàng chē get into a vehicle
上船 shàng chuán board a ship
上飞机 shàng fēijī get on the plane

3 attend (school), go to (work)

上大学 shàng dàxué go to university

上班 shàngbān v go to work

上报 shàngbào v 1 report to a higher body
2 appear in the newspapers

上当 shàngdàng v be fooled, be duped

上课 shàngkè v go to class, have classes

上任 shàngrèn v assume office, take up a post

上市 shàngshì v be available on the market

上市公司 shàngshì gōngsī listed company

上台 shàngtái v **1** go on stage **2** come to power

上网 shàngwǎng v get on the Internet, surf the Internet

上学 shàngxué v go to school

尚 shàng v worship, revere

裳 shang n clothing (See 衣裳 yīshang)

烧 shāo TRAD 燒 v **1** burn **2** cook **3** have a fever

烧饼 shāobǐng n sesame seed cake (块 kuài)

烧毁 shāohuǐ v burn up

捎 shāo v take (something) along for (someone)

捎个话儿 shāo gè huàr take an (oral) message, relay a message

梢 shāo n the thin tip of a long-shaped object

树梢儿 shùshāor treetops

稍 shāo ADV Same as 稍微 shāowéi. Often used in written Chinese.

稍微 shāowéi ADV slightly, just a little bit

勺 sháo n spoon

勺子 sháozi n ladle, spoon (把 bǎ)

少 shǎo **I** ADJ small in amount, few, little **II** ADV not often, seldom **III** v be short, be missing

少量 shǎoliàng n small amount, little, few

少数 shǎoshù n minority

少数民族 shǎoshù mínzú minority nationality (non-Han ethnic group in China)

少 shào ADJ young

少年 shàonián n young man (from around 10 to 16 years old), adolescent

NOTE: (1) A young woman of around 10 to 16 years old is called 少女 shàonǚ. (2) The word 青少年 qīngshàonián is often used to mean *young people* collectively.

少女 shàonǚ n teenage girl

少先队 Shàoxiānduì n the Young Pioneers

NOTE: 少先队 Shàoxiānduì is the shortened form of 少年先锋队 Shàonián Xiānfēngduì.

绍 shào TRAD 紹 v connect (See 介绍 jièshào.)

哨 shào n **1** sentry **2** whistle

哨兵 shàobīng n sentry, armed guard (名 míng)

哨子 shàozi n whistle

吹哨子 chuī shàozi blow a whistle

奢 shē ADJ excessive, luxurious

奢侈 shēchǐ ADJ luxurious

奢侈品 shēchǐpǐn luxury item

舌 shé n tongue

舌头 shétou n the tongue

蛇 shé n snake (条 tiáo)

舍 shě v give up

舍不得 shěbude v unwilling to give up, hate to part with

舍得 shěde v be willing to part with, not grudge

设 shè TRAD 設 v equip, set up

设备 shèbèi n equipment, installation (件 jiàn, 套 tào)

设法 shèfǎ v try to find a way, attempt to

设计 shèjì **I** v design **II** n design, plan

设立 shèlì v establish, set up

设施 shèshī n facilities, equipment

设想 shèxiǎng v conceive, envision

不堪设想的后果 bùkān shèxiǎng de hòuguǒ inconceivable consequences

设置 shèzhì v set up, establish

社 shè N association

社会 shèhuì N society
社会上 shèhuì shang in society, the general public

社会学 shèhuìxué N sociology

社会主义 shèhuì zhǔyì N socialism

社交 shèjiāo N social life, social intercourse

社论 shèlùn N editorial (篇 piān)

舍 shè N hut, shed (See 宿舍 sùshè.)

摄 shè TRAD 攝 V photograph, shoot (movies, etc)

摄氏 shèshì N Celsius, centigrade
摄氏温度计 shèshì wēndùjì centigrade thermometer

NOTE: China uses Celsius (摄氏 shèshì), not Fahrenheit (华氏 huáshì). In everyday speech, people usually do not mention 摄氏 shèshì. So if a Chinese person says 今天最高气温二十八度。Jīntiān zuìgāo qìwēn èrshíbā dù, it automatically means *The highest temperature today will be 28 degrees Celsius.*

摄像 shèxiàng V make a video recording
摄像机 shèxiàngjī camcorder

摄影 shèyǐng N photography
摄影家 shèyǐngjiā accomplished photographer
摄影师 shèyǐngshī photographer
摄影作品 shèyǐng zuòpǐn a work of photography

射 shè V shoot (a gun, an arrow etc.)

射击 shèjī V shoot, fire

涉 shè V involve (See 干涉 gānshè.)

涉及 shèjí V involve, touch on, have something to do with

谁 shéi TRAD 誰 PRON Same as 谁 shuí. Used colloquially.

身 shēn I N human body II M. WD (for clothes)
一身新衣服 yì shēn xīn yīfu a suit of new clothes

身边 shēnbiān N close by one's side, on one's person

身材 shēncái N stature, figure
身材苗条 shēncái miáotiáo with a slender figure

身分(份) shēnfen N social status, identity
身分不明 shēnfen bùmíng unknown identity

身分证 shēnfenzhèng N I.D. card

身体 shēntǐ N 1 human body 2 health

NOTE: Although its original meaning is the *body*, 身体 shēntǐ is often used in colloquial Chinese to mean *health*. Friends often ask about each other's health in greeting: 你最近身体怎么样? Nǐ zuìjìn shēntǐ zěnmeyàng? *How's your health been recently?*

深 shēn ADJ 1 deep 2 difficult to understand, profound

深奥 shēn'ào ADJ profound, abstruse

深沉 shēnchén ADJ deep, heavy
深沉的爱 shēnchén de ài deep love

深处 shēnchù N depths, recesses
内心深处 nèixīn shēnchù one's innermost heart, one's most private feelings and thoughts

深度 shēndù N depth, how deep something is

深厚 shēnhòu ADJ deep, profound

深化 shēnhuà V deepen

深刻 shēnkè ADJ incisive, insightful, profound

深浅 shēnqiǎn N 1 Same as 深度 shēndù 2 proper limit for speech or action, propriety

深切 shēnqiè ADJ heartfelt, earnest

深情 shēnqíng N deep feelings

深入 shēnrù V enter deeply into
深入浅出 shēn-rù-qiǎn-chū IDIOM explain complicated theories or phenomena in simple, easy-to-understand language.

深信 shēnxìn V firmly believe, be deeply convinced

深远 shēnyuǎn ADJ profound and lasting, far-reaching

深重 shēnzhòng ADJ extremely serious, extremely grave

申 shēn V explain, state

申报 shēnbào V 1 declare (at customs) 2 submit an official report

申请 shēnqǐng V apply for (a visa, job, permit, etc.)

申请表 shēnqǐngbiǎo application form

申请人 shēnqǐngrén applicant

申请书 shēnqǐngshū letter of application

申述 shēnshù V give an official explanation

伸 shēn V stretch out, extend

伸展 shēnzhǎn V extend, stretch

绅 shēn TRAD 紳 as in 绅士 shēnshì

绅士 shēnshì N gentleman, gentry

呻 shēn as in 呻吟 shēnyín

呻吟 shēnyín V groan, moan

神 shén I N god, supernatural being

财神爷 cáishényé the god of money, Mammon

II ADJ magical, wondrous

神话 shénhuà N mythology, myth

神经 shénjīng N 1 nerve 2 the mind, mental state

神经病 shénjīngbìng neuropathy, mental disorder, crazy

NOTE: The formal word for *mental disorder* is 精神病 jīngshénbìng but 神经病 shénjīngbing may be used in everyday Chinese.

神秘 shénmì ADJ mysterious

神奇 shénqí ADJ miraculous, mystical

神气 shénqì ADJ 1 arrogant and cocky 2 spirited and vigorous

神情 shénqíng N (facial) expression, look

神色 shénsè N appearance, expression

神圣 shénshèng ADJ sacred, holy

神态 shéntài N bearing, appearance

神仙 shénxiān N immortal, celestial being (位 wèi)

什 shén PRON what

什么 shénme PRON what

什么的 shénmede PRON and so on, and so forth

审 shěn V 1 examine 2 interrogate

审查 shěnchá V examine, investigate

审定 shěndìng V examine and approve (a proposal, a plan, etc.)

审计 shěnjì V audit

审计员 shěnjìyuán auditor

审理 shěnlǐ V try (a legal case), handle (a legal case)

审美 shěnměi N appreciation of what is beautiful

审判 shěnpàn V bring to trial, try

审批 shěnpī V examine and approve

审问 shěnwèn V Same as 审讯 shěnxùn

审讯 shěnxùn V interrogate (by the police)

审议 shěnyì V deliberate, consider

婶 shěn N wife of one's father's younger brother

婶母 shěnmǔ wife of one's father's younger brother

婶婶 shěnshen Same as 婶母 shěnmǔ. Used as a form of address

肾 shèn N kidney

肾炎 shènyán N nephritis

甚 shèn ADV much, very much

甚至 shènzhì ADV even, so much so

慎 shèn ADJ cautious

慎重 shènzhòng ADJ very cautious, discreet

渗 shèn V seep, ooze

渗透 shèntòu V seep into, permeate

升 shēng V rise, go up

生 shēng 1 shēng I V 1 give birth to, grow 2 be born 3 live, grow II ADJ alive, living

生病 shēngbìng V fall ill

生产 shēngchǎn V produce, manufacture

生产力 shēngchǎnlì N productive force

生产率 shēngchǎnlǜ N productivity

生存 shēngcún I V survive, be alive II N survival

生动 shēngdòng ADJ vivid, lively

生活 shēnghuó I N life

  日常生活 rìcháng shēnghuó daily life II V live, lead (a life)

生活费 shēnghuófèi N living allowance, stipend

生活费用 shēnghuó fèiyòng N cost of living

生活水平 shēnghuó shuǐpíng N living standards

  提高生活水平 tígāo shēnghuó shuǐpíng raise living standards

生机 shēngjī N **1** chance of survival, lease of life

  一线生机 yíxiàn shēngjī a slim chance of survival

  2 vitality

生机勃勃 shēngjī bóbó full of vigor and vitality

生理 shēnglǐ N the physical aspect of human life

  生理上 shēnglǐ shàng physical, physically

生理学 shēnglǐxué physiology

生命 shēngmìng N life (条 tiáo)

  生命科学 shēngmìng kēxué life science

生命力 shēngmìnglì N life force

生怕 shēngpà CONJ for fear of, so as not to

生气 shēngqì V get angry, be offended

生前 shēngqián N (of a dead person) during his/her lifetime

生日 shēngrì N birthday

  过生日 guò shēngrì celebrate a birthday

生日贺卡 shēngrì hékǎ birthday card

生日礼物 shēngrì lǐwù birthday present

生态 shēngtài N ecology

生态学家 shēngtàixuéjiā ecologist

生态旅游 shēngtài lǚyóu ecotourism

生物 shēngwù N living things

生物学 shēngwùxué biology

生物化学 shēngwù huàxué chemical biology, biochemistry

生效 shēngxiào V come into effect, become effective

生意 shēngyi N business, trade

生育 shēngyù V give birth to, bear

生长 shēngzhǎng V grow, grow up

生殖 shēngzhí V reproduce

生殖系统 shēngzhí xìtǒng reproductive system

生 2 shēng ADJ **1** raw, not cooked **2** unripe **3** unfamiliar

生词 shēngcí N new words and phrases (in a language lesson)

  记生词 jì shēngcí memorize new words

生人 shēngrén N stranger

生疏 shēngshū ADJ unfamiliar

  人地生疏 réndìshēngshū unfamiliar with the place and the people, be a stranger in a place

甥 shēng N one's sister's child (See 外甥 wàishēng)

牲 shēng N domesticated animal

牲畜 shēngchù N livestock, domestic animal (头 tóu)

牲口 shēngkou N pack animal, draught animal (e.g. horse, buffalo) (头 tóu)

声 shēng TRAD 聲 N sound, noise, voice

声调 shēngdiào N tone of a Chinese character

声明 shēngmíng I N formal statement II V make a statement, publicly declare

声势 shēngshì N power and influence, momentum

声音 shēngyīn N voice, sound

声誉 shēngyù N reputation, prestige

绳 shéng TRAD 繩 N string, rope

绳子 shéngzi rope, cord (根 gēn, 条 tiáo)

省 1 shěng N province

省会 shěnghuì N provincial capital

省长 shěngzhǎng N governor of a province

省 2 shěng V **1** save, economize **2** leave out, omit

省得 shěngde CONJ in case, so as not to

省略 shěnglüè V omit, leave out

省略号 shěnglüèhào N (punctuation mark to indicate ellipsis ...), ellipsis

胜 **shèng** TRAD 勝 v triumph (over), be victorious, defeat

胜利 **shènglì** I v win a victory II N victory

剩 **shèng** v be left over, have as surplus

剩菜 **shèng cài** N leftovers

剩余 **shèngyú** I N surplus, remainder II v Same as 剩 **shèng**

盛 **shèng** ADJ 1 flourishing, prosperous 2 magnificent, grand 3 popular, common

盛产 **shènchǎn** v produce an abundance of, abound in

盛大 **shèngdà** ADJ grand, magnificent

盛大的典礼 **shèngdà de diǎnlǐ** a grand and elaborate ceremony

盛开 **shèngkāi** v bloom luxuriantly

盛情 **shèngqíng** N great kindness, lavish hospitality

盛行 **shèngxíng** v be in vogue, be very popular

圣 **shèng** TRAD 聖 ADJ sacred, holy

圣诞节 **shèngdànjié** N Christmas

圣诞夜 **shèngdànyè** Christmas eve

失 **shī** I v 1 lose 2 err, make mistakes II N slip, mishap, mistake

失败 **shībài** I v be defeated, lose, fail II N defeat, loss, failure

失眠 **shīmián** I N insomnia II v suffer from insomnia

失去 **shīqù** v lose (something valuable)

失事 **shīshì** v have an accident

失望 **shīwàng** ADJ disappointed

对…失望 **duì…shīwàng** be disappointed with …

失误 **shīwù** I v make a mistake, muff II N fault, error, miscalculation

失效 **shīxiào** v (of documents) become invalid, expire, (of medicines) cease to be effective

失学 **shīxué** v be unable to go to school, be deprived of education

失业 **shīyè** v lose one's job, become unemployed

失约 **shīyuē** v fail to keep an appointment

失踪 **shīzōng** v be missing, disappear

失踪人员 **shīzōng rényuán** missing person

师 **shī** TRAD 師 N master, teacher

师范 **shīfàn** teachers' education

师范学院 **shīfàn xuéyuàn** teachers' college, college of education

师傅 **shīfu** N master worker (位 **wèi**)

NOTE: 师傅 **shīfu** is also a polite form of address for *a worker*. For example, an electrician or mechanic can be addressed as 师傅 **shīfu** or, if his family name is 李 **Lǐ**, 李师傅 **Lǐ shīfu**.

师长 **shīzhǎng** N 1 teacher 2 division commander (in the army)

诗 **shī** N poem, poetry (首 **shǒu**)

诗歌 **shīgē** N poem, poetry (首 **shǒu**)

诗人 **shīrén** N poet (名 **míng**)

施 **shī** v carry out, execute

施肥 **shīféi** v apply fertilizer

施工 **shīgōng** v (construction work) be underway, be in progress

施加 **shījiā** v exert, bring to bear on

对…施加压力 **duì…shījiā yālì** put pressure on …

施行 **shīxíng** v (of regulations, laws, etc.) put into force, implement, enforce

施展 **shīzhǎn** v put out to good use, give free play to

狮 **shī** TRAD 獅 N lion

狮子 **shīzi** lion (头 **tóu**)

湿 **shī** TRAD 濕 ADJ damp, wet

湿度 **shīdù** N humidity, moisture

湿润 **shīrùn** ADJ moist

尸 **shī** TRAD 屍 N dead body, corpse

尸体 **shītǐ** dead body, corpse (具 **jù**)

十 **shí** NUM ten

十五 **shíwǔ** fifteen, 15

五十 **wǔshí** fifty, 50

十分 **shífēn** ADV one hundred percent, totally, fully

十全十美 **shíquán shíměi** IDIOM perfect in every way

十足 **shízú** ADV 100 percent, out-and-out

拾 1 **shí** NUM ten

拾 2 **shí** V pick up (from the ground)

石 **shí** N stone, rock

石灰 **shíhuī** N lime
　石灰石 **shíhuīshí** limestone

石头 **shítou** N stone, rock (块 kuài)

石油 **shíyóu** N petroleum, oil

蚀 **shí** V lose

蚀本 **shíběn** V lose one's capital (in business ventures)

识 **shí** TRAD 識 V know (See 认识 rènshi, 知识 zhīshi.)

识别 **shíbié** V distinguish, identify, recognize

识别敌友 **shíbié dí yǒu** tell enemies from friends

识字 **shízì** V learn to to read, become literate

时 **shí** TRAD 時 N Same as 点钟 diǎnzhōng. Used only in writing.

时常 **shícháng** ADV often, frequently

时代 **shídài** N a historical period, epoch, age

时而 **shí'ér** ADV occasionally, sometimes

时光 **shíguāng** N time

时候 **shíhou** N a certain point in time, (the time) when

时机 **shíjī** N opportunity, opportune moment

时间 **shíjiān** N a period of time

时节 **shíjié** N occasion, season
　荷花盛开的时节 **héhuā shèngkāi de shíjié** the season when lotus flowers are in full bloom

时刻 **shíkè** N at a particular point in time
　时刻表 **shíkèbiǎo** (railway, coach, etc.) timetable

时髦 **shímáo** ADJ fashionable, in vogue

时期 **shíqī** N period of time, stage

时时 **shíshí** ADV constantly, at all times

时事 **shíshì** N current affairs, current events

时装 **shízhuāng** N the latest fashion
　时装表演 **shízhuāng biǎoyǎn** fashion show
　时装设计 **shízhuāng shèjì** fashion design

实 **shí** TRAD 實 I ADJ real, true II N reality, fact

实话 **shíhuà** N true fact, truth
　实话实说 **shíhuà shíshuō** tell the truth

实惠 **shíhuì** I N real benefit II ADJ substantial

实际 **shíjì** I N reality, actual situation II ADJ practical, realistic

实践 **shíjiàn** I V put into practice, apply II N practice

实况 **shíkuàng** N what is really happening
　实况转播 **shíkuàng zhuǎnbō** live broadcast

实力 **shílì** N actual strength, strength
　军事实力 **jūnshì shílì** military strength

实施 **shíshī** V put into effect, carry out

实事求是 **shíshìqiúshì** IDIOM find out truth from the facts, be realistic

实体 **shítǐ** N 1 entity 2 substance

实物 **shíwù** N real object
　实物交易 **shíwù jiāoyì** barter

实习 **shíxí** N practice, fieldwork

实现 **shíxiàn** V materialize, realize

实行 **shíxíng** V put into practice, take effect, implement, carry out, institute

实验 **shíyàn** N experiment, test (项 xiàng, 次 cì)
　实验室 **shíyànshì** laboratory
　实验员 **shíyànyuán** laboratory technician

实业 **shíyè** N industry and commerce, industry
　实业家 **shíyèjiā** entrepreneur, industrialist

实用 **shíyòng** ADJ practical (for use), useful, handy

实在 **shízài** I ADJ honest, truthful II ADV indeed, really

实质 **shízhì** N substance, essence
　实质上 **shízhìshang** in essence, practically, virtually

食 **shí** N food, meal

食品 **shípǐn** N foodstuff (as commodities) (件 jiàn)

食品工业 **shípǐn gōngyè** food industry

食品加工 **shípǐn jiāgōng** food processing

食品商店 **shípǐn shāngdiàn** provision shop, grocery

食堂 **shítáng** N dining hall

食物 **shíwù** N food

食用 **shíyòng** ADJ used as food, edible

食欲 **shíyù** N appetite

没有食欲 **méiyǒu shíyù** have no appetite

史 **shǐ** N history (See 历史 lìshǐ)

史料 **shǐliào** N historical data, historical materials

屎 **shǐ** N excrement

使 **shǐ** V 1 make, enable 2 make use of, apply

使得 **shǐdé** V Same as 使 shǐ 1

使劲 **shǐjìn** V exert all one's strength

使命 **shǐmìng** N mission

不辱使命 **bùrǔ shǐmìng** mission accomplished

使用 **shǐyòng** V use, apply

驶 **shǐ** V sail, drive

始 **shǐ** V begin, start (See 开始 kāishǐ)

始终 **shǐzhōng** ADV from beginning to end, throughout, ever

示 **shì** V show, indicate

示范 **shìfàn** V set an example, demonstrate

教学示范 **jiàoxué shìfàn** teaching demonstration

示弱 **shìruò** V show signs of weakness

示威 **shìwēi** V put on a show of force, demonstrate

抗议示威 **kàngyì shìwēi** protest demonstration

示意图 **shìyìtú** N sketch map

士 **shì** N 1 scholar, gentleman (See 博士 bóshì, 护士 hùshì, 女士 nǚshì, 硕士 shuòshì, 学士 xuéshì, 战士 zhànshì.)

2 non-commisioned officer

士兵 **shìbīng** N rank-and-file soldier, private

誓 **shì** V vow, pledge

发誓 **fāshì** vow, swear, take an oath

誓言 **shìyán** N oath, pledge

氏 **shì** N family name

侍 **shì** V wait on, serve

侍女 **shìnǚ** N maid

侍候 **shìhòu** V wait on, look after

释 **shì** TRAD 釋 V 1 explain (See 解释 jiěshì) **2** let go, be relieved of

释放 **shìfàng** V release, set free

世 **shì** N 1 the world **2** lifetime **3** generation, era

世代 **shìdài** N generations

世代经商 **shìdài jīngshāng** have been businessmen for generations

世纪 **shìjì** N century

世界 **shìjiè** N the world

世界上 **shìjiè shang** in the world

世界博览会 **Shìjiè Bólǎnhuì** the World Exposition

世界贸易组织 **Shìjiè Màoyì Zǔzhī** the World Trade Organization (WTO)

世界卫生组织 **Shìjiè Wèishēng Zǔzhī** the World Health Organization (WHO)

世界观 **shìjièguān** N the way one looks at the world, world outlook, ideology

市 **shì** N 1 municipality, city **2** market

市场 **shìchǎng** N marketplace, market

市场经济 **shìchǎng jīngjì** market economy

菜市场 **cài shìchǎng** vegetable market, food market

市价 **shìjià** N market price

市民 **shìmín** N resident of a city, townsfolk

市长 **shìzhǎng** N mayor

式 **shì** N form, pattern

式样 **shìyàng** N style, type

事 **shì** N 1 affair, matter (件 jiàn) **2** job, work

找个事做 zhǎo ge shì zuò try to find something to do, try to find a job

3 accident, something bad

事变 shìbiàn N military or political incident of historical significance

事故 shìgù N accident, mishap (件 jiàn)

事故现场 shìgù xiànchǎng scene of an accident

工伤事故 gōngshāng shìgù industrial accident

交通事故 jiāotōng shìgù traffic accident, road accident

事迹 shìjì N deed, achievement

英雄事迹 yīngxióng shìjì heroic deeds

事件 shìjiàn N (historic) event, incident

事例 shìlì N example, case

事情 shìqing N Same as 事 shì

NOTE: (1) In many cases, 事 shì may be replaced by 事情 shìqing, e.g.: 这件事情很重要，一定要办好。Zhè jiàn shìqing hěn zhòngyào, yídìng yào bànhǎo. *This is an important matter and must be done well.*

找个事情做 zhǎo ge shìqing zuò try to find something to do, try to find a job.

(2) 事 shì or 事情 shìqing is a noun that can be applied widely, denoting *any affair, matter or business to be done or considered.* Here is another example: 我今天晚上没有事情做。Wǒ jīntiān wǎnshang méiyǒu shìqing zuò. *I've nothing to do this evening.*

事实 shìshí N fact (件 jiàn)

事实上 shìshí shang in fact, as a matter of fact

事态 shìtài N state of affairs, situation

事先 shìxiān ADV beforehand, in advance

事务 shìwù N matters to attend to, work

事务工作 shìwù gōngzuò routine work

事项 shìxiàng N item, matter

注意事项 zhùyì shìxiàng points for attention

事业 shìyè N **1** career **2** cause, undertaking

视 shì TRAD 視 V watch (See 电视 diànshì)

视察 shìchá V (of a high-ranking official) inspect, observe

视觉 shìjué N the sense of sight

视力 shìlì N eyesight, sight

视力测验 shìlì cèyàn eyesight test

视频光盘 shìpín guāngpán video compact disc, VCD

视线 shìxiàn N line of sight

挡住了视线 dǎngzhù le shìxiàn block one's view

视野 shìyě N field of vision

是 shì V **1** be, yes **2** (indicating existence of), (there) be **3** (used to emphasize the words following it)

是非 shìfēi N **1** right and wrong, truth and falsehood

明辨是非 míngbiàn shìfēi distinguish clearly between right and wrong

2 trouble, quarrel

搬弄是非 bānnòng shìfēi sow discord, tell tales

饰 shì TRAD 飾 V decorate (See 装饰 zhuāngshì)

室 shì N room (See 办公室 bàngōngshì, 教室 jiàoshì, 浴室 yùshì.)

柿 shì N persimmon (See 西红柿 xīhóngshì.)

适 shì TRAD 適 V suit, fit

适当 shìdàng ADJ appropriate, suitable

适合 shìhé V suit, fit

适宜 shìyí ADJ suitable, appropriate

适应 shìyìng V adapt to

适用 shìyòng ADJ applicable, suitable

逝 shì V pass, leave

逝世 shìshì V pass away, die

NOTE: See note on 去世 qùshì.

试 shì TRAD 試 V test, try

试试/试一下 shìshì/shì yíxià have a try

试卷 shìjuàn N examination paper, test paper (份 fèn)

试行 shìxíng V try out

试验 shìyàn V test, experiment (项 xiàng, 次 cì)

试用 shìyòng V try out, be on probation

试用人员 shìyòng rényuán staff on probation

试用期 shìyòngqī probation period

势 **shì** TRAD 勢 N 1 power, force 2 situation, circumstances

势必 shìbì ADV be bound to, be sure to

势力 shìlì N (social) force

匙 **shi** N spoon (See 钥匙 yàoshi.)

收 **shōu** V 1 receive, accept

收到 shōudao receive

收下 shōuxia accept

2 collect (fee), charge

收藏 shōucáng V collect (antiques, collectibles, etc.)

收藏中国明代花瓶 shōucáng Zhōngguó Míngdài huāpíng collect Chinese Ming vases

收成 shōucheng N harvest (of crops)

收复 shōufù V recover (lost territory)

收购 shōugòu V purchase, buy

收购价格 shōugòu jiàgé purchasing price

收回 shōuhuí V take back, recall

收回贷款 shōuhuí dàikuǎn recall a loan, call in a loan

收获 shōuhuò I V gather in crops, harvest II N gain (of work), achievement, reward

收集 shōují V collect, gather

收买 shōumǎi V buy over, buy in

收入 shōurù I V earn, receive II N income

收拾 shōushí V put in order, tidy up

收缩 shōusuō V contract, shrink

收益 shōuyì N profit, earnings

收音机 shōuyīnjī N radio (台 tái, 架 jià)

手 **shǒu** N hand (只 zhī, 双 shuāng)

手上 shǒu shang in the hand

右手 yòushǒu the right hand

左手 zuǒshǒu the left hand

手表 shǒubiǎo N wristwatch (块 kuài)

NOTE: In everyday usage, 手表 shǒubiǎo is often shortened to 表 biǎo: 我的表慢了，你的表几点? Wǒ de biǎo màn le, nǐ de biǎo jǐ diǎn? *My watch is slow. What time is it by your watch?*

手电筒 shǒudiàntǒng N flashlight, torch (只 zhī)

手段 shǒuduàn N means, measure

手法 shǒufǎ N trick, gimmick

手工 shǒugōng ADJ done by hand, made by hand, manual

手工业 shǒugōngyè handicraft industry

手工艺品 shǒugōngyìpǐn handicraft item

手机 shǒujī N cell phone, mobile telephone (只 zhī)

手巾 shǒujin N face towel, towel (条 tiáo)

手绢 shǒujuàn N handkerchief (块 kuài)

手枪 shǒuqiāng N pistol (把 bǎ)

手势 shǒushì N gesture, signal, sign

打手势 dǎ shǒushì make a gesture

手术 shǒushù N operation

手术间 shǒushùjiān operating room, surgery room

做手术 zuò shǒushù perform an operation, operate

手套 shǒutào N glove (只 zhī, 副 fù)

手续 shǒuxù N formalities, procedures

办手续 bàn shǒuxù go through the formalities

手艺 shǒuyì N craftsmanship, workmanship

手指 shǒuzhǐ N finger, thumb

手镯 shǒuzhuó N bracelet

守 **shǒu** V 1 observe, abide by 2 guard, defend

守财奴 shǒucáinú N miser

守法 shǒufǎ V observe the law

守卫 shǒuwèi V guard, defend

首 **shǒu** I N the head II ADJ first

首创 shǒuchuàng V initiate, pioneer

首创精神 shǒuchuàng jīngshén pioneering spirit

首都 shǒudū N capital city

首领 shǒulǐng N leader, chieftain, chief

首脑 shǒunǎo N head

首脑会议 shǒunǎo huìyì summit meeting, summit

首席 shǒuxí ADJ chief, principal

首席小提琴手 shǒuxí xiǎotíqínshǒu the first violinist (of an orchestra)

首席执行官 shǒuxí zhíxíngguān chief executive officer (CEO)

首先 shǒuxiān ADV first, first of all

首相 shǒuxiàng N prime minister
  英国首相 Yīngguó shǒuxiàng the British
  Prime Minister
首要 shǒuyào ADJ of primary importance
首长 shǒuzhǎng N senior official, ranking
  officer

首 2 shǒu M. WD (for songs and
  poems)
  一首歌 yì shǒu gē a song

寿 shòu TRAD 壽 N life, lifespan

  长寿 chángshòu longevity
寿命 shòumìng N lifespan
  寿星 shòuxing birthday boy, birthday
  girl

受 shòu V 1 receive, accept 2 suffer,
  be subject to
  受苦 shòukǔ suffer from hardship
受罚 shòufá V be punished, be penalized
受理 shòulǐ V (of law courts or lawyers)
  accept and handle a case
受聘 shòupìn V be appointed for a position
  受聘担任首席法律顾问 shòupìn dānrèn
  shǒuxí fǎlǜ gùwèn be appointed as
  chief legal advisor
受伤 shòushāng V be wounded, be injured

授 shòu V give, award

授予 shòuyǔ V confer, award
  授予学位 shòuyǔ xuéwèi confer an
  academic degree

瘦 shòu ADJ thin, lean

瘦肉 shòuròu N lean meat
瘦子 shòuzi lean or thin person

售 shòu V sell

售货员 shòuhuòyuán N shop assistant,
  sales clerk

兽 shòu TRAD 獸 N beast, animal

  人面兽心 rénmiàn shòuxīn a human
  face with a beast's heart—a beast in human shape
兽医 shòuyī N 1 veterinary science
  2 veterinary surgeon, veterinarian

殊 shū ADJ different (See 特殊 tèshū)

书 shū TRAD 書 I N 1 book (本 běn) 2
  style of calligraphy 3 letter II V write
  看书 kàn shū read, do reading
书包 shūbāo N schoolbag (只 zhī)
书本 shūběn N book
书呆子 shūdāizi N bookworm, nerd
书店 shūdiàn N bookstore, bookshop (家
  jiā)
书法 shūfǎ N calligraphy
  书法家 shūfǎjiā calligrapher
书籍 shūjí N books (collectively)
书记 shūjì N secretary of the Chinese
  Communist Party organizations
书架 shūjià N bookshelf
书刊 shūkān N books and periodicals
书面 shūmiàn ADJ in written form, written
  书面邀请 shūmiàn yāoqǐng written
  invitation
书目 shūmù N booklist, (book) catalogue
  参考书目 cānkǎo shūmù list of reference
  books, bibliography
书评 shūpíng N book review
书市 shūshì N book fair, book market
书写 shūxiě V write
书信 shūxìn N letter
书展 shūzhǎn N book fair

NOTE: 书展 shūzhǎn is the shortening of
图书展销 túshū zhǎnxiāo.

叔 shū N father's younger brother

叔叔 shūshu N father's younger brother,
uncle

NOTE: 叔叔 shūshu is a form of address
used by a child for a man around his/her
father's age. It is common to put a family
name before 叔叔 shūshu e.g. 张叔叔
Zhāng shūshu. Also see note on 阿姨 āyí.

梳 shū N comb

梳子 shūzi comb (把 bǎ)

舒 shū I ADJ relaxing, leisurely
II V stretch, unfold
舒畅 shūchàng ADJ free from worry

心情舒畅 xīnqíng shūchàng feel care-free

舒服 shūfu ADJ comfortable

不舒服 bù shūfu (of a person) not very well, be under the weather

舒适 shūshì ADJ comfortable, cosy

疏 shū I ADJ 1 sparse, scattered 2 (of relationships) not intimate, distant II v neglect, overlook

疏忽 shūhu I v neglect, overlook II N oversight, omission

疏漏 shūlòu N careless omission, slip

疏远 shūyuǎn ADJ (of relationships) not close, estranged

蔬 shū N vegetable

蔬菜 shūcài vegetable, greens

输 1 shū TRAD 輸 v lose (a game, a bet)

输 2 shū TRAD 輸 v transport

输出 shūchū v export

输送 shūsòng v transport, convey

输血 shūxuè N blood transfusion

熟 shú ADJ 1 ripe, cooked 2 familiar with, well acquainted

熟练 shúliàn ADJ skilful, skilled

熟悉 shúxī ADJ familiar with, well ac-quainted with

数 shǔ TRAD 數 v count

暑 shǔ N heat, hot season

暑假 shǔjià N summer holiday, summer vacation

薯 shǔ N potato, yam

署 shǔ N government office

属 shǔ TRAD 屬 v 1 belong to 2 be born in the year of ...

属相 shǔxiang N (lunar calendar) the traditional twelve animals that mark the cycle of years

属于 shǔyú v belong to

鼠 shǔ N rat, mouse

老鼠 lǎoshǔ rat, mouse (只 zhī)

术 shù TRAD 術 N craft, skill

术语 shùyǔ N technical term, terminology

束 shù N knot

束缚 shùfù v bind up, fetter

述 shù v narrate

述评 shùpíng N commentary, review

树 shù TRAD 樹 I N tree (棵 kē) II v set up

树干 shùgàn N tree trunk

树立 shùlì v set up, establish

树林 shùlín N woods

树木 shùmù N trees (collectively)

树皮 shùpí N bark

数 shù TRAD 數 I N number, figure II ADJ a few, several

数额 shù'é N amount, quota

数据 shùjù N data

数据库 shùjùkù data base

数目 shùmù N number, figure

确切的数目 quèqiè de shùmù precise number

数量 shùliàng N quantity, amount

数学 shùxué N mathematics

数学家 shùxuéjiā mathematician

数字 shùzì N 1 numeral, digit (in writing) 2 figure, number

数字相机 shùzì xiàngjī digital camera

数字摄像机 shùzì shèxiàngjī digital camcorder

竖 shù ADJ vertical

竖立 shùlì v erect, set upright

刷 shuā v brush

耍 shuǎ v play

摔 shuāi v 1 fall, fumble 2 fall and break, cause to fall and break

衰 shuāi v decline, decay

衰老 shuāilǎo ADJ old and in declining health

衰弱 shuāiruò ADJ feeble, very weak

衰退 shuāituì v become weaker, decline
经济衰退 jīngjì shuāituì economic recession

甩 shuǎi v swing, throw

帅 shuài TRAD 帥 I N commander in chief
元帅 yuánshuài marshal
II ADJ beautiful, handsome

率 shuài v lead, command
率领 shuàilǐng v lead, command (troops)

拴 shuān v tie, fasten

双 shuāng TRAD 雙 M. WD 1 two, double 2 a pair of (shoes, chopsticks, etc.)
一双鞋 yì shuāng xié a pair of shoes
两双筷子 liǎng shuāng kuàizi two pairs of chopsticks
双胞胎 shuāngbāotāi N twins
双方 shuāngfāng N both sides, both parties
双人床 shuāngrénchuáng N double bed

霜 shuāng N frost, frostlike powder

爽 shuǎng ADJ 1 crisp, freshing 2 straightforward, open-hearted
爽快 shuǎngkuài 1 straightforward, frank 3 readily, without hesitation

谁 shuí TRAD 誰 PRON 1 who, whom 2 everyone, anybody, whoever, no matter who

水 shuǐ N water
自来水 zìláishuǐ running water, tap water
开水 kāishuǐ boiled water
水产 shuǐchǎn N aquatic product
水产品 shuǐchǎnpǐn aquatic product
水稻 shuǐdào N paddy rice, rice
水电 shuǐdiàn N Same as 水力发电 shuǐlì fādiàn
水电供应 shuǐdiàn gōngyìng water and electricity supply
水电站 shuǐdiànzhàn N Same as 水力发电站 shuǐlì fādiànzhàn

水分 shuǐfèn N moisture content
水果 shuǐguǒ N fruit
水果刀 shuǐguǒ dāo penknife
水果店 shuǐguǒ diàn fruit shop, fruiterer
水库 shuǐkù N reservoir
水利 shuǐlì N water conservancy, irrigation works
水利工程 shuǐlì gōngchéng water conservancy project
水力 shuǐlì N waterpower, hydraulic power
水力发电 shuǐlì fādiàn N hydraulic electricity
水力发电站 shuǐlì fādiànzhàn hydroelectric station, hydropower station
水泥 shuǐní N cement
水平 shuǐpíng N 1 level, standard 2 proficiency (in language)
生活水平 shēnghuó shuǐpíng living standard
提高生活水平 tígāo shēnghuó shuǐpíng raise the standard of living
文化水平 wénhuà shuǐpíng cultural level, educational experience
水土 shuǐtǔ N water and soil
水土流失 shuǐtǔ liúshī soil erosion
水银 shuǐyín N mercury
水源 shuǐyuán N source of a river, headwater
水灾 shuǐzāi N flood, inundation
水蒸气 shuǐzhēngqì N water vapor, steam
水准 shuǐzhǔn N Same as 水平 shuǐpíng

税 shuì N tax, duty
税务局 shuìwùjú tax bureau, Inland Revenue Service
关税 guānshuì tariff, customs duty
税率 shuìlǜ N tax rate
税收 shuìshōu N tax revenue

睡 shuì v sleep
睡觉 shuìjiào v sleep, go to bed

NOTE: (1) 睡 shuì and 睡觉 shuìjiào are often interchangeable. (2) 觉 is pronounced jiào in 睡觉 shuìjiào, but jué in 觉得 juéde.

睡眠 shuìmián N sleep

睡眠不足 **shuìmián bùzú** sleep deficiency

睡衣 **shuìyī** N pajamas, dressing gown

睡着 **shuìzháo** V fall asleep

顺 **shùn** TRAD 順 I ADJ smooth II V 1 arrange, plan 2 do at one's convenience

顺便 **shùnbiàn** ADV in passing, incidentally

顺利 **shùnlì** ADJ smooth, without a hitch, successful

顺手 **shùnshǒu** ADJ 1 smooth, without hitches 2 convenient, without much trouble

顺序 **shùnxù** N sequence, order

说 **shuō** TRAD 說 V 1 say, speak 2 explain, tell

说笑话 **shuō xiàohua** tell a joke

说法 **shuōfǎ** N 1 wording 2 statement, version

说服 **shuōfú** V 1 persuade 2 convince

说谎 **shuōhuǎng** V tell lies, lie

说理 **shuōlǐ** V reason things out, argue

说明 **shuōmíng** I V 1 explain 2 prove, show II N explanation, manual

说情 **shuōqíng** V plead for mercy (for someone)

烁 **shuò** TRAD 爍 V glitter (See 闪烁 **shǎnshuò**)

硕 **shuò** TRAD 碩 ADJ large, big

硕士 **shuòshì** N holder of a master's degree

硕士学位 **shuòshì xuéwèi** master's degree, masterate

司 **sī** V take charge of

司法 **sīfǎ** N administration of justice, judicature

司法机关 **sīfǎ jīguān** judicial office, judicial system

司机 **sījī** N (professional) automobile driver, train driver

司令 **sīlìng** N commander, commanding officer

司令部 **sīlìngbù** N (military) headquarters

斯 **sī** PRON this

NOTE: This character was used in Classical Chinese to mean *this*. In Modern Chinese it is normally used just to transliterate foreign names, e.g. 查尔斯 **Chá'ěrsī** for the English name *Charles*.

撕 **sī** V tear (a piece of paper)

撕得粉碎 **sī dé fěnsuì** tear into tiny pieces, tear up

私 **sī** ADJ private

私人 **sīrén** I ADJ private, personal II N personal relationship

私营 **sīyíng** ADJ privately operated, private owned

私有 **sīyǒu** ADJ privately owned, private

私自 **sīzì** ADV without permission, secretly
私自决定 **sīzì juédìng** make a decision all by oneself and without permission from the authorities

思 **sī** V think

思潮 **sīcháo** N trend of thought, ideological trend

思考 **sīkǎo** V ponder over, think seriously

思念 **sīniàn** V miss, think of longingly

思前想后 **sīqián xiǎnghòu** ponder over, weigh pros and cons

思索 **sīsuǒ** V think hard, beat one's brains

思维 **sīwéi** N thought, thinking, the process of thinking

思想 **sīxiǎng** N thought, thinking
思想家 **sīxiǎngjiā** thinker

思绪 **sīxù** N train of thought, thinking

丝 **sī** TRAD 絲 N 1 silk 2 threadlike things

丝绸 **sīchóu** N silk, silk cloth

丝毫 **sīháo** N the slightest, in the least
没有丝毫变化 **méiyǒu sīháo biànhuà** without the slightest change, haven't changed in the least

NOTE: 丝毫 **sīháo** is usually used alongside with a negative word.

死 sǐ v die

NOTE: See note on 去世 qùshì.

死亡 sǐwáng N death
死亡证 sǐwáng zhèng death certificate
死刑 sǐxíng N death sentence

四 sì NUM four

四十四 sìshí sì forty-four, 44
四处 sìchù ADV here and there, in all directions, everywhere
四方 sìfāng N the four directions of east, west, north and south, all sides
四季 sìjì N the four seasons, all the year round
四季如春 sìjì rú chūn (warm and pleasant) like spring all the year round
四面八方 sìmiàn bāfāng IDIOM in all directions, from all over
四肢 sìzhī N four limbs, arms and legs
四肢发达 sìzhī fādá physically strong
四周 sìzhōu ADV all around, on all sides

肆 sì NUM four

饲 sì v TRAD 飼 raise (animals)

饲料 sìliào N (animal) feed, fodder
饲养 sìyǎng v raise (animals)

伺 sì v watch, await

伺机 sìjī v wait for one's chances

似 sì v seem

似乎 sìhū ADV it seems, as if
似是而非 sìshì'érfēi IDIOM sound right but is actually wrong
似是而非的理论 sìshì'érfēi de lǐlùn a plausibly deceptive theory, a specious theory

寺 sì N monastery, temple

清真寺 qīngzhēnsì mosque

松 1 sōng TRAD 鬆 I ADJ lax, weak II v loosen, slacken (See 放松 fàngsōng)

松 2 sōng N pine

松树 sōngshù pine tree (棵 kē)

耸 sǒng TRAD 聳 v 1 alarm, alert 2 rise up

耸耸肩膀 sǒngsǒng jiānbǎng shrug one's shoulders
耸人听闻 sǒngrén tīngwén IDIOM exaggerate (news) in order to sensationalize

颂 sòng TRAD 頌 v praise, extol

颂扬 sòngyáng v sing praises of, eulogize

讼 sòng TRAD 訟 v file a lawsuit (See 诉讼 sùsòng)

送 sòng v 1 give as a gift 2 deliver 3 accompany, take, escort

送礼 sònglǐ v present a gift to
送大礼 sòng dà lǐ give an expensive gift
送行 sòngxíng v see off
到机场送行 dào jīchǎng sòngxíng see ... off at the airport

诵 sòng TRAD 誦 v chant, recite (See 背诵 bèisòng.)

艘 sōu M. WD (used with nouns denoting boats and ships)

一艘渔轮 yì sōu yúlún a fishing boat

搜 sōu v search

搜查 sōuchá v search, ransack
搜查证 sōucházhèng search warrant
搜集 sōují v collect, gather
搜集资料 sōují zīliào collect data, data-gathering
搜索 sōusuǒ v search
搜索队 sōusuǒduì search party
搜索引擎 sōusuǒ yǐnqíng search engine

嗽 sòu N cough (See 咳嗽 késou.)

苏 sū TRAD 蘇 v revive

苏打 sūdá N soda
苏醒 sūxǐng v regain consciousness, come to

俗 sú N custom, convention

俗话 súhuà N traditional saying, saying

诉 sù TRAD 訴 v tell (See 告诉 gàosu.)

诉讼 sùsòng v lawsuit, litigation

对··提出诉讼 duì...tíchū sùsòng file a lawsuit against

肃 **sù** TRAD 肅 I ADJ solemn (See 严肃 yánsù.) II V clean up, eliminate

肃清 **sùqīng** V eliminate, clean up

速 **sù** N speed

速度 **sùdù** N speed, velocity

素 **sù** ADJ 1 plain, simple (See 朴素 pǔsù) 2 vegetarian

吃素 **chīsù** eat vegetarian food only, be a vegetarian

素菜 **sùcài** N vegetarian dish, vegetarian food

素食 **sùshí** N vegetarian food

素食主义 **sùshí zhǔyì** vegetarianism

素食主义者 **sùshí zhǔyìzhě** vegetarian (a person)

素质 **sùzhì** N (of a person) true quality, basic nature

宿 **sù** V stay overnight

宿舍 **sùshè** N hostel, dormitory

学生宿舍 **xuésheng sùshè** students' hostel (dormitory)

塑 **sù** V mold

塑料 **sùliào** N plastic

塑造 **sùzào** V sculpture, portray

酸 **suān** ADJ sour

算 **suàn** V 1 calculate 2 regard, consider

算了 **suànle** V forget about it, let it pass

算盘 **suànpán** N abacus (把 bǎ)

算是 **suànshì** ADV at last

算术 **suànshù** N arithmetic

算数 **suànshù** V count

蒜 **suàn** N garlic

大蒜 **dàsuàn** garlic

虽 **suī** TRAD 雖 CONJ although

虽然 **suīrán** CONJ although, though

虽说 **suīshuō** Same as 虽然 **suīrán**, used colloquially

随 **suí** TRAD 隨 V let (somebody do as he pleases), as you wish

随便 **suíbiàn** ADJ casual, informal

NOTE: 随便 **suíbiàn** is often used in casual conversation to mean *like as you wish, anything you like,* or *I have no objection whatsoever.* e.g.: "你喝红茶还是绿茶?" "随便。" "Nǐ hē hóngchá háishì lǜchá?" "Suíbiàn." "Do you want to drink black tea or green tea?" "Anything's fine with me."

随后 **suíhòu** ADV immediately afterwards

随即 **suíjí** ADV immediately, soon after

随时 **suíshí** ADV whenever, at any moment

随时随地 **suíshí suídì** IDIOM anytime and anywhere, ever

随手 **suíshǒu** ADV 1 immediately 2 casually, without much thought

随手乱放 **suíshǒu luàn fàng** put ... somewhere casually and without much thought

随意 **suíyì** I ADV as one pleases, casually II ADJ random

随意抽样 **suíyì chōuyàng** random sampling

随着 **suízhe** PREP along with, in the wake of

岁 **suì** TRAD 歲 M. WD year (of age)

NOTE: See 年纪 **niánjì**.

岁数 **suìshu** N years of age

上了岁数的人 **shàngle suìshu de rén** elderly person

岁月 **suìyuè** N years

碎 **suì** ADJ broken, fragmentary (See 破碎 pòsuì)

穗 **suì** N the ear of grain

麦穗 **màisuì** ear of wheat, wheat head

隧 **suì** N tunnel

隧道 **suìdào** N tunnel

孙 **sūn** TRAD 孫 N grandchild

孙女 **sūnnǚ** N granddaughter

孙子 **sūnzi** N grandson

笋 sǔn

笋 sǔn N bamboo shoot

竹笋 zhúsǔn bamboo shoot

损 sǔn TRAD 損 v damage

损害 sǔnhài v harm, damage, injure

损耗 sǔnhào I v undergo wear and tear, deplete II N loss

损坏 sǔnhuài v damage as to render unusable, damage

损坏公物 sǔnhuài gōngwù damage public property

损人利己 sǔnrénlìjǐ IDIOM harm others to benefit oneself

损伤 sǔnshāng v damage, harm, hurt

损失 sǔnshī I v lose, suffer from damage and/or loss II N loss, damage

唆 suō v instigate, abet

唆使 suōshǐ v abet, instigate

缩 suō TRAD 縮 v shrink

缩短 suōduǎn v shorten, cut down

缩小 suōxiǎo v reduce in size, shrink

所 1 suǒ M. WD (for houses or institutions housed in a building)

一所医院 yì suǒ yīyuàn a hospital

两所大学 liǎng suǒ dàxué two universities

所 2 suǒ I N place II PARTICLE indicating passive voice

所得 suǒdé N income, earnings

所得税 suǒdéshuì income tax

所谓 suǒwèi ADJ what is called, so-called

所以 suǒyǐ CONJ therefore, so

所有 suǒyǒu IDIOM ADJ all

NOTE: 所有 suǒyǒu is (1) used only as an attribute, (2) always followed by 的 de and (3) often used together with 都 dōu.

所有制 suǒyǒuzhì N ownership

所在 suǒzài N place, location

索 suǒ v search, search for (See 探索 tànsuǒ)

索赔 suǒpéi v claim indemnity

索取 suǒqǔ v ask for, exact

索取报名单 suǒqǔ bàomíngdān ask for an application form

索性 suǒxìng ADV might as well, simply

锁 suǒ TRAD 鎖 I N lock II v lock

嗦 suo as in 罗嗦 luósuo

T

他 tā PRON he, him

他们 tāmen PRON they, them

他人 tārén PRON another person, other people

它 tā PRON it

它们 tāmen PRON (non-human) they, them (plural form of 它 tā)

她 tā PRON she, her

她们 tāmen PRON (female) they, them

塌 tā v collapse, cave in

踏 tā as in 踏实 tāshi

踏实 tāshi ADJ 1 reliable 2 free from anxiety, reassured

塔 tǎ N pagoda, tower (座 zuò)

踏 tà v step on, tread

蹋 tà v as in 糟蹋 zāota

台 tái TRAD 檯 I N table, desk (张 zhāng) II M. WD (for machines, big instruments, etc.)

一台机器 yì tái jīqì a machine

台风 táifēng N typhoon (场 cháng)

台阶 táijiē N flight of steps, steps

台湾 Táiwān N Taiwan

抬 tái TRAD 擡 v lift, raise

抬高 (物价) táigāo (wùjià) raise (prices)

泰 tài ADJ peaceful

170

泰然 tàirán ADJ calm, composed
泰然自若 tàirán zìruò behave with great composure

太 tài ADV 1 excessively, too 2 extremely, really
太空 tàikōng N outer space
太平 tàipíng ADJ peaceful and orderly
太平间 tàipíngjiān N mortuary
太平洋 Tàipíngyáng N the Pacific Ocean
太太 tàitai N 1 Mrs, Madam 2 wife

NOTE: (1) While Mrs is used in English-speaking countries regardless of class or social status, its counterpart 太太 tàitai meaning wife is only used in middle-class or upper-class circles. (2) Although Chinese women often retain their family names after marriage, 太太 tàitai as a form of address must be prefixed by the husband's family name: 王太太 Wáng tàitai Mrs Wang (the wife of Mr Wang).

太阳 tàiyang N the sun, sunshine
太阳能 tàiyángnéng N solar energy
态 tài TRAD 態 N stance
态度 tàidu N attitude, approach

NOTE: Though 态度 tàidu is glossed as attitude or approach, it is more commonly used in Chinese than its equivalents in English.

汰 tài v eliminate (See 淘汰 táotài)
摊 tān TRAD 攤 N trader's stand, stall
滩 tān TRAD 灘 N beach, shoal (See 沙滩 shātān)
瘫 tān TRAD 癱 v be paralyzed
瘫痪 tānhuàn I v be paralyzed
II N paralysis
全身瘫痪 quánshēn tānhuàn complete paralysis
贪 tān v 1 be greedy 2 be corrupt, practice graft
贪官 tānguān corrupt official
3 covet, hanker after

贪婪 tānlán ADJ greedy, avaricious
贪图 tāntú v hanker after, covet
贪污 tānwū I v embezzle, be involved in corruption
贪污公款 tānwū gōngkuǎn embezzle public funds
II N graft, corruption
贪污犯 tānwūfàn embezzler, grafter
贪心 tānxīn N greed, avarice
贪嘴 tānzuǐ ADJ greedy for food
坛 tán TRAD 壇 N altar
天坛 Tiāntán the Temple of Heaven (in Beijing)
潭 tán N deep pool
痰 tán N phlegm, sputum
吐痰 tǔtán spit
谈 tán TRAD 談 v talk, discuss
谈一下 tán yíxià talk briefly about, give a brief talk about
谈话 tánhuà v have a (serious, formal) talk
谈论 tánlùn v talk about
谈判 tánpàn I v negotiate, hold talks
II N negotiation (项 xiàng)
谈天 tántiān v talk about everything under the sun, shoot the breeze, chitchat
毯 tǎn N carpet, rug, blanket
地毯 dìtǎn carpet, rug
挂毯 guàtǎn tapestry
毯子 tǎnzi N blanket (条 tiáo)
坦 tǎn ADJ 1 candid, frank 2 level, smooth
平坦 píngtǎn (of land) level, flat
坦白 tǎnbái v 1 confess to (crimes or wrongdoing) 2 be frank, be candid
坦白地说 tǎnbáide shuō to be frank with you, to tell the truth
坦克 tǎnkè N tank (military vehicle)
炭 tàn N charcoal
碳 tàn N carbon (C)
二氧化碳 èryǎnghuàtàn carbon dioxide

叹 **tàn** TRAD 嘆 v sigh

叹气 **tànqì** v heave a sigh

探 **tàn** v **1** explore **2** spy **3** visit

探测 **tàncè** v survey, probe

探亲 **tànqīn** v visit one's parents, visit relatives

探索 **tànsuǒ** v explore, seek, search for

探讨 **tàntǎo** v explore and discuss, inquire into

探讨…的可行性 **tàntǎo...de kěxíngxìng** explore the feasibility of ...

探望 **tànwàng** v go to see, visit

探望病人 **tànwàng bìngrén** visit someone who is sick, visit a patient

探险 **tànxiǎn** v venture into, explore

探险队 **tànxiǎnduì** exploration team

探险家 **tànxiǎnjiā** explorer

汤 **tāng** TRAD 湯 N soup (碗 wǎn)

喝汤 **hē tāng** eat soup

汤匙 **tāngchí** N tablespoon (把 bǎ)

汤圆 **tāngyuán** N stuffed dumpling made of glutinous rice

堂 **táng** I N **1** main room, hall (See 食堂 shítáng.) **2** relationship between cousins of the same paternal grandfather

堂兄弟 **tángxiōngdì** male children of one's father's brothers

II M. WD (for a period of lessons)

上午有三堂课 **shàngwǔ yǒu sān táng kè** three classes in the morning

膛 **táng** N chest

唐 **táng** N the Tang Dynasty (AD 618–907)

唐人街 **tángrénjiē** N Chinatown

塘 **táng** N dyke, embankment

糖 **táng** N sugar, candy (块 kuài)

糖果 **tángguǒ** N candy, sweets

倘 **tǎng** CONJ if, in case

倘若 **tǎngruò** CONJ if, in case

躺 **tǎng** v lie

趟 **tàng** M. WD (for trips)

烫 **tàng** TRAD 燙 ADJ boiling hot, scalding hot, burning hot

涛 **tāo** N big waves

滔 **tāo** v inundate, flood

滔滔不绝 **tāotāo bùjué** ADJ talking on and on in a flow of eloquence

掏 **tāo** v pull out, draw out

掏耳朵 **tāo ěrduo** pick one's ears

陶 **táo** N pottery

陶瓷 **táocí** N pottery and porcelain, ceramics

萄 **táo** N as in 葡萄 pútao

淘 **táo** v wash in a pan or basket

淘金 **táojīn** pan for gold

淘气 **táoqì** ADJ naughty, mischievous

淘气鬼 **táoqìguǐ** a naughty child, an imp

淘汰 **táotài** v eliminate through competition

淘汰赛 **táotàisài** (in sports) elimination series

桃 **táo** N peach

桃花 **táohuā** peach blossom

桃树 **táoshù** peach tree

桃子 **táozi** peach (只 zhī)

逃 **táo** v **1** flee, run away (from danger, punishment, etc.) **2** evade, escape

逃避 **táobì** v evade, shirk

逃避责任 **táobì zérèn** evade responsibility

逃跑 **táopǎo** v run way, take flight

逃税 **táoshuì** I v evade paying taxes

II N tax evasion

逃学 **táoxué** v play truant

逃走 **táozǒu** Same as 逃跑 táopǎo

讨 **tǎo** TRAD 討 v ask for, demand

讨好 tǎohǎo v **1** fawn on, toady to **2** be rewarded with good results
吃力不讨好 chīlì bù tǎohǎo work hard only to get negative results, do a thankless job
讨价还价 tǎojià huánjià v haggle over prices, bargain
讨论 tǎolùn **I** v discuss, talk over **II** N discussion (次 cì)
讨厌 tǎoyàn **I** ADJ vexing, disgusting **II** v find vexing, find disgusting
讨债 tǎozhài v press for repayment of a debt

套 tào M. WD set, suit, suite (for a collection of things)
一套衣服 yí tào yīfu a suit of clothes
两套家具 liǎng tào jiājù two sets of furniture

特 tè ADV particularly, especially
特别 tèbié **I** ADJ special **II** ADV especially
特别行政区 tèbié xíngzhèngqū special administrative region
特产 tèchǎn N special local product or produce
特此 tècǐ ADV hereby
特点 tèdiǎn N special features, characteristics
特定 tèdìng ADJ specific, specified, special
特定的条件 tèdìngde tiáojiàn special condition
特快 tèkuài ADJ express
特快火车 tèkuài huǒchē express train
特快专递 tèkuài zhuāndì express delivery
特区 tèqū N special zone
特权 tèquán N privilege
特色 tèsè N distinguishing feature
特殊 tèshū ADJ special, unusual, exceptional
特殊教育 tèshū jiàoyù special education
特务 tèwù N special agent, spy
特意 tèyì ADV for a special purpose, specially
特征 tèzhēng N salient feature

藤 téng N vine, rattan
藤椅 téngyǐ rattan chair

葡萄藤 pútaoténg grape vine

腾 téng v gallop, jump

疼 téng v **1** ache, hurt
头疼 tóu téng headache, have a headache **2** love dearly, dote on

NOTE: 疼 téng in the sense of *ache, hurt* is a colloquial word. You can use 痛 tòng instead of 疼 téng to mean *ache, hurt*.

疼痛 téngtòng ADJ pain, ache, soreness
全身疼痛 quánshēn téngtòng aches and pains all over

梯 tī N ladder, steps (See 电梯 diàntī, 楼梯 lóutī.)

踢 tī v kick
踢球 tī qiú play soccer
踢足球 tī zúqiú play soccer

提 tí v **1** carry in the hand (with the arm down) **2** mention, raise
提建议 tí jiànyì put forward a proposal, make a suggestion
提问题 tí wèntí raise a question
提案 tí'àn N proposal (份 fèn)
提拔 tíbá v promote (to a higher position)
提拔为部门经理 tíbá wéi bùmén jīnglǐ be promoted to branch manager
提包 tíbāo N handbag, shopping bag (只 zhī)
提倡 tíchàng v advocate, recommend
提纲 tígāng N outline
提高 tígāo v raise, advance, improve
提供 tígōng v provide, supply
提交 tíjiāo v submit to, refer to
提炼 tíliàn v extract and purify, refine
提名 tímíng v nominate (for a/an position/election)
提前 tíqián v put ahead of schedule, advance, bring forward
提取 tíqǔ v withdraw, collect
提取存款 tíqǔ cúnkuǎn withdraw money from a bank account
提取行李 tíqǔ xínglǐ collect luggage
提升 tíshēng v promote (to a higher position)

提示 tíshì v hint, tip

提问 tíwèn v put questions to

提醒 tíxǐng v remind, call attention to

提要 tíyào n abstract, synopsis

提议 tíyì I v propose II n proposal

提早 tízǎo v Same as 提前 tíqián

题 tí TRAD 題 n 1 topic, title 2 question, problem

题材 tícái n subject matter, theme

题目 tímù n 1 question for an examination, school exercises, etc. (道 dào) 2 title, subject

蹄 tí n hoof

体 tǐ TRAD 體 I n 1 body 2 substance II v personally do or experience

体操 tǐcāo n gymnastics

体会 tǐhuì I v learn, realize, gain intimate knowledge through personal experience II n personal understanding

体积 tǐjī n volume (mathematics)

体力 tǐlì n physical strength

体谅 tǐliàng v show understanding towards, be sympathetic to, make allowance for

体谅别人的难处 tǐliàng tārén de nánchu understand and sympathize with other people's difficulties, empathize

体面 tǐmiàn I ADJ respectable, decent II n dignity, face

体贴 tǐtiē v give every consideration to, give loving care to

体温 tǐwēn n body temperature, temperature

体现 tǐxiàn v give expression to, embody

体验 tǐyàn n personal experience I v learn through one's personal experience

体育 tǐyù n physical education, sports

体育场 tǐyùchǎng n stadium, sports field

体育馆 tǐyùguǎn n gymnasium

体育课 tǐyù kè n physical education (PE) lesson

体制 tǐzhì n (organizational) system, structure

体质 tǐzhì n physique, constitution

体重 tǐzhòng n (body) weight

惕 tì ADJ be on the alert (See 警惕 jǐngtì)

剃 tì v shave

剃胡子 tì húzi shave one's beard

涕 tì n 1 tears 2 snivel (See 鼻涕 bítì)

屉 tì n drawer (See 抽屉 chōutì)

替 tì v 1 replace, substitute 2 Same as 给 gěi PREP

替代 tìdài v substitute for, replace

替换 tìhuàn v replace, displace

天 tiān n 1 sky, heaven 2 day 3 weather

老天爷 Lǎotiānyé Heavens (a colloquial term that denotes "God" or "Nature")

天才 tiāncái n genius

天地 tiāndì n field of activity, scope of operation

天空 tiānkōng n sky

天气 tiānqì n weather

天然 tiānrán ADJ natural

天然气 tiānránqì natural gas

天色 tiānsè n time of the day

天上 tiānshang n in the sky

天生 tiānshēng ADJ inherent, natural

天堂 tiāntáng n paradise

天天 tiāntiān n every day

天天向上 tiāntiān xiàngshàng make progress every day

天文 tiānwén n astronomy

天文台 tiānwéntái astronomical observatory

天文学家 tiānwénxuéjiā astronomer

天下 tiān xià n under heaven, in the world, on earth

天线 tiānxiàn n antenna

天知道! Tiān zhīdao! IDIOM Only God knows!

天真 tiānzhēn ADJ 1 simple and unaffected, ingenuous 2 naïve, gullible

天主教 tiānzhǔjiào n the Catholic Church, Catholicism

天主教徒 Tiānzhǔjiàotú member of the Catholic Church, Catholic

添 tiān v add

田 **tián** N farmland (esp. paddy fields), fields
　种田 **zhòngtián** grow crops, farm
田地 **tiándì** N farmland, field
田野 **tiányě** N farmland and open country

填 **tián** v fill in (a form, blanks as in an exercise)
填补 **tiánbǔ** v fill, fill up
填写 **tiánxiě** v fill out (a document)

挑 **tiāo** v take one's pick, choose, select
　东挑西拣 **dōng-tiāo-xī-jiǎn** choose this and pick that, spend a long time choosing, be very choosy
挑选 **tiāoxuǎn** v select

条 **tiáo** TRAD 條 I M. WD (for things with a long, narrow shape)
　一条河 **yì tiáo hé** a river
　两条鱼 **liǎng tiáo yú** two fish
II N 1 strip 2 item, article
条件 **tiáojiàn** N 1 condition
　生活条件 **shēnghuó tiáojiàn** living conditions
　工作条件 **gōngzuò tiáojiàn** working conditions
　2 requirement, prerequisite
条款 **tiáokuǎn** N clause (in a contract, an agreement, etc.) (项 **xiàng**)
条理 **tiáolǐ** N orderliness
　有条理 **yǒu tiáolǐ** well-organized
条例 **tiáolì** N regulation, rule
条文 **tiáowén** N clause, article, item
条约 **tiáoyuē** N treaty, pact (份 **fèn**)
条子 **tiáozi** N informal note
　给他留一张条子 **gěi tā liú yì zhāng tiáozi** leave a brief note for him

调 **tiáo** TRAD 調 v 1 adjust 2 mediate 3 provoke, tease
调和 **tiáohé** v 1 mediate, reconcile 2 compromise
调剂 **tiáojì** v adjust, regulate
调节 **tiáojié** v regulate, moderate
　调节器 **tiáojiéqì** regulator, conditioner
调解 **tiáojiě** v mediate, make peace
　调解纠纷 **tiáojiě jiūfēn** mediate disputes
调皮 **tiáopí** ADJ naughty, mischievous
调整 **tiáozhěng** v adjust, rectify

挑 **tiāo** v 1 poke, pick up 2 stir up, instigate
挑拨 **tiǎobō** v instigate, sow discord
　挑拨同事之间的关系 **tiǎobō tóngshì zhījiān de guānxi** sow discord among colleagues
挑衅 **tiǎoxìn** I v provoke II N provocation
　故意挑衅 **gùyì tiǎoxìn** deliberate provocation
挑战 **tiǎozhàn** v challenge to battle, challenge to a contest, throw down the gauntlet

跳 **tiào** v jump, leap, hop
跳动 **tiàodòng** v move up and down, beat
跳高 **tiào gāo** N high jump
　撑竿跳高 **chēnggān tiàogāo** pole vault, pole jump
跳绳 **tiào shéng** N rope-skipping, rope-jumping
跳水 **tiào shuǐ** N diving
　跳板跳水 **tiàobǎn tiàoshuǐ** springboard diving
　跳台跳水 **tiàotái tiàoshuǐ** platform diving
跳远 **tiào yuǎn** N long jump
　三级跳远 **sānjí tiàoyuǎn** hop, step and jump, triple jump
跳舞 **tiàowǔ** v dance
跳跃 **tiàoyuè** v jump, leap
跳蚤 **tiàozǎo** N flea (只 **zhī**)

贴 **tiē** TRAD 貼 v paste, stick

帖 **tiě** N invitation card
　请帖 **qǐngtiě** invitation card

铁 **tiě** TRAD 鐵 N iron
铁道 **tiědào** N Same as 铁路 **tiělù**
铁路 **tiělù** N railway (条 **tiáo**)

厅 **tīng** TRAD 廳 N hall (See 餐厅 **cāntīng**.)

听 **tīng** TRAD 聽 v 1 listen
听见 **tīngjiàn** hear
　2 heed, obey
听话 **tīnghuà** v heed, be obedient
听讲 **tīngjiǎng** v listen to a talk (or lecture)

听取 tīngqǔ v hear (one's subordinate's report, complaint, etc.)

听说 tīngshuō v hear of, it is said

听写 tīngxiě N dictation, do dictation

听众 tīngzhòng N audience (of a radio, a concert, etc.)

亭 tíng N pavilion, kiosk

亭子 tíngzi pavilion, kiosk

停 tíng v 1 stop, park (a vehicle)

停下来 tíng xiàlai come to a stop **2** stay over

停泊 tíngbó v (of ships) lie at anchor, anchor

停车 tíngchē v stop a car, park a car

停车场 tíngchēchǎng parking lot, car park

停顿 tíngdùn v pause

停留 tíngliú v stop and stay for a short while, stop over

停职 tíngzhí v suspend from one's duties (as a disciplinary action)

停止 tíngzhǐ v stop, cease

停滞 tíngzhì v stagnate, be at a standstill

庭 tíng N front courtyard

庭院 tíngyuàn N courtyard and garden

艇 tíng N light boat (艘 sōu)

救生艇 jiùshēngtíng lifeboat

挺 tíng I ADV very II ADJ tall, upright, erect

NOTE: 挺 tǐng and 很 hěn share the same meaning, but 挺 tǐng is a colloquial word.

挺拔 tǐngbá ADJ tall and straight

挺立 tǐnglì v stand upright

通 tōng I v 1 (of roads, railways) lead to, go to **2** go through without blockage **3** understand, comprehend **4** notify, give notice II ADJ 1 (of language) grammatical, logical **2** in general use

通报 tōngbào I v (of government offices) circulate a notice II N circular, bulletin

通常 tōngcháng ADJ general, usual

通道 tōngdào N thoroughfare, passageway

通风 tōngfēng N ventilation

通风口 tōngfēngkǒu ventilation opening

通风系统 tōngfēng xì tǒng ventilation system

通告 tōnggào I v give public notice, announce II N public notice, announcement

通过 tōngguò I v pass through II PREP through, as a result of

通航 tōngháng v be open to navigation or air traffic

通红 tōnghóng ADJ very red

通货膨胀 tōnghuò péngzhàng N inflation

抑制通货膨胀 yīzhì tōnghuò péngzhàng check inflation

通奸 tōngjiān v commit adultery

通商 tōngshāng v (of countries) have trade relations

通顺 tōngshùn ADJ (of writing) coherent and smooth

通俗 tōngsú ADJ easily understood and accepted by common folks, popular

通俗读物 tōngsúdúwù light reading, popular literature

通信 tōngxìn v exchange letters with, correspond

通行 tōngxíng v pass through

通行证 tōngxíngzhèng pass, permit

通讯 tōngxùn N communication

通讯社 tōngxùn shè N news service

通用 tōngyòng v be in general use

通知 tōngzhī I v notify, inform II N notice

童 tóng N child

童年 tóngnián N childhood

同 tóng I ADV together, in common II PREP with, along with III ADJ same, alike IV CONJ and

同伴 tóngbàn N companion

同胞 tóngbāo N fellow countryman, compatriot

同步 tóngbù ADJ at the same time, synchronic, simultaneous

同步卫星 tóngbùwèixīng synchronous satellite

同等 tóngděng ADJ of the same rank (status, grade, etc.)

同行 tóngháng ADJ of the same trade or occupation

同类 tónglèi ADJ of the same category (kind)

同盟 tóngméng N alliance, league

同情 tóngqíng I v sympathize with II N sympathy

同时 tóngshí ADV at the same time, simultaneously

同事 tóngshì N colleague, co-worker

同屋 tóngwū N roommate, flatmate

同性恋 tóngxìngliàn N 1 homosexuality, homosexual love 2 (a person) homosexual, gay, lesbian

同学 tóngxué N classmate, schoolmate

老同学 lǎotóngxué former schoolmate

NOTE: In Chinese schools, teachers address students as 同学们 tóngxuémen, e.g.: 同学们, 我们现在上课了。Tóngxuémen, wǒmen xiànzài shàngkè le. *Class, we're starting class now.*

同样 tóngyàng ADJ same, similar

同一 tóngyī ADJ identical, same

同意 tóngyì v agree, approve

同志 tóngzhì N comrade

NOTE: 同志 tóngzhì used to be the most common form of address in China before 1980. Now it is seldom used. The common forms of address in China today are 先生 xiānsheng (to men) and 小姐 xiǎojiě (to women, especially young women).

铜 tóng TRAD 銅 N copper, bronze

筒 tǒng N section of thick bamboo

竹筒 zhútǒng a thick bamboo tube

捅 tǒng v poke, stab

桶 tǒng N bucket, pail (只 zhī)

统 tǒng TRAD 統 ADV together

统称 tǒngchēng v generally be known as

统筹 tǒngchóu v plan as a whole

统计 tǒngjì I v add up II N statistics

统一 tǒngyī I v unify, integrate II ADJ unified

统治 tǒngzhì v rule

统治阶级 tǒngzhì jiējí ruling class

痛 tòng v Same as 疼 téng v 1

痛苦 tòngkǔ ADJ painful, tortuous

痛快 tòngkuai ADJ overjoyed, very delighted

偷 tōu v steal, pilfer

偷窃 tōuqiè v steal, pilfer

偷税 tōushuì v evade taxes

偷偷 tōutōu ADV stealthily, on the quiet

头 tóu TRAD 頭 I N 1 the head 2 head, chief, leader II ADJ first, first few III M. WD (for cattle or sheep)

一头牛 yì tóu niú a head of cattle (or buffalo/cow)

两头羊 liǎng tóu yáng two sheep

头发 tóufa N hair (on the human head) (根 gēn)

头脑 tóunǎo N brains

头脑简单 tóunǎo jiǎndān simple-minded

投 tóu v 1 throw, toss 2 join

投标 tóubiāo v make a bid, lodge a tender

投产 tóuchǎn v go into production

投放 tóufàng v 1 throw in, put in 2 put (goods, funds) on the market

投机 tóujī I v 1 engage in speculation

货币投机 huòbì tóujī currency speculation

2 be opportunistic II ADJ opportunistic

投机分子 tóujīfènzǐ opportunist

投机 tóujī ADJ agreeable, of the same mind

谈得很投机 tán de hěn tóujī have a most agreeable conversation

投票 tóupiào v cast a vote, vote

投入 tóurù v put into, invest

投诉 tóusù I v complain formally II N formal complaint

投降 tóuxiáng v surrender, capitulate

投掷 tóuzhì v throw, hurl

投资 tóuzī I v invest

投资在一家合资企业 tóu zī zài yì jiā hézī qǐyè invest in a joint venture

II N investment
投资的回报 tóuzī de huíbào return on an investment

透 **tòu** **I** V penetrate, pass through **II** ADJ thorough
透明 tòumíng ADJ transparent
透明度 tòumíngdù transparency

凸 **tū** ADJ protruding

秃 **tū** ADJ bald, bare

突 1 **tū** ADJ protruding
突出 tūchū **I** V give prominence, highlight, emphasize **II** ADJ prominent, conspicuous

突 2 **tū** ADV suddenly, unexpectedly
突击 tūjī **I** N sudden attack **II** V make a sudden attack
突破 tūpò **I** N breakthrough **II** V achieve a breakthrough
突然 tūrán ADJ sudden, abrupt, unexpected

图 **tú** TRAD 圖 N **1** picture **2** chart, diagram (张 zhāng)
图案 tú'àn N pattern, design
图表 túbiǎo N chart, diagram, graph (张 zhāng)
图画 túhuà N picture, painting, drawing (张 zhāng)
图片 túpiàn N picture, photograph
图书 túshū N books
图书馆 túshūguǎn N library (座 zuò)
图像 túxiàng N picture, image
图形 túxíng N graph
图纸 túzhǐ N blueprint

徒 **tú** N apprentice
徒弟 túdì N apprentice, pupil

屠 **tú** V slaughter
屠夫 túfū N butcher
屠杀 túshā N massacre

涂 **tú** TRAD 塗 V smear, spread on

途 **tú** N way, route
途径 tújìng N way, channel

土 **tǔ** N soil, earth
土地 tǔdì N land
土豆 tǔdòu N potato (只 zhī, 块 kuài)
土壤 tǔrǎng N soil
肥沃的土壤 féiwò de tǔrǎng fertile soil

吐 **tǔ** V spit, exhale

吐 **tù** V vomit, throw up

兔 **tù** N rabbit, hare
兔子 tùzi rabbit, hare (只 zhī)

团 **tuán** TRAD 團 **I** N **1** (military) regiment, group, team
代表团 dàibiǎotuán delegation
歌舞团 gēwǔtuán song and dance troupe
旅行团 lǚxíngtuán tour group
II V unite, get together
团结 tuánjié V unite, be in solidarity with
团聚 tuánjù V reunite
和老同学团聚 hé lǎo tóngxué tuánjù reunite with old classmates
团体 tuántǐ N organization, group
团员 tuányuán N **1** member of a delegation, group, etc. **2** member of the Chinese Communist Youth League
团圆 tuányuán N reunite with family members
团长 tuánzhǎng N **1** head of a delegation **2** (in the army) regiment commander

推 **tuī** V **1** push, shove **2** shirk, shift **3** infer, reason **4** put off, defer
推测 tuīcè V infer, suppose
推迟 tuīchí V postpone
推动 tuīdòng V push forward, promote
推翻 tuīfān V overturn, overthrow
推广 tuīguǎng V popularize, spread
推荐 tuījiàn V recommend
推进 tuījìn V promote, advance
推理 tuīlǐ **I** V infer, reason **II** N reasoning by way of inference, inference
推论 tuīlùn **I** V infer, deduce **II** N conclusion based on inference

推算 tuīsuàn **I** v work out (with figures), calculate **II** N calculation

推特 tuītè N (microblogging service) Twitter

推销 tuīxiāo v promote (sale), market

推销新产品 tuīxiāo xīnchǎnpǐn promote a new product

推行 tuīxíng v carry out, pursue, implement

推选 tuīxuǎn v elect, choose

腿 tuǐ N leg (条 tiáo)

退 tuì v move back, retreat

退步 tuìbù v retrogress, fall behind

退还 tuìhuán v return

退还礼物 tuìhuán lǐwù return a gift

退款 tuìkuǎn v refund, ask for refund

退休 tuìxiū **I** v retire **II** N retirement

退休金 tuìxiūjīn N pension

吞 tūn v swallow

屯 tún N village

托 tuō v entrust, ask

托儿所 tuō'érsuǒ N nursery, child-care center (所 suǒ)

拖 tuō v drag on, defer, procrastinate

拖延 tuōyán v delay, put off

脱 tuō v **1** take off (clothes, shoes, etc.)

脱衣服 tuō yīfu take off clothes
脱帽子 tuō màozi take off one's hat
脱鞋 tuō xié take off one's shoes
2 get out of (See 摆脱 bǎituō)

脱离 tuōlí v break away from, sever

脱落 tuōluò v drop, come off

驼 tuó N camel

椭 tuǒ as in 椭圆 tuǒyuán

椭圆 tuǒyuán N oval

椭圆形 tuǒyuánxíng oval shape

妥 tuǒ ADJ appropriate, proper

妥当 tuǒdàng ADJ appropriate, proper

妥善 tuǒshàn ADJ appropriate and satisfactory

妥协 tuǒxié v, N compromise

拓 tuò v open up (See 开拓 kāituò)

唾 tuò N saliva

唾沫 tuòmo saliva, spittle

W

挖 wā v dig, scoop, excavate

挖掘 wājué v dig, excavate, unearth

哇 wā PARTICLE Same as 啊 a **II**

蛙 wā N frog (See 青蛙 qīngwā.)

娃 wá N baby, child

娃娃 wáwa baby, child (个 gè)

瓦 wǎ N tile (片 piàn)

瓦解 wǎjiě v disintegrate, collapse

袜 wà TRAD 襪 N sock, stocking

袜子 wàzi stocking, sock (只 zhī, 双 shuāng)
穿袜子 chuān wàzi put on socks, wear socks
脱袜子 tuō wàzi take off socks

歪 wāi ADJ not straight, askew, crooked

歪曲 wāiqū v distort, misinterpret

外 wài N outside

外边 wàibian N outside

外表 wàibiǎo N outward appearance, exterior

外宾 wàibīn N foreign guest, foreign visitor (位 wèi)

外部 wàibù N exterior, what is external

外出 wàichū v go outside, leave town

外地 wàidì N parts of the country other than where one is

外地人 wàidìrén one who is from other parts of the country, not a native

外观 wàiguān N exterior, surface, outward appearance

外国 wàiguó N foreign country

外国货 wàiguóhuò foreign products, foreign goods

外国人 wàiguórén foreigner

外行 wàiháng I ADJ lay, not trained II N layman

外汇 wàihuì N foreign exchange

外汇储备 wàihuì chǔbèi foreign currency reserve

外汇兑换率 wàihuì duìhuànlǜ exchange rate

外交 wàijiāo N foreign affairs, diplomacy

外交部 Wàijiāo bù Ministry of Foreign Affairs

外交官 wàijiāo guān diplomat

外界 wàijiè N the external world

外科 wàikē N department of external medicine, surgery

外科医生 wàikē yīshēng surgeon

外力 wàilì N external force

外流 wàiliú V outflow

人才外流 réncái wàiliú brain drain

外面 wàimiàn N Same as 外边 wàibian

外婆 wàipó N (maternal) grandma

外甥 wàishēng N one's sister's son

外甥女 wàishēngnǚ N one's sister's daughter

外事 wàishì N foreign affairs

外事处 wàishìchù foreign affairs office

外头 wàitou N outside, outdoors

外文 wàiwén N foreign language (especially its writing) (门 mén)

外向型 wàixiàngxíng ADJ export-oriented

外向型经济 wàixiàngxíng jīngjì export-oriented economy

外形 wàixíng N appearance, external form

外衣 wàiyī N coat, outer clothing

外语 wàiyǔ N foreign language (门 mén)

外资 wàizī N foreign capital, foreign investment

外祖父 wàizǔfù N (maternal) grandfather

外祖母 wàizǔmǔ N (maternal) grandmother

豌 wān as in 豌豆 wāndòu

豌豆 wāndòu N pea

弯 wān TRAD 彎 ADJ curved, tortuous

弯曲 wānqū ADJ curved, zigzagging

湾 wān TRAD 灣 N bay, gulf (See 台湾 Táiwān.)

顽 wán ADJ naughty, stubborn

顽固 wángù ADJ 1 stubborn, pig-headed 2 difficult to cure

顽皮 wánpí ADJ naughty, impish

顽强 wánqiáng ADJ indomitable, tenacious

丸 wán N bolus, pill (粒 lì, 颗 kē)

完 wán V finish, end

吃完 chīwán finish eating, eat up

看完 kànwán finish reading/watching

用完 yòngwán use up

做完 zuòwán finish doing

完备 wánbèi ADJ perfect, complete

完毕 wánbì V complete, finish

完成 wánchéng V accomplish, fulfill

完蛋 wándàn V be done for, be finished

完全 wánquán ADJ complete

完善 wánshàn V make perfect, perfect

完整 wánzhěng ADJ complete, integrated

玩 wán V have fun, play

玩具 wánjù N toy (个 gè)

玩弄 wánnòng V play with

玩儿 wánr V play, have fun

NOTE: Though 玩儿 wánr is often glossed as to play, its basic meaning is to have fun or to have a good time. It can refer to many kinds of activities and therefore has a very wide application. An example: 上星期天我们在海边玩儿得真高兴! Shàng Xīngqītiān wǒmen zài hǎibiān wánr de zhēn gāoxìng. We had a wonderful time by the seaside last Sunday.

玩笑 wánxiào N joke, jest

开玩笑 kāi wánxiào play a prank, crack a joke, pull someone's leg

玩意儿 wányìr N 1 plaything 2 stuff, thing

NOTE: 玩意儿 wányìr is normally used with some contempt to suggest "insignificance" or "unworthiness", similar to 东西 dōngxi. The expletives 什么玩意儿? Shénme wányìr? and 他是个什么玩意儿? Tā shì ge shénme wányìr? may be roughly translated respectively into *What trash!* and *Who does he think himself is?*

挽 wǎn v salvage, draw, pull

挽救 wǎnjiù v rescue, save

晚 wǎn I ADJ late, not on time II N evening, night

晚报 wǎnbào N evening paper (份 fèn)

晚餐 wǎncān N Same as 晚饭 wǎnfàn, used formally.

晚饭 wǎnfàn N evening meal, dinner, supper (顿 dùn)

做晚饭 zuò wǎnfàn prepare supper

晚会 wǎnhuì N evening party, an evening of entertainment

晚年 wǎnnián N old age

晚上 wǎnshang N evening

今天晚上 (今晚) jīntiān wǎnshang (jīnwǎn) this evening

昨天晚上 (昨晚) zuótiān wǎnshang (zuówǎn) yesterday evening

惋 wǎn v be sorry for, sigh

惋惜 wǎnxī v feel sorry (for someone or about something)

为浪费人才而惋惜 wéi làngfèi réncái ér wǎnxī feel sorry about the waste of talents

碗 wǎn N bowl (只 zhī)

...碗饭 ...wǎnfàn ... bowl(s) of rice

菜碗 càiwǎn a dish bowl, big bowl

饭碗 fànwǎn rice bowl, livelihood, job

万 wàn TRAD 萬 I NUM ten thousand

一万两千三百 yíwàn liǎngqiān sānbǎi twelve thousand and three hundred, 12,300

二十万 èr shí wàn two hundred thousand, 200,000

II N a very large number III ADV (negative sense) absolutely

NOTE: 万 wàn (ten thousand) is an important number in Chinese. While English has four basic digits (one, ten, hundred and thousand) Chinese has five (个 gè one, 十 shí ten, 百 bǎi hundred, 千 qiān thousand, 万 wàn ten thousand). The Chinese use 万 wàn to mean ten thousand. Therefore *a hundred thousand* is 十万 shí wàn. In Chinese-speaking communities in Southeast Asia, some people use 十千 shíqiān for *ten thousand*, e.g. 三十千 sānshíqiān 30,000. This is, however, not acceptable in standard Chinese.

万分 wànfēn ADV extremely

万岁 wànsuì INTERJ Long Live

万万 wànwàn ADV under no circumstances, never ever

万一 wànyī I CONJ in the unlikely event of, in case II N a possible but unlikely event, contingency

对付万一的情况 duìfu wànyī de qíngkuàng cope with a contingency

万维网 wànwéiwǎng N World Wide Web (www)

汪 wāng ADJ (of water) vast

汪洋 wāngyáng N vast expanse of water

王 1 wáng N king

王国 wángguó N kingdom

丹麦王国 Dānmài wángguó the Kingdom of Denmark

王 2 Wáng N (a family name)

亡 wáng v perish, die

枉 wǎng v treat unfairly, wrong (See 冤枉 yuānwang)

网 wǎng TRAD 網 N net, network

网吧 wǎngbā N Internet café (座 zuò, 家 jiā)

网络 **wǎngluò** N Internet
  网络电话 wǎngluò diànhuà Internet phone
  网络电视 wǎngluò diànshì Internet TV
  网络警察 (网警) wǎngluò jǐngchá (wǎngjǐng) Internet police

网球 **wǎngqiú** N tennis
  网球场 wǎngqiúchǎng tennis court

网页 **wǎngyè** N web page

网站 **wǎngzhàn** N website

往 **wǎng** I PREP towards, in the direction of II V go III ADJ previous, past

往常 **wǎngcháng** ADV habitually in the past, used to

往返 **wǎngfǎn** V journey to and from, make a round trip

往后 **wǎnghòu** ADV from now on
  往后的日子 wǎnghòu de rìzi the days to come

往来 **wǎnglái** I V come and go II N contact, dealings
  业务往来 yèwù wǎnglái business dealings

往年 **wǎngnián** N (in) former years

往日 **wǎngrì** N in former times, in the past

往事 **wǎngshì** N past events, the past
  回忆往事 huíyì wǎngshì recollect past events, reflect upon the past

往往 **wǎngwǎng** ADV very often, usually

旺 **wàng** ADJ flourishing

妄 **wàng** ADJ preposterous

妄图 **wàngtú** V try in vain

妄想 **wàngxiǎng** I V attempt in vain II N vain hope

忘 **wàng** V forget, overlook

忘记 **wàngjì** V forget, overlook

忘却 **wàngquè** V forget

望 **wàng** V look at, gaze into the distance

望远镜 **wàngyuǎnjìng** N telescope, binoculars

危 **wēi** I ADJ perilous II ADV by force

危害 **wēihài** I V harm severely, jeopardize II N severe harm, damage

危机 **wēijī** N crisis

危急 **wēijí** ADJ in acute danger, critical, perilous

危险 **wēixiǎn** I ADJ dangerous, risky II N danger, risk

威 **wēi** N awesome force

威风 **wēifēng** N power and prestige, manner or style showing power and prestige
  耍威风 shuǎ wēifēng throw one's weight around

威力 **wēilì** N formidable force, power

威望 **wēiwàng** N enormous prestige

威胁 **wēixié** I V threaten II N threat
  构成威胁 gòuchéng wēixié pose a threat

威信 **wēixìn** N popular trust, prestige
  在同事中享有很高威信 zài tóngshì zhōng xiǎngyǒu hěn gāo wēixìn enjoy high prestige among colleagues

微 **wēi** ADJ tiny, of extremely small amounts, minute

微不足道 **wēi bùzú dào** IDIOM negligibly small, extremely tiny

微观 **wēiguān** ADJ microcosmic, microscopic

微小 **wēixiǎo** ADJ tiny, of very small amounts

微笑 **wēixiào** V smile

桅 **wéi** as in 桅杆 wéigān

桅杆 **wéigān** N mast

围 **wéi** TRAD 圍 V enclose, surround

围攻 **wéigōng** V besiege, lay siege to

围巾 **wéijīn** N scarf (条 tiáo)

围棋 **wéiqí** N weiqi (a Chinese chess game, also known as go)
  下围棋 xiàwéiqí play weiqi

围绕 **wéirào** V 1 move around, encircle 2 center on, focus on

唯 **wéi** ADV only

NOTE: In some cases, 唯 is also written as 惟 wéi.

唯独 **wéidú** ADV only, alone

唯物论 **wéiwùlùn** N materialism

唯心论 **wéixīnlùn** N idealism

唯一 **wéiyī** ADJ the only one, sole

维 **wéi** TRAD 維 v preserve, safeguard

维护 wéihù v safeguard, defend
维生素 wéishēngsù N vitamin
维修 wéixiū v keep in good repair, maintain (a machine, a house, etc.)

违 **wéi** TRAD 違 v disobey, violate

违背 wéibèi v go against, violate
违法 wéifǎ v violate the law, break the law
违反 wéifǎn v run counter to, violate
违犯 wéifàn v break (the law, regulations, etc.)
违犯财务规定 wéifàn cáiwù guīdìng breach financial regulations

为 **wéi** TRAD 為 v **1** be, become **2** do, act

为难 wéinán v **1** make things difficult for **2** feel awkward
为难的事情 wéinán de shìqíng something one finds difficult to cope with, some perplexing matter
为期 wéiqī ADV (to be completed) by a definite date
为期不远 wéi qī bù yuǎn will take place soon
为期一星期 wéiqī yì xīngqī will last a week
为首 wéishǒu v be headed by
以董事长为首的代表团 yǐ dǒngshìzhǎng wéishǒu de dàibiǎotuán a delegation headed by the chairman of the Board of Trustees
为止 wéizhǐ v up to, till
到…为止 dào…wéizhǐ up to, until

尾 **wěi** N tail, end

尾巴 wěiba N tail (条 tiáo)

委 **wěi** v entrust

委屈 wěiqu v **1** feel wronged, nurse a grievance **2** inconvenience someone
委托 wěituō v entrust
委员会 wěiyuánhuì N committee (个 gè)

伟 **wěi** TRAD 偉 ADJ big

伟大 wěidà ADJ great

伪 **wěi** ADJ false

伪造 wěizào v forge, counterfeit
一份伪造的文件 yí fèn wěizào de wénjiàn a forged document

卫 **wèi** TRAD 衛 v defend, protect

卫生 wèishēng N hygiene, sanitation
个人卫生 gèrén wèishēng hygiene, personal hygiene
公共卫生 gōnggòng wèishēng sanitation, public sanitation
环境卫生 huánjìng wèishēng environmental sanitation
卫生间 wèishēngjiān N bathroom, (private) toilet
卫生局 wèishēngjú N (government) health department
卫星 wèixīng N satellite
卫星电视 wèixīng diànshì satellite TV
人造卫星 rénzào wèixīng man-made satellite

为 **wèi** TRAD 為 PREP (do, work) for the benefit of, in the interest of

为何 wèihé ADV what for, why
为了 wèile PREP for the purpose of

NOTE: Both 为 wèi and 为了 wèile can be used as prepositions and have similar meanings, but 为了 wèile is more commonly used in everyday Chinese.

为什么 wèishénme ADV why, what for

未 **wèi** ADV have not, did not

NOTE: 未 wèi is only used in rather formal, written styles. In everyday Chinese, 没有 méiyǒu is used instead.

未必 wèibì ADV not necessarily, may not
未来 wèilái N future
未免 wèimiǎn ADV rather, a bit too

位 **wèi** I M. WD (polite term used for people)
一位老师 yí wèi lǎoshī a teacher
II N position, location
位于 wèiyú v be situated in, be located in

位置 **wèizhi** N **1** place, location **2** (abstract) position

味 **wèi** N taste, flavor

味道 **wèidao** N taste

味精 **wèijīng** N monosodium glutamate (MSG), gourmet powder

胃 **wèi** N stomach

谓 **wèi** V be called (See 所谓 suǒwèi)

慰 **wèi** V console (See 安慰 ānwèi)

慰问 **wèiwèn** V express sympathy and solicitude for

畏 **wèi** V fear

畏惧 **wèijù** V fear, dread

喂[1] **wèi** INTERJ **1** hey **2** hello, hi

NOTE: In telephone conversations 喂 wèi is equivalent to *hello*. In other contexts, 喂 wèi is a rude way of getting people's attention. It is more polite to say 对不起 duìbuqǐ, e.g.: 对不起，先生，您的票呢? Duìbuqǐ, xiānsheng, nín de piào ne? *Excuse me, sir, where's your ticket?*

喂[2] **wèi** V feed

温 **wēn** I ADJ warm II V **1** warm up **2** review (one's lessons)

温带 **wēndài** N temperate zone

温度 **wēndù** N temperature (atmospheric)

NOTE: 温度 wēndù generally refers to *atmospheric temperature* only. For *body temperature* the expression is 体温 tǐwēn, e.g.: 人的正常体温是多少? Rénde zhèngcháng tǐwēn shì duōshǎo? *What is the normal temperature of a human being?* When a person has a fever, however, 热度 rèdù is used to refer to his/her temperature, e.g.: 他今天热度还很高。Tā jīntiān rèdù hái hěn gāo. *He is still running a fever.*

温度计 **wēndùjì** N thermometer

温和 **wēnhé** ADJ **1** (of climate) temperate, without extreme temperatures

温和的气候 **wēnhé de qìhòu** mild, intemperate climate

2 (of people) gentle, mild

语气温和 **yǔqì wēnhé** mild tone

温暖 **wēnnuǎn** ADJ warm

温柔 **wēnróu** ADJ (of people) gentle and soft, soothing

瘟 **wēn** N plague

瘟疫 **wēnyì** N epidemic, pandemic (场 cháng)

文 **wén** N **1** writing, script **2** culture

文化 **wénhuà** N culture

文化部 **Wénhuàbù** Ministry of Culture

文件 **wénjiàn** N **1** document (份 fèn) **2** (computer) file

文盲 **wénmáng** N illiterate person

文明 **wénmíng** I N civilization, culture II ADJ civilized

文凭 **wénpíng** N diploma, certificate of academic achievements (张 zhāng)

文人 **wénrén** N man of letters, literati

文物 **wénwù** N cultural relic, historical relic

文物商店 **wénwù shāngdiàn** antique shop

文献 **wénxiàn** N document, literature

文学 **wénxué** N literature

文学家 **wénxué jiā** (great) writer

文雅 **wényǎ** ADJ refined and elegant

文言 **wényán** N Classical Chinese

文言文 **wényánwén** Classical Chinese writing

NOTE: Before the 20th century mainstream Chinese writing was done in 文言 wényán Classical Chinese, which was based on ancient Chinese and divorced from everyday speech of the time. A literate revolution took place in early 20th century, which succeeded in replacing 文言 wényán with 白话 báihua, plain speech, vernacular.

文艺 **wényì** N literature and art, performing arts

文艺晚会 wényì wǎnhuì an evening of entertainment, soirée

文章 wénzhāng N essay, article (篇 piān)

文字 wénzì N written language, script, character

文字处理 wénzì chǔlǐ word processing

纹 wén TRAD 紋 N ripple (See 皱纹 zhòuwén)

蚊 wén N mosquito

蚊子 wénzi mosquito (只 zhī)

闻 wén TRAD 聞 N what is heard

闻名 wénmíng ADJ well-known

吻 wěn v, N kiss

稳 wěn TRAD 穩 ADJ steady, stable

稳当 wěndang ADJ reliable, safe
一个稳当的办法 yí ge wěndang de bànfǎ a reliable method

稳定 wěndìng ADJ stable

稳妥 wěntuǒ ADJ safe and appropriate

问 wèn TRAD 問 v 1 ask (a question), inquire 2 ask after, send regards

问答 wèndá N questions and answers

问答题 wèndátí (in tests, exercises, etc.) question requiring an answer in writing (not a multiple-choice question)

问好 wèn hǎo v ask after, give greetings to

问候 wènhòu v give regards to, ask after

问路 wèn lù v ask the way

问世 wènshì v be published, come into being

问题 wèntí N 1 question (道 dào, for school examinations only) 2 problem
没有问题 méiyǒu wèntí no problem

翁 wēng N old man

嗡 wēng ONOMATOPOEIA buzz

窝 wō N nest, lair

鸟窝 niǎowō bird's nest

窝囊 wōnang I v feel vexed and annoyed
受窝囊气 shòu wōnangqì be subject to petty annoyances

II ADJ (of people) useless, good-for-nothing

我 wǒ PRON I, me

我们 wǒmen PRON we, us

卧 wò v lie

卧床休息 wòchuáng xiūxi lie in bed and rest

卧室 wòshì N bedroom (间 jiān)

沃 wò ADJ (of land) fertile (See 肥沃 féiwò)

握 wò v hold, grasp (See 把握 bǎwò)

握手 wòshǒu v shake hands

乌 wū ADJ black, dark

乌鸦 wūyā N crow (只 zhī)

乌云 wūyún N dark clouds

呜 wū v toot, hoot

呜咽 wūyè v sob

污 wū I N filth II v smear, defile

污蔑 wūmiè v slander

污染 wūrǎn I v pollute II N pollution

巫 wū N witch

巫术 wūshù witchcraft

巫婆 wūpó N witch

诬 wū TRAD 誣 v accuse falsely

诬告 wūgào v file a false charge against

诬蔑 wūmiè I v slander, vilify II N slander

诬陷 wūxiàn v frame
诬陷好人 wūxiàn hǎorén frame an innocent person

屋 wū N house, room

屋子 wūzi N room (间 jiān)

NOTE: 屋子 wūzi in the sense of *room* is only used in north China. To southern Chinese 屋子 wūzi may mean *house*. To avoid ambiguity, it is better to use the word 房间 fángjiān for *room*.

无 wú TRAD 無 I N nothing, nil

无比 wúbǐ

从无到有 cóng wú dào yǒu grow out of nothing
II v have no

无比 wúbǐ ADJ matchless, unparalleled

无偿 wúcháng ADJ free, gratis
无偿服务 wúcháng fúwù voluntary service

无耻 wúchǐ ADJ shameless, brazen

无从 wúcóng ADV having no way (of doing something), being in no position to
无从说起 wúcóng shuōqǐ don't know where to begin

无法 wúfǎ MODAL V unable to

无非 wúfēi ADV nothing but, no more than

无话可说 wú huà kě shuō IDIOM have nothing to say

无可奉告 wú kě fènggào IDIOM No comment

无可奈何 wú kě nàihé IDIOM have no alternative (but)

无理 wúlǐ ADJ unreasonable, unjustifiable
无理取闹 wúlǐ qǔnào make trouble without any justification, provoke deliberately

无聊 wúliáo ADJ **1** bored **2** silly, meaningless

无论 wúlùn CONJ Same as 不管 bùguǎn. Tends to be used in writing.

无论如何 wúlùn rúhé IDIOM no matter what, at any rate

无能为力 wú néng wéi lì IDIOM be totally powerless

无情 wúqíng ADJ ruthless, heartless
无情无义 wú qíng wú yì IDIOM cold-hearted and merciless

无穷 wúqióng ADJ infinite, boundless

无绳电话 wú shéng diànhuà N cordless telephone

无数 wúshù ADJ innumerable, countless

无所谓 wúsuǒwèi v doesn't matter

无所作为 wú suǒ zuòwéi IDIOM make no effort, be in a state of inertia

无微不至 wú wēi bú zhì IDIOM meticulous, sparing no effort, paying attention to every detail
无微不至的照顾 wú wēi bú zhì de zhàogù meticulous care and attention

无限 wúxiàn ADJ infinite, limitless

无线电 wúxiàndiàn N (wireless) radio
无线因特网 wúxiàn yīntèwǎng wireless Internet

无效 wúxiào ADJ invalid

无疑 wúyí ADV undoubtedly, beyond any doubt

无意 wúyì ADJ unintentional
无意之中发现 wúyì zhīzhōng fāxiàn discover by chance

五 WǓ NUM five, 5
五星红旗 wǔ xīng hóng qí the five-star red flag (the Chinese national flag)

伍 WǓ NUM five, 5

午 WǓ N noon
午饭 wǔfàn N lunch (顿 dùn)
午间 wǔjiān N lunchtime
午间休息 wǔjiān xiūxi lunchtime break

武 WǓ N military
武力 wǔlì N military force
武力解决 wǔlì jiějué deal with (a situation) by force
武器 wǔqì N weapon (件 jiàn)
大规模杀伤武器 dàguīmó shāshāng wǔqì weapon of mass destruction (WMD)
武术 wǔshù N martial arts
武术大师 wǔshù dàshī martial arts master
武术馆 wǔshù guǎn martial arts school
武装 wǔzhuāng **I** v arm, equip
武装到牙齿 wǔzhuāng dào yáchǐ be armed to the teeth
II N arms
解除武装 jiěchú wǔzhuāng lay down arms, be disarmed

侮 WǓ v insult
侮辱 wǔrǔ **I** v insult, humiliate **II** N insult

舞 WǓ N dance
舞弊 wǔbì **I** N fraud, fraudulent practice
舞弊案 wǔbì àn a case of fraud
II v commit a fraud

舞蹈 wǔdǎo N dance

舞会 wǔhuì N ball

化装舞会 huàzhuāng wǔhuì fancy dress party

舞台 wǔtái N stage, theater

舞厅 wǔtīng N dance hall

迪斯科舞厅 dísīkē wǔtīng discothèque, disco

晤 **wù** V meet (people)

勿 **wù** ADV do not, don't

物 **wù** N 1 things, objects 2 material

物价 wùjià N price, commodity price

物理 wùlǐ N physics

物力 wùlì N material resources

物品 wùpǐn N article, goods

物体 wùtǐ N object, substance

物业 wùyè N real estate, property

物业管理 wùyè guǎnlǐ property management

物资 wùzī N goods and materials, supplies

务 **wù** TRAD 務 I V work, to spend one's efforts on II ADV must, be sure to

务必 wùbì ADV must, be sure to

雾 **wù** TRAD 霧 N fog, mist

悟 **wù** V realize

悟出了道理 wùchūle dàolǐ come to see the light, begin to understand

顿悟 dùnwù epiphany

误 **wù** TRAD 誤 ADJ erroneous (See 错误 cuòwù)

误差 wùchā N (in physics) error

误会 wùhuì I V misunderstand, misconstrue II N misunderstanding

误解 wùjiě V misunderstanding

恶 **wù** V loathe (See 厌恶 yànwù)

X

西 **XĪ** N west, western

西北 xīběi N northwest, the Northwest

西边 xībian N west side, to the west, in the west

西餐 xīcān N Western-style meal

西餐馆 xīcānguǎn N Western-style restaurant

西方 xīfāng N the West, Occident

西服 xīfú N Western-style clothes, men's suit

西瓜 xīguā N watermelon (只 zhī)

西红柿 xīhóngshì N tomato (只 zhī)

西面 xīmiàn Same as 西边 xībian

西南 xīnán N southwest, the Southwest

西医 xīyī N 1 Western medicine 2 doctor trained in Western medicine (位 wèi)

中西医结合治疗 Zhōngxīyī jiéhé zhìliáo treat (patients) with a combination of Chinese and Western medicine

晰 **XĪ** ADJ clear, distinct (See 清晰 qīngxī)

锡 **XĪ** N (metal) tin (Sn)

吸 **XĪ** V 1 inhale, suck (See 呼吸 hūxī) 2 absorb, suck up

吸毒 xīdú I V take drugs II N drug-taking, substance abuse

吸取 xīqǔ V absorb, draw in

吸取教训 xīqǔ jiàoxun learn a lesson (from past experience)

吸收 xīshōu V suck up, absorb

吸烟 xīyān I V smoke II N smoking

吸引 xīyǐn V attract

吸引力 xīyǐnlì N attraction

有吸引力 yǒu xīyǐnlì attractive

希 **XĪ** V wish, hope

希望 xīwàng I V hope, wish II N hope

稀 **XĪ** ADJ 1 rare, scarce 2 watery

稀饭 xīfàn N rice porridge

稀少 xīshǎo ADJ scarce, few and far between

人烟稀少 rényān xīshǎo sparsely populated

稀有 xīyǒu ADJ rare

稀有金属 xīyǒujīnshǔ a rare metal

夕 XĪ N dusk, twilight

夕阳 xīyáng the setting sun

惜 XĪ V **1** cherish, treasure (See 珍惜 zhēnxī) **2** have pity on (See 可惜 kěxī)

牺 XĪ TRAD 犧 N sacrifice

牺牲 xīshēng I V sacrifice, give up II N sacrifice

悉 XĪ V know (See 熟悉 shúxī.)

溪 XĪ N small stream

小溪 xiǎoxī a small stream

膝 XĪ N knee

膝盖 xīgài knee

息 XĪ V cease (See 消息 xiāoxi, 休息 xiūxi.)

熄 XĪ V extinguish (fire)

熄灭 xīmiè V (of fire) die out, be extinguished

媳 XÍ daughter-in-law

媳妇 xífù N daughter-in-law
儿媳妇 érxífù daughter-in-law

NOTE: In some dialects, 媳妇 xífu may also refer to *a wife*, e.g. 娶媳妇 qǔ xífu *to get a wife, (for men) to get married*.

袭 XÍ TRAD 襲 V attack, raid

袭击 xíjī V (of troops) attack, raid
突然袭击 tūrán xíjī sudden attack, launch a sudden attack

习 XÍ TRAD 習 I V practice, exercise (See 练习 liànxí, 学习 xuéxí.) II N custom, habit

习惯 xíguàn I N habit II V be accustomed to, be used to
习惯上 xíguàn shang habitually

习俗 xísú N accepted custom, custom

习题 xítí N exercises (in school work)

席 XÍ N seat

来宾席 láibīnxí visitors' seats

席位 xíwèi N seat

洗 XĪ V wash, bathe

洗尘 xǐchén V give a welcome dinner

洗涤 xǐdí V wash, cleanse
洗涤剂 xǐdíjì detergent

洗手间 xǐshǒujiān N toilet, restroom, washroom

NOTE: 洗手间 xǐshǒujiān is a common euphemism for *toilet*. The formal word for *toilet* is 厕所 cèsuǒ.

洗衣机 xǐyījī N washing machine (台 tái)

洗澡 xǐzǎo V take a bath, take a shower
洗澡间 xǐzǎojiān bathroom, shower room (Same as 浴室 yùshì.)

喜 XǏ I V be fond of II ADJ happy, glad

喜爱 xǐ'ài V be fond of, love

喜欢 xǐhuan V like, be fond of

喜鹊 xǐque N magpie (只 zhī)

NOTE: In Chinese folklore, 喜鹊 xǐque *the magpie* is an auspicious bird, the harbinger of good tidings, hence 喜鹊 xǐque.

喜事 xǐshì N happy event (especially a wedding)

办喜事 bànxǐshì arrange a wedding

喜讯 xǐxùn N good news, good tidings

喜悦 xǐyuè ADJ happy, joyful

隙 XÌ N narrow gap (See 空隙 kòngxì.)

戏 XÌ TRAD 戲 N drama, play (出 chū)

戏剧 xìjù N drama

系 XÌ N department (of a university)

系主任 xì zhǔrèn chair of a (university) department

系列 xìliè N series
一系列 yíxìliè a series of

系统 xìtǒng N a group of items serving a common purpose, system (套 tào)

细 xì TRAD 細 ADJ **1** thin, slender (of objects shaped like a strip) **2** small, tiny

细沙 xìshā fine sand

3 meticulous (See 详细 xiángxì)

细胞 xìbāo N (in biology) cell

细节 xìjié N details

细菌 xìjūn N bacterium, germ

细小 xìxiǎo ADJ tiny

细心 xìxīn ADJ very careful, meticulous

细致 xìzhì ADJ careful, meticulous

瞎 xiā ADJ blind

虾 xiā TRAD 蝦 N prawn, shrimp (只 zhī)

峡 xiá N gorge

峡谷 xiágǔ N gorge, canyon

狭 xiá ADJ narrow

狭隘 xiá'ài ADJ narrow

狭窄 xiázhǎi ADJ narrow, narrow and limited

心胸狭窄 xīnxiōng xiázhǎi narrow-minded, intolerant

霞 xiá N rosy clouds, morning or evening glow

辖 xiá TRAD 轄 V govern (See 管辖 guǎnxiá)

下 1 xià I PREP below, under, underneath

山下 shānxia at the foot of a mountain or hills II V **1** go/come down **2** leave off, finish **3** issue, deliver III ADJ low, inferior

下班 xiàbān V get off work

下边 xiàbian N below, under

下车 xiàchē V get off a vehicle

下达 xiàdá V make known to lower levels

下岗 xiàgǎng V be laid off, be unemployed

下岗工人 xiàgǎng gōngrén a worker who has been laid off, an unemployed worker

下级 xiàjí N lower level, subordinate

下降 xiàjiàng V fall, descend

下课 xiàkè V finish class

下来 xiàlái V come down

下列 xiàliè ADJ listed below

下令 xiàlìng V issue an order

下落 xiàluò N what has happened (to someone), whereabouts

打听…的下落 dǎtīng…de xiàluò inquire about (someone's) whereabouts, try to find what has happened to (someone)

下面 xiàmiàn Same as 下边 xiàbian

下去 xiàqu V go down

下台 xiàtái V **1** step down from the stage **2** lose a position, fall from power

下午 xiàwǔ N afternoon

下乡 xiàxiāng V go to the countryside

下旬 xiàxún N the last ten days of a month

下游 xiàyóu N lower reaches (of a river)

下载 xià zài V download

下 2 xià M. WD (used with certain verbs to indicate the number of times the action is done)

吓 xià TRAD 嚇 V **1** frighten, scare **2** be frightened, be scared

吓人 xiàrén ADJ frightening, terrible

夏 xià N summer

夏天 xiàtiān N summer

掀 xiān V lift, lift up

掀起 xiānqǐ V set off, start

先 xiān ADV first (in time sequence)

先…再… xiān…zài… first … and then …

先锋 xiānfēng N pioneer

先后 xiānhòu ADV one after another, successively

先进 xiānjìn ADJ advanced

先前 xiānqián ADV previously

先生 xiānsheng N **1** teacher **2** Mister (Mr) **3** sir, gentleman **4** husband

先行 xiānxíng V go ahead, precede

鲜 xiān TRAD 鮮 ADJ **1** fresh **2** bright, brightly-colored **3** delicious

鲜红 xiānhóng N bright red, scarlet

鲜花 xiānhuā N fresh flower, flower (朵 duǒ)

鲜明 xiānmíng ADJ bright, clear, distinct

鲜血 xiānxuè N blood

鲜艳 **xiānyàn** ADJ gaily-colored

纤 **xiān** TRAD 纖 N fiber

纤维 **xiānwéi** N fiber

仙 **xiān** N fairy, immortal

仙女 **xiānnǚ** N fairy maiden

仙人 **xiānrén** N immortal, celestial

贤 **xián** TRAD 賢 ADJ virtuous

贤惠 **xiánhuì** ADJ (of women) kind and wise, virtuous

衔 **xián** TRAD 啣 I V 1 hold in the mouth 2 join, link up II N rank, title

军衔 **jūnxián** military rank

衔接 **xiánjiē** V link up, join

弦 **xián** N string (of a musical instrument), bowstring

咸 **xián** TRAD 鹹 ADJ salty

闲 **xián** TRAD 閑 ADJ idle, unoccupied

清闲 **qīngxián** leisurely, carefree

闲话 **xiánhuà** N chat, gossip

闲人 **xiánrén** N idler, uninvolved person

闲事 **xiánshì** N matter that does not concern you

嫌 **xián** I V dislike, complain II N suspicion

避嫌 **bìxián** avoid suspicion

嫌疑 **xiányí** N suspicion

显 **xiǎn** TRAD 顯 V appear, look

显得 **xiǎnde** V appear to be, seem to be

显然 **xiǎnrán** ADV clearly, obviously

显示 **xiǎnshì** V show, manifest

显著 **xiǎnzhù** ADJ remarkable, outstanding, notable

险 **xiǎn** TRAD 險 ADJ dangerous (See 危险 wēixiǎn.)

县 **xiàn** TRAD 縣 N (rural) county

县城 **xiànchéng** N county town, county seat

县长 **xiànzhǎng** N mayor of a county

现 **xiàn** TRAD 現 N now, at present

现场 **xiànchǎng** N 1 (crime, disaster, etc.) scene 2 on the site, on the spot

事故现场 **shìgù xiànchǎng** accident scene

现成 **xiànchéng** ADJ ready-made

现代 **xiàndài** N modern times, the contemporary age

现代化 **xiàndàihuà** I V modernize II N modernization

现金 **xiànjīn** N cash

现钱 **xiànqián** Same as 现金 **xiànjīn**

现实 **xiànshí** I N what is real, reality, actuality II ADJ realistic

现象 **xiànxiàng** N phenomenon

现行 **xiànxíng** ADJ currently in effect, in effect

现行法令 **xiànxíngfǎlìng** decrees in effect, current laws

现在 **xiànzài** N the present time, now

现状 **xiànzhuàng** N current situation

陷 **xiàn** V 1 get bogged down 2 get trapped, be framed

陷害 **xiànhài** V make a trumped-up charge against, frame

陷入 **xiànrù** V get trapped, be caught in

馅 **xiàn** N filling, stuffing

馅儿 **xiànr** filling, stuffing

线 **xiàn** TRAD 線 N string, thread, wire (根 **gēn**)

线路 **xiànlù** N circuit, route

线索 **xiànsuǒ** N clue, lead (in a police case)

发现线索 **fāxiàn xiànsuǒ** discover a clue, find a lead

限 **xiàn** V limit

限度 **xiàndù** N limitation, limit

超过限度 **chāoguò xiàndù** exceed the limit

限期 **xiànqī** I N time limit, deadline II V set a time limit, impose a deadline

限期完成 **xiànqī wánchéng** must be done (finished, completed, etc.) by the deadline

限于 **xiànyú** V be confined to, be limited to

限于时间关系 **xiànyú shíjiān guānxi** owing to the time limitation

限制 xiànzhì v limit, restrict, confine

宪 **xiàn** TRAD 憲 N statute

宪兵 xiànbīng N military police

宪法 xiànfǎ N constitution

羡 **xiàn** v admire, envy

羡慕 xiànmù v envy

献 **xiàn** TRAD 獻 v offer, dedicate (See 贡献 gòngxiàn)

献身 xiànshēn v give one's life for, devote oneself to

乡 **xiāng** TRAD 鄉 N rural town

乡村 xiāngcūn N rural area, countryside

乡下 xiāngxia N countryside, rural area

乡镇 xiāngzhèn N townships and villages

乡镇企业 xiāngzhèn qǐyè township and village enterprise, rural industry

相 **xiāng** ADV each other, mutually

相比 xiāngbǐ v compare

相差 xiāngchà v differ, differ from

相当 xiāngdāng I ADJ suitable, appropriate II ADV fairly, rather, quite

相等 xiāngděng v be equal

相对 xiāngduì ADV relatively, comparatively

相对来说 xiāngduì láishuō relatively speaking

相对论 xiāngduìlùn theory of relativity

相反 xiāngfǎn ADJ opposite, contrary

相符 xiāngfú v conform to, agree with, tally with

与事实相符 yǔ shìshí xiāngfú conform with the facts

相关 xiāngguān v be related to, be interrelated

相互 xiānghù ADJ mutual, each other

相继 xiāngjì ADV in succession, one after another

相交 xiāngjiāo v intersect

相识 xiāngshí v be acquainted with, come to know

老相识 lǎoxiāngshí someone you have known for a long time, an old acquaintance

相似 xiāngsì ADJ similar to, be alike

相通 xiāngtōng I v be linked with each other II ADJ mutually comprehensible, compatible with

相同 xiāngtóng ADJ identical, same

相信 xiāngxìn v believe, believe in

相应 xiāngyìng ADJ corresponding, relevant

相应措施 xiāngyìng cuòshī appropriate measures

镶 **xiāng** TRAD 鑲 v 1 set into, set 2 mount

香 **xiāng** ADJ 1 fragrant, sweet-smelling, aromatic 2 savoury, appetizing

香肠 xiāngcháng N sausage (根 gēn)

香港 Xiānggǎng N Hong Kong

香蕉 xiāngjiāo N banana (根 gēn)

香味 xiāngwèi N sweet smell, fragrance

香烟 xiāngyān N cigarette (支 zhī)

香皂 xiāngzào N toilet soap, bath soap (块 kuài)

箱 **xiāng** N box, chest, trunk

箱子 xiāngzi N trunk, box, suitcase (只 zhī)

厢 **xiāng** N wing (of a house), wing room

车厢 chēxiāng (train) carriage

详 **xiáng** TRAD 詳 ADJ detailed

详细 xiángxì ADJ in detail, detailed

祥 **xiáng** ADJ auspicious (See 吉祥 jíxiáng)

翔 **xiáng** v circle in the air, fly (See 飞翔 fēixiáng)

享 **xiǎng** v enjoy

享福 xiǎngfú v enjoy a happy life, live a blessed life

享乐 xiǎnglè v indulge in material comfort

享乐主义 xiǎnglè zhǔyì hedonism

享受 xiǎngshòu I v enjoy II N enjoyment, pleasure

精神享受 jīngshén xiǎngshòu spiritual pleasure

享有 xiǎngyǒu v enjoy (rights, prestige, etc.)

响 **xiǎng** TRAD 響 I ADJ loud, noisy II N sound, noise

响亮 **xiǎngliàng** ADJ loud and clear, resounding

响声 **xiǎngshēng** N sound (especially loud sounds)

响应 **xiǎngyìng** V respond, answer

想 **xiǎng** V 1 think

想一下 **xiǎng yíxià** think for a while, give ... some thought
2 think back, recall 3 miss, remember with longing

想办法 **xiǎng bànfǎ** V think of a way (to do something)

想法 **xiǎngfa** N what one thinks, idea, opinion

想方设法 **xiǎng fāng shè fǎ** IDIOM try every means, do all one can

想念 **xiǎngniàn** V miss, remember with longing

想像 **xiǎngxiàng** V imagine

想像力 **xiǎngxiànglì** imaginative power

相 **xiàng** as in 相声 xiàngsheng

相声 **xiàngsheng** N comic dialogue, comic cross-talk

巷 **xiàng** N narrow street, alley (条 tiáo)

一条深巷 **yìtiáo shēn xiàng** a long alley

项 1 **xiàng** TRAD 項 N the neck

项链 **xiàngliàn** N necklace (条 tiáo)
戴一条珍珠项链 **dài yì tiáo zhēnzhū xiàngliàn** wear a pearl necklace

项 2 **xiàng** TRAD 項 M. WD item of something (for things that are composed of items or things considered to be components)

一项任务 **yí xiàng rènwù** a mission

项目 **xiàngmù** N item

象 1 **xiàng** N elephant (头 tóu, 只 zhī)

NOTE: Chinese often fondly refer to elephants as 大象 dàxiàng.

象棋 **xiàngqí** N chess (副 fù, 盘 pán)

国际象棋 **guójì xiàngqí** Western chess

中国象棋 **Zhōngguó xiàngqí** Chinese chess

下一盘象棋 **xià yì pán xiàngqí** play a game of chess

象 2 **xiàng** Same as 像 xiàng I V

象征 **xiàngzhēng** I N symbol II V symbolize

像 **xiàng** I V resemble, take after, be like II N likeness of (a human being), portrait (幅 fú)

像样 **xiàngyàng** ADJ presentable, up to the standard

橡 **xiàng** N rubber, rubber tree, oak, oak tree

橡胶 **xiàngjiāo** N rubber

橡胶树 **xiàngjiāoshù** rubber tree

橡皮 **xiàngpí** N eraser (块 kuài)

向 **xiàng** I V face II PREP in the direction of, towards III ADV all along, always

向导 **xiàngdǎo** N guide

旅游向导 **lǚyóu xiàngdǎo** tourist guide

向来 **xiànglái** ADV always, all along

向往 **xiàngwǎng** V yearn for, look forward to

消 **xiāo** V 1 vanish, disappear 2 dispel, remove

消除 **xiāochú** V clear up, dispel

消毒 **xiāodú** V disinfect, sterilize

消费 **xiāofèi** V consume

消费品 **xiāofèipǐn** consumer commodities, consumer goods

消费者 **xiāofèizhě** consumer

消化 **xiāohuà** V digest

消化不良 **xiāohuà bùliáng** indigestion

消化系统 **xiāohuà xìtǒng** digestive system

消极 **xiāojí** ADJ lacking enthusiasm, passive

消灭 **xiāomiè** V eliminate, wipe out

消失 **xiāoshī** V disappear, vanish

消息 **xiāoxi** N news (条 tiáo)

宵 **xiāo** N night (See 元宵 yuánxiāo)

销 **xiāo** TRAD 銷 V 1 sell, market

畅销书 chàngxiāoshū bestseller (book) **2** cancel, annual

销毁 xiāohuǐ v destroy (especially by burning)

销毁罪证 xiāohuǐ zuìzhèng destroy incriminating evidence

销路 xiāolù N market, sale

销路很好 xiāolù hěn hǎo (of a commodity) have a good market

销售 xiāoshòu N sale, market

销售部 xiāoshòubù sales department

销售额 xiāoshòu'é revenue from sales, sales takings

销售量 xiāoshòuliàng sales volume

削 **xiāo** v peel with a knife

削苹果 xiāo píngguǒ peel an apple

淆 **xiáo** v confuse (See 混淆 hùnxiáo)

小 **xiǎo** ADJ **1** small, little **2** being a child, young

小孩儿 xiǎoháir young child, child

NOTE: "小 xiǎo + family name," like 小 李 Xiǎo Lǐ, is a casual, friendly form of address to a person younger than oneself. See note on 老 lǎo for forms of address like 老李 Lǎo Lǐ.

小便 xiǎobiàn **I** N urine

小便池 xiǎobiànchí urinal

II v urinate

小费 xiǎofèi N tip, gratuity

小伙子 xiǎohuǒzi N young man, lad

NOTE: See note on 姑娘 gūniang.

小姐 xiǎojiě N **1** young lady **2** Miss

NOTE: 小姐 xiǎojiě is a common form of address to a young (or not so young) woman. If her family name is not known, just use 小姐 xiǎojiě. 小姐 xiǎojiě is also the form of address for a waitress or female attendant.

小康 xiǎokāng ADJ fairly prosperous, well-off, well-to-do

小康社会 xiǎokāng shèhuì a well-off society

小麦 xiǎomài N wheat

小米 xiǎomǐ N millet

小朋友 xiǎopéngyou N (a friendly form of address or reference) child

小气 xiǎoqì ADJ stingy, miserly

小区 xiǎoqū N residential community, neighborhood

小时 xiǎoshí N hour

半小时 bàn xiǎoshí half an hour

小时工 xiǎoshígōng N (domestic) worker paid on an hourly basis

小数 xiǎoshù N decimal

小说 xiǎoshuō N novel (本 běn, 篇 piān)

小说家 xiǎoshuōjiā (accomplished) novelist

爱情小说 àiqíng xiǎoshuō romance novel

长篇小说 chángpiān xiǎoshuō novel

短篇小说 duǎnpiān xiǎoshuō short story, story

历史小说 lìshǐ xiǎoshuō historical novel

小提琴 xiǎotíqín N violin

小提琴手 xiǎotíqínshǒu violinist

拉小提琴 lā xiǎotíqín play the violin

小偷 xiǎotōu N thief, pickpocket

小心 xiǎoxīn ADJ careful, cautious

小型 xiǎoxíng ADJ small-sized

小学 xiǎoxué N primary school (座 zuò, 所 suǒ)

小学生 xiǎoxuésheng primary school student, pupil

小子 xiǎozi N son, boy

小组 xiǎozǔ N small group

晓 **xiǎo** TRAD 曉 v know

晓得 xiǎode v Same as 知道 zhīdào. Only used in colloquial Chinese.

孝 **xiào** N filial piety

孝顺 xiàoshùn v perform one's filial duties faithfully, be obedient and considerate of one's parents

效 **xiào** N effect

效果 xiàoguǒ N effect, result

效力 xiàolì N desired effects, intended results

效率 xiàolǜ N efficiency

效益 xiàoyì N beneficial (economic) results, economic benefits

校 xiào N school

校徽 xiàohuī N school badge

校园 xiàoyuán N school ground, campus

校长 xiàozhǎng N headmaster, principal, university president, university vice chancellor

NOTES: (1) While in Chinese the chief of any school is called 校长 xiàozhǎng, different terms are required in English. (2) In an English-system university, the vice-chancellor is its chief executive officer. Vice-chancellor should therefore be translated as 校长 xiàozhǎng while chancellor, being largely an honorary position, should be 名誉校长 míngyù xiàozhǎng.

笑 xiào V 1 laugh, smile

大笑 dàxiào laugh
2 laugh at, make fun of

笑话 xiàohua I N joke II V laugh at

笑容 xiàoróng N smiling expression, smile
笑容满面 xiàoróng mǎnmiàn be all smiles

肖 xiào V resemble, be like

肖像 xiàoxiàng N portrait (幅 fú)

啸 xiào V howl, roar

些 xiē M. WD some, a few, a little

好些 hǎoxiē quite a few, lots of

歇 xiē V take a rest

协 xié TRAD 協 V 1 join 2 assist

协定 xiédìng N agreement, treaty

协会 xiéhuì N association (an organization)
环境保护者协会 huánjìng bǎohùzhě xiéhuì Environmentalists Association

协力 xiélì V join in a common effort, work together

协商 xiéshāng V discuss and seek advice, consult

协调 xiétiáo V coordinate, harmonize

协议 xiéyì N agreement (a document)

协议书 xiéyìshū agreement (a document) (份 fèn)
达成协议 dáchéng xiéyì reach an agreement

协助 xiézhù N in assistance

协作 xiézuò V cooperate

胁 xié TRAD 脅 V threaten (See 威胁 wēixié)

斜 xié ADJ oblique, slanting

挟 xié V hold under the arm

挟持 xiéchí V 1 seize by force 2 detain under duress

携 xié V 1 carry, take along with 2 take by the hand

携带 xiédài V carry, take along

携手 xiéshǒu ADV hand in hand
携手并进 xiéshǒu bìngjìn go forward hand in hand, advance side by side

邪 xié ADJ evil, heretical

邪教 xiéjiào N religious cult, cult

鞋 xié N shoe (只 zhī, 双 shuāng)

凉鞋 liáng xié sandals
皮鞋 pí xié leather shoes
拖鞋 tuō xié slippers
雨鞋 yǔ xié rubber boots
运动鞋 yùndòng xié sports shoes

鞋带 xiédài N shoelace, shoestring (根 gēn, 副 fù)
系鞋带 jì xiédài tie shoelace

谐 xié TRAD 諧 ADJ harmonious (See 和谐 héxié)

血 xié N Same as 血 xuè. Used only in colloquial Chinese.

写 xié TRAD 寫 V write, write with a pen

写作 xiězuò V write as a professional writer, compose essays

泻 xiè V flow swiftly

腹泻 fùxiè have diarrhea

卸 **xiè** v **1** unload **2** remove, strip (See 装卸 zhuāngxiè)

泄 **xiè** v allow air or liquid to escape, let out, leak
世露 xièlòu v leak (information)
世气 xièqì v lose heart, be discouraged

谢 **xiè** TRAD 謝 v **1** thank **2** decline
射谢 xièxiè v thank

NOTE: There are many ways of replying to 谢谢你 xièxiè nǐ, e.g.: 不客气。Bú kèqì. *You don't have to be so polite.*; 不用谢。Bú yòng xiè. *You don't have to thank me.*

射绝 xièjué v decline (an invitation, an offer, etc.), refuse politely

械 **xiè** N tool (See 机械 jīxiè.)

屑 **xiè** N butts, scraps
面包屑 miànbāo xiè crumbs (of bread)

心 **xīn** N **1** the heart
用心 yòngxīn apply oneself to
放心 fàngxīn feel relieved, be assured, at ease
开心 kāixīn be joyous
痛心 tòngxīn pained, agonized
2 mind, feeling **3** core, center
心爱 xīn'ài ADJ beloved, treasured
心得 xīndé N what one has learned from work, study, etc, gain in understanding
心理 xīnlǐ N mentality, psychology
心理分析 xīnlǐ fēnxi psychoanalysis
心理学 xīnlǐxué (the science of) psychology
心理咨询 xīnlǐ zīxún psychological consultation
心里 xīnli ADV in the heart, in the mind
心里有事 xīnli yǒushì have something on one's mind
心灵 xīnlíng I N soul, spirit
心灵深处 xīnlíng shēnchù deep down in one's heart
II ADJ quick-witted, agile-minded, bright
心灵手巧 xīnlíng shǒuqiǎo intelligent and capable, clever and deft

心目 xīnmù N mental view, mind
在他的心目中 zài tāde xīnmùzhōng in his eyes, in his opinion and judgment
心情 xīnqíng N state of mind, mood
心事 xīnshì N worry, something on one's mind
心思 xīnsi N idea, thought **2** state of mind, mood
没有心思出去玩儿 méiyǒu xīnsi chūqu wánr not in a mood to go out
心疼 xīnténg V **1** love dearly **2** feel sorry
心头 xīntóu N mind, heart
牢记心头 láojì xīntóu bear firmly in mind
心血 xīnxuè N painstaking effort
付出很大心血 fùchū hěn dà xīnxuè put a great deal of painstaking efforts
心血来潮 xīnxuè láicháo IDIOM be seized by an impulse, have a brainstorm
心眼儿 xīnyǎnr N heart, mind, intention
没安什么好心眼儿 méi ān shénme hǎo xīnyǎnr do not mean well, have some bad intention
心意 xīnyì N regard, warm feelings, good intention
心愿 xīnyuàn N wish, aspiration
心脏 xīnzàng N the heart (as a medical term)
心直口快 xīnzhí kǒukuài ADJ frank and outspoken

欣 **xīn** ADJ joyful
欣赏 xīnshǎng v admire, appreciate
欣欣向荣 xīnxīn xiàng róng IDIOM flourishing, prosperous

辛 **xīn** ADJ **1** spicy hot **2** laborious, hard
辛苦 xīnkǔ I ADJ **1** hard and toilsome (job) **2** harsh, difficult (life) II V (used to request somebody's service)

NOTE: "你们辛苦了!" "Nǐmen xīnkǔ le!" is used by a superior to express appreciation of hard work done by subordinate(s). When somebody has done you a service, you can say: "辛苦你了!" "Xīnkǔ nǐ le!"

辛勤 xīnqín ADJ industrious

锌 xīn N zinc (Zn)

新 xīn I ADJ new **II** ADV newly, recently

新陈代谢 xīnchéndàixiè IDIOM metabolism

新房 xīnfáng N bridal bedroom

新近 xīnjìn ADV recently, lately

新加坡 Xīnjiāpō N Singapore

新郎 xīnláng N bridegroom

新年 xīnnián N New Year

　新年贺卡 xīnnián hèkǎ New Year card

新娘 xīnniáng N bride

新生 xīnshēng N **1** newborn

　新生儿 xīnshēng'ér newborn baby

　2 new student

　新生报到 xīnshēng bàodào new students registration

　3 new life, a new leaf (in one's life)

　开始新生 kāishǐ xīnshēng turn over a new leaf

新式 xīnshì N new type, new style

新闻 xīnwén N news (of current affairs) (条 tiáo)

新西兰 Xīnxīlán N New Zealand

新鲜 xīnxiān ADJ fresh

新兴 xīnxīng ADJ new and fast developing, burgeoning

　新兴产业 xīnxīng chǎnyè fast growing industry, sunrise industry

新型 xīnxíng N new type, new pattern

新颖 xīnyǐng ADJ new and original

薪 xīn N **1** firewood **2** salary

　高薪养廉 gāoxīn yǎnglián the policy of high salary for civil servants in order to cultivate a clean government

薪金 xīnjīn Same as 薪水 xīnshui

薪水 xīnshui N salary, wages

信 xīn ¹ **I** N **I** V believe, trust **II** N **1** trust

　信贷 xìndài N (in banking) credit

信赖 xìnlài V trust, have faith in

　可以信赖的 kěyǐ xìnlài de trustworthy, reliable

信念 xìnniàn N faith, conviction

信任 xìnrèn **I** V trust, have confidence in **II** N trust, confidence

信心 xìnxīn N confidence, faith

信用 xìnyòng N **1** trustworthiness

　讲信用 jiǎngxìnyòng keep one's word, be trustworthy

　2 credit

信用卡 xìnyòngkǎ credit card

信誉 xìnyù N reputation, prestige

信 xīn ² N **1** letter, mail

　寄信 jì xìn post a letter

　介绍信 jièshàoxìn letter of recommendation, reference

　收到信 shōudào xìn receive a letter

　祝贺信 zhùhèxìn letter of congratulation

　2 sign, evidence

信封 xìnfēng N envelope

信号 xìnhào N signal

信件 xìnjiàn N letters, mail

信息 xìnxī N information

信息产业 xìnxī chǎnyè N information industry

衅 xìn N quarrel, dispute

挑衅 tiǎoxìn provoke

兴 xīng TRAD 興 **I** V **1** promote **2** start, begin **II** ADJ flourishing

兴办 xīngbàn V set up, initiate

兴奋 xīngfèn ADJ excited, overjoyed

兴奋剂 xīngfènjì N stimulant

兴建 xīngjiàn V build, construct

兴起 xīngqǐ V start and become popular, rise

兴旺 xīngwàng ADJ prosperous, thriving

星 xīng N star (颗 kē)

行星 xíngxīng planet

NOTE: In everyday Chinese 星星 xīngxing is normally used instead of 星 xīng, e.g.: 今天晚上的星星真亮。 Jīntiān wǎnshang de xīngxing zhēn liàng. *Tonight the stars are really bright.*

星期 xīngqī N week (个 gè)

星期一 Xīngqīyī Monday

星期二 Xīngqī'èr Tuesday

星期三 Xīngqīsān Wednesday

星期四 Xīngqīsì Thursday

星期五 Xīngqīwǔ Friday

星期六 Xīngqīliù Saturday

星期日/ 星期天 Xīngqīrì/ Xīngqītiān Sunday

上星期 shàng xīngqī last week

下星期 xià xīngqī next week

腥 **xīng** N fishy smell

行 1 **xíng** I v 1 travel, go 2 practice, carry out II N 1 trip, travel 2 act, behavior

行程 xíngchéng N route, distance traveled

行动 xíngdòng I v move around II N action, behavior

行贿 xínghuì v offer a bribe, bribe

行径 xíngjìng N disgraceful conduct, deviant behavior

行军 xíng jūn v (of troops) march

行李 xíngli N luggage, baggage (件 jiàn)

行人 xíngrén N pedestrian

行人道 xíngréndào sidewalk

行人横道线 xíngrén héngdàoxiàn pedestrian crossing

行使 xíngshǐ v exercise (rights, power, etc.)

行使公民权利 xíngshǐ gōngmín quánlì exercise one's civil rights

行驶 xíngshǐ v (of a vehicle or ship) travel

行为 xíngwéi N behavior, conduct, act

行政 xíngzhèng N administration

行政部门 xíngzhèng bùmén administrative department

行政命令 xíngzhèng mìnglìng executive order

行 2 **xíng** I v all right, OK, (that) will do II ADJ competent, capable

刑 **xíng** ADJ penal, criminal

刑场 xíngchǎng N execution ground

刑罚 xíngfá N torture

上刑罚 shàngxíng fá torture

刑法 xíngfǎ N penal code, criminal law

刑事 xíngshì ADJ criminal, penal

刑事犯 xíngshìfàn criminal offender, convict

刑事案件 xíngshì ànjiàn criminal case

形 **xíng** N form, shape

形成 xíngchéng v take shape, form

形容 xíngróng v describe

形式 xíngshì N form, shape

形势 xíngshì N situation

形态 xíngtài N form, pattern

形象 xíngxiàng N image

形状 xíngzhuàng N appearance, shape, form

型 **xíng** N model, type

型号 xínghào N model (of a car, airplane, etc.)

醒 **xǐng** v wake, wake up

睡醒 shuìxǐng have enough sleep

叫醒 jiàoxǐng wake somebody up

兴 **xìng** TRAD 興 ADJ joyful

兴趣 xìngqù N interest

对… (不) 感兴趣 duì...(bù) gǎn xìngqù be (un)interested in ...

对… (没) 有兴趣 duì...(méi) yǒu xìngqù be (un)interested in ...

杏 **xìng** N apricot

杏花 xìnghuā apricot blossom (朵 duǒ)

杏树 xìngshù apricot tree

杏子 xìngzi apricot (个 gè)

性 **xìng** N 1 nature, character

本性 běnxìng (of a human being) innate quality, character

2 sex, gender

男性 nánxìng male

性别 xìngbié N gender, sex

性病 xìngbìng N sexually transmitted disease (STD)

性格 xìnggé N person's character, disposition

性工作者 xìng gōngzuòzhě N sex worker

性交 xìngjiāo N sexual intercourse

性命 xìngmìng N (human) life

性能 xìngnéng N function, performance

性能良好 xìngnéng liánghǎo (of a machine) perform well, with satisfactory performance

性情 xìngqíng N temperament

性情温和 xìngqíng wēnhé with a gentle, mild temperament

性骚扰 xìng sāorǎo N sexual harassment

性质 xìngzhì N nature (of a matter, an event, etc.), basic quality

幸 xìng N good fortune

幸福 xìngfú ADJ happy, fortunate

NOTE: 幸福 xìngfú is used in a sublime sense, denoting *a profound and almost perfect happiness*. So it has a much more limited use than its English equivalents *happy* or *fortunate*. The usual Chinese word for *happy*, as in "I'm happy to hear the news," is 高兴 gāoxìng, e.g.: 听到这个消息, 我很高兴。Tīngdào zhège xiāoxi, wǒ hěn gāoxìng. *I'm happy to hear this news.*

幸好 xìnghǎo ADV fortunately, luckily

幸亏 xìngkuī ADV fortunately, luckily

幸运 xìngyùn ADJ fortunate, lucky

姓 xìng N family name

贵姓 guìxìng your family name (polite usage, normally in a question)

NOTE: The character 姓 xìng has 女 nǚ, meaning *female*, in it — an indication that the Chinese once had a matriarchal society.

姓名 xìngmíng N full name

兄 xiōng N elder brother

兄弟 xiōngdì N brother(s)

胸 xiōng N chest, thorax

胸怀 xiōnghuái I N mind, heart
胸怀宽广 xiōnghuái kuānguǎng be broad-minded
II V cherish, harbor
胸怀大志 xiōnghuái dàzhì cherish great ambition

胸膛 xiōngtáng N chest (of the human body)

凶 xiōng TRAD 兇 ADJ ferocious, fierce

凶恶 xiōng'è ADJ ferocious, fierce

凶狠 xiōnghěn ADJ fierce and malicious

凶猛 xiōngměng ADJ ferocious, violent

汹 xiōng TRAD 洶 as in 汹涌
xiōngyǒng

汹涌 xiōngyǒng ADJ turbulent

雄 xióng ADJ 1 male (of animals)
2 grand, imposing

雄厚 xiónghòu ADJ abundant, rich
资金雄厚 zījīnxiónghòu with abundant funds, very well-financed

雄伟 xióngwěi ADJ grand, magnificent

雄壮 xióngzhuàng ADJ full of power and grandeur, magnificent

熊 xióng N bear (只 zhī)

熊猫 xióngmāo N (giant) panda (只 zhī)

修 xiū V 1 Same as 修理 xiūlǐ 2 build, construct (a building, bridge, road, etc.) 3 study, cultivate

修订 xiūdìng V revise
修订版 xiūdìngbǎn revised edition

修复 xiūfù V restore (a work of art)

修改 xiūgǎi V amend, revise

修建 xiūjiàn V build, construct

修理 xiūlǐ V repair, fix

修养 xiūyǎng N 1 accomplishment, training
文化修养 wénhuà xiūyǎng cultural accomplishment
2 self-cultivation, good behavior and manners

修正 xiūzhèng V amend, revise

修筑 xiūzhù V build, construct

羞 xiū V be shy, be bashful

羞耻 xiūchǐ N sense of shame

羞耻心 xiūchǐ xīn sense of shame
不知羞耻 bùzhī xiūchǐ have no sense of shame, shameless

休 xiū I N leisure II V stop, cease, rest

休息 xiūxi V rest, take a rest, have a day off

休闲 xiūxián N leisure

休闲服 xiūxiánfú casual clothes

休养 xiūyǎng V recuperate, convalesce

朽 **xiǔ** v decay
不朽 bùxiǔ v immortal

嗅 **xiù** v smell, sniff

秀 **xiù** ADJ elegant
秀丽 xiùlì ADJ elegantly beautiful

锈 **xiù** TRAD 鏽 N rust

绣 **xiù** TRAD 繡 v embroider

袖 **xiù** N sleeve
袖子 xiùzi sleeve

须 **xū** TRAD 須 MODAL v must
须知 xūzhī N (important) notice, essential information
考生须知 kǎoshēng xūzhī important notice to examinees

虚 **xū** ADJ 1 void 2 of frail health 3 false 4 modest
虚假 xūjiǎ ADJ false, sham
虚拟 xūnǐ ADJ invented, fictitious
虚拟现实 xūnǐ xiànshí virtual reality
虚弱 xūruò ADJ debilitated, weak
虚伪 xūwěi I ADJ hypocritical II N hypocrisy
虚伪的人 xūwěi de rén hypocrite
虚心 xūxīn ADJ open-minded and modest

墟 **xū** N ruins (See 废墟 fèixū)

需 **xū** v need
需求 xūqiú N demand, requirement
需要 xūyào v need, be in need of

许 **xǔ** TRAD 許 I v 1 promise 2 allow II ADJ approximate, rough
许多 xǔduō ADJ many, much
许可 xǔkě v permit, allow

序 **xù** N 1 sequence, order 2 preface
序言 xùyán N preface

续 **xù** TRAD 續 v continue (See 继续 jìxù, 连续 liánxù, 陆续 lùxù, 手续 shǒuxù.)

绪 **xù** TRAD 緒 N mood (See 情绪 qíngxù)

絮 **xù** as in 絮叨 xùdao
絮叨 xùdao I ADJ garrulous, long-winded II v talk too much, be a chatterbox

畜 **xù** v keep domesticated animals
畜产品 xùchǎnpǐn N animal products
畜牧 xùmù v raise livestock
畜牧业 xùmùyè animal husbandry

蓄 **xù** v save up
蓄电池 xùdiànchí N battery

酗 **xù** as in 酗酒 xùjiǔ
酗酒 xùjiǔ v drink excessively, get drunk

叙 **xù** 1 chat 2 narrate
叙述 xùshù v narrate, recount
叙谈 xùtán v chat

宣 **xuān** v declare, announce
宣布 xuānbù v declare, announce
宣称 xuānchēng v assert, profess
宣传 xuānchuán I v 1 disseminate, publicize 2 propagandize II N 1 dissemination 2 propaganda
宣读 xuāndú v read out in public
宣告 xuāngào v declare, proclaim
宣誓 xuānshì v swear an oath
宣誓仪式 xuānshì yíshì swearing-in ceremony
宣言 xuānyán N declaration, manifesto
宣言书 xuānyánshū declaration (份 fèn)
宣扬 xuānyáng v publicize, promote

喧 **xuān** ADJ noisy
喧闹 xuānnào ADJ noisy and full of activities, very noisy

悬 **xuán** TRAD 懸 v hang, suspend
悬案 xuán'àn N unsettled case, cold case
悬挂 xuánguà v hang
悬念 xuánniàn N suspense
悬崖 xuányá N overhanging cliff, precipice
悬崖勒马 xuányá lèmǎ rein in at the

199

旋 xuán

brink of the precipice (→ avoid an imminent danger at the last moment)

旋 xuán v circle, spin

旋律 xuánlǜ N melody
旋转 xuánzhuǎn v revolve, spin

选 xuǎn TRAD 選 v 1 Same as 选举 xuǎnjǔ 2 select, choose

选拔 xuǎnbá v select, choose
选定 xuǎndìng v select, decide on
选购 xuǎngòu v choose and buy
　选购年货 xuǎngòu niánhuò shop for the Chinese New Year
选举 xuǎnjǔ I v elect, vote II N election, voting
选民 xuǎnmín N voter, electorate
选手 xuǎnshǒu N (of sports) selected contestant, player, athlete, competing athlete
选用 xuǎnyòng v select for use
选择 xuǎnzé I v select, choose II N choice

削 xuē v cut, pare

削减 xuējiǎn v cut down, reduce
削弱 xuēruò v weaken

靴 xuē N boots

靴子 xuēzi boots (只 zhī, 双 shuāng)

穴 xué N cave

学 xué TRAD 學 I v learn, study II N 1 learning, knowledge 2 school, course of study

学费 xué fèi N tuition, tuition fee
学会 xuéhuì I v learn (to do something), master
学科 xuékē N subject for study, discipline
学年 xuénián N academic year
学派 xuépài N school of thought
学期 xuéqī N semester, term
学生 xuésheng N student, pupil (个 gè, 名 míng)
学时 xuéshí N class hour, period
学术 xuéshù N learning, scholarship
　学术会议 xuéshù huìyì (scholarly or scientific) conference, symposium
学说 xuéshuō N theory, doctrine
学位 xuéwèi N academic degree

学士学位 xuéshì xuéwèi bachelor degree
硕士学位 shuòshì xuéwèi master's degree, masterate
博士学位 bóshì xuéwèi PhD degree, doctorate
学问 xuéwen N learning, knowledge
学习 xuéxí I v study, learn
　向…学习 xiàng…xuéxí learn from …, emulate …
　II N study
学校 xuéxiào N school (座 zuò)
学院 xuéyuàn N college, institute
学者 xuézhě N scholar
学制 xuézhì N 1 educational system 2 term of study

雪 xuě N snow

下雪 xià xuě to snow
雪白 xuě bái ADJ snow-white
雪花 xuěhuā N snowflake (片 piàn)

血 xuè N blood

输血 shūxuè blood transfusion
血管 xuèguǎn N blood vessel
　动脉血管 dòngmài xuèguǎn artery
　静脉血管 jìngmài xuèguǎn vein
血汗 xuèhàn N blood and sweat, sweat and toil
　血汗工厂 xuèhàn gōngchǎng sweatshop
血库 xuèkù N blood bank
血型 xuèxíng N blood type
血压 xuèyā N blood pressure
　高血压 gāoxuèyā high blood pressure, hypertension
　低血压 dīxuèyā low blood pressure, hypotension
血液 xuèyè N blood (as a technical term)

熏 xūn v treat with smoke, smoke

熏肉 xūnròu smoked meat
熏鱼 xūnyú smoked fish

循 xún v abide by, follow

循环 xúnhuán v circulate
　血液循环 xuèyè xúnhuán blood circulation

循序渐进 xúnxù jiànjìn IDIOM proceed step by step in an orderly way

寻 xún TRAD 尋 v seek, search

探寻 tànxún search, explore
追寻 zhuīxún pursue, track down
寻宝 xúnbǎo N treasure hunt
寻常 xúncháng ADJ usual, common
寻求 xúnqiú v seek, go in quest of
寻死 xúnsǐ v commit suicide
寻找 xúnzhǎo v look for, seek

旬 xún N a period of ten days in a month

上旬 shàngxún the first ten days in a month
中旬 zhōngxún the second ten days in a month
下旬 xiàxún the last ten days in a month

询 xún TRAD 詢 v inquire (See 咨询 zīxún.)

询问 xúnwèn v inquire, ask about

巡 xún v patrol

巡逻 xúnluó v patrol, go on patrol
巡逻艇 xúnluótǐng patrol boat

讯 xùn N message (See 通讯 tōngxùn.)

迅 xùn ADJ rapid

迅速 xùnsù ADJ rapid, speedy, swift

训 xùn v train

军训 jūnxùn military training
训练 xùnliàn v train

逊 xùn ADJ modest (See 谦逊 qiānxùn.)

Y

压 yā TRAD 壓 v press, push down

压价 yājià v undersell with reduced prices
压力 yālì N pressure
压迫 yāpò I v oppress II N oppression
压缩 yāsuō v compress, condense
空气压缩机 kōngqì yāsuōjī air compressor

压抑 yāyì v suppress, bottle up
压抑自己的愤怒 yāyì zìjǐ de fènnù bottle up one's anger
压制 yāzhì v repress, stifle

呀 yā INTERJ oh, ah (expressing surprise)

鸦 yā N crow (See 乌鸦 wūyā)

鸦片 yāpiàn N opium
抽鸦片 chōu yāpiàn smoke opium

鸭 yā TRAD 鴨 N duck

鸭子 yāzi duck (只 zhī)

押 yā v 1 escort (goods, criminal) 2 pawn, pledge as security (See 抵押 dǐyā)

牙 yá N tooth, teeth (颗 kē)

牙齿 yáchǐ N tooth, teeth (颗 kē)
牙膏 yágāo N toothpaste (管 guǎn)
牙科 yákē N dentistry
牙科医生 yákē yīshēng dentist (位 wèi)
牙刷 yáshuā N toothbrush (把 bǎ)
牙医 yáyī N Same as 牙科医生 yákē yīshēng

芽 yá N sprout, bud

发芽 fāyá germinate, to bud, to sprout

崖 yá N cliff (See 悬崖 xuányá)

雅 yǎ ADJ elegant, cultured (See 文雅 wényǎ)

雅思 Yǎsī N International English Language Testing System (IELTS)

哑 yǎ TRAD 啞 ADJ dumb, mute

哑巴 yǎba N mute person, mute
哑语 yǎyǔ N sign language

亚 yà ADJ second

亚军 yàjūn N (in sports) second place, runner-up
亚洲 Yàzhōu N Asia

讶 yà v be surprised (See 惊讶 jīngyà)

轧 yà TRAD 軋 v run over, roll

呀 ya

呀 ya PARTICLE Same as 啊 ā 2 PARTICLE (Used after a, e, i, o, u)

淹 yān v submerge, inundate
淹没 yānmò v submerge, flood

烟 yān N 1 smoke 2 Same as 香烟 xiāngyān
禁烟区 jìnyānqū smoke-free area, "No Smoking" area
烟草 yāncǎo N tabacco
烟囱 yāncōng N chimney
烟雾 yānwù N mist, smoke, smog

严 yán TRAD 嚴 ADJ strict, severe

严格 yángé I ADJ strict, stringent, rigorous II v make ... strict, make ... stringent
严寒 yánhán v severe cold
严禁 yánjìn v strictly forbid
严厉 yánlì ADJ stern, severe
严厉的警告 yánlì de jǐnggào a stern warning
严密 yánmì ADJ tight, watertight
严肃 yánsù ADJ serious, solemn
严重 yánzhòng ADJ serious, critical

岩 yán N rock
岩石 yánshí rock (块 kuài)

炎 yán ADJ scorching
炎热 yánrè ADJ scorching hot

延 yán v extend, delay, postpone

延长 yáncháng v prolong, extend
延缓 yánhuǎn v put off, delay
延期 yánqī v postpone, defer
延伸 yánshēn v stretch, extend
延续 yánxù v 1 continue, go on 2 last

言 yán I N speech II v talk, say
言论 yánlùn N remark, expression of opinion
言论自由 yánlùn zìyóu freedom of speech
言语 yányǔ v speak, reply

沿 yán PREP along
沿儿 yánr N edge, border

沿岸 yán'àn N bank, coast
沿海 yánhǎi N coast
沿海城市 yánhǎi chéngshì coastal city
沿途 yántú N (places) on the way
沿途的见闻 yántú de jiànwén what one sees and learns on the way

研 yán v study, research
研究 yánjiū I v research, study, consider carefully II N research, study (项 xiàng)
做气候变化的研究 zuò qìhou biànhuà de yánjiū do research on climate change
研究生 yánjiūshēng N graduate student, post-graduate student
研究生院 yánjiūshēng yuàn graduate school (of a university)
研究所 yánjiūsuǒ N research institute, research unit

NOTE: The difference between 研究所 yánjiūsuǒ and 研究院 yánjiūyuàn is that the former is usually smaller in scale.

研究院 yánjiūyuàn N research institute
研制 yánzhì N research and development, R&D

盐 yán TRAD 鹽 N salt

颜 yán TRAD 顏 N complexion, color
颜色 yánsè N color

掩 yǎn v cover, cover up
掩盖 yǎngài v cover, cover up
掩护 yǎnhù v cover, shield
掩饰 yǎnshì v cover up, gloss over, conceal
掩饰错误 yǎnshì cuòwù gloss over a mistake

眼 yǎn N eye
左眼 zuǒyǎn the left eye
右眼 yòuyǎn the right eye
眼光 yǎnguāng N eye, way of looking at things, point of view
很有审美眼光 hěn yǒu shěnměi yǎn-guāng have an eye for what is beautiful
用老眼光看新问题 yòng lǎo yǎnguāng

kàn xīn wèntí look at a new problem from an old point of view

眼镜 yǎnjìng N glasses, spectacles (副 fù)

太阳眼镜 tàiyáng yǎnjìng sunglasses

眼镜店 yǎnjìngdiàn N optician's shop

眼镜盒 yǎnjìnghé N glasses case

眼睛 yǎnjing N eye

眼看 yǎnkàn ADV soon, in a moment

眼科 yǎnkē N department of ophthalmology

眼科医生 yǎnkē yīshēng ophthalmologist

眼泪 yǎnlèi N tear (滴 dī)

流下一滴眼泪 liúxià yì dī yǎnlèi shed a drop of tear

眼力 yǎnlì N 1 eyesight

眼力好 yǎnlì hǎo good eyesight

2 discerning power, judgment

有眼力 yǒu yǎnlì be discerning

眼前 yǎnqián ADV 1 before one's eyes 2 at present, at this moment

眼色 yǎnsè N meaningful glance

交换眼色 jiāohuàn yǎnsè exchange meaningful glances

眼神 yǎnshén N expression in one's eyes

眼下 yǎnxià ADV at the moment, now

演 yǎn I v act, perform, show II N show (a film)

演变 yǎnbiàn v evolve, unfold

演出 yǎnchū I v put on a theatrical performance, perform II N theatrical performance

演说 yǎnshuō v deliver a formal speech

演算 yǎnsuàn v perform mathematical calculations

演习 yǎnxí N exercise, drill

军事演习 jūnshì yǎnxí military exercise

演员 yǎnyuán N actor, actress, performer

演奏 yǎnzòu v give an instrument performance

衍 yǎn v spread out (See 敷衍 fūyan)

厌 yàn TRAD 厭 v detest, loathe

厌恶 yànwù v detest, be disgusted with

艳 yàn ADJ fresh and attractive (See 鲜艳 xiānyàn)

燕 yàn N (bird) swallow

燕子 yànzi swallow (只 zhī)

雁 yàn N wild goose

大雁 dàyàn wild goose

焰 yàn N flame (See 火焰 huǒyàn)

咽 yàn v swallow

宴 yàn I N feast II v entertain

宴会 yànhuì N banquet, feast

参加宴会 cānjiā yànhuì attend a banquet

告别（欢迎）宴会 gàobié (huānyíng) yànhuì farewell (welcome) banquet

结婚宴会 jiéhūn yànhuì wedding banquet

宴请 yànqǐng v entertain with a feast

宴席 yànxí N banquet, feast

验 yàn TRAD 驗 v examine

验光 yànguāng N optometry

验光师 yànguāngshī optometrist

验收 yànshōu v check and accept, check upon delivery

验证 yànzhèng v test to verify

央 yāng N center (See 中央 zhōngyāng)

秧 yāng N seedling

插秧 chāyāng transplant rice seedlings

秧苗 yāngmiáo N rice seedling

殃 yāng N calamity (See 遭殃 zāoyāng)

羊 yáng N sheep, goat, lamb (头 tóu)

山羊 shānyáng goat

小羊 xiǎoyáng lamb

羊毛 yángmáo N wool

羊皮 yángpí N sheepskin

羊肉 yángròu N mutton

阳 yáng TRAD 陽 N what is open, overt, masculine, the sun

阳光 yángguāng N sunshine, sunlight

阳性 yángxìng ADJ (of medical test) positive

扬 yáng TRAD 揚 v raise, make known (See 表扬 biǎoyáng, 发扬 fāyáng.)

杨 yáng N poplar

杨树 yángshù poplar tree (棵 kē)

洋 yáng N ocean (See 大洋洲 Dàyángzhōu, 海洋 hǎiyáng.)

养 yáng TRAD 養 V 1 provide for, support 2 raise, keep as pet 3 form, cultivate 4 recuperate one's health

养成 yángchéng V form (a habit)
养成每天锻炼的好习惯 yángchéng měitiān duànliàn de hǎo xíguàn form the good habit of doing exercises every day

养活 yǎnghuo V provide for, support, sustain

养料 yǎngliào N nourishment, nutriment

养育 yǎngyù V bring up (a child), rear

养殖 yǎngzhí N breed or cultivate (aquatic products, plants, etc.)
水产养殖场 shuǐchǎn yǎngzhíchǎng aquatic farm

氧 yǎng N oxygen (O₂)

氧气 yǎngqì oxygen
氧化 yǎnghuà V oxidize, oxidate

痒 yǎng V itch, tickle

发痒 fāyǎng itch

仰 yǎng V face upward

仰望 yǎngwàng V 1 look up to 2 revere

样 yàng TRAD 樣 I M. WD kind, category, type II N appearance, looks
样子 yàngzi N appearance, manner

要 yāo as in 要求 yāoqiú

要求 yāoqiú I V ask, demand, require II N demand, requirement

腰 yāo N waist, small of the back

妖 yāo N evil spirit

妖怪 yāoguài N monster, bogey man

邀 yāo V invite

邀请 yāoqǐng I V invite II N invitation
邀请信 yāoqǐngxìn letter of invitation

摇 yáo V shake, wave

摇头丸 yáotóuwán N Ecstasy pill (an addictive drug)

谣 yáo TRAD 謠 N 1 rumor 2 ballad, rhyme

民谣 mínyáo folk ballad, ballad
谣言 yáoyán N malicious rumor, rumor

遥 yáo ADJ faraway

遥远 yáoyuǎn ADJ faraway, remote

窑 yáo N kiln

砖窑 zhuānyáo brick kiln (座 zuò)

咬 yǎo V bite

药 yào TRAD 藥 N medicine, drug

草药 cǎoyào herbal medicine
吃药 chī yào take medicine
西药 xīyào Western medicine
中药 Zhōngyào traditional Chinese medicine
药方 yàofāng N prescription
药房 yàofáng N pharmacist's, pharmacy
药片 yàopiàn N pill
药水 yàoshuǐ N liquid medicine

耀 yào V shine, dazzle (See 照耀 zhàoyào)

要 yào I V 1 want, would like 2 ask (somebody to do something) II ADJ important
要人 yàorén important person, VIP III MODAL V should, must IV CONJ suppose, if
要点 yàodiǎn N key point, major point
要好 yàohǎo ADJ on very good terms, very close
要紧 yàojǐn ADJ important, urgent, serious
不要紧 búyàojǐn it doesn't matter
要领 yàolǐng N main points, gist
要么 yàome CONJ either ... (or)
要命 yàomìng ADV extremely
要是 yàoshì CONJ if

NOTE: Both 如果 rúguǒ and 要是 yàoshì mean *if*. While 如果 rúguǒ is for general use, 要是 yàoshì is a colloquialism.

要素 yàosù N essential element

钥 yào TRAD 鑰 as in 钥匙 yàoshi

钥匙 yàoshi N key (把 bǎ)

爷 yé TRAD 爺 N paternal grandfather

爷爷 yéye N Same as 祖父 zǔfù. Used in colloquial Chinese.

也 yě ADV 1 also, too 2 neither, nor

也许 yěxǔ ADV perhaps, maybe

NOTE: See note on 恐怕 kǒngpà.

野 yě I N open country II ADJ wild

野蛮 yěmán ADJ savage, barbaric
野生 yěshēng ADJ wild (animal or plant)
野生动物 yěshēng dòngwù wildlife
野兽 yěshòu N wild beast
野外 yěwài N open country, field
野外作业 yěwài zuòyè field work
野心 yěxīn N wild ambition

冶 yě V smelt

冶炼 yěliàn smelt
冶金 yějīn N metallurgy

业 yè TRAD 業 N industry

业务 yèwù N 1 professional work, vocational work 2 business
业余 yèyú I N spare time II ADJ amateur

叶 yè TRAD 葉 N leaf

叶子 yèzi leaf (片 piàn)

页 yè TRAD 頁 N page

夜 yè N night, evening

半夜 bànyè midnight
夜班 yèbān N night shift
上夜班 shàng yèbān be on a night shift
夜车 yèchē N night train
夜里 yèlǐ N at night
夜晚 yèwǎn N Same as 夜里 yèlǐ
液 yè N liquid, fluid

液体 yètǐ N liquid

一 yī NUM one

NOTE: (1) 一 undergoes tone changes (tone sandhi). When standing alone, 一 is pronounced with the first tone, i.e. yī. When followed by a sound in the fourth tone, 一 changes to the second tone, e.g. 一定 yídìng. 一 is pronounced in the fourth tone in all other circumstances, e.g. 一般 yìbān, 一同 yìtóng, 一起 yìqǐ. Pay attention to the various tones of 一 here and in the following words. (2) When saying a number (e.g. a telephone number) people pronounce 一 as yāo for clarity, e.g.: 我的电话号码是五八一三九。Wǒ de diànhuà hàomǎ shì wǔ-bā-yāo-sān-jiǔ. *My telephone number is 58139.*

一般 yìbān ADJ 1 generally speaking, normal 2 average, commonplace 3 same as, as … as
一半 yíbàn N half, one half
一辈子 yíbèizi N one's entire life
一边 yìbiān N one side
一边…一边… yìbiān…yìbiān… CONJ while …, at the same time

NOTE: 一边…一边… yìbiān…yìbiān… links two verbs to indicate that the two actions denoted by the verbs take place simultaneously. An example: 他常常一边做作业一边听音乐。Tā chángcháng yìbiān zuò zuòyè yìbiān tīng yīnyuè. *He often does his homework while listening to music.* When the verbs are monosyllabic, 边…边… biān…biān… may be used instead of 一边…一边… yìbiān…yìbiān…, e.g.: 孩子们边走边唱。Háizimen biān zǒu biān chàng. *The children sang while walking.*

一旦 yídàn CONJ once, in case
一道 yídào ADV Same as 一起 yìqǐ
一点儿 yìdiǎnr N a tiny amount, a bit
一定 yídìng I ADJ 1 fixed, specified 2 to a certain degree, fair, limited II ADV certainly, definitely
一度 yídù ADV for a time, on one occasion
一帆风顺 yìfān fēng shun IDIOM plain sailing

一方面…一方面… yìfāngmiàn…yìfāng-
miàn… CONJ on the one hand ... on the
other hand ...

一概 yígài ADV all, without exception

一概而论 yígài ér lùn IDIOM lump
everything together, make sweeping
generalization

一共 yígòng ADV in all, total, altogether

一贯 yíguàn ADV all along, always

一会儿 yíhuìr ADV in a very short time

一会儿…一会儿 yíhuìr…yíhuìr CONJ one
moment ... the next (moment)

一…就… yī…jiù… CONJ as soon as, no
sooner ... than ...

一口气 yìkǒuqì ADV (do something) in one
breath, without a break

一块儿 yíkuàir ADV Same as 一起 yìqǐ.
Tends to be used in colloquial Chinese.

一连 yìlián ADV in a row, successively

一路平安 yílù píng'ān IDIOM have a good
journey

一路顺风 yílù shùnfēng IDIOM Have a
good trip!

一律 yílǜ ADV all, without exception

一毛不拔 yìmáo bù bá IDIOM unwilling to
give even a hair, very stingy

一旁 yìpáng N one side

一面…一面 yímiàn…yímiàn CONJ at the
same time, while

一齐 yìqí ADV Same as 一起 yìqǐ

一起 yìqǐ ADV together

一切 yíqiè I ADJ all, every and each without exception II PRON all, everything

一生 yìshēng N all one's life, lifetime

一时 yìshí ADV for the time being, mo-
mentarily

一手 yìshǒu ADV single-handedly, all by
oneself

一同 yìtóng ADV Same as 一起 yìqǐ

一系列 yíxìliè N a series of

一下 yíxià ADV (used after a verb to
indicate the action is done briefly or
casually) for a short while

NOTE: It is very common in spoken
Chinese to use 一下 yíxià after a verb,
especially as an informal request. Some

Northern Chinese speakers use 一下儿
yíxiàr instead of 一下 yíxià. An example:
我们在这儿停一下儿吧。Wǒmen zài zhèr
tíng yíxiàr ba. *Let's stop here for a while.*

一下子 yíxiàzi ADV all at once, all of a
sudden

一向 yíxiàng ADV all along, always

一些 yìxiē M WD a small amount of, a
bit of

一心 yìxīn ADV single-mindedly, whole-
heartedly

一样 yíyàng ADJ same, identical

一再 yízài ADV time and again, repeatedly

一直 yìzhí ADV always, all the time

一致 yízhì ADJ unanimous, identical

壹 yī N one

衣 yī N clothing

衣服 yīfu N clothes, pieces of clothing
(件 jiàn)

NOTE: 衣服 yīfu may denote *clothes* or
pieces of clothing. 一件衣服 yí jiàn yīfu
may be a *jacket*, a *coat*, a *dress* or a
sweater, but not a *pair of trousers*, which is
一条裤子 yì tiáo kùzi.

衣裳 yīshang N Same as 衣服 yīfu

伊 yī PRON she, her, he, his

伊斯兰教 Yīsīlánjiào N Islam

医 yī TRAD 醫 I V heal, cure II N
medicine

医疗 yīliáo N medical care
公费医疗 gōngfèi yīliáo public health
service

医生 yīshēng N medical doctor (位 wèi)

医务室 yīwùshì N clinic (in a school, factory, etc.)

医学 yīxué N medical science, medicine

医学院 yīxuéyuàn N medical school

医药 yīyào N medicine

医药费 yīyàofèi medical expenses

医院 yīyuàn N hospital (座 zuò)
送…去医院 sòng…qù yīyuàn take ... to
the hospital

住(医)院 zhù (yī) yuàn be hospitalized

医治 yīzhì v treat (a patient)

依 yī v **1** rely on **2** according to

依次 yīcì ADV in order, successively

依旧 yījiù ADV as before, still

依据 yījù v be based on
依据最新资料 yījù zuìxīn zīliào based on the latest data
II N basis, foundation
没有依据的指控 méiyǒu yījù de zhǐkòng unfounded allegation

依靠 yīkào v rely on, depend on

依赖 yīlài v rely on, be dependent on

依然 yīrán ADV still, as before

依照 yīzhào PREP according to, based on

姨 yí N one's mother's sister (See 阿姨 āyí)

仪 yí TRAD 儀 N instrument, appearance

仪表 yíbiǎo N **1** appearance, bearing
仪表堂堂 yíbiǎo tángtáng look dignified, with imposing presence
2 gauge, meter

仪器 yíqì N instrument (件 jiàn)

仪式 yíshì N ceremony
举行仪式 jǔxíng yíshì hold a ceremony

宜 yí ADJ suitable (See 便宜 piányi.)

移 yí v move, shift

移动 yídòng v move, shift
移动电话 yídòng diànhuà mobile telephone

移民 yímín **I** v immigrate, emigrate
II N immigrant, emigrant, immigration
移民局 Yímínjú Immigration Services
新移民 xīn yímín new immigrant

疑 yí v doubt, disbelief

疑惑 yíhuò v feel uncertain, wonder

疑问 yíwèn N doubt

疑心 yíxīn N Same as 怀疑 huáiyí

遗 yí TRAD 遺 v **1** leave behind as legacy, inheritance **2** bequeath, hand down **3** lose, omit

遗产 yíchǎn N inheritance, legacy

遗传 yíchuán v pass to the next generation, be hereditary
遗传病 yíchuánbìng hereditary disease

遗憾 yíhàn **I** v regret **II** ADJ regretful

遗留 yíliú v leave behind, hand down

遗失 yíshī v lose, be lost

遗体 yítǐ N body of a dead person, remains
向遗体告别 xiàng yítǐ gàobié pay last tribute to a dead person

遗址 yízhǐ N remains (of a building), ruins

已 yǐ ADJ Same as 已经 yǐjīng. Used in written Chinese.

已经 yǐjīng ADV already

乙 yǐ **I** N the second of the ten Heavenly Stems **II** ADJ second

以 yǐ PREP **1** with, in the manner of
2 for, because of
2 yǐ CONJ in order to, so as to

以便 yǐbiàn CONJ so that, in order that

以后 yǐhòu N after, later

以及 yǐjí CONJ Same as 和 hé **2** CONJ, used in formal Chinese.

以来 yǐlái N since, in the past ...

以免 yǐmiǎn CONJ in order to avoid, so as not to

以内 yǐnèi N within, during

以前 yǐqián N before, some time ago
不久以前 bùjiǔ yǐqián not long ago

以上 yǐshàng N over, more than

以身作则 yǐshēn zuòzé IDIOM set a good example (for others to follow)

以外 yǐwài N beyond, outside, other than

以往 yǐwǎng N formerly, in the past

以为 yǐwéi v think (usually incorrectly)

以下 yǐxià N below, less than

以至 yǐzhì CONJ **1** up to **2** so as to, so ... that

以至于 yǐzhìyú CONJ Same as 以至 yǐzhì

椅 yǐ N chair
椅子 yǐzi chair (把 bǎ)

倚 yǐ v lean on or against, rest on or against

蚁 yǐ N ant (See 蚂蚁 mǎyǐ)

亿 yì TRAD 億 NUM one hundred million

十亿 shíyì billion

亿万 yìwàn NUM millions upon millions, an astronomical number of

亿万富翁 yìwàn fùwēng billionaire, super-rich

艺 yì TRAD 藝 N art

艺术 yìshù N art

艺术家 yìshùjiā N (accomplished, recognized) artist

艺术作品 yìshù zuòpǐn N a work of art

忆 yì TRAD 憶 V recall (See 回忆 huíyì, 记忆 jìyì.)

异 yì TRAD 異 ADJ different, unusual

异常 yìcháng ADJ abnormal, unusual

毅 yì ADJ firm, resolute

毅力 yìlì N indomitable will, strong willpower

毅然 yìrán ADV resolutely

抑 yì V repress (See 压抑 yāyì)

役 yì N military campaign (See 战役 zhànyì)

疫 yì N epidemic (See 瘟疫 wēnyì)

亦 yì ADV also

译 yì TRAD 譯 V translate, interpret

译员 yìyuán N interpreter, translator (位 wèi, 名 míng)

易 yì I ADJ easy (See 容易 róngyì) II V exchange (See 贸易 màoyì)

益 yì N benefit (See 利益 lìyì.)

谊 yì TRAD 誼 N friendship (See 友谊 yǒuyì.)

意 yì N 1 idea, meaning 2 expectation, wish

意见 yìjiàn N 1 opinion, view (条 tiáo) 2 complaint, objection

提意见 tí yìjiàn make a comment (on an issue, a proposal etc.), make a complaint

意料 yìliào V expect, anticipate

意料之中 yìliào zhīzhōng in line with expectations

出乎意料 chūhū yìliào out of expectations, not anticipated

意识 yìshí N consciousness II V be conscious of, be aware of

意思 yìsi N meaning

意图 yìtú N intention

了解他们的意图 liǎojiě tāmende yìtú find out their intentions

意外 yìwài I ADJ unexpected, unforeseen II N mishap, accident

意味着 yìwèizhe V mean, imply

意向 yìxiàng N intent, purpose

意向书 yìxiàngshū letter of intent, agreement of intent

意义 yìyì N significance

意愿 yìyuàn N will, wish

意志 yìzhì N will, willpower

义 yì TRAD 義 I ADJ righteous II N righteousness, justice

义务 yìwù N duty, obligation

义务工作(义工) yìwù gōngzuò (yìgōng) N voluntary work, voluntary worker

义务教育 yìwù jiàoyù N compulsory education

议 yì TRAD 議 V discuss, exchange views

议案 yì'àn N proposal, motion (份 fèn)

议程 yìchéng N agenda

议定书 yìdìngshū N protocol (a diplomatic document) (份 fèn)

议会 yìhuì N parliament

议论 yìlùn V comment, discuss, talk

议员 yìyuán N member of parliament (MP)

翼 yì N wing

因 yīn CONJ because

因此 yīncǐ CONJ therefore, so

因而 yīn'ér CONJ Same as 因此 yīncǐ

因素 yīnsù N factor, element

因特网 yīntèwǎng N Internet

因为 yīnwèi CONJ because

NOTE: 因为 yīnwèi *because* is usually followed by 所以 suǒyǐ *therefore*: 因为大多数人都反对，所以这个计划放弃了。 Yīnwèi dàduōshù rén dōu fǎnduì, suǒyǐ zhège jìhuà fàngqì le. *Because the majority opposed the plan, it was abandoned.*

阴 **yīn** TRAD 陰 ADJ **1** cloudy, overcast **2** hidden

阴暗 yīn'àn ADJ gloomy
生活中的阴暗面 shēnghuó zhōngde yīn'ànmiàn the seamy side of life
阴谋 yīnmóu N conspiracy
揭露一项国际阴谋 jiēlù yí xiàng guójì yīnmóu uncover an international conspiracy
阴天 yīntiān cloudy day
阴性 yīnxìng ADJ (of medical test) negative

姻 **yīn** N marriage (See 婚姻 hūnyīn.)

音 **yīn** N sound

音响 yīnxiǎng N sound, acoustics
音响设备 yīnxiǎng shèbèi sound system
音响效果 yīnxiǎng xiàoguǒ acoustic effects
音像 yīnxiàng N audio-video
音乐 yīnyuè N music
古典音乐 gǔdiǎn yīnyuè classical music
流行音乐 liúxíng yīnyuè pop music
轻音乐 qīng yīnyuè light music, easy listening
音乐会 yīnyuè huì concert (场 cháng)
露天音乐会 lùtiān yīnyuèhuì open-air concert
音乐家 yīnyuè jiā musician
音乐学院 yīnyuè xuéyuàn (music) conservatory

银 **yín** TRAD 銀 I N silver II ADJ relating to money or currency

银行 yínháng N bank (家 jiā)
银行家 yínhángjiā banker
储备银行 chǔbèi yínháng reserve bank
商业银行 shāngyè yínháng commercial bank
投资银行 tóuzī yínháng investment bank
银幕 yínmù N projection screen, screen

淫 **yín** ADJ **1** pornographic **2** excessive

淫秽 yínhuì ADJ pornographic, obscene

引 **yǐn** V lead, provoke

引导 yǐndǎo V guide, lead
引进 yǐnjìn V introduce, import
引起 yǐnqǐ V give rise to, lead to, cause, arouse
引人注目 yǐnrén zhùmù IDIOM eye-catching, conspicuous
引入 yǐnrù V lead into, introduce
引用 yǐnyòng V quote, cite
引诱 yǐnyòu V lure, seduce

隐 **yǐn** TRAD 隱 V hide, conceal

隐蔽 yǐnbì V take cover, conceal
隐藏 yǐncáng V hide
隐藏的地方 yǐncáng de dìfāng hideaway
隐瞒 yǐnmán V conceal (facts)
隐瞒真相 yǐnmán zhēnxiàng cover up the truth
隐约 yǐnyuē ADJ **1** indistinct, faint **2** vague

饮 **yǐn** TRAD 飲 V drink

饮料 yǐnliào N drink, beverage
饮食 yǐnshí N food and drink
饮食业 yǐnshíyè catering industry, catering
饮用水 yǐnyòngshuǐ N drinking water
非饮用水 fēi yǐnyòngshuǐ non-drinking water

印 **yìn** V print

影印 yǐngyìn photocopy
影印机 yǐngyìnjī photocopier
印染 yìnrǎn V print and dye (textiles)
印刷 yìnshuā V print (books, pamphlets, etc.)
印刷厂 yìnshuāchǎng N print shop, printing press
印刷机 yìnshuājī N printing machine, press
印刷品 yìnshuāpǐn N printed matter
印象 yìnxiàng N impression
给…留下印象 gěi…liúxià yìnxiàng leave an impression on ...

应 **yīng** TRAD 應 MODAL V Same as 应该 yīnggāi

应当 yīngdāng MODAL V Same as 应该 yīnggāi

应该 yīnggāi MODAL V should, ought to

英 **yīng** ADJ outstanding

英国 Yīngguó N England, Britain, the UK

英俊 yīngjùn ADJ (of men) handsome, attractive

英俊青年 yīngjùn qīngnián handsome young man

英明 yīngmíng ADJ wise, brilliant

英文 Yīngwén N the English language (especially the writing)

英雄 yīngxióng N hero

英勇 yīngyǒng ADJ heroic

英语 Yīngyǔ N the English language

婴 **yīng** TRAD 嬰 N baby

婴儿 yīng'ér baby (个 gè)

樱 **yīng** N oriental cherry

樱花 yīnghuā cherry blossom

鹰 **yīng** N eagle

老鹰 lǎoyīng eagle (只 zhī)

秃鹰 tūyīng bald eagle

迎 **yíng** V meet, receive, welcome (See 欢迎 huānyíng)

迎接 yíngjiē V meet, greet

营 **yíng** TRAD 營 I V operate II N (military) battalion

营长 yíngzhǎng battalion commander

营养 yíngyǎng N nutrition, nourishment

营业 yíngyè V (of a commercial or service establishment) do business

营业员 yíngyèyuán N shop assistant, salesperson

营业时间 yíngyè shíjiān N business hours

盈 **yíng** N surplus

盈利 yínglì I V make profit, reap profit II N profit

蝇 **yíng** TRAD 蠅 N fly (See 苍蝇 cāngying.)

赢 **yíng** TRAD 贏 V win (a game), beat (a rival)

影 **yǐng** N 1 shadow

影子 yǐngzi shadow

2 image, reflection

影片 yǐngpiàn N movie, film (部 bù)

影响 yǐngxiǎng I V influence, affect II N influence

颖 **yǐng** ADJ clever (See 新颖 xīnyǐng)

应 **yìng** TRAD 應 V respond

应酬 yìngchou V engage in social activities, entertain

应付 yìngfu V 1 cope with 2 do perfunctorily

应邀 yìngyāo ADJ at the invitation of, on invitation

应用 yìngyòng V apply

应用科学 yìngyòng kēxué N applied science

映 **yìng** V reflect (See 反映 fǎnyìng.)

硬 **yìng** ADJ (of substance) hard, tough

硬件 yìngjiàn N (in computing) hardware

拥 **yōng** TRAD 擁 V 1 embrace 2 crowd, swarm 3 own, possess

拥抱 yōngbào V embrace, hug

拥挤 yōngjǐ I V push, push and shove II ADJ crowded

拥有 yōngyǒu V possess, own

佣 **yōng** N servant

女佣 nǔyōng woman servant

佣人 yōngrén N servant

庸 **yōng** ADJ 1 mediocre 2 second-rate, inferior

平庸 píngyōng mediocre, commonplace

庸俗 yōngsú ADJ vulgar

永 **yǒng** ADV forever

永久 yǒngjiǔ ADJ perpetual, everlasting

永远 yǒngyuǎn ADV forever

咏 **yǒng** V sing (See 歌咏 gēyǒng)

泳 **yǒng** V swim (See 游泳 yóuyǒng)

勇 **yǒng** ADJ courageous, bold, brave

勇敢 yǒnggǎn ADJ brave, bold, fearless

勇气 yǒngqì N courage

勇士 yǒngshì N heroic warrior, hero

勇于认错 yǒngyú have the courage to

勇于认错 yǒngyú rèncuò have the courage to admit one's mistake

涌 **yǒng** V gush, surge

涌现 yǒngxiàn V emerge in large numbers

用 **yòng** I V 1 use, (do something) with 2 need II N use, usefulness

用不着 yòngbuzháo IDIOM 1 there is no need to 2 useless

用处 yòngchu N use

用法 yòngfǎ N the way to use, use, usage

用功 yònggōng ADJ hardworking, diligent (student)

用户 yònghù N user (of a product), consumer

用具 yòngjù N utensil, appliance

用力 yònglì V exert oneself (physically)

用人 yòngrén N Same as 佣人 yōngrén

用途 yòngtú N use, function

用意 yòngyì N intention, purpose

幽 **yōu** ADJ 1 quiet, serene 2 dim, secluded

幽暗 yōu'àn ADJ dim, gloomy

幽静 yōujìng ADJ quiet and secluded, serene

幽默 yōumò N humor

悠 **yōu** ADJ remote

悠久 yōujiǔ ADJ very long, long-standing, time-honored

优 **yōu** TRAD 優 ADJ excellent, superior

优点 yōudiǎn N strong point, merit

优惠 yōuhuì ADJ preferential, favorable

优惠价 yōuhuìjià preferential price

优良 yōuliáng ADJ fine, good

优美 yōuměi ADJ beautiful, graceful

优胜 yōushèng ADJ winning

优胜者 yōushèngzhě winner

优势 yōushì N superiority, advantage

优先 yōuxiān ADJ taking precedence, having priority

优秀 yōuxiù ADJ outstanding, excellent

优异 yōuyì ADJ outstanding, exceptional

优越 yōuyuè ADJ superior

优越感 yōuyuègǎn superiority complex

优质 yōuzhì N superior quality, excellent quality

忧 **yōu** TRAD 憂 I V worry II N sorrow, anxiety

忧虑 yōulǜ V feel anxious, worry

忧郁 yōuyù ADJ melancholy, heavy-hearted

尤 **yóu** ADV especially

尤其 yóuqí ADV especially

由 **yóu** PREP 1 (introducing the agent of an action) by 2 (introducing manner or cause of an action) with

由此可见 yóu cǐ kě jiàn IDIOM it can be seen that, this shows

由于 yóuyú I PREP because of, owing to, due to II CONJ because

油 **yóu** I N oil II ADJ greasy (food)

食油 shíyóu edible oil, cooking oil

石油 shíyóu petroleum, oil

油画 yóuhuà N oil painting (幅 fú)

油料 yóuliào N oil material

油料作物 yóuliàozuòwù oil-bearing crops

油腻 yóunì ADJ greasy

油田 yóutián N oilfield

铀 **yóu** N uranium (U)

邮 **yóu** TRAD 郵 N mail, post

邮包 yóubāo N mailbag

邮购 yóugòu N mail order

邮寄 yóujì V mail, post

邮局 yóujú N post office

邮票 yóupiào N postal stamp (张 zhāng)

邮政 yóuzhèng N mail service, postal service

犹 **yóu** TRAD 猶 PREP like, as

犹如 yóurú PREP just like, just as

犹豫 yóuyù ADJ hesitant, wavering, procrastinating

游 **yóu** V 1 play 2 tour

游击 yóujī V be engaged in guerrilla warfare

游击战 yóujīzhàn guerrilla warfare

游客 yóukè N tourist, visitor (to a tourist attraction)

游览 yóulǎn V go sightseeing, tour for pleasure

　游览者 yóulǎnzhě tourist

游人 yóurén N Same as 游客 yóukè

游戏 yóuxì N game

　(电脑) 游戏机 (diànnǎo) yóuxìjī (computer) play station, (electronic game) console

　(儿童) 游戏室 (értóng) yóuxìshì (kids') playing room

　电子游戏 diànzǐ yóuxì video game, electronic game

游行 yóuxíng N **1** (celebratory) parade **2** (protest) demonstration

　举行游行 jǔxíng yóuxíng hold a parade, hold demonstrations

游泳 yóuyǒng V swim

　蛙式游泳 (蛙泳) wāshì yóuyǒng (wāyǒng) breaststroke

　自由式游泳 (自由泳) zìyóushì yóuyǒng (zìyóuyǒng) freestyle

游泳池 yóuyǒngchí N swimming pool

　室内游泳池 shìnèi yóuyǒngchí indoor swimming pool (座 zuò)

游泳裤 yóuyǒngkù N swimming trunks (条 tiáo)

游泳衣 yóuyǒngyī N swimsuit (件 jiàn)

友 **yǒu** N friend

友爱 yǒu'ài N friendly affection

友好 yǒuhǎo ADJ friendly

友情 yǒuqíng N friendly sentiments

友人 yǒurén N friend

友谊 yǒuyì N friendship

有 **yǒu** V **1** possess, have **2** exist, there is (are)

　没有 méiyǒu do not possess, have no, do not exist, there is no

有待 yǒudài V remain, await

有的 yǒude PRON some

　有的是 yǒudeshì V be plenty of, be abundant, not in short supply

有(一)点儿 yǒu(yì)diǎnr ADV slightly, a little, somewhat

NOTE: 有点 yǒudiǎn, 有点儿 yǒudiǎnr, 有一点 yǒuyìdiǎn, 有一点儿 yǒuyìdiǎnr mean the same thing. 有点儿 yǒudiǎnr and 有一点儿 yǒuyìdiǎnr are only used in colloquial Chinese.

有关 yǒuguān V have bearing on, have something to do with, be related to

有害 yǒuhài ADJ harmful

有机 yǒujī ADJ organic

有力 yǒulì ADJ forceful, powerful, strong

有利 yǒulì ADJ favorable, advantageous

有名 yǒumíng ADJ famous, well-known

有钱 yǒuqián ADJ rich, wealthy

NOTE: See note on 富 fù.

有趣 yǒuqù ADJ interesting, amusing

有时 yǒushí ADV Same as 有时候 yǒushíhou

有时候 yǒushíhou ADV sometimes

有效 yǒuxiào ADJ **1** effective, efficacious **2** valid

　有效期 yǒuxiàoqī term of validity, expiration date

有些 yǒuxiē PRON Same as 有的 yǒude

有氧运动 yǒuyǎng yùndòng N aerobic exercise

有意 yǒuyì V **1** have a mind to, be inclined **2** Same as 故意 gùyì

有意思 yǒu yìsi ADJ meaningful, interesting

　没有意思 méiyǒu yìsi uninteresting, meaningless

有益 yǒuyì ADJ beneficial

有用 yǒuyòng ADJ useful

　没有用 méiyǒu yòng useless

诱 **yòu** V induce, seduce

诱惑 yòuhuò V entice, seduce

右 **yòu** N the right side

右边 yòubian N the right side, the right-hand side

幼 **yòu** ADJ very young

幼儿 yòu'ér N young child between 2 and 6 years old

幼儿园 yòu'éryuán N kindergarten

幼稚 yòuzhì ADJ naïve, childish

又 yòu ADV 1 again 2 moreover, additionally

又…又… yòu...yòu... CONJ ... and also ..., both ... and ...

NOTE: See note on 再 zài.

愚 yú ADJ foolish

愚蠢 yúchǔn ADJ foolish, stupid

愚昧 yúmèi ADJ ignorant and foolish

與 yú N chariot

舆论 yúlùn N public opinion

余 yú TRAD 餘 V spare (See 其余 qíyú, 业余 yèyú.)

鱼 yú TRAD 魚 N fish (条 tiáo)

渔 yú N fishing

渔船 yúchuán N fishing boat (艘 sōu)

渔民 yúmín N fisherman

渔网 yúwǎng N fishing net (张 zhāng)

渔业 yúyè N fishery

娱 yú V amuse, give pleasure to

娱乐 yúlè I V entertain, amuse II N entertainment, amusement

娱乐活动 yúlè huódòng recreation, recreational activities

愉 yú N pleasure

愉快 yúkuài ADJ 1 pleasant, joyful 2 pleased, happy

于 yú TRAD 於 PREP in, at (only used in written Chinese)

于是 yúshì CONJ as a result, hence

予 yǔ V give

予以 yǔyǐ give

宇 yǔ N 1 space 2 building

宇宙 yǔzhòu N the universe

与 yǔ TRAD 與 Same as 和 hé and 跟 gēn. Only used in written Chinese.

与此同时 yǔ cǐ tóngshí IDIOM at the same time

与其…不如 yǔqí...bùrú CONJ would rather ... than

与其坐着谈, 不如起而行 yǔqí zuòzhe tán, bùrú qǐ ér xíng would rather get up and do something than sit here talking

NOTE: Pay attention to the different word orders of 与其…不如 yǔqí...bùrú and would rather ... than; while it is 与其A不如B in Chinese, in English it is would rather B than A.

屿 yǔ TRAD 嶼 N islet (See 岛屿 dǎoyǔ)

雨 yǔ N rain

下雨 xià yǔ to rain

雨天 yǔtiān rainy day

雨水 yǔshuǐ N rainwater, rainfall

雨衣 yǔyī N raincoat

羽 yǔ N feather

羽毛 yǔmáo N feather (根 gēn)

羽毛球 yǔmáoqiú N badminton, shuttlecock (只 zhī)

羽绒 yǔróng N eiderdown

羽绒衣 yǔróngyī eiderdown clothes, eiderdown coat

语 yǔ TRAD 語 I N language, words II V speak, say

语调 yǔdiào N intonation

语法 yǔfǎ N grammar

语气 yǔqì N tone, manner of speaking

语文 yǔwén N speech and writing, language

语言 yǔyán N language (门 mén, 种 zhǒng)

与 yù TRAD 與 V take part, participate

与会 yùhuì V be present at a meeting (conference)

域 yù N territory (See 领域 lǐngyù)

郁 yù TRAD 鬱 ADJ gloomy (See 忧郁 yōuyù)

吁 yù TRAD 籲 V appeal (See 呼吁 hūyù)

玉 yù N jade

玉手镯 yùshǒuzhuó jade bracelet

玉米 yùmǐ N corn, maize (根 gēn)

育 yù v educate, nurture (See 教育 jiàoyù, 体育 tǐyù, 体育场 tǐyùchǎng, 体育馆 tǐyùguǎn, 养育 yǎngyù)

浴 yù v bathe

浴室 yùshì N bathroom (间 jiān)

遇 yù v encounter

遇到 yùdào v encounter, come across

遇见 yùjiàn v meet (someone) unexpectedly, come across, run into

喻 yù v explain (See 比喻 bǐyù)

愈 yù I v recover from illness

大病处愈 dàbìng chù yù have just recovered from a serious illness

II ADV more

欲 yù N desire

食欲 shíyù desire for food, appetite

性欲 xìngyù sex desire

欲望 yùwàng N desire

求知的欲望 qiúzhī de yùwàng desire to have more knowledge, hunger for knowledge

预 yù TRAD 預 ADV in advance

预报 yùbào N forecast, prediction

预备 yùbèi v prepare, get ready

预备会议 yùbèi huìyì preparatory meeting

预备学校 yùbèi xuéxiào preparatory school

预测 yùcè v forecast, predict

预定 yùdìng v schedule, fix in advance

预订 yùdìng v book, place an order

预防 yùfáng v take precautionary measures to prevent, prevent

预告 yùgào v announce in advance

预计 yùjì v project

预见 yùjiàn v foresee

预期 yùqī v expect, anticipate

预赛 yùsài v trial match, preliminary contest

预算 yùsuàn N budget

预习 yùxí v prepare lessons before class, preview

预先 yùxiān ADV in advance, beforehand

预言 yùyán I v predict II N prediction, prophecy

古代圣人的预言 gǔdài shèngrén de yùyán prophecy made by ancient sages

预约 yùyuē v make an appointment

狱 yù TRAD 獄 N prison (See 监狱 jiānyù)

誉 yù TRAD 譽 N honor (See 荣誉 róngyù)

裕 yù ADJ abundant (See 宽裕 kuānyù)

寓 yù I v imply II reside

公寓 gōngyù apartment, apartment building

寓言 yùyán N fable

豫 yù N comfort (See 犹豫 yóuyù.)

冤 yuān N injustice, wrong

冤枉 yuānwang v treat unfairly, wrong

猿 yuán N ape

猿人 yuánrén N apeman

北京猿人 Běijīng Yuánrén Peking man

缘 yuán N reason

缘故 yuángù N reason, cause

元 1 yuán ADJ first, primary

元旦 yuándàn N New Year's Day

元件 yuánjiàn N component part, component

元首 yuánshǒu N head of state

元素 yuánsù N (chemical) element

元宵 yuánxiāo N 1 元宵节 Yuánxiāojié, the Lantern Festival (the 15th of the first month in the Chinese lunar calendar) 2 the traditional sweet dumpling for the Lantern Festival

元 2 yuán M. WD (the basic unit of Chinese currency 1 元 yuán = 10 角 jiǎo/毛 máo = 100 分 fēn), yuan, dollar

美元 Měiyuán U.S. dollar
日元 Rìyuán Japanese yen

NOTE: 元 yuán is the formal word for the basic unit of Chinese currency. In spoken Chinese 块 kuài is more common. For instance, the sum of 50 yuan is usually written as 五十元 wǔshí yuán, but spoken of as 五十块 wǔshí kuài or 五十块钱 wǔshí kuài qián.

员 yuán TRAD 員 N member (See 党员 dǎngyuán, 服务员 fúwùyuán, 官员 guānyuán, 技术员 jìshùyuán, 教员 jiàoyuán, 人员 rényuán, 售货员 shòuhuòyuán, 委员会 wěiyuánhuì, 演员 yǎnyuán, 运动员 yùndòngyuán.)

园 yuán TRAD 園 N garden (See 动物园 dòngwùyuán, 公园 gōngyuán, 花园 huāyuán.)

原 yuán ADJ original, former
原材料 yuáncáiliào N raw material
原告 yuángào N plaintiff, prosecutor
原来 yuánlái ADJ original, former
原理 yuánlǐ N principle, tenet
　生物学原理 shēngwùxué yuánlǐ principles of biology
原谅 yuánliàng V pardon, excuse, forgive
原料 yuánliào N raw material
原始 yuánshǐ ADJ primitive
原因 yuányīn N cause, reason
原油 yuányóu N crude oil
原则 yuánzé N principle
原子 yuánzǐ N atom
原子弹 yuánzǐdàn atomic bomb
原子能 yuánzǐnéng atomic energy

源 yuán N source, fountainhead
源泉 yuánquán N source, fountainhead

圆 yuán TRAD 圓 ADJ round, circular
圆满 yuánmǎn ADJ totally satisfactory, perfect

援 yuán V help
援助 yuánzhù V aid, support

远 yuǎn TRAD 遠 ADJ far, distant, remote (See 遥远 yáoyuǎn)
　离…远… lí…yuǎn… … is far from …
远方 yuǎnfāng N distant place
远景 yuǎnjǐng N distant view, prospect

院 yuàn N courtyard
院子 yuànzi N courtyard, compound

愿 yuàn TRAD 願 V wish, hope (See 心愿 xīnyuàn)
愿望 yuànwàng N wish, aspiration, desire
愿意 yuànyì I MODAL V be willing, will II V wish, want

怨 yuàn V resent, complain (See 抱怨 bàoyuàn, 埋怨 mányuàn)

约 yuē TRAD 約 ADV Same as 大约 dàyuē. Used in written Chinese.
约会 yuēhuì N (social) appointment, engagement, date
约束 yuēshù V restrain, bind

月 yuè N 1 month 2 the moon
　一月 yīyuè January
　十二月 shí'èryuè December
月份 yuèfèn N month
　四月份 sìyuèfèn April
月光 yuèguāng N moonlight
月亮 yuèliang N the moon
月球 yuèqiú N the Moon (as a scientific term)

乐 yuè TRAD 樂 N music
乐队 yuèduì N band, orchestra
乐器 yuèqì N musical instrument
乐曲 yuèqǔ N melody

越 yuè I ADV even more II V get over, jump
越过 yuèguò V cross, surmount
越来越 yuèláiyuè… ADV more and more
越…越… yuè…yuè… ADV the more … the more …

悦 yuè ADJ pleased (See 喜悦 xǐyuè)

阅 yuè TRAD 閱 V read
阅读 yuèdú V read seriously
阅览室 yuèlǎnshì N reading room (间 jiān)

跃 yuè TRAD 躍 V leap

跃进 yuèjìn V leap forward

粤 yuè N a shortened form for 广东 Guǎngdōng
粤语 Yuèyǔ Guangdong dialect, Cantonese

匀 yún V divide evenly, even up

云 yún TRAD 雲 N cloud

多云 duōyún N cloudy
云彩 yúncai N clouds

允 yún V allow

允许 yǔnxǔ V allow, permit

运[1] yùn TRAD 運 V transport, carry

运动 yùndòng I V do physical exercises
II N physical exercises
运动会 yùndònghuì N sports meet, games
奥林匹克运动会 Àolínpǐkè yùndònghuì
the Olympic Games
运动鞋 yùndòngxié N sport shoes
运动员 yùndòngyuán N athlete, sportsman, sportswoman
运输 yùnshū I V transport, carry II N
transportation
运送 yùnsòng V transport, ship
运算 yùnsuàn V operate (a mathematical problem)
运行 yùnxíng V move, be in motion
运用 yùnyòng V use, apply, put into use
运转 yùnzhuǎn V revolve, turn around

运[2] yùn TRAD 運 N fortune, luck

运气 yùnqì N good luck

蕴 yùn TRAD 蘊 V hold in store

蕴藏 yùncáng V hold in store, contain
石油蕴藏量 shíyóu yùncángliàng oil
reserves

酝 yùn TRAD 醞 V brew, make wine

酝酿 yùnniàng V 1 brew, ferment 2 deliberate, prepare mentally

晕 yùn TRAD 暈 ADJ dizzy, giddy

韵 yùn N rhyme

韵母 yùnmǔ N vowel

孕 yùn N pregnancy (See 怀孕 huáiyùn)

Z

砸 zá V smash, break

杂 zá TRAD 雜 ADJ 1 miscellaneous,
sundry 2 mixed, mingled, disorderly
杂费 záfèi sundry charges
杂技 zájì N acrobatics
杂技团 zájìtuán acrobatic troupe
杂技演员 zájì yǎnyuán acrobat
杂交 zájiāo V hybridize, cross
杂乱 záluàn ADJ disorderly, in a jumble
杂事 záshì N miscellaneous matters, odd
jobs
杂文 záwén N essay of social commentary
杂志 zázhì N magazine (本 běn, 种 zhǒng)
杂质 zázhì N (in chemistry) foreign
substance

咋 zǎ ADV how, why (a Northern
dialectal word)

栽 zāi V plant

栽培 zāipéi V cultivate and grow

灾 zāi TRAD 災 N disaster, calamity

旱灾 hànzāi drought
火灾 huǒzāi fire
水灾 shuǐzāi flooding, floods
灾害 zāihài N disaster, calamity
自然灾害 zìrán zāihài natural disaster
灾荒 zāihuāng N famine caused by a
natural disaster
灾难 zāinàn N great suffering caused by a
natural disaster, calamity (场 cháng)
灾难性后果 zāinànxìng hòuguǒ disastrous consequences

宰 zǎi V slaughter

屠宰 túzǎi butcher, slaughter

载 **zài** v carry, be loaded with

载重 zàizhòng N load, carrying capacity

再 **zài** ADV again, once more

NOTE: 再 zài and 又 yòu are both glossed as *again*, but they have different usage: 又 yòu is used in the context of a past situation while 再 zài is used for a future situation. Here is a pair of examples: 她昨天又迟到了。 Tā zuótiān yòu chídào le. *She was late (for work, school, etc.) again yesterday.*; 明天你不要再迟到了。 Míngtiān nǐ bú yào zài chídào le. *Please do not be late again tomorrow.*

再见 zàijiàn v see you again, goodbye

再三 zàisān ADV over and over again

再说 zàishuō ADV 1 what's more, besides 2 later, some other time

在 1 **zài** I PREP in, on, at

在…里 zài…li in
在…上 zài…shang on
在…下 zài…xia under …
在…之间 zài…zhī jiān between

II v be in

在乎 zàihu v care, care about

NOTE: 在乎 zàihu is normally used in a negative sentence, or a question. The same is true with 在意 zàiyì.

在意 zàiyì v take notice of, mind, care

NOTE: See note on 在乎 zàihu.

在于 zàiyú v lie in, rest with

在座 zàizuò v be present (at a meeting)

在 2 **zài** ADV (used to indicate an action in progress)

咱 **zán** PRON Same as 咱们 zánmen

咱们 zánmen PRON we, us (including the person or persons spoken to)

NOTE: 咱们 zánmen is only used in colloquial Chinese, and has a Northern dialect flavor. You can always just use 我

们 wǒmen, even to include the person(s) spoken to. The following example is perfectly acceptable: 你在学中文, 我也在学中文, 我们 [咱们] 都在学中文。 Nǐ zài xué Zhōngwén, wǒ yě zài xué Zhōngwén, wǒmen [zánmen] dōu zài xué Zhōngwén. *You're learning Chinese. I'm learning Chinese. We're both learning Chinese.*

攒 **zǎn** TRAD 攢 v save (money)

攒钱 zǎnqián save money

暂 **zàn** TRAD 暫 ADJ temporary

暂且 zànqiě ADV for the time being, for the moment

暂时 zànshí ADV temporarily, for the time being

赞 **zàn** TRAD 贊 v 1 support, favor 2 praise, commend

赞成 zànchéng v approve of, support, be in favor of

赞美 zànměi v eulogize, praise highly

赞赏 zànshǎng v appreciate, admire

赞叹 zàntàn v gasp in admiration

赞同 zàntóng v endorse, approve of

赞扬 zànyáng v praise publicly

赞助 zànzhù v support, sponsor

脏 **zāng** TRAD 髒 ADJ dirty (See 肮脏 āngzāng)

肮脏 āngzāng filthy, dirty

脏 **zàng** TRAD 臟 N internal organs (See 心脏 xīnzàng)

葬 **zàng** v bury (a human body)

葬礼 zànglǐ N funeral

遭 **zāo** v meet with (misfortune)

遭到 zāodào v suffer, encounter, meet with

遭受 zāoshòu v suffer, be subjected to

遭殃 zāoyāng v suffer disasters, be subject to terrible suffering

遭遇 zāoyù v encounter, meet with

糟 **zāo** ADJ messy, wretched

糟糕 **zāogāo** I ADJ in a mess, terrible, very bad II INTERJ How terrible! What bad luck!

糟蹋 **zāota** V 1 ruin, waste, spoil 2 abuse, violate

凿 **záo** V chisel

枣 **zǎo** N date (a fruit)

枣树 **zǎoshù** date tree
枣子 **zǎozi** date (颗 kē)
蜜枣 **mìzǎo** candied date

早 **zǎo** I ADJ early II good morning (See note below)

NOTE: A common greeting among the Chinese when they meet in the morning is 早 **zǎo** or 你早 **Nǐ zǎo**.

早晨 **zǎochén** N early morning (approximately 6–9 a.m.)
早点 **zǎodiǎn** Same as 早饭 **zǎofàn**
早饭 **zǎofàn** N breakfast (顿 dùn)
早期 **zǎoqī** N early stage, early phase
早日 **zǎorì** N at an early date, soon
早上 **zǎoshang** N Same as 早晨 **zǎochén**
早晚 **zǎowǎn** I N morning and evening II ADV sooner or later
早已 **zǎoyǐ** ADV long ago, for a long time

澡 **zǎo** N bath (See 洗澡 **xǐzǎo**.)

躁 **zào** ADJ rash, impetuous (See 急躁 **jízào**)

噪 **zào** ADJ noisy

噪音 **zàoyīn** N noise
噪音污染 **zàoyīnwūrǎn** noise pollution, white pollution

燥 **zào** ADJ dry (See 干燥 **gānzào**.)

皂 **zào** N soap (See 香皂 **xiāngzào**.)

造 **zào** V 1 make, build 2 invent, fabricate

造成 **zàochéng** V result in, give rise to
造反 **zàofǎn** V rise in rebellion, rebel
造价 **zàojià** N cost (of building or manufacturing)

造句 **zàojù** I V make sentences
用所给的词语造句 **yòng suǒ gěi de cíyǔ zàojù** make sentences with the given words
II N sentence-making

造型 **zàoxíng** N modelling

灶 **zào** N stove

则 **zé** TRAD 則 CONJ in that case, then

NOTE: 则 **zé** is only used in formal Chinese. In everyday Chinese, use 那 **nà** or 那么 **nàme** instead. See note on 那么 **nàme**.

责 **zé** TRAD 責 I N duty II V scold

责备 **zébèi** V reproach, blame
责备的口气 **zébèi de kǒuqì** a reproachful tone
责怪 **zéguài** V blame
责任 **zérèn** N 1 responsibility, duty 2 responsibility for a fault or mistake
责任感 **zérèngǎn** N sense of responsibility

择 **zé** TRAD 擇 V choose (See 选择 **xuǎnzé**.)

泽 **zé** TRAD 澤 N pool, pond (See 沼泽 **zhǎozé**)

贼 **zéi** TRAD 賊 N thief

怎 **zěn** ADV how, why

怎么 **zěnme** ADV 1 how, in what manner 2 no matter how (used with 都 dōu or 也 yě) 3 why, how come 4 how can ...
怎么办 **zěnmebàn** ADV what's to be done?
怎么了 **zěnmele** ADV what happened?
怎么样 **zěnmeyàng** ADV 1 Same as 怎么 **zěnme** 1 (= how) 2 how 3 how's that? is it OK?
怎样 **zěnyàng** ADV Same as 怎么样 **zěnmeyàng**. Used in writing.

增 **zēng** V add, increase

增产 **zēngchǎn** V increase production
增加 **zēngjiā** V increase
增进 **zēngjìn** V promote, enhance
增强 **zēngqiáng** V strengthen

增设 zēngshè v add (a new office, a new department, etc.), introduce (a new course of study)

增添 zēngtiān v provide (additional equipment, evidence, etc.)
增添人员和设备 zēngtiān rényuán hé shèbèi provide more personnel and equipment

增援 zēngyuán I N (military) reinforcements II v send reinforcements

增长 zēngzhǎng v increase, grow

赠 zèng v present a gift

赠送 zèngsòng v present as a gift
向主人赠送礼物 xiàng zhǔrén zèngsòng lǐwù present a gift to the host
赠阅 zèngyuè v give (a book, a publication) as a complimentary copy

扎 zhā v prick, stab

扎实 zhāshí ADJ solid, sturdy

渣 zhā N dregs, residue
煤渣 méizhā coal cinders
渣滓 zhāzǐ N sediment, dregs, residue

闸 zhá N floodgate
闸门 zhámén N 1 sluice gate 2 throttle valve

眨 zhǎ v blink, wink
向我眨了眨眼 xiàng wǒ zhǎ le zhǎ yǎn winked at me

炸 zhà v explode, burst
炸弹 zhàdàn N bomb (枚 méi)
扔炸弹 rēng zhàdàn drop a bomb
炸药 zhàyào N dynamite, explosives
引爆炸药 yǐnbào zhàyào set off an explosive

诈 zhà v cheat, swindle
诈骗 zhàpiàn v defraud, swindle
诈骗犯 zhàpiànfàn swindler

榨 zhà v press, extract
榨菜 zhàcài N hot pickled mustard tuber

摘 zhāi v pick, pluck

摘要 zhāiyào I N abstract, summary
论文摘要 lùnwén zhāiyào abstract of an academic or scholarly paper
II v make a summary

宅 zhái N residence, house. (See 住宅 zhùzhái)

窄 zhǎi ADJ narrow (See 狭窄 xiázhǎi)

债 zhài N debt
还债 huánzhài to pay off/settle a debt
借债 jièzhài to borrow money, to get a loan
欠债 qiànzhài to owe a debt
要债 yào zhài to demand repayment of a debt
债务 zhàiwù N debt, liabilities
债务人 zhàiwùrén debtor
债主 zhàizhǔ N creditor

寨 zhài N stockade, stockaded village

瞻 zhān v look up or forward
瞻仰 zhānyǎng v look at with reverence

沾 zhān v be stained with
沾光 zhānguāng v benefit from association, sponge off

展 zhǎn v display
展出 zhǎnchū v be on show, put on display
展开 zhǎnkāi v carry out, launch
展览 zhǎnlǎn I v put on display, exhibit II N exhibition, show
展览会 zhǎnlǎnhuì Same as 展览 II N
展示 zhǎnshì v display, show
展望 zhǎnwàng I v look into the distance, look into the future
展望未来 zhǎnwàngwèilái foresee the future, predict the future
II N general view regarding future developments
展现 zhǎnxiàn v present before one's eyes

展销 zhǎnxiāo

展销 zhǎnxiāo v show and advertise (products)
汽车展销会 qìchē zhǎnxiāohuì automobile fair, auto fair

盏 zhǎn TRAD 盞 M. WD (for lamps)

斩 zhǎn TRAD 斬 v chop, cut

斩草除根 zhǎn cǎo chú gēn IDIOM cut the weeds and dig up the roots (→ destroy root and branch, remove the root of trouble completely)

崭 zhǎn TRAD 嶄 as in 崭新 zhǎnxīn

崭新 zhǎnxīn ADJ brand-new

占 zhàn v occupy

占领 zhànlǐng v occupy, seize
占领军 zhànlǐngjūn occupation troops
占便宜 zhàn piányi v gain additional advantage at others' expenses
占有 zhànyǒu v possess, own
占有有利地位 zhànyǒu yǒulì dìwèi occupy an advantageous position

战 zhàn TRAD 戰 N 1 war, warfare 2 fight, battle

战场 zhànchǎng N battleground, battlefield
战斗 zhàndòu v combat, fight
战略 zhànlüè N military strategy, strategy
战胜 zhànshèng v triumph over, defeat
战士 zhànshì N soldier, fighter
战术 zhànshù N military tactics
战线 zhànxiàn N battle line
战役 zhànyì N military campaign
战友 zhànyǒu N army buddy
战争 zhànzhēng N war

站 zhàn v stand

站起来 zhàn qǐlai stand up
站岗 zhàngǎng v stand guard, be on sentry duty

站 zhàn N station, stop

出租汽车站 chūzū qìchē zhàn taxi stand
火车站 huǒchē zhàn railway station
汽车站 qìchē zhàn coach/bus station, bus stop

站长 zhànzhǎng N railway/coach station-master

长 zhāng TRAD 張 v open, spread

张望 zhāngwàng v look around

长 zhāng TRAD 張 M. WD (for paper, bed, table etc.)

一张纸 yì zhāng zhǐ a piece of paper
两张床 liǎng zhāng chuáng two beds
三张桌子 sān zhāng zhuōzi three tables/desks

长 Zhāng TRAD 張 N a common family name

张先生/太太/小姐 Zhāng xiānsheng/tàitai/xiǎojiě Mr/Mrs/Miss Zhang

章 zhāng N chapter (See 文章 wénzhāng)

章程 zhāngchéng N regulations (for an organization)

彰 zhāng v clear, evident (See 表彰 biǎozhāng)

掌 zhǎng N hand, palm

了如指掌 liǎo rú zhǐzhǎng know ... like the back of one's hand
掌管 zhǎngguǎn v be in charge of
掌上电脑 zhǎngshàng diànnǎo N palmtop, hand-held computer
掌声 zhǎngshēng N clapping, applause
掌握 zhǎngwò v have a good command of, know well

长 zhǎng TRAD 長 v 1 grow 2 grow to be, look

长 zhǎng TRAD 長 N chief (See 校长 xiàozhǎng)

涨 zhǎng TRAD 漲 v rise, go up

涨价 zhǎngjià v (of prices) rise

帐 zhàng TRAD 帳 N curtain, canopy

帐篷 zhàngpeng N tent
搭帐篷 dā zhàngpeng pitch a tent

帐 zhàng TRAD 賬 N account

查帐 chá zhàng examine an account, audit
算帐 suàn zhàng compute income and

220

expense, settle accounts

NOTE: 帐 zhàng *account* is also written as 账, e.g. 查账, 算账.

帐单(账单) zhàngdān N bill
付电话帐单 fù diànhuà zhàngdān pay the phone bill
帐目(账目) zhàngmù N items of an account
帐目不清 zhàngmù bùqīng accounts not in order

胀 zhàng TRAD 脹 v swell

障 zhàng v hinder, obstruct

障碍 zhàng'ài N obstacle, barrier
排除障碍 páichú zhàng'ài clear an obstacle

丈 zhàng N 1 senior 2 husband

丈夫 zhàngfu N husband

招 zhāo v beckon, attract

招待 zhāodài v receive or entertain (a guest)
招待会 zhāodàihuì N reception (a social function)
记者招待会 jìzhě zhāodàihuì press conference
招呼 zhāohu v call, shout at
打招呼 dǎ zhāohu 1 greet 2 inform casually, tell
招聘 zhāopìn v advertise for a position, recruit (employees)
招聘广告 zhāopìn guǎnggào advertisement for employment
招生 zhāoshēng v enrol new students, recruit students
招生办公室 zhāoshēng bàngōngshì (college and university) enrolment office
招收 zhāoshōu v recruit
招收工人 zhāoshōu gōngrén recruit workers
招收学生 zhāoshōu xuésheng enroll new students
招手 zhāoshǒu v wave (one's hand), beckon

朝 zhāo N early morning

朝气 zhāoqì N youthful spirit
朝气蓬勃 zhāoqì péngbó full of youthful spirit, full of vigor and vitality
朝夕 zhāoxī N morning and evening, daily
朝夕相处 zhāoxī xiāngchǔ be together from morning till night

着 zháo v catch

着急 zháojí v be anxious, be worried
着凉 zháoliáng v catch a cold

找 zhǎo v look for, search for

找到 zhǎodào v find

沼 zhǎo N pond

沼泽 zhǎozé N swamp, marsh
沼泽地 zhǎozédì swamp, marshland

召 zhào v summon

召集 zhàojí v call, convene
召集紧急会议 zhàojí jǐnjí huìyì convene an emergency meeting
召开 zhàokāi v convene (a conference)

照 1 zhào v 1 take a photo 2 look in a mirror 3 shine, light up

照顾 zhàogu v look after, care for
照会 zhàohuì N (diplomatic) note
照料 zhàoliào v take care of, attend to
照料日常事务 zhàoliào rìcháng shìwù take care of day-to-day affairs
照明 zhàomíng N lighting, illumination
照明设备 zhàomíng shèbèi lighting equipment
照片 zhàopiàn N photograph, picture, snapshot (张 zhāng)
照射 zhàoshè v shine on, light up
照相 zhàoxiàng v take a picture
照相馆 zhàoxiàngguǎn N photographic studio
照相机 zhàoxiàngjī N camera (架 jià, 台 tái)
数码照相机 shùmǎ zhàoxiàngjī digital camera
照耀 zhàoyào v shine, illuminate
照应 zhàoyìng v look after, take care of

照 2 zhào PREP according to, in the manner of

照常 zhàocháng ADV as usual
照例 zhàolì ADV as usual, as a rule
照样 zhàoyàng ADV in the same old way

罩 zhào V cover, overspread

兆 zhào N sign, omen

预兆 yùzhào omen, presage

遮 zhē V hide from view

折 zhē as in 折腾 zhēteng

折腾 zhēteng V **1** do over and over again **2** cause suffering

折 zhé I V convert to, amount to II N discount, reduction (in price)

折合 zhéhé V convert to, amount to
折磨 zhémó I V cause much mental or physical suffering II N suffering
受病痛的折磨 shòu bìngtòng de zhémó suffer terribly from the disease

哲 zhé ADJ wise

哲学 zhéxué N philosophy
哲学家 zhéxuéjiā philosopher

者 zhě SUFFIX (a nominal suffix denoting a person or people) (See 读者 dúzhě, 记者 jìzhě, 作者 zuòzhě.)

这 zhè TRAD 這 PRON this

这个 zhège PRON this one, this
这会儿 zhèhuìr N now, this time
这里 zhèlǐ N this place, here

NOTE: In spoken Chinese 这里 zhèlǐ can be replaced by 这儿 zhèr.

这么 zhème ADV like this, in this manner
这么着 zhèmezhe ADV like this, so
这些 zhèxiē PRON these
这样 zhèyàng ADJ **1** such **2** Same as 这么 zhème. Used only in writing.
这样一来 zhèyàng yìlái ADV consequently

蔗 zhè N sugarcane (See 甘蔗 gānzhe)

着 zhe PARTICLE (used after a verb to indicate the action or state is going on)

这 zhèi TRAD 這 PRON. Same as 这 zhè. Used colloquially.

珍 zhēn ADJ valuable

珍贵 zhēnguì ADJ precious, valuable
珍惜 zhēnxī V cherish dearly, value highly
珍珠 zhēnzhū N pearl (颗 kē)
珍珠项链 zhēnzhū xiàngliàn pearl necklace

真 zhēn ADJ true, real

真诚 zhēnchéng ADJ sincere, genuine
真话 zhēnhuà N truth
真空 zhēnkōng vacuum
真理 zhēnlǐ N truth
真实 zhēnshí ADJ true, real, authentic
真相 zhēnxiàng N the real situation, actual facts
真心 zhēnxīn N sincerity
真正 zhēnzhèng ADJ true, real, genuine

针 zhēn N **1** needle (根 gēn) **2** injection

打针 dǎzhēn give an injection, get an injection
针对 zhēnduì V aim at, be aimed at
针灸 zhēnjiǔ I N acupuncture and moxibustion II V give or receive acupuncture and moxibustion treatment

贞 zhēn TRAD 貞 ADJ loyal, faithful

侦 zhēn TRAD 偵 V detect

侦察 zhēnchá V reconnoiter, scout
侦察卫星 zhēnchá wèixīng reconnaissance (spy) satellite
侦探 zhēntàn N detective
私人侦探 sīrén zhēntàn private detective, private eye

诊 zhěn TRAD 診 V examine (a patient)

诊断 zhěnduàn I V diagnose
诊断为良性肿瘤 zhěnduàn wéi liángxìng zhǒngliú diagnosed as a benign tumor
II N diagnosis
做出诊断 zuòchū zhěnduàn make a diagnosis

枕 zhěn N pillow

枕头 zhěntou pillow (只 zhī)

阵 1 zhèn TRAD 陣 N column or row of troops

阵地 zhèndì N (military) position

阵容 zhènróng N layout of troops

阵线 zhènxiàn N (military) front

阵营 zhènyíng N military camp

阵 2 zhèn TRAD 陣 M. WD (for an action or event that lasts for some time)

阵雨 zhènyǔ shower

振 zhèn v arouse to action

振动 zhèndòng v vibrate

振奋 zhènfèn v stimulate, excite

令人振奋的消息 lìngrén zhènfèn de xiāoxi exciting news

振兴 zhènxīng v promote, develop

镇 zhèn I N rural town II v suppress

镇定 zhèndìng ADJ composed, calm

镇定剂 zhèndìng jì sedative (a medicine)

镇静 zhènjìng ADJ calm, composed

镇痛 zhèntòng I v ease pain II N analgesia

镇痛药 zhèntòngyào analgesic medicine, pain-killer

镇压 zhènyā v suppress, put down

震 zhèn v shake

地震 dìzhèn earthquake

震荡 zhèndàng v vibrate

震动 zhèndòng v shake, quake

震惊 zhènjīng v be greatly surprised, be shocked

正 zhēng as in 正月 zhēngyuè

正月 zhēngyuè N the first month of the lunar year

蒸 zhēng v steam

蒸发 zhēngfā v evaporate

蒸汽 zhēngqì N steam

蒸汽机 zhēngqì jī N steam engine

蒸气浴 zhēngqì yù N sauna

挣 zhēng as in 挣扎 zhēngzhá

挣扎 zhēngzhá v struggle desperately

征 zhēng TRAD 徵 v solicit

征求 zhēngqiú v solicit, ask for

争 zhēng v 1 strive 2 argue

争论 zhēnglùn v dispute, debate

争气 zhēngqì v work hard to win honor

为父母争气 wéi fùmǔ zhēngqì work hard to win honor for one's parents

争取 zhēngqǔ v strive for, fight for

争议 zhēngyì N dispute

有争议的问题 yǒu zhēngyì de wèntí issue in dispute, a controversial matter

筝 zhēng N 1 a musical instrument, zheng 2 kite

风筝 fēngzheng kite

睁 zhēng v open (the eyes)

整 1 zhěng ADJ whole, full, entire

整个 zhěngge ADJ whole, entire

整数 zhěngshù N (in maths) whole number, integer

整体 zhěngtǐ N whole, entirety, (something) as a whole

从整体上说 cóng zhěngtǐ shàng shuō on the whole

整天 zhěngtiān N the whole day, all the time

整天抱怨 zhěngtiān bàoyuàn grumble all the time

整整 zhěngzhěng ADJ whole, full

整整一个星期 zhěngzhěng yí ge xīngqī a full week, the entire week

整 2 zhěng I ADJ in good order, neat, tidy II v put in order

整顿 zhěngdùn v put in order, improve, re-organize

整顿纪律 zhěngdùn jìlù enforce discipline

整洁 zhěngjié ADJ clean and tidy

整理 zhěnglǐ v put in order, tidy up

整齐 zhěngqí ADJ in good order, neat and tidy

整整齐齐 zhěng-zhěng-qí-qí (an emphatic form of 整齐 zhěngqí)

正 zhèng I ADJ 1 straight, upright 2 standard, normal, regular II ADV Same as 正在 zhèngzài

正常 zhèngcháng ADJ normal, regular

正当 zhèngdāng CONJ just when, just as

正当 zhèngdàng ADJ proper, legitimate
正当权益 zhèngdàng quányì legitimate rights and interests

正规 zhèngguī ADJ regular, standard

正好 zhènghǎo I ADJ just right II ADV chance to, by coincidence

正经 zhèngjing ADJ 1 decent, proper 2 serious, not frivolous
一本正经 yì běn zhèngjing in all seriousness, sanctimonious

正面 zhèngmiàn I N facade, the obverse side II ADJ positive

正派 zhèngpài ADJ upright, decent
正派人 zhèngpàirén a decent person

正巧 zhèngqiǎo ADV as it happens, just at the right moment

正确 zhèngquè ADJ correct, accurate

正式 zhèngshì ADJ formal, official

正在 zhèngzài ADV (used before a verb to indicate the action is in progress)

正在…呢 zhèngzài...ne Same as 正在 zhèngzài but with a casual, friendly tone

证 zhèng TRAD 證 N proof, certificate
身分证 shēnfen zhèng ID card
学生证 xuéshengzhèng student ID card

证件 zhèngjiàn N paper or document proving one's identity, e.g a passport, an ID card

证据 zhèngjù N evidence, proof

证明 zhèngmíng I V prove, testify II N certificate
出证明 chū zhèngmíng issue a certificate
出生证明 chūshēng zhèngmíng birth certificate

证书 zhèngshū N certificate (份 fèn, 张 zhāng)
毕业证书 bìyè zhèngshū diploma
结婚证书 jiéhūn zhèngshū marriage license, marriage certificate

政 zhèng N governance, government

政变 zhèngbiàn N coup d'etat

政策 zhèngcè N government policy

政党 zhèngdǎng N political party

政府 zhèngfǔ N government

政权 zhèngquán N 1 political power 2 government, regime

政治 zhèngzhì N politics, governance

症 zhèng N disease

急症 jízhèng acute disease, (medical) emergency
急症室 jízhèng shì emergency room (ER)

症状 zhèngzhuàng N symptom

挣 zhèng V work to earn (money)
挣钱养活全家 zhèngqián yǎnghuo quánjiā to work to earn money so as to provide for the family

郑 zhèng TRAD 鄭 as in 郑重 zhèngzhòng

郑重 zhèngzhòng ADJ solemn, serious

之 zhī PARTICLE Same as 的 de. Used in written Chinese or certain set expressions.

之后 zhī hòu PREP after, behind

之间 zhī jiān PREP between

之前 zhī qián PREP before

之外 zhī wài PREP outside, apart from

之下 zhī xià PREP below, under

之一 zhī yī N one of

之中 zhī zhōng PREP between, among

芝 zhī as in 芝麻 zhīma

芝麻 zhīma N sesame (粒 lì)

支 1 zhī I V 1 prop up, sustain 2 send away II N branch

支部 zhībù N branch (of a political party)

支撑 zhīchēng V prop up, shore up

支持 zhīchí V support

支出 zhīchū I V pay, expend II N expenditure, expenses

支付 zhīfù V pay

支流 zhīliú N tributary

支配 zhīpèi V 1 allocate, arrange

合理支配有限的资金 hélǐ zhīpèi yǒuxiàn de zījīn rationally allocate limited funds **2** control, determine

支票 zhīpiào **N** (in banking) check, cheque (张 zhāng)

兑现支票 duìxiàn zhīpiào cash a check

支援 zhīyuán **V**, **N** support, aid

支柱 zhīzhù **N** mainstay, pillar

支 **2** zhī **M. WD** (for stick-like things)

一支笔 yì zhī bǐ a pen

枝 zhī **N** twig, branch (根 gēn)

肢 zhī **N** limb

上肢 shàngzhī upper limbs

下肢 xiàzhī lower limbs

只 zhī **TRAD** 隻 **M. WD** (for animals, utensils, objects normally occurring in pairs, etc.)

一只手 yì zhī shǒu a hand

两只狗 liǎng zhī gǒu two dogs

知 zhī **V** know, be aware of

知道 zhīdào **V** know

知觉 zhījué **N** consciousness, senses

知识 zhīshi **N** knowledge

知识经济 zhīshi jīngjì knowledge economy

蜘 zhī as in 蜘蛛 zhīzhū

蜘蛛 zhīzhū **N** spider (只 zhī)

蜘蛛网 zhīzhūwǎng spider web

脂 zhī **N** fat, grease

脂肪 zhīfáng **N** fat

汁 zhī **N** juice

果汁 guǒzhī fruit juice

织 zhī **TRAD** 織 **V** weave (See 纺织 fǎngzhī, 组织 zǔzhī.)

执 zhī **TRAD** 執 **V 1** grasp, persist **2** take charge, manage

执法 zhīfǎ **V** enforce the law

执行 zhīxíng **V** carry out, implement, execute

执行总公司的指示 zhīxíng zǒnggōngsī de zhǐshì carry out instructions from the company HQ

执照 zhīzhào **N** license, permit

驾驶执照 jiàshǐ zhízhào driver's license

营业执照 yíngyè zhízhào business permit

执政 zhízhèng **V** (of a political party) govern, be in power

执政党 zhízhèngdǎng ruling party

直 zhí **ADJ** straight, direct

直达 zhídá **ADV** nonstop, through

直到 zhídào **PREP** until, till

直接 zhíjiē **ADJ** direct

直径 zhíjìng **N** diameter

直辖市 zhíxiáshì **N** metropolis under the direct jurisdiction of the central government (the metropolises of Beijing, Shanghai, Tianjin and Chongqing)

直线 zhíxiàn **N** straight line (条 tiáo)

直至 zhízhì **CONJ** until

值 zhí **I N** value **II V 1** be worth **2** be on duty

值班 zhíbān **V** be on duty

值得 zhíde **V** be worth

植 zhí **V** plant, grow

植物 zhíwù **N** plant, flora

植物学 zhíwùxué **N** botany

植物学家 zhíwùxuéjiā botanist

植物园 zhíwùyuán botanical garden

殖 zhí **V** breed

殖民 zhímín **V** colonize

殖民地 zhímíndì colony

殖民主义 zhímín zhǔyì colonialism

侄 zhí **N** one's brother's child

侄女 zhínǚ **N** one's brother's daughter

侄子 zhízi **N** one's brother's son

职 zhí **TRAD** 職 **N** job, profession, office

职称 zhíchēng **N** professional title

职工 zhígōng **N** staff (of a factory, a company, an enterprise, etc.), employee(s)

职能 zhínéng **N** function

职权 zhíquán **N** authority of office

职务 zhíwù N official duties and obligations, post

职业 zhíyè N occupation, profession, vocation

职业病 zhíyèbìng N occupational disease

职业介绍所 zhíyè jièshàosuǒ N employment agency

职员 zhíyuán N office worker, clerk (名 míng)

止 **zhǐ** V stop (pain, cough, thirst, etc.)

只 **zhǐ** TRAD 祇 ADV only

只得 zhǐděi V have got to, have to
　只得照他说的做 zhǐdéi zhào tā shuōde zuò have got no choice but do as he told

只顾 zhǐgù V care only about, be absorbed in
　只顾赚钱 zhǐgù zhuànqián only care about making money

只管 zhǐguǎn V do as you wish, do not hesitate to

只好 zhǐhǎo ADV have no choice but

只是 zhǐshì ADV only, just

只要 zhǐyào CONJ so long as, provided that, if only

只有 zhǐyǒu I ADV can only, have no choice but II CONJ only, only if

指 1 **zhǐ** I N finger
　手指 shǒuzhǐ finger (根 gēn, 个 gè)
　II V 1 point at, point to 2 refer to, allude to, mean

指头(手指头) zhǐtou (shǒuzhítou) N Same as 手指 shǒuzhǐ

指标 zhǐbiāo N target, quota

指出 zhǐchū V point out

指甲 zhǐjia N fingernail
　修指甲 xiū zhǐjia do fingernails, manicure fingernails

指 2 **zhǐ** V 1 guide, refer to 2 reply on, count on

指导 zhǐdǎo V guide, direct, supervise

指导员 zhǐdǎoyuán N political instructor (in the Chinese People's Liberation Army)

指导思想 zhǐdǎo sīxiǎng N guiding principle

指定 zhǐdìng V appoint, designate
　指定法律代表 zhǐdìng fǎlǜ dàibiǎo appoint a legal representative

指挥 zhǐhuī V command, direct, conduct

指挥部 zhǐhuībù N headquarters

指令 zhǐlìng N instruction, order

指明 zhǐmíng V point out, show clearly

指南针 zhǐnánzhēn N compass

指示 zhǐshì I V 1 instruct 2 indicate II N 1 instruction 2 indication

指数 zhǐshù N index
　琼斯指数 Dào Qióngsī zhǐshù Dow Jones Index

指望 zhǐwàng V count on, expect

指针 zhǐzhēn N (needle) indicator, pointer

纸 **zhǐ** TRAD 紙 N paper (张 zhāng)

纸张 zhǐzhāng N paper

址 **zhǐ** N location (See 地址 dìzhǐ)

旨 **zhǐ** N purpose (See 宗旨 zōngzhǐ)

挚 **zhì** ADJ sincere (See 诚挚 chéngzhì)

至 **zhì** PREP to, until (only used in written Chinese)

至多 zhìduō ADV at most, maximum

至今 zhìjīn ADV till now, to this day, so far

至少 zhìshǎo ADV at least, minimum

至于 zhìyú CONJ as to, as for

志 1 **zhì** TRAD 誌 N record (See 杂志 zázhì.)

志 2 **zhì** N will, aspiration

志气 zhìqì N aspiration, ambition
　有志气 yǒu zhìqì have lofty aspirations

志愿 zhìyuàn I V volunteer
　志愿者 zhìyuànzhě volunteer (a person)
　II N wish, ideal

致 **zhì** V 1 send, extend 2 devote (time, efforts, etc)

致词 zhìcí V make a (short formal) speech

致富 zhìfù V become rich
　勤劳致富 qínláo zhìfù become rich by working hard

致敬 zhìjìng V salute

治 **zhì** v **1** treat (disease) **2** rule, govern
治安 zhì'ān N public order, public security
治理 zhìlǐ v govern, administrate
治疗 zhìliáo **I** v treat (a patient, a disease) **II** N medical treatment

制 **zhì** TRAD 製 v **1** make, work out **2** control, restrict
制裁 zhìcái N sanction
　制裁那个国家 zhìcái nàge guójiā establish sanctions against that country
制定 zhìdìng v lay down, draw up
制度 zhìdù N system
制服 zhìfú N uniform (件 jiàn, 套 tào)
制品 zhìpǐn N products
　乳制品 rǔzhìpǐn dairy product
制约 zhìyuē v constrain, restrain
　受条件的制约 shòu tiáojiàn de zhìyuē constrained by one's circumstances
制造 zhìzào v make, manufacture
制造业 zhìzàoyè manufacturing industry
制止 zhìzhǐ v stop, curb

帜 **zhì** TRAD 幟 N banner (See 旗帜 qízhì)

质 **zhì** TRAD 質 N nature, character (See 性质 xìngzhì)
质变 zhìbiàn N qualitative change
质量 zhìliàng N qualit
质朴 zhìpǔ ADJ unaffected, ingenuous

秩 **zhì** N order, rank
秩序 zhìxù N order, proper sequence

置 **zhì** v place, put (See 布置 bùzhì)

掷 **zhì** TRAD 擲 v throw, hurl

智 **zhì** ADJ wise, intelligent
　智者 zhìzhě wise man
智慧 zhìhuì N wisdom, intelligence
智力 zhìlì N intelligence, intellect
　智力发达 zhìlì fādá highly intelligent
智谋 zhìmóu N tactic, clever scheme
智能 zhìnéng N intelligence and capability
　人工智能 réngōng zhìnéng artificial intelligence
智商 zhìshāng N intelligence quotient (IQ)

稚 **zhì** ADJ childish (See 幼稚 yòuzhì)

滞 **zhì** v stagnate (See 停滞 tíngzhì)

终 **zhōng** TRAD 終 v end, finish
终点 zhōngdiǎn N end point, destination
终端 zhōngduān N terminal
终究 zhōngjiū ADV after all, in the end
终年 zhōngnián ADV all the year round, throughout the year
终身 zhōngshēn ADJ all one's life, lifelong
　终生大事 zhōngshēng dàshì marriage
终于 zhōngyú ADV finally, at last
终止 zhōngzhǐ v terminate, end

中 **zhōng I** N center, middle
　东南西北中 dōng, nán, xī, běi, zhōng the east, the south, the west, the north and the center
II ADJ **1** middle, medium **2** Chinese
中餐 zhōngcān N Chinese cuisine, Chinese food
中餐馆 zhōngcānguǎn Chinese restaurant
中餐厅 zhōngcāntīng Chinese restaurant (in a hotel, etc.)
中国 Zhōngguó N China
中华 Zhōnghuá N China, Chinese

NOTE: Both 中国 Zhōngguó and 中华 Zhōnghuá may refer to *China*, but 中华 Zhōngghuá has historical and cultural connotations.

中间 zhōngjiān **I** N center, middle **II** PREP among
中立 zhōnglì ADJ neutral
　中立国 zhōnglìguó a neutral state
中年 zhōngnián N middle age
　中年人 zhōngniánrén middle-aged person
中秋节 Zhōngqiūjié N Mid-Autumn Festival (the fifteenth day of the eighth lunar month)
中途 zhōngtú N halfway, mid-way
中文 Zhōngwén N the Chinese language (especially the writing)

中午 zhōngwǔ

NOTE: See note on 汉语 Hànyǔ.

中午 zhōngwǔ N noon
中心 zhōngxīn N central part, center
 市中心 shìzhōngxīn city center
 研究中心 yánjiū zhōngxīn research center
中型 zhōngxíng ADJ medium-sized
中学 zhōngxué N secondary school, high school, middle school (座 zuò, 所 suǒ)
中药 zhōngyào N traditional Chinese medicine (e.g. herbs)
中医 zhōngyī N 1 traditional Chinese medicine (TCM) 2 traditional Chinese medical doctor
中游 zhōngyóu N middle-reaches (of a river)

忠 zhōng ADJ loyal

忠诚 zhōngchéng ADJ loyal, faithful
忠实 zhōngshí ADJ loyal and faithful
忠于 zhōngyú V be loyal to
 忠于祖国 zhōngyú zǔguó be loyal to one's motherland
忠贞 zhōngzhēn ADJ loyal (to one's country, spouse, etc.)

衷 zhōng N innermost feelings

言不由衷 yánbùyóuzhōng speak insincerely
衷心 zhōngxīn ADJ sincere, whole-hearted

钟 zhōng TRAD 鐘 N clock (座 zuò)

钟表 zhōngbiǎo N clocks and watches, time-piece
 钟表店 zhōngbiǎodiàn watchmaker's shop
钟点 zhōngdiǎn N time, hour
钟点工 zhōngdiǎngōng Same as 小时工 xiǎoshígōng
钟楼 zhōnglóu N clock tower
钟头 zhōngtóu N Same as 小时 xiǎoshí. Used in spoken Chinese.

肿 zhǒng TRAD 腫 N swell

肿瘤 zhǒngliú N tumor
 恶性肿瘤 èxìng zhǒngliú malignant tumor, cancer

良性肿瘤 liángxìng zhǒngliú benign tumor

种 zhǒng TRAD 種 I M. WD kind, sort, type
 各种各样 gè zhǒng gè yàng all sorts of, all kinds of
II N 1 seed, breed 2 racial group
种类 zhǒnglèi N kind, category
种种 zhǒngzhǒng ADJ all sorts of
种子 zhǒngzi N seed
种族 zhǒngzú N race
 种族主义 zhǒngzúzhǔyì racism

种 zhòng TRAD 種 V plant

种地 zhòngdì V grow crops, farm
种植 zhòngzhí V grow (crops)

重 zhòng ADJ 1 heavy 2 considerable in value or quantity
重大 zhòngdà ADJ major, great
重点 zhòngdiǎn N main point, focal point, emphasis
重工业 zhònggōngyè N heavy industry
重量 zhòngliàng N weight
重视 zhòngshì V attach importance to, value
重心 zhòngxīn N 1 center of gravity 2 focus, point of emphasis
重型 zhòngxíng ADJ heavy-duty
重要 zhòngyào ADJ important

众 zhòng TRAD 眾 I N crowd (See 观众 guānzhòng, 听众 tīngzhòng) II ADJ numerous
众多 zhòngduō ADJ numerous
众人 zhòngrén N all the people, everybody
众议院 Zhòngyìyuàn N (U.S.) House of Representatives

舟 zhōu N boat

周 I zhōu I N 1 week 2 circumference, cycle II ADV all around, all over

NOTES: (1) 周 zhōu and 星期 xīngqī both mean week, but 周 zhōu is usually used in writing only. Normally 星期 xīngqī is the word to use. (2) 周 zhōu is not used with any measure words.

周到 zhōudào ADJ thorough, thoughtful

周密 zhōumì ADJ careful and thorough, attentive to every detail

周末 zhōumò N weekend

周年 zhōunián N anniversary

结婚十周年 jiéhūn shí zhōunián the tenth anniversary of one's wedding

周期 zhōuqī N cycle, period

周围 zhōuwéi N surrounding area, all around

周折 zhōuzhé N twists and turns, setbacks

周转 zhōuzhuǎn N (of funds) flow, cash flow

周转不灵 zhōuzhuǎnbùlíng not have enough cash for business operation, have cashflow problems

周 2 Zhōu N a common family name

周先生/太太/小姐 Zhōu xiānsheng/tàitai/xiǎojiě Mr/Mrs/Miss Zhou

州 zhōu N 1 administrative district in ancient China 2 state (in the U.S.)

纽约州 Niǔyuēzhōu the State of New York

洲 zhōu N 1 island in a river 2 continent (See 大洋洲 Dàyángzhōu, 欧洲 Ōuzhōu, 亚洲 Yàzhōu.)

粥 zhōu N porridge, gruel

小米粥 xiǎomǐzhōu millet gruel

喝了半碗粥 hēle bàn wǎn zhōu ate half a bowl of gruel

皱 zhòu TRAD 皺 V wrinkle, crease

皱纹 zhòuwén N wrinkle (on skin), lines

昼 zhòu N daytime

昼夜 zhòuyè N day and night, round the clock

昼夜服务 zhòuyè fúwù round-the-clock (7/24) service

宙 zhòu N time (See 宇宙 yǔzhòu)

骤 zhòu N trot (See 步骤 bùzhòu)

猪 zhū N pig (头 tóu)

诸 zhū ADJ all, various

诸位 zhūwèi PRON everybody, all of you

朱 zhū N 1 red 2 a common family name

珠 zhū N pearl (See 珍珠 zhēnzhū)

株 zhū M. WD (for plants and small trees)

竹 zhú N bamboo

竹子 zhúzi bamboo (棵 kē)

逐 zhú ADV one after another, one by one

逐步 zhúbù ADV step by step, progressively, gradually

逐渐 zhújiàn ADV gradually, step by step

逐年 zhúnián ADV one year after another, year by year

烛 zhú TRAD 燭 N candle (See 蜡烛 làzhú)

主 zhǔ I N 1 master, owner 2 host II ADJ dominant, principal

主办 zhǔbàn V host (a conference, an event, etc.)

主编 zhǔbiān N editor-in-chief, editor

主持 zhǔchí V be in charge of, host (a TV program), chair (a meeting)

节目主持人 jiémù zhǔchírén host/hostess of a TV/radio show

主导 zhǔdǎo ADJ guiding, dominant

主动 zhǔdòng ADJ of one's own accord, taking the initiative

主观 zhǔguān ADJ subjective

主管 zhǔguǎn I V be in charge, be responsible for II N person in charge

主力 zhǔlì N main force

主流 zhǔliú N mainstream

主权 zhǔquán N sovereign rights, sovereignty

主人 zhǔrén N 1 host 2 owner, proprietor

主人翁 zhǔrénwēng N master (of one's country, a society, etc.)

主任 zhǔrèn N chairman (of a committee), director (of a department)

办公室主任 bàngōngshì zhǔrèn office manager

车间主任 chējiān zhǔrèn head of a workshop (in a factory)

主任医生 zhǔrèn yīshēng N chief physician, chief surgeon

主食 zhǔshí N staple food

主题 zhǔtí N theme

(电影的) 主题歌 (diànyǐng de) zhǔtígē theme song (of a movie)

主体 zhǔtǐ N main body

主席 zhǔxí N chairman, chairperson

大会主席 dàhuì zhǔxí chairperson of an assembly

主要 zhǔyào ADJ major, chief, main

主义 zhǔyì N doctrine, -ism

主意 zhǔyi N definite view, idea

主张 zhǔzhāng I V advocate, stand for II N proposition, idea, what one stands for

煮 zhǔ V boil, cook

煮煮 pēngzhǔ boil vegetables

煮水 zhǔshuǐ boil water

嘱 zhǔ TRAD 囑 V advise

嘱咐 zhǔfù V exhort, tell (somebody to do something) earnestly, advise

嘱托 zhǔtuō V entrust

住 zhù V reside, stay

住房 zhùfáng N housing, accommodation

住所 zhùsuǒ N where one lives, lodge, residence

住院 zhùyuàn V be hospitalized

住宅 zhùzhái N residence, home

住宅区 zhùzháiqū residential quarters

助 zhù V assist, help

助理 zhùlǐ N assistant

助理局长 zhùlǐ júzhǎng assistant director of the bureau

局长助理 júzhǎng zhùlǐ assistant to the director of the bureau

助手 zhùshǒu N assistant

助长 zhùzhǎng V encourage, promote

注 zhù V 1 add, pour 2 fix, focus on 3 register, record 4 annotate, explain

注册 zhùcè V register

注册商标 zhùcè shāngbiāo registered trademark

注解 zhùjiě I V annotate, explain with notes II N explanatory note, note

注目 zhùmù V fix one's eyes on

引人注目 yǐnrén zhùmù eye-catching

注射 zhùshè V inject

注射器 zhùshèqì N syringe

注射针 zhùshèzhēn N hypodermic needle

注释 zhùshì Same as 注解 zhùjiě

注视 zhùshì V look attentively, gaze at

注意 zhùyì V pay attention to, take notice of

注重 zhùzhòng V 1 emphasize, stress 2 pay great attention to, attach importance to

注重售后服务 zhùzhòng shòuhòufúwù pay much attention to after-sale service

驻 zhù TRAD 駐 V stay

驻扎 zhùzhá V (of troops) be stationed

蛀 zhù V (of insects) eat into, bore through

蛀虫 zhùchóng N bookworm, termite

祝 zhù V express good wishes, wish

祝福 zhùfú V give one's blessing to, wish somebody happiness

祝贺 zhùhè V congratulate

祝愿 zhùyuàn I V wish II N good wishes

著 zhù V write

著名 zhùmíng ADJ famous, well-known

著作 zhùzuò N writings, (literary) work

筑 zhù TRAD 築 V build, construct (See 建筑 jiànzhù.)

柱 zhù N pillar, column

柱子 zhùzi pillar, column (根 gēn)

铸 zhù V cast

铸造 zhùzào cast, foundry

抓 zhuā V grab, seize

抓紧 zhuājǐn V grasp firmly

爪 zhuǎ N paw, claw

爪子 zhuǎzi paw, claw (只 zhī)

拽 zhuài v fling, throw

专 zhuān TRAD 專 ADJ special, specific

专长 zhuāncháng N special skill, specialist field, expertise

专程 zhuānchéng ADV (make a trip) specially for

专家 zhuānjiā N expert, specialist

专科 zhuānkē N school (or college) for vocational training

专科学校 zhuānkē xuéxiào school (or college) for vocational training

专利 zhuānlì N patent

申请专利 shēnqǐng zhuānlì apply for a patent

专门 zhuānmén ADJ, N specialized, specialist

专心 zhuānxīn ADJ concentrate on, be absorbed in

专业 zhuānyè N specialist field of study, specialty

专用 zhuānyòng v use for a special purpose

专款专用 zhuānkuǎn zhuānyòng earmark a fund for a specific purpose

专政 zhuānzhèng N dictatorship

专制 zhuānzhì N autocracy

砖 zhuān TRAD 磚 N brick

砖头 zhuāntóu brick (块 kuài)

转 zhuǎn TRAD 轉 v **1** turn, change **2** pass on, forward

转变 zhuǎnbiàn v change, transform (usually for the better)

转播 zhuǎnbō v relay a radio or TV broadcast

转车 zhuǎnchē v transfer to another train (or bus)

转达 zhuǎndá v pass on (a piece of information)

转动 zhuǎndòng v turn around, turn

转告 zhuǎngào v pass along (word)

转化 zhuǎnhuà v transform

转换 zhuǎnhuàn v transform, change

转基因 zhuǎn jīyīn N genetic modification, GM

转基因食品 zhuǎnjīyīn shípǐn transgenic food

转交 zhuǎnjiāo v pass on (something)

转让 zhuǎnràng v transfer (a property, rights, etc.)

转入 zhuǎnrù v switch over, turn to

转弯 zhuǎnwān v turn a corner, turn
向左转弯 xiàngzuǒ zhuǎnwān turn left

转向 zhuǎnxiàng v change direction

转学 zhuǎnxué v transfer to another school

转折 zhuǎnzhé N a turn in the course of events

转移 zhuǎnyí v shift, transfer

传 zhuàn TRAD 傳 N biography

自传 zìzhuàn autobiography

传记 zhuànjì N biography

赚 zhuàn TRAD 賺 v make money, make a profit

庄 zhuāng TRAD 莊 I N village II ADJ serious, grave

庄稼 zhuāngjia N crop

庄稼地 zhuāngjiadì N farmland

庄稼人 zhuāngjiarén N farmer (especially one that grows crops)

庄严 zhuāngyán ADJ solemn, imposing

庄重 zhuāngzhòng ADJ serious, solemn

妆 zhuāng TRAD 妝 v apply make-up (See 化妆 huàzhuāng, 化妆品 huàzhuāngpǐn)

装 zhuāng TRAD 裝 I v **1** pretend **2** load and unload **3** fit, install II N clothing

装备 zhuāngbèi I v equip II N equipment
军事装备 jūnshì zhuāngbèi armament

装配 zhuāngpèi v assemble (parts)

装配线 zhuāngpèixiàn assembly line

装饰 zhuāngshì I v decorate II N decoration

装饰品 zhuāngshìpǐn article for decoration, ornament

装卸 zhuāngxiè v load and unload

装置 zhuāngzhì I v install II N installation, device
节能装置 jiénéng zhuāngzhì energy-saving device

壮 zhuàng TRAD 壯 ADJ **1** robust, sturdy **2** magnificent

壮大 zhuàngdà v grow in strength

壮观 zhuàngguān N magnificent sight

壮丽 zhuànglì ADJ beautiful and magnificent

壮烈 zhuàngliè ADJ heroic

壮志 zhuàngzhì N high aspirations

状 zhuàng TRAD 狀 N form, shape

状况 zhuàngkuàng N shape (of things), situation, condition

状态 zhuàngtài N state (of affairs), appearance

撞 zhuàng v bump against, collide

撞运气 zhuàng yùnqì try one's luck

幢 zhuàng M. WD (for houses)

一幢大楼 yí zhuàng dàlóu a big (multi-storied) building

追 zhuī v **1** chase, run after **2** look into, get to the roots of

追查 zhuīchá v trace, investigate

追查谣言 zhuīchá yáoyán try to find out the source of a rumor

追悼 zhuīdào v mourn over (the death of somebody)

追悼会 zhuīdàohuì memorial service, memorial meeting

追赶 zhuīgǎn v run after, pursue

追究 zhuījiū v get to the roots, investigate the origin

追究责任 zhuījiū zérèn investigate to find out who is responsible for an accident

追求 zhuīqiú v pursue, seek

追上 zhuīshang v catch up with, catch

追问 zhuīwèn v inquire in great details

缀 zhuì v sew, stitch (See 点缀 diǎnzhui)

准 zhǔn TRAD 準 I ADJ accurate, exact II v permit, allow III N norm, standard

准备 zhǔnbèi I v prepare

准备好 zhǔnbèi hǎo be well prepared II N preparation

准确 zhǔnquè ADJ accurate, exact

准时 zhùnshí ADJ punctual, on time

准许 zhǔnxǔ v permit, allow

准则 zhǔnzé N norm, standard

行为准则 xíngwéi zhǔnzé code of conduct

捉 zhuō v catch, capture

拙 zhuō ADJ clumsy (See 笨拙 bènzhuō)

桌 zhuō N table

桌子 zhuōzi table, desk (张 zhāng)

卓 zhuó ADJ outstanding

卓越 zhuóyuè ADJ brilliant, exceptional

啄 zhuó v peck

啄木鸟 zhuómùniǎo woodpecker

酌 zhuó v **1** weigh and consider **2** drink (wine)

酌情 zhuóqíng v take the circumstances into consideration

酌情处理 zhuóqíng chǔlǐ settle a matter as one sees fit

着 zhuó v apply, use

着手 zhuóshǒu v begin, set out

着想 zhuóxiǎng v consider (somebody's interest)

浊 zhuó TRAD 濁 ADJ turbid, muddy (See 浑浊 húnzhuó)

镯 zhuó N bracelet (See 手镯 shǒuzhuó)

姿 zī N looks, appearance

姿势 zīshì N posture

姿态 zītài N **1** posture **2** attitude, pose

保持低姿态 bǎochí dīzītài keep a low profile

咨 zī consult

咨询 zīxún v seek advice, consult

资 zī TRAD 資 N money, capital

资本 zīběn N capital

资本家 zīběnjiā N capitalist

资本主义 zīběn zhǔyì N capitalism

资产 zīchǎn N asset, property

资产阶级 zīchǎnjiējí N bourgeoisie

资格 zīgé N qualification

资金 zījīn N fund

资料 zīliào N **1** material, data **2** means (of production)

资源 zīyuán N natural resources

资助 zīzhù V provide financial support, fund

滋 Zī V grow

滋味 zīwèi N taste, flavor

滋长 zīzhǎng V grow, develop

子 Zǐ N **1** son, child

长子 zhǎngzǐ the first son

2 something small and hard

子弹 zǐdàn N bullets

子弟 zǐdì N sons and younger brothers, children

高干子弟 gāogàn zǐdì children of high-ranking officials, "princelings"

子女 zǐnǚ sons and daughters, children

子孙 zǐsūn N children and grandchildren, descendants

子孙后代 zǐsūn hòudài descendants, posterity

籽 Zǐ N seed

仔 Zǐ ADJ as in 仔细 zǐxì

仔细 zǐxì ADJ very careful, paying attention to details

紫 Zǐ ADJ purple

自 1 Zì PRON self, one's own

自卑 zìbēi V feel oneself inferior

自卑感 zìbēigǎn inferiority complex, sense of inferiority

自动 zìdòng ADJ automatic

自动扶梯 zìdòng fútī escalator

自动化 zìdònghuà automatic, automation

自动柜员机 zìdòng guìyuánjī N automated teller machine (ATM)

NOTE: ATM can also be called 自动取款机 zìdòng qǔkuǎnjī or 自动提款机 zìdòng tíkuǎnjī.

自发 zìfā ADJ spontaneous

自费 zìfèi ADJ self-supporting, paid by myself

自费留学生 zìfèi liúxuéshēng self-supporting foreign student, fee-paying foreign student

自豪 zìháo V be very proud of oneself

自己 zìjǐ PRON self, one's own

你自己 nǐ zìjǐ yourself

你们自己 nǐmen zìjǐ yourselves

他自己 tā zìjǐ himself

他们自己 tāmen zìjǐ themselves

我自己 wǒ zìjǐ myself

我们自己 wǒmen zìjǐ ourselves

自觉 zìjué ADJ being aware of, being conscious of, voluntary, conscientious

自来水 zìláishuǐ N running water

自满 zìmǎn ADJ complacent

自然 zìrán I N nature

自然保护区 zìrán bǎohùqū nature reserve

II ADJ natural

自杀 zìshā I V commit suicide II N suicide

自身 zìshēn N self, oneself

自私 zìsī ADJ selfish, egoistic

自私自利 zìsī zìlì IDIOM selfish, self-seeking

自卫 zìwèi N self-defense

自我 zìwǒ N oneself

自相矛盾 zìxiāng máodùn IDIOM self-contradictory

自信 zìxìn ADJ self-confident

缺乏自信 quēfá zìxìn lacking in self-confidence

自行 zìxíng ADV by oneself

自行车 zìxíngchē N bicycle (辆 liàng)

自学 zìxué V study independently, teach oneself

自由 zìyóu I N freedom, liberty II ADJ free, unrestrained

自愿 zìyuàn V volunteer, of one's own accord

自治 zìzhì N autonomy

自治区 zìzhìqū N autonomous region

广西壮族自治区 Guǎngxī Zhuàngzú Zìzhìqū Guangxi Zhuang Autonomous Region

自主 zìzhǔ V act on one's own, keep the initiative in one's own hands

自助餐 zìzhùcān N buffet dinner

自 2 zì PREP Same as 从 cóng. Only used in written Chinese.

自从 zìcóng PREP from, since

自古 zìgǔ ADV since ancient times

自始至终 zì shǐ zhì zhōng IDIOM from start to finish

字 zì N Chinese character, sinogram

汉字 Hànzì Chinese character

字典 zìdiǎn N dictionary (本 běn)

字母 zìmǔ N letter (of an alphabet)

字母表 zìmǔbiǎo alphabet

子 zi PARTICLE (a nominal suffix) (See 杯子 bēizi, 被子 bèizi, 本子 běnzi, 鼻子 bízi, 脖子 bózi, 叉子 chāzi, 虫子 chóngzi, 村子 cūnzi, 刀子 dāozi, 电子 diànzi, 儿子 érzi, 房子 fángzi, 个子 gèzi, 孩子 háizi, 盒子 hézi, 猴子 hóuzi, 胡子 húzi, 饺子 jiǎozi, 橘子 júzi, 句子 jùzi, 裤子 kùzi, 筷子 kuàizi, 例子 lìzi, 帽子 màozi, 脑子 nǎozi, 牌子 páizi, 盘子 pánzi, 妻子 qīzi, 旗子 qízi, 裙子 qúnzi, 日子 rìzi, 嗓子 sǎngzi, 嫂子 sǎozi, 沙子 shāzi, 勺子 sháozi, 绳子 shéngzi, 狮子 shīzi, 毯子 tǎnzi, 兔子 tùzi, 袜子 wàzi, 蚊子 wénzi, 屋子 wūzi, 箱子 xiāngzi, 小伙子 xiǎohuǒzi, 样子 yàngzi, 叶子 yèzi, 一下子 yíxiàzi, 椅子 yǐzi, 院子 yuànzi, 种子 zhǒngzi, 竹子 zhúzi, 桌子 zhuōzi.)

宗 zōng N ancestor

宗教 zōngjiào N religion

宗教信仰 zōngjiào xìnyǎng religious belief

宗派 zōngpài N faction, sect

宗旨 zōngzhǐ N primary purpose, aim

棕 zōng N palm, palm fiber

棕色 zōngsè N brown

综 zōng ADJ comprehensive

综合 zōnghé ADJ comprehensive, synthetical

踪 zōng N footprint

跟踪 gēnzōng follow the tracks of, shadow (somebody)

踪迹 zōngjì N trace, track

总 zǒng TRAD 總 I ADJ 1 overall, total

总开关 zǒngkāiguān switch

2 chief, head

总书记 Zǒngshūjì Secretary-General

II ADV 1 always, invariably 2 anyway, after all

总得 zǒngděi MODAL V have got to, have to, must

总的来说 zǒngdeláishuō IDIOM generally speaking, on the whole

总督 zǒngdū N governor-general, governor

总额 zǒng'é N total (a sum of fund)

总而言之 zǒng'éryánzhī IDIOM Same as 总之 zǒngzhī

总共 zǒnggòng ADV in all, altogether

总和 zǒnghé N sum total

总计 zǒngjì N grand total

总结 zǒngjié I V sum up, do a review of one's past work or life experiences II N summary, a general view of one's past work or life experiences

总理 zǒnglǐ N premier, prime minister

总是 zǒngshì ADV Same as 总 II ADV 1

总数 zǒngshù N sum total

总司令 zǒngsīlìng N commander-in-chief

总算 zǒngsuàn ADV at long last, finally

总统 zǒngtǒng N president (of a country)

总务 zǒngwù N general affairs

总务科 zǒngwùkē general affairs section

总之 zǒngzhī ADV in a word, in short

纵 zòng ADV 1 from north to south 2 vertical, lengthwise

纵横 zònghéng ADJ in length and breadth

走 zǒu V 1 walk 2 leave 3 visit

4 escape, leak out

走亲戚 zǒu qīnqi visit a relative

走道 zǒudào N sidewalk, footpath

走访 zǒufǎng V visit and interview, interview

走狗 zǒugǒu N running dog, flunkey

走廊 zǒuláng N corridor, hallway

走漏 zǒulòu V leak (information)

走私 zǒusī V smuggle

走私犯 zǒusīfàn smuggler

走弯路 zǒuwānlù v take a roundabout course

走向 zǒuxiàng N 1 alignment 2 trend
明年市场的走向 míngnián shìchǎng de zǒuxiàng the market trend next year

奏 zòu v play music (See 演奏 yǎnzòu)

揍 zòu v beat, hit

挨揍 áizòu get a thrashing

租 zū I v rent, hire II N rent (money)

房租 fángzū (housing) rent
租金 zūjīn N rent

足 zú I N foot II ADJ sufficient, enough

足球 zúqiú N soccer
踢足球 tī zúqiú play soccer
足以 zúyǐ ADJ enough, sufficient

族 zú N clan, nationality (See 民族 mínzú.)

阻 zǔ v 1 resist, prevent 2 hinder, block

阻碍 zǔ'ài v hinder, obstruct
阻挡 zǔdǎng v block, stop
阻拦 zǔlán v bar the way, stop
阻力 zǔlì N resistance, obstacle
阻扰 zǔrǎo v obstruct, stand in the way

NOTE: 阻扰 zǔrǎo may also be 阻挠 zǔnáo. They are interchangeable.

阻止 zǔzhǐ v stop, hold back

祖 zǔ N ancestor

祖父 zǔfù N grandfather
祖国 zǔguó N motherland, fatherland
祖母 zǔmǔ N grandmother
祖先 zǔxiān N ancestor, ancestry

组 zǔ TRAD 組 I N group II v form, organize

组成 zǔchéng v make up, compose
组合 zǔhé v compose, combine
组织 zǔzhī I v organize II N organization

钻 zuān TRAD 鑽 N drill

钻研 zuānyán v study in great depth, study intensively

钻 zuàn TRAD 鑽 N diamond

钻石 zuànshí diamond (粒 lì, 颗 kē)
一枚三克拉的钻石戒指 yìméi sān kèlā de zuànshí jièzhi a 3-carat diamond ring

嘴 zuǐ N mouth

嘴巴 zuǐba N mouth
张开嘴巴 zhāngkāi zuǐba open one's mouth
嘴馋 zuǐchán ADJ too fond of eating
嘴唇 zuǐchún N lip

最 zuì ADV most (used before an adjective or a verb to indicate the superlative degree)

最初 zuìchū ADV in the initial stage, initially
最好 zuìhǎo I ADJ best, top-rate II ADV had better
最后 zuìhòu ADV in the final stage, finally
最近 zuìjìn ADV recently, in recent times

罪 zuì N crime, offense

罪恶 zuì'è N crime, evil
罪犯 zuìfàn N criminal, convict
罪名 zuìmíng N charge, accusation
逃税的罪名 táoshuì de zuìmíng tax evasion charge
罪行 zuìxíng N crime, offense
罪状 zuìzhuàng N facts about a crime, indictment

醉 zuì v get drunk, be intoxicated

尊 zūn v respect, esteem

自尊心 zìzūnxīn self-esteem
敬老尊贤 jìnglǎo zūnxián respect the wise and venerate the worthy
尊敬 zūnjìng v respect, honor
尊严 zūnyán N dignity, honor
尊重 zūnzhòng v respect, esteem

遵 zūn v obey

遵命 zūnmìng v follow orders
遵守 zūnshǒu v observe, abide by
遵行 zūnxíng v obey, comply with
遵循 zūnxún v follow faithfully, adhere to

遵依 zūnyī v act accordingly, obey

遵照 zūnzhào v act in accordance with

昨 **zuó** N yesterday

昨天 zuótiān N yesterday

琢 **zuó** as in 琢磨 zuómó

琢磨 zuómó v turn over in one's mind, ponder

左 **zuǒ** N the left side

左边 zuǒbian N the left side, the left-hand side

左邻右舍 zuǒlín-yòushè N neighbors

左撇子 zuǒpiězi N left-handed person

左思右想 zuǒsī-yòuxiǎng IDIOM turn sth over in one's mind, to consider from different perspectives

左右 zuǒyòu ADV approximately, nearly, about

做 **zuò** v 1 do 2 make

做工 zuògōng do manual work, work

做法 zuòfǎ N way of doing things, method, practice

做饭 zuòfàn cook, prepare a meal

做客 zuòkè v be a guest, visit

做梦 zuòmèng v dream

做主 zuòzhǔ v be one's own master

作 **zuò** v Same as 做 zuò

NOTE: 做 zuò and 作 zuò have the same pronunciation and often the same meaning, but 做 zuò is much more commonly used while 作 zuò occurs only in certain set expressions.

作案 zuò'àn v commit a crime

作废 zuòfèi v become invalid

作风 zuòfēng N way of behavior, way of working, style

独断独行的领导作风 dúduàndúxíng de lǐngdǎo zuòfēng autocratic style of leadership

作怪 zuòguài v make mischief, create trouble

作家 zuòjiā N writer (especially of literary works, e.g. novels, stories)

作家协会 Zuòjiā Xiéhuì Writers' Association

作弄 zuònòng v tease, make fun of, pull a trick on

作品 zuòpǐn N literary or artistic work

作为 zuòwéi PREP as, in the capacity of

作文 zuòwén N (student's) composition

作物 zuòwù N crop

作业 zuòyè N school assignment, homework

作用 zuòyòng N function, role

在…中起作用 zài...zhōng qǐ zuòyòng play a role in ..., perform a function in ...

作者 zuòzhě N author

坐 **zuò** v sit

座 **zuò** I M. WD (for large and solid objects, such as a large building)

一座大楼 yí zuò dàlóu a big building

一座山 yí zuò shān a mountain, a hill

一座工厂 yí zuò gōngchǎng a factory

一座大学 yí zuò dàxué a university

一座桥 yí zuò qiáo a bridge

一座城市 yí zuò chéngshì a city

II N seat

座儿 zuòr N seat

座谈 zuòtán v have an informal discussion, have an informal meeting

座谈会 zuòtánhuì an informal discussion, forum

座位 zuòwèi N seat

座右铭 zuòyòumíng N motto

English–Chinese

A

A N 优, 优等 yōuděng

a, an ART 一, 一个 yí ge
　a boy 一个男孩 yí ge nánhái
　an hour 一个小时 yí ge xiǎoshí

abacus N 算盘 suànpán [M. WD 只 zhī]

abandon V 遗弃 yíqì, 抛弃 fàngqì, 中止 zhōngzhǐ

abashed ADJ 惭愧的 cánkuì de, 难为情的 nánwéiqíng de

abate V 减轻 jiǎnqīng, 减少 jiǎnshǎo

abbey N 修道院 xiūdàoyuàn, 寺院 sìyuàn [M. WD 座 zuò]

abbreviate V 省略 shěnglüè, 缩略 suōlüè

abdomen N 腹部 fùbù, 肚子 dùzi

abduct V 劫持 jiéchí, 绑架 bǎngjià

aberration N 异常 yìcháng

abet V 唆使 suōshǐ, 教唆 jiàosuō

abhor V 厌恶 yàn'è, 憎恶 zēng'è

abide (PT & PP **abided/abode**) V (abide by) 遵守 zūnshǒu, 信守 xìnshǒu

abiding ADJ 永久的 yǒngjiǔ de, 持久的 chíjiǔ de

ability N 能力 nénglì, 才能 cáinéng

abject ADJ 卑躬屈膝的 [+行为] bēigōng qūxī de [+xíngwéi]; 低声下气的 [+道歉] dīshēng xiàqì de [+dàoqiàn]
　abject poverty 赤贫 chìpín

ablaze ADJ 燃烧 ránshāo, 熊熊燃烧 xióngxióng ránshāo

able ADJ 能 néng, 能够 nénggòu

abnormal ADJ 不正常的 bú zhèngcháng de, 反常的 fǎncháng de

aboard ADV 在飞机／火车／轮船上 zài fēijī/huǒchē/lúnchuán shang, 上飞机／火车／轮船 shàng fēijī/huǒchē/lúnchuán

abode I N 住所 zhùsuǒ II See **abide**

abolish V 废除 fèichú

Aborigine N（澳大利亚）原住民 (Àodàlìyà) yuánzhùmín

abort V 1 使 [+怀孕的妇女] 流产 shǐ [+huáiyùn de fùnǚ] liúchǎn, 堕胎 duòtāi, 使堕胎 shǐ duòtāi 2 中止 [+行动／计划] zhōngzhǐ [+xíngdòng/jìhuà]

abortion N 堕胎 duòtāi, 人工流产 réngōng liúchǎn

abound V 大量存在 dàliàng cúnzài

about I PREP 关于 guānyú
　How about/what about …? …, 怎么样 …, zěnmeyàng, …, 好不好? …, hǎobuhǎo?
　II ADV 大约 dàyuē, 大概 dàgài
　to be about to do sth 刚要 gāng yào, 正要 zhèngyào, 马上要 mǎshàng yào

above I PREP 1 在…上边 zài…shàngbian, 在…上面 zài…shàngmian
　above all 首先 shǒuxiān, 最重要的 zuì zhòngyào de
　2 超过 chāoguò II ADV 1 在上面 zài shàngmian
　prices listed above 上面列出的价格 shàngmian lièchū de jiàgé
　2 超过 chāoguò
　families with above average incomes 超过平均收入的家庭 chāoguò píngjūn shōurù de jiātíng
　III ADJ 上述的 shàngshù de

abrasive ADJ 生硬的 shēngyìng de, 鲁莽的 lǔmǎng de

abreast ADV 并排的 bìngpái de
　to keep abreast of … 了解…的最新情况 liǎojiě…de zuìxīn qíngkuàng

abridged ADJ 删节的 shānjié de, 节缩的 jié suō de

abroad ADV 到／在国外 dào/zài guówài

237

abrupt ADJ 突然的 tūrán de, 粗鲁的 [+态度] cūlǔ de [+tàidu]

abscess N 脓肿 nóngzhǒng

abscond V 携款潜逃 xiékuǎn qiántáo, 潜逃 qiántáo

absence N 不在 bú zài, 缺席 quēxí

absent ADJ 不在 búzài, 缺席 quēxí
absent-minded 心不在焉的 xīn bú zài yān de

absolute ADJ 绝对 juéduì, 完全 wánquán

absolve V 宣布无罪 xuānbù wúzuì

absorb V 吸收 xīshōu

absorbent ADJ 易吸水的 yì xīshuǐ de

abstain V 1 放弃投票权 fàngqì tóupiào quán, 弃权 qìquán 2 避免 bìmiǎn, 戒除 jièchú
to abstain from sex before marriage 避免婚前性生活 bìmiǎn hūnqián xìng shēnghuó

abstinence N 禁欲 jìnyù, 戒酒戒烟 jièjiǔ jièyān

abstract[1] ADJ 抽象的 chōuxiàng de

abstract[2] N（论文）摘要（lùnwén）zhāiyào [M. WD 篇 piān]

absurd ADJ 荒谬 huāngmiù, 荒唐 huāngtang

abundant ADJ 丰富 fēngfù, 充沛 chōngpèi

abuse I N 1 滥用 lànyòng
drug/alchohol abuse 吸毒／酗酒（现象）xīdú/xùjiǔ（xiànxiàng）2 虐待 nüèdài 3 谩骂 mànmà, 辱骂 rǔmà II V 虐待 nüèdài
physical abuse 殴打 ōudǎ
verbal abuse 辱骂 rǔmà

abusive ADJ 虐待的 nüèdài de

abyss N 1 深渊 shēnyuān 2 极其危险的境地 jíqí wēixiǎn de jìngdì

academic ADJ 学校的 xuéxiào de
academic degree 学位 xuéwèi
academic year 学年 xuénián

academy N 1 专科学院 zhuānkē xuéyuàn 2 研究院 yánjiūyuàn, 学会 xuéhuì 3 私立学院 sīlì xuéyuàn

acccelerate V 加速 jiāsù, 使…加速 shǐ…jiāsù, 提前 tíqián, 使…提前 shǐ…tíqián

accelerator N 加速器 jiāsùqì, 油门 yóumén

accent I N 口音 kǒuyīn

to speak Chinese with an English accent 讲中文带有英语口音 jiǎng Zhōngwén dàiyǒu Yīngyǔ kǒuyīn II V 强调 qiángdiào, 突出 tūchū

accept V 接受 jiēshòu

acceptable ADJ 可以接受的 kěyǐ jiēshòude, 还不错的 hái búcuò de

acceptance N 接受 jiēshòu, 认可 rènkě

access I N 达到 dádào, 进入 jìnrù II V 获取 [+信息] huòqǔ [+xìnxī] 2 进入 [+贮藏室] jìnrù [+zhùcángshì]
access time（计算机）读取（信息）时间 (jìsuànjī) dú qǔ (xìnxī) shíjiān

accessible ADJ 容易进入的 róngyì jìnrù de, 容易得到的 róngyì dédào de

accessory N 1 装饰品 zhuāngshìpǐn, 附件 fùjiàn 2 从犯 cóngfàn, 帮凶 bāngxiōng

accident N 事故 shìgù 件 jiàn]
car accident 交通事故 jiāotōng shìgù
by accident 不是故意的 búshì gùyì de, 意外的 yìwài de

accidental ADJ 意外的 yìwài de, 偶然的 ǒurán de

acclaim I V 称赞 chēngzàn, 叫好 jiàohǎo II N 称赞 chēngzàn, 赞誉 zànyù

accolade N 高度赞扬 gāodù zànyáng

accommodate V 1 提供住宿 tígōng zhùsù 2 适应 shìyìng, 迎合 yínghé

accommodation N 住宿 zhùsù, 住宿的地方 zhùsù de dìfang

accompaniment N（音乐）伴奏 (yīnyuè) bànzòu
with piano accompaniment 钢琴伴奏 gāngqín bànzòu

accompany V 1 陪同 péitóng 2 为…伴奏 wéi…bànzòu
to accompany her on a trip to China 陪同她去中国 péitóng tā qù Zhōngguó

accomplice N 帮凶 bāngxiōng, 同谋 tóngmóu

accomplished ADJ 很有才华的 hěn yǒu cáihuá de, 有造诣的 yǒu zàoyì de
an accomplished fact 既成事实 jìchéng shìshí

accomplishment N 1 成就 chéngjiù, 成绩 chéngjì 2 技能 jìnéng, 技巧 jìqiǎo
a high level of accomplishment in

figure skating 非常高的花样滑冰技巧 fēicháng gāo de huāyàng huábīng jìqiǎo

accord I N 1 符合 fúhé, 一致 yízhì 2 协定 xiédìng [M. WD 项 xiàng]
of one's own accord 自愿地 zìyuànde
to reach an accord 达成协议 dáchéng xiéyì
II v 给与 jǐyǔ

accordance N (in accordance with) 与… 一致 yǔ...yīzhì, 根据 genjù
in accordance with his will 根据他的 遗嘱 gēnjù tāde yízhǔ

according to PREP 根据 gēnjù, 按照 ànzhào

accost v 走上去与…主动讲话 zǒushang qù yǔ...zhǔdòng jiǎnghuà, 与…搭讪 yǔ...dāshàn

account I N 1 叙述 xùshù, 描写 miáoxiě
to give an account of … 讲述 jiǎngshù
2 帐 zhàng, 账户 zhànghù, 账目 zhàngmù
checking account 活期账户 huóqī zhànghù
savings account 储蓄账户 chǔxù zhànghù
3 考虑 kǎolǜ, 想法 xiǎngfǎ
to take … into account/take account of 考虑 kǎolǜ
II v (to account for) 说明 shuōmíng, 解释 jiěshì

accountability N 负责 fùzé, 责任制 zérènzhì

accountable ADJ 负有责任的 fùyǒu zérèn de

accountant N 会计 kuàijì, 会计师 kuàijìshī

accredited ADJ 得到正式认可的 [+教师] dédào zhèngshì rènkě de [+jiàoshī], 有正式资格的 [+专业工作者] yǒu zhèngshì zīge de [+zhuānyè gōngzuòzhě]
an accredited accountant 有资格开业 的会计师 yǒu zīgé kāiyè de kuàijìshī

accumulate v 积累 jīlěi, 集聚 jíjù

accuracy N 准确性 zhǔnquèxìng, 精确度 jīngquèdù

accurate ADJ 准确 zhǔnquè, 精确 jīngquè

accusation N 控告 kònggào, 指控 zhǐkòng

accuse v 控告 kònggào, 控诉 kòngsù
to accuse him of sex harassment 控告他性骚扰 kònggào tā xìngsāorǎo

accused N 被告 bèigào [M. WD 名 míng]

accustomed ADJ 习惯 xíguàn, 习惯于 xíguàn yú
be accustomed to a vegetarian diet 习惯于吃素食 xíguàn yú chīsù shí

ace I N 1 （扑克牌）A 牌（pūkèpái）ēi pái 2 王牌 wángpái, 高手 gāoshǒu II ADJ 第一流的 dìyīliú de, 棒极的 bàng jí de
an ace pitcher 王牌投球手 wángpái tóuqiú shǒu

acerbic ADJ 尖刻的 jiānkè de, 刻毒的 kèdú de

ache N 疼 téng, 痛 tòng

achieve v 1 取得 [+平等地位] qǔdé [+píngděng dìwèi], 获得 huòdé 2 实现 [+目标] shíxiàn [+mùbiāo]

achievement N 成就 chéngjiù, 成绩 chéngjì

acid N 酸 suān
acid rain 酸雨 suānyǔ

acknowledge v 1 承认 chéngrèn, 确认 quèrèn 2 表示感谢 biǎoshì gǎnxiè, 鸣谢 míngxiè, 致谢 zhìxiè

acknowledgment N 1 承认 chéngrèn, 确认 quèrèn 2 感谢 gǎnxiè, 鸣谢 míngxiè
in acknowledgment of 确认 quèrèn, 表彰 biǎozhāng

acne N 粉刺 fěncì

acorn N 橡树的果子 xiàngshù de guǒzi

acoustics N 1 音响效果 yīnxiǎng xiàoguǒ 2 声学 shēngxué

acquaint v 认识 rènshi, 知晓 zhīxiǎo
to be acquainted with 认识 rènshi, 了解 liǎojiě

acquaintance N 认识的人 rènshì de rén, 熟人 shúrén
to make sb's acquaintance 认识 rènshi, 结识 jiéshí

acquiesce v 默许 mòxǔ, 勉强同意 miǎnqiǎng tóngyì

acquire v 取得 qǔdé, 获得 huòdé

acquisition N 1 获得 huòdé, 得到 dédào 2 获得的东西 huòdé de dōngxi, 得到的东西 dédào de dōngxi mergers and acquisitions 公司并购 gōngsī bìnggòu

acquit v 宣布无罪 xuānbù wúzuì

acre N 英亩 yīngmǔ

acrid ADJ **1** 刺鼻的 [+气味] cìbí de [+qìwèi] **2** 刻薄的 [+话] kèbó de [+huà]

acrimonious ADJ 充满敌意的 chōngmǎn díyì de, 激烈的 jīliè de

acrobat N 杂技演员 zájì yǎnyuán

across I PREP **1** 通过, 穿过 chuānguo **2** 在…的对面 zài…de duìmiàn II ADV 过去, 穿过 chuānguò

act I v **1** [迅速+] 行动 [xùnsù+] xíngdòng **2** 演 [+主角] yǎn [+zhǔjué], 扮演 [+一个角色] bànyǎn [+yí ge juésè] **3** 假装 jiǎzhuāng

to act as 当 [+中间人] dāng [+zhōngjiānrén], 担任 dānrèn

II N **1** 行动 xíngdòng, 行为 xíngwéi **2** [通过+] 法令 [tōngguò+] fǎlìng

acting I ADJ 代理的 dàilǐ de II N 表演 biǎoyǎn

action N 行动 xíngdòng, 行为 xíngwéi

Actions speak louder than words. 行动重于言辞。Xíngdòng zhòngyú yáncí.

to take action 采取行动 cǎiqǔ xíngdòng

activate v [+警报] 使活动 [+jǐngbào] shǐ húodòng

active I ADJ 活跃 huóyuè, 积极 jījí II N 主动语态 zhǔdòng yǔtài

activity N 活动 húodòng [M. WD 项 xiàng]

after-school activities 课外活动 kè wài húodòng

terrorist activities 恐怖主义活动 kǒngbù zhǔyì húodòng

actor N（男）演员 (nán) yǎnyuán

actress N（女）演员 (nǚ) yǎnyuán

actual ADJ 实际的 shíjì de, 真实的 zhēnshí de

actually ADV 事实上 shìshíshang, 其实 qíshí

acumen N 机敏 jīmǐn, 敏锐 mǐnruì

acupuncture N 针灸 zhēnjiǔ, 针灸疗法 zhēnjiǔliáofǎ

acute ADJ **1** 严重的 yánzhòng de **2** 急性的 jíxìng de

acute disease 急性病 jíxìngbìng

acute pain 剧烈疼痛 jùliè téngtòng

AD ABBREV (= *Anno Domini*) 公元 gōngyuán

adamant ADJ 坚持 jiānchí, 坚决 jiānjué

adapt v **1** 改变…以适应 gǎibiàn…yǐ shìyìng **2** 改编 [+小说] gǎibiān [+xiǎoshuō]

adapter N 转接器 zhuǎnjiēqì, 插座 chāzuò

add v **1** 加 jiā **2** 补充 bǔchōng

addict N **1** 吸毒上瘾的人 xīdú shàngyǐn de rén **2** 上瘾的人 shàngyǐn de rén

cocaine addict 可卡因上瘾者 kěkǎyīn shàngyǐn zhě

addicted ADJ 上瘾的 xīdú shàngyǐn de

addicted to gambling 赌博上瘾的 dǔbó shàngyǐn de

addictive ADJ 使人上瘾的 shǐrén shàngyǐn de

addition N 加 jiā, 加法 jiāfǎ

in addition 另外 lìngwài, 此外 cǐwài

in addition to 除了…以外 chúle…yǐwài

additional ADJ 额外的 éwàide, 附加的 fùjiāde

additive N 添加剂 tiānjiājì

address I N **1** 地址 dìzhǐ **2** 演说 yǎnshuō, 讲话 jiǎnghuà

to deliver an opening address 致开幕词 zhì kāimùcí

II v **1**（在邮件上）写姓名地址 (zài yóujiàn shàng) xiě xìngmíng dìzhǐ, 开信封 kāi xìnfēng **2** 演讲 yǎnjiǎng, 发表演说 fābiǎo yǎnshuō **3** 称呼 chēnghu

form of address 称呼方式 chēnghu fāngshì

adept I ADJ 擅长的 shàncháng de, 熟练的 shúliàn de II N 能手 néngshǒu, 内行 nèiháng

adequate ADJ 充分的 chōngfèn de, 足够的 zúgòu de

adhere v 黏附 niánfù

to adhere to 坚持 jiānchí

adhesive ADJ 有粘性的 yǒu zhānxìng de

adhesive tape 胶布 jiāobù, 胶带 jiāodài

ad hoc ADJ 专门的 zhuānmén de, 特地 tèdì

an ad hoc committee 专门委员会 zhuānmén wěiyuánhuì

adjacent ADJ 邻近的 línjìn de, 相连的 xiānglián de

adjective N 形容词 xíngróngcí

adjoining ADJ 相邻的 xiānglín de, 紧挨着的 jǐn'āizhe de

adjourn V 暂停 zàntíng, 休会 xiūhuì

adjudicate V 裁定 cáidìng, 评审 píngshěn

adjunct N 附属物 fùshǔwù, 附件 fùjiàn

adjust V 1 调整 tiáozhěng, 调节 tiáojié **2** 适应 shìyìng
well-adjusted 身心健全的 shēnxīnjiànquán de, 能对付生活中的问题的 néng duìfu shēnghuó zhōngde wèntíde

adjustment N 调整 tiáozhěng, 调节 tiáojié

administer V 1 管理 [+医院] guǎnlǐ [+yīyuàn], 治理 zhìlǐ 2 执行 [+规定] zhíxíng [+guīdìng]

administration N 1 管理 guǎnlǐ, 行政 xíngzhèng 2 政府 zhèngfǔ

admirable ADJ 令人敬佩的 lìngrén jìng pèi de, 出色的 chūsè de

admiral N 舰队司令 jiànduì sīlìng, 海军上将 hǎijūn shàngjiàng [M. WD 位 wèi]

admiration N 敬佩 jìngpèi, 佩服 pèifu

admire V 1 敬佩 jìngpèi, 钦佩 qīnpèi, 佩服 pèifu 2 欣赏 [+美景] xīnshǎng [+měijǐng], 观赏 [+风景] guānshǎng [+fēngjǐng]

admissible ADJ 可接受的 kě jiēshòu de, 可采纳的 kě cǎinà de
admissible evidence 可接受的证词 kě jiēshòu dí zhèngcí

admission N 1 承认 chéngrèn 2 门票 ménpiào
No admission 不准入内 bùzhǔn rùnèi

admit V 1 承认 chéngrèn 2 允许加入 yǔnxǔ jiārù, 接纳 jiēnà
to be admitted to the country club 被接纳加入乡村俱乐部 bèi jiēnà jiārù xiāngcūn jùlèbù
3 接收入医院 jiē shōu rù yīyuàn
to be admitted to the intensive care 送往医院特别护理部 sòngjìn yīyuàn tèbié hùlì bù

admittance N 进入 jìnrù
to gain admittance to Harvard 进入哈佛大学学习 jìnrù Hāfó Dàxué xuéxí, 被哈佛大学录取 bèi Hāfó Dàxué lùqǔ

admonish V 劝告 quàngào, 告诫 gàojiè

adolescent I ADJ 青少年的 qīngshàonián de, 青春期的 qīngchūnqī de II N 青少年 qīngshàonián

adopt V 1 领养 lǐngyǎng 2 采用 cǎiyòng, 采纳 cǎinà

adoptive ADJ 领养的 lǐngyǎng de
an adoptive father 领养孩子的父亲 lǐngyǎng háizi de fùqin, 养父 yǎngfù

adorable ADJ 非常可爱的 fēicháng kě'ài de

adoration N 爱慕 àimù, 敬慕 jìngmù

adore V 爱慕 àimù, 敬慕 jìngmù

adorn V 装饰 zhuāngshì

adornment N 装饰品 zhuāngshìpǐn

adrift ADJ 漂流的 piāoliú de

adroit ADJ 1 灵巧的 [+手] líng qiǎo de [+shǒu] 2 口齿伶俐的 [+外交家] kǒuchǐ línglì de [+wàijiāojiā]

adult I N 成年人 chéngniánrén, 成人 chéngrén II ADJ 1 成人的 chéngrén de 2 适合成年的 shìhé chéngnián de

adulterate V 掺假 chān jiǎ

adultery N 通奸 tōngjiān

advance I V 1 进展 jìnzhǎn, 发展 fāzhǎn 2 提出 [+计划、理论等] tíchū [+jìhuà, lǐlùn děng] 3 预支 [+工资、报酬等] yùzhī [gōngzī, bàochou děng] II N 1 预先 yùxiān 2 进展 jìnzhǎn, 发展 fāzhǎn 3 预付款 yùfùkuǎn

advanced ADJ 1 先进的 [+技术] xiānjìn de [+jìshù] 2 高级（的）[+数学] gāojí (de) [+shùxué]

advances N 挑逗 tiǎodòu, 勾引 gōuyǐn
to make advances to sb 挑逗某人 tiǎodòu mǒurén, 对某人性骚扰 duì mǒurén xìngsāorǎo

advantage N 1 好处 hǎochù, 益处 yìchù 2 有利条件 yǒulì tiáojiàn
to have an advantage over 对…占有优势 duì…zhànyǒu yōushì
to take advantage of sb 占某人的便宜 zhàn mǒurén piányi

advent N 出现 chūxiàn, 来临 láilín

adventure N 冒险 màoxiǎn
adventure tour 冒险旅游 màoxiǎn lǚyóu

adverb N 副词 fùcí

adversary N 敌手 díshǒu, 对手 duìshǒu
adverse ADJ 不利的 búlì de, 反面的 fǎnmiàn de
advertise V 1 做广告 zuò guǎnggào, 登广告 dēng guǎnggào 2 招聘 [+职员] zhāopìn [+zhíyuán]
advertisement N 广告 guǎnggào
advertising N 广告业 guǎnggàoyè
  advertising agency 广告公司 guǎnggào gōngsī
advice N 劝告 quàngào, 意见 yìjiàn
advise V 1 劝 quàn 2 提供咨询 tígōng zīxún
adviser, advisor N 顾问 gùwèn
advisory ADJ 顾问的 gùwèn de, 咨询的 zīxún de
  an advisory committee 顾问委员会 gùwèn wěiyuánhuì, 咨询委员会 zīxún wěiyuánhuì
advocate N, V 提倡 tíchàng, 主张 zhǔzhāng
aerial ADJ 从飞机上来的 cóng fēijī shànglái de
  an aerial photograph 空中拍摄的照片 kōngzhōng pāishè de zhàopiàn
aerobics N 有氧健身操 yǒu yǎng jiànshēncāo
aerospace ADJ 航空和航天工业 hángkōng hé hángtiān gōngyè
aesthetics N 美学 měixué
afar ADV 从远方 cóng yuǎnfāng
affable ADJ 和蔼可亲的 hé'ǎi kěqīn de, 友好的 yǒuhǎo de
affair N 1 事 shì, 事情 shìqing [M. WD 件 jiàn], 事件 shìjiàn 2 事务 shìwù [M. WD 件 jiàn]
  foreign affairs 外交事务 wàijiāo shìwù, 外事 wàishì
  3 婚外恋 hūnwài liàn
affect V 1 影响 yǐngxiǎng 2 假装 jiǎzhuāng
affected ADJ 做作的 zuòzuo de, 装出来的 zhuāngchū láide
affection N 爱 ài, 喜爱 xǐ'ài
affectionate ADJ 充满爱意的 chōngmǎn àiyì de
affiliate I N 附属机构 fùshǔ jīgòu II V 使附属 shǐ fùshǔ

affinity N 情投意合 qíngtóuyìhé, 生性喜好 shēngxìng xǐhào
affirm V 确认 quèrèn, 断定 duàndìng
affirmative ADJ 肯定的 kěndìng de
  an affirmative sentence 肯定句 kěndìng jù
  affirmative action 积极措施 jījí cuòshī
affix V 使固定 shǐ gùdìng, 贴上 tiēshang
afflict V 使 [+病人] 经受痛苦 shǐ [+bìngrén] jīngshòu tòngkǔ, 折磨 zhémo
  be afflicted with a disease 患上病 huànshang bìng
affluent ADJ 富裕的 fùyù de
  affluent lifestyle 富裕的生活方式 fùyù de shēnghuó fāngshì
afford V 1 买得起 mǎideqǐ 2 …得起 …dé qǐ
  cannot afford to offend sb 得罪不起某人 dézuì bùqǐ mǒurén
affordable ADJ 买得起的 mǎideqǐ de, 支付得起的 zhīfù dé qǐ de
affront N 侮辱性言行 wǔrǔ xìng yánxíng, 侮辱 wǔrǔ
afloat ADJ 资金周转良好的 zījīn zhōuzhuǎn liánghǎo de
afraid ADJ 1 怕 pà, 害怕 hàipà 2 恐怕 kǒngpà
afresh ADV 重新 chóngxīn, 新 xīn
Africa N 非洲 Fēizhōu
African I ADJ 非洲的 Fēizhōu de II N 非洲人 Fēizhōu rén
after I PREP, CONJ 在…以后 zài…yǐhòu
  After you. 您先请。Nín xiān qǐng.
  day after tomorrow 后天 hòutiān
  after all 毕竟 bìjìng, 不管怎么说 bùguǎn zěnme shuō
  II ADV 以后 yǐhòu
  not long after 不久以后 bùjiǔ yǐhòu
after-effect N 后遗症 hòuyízhèng, 副作用 fùzuòyòng
afterlife N 来生 láishēng, 来世 láishì
aftermath N 后果 hòuguǒ, 余波 yúbō
afternoon N 下午 xiàwǔ
aftershave N 剃须后用的润肤油 tìxū hòu yòng de rùn fū yóu, 须后蜜 xūhòumì
aftertaste N 余味 yúwèi
afterthought N 事后的想法 shìhòu de

xiǎngfǎ, 后来想起的事 hòulái xiǎngqǐ de shì

afterward, afterwards ADV 后来 hòulái

again ADV 又 yòu, 再 zài
Try it again! 再试一下! Zài shì yí xià!
now and again 常常 chángcháng

against PREP 反对 fǎnduì

age I N 1 年龄 niánlíng, 年纪 niánjì 2 时代 shídài, 时期 shíqī
for ages 很长时间 hěn cháng shíjiān
II V 变老 biànlǎo

aged ADJ 年老的 niánlǎo de
the aged 老年人 lǎoniánrén

ageless ADJ 永不变老的 yǒngbú biànlǎo de, 永葆青春的 yǒngbǎoqīngchūn de

agency N (代理) 公司 (dàilǐ) gōngsī
dating agency 婚姻介绍所 hūnyīn jièshàosuǒ
employment agency 就业公司 jiùyè gōngsī, 职业介绍所 zhíyè jièshàosuǒ

agenda N 1 会议议程 huìyì yìchéng 2 要做的事情 yào zuò de shìqing
high on the agenda 优先办的事情 yōuxiān bàn de shìqing, 急需解决的问题 jíxū jiějué de wèntí
hidden agenda 隐秘的动机 yǐnmì de dòngjī, 不可告人的目的 bùkěgàorén de mùdì

agent N 1 代理人 dàilǐrén, 经纪人 jīngjìrén 2 特工人员 tègōng rényuán
FBI agent 联邦调查局特工 liánbāng diàochájú tègōng

aggravate V 使恶化 shǐ èhuà, 加剧 jiājù

aggressive ADJ 1 侵略的 qīnlüè de 2 好斗的 hào dǒu de 3 有进取心的 yǒu jìnqǔxīn de, 冲劲十足的 chōng jìn shízú de

aggrieved ADJ 深感委屈的 shēngǎn wěiqu de, 愤懑的 fènmèn de

aghast ADJ 吓呆了的 xiàdāile de, 大为震惊的 dàwéi zhènjīng de

agile ADJ 灵活的 línghuó de, 敏捷的 mǐnjié de

agitate V 煽动 shāndòng, 鼓动 gǔdòng

agnostic N 不可知论者 bùkězhīlùnzhě

ago ADV 前 qián, 以前 yǐqián

agonize V 痛苦 tòngkǔ, 苦恼 kǔnǎo

to agonize over sth 为 [+一项困难的决定] 苦恼 wéi [+yí xiàng kùnnan de juédìng] kǔnǎo, 难作决定 nán zuò juédìng

agonizing ADJ 极其痛苦的 jíqí tòngkǔ de, 极为苦恼的 jíwéi kǔnǎo de

agony N 剧烈的疼痛 jùliè de téngtòng, 痛苦 tòngkǔ
in agony 极其痛苦地 jíqí tòngkǔ de

agree V 1 同意 tóngyì 2 约定 yuēdìng, 决定 juédìng 3 相符合 xiāngfú hé, 一致 yízhì
not to agree with sb 不对某人胃口 búduì mǒurén wèikǒu

agreeable ADJ 1 可以同意的 kěyǐ tóngyì de 2 讨人喜欢的 tǎorén xǐhuan de

agreement N 1 同意 tóngyì 2 协议 xiéyì

agriculture N 农业 nóngyè

ahead ADV 前面 qiánmian, 在前面 zài qiánmiàn
ahead of schedule 提前 tíqián

aid N, V 援助 yuánzhù, 帮助 bāngzhù

aide N 助理人员 zhùlǐ rényuán, 助理 zhùlǐ, 助手 zhùshǒu

AIDS N 艾滋病 àizībìng

ailment N 小病 xiǎo bìng, 不舒服 bùshūfú

aim I V 1 打算 dǎsuan, 准备 zhǔnbèi 2 针对 zhēnduì 3 瞄准 miáozhǔn II N 目标 mùbiāo
to take aim 瞄准 miáozhǔn

air I N 1 空气 kōngqì 2 空中 kōngzhōng, 天空 tiānkōng
air strike 空中打击 kōngzhōng dǎjī, 空袭 kōngxí
air time (广播电视) 播放时间 (guǎngbō diànshì) bōfàng shíjiān
by air 坐飞机 zuò fēijī
to be on air (电台) 正在广播 (diàntái) zhèng zài guǎngbō
II V 1 晾干 [+衣服] liànggān [+yīfu] 2 表达 [+意见] biǎodá [+yìjiàn]

airbag N 安全气囊 ānquán qìnáng

airbase N 空军基地 kōngjūn jīdì

airborne ADJ 1 在飞行中 zài fēixíng zhōng 2 空降的 kōngjiàng de

air conditioner N 空气调节器 kōngqì tiáojié qì, 空调器 kōngtiáoqì

airfare N 飞机票价 fēijī piàojià

airfield N （空军）机场 (kōngjūn) jīchǎng

air force N 空军 kōngjūn

airline N 航空公司 hángkōng gōngsī [M.
WD 家 jiā]
   budget airline 廉价航空公司 liánjià
   hángkōng gōngsī

airliner N 班机 bānjī [M. WD 架 jià], 大型
客机 dàxíng kèjī [M. WD 架 jià]

airmail N 航空邮件 hángkōng yóujiàn

airplane N 飞机 fēijī [M. WD 架 jià]

airport N 飞机场 fēijīchǎng [M. WD 座
zuò], 机场 jīchǎng [M. WD 座 zuò]

airspace N 领空 lǐngkōng
   Japanese airspace 日本领空 Rìběn
   lǐngkōng

airtight ADJ 密封的 mìfēng de

airy ADJ 通风良好的 tōngfēng liánghǎo de

aisle N 通道 tōngdào
   to walk down the aisle 结婚 jiéhūn

ajar ADJ （门）微开的 (mén) wēi kāi de,
半开的 bàn kāi de

a.k.a. (= also known as) ABBREV 又名
yòumíng, 又叫 yòujiào
   Halsey, a.k.a. raging bull 海尔塞，又名
   "蛮牛" Hǎi'ěr sāi, yòumíng "mánniú"

akin ADJ 极为类似 jíwéi lèisì
   akin to sth 和（某物）极为类似 hé
   (mǒu wù) jíwéi lèisì, 和（某物）十分相
   似 hé (mǒu wù) shífēn xiāngsì

à la carte ADJ （从菜单上）点菜 (cóng
càidān shàng) diǎncài
   to order à la carte 从菜单上点菜 cóng
   càidān shàng diǎncài

alacrity N 快捷 kuàijié

alarm I N 1 警报 jǐngbào, 警报器
jǐngbàoqì 2 闹钟 nàozhōng 3 惊恐
jīngkǒng II v 警觉 jǐngjué
   alarm clock 闹钟 nàozhōng
   false alarm 一场虚惊 yì cháng xūjīng
   to raise the alarm 发出警报 fāchū
   jǐngbào, 发出警告 fāchū jǐnggào

alarming ADJ 令人担忧的 lìng rén dānyōu
de, 令人恐慌的 lìngrén kǒnghuāng de

alas INTERJ 哎呀 āiyā

albino N 白化病病人 báihuàbìng bìngrén,
患白化病的动物 huàn báihuàbìng de
dòngwù

album N 1 唱片 chàngpiàn, 音乐专辑
yīnyuè zhuānjí 2 照相簿 zhàoxiàngbù
3 集邮册 jíyóucè

alcohol N 酒 jiǔ, 酒精 jiǔjīng
   alcohol abuse 酗酒 xùjiǔ

alcoholic I ADJ 含有酒精的 hányǒu
jiǔjīng de
   alcoholic beverage 含有酒精的饮料
   hányǒu jiǔjīng de yǐnliào, 酒类 jiǔlèi
II N 酒鬼 jiǔguǐ, 酗酒者 xùjiǔzhě

ale N 浓啤酒 nóngpíjiǔ, 麦芽酒 màiyá jiǔ

alert I ADJ 机敏的 jīmǐn de, 机警的
jīngjué de II v 1 提醒 tíxǐng 2 发出警报 fāchū
jǐngbào III N 警报 jǐngbào
   to be on the alert 保持警觉 bǎochí
   jǐngjué

algebra N 代数 dàishù

alias I ADV 又名 yòumíng, 又叫 yòujiào
II N 化名 huàmíng, 假名 jiǎmíng

alibi N 不在犯罪现场的证明 búzài fànzuì
xiànchǎng de zhèngmíng [M. WD 份 fèn]

alien N 1 外国人 wàiguórén, 侨民
qiáomín, (an illegal alien) 非法外侨
fēifǎ wàiqiáo 2 外星人 wàixīngrén

alienate v 1 离间 líjiàn, 使疏远 shǐ
shūyuǎn 2 转让 [+土地] zhuǎnràng
[+tǔdì]

alight¹ ADJ 燃烧着的 ránshāozhe de

alight² v 1 从 [+飞机／汽车上] 下来 cóng
[+fēijī/qìchē shàng] xiàlai 2 [鸟+] 飞落
[niǎo+] fēi luò

align v 1 与 [+大多数人] 一致 yǔ [+dàduō-
shù rén] yízhì 2 使 [+车轮] 排成直线 shǐ
[+chēlún] pái chéng zhíxiàn

alike I ADJ 相像 xiāngxiàng II ADV 同样
tóngyàng

alimony N （离婚）赡养费 (líhūn)
shànyǎngfèi [M. WD 笔 bǐ]

alive ADJ 1 活着的 huózhāo de 2 仍然存在
的 réngrán cúnzài de
   alive and well 活得好好的 huó dé
   hǎohǎode

alkaline ADJ 含有碱的 hányǒu jiǎn de

all I ADJ 所有的 suǒyǒu de, 全部的 quánbù de II ADV 完全 wánquán III PRON 全部
quánbù, 一切 yíqiè
   all along 一直 yìzhí

all-around 全能的 quánnéng de

all right 行 xíng, 可以 kěyǐ

all the time 总是 zǒngshì, 老是 lǎoshi

Allah N 真主 Zhēnzhǔ, 安拉 Ānlā

allay v 减轻 jiǎnqīng
to allay suspicion 减轻怀疑 jiǎnqīng huáiyí

allegation N 指控 zhǐkòng
allegation of tax evasion 逃税的指控 táoshuì de zhǐkòng

allegiance N 效忠 xiàozhōng, 忠诚 zhōngchéng
to pledge allegiance to 向…宣誓效忠 xiàng...xuānshì xiàozhōng

allergic ADJ 过敏的 guòmǐn de
to be allergic to 对…过敏 duì...guòmǐn

allergy N 过敏 guòmǐn, 过敏反应 guòmǐnfǎnyìng

alleviate v 缓解 huǎnjiě, 减轻 jiǎnqīng
to alleviate hardship for the rural poor 减轻农村贫穷人口的艰难生活 jiǎnqīng nóngcūn pínqióng rénkǒu de jiānnán shēnghuó

alley N 小巷 xiǎoxiàng [M. WD 条 tiáo]

alliance N 联盟 liánméng, 同盟 tóngméng

alligator N （短吻）鳄鱼 (duǎnwěn) èyú [M. WD 条 tiáo]

all-inclusive ADJ 全部包括的 quánbù bāokuò de, 费用全包的 fèiyòng quán bāo de

allocate v 分配 fēnpèi, 拨给 bōgěi
to allocate 200,000 dollars for a literacy program 拨给扫盲计划二十万美元 bō gěi sǎománg jìhuà èrshí wàn Měiyuán

allocation N 1 分配 fēnpèi, 拨款 bōkuǎn 2 配给量 pèijǐ liáng

allot v 分配 fēnpèi, 配给 pèijǐ
to allot 10 minutes for a quiz 安排十分钟做小测验 ānpái shífēn zhōng zuò xiǎo cèyàn

allow v 允许 yǔnxǔ, 准许 zhǔnxǔ
Allow me! 让我来帮你! Ràng wǒ lái bāng nǐ!

allowance N 1 限额 xiàn'é
baggage allowance 行李限重 xíngli xiàn zhòng
2 [住房+] 津贴 [zhùfáng] jīntiē, [旅差+] 补助 [lǚchà+] bǔzhù

alloy N 合金 héjīn

allure N 诱惑 yòuhuò, 魅力 mèilì, 吸引力 xīyǐnlì

ally I N 盟国 méngguó, 盟友 méngyǒu II v 与…结盟 yǔ...jiéméng
to ally oneself with 与…结盟 yǔ...jiéméng, 与…联手 yǔ...liánshǒu

almanac N 历书 lìshū, 年鉴 niánjiàn

almighty ADJ 全能的（上帝） quánnéng de (Shàngdì)
Almighty God 全能的上帝 quánnéng de Shàngdì

almond N 杏仁 xìngrén [M. WD 颗 kē]

almost ADV 几乎 jīhū, 差不多 chàbuduō

alms N 救济品 jiùjì pǐn, 施舍 shīshě

aloft ADV 在高处 zài gāo chù

alone ADJ 单独的 dāndú de, 孤独的 gūdú de
Leave me alone. 让我一个人待着。 Ràng wǒ yí gè rén dāizhe.
to go it alone 独自干 dúzì gàn, 单干 dāngàn

along PREP 沿着 yánzhe

alongside ADV 1 在一起 zài yìqǐ 2 靠着 kàozhe

aloof ADJ 冷淡的 lěngdàn de
to stay aloof from 远离 yuǎnlí, 不参与 bù cānyù

aloud ADV 大声地 dàshēng de

alphabet N 字母表 zìmǔ biǎo, 字母 zìmǔ

already ADV 已经 yǐjīng

also ADV 也 yě

altar N 祭台 jìtái
altar boy 祭台助手 jìtái zhùshǒu

alter v 改 gǎi, 改变 gǎibiàn

alteration N 改变 gǎibiàn, 变动 biàndòng

alternate I v 轮流 lúnliú, 交替 jiāotì II ADJ 1 轮流的 lúnliú de, 交替的 jiāotì de 2 候补的 [+委员] hòubǔ de [+wěiyuán], 后备的 [+球员] hòubèi de [+qiúyuán]

alternative I ADJ 另一个 lìng yí ge, 可选择的 kě xuǎnzé de II N 选择
to have no alternative but ... 没有别的办法 méiyǒu biéde bànfǎ, 只能 zhǐ néng

although CONJ 虽然 suīrán

altitude N 高度 gāodù, 海拔 hǎibá

altogether ADV 一共 yígòng, 总共 zǒnggòng

altruism N 利他主义 lìtāzhǔyì

aluminum (AI) N 铝 lǚ

always ADV 总是 zǒngshì, 一直 yìzhí, 一向 yíxiàng

am V See be

amalgamate V 合并 hébìng, 联合 liánhé

amass V 积聚 jījù, 积累 jīlěi

amateur I ADJ 业余的 yèyú de **II** N 1 业余爱好者 yèyú àihàozhě 2 生手 shēngshǒu

amaze V 使…十分惊奇 shǐ...shífēn jīngqí

amazement N 惊奇 jīngqí

amazing ADJ 令人惊奇的 lìngrén jīngqí de, 令人惊讶的 lìngrén jīngyà de

ambassador N 大使 dàshǐ [M. WD 位 wèi] the Chinese ambassador to the U.S. 中国驻美国大使 Zhōngguó zhù Měiguó dàshǐ

ambiguous ADJ 含义不清的 hányì bùqīng de, 模棱两可的 móléngliǎngkě de

ambition N 雄心 xióngxīn, 抱负 bàofù

ambitious ADJ 有雄心的 yǒu xióngxīn de, 有抱负的 yǒu bàofù de

ambivalent ADJ 内心矛盾的 nèixīn máodùn de

amble V 慢慢地走 mànmàn de zǒu

ambulance N 救护车 jiùhùchē

ambush N, V 伏击 fújī

ameliorate V 改善 gǎishàn, 改进 gǎijìn

amen INTERJ 阿门 āmén
Amen to that. 同意 tóngyì, 赞成 zànchéng

amenable ADJ 愿意听从的 yuànyì tīngcóng de, 顺从的 shùncóng de
to be amenable to a compromise 愿意妥协 yuànyì tuǒxié

amend V 修正 xiūzhèng, 修改 xiūgǎi

amendment N 1 修正 xiūzhèng, 修改 xiūgǎi 2 修正案 xiūzhèng'àn

amends N 道歉 dàoqiàn, 赔偿 péicháng
to make amends 道歉 dàoqiàn, 赔偿 péicháng

amenities N 公益设施 gōngyì shèshī

American I ADJ 美国的 Měiguó de, 美洲的 Měizhōu de **II** N 美国人 Měiguórén

amiable ADJ 友好的 yǒuhǎo de, 亲切友好的 qīnqiè yǒuhǎo de

amicable ADJ 友好的 yǒuhǎo de, 和睦的 hémù de
an amicable out-of-court settlement 法庭外友好和解 fǎtíng wài yǒuhǎo héjiě

amid PREP 在…中间 zài...zhōngjiān

amiss ADJ 有差错的 yǒu chācuò de
to see something amiss 发现有差错 fāxiàn yǒu chācuò, 发现有问题 fāxiàn yǒu wèntí

ammunition N 弹药 dànyào

amnesia N 1 记忆丧失 jìyì sàngshī 2 健忘 jiànwàng, 健忘症 jiànwàngzhèng

amnesty N 赦免 shèmiǎn, 不予追究 bùyǔ zhuījiū

among PREP 在…中间 zài...zhōngjiān

amoral ADJ 不道德的 bú dàodé de

amorous ADJ 色情的 sèqíng de, 男女情爱的 nánnǚ qíng'ài de

amorphous ADJ 不定形的 búdìngxíng de

amount N 数量 shùliàng

amphibian N 水陆两栖动物 shuǐlù liǎngqīdòngwù

amphitheater N 圆形露天剧场 yuánxíng lùtiānjùchǎng, 圆形露天竞技场 yuánxíng lùtiān jìngjìchǎng [M. WD 座 zuò]

ample ADJ 充足的 chōngzú de

amplifier N 扩音器 kuòyīnqì, 扬声器 yángshēngqì

amplify V 放大 fàngdà

amputate V 切除 [+肢趾] qiēchú [+jiǎozhǐ], 截肢 jiézhī

amputee N 被截肢者 bèi jiézhī zhě

amuse V 使…快乐 shǐ...kuàilè, 让…高兴 ràng...gāoxìng

amusement N 娱乐 yúlè
amusement park 娱乐场 yúlè chǎng

an See a

anachronism N 1 不合时代的人（事）bùhé shídài de rén (shì) 2 年代错乱 niándài cuòluàn

anal ADJ 1 肛门的 gāngmén de 2 吹毛求疵的 chuī máo qiú cī de

analgesic N 止痛药 zhǐtòngyào

analogous ADJ 类似的 lèisì de, 相似的 xiāngsì de

analogy N 类比 lèibǐ, 类似 lèisì

analysis N 分析 fēnxī

analyst N 分析员 fēnxī yuán
stock market analyst 股票市场分析员 gǔpiào shìchǎng fēnxī yuán

analytic, analytical ADJ 分析的 fēnxī de
analytic chemistry 分析化学 fēnxīhuàxué

analyze V 分析 fēnxī

anarchy N 混乱状态 hùnluàn zhuàngtài, 无政府状态 wúzhèngfǔ zhuàngtài

anatomy N 1 解剖 jiěpōu 2 解剖学 jiěpōuxué 3 解剖构造 jiěpōu gòuzào

ancestor N 1 祖先 zǔxiān, 祖宗 zǔzōng 2 原型 yuánxíng

ancestry N 祖先 zǔxiān, 祖宗 zǔzōng

anchor I N 1 （船）锚 (chuán) máo 2 电视新闻节目主持人 diànshì xīnwén jiémù zhǔchírén 3 精神支柱 jīngshén zhīzhù II V 1 抛锚 pāomáo, 停船 tíngchuán 2 主持电视节目 zhǔchí diànshì jiémù 3 扎根于 zhāgēn yú 4 支持 zhīchí
anchorman 男电视节目主持人 nán diànshì jiémù zhǔchírén

ancient ADJ 古代的 gǔdài de

and CONJ 1 和 hé, 与 yǔ, 以及 yǐjí 2 然后 ránhòu 3 而且 érqiě

android N （似人的）机器人 (sì rén de) jīqìrén

anecdote N 趣闻轶事 qùwén yìshi

anemia N 贫血 pínxuè, 贫血症 pínxuè-zhèng

anesthesia N 1 麻醉 mázuì, 麻醉法 mázuìfǎ 2 麻醉状态 mázuì zhuàngtài

anew ADV 重新 chóngxīn
to start life anew 开始新生活 kāishǐ xīn shēnghuó

angel N 天使 tiānshǐ

anger N 愤怒 fènnù

angle N 角 jiǎo, 角度 jiǎodù

Anglican ADJ 英国圣公会教徒 Yīngguó Shènggōnghuì jiàotú

angry ADJ 愤怒 fènnù, 生气 shēngqì

angst N 切的忧虑 shēnqiè de yōulǜ

anguish N 极度痛苦 jídù tòngkǔ, 极度焦虑 jídù jiāolǜ

angular ADJ 1 骨瘦如柴的 [+老人] gǔ

shòu rú chái de [+lǎorén] 2 有尖角的 [+图案] yǒu jiān jiǎo de [+tú'àn]

animal N 动物 dòngwù
party animal 喜欢参加社交聚会的人 xǐhuan cānjiā shèjiāo jùhuì de rén

animated ADJ 1 动画的 dònghuà de
an animated cartoon 动画片 dònghuàpiàn 2 活跃的 [+讨论] huóyuè de [+tǎolùn]

animation N 动画片制作 dònghuàpiàn zhìzuò

animosity N 仇恨 chóuhèn, 深深的敌意 shēnshēn de díyì

ankle N 踝 huái, 踝骨 huáigǔ

annals N 历史记载 lìshǐ jìzǎi

annex[1] N 并吞 bìngtūn, 兼并 jiānbìng

annex[2] N 附属建筑 fùshǔ jiànzhù

annihilate V 彻底消灭 chèdǐ xiāomiè, 彻底摧毁 chèdǐ cuīhuǐ

anniversary N [结婚+] 周年 [jiéhūn+] zhōunián, 纪念日 jìniànrì

announce V 宣布 xuānbù, 宣告 xuāngào

announcement N 告示 gàoshi, 启事 qǐshì
wedding announcement 结婚启事 jiéhūn qǐshì

annoy V 使 [+人] 恼怒 shǐ [+rén] nǎonù, 使 [+人] 生气 shǐ [+rén] shēngqì

annoyance N 恼怒 nǎonù, 生气 shēngqì

annoyed ADJ （感到）恼怒 (gǎndào) nǎonù

annual I ADJ 每年的 měinián de, 年度的 [+全体会议] niándù de [+quántǐ huìyì] II N 一年生植物 yìniánshēng zhíwù

annuity N [优厚的+] 年金 [yōuhòu de+] niánjīn

annul V 解除 jiěchú, 废止 fèizhǐ

anomaly N 异常 yìcháng, 反常 fǎncháng

anonymity N 匿名 nìmíng

anonymous ADJ 匿名的 nìmíng de
an anonymous phone call 匿名电话 nìmíng diànhuà

anorexia N 厌食症 yànshízhèng

another PRON 1 又一（个）yòu yí (ge), 再一（个）zàiyí (ge) 2 另一（个）lìng yí (ge), 别的 biéde

answer I V 1 回答 huídá 2 回应 huíyìng
to answer a letter 回信 huíxìn

to answer the telephone 接电话 jiē diànhuà

II N 回答 huídá, 答案 dá'àn

answerable ADJ 必须承担责任的 bìxū chéngdān zérèn de, 对…负责的 duì… fùzé de

ant N 蚂蚁 mǎyǐ [M. WD 只 zhǐ]

antagonism N 敌对 díduì, 对抗 duìkàng

antagonize V 使…愤怒 shǐ…fènnù, 和…对抗 hé…duìkàng

Antarctic N 南极 Nánjí

Antarctica N 南极洲 Nánjízhōu, 南极大陆 Nánjí dàlù

ante N 赌注 dǔzhù

to up the ante 增加赌注 zēngjiā dǔzhù

antecedent N 以前类似的事 yǐqián lèisì de shì [M. WD 件 jiàn], 前例 qiánlì

antechamber N [主人卧室的+] 前厅 [zhǔrén wòshì de+] qiántīng

antelope N 羚羊 língyáng [M. WD 只 zhǐ/头 tóu]

antenna N 天线 tiānxiàn

anteroom N 前室 qiánshì, 接待室 jiēdàishì

anthem N 赞歌 zàngē [M. WD 首 shǒu] national anthem 国歌 guógē [M. WD 首 shǒu]

anthology N 选集 xuǎnjí

anthropology N 人类学 rénlèixué

antiaircraft ADJ 防空的 fángkōng de antiaircraft missile 防空导弹 fángkōng dǎodàn

antibiotic N 抗生素 kàngshēngsù

antibody N 抗体 kàngtǐ

anticipate V 预期 yùqī, 预料 yùliào

anticipation N 预期 yùqī, 预料 yùliào

anticlimax N 远远没有预期好的情况 yuǎnyuǎn méiyǒu yùqī hǎode qíngkuàng, 令人扫兴的事 lìngrén sǎoxìng de shì

antics N 可笑的举动 kěxiào de jǔdòng

antidote N 解毒药 jiě dúyào

antipathy N 强烈的反感 qiángliè de fǎngǎn

antique N 古董 gǔdǒng, 古玩 gǔwán antique dealer 古董商人 gǔdǒngshāng rén

antiquity N **1** 古代 gǔdài **2** 古建筑 gǔ jiànzhù, 文物 wénwù

antiseptic N 消毒药品 xiāodúyào pǐn, 防腐剂 fángfǔjì

antisocial ADJ **1** 反社会的 fǎn shèhuì de **2** 不合群的 bùhé qún de

antler N 鹿角 lùjiǎo [M. WD 只 zhǐ]

antonym N 反义词 fǎnyìcí

anus N 肛门 gāngmén

anvil N 铁砧 tiězhēn

anxiety N 焦虑 jiāolǜ

anxious ADJ 焦虑 jiāolǜ, 非常担忧 fēicháng dānyōu

any **I** ADJ 什么 shénme, 任何 rènhé **II** ADV 一点儿 yìdiǎnr **III** PRON 哪个 nǎ ge, 哪些 nǎ xiē

anybody PRON 任何人 rènhérén, 谁 shéi

anyhow ADV 不管怎么 bùguǎn zěnme, 无论如何 wúlùn rúhé

anymore ADV 再 zài not anymore 不再 búzài

anyone PRON 任何人 rènhé rén, 谁 shéi

anyplace ADV 任何地方 rènhé dìfang

anything PRON 任何事 rènhé shì, 什么事 shénme shì

anyway ADV 不管怎么说 bùguǎn zěnme shuō, 反正 fǎnzhèng

anywhere ADV 任何地方 rènhé dìfang, 无论哪里 wúlùn nǎli

apart ADV **1** 相隔 xiānggé **2** 分开 fēnkāi, 隔离 gélí apart from 除了 chúle

apartheid N（南非的）种族隔离制度（Nánfēi de）zhǒngzú gélí zhìdù

apartment N 一套房间 yí tào fángjiān, 公寓 gōngyù [M. WD 套 tào] apartment complex 住宅小区 zhùzhái xiǎoqū

apathetic ADJ 不感兴趣的 bù gǎn xìngqù de, 冷淡的 lěngdàn de

ape **I** N 猿 yuán [M. WD 只 zhǐ] **II** V 模仿 mófǎng

aperture N 孔 kǒng, 洞 dòng

apex N 顶点 dǐngdiǎn, 最高点 zuìgāo diǎn

aphrodisiac N 激发性欲的药 jīfā xìngyù de yào, 春药 chūnyào

apiece ADV 每一个 měi yí gè, 每个 měige

aplomb N 自信 zìxìn, 自信力 zìxìn lì

apocalypse N 世界末日 shìjiè mòrì, 巨大

灾难 jùdà zāinàn

apolitical ADJ 非政治的 fēi zhèngzhì de

apologetic ADJ 道歉的 dàoqiàn de, 有歉意的 yǒu qiànyì de

apologize V 道歉 dàoqiàn, 认错 rèncuò

apology N 道歉 dàoqiàn, 歉意 qiànyì

apoplexy N 中风 zhòngfēng

apostle N 耶稣基督的门徒 Yēsū Jīdū de méntú, 传道者 chuándào zhě

apostrophe N 撇号 piēhào (')

appall V 使…大为震惊 shǐ…dàwéi zhènjīng, 使…深感痛恨 shǐ…shēngǎn tònghèn
to be appalled 感到震惊 gǎndào zhènjīng, 感到极大的愤怒 gǎndào jídà de fènnù

appalling ADJ 1 坏极了 huài jíle, 糟糕透了 zāogāo tòu le 2 极其可怕 jíqí kěpà

apparatus N 器械 qìxiè, 设备 shèbèi

apparel N 服装 fúzhuāng, 服饰 fúshì
ready-to-wear apparel 现成时装 xiànchéng shízhuāng, 成衣 chéngyī

apparent ADJ 明显 míngxiǎn, 明白 míngbái

apparently ADV 明显地 míngxiǎn de, 显然地 xiǎnrán de

apparition N 鬼 (魂) guǐ (hún)

appeal V 1 呼吁 hūyù, 请求 qǐngqiú 2 有吸引力 yǒu xīyǐnlì, 使…感兴趣 shǐ…gǎn xìngqu

appear V 1 看来 kànlái, 好像 hǎoxiàng 2 出现 chūxiàn

appearance N 1 外貌 wàimào 2 出现 chūxiàn

appease V 平息 píngxī

append V 附上 fùshàng, 附加 fùjiā

appendicitis N 阑尾炎 lánwěiyán, 盲肠炎 mángchángyán

appendix N 1 附录 fùlù 2 阑尾 lánwěi, 盲肠 mángcháng

appetite N 胃口 wèikǒu

appetizer N 开胃菜 kāiwèicài

applaud V 鼓掌 gǔzhǎng

applause N 掌声 zhǎngshēng

apple N 苹果 píngguǒ [M. WD 只 zhī]
apple pie 苹果馅饼 píngguǒ xiànbǐng

appliance N 1 器具 qìjù 2 家用电器 jiāyòng diànqì

applicable ADJ 生效的 shēngxiào de, 有效的 yǒuxiào de

applicant N 申请人 shēnqǐngrén

application N 1 申请 shēnqǐng 2 申请书 shēnqǐngshū, 申请表 shēnqǐng biǎo

apply V 1 申请 [+工作／签证] shēnqǐng [+gōngzuò/qiānzhèng] 2 运用 [+新技术] yùnyòng [+xīn jìshù], 适用 shìyòng 3 涂 [+一层油漆] tú [+yì céng yóu qī]

appoint V 1 任命 rènmìng, 委派 wěipài 2 约定 yuēdìng, 指定 zhǐdìng

appointment N 1 (朋友的) 约会 (péngyoude) yuēhuì [M. WD 次 cì] 2 (医生的) 预约 yùyuē 3 (职务) 任命 (zhíwù) rènmìng, 委任 wěirèn

apportion V 分配 fēnpèi, 分摊 fēntān

appraisal N 估价 gūjià, 鉴定 jiàndìng

appreciate V 1 感谢 gǎnxiè, 领情 lǐngqíng 2 理解 lǐjiě 3 [房产+] 增值 [fángchǎn+] zēngzhí

appreciation N 1 感谢 gǎnxiè 2 理解 lǐjiě, 欣赏 xīnshǎng 3 增值 zēngzhí

apprehend V 逮捕 dàibǔ, 拘捕 jūbǔ

apprehensive ADJ 担忧的 dānyōu de, 忧虑的 yōulǜ de

apprentice I N 学徒 xuétú, 徒弟 túdì
II V 当学徒 dāng xuétú

approach I V 1 走近 zǒujìn, [新年+] 临近 [xīnnián+] línjìn 2 接近 [+去年的水平] jiējìn [+qùnián de shuǐpíng] 3 与 [+政府部门] 交涉 yǔ [+zhèngfǔ bùmén] jiāoshè 4 处理 [+问题] chǔlǐ [+wèntí], 对付 duìfu II N 1 [教学+] 方法 [jiàoxué+] fāngfǎ 2 要求 yāoqiú, 请求 qǐngqiú 3 通道 tōngdào, 入口 rùkǒu 4 来临 láilín
to make approaches 主动接近 zhǔdòng jiējìn, 求爱 qiú'ài

approachable ADJ 1 可接近的 kě jiējìn de 2 可亲近的 kěqīn jìn de

approbation N 1 批准 pīzhǔn 2 称赞 chēngzàn

appropriate¹ ADJ 合适的 héshì de, 适合 shìhé

appropriate² V 1 [局长+] 挪用 [júzhǎng+] nuó yòng 2 [政府+] 拨款 [zhèngfǔ+] bōkuǎn

approval N 批准 pīzhǔn, 同意 tóngyì

249

approve v 1 批准 pīzhǔn
to approve of 赞成 zànchéng

approximate I ADJ 大约的 dàyuē de
II v 近似 jìnsì, 接近 jiējìn

apricot N 杏 xìng [M. WD 只 zhī], 杏子
xìngzi [M. WD 只 zhī]

April N 四月 sìyuè

apron N 围裙 wéiqún [M. WD 条 tiáo]

apt ADJ 恰当的 qiàdàng de
apt to 容易…的 róngyì…de

aptitude N [学语言的+] 才能 [xuéyú yán
de+] cáinéng, 能力 nénglì

aquarium N 水族馆 shuǐzúguǎn [M. WD
座 zuò]

aquatic ADJ 水生的 shuǐshēng de
an aquatic product 水产品 shuǐchǎnpǐn

aqueduct N 高架渠 gāo jià qú, 渡槽
dùcáo [M. WD 道/条 tiáo]

Arabic I ADJ 阿拉伯的 Ālābó de
Arabic numeral 阿拉伯数字 Ālābó shùzì
II N 阿拉伯语 Ālābóyǔ

arable ADJ 可以耕种的 kěyǐ gēngzhòng de
arable land 可耕地 kěgēngdì

arbitrary ADJ 主观武断的 zhǔguān
wǔduàn de
an arbitrary decision 主观武断的决定
zhǔguān wǔduàn de juédìng

arbitration N 仲裁 zhòngcái, 公断
gōngduàn
to be settled by arbitration 通过仲
裁得到解决 tōngguò zhòngcái dédào
jiějué

arc N 弧线 húxiàn, 弧形 húxíng

arcade N 拱廊 gǒng láng [M. WD 条 tiáo]

arch I N 拱门 gǒngmén [M. WD 座 zuò],
拱顶 gǒngdǐng II v 使成弓形 shǐchéng
gōngxíng, 拱起 gǒng qǐ

archaic ADJ 1 古老的 gǔlǎo de 2 古体的
gǔtǐ de, 不通用的 bù tōngyòng de
an archaic word 古词 gǔ cí, 古语 gǔyǔ

archbishop N 大主教 dàzhǔjiào

archeology N 考古 kǎogǔ, 考古学
kǎogǔxué

archipelago N 群岛 qúndǎo

architect N 建筑师 jiànzhùshī
landscape architect 园林设计师 yuán-
lín shèjìshī

architecture N 建筑学 jiànzhùxué
marine architecture 造船学 zào-
chuánxué

archive N 档案 dàng'àn
archives 档案馆 dàng'ànguǎn

Arctic N 北极 Běijí, 北极区 Běijíqū

ardent ADJ 热情的 [+支持] rèqíng de
[+zhīchí], 热烈的 rèliè de

ardor N 热情 rèqíng, 激情 jīqíng

arduous ADJ 艰巨的 jiānjù de, 艰难的
jiānnán de

are See be

area N 1 地区 dìqū 2 面积 miànjī
area code 分区电话号码 fēnqū diànhuà
hàomǎ

arena N 1 室内运动场 shìnèiyùndòng
chǎng 2（搏斗）场所（bódòu）
chǎngsuǒ

argue v 争论 zhēnglùn

argument N 1 争论 zhēnglùn, 争吵
zhēngchǎo. 2 理由 lǐyóu, 论点 lùndiǎn

arid ADJ 干旱的 gānhàn de 2 枯燥乏味
的 kūzào fáwèi de

arise (PT **arose**; PP **arisen**) v 1 起立 qǐlì
2 出现 chūxiàn 3 引起 yǐnqǐ

arisen See **arise**

aristocrat N 贵族 guìzú [M. WD 位 wèi]

arithmetic N 算术 suànshù
mental arithmetic 心算 xīnsuàn

arm I N 手臂 shǒubì [M. WD 条 tiáo] II v 给
…武器 gěi…wǔqì, 武装 wǔzhuāng

armament N 1 武器 wǔqì [M. WD 件 jiàn]
2 (armaments) 军备 jūnbèi

armchair N 扶手椅 fúshǒuyǐ [M. WD 把 bǎ]

armed ADJ 有武器的 yǒu wǔqì de, 武装的
wǔzhuāng de
armed forces 武装部队 wǔzhuāng
bùduì, 军队 jūnduì

armor N 1 铁甲 tiějiǎ, 装甲钢板 zhuāngjiǎ
gāng bǎn 2 装甲兵 zhuāngjiǎbīng, 装甲
部队 zhuāngjiǎ bùduì
armored division 装甲师 zhuāngjiǎshī

arms N 武器 wǔqì
to take up arms 拿起武器 náqǐ wǔqì,
准备战斗 zhǔnbèi zhàndòu

army N 陆军 lùjūn, 军队 jūnduì

aroma N [香料的+] 芳香 [xiāngliào de+]

fāngxiāng, [咖啡的+] 香气 [kāfēi de+] xiāngqì

aromatherapy N 芳香疗法 fāngxiāng liáofǎ

arose See **arise**

around I PREP 1 在…周围 zài...zhōuwéi, 围绕 wéirào 2 在…各地 zài...gèdì 3 大约 dàyuē II ADV 周围 zhōuwéi

arouse V 引起 yǐnqǐ, 激起 jīqǐ

arraign V 传讯 [+嫌疑犯] chuánxùn [+xiányífàn], 指控 zhǐkòng

arrange V 1 安排 [+会议] ānpái [+huìyì], 约定 yuēdìng 2 布置 [+陈列品] bùzhì [+chénlièpǐn], 排列 páiliè

arrangement N 1 安排 ānpái, 约定 yuēdìng 2 布置 bùzhì, 排列 páiliè

array N 1 一系列 yíxìliè, 大量 dàliàng II V 部署 bùshǔ, 制定 zhìdìng

arrears N 1 积压 jīyā 2 应付欠款 yìngfù qiànkuǎn
  in arrears 拖欠的 [+房租] tuōqiàn de [+fángzū]

arrest V 逮捕 dàibǔ

arrival N 到达 dàodá

arrive V 到达 dàodá, 抵达 dǐdá

arrogance N 傲慢 àomàn, 妄自尊大 wàng zì zūn dà

arrow N 箭头 jiàntóu

arsenal N 军火库 jūnhuǒkù, 兵工厂 bīnggōngchǎng [m. wɒ 座 zuò]

arson N 放火 fànghuǒ, 纵火罪 zònghuǒ zuì

art N 艺术 yìshù, 美术 měishù
  the arts 文艺 wényì

artery N 1 [人的+] 动脉 [rén de+] dòng-mài 2 [交通+] 干线 [jiāotōng+] gànxiàn, 干道 gàndào

arthritis N 关节炎 guānjiéyán

article N 1 文章 wénzhāng 2 物件 wùjiàn

articulate I ADJ 表达力强的 biǎodálì qiáng de, 口才好的 kǒucái hǎode II V 清晰地说 qīngxī de shuō

artifact N 人工制品 réngōng zhìpǐn

artificial ADJ 人造的 rénzào de, 人工的 réngōng de
  artificial intelligence 人工智能 réngōng zhìnéng

artificial respiration 人工呼吸 réngōng hūxī

artillery N 炮兵 pàobīng

artisan N 手艺人 shǒuyìrén

artist N 艺术家 yìshùjiā [m. wɒ 位 wèi]

as I PREP 作为 zuòwéi II CONJ 1 当 dāng, 在…的时候 zài...de shíhou 2 由于 yóuyú III ADV 1 像…一样 xiàng...yíyàng 2 (as well) 也 yě

ascend V 上升 shàngshēng, 登高 dēnggāo

ascent N 上升 shàngshēng, 登高 dēnggāo

ascertain V 确定 quèdìng, 查明 chámíng

ascetic ADJ 苦行的 kǔxíng de, 禁欲的 jìnyù de

ascribe V 把…归因于 bǎ...guīyīnyú

asexual ADJ 无性的 wúxìng de, 无性器官 的 wúxìng qìguān de
  asexual reproduction 无性繁殖 wúxìng fánzhí

ash N 灰 huī, 灰烬 huījìn
  volcanic ashes 火山灰 huǒshānhuī

ashamed ADJ 惭愧 cánkuì, 羞愧 xiūkuì

ashen ADJ 灰白色的 [+脸色] huībáisè de [+liǎnsè], 苍白 cāngbái

ashore ADV 上岸 shàng'àn

Asia N 亚洲 Yàzhōu

Asian I N 亚洲人 Yàzhōurén II ADJ 亚洲 （的）Yàzhōu (de)

aside I ADV 向边上 xiàng biānshàng, 在旁 边 zài pángbiān II N 悄悄话 qiāoqiāohuà

ask V 1 问 wèn 2 请求 qǐngqiú, 请 qǐng 3 邀请 yāoqǐng, 请 qǐng
  to ask after 问候 wènhòu
  to ask the way 问路 wènlù

askew ADV 歪斜 wāixié

asleep ADJ 睡着 shuìzháo
  to fall asleep 睡着 shuìzháo, 入睡 rùshuì

asparagus N 芦笋 lúsǔn

aspect N 1 外表 wàibiǎo, 面貌 miànmào 2 方面 fāngmiàn 3 方向 fāngxiàng, 方 位 fāngwèi
  to study a problem from all aspects 全面地研究问题 quánmiàn de yánjiū wèntí

aspersion N 诽谤 fěibàng, 中伤 zhòngshāng

asphalt N 沥青 lìqīng, 柏油 bǎiyóu

aspiration N 志向 zhìxiàng, 抱负 bàofù
aspirin N 阿司匹林 āsīpǐlín
ass N 1 驴 lǘ [M. wD 头 tóu], 驴子 lǘzi 2 傻瓜 shǎguā 3 屁股 pìgu
  to make an ass of oneself 干傻事 gān shǎshì
assailant N 攻击者 gōngjīzhě
assassin N 暗杀者 àn shā zhě, 刺客 cìkè
assault N, V 攻击 gōngjī
  sexual assault 强暴 qiángbào, 强奸 qiángjiān
assemble V 1 集会 jíhuì 2 收集 shōují 3 装配 zhuāngpèi
assembly N 1 集会 jíhuì 2 参加聚会的人 cānjiā jùhuì de rén 3 装配 zhuāngpèi
  assembly line 装配线 zhuāngpèixiàn
assent N 同意 tóngyì, 赞同 zàntóng
assert V 主张 zhǔzhāng, 坚称 jiānchēng
  to assert oneself 坚持自己的权利 jiānchí zìjǐ de quánlì, 显示自己的地位 xiǎnshì zìjǐ de dìwèi
assertion N 1 主张 zhǔzhāng 2 断言 duànyán
assess V 测算 cèsuàn, 估价 gūjià
asset N 1 资产 zīchǎn 2 有价值的人（或物）yǒu jiàzhí de rén (huò wù)
  liquid assets 流动资金 liúdòng zījīn
asshole N 1 屁眼 pìyǎn 2 笨蛋 bèndàn
assign V 1 分配 [+任务] fēnpèi [+rènwu] 2 指派 zhǐpài
  to assign sb to do sth 指派某人担任某职 zhǐpài mǒurén dānrèn mǒu zhí
assignment N 任务 rènwu
  homework assignment 作业 zuòyè
assimilate V 融入 róng rù, 同化 tónghuà
assist V 帮助 bāngzhù, 协助 xiézhù
assistance N 帮助 bāngzhù, 协助 xiézhù
assistant N 助理 zhùlǐ, 助理人员 zhùlǐ rényuán
associate I V 联系 liánxì
  to associate with sb 与某人交往 yǔ mǒurén jiāowǎng
  II N 1 伙伴 huǒbàn, 同事 tóngshì 2 准学位获得者 zhǔn xuéwèi huòdézhě
  Associate of Arts 准文学士 zhǔn wénxuéshì
  III ADJ 副 fù, 准 zhǔn

associate professor 副教授 fùjiàoshòu
association N 协会 xiéhuì, 社团 shètuán
assorted ADJ 各种各样的 gèzhǒng gèyàng de
assortment N 混合物 hùnhéwù, 什锦 shíjǐn
  an assortment of desserts 什锦甜点 shíjǐn tiándiǎn
assume V 假定 jiǎdìng
  an assumed name 假名 jiǎmíng
assumption N 假设 jiǎshè, 假定 jiǎdìng
assurance N 自信 zìxìn
assure V 担保 dānbǎo, 保证 bǎozhèng
asterisk N 星号 xīnghào (*)
asteroid N 小行星 xiǎoxíngxīng
asthma N 哮喘病 xiàochuǎnbìng, 气喘 qìchuǎn
astonish V 使…吃惊 shǐ…chījīng
astonishing ADJ 让人吃惊的 ràng rén chījīng de
astound V 使…非常吃惊 shǐ…fēicháng chījīng
astounding ADJ 让人非常吃惊的 ràng rén fēicháng chījīng de
astray ADV 迷失 míshī
  to go astray 不务正业 bú wù zhèngyè
astride ADV 跨坐地 kuà zuò de
astringent ADJ 1 严厉的 [+批评] yánlì de [+pīpíng] 2 止血的 zhǐxuè de
astrology N 占星术 zhānxīngshù
astronaut N 宇航员 yǔhángyuán
astronomical ADJ 1 天文学的 tiānwénxué de 2 巨大的 [+数字] jùdà de [+shùzì], 天文数字的 tiānwén shùzì de
astronomy N 天文学 tiānwénxué
astute ADJ 精明的 [+投资者] jīngmíng de [+tóuzīzhě]
asylum N 避难 bìnàn, 庇护 bìhù
  political asylum 政治避难 zhèngzhì bìnàn
at PREP 1 在… (地方／时间) zài…(dìfang/shíjiān) 2 对 duì, 向 xiàng
atheist N 无神论者 wúshénlùnzhě
athletic ADJ 1 体育运动的 [+学校] tǐyù yùndòng de [+xuéxiào] 2 健壮的 [+青年], jiànzhuàng de [+qīngnián], 擅长体育的 shàncháng tǐyù de
athletics N 体育运动 tǐyù yùndòng

Atlantic Ocean N 大西洋 Dàxīyáng

atlas N 地图册 dìtúcè [M. WD 张 zhāng], 地图册 dìtúcè [M. WD 本 běn]

ATM (= Automated Teller Machine) AB-BREV 自动提款机 zìdòng tíkuǎnjī

atmosphere N 1 气氛 qìfen 2 大气 dàqì, 大气层 dàqìcéng

atom N 原子 yuánzǐ

atone V 赎罪 shúzuì, 弥补 [过失] míbǔ [+guòshī]

atrocious ADJ 坏极了的 huài jíle de, 糟透了的 zāotòu le de

attach V 附上 fùshàng
to be attached to 喜爱 xǐ'ài, 依恋 yīliàn

attaché N [大使馆的+] 随员 [dàshǐguǎn de+] suíyuán
a military attaché (大使馆的) 武官 (dàshǐguǎn de) wǔguān

attachment N 附件 fùjiàn

attack I V 攻击 gōngjī II N 1 攻击 gōngjī 2 (疾病) 发作 (jíbìng) fāzuò
heart attack 心脏病发作 xīnzàngbìng fāzuò

attain V 实现 shíxiàn, 获得 huòdé

attempt I V 试图 shìtú, 想要 xiǎngyào II N 试图 shìtú

attend V 出席 chūxí, 参加 cānjiā

attendance N 出席 chūxí, 出席人数 chūxí rénshù

attendant N 服务员 fúwùyuán
parking-lot attendant 停车场服务员 tíngchēchǎng fúwùyuán

attention N 注意 zhùyì
to pay attention to 注意 zhùyì, 留意 liúyì

attentive ADJ 关注的 [+老师] guānzhù de [+lǎoshī] 2 周到的 [+服务] zhōudao de [+fúwù]

attest V 证明 zhèngmíng

attic N 阁楼 gélóu [M. WD 层 céng]

attire N 服装 fúzhuāng

attitude N 态度 tàidu, 心态 xīntài

attorney N 律师 lǜshī
attorney general 首席检察官 shǒuxí jiǎncháguān [M. WD 位 wèi]

attraction N 吸引力 xīyǐnlì
tourist attraction 旅游点 lǚyóudiǎn

attractive ADJ 有吸引力的 yǒu xīyǐnlì de, 漂亮的 piàoliang de

attribute I V (to attribute to) 归因于 guīyīnyú II N 特性 tèxìng, 品质 pǐnzhì

attrition N 1 消耗 [+战] xiāohào [+zhàn] 2 [公司的+] 自然减员 [gōngsī de+] zìrán jiǎnyuán
natural attrition 自然缩减 zìrán suōjiǎn

attuned ADJ 适应的 shìyìng de

auburn N 红褐色 hóng hèsè

auction N, V 拍卖 pāimài
to put sth up for auction 把某物拿去拍卖 bǎ mǒuwù ná qù pāimài

auctioneer N 拍卖人 pāimài rén

audacious ADJ 大胆的 dàdǎn de, 鲁莽的 lǔmǎng de

audible ADJ 听得见的 tīngdé jiàn de

audience N [+电影] 观众 [+diànyǐng] guānzhòng, [音乐会+] 听众 [+yīnyuèhuì+] tīngzhòng

audio ADJ 音响的 yīnxiǎng de

audiotape N 录音磁带 lùyīn cídài

audiovisual ADJ 视听的 shìtīng de
audiovisual equipment 视听设备 shìtīng shèbèi

audit N, V 审计 shěnjì, 查账 cházhàng
to audit company accounts 审计公司账目 shěnjì gōngsī zhàngmù

audition N, V 试唱 shì chàng, 试演 shìyǎn
to audition for a musical 参加一处音乐剧的试演 cānjiā yíchù yīnyuè jù de shìyǎn

auditorium N 礼堂 lǐtáng

augment V 增加 zēngjiā, 扩大 kuòdà

August N 八月 bāyuè

aunt N 阿姨 āyí (mother's sister), 姑姑 gūgu (father's sister), 舅妈 jiùmā (maternal uncle's wife), 伯母 bómǔ (father's elder brother's wife), 婶婶 shěnshen (father's younger brother's wife)

auspices N 赞助 zànzhù
under the auspices of 由…赞助 yóu… zànzhù

auspicious ADJ 吉祥的 jíxiáng de, 吉利的 jílì de

austere ADJ 1 严厉的 yánlì de 2 简朴的 jiǎnpǔ de

austerity N [+经济上] 紧缩 [+jīngjìshang] jǐnsuō, 节省 jiéshěng

Australia N 澳大利亚 Àodàlìyà

authentic ADJ 1 正宗的 [+法国香槟酒] zhèngzōng de [+Fǎguó xiāngbīnjiǔ] 2 原作的 yuánzuò de, 真的 zhēnde
an authentic painting of Piccaso 一幅毕加索的原画 yìfú Bìjiāsuǒ de yuánhuà

authenticate V 1 鉴定…是真的 jiàndìng…shì zhēnde 2 证实 zhèngshí

authenticity N 真实性 zhēnshíxìng

author N 作者 zuòzhě

authoritative ADJ 权威性的 quánwēi xìng de

authority N 权威 quánwēi, 权力 quánlì
the authorities 当局 dāngjú

autism N 自闭症 zìbìzhèng

autobiography N 自传 zìzhuàn [M. WD 篇 piān/本 běn]

autocratic ADJ 独裁的 dúcái de, 专制的 zhuānzhì de

autograph I N [名人的+] 签名 [míngrén de+] qiānmíng II V 签名 qiānmíng

automatic I ADJ 自动的 zìdòng de, 自动化的 zìdònghuà de
automatic transmission 自动排档 zìdòng pái dàng
II N 自动变速汽车 zìdòng biànsù qìchē

automobile N 汽车 qìchē [M. WD 辆 liàng]
automobile industry 汽车工业 qìchē gōngyè

autonomous ADJ 自治的 zìzhì de

autonomy N 自治 zìzhì

autopsy N 尸体检验 shītǐ jiǎnyàn

autumn N 秋天 qiūtiān, 秋季 qiūjì

auxiliary ADJ 辅助的 fǔzhù de 2 备用的 bèiyòng de

avail V 有利于 yǒu lìyú
to avail oneself of 利用 lìyòng

available ADJ 能得到的 néng dédào de

avalanche N 雪崩 xuěbēng [M. WD 场 cháng]

avarice N 贪婪 tānlán, 贪心 tānxīn

avenue N 大街 dà jiē, 街 jiē [M. WD 条 tiáo]

average I ADJ 平均 píngjūn, 通常 tōngcháng II N 平均数 píngjūnshù, 一般水平 yìbān shuǐpíng III V 平均是 píngjūn shì

averse ADJ 厌恶 yànwù, 很不喜欢 hěn bù xǐhuan

avert V 避免 bìmiǎn, 防止 fángzhǐ

aviation N 避免 bìmiǎn, 防止 fángzhǐ

aviator N 飞行员 fēixíngyuán

avid ADJ 热心的 rèxīn de, 狂热的 kuángrè de

avocado N 鳄梨 èlí

avoid V 避免 bìmiǎn

avow V 公开承认 gōngkāi chéngrèn, 声明 shēngmíng

awake I V (PT awoke; PP awaken) 叫醒 jiàoxǐng II ADJ 醒着 xǐngzhe

awaken¹ V 1 叫醒 jiàoxǐng 2 唤醒 huànxǐng

awaken² See **awake**

awakening N 觉醒 juéxǐng

award I N 1 奖 jiǎng, 奖章 jiǎngzhāng [M. WD 枚 méi] 2 奖金 jiǎngjīn [M. WD 笔 bǐ] II V 授奖 shòujiǎng, 颁奖 bānjiǎng

aware ADJ 意识到 yìshìdào, 知道 zhīdào

awareness N 意识 yìshi, 认识 rènshi

awash ADJ 充斥的 chōngchì de, 泛滥的 fànlàn de

away ADV 1 离开 líkāi
Go away! 走开! Zǒukāi! 滚! Gǔn! 2 不在 (家，办公室) bú zài (jiā, bàngōngshì)
to put sth away 把…收起来 bǎ…shōuqǐlai

awe N 敬畏 jìngwèi, 畏惧 wèijù

awesome ADJ 1 令人敬畏的 [+高山] lìngrén jìngwèi de [+gāoshān] 2 好极了 hǎo jí le

awful I ADJ 1 坏极了 huài jíle, 糟透了 zāotòu le II 糟糕透了的 zāogāo tòu le 2 非常 fēicháng

awfully ADV 非常 fēicháng

awhile ADV 一会儿 yíhuìr

awkward ADJ 1 笨拙的 [+男孩] bènzhuō de [+nánhái], 不灵活 bùlínghuó 2 尴尬的 [+场面] gāngà de [+chǎngmiàn]

awning N 遮蓬 zhēpéng, 雨蓬 yǔpéng

awoke See **awake**

awry ADJ 歪的 wāi de, 斜的 xié de
to go awry 出岔子 chūchàzi

ax I N 斧头 fǔtou [M. WD 把 bǎ]
to get the ax 解雇 jiěgù, 砍掉 kǎndiào

to have an ax to grind 抱有个人目的 bàoyǒu gèrén mùdì
II v 解雇 jiěgù, 砍掉 kǎndiào
axis N 轴 zhóu, 轴线 zhóuxiàn
axle N 车轴 chēzhóu
aye INTERJ 是 shì, 赞成 zànchéng

B

babble v 1 [婴儿+] 牙牙学语 [yīng'ér+] yáyáxuéyǔ 2 [老太太+] 喋喋不休 [lǎotàitai+] diédié bùxiū
babe N 婴儿 yīng'ér
baby N 1 婴儿 yīng'ér, 小宝宝 xiǎobǎobao 2 (男子对心爱的女人) 宝贝 (nánzǐ duìxīn ài de nǚrén) bǎobèi
baby carriage 童车 tóngchē
baby talk 幼儿语 yòu'ér yǔ
baby boomer N 生育高峰期出生的人 shēngyù gāofēngqī chūshēng de rén, 1948–64年出生的人 1948–64 nián chūshēng de rén
babysat See **babysit**
babysit (PT & PP **babysat**) v 照看小孩 zhàokàn xiǎohái
bachelor N 单身男子 dānshēn nánzǐ, 未婚男子 wèihūn nánzǐ
bachelor party 单身汉聚会 dānshēnhàn jùhuì
back I N 背 bèi, 背部 bèibù II ADJ 背后 bèihòu, 后面 hòumian III ADV 1 后面 hòumian
Step back! 往后退! Wàng hòu tuì!
2 回 huí, 原处 yuánchù
behind one's back 瞒着… mánzhe…
back and forth 来来回回 láilái huíhuí
backache N 腰酸背疼 yāosuān bèiténg
backbone N 1 脊柱 jǐzhù 2 骨干 gǔgàn
backbreaking ADJ 艰苦繁重的 [+体力劳动] jiānkǔ fánzhòng de [+ tǐlì láodòng]
backdate v 1 写上比实际时间早的日期 xiě shàng bǐ shíjì shíjiān zǎo de rìqī 2 追溯到 zhuīsù dào
backdrop N 背景 bèijǐng
backfire v 1 [汽车引擎+] 逆火 [qìchē yǐnqíng+] nìhuǒ 2 [计划+] 发生意外 [jìhuà+] fāshēng yìwài, 产生与预料相

反的效果 chǎnshēng yǔ yùjì xiāngfǎn de xiàoguǒ
backgammon N 十五子棋 shíwǔ zi qí [M. WD 盘 pán/副 fù]
background N 背景 bèijǐng
backhanded ADJ 1 反手的 [+击球] fǎnshǒu de [+jīqiú] 2 讽刺挖苦的 [+赞扬] fěngcì wākǔ de [+zànyáng], 反话的 fǎnhuà de
a backhanded compliment 挖苦的恭维话 wākǔ de gōngweihuà
backing N 1 支持 zhīchí 2 后退 hòutuì
backlash N 反弹 fǎntán, 强烈反对 qiángliè fǎnduì
backlog N 积压（的工作）jīyā (de gōngzuò)
a backlog of criminal cases 积压的刑事案件 jīyā de xíngshì ànjiàn
backpack N 背包 bēibāo [M. WD 只 zhī]
backseat N 后座 hòu zuò
to take a back seat 接受次要的地位 jiēshòu cìyào de dìwèi
backside N 屁股 pìgǔ
backstage ADV 在后台 zàihòu tái, 往后台 wǎnghòu tái
backtrack v 1 原路返回 yuánlù fǎnhuí 2 退缩 tuìsuō
backup N 1 备份 bèifèn, 备用品 bèiyòng pǐn
backup generator 备用发电机 bèiyòng fādiànjī
2 后备人员 hòubèi rényuán
backward I ADJ 1 向后的 xiànghòu de 2 落后的 [+地区] luòhòude [+dìqū]
II ADV 向后 xiànghòu
backwater N 1 闭塞的地方 bìsè de dìfang 2 [小河的+] 死水 [xiǎo hé de+] sǐshuǐ
backyard N 后院 hòuyuàn
bacon N 咸肉 xiánròu
to bring home the bacon 挣钱养家 zhèngqián yǎngjiā
bacteria N 细菌 xìjūn
bad ADJ 1 坏 huài, 糟糕 zāogāo, 不行 bùxíng
That's too bad! 那太糟了! Nà tài zāo le!
to feel bad about 感到很不开心 gǎndào hěn bù kāixīn
2 有害 yǒuhài

badge N 徽章 huīzhāng [M. WD 枚 méi]

badly ADV 1 很不好 hěn bùhǎo, 很糟 hěn zāo 2 极其 jíqí, 非常 fēicháng

badminton N 羽毛球运动 yǔmáoqiú yùndòng

badmouth v 说…坏话 shuō...huàihuà

baffled ADJ 被难住了 bèinàn zhù le, 感到困惑不解 gǎndào kùnhuò bùjiě

bag N 包 bāo, 袋 dài
bag lady 无家可归的女人 wú jiā kě guī de nǚrén
school bag 书包 shūbāo

bagel N 圆形硬面包 yuánxíng yìng miànbāo [M. WD 块 kuài]

bagful N 一袋的 yí dài de

baggage N 行李 xínglǐ [M. WD 件 jiàn]
baggage car 火车的行李车 huǒchē de xínglǐchē
baggage room 行李寄存处 xínglǐ jìcúnchù

bail I N 保释金 bǎoshìjīn [M. WD 笔 bǐ]
to stand bail 交保释金 jiāobǎo shì jīn
II v 1 保释 bǎoshì 2 脱身 tuōshēn
to bail out 帮助 [+厂商] 脱离经济困境 bāngzhù [+chǎng shāng] tuōlí jīngjì kùnjìng

bait I N 诱饵 yòu'ěr
to take the bait 受诱惑上当 shòu yòuhuò shàngdàng
II v 装上诱饵 zhuāngshàng yòu'ěr

bake v 烤 [+牛肉] kǎo [+niúròu], 烘 [+面包] hōng [+miànbāo]
bake sale 糕点义卖 gāodiǎn yìmài

baker N 面包师 miànbāoshī, 糕点师傅 gāodiǎn shīfu

balance I N 平衡 pínghéng
balance of international payments 国际收支平衡 guójì shōuzhī pínghéng
balance sheet 资产负债表 zīchǎn fùzhàibiǎo, 决算表 juésuànbiǎo
II v 掂量 diānliang, 权衡 quánhéng

balanced ADJ 平衡的 pínghéng de, 均衡的 jūnhéng de
balanced diet 均衡饮食 jūnhéng yǐnshí

balcony N 阳台 yángtái

bald ADJ 秃的 tū de, 秃头的 [+男人] tūtóu de [+nánren]

baleful ADJ 邪恶的 [+意图] xié'è de [+yìtú], 阴毒的 [+目光] yīndú de [+mùguāng]

ball[1] N [打+] 球 [dǎ+] qiú [M. WD 只 zhī]
ball game 球赛 qiúsài
ball park 球场 qiúchǎng

ball[2] N 舞会 wǔhuì [M. WD 次 cì/场 cháng]
to open the ball 带头跳第一场舞 dàitóu tiào dì yì cháng wǔ

ballad N 歌谣 gēyáo [M. WD 首 shǒu]

ballerina N 芭蕾舞女演员 bālěiwǔ nǚyǎnyuán

ballet N 芭蕾舞 bālěiwǔ

balloon N 气球 qìqiú [M. WD 只 zhī]
hot air balloon 热气球 rèqìqiú

ballot N 选票 xuǎnpiào [M. WD 张 zhāng]
ballot box 投票箱 tóupiàoxiāng

ballpoint pen N 圆珠笔 yuánzhūbǐ

ballroom N 舞厅 wǔtīng
ballroom dancing 交谊舞 jiāoyìwǔ, 交际舞 jiāojìwǔ

balm N（镇痛）油膏 (zhèntòng) yóugāo [M. WD 盒 hé]

bamboo N 竹 zhú, 竹子 zhúzi

ban v 禁止 [+非法交易] jìnzhǐ [+fēifǎ jiāoyì]

banal ADJ 陈腐的 chénfǔ de, 乏味的 fáwèi de, 没有特色的 méiyǒu tèsè de

banana N 香蕉 xiāngjiāo [M. WD 根 gēn]

band I N 1 带子 dàizi [M. WD 条 tiáo]
rubber band 橡皮筋 xiàngpíjīn
2 群 qún
a band of wild dogs 一群野狗 yìqún yěgǒu
3 乐队 yuèduì
bandstand 乐池 yuèchí
II v 聚集 jùjí

bandage I N 绷带 bēngdài [M. WD 条 tiáo/卷 juàn] II v 用绷带扎 yòng bēngdài bāozā

bandit N 土匪 tǔfěi, 匪徒 fěitú

bandwagon N 1 乐队彩车 yuèduì cǎichē 2 得势的一派 déshì de yīpài
to jump on the bandwagon 投入得势的一派 tóurù déshì de yípài, 赶浪头 gǎn làngtou

bane N 灾星 zāixīng, 祸根 huògēn
more of a bane than a boom 与其说

是福音，还不如说是祸根 yǔqí shuō shì fúyīn, hái bùrú shuō shì huògēn

bang I v 发出砰的一声 fāchū pēng de yìshēng II N 1 砰的一声 pēng de yìshēng 2 一声巨响 yì shēng jùxiǎng

banish v 把 [+政治犯] 流放 bǎ [+zhèng-zhìfàn] liúfàng

banister N [楼梯的+] 扶手 [lóutī de+] fúshou, 栏杆 lángān

bank[1] I N 1 银行 yínháng [M. WD 家 jiā]
bank account 银行账户 yínháng zhànghù
data bank 资料库 zīliàokù
II v 把钱存入银行 bǎ qián cún rù yínháng

bank[2] N 岸 àn, 河岸 hé'àn, 湖岸 hú'àn

banker N 银行家 yínhángjiā, 银行高级职员 yínháng gāojí zhíyuán [M. WD 位 wèi]

bankrupt ADJ 破产的 [+商人] pòchǎn de [+shāngrén]

banner N 旗 qí, 旗帜 qízhì
banner headline 通栏大标题 tōnglán dà biāotí

banquet N 宴会 yànhuì [M. WD 次 cì]

banter N 善意的取笑 shànyì de qǔxiào

baptism N 洗礼 xǐlǐ, 浸礼 jìnlǐ

Baptist N 浸礼会教友 jìnlǐhuì jiàoyǒu

bar I N 1 酒吧 jiǔbā, 酒吧间 jiǔbājiān [M. WD 家 jiā] 2 块 kuài
a bar of chocolate 一块巧克力 yí kuài qiǎokèlì
3 线条 xiàntiáo, 条纹 tiáowén
bar code 条形码 tiáoxíngmǎ
II v 阻挡 zǔdǎng

barbaric ADJ 野蛮的 [+部落] yěmán de [+bùluò]

barbecue, BBQ N 烧烤野餐 shāokǎo yěcān

barbed ADJ 有倒勾的 yǒu dǎo gōu de, 有倒刺的 yǒu dàocì de
barbed wire 有刺铁丝网 yǒucì tiěsīwǎng

barber N 理发师 lǐfàshī

bare I ADJ 赤裸 chìluǒ, 不穿衣服的 bù chuān yīfu de II v 露出 lòuchu

bareback ADJ [骑马+] 不用鞍具的 [qímǎ+] búyòng ānjù de

bare-bone ADJ 少到不能再少的 shǎo dào bùnéng zài zài de

bare-foot ADJ 赤脚的 chìjiǎo de

barely ADV 勉强 miǎnqiǎng

bargain I N 1 便宜货 piányíhuò [M. WD 件 jiàn] II v 讨价还价 tǎojià huánjià

barge I N 大型平底船 dàxíng píngdǐchuán, 驳船 bóchuán [M. WD 艘 sōu] II v 冲撞 chōngzhuàng

bark I N v (狗) 叫 (gǒu) jiào, 汪汪叫 wāngwāng jiào II N 狗叫声 gǒujiào, 狗叫声 gǒujiào shēng

barley N 大麦 dàmài

barn N 谷仓 gǔcāng, 粮仓 liángcāng [M. WD 座 zuò]

barometer N 气压表 qìyābiǎo, 气压计 qìyājì, 晴雨表 qíngyǔbiǎo

barracks N 营房 yíngfáng [M. WD 座 zuò]

barrage N 1 火力网 huǒlìwǎng 2 连珠炮似的问题 liánzhūpào shìde wèntí

barrel I N 桶 tǒng II v 装桶 zhuāng tǒng

barren ADJ 1 贫瘠的 [+土地] pínjí de [+tǔdì] 2 不生育的 [+妇女] bù shēngyù de [+fùnǚ]
a barren mine 贫化矿 pínhuà kuàng

barricade I N 路障 lùzhàng, 街垒 jiēlěi II v 设置路障 shèzhì lùzhàng

barrier N 屏障 píngzhàng, 障碍物 zhàng'àiwù

barring PREP 除了 [+意外情况] 以外 chú le [+yìwài qíngkuàng] yǐwài

bartender N 酒吧间服务员 jiǔbājiān fúwùyuán [M. WD 位 wèi]

barter I v 做易货贸易 zuò yìhuò màoyì, 以货易货 yǐ huò yì huò II N 易货贸易 yìhuò màoyì

base I N 1 底部 dǐbù, 基础 jīchǔ 2 基地 jīdì
military base 军事基地 jūnshì jīdì
II v 基于 jīyú, 以…为基础 yǐ...wéi jīchǔ

baseball N 棒球 bàngqiú

basement N 地下室 dìxiàshì

bash I v 打 dǎ, 痛打 tòngdǎ II N 猛击 měngjī

bashful ADJ 害羞的 [+女孩] hàixiū de [+nǚ hái]

basic ADJ 基本的 [+问题] jīběn de [+wèntí]

basin N 1 盆 pén 2 水池 shuǐchí 3 盆地 péndì

basis N 基础 jīchǔ

bask v 晒太阳 shài tàiyáng

basket N 篮 lán, 篮子 lánzi [M. WD 只 zhī]
Don't put all your eggs in one basket. 不要把所有的鸡蛋都放在一个篮子里。(→ 不要把一切希望都寄托在一件事情上。) Bú yào bǎ suǒyǒu de jīdàn dōu fàng zài yí ge lánzi lǐ. (→ Bú yào bǎ yíqiè xīwàng dōu jìtuō zài yí jiàn shìqingshang.)

basketball N 篮球 lánqiú
basketball court 篮球场 lánqiúchǎng

basketcase N 1 失去行动能力的人 shīqù xíngdòng nénglì de rén 2 精神崩溃的人 jīngshén bēngkuì de rén

bass I N 1 [音乐+] 低音 [yīnyuè+] dīyīn 2 男低音 nándīyīn II ADJ [音乐+] 低音的 [yīnyuè+] dīyīn de

bastard N 1 私生子 sīshēngzǐ 2 混蛋 húndàn, 王八蛋 wángbādàn

bat[1] N 蝙蝠 biānfú [M. WD 只 zhī]

bat[2] I N 球棒 qiúbàng [M. WD 根 gēn]
at bat (棒球) 轮到击球 (bàngqiú) lúndào jīqiú
II v 1 用棒击 yòng bàng jī 2 当 (棒球) 投球手 dāng (bàngqiú) tóuqiúshǒu

batch N [一+] 批 [yì+] pī, [一+] 捆 [yì+] kǔn

bated ADJ 抑制 yìzhì
with bated breath 屏息 bǐngxī, 不敢大声出气 bùgǎn dàshēng chūqì

bath N 1 洗澡 xǐ zǎo 2 洗澡水 xǐ zǎo shuǐ
Don't throw out the baby with the bathwater. 不要把婴儿连同洗澡水一起倒掉。Bú yào bǎ yīng'ér liántóng xǐzǎo shuǐ yìqǐ dàodiào. (→ 不要把珍贵的东西跟废物一起扔掉。Bú yào bǎ zhēnguì de dōngxi gēn fèiwù yìqǐ rēngdiào.)

bathe v 1 洗澡 xǐzǎo 2 沐浴 mùyù

bathrobe N 浴衣 yùyī [M. WD 件 jiàn]

bathroom N 浴室 yùshì, 洗澡间 xǐzǎojiān

bathtub N 浴缸 yùgāng

baton N 指挥棒 zhǐhuībàng

battalion N 营 yíng
battalion commander 营长 yíngzhǎng

batter I N [面粉、鸡蛋、牛奶调成的+] 面糊 [miànfěn, jīdàn, niúnǎi tiáo chéng de+] miànhú II v 连续猛打 liánxù měngdǎ

battery N 电池 diànchí

battle N, v 战斗 zhàndòu, 斗争 dòuzhēng

battleground N 战场 zhànchǎng

bawdy ADJ 猥亵的 [+笑话] wěixiè de [+xiàohua], 下流的 [+故事] xiàliú de [+gùshi]

bawl v 粗野地喊叫 cūyě de hǎnjiào, 咆哮 páoxiào

bay N 海湾 hǎiwān

bayonet N [枪上的+] 刺刀 [qiāng shàng de+] cìdāo

bazaar N 市场 shìchǎng, 集市 jíshì

B.C. (= Before Christ) ABBREV 公元前 gōngyuánqián, 元前 yuán qian

be (am, are, is; PT was, were; PP been) [NEG is not/isn't; are not/aren't; was not/wasn't; were not/weren't] I v 1 (used with complement) 是 shì 2 (asking about time/age/location) 3 (talking about daily occurrences) 4 (exist, happen, etc) 5 (price, cost) II AUX v 1 (used with continuous tenses) 2 (with to-infinitive verbs) 3 (with passive verbs) 4 (with question endings)

beach N 沙滩 shātān, 海滩 hǎitān
beach ball 浮水气球 fúshuǐ qìqiú

beacon N 指路明灯 zhǐlùmíngdēng, 灯标 dēngbiāo

bead N 珠子 zhūzi
a string of beads 一串珠子 yíchuàn zhūzi

beak N 鸟嘴 niǎozuǐ

beaker N 1 烧杯 shāobēi 2 大酒杯 dà jiǔbēi

beam I N 1 (房) 梁 (fáng) liáng 2 光线 guāngxiàn 3 笑容 xiàoróng, 喜色 xǐsè
with a beam of welcome 喜笑颜开地欢迎 xǐxiào yánkāi de huānyíng
II v 1 发射出光芒 (或热量) fāshè chū guāngmáng (huò rèliàng) 2 喜笑颜开 xǐxiào yánkāi

bean N 豆 dòu [M. WD 棵 kē/粒 lì]
coffee beans 咖啡豆 kāfēi dòu
to spill the beans 无意中泄露秘密 wúyìzhōng xièlòu mìmì

bear[1] (PT bore; PP borne) v 1 忍受 rěnshòu

to bear with 容忍 róngrěn, 宽容 kuānróng

2 生 shēng, 产 chǎn, 结（果）jié (guǒ)

to bear out 证明 zhèngmíng, 证实 zhèngshí

to bear a baby boy 生一个男孩 shēng yí ge nánhái

3 携带 xiédài

bear² N 熊 xióng [M. WD 头 tóu/只 zhī]

bear market 熊市 xióng shì

grizzly bear 大灰熊 dà huī xióng

bearable ADJ 可以忍受的 kěyǐ rěnshòu de

beard N 胡子 húzi, 胡须 húxū

bearer N **1** 携带者 xiédàizhě **2** 抬棺人 tái guān rén

bearing N 举止 jǔzhǐ

bearish ADJ **1** 像熊一样的 xiàng xióng yíyàng de, 粗鲁的 cūlǔ de, 笨拙的 bènzhuō de **2** 熊市的 xióng shì de, 行情下跌的 hángqíng xiàdiē de

beast N **1** 野兽 yěshòu, 畜牲 chùshēng **2** 叫人讨厌的人（或物）jiào rén tǎoyàn de rén (huò wù)

beat (PT beat; PP beaten) V **1** 打败 dǎbài **2** 打 dǎ

Beat it! 滚开! Gǔnkāi

beaten See **beat**

beater N 搅拌器 jiǎobànqì

egg beater 打蛋器 dǎdànqì

beautician N 美容师 měiróngshī

beautiful ADJ 美丽的 měilì de, 美的 měi de

beauty N **1** 美 měi, 美丽 měilì **2** 美人 měirén **3** 美丽的东西 měilì de dōngxi

beauty salon 美容院 měiróngyuàn

beaver N 海狸 hǎilí [M. WD 只 zhī]

became See **become**

because CONJ 因为 yīnwèi

become (PT became; PP become) V 成为 chéngwéi, 变成 biànchéng

bed I N 床 chuáng [M. WD 张 zhāng]

to go to bed 上床睡觉 shàngchuáng shuìjiào

II V 安置 ānzhì

bed and board N 伙食和住宿 huǒshí hé zhùsù, 食宿 shísù

bedclothes N 床上用品 chuáng shàng yòngpǐn

bedlam N 吵吵闹闹的地方（或活动）chǎochǎo nàonào de dìfang (huò huódòng)

bedraggled ADJ 凌乱不堪的 [+衣服和头发] língluànbùkān de [+yīfu hé tóufa]

bedridden ADJ [因生病或年老+] 卧床不起的 [yīn shēngbìng huò niánlǎo+] wòchuáng bùqǐ de

bedroom N 卧室 wòshì, 睡房 shuìfáng [M. WD 间 jiān]

bedside N 床边 chuáng biān

bedside lamp 床头灯 chuángtóudēng

bedside table 床头柜 chuángtóuguì

bedtime N 睡觉时间 shuìjiào shíjiān

bee N 蜜蜂 mìfēng [M. WD 只 zhī]

to have a bee in one's bonnet 老是想着一件事 lǎo shì xiǎngzhe yí jiàn shì

beef I N 牛肉 niúròu II V 发牢骚 fāláosāo

beefy ADJ 身材粗壮的 shēncái cūzhuàng de

beehive N 蜂窝 fēngwō

beeline N 直线 zhíxiàn

to make a beeline for 朝…直奔过去 cháo…zhíbēn guòqù

beep V 发出嘟嘟声 fāchū dūdū shēng

beer N 啤酒 píjiǔ [M. WD 瓶 píng/罐 guàn/杯 bēi]

beer belly 啤酒肚 píjiǔ dù, 大肚子 dàdùzi

beet N 甜菜 tiáncài [M. WD 棵 kē]

beetle N 甲壳虫 jiǎqiàochóng

before CONJ, PREP 在…以前 zài…yǐqián II ADV 以前 yǐqián

beforehand ADV 事先 shìxiān, 预先 yùxiān

befriend V 友好对待 yǒuhǎo duìdài

beg V **1** 讨 tǎo, 乞讨 qǐtǎo **2** 乞求 qǐqiú, 苦苦哀求 kǔkǔ āiqiú

I beg your pardon. ① 对不起 duìbuqǐ ② 对不起，您说什么? Duìbuqǐ, nín shuō shénme?

began See **begin**

beggar N 乞丐 qǐgài, 叫花子 jiàohuāzi

begin (PT began; PP begun) V 开始 kāishǐ

beginning N 开始 kāishǐ, 开始的时候 kāishǐ de shíhou

begrudge v 不情愿 bùqíngyuàn, 不情愿给 bùqíngyuàn gěi

beguile v 欺骗 qīpiàn, 诱骗 yòupiàn

begun See begin

behalf N (in/on behalf of) 代表 dàibiǎo, 代表…的利益 dàibiǎo…de lìyì

behave v 举止 jǔzhǐ, 行为 xíngwéi
Behave yourself! 规矩点! Guījù diǎn!

behavior N 行为 xíngwéi, 举止 jǔzhǐ
to be on one's best behavior 行为规规矩矩 xíngwéi guīguī jǔjū

beheld See behold

behind I PREP 1 在…后面 zài…hòumian 2 落后 luòhòu 3 支持 zhīchí II ADV 在后面 zàihòumiàn
to leave behind 把…留在 bǎ…liú zài, 留下 liúxià
III N 臀部 túnbù

behold (PT & PP **beheld**) v 目睹 mùdǔ, 看到 kàndào

beige N 米黄色 mǐhuángsè

being N 1 存在 cúnzài
to come into being 开始存在 kāishǐ cúnzài, 形成 xíngchéng
2 生命 shēngmìng
human being 人 rén, 人类 rénlèi

belated ADJ 被耽误的 bèi dānwù de, 迟到的 [+祝贺] chídào de [+zhùhè]

belch v 打嗝 dǎ gé

belief N 1 相信 xiāngxìn, 信心 xìnxīn 2（宗教）信仰（zōngjiào）xìnyǎng

believable ADJ 可以相信的 kěyǐ xiāngxìn de

believe v 相信 xiāngxìn
Believe it or not! 信不信由你! Xìn bú xìn yóu nǐ!
to believe in 信任 xìnrèn, 信仰 xìnyǎng

believer N 信徒 xìntú

belittle v 轻视 qīngshì, 贬低 biǎndī

bell N 铃 líng, 钟 zhōng

belligerent ADJ 怒气冲冲准备打架的 nùqì chōngchōng zhǔnbèi dǎjià de, 好斗的 hǎo dǒu de

bellow N [公牛+] 吼叫 [gōngniú+] hǒujiào

belly N 肚子 dùzi, 肚皮 dùpí
belly button 肚脐眼 dùqíyǎn

belong v 属于 shǔyú

belongings N 个人物件 gèrén wùjiàn, 财物 cáiwù, 动产 dòngchǎn

beloved ADJ 亲爱的 qīn'ài de, 受到爱戴的 shòudào àidài de

below I PREP 1 在…下面 zài…xiàmian 2 在…以下 zài…yǐxià II ADV 在下面 zài xiàmian

belt N 带 dài, 皮带 pídài [M. WD 条 tiáo]
to hit below the belt 用不正当手段攻击 yòng búzhèngdāng shǒuduàn gōngjī
to tighten the belt 勒紧裤带 lēijǐnkùdài, 紧缩开支 jǐnsuō kāizhī

bench N 长椅 cháng yǐ, 长凳 chángdèng

benchmark N 基准 jīzhǔn

bend I v (PT & PP **bent**) 弯曲 wānqū
II N 弯曲形 wānqū xíng, [道路+] 转弯 [dàolù+] zhuǎnwān

beneath I PREP 在…下方 zài…xiàfāng II ADV 在下面 zàixià miàn

benediction N 祝福 zhùfú, 祝祷 zhùdǎo

benefactor N 捐助人 juānzhù rén, 赞助人 zànzhùrén

beneficial ADJ 有益的 yǒuyì de, 有利的 yǒulì de
to be beneficial to 对…有益 duì…yǒuyì, 对…有利 duì…yǒulì

beneficiary N 受益者 shòuyìzhě

benefit I v 对…有利 duì…yǒulì II N 利益 lìyì, 好处 hǎochu
benefit of the doubt（在证据不足的情况下）假定无罪 (zài zhèngjù bùzú de qíngkuàng xià) jiǎdìng wúzuì, 暂时相信 zànshí xiāngxìn

benevolent ADJ 仁慈的 réncí de, 善良的 shànliáng de

benign ADJ 仁爱的 rén'ài de
benign tumor 良性肿瘤 liángxìng-zhǒngliú

bent¹ See bend

bent² I ADJ 1 弯曲的 wānqū de 2 决意的 juéyì de II N 爱好 àihào, 天生的才能 tiānshēng de cáinéng
a bent for music 音乐天赋 yīnyuè tiānfù

bequeath v 遗赠给 yízèng gěi

bequest N 遗留 yíliú, 遗产 yíchǎn
a bequest of $750,000 一笔七十五万

美元的遗产 yìbǐ qīshíwǔwàn Měiyuán de yíchǎn

berate v 训斥 xùnchì, 痛骂 tòngmà

bereaved ADJ 丧失亲人的 sàngshī qīnrén de

a bereaved mother 失去孩子的母亲 shīqù háizi de mǔqin

bereft ADJ **1** 丧失了亲人的 sàngshī le qīnrén de **2** 缺乏的 quēfá de

berry N 浆果 jiāngguǒ

berserk ADJ 狂怒的 kuángnù de

to go berserk 变得狂怒 biàn de kuángnù, [气得+] 发疯 [qì dé+] fāfēng

berth N **1** 停泊位 tíngbó wèi, 锚地 máodì **2** 卧铺 wòpù

beset (PT & PP **beset**) v 不断困扰 búduàn kùnrǎo

to be beset with difficulties 困难重重 kùnnan chóngchóng

beside PREP 在…旁边 zài…pángbiān

besides I PREP 除了 chúle II ADV 而且 érqiě

besiege v 围困 wéikùn

best I ADJ 最好的 zuìhǎo de

best man 男傧相 nánbīnxiàng

II ADV 最好地 zuìhǎo de

as best as one can 尽可能 jìnkěnéng

III N 最好的人（或事）zuìhǎo de rén (huò shì)

All the best! 祝你万事如意! Zhù nǐ wànshì rúyì!

bestial ADJ 像禽兽一样的 xiàng qínshòu yíyàng de, 极其残忍的 jíqí cánrěn de

bestow v 给予 jǐyǔ, 授予 [+名誉学位] shòuyǔ [+míngyù xuéwèi]

bestseller N 畅销书 chàngxiāoshū, 畅销货 chàngxiāohuò

bet (PT & PP **bet**) v（打）赌（dǎ）dǔ

betray v 背叛 [+朋友] bèipàn [+péngyou]

better I ADJ 比较好 bǐjiào hǎo, 更好 gènghǎo

one's better half 妻子（或丈夫）qīzi (huò zhàngfu)

Better late than never. 晚做比不做好。Wǎn zuò bǐ bú zuò hǎo.

II N 比较好的人（或事）bǐjiào hǎode (rén huò shì)

a change for the better 好转 hǎozhuǎn

between I PREP 在…之间 zài…zhījiān II ADV 在中间 zài zhōngjiān

beverage N 饮料 [+茶、咖啡等] yǐnliào [+chá, kāfēi děng] [M. WD 杯 bēi]

beware v 谨防 [+骗子] jǐnfáng [+piànzi]

Beware of pickpockets. 谨防扒手。Jǐnfáng páshǒu.

bewilder v 使迷惑 shǐ míhuo, 使糊涂 shǐ hútu

bewitch ADJ 施魔力 shǐ mólì, 使着迷 shǐzháo mí

beyond I PREP 在 [+大墙以外] zài [+dà qiáng yǐwài] II ADV 更远 gèng yuǎn, 再往前 zài wǎngqián

biased ADJ 偏袒的 piāntǎn de, 有偏见的 yǒupiān jiàn de

bib N 围嘴 wéi zuǐ

Bible N 圣经 Shèngjīng [M. WD 本 běn]

bibliography N 书目 shūmù, 参考书目 cānkǎo shūmù [M. WD 份 fèn]

bicker v 吵嘴 chǎozuǐ, 口角 kǒujué

bicycle I N 自行车 zìxíngchē [M. WD 辆 liàng] II v 骑自行车 qí zìxíngchē

bid I N **1** 出价 chūjià

a bid for \$200 for the antique chair 出价两百元买一把古董椅子 chūjià liǎngbǎi yuán mǎi yì bǎ gǔdǒng yǐzi

2 投标 tóubiāo II v (PT & PP **bid**) **1** 出价 chūjià

to bid \$200 for the antique chair 出价两百元买一把古董椅子 chūjià liǎngbǎi yuán mǎi yì bǎ gǔdǒng yǐzi

2 叫牌 jiàopái

bide v 等待 děngdài

to bide one's time 等待机会 děngdài jīhuì

biennial ADJ 两年一次的 liǎng nián yícì de

bifocals N 双光眼镜 shuāngguāng yǎnjìng [M. WD 副 fù]

big ADJ 大 dà

big mouth 多嘴多舌的人 duō zuǐ duō shé de rén

big name 大名鼎鼎的人 dàmíng dǐngdǐng de rén

bigamy N 重婚（罪）chónghūn (zuì)

bighead N 妄自尊大的人 wàng zì zūn dà de rén

bigot N 盲从的人 mángcóng de rén, 偏执的人 piānzhí de rén

bike I N 1 自行车 qí zìxíngchē [M. WD 辆 liàng], 摩托车 qí mótuōchē [M. WD 辆 liàng] II V 骑自行车 qí zìxíngchē, 骑摩托车 qí mótuōchē

bikini N 比基尼游泳服 Bǐjīní yóuyǒng fú [M. WD 件 jiàn], 三点式泳装 sāndiǎnshì yǒngzhuāng [M. WD 件 jiàn]

bilateral ADJ 双边的 shuāngbiān de

bile N 1 胆汁 dǎnzhī 2 坏脾气 huài píqi

bilingual ADJ 1 双语的 shuāngyǔ de [+儿童] shuāngyǔ de [+értóng] 2 会两种语言的 huì liǎng zhǒng yǔyán de
a bilingual dictionary 双语词典 shuāngyǔ cídiǎn

bill I N 1 账单 zhàngdān [M. WD 张 zhāng] to foot the bill 负担费用 fùdān fèiyòng, 付款 fùkuǎn
2 钞票 chāopiào [M. WD 张 zhāng] 3 法案 fǎ'àn, 议案 yì'àn [M. WD 件 jiàn] II V 给···帐单 gěi···zhàngdān

billboard N 广告牌 guǎnggàopái

billfold N 皮夹子 píjiāzi [M. WD 只 zhī], 钱包 qiánbāo [M. WD 只 zhī]

billiards N 桌球 zhuōqiú, 台球 táiqiú

billion N 十亿 shíyì

billow N 巨浪 jùlàng

bimonthly I ADJ 1 两个月一次的 liǎng gè yuè yícì de, 双月的 shuāngyuè de II N 双月刊 shuāngyuèkān

bin N 大箱子 dà xiāngzi

binary ADJ 由两部分组成的 yóu liǎng bù fēnzǔ chéng de, 双重的 shuāngchóng de

bind I V (PT & PP **bound**) 1 捆绑 [+受害人] kǔnbǎng [+shòuhàirén] 2 [条约+] 约束 [tiáoyuē+] yuēshù II N 困境 kùnjìng
in a bind 处于困境 chǔyú kùnjìng

binder N 1 装订机 zhuāngdìngjī 2 装订工 zhuāngdìng gōng 3 活页夹 huóyèjiā
four-ring binder 四眼活页夹 sì yǎn huóyèjiā

binding I ADJ 1 粘合的 zhānhé de 2 有约束力的 [+合同] yǒu yuēshùlì de [+hétong] II N 1 [书的+] 封面 [shū de+] fēngmiàn 2 镶边 xiāngbiān

binge N 1 狂饮 kuángyǐn 2 狂热行为 kuángrè xíngwéi
shopping binge 疯狂大采购 fēngkuáng dà cǎigòu

bingo N 宾戈（游戏）bīngē (yóuxì)
Bingo! 你瞧！Nǐ qiáo! 嘿！Hēi!

binoculars N 望远镜 wàngyuǎnjìng [M. WD 副 fù]

biochemistry N 生物化学 shēngwù huàxué, 生化 shēnghuà

biodegradable ADJ 会自然分解的 huì zìrán fēnjiě de, 会腐烂的 huì fǔlàn de

biography N 传记 zhuànjì [M. WD 本 běn]

biological ADJ 生物的 shēngwù de
biological warfare 生物战 shēngwùzhàn

biology N 生物学 shēngwùxué

biopic N 传记电影 zhuànjì diànyǐng, 传记片 zhuànjìpiàn [M. WD 部 bù]

biopsy N 活体组织检查 huótǐ zǔzhī jiǎnchá

biotechnology N 生物工程 shēngwù gōngchéng

bioterrorism N 生物恐怖主义（行为）shēngwù kǒngbùzhǔyì (xíngwéi)

bird N 鸟 niǎo [M. WD 只 zhī], 禽类 qínlèi
bird flu 禽流感 qínliúgǎn
bird's eye view 鸟瞰 niǎokàn
to kill two birds with one stone 一举两得 yìjǔ liǎngdé

birth N 出生 chūshēng
birth certificate 出生证 chūshēng zhèng
birth control 计划生育 jìhuà shēngyù
date of birth 出生日期 chūshēng rìqī

birthday N 生日 shēngrì

birthmark N 胎记 tāijì

biscuit N 1 烤饼 kǎobǐng [M. WD 块 kuài] 2 饼干 bǐnggān [M. WD 块 kuài/盒 hé]

bisect V 平分为二 píngfēn wéi èr

bisexual ADJ 具有两性特征的 [+生物] jùyǒu liǎngxìng tèzhēng de [+shēngwù], 对男女两性都感兴趣的 duì nánnǚ liǎngxìng dōu gǎn xìngqu de

bishop N 主教 zhǔjiào [M. WD 位 wèi]

bit[1] N 一点儿 yìdiǎnr

bit[2] See **bite**

bitch I N 母狗 mǔgǒu [M. WD 只 zhī] **2** 坏女人 huài nǚrén
son of a bitch 狗养的 gǒuyǎngde
II V 发牢骚 fāláosāo

bite I V (PT bit; PP bitten) [虫子+] 咬 [chóngzi+] yǎo, [蚊子+] 叮 [wénzi+] dīng **II** N 咬 yǎo, 叮 dīng

bitten See **bite**

bitter ADJ **1** 苦 kǔ
Good medicine tastes bitter. 良药苦口。Liáng yào kǔ kǒu
2 痛苦的 [+经历] tòngkǔ de [+jīnglì]
to the bitter end 坚持到最后 jiānchí dào zuìhòu

bittersweet ADJ **1** 甜酸的 tián suān de **2** 甜蜜而又辛酸的 [+爱情] tiánmì ér yòu xīnsuān de [+àiqíng], 有快乐也有痛苦的 yǒu kuàilè yě yǒu tòngkǔ de

biweekly ADJ 双周的 shuāng zhōu de

bizarre ADJ 奇怪的 [+现象] qíguài de [+xiànxiàng], 稀奇古怪的 xīqí gǔguài de

blab V 泄露秘密 xièlòu mìmì

black I ADJ **1** 黑色的 hēisè de **II** N 黑色 hēisè
black and white 黑白的 hēibái de
III V (to black out) 昏倒 hūndǎo, 失去知觉 shīqù zhījué

blackboard N 黑板 hēibǎn

blacken V **1** 变黑 biàn hēi **2** 破坏 [+名誉] pòhuài [+míngyù]

blackhead N 黑头粉刺 hēitóu fěncì

blackjack N 二十一点（纸牌游戏）èrshí yì diǎn (zhǐpái yóuxì)

blacklist I N 黑名单 hēimíngdān **II** V 上黑名单 shàng hēimíngdān

blackmail N, V 讹诈 ézhà, 勒索 lèsuǒ

blackout N **1** 灯火管制 dēnghuǒguǎnzhì **2** 晕倒 yūndǎo

blacksmith N 铁匠 tiějiang

bladder N 膀胱 pángguāng

blade N 刀刃 dāorèn, 刀口 dāokǒu

blame I V 责怪 zéguài, 责备 zébèi
A bad workman blames his tools. 蹩脚工匠，责怪工具。Biéjiǎo gōngjiàng, zéguài gōngjù.
II N 责任 zérèn

blanch V **1** 变白 biànbái **2** 去皮 qùpí

bland ADJ 清淡的 [+食物] qīngdàn de [+shíwù], 无味的 [+汤] wúwèi de [+tāng]

blank I ADJ 空白的 [+支票] kòngbái de [+zhīpiào]
blank verse 无韵诗 wúyùnshī
II N 空白处 kòngbái chù, 空格 kònggé

blanket I N 毛毯 máotǎn [M. WD 条 tiáo], 毯子 tǎnzi [M. WD 条 tiáo] **II** ADJ 包括一切的 bāo kuò yíqiè de

blasé ADJ（享受过度而）感到厌倦的 [+富家子] (xiǎngshòu guòdù ér) gǎndào yànjuàn de [+fùjiāzǐ]

blasphemy N 亵渎神明 xiè dú shénmíng

blast I N **1** 爆炸 bàozhà **2** 强劲的风 qiángjìn de fēng
blast furnace 鼓风炉 gǔfēnglú
II V 爆破 bàopò

blast-off N 起飞 qǐfēi

blatant ADJ 公然的 gōngrán de

blaze I N **1** 大火 dàhuǒ, 熊熊大火 xióngxióng dàhuǒ **2** 熊熊燃烧 xióngxióng ránshāo

bleach I V 漂白 piǎobái, 变白 biànbái **II** N 漂白剂 piǎobáijì

bleak ADJ **1** 阴冷的 [+天气] yīnlěng de [+tiānqì] **2** 暗淡的 [+前途] àndàn de [+qiántú]

bleary ADJ（眼睛）红肿的 (yǎnjing) hóngzhǒng de, 视力模糊的 shìlì móhu de

bleat V（羊或小牛）叫 (yáng huò xiǎoniú) jiào

bled See **bleed**

bleed (PT & PP bled) V 流血 liúxuè

bleep I N（机器的）嘟嘟声 (jīqì de) dūdū shēng **II** V 发出嘟嘟声 fāchū dūdū shēng

blemish I N [声誉+] 污点 [shēngyù+] wūdiǎn, 瑕疵 xiácī **2** 损害 [+性格] 的完美 sǔnhài [+xìnggé] de wánměi

blend I V **1** 混合 hùnhé, 掺合 chānhé **2** 调和 tiáohé **II** N 混合物 hùnhéwù

blender N 搅拌机 jiǎobànjī [M. WD 台 tái]

bless V 祝福 zhùfú, 保佑 bǎoyòu

blessing N **1** 祝福 zhùfú **2** 批准 pīzhǔn, 允许 yǔnxǔ

blew See **blow**

blight I N 1 毁坏 huǐhuài 2（植物）枯萎病 (zhíwù) kūwěi bìng II v 毁坏 huǐhuài, 折磨 zhémó

blind¹ ADJ 瞎的 xiā de, 看不见的 kànbujiàn de, 盲的 máng de
No one is more blind than those who refuse to see. 没有谁比拒绝看的人更瞎。Méiyǒu shéi bǐ jùjué kàn de rén gèngxiā.
blind date 与从未见过面的人约会 yǔ cóngwèi jiàn guò miàndì rén yuēhuì, 初次约会谈 chūcì yuēhuì

blind² N 窗帘 chuānglián, 帘子 liánzi

blinders N（马的）眼罩 (mǎ de) yǎnzhào

blindfold I N 眼罩 yǎnzhào, 蒙眼布 méng yǎn bù II v 蒙住眼睛 méngzhùyǎnjing

blindspot N 盲点 mángdiǎn

blink v 眨眼睛 zhǎyǎn jīng

blinkers N [马的+] 眼罩 [mǎ de+] yǎnzhào

blip I N [机器+] 哔哔声 [jīqì+] bìbì shēng II v 发出哔哔声 fāchū bìbì shēng

bliss N 极乐 jí lè, 至上的幸福 zhìshàng de xìngfú

blissful ADJ 快乐极了 kuàilè jíle, 无忧无虑的 wúyōu wúlǜ de

blister I N 水疱 shuǐpào II v 起水疱 qǐshuǐ pào

blithe ADJ 欢乐的 huānlè de

blitz N 1 闪电战 shǎndiànzhàn 2 突然的大规模袭击 tūrán de dàguīmó xíjī

blizzard N 暴风雪 bàofēngxuě [M. WD 场 cháng]

bloated ADJ 肿胀的 zhǒngzhàng de, 膨胀的 péngzhàng de

blob N 一滴 yìdī

bloc N 集团 jítuán

block I N 1 大块 dà kuài
a block of wood 一大块木头 yí dà kuài mùtou
2 街区 jiēqū II v 阻塞 zǔsè, 堵住 dǔzhù

blockade I N 封锁 fēngsuǒ II v 封锁 fēngsuǒ

blockage N 堵塞物 dǔsè wù

blockbuster N 1 大片 dàpiān [M. WD 部 bù] 2 成功的畅销书 chénggōng de chàngxiāoshū

blockhead N 傻瓜 shǎguā, 笨蛋 bèndàn

blog I N 互联网网页 hùliánwǎng wǎngyè II v 在互联网网页发表文章 zài hùliánwǎng wǎngyè fābiǎo wénzhāng

blogger N 博客 bókè, 在互联网网页发表文章的人 zài hùliánwǎng wǎngyè fābiǎo wénzhāng de rén

blond, blonde N 有金黄头发的人 yǒu jīnhuáng tóufa de rén, 金发女郎 jīnfā nǚláng

blood N 血 xuè [M. WD 滴 dī]
blood pressure 血压 xuèyā
blood type 血型 xuèxíng

bloodshed N 流血 liúxuè

bloodshot ADJ 充血的 chōngxuè de, 带血丝的 dài xuèsī de

bloody ADJ 1 带血的 dàixuè de 2 残酷的 cánkù de

bloom I N 花朵 huāduǒ, 花 huā [M. WD 朵 duǒ] II v 开花 kāihuā

blossom I N 花 huā, 花儿 huār [M. WD 朵 duǒ] II v 开花 kāihuā

blot I N 污迹 wūjì, 污点 wūdiǎn II v 留下污迹 liúxià wūjì

blotch N 1 大片污迹 dàpiàn wūji 2（皮肤）红斑 (pífū) hóngbān

blotter N 1 吸墨纸 xīmòzhǐ [M. WD 张 zhāng] 2 记录簿 jìlùbù [M. WD 本 běn]

blouse N 女式衬衫 nǚshì chènshān [M. WD 件 jiàn]

blow I v (PT **blew**; PP **blown**) 吹 chuī, 刮 guā
to blow one's own horn 自吹自擂 zìchuī zìléi
to blow sb a kiss 给…一个飞吻 gěi...yí ge fēiwěn
to blow the whistle on 揭发 jiēfā
II N 1 吹 chuī, 吹动 chuīdòng 2 重击 zhòngjī
to come to blows 打起来 dǎqǐlái
3（心理上的）打击 (xīnlǐ shàng de) dǎjī
to deal sb a heavy blow 给某人打击 gěi mǒurén dǎjī

blown See **blow**

blowout N 1 轻而易举的胜利 qīng ér yìjǔ de shènglì 2 盛大宴会 shèngdà yànhuì 3 [轮胎+] 爆裂 [lúntāi+] bàoliè

blowtorch N 喷灯 pēndēng

blow-up N 1 放大的照片 fàngdà de zhàopiàn 2 突然发生的吵架 tūrán fāshēng de chǎojià

blubber[1] N [鲸鱼／人的+] 脂肪 [jīngyú/rén de+] zhīfáng

blubber[2] V (让人讨厌地) 哇哇大哭 (ràng rén tǎoyàn de) wāwā dàkū

blue I ADJ 1 蓝色的 [+天空] lánsè de [+tiānkōng]
blue chip 蓝筹股的 lánchóugǔ de, 稳赚的 wěn zhuàn de
2 色情的 sèqíng de 3 悲观的 bēiguān de II N 1 蓝色 lánsè 2 天空 tiānkōng, 海洋 hǎiyáng
out of the blue 突然的 tūrán de, 出人意料的 chūrén yìliào de

blue-blood ADJ 血统高贵的 [+家族] xuètǒng gāoguì de [+jiāzú], 出生名门豪族的 chūshēng míngmén háozú de

blue-collar ADJ 蓝领阶层的 [+工人] lánlíng jiēcéng de [+gōngrén]

bluejeans N 牛仔裤 niúzǎikù [M. WD 条 tiáo]

blueprint N 蓝图 lántú [M. WD 幅 fú/张 zhāng]

blues N 1 布鲁斯音乐 bùlǔsī yīnyuè 2 (the blues) 忧郁 yōuyù

bluff N, V 虚张声势 xūzhāng shēngshì, 吓唬 xiàhu

blunder I N 愚蠢的错误 yúchǔn de cuòwù, 重大的疏忽 zhòngdà de shūhu II V 1 犯愚蠢的错误 fàn yúchǔn de cuòwù 2 误入 wùrù

blunt ADJ 1 钝的 [+刀] dùn de [+dāo], 不锋利的 bù fēnglì de 2 直言不讳的 [+话] zhíyán búhuì de [+huà], 毫不客气的 [+批评] háobú kèqi de [+pīpíng]

blur I N 一片模糊 yípiàn móhu II V 使 [+景象] 模糊 shǐ [+jǐngxiàng] móhu

blurb N [书 de+] 内容提要 [shū de+] nèiróngtíyào

blurt V 不假思索地说出来 bù jiǎ sīsuǒ de shuōchulai

blush I V [脸+] 红 [liǎn+] hóng II N 脸红 liǎnhóng

bluster I V [人+] 神气活现地叫嚷 [rén

+] shénqi huóxiàn de jiàorǎng, 咆哮 páoxiào II N 夸夸其谈 kuākuā qí tán, 吹牛 chuīniú

BO, B.O. (= body odor) ABBREV 体臭 tǐ chòu

boar N 公猪 gōngzhū, 野猪 yězhū

board I N 木板 mùbǎn [M. WD 块 kuài]
bulletin board 布告牌 bùgàopái
2 董事会 dǒngshìhuì, 理事会 lǐshìhuì
chairman of the board (公司) 董事长 (gōngsī) dǒngshìzhǎng
3 伙食 huǒshí, 伙食费 huǒshífèi II V 登上 [+飞机／公共汽车／火车] dēngshàng [+fēijī/gōnggòng qìchē/huǒchē]

boarder N 寄宿生 jìsùshēng, 寄膳房客 jì shàn fángkè

boarding school N 寄宿学校 jìsùxuéxiào

boast I V 吹嘘 [+自己] chuīxū [+zìjǐ], 吹牛 chuīniú II N 吹嘘 chuīxū, 自吹 zìchuī

boastful ADJ 自吹自擂的 zìchuī zìléi de

boat N 船 chuán [M. WD 条 tiáo/艘 sōu], 小船 xiǎochuán [M. WD 条 tiáo/艘 sōu]
in the same boat 共患难 gòng huànnàn, 同舟共济 tóngzhōu gòngjì
to rock the boat 唱反调捣乱 chàng fǎndiào dǎoluàn

bob V 上下摇动 shàngxià yáodòng

bode V 预示 yùshì

bodice N 紧身胸衣 jǐnshēn xiōngyī

bodily I ADJ 身体的 shēntǐ de, 肉体的 ròutǐ de II ADV 全体 quántǐ, 整个 zhěnggè

body N 1 身体 shēntǐ, 身躯 shēnqū
body language 体态语言 tǐtài yǔyán
2 (dead body) 尸体 shītǐ [M. WD 具 jù]
3 团体 tuántǐ 4 物体 wùtǐ [M. WD 件 jiàn]

bodyguard N 保镖 bǎobiāo, 警卫 jǐngwèi

body odor See BO

bog N 沼泽 zhǎozé [M. WD 片 piàn]

bogeyman N 妖怪 yāoguài

boggle V 惊恐 jīngkǒng, 大为恐惧 dàwéi kǒngjù

bogus ADJ 假的 jiǎ de, 伪装的 wěizhuāng de

boil V 1 [水+] 沸腾 [shuǐ+] fèiténg 2 烧开 [+水] shāokāi [+shuǐ] 3 煮 [+土豆] zhǔ [+tǔdòu]
boiled water 开水 kāishuǐ

boiler N 锅炉 guōlú

boiling point N 沸点 fèidiǎn

boisterous ADJ 吵吵闹闹的 chǎochǎo nàonào de

bold ADJ 勇敢的 yǒnggǎn de, 大胆的 dàdǎn de

bolster I V 增强 zēngqiáng, 支持 zhīchí II N 1 垫枕 diàn zhěn 2 垫木 diànmù

bolt I N 1 螺栓 luóshuān, 螺丝钉 luósīdīng 2 门拴 ménshuān, 窗拴 chuāng shuān II V 1 把…拴在一起 bǎ…shuān zài yìqǐ 2 [马+] 逃跑 [mǎ+] táopǎo 3 匆匆吞下 cōngcōng tūnxià III ADV 笔直 bǐzhí

bomb I N 炸弹 zhàdàn [M. WD 枚 méi] II V 1 轰炸 hōngzhà, [用炸弹+] 爆炸 [yòng zhàdàn+] bàozhà 2 失败 shībài

bombard V 1 对 [+敌人的阵地] 狂轰滥炸 duì [+dírén de zhèndì] kuánghōng lànzhà 2 对 [+市长] 提出一连串问题 duì [+shìzhǎng] tíchū yìliánchuàn wèntí

bombed ADJ 喝醉了 (酒) hēzuìle (jiǔ)

bomber N 1 投放炸弹的人 tóufàng zhàdàn de rén 2 轰炸机 hōngzhàjī

bombshell 1 N 惊人事件 jīngrén shìjiàn 2 炸弹 zhàdàn [M. WD 枚 méi]

bona fide ADJ 真正的 zhēnzhèng de, 真诚的 zhēnchéng de

bonanza N 1 财源 cáiyuán 2 繁荣兴旺 fánróng xīngwàng 3 富矿 fùkuàng

bond I N 1 债券 zhàiquàn

U.S. savings bond 美国储蓄债券 Měiguó chǔxù zhàiquàn

2 保释金 bǎoshìjīn 3 纽带 niǔdài, 联系 liánxì II V 培养亲密关系 péiyǎng qīnmì guānxi

bondage N 1 奴役 núyì 2 束缚 shùfù

bone I N 1 骨头 gǔtou [M. WD 根 gēn]

to make no bones about 对…毫无顾忌 duì…háo wú gùjì

to have a bone to pick with 对…有意见 duì…yǒu yìjiàn

to feel sth in one's bones 确信 quèxìn II V 去骨 [+鸡] 的骨头 qùdiào [+jī] de gǔtou

bonus N 奖金 jiǎngjīn, 红利 hónglì

bony ADJ 皮包骨头的 [+饥民] píbāo gǔtou de [+jīmín]

boo V 发出嘘声 fāchū xū shēng, 向 [+演员] 喝倒彩 xiàng [+yǎnyuán] hèdàocǎi

boob N 乳房 rǔfáng, 奶头 nǎitou

boo-boo N 犯傻 fànshǎ

booby prize N 倒数第一名奖 dàoshǔ dìyīmíng jiǎng

booby trap N 1 伪装地雷 wěizhuāng dìléi [M. WD 枚 méi] 2 恶作剧 èzuòjù

book I N 1 书 shū, 图书 túshū 2 本子 běnzi, 簿子 bùzi [M. WD 本 běn]

address book 地址簿 dìzhǐbù

notebook 笔记本 bǐjìběn

3 账本 zhàngběn, 账目 zhàngmù [M. WD 本 běn]

by the book 严格照章办事 yángé zhàozhāngbànshì

II V 预定 [+旅馆房间] yùdìng [+lǚguǎn fángjiān]

bookcase N 书橱 shūchú

bookmark N 书签 shūqiān

bookshelf N 书架 shūjià

bookstore N 书店 shūdiàn [M. WD 家 jiā]

boom I N 1 [生意+] 兴隆 [shēngyì+] xīnglóng

boom town 兴旺发达的城市 xīngwàng fādá de chéngshì

2 隆隆声 lónglóng shēng II V 1 [生意+] 兴隆 [shēngyì+] xīnglóng, 兴旺 xīngwàng 2 发出隆隆声 fāchū lónglóng shēng

boomerang I N 回飞镖 huí fēibiāo II V 自食其咎 zìshí qízhòu

boon N 带来极大好处的事物 dàilái jídá hǎochu de shìwù, 恩物 ēnwù

boor N 粗鲁的男子 cūlǔ de nánzǐ

boost I N 激励 jīlì, 鼓励 gǔlì II V 激励 [+士气] jīlì [+shìqì], 鼓励 gǔlì

booster N 1 增效药剂 zēng xiào yàojì 2 起鼓励作用的事物 qǐ gǔlì zuòyòng de shìwù

moral booster 鼓舞士气的事 gǔlì shìqì de shì

3 助推器 zhùtuīqì

boot I N 1 靴子 xuēzi

boot camp 新兵训练营 xīnbīng xùnliàn yíng

II V 1 使 [+电脑] 启动 shǐ [+diànnǎo] qǐdòng 2 赶走 [+捣乱的人] gǎnzǒu [+dǎoluàn de rén]

booth N 1 小亭 xiǎo tíng
ticket booth 售票亭 shòupiào tíng
2（餐馆）火车座（cānguǎn）huǒchēzuò
3 售货摊位 shòuhuò tānwèi

bootleg I ADJ 盗制的 dào zhì de, 走私的 zǒusī de II N 盗制 [+电脑软件等] dào zhì [+diànnǎo ruǎnjiàn děng]

bootstraps N 拔靴带 bá xuē dài
to pull oneself up by one's boot-straps 自强不息改善处境 zìqiáng bùxī gǎishàn chǔjìng

booty N 战利品 zhànlìpǐn [M. WD 件 jiàn]

booze I N 酒 jiǔ II V 豪饮 háoyǐn, 酗酒 xùjiǔ

border I N 1 边儿 biānr 2 国界 guójiè, 国境线 guójìngxiàn II V 与…接壤 yǔ…jiērǎng

borderline I N 分界线 fēnjièxiàn [M. WD 道 dào/条 tiáo] II ADJ 几乎 jīhū

bore¹ See **bear¹**

bore² I V 1 使…厌烦 shǐ…yànfán, 使…厌倦 shǐ…yànjuàn
to bore sb to death 使…厌烦得要死 shǐ…yànfán deyàosǐ
2 钻孔 zuānkǒng II N 1 令人厌烦的人 [+或事] lìngrén yànfán de rén [+huò shì] 2 口径 kǒujìng

bored ADJ 厌烦 yànfán, 厌倦 yànjuàn

boring ADJ 让人厌烦 ràng rén yànfán, 枯燥 kūzào

born ADJ 出生 chūshēng
be born with a silver spoon in one's mouth 生在富贵人家 shēng zài fùguì rénjiā

born-again ADJ 新近开始的 xīnjìn kāishǐ de
a born-again Christian 基督教再生教徒 Jīdūjiào zàishēng jiàotú

borne See **bear¹**

borough N （城市里的）区 (chéngshì lǐ de) qū

borrow V 借 jiè, 借用 jièyòng

borrowing N 1 借款 jièkuǎn, 贷款 dàikuǎn 2 外来语 wàiláiyǔ
borrowing powers 借款限额 jièkuǎn xiàn'é

bosom N 胸部 xiōngbù

a bosom friend 心腹之交 xīnfù zhī jiāo, 知己朋友 zhījǐ péngyou

boss I N 1 老板 lǎobǎn 2 领袖 lǐngxiù [M. WD 位 wèi], 头目 tóumù
party boss 政党领袖 zhèngdǎng lǐngxiù
crime boss 犯罪分子头目 fànzuì fènzǐ tóumù
II V (to boss sb around) 对…发号施令 duì…fāhào shīlìng

botany N 植物学 zhíwù xué

botch V 把…搞糟 bǎ…gǎozāo

both I ADJ 两 liǎng II PRON 两个…都 liǎng ge…dōu
both … and … 既…又… jì…yòu…

bother I V 1 打搅 dǎjiǎo 2 烦恼 fánnǎo, 发愁 fāchóu 3 麻烦 máfan II N 麻烦 máfan
no bother 没关系 méi guānxi, 不费事 bú fèishì

bottle I N 瓶 píng [M. WD 只 zhī], 瓶子 píngzi II V 装瓶 zhuāng píng

bottlefed See **bottlefeed**

bottlefeed (PT & PP **bottlefed**) V 人工喂养 réngōng wèiyǎng

bottleneck N 1 瓶颈 píngjǐng, 瓶颈路段 píngjǐng lùduàn 2 障碍 zhàng'ài

bottom I N 1 底 dǐ, 底部 dǐbù 2 最后的位置 zuìhòu de wèizhi, 末尾 mòwěi 3 最底下的 zuì dǐxia de II ADJ 最底层的 zuì dǐcéng de
bottom line ① 最基本的事实 zuì jīběn de shìshí ② 底线 dǐxiàn
III V (to bottom out) 降到最低点 jiàng dào zuì dīdiǎn

bough N 主要的树叉 zhǔyào de shùchā

bought See **buy**

boulder N 巨石 jù shí [M. WD 块 kuài]

boulevard N 林荫大道 lín yìn dàdào [M. WD 条 tiáo], 大道 dàdào [M. WD 条 tiáo]

bounce I V 1 跳跃 tiào, 弹跳 tántiào 2 退回 tuìhuí
to bounce back 恢复元气 huīfù yuánqì
II N 1 跳跃 tiào, 弹跳 tántiào 2 活力 huólì

bouncer N 门卫 ménwèi

bouncy ADJ 1 弹性很足的 [+椅子] tánxìng hěn zú de [+yǐzi] 2 精神饱满的 [+音乐] jīngshén bǎomǎn de [+yīnyuè], 快乐的 [+人] kuàilè de [+rén]

bound I ADJ **1** 肯定 kěndìng
be bound to 肯定会 kěndìng huì, 注定
会 zhùdìng huì
2 有义务的 yǒu yìwù de **3** 订制好的
zhuāngdìng hǎode **II** v 以…为界 yǐ…wéi
jiè **III** N 界限 jièxiàn
bound See **bind**
boundary N 分界线 fēnjièxiàn
to push the boundary 开拓思路 kāituò
sīlù
bountiful ADJ 充裕的 chōngyù de
bounty N 奖金 jiǎngjīn [M. WD 笔 bǐ], 悬赏
金 xuánshǎng jīn [M. WD 笔 bǐ]
bouquet N **1** 花束 huāshù
a bouquet of roses 一束玫瑰花 yíshù
méiguīhuā
2 (酒) 香 (jiǔ) xiāng
bout N [疾病+] 发作 [jíbìng+] fāzuò
boutique N 小精品店 xiǎo jīngpǐndiàn
bow I v **1** 鞠躬 [+谢幕] jūgōng [+xièmù]
2 低头 [+祷告] dītóu [+dǎogào] **II** N **1** 鞠
躬 jūgōng **2** 弓 gōng, 琴弓 qín gōng **3** 蝴
蝶结 húdiéjié
bowel N 肠 cháng
to move bowels 解大便 jiě páidàbiàn,
大便 dàbiàn
bowl I N 碗 wǎn [M. WD 只 zhī]
fish bowl 鱼缸 yúgāng [M. WD 只 zhī]
II v 打保龄球 dǎ bǎolíngqiú
bow-legged ADJ 罗圈腿的 luóquāntuǐ de
bowling N 保龄球 (运动) bǎolíngqiú
(yùndòng)
bowling alley 保龄球馆 bǎolíngqiú guǎn
box I N 盒 hé, 箱 xiāng [M. WD 只 zhī] **2** 方
框 fāngkuàng, 选项框 xuǎn xiàng kuàng
to check the box 在选项框内打勾 zài
xuǎn xiàng kuàng nèi dǎ gōu
to think outside the box 想出新花招
xiǎngchū xīn huāzhāo
3 包厢 bāoxiāng **4** 电视机 diànshìjī
box office 票房 piàofáng
II v **1** 把…装入箱内 bǎ…zhuāngrù xiāng
nèi **2** 与…比赛拳击 yú…bǐsài quánjī
3 打…耳光 dǎ…ěrguāng
boxer N 拳击手 quánjīshǒu
boxer shorts (男用) 平脚短裤 (nán
yòng) píng jiǎo duǎnkù

boxing N 拳击 quánjī, 拳击运动 quánjī
yùndòng
boy I N 男孩 nánhái
Boy Scouts 童子军 tóngzǐjūn
2 儿子 érzi **3** 年轻人 niánqīngrén
II INTERJ 好家伙!
Oh boy! 啊哟! Āyā!
boycott I v 抵制 dǐzhì **II** N 抵制 dǐzhì
bozo N 傻瓜 shǎguā
bra N 胸罩 xiōngzhào
brace I v **1** 做好准备对付困难 zuò hǎo
zhǔnbèi duìfu kùnnan **2** 加固 jiāgù, 支撑
zhī chēng **II** N 支撑物 zhīchēngwù
braces 矫正牙箍 jiǎozhèng yá gū
neck brace 颈托 jǐng tuō
bracelet N 手镯 shǒuzhuó
bracket N **1** 括号 kuòhào **2** 等级段
děngjíduàn, 组组
income bracket 收入等级 shōurù
děngjí
II v **1** 把…放入括号内 bǎ…fàngrù
kuòhào nèi **2** 把…放入同一等级段 bǎ…
fàngrù tóngyī děngjí duàn
brag N 吹嘘 chuī xū
braid I N **1** 发辫 fàbiàn, 辫子 biànzi [M. WD
条 tiáo] **2** 穗带 suì dài [M. WD 条 tiáo]
II v **1** 编成辫子 biānchéng biànzi **2** 编成
穗带 biānchéng suì dài
brain N **1** 脑 nǎo, 脑子 nǎozi
brain damage 脑损伤 nǎo sǔnshāng
2 脑力 nǎolì, 能力 nénglì
brain drain 人才外流 réncái wàiliú
brainstorming N [一群人+] 共同出主意
[yìqún rén+] gòngtóng chū zhǔyì, 群策
群力 qún cè qún lì
brainwash v 洗脑 xǐnǎo
braise v 用文火慢煮 yòng wénhuǒ màn
zhǔ, 炖 dùn
brake I N 刹车 shāchē, 制动器 zhìdòngqì
II v 踩刹车 cǎi shāchē
bran N 麦麸 màifū, 糠 kāng
branch I N **1** 树枝 shùzhī **2** 分部 fēnbù
3 支流 zhīliú **II** v 分支 fēnzhī, 分道 fēndào
to branch out 扩大领域 kuòdà lǐngyù
brand I N **1** 牌子 páizi, 商标 shāngbiāo
brand name 商标名称 shāngbiāo
míngchēng, 名牌 míngpái

ll v 1 给…打上烙印 gěi...dǎshànglàoyìn 2 给…坏名声 gěi...huài míngshēng

brand-new ADJ 崭新的 zhǎnxīn de

brandy N 白兰地 [+酒] báilándì [+jiǔ]

brash ll ADJ 1 自以为是的 zìyǐwéishì de, 傲慢粗鲁的 àomàn cūlǔ de 2 刺耳的 cì'ěr de, 刺眼的 cìyǎn de

brass 1 N 1 黄铜 huángtóng 2 铜管乐器 tóngguǎnyuèqì
    brass band 铜管乐队 tóngguǎn yuèduì
3 重要人物 zhòngyào rénwù

brasserie N（法式）小餐馆 (Fǎshì) xiǎo cānguǎn [M. wD jiā]

brassy ADJ 1 黄铜的 huángtóng de 2 打扮艳丽举止粗俗的 dǎban yànlì jǔzhǐ cūsú de [+女人] [+nǚrén]

brat N 没有教养的小孩 méiyǒu jiàoyǎng de xiǎohái, 小坏蛋 xiǎo huàidàn

bravado N 虚张声势 xūzhāng shēngshì, 逞强的姿态 chěngqiáng de zītài

brave l ADJ 1 勇敢的 [+士兵] yǒnggǎn de [+shìbīng] 2 美好的 [+新世界] měihǎo de [+xīn shìjiè] ll v 勇敢面对 yǒnggǎn miànduì

bravo INTERJ 好哇, 妙哉, 高 gāo

brawl N, v 打群架 dǎ qúnjià

bray N 发出叫声 [驴+] fāchū jiàoshēng, [驴+] 叫 [lǘ+] jiào

brazen ADJ 厚颜无耻的 hòuyán wúchǐ de

brazier N 火盆 huǒpén [M. wD 只 zhī]

breach N 1 违反 wéifǎn
    breach of security 违反安全规定 wéifǎn ānquán guīdìng
2 破裂 pòliè

bread N 面包 miànbāo [M. wD 块 kuài]

breadth N 宽度 kuāndù, 广度 guǎngdù

breadwinner N 挣钱养家的人 zhèngqián yǎngjiā de rén

break l v (PT broke; PP broken) 1 打破 dǎpò, 破损 pòsǔn
    to break a record 打破纪录 dǎpò jìlù
2 摔坏 shuāi huài, 摔伤 shuāi shāng
3 折断 shuāiduàn
    to break in/into 私自闯入 sīzì chuǎngrù
    to break a promise 违背承诺 wéibèi chéngnuò, 食言 shíyán
    to break a rule 犯规 fànguī

to break up 断绝来往 duànjué láiwǎng, 断交 duànjiāo
ll N 1 [+谈话] 中断 [+tánhuà] zhōngduàn 2 [+午餐] 休息 [+wǔcān] xiūxi 3 骨折 gǔzhé 4 [+电影] 间歇 [+diànyǐng] jiānxiē

breakable ADJ 易破碎的 yì pòsuì de

breakage N 破损 pòsǔn

breakdown N 失败 shībài, 破裂 pòliè

break-even ADJ 收支平衡的 shōuzhī pínghéng de

breakfast N 早饭 zǎofàn, 早餐 zǎocān

breakneck ADJ 超高速的 chāogāosù de

breakthrough N 突破 tūpò

breast N 1 乳房 rǔfáng 2 胸 xiōng, 胸部 xiōngbù

breastfed See **breastfeed**

breastfed (PT & PP **breastfed**) v 用母乳喂养 yòng mǔrǔ wèiyǎng

breaststroke N 蛙式游泳 wāshì yóuyǒng, 蛙泳 wāyǒng

breath N 呼吸 hūxī
    out of breath 喘不过气 chuǎnbúguò qì
    to take a deep breath 深吸一口气 shēn xī yì kǒu qì

breathalyze v 做酒精检测 zuò jiǔjīng jiǎncè

breathe v 呼吸 hūxī
    not to breathe a word 一句话也不说 yí jù huà yě bù shuō, 只字不露 zhīzì bùlù
    breathe in 吸气 xīqì
    breathe out 呼气 hūqì

breathless ADJ 气喘吁吁的 qìchuǎn xūxū de

breathtaking ADJ 令人惊叹的 lìngrén jīngtàn de

bred See **breed**

breed l N [动物的+] 品种 [dòngwù de+] pǐnzhǒng ll v (PT & PP **bred**) 1 繁殖 [+名种狗] fánzhí [+míng zhǒng gǒu], 培育 péiyù 2 [动物+] 交配 [dòngwù+] jiāopèi 3 滋生 [+犯罪] zīshēng [+fànzuì], 引起 yǐnqǐ

breeding N 繁殖 fánzhí, 培育 péiyù
    breeding ground 繁殖场 fánzhí chǎng, 孳生地 zīshēng dì

breeze l N 微风 wēifēng ll v 飘然而来 piāorán érlái

breezy ADJ 1 有微风的 [+天气] yǒu

269

wēifēng de [+tiānqì] **2** 轻松自信的 [+青年] qīngsōng zìxìn de [+qīngnián]，快活的 kuàihuo de

brethren N 教友 jiàoyǒu

brevity N 简洁 jiǎnjié

brew I v **1** 酿造 [+酒] niàngzào [+jiǔ] **2** 冲泡 [+红茶] chōngpào [+hóngchá] II N **1** 啤酒 píjiǔ **2**（酿造或冲泡的）饮料 (niàngzào huò chōngpào de) yǐnliào
home brew 家酿啤酒 jiāniàng píjiǔ

brewery N 啤酒厂 píjiǔchǎng

bribe I N 贿赂 huìlù
to take bribes 接受贿赂 jiēshòu huìlù，受贿 shòuhuì
II v 贿赂 huìlù，行贿 xínghuì

bribery N 贿赂的行为 huìlù de xíngwéi，行贿 xínghuì，受贿 shòuhuì

brick I N 砖 zhuān，砖头 zhuāntóu [M. WD 块 kuài] II v 用砖砌 yòng zhuān qì

brickyard N 制砖厂 zhì zhuānchǎng

bridal ADJ 婚礼的 hūnlǐ de，新娘的 xīnniáng de
bridal gown 婚纱 hūnshā

bride N 新娘 xīnniáng

bridegroom N 新郎 xīnláng

bridesmaid N 女傧相 nǚbīnxiàng

bridge I N **1** 桥 qiáo [M. WD 座 zuò] **2** 桥牌 qiápái II v 缩小 [+差异] suōxiǎo [+chāyì]，消除 [+分歧] xiāochú [+fēnqí]

bridle N 马笼头 mǎlóngtóu

brief I ADJ **1** 短暂的 duǎnzàn de **2** 简洁的 jiǎnjié de，简明的 jiǎnmíng de II N **1** 简报 jiǎnbào，摘要 zhāiyào **2** 案情摘要 ànqíng zhāiyào，诉讼要点 sùsòng yàodiǎn
to file a brief [+向法院] 提交诉讼 [+xiàng fǎyuàn] tíjiāo sùsòng
III v 向…介绍情况 xiàng…jièshào qíngkuàng

briefcase N 公事包 gōngshìbāo

briefing N **1** 简要情况 jiǎnyào qíngkuàng **2** 简报会 jiǎnbàohuì

briefs N 三角裤 sānjiǎokù [M. WD 条 tiáo]

brigade N **1**（军队的）旅 (jūnduì de) lǚ **2** 一队 yíduì，一帮 yìbāng，一群 yìqún

bright ADJ **1** 明亮的 míngliàng de **2** 聪明的 cōngming de **3** 欢快的 huānkuài de，高兴的 gāoxìng de

brighten v **1** 使 [+环境] 更美丽 shǐ [+huánjìng] gèng měilì **2** 使 [+形势] 变得明亮 shǐ [+xíngshì] biàn de míngliàng

brilliance N **1** [艺术家的+] 才华 [yìshùjiā de+] cáihuá **2** 亮光 guāngliàng

brilliant ADJ **1** 明亮的 [+灯光] míngliàng de [+dēngguāng]，光辉的 guānghuī de **2** 才华洋溢的 [+艺术家] cáihuá yángyì de [+yìshùjiā] **3** 绝妙的 [+主意] juémiào de [+zhǔyì]

brim I N 边 biān，边沿 biānyán，边缘 biānyuán II v 充满 chōngmǎn，洋溢 yángyì
to brim over ① [水池+] 满到溢出来 [shuǐchí+] mǎn dào yìchū lái ② 充满 [+信心] chōngmǎn [+xìnxīn]

brine N 浓盐水 nóng yánshuǐ

bring (PT & PP **brought**) v **1** 带来 dàilai，拿来 nálái **2** 造成 zàochéng
to bring about 造成 zàochéng
to bring … to an end 使…结束 shǐ…jiéshù，结束 jiéshù
to bring up 抚养 [+孩子] fǔyǎng [+háizi]

brink N 边缘 biānyuán

brisk ADJ **1** 轻快的 [+步子] qīngkuài de [+bùzi] **2** 兴隆的 [+生意] xīnglóng de [+shēngyì]，繁忙活跃的 fánmáng huóyuè de

bristle v **1** 被激怒 bèi jīnù，怒气冲冲 nùqì chōngchōng **2** [动物+] 毛发竖立 [dòngwù+] máofà shùlì

British I ADJ 英国的 Yīngguó de II N 英国人 Yīngguórén

brittle ADJ 脆的 cuì de，易碎的 yì suì de

broach v 提出 tíchū，提到 tídào

broad ADJ **1** 宽阔的 [+街道] kuānkuò de [+jiēdào]，宽的 kuān de **2** 简要的 [+说明] jiǎnyào de [+shuōmíng]
in broad daylight 大白天 dàbáitiān，光天化日之下 guāngtiānhuàrì zhīxià

broadband N 宽带 kuāndài

broadcast I v (PT & PP **broadcast**) 广播 guǎngbō，转播 zhuǎnbō II N 广播 guǎngbō
live broadcast 现场直播 xiànchǎng zhíbō

broadly ADV 大体上 dàtǐshàng，总体上 zǒngtǐ shàng

broadly speaking 大体上说 dàtǐshàng shuō

broadminded ADJ 心胸开阔的 xīnxiōngkāikuò de

Broadway N（美国）百老汇大街 (Měiguó) Bǎilǎohuì Dàjiē

brocade N 织锦 zhījǐn, 锦缎 jǐnduàn

broccoli N 花椰菜 huāyēcài [M. WD 棵 kē], 花茎甘蓝 huājīng gānlán [M. WD 棵 kē]

brochure N 小册子 xiǎocèzi

brogue N 1 厚底拷花皮鞋 hòudǐ kǎohuā píxie [M. WD 只 zhī/双 shuāng] 2 浓重的地方口音 nóngzhòng de dìfang kǒuyīn

broil V 烤烤 kǎo, 烧烤 shāokǎo

broke[1] ADJ 没有钱的 méiyǒu qián de, 身无分文的 shēn wú fēnwén de
to go broke 破产 pòchǎn

broke[2] See **break**

broken I See **break** II ADJ 1 破的 [+花瓶] pòde [+huāpíng], 破碎的 pòsuì de 2 坏了的 [+沙发] huàile de [+shāfā] 3 破裂的 [+婚姻] pòliè de [+hūnyīn]

broker I N 经纪人 jīngjìrén, 掮客 qiánkè, 代理人 dàilǐrén II V 促成 cùchéng
to broker a deal 促成交易 cùchéng jiāoyì

bronchitis N 支气管炎 zhīqìguǎnyán

bronze N 青铜 qīngtóng, 古铜 gǔtóng
bronze medal 铜牌 tóngpái

brooch I V 1 沉思 chénsī, 深思 shēnsī 2 孵卵 fūluǎn II N 一窝 [+小鸟] yìwō [+xiǎoniǎo]

broom N 扫帚 sàozhou [M. WD 把 bǎ]

broomstick N 扫帚柄 sàozhoubǐng

brother N 兄弟 xiōngdì, 哥哥 gēge, 弟弟 dìdi

brotherhood N 1 兄弟情谊 xiōngdì qíngyì, 手足之情 shǒuzú zhī qíng 2（宗教）兄弟会 (zōngjiào) xiōngdìhuì

brother-in-law N 大伯 dàbó (husband's elder brother), 小叔 xiǎoshū (husband's young brother), 内兄 nèixiōng (wife's elder brother), 内弟 nèidì (wife's younger brother), 姐夫 jiěfū (elder sister's husband), 妹夫 mèifū (younger sister's husband)

brotherly ADJ 兄弟情谊的 xiōngdì qíngyì de, 手足之情的 shǒuzú zhī qíng de

brought See **bring**

brow N 额 é, 额头 étóu
to knit one's brow 紧锁眉头 jǐnsuǒ méitóu, 愁眉不展 chóu méi bù zhǎn

browbeat (PT **browbeat**; PP **browbeaten**) V 对…吹胡子瞪眼睛 duì…chuīhúzi dèngyǎn jīng, 威逼 wēibī

browbeaten See **browbeat**

brown N, ADJ 棕色（的）zōngsè (de), 咖啡色（的）kāfēisè (de)

brownstone N 褐砂石 hèshāshí

browse V 随便翻阅 suíbiàn fānyuè, 浏览 liúlǎn

browser N 浏览器 liúlǎnqì

bruise I N 擦伤 cāshāng, 伤痕 shānghén II V 擦伤 cāshāng

brunch N 早午餐 zǎowǔcān

brunette N 深褐色头发的女子 shēn hèsè tóufa de nǔzǐ, 黑发女郎 hēi fā nǔláng

brunt N 重击 zhòngjī, 猛攻 měnggōng
to bear the brunt of 受到最猛烈的攻击 shòudàozuì měngliè de gōngjī, 首当其冲 shǒudāngqíchōng

brush I V 刷 shuā
to brush aside 不理会 bùlǐhuì
to brush up (on) 温习 wēnxí
II N 刷子 shuāzi

brush-off N 不理睬 bù lǐcǎi
to give sb the brush-off 让…碰一鼻子灰 ràng…pèng yì bízi huī

brusque ADJ 粗鲁的 cūlǔ de, 简慢的 jiǎnmàn de

brutal ADJ 野蛮的 yěmán de, 凶暴的 xiōngbào de

brute I N 1 野兽 yěshòu 2 粗野汉子 cūyě hànzi, 凶残的人 xiōngcán de rén II ADJ 野蛮的 yěmán de
brute force 野蛮暴力 yěmán bàolì, 暴力 bàolì

bubble I N 泡沫 pàomò, 气泡 qìpào
bubble gum 泡泡糖 pàopaotáng
II V 起泡 qǐpào, 冒泡 mào pào

bubbly I ADJ 1 充满泡沫的 chōngmǎn pàomò de 2 生气勃勃的 shēngqì bóbó de II N 香槟酒 xiāngbīnjiǔ

buck I N 1 美元 Měiyuán, 钱 qián to feel like a million bucks 感觉精神焕发 gǎnjué jīngshén huànfā 2 庄家标志 zhuāngjiā biāozhì 3 雄性动物 xióngxìng dòngwù II v 1 [马+] 弓背跃起 [mǎ+] gōngbèi yuèqǐ 2 [汽车+] 颠簸行驶 [qìchē+] diānbǒ xíngshǐ 3 反对 fǎnduì

bucket N 水桶 shuǐtǒng

buckle I N 扣子 kòuzi, 带扣 dàikòu II v 1 系上扣子 jìshang kòuzi Buckle up. 请系上安全带。Qǐng jìshang ānquándài. 2 腿软 tuǐ ruǎn, 站不直 zhàn bù zhí to buckle under pressure 屈服压力 qūfú yālì 3 弯曲变形 wānqū biànxíng

bud N 花苞 huābāo, 芽 yá II v 长出花苞 zhǎng chū huābāo, 发芽 fāyá

Buddhism N 佛教 Fójiào

budding ADJ 崭露头角的 zhǎnlù tóujiǎo de, 开始发展的 kāishǐ fāzhǎn de

budge v 1 移动 yídòng, 挪动 nuódòng not to budge an inch 一点儿都动不了 yìdiǎnr dōu dòngbuliǎo 2 改变注意 gǎibiàn zhùyì

budget I N 预算 yùsuàn II v 1 计划用钱 jìhuà yòngqián, 省钱 shěngqián 2 作预算 zuò yùsuàn, 编制预算 biānzhì yùsuàn 3 精打细算 jīngdǎ xìsuàn III ADJ 经济的 jīngjì de, 便宜的 piányi de

buff I N 爱好者 àihàozhě, 迷 mí movie buff 电影迷 diànyǐngmí, 影迷 yǐngmí 2 米黄色 mǐhuángsè II v 擦亮 cāliàng

buffalo N 牛 niú, 水牛 shuǐniú

buffer N 缓冲物 huǎnchōngwù, 缓冲国 huǎnchōngguó, 缓冲储存器 huǎnchōng chǔcúnqì

buffet N 1 自助餐 zìzhùcān 2 餐具柜 cānjù guì

buffoon N 丑角 chǒujué, 小丑 xiǎochǒu

bug I N 1 小虫子 xiǎo chóngzi stomach bug 肚子不舒服 dùzi bùshūfu 2 细菌 xìjūn, 病毒 bìngdú II v 1 安装窃听器 ānzhuāng qiètīngqì, 窃听 qiètīng 2 烦扰 fánrǎo

build I v (PT & PP **built**) 建 jiàn, 建造 jiànzào II N 体格 tǐgé, 体形 tǐxíng

building N 建筑物 jiànzhùwù building industry 建筑业 jiànzhùyè

building block N 1 砌块 qìkuài 2 基本要素 jīběn yàosù 3 积木 jīmù

build-up N 增长 zēngzhǎng

built See **build**

built-up ADJ 盖了很多房子的 gàile hěn duō fángzi de

bulb N 1 灯泡 dēngpào 2 球茎 qiújīng

bulge I N 膨胀 péngzhàng, 鼓出的地方 gǔ chū de dìfang II v 膨胀 péngzhàng, 鼓起 gǔqǐ

bulimia N 食欲过盛 shíyù guòshèng, 易饥症 yìjīzhēng

bulk N 大批 dàpī, 大量 dàliàng, 大宗 dàzōng bulk buying 大量购买 dàliàng gòumǎi

bulky ADJ 体积大的 tǐjī dà de, 又大又重的 yòu dà yòu zhòng de

bull N 1 公牛 gōngniú [M. WD 头 tóu] 2 雄性动物 xióngxìng dòngwù

bulldog N 斗牛狗 dòuniú gǒu

bulldoze v [用推土机+] 推平 [yòng tuītǔjī+] tuī píng, [用推土机+] 推倒 [yòng tuītǔjī+] tuīdǎo

bulldozer N 推土机 tuītǔjī

bullet N 子弹 zǐdàn [M. WD 枚 méi] to bite the bullet 咬紧牙关忍受痛苦 yǎojǐn yáguān rěnshòu tòngkǔ, 忍痛 rěntòng

bulletin N 布告 bùgào, 公告 gōnggào

bullfight, bullfighting N 斗牛 dòuniú

bullion N 金 [或银+] 块 jīn [huò yín+] kuài, 金 [或银+] 条 jīn [+huò yín] tiáo

bullish ADJ 1 [股票市场+] 看涨的 [gǔpiào shìchǎng+] kànzhǎng de 2 乐观自信的 [+投资者] lèguān zìxìn de [+tóuzīzhě]

bullpen N (棒球) 投球区 [bàngqiú+] tóuqiú qū

bull's eye N 靶心 bǎxīn

bullshit INTERJ 狗屁 gǒupì, 胡说八道 húshuō bādào

bully I N 持强凌弱者 chíqiáng língruò zhě, 欺负人的恶棍 qīfù rén de ègùn II v 欺负 [+小同学] qīfù [+xiǎo tóngxué], 威胁 wēihè

bum I N 不务正业的人 bú wù zhèngyè de rén, 无用的人 wúyòng de rén **II** v 乞讨 qǐtǎo, 乞求 qǐqiú **III** ADJ 1 没有用处的 [+建议] méiyǒu yòng chù de [+jiànyì], 蹩脚货 biéjiǎohuò 2 受伤的 [+脚] shòushāng de [+jiǎo]

bumblebee N 大黄蜂 dàhuángfēng

bummer N 叫人扫兴的事 jiào rén sǎoxìng de shì

bump I v 1 撞 zhuàng, 碰 pèng 2 颠簸 diānbǒ **II** N 1 碰撞 pèngzhuàng 2 肿块 zhǒng kuài 3 凸起部分 tūqǐ bùfen

bumper I N 保险杠 bǎoxiǎngàng
bumper sticker（贴在汽车保险杠上的）小标语 (tiē zài qìchē bǎoxiǎngàng shàng de) xiǎo biāoyǔ
II v 大量的 dàliàng de
bumper harvest 大丰收 dà fēngshōu

bumper-to-bumper ADV（汽车）一辆挨一辆 (qìchē) yíliàng ái yíliàng

bumpy ADJ 1 高低不平的 gāodī bùpíng de 2 颠簸的 diānbǒ de

bun N 小圆面包 xiǎo yuán miànbāo

bunch I N 束 shù, 串 chuàn
a bunch of flowers 一束花 yí shù huā
II v 扎成一束 zhā chéng yí shù

bundle I N 1 一捆 yìkǔn, 一扎 yì zhā 2 包裹 bāoguǒ, 一包 yìbāo 3 捆绑销售的商品 kǔnbǎng xiāoshòu de shāngpǐn **II** v 捆绑销售 kǔnbǎng xiāoshòu

bungalow N 平房 píngfáng [M. WD 栋 dòng]

bungle v 搞糟 gǎozāo, 一再出错 yízài chūcuò

bunk I N 床铺 chuángpù, 铺位 pùwèi
bunk beds 双层床 shuāngcéngchuáng
II v（在别人家）过夜 (zài biéren jiā) guòyè

bunny N 兔子 tùzi [M. WD 只 zhī]

buoy I N 浮标 fúbiāo, 航标 hángbiāo **II** v 1 鼓舞 [+士气] gǔwǔ [+shìqì], 振奋 [+精神] zhènfèn [+jīngshén] 2 维持 [+价格的高水平] wéichí [+jiàgé de gāoshuǐpíng]

buoyant ADJ 1 轻松愉快的 [+喜剧演员] qīngsōng yúkuài de [+xǐjù yǎnyuán], 充满自信的 chōngmǎn zìxìn de 2 欣欣向荣的 [+经济] xīnxīn xiàng róng de

[+泡沫塑料] yǒu fúlì de [+pàomò sùliào]

burden I N 负担 fùdàn, 重担 zhòngdàn
burden of proof 举证责任 jǔ zhèng zérèn
II v 使…负担 shǐ…fùdān
to be burdened with 承受…的重负 chéngshòu…de zhòngfù

bureau N 局 jú, 司 sī
the Federal Bureau of Investigation (FBI)（美国）联邦调查局 (Měiguó) Liánbāng Diàochájú

bureaucratic ADJ 官僚的 guānliáo de, 官僚主义的 guānliáo zhǔyì de

burgeoning ADJ 迅速增长的 xùnsù zēngzhǎng de

burger N 圆牛肉饼 yuán niúròubǐng

burglar N 破门盗窃者 pòmén dàoqiè zhě, 盗贼 dàozéi

burglary N 破门盗窃罪 pòmén dàoqièzuì

burial N 埋葬 máizàng, 葬礼 zànglǐ

burly ADJ 高大粗壮的 gāodà cūzhuàng de, 魁梧的 kuíwú de

burn I v (PT & PP **burned, burnt**) 1 烧 shāo, 燃烧 ránshāo
to burn to the ground 烧成灰烬 shāo chéng huījìn
2 烧伤 shāoshāng 3 晒伤 shàishāng 4 照亮 zhàoliàng
to burn the midnight oil 熬夜工作 áoyè gōngzuò, 开夜车 kāiyèchē
to be burned out ① 精疲力尽 jīngpí lìjìn, 身心疲惫 shēnxīn píbèi ② 烧毁 shāohuǐ, 烧尽 shāo jìn ③ 使…非常气愤 shǐ…fēicháng qìfèn
5 复制 [+光碟] fùzhì [+guāngdié], 拷贝 kǎobèi **II** N 烧伤 shāoshāng, 烫伤 tàngshāng

burner N 灶火头 zàohuo tóu, 火眼 huǒyǎn
to put sth on the back burner 推迟做某事 tuīchí zuò mǒushì, 暂时不考虑 zànshí bù kǎolǜ

burnish v 擦亮 cāliàng

burned, burnt See burn

burnt ADJ 烧焦的 shāojiāo de

burp v 打嗝 dǎ gé

burrow I v [动物+] 打洞 [dòngwù+] dǎ dòng II N 洞穴 dòngxué

bursar N 财务主管 cáiwù zhǔguǎn

burst I v (PT & PP **burst**) 1 爆裂 bàoliè
to burst out laughing/crying 突然大笑／大哭起来 tūrán dàxiào/dàkū qǐlai
to burst into tears 放声大哭 fàngshēng dàkū
2 闯 chuǎng, 闯入 chuǎngrù II N 破裂 pòliè, 爆裂 bàoliè

bury v 埋 mái, 埋葬 máizàng

bus I N 公共汽车 gōnggòng qìchē
bus conductor 公共汽车售票员 gōnggòng qìchē shòupiàoyuán
bus terminus 公共汽车总站 gōnggòng qìchē zǒngzhàn, 公共汽车终点站 gōnggòng qìchē zhōngdiǎnzhàn
II v 1 用大客车运送 yòng dàkèchē yùnsòng 2 [餐馆里+] 收拾脏餐具 [cānguǎn lǐ+] shōushi zàng cānjù

bush N 灌木丛 guànmùcóng

bushel N (容量单位) 蒲式耳 (róngliàng dānwèi) púshì'ěr (= 36.4 liters)

bushy ADJ [毛发+] 浓密的 [máofà+] nóngmì de

business N 1 商业 shāngyè, 生意 shēngyì
business class [飞机+] 商务舱 [fēijī+] shāngwùcāng
2 商店 shāngdiàn, 商行 shāngháng, 企业 qǐyè [M. WD 家 jiā]
business card 名片 míngpiàn
business hours 营业时间 yíngyè shíjiān
Master of Business Administration (M.B.A.) 商业管理硕士 shāngyè guǎnlǐ shuòshì
3 工作 gōngzuò, 任务 rènwù
business lunch 工作午餐 gōngzuò wǔcān
business trip 出差 chūchāi

bust I v 1 打破 dǎpò 2 [警察+] 指控 [jǐngchá+] zhǐkòng 3 超支 chāozhī II N 1 胸部 xiōngbù, 胸围 xiōngwéi 2 半身塑像 bànshēn sùxiàng

buster N 小子 xiǎozǐ, 讨厌鬼 tǎoyànguǐ

bustle I v 忙乱 mángluàn, 奔忙 bēnmáng II N 忙乱 mángluàn, 喧闹 xuānnào

bustling ADJ 繁忙喧闹的 fánmáng xuānnào de

busy ADJ 1 忙 máng, 繁忙 fánmáng 2 [电话+] 占线的 [diànhuà+] zhànxiàn de

busybody N 爱管闲事的人 ài guǎn xiánshì de rén

but I CONJ 但是 dànshì, 可是 kěshì II PREP 除了 chúle III ADV 仅仅 jǐnjǐn, 只不过 zhǐbúguò

butcher I N 1 肉商 ròu shāng 2 屠夫 túfū II v 屠宰 túzǎi

butler N 男管家 nánguǎnjiā

butt I N 1 屁股 pìgu 2 烟头 yāntóu, 烟蒂 yāndì 3 枪托 qiāngtuō II v 用头顶撞 yòngtóu dǐngzhuàng

butter I N 黄油 huángyóu, 牛油 niúyóu II v 涂黄油 tú huángyóu

butterfly N 1 蝴蝶 húdié [M. WD 只 zhī] 2 蝶泳 diéyǒng

buttock N 屁股 pìgu

button I N 1 纽扣 niǔkòu 2 按钮 ànniǔ 3 胸针 xiōngzhēn [M. WD 枚 méi] II v 上纽扣 kòushang niǔkòu

buttress I N 扶璧 fú bì, 撑墙 chēng qiáng II v 支持 zhīchí

buxom ADJ 丰满健美的 [+女子] fēngmǎn jiànměi de [+nǚzǐ]

buy I v (PT & PP **bought**) 1 买 mǎi
to buy into 收购 shōugòu
to buy out 全部收购 quánbù shōugòu
to buy time 争取时间 zhēngqǔ shíjiān
2 相信 xiāngxìn, 接受 jiēshòu II N 购买 gòumǎi
to be a good buy 买得合算 mǎi dé hésuàn

buyer N 购买者 gòumǎizhě, 买主 mǎizhǔ

buzz I N 嗡嗡声 wēngwēng shēng II v 发出嗡嗡声 fāchū wēngwēng shēng

buzzer N 蜂鸣器 fēngmíngqì

buzzword N 术语 shùyǔ, 行话 hánghuà

by I PREP 1 在…旁边 zài...pángbiān 2 经过 jīngguò 3 在…以前 zài...yǐqián II ADV 经过 jīngguò
by and large 大体上 dàtǐshàng, 大致 dàzhì

bye INTERJ 再见 zàijiàn

bygone ADJ 过去的 guòqù de, 以往的 yǐwǎng de

bylaw N [内部+] 章程 [nèibù+] zhāngchéng

byline N 1 作者署名行 zuòzhě shǔmíng háng 2 球门线 qiúménxiàn

bypass N 旁道 pángdào 2 心脏搭桥手术 xīnzàng dāqiáo shǒushù II v 绕过 ràoguò

by-product N 副产品 fùchǎnpǐn

bystander N 旁观者 pángguānzhě

byte N 字节 zìjié

byway N 偏僻小路 piānpì xiǎolù

byword N 代名词 dàimíngcí

C

C (= Celsius, Centigrade) ABBREV 摄氏 shèshì

cab N 出租汽车 chūzū qìchē

　to hail a cab 叫出租汽车 jiào chūzū qìchē

cabaret N（夜总会或餐馆的）歌舞表演（yèzǒnghuì huò cānguǎn de) gēwǔ biǎoyǎn

cabbage N 卷心菜 juǎnxīncài

cabbie, cabby N 出租汽车司机 chūzū qìchē sījī

cabin N 1 小木屋 xiǎo mùwū [M. WD 间 jiān/栋 dòng] 2 [轮船／飞机+] 客舱 [lún chuán/fēijī+] kècāng [M. WD 间 jiān]

cabinet N 1 柜子 guìzi [M. WD 只 zhī]　display cabinet 陈列柜 chénlièguì 2 [政府] 内阁 [zhèngfǔ] nèigé

cable N 电缆 diànlǎn [M. WD 条 tiáo]　cable car 电缆车 diànlǎnchē 2 有线电视 yǒuxiàn diànshì　cable television 有线电视 yǒuxiàn diànshì

cache N 隐藏物 yǐncángwù, 隐藏处 yǐncángchù

cackle v 1 [母鸡+] 咯咯叫 [mǔjī+] gēgē jiào 2 发出刺耳的笑声 fāchū cì'ěr de xiàoshēng

caddy N（为高尔夫球手服务的）球童 (wéi gāo'ěrfūqiú shǒu fúwù de) qiútóng

cadet N（军官学校或警官学校）学生 (jūnguān xuéxiào huò jǐngguān xué-xiào) xuésheng

cadre N 骨干队伍 gǔgànduìwǔ, 干部 gànbù

Caesarean N 剖腹产手术 pōufùchǎn shǒushù

café N 咖啡馆 kāfēiguǎn [M. WD 家 jiā]

cafeteria N 自助餐厅 zìzhù cāntīng [M. WD 家 jiā], 食堂 shítáng

caffeine N 咖啡因 kāfēiyīn

cage I N 笼子 lóngzi II v 放进笼子 fàngjìn lóngzi

　to feel caged in 感到失去自由 gǎndào shīqù zìyóu

cahoots N 同伙 tónghuǒ

　to be in cahoots with 与…同伙 yǔ… tónghuǒ

cajole v 哄骗 hǒngpiàn

cake N 糕 gāo, 蛋糕 dàngāo

　birthday cake 生日蛋糕 shēngrì dàngāo

　to be a piece of cake 轻而易举的事 qīng ér yì jǔ de shì

　to have your cake and eat it too 两者兼得 liǎngzhě jiān dé

calamity N 灾难 zāinàn [M. WD 场 cháng], 灾祸 zāihuò [M. WD 场 cháng]

calcium N 钙 gài

calculate v 计算 jìsuàn

calculated ADJ 预料中的 yùliào zhòngdì, 预计的 yùjì de

　calculated risk 预计的风险 yùjì de fēngxiǎn

　be calculated to do sth 目的在于 mùdì zàiyú

calculator N 计算器 jìsuànqì

calculus N 微积分 wēijīfēn

calendar N 日历 rìlì

calf N 1 小牛 xiǎoniú 2 小腿 xiǎotuǐ

caliber N 1 [人的+] 才干能力 [rén de+] cáigàn nénglì 2 [事物的+] 质量 [shìwù de+] zhìliàng

calibration N 刻度 kèdù

call I v 1 打电话 dǎ diànhuà

　to call back 回电话 huí diànhuà

　to call collect 打对方付费的电话 dǎ duìfāng fùfèi de diànhuà

2 叫 jiào, 喊 hǎn

　to call for 要求 yāoqiú, 请求 qǐngqiú

3 把…叫作 bǎ…jiàozuo, 叫 jiào 4 拜访 bàifǎng

　to call on 拜访 bàifǎng

to call the shots 发号施令 fāhào shīlìng
II N 1 电话 diànhuà

call box 路边紧急求援电话 lùbiān jǐnjí qiúyuán diànhuà

2 叫喊声 jiàohǎnshēng 3 拜访 bàifǎng

the call of nature 要小便 yào xiǎobiàn

to be on call 随叫随到 suíjiào suídào

caller N 打电话来的人 dǎ diànhuà láide rén

caller ID（电话）来电显示 (diànhuà) láidiàn xiǎnshì

calligraphy N 书法（艺术）shūfǎ (yìshù)

call-in N 电话热线节目 diànhuà rèxiàn jiémù, 叫应节目 kòuyìng jiémù

calling N 使命感 shǐmìnggǎn

callous ADJ 冷漠的 lěngmò de, 冷酷的 lěngkù de

callus N [手脚上的+] 硬皮 [shǒujiǎo shàng de+] yìng pí, 老茧 lǎojiǎn

calm I ADJ 镇静的 zhènjìng de, 镇定的 zhèndìng de II V 使…镇静 shǐ…zhènjìng

calorie N 卡路里 kǎlùlǐ, 卡 kǎ

camaraderie N 同志情谊 tóngzhì qíngyì

camcorder N 便携式摄像机 biànxiéshì shèlùxiàngjī [M. WD 只 zhī/台 tái]

came See **come**

camel N 骆驼 luòtuo [M. WD 只 zhī/头 tóu]

camera N 照相机 zhàoxiàngjī

digital camera 数码照相机 shùmǎ zhàoxiàngjī

surveillance camera 监控摄像机 jiānkòng shèxiàngjī

camouflage I N 1 伪装 wěizhuāng 2 迷彩服 mícǎifú II V 用伪装隐蔽 yòng wěizhuāng yǐnbì

camp I N 营 yíng, 营地 yíngdì

campfire 营火 yínghuǒ, 篝火 gōuhuǒ

campsite 露营地 lùyíngdì

II V 露营 lùyíng

campaign I N [一系列的+] 活动／运动 [yíxìliè de+] huódòng/yùndòng II V 发起或参与（一系列）活动、运动 fāqǐ huò cānyù (yíxìliè de) huódòng, yùndòng

camper N 1 露营者 lùyíng zhě 2 野营车 yěyíng chē [M. WD 辆 liàng]

campus N（大学）校园 (dàxué) xiàoyuán

can[1] MODAL V [NEG cannot ABBREV can't] (PT could; NEG could not ABBREV couldn't) 1 能 néng, 能够 nénggòu 2 可以 kěyǐ

can[2] I N 1 罐头 guàntou 2 桶 tǒng

can opener 开罐器 kāiguànqì

garbage can 垃圾桶 lājītǒng

II V 把（食物）装罐 bǎ (shíwù) zhuāngguàn

Canada N 加拿大 Jiānádà

canal N 运河 yùnhé, 水渠 shuǐqú

cancel V 取消 qǔxiāo

to cancel out 抵消 dǐxiāo

cancellation N 取消 qǔxiāo, 作废 zuòfèi

cancer N 癌 ái, 癌症 áizhèng

candidate N 候选人 hòuxuǎnrén

candidly ADV 直言不讳地 zhíyán búhuì de, 坦率地 tǎnshuài de

candle N 蜡烛 làzhú [M. WD 支 zhī]

to burn the candle at both ends 起早摸黑地工作 qǐzǎomōhēi de gōngzuò

candor N 坦率 tǎnshuài, 坦诚 tǎnchéng

candy N 糖果 tángguǒ

cane I N 1 拐杖 guǎizhàng [M. WD 根 gēn] 手杖 shǒuzhàng [M. WD 根 gēn] II V 用藤鞭抽打 yòng téngbiān chōudǎ

canine ADJ 犬类的 quǎn lèi de, 狗的 gǒu de

police canine unit 警犬小组 jǐngquǎn xiǎozǔ

canister N 方形圆顶罐桶 fāngxíng yuándǐng guàn tǒng, 罐、罐 guàn, 桶 tǒng

canker N 口（角）疮 kǒu (jué) chuāng

canker sore 植物溃疡 zhíwù kuìyáng

canned ADJ 1 罐装的 guànzhuāng de 2 预先录音的 [+笑声／音乐] yùxiān lùyīn de [xiàoshēng, yīnyuè]

canned laughter 预先录制的笑声 yùxiān lùzhì de xiàoshēng

cannibal N 食人肉者 shí rénròu zhě

cannon N 大炮 dàpào [M. WD 门 mén], 加农炮 jiānóngpào [M. WD 门 mén]

canny ADJ 精明的 jīngmíng de, 不容易上当的 bù róngyì shàngdàng de

canoe N 独木舟 dúmùzhōu

canopy N 1 树冠 shùguān 2 顶罩 dǐng zhào

can't See **can**

canteen N 1 食堂 shítáng [M. WD 间 jiān], 行军水壶 xíngjūn shuǐhú

canter V（骑马）中速跑 (qímǎ) zhōng sù pǎo

Cantonese N 1 广东话 Guǎngdōnghuà 2 广东人 Guǎngdōng rén

canvas N 1 帆布 fānbù 2 油画布 yóuhuàbù, 油画 yóuhuà [M. WD 块 kuài]

canvass V 征求意见 zhēngqiú yìjiàn, 了解情况 liǎojiě qíngkuàng, 游说 yóushuì

canyon N 峡谷 xiágǔ

cap N 帽子 màozi, 鸭舌帽 yāshémào

capability N 能力 nénglì, 才能 cáinéng

capable ADJ 能干的 nénggàn de, 有能力的 yǒu nénglì de
to be capable of 能够 nénggòu

capacity N 1 能力 nénglì 2 容量 róngliàng

cape N 1 海角 hǎijiǎo 2 斗篷 dǒupéng [M. WD 件 jiàn], 披风 pīfēng [M. WD 件 jiàn]

caper I N 1 不法勾当 bùfǎ gòudang, 冒险举动 màoxiǎn jǔdòng 2 动作片 dòngzuò piàn II V 兴奋地跳跃 xīngfèn de tiàoyuè

capillary N 毛细血管 máoxì xuèguǎn

capital I N 1 首都 shǒudū 2 资本 zīběn
capital assets 固定资产 gùdìng zīchǎn
II ADJ 1 大写的 dàxiě de
capital letter 大写字母 dàxiězìmǔ
2 死刑的 sǐxíng de
capital punishment 死刑 sǐxíng

capitalist I N 资本家 zīběnjiā II ADJ 资本主义的 zīběn zhǔyì de

capitalize V 1 提供资金 tígōng zījīn 2 大写 [+第一个字母] dàxiě [dìyīgè zìmǔ] 3 利用 [+机会] lìyòng [+jīhuì]

Capitol（美国）国会大厦 (Měiguó) Guóhuì dàshà

capitulate V 屈服 qūfú, 投降 tóuxiáng

cappuccino N 卡普奇诺咖啡 kǎpǔqínuò kāfēi

capricious ADJ 1 任性的 rèn xìng de 2 不合理的 bùhélǐ de

capsize V [船+] 倾覆 [chuán+] qīngfù, 翻船 fānchuán

capsule N 1 胶囊 jiāonáng [M. WD 粒 lì] 2 航天舱 hángtiāncāng [M. WD 间 jiān], 密封舱 mìfēngcāng [M. WD 间 jiān]

captain N 船长 chuánzhǎng, 机长

jīzhǎng 2（球队等）队长 (qiúduì děng) duìzhǎng

caption N 1 [图片+] 说明文字 [túpiàn+] shuōmíng wénzì 2 [电影／电视+] 字幕 [diànyǐng/diànshì+] zìmù

captivate V 迷住 mízhù, 吸引 xīyǐn

captivating ADJ 迷人的 mírén de, 非常吸引人的 fēicháng xīyǐnrén de

captive I ADJ 被关押的 bèi guānyā de
to take sb captive 关押某人 guānyā mǒurén
II N 囚徒 qiútú, 战俘 zhànfú

captivity N 囚禁 qiújìn, 关押 guānyā

captor N 捕捉者 bǔzhuōzhě

capture I V 1 捕获 [+罪犯] bǔhuò [+zuìfàn] 2 攻占 [+城市] gōngzhàn [chéngshì] 3 夺取 [+市场] duóqǔ [+shìchǎng], 赢得 yíngdé
to capture sb's imagination 唤起某人的想象 huànqǐ mǒurén de xiǎngxiàng
II N 捕获 bǔhuò

car N 汽车 qìchē [M. WD 辆 liàng]
car pool 合伙用车的人 héhuǒ yòng chē de rén
sports car 赛车 sàichē
used car 二手车 èrshǒuchē, 旧车 jiùchē

carafe N 饮料瓶 yǐnliàopíng

carat N 克拉 kèlā

caravan N 长途旅行车队 chángtú lǚxíng chēduì

carbohydrate N 碳水化合物 tànshuǐ huàhéwù

carbon (C) N 碳 tàn
carbon copy 复写本 fùxiěběn
carbon dating 碳年代测定法 tàn niándài cèdìngfǎ
carbon dioxide 二氧化碳 $èryǎng huàtàn$
carbon monoxide 一氧化碳 yìyǎng huàtàn
carbon footprint 消耗能源的纪录 xiāohào néngyuán de jìlù

carbonated ADJ 含有二氧化碳的 hányǒu èryǎnghuàtàn de

carburettor N（汽车）汽化器 (qìchē) qìhuàqì

carcass N（动物）尸体 (dòngwù) shītǐ

carcinogen N 致癌物质 zhì'ái wùzhì

carcinogenic ADJ 致癌的 zhì'ái de

card N 1 卡 kǎ, 卡片 kǎpiàn 2 贺卡 hèkǎ 3 银行卡 yínhángkǎ 4 扑克牌 pūkèpái, 纸牌 zhǐpái [M. WD 张 zhāng]

　card table 牌桌 pái zhuō

　card shark 靠作弊赢牌的人 kào zuòbì yíng pái de rén

　birthday card 生日贺卡 shēngrì hèkǎ

　Christmas card 圣诞贺卡 shèngdàn hèkǎ

　credit card 信用卡 xìnyòngkǎ

　ID card 身份证 shēnfènzhèng

cardboard N 硬纸板 yìngzhǐbǎn

cardiac ADJ 心脏的 xīnzàng de

　cardiac arrest 心脏停搏 xīnzàng tíng bó

cardigan N 对襟羊毛衫 duìjīn yángmáoshān [M. WD 件 jiàn]

cardinal I ADJ 基本的 jīběn de, 主要的 zhǔyào de

　cardinal number 基数 jīshù

　II N 枢机主教 Shūjī Zhǔjiào, 红衣主教 Hóngyī Zhǔjiào

cardiology N 心脏病学 xīnzàngbìngxué

cardiovascular ADJ 心血管的 xīnxuèguǎn de

care I V 1 关心 guānxīn, 关怀 guānhuái 2 照顾 zhàogù, 照料 zhàoliào 3 喜欢 xǐhuan 4 在乎 zàihu II N 注意 zhùyì, 小心 xiǎoxīn

　Handle with care! 小心轻放! Xiǎoxīn qīngfàng!

　to take care of ① 照顾 zhàogù, 照料 zhàoliào ② 处理 chǔlǐ, 料理 liàolǐ

　care package [寄给学生／军人的+] 食品包裹 [jìgěi xuésheng/jūnrén de+] shípǐn bāoguǒ

careen V 歪歪扭扭地疾驶向前 wāiwāi niǔniǔ de jíshǐ xiàngqián

career I N [个人的+] 事业 [gèrén de+] shìyè

　career counsellor 就业指导员 jiùyè zhǐdǎoyuán

　II ADJ 职业的 zhíyè de, 专业的 zhuānyè de

　career woman 职业妇女 zhíyè fùnǚ

carefree ADJ 无忧无虑 wúyōu wúlǜ

careful ADJ 小心的 xiǎoxīn de, 仔细的 zǐxì de

　to be careful with money 花钱很谨慎 huāqián hěn jǐnshèn

caregiver N 照看儿童或病人的人 zhàokàn értóng huò bìngrén de rén

careless ADJ 粗心的 cūxīn de

caress V 爱抚 àifǔ, 抚摸 fǔmō

caretaker N 看管人 kānguǎn rén, 管理员 guǎnlǐyuán

cargo N 货物 huòwù

Caribbean ADJ 加勒比海的 Jiālèbǐhǎi de

　Caribbean Sea 加勒比海 Jiālèbǐhǎi

caricature I N 1 漫画 mànhuà, 讽刺画 fěngcìhuà 2 讽刺文章 fěngcì wénzhāng II V 把…画成漫画 bǎ...huà chéng mànhuà

caring ADJ 关心别人的 guānxīn biéren de, 关爱的 guān'ài de

carjacking N 劫持汽车 jiéchí qìchē

carnage N 大屠杀 dà túshā

carnal ADJ 肉欲的 ròuyù de, 肉体的 ròutǐ de

carnation N 麝香石竹 shèxiāng shízhú, 康乃馨 kāngnǎixīn [M. WD 朵 duǒ/株 zhū]

carnival N 1 狂欢节 kuánghuānjié 2 流动游艺团 liúdòng yóuyìtuán

carnivore N 食肉动物 shíròu dòngwù

carnivorous ADJ 食肉的 shíròu de

carol N 圣诞颂歌 Shèngdàn sònggē

carousel N 旋转木马 xuánzhuàn mùmǎ

carp[1] N 鲤鱼 lǐyú

carp[2] V 挑剔 tiāoti, 吹毛求疵 chuī máo qiú cī

carpenter N 木工 mùgōng, 木工师傅 mùgōng shīfu

carpet N 地毯 dìtǎn [M. WD 块 kuài]

carport N 停车棚 tíngchēpéng

carriage N 车厢 chēxiāng

carrier N 1 航空运输公司 hángkōng yùnshū gōngsī 2 航空母舰 hángkōng-mǔjiàn 3 送递人 yùnsòngrén

carrot N 1 胡萝卜 húluóbo [M. WD 根 gēn] 2 许诺 xǔnuò

　a carrot-and-stick approach 胡萝卜加大棒的方法 húluóbo jiā dàbàng de fāngfǎ

carry V 1 运送 yùnsòng 2 随身带 suíshēn dài, 携带 xiédài

　to carry out 实行 shíxíng, 进行 jìnxíng

to get/be carried away 激动得失去控制 jīdòng de shīqù kòngzhì

carsickness N 晕车 yùnchē

cart I N 推车 tuīchē
  shopping cart 购物车 gòuwùchē
  II v 搬运 bānyùn, 装运 zhuāngyùn

cartel N 卡特尔 kǎtè'ěr, 同业联盟 tóngyè liánméng

cartilage N 软骨组织 ruǎngǔ zǔzhī

cartography N 地图绘制 dìtú huìzhì

carton N 纸板箱 zhǐbǎnxiāng

cartoon N 1 漫画 mànhuà 2 (animated cartoon) 动画片 dònghuàpiàn

cartridge N 1 小盒子 xiǎohézi [M. WD 只 zhī] 2 子弹 zǐdàn [M. WD 颗 kē/枚 méi]
  computer game cartridge 电脑游戏卡 diànnǎo yóuxìkǎ

cartwheel N 侧手翻 cèshǒufān

carve v 雕刻 diāokè

cascade I N 小瀑布 xiǎopùbù II v 瀑布一样地落下 pùbù yīyàng de luòxia

case N 1 事例 shìlì 2 (法律) 案件 (fǎlǜ) ànjiàn 3 病例 bìnglì
  case study 个案研究 gè'àn yánjiū
  in case 万一 wànyī
  in any case 无论如何 wúlùn rúhé, 不管怎样 bùguǎn zěnyàng

caseload N 工作量 gōngzuòliàng

cash I N 现金 xiànjīn II v 兑换现金 duìhuàn xiànjīn
  cash cow 摇钱树 yáoqiánshù
  cash crop 经济作物 jīngjì zuòwù
  cash flow 现金流通 xiànjīn liútōng

cashew N 腰果 yāoguǒ [M. WD 粒 lì]

cashier N 出纳 chūnà (员 yuán)

cashmere N (山) 羊绒 (shān) yángróng

cash-strapped ADJ 资金困难的 zījīn kùnnan de

casing N 套套 tàotào, 罩 zhào

casino N 赌场 dǔchǎng

cask N (装酒的) 木桶 (zhuāng jiǔ de) mùtǒng

casket N 1 棺材 guāncai 2 首饰盒 shǒushìhé

casserole N 1 砂锅 shāguō, 炖锅 dùnguō 2 砂锅菜 shāguōcài, 炖锅菜 dùnguōcài
  beef casserole 砂锅牛肉 shāguō niúròu

cassette N 盒式磁带 hé shì cídài
  audio cassette 盒式录音带 héshì lùyīndài
  video cassette 盒式录像带 héshì lùxiàngdài

cast I v (PT & PP cast) 1 投 tóu, 掷 zhì 2 清除 qīngchú, 扔掉 rēngdiào 3 投射 tóushè
  to cast a vote 投票 tóupiào
  to cast a shadow 投下阴影 tóuxià yīnyǐng
  II N 1 全体演员 quántǐ yǎnyuán 2 人物 rénwù, 角色 juésè

castaway N [沉船后+] 漂流到荒岛的人 [chénchuán hòu+] piāoliú dào huāngdǎo de rén

caste N (印度的) 种姓制度 (Yìndù de) zhǒngxìng zhìdù

castigate v 严厉批评 yánlì pīpíng, 严惩 yánchéng

castle N 城堡 chéngbǎo [M. WD 座 zuò]

castoff N 丢弃的 [+衣服] diūqì de [+yīfu]

castrate v 阉割 yāngē

casual ADJ 1 非正式的 fēizhèngshì de 2 随意的 suíyì de, 漫不经心的 màn bù jīngxīn de 3 不是经常的 bú shì jīngcháng de, 偶然的 ǒurán de
  casual clothes 休闲服装 xiūxián fúzhuāng
  a casual remark 随口说的一句话 suíkǒu shuōde yíjù huà
  casual worker 临时工 línshígōng

casualty N 伤亡人员 shāngwáng rényuán, 伤亡人数 shāngwáng rénshù

cat N 猫 māo [M. WD 只 zhī]
  like a cat on a hot tin roof 像热锅上的蚂蚁 xiàng règuōshàng de mǎyǐ

cataclysmic ADJ 剧变的 jùbiàn de

catalog N 1 商品目录 shāngpǐn mùlù, 样品簿 yàngpǐnbù 2 图书目录 túshūmùlù, 索引 suǒyǐn

catalysis N 催化作用 cuīhuà zuòyòng

catalyst N 1 催化剂 cuīhuàjì 2 促使巨变的人 (或事) cùshǐ jùbiàn de rén (huò shì)

catapult I N 1 弹弓 dàngōng 2 飞机弹射器 fēijī tánshèqì II v 把…弹出去 bǎ…dàn chūqu

cataract N 白内障 báinèizhàng

catastrophe N 巨大灾难 jùdà zāinàn

catch I v (PT & PP **caught**) 1 抓住 zhuāzhù, 抓获 zhuāhuò 2 赶上 gǎn shàng 3 感染上 gǎnrǎn shàng

to be caught up in sth 被卷入某事 bèijuǎn rù mǒu shì

to catch on 开始明白 kāishǐ míngbai

to catch one's breath 喘过气来 chuǎn guòqì lái, 喘气 chuǎnqì

to catch sb's eye 吸引某人的注意 xīyǐn mǒurén de zhùyì

II N 1 抓住 zhuāzhù, 接住 jiēzhù 2 (隐藏的) 问题 (yǐncáng de) wèntí, 隐患 yǐnhuàn 3 圈套 quāntào, 诡计 guǐjì 4 [海产的+] 捕获量 [hǎichǎn de+] bǔhuòliàng 5 [项链+] 扣子 [xiàngliàn+] kòuzi

catch phrase 流行语 liúxíng yǔ, 口头禅 kǒutóuchán

catching ADJ 传染性的 chuánrǎnxìng de

catchword N 口号标记 kǒuhào, 标语 biāoyǔ

catchy ADJ 朗朗上口的 lǎnglǎng shàngkǒu de, 顺口的 shùnkǒu de

catechism N (基督教的) 教理问答 (Jīdūjiào de) jiàolǐ wèndá

categorical ADJ 明确的 míngquè de

categorize v 把…分类 bǎ…fēnlèi

category N 种类 zhǒnglèi, 类别 lèibié

cater v 提供饮食服务 tígōng yǐnshí fúwù, 办酒席 bànjiǔxí

to cater to/for 满足 [顾客+] 的需要 mǎnzú [gùkè+] de xūyào

catering N 提供饮食 tígōng yǐnshí, 承办酒席 chéngbàn jiǔxí

catering industry 饮食行业 yǐnshí hángyè

caterpillar N 毛虫 máochóng

cathedral N 大教堂 dàjiàotáng

Catholic N 天主教 Tiānzhǔjiào

catnap N 小睡 xiǎoshuì

to take catnaps 小睡一会儿 xiǎoshuì yíhuir, 打盹儿 dǎdǔnr

cattle N 牛群 niúqún, 牛 niú

catty ADJ 恶毒的 èdú de, 歹毒的 dǎidú de

catwalk N (时装表演) 步行台 (shízhuāng biǎoyǎn) bùxíngtái, T 形台 tīxíngtái

Caucasian N, ADJ 白种人 (的) báizhǒngrén (de)

caucus N 政党地区会议 zhèngdǎng dìqū huìyì

caught See **catch**

cauliflower N 花椰菜 huāyēcài [M. WD 颗 kē], 花菜 huācài [M. WD 颗 kē]

cause I N 1 原因 yuányīn, 理由 lǐyóu

with good cause 有充分理由 yǒu chōngfèn lǐyóu

2 事业 shìyè II v 因某事 yīnqí, 造成 zàochéng

caustic ADJ 1 刻薄的 [+言词] kèbó de [+yáncí], 尖刻的 jiānkè de 2 腐蚀性的 [+物质] fǔshíxìng de [+wùzhì]

caution I N 谨慎 jǐnshèn II v 告诫 gàojiè, 提醒 tíxǐng

cautionary ADJ 警告的 jǐnggào de

a cautionary tale 有警示意义的事例 yǒu jǐngshì yìyì de shìlì

cautious ADJ 谨慎的 jǐnshèn de

cave¹ N 洞 dòng, 洞穴 dòngxuě

cave² v (to cave in) 1 [煤矿+] 塌方 [méikuàng+] tāfāng 2 停止抵抗 tíngzhǐ dǐkàng, 屈从 qūcóng

cavern N 大山洞 dà shāndòng, 大洞穴 dà dòngxuě

caviar N 鱼子酱 yúzǐjiàng

cavity N 1 蛀牙洞 zhùyá dòng 2 腔 qiāng, 洞 dòng

cavort v 欢腾 huānténg, 欢闹 huān nào

cc (= cubic centimeter) ABBREV 立方厘米 lìfānglímǐ

CCTV (= closed-circuit televison) ABBREV 闭路电视 bìlù diànshì

CD (= compact disk) ABBREV 光碟 guāngdié [M. WD 张 zhāng/盘 pán]

cease v 终止 zhōngzhǐ, 停止 tíngzhǐ

ceasefire N 停火 tínghuǒ

ceaseless ADJ 不停的 bùtíng de

cedar N 西洋杉 Xīyáng shān, 雪松 xuěsōng

cede v 割让 gēràng, 交出 jiāochū

ceiling N 1 天花板 tiānhuābǎn 2 上限 shàngxiàn

celebrate v 1 庆祝 [+新年] qìngzhù [+xīnnián] 2 赞美 [+大自然] zànměi [+dàzìrán], 颂扬 sòngyáng

celebrated ADJ 著名的 zhùmíng de, 闻名的 wénmíng de

celebration N 1 庆祝 qìngzhù 2 颂扬 sòngyáng

celebrity N 名人 míngrén

celery N 芹菜 qíncài

celestial ADJ 天上的 tiānshàng de, 天堂的 tiāntáng de

celibate ADJ (因宗教而) 禁欲的 (yīn zōngjiào ér) jìnyù de

cell N 1 牢房 láofáng [M. WD 间 jiān] 2 细胞 xìbāo 3 电池 diànchí [M. WD 节 jié]

cellar N 地窖 dìjiào
wine cellar 酒窖 jiǔjiào, 储藏在地窖的酒 chǔcáng zài dìjiào de jiǔ

cellist N 大提琴演奏者 dàtíqín yǎnzòuzhě

cello N 大提琴 dàtíqín [M. WD 把 bǎ]

cellophane N 玻璃纸 bōlizhǐ

cell phone N 手机 shǒujī, 移动电话 yídòng diànhuà

cellular ADJ 1 细胞的 xìbāo de 2 移动电话的 yídòng diànhuà de

cellulite N 皮下脂肪 pí xià zhīfáng

celluloid N (早期) 电影的 (zǎoqī) diànyǐng de

Celsius N See C

cement I N 1 水泥 shuǐní 2 胶合剂 jiāohéjì II V 1 涂上水泥 tú shàngshuǐ ní 2 巩固 gǒnggù

cemetery N 公墓 gōngmù, 墓地 mùdì

censor I V 审查 shěnchá II N 审查人员 shěnchá rényuán

censorship N 审查 shěnchá, 审查制度 shěnchá zhìdù

censure V 正式批评 zhèngshì pīpíng, 公开谴责 gōngkāi qiǎnzé

census N 人口普查 rénkǒu pǔchá

cent N [钱] 分 [qián] fēn

centennial, centenary N 一百周年 yìbǎi zhōunián, 一百周年纪念 yìbǎi zhōunián jìniàn

center N 中间 zhōngjiān, 中心 zhōngxīn
center of gravity 重心 zhòngxīn
shopping center 购物中心 gòuwù zhōngxīn

centerfold N (杂志中页的) 裸女照片 (zázhì zhōng yè de) luǒnǚ zhàopiàn

centerpiece N 1 餐桌中央的装饰品 cānzhuō zhōngyāng de zhuāngshìpǐn 2 最重要的部分 zuì zhòngyào de bùfen

Centigrade N 摄氏 Shèshì

centimeter, cm N 厘米 límǐ, 公分 gōngfēn

centipede N 百足虫 bǎizúchóng, 蜈蚣 wúgōng

central ADJ 中心的 zhōngxīn de, 中央的 zhōngyāng de
(New York) Central Park (纽约) 中央公园 (Niǔyuē) zhōngyāng gōngyuán

century N 世纪 shìjì

CEO (= Chief of Executive Officer) AB-BREV 首席执行官 shǒuxí zhíxíngguān, 总经理 zǒngjīnglǐ [M. WD 位 wèi]

ceramics N 陶瓷器 (制作) táocíqì (zhìzuò)

cereal N 早餐谷物食品 zǎocān gǔwù shípǐn, 麦片 màipiàn

cerebral ADJ 1 大脑的 dànǎo de 2 需要大脑思考的 xūyào dànǎo sīkǎo de, 深奥的 shēn'ào de

ceremonial ADJ 礼仪的 lǐyí de, 典礼的 diǎnlǐ de

ceremony N 仪式 yíshì, 典礼 diǎnlǐ
marriage ceremony 结婚仪式 jiéhūn yíshì

certain ADJ 1 肯定的 kěndìng de 2 某个 mǒu ge, 某些 mǒuxiē

certainly ADV 1 肯定地 kěndìng de 2 当然 dāngrán

certainty N 确定性 quèdìngxìng, 确定的事 quèdìng de shì
to say with (any) certainty 确切地说 quèqiè de shuō

certifiable ADJ 1 可以证明的 kěyǐ zhèngmíng de 2 可以通过的 kěyǐ tōngguò de

certificate N 证书 zhèngshū, 证明 zhèngmíng [M. WD 份 fèn, 张 zhāng]
birth certificate 出生证 chūshēngzhèng
certificate of deposit 存款单 cúnkuǎndān
death certificate 死亡证 sǐwángzhèng

certified ADJ 完成专业培训的 wánchéng zhuānyè péixùn de, 合格的 hégé de

certified public accountant 合格的开业会计 hégé de kāiyè kuàijì, 执业会计 zhíyè kuàijì
2 被核准的 bèi hézhǔn de
a certified copy 经鉴定核准的副本 jīng jiàndìng hézhǔn de fùběn

certify v 正式证明 zhèngshì zhèngmíng

cervical ADJ 子宫颈的 zǐgōngjǐng de
cervical cancer 子宫颈癌 zǐgōngjǐng ái

cessation N 停止 tíngzhǐ, 中断 zhōngduàn

cesspool N 污秽的场所 wūhuì de chǎngsuǒ

chafe v 恼火 nǎohuǒ, 焦躁 jiāozào

chagrin I N 懊恼 àonǎo, 失望 shīwàng
II v 使（某人）懊恼 shǐ (mǒurén) àonǎo, 使（某人）失望 shǐ (mǒurén) shīwàng

chain I N **1** 链条 liàntiáo **2** 一系列 yíxìliè **3** 连锁商店 liánsuǒshāngdiàn/餐馆 cānguǎn/旅馆 lǚguǎn II v 用链条栓住 yòng liàntiáo shuānzhù
chain letter 连锁信 liánsuǒ xìn
chain reaction 连锁反应 liánsuǒ fǎnyìng

chainsaw N 链锯 liànjù [M. WD 把 bǎ]

chainsmoker N 一支接一支地吸烟的人 yìzhī jiē yìzhī de xīyān de rén, 烟鬼 yānguǐ

chair N 椅子 yǐzi [M. WD 把 bǎ]
armchair 扶手椅 fúshǒuyǐ [M. WD 把 bǎ]
wheelchair 轮椅 lúnyǐ [M. WD 辆 liàng]

chairperson N 主席 zhǔxí [M. WD 位 wèi]
chairman of a company 公司董事长 gōngsī dǒngshìzhǎng

chalet N（瑞士）小屋 (Ruìshì) xiǎo wū

chalk I N **1** 粉笔 fěnbǐ [M. WD 支 zhī] **2** 白垩 bái'è II v 用粉笔写 yòng fěnbǐ xiě
to chalk up 获分 huò fēn

chalkboard N 黑板 hēibǎn

challenge I v **1** 挑战 [+权威] tiǎozhàn [+quánwēi] **2** 要求 [+做困难的事] yāoqiú [+zuò kùnnáo de shì] II N **1** 挑战 tiǎozhàn, 挑战书 tiǎozhànshū **2** 很难对付的人（或事）hěn nán duìfu de rén (huò shì) **3** 质疑 zhìyí

chamber N **1** 房间 fángjiān **2** 室 shì, 腔 qiāng
chamber music 室内（音）乐 shìnèi (yīn) yuè
chamber of commerce 商会 shānghuì

chameleon N **1** 变色蜥蜴 biànsè xīyì **2** 见风使舵的人 jiàn fēng shǐ duò de rén, 变色龙 biànsèlóng

champagne N 香槟酒 xiāngbīnjiǔ

champion N 冠军 guànjūn [M. WD 位 wèi]

championship N 锦标赛 jǐnbiāosài

chance I N 机会 jīhuì
to take a chance, to take chances 冒险 màoxiǎn, 冒风险 mào fēngxiǎn
fat chance 不可能 bùkěnéng
by chance 偶然 ǒurán, 正巧 zhèngqiǎo
to leave nothing to chance 毫不疏忽 háobù shūhu
II v **1** 冒险 màoxiǎn **2** 碰巧 pèngqiǎo
III ADJ 偶然的 ǒurán de

chancellor N **1**（某些大学的）校长 (mǒuxiē dàxué de) xiàozhǎng **2**（德国）总理 (Déguó) Zǒnglǐ

chandelier N 枝形吊灯 zhīxíng diàodēng

change I v **1** 变化 biànhuà **2** 改变 gǎibiàn **3** 换乘（火车、飞机等）huàn chéng (huǒchē、fēijī děng) II N **1** 变化 biànhuà **2** 找头 zhǎotou **3** 零钱 língqián
small change 零钱 língqián
a change of clothes 备换的衣服 bèi huàn de yīfu

changeable ADJ 常常变化的 chángcháng biànhuà de

channel I N **1** 电视频道 diànshì píndào **2** 海峡 hǎixiá **3** [供水+] 管道 [gōngshuǐ+] guǎndào **4** [获取信息的+] 途径 tújìng, 渠道 qúdào
to go through diplomatic channels 通过外交渠道 tōngguò wàijiāo qúdào
II v 把（金钱、精力）用于 bǎ (jīnqián, jīnglì) yòng yú
to channel resources into research and development 把资源用于开发研究 bǎ zīyuán yòng yú kāifā yánjiū

chant I v **1** 反复地喊叫 fǎnfù de hǎnjiào **2** 吟唱 [+宗教歌曲] yínchàng [+zōngjiào gēqǔ] II N **1** 一再重复的话 yízài chóngfù dehuà **2** 宗教歌曲 zōngjiào gēqǔ

chaos N 混乱 hùnluàn, 无序状态 wú xù zhuàngtài

chaotic ADJ 极其混乱的 jíqí hùnluàn de, 紊乱不堪的 wěnluàn bùkān de

chapel N 小教堂 xiǎojiàotáng
  wedding chapel 婚礼教堂 hūnlǐ jiàotáng

chaperone I N （未成年人在社交场合的）
  监护人 (wèi chēngnián rén zài shèjiāo
  chǎnghé de) jiānhùrén II V 当监护人
  dāng jiānhùrén

chaplain N （军队、医院等地的）牧师
  (jūnduì, yīyuàn děng dì de) mùshī

chapped ADJ 皲裂的 jūnliè de, 干燥的
  gānzào de

chapter N 1 章 zhāng, 章节 zhāngjié 2 时
  期 shíqī, 事件 shìjiàn 3 分会 fēnhuì

char V 烧焦 shāojiāo

character N 1 [电影 / 小说+] 人物 / 角色
  [diànyǐng/xiǎoshuō+] rénwù/juésè
  2 性格 xìnggé 3 特征 tèzhēng 4 书写符
  号 shūxiě fúhào
  Chinese character 汉字 Hànzì

characteristic I N 特点 tèdiǎn, 特性
  tèxìng II ADJ 独特的 dútè de, 显著的
  xiǎnzhe de

characterize V 把…说成 bǎ…shuōchéng,
  描绘…的特征 miáohuì…de tèzhēng
  to characterize the economic situation as dire 把经济形势说成是极其糟糕
  的 bǎ jīngjì xíngshì shuōchéng shì jíqí
  zāogāo de

charades N 猜字游戏 cāizì yóuxì

charcoal N 炭 tàn, 木炭 mùtàn

charge I V 1 要价 yàojià 2 记账 jìzhàng
  3 指控 zhǐkòng 4 猛冲 měngchōng II N
  1 费用 fèiyòng
  free of charge 免费 miǎnfèi
  2 指控 zhǐkòng, 罪名 zuìmíng 3 负责
  fùzé 4 突然猛冲 tūrán měngchōng 5 充
  电 chōngdiàn

charger N 充电器 chōngdiànqì

chariot N （古代）战车 (gǔdài) zhànchē

charisma N 魅力 mèilì, 个人魅力 gèrén
  mèilì

charitable ADJ 1 慈善的 císhàn de, 慈
  善事业的 císhàn shìyè de 2 宽容的
  kuānróng de, 同情的 tóngqíng de

charity N 1 慈善 císhàn, 慈善事业 císhàn
  shìyè
  charity concert 为慈善事业募捐的

音乐会 wéi císhàn shìyè mùjuān de
  yīnyuèhuì, 义演音乐会 yìyǎn yīnyuèhuì
  2 施舍物 shīshě wù

charlatan N 冒充内行的骗子 màochōng
  nèiháng de piànzi

charm N 1 迷人之处 mírén zhī chù, 魅力
  mèilì 2 装饰挂件 zhuāngshì guàjiàn
  lucky charm 护身符 hùshēnfú [M. WD
  件 jiàn]

charmed ADJ 好像有魔法保护的 hǎoxiàng
  yǒu mófǎ bǎohù de, 幸运的 xìngyùn de
  to lead a charmed life 生活一直很幸福
  shēnghuó yìzhí hěn xìngfú

charred ADJ 烧焦的 shāojiāo de

chart I N 图表 túbiǎo
  pie chart 饼形分析图 bǐngxíng fēnxī tú
  II V 1 记录 jìlù 2 制订计划 zhìdìng jìhuà

charter I N 1 [飞机 / 船只+] 包租 [fēijī/
  chuánzhǐ+] bāozū 2 纲领 gānglǐng
  charter flight 包机旅行 bāojī lǚxíng
  II V 包租 [+飞机 / 船只] bāozū [+fēijī/
  chuánzhǐ]

chase V 1 追 zhuī, 追赶 zhuīgǎn 2 追求
  zhuīqiú
  to chase down 找到 zhǎodào, 追捕到
  zhuībǔdào

chasm N 1 深渊 shēnyuān 2 巨大的分歧
  jùdà de fēnqí

chassis N （汽车）底盘 (qìchē) dǐpán

chaste ADJ 贞洁的 zhēnjié de, 纯洁的
  chúnjié de

chasten V 惩戒 chéngjiè, 使…接受教训
  shǐ…jiēshòu jiàoxùn

chat N, V 闲谈 xiántán, 聊天 liáotiān
  2 网上聊天 wǎngshàng liáotiān
  chat room 网上聊天室 wǎngshàng
  liáotiānshì

chateau N （法国的）城堡 (Fǎguó de)
  chéngbǎo

chatter I V 1 [人+] 唠叨 [ren+] láodao, 喋
  喋不休 diédié bùxiū 2 [猴子 / 鸟+] 鸣叫
  [hóuzi/niǎo+] míngjiào 3 [牙齿+] 打战
  [yáchǐ+] dǎzhàn

chatterbox N 喋喋不休的人 diédié bùxiū
  de rén

chauffeur I N （私人）司机 (sīrén) sījī
  II V 当私人司机 dāng sīrén sījī

a chauffeured limousine 配有私人司机的豪华轿车 pèiyǒu sīrén sījī de háohuá jiàochē

chauvinism N 沙文主义 Shāwén zhǔyì
male chauvinsim 大男子主义 dànánzǐ zhǔyì

cheap ADJ 1 便宜的 piányi de, 廉价的 liánjià de 2 劣质的 lièzhì de 3 不尊重的 bù zūnzhòng de
cheap remarks 不公平的批评 bùgōngpíng de pīpíng

cheapen V 使…降低身份 shǐ…jiàngdī shēnfèn

cheapskate N 小气鬼 xiǎoqìguǐ

cheat I V 1 骗 piàn, 欺骗 qīpiàn 2 作弊 zuòbì II N 骗子 piànzi, 作弊者 zuòbìzhě

check I V 1 检查 jiǎnchá, 核对 héduì 2 托运 tuōyùn
to check in ① [在旅馆 / 医院+] 登记入住 [zài lǚguǎn/yīyuàn+] dēngjì rùzhù ② 办登飞机手续 bàn dēng fēijī shǒuxù
to check out ① [在旅馆 / 医院+] 结账离开 [zài lǚguǎn/yīyuàn+] jiézhàng líkāi ② 从图书馆借书 cóng túshūguǎn jiè shū 3 核实 [+信息] héshí [+xìnxī] 4 检查 jiǎnchá II N 1 检查 jiǎnchá, 核对 héduì
security check 安全检查 ānquán jiǎnchá 2 控制 kòngzhì, 抑制 yìzhì 3 支票 zhīpiào 4 [餐馆+] 账单 [cānguǎn+] zhàngdān

checkbook N 支票簿 zhīpiàobù [M. WD 本 běn]

checked ADJ 彩色方格图案的 cǎisè fānggé tú'àn de

checker N 1 (超市) 收银员 (chāoshì) shōuyínyuán 2 检查员 jiǎncháyuán
spelling checker (电脑) 拼写检查程序 (diànnǎo) pīnxiě jiǎnchá chéngxù

checkers N 西洋跳棋 Xīyáng tiàoqí

check-in N 1 [旅馆+] 入住手续 [lǚguǎn+] rùzhù shǒuxù 2 登机手续 dēngjī shǒuxù
check-in counter [旅馆+] 入住手续处 [lǚguǎn+] rùzhù shǒuxùchù, [机场+] 登机手续柜台 [jīchǎng+] dēngjī shǒuxùguìtái

checklist N (核对用的) 清单 (héduì yòng de) qīngdān [M. WD 份 fèn]

checkout N 1 付款处 fùkuǎnchù, 收银台

shōuyíntái 2 [旅馆+] 退房时间 [lǚguǎn+] tuìfáng shíjiān

checkpoint N 检查站 jiǎncházhàn

check-up N 体格检查 tǐgé jiǎnchá

cheek N 面颊 miànjiá

cheer N, V 欢呼 huānhū
to cheer … on 为…加油 wéi …jiāyóu
to cheer up 振作起来 zhènzuòqǐlái, 高兴起来 gāoxìng qǐlái
Cheer up! 振作起来! Zhènzuòqǐlái! 高兴一点儿! Gāoxìng yìdiǎnr!

cheerful ADJ 快活的 kuàihuo de, 令人愉快的 lìngrén yúkuài de

cheerleader N 1 [橄榄球+] 啦啦队员 [gǎnlǎnqiú+] lālāduìyuán 2 鼓励者 gǔlì zhě

cheese N 奶酪 nǎilào
Say cheese! (照相时) 笑一笑! (zhàoxiàng shí) Xiào yí xiào! 说 "茄子"! Shuo "qiézi"!

cheetah N 猎豹 lièbào [M. WD 头 tóu]

chef N 大厨师 dàchúshī [M. WD 位 wèi]
pastry chef 点心师傅 diǎnxin shīfu

chemical I N 化学制品 huàxué zhìpǐn II ADJ 化学的 huàxué de, 化工的 huàgōng de
chemical plant 化工厂 huàgōngchǎng
chemical engineer 化工工程师 huàgōng gōngchéngshī

chemist N 化学家 huàxuéjiā

chemistry N 化学 huàxué

chemotherapy N 化学疗法 huàxué liáofǎ, 化疗 huàliáo

cherish V 珍视 zhēnshì

cherry N 樱桃 yīngtáo [M. WD 颗 kē/粒 lì]
cherry blossom 樱花 yīnghuā

cherub N 小天使 xiǎotiānshǐ

chess N 象棋 xiàngqí, 国际象棋 guójì xiàngqí [M. WD 副 fù/盘 pán]

chest N 1 胸 xiōng, 胸口 xiōngkǒu 2 大箱子 dàxiāngzi
medicine chest 药品橱 yàopǐnchú
chest of drawers 五斗橱 wǔdǒuchú

chestnut N 栗子 lìzi [M. WD 粒 lì/颗 kē]

chew V 嚼 jiáo, 咀嚼 jǔjué
to chew on 深思 shēnsī
to chew out 严厉责备 yánlì zébèi

chewing gum N 口香糖 kǒuxiāngtáng

chic ADJ 时髦漂亮的 shímáo piàoliang de

chick N 1 小鸡 xiǎojī [M. WD 只 zhī], 小鸟 xiǎoniǎo 2 小妞 xiǎoniū

chicken I N 1 鸡 jī [M. WD 只 zhī]
a chicken-and-egg situation 先有鸡还是先有蛋的问题 xiān yǒu jī háishi xiān yǒu dàn de wèntí
2 鸡肉 jīròu II ADJ 胆小的 dǎnxiǎo de

chickenpox N 水痘 shuǐdòu

chide V 斥责 chìzé, 怒骂 nùmà

chief I ADJ 主要的 zhǔyào de
the Chief Executive 美国总统 Měiguó zǒngtǒng
chief justice 首席法官 shǒuxí fǎguān
II N 主管 zhǔguǎn, 头儿 tóur
chief of staff 参谋长 cānmóuzhǎng
police chief 警长 jǐngzhǎng

chiefly ADV 主要 zhǔyào, 大部分 dàbùfen

chieftain N 酋长 qiúzhǎng, 族长 zúzhǎng

chiffon N 雪纺绸 xuěfǎngchóu

child N (PL **children**) 1 儿童 értóng, 孩子 háizi 2 子女 zǐnǚ, 孩子 háizi
child support 子女抚养费 zǐnǚ fǔyǎngfèi

childbearing N 生孩子 shēng háizi, 分娩 fēnmiǎn
childbearing age 育龄 yùlíng

childbirth N 分娩 fēnmiǎn, 生孩子 shēng háizi

childcare N 儿童照管 értóng zhàoguǎn
childcare center 儿童照管中心 értóng zhàoguǎn zhōngxīn, 托儿所 tuō'érsuǒ

childhood N 童年 tóngnián

childish ADJ 孩子气的 háiziqì de, 幼稚的 yòuzhì de

childless ADJ 无子女的 wú zǐnǚ de

childlike ADJ 孩子般的 háizi bān de, 天真的 tiānzhēn de

childproof ADJ 儿童不能开启的 értóng bù néng kāiqǐ de, 对儿童无害的 duì értóng wúhài de

children See **child**

chili, chilli N 辣椒 làjiāo

chill I V 使…冷却 shǐ…lěngquè, 使…变冷 shǐ…biàn lěng II N 1 寒意 hányì 2 害怕 hàipà, 胆战心惊 dǎnzhàn xīnjīng III ADJ 非常冷的 fēicháng lěng de

chilling ADJ 令人极其害怕的 lìngrén jíqí hàipà de, 令人毛骨悚然的 lìngrén máogǔ sǒngrán de

chilly ADJ 寒冷的 hánlěng de

chime I N 编钟 biānzhōng II V [钟+] 响 [zhōng+] xiǎng
to chime in 插话 [+表示赞同] chāhuà [+biǎoshì zàntóng]

chimney N 烟囱 yāncōng

chimpanzee N 黑猩猩 hēixīngxīng

chin N 下巴 xiàba
chin up 引体向上 yǐntǐxiàngshàng
to take it on the chin 承受 [+不公正对待] chéngshòu [+bù gōngzhèng duìdài]

china N 瓷器 cíqì

China N 中国 Zhōngguó

Chinatown N 唐人街 Tángrénjiē, 华人区 Huárén qū

Chinese I ADJ 中国的 Zhōngguó de II N 1 中国人 Zhōngguórén 2 中文 Zhōngwén, 汉语 Hànyǔ, 华语 Huáyǔ

chink N 缝隙 fèngxì, 漏洞 lòudòng

chip N 1 炸土豆条 zhá tǔdòutiáo, 炸薯条 zhá shǔtiáo 2 (计算机) 集成电路片 (jìsuànjī) jíchéng diànlù piàn 3 (碗) 豁口 (wǎn) huōkǒu, 缺口 quēkǒu 4 (赌场) 筹码 (dǔchǎng) chóumǎ

chipmuck N 花鼠 huāshǔ [M. WD 只 zhī], 金花鼠 jīnhuā shǔ

chiropractor N 背部按摩师 bèibù ànmóshī

chirp V [鸟或昆虫+] 叫 [niǎo huò kūnchóng+] jiào, 唧唧喳喳地叫 jījīzhāzhā de jiào

chisel I N 凿子 záozi, 凿刀 záo dāo [M. WD 把 bǎ] II V (用凿子) 凿 (yòng záozi) záo

chit N 借贷字据 jièdài zìjù, 欠账单 qiànzhàng dān

chit-chat N 闲聊 xiánliáo

chivalry N 骑士风度 qíshì fēngdù

chives N 细香葱 xìxiāngcōng

chlorine N 氯 lù, 氯气 lùqì

chock-a-block ADJ 满满的 mǎnmǎn de, 爆满的 bàomǎn de

chock-full ADJ 装满的 zhuāngmǎn de, 塞满的 sāimǎn de

chocoholic, chocaholic N 特别爱吃巧克力的人 tèbié ài chī qiǎokèlì de rén

chocolate N 巧克力 qiǎokèlì
hot chocolate 热巧克力饮料 rè qiǎokèlì yǐnliào

choice I N 选择 xuǎnzé
by choice 自己选择的 zìjǐ xuǎnzé de, 自愿的 zìyuàn de
II ADJ 精选的 jīngxuǎn de, 优质的 yōuzhì de

choir N (教会) 唱诗班 (jiàohuì) chàngshībān, (学校) 合唱团 (xuéxiào) héchàngtuán

choke I v 1 使…窒息 shǐ...zhìxī 2 堵塞 dǔsè 3 (因激动) 说不出话来 (yīn jīdòng) shuōbuchū huà lái II N 1 窒息 zhìxī 2 阻门器 zǔ mén qì
choke collar (狗) 项圈 (gǒu) xiàngquān

cholera N 霍乱 huòluàn

cholesterol N 胆固醇 dǎngùchún

choose (PT **chose**; PP **chosen**) v 1 选择 xuǎnzé, 挑选 tiāoxuǎn 2 决定 juédìng

choosy ADJ 十分挑剔的 shífēn tiāoti de

chop I v 1 劈开 pī kāi, 切成小块 qiēchéng xiǎo kuài 2 砍缺 kǎn 3 削减 xuējiǎn
to chop down 砍倒 kǎn dǎo
II N 1 排骨 páigǔ
pork chop 猪排 zhūpái
2 劈 pī, 砍 kǎn
to get the chop 被解雇 bèi jiěgù

chopper N 直升飞机 zhíshēng fēijī

choppy ADJ 波浪起伏的 bōlàng qǐfú de

chopsticks N 筷子 kuàizi [M. WD 根 gēn/双 shuāng]

choral ADJ (教会) 唱诗班的 (jiàohuì) chàngshībān de, (学校) 合唱团的 (xuéxiào) héchàngtuán de

chord N 和音 héyīn, 和弦 héxián
to strike a chord 引起共鸣 yǐnqǐ gòngmíng

chore N 1 家务杂事 jiāwù záshì 2 乏味的工作 fáwèi de gōngzuò, 烦人的杂事 fánrén de záshì

choreography N 舞蹈设计 wǔdǎo shèjì

chortle I v 咯咯地笑个不停 gēgē de xiào gè bùtíng II N 咯咯的笑声 gēgē de xiàoshēng

chorus N 1 合唱队 héchàngduì 2 合唱部分 héchàng bùfen

in chorus 齐声说 qíshēngshuō

chose See **choose**

chosen I v See **choose** II ADJ 被选中的 bèi xuǎnzhòng de
God's chosen people 上帝的子民 Shàngdì de zǐmín

chow I N 1 食物 shíwù 2 狮子狗 shīzigǒu II v (to chow down) 狼吞虎咽地吃 lángtūn hǔyàn de chī

Christ N 基督 Jīdū, 耶稣 Yēsū

christening N 洗礼命名仪式 xǐlǐ mìngmíng yíshì

Christian N 基督教徒 Jīdū jiàotú

Christianity N 基督教 Jīdūjiào

Christmas N 圣诞节 Shèngdànjié
Christmas carol 圣诞赞歌 Shèngdàn zàngē
Christmas Day 圣诞节 Shèngdànjié
Christmas eve 圣诞夜 Shèngdànyè, 平安夜 píng'ān yè

chromosome N 染色体 rǎnsètǐ

chronic ADJ 1 慢性的 mànxìng de 2 长期的 chángqī de, 反复发作的 fǎnfù fāzuò de
a chronic gambler 赌棍 dǔgùn, 赌徒 dǔtú

chronically ADV 长期地 chángqī de
the chronically ill 长期患病的人 chángqī huànbìng de rén

chronicle I N 编年史 biān niánshǐ II v 记载入历史 jìzǎi rù lìshǐ

chronological ADJ 按照年代/时间顺序排列的 ànzhào niándài/shíjiān shùnxù páilìe de

chronology N 大事年表 dàshì niánbiǎo

chrysanthemum N 菊花 júhuā

chubby ADJ 胖嘟嘟的 pàngdūdū de

chuck v 随手扔 suíshǒu rēng

chuckle I v 低声地笑 dīshēng de xiào II N 低声的笑 dīshēng de xiào, 暗笑 ànxiào

chug v 缓慢行驶 huǎnmàn xíngshǐ

chump N 傻瓜 shǎguā

chunk N 一大块 yí dà kuài

chunky ADJ 大块的 dà kuài de

church N 1 教会 jiàohuì 2 教堂 jiàotáng

churlish ADJ 粗鲁的 cūlǔ de, 不友好的 bù yǒuhǎo de

churn V [胃里+] 剧烈搅动 [wèi lǐ+] jùliè jiǎodòng
to churn up 剧烈翻腾 jùliè fānténg

chute N 滑运道 huáyùndào, 斜槽 xié zāo

CIA (= Central Intelligence Agency) ABBREV（美国）中央情报局 (Měiguó) Zhōngyāng Qíngbàojú

cider N 苹果汁 píngguǒzhī, 苹果酒 píngguǒjiǔ

cigar N 雪茄（烟）xuějiā (yān)

cigarette N 香烟 xiāngyān [M. WD 支 zhī]
a pack of cigarettes 一包香烟 yì bāo xiāngyān

cinch I N 1 一定会发生的事 yídìng huì fāshēng de shì, 非常容易做的事 fēicháng róngyì zuò de shì 2 一定会做某事的人 yídìng huì zuò mǒu shì de rén II V 1 确保 quèbǎo 2 系紧带子 jì jǐn dàizi

cinder N 煤渣 méizhā, 炭渣 tànzhā

cinema N 电影院 diànyǐngyuàn

cinematography N 电影摄影艺术 diànyǐng shèyǐng yìshù

cinnamon N 肉桂 ròuguì

cipher, cypher N 1 密码 mìmǎ 2 无足轻重的人 wúzú qīngzhòng de rén

circle I N 圆圈 yuánquān
to draw a circle 划圆圈 huà yuánquān II V 在…上画圆圈 zài…shàng huà yuánquān

circuit N 1 电路 diànlù 2 巡回演出（讲座、比赛等）xúnhuí yǎnchū (jiǎngzuò, bǐsài děng)
circuit board 电路板 diànlùbǎn, 印刷电路 yìnshuā diànlù
circuit breaker 断路器 duànlùqì

circular¹ ADJ 圆（形）的 yuán (xíng) de
circular saw 电动圆锯 diàndòng yuánjù

circular² N 1 广告纸 guǎnggàozhǐ 2 通知 tōngzhī

circulate V 1 流通 liútōng 2 流传 liúchuán

circulation N 1 血液循环 xuèyè xúnhuán 2 流通 liútōng

circumcision N 1 包皮环切 bāopí huánqiē 2 阴蒂切除 yīndì qiēchú

circumference N 周长 zhōucháng

circumscribe V 约束 yuēshù, 限制 xiànzhì

circumspect ADJ 谨慎 jǐnshèn, 考虑周到的 kǎolǜzhōudào de

circumstance N 情况 qíngkuàng, 处境 chǔjìng
under no circumstances 绝不 juébù

circumstantial ADJ 间接的 jiànjiē de
circumstantial evidence 间接证据 jiànjiē zhèngjù

circus N 马戏团 mǎxìtuán, 马戏 mǎxì

cistern N 储水箱 chǔ shuǐxiāng

citation N 1 [法庭+] 传票 [fǎtíng+] chuánpiào 2 [违章停车+] 罚款单 [wéizhāng tíngchē+] fákuǎndān 3 嘉奖状 jiājiǎngzhuàng 4 引文 yǐnwén

cite V 1 传讯 chuánxùn 2 嘉奖 jiājiǎng 3 引证 yǐnzhèng

citizen N 1 公民 gōngmín 2 市民 shìmín

citizenship N 公民身份 gōngmín shēnfen, 公民权 gōngmínquán

citrus ADJ 柑橘类水果 gānjú lèi shuǐguǒ

city N 城 chéng, 城市 chéngshì
city council 市政议会 shìzhèng yìhuì
city hall 市政厅 shìzhèngtīng

civic ADJ 1 公民的 gōngmín de 2 市政的 shìzhèng de

civics N 公民课 gōngmín kè

civil ADJ 公民的 gōngmín de, 民用的 mínyòng de
civil engineering 土木工程 tǔmù gōngchéng
civil lawsuit 民事案件 mínshì ànjiàn
civil rights 公民权利 gōngmín quánlì
civil service 政府文职部门 zhèngfǔ wénzhí bùmén

civilian N 平民 píngmín

civilization N 文明 wénmíng

civilized ADJ 文明的 wénmíng de

clad ADJ 穿…衣服的 chuān…yīfu de

claim I V 1 认领 rènlǐng 2 声称 shēngchēng 3 索取 [+赔偿] suǒqǔ [+péicháng] II N 1 索赔 suǒpéi
claim form 索赔申请表 suǒpéi shēnqǐngbiǎo
2 声称 shēngchēng, 声明 shēngmíng 3 权利 quánlì

claimant N [索赔+] 申请人 [suǒpéi+] shēnqǐngrén

clairvoyant N 声称有超人洞察力的人 shēngchēng yǒu chāorén dòngchálì de rén

clam I N 1 蛤蜊 gélí 2 沉默寡言的人 chénmò guǎyán de rén II v 闭口不言 bìkǒu bùyán

clamber v 攀登 pāndēng

clamor N 1 吵嚷声 chǎo rǎng shēng 2 强烈要求 qiángliè yàoqiú

clamp I N 1 夹具 jiājù, 夹钳 jiāqián II v 夹紧 jiā jǐn

clampdown N 取缔 qǔdì, 严禁 yánjìn

clan N 1 大家族 dà jiāzú 2 宗族 zōngzú

clandestine ADJ 秘密的 mìmì de

clang v 发出叮当声 fāchū dīngdāngshēng

clank v 发出当啷声 fāchū dānglāngshēng

clap I v 拍手 pāishǒu, 鼓掌 gǔzhǎng II N 拍手声 pāishǒushēng, 鼓掌声 gǔzhǎngshēng 2 响声 xiǎngshēng
a clap of thunder 轰隆的雷声 hōnglōng de léishēng

clarification N 澄清 chéngqīng

clarify v 澄清 chéngqīng

clash I v 1 发生冲突 fāshēng chōngtū 2 不相配 bù xiāngpèi II N 1 冲突 chōngtū 2 争论 zhēnglùn

clasp I N 1 钩子 gōuzi, 扣环 kòuhuán 2 紧握 jǐnwò II v 紧紧握住 jǐnjǐn wòzhù, 扣住 kòuzhù

class N 1 [学校] 班 [xuéxiào] bān, 级 jí, 班级 bānjí 2 课（程）kè (chéng) 3 阶级 jiējí
middle class 中产阶级 zhōngchǎn jiējí
4 等级 děngjí
to travel first class 乘头等舱飞机（或轮船）chéng tóuděngcāng fēijī (huò lúnchuán)

classic I ADJ 经典的 jīngdiǎn de, 典型的 diǎnxíng de
a classic case 典型实例 diǎnxíng shílì
II N 经典作品 jīngdiǎn zuòpǐn

classical ADJ [文学／艺术+] 经典的 [wénxué/yìshù+] jīngdiǎn de, 古典的 gǔdiǎn de
classical music 古典音乐 gǔdiǎn yīnyuè

classification N 1 分类 fēnlèi 2 类别 lèibié, 等级 děngjí

classified ADJ 1 分类的 fēnlèi de 2 保密的 bǎomì de, 机密的 jīmì de
classified ad 分类广告 fēnlèi guǎnggào

classroom N 教室 jiàoshì [M. WD 间 jiān], 课堂 kètáng [M. WD 间 jiān]

classy ADJ 高档的 gāodàng de, 高级的 gāojí de

clatter I v 发出咔嗒声 fāchū kǎdā shēng II N 咔嗒声 kǎdā shēng

clause N 1 （法律）条款 (fǎlǜ) tiáokuǎn 2 从句 cóngjù, 分句 fēnjù

claustrophobia N 幽闭恐惧症 yōubì kǒngjùzhèng

claw N 1 爪 zhuǎ, 鸟爪 niǎozhuǎ 2 起钉器 qǐdīngqì

clean I ADJ 1 干净的 gānjìng de, 清洁的 qīngjié de 2 守法的（不吸毒、不带武器等）shǒufǎ de (bù xīdú, bù dài wǔqì děng) 3 公平的 gōngpíng de, 廉洁的 liánjié de
a clean bill of health 健康证明 jiànkāng zhèngmíng,（机器、建筑物等）安全证明 (jīqì, jiànzhùwù děng) ānquán zhèngmíng
to come clean 坦白认罪 tǎnbái rènzuì
II v 弄干净 nòng gānjìng III ADV 完全（地）wánquán (de)

cleaner N 清洁工 qīngjiégōng

cleanse v 清洗 qīngxǐ

cleanser N 清洗剂 qīngxǐjì

clean-shaven ADJ 胡子刮得很干净的 húzi guā de hěn gānjìng de

cleanup N 大扫除 dàsǎochú

clear I ADJ 1 清澈的 qīngchè de, 明亮的 míngliàng de 2 清楚的 qīngchu de, 明白的 míngbai de II v 收拾干净 shōushí gānjìng

clearance N 1 许可 xǔkě
security clearance 安全审查 ānquán shěnchá
2 清理 qīnglǐ
clearance sale 清仓拍卖 qīngcāng pāimài

clear-cut ADJ 明显的 míngxiǎn de, 显著的 xiǎnzhù de

clear-headed ADJ 头脑清醒的 tóunǎo qīngxǐng de

clearing N (树林中) 小块空地 (shùlín zhōng) xiǎo kuài kòngdì

clearly ADV 1 清楚地 qīngchu de 2 明显地 míngxiǎn de, 显然地 xiǎnrán de

clear-sighted ADJ 有见识的 yǒu jiànshi de

cleat N 1 防滑鞋 fánghuáxié 2 防滑条 fánghuátiáo [M. WD 条 tiáo]

cleavage N 1 分歧 fēnqí 2 乳沟 rǔgōu

cleaver N 剁肉刀 duòròudāo

clef N 谱号 pǔhào

cleft N 1 裂缝 lièfèng 2 凹痕 āohén

clemency N [对罪行+] 从宽处理 [duì zuìxíng+] cóngkuān chǔlí, 宽大 kuāndà

clench V 握紧拳头 wòjǐn quántou
to clench one's teeth 咬紧牙关 yǎojǐn yáguān

clergy N 神职人员 shénzhí rényuán

clerical ADJ 1 神职人员的 shénzhí rényuán de 2 办事员的 bànshìyuán de, 文书的 wénshū de

clerk N 办事员 bànshìyuán, 职员 zhíyuán
file clerk 档案管理员 dàng'àn guǎnlí yuán

clever ADJ 聪明的 cōngming de

cliché N 1 老一套的话 lǎoyítào de huà, 陈词滥调 chéncí làndiào 2 陈腐的想法 chénfǔ de xiǎngfǎ, 老生常谈 lǎoshēng chángtán

click I V 1 发出咔嗒声 fāchū kǎdāshēng 2 (电脑鼠标) 点击 (diànnǎo shǔbiāo) diǎnjī 3 突然明白 tūrán míngbai, 开窍 kāiqiào II N 咔嗒声 kǎdāshēng

client N 1 客户 kèhù, 顾客 gùkè 2 救济对象 jiùjì duìxiàng

cliff N 悬崖 xuányá

climactic ADJ 高潮的 gāocháo de

climate N 1 [温带+] 气候 [wēndài+] qìhòu 2 [保守的+] 风气 [bǎoshǒu de+] fēngqì

climax I N 高潮 gāocháo II V 达到高潮 dádào gāocháo

climb V 1 攀登 pāndēng, 爬 pá 2 [价格+] 攀升 [jiàgé+] pānshēng, 上升 shàngshēng

clinch V 最终赢得 zuìzhōng yíngdé
to clinch a deal 敲定交易 qiāodìng jiāoyì

clincher N 关键的事实论点 / 行动 guānjiàn de shìshí lùndiǎn/xíngdòng

cling (PT & PP **clung**) V 拼命地抓住 pīnmìng de zhuāzhù

clingy ADJ 过于依赖他人的 guòyú yīlài tārén de, 依赖性特强的 yīlàixìng tè qiáng de

clinic N 门诊所 ménzhěnsuǒ

clinical ADJ 1 临床的 [+试验] línchuáng de [+shìyàn] 2 诊所的 [+管理] zhěnsuǒ de [+guǎnlǐ] 3 绝对冷静的 [+观点] juéduì lěngjìng de [+guāndiǎn]

clink V 发出叮当声 fāchū dīngdāng shēng
to clink their glasses 碰杯 pèngbēi

clip N 1 回形针 huíxíngzhēn 2 夹子 jiāzi 3 电影（电视）片段 diànyǐng (diànshì) piànduàn II V 1 夹住 jiāzhù 2 剪下 [+报上的文章] jiǎn xià [+bàoshang de wénzhāng]

clipboard N 1 [电脑+] 剪贴板 [diànnǎo+] jiǎntiēbǎn 2 有夹子的书写板 yǒu jiāzi de shūxiě bǎn

clippers N 修剪器 xiūjiǎnqì

clipping N 剪报 jiǎnbào

clique N 小集团 xiǎojítuán

clitoris N 阴蒂 yīndì

cloak I N 1 披风 pīfēng [M. WD 件 jiàn] 2 幌子 huǎngzi, 掩盖 yǎngài
under the cloak of 打着…的幌子 dǎzhe...de huǎngzi
II V 掩盖 yǎngài

cloakroom N 衣帽间 yīmàojiān

clobber V 猛揍 měng zòu, 狠打 hěn dǎ

clock I N 钟 zhōng [M. WD 座 zuò/只 zhī]
clock radio 收音机闹钟 shōuyīnjī nàozhōng
around the clock 日夜 rìyè
to set one's clock for 把闹钟开到… bǎ nàozhōng kāidào...
II V 记下…的速度 / 时间 jìxià...de sùdù/shíjiān
to clock in/out 打卡上班 / 下班 dǎkǎ shàngbān/xiàbān

clockwise ADJ, ADV 按顺时钟方向 àn shùn shízhōng fāngxiàng
anti-clockwise 按反时钟方向 àn fǎn shízhōng fāngxiàng

clog V 阻塞 zǔsè, 堵塞 dǔsè

clogs N 木拖鞋 mù tuōxié

clone I N 1 无性繁殖 wúxìng fánzhí, 克隆 kèlóng 2 仿制机 fǎngzhì jī II V 1 使…无性繁殖 shǐ...wúxìng fánzhí, 克隆 kèlóng 2 盗用 [+手机号码] dàoyòng [+shǒujī hàomǎ]

close I ADJ 1 近 jìn, 接近 jiējìn
in close quarters [住得+] 很靠近 [zhù dé+] hěn kàojìn
2 亲密的 qīnmì de II V 1 关 guān, 关闭 guānbì 2 结束 jiéshù
to close ranks 团结起来 tuánjié qǐlái
3 收盘 shōupán III ADV 接近地 jiējìn de
close by 在附近 zài fùjìn
IV N 1 结尾 jiéwěi
to come to a close 结束 jiéshù

closed ADJ 1 仅限特定的人 [+会议] jǐn xiàn tèdìng de rén [+huìyì]
behind closed doors 不公开地 bù gōngkāi de, 秘密地 mìmì de
2 关闭的 guānbì de, 封闭的 fēngbì de

closely ADV 1 密切地 [+关注] mìqiè de [+guānzhù], 严密地 yánmì de 2 紧挨着 jǐn'āizhe, 紧接着 jǐnjiēzhe

close-mouthed ADJ 守口如瓶的 shǒu kǒu rú píng de

closet N 壁橱 bìchú
to be in the closet 否认自己是同性恋者 fǒurèn zìjǐ shì tóngxìngliànzhě
to come out of the closet 承认自己是同性恋者 chéngrèn zìjǐ shì tóngxìngliànzhě

close-up N 特写照片 tèxiě zhàopiàn

closure N 1 关闭 guānbì 2 封闭 fēngbì

clot I N (血、牛奶等) 凝块 (xuè, niúnǎi děng) níngkuài II V (血、牛奶等) 凝结成块 (xuè, niúnǎi děng) níngjié chéng kuài

cloth N 布料 bùliào, 毛料 máoliào

clothe V 1 为…提供衣服 wéi...tígōng yīfu 2 给…穿衣 gěi...chuān yī

clothes N 衣服 yīfu [M. WD 件 jiàn]
work clothes 工作服 gōngzuòfú

clothesline N 晾衣绳 liàngyīshéng

clothing N 服装 fúzhuāng

cloud I N 云 yún [M. WD 朵 duǒ]
under a cloud 受到怀疑 shòudào cāiyí
II V 1 使…变得模糊不清 shǐ...biàn de

móhu bùqīng 2 使…糊涂 shǐ...hútu 3 使…蒙上阴影 shǐ...méng shàng yīnyǐng

cloudy ADJ 1 多云的 duōyún de, 阴 yīn 2 模糊的 móhu de

clout N [经济+] 权势 [jīngjì+] quánshì, [政治+] 影响力 [zhèngzhi+] yǐngxiǎnglì

clover N 三叶草 sānyècǎo, 苜蓿 mùxu

clown N 1 小丑 xiǎochǒu, 丑角 chǒujué 2 讨厌家伙 tǎoyàn jiāhuo

club I N 1 俱乐部 jùlèbù 2 (纸牌) 梅花 (zhǐpái) méihuā 3 大棒 dàbàng [M. WD 根 gēn] II V 用棍棒打 yòng gùnbàng dǎ

clubhouse N 1 俱乐部会所 jùlèbù huìsuǒ 2 (体育场) 更衣室 (tǐyùchǎng) gēngyīshì

cluck V 1 [母鸡+] 发出咯咯声 [mǔjī+] fāchū gēgē shēng 2 [人+] 发出啧啧声 [rén +] fāchū zézé shēng

clue I N 1 线索 xiànsuǒ [M. WD 条 tiáo]
to have no clue 一无所知 yīwúsuǒzhī
2 提示 tíshì II V 提供线索 tígōng xiànsuǒ

clump I N 1 一簇树木 yí cù shùmù 2 一块泥土 yí kuài nítǔ II V 凝集成块 níngjí chéng kuài

clumsy ADJ 1 笨拙的 [+男人] bènzhuō de [+nánren] 2 粗制滥造的 [+文章] cūzhì lànzào de [+wénzhāng]

clung See **cling**

clunky ADJ 笨重的 bènzhòng de

cluster I N 串 chuàn, 组 zǔ, 群 qún II V 成群 chéngqún

clutch I V 紧紧握住 jǐnjǐn wòzhù II N 1 (汽车) 离合器 (qìchē) líhéqì 2 紧握 jǐnwò 3 一小簇 yì xiǎo cù

clutter I V 堆满 duīmǎn, 塞满 sāimǎn II N 杂乱无章的东西 záluàn wúzhāng de dōngxi
free of clutter 没有杂乱无章的东西 méiyǒu záluàn wú zhāng de dōngxi

cm (= centimeter) See **centimeter**

coach[1] I N 教练 jiàoliàn II V 辅导 fǔdǎo, 训练 xùnliàn

coach[2] N 1 长途汽车 chángtú qìchē 2 (飞机) 经济舱 (fēijī) jīngjìcāng

coagulate V 使…凝结 shǐ...níngjié

coal N 煤 méi [M. WD 块 kuài]
coal mine 煤矿 méikuàng

coal tar 煤焦油 méijiāoyóu

coalfield N 煤田 méitián

coalition N 联盟 liánméng, 同盟 tóngméng

  coalition government 联合政府 liánhé zhèngfǔ

coarse ADJ 1 粗糙的 [+衣料] cūcāo de [+yīliào] 2 粗俗的 [+语言] cūsú de [+yǔyán]

coast I N 海岸 hǎi'àn

  Coast Guard（美国）海岸警卫队 (Měiguó) Hǎi'àn Jǐngwèiduì

  II V（汽车或自行车）滑行 (qìchē huò zìxíngchē) huáxíng

coastal ADJ 近海的 jìnhǎi de, 沿海的 yánhǎi de

coaster N 1 杯垫 bēidiàn 2 沿海航行的船只 yánhǎi jīn hángxíng de chuánzhī

coastline N 海岸线 hǎi'ànxiàn

coat I N 1 外衣 wàiyī, 大衣 dàyī 2 上装 shàngzhuāng

  coat of arms 纹章 wénzhāng, 盾徽 dùnhuī

  coat rack 挂衣架 guàyījià

  II V 涂一层 tú yìcéng

coax V 劝诱 quànyòu, 哄 hōng

cob N 玉米棒子芯 yùmǐ bàngzi xīn

  corn on the cob 玉米棒子 yùmǐ bàngzi

cobbled ADJ 铺鹅卵石的 pū éluǎnshí de

cobbler N 1 水果馅饼 shuǐguǒ xiànbǐng 2 修鞋匠 xiūxiéjiàng

cobblestone N 鹅卵石 éluǎnshí

cobra N 眼镜蛇 yǎnjìngshé

cobweb N 蜘蛛网 zhīzhūwǎng

Coca-Cola N 可口可乐 Kěkǒukělè

cocaine N 可卡因 kěkǎyīn

cock I N 1 公鸡 gōngjī [M. WD 只 zhī] 2 雄鸟 xióng niǎo [M. WD 只 zhī] 3 鸡巴 jība

  cock-and-bull story 荒唐的故事／借口 huāngtang de gùshi/jièkǒu

cockeyed ADJ 1 歪的 wāi de, 倾斜的 qīngxié de 2 荒谬的 huāngmiù de, 不切实际的 bù qiè shíjì de

cockpit N（飞机）驾驶舱 (fēijī) jiàshǐ cāng,（赛车）驾驶座 (sàichē) jiàshǐ zuò

cockroach N 蟑螂 zhāngláng

cocktail N 鸡尾酒 jīwěijiǔ

  cocktail party 鸡尾酒会 jīwěi jiǔhuì

  2 冷盘 lěngpán [M. WD 道 dào], 开胃菜 lěngpán

  seafood cocktail 海鲜冷盘 hǎixiān lěngpán

  3 危险的混合物 wēixiǎn de hùnhéwù

  Molotov cocktail 莫洛托夫汽油弹 Mòluòtuōfū qìyóudàn

cocky ADJ 自高自大的 zìgāo zìdà de

cocoa N 可可粉 kěkěfěn

coconut N 椰子 yēzi [M. WD 只 zhī]

cocoon I N 1 蚕茧 cánjiǎn, 茧 jiǎn 2 舒适安全的地方 shūshì ānquán de dìfang II V 将…严密保护 jiāng...yánmì bǎohù

C.O.D. (= cash on delivery, collect on delivery) ABBREV 货到付款 huòdàofùkuǎn

cod N 雪鱼 xuěyú [M. WD 条 tiáo]

code I N 1 编码 biānmǎ, 密码 mìmǎ 2（电脑）编码 yóuzhèng biānmǎ 2（电脑）编码 biānmǎ 3 行为准则 xíngwéi zhǔnzé

  code of conduct/ethics 行为准则 xíngwéi zhǔnzé

  code of practice 行业准则 hángyè zhǔnzé

  code word 代码 dàimǎ, 代称 dài chēng

  II V 编码 biānmǎ

co-ed ADJ 男女同校的 nánnǚ tóngxiào de

coerce V 强迫 qiángpò, 迫使 pòshǐ

coexist V （和平地）共存 (hépíng de) gòngcún

coffee N 咖啡 kāfēi [M. WD 杯 bēi]

  black coffee 不加牛奶的咖啡 bù jiā niúnǎi de kāfēi

  coffee break 工间休息 gōngjiān xiūxi

coffin N 棺材 guāncai

cog N 齿轮 chǐlún

cogent ADJ 令人信服的 lìngrén xìnfú de

cognac N（干邑）白兰地 (gānyì) báilándì

cohabit V 未婚同居 wèihūn tóngjū

cohabitation N 未婚同居 wèihūn tóngjū

coherence N 1 条理性 tiáolǐxìng 2 凝聚力 níngjùlì

coherent ADJ 有条理的 yǒu tiáolǐ de

cohesion N 凝聚力 níngjùlì

coil I V (to coil up) 盘绕 pánrào, 缠绕 chánrào II N 1 [电路+] 线圈 [diànlù+] xiànquān 2,一卷 yì juàn

coin I N 1 硬币 yìngbì [M. WD 枚 méi] II V 创造 [+新词语] chuàngzào [+xīncíyǔ]

coincide v **1** 同时发生 tóngshí fāshēng **2** 一致 yízhì, 相符 xiāngfú

coincidence N 巧合 qiǎohé
by coincidence 碰巧 pèngqiǎo

coincidental ADJ 巧合的 qiǎohé de

coke N 焦炭 jiāotàn, 焦煤 jiāoméi

Coke See Coca-cola

colander N 滤盆 lùpén

cold I ADJ **1** 冷 lěng, 寒冷 hánlěng
cold sore 冻疮 dòngchuāng
cold war 冷战 lěngzhàn
2 冷漠的 lěngmò de, 不友好的 bù yǒuhǎo de II N **1** 感冒 gǎnmào, 伤风 shāngfēng **2** 寒冷 hánlěng

cold-blooded ADJ **1** 冷酷的 [+人] lěngkù de [+rén], 毫不留情的 háobù liúqíng de **2** 冷血的 [+动物] lěngxuè de [+dòngwù]

cold-hearted ADJ 铁石心肠的 tiěshí xīncháng de, 毫无同情心的 háowú tóngqíngxīn de

coleslaw N 凉拌卷心菜丝 liángbàn juǎnxīncàisī

colic N 腹绞痛 fù jiǎotòng

collaborate v **1** 合作 hézuò **2** 与敌人合作 yǔ dírén hézuò, 通敌 tōngdí

collaboration N **1** 合作 hézuò **2** 通敌 tōngdí

collage N 拼贴画 pīntiēhuà

collapse I v **1** 突然倒下 tūrán dǎoxià, 倒塌 dǎotā **2** 崩溃 bēngkuì, 垮掉 kuǎdiào II N **1** 崩溃 bēngkuì, 垮掉 kuǎdiào **2** 倒塌 dǎotā **3** 昏倒 hūndǎo

collapsible ADJ 可折叠的 kě zhédié de
a collapsible chair 折叠椅 zhédiéyǐ

collar I N **1** 领子 lǐngzi, 衣领 yīlǐng **2** 颈圈 jǐngquān **3** (给动物) 戴颈圈 (gěi dòngwù) dài jǐngquān **2** 逮住 dài zhù, 抓捕 zhuābǔ

collarbone N 锁骨 suǒgǔ

collate v 校对 jiàoduì, 核对 héduì

collateral N 抵押品 dǐyāpǐn

colleague N 同事 tóngshì

collect v **1** 收集 shōují **2** 聚集 jùjí

collected ADJ **1** 收集成的 [+作品] shōují chéng de [+zuòpǐn] **2** 镇定的 zhèndìng de, 不慌不忙的 bùhuāng bùmáng de

collectible, collectable N 有收藏价值的

东西 yǒu shōucáng jiàzhí de dōngxi, 收藏品 shōucángpǐn [M. WD 件 jiàn]

collection N **1** 收藏 shōucáng **2** 捐款 juānkuǎn

collective ADJ 集体的 jítǐ de, 共同的 gòngtóng de
collective bargaining 集体谈判 jítǐ tánpàn

collector N **1** 收款人 shōukuǎnrén, 检票员 jiǎnpiàoyuán **2** 收藏者 shōucángzhě, 藏家 shōucángjiā

college N **1** 大学 dàxué **2** 学院 xuéyuàn
college of the arts and humanities 人文艺术学院 rénwén yìshù xuéyuàn

collide v **1** 相撞 xiāngzhuàng
to collide head-on 迎面相撞 yíngmiàn xiāngzhuàng **2** 冲突 chōngtū

collie N 克里牧羊犬 kè lǐ mùyángquǎn

collision N **1** [车辆+] 相撞 [chēliàng+] xiāngzhuàng **2** [两派+] 冲突 [liǎng pài+] chōngtū
on a collision course 有发生冲突的趋势 yǒu fāshēng chōngtū de qūshì

colloquial ADJ 口语的 kǒuyǔ de

colloquialism N 口语词语 kǒuyǔ cíyǔ, 口语体 kǒuyǔtǐ

collude v 勾结 gōujié, 共谋 gòngmóu

collusion N 勾结 gōujié, 共谋 gòngmóu

colon N **1** 结肠 jiécháng **2** 冒号 màohào (:)

colonel N 上校 shàngxiào [M. WD 位 wéi]

colonial ADJ 殖民的 zhímín de, 殖民时期的 zhímín shíqī de

colonize v 开拓…为殖民地 kāituò…wéi zhímín dì

colony N 殖民地 zhímíndì

color N 颜色 yánsè
color scheme 色彩设计 sècǎi shèjì **2** 脸色 liǎnsè II v 给…涂上颜色 gěi…tú shàng yánsè, 上色 shàngsè III ADJ 彩色的 cǎisè de
color TV 彩色电视 cǎisè diànshì

colorblind ADJ 色盲的 sèmáng de

color-coordinated ADJ 颜色协调的 yánsè xiétiáo de

colorfast ADJ 不褪色的 bù tuìsè de

colorful ADJ **1** 色彩鲜艳的 [+服装] sècǎi xiānyàn de [+fúzhuāng] **2** 丰富多彩的

[+生活] fēngfù duōcǎi de [+shēnghuó], 生动有趣的 shēngdòng yǒuqù de

coloring N 1 填色 tiánsè, 上色 shàngsè 2 食用色素 shíyòngsèsù
coloring book 填色书 tiánsèshū

colorless ADJ 无色的 wúsè de, 无趣味的 wú qùwèi de, 没有生气的 méiyǒu shēngqì de

colossal ADJ 巨大的 jùdà de

colossus N 庞然大物 pángrán dàwù, 巨人 jùrén

colt N 小公马 xiǎo gōngmǎ [M. WD 匹 pǐ], 雄马驹 xióng mǎjū [M. WD 匹 pǐ]

column N 1 圆柱 yuánzhù, 柱子 zhùzi 2 (报纸) 专栏 (bàozhǐ) zhuānlán 3 (军事) 纵队 (jūnshì) zòngduì

columnist N 专栏作家 zhuānlán zuòjiā

coma N 昏迷 hūnmí
in a coma 处于昏迷状态 chù yú hūnmí zhuàngtài, 昏迷之中 hūnmí zhīzhōng

comatose ADJ 1 昏迷的 [+病人] hūnmí de [+bìngrén] 2 极其疲倦 jíqí píjuàn, 呆滞的 dāizhì de

comb I N 1 梳子 shūzi 2 (公鸡的) 鸡冠 (gōngjī de) jīguān 3 蜂巢 fēngcháo, 蜂房 fēngfáng II v 梳 shū, 梳理 shūlǐ

combat I N 战斗 zhàndòu
killed in combat 死于战斗 sǐ yú zhàndòu, 阵亡 zhènwáng
II v 与…作战 yǔ…zuòzhàn

combination N 1 联合 liánhé 2 组合 zǔhé
a winning combination 成功的组合 chénggōng de zǔhé
combination lock 密码锁 mìmǎsuǒ

combine v 1 结合 jiéhé, 组合 zǔhé 2 混合 hùnhé, 化合 huàhé

combustion N 燃烧 ránshāo

come (PT **came**; PP **come**) v 来 lái, 到来 dàolái
to come across 碰见 pèngjiàn, 遇到 yùdào
come on! 快点儿! Kuài diǎnr! 行了! Xíngle!

comeback N 复活 fùhuó, 东山再起 dōngshān zài qǐ

comedian N 喜剧演员 xǐjù yǎnyuán, 谐星 xiéxīng

comedown N 失落 shīluò, 失势 shīshì

comedy N 喜剧 xǐjù

come-on N 勾引 gōuyǐn, 挑逗 tiǎodòu

comet N 彗星 huìxīng

comfort I N 1 安慰 ānwèi 2 舒适 shūshì
in comfort 舒适 shūshì
3 (creature comforts) 使生活舒适的东西 shǐ shēnghuó shūshì de dōngxi II v 安慰 ānwèi

comfortable ADJ 1 舒服 shūfu, 舒适 shūshì 2 自在 zìzài, 不拘束 bù jūshù

comforter N 被子 bèizi [M. WD 条 tiáo]

comfy ADJ 舒适的 shūshì de

comic I ADJ 滑稽的 huájī de
comic book 儿童连环画 értóng liánhuánhuà
comic strip 连环漫画 liánhuán mànhuà II N 1 喜剧演员 xǐjù yǎnyuán 2 儿童连环画 értóng liánhuánhuà

comical ADJ 滑稽的 huájī de, 可笑的 kěxiào de

comma N 逗号 dòuhào (,)

command I v 1 指挥 zhǐhuī 2 命令 mìnglìng II N 1 指挥 zhǐhuī 2 命令 mìnglìng 3 兵团 bīngtuán 4 掌握 zhǎngwò, 运用能力 yùnyòng nénglì
to have a good command of Chinese 具有很好的中文能力 jùyǒu hěn hǎode Zhōngwén nénglì

commandant N 司令官 sīlìngguān, 指挥官 zhǐhuīguān [M. WD 位 wéi/名 míng]

commanding ADJ 1 指挥的 [+军官] zhǐhuī de [+jūnguān] 2 威严的 [+口气] wēiyán de [+kǒuqì] 3 居高临下的 [+山峰] jūgāo línxià de [+shānfēng] 4 遥遥领先的 yáoyáo lǐng xiān de

commandment N 戒律 jièlǜ
the Ten Commandments (圣经) 十戒 (Shèngjīng) shíjiè

commando N 突击队 tūjīduì, 特种部队 tèzhǒng bùduì

commemorate v 纪念 jìniàn

commemorative ADJ 纪念的 jìniàn de

commence v 开始 kāishǐ

commencement N 1 开始 kāishǐ 2 毕业典礼 bìyè diǎnlǐ

commend v 公开表扬 gōngkāi biǎoyáng,

赞扬 zànyáng

commendable ADJ 值得赞扬的 zhíde zànyáng de

commensurate ADJ 相称的 xiāngchèn de, 相应的 xiāngyìng de

comment I v 议论 yìlùn, 评论 pínglùn
II N 议论 yìlùn, 评论 pínglùn

commentary N [球赛的+] 现场解说 [qiúsài de+] xiànchǎng jiěshuō, [新闻的+] 实况报道 [xīnwén de+] shíkuàng bàodào
running commentary 现场评论 xiànchǎng píngjiè

commentator N 解说员 jiěshuōyuán

commerce N 商业 shāngyè, 商务 shāngwù

commercial I ADJ 商业的 shāngyè de
commercial break 广告时间 guǎnggào shíjiān
II N 电视广告 diànshì guǎnggào

commercialize v 商业化 shāngyèhuà

commiserate v 表示同情 biǎoshì tóngqíng

commission I N 1 [税务+] 委员会 [shuìwù+] wěiyuánhuì 2 [代理人+] 佣金 [dàilǐrén+] yòngjīn 3 [专门定做的+] 艺术品 [zhuānmén dìngzuò de] yìshùpǐn
in commission 仍在服役的 [+军舰] réng zài fúyì de [+jūnjiàn]
II v 1 委托 [+制作艺术品] wěituō [+zhìzuò yìshùpǐn] 2 授予军衔 shòuyǔ jūnxián

commissioner N 负责长官 fùzé zhǎngguān

commit v 1 保证 bǎozhèng, 承担 chéngdān
to commit oneself to 保证 bǎozhèng
2 付出 fùchū 3 犯 (罪/错误) fàn (zuì/cuòwù)
to committ a felony 犯重罪 fàn zhòngzuì

commitment N 1 承诺 chéngnuò 2 奉献 fèngxiàn, 敬业精神 jìngyè jīngshén

committed ADJ 献身的 xiànshēn de, 尽职的 jìnzhí de

committee N 委员会 wěiyuánhuì

commodity N 商品 shāngpǐn

common ADJ 1 共同的 gòngtóng de 2 普通的 pǔtōng de
to have something/nothing in com-

mon with 和…有些/没有共同点 hé… yǒuxiē/méiyǒu gòngtóngdiǎn
common sense 常识 chángshí
3 常见的 chángjiàn de
common cold 感冒 gǎnmào

common-law ADJ 普通法 pǔtōngfǎ
common-law marriage 事实婚姻 shìshí hūnyīn, 同居关系 tóngjū guānxi

commonplace ADJ 平常的 píngcháng de, 不足为奇的 bùzú wéi qí de

commonwealth N 联合体 liánhétǐ, 联邦 liánbāng
British Commonwealth（大）英联邦 (Dà) Yīng liánbāng

commotion N 吵闹 chǎonào, 混乱 hùnluàn

communal ADJ 公共的 gōnggòng de, 共用的 gòngyòng de

commune I N 公社 gōngshè II v 交流 jiāoliú

communicate v 1 沟通 gōutōng, 交流 jiāoliú 2 [痢疾+] 传染 [lìji+] chuánrǎn

communications N 1 [现代+] 通讯手段 [xiàndài+] tōngxùn shǒuduàn 2 [学习+] 传媒学 [xuéxí+] chuánméixué

communion N 1 情感思想交流 qínggǎn sīxiǎng jiāoliú 2 圣餐仪式 Shèngcān yíshì
Holy Communion 圣餐仪式 Shèngcān yíshì

communique N 公报 gōngbào

communist N 共产主义者 Gòngchǎn zhǔyìzhě, 共产党党员 Gòngchǎndǎng dǎngyuán

community N 1 社区 shèqū
community service 社区服务 shèqū fúwù
2 群体 qúntǐ, 公众 gōngzhòng
community property 夫妻共有财产 fūqī gòngyǒu cáichǎn

commute I v 远距离上下班 yuǎnjùlí shàngxiàbān II N（远距离）上下班的时间 (yuǎnjùlí) shàngxiàbān de shíjiān

commuter N 远距离上下班的人 yuǎnjùlí shàngxiàbān de rén

compact I ADJ 小而紧凑的 xiǎo ér jǐncòu de II N 1 小型汽车 xiǎoxíng qìchē [M. WD 辆 liàng] 2 化妆粉盒 huàzhuāng fěnhé III v 压紧 yā jǐn

companion N 1 同伴 tóngbàn 2 [旅游+] 手册 [lǚyóu+] shǒucè

companionship ADJ 友伴 yǒubàn, 友好往来 yǒuhǎowǎnglái

company N 1 公司 gōngsī [M. WD 家 jiā] listed company 上市公司 shàngshì gōngsī
2 交往 jiāowǎng, 陪伴 péibàn 3 同伴 tóngbàn, 朋友 péngyou
to fall into bad company 交了坏朋友 jiāole huài péngyou
4 客人 kèrén, 访客 fǎngkè
to expect company 等客人到来 děng kèrén dàolái

comparable ADJ 类似的 lèisì de, 可相提并论的 kě xiāngtí bìnglùn de

comparative ADJ 1 相对的 xiāngduì de 2 (学术研究方面) 比较的 (xuéshù yánjiū fāngmiàn) bǐjiào de
comparative literature 比较文学 (研究) bǐjiào wénxué (yánjiū)

compare V 比 bǐ, 比较 bǐjiào

comparison N 比较 bǐjiào
by comparison 相之下 xiāngbǐ zhī xià

compartment N 1 分隔间 fēngé jiān 2 (飞机 / 火车等) 舱 (fēijī/huǒchē děng) cāng
first-class compartment 头等舱 tóuděngcāng

compass N 1 指南针 [+指路] zhǐnánzhēn [+zhǐlù] 2 圆规 yuánguī

compassion N 强烈的 同情心 qiángliè de tóngqíngxīn

compassionate ADJ 有同情心的 yǒu tóngqíngxīn de
compassionate leave 私事假 sīshìjià, 丧假 sāngjià

compatibility N 兼容性 jiānróngxìng

compatible I ADJ 兼容的 jiānróng de, 一致的 yízhì de II N 兼容机 jiānróng jī

compatriot N 同胞 tóngbāo

compel V 强迫 qiǎngpò

compelling ADJ 令人不得不注意的 lìngrén bùdébù zhùyì de, 极为有趣的 jíwéi yǒuqù de
a compelling reason 强烈的理由 qiángliè de lǐyóu

compendium N 大全 dàquán

compensate V 赔偿 péicháng 2 弥补 míbǔ

compensation N 赔偿 péicháng [M. WD 笔 bǐ], 赔偿金 péichángjīn [M. WD 笔 bǐ]

compete N 1 竞争 jìngzhēng 2 参加比赛 cānjiā bǐsài

competence N 能力 nénglì

competent ADJ 有能力的 yǒu nénglì de, 能胜任的 néng shèngrèn de

competition N 1 竞争 jìngzhēng 2 比赛 bǐsài

competitive ADJ 有竞争力的 yǒu jìngzhēnglì de

competitor N 竞争者 jìngzhēngzhě, 参赛者 cānsàizhě

compilation N 汇编集 huìbiānjí

compile V 汇编 huìbiān, 编辑 biānjí

complacent ADJ 自满的 zìmǎn de, 心满意得的 xīn mǎnyì dé de

complain V 1 投诉 tóusù 2 抱怨 bàoyuàn
I can't complain. 还算不错。Háisuàn bùcuò.

complaint N 1 抱怨 bàoyuàn 2 投诉 tóusù 3 (病人的) 主诉 (bìngrén de) zhǔsù

complement I N 1 补充物 (或人) bǔchōng wù (huò rén) 2 全数 quánshù II V 衬托 chèntuō

complementary ADJ 补充的 bǔchōng de

complete I ADJ 完全的 wánquán de, 全部的 quánbù de II V 完成 wánchéng

completely ADV 完全地 wánquán de, 彻底地 chèdǐ de

completion N 完成 wánchéng

complex I ADJ 复杂 fùzá II N 综合建筑群 zōnghé jiànzhùqún
movie complex 综合影院 zōnghé yǐngjùyuàn

complexion N 面色 miànsè

complexity N 复杂性 fùzáxìng

compliant ADJ 服从的 fúcóng de, 顺从的 shùncóng de

complicate V 使…复杂 shǐ…fùzá

complicated ADJ 复杂的 fùzá de

complication N 1 复杂性 fùzáxìng 2 并发症 bìngfāzhèng

compliment N, V 称赞 chēngzàn, 赞美 zànměi

complimentary ADJ **1** 称赞的 chēngzàn de **2** 赠送的 zèngsòng de, 免费的 miǎnfèi de

compliments N 问候 wènhòu, 致意 zhìyì

comply V 遵守 zūnshǒu, 服从 fúcóng

component N 组成部分 zǔchéng bùfen

compose V **1** 组成 zǔchéng
to be composed of 由…组成 yóu… zǔchéng
2 写 xiě, 谱写 pǔxiě

composed ADJ 平静的 píngjìng de

composer N 作曲者 zuòqǔzhě, 作曲家 zuòqǔjiā

composite I ADJ 拼合成的 pīnhéchéng de II N 混合物 hùnhéwù

composition N **1** [化学成份+] 组成 [huà-xué chéngfèn+] zǔchéng **2** [学生的+] 作文 [xuésheng de+] zuòwén **3** [音乐+] 作品 [yīnyuè+] zuòpǐn

compost N 堆肥 duīféi

composure N 镇定 zhèndìng, 冷静 lěngjìng

compound I N **1** 大院 dàyuàn, 场地 chǎngdì **2** 化合物 huàhéwù, 混合物 hùnhéwù **3** 复合词 fùhécí II V **1** 使混合 shǐ hùnhé **2** 使恶化 shǐ èhuà **3** 计算复利 jìsuàn fùlì III ADJ **1** 复合的 fùhé de **2** 重复的 chóngfù de
compound interest 复利 fùlì

comprehend V 理解 lǐjiě, 领悟 lǐngwù

comprehension N 理解 lǐjiě, 领悟 lǐngwù

comprehensive ADJ 综合的 zōnghé de, 全面的 quánmiàn de

compress V 压缩 yāsuō, 压紧 yā jǐn

comprise V 由…组成 yóu…zǔchéng

compromise I N 妥协 tuǒxié
to make compromises 让步 ràngbù
II V **1** 妥协 tuǒxié, 让步 ràngbù **2** 损害 sǔnhài
to compromise oneself 损害自己 sǔnhài zìjǐ, 损害自己的形象 sǔnhài zìjǐ de xíngxiàng

compromising ADJ 不光彩的 bùguāngcǎi de, 有失体面的 yǒu shī tǐmiàn de

compulsion N **1** 强烈冲动 qiángliè chōngdòng **2** 强迫 qiǎngpò

compulsive ADJ 有强烈冲动的 yǒu qiángliè chōngdòng de, 强迫性的 qiǎngpò xìng de
a compulsive gambler 赌博成性的人 dǔbó chéngxìng de rén

compulsory ADJ 必须做的 bìxū zuò de, 强迫性的 qiǎngpò xìng de
compulsory (school) subject 学校必修课目 xuéxiào bìxiūkè mù

compunction N 内疚 nèijiù, 后悔 hòuhuǐ

computation N 计算 jìsuàn, 计算的技能 jìsuàn de jìnéng

compute V 计算 jìsuàn

computer N 计算机 jìsuànjī, 电脑 diànnǎo
computer game 电脑游戏 diànnǎo yóuxì
computer literate 会使用计算机的 huì shǐyòng jìsuànjī de

computing N 计算机操作 jìsuànjī cāozuò

comrade N 同志 tóngzhì

con I V 欺骗 qīpiàn, 诈骗 zhàpiàn II N 欺骗 qīpiàn, 诈骗 zhàpiàn
con artist 骗子 piànzi

concave ADJ 凹面的 āomiàn de
a concave mirror 凹透镜 āotòujìng

conceal V 隐藏 yǐncáng

concealment N 隐藏 yǐncáng

concede V（勉强）承认 (miǎnqiǎng) chéngrèn

conceit N 自负 zìfù, 骄傲 jiāo'ào

conceited ADJ 自负的 zìfù de, 自高自大的 zìgāo zìdà de

conceivable ADJ 可以想象的 kěyǐ xiǎngxiàng de

conceive V **1** 想象 [+状况] xiǎngxiàng [+zhuàngkuàng], 相信 xiāngxìn **2** 设想 [+新方法] shèxiǎng [+xīn fāngfǎ], 构想 gòuxiǎng **3** 怀胎 huáitāi

concentrate I V **1** 集中 jízhōng **2** 专心 zhuānxīn, 集中注意力 jízhōng zhùyìlì II N 浓缩液 nóngsuōyè, 浓缩物 nóngsuōwù

concentrated ADJ **1** 浓缩的 [+水果汁] nóngsuō de [+shuǐguǒzhī] **2** 全神贯注的 quánshén guànzhù de
to make a concentrated effort 全力以赴地 quánlì yǐfù de

concentration N 1 专心致志 zhuānxīn zhìzhì 2 集中 jízhōng 3 浓度 nóngdù

concentric ADJ 同心的 tóngxīn de

concept N 概念 gàiniàn, 观念 guānniàn

conception N 1 概念 gàiniàn, 观念 guānniàn 2 构想 gòuxiǎng 3 怀胎 huáitāi

conceptual ADJ 概念的 gàiniàn de, 观念的 guānniàn de

concern I V 1 和…有关系 hé...yǒu guānxi 2 使…担心 shǐ...dānxīn
to be concerned with 关注 guānzhù, 担心 dānxīn
II N 1 关心 guānxīn, 担心 dānxīn 2 关心的事 guānxīn de shì 3 公司 gōngsī, 企业 qǐyè

concerned ADJ 1 焦虑的 jiāolǜ de, 担心的 dānxīn de 2 有关的 yǒuguān de
as far as … is concerned 就…而言 jiù...éryán

concerning PREP 关于 guānyú

concert N 音乐会 yīnyuèhuì
concert grand 平台大钢琴 píngtái dàgāngqín
in concert with 共同行动 gòngtóng xíngdòng

concerted ADJ 共同的 gòngtóng de, 一致的 yízhì de

concession N 1 让步 ràngbù 2 特许权 tèxǔquán
concession stand 小食品摊 xiǎo shípǐn tān

concierge N 旅馆服务台职员 lǚguǎn fúwùtái zhíyuán

conciliation N 调停 tiáotíng, 调解 tiáojiě

concise ADJ 简明的 jiǎnmíng de, 简洁的 jiǎnjié de

conclude V 1 结束 jiéshù 2 下结论 xiàjiélùn, 得出结论 déchū jiélùn

conclusion N 1 结束 jiéshù, 结局 jiéjú 2 结论 jiélùn, 断言 duànyán
to jump to conclusions 轻易下结论 qīngyì xiàjiélùn

conclusive ADJ 确信无意的 quèxìn wúyì de, 毫无疑问的 háo wúyí wèn de

concoct V 1 编造 [+谎言] biānzào [+huǎngyán], 虚构 xūgòu 2 配制 [+食谱] pèizhì [+shípǔ], 拼凑 pīncòu

concoction N 调制品 tiáozhì pǐn

concourse N 大厅 dàtīng

concrete I N 混凝土 hùnníngtǔ II ADJ 1 混凝土的 [+大桥] hùnníngtǔ de [+dàqiáo] 2 具体的 [+计划] jùtǐ de [+jìhuà]

concur V 与…意见一致 yǔ...yìjiàn yízhì, 完全赞同 wánquán zàntóng

concurrent ADJ 1 同意的 tóngyì de 2 同时发生的 tóngshí fāshēng de

concussion N 1 震荡 zhèndàng 2 脑震荡 nǎozhèndàng

condemnation N 谴责 qiǎnzé

condensation N 1 凝结 níngjié 2 水滴 shuǐdī 3 压缩 yāsuō

condense V 1 凝结 níngjié 2 压缩 yāsuō

condescending ADJ 居高临下的 jūgāo línxià de, 带有优越感的 dàiyǒu yōuyuègǎn de

condiment N 调味品 tiáowèipǐn

condition I N 1 条件 tiáojiàn 2 情况 qíngkuàng, 条件 tiáojiàn 3 健康状况 jiànkāng zhuàngkuàng 4 疾病 jíbìng
a skin condition 皮肤病 pífūbìng
II V 1 使…习惯 shǐ...xíguàn, 使…适应 shǐ...shìyìng 2 支配 zhīpèi, 训练 xùnliàn

conditional ADJ 有条件的 yǒu tiáojiàn de
conditional upon 以…为前提 yǐ...wéi qiántí

condolence N 吊唁 diàoyàn, 慰问 wèiwèn

condom N 避孕套 bìyùntào

condominium N 公寓 gōngyù, 公寓楼 gōngyù lóu

condone V 纵容 zòngróng, 宽容 kuānróng

conducive ADJ 有助于的 yǒuzhù yú de

conduct I V 1 进行 jìnxíng 2 带领 dàilǐng 3 指挥 [+乐队] zhǐhuī [+yuèduì] 4 传导 [+电／热] chuán dǎo [+diàn/rè]
to conduct oneself 举止 jǔzhǐ, 表现 biǎoxiàn
II N 1 行为 xíngwéi, 举止 jǔzhǐ 2 经营 jīngyíng

conductive ADJ 导电（或热）性能强的 dǎo diàn (huò rè) xìngnéng qiáng de

conductor N 1 [音乐+] 指挥 [yīnyuè+] zhǐhuī 2 [火车+] 列车员 [huǒchē+] lièchēyuán 3 导体 dǎotǐ

cone N 1 圆锥体 yuánzhuītǐ 2 冰淇淋蛋卷筒 bīngqílín dànjuǎntǒng 3 球状 qiúguǒ

confectioner N 糖果商 tángguǒ shāng

confederation N 联盟 liánméng

confer v 1 [与顾问+] 商议 [yǔ gùwèn+] shāngyì 2 授予 [+奖章] shòuyǔ [+jiǎngzhāng]

conference N 会议 huìyì

confess v 坦白 tǎnbái, 承认 [+错误] chéngrèn [+cuòwù]

confession N 1 坦白 tǎnbái, 供认 gòngrèn 2 (天主教) 忏悔 (Tiānzhǔjiào) chànhuǐ

confetti N 彩色纸屑 cǎisè zhǐxiè

confidant, confidante N 知心密友 zhīxīn mìyǒu

confide v 吐露 [+私人秘密] tǔlù [+sīrén mìmì]

confidence N 1 信心 xìnxīn
to have confidence in 对…有信心 duì…yǒu xìnxīn
2 确信 quèxìn 3 信任感 xìnrèngǎn

confident ADJ 有信心的 yǒu xìnxīn de

confidential ADJ 机密的 jīmì de

confidentiality N 机密 jīmì
breach of confidentiality 违反保密原则 wéifǎn bǎomì yuánzé

configuration N 1 外形 wàixíng 2 构造 gòuzào 3 (计算机) 配置 (jìsuànjī) pèizhì

configure v (计算机) 配置 (jìsuànjī) pèizhì

confine v 1 监禁 [+嫌疑犯] jiānjìn [+xiányífàn], 关押 guānyā 2 控制 [+传染病] kòngzhì [+chuánrǎnbìng], 限制 xiànzhì

confinement N 1 (产妇的) 分娩期 (chǎnfù de) fēnmiǎn qī 2 监禁 jiānjìn, 关押 guānyā

confirm v 1 确定 quèdìng 2 证实 zhèngshí
neither confirm nor deny 既不证实, 也不否认 jì bú zhèngshí, yě bù fǒurèn, 不置可否 bú zhì kě fǒu

confirmation N 1 确定 quèdìng 2 证实 zhèngshí

confirmed ADJ 坚定的 jiāndìng de
a confirmed bachelor 坚定的单身汉

jiāndìng de dānshēnhàn, 决心打光棍的人 juéxīn dǎguānggùn de rén

confiscate v 没收 mòshōu, 把…充公 bǎ…chōnggōng

conflict I N 冲突 chōngtū, 矛盾 máodùn
conflict of interest 利益冲突 lìyì chōngtū
II v 冲突 chōngtū

conform v 1 保持一致 bǎochí yízhì 2 遵循 zūnxún

conformist ADJ 墨守成规的 mòshǒu chéngguī de, 循规蹈矩的 xúnguī dǎojǔ de

confound v 使…困惑 shǐ…kùnhuò, 使…惊讶 shǐ…jīngyà

confront v 1 面临 miànlín, 遭遇 zāoyù 2 面对 [+问题] miànduì [+wèntí], 对抗 duìkàng

confrontation N 对抗 duìkàng, 冲突 chōngtū

confuse v 使…糊涂 shǐ…hútu, 把…搞错 bǎ…gǎocuò

confused ADJ 搞糊涂了 gǎo hútu le

confusing ADJ 使人糊涂的 shǐrén hútu de

confusion N 1 困惑 kùnhuò 2 混乱 hùnluàn

congeal v 凝结 níngjié

congenial ADJ 1 令人舒适轻松的 lìngrén shūshì qīngsōng de 2 和善的 héshàn de

congenital ADJ 1 先天的 xiāntiān de 2 天生的 tiānshēng de

congested ADJ 1 拥挤的 yōngjǐ de 2 堵塞的 dǔsè de

congestion N 1 [交通+] 拥挤 [jiāotōng+] yōngjǐ 2 [鼻子+] 堵塞 [bízi+] dǔsè

conglomerate N 1 大型企业集团 dàxíng qìyè jítuán 2 混合体 hùnhé tǐ

congratulate v 祝贺 zhùhè
to congratulate oneself 自我满足 zìwǒ mǎnzú, 自豪 zìháo

congratulations N 祝贺 zhùhè
Congratulations! 恭喜恭喜! Gōngxǐ gōngxǐ! 祝贺你(们)! Zhùhè nǐ (men)!

congregate v 聚集 jùjí, 聚合 jùhé

congregation N (教堂) 会众 (jiàotáng) huìzhòng

congress N 1 代表大会 dàibiǎo dàhuì

2（美国）国会 (Měiguó) Guóhuì,（美国）国会众议院 (Měiguó) Guóhuì zhòngyìyuàn

conical, conic ADJ 圆锥形的 yuánzhuī xíng de

conifer N 针叶树 zhēnyèshù

conjecture N, V 猜测 cāicè

conjugal ADJ 婚姻的 hūnyīn de, 夫妻之间的 fūqī zhījiān de
conjugal visit 配偶探监同房 pèi ǒu tànjiān tóngfáng

conjunction N 1 结合 jiéhé, 连接 liánjiē
in conjunction with 与…结合起来与yǔ…jiéhéqǐlái
2 同时发生 tóngshí fāshēng 3 连接词 liánjiēcí

conjure V 变魔术 biàn móshù, 变出 biàn chū

conman N 骗子 piànzi

connect V 连接 liánjiē

connection N 1 关系 guānxi, 联系 liánxì 2 连接 liánjiē

connive V 默许 mòxǔ, 纵容 zòngróng
to connive to do sth 串通起来 chuàntōng qǐlái, 合谋 hémóu

connoisseur N 鉴赏家 jiànshǎngjiā

connotation N 隐含意义 yǐnhán yìyì

conquest N 征服 zhēngfú

conscience N 良心 liángxīn, 是非感 shìfēigǎn
a guilty conscience 负罪感 fùzuìgǎn

conscientious ADJ 认真的 rènzhēn de

conscious ADJ 感觉到的 gǎnjuédào de, 有感觉的 yǒu gǎnjué de

consciousness N 知觉 zhījué, 感觉 gǎnjué
to lose (regain) consciousness 失去（恢复）知觉 shīqù (huīfù) zhījué

conscript I V 征召 zhēngzhāo II N 应征入伍的士兵 yìngzhēngrùwǔ de shìbīng

consecrate V 宣布…为神圣 xuānbù…wéi shénshèng

consecutive ADJ 连续的 liánxù de

consensus N 共识 gòngshí, 一致意见 yízhì yìjiàn

consent N, V 同意 tóngyì, 允许 yǔnxǔ

consequence N 后果 hòuguǒ

consequential ADJ 1 意义重大的 yìyì zhòngdà de 2 随后发生的 suíhòu fāshēng de

consequently ADV 因此 yīncǐ, 所以 suǒyǐ

conservation N 保护 bǎohù, 保存 bǎocún
wildlife conservation 野生动物保护 yěshēng dòngwù bǎohù

conservative ADJ 保守的 bǎoshǒude

conservatory N 1 音乐学院 yīnyuè xuéyuàn 2 温室 wēnshì

conserve V 保护 bǎohù, 保存 bǎocún

consider V 1 考虑 kǎolǜ 2 认为 rènwéi

considerable ADJ 相当多的 xiāngdāng duō de, 相当大的 xiāngdāng dà de

considerate ADJ 考虑周到的 kǎolǜ zhōudào de, 体贴的 tǐtiē de

consideration N 1 考虑 kǎolǜ 2 需要考虑的事 xūyào kǎolǜ de shì, 因素 yīnsù 3 体谅 tǐliang

considering PREP 考虑到 kǎolǜdào, 由于 yóuyú

consign V 1 使…陷于 shǐ…xiànyú, 使…处于 shǐ…chǔyú 2 运送 yùnsòng

consignment N 1 运送 yùnsòng 2 运送的货物 yùnsòng de huòwù

consist V 组成 zǔchéng
to consist in 在于 zàiyú
to consist of 由…组成 yóu…zǔchéng, 包括 bāokuò

consistent ADJ 一贯的 yíguàn de
consistent with 与…一致 yǔ…yízhì

consolation N 安慰 ānwèi
consolation prize 安慰奖 ānwèijiǎng

console I V 安慰 ānwèi II N 控制台 kòngzhìtái, 仪表板 yíbiǎobǎn

consolidate V 1 合并 hébìng 2 巩固 gǒnggù

consonant N 辅音 fǔyīn

consortium N 财团 cáituán

conspicuous ADJ 显眼的 xiǎnyǎn de, 引人注目的 yǐnrén zhùmù de

conspiracy N 阴谋 yīnmóu

conspire V 搞阴谋 gǎo yīnmóu, 密谋 mìmóu

constant I ADJ 经常的 jīngcháng de, 不变的 búbiàn de II N 不变的事 búbiàn de shì, 常数 chángshù

constellation N 星座 xīngzuò

consternation N 惊慌失措 jīnghuāng shīcuò, 惊恐 jīngkǒng

constipation N 便秘 biànbì

constituency N 1 选区 xuǎnqū 2 支持者 zhīchízhě

constituent N 成分 chéngfèn

constitute V 组成 zǔchéng, 构成 gòuchéng

constitution N 1 [美国+] 宪法 [Měiguó+] xiànfǎ 2 [强壮的+] 体质 [qiángzhuàng de+] tǐzhì

constrain V 约束 yuēshù, 限制 xiànzhì

constraint N 约束 yuēshù, 限制 xiànzhì

constrict V 压缩 yāsuō, 收紧 shōujǐn

construct V 建筑 jiànzhù, 建造 jiànzào

construction N 建造 jiànzào, 建设 jiànshè

　construction paper 彩色厚纸 cǎisè hòuzhǐ

constructive ADJ 建设性的 jiànshèxìng de

construe V 理解为 lǐjiě wéi

consul N 领事 lǐngshì

consulate N 领事馆 lǐngshìguǎn

consult V 1 咨询 [+专家] zīxún [+zhuānjiā], 请教 qǐngjiào 2 [与同事+] 磋商 [yǔ tóngshì+] cuōshāng 3 查阅 [+参考资料] cháyuè [+cānkǎo zīliào]

consultancy N 咨询公司 zīxún gōngsī

consultant N 顾问 gùwèn [M. WD 位 wéi]

consultation N 1 咨询 zīxún 2 磋商 cuōshāng 3 查阅 cháyuè

consume V 1 耗费 [+汽油] hàofèi [+qìyóu] 2 吃喝 chīhē

consumer N 消费者 xiāofèizhě

consumerism N 消费主义 xiāofèi zhǔyì

consummate I ADJ 1 技艺高超的 [+球员] jìyì gāochāo de [+qiúyuán] 2 完美的 [+艺术作品] wánměi de [+yìshù zuòpǐn], 无暇可击的 wúxiá kě jī de II V 1 使…圆满成功 shǐ...yuánmǎn chénggōng 2 完婚 wánhūn, 做成夫妻 zuòchéng fūqī

consumption N 1 消费量 xiāofèiliàng 2 消耗量 xiāohàoliàng 3 吃 chī, 喝 hē

contact I V 联系 liánxì II N 1 联系 liánxì 2 接触 jiēchù 3 熟人 shúrén

　contact lens 隐形眼镜 yǐnxíng yǎnjìng

to come into (lose) contact with 跟…发生（失去）联系 gēn...fāshēng (shīqù) liánxì

contagious ADJ 接触传染的 jiēchù chuánrǎn de

contain V 1 容纳 róngnà, 包含 bāohán 2 克制 [+愤怒的情绪] kèzhì [+fènnù de qíngxù]

container N 1 容器 róngqì 2 集装箱 jízhuāngxiāng

　container ship 集装箱货轮 jízhuāngxiāng huòlún

contaminate V 把…弄脏 bǎ...nòngzāng, 污染 wūrǎn, 毒害 dúhài

contamination N 污染 wūrǎn, 毒害 dúhài

contemplate V 打算 dǎsuan, 认真考虑 rènzhēn kǎolǜ

contemplation N 思考 sīkǎo, 深思 shēnsī

contemporary I ADJ 1 当代的 dāngdài de 2 同时代的 tóngshí dài de II N 同时代的人 tóngshí dài de rén

contempt N 蔑视 mièshì, 轻蔑 qīngmiè

　contempt of court 蔑视法庭 mièshì fǎtíng

contemptible ADJ 可蔑视的 kě mièshì de, 可耻的 kěchǐ de

contemptuous ADJ 轻蔑的 qīngmiè de, 看不起的 kànbuqǐ de

contend V 竞争 jìngzhēng

contender N 竞争者 jìngzhēngzhě

content I N 1 内容 nèiróng 2 满足 mǎnzú

　to one's heart's content 尽情地 jìnqíng de

II ADJ 满足的 mǎnzú de, 满意的 mǎnyì de III V 使…满足 shǐ...mǎnzú

contention N 主张 zhǔzhāng, 论点 lùndiǎn

contents N 内容 nèiróng

　table of contents 目录 mùlù

contest N, V 竞赛 jìngsài, 比赛 bǐsài

contestant N 竞争者 jìngzhēngzhě, 参赛者 cānsàizhě

context N 上下文 shàngxiàwén

　to take sth out of context 断章取义 duànzhāng qǔyì

contiguous ADJ 相邻的 xiānglín de

continent N 洲 zhōu, 大陆 dàlù

continental ADJ 大陆的 dàlù de

continental breakfast 欧洲大陆式早餐 Ōuzhōu dàlù shì zǎocān

contingency N 意外事件 yìwài shìjiàn

contingent I ADJ 视将来情况而定的 shì jiānglái qíngkuàng ér dìng de
contingent upon 取决于… qǔjuéyú…
II N 特遣部队 tèqiǎnbùduì

continual ADJ 一再重复的 yízài chóngfù de, 没完没了的 méiwán méiliǎo de

continuation N 继续 jìxù

continue V 继续 jìxù

continuity N 连续 liánxù, 连续性 liánxùxìng

continuous ADJ 1 连续的 liánxù de 2 正在进行的 zhèngzài jìnxíng de

contort V 使…扭曲 shǐ…niǔqū

contour N 轮廓 lúnkuò, 外形 wàixíng

contraband N 走私货 zǒusīhuò [M. WD 件 jiàn/批 pī]

contraception N 避孕 bìyùn

contraceptive N 避孕药 bìyùnyào, 避孕用具 bìyùn yòngjù

contract N 合同 hétong [M. WD 份 fèn]
to bid/tender for a contract 为合同投标 wéi hétong tóubiāo
to enter into (terminate) a contract 签订（终止）合同 qiāndìng (zhōngzhǐ) hétong
II V 1 签订合同 qiāndìng hétong 2 紧缩 jǐnsuō 3 感染 [+病] gǎnrǎn [+bìng]

contraction N 收缩 shōusuō, 缩小 suōxiǎo

contractor N 承包商 chéngbāoshāng

contractual ADJ 合同规定的 hétong guīdìng de

contradict V 与…相矛盾 yǔ…xiāng máodùn
to contradict oneself 自相矛盾 zìxiāng máodùn

contraption N（不好的）新发明 (bùhǎo de) xīn fāmíng

contrary I N 相反 xiāngfǎn
on the contrary 正相反 zhèngxiāngfǎn
II ADJ 相反的 xiāngfǎn de

contrast V, N 对比 duìbǐ
in contrast 相比之下 xiāngbǐ zhī xià

contravene V 相抵触 xiāngdǐ chù

contribute V 1 贡献 gòngxiàn 2 捐款 juānkuǎn 3 促成 cùchéng

contribution N 1 贡献 gòngxiàn 2 [慈善事业+] 捐款 [císhàn shìyè+] juānkuǎn

contrite ADJ 认错的 rèncuò de, 痛悔的 tònghuǐ de

contrive V 1 设法 shèfǎ 2 创造出 chuàngzàochū 3 谋划 móuhuà

control V, N 控制 kòngzhì
to control costs 控制成本 kòngzhì chéngběn
to control one's temper 控制自己的脾气 kòngzhì zìjǐ de píqi
control key（计算机）控制键 (jìsuànjī) kòngzhìjiàn
control freak 控制狂 kòngzhìkuáng
control tower 控制塔 kòngzhìtǎ

controller N 审计人员 shěnjì rényuán

controversy N 争议 zhēngyì, 争论 zhēnglùn

convalesce V 疗养 liáoyǎng, 恢复健康 huīfù jiànkāng, 康复 kāngfù

convalescence N 康复期 kāngfù qī

convalescent I ADJ 康复的 kāngfù de 2 II N 康复病人 kāngfù bìngrén

convene V 召集 zhàojí, 召开 zhàokāi

convenience N 方便 fāngbiàn
convenience food 方便食品 fāngbiàn shípǐn
convenience store 便民店 biànmíndiàn, 方便店 fāngbiàndiàn

convenient ADJ 方便的 fāngbiàn de, 便利的 biànlì de

convent N 女修道院 nǚxiūdàoyuàn

convention N 1 惯例 guànlì, 习俗 xísú 2 大会 dàhuì 3 公约 gōngyuē, 协定 xiédìng
the Geneva Convention 日内瓦公约 Rìnèiwǎ Gōngyuē

conventional ADJ 传统的 chuántǒng de, 常规的 chángguī de
conventional wisdom 普遍的看法 pǔbiàn de kànfǎ

converge V 聚集 jùjí, 汇集 huìjí

convergence N 聚集 jùjí, 汇集 huìjí

conversant ADJ 熟悉的 shúxī de, 有经验的 yǒu jīngyàn de

conversation N 会话 huìhuà, 谈话 tánhuà
to make conversation 没话找话说 méi huà zhǎo huà shuō

converse¹ v 交谈 jiāotán

converse² ADJ 相反的 xiāngfǎn de
the converse 相反情况 xiāngfǎn qíngkuàng

conversion N 1 转换 zhuǎnhuàn, 转化
zhuǎnhuà 2 皈依 guīyī 3 (橄榄球) 附加
得分 (gǎnlǎnqiú) fùjiā défēn

convert I v 1 转换 [+为美元] zhuǎnhuàn
[+wéi Měiyuán], 转化 [+为能量]
zhuǎnhuà [+wéi néngliàng] 2 使…皈依
[+基督教] shǐ…guīyī [+Jīdūjiào] 3 改变
gǎibiàn II N 改变信仰者 gǎibiàn
xìnyǎngzhě

convertible I ADJ 1 可兑换的 [+货币]
kěduìhuàn de [+huòbì] 2 可折叠的 [+的
沙发] kě zhédié de [+de shāfā] II N 折
蓬轿车 zhé péng jiàochē

convex ADJ 凸出的 tūchū de, 凸的 tū de

convey v 1 转达 chuándá 2 传送 chuánsòng

convict I v 被判有罪 bèi pàn yǒuzuì II N
囚犯 qiúfàn, 罪人 fànrén

conviction N 1 坚定的信仰 jiāndìng de
xìnyǎng, 坚信 jiānxìn 2 有罪判决 yǒuzuì
pànjué, 定罪 dìngzuì

convince v 使…相信 shǐ…xiāngxìn

convinced ADJ 相信 xiāngxìn, 确信 quèxìn

convivial ADJ 友好的 yǒuhǎo de, 轻松愉
快的 qīngsōng yúkuài de

convoluted ADJ 复杂的 fùzá de, 很难懂的
hěn nándǒng de

convoy N 车队 chēduì, 船队 chuánduì

convulse v 1 使…动乱 shǐ…dòngluàn
2 痉挛 jìngluán, 抽搐 chōuchù

convulsion N 1 痉挛 jìngluán, 抽搐
chōuchù 2 动乱 dòngluàn

coo v 1 [鸽子+] 咕咕叫 [gēzi+] gūgū
jiào 2 [情人+] 轻声柔语 [qíngrén+]
qīngshēng róuyǔ

cook I v 做饭 zuòfàn
to cook the book 做假账 zuò jiǎzhàng
II N 厨师 chúshī, 炊事员 chuīshìyuán

cookie N 1 甜饼干 tián bǐnggān 2 网络跟
踪文件 wǎngluò gēnzōng wénjiàn

cool I ADJ 1 好凉 hǎo, 棒 bàng, 酷 kù 2 凉
凉快 liángkuai II v 变冷 biàn lěng,
冷下来 lěng xiàlai

Cool it! 别着急, 慢慢来。Bié zháojí,
mànmànlái.
III N 冷静 lěngjìng
to keep one's cool 保持冷静 bǎochí
lěngjìng
IV ADV 冷静地 lěngjìng de
to play it cool 冷静对待 lěngjìng duìdài

cooler N 冷却器 lěngquèqì, 冰桶 bīngtǒng

coop I N 鸡笼 jīlóng II v (be cooped up) 被
困在 bèi kùn zài, 被关在 bèi guān zài

cooperate v 合作 hézuò, 同心协力
tóngxīn xiélì

cooperative I ADJ 合作的 hézuò de II N
1 合作社 hézuòshè 2 合作公寓 hézuò
gōngyù

co-opt v 1 收买 shōumǎi, 拉拢 lālong
2 强行吸纳 qiángxíng xīnà

coordinate I v 协调 xiétiáo II N 坐标
zuòbiāo

coordination N 协调 xiétiáo

cope v 1 应付 yìngfu 2 处理 chǔlǐ

copier N 复印机 fùyìnjī [M. WD 台 tái]

co-pilot N (飞机) 副驾驶员 (fēijī)
fùjiàshǐyuán

copious ADJ 丰富的 fēngfù de, 大量的
dàliàng de

copper (Cu) N 铜 tóng

copter N See **helicopter**

copulate v 交配 jiāopèi

copy I v 1 复印 [+书] fùyìn [+shū], 复制
[+产品] fùzhì [+chǎnpǐn] 2 用手 [+抄写
[+yòng shǒu+] chāoxiě 3 模仿 mófǎng,
仿效 fǎngxiào II N 1 复印本 fùyìn běn,
副本 fùběn 2 本 běn, 册 cè 3 文字稿
wénzì gǎo

copycat N 只会模仿的人 zhǐ huì mófǎng
de rén
a copycat crime 模仿性犯罪 mófǎng
xìng fànzuì

copyright N 版权 bǎnquán

copywriter N 广告撰稿人 guǎnggào
zhuàngǎorén

coral N 珊瑚 shānhú

cord N 1 电线 diànxiàn 2 绳子 shéngzi

cordial ADJ 亲切的 qīnqiè de, 热忱的
rèchén de

cordless ADJ 无绳的 wú shéng de

cordless telephone 无绳电话 wú shéng diànhuà

cordon I N 警戒线 jǐngjièxiàn II v (to cordon off) 设置警戒线 shèzhì jǐngjièxiàn, 封锁 fēngsuǒ

corduroy N 灯芯绒 dēngxīn róng

core I N 核 hé, 核心 héxīn II v 挖去 [+水果的] 核 wā qù [+shuǐguǒ de] hé

cork I N 软木（塞）ruǎnmù (sāi) II v（用软木塞）塞紧 (yòng ruǎnmùsāi) sāijǐn

corkscrew N 螺丝起子 luósīqǐzi, 瓶塞钻 píngsāizuān

corn I N 玉米 yùmǐ

corn on the cob 玉米棒子 yùmǐ bàngzi

2 鸡眼 jīyǎn

cornea N（眼睛）角膜 (yǎnjing) jiǎomó

corner I N 1 拐角 guǎijiǎo 2 角落 jiǎoluò 3（足球的）角球 (zúqiú de) jiǎoqiú II v 使…陷入绝境 shǐ...xiànrù juéjìng

cornstarch N 玉米淀粉 yùmǐ diànfěn, 勾芡粉 gōuqiàn fěn

corny ADJ 过时的 guòshí de, 老掉牙的 lǎodiàoyá de

coronary ADJ 心脏的 xīnzàng de

coronation N 加冕 jiāmiǎn, 加冕典礼 jiāmiǎn diǎnlǐ

coroner N 验尸官 yànshīguān

corporal I N 下士 xiàshì II ADJ 肉体的 ròutǐ de

corporal punishment 体罚 tǐfá

corporate ADJ 1 公司的 gōngsī de

corporate hospitality 公司招待客户 gōngsī zhāodài kèhù

2 团体的 tuántǐ de, 共同的 gòngtóng de

corporation N 大公司 dàgōng sī, 股份公司 gǔfèn gōngsī

multinational corporation (MNC) 跨国公司 kuàguógōngsī

corps N 1 军团 jūntuán 2 部队 bùduì

Marine Corps 海军陆战队 hǎijūn lùzhànduì

corpse N 尸体 shītǐ

corpulent ADJ 肥胖的 féipàng de

corral N 畜栏 chùlán

correct I ADJ 1 正确 zhèngquè, 对 duì 2 恰当的 qiàdàng de II v 纠正 jiūzhèng, 改正 gǎizhèng

I stand corrected. 我承认有错。Wǒ chéngrèn yǒu cuò.

correction N 改正 gǎizhèng, 纠正 jiūzhèng

correction fluid 改正液 gǎizhèngyè

corrective ADJ 改正的 gǎizhèng de, 纠正的 jiū zhèngde

correlate v 与…相关联 yǔ...xiāngguān lián

correspond v 1 与 … 相对应 yǔ...xiāngduì yìng 2 通信 tōngxìn

correspondence N 1 关系 guānxì, 对应 duìyìng 2 通信 tōngxìn 3 信件 xìnjiàn, 函件 hánjiàn

correspondent N 1 记者 jìzhě

a foreign correspondent 驻外记者 zhùwài jìzhě

2 通信者 tōngxìnzhě

corresponding ADJ 相应的 xiāngyìng de, 相关联的 xiāngguānlián de

corridor N 走廊 zǒuláng [M. WD 条 tiáo]

corroborate v 证实 zhèngshí

corrode v 腐蚀 fǔshí, 侵蚀 qīnshí

corrosion N 腐蚀 fǔshí, 侵蚀 qīnshí

corrugated ADJ 瓦楞的 wǎléng de

a corrugated iron roof 瓦楞铁制屋顶 wǎléng tiězhì wūdǐng

corrupt I ADJ 腐败的 fǔbài de, 道德败坏的 dàodé bàihuài de II v 使…腐败 shǐ...fǔbài, 使…道德败坏 shǐ...dàodé bàihuài

cosmetic I N 化妆用的 huàzhuāng yòng de 2 表面的 biǎomiàn de, 装饰门面的 zhuāngshì ménmian de

cosmetics N 1 化妆品 huàzhuāngpǐn 2 装饰门面的东西 zhuāngshì ménmian de dōngxi

cosmic ADJ 1 宇宙的 yǔzhòu de 2 特大的 tèdà de

cosmonaut N 宇航员 yǔhángyuán

cosmopolitan ADJ 1 世界性的 shìjièxìng de 2 见多识广的 jiàn duō shí guǎng de

cosmos N 宇宙 yǔzhòu

cost I v（PT & PP cost）花费 huāfèi, 花（多少钱）huā (duōshaoqián) II N 1 费用 fèiyòng, 成本 chéngběn 2 代价 dàijià

at any cost/at all costs 不惜代价 bùxī dàijià

cost-effective ADJ 效益高的 xiàoyì gāo de

costly ADJ 昂贵的 ángguì de, 花很多钱的 huā hěn duō qián de

costume N（某一时期或某一地区的）服装 (mǒu yì shíqī huò mǒu yí dìqū de) fúzhuāng
costume jewelry 人造首饰 rénzào shǒushi

cot N 轻便折叠床 qīngbiàn zhédiéchuáng

cottage N 小屋 xiǎo wū

cotton N 棉花 miánhua

couch N（长）沙发 (cháng) shā fā
couch potato 老是坐在沙发上看电视的人 lǎoshi zuò zài shāfā shàng kàn diànshì de rén

cough N 咳嗽 késou
cough drop 润喉糖 rùnhóutáng
cough syrup 止咳糖浆 zhǐké tángjiāng

could MODEL V (PT OF **can**)

couldn't See **can**

council N（市）议会 (shì) yìhuì, 理事会 lǐshìhuì
the Security Council of the U.N. 联合国安全理事会 Liánhéguó Ānquán Lǐshìhuì

counsel I N 1 辩护律师 biànhù lǜshī 2 法律顾问 fǎlǜ gùwèn 3 忠告 zhōnggào
to keep one's own counsel 不透露自己的想法 bú tòulù zìjǐ de xiǎngfǎ
II V 提供咨询 tígōng zīxún, 辅导 fǔdǎo

counseling N 咨询（服务）zīxún (fúwù)

counselor N 咨询人员 zīxún rényuán, 辅导人员 fǔdǎo rényuán

count I V 1 数 shǔ, 计数 jìshù
Don't count your chickens before they are hatched. 蛋未孵出莫数小鸡。(→ 好事不要指望过早。) Dàn wèi fūchū mò shǔ xiǎojī. (→ Hǎoshì bú yào zhǐwàng guòzǎo.)
2 算数 suànshù, 有效 yǒuxiào 3 很重要 hěn zhòng yào
to count on 指望 zhǐwàng, 依靠 yīkào
II N 1 总数 zǒngshù
to keep count 记录 jìlù, 记录数字 jìlù shùzì
to lose count 记不清数字 jìbuqīng shùzì

2 计量 jìliàng 3 罪状 zuìzhuàng

countable ADJ 可数的 kěshù de

countdown N 倒计时 dǎojìshí

countenance N 面容 miànróng, 面部表情 miànbù biǎoqíng

counter I N 1 [商店+] 柜台 [shāngdiàn+] guìtái 2 [厨房+] 操作台 [chúfáng+] cāozuò tái
under the counter 暗地里 àndìli
II V 反驳 fǎnbó III ADV 相反 xiāngfǎn

counteract V 抵消 dǐxiāo

counterattack V, N 反击 fǎnjī, 反攻 fǎngōng

counterbalance I V 抵消 dǐxiāo II N 抵消 dǐxiāo

counterclockwise ADJ, ADV 反时针方向的 / 地 fǎn shízhēn fāngxiàng de

counterfeit I ADJ 伪造的 wěizào de
a counterfeit bill 一张假钞票 yìzhāng jiǎ chāopiào, 一张假币 yìzhāng jiǎbì
II V 伪造 wěizào

counterpart N 地位相当的人（或物）dìwèi xiāngdāng de rén (huò wù)

counterproductive ADJ 起反作用的 qǐ fǎnzuòyòng de, 效果适得其反的 xiàoguǒ shìdé qífǎn de

countersign V 联署 liánshǔ

countless ADJ 无数的 wúshù de

country N 1 国家 guójiā 2 乡下 xiāngxia
country club 乡村俱乐部 xiāngcūn jùlèbù

countryman N 同胞 tóngbāo

countryside N 乡下 xiāngxia, 农村 nóngcūn

county N 县 xiàn
county fair 农村集市 nóngcūn jíshì

coup N 1（军事）政变 (jūnshì) zhèngbiàn 2 成功的行动 chénggōng de xíngdòng

couple I N 1 一对夫妻 yíduì fūqī, 一对情人 yíduì qíngrén 2 两个 liǎng ge, 两三个 liǎng sān ge II V 结合 jiéhé, 连接 liánjiē

coupon N 优惠券 yōuhuìquàn [M. WD 张 zhāng], 礼券 lǐquàn [M. WD 张 zhāng]

courage N 勇气 yǒngqì, 勇敢 yǒnggǎn

courageous ADJ 勇敢的 yǒnggǎn de, 有勇气的 yǒu yǒngqì de

courier N 信使 xìnshǐ [M. WD 名 míng]

course I N 1 路程 lùchéng, 过程 guòchéng 2 课程 kèchéng 3 道（菜）dào (cài) of course 当然 dāngrán II V 流liú, 流动 liúdòng

court I N 1 法庭 fǎtíng 2 球场 qiú chǎng 3 宫廷 gōngtíng, 王室 wángshì II V 讨好 tǎohǎo, 追求 zhuīqiú

courteous ADJ 有礼貌的 yǒulǐmào de, 彬彬有礼 bīnbīn yǒulǐ

courtesy N 礼貌 lǐmào, 好意 hǎoyì courtesy of 承蒙…的好意 chéng-méng…de hǎoyì courtesy call 礼节性拜访 lǐjiéxìng bàifǎng

courthouse N 法院 fǎyuàn

courtmartial N 1 军事法庭 jūnshì fǎtíng 2 军法审判 jūnfǎ shěnpàn

courtroom N 法庭 fǎtíng

courtship N 恋爱 liàn'ài, 恋爱期 liàn'àiqī

courtyard N 院子 yuànzi

cousin N 堂弟/哥 táng gē/dì (paternal uncle's son, younger/older than yourself), 堂姐/妹 tángjiě/mèi (paternal uncle's daughter, older/younger than yourself), 表哥/弟 biǎogē/dì (maternal uncle or aunt's son, paternal uncle, older/ younger than yourself), 表姐/妹 biǎojiě/mèi (maternal uncle or aunt's daughter, paternal aunt's daughter, older/younger than yourself)

cove N 小海湾 xiǎo hǎiwān

covenant N 契约 qìyuē

cover I V 1 盖 gài, 覆盖 fùgài to cover up 掩盖 yǎngài 2 涉及 shèjí, 包括 bāokuò 3 给…保险 gěi…bǎoxiǎn, 承保 chéngbǎo not to cover cosmetic surgery 不承保整容手术 bù chéngbǎo zhěngróng shǒushù 4 有钱支付 yǒuqián zhīfù to cover all expenses 有钱支付所有的费用 yǒuqián zhīfù suǒyǒu de fèiyòng 5 走完 [+距离] zǒu wán [+jùlí] II N 1 盖 gài, 盖子 gàizi 2（书、杂志）封面 (shū, zázhì) fēngmiàn 3 掩护 yǎnhù 4 保险范围 bǎoxiǎn fànwéi cover charge 服务费 fúwùfèi

coverage N 1 报道 bàodào, 新闻报道 xīnwén bàodào 2 保险 bǎoxiǎn, 保险范围 bǎoxiǎn fànwéi

covert ADJ 秘密的 mìmì de

cover-up N 隐瞒 yǐnmán

covet V 贪求 tānqiú, 对…垂涎三尺 duì…chuíxián sānchǐ

cow N 1 母牛 mǔniú 2 大型雌性哺乳动物 dàxíng cíxìng bǔrǔ dòngwù

coward N 胆小鬼 dǎnxiǎoguǐ, 懦夫 nuòfū

cowardice N 胆小 dǎnxiǎo, 怯懦 qiènuò

cowardly ADJ 胆小的 dǎnxiǎo de, 怯懦的 qiènuò de

cower V 畏缩 wèisuō, 蜷缩 quánsuō

co-worker N 同事 tóngshì

coy ADJ 1 装作害羞的 zhuāngzuò hàixiū de, 故作忸怩的 gùzuò niǔní de 2 含糊其词的 hánhú qí cí de

coyote N 丛林狼 cónglínláng

cozy ADJ 温暖舒适的 wēnnuǎn shūshì de

CPR (= cardiopulmonary resuscitation) ABBREV 人工呼吸抢救 réngōng hūxī qiǎngjiù

crab N 蟹 xiè [M. WD 只 zhī]

crabby ADJ 暴躁的 bàozao de

crack I V 1 破裂 pòliè 2 精神崩溃 jīngshén bēngkuì, 崩溃 bēngkuì 3 [嗓音+] 变嘶哑 [sǎngyīn+] biàn sīyǎ 4 破解 [+密码] pòjiě [+mìmǎ] II N 1 裂缝 lièfèng 2 强效可卡因 qiáng xiào kěkǎyīn III ADJ 第一流的 dìyīliú de

crackdown N 镇压 zhènyā, 取缔 qǔdì

cracked ADJ 1 有裂缝的 yǒu lièfèng de 2 [嗓音+] 嘶哑的 [sǎngyīn+] sīyǎ de

cracker N 薄脆饼干 báo cuì bǐnggān, 梳打饼干 shūdǎ bǐnggān

crackle V 发出噼啪声 fāchū pīpāshēng

crackpot N 有古怪离奇念头的人 yǒu gǔguài líqí niàntou de rén

cradle I N 摇篮 yáolán II V 小心翼翼地抱着 xiǎoxīn yìyì de bàozhe

craft N 手（工）艺 shǒu (gōng) yì

craftsman N 手工艺人 shǒugōngyìrén

craftsmanship N 手工技能 shǒugōngyì jìnéng

crafty ADJ 足智多谋的 zú zhì duō móu de, 狡猾的 jiǎohuá de

craggy ADJ 陡峭多石的 dǒuqiào duō shí de

cram V 1 把…塞进 bǎ…sāijìn 2 (考试前) 死记硬背 (kǎoshì qián) sǐjì yìngbèi
to cram for a test 在考试前死记硬背 zài kǎoshì qián sǐjì yìngbèi

cramp I N 1 痉挛 jìngluán, 抽筋 chōujīn 2 约束 yuēshù, 限制 xiànzhì II N 痉挛 jìngluán, 抽筋 chōujīn

cramped ADJ 狭小的 xiáxiǎo de

cramps N [腹部+] 绞痛 [fùbù+] jiǎotòng, [妇女+] 经痛 [fùnǚ+] jīngtòng

crane I N 1 起重机 qǐzhòngjī [M. WD 台 tái] 2 鹤 hè, 仙鹤 xiānhè [M. WD 只 zhī] II V 伸长脖子看 shēncháng bózi kàn

cranium N 头颅 tóulú

crank I N 曲柄 qūbǐng II V (用曲柄) 转动 (yòng qūbǐng) zhuàndòng

cranky ADJ 易怒的 yì nù de

crap N 1 胡扯 húchě, 废话 fèihuà 2 劣质品 lièzhìpǐn, 破坏玩意儿 pòhuàiwányìr 3 粪便 fènbiàn

crash I V 1 撞 zhuàng, 碰撞 pèngzhuàng 2 (电脑) 死机 (diànnǎo) sǐjī 3 猛撞发出巨响 měngzhuàng fāchū jùxiǎng 4 [股市+] 崩盘 [gǔshì+] bēngpán
to crash and burn 突然垮台 tūrán kuǎtái II N [飞机／火车+] 相撞 [fēijī/huǒchē+] xiāngzhuàng, 失事 shīshì
crash landing 强行着陆 qiángxíng zhuólù
III ADJ 快速的 kuàisù de
crash diet 快速减肥食谱 kuàisù jiǎnféi shípǔ

crass ADJ 粗鲁的 cūlǔ de, 令人厌恶的 lìngrén yàn è de

crate N 大装货箱 dà zhuānghuò xiāng

crater N 1 火山口 huǒshānkǒu 2 坑 kēng

crave V 渴望 kěwàng, 渴求 kěqiú

craving N 渴望 kěwàng

crawl I N V 爬 pá, 爬行 páxíng II N 缓慢移动 huǎnmàn yídòng

crayfish N 淡水螯虾 dànshuǐ áoxiā

crayon N 彩色蜡笔 cǎisè làbǐ

craze N 时尚 shíshàng, 热 rè
Chinese craze 学中文热 xué Zhōngwén rè

crazy ADJ 1 疯 fēng, 发疯 fāfēng 2 喜欢得要命 xǐhuan deyàomìng 3 古怪的 gǔguài de
crazy code 乱码 luànmǎ

creak I V 发出嘎吱嘎吱的声响 fāchū gāzhī gāzhī de shēngxiǎng II N 嘎吱嘎吱的声响 gāzhī gāzhī de shēngxiǎng

creaky ADJ 1 发出嘎吱嘎吱的声响的 fāchū gāzhī gāzhī de shēngxiǎng de 2 老旧的 lǎojiù de

cream N 1 奶油 nǎiyóu 2 油膏 yóugāo face cream 面霜 miànshuāng
the cream of the crop (一群人中的) 精英 (yìqún rénzhōng de) jīngyīng, 佼佼者 jiǎojiǎozhě

creamer N 1 代用奶油 dàiyòng nǎiyóu 2 奶油壶 nǎiyóu hú

crease I N 1 皱褶 zhòuzhě, 折缝 zhé féng II V 使…起皱 shǐ…qǐzhòu

create V 1 创造 chuàngzào, 创建 chuàngjiàn 2 发明 fāmíng, 设计 shèjì

creation N 1 创造 chuàngzào 2 创物 chuàngzào wù
the Creation (上帝) 创世 (Shàngdì) chuàngshì, 创造世界 chuàngzào shìjiè

creative ADJ 有创造性的 yǒu chuàng-zàoxìng de

creator N 创作者 chuàngzuòzhě
the Creator 造物主 Zàowùzhǔ

creature N 动物 (包括人) dòngwù (bāokuò rén)

credentials N 1 资格证书 zīgé zhèngshū 2 资格 zīgé, 能力 nénglì

credibility N 可信性 kěxìnxìng, 信赖 xìnlài

credible ADJ 可信的 kěxìn de, 可靠的 kěkào de

credit I N 1 信贷 xìndài, 借款 jièkuǎn
credit rating 信用等级 xìnyòng děngjí
credit report 信用报告 xìnyòng bàogào 2 信誉 xìnyù, 声望 shēngwàng
to do sb credit 使某人赢得声誉 shǐ mǒurén yíngdé shēngyù
to take credit 归功于己 guī gōng yú jǐ 3 带来荣耀／好名声的人 (或事) dàilai róngyào/hǎo míngshēng de rén (huò shì) II V 1 存入 [+钱] cúnrù [+qián] 2 归功于 guī gōng yú

creditable ADJ 值得赞扬的 zhídé zànyáng de

creditor N 债权人 zhàiquánrén

credulous ADJ 轻信的 qīngxìn de

creed N 信条 xìntiáo, 信仰 xìnyǎng

creek N 小溪 xiǎoxī, 溪流 xīliú

creep I v (PT & PP **crept**) 1 爬, 爬行 páxíng 2 蔓生 mànshēng II N 讨厌的人 tǎoyàn de rén
　　to give sb the creeps 叫…毛骨悚然 jiào…máogǔ sǒngrán

cremate v 火化 huǒhuà, 火葬 huǒzàng

crematorium N 火葬场 huǒzàngchǎng

crêpe N 绉纱 zhòushā, 绉绸 zhòuchóu

crept See **creep**

crescendo N [声音+] 渐强 [shēngyīn+] jiàn qiáng

crescent N 新月 xīnyuè

crest N 1 山顶 shāndǐng, 浪峰 làngfēng 2 鸟冠 niǎoguān

crestfallen ADJ 沮丧的 jǔsàng de, 垂头丧气的 chuítóu sàngqì de

crevice N 裂缝 lièfèng, 缺口 quēkǒu

crew N 1 （飞机）机组人员 (fēijī) jīzǔ rényuán,（轮船）船员 (lúnchuán) chuányuán 2 工作人员 gōngzuò rényuán
　　crew cut 板刷头 bǎnshuātóu

crib N 婴儿床 yīng'ér chuáng

cricket N 1 蟋蟀 xīshuài 2 板球 bǎnqiú

crime N 罪 zuì, 罪行 zuìxíng
　　Crime does not pay. 犯罪是不值得的。Fànzuì shì bù zhídé de.

criminal I ADJ 犯罪的 fànzuì de II N 罪犯 zuìfàn
　　criminal law 刑法 xíngfǎ

crimson N, ADJ 深红色（的）shēnhóngsè (de)

cringe v 1 退缩 tuìsuō 2 感到难堪 gǎndào nánkān

crinkle v 起皱 qǐzhòu

cripple N 残疾人 cánjírén, 跛子 bǒzi

crisis N 危机 wēijī

crisp ADJ 1 [食品+] 脆的 [shípǐn+] cuì de 2 易碎的 yì suì de 3 [天气+] 干冷的 [tiānqì+] gānlěng de

crispy ADJ 松脆的 sōngcuì de

crisscross v 1 往返 wǎngfǎn, 来回奔波 láihuí bēnbō 2 画交错的直线 huà jiāocuò de zhíxiàn, 纵横交错 zònghéng jiāocuò

criterion N (PL **criteria**) 标准 biāozhǔn

critic N 1 批评者 pīpíngzhě, 反对者 fǎnduìzhě 2 评论员 pínglùnyuán, 批评家 pīpíngjiā

critical ADJ 1 批判的 pīpàn de, 批评的 pīpíng de 2 关键的 guānjiàn de, 危险的 wēixiǎnde

criticism N 批评 pīpíng, 评论 pínglùn

critique N, V 评论 pínglùn

croak I v 1 用低沉沙哑的声音说 yòng dī chén shāyǎ de shēngyīn shuō 2 [青蛙+] 鸣叫 [qīngwā+] míngjiào II N 1 低沉沙哑的声音 dīchén shāyǎ de shēngyīn 2 （青蛙）鸣叫 (qīngwā) míngjiào

crochet v 用钩针编结 yòng gōuzhēn biānjié

crockery N 陶器 táoqì

crocodile N 鳄鱼 èyú [M. WD 条 tiáo]
　　to shed crocodile tears 掉几滴鳄鱼的眼泪 diào jǐ dī èyú de yǎnlèi

crocus N 藏红花 zànghónghuā

croissant N 羊角面包 yángjiǎo miànbāo

crony N 亲密的朋友 qīnmì de péngyou

crook I N 1 骗子 piànzi, 贼 zéi 2 弯曲 II v 1 使…弯曲 shǐ…wānqū 2 弯 wān, 勾 gōu

crooked ADJ 弯曲的 wānqū de 2 狡诈的 jiǎozhà de

croon v 轻柔地歌唱（或说话）qīngróu de gēchàng (huò shuōhuà)

crop I N 1 庄稼 zhuāngjia, 农作物 nóngzuòwù 2 收成 shōuchéng 3 平头发型 píngtóu fàxíng, 短头发 duǎn tóu fà II v 剪断 [头发] jiǎnduàn [+tóufa]

cross I N 1 十字架 shízìjià 2 十字形 shízì xíng, 叉 chā
　　the Red Cross 红十字 Hóngshízì 3 混合物 hùnhéwù, 杂交品种 zájiāo pǐnzhǒng II v 1 穿越 chuānyuè, 度过 dùguò 2 交叉 jiāochā
　　to cross one's fingers 但愿有好运 dànyuàn yǒu hǎoyùn 3 杂交 zájiāo III ADJ 生气的 shēngqì de

cross-country ADJ 越野的 yuèyě de
cross-country running 越野赛跑 yuèyěsàipǎo

cross-cultural ADJ 跨文化的 kuà wénhuà de

cross-examine V 反复盘问 fǎnfù pánwèn

cross-eyed ADJ 内斜视的 nèixiéshì de, 斗鸡眼的 dòujīyǎn de

crossfire N 交叉火力 jiāochā huǒlì

crossing N 1 (铁路) 过道 (tiělù) guòdào 2 十字路口 shízì lùkǒu 3 跨海旅程 kuà hǎi lǚchéng

cross-legged ADV 盘腿而坐 pántuǐ ér zuò

cross-purposes N 相反目的 xiāngfǎn mùdì
at cross purposes 相互矛盾 xiānghù máodùn

cross-reference N 相互参照 xiānghù cānzhào, 互见 hùjiàn

crossroads N 十字路口 shízì lùkǒu

cross-section N 1 横剖面 héngpōumiàn 2 一组有代表性的人 yìzǔ yǒu dàibiǎoxìng de rén

crotch N 胯部 kuàbù

crouch V 蹲 (下) dūn (xià)

crow I N 1 乌鸦 wūyā 2 (公鸡) 鸣叫 (gōngjī) míngjiào II V [公鸡+] 叫 [gōngjī+] jiào

crowd I N 人群 rénqún, 一群人 yìqún rén II V 1 群集 qúnjí, 群聚 qúnjù 2 挤 jǐ, 推挤 tuījǐ 3 催 cuī, 催促 cuīcù

crowded ADJ 拥挤的 yōngjǐ de

crown I N 1 王冠 wángguān, 冕 miǎn 2 王国政府 wángguó zhèngfǔ 3 [牙齿+] 人造冠 [yáchǐ+] rénzào guān II V 1 为 [+国王] 加冕 wéi [+guówáng] jiāmiǎn 2 为…镶假牙冠 wéi…xiāng jiǎ yáguān 3 达到顶峰 dádào dǐngfēng

crucial ADJ 决定性的 juédìngxìng de, 关键的 guānjiàn de

crucifix N 有耶稣像的十字架 yǒu Yēsū xiàng de shízìjià

crucifixion N 耶稣被钉在十字架上 Yēsū bèi dīng zài shízìjià shàng, 耶稣受难 Yēsū shòunàn

crud N 令人恶心的东西／人 lìngrén èxīn de dōngxi/rén

crude ADJ 1 粗俗的 [+语言] cūsú de

[+yǔyán] 2 未经提炼的 [+石油] wèijīng tíliàn de [+shíyóu]
crude oil 原油 yuányóu

cruel ADJ 残酷 cánkù

cruelty N 1 残酷 cánkù 2 虐待 (的行为) nüèdài (de xíngwéi)

cruise V 1 [乘船+] 巡游 [chéngchuán+] xúnyóu 2 [汽车+] 稳速行驶 [qìchē+] wěn sù xíngshǐ 3 (乘车) 兜风 (chéngchē) dōufēng
cruise ship 大游轮 dà yóulún

cruiser N 巡洋舰 xúnyángjiàn

crumb N 食物碎屑 shíwù suìxiè, 面包屑 miànbāo xiè

crumble V 1 把…弄成碎屑 bǎ…nòngchéng suìxiè 2 [建筑物+] 年久倒塌 [jiànzhùwù+] niánjiǔ dǎotā 3 瓦解 wǎjiě

crumple V 1 弄皱 nòng zhòu, 弄皱 …nòng zhòu 2 晕倒 yūndǎo

crunch I V 1 发出嘎吱嘎吱的声响 fāchū gāzhī gāzhī de shēngxiǎng 2 嘎吱嘎吱地吃 gāzhī gāzhī de chī
to crunch the numbers 作大量计算 zuò dàliàng jìsuàn
II N 1 嘎吱嘎吱的声响 gāzhī gāzhī de shēngxiǎn 2 困境 kùnjìng, 危机 wēijī
credit crunch 信贷危机 xìndài wēijī

crunchy ADJ 脆的 cuìde

crusade I N 1 改革运动 gǎigé yùndòng 2 十字军东征 Shízìjūn dōngzhēng II V 致力于改革 zhìlì yú gǎigé

crush I V 1 压碎 yāsuì, 粉碎 fěnsuì II N 迷恋 míliàn, 强烈的暗恋 qiángliè de ànliàn
to have a crush on 暗暗的迷恋上 àn'àn de míliàn shàng

crust N 1 面包皮 miànbāopí, 比萨饼皮 bǐsàbǐngpí 2 硬壳 yìngké
Earth's crust 地壳 dìqiào

crustacean N 甲壳纲动物 jiǎqiàogāng dòngwù

crutch N 拐杖 guǎizhàng

crux N 中心 zhōngxīn, 症结 zhēngjié

cry I V 1 喊叫 hǎnjiào
to cry foul (大声) 抗议 (dàshēng) kàngyì
to cry over spilled milk 作无益的悔恨 zuò wúyì de huǐhèn

to cry wolf ① 叫 "狼来了" jiào "láng lái le" ② 发假警报 fā jiǎ jǐngbào
2 哭 kū **II** N **1** 叫喊（声）jiàohǎn (shēng) **2** 哭（声）kū (shēng) **3**（动物的）叫声（dòngwù de) jiàoshēng
to be a far cry from 与…相差很远 yǔ…xiāngchà hěn yuǎn

cryptic ADJ 神秘的 shénmì de, 难懂的 nándǒng de

crystal N 水晶 shuǐjīng
crystal clear 明白易懂的 míngbai yìdǒng de, 明摆着的 míngbǎizhe de

crystallize v **1** [盐+] 结晶 [yán+] jiéjīng **2** 使 [+思路] 变得明朗清晰 shǐ [+sīlù] biàn de mínglǎng qīngxī

cub N 小熊 xiǎoxióng, 小老虎 xiǎolǎohǔ, 小狮子 xiǎoshīzi

cube I N **1** 立方体 lìfāngtǐ
ice cube 冰块 bīngkuài
2 立方 lìfāng

cubic ADJ 立方的 lìfāng de
cubic inch/feet/yard 立方英寸／英尺／码 lìfāng yīngcùn/yīngchǐ/mǎ

cubicle N 小隔间 xiǎo géjiān

cuckoo N 杜鹃 dùjuān, 布谷鸟 bùgǔniǎo [M. WD 只 zhī]

cucumber N 黄瓜 huángguā

cuddle I v 拥抱 yōngbào, 搂搂抱抱 lǒulǒubàobào **II** N 拥抱 yōngbào

cue N **1** 提示 tíshì
on cue 恰好这时候 qiàhǎo zhè shíhou
to take one's cue from 学…的样 xué…de yàng, 仿效 fǎngxiào
2 球杆 qiú gǎn

cuff I N 袖口 xiùkǒu
off the cuff 未经考虑的 [+讲话] wèi jīng kǎolǜ de [+jiǎnghuà]
II v 给 [+犯人] 戴手铐 gěi [+fànrén] dài shǒukào

cuffs N 手铐 shǒukào [M. WD 副 fù]

cuisine N 烹饪法 pēngrènfǎ, 烹饪风味 pēngrèn fēng wèi **2** 菜肴 càiyáo

culinary ADJ 烹饪的 pēngrèn de

cull I v **1** 挑选 tiāoxuǎn, 选用 xuǎnyòng **2** 宰杀 zǎishā **II** N 宰杀 zǎishā

culminate v **1** 告终 gàozhōng, 结束 jiéshù **2** 达到顶峰 dádào dǐngfēng

culpable ADJ 应负责任的 yìng fù zérèn de
culpable negligence 失职罪 shīzhízuì

culprit N 罪犯 zuìfàn, 有过失的人 yǒuguò shī de rén

cult N **1** 异教 yìjiào, 邪教 xiéjiào **2** 时尚观念 shíshàng guānniàn

cultivate v **1** 耕作 gēngzuò **2** 培育 péiyù, 培养 péiyǎng

cultivated ADJ **1** 有教养的 yǒu jiàoyǎng de **2** 养殖的 yǎngzhí de

cultural ADJ 文化的 wénhuà de

culture N **1** 文化 wénhuà **2** 文明 wénmíng **3** 细菌培养 xìjūn péiyǎng

cumbersome ADJ 运转不灵的 yùnzhuǎn bù líng de, 笨重的 bènzhòng de

cumulative ADJ 积累的 jīlěi de

cunning I ADJ 狡猾的 jiǎohuá de **II** N 狡猾 jiǎohuá

cup I N **1** 杯子 bēizi **2** 奖杯 jiǎngbēi **II** v 捧 pěng, 托 tuō

cupboard N 柜子 guìzi, 食柜 shíguì, 碗柜 wǎnguì

cupcake N 杯形蛋糕 bēixíng dàngāo

curable ADJ 可以医好的 kěyǐ yīhǎo de, 医得好的 yī dé hǎode

curator N [博物馆+] 馆长 [bówùguǎn+] guǎnzhǎng

curb I N **1** 路沿 lù yán **2** 抑制 yìzhì, 控制 kòngzhì **II** v 抑制 yìzhì, 控制 kòngzhì

curd N 凝乳 níngrǔ

curdle v 凝结 níngjié

cure I v **1** 治愈 [+病] zhìyù [+病], 治好 zhìhǎo **2** 烟熏 [+火腿] yānxūn [+huǒtuǐ], 腌制 yānzhì **II** N **1** 治疗 zhìliáo **2** 治愈 zhìyù, 治好 zhìhǎo

curfew N 宵禁 xiāojìn

curio N 古董 gǔdǒng, 古玩 gǔwán

curiosity N 好奇心 hàoqíxīn

curious ADJ **1** 好奇的 hàoqí de **2** 奇怪的 qíguài

curl I N **1** 卷发 juǎnfà **2** 卷曲的东西 juǎnqǔ de dōngxi **II** v **1** 缠绕 chánrǎo **2** 卷曲 juǎnqū, 卷发 juǎnfà

currant N 醋栗 cùlì

currency N **1** 货币 huòbì **2** 流通 liútōng

current N **1** 水流 shuǐliú **2** 电流 diànliú

II ADJ 当前的 dāngqián de, 当今的 dāngjīn de
current events 时事 shíshì
curriculum N 课程 kèchéng
curriculum vitae (ABBREV CV) N （个人）简历 (gèrén) jiǎnlì, 履历 lǚlì
curry N 加哩（粉）jiālī (fěn)
curse V, N 1 骂 mà, 咒骂 zhòumà 2 诅咒 zǔzhòu
cursed ADJ 1 遭诅咒的 zāo zǔzhòu de 2 受到折磨无法摆脱的 shòudào zhémo wúfǎ jiětuō de
cursor N 光标 guāngbiāo
cursory ADJ 粗略的 cūlüè de, 草草了事的 cǎocǎo liǎoshì de
curt ADJ 简短而不礼貌的 jiǎnduǎn ér bù lǐmào de
curtail V 削减 xuējiǎn, 减少 jiǎnshǎo
curtailment N 削减 xuējiǎn, 减少 jiǎnshǎo
curtain N 1 窗帘 chuānglián 2 幕布 mùbù
curtsy, curtsey V 行屈膝礼 xíng qūxīlǐ
curve I N 曲线 qūxiàn, 弯曲 wānqū II V 弯曲 wānqū
cushion I N 垫子 diànzi, 靠垫 kàodiàn II V 缓冲 huǎnchōng
cuss V 咒骂 zhòumà
custard N 乳蛋糕 rǔ dàngāo
custody N 1 监护（权）jiānhù (quán) 2 拘留 jūliú
in custody 被拘留 bèi jūliú, 被监禁 bèi jiānjìn
custom I N 风俗 fēngsú II ADJ 定做的 dìngzuò de
customary ADJ 1 习俗的 xísú de 2 习惯性的 xíguànxìng de
customer N 顾客 gùkè
customize V 定做 dìngzuò, 定制 dìngzhì
customs N 海关 hǎiguān
cut I V (PT & PP cut) 1 切 qiē, 剪 jiǎn 2 划破 huápò 3 打断 dǎduàn 4 切牌 qiē pái
to cut corners 偷工减料 tōu gōng jiǎn liào
cut and dried 已成定局的 yǐ chéng dìngjú de
II N 1 伤口 shāngkǒu 2 减少 jiǎnshǎo 3 剪头发 jiǎntóufà, 理发 lǐfà
cutback N 削减 xuējiǎn

cute ADJ 可爱的 kě'ài de, 漂亮的 piàoliang de
cutlery N 餐具（刀叉等）cānjù (dāochā děng)
cutlet N 肉排 ròupái [M. WD 块 kuài]
cutoff N 截止点 jiézhǐ diǎn
cutting I ADJ 1 尖刻的 jiānkè de 2 刺骨的 cìgǔ de
at the cutting edge of 处于领先地位 chǔyú lǐngxiān dìwèi
II N 插枝 chāzhī
cyanide N 氰化物 qínghuàwù
cybercafe N 网吧 wǎngbā [M. WD 间 jiān]
cyberspace N 计算机空间 jìsuànjī kōngjiān, 网络空间 wǎngluò kōngjiān
cycle I N 1 周期 zhōuqī
life cycle 生命周期 shēngmìng zhōuqī 2 循环 xúnhuán
a vicious cycle 恶性循环 èxìng xúnhuán
II V 骑自行车 qí zìxíngchē
cyclic(al) ADJ 周期性的 zhōuqīxìng de
cyclone N 龙卷风 lóngjuǎnfēng [M. WD 场 cháng]
cylinder N 1 圆柱（体）yuánzhù (tǐ) 2 圆筒 yuántǒng, 圆罐 yuán guan
gas cylinder 煤气罐 méiqìguàn 3 气缸 qìgāng
cymbal N 钹 bó, 铙钹 náobó
cynic N 认为人性恶的人 rènwéi rénxìng è de rén, 犬儒 quǎnrú
cynical ADJ 1 认为人性恶的 rènwéi rénxìng è de 2 不讲道德的 bù jiǎngdào dé de
cyst N 囊肿 nángzhǒng
czar N 沙皇 shāhuáng

D

dab I N 1 少量 [+黄油] shǎoliàng [+huángyóu], 一点儿 yìdiǎnr 2 轻拍 qīng pāi II V 轻拍 qīng pāi, 轻触 qīngchù
dad, daddy N 爸爸 bàba, 多多 diēdie
dagger N 匕首 bǐshǒu, 短剑 duǎnjiàn
daily ADJ, ADV 每天 měitiān, 每日 měirì
dainty ADJ 1 精致的 [+小点心] jīngzhì de [+xiǎo diǎnxin] 2 优雅的 [+举止] yōuyǎ de [+jǔzhǐ]

dairy N 牛奶场 niúnǎi chǎng
dairy product 乳制品 rǔzhìpǐn

dally v 浪费时间 làngfèi shíjiān, 磨蹭 móceng

dam N 水坝 shuǐbà [M. WD 座 zuò]

damage I N 损害 sǔnhài, 损伤 sǔnshāng
damages 损害赔偿金 sǔnhài péichángjīn
II v 损坏 sǔnhuài, 损害 sǔnhài

damn I ADJ 该死的 gāisǐ de II ADV 非常 fēicháng, 很 hěn
damn well 非常地 fēicháng de
III INTERJ 该死 gāisǐ, 天哪 tiānna
Damn it! 该死的! Gāisǐ de!
Damn you! 你这个混蛋! Nǐ zhège húndàn! 混蛋! Húndàn!

damning ADJ 极其不利的 jíqí búlì de

damp I ADJ 潮湿的 cháoshī de II 使… 削弱／减少 shǐ... xuēruò/jiǎnshǎo, 抑制 yìzhì
to damp one's interest 使兴趣减少 shǐ xìngqù jiǎnshǎo

dampen v 1 使 [+一块布] 潮湿 shǐ [+yí kuài bù] cháoshī 2 削弱 [+热情] xuēruò [+rèqíng] 3 使扫兴 shǐ sǎoxìng

damper N 令人扫兴的人／事 lìngrén sǎoxìng de rén/shì
to put a damper on 让人扫兴 ràng rén sǎoxìng

damsel N 未婚少女 wèihūn shàonǚ

dance I N 1 跳舞 tiàowǔ 2 跳动 tiàodòng II N 1 舞蹈 wǔdǎo 2 舞会 wǔhuì
school dances 学校舞会 xuéxiào wǔhuì
3 舞曲 wǔqǔ [M. WD 首 shǒu]

dancer N 舞蹈演员 wǔdǎo yǎnyuán

dandruff N 头皮屑 tóupíxiè

Dane N 丹麦人 Dānmàirén

danger N 危险 wēixiǎn
in danger of 有危险 yǒu wēixiǎn, 处于危险之中 chǔyú wēixiǎn zhīzhōng
out of danger 脱离危险 tuōlí wēixiǎn

dangerous ADJ 危险的 wēixiǎn de

dangle v 挂着来回摆动 guàzhe láihuí bǎidòng, 悬吊 xuándiào

Danish I ADJ 丹麦的 Dānmài de, 丹麦语的 Dānmàiyǔ de, 丹麦人的 Dānmàirén de II 丹麦语 Dānmàiyǔ

dank ADJ 湿冷的 shīlěng de, 阴冷的 yīnlěng de

dapper ADJ 衣冠楚楚的 yīguān chǔchǔ de, 矮小而精悍的 ǎixiǎo ér jīnghàn de

dare I v 1 敢 gǎn 2 激将 jījiàng, 挑战 tiǎozhàn
I dare you! 我谅你不敢! Wǒ liàng nǐ bù gǎn!
II N 挑战 tiǎozhàn

daring I ADJ 大胆的 dàdǎn de II N 勇气 yǒngqì, 胆量 dǎnliàng

dark I ADJ 1 黑暗的 hēi'àn de, 黑色的 hēisè de 2 深颜色的 shēn yánsè de 3 邪恶的 [+势力] xié'è de [+shìlì] 4 苦难的 [+岁月] kǔnàn de [+suìyuè] II N 1 天黑 tiānhēi 2 黑暗 hēi'àn
in the dark 完全不知道 wánquán bùzhīdào

darken v 使 [+前景] 变得暗淡 shǐ [+qiánjǐng] biàn de àndàn, 变暗 biàn àn

darkroom N 暗房 ànfáng, 暗室 ànshì

darling I ADJ 亲爱的 qīn'ài de II N 亲爱的 (人) qīn'ài de (rén), 宝贝儿 bǎobèir

darn I v 缝补 féngbǔ II ADJ 该死的 gāisǐ de, 讨厌的 tǎoyàn de
Darn it! 该死! Gāisǐ! 真倒霉! Zhēn dǎoméi!
III ADV 非常 fēicháng

dart I N 1 镖 biāo, 飞镖 fēibiāo
darts 掷镖游戏 zhìbiāo yóuxì
II v 1 投镖 tóuzhì 2 猛冲 měngchōng

dash I v 猛冲 měngchōng, 疾奔 jí bēn
to dash sb's dream 使某人的希望落空 shǐ mǒurén de xīwàng luòkōng
II N 1 短跑 duǎnpǎo 2 破折号 pòzhéhào (—) 3 少量 shǎoliàng, 一点点 yìdiǎndiǎn
a dash of pepper 一点点胡椒 yìdiǎndiǎn hújiāo

dashboard N (汽车) 仪表板 (qìchē) yíbiǎobǎn

data N 数据 shùjù, 资料 zīliào
data processing 数据处理 shùjù chǔlǐ

database, databank N 数据库 shùjùkù, 资料库 zīliàokù

date¹ I N 1 日期 rìqī
to date 至今 zhìjīn

out of date 过期了的 guòqīle de, 陈旧的 chénjiù de

2 约会 yuēhuì **3** 约会的对象 yuēhuì de duìxiàng, 男／女朋友 nán/nǚ péngyou **II** v **1** 写上日期 xiěshàng rìqī **2** 和 [+一个女孩子] 约会 hé [+yí ge nǚháizi] yuēhuì **3** [科学家+] 鉴定…的年代 [kēxuéjiā+] jiàndìng...de niándài

date² N 海枣 hǎizǎo, 枣子 zǎozi

daughter N 女儿 nǚ'ér

daughter-in-law 媳妇 xífu, 儿媳 érxí

daunting ADJ 使人胆怯的 shǐrén dǎnqiè de

dawdle ADJ 磨蹭 móceng

dawn I N **1** 黎明 límíng, 天亮 tiānliàng **2** 开端 kāiduān, 开始 kāishǐ **II** v **1** 破晓 pòxiǎo, 天亮 tiānliàng **2** 开始 kāishǐ

to dawn on 开始明白 kāishǐ míngbai, 想到 xiǎngdào

daybreak N 黎明 límíng

daycare N 日托 rìtuō

daycare center 托儿所 tuō'érsuǒ

daydream I v 做白日梦 zuò báirìmèng, 想入非非 xiǎng rù fēifēi **II** N 白日梦 báirìmèng

daylight N **1** 日光 rìguāng **2** 大白天 dàbáitiān

daylight saving time 夏令时间 xiàlìng shíjiān

daytime N 白天 báitiān, 日间 rìjiān

day-to-day ADJ 日常的 rìcháng de, 日复一日的 rì fù yí rì de

daze I v 使…发昏 shǐ...fāhūn **II** N 迷茫 mímáng, 迷乱 míluàn

dazzle v 使…惊讶 shǐ...jīngyà, 使…赞叹不已 shǐ...zàntàn bùyǐ

dazzling ADJ 令人赞叹不已的 lìng rén zàntàn bùyǐ de, 令人眼花缭乱的 lìng rén yǎnhuā liáoluàn de

dead I ADJ **1** 死的 sǐ de, 死去 qùshì **2** 用

完了 yòngwán le **3** 死气沉沉的 sǐqì chénchén de

dead center 正中 zhèngzhōng

dead end 死胡同 sǐhútòng, 绝境 juéjìng

dead wood 没有用的人／东西 méiyǒu yòng de rén/dōngxi

II N 死人 sǐrén, 死者 sǐzhě **III** ADV 完全地 wánquán de

be dead against 完全反对 wánquán fǎnduì

deadline N 截至时间 jiézhì shíjiān

deadlock N 僵局 jiāngjú

deadly I ADJ 致命的 zhìmìng de

a deadly enemy 不共戴天的仇敌 bú gòng dài tiān de chóudí

II ADV 极其 jíqí, 非常 fēicháng

deaf ADJ 聋的 lóng de

the deaf 耳聋的人 ěrlóng de rén

the deaf and mute 聋哑人 lóngyǎrén

deafening ADJ 震耳欲聋的 zhèn ěr yù lóng de

deal I N **1** 交易 jiāoyì, 买卖 mǎimai

It's a deal! 就这么讲定了! Jiù zhème jiǎngdìng le!

2 协议 xiéyì [M. WD 项 xiàng]

to strike a deal 达成协议 dáchéng xiéyì **3** 待遇 dàiyù, 待遇 dàiyù

a great deal 大量 dàliàng

a rough deal 不公平待遇 bù gōngpíng dàiyù

II v (PT & PP dealt) **1** 做买卖 zuò mǎimai, 经营 jīngyíng **2** 发牌 fā pái

to deal with 和…打交道 hé...dǎ jiāodào, 处理 chǔlǐ

dealer N **1** 经销商 jīngxiāoshāng, [毒品+] 贩子 [dúpǐn+] fànzi **2** [扑克牌+] 发牌人 [pūkèpái+] fāpáirén

dealt See deal

dean N（大学）学院院长 (dàxué) xuéyuàn yuànzhǎng, 学监 xuéjiān

dear I ADJ **1** 亲爱的 qīn'ài de **2** 珍贵的 zhēnguì de, 昂贵的 ánggui de **II** N 亲爱的（人）qīn'ài de (rén)

Oh dear! 天哪! Tiānna!

dearth N 稀少 xīshǎo

death N 死亡 sǐwáng, 去世 qùshì

(the angel of) Death 死神 Sǐshén

death penalty 死刑 sǐxíng
death row 死囚牢房 sǐqiú láofáng
death trap 死亡陷井 sǐwáng xiànjǐng

deathbed N 死亡时睡的床 sǐwáng shí shuì de chuáng
on one's deathbed 临死时 línsǐ shí, 临终时 línzhōng shí

debacle N 惨败 cǎnbài, 崩溃 bēngkuì

debase V 降低品质 jiàngdī pǐnzhì, 降低价值 jiàngdī jiàzhí

debate I v 1 辩论 biànlùn 2 反复考虑 fǎnfù kǎolǜ II N 1 辩论 biànlùn 2 正式讨论 zhèngshì tǎolùn

debauchery N 放荡 fàngdàng, 纵情声色 zòngqíng shēngsè

debilitate V 使…虚弱 shǐ…xūruò

debilitating ADJ 导致虚弱的 dǎozhì xūruò de

debit I N 借项 jièxiàng II v 取款 qǔkuǎn
debit card 借记卡 jièjìkǎ

debrief V 听取汇报 tīngqǔ huìbào, 询问情况 xúnwèn qíngkuàng

debriefing N 听取汇报 tīngqǔ huìbào

debris N 碎片垃圾 suìpiàn lājī

debt N 债 zhài, 债务 zhàiwù [M. WD 笔 bǐ]
to be in sb's debt 深欠某人的情 shēn qiàn mǒurén de qíng
to be in debt 欠债 qiànzhài
to pay off debts 还清债务 huánqīng zhàiwù

debtor N 债务人 zhàiwùrén

debug V 1 拆除窃听器 chāichú qiètīngqì 2 排除计算机程序中的错误 páichú jìsuànjī chéngxù zhòng de cuòwù 3 排除故障 páichúgùzhàng

debunk V 证明…是错误的 zhèngmíng…shì cuòwù de

debut N, V 首次登场 shǒucì dēngchǎng, 首次登台 shǒucì dēngtái

debutante N 初进社交界的女子 chū jìn shèjiāo jiè de nǚzǐ

decade N 十年 shí nián

decadent ADJ 颓废的 tuífèi de, 堕落的 duòluò de

decaffeinated ADJ 脱去咖啡因的 [+茶／咖啡] tuōqù kāfēiyīn de [+chá/kāfēi]

decanter N 玻璃酒瓶 bōli jiǔ píng

decathlon N 十项全能运动 shíxiàng quánnéng yùndòng

decay I v 1 腐烂 fǔlàn 2 [文明+] 衰亡 [wénmíng+] shuāiwáng II N 1 腐烂 fǔlàn 2 衰亡 shuāiwáng

deceased I ADJ 已死亡的 yǐ sǐwáng de, 已故世的 yǐ gùshì de II N 死者 sǐzhě, 故亡者 gùwángzhě

deceit N 欺骗 qīpiàn

deceitful ADJ 欺骗的 qīpiàn de

deceive V 欺骗 qīpiàn
to deceive oneself 自欺欺人 zì qī qī rén

December N 十二月 shí'èryuè

decency N 起码的尊严 qǐmǎ de zūnyán, 体面 tǐmian
human decency 做人的起码标准 zuòrén de qǐmǎ biāozhǔn
to have the decency to 懂得起码的礼仪 dǒngde qǐmǎ de lǐyí

decent 1 ADJ 正派的 [+人] zhèngpài de [+rén], 体面的 tǐmian de 2 像样的 [+衣服] xiàngyàng de [+yīfu], 可以接受的 kěyǐ jiēshòu de

decentralization N 下放权力 xiàfàng quánlì

deceptive ADJ 欺骗的 qīpiàn de, 欺诈的 qīzhà de

decibel N 分贝 fēnbèi

decide V 决定 juédìng

deciduous ADJ 落叶的 luòyè de

decimal I ADJ 十进位的 shíjìnwèi de II N 小数 (比如 0.8, 0.45, 0.3536)
decimal point 小数点 xiǎoshùdiǎn

decimate V 大量毁灭 dàliàng huǐmiè

decipher V 破译 pòyì

decision N 决定 juédìng

decisive ADJ 1 决定性的 [+胜利] juédìng-xìng de [+shènglì] 2 果断的 [+领导人] guǒduàn de [+lǐngdǎorén] 3 明确的 [+回答] míngquè de [+huídá]

deck I N 1 甲板 jiǎbǎn 2 露天木平台 lùtiān mù píngtái 3 一副 [+扑克牌] yífù [+pūkèpái] II v 装饰 zhuāngshì

declaration N 宣言 xuānyán, 声明 shēngmíng

declare V 1 宣布 xuānbù 2 申报 shēnbào

decline I v 1 变小 biàn xiǎo, 变弱 biàn

ruò, 衰弱 shuāiruò **2** 拒绝 [+邀请] jùjué [+yāoqǐng] **II** v 消减 xiāojiǎn, 衰落 shuāiluò

decode v 解码 jiěmǎ

decoder N 解码器 jiěmǎ qì

decompose v **1** 使…腐烂 shǐ…fǔlàn **2** 分解 fēnjiě

décor N 装饰 zhuāngshì

decorate v **1** 装饰 zhuāngshì **2** 授予…勋章 shòuyǔ…xūnzhāng
a much decorated veteran 一位获得多枚勋章的老兵 yíwèi huòdé duō méi xūnzhāng de lǎobīng

decoration N **1** 装饰 zhuāngshì, 装修 zhuāngxiū **2** 装饰品 zhuāngshìpǐn **3** 勋章 xūnzhāng [M. WD 枚 méi]

decorative ADJ 装饰的 zhuāngshì de

decorator N 室内设计师 shìnèi shèjì shī

decorum N 有礼 yǒulǐ, 得体 détǐ

decoy I N 诱饵 yòu'ěr, 诱惑物 yòuhuò wù **II** v 诱骗 yòupiàn

decrease I v 减少 jiǎnshǎo, [数量+] 下降 [shùliàng+] xiàjiàng **II** v 减少 jiǎnshǎo, (数量) 下降 (shùliàng) xiàjiàng

decree I N 法令 fǎlìng, 命令 mìnglìng **II** v 规定 guīdìng, 命令 mìnglìng

decrepit ADJ 破旧的 pòjiù de, 老朽的 lǎoxiǔ de

decry v 公开反对 gōngkāi fǎnduì, 谴责 qiǎnzé

dedicate v **1** 把…献给 bǎ…xiàngěi **2** 以…命名 yǐ…mìngmíng
to dedicate oneself to 献身于 xiànshēn yú

dedicated ADJ **1** 有献身精神的 yǒu xiànshēn jīngshén de, 敬业的 jìngyè de **2** 致力于…的 zhìlì yú…de **3** 专用的 zhuānyòng de

dedication N 献身精神 xiànshēn jīngshén, 奉献 fèngxiàn

deduce v 推断 tuīduàn, 推理 tuīlǐ

deduct v 扣除 kòuchú, 减去 jiǎnqù

deductible ADJ 可减免的 kě jiǎnmiǎn de

deduction N **1** 扣除 kòuchú, 减去 jiǎnqù **2** 推理 tuīlǐ, 演绎 yǎnyì

deed N **1** 行为 xíngwéi, 事迹 shìjì **2** (房地产) 契约 (fángdìchǎn) qìyuē

in deed 事实上 shìshíshang, 确实 quèshí

deem v 认为 rènwéi, 看作 kànzuò

deep I ADJ **1** 深邃
deep sleep 沈睡 chénshuì, 酣睡 hānshuì **2** 深刻 shēnkè, 深奥 shēn'ào **3** 专心 zhuānxīn
deep in thought 沉思 chénsī **II** ADV 深深地 shēnshēn de
deep down 内心深处 nèixīn shēnchù

deepen v 加深 jiāshēn, 加剧 jiājù

deer N 鹿 lù [M. WD 头 zhī/头 tóu]

deface v 毁坏…的容貌 huǐhuài…de róngmào, 涂污 túwū

de facto ADJ 实际上的 shíjì shang de

defamatory ADJ 诋毁的 dǐhuǐ de, 中伤的 zhòngshāng de

defame v 破坏…的声誉 pòhuài…de shēngyù, 诋毁 dǐhuǐ

default I N **1** 未履行 wèi lǚxíng **2** 缺席 quēxí
by default 因对手缺席而赢 yīn duìshǒu quēxí ér yíng **3** 缺乏 quēfá
in default of 因为没有 yīnwèi méiyǒu **4** 默认 (值) mòrèn (zhí), 预设 (值) yùshè (zhí) **II** v 不履行 bùlǚxíng, 拖欠 tuōqiàn
to default on a loan 不还贷款 bù huán dàikuǎn

defeat I v 打败 dǎbài **II** N 失败 shībài, 输 shū

defecate v (排) 大便 (pái) dàbiàn

defect I N 缺点 quēdiǎn, 缺陷 quēxiàn **II** v 背叛 bèipàn, 投敌 tóudí

defective ADJ 有缺陷的 yǒu quēxiàn de, 有毛病的 yǒu máobìng de

defend v **1** 保卫 [+国土] bǎowèi [+guótǔ], 捍卫 hànwèi **2** 为 [+被告] 辩护 wéi [+bèigào] biànhù **3** 防守 fángshǒu

defendant N 被告 bèigào

defense N **1** 防御 fángyù, 抵御 dǐyù
self-defense 自卫 zìwèi **2** 国防 guófáng
national defense 国防 guófáng

defenseless ADJ 无防卫能力的 wú fángwèi nénglì de

defensive ADJ **1** 防御性的 fángyùxìng de

2 防备的 fángbèi de

on the defensive 采取守势的 cǎiqǔ shǒushì de, 防备的 fángbèi de

defensive driving 防御性驾驶 fángyùxìng jiàshǐ

3 防守的 fángshǒu de

defer v **1** 推迟 tuīchí, 拖延 tuōyán **2** 遵从 zūncóng, 顺从 shùncóng

deferential ADJ 恭敬的 gōngjìng de

defiance N 对抗 duìkàng, 蔑视 miǎoshì

in defiance of 不顾 búgù

defiant ADJ 对抗的 duìkàng de, 蔑视的 miǎoshì de

deficient ADJ 缺乏的 quēfá de, 不足的 bùzú de

deficit N 赤字 chìzì, 亏损 kuīsǔn

defile v 污损 wūsǔn, 污染 wūrǎn

define v **1** 给…下定义 gěi…xià dìngyì **2** 规定 guīdìng **3** 标明…的界限 biāomíng…de jièxiàn

definite ADJ **1** 确定的 quèdìng de, 明确的 míngquè de **2** 肯定的 kěndìng de, 一定的 yídìng de

definition N **1** 定义 dìngyì **2** 清晰度 qīngxīdù

definitive ADJ **1** 权威的 [+著作] quánwēi de [+zhùzuò], 最可靠的 zuì kěkào de **2** 最终的 [+判决] zuìzhōng de [+pànjué], 结论性的 jiélùn xìng de

deflate v **1** 放掉 [+轮胎] 的气 fàngdiào [+lúntāi] de qì **2** 使 [+人] 泄气 shǐ [+rén] xièqì **3** 揭穿 [+论点] jiēchuān [+lùndiǎn]

deflation N **1** [轮胎+] 漏气 [lúntāi+] lòuqì **2** 泄气 xièqì **3** 通货紧缩 tōnghuò jǐnsuō

deflect v 使…转向 shǐ…zhuǎnxiàng

to deflect attention 转移注意力 zhuǎnyí zhùyìlì

deform v 使…变形 shǐ…biànxíng

deformed ADJ 畸形的 jīxíng de

deformity N 畸形 jīxíng, 变形 biànxíng

defraud v 骗取 piànqǔ, 欺诈 qīzhà

defrost v 解冻 jiědòng

deft ADJ 熟练的 shúliàn de, 灵巧的 língqiǎo de

defunct ADJ **1** 不再存在的 [+团体] búzài cúnzài de [+tuántǐ], 解散的 jiěsàn de

2 不再使用的 [+方法] búzài shǐyòng de [+fāngfǎ]

defuse v 缓解 huǎnjiě, 改善 gǎishàn

defy v 违抗 wéikàng, 蔑视 mièshì

to defy explanation 无法解释 wúfǎ jiěshì

degenerate I v 堕落 duòluò, 退化 tuìhuà **II** ADJ 堕落的 duòluò de, 败坏的 bàihuài de **III** N 堕落的人 duòluò de rén

degeneration N 退化 tuìhuà, 堕落 duòluò

degradation N 贬低 biǎndī, 侮辱 wǔrǔ

degrade v 贬低 biǎndī, 侮辱 wǔrǔ

degrading ADJ 有辱人格的 yǒu rǔ rénggé de, 有失身份的 yǒu shīshēn fèn de

degree N **1** 程度 chéngdù **2** 学位 xuéwèi **3** (气温等) 度 (qìwēn děng) dù

dehumanize v 使…丧失人性 shǐ…sàngshī rénxìng

dehydration N 脱水 tuōshuǐ

deign v 降低身份 jiàngdī shēnfen, 屈尊 qūzūn

to deign to do 降低身份 (做某事) jiàngdī shēnfen (zuò mǒu shì)

deity N 神 shén, 女神 nǚshén

the Deity 上帝 Shàngdì

déjà vu N 似曾相识 sì céng xiāngshí, 似曾经历 sì céng jīnglì

dejected ADJ 情绪低落的 qíngxù dīluò de, 忧郁的 yōuyù de

dejection N 情绪低落 qíngxù dīluò, 忧郁 yōuyù

delay I v 耽误 dānwù, 耽搁 dāngé **II** N 耽误 dānwù, 耽搁 dāngé

without delay 马上 mǎshàng, 立即 lìjí

delectable ADJ 美味的 měiwèi de, 香喷喷的 xiāngpēnpēn de

delegate I N 代表 dàibiǎo [M. WD 名 míng] **II** v 授权 shòuquán, 委托 wěituō

delete v 删除 shānchú

deletion N 删除 shānchú

deli, delicatessen N 熟食店 shúshídiàn

deliberate I ADJ **1** 故意的 gùyì de **2** 深思熟虑的 shēnsī shúlǜ de **II** v 仔细考虑 zǐxì kǎolǜ

deliberation N **1** 仔细考虑 zǐxì kǎolǜ **2** 谨慎 jǐnshèn, 从容 cóngróng

delicacy N **1** 敏感 mǐngǎn, 谨慎 jǐnshèn

2 精美 jīngměi, 雅致 yǎzhì 3 美味佳肴 měiwèi jiāyáo

delicate ADJ 1 脆弱的 cuìruò de, 易碎的 yìsuì de 2 敏感的 mǐngǎn de, 微妙的 wēimiào de

delicious ADJ 好吃的 hǎochī de, 美味的 měiwèi de

delight I N 高兴 gāoxìng, 快乐 kuàilè II V 使…高兴 shǐ…gāoxìng, 使…快乐 shǐ…kuàilè

delightful ADJ 令人愉快的 lìng rén yúkuài de, 惹人喜爱的 rě rén xǐ'ài de

delineate V 描写 miáoxiě, 描绘 miáohuì

delinquency N 1 违法 wéifǎ, (青少年) 犯罪 (qīngshàonián) fànzuì juvenile delinquency 青少年犯罪 qīngshàonián fànzuì 2 拖欠款 tuō qiànkuǎn

delinquent I ADJ 1 违法的 wéifǎ de 2 拖欠不付的 tuōqiàn bú fù de II N 少年犯 shàoniánfàn

delirious ADJ 昏迷的 hūnmí de

deliver V 1 送交 sòngjiāo, 递交 dìjiāo 2 发表 fābiǎo 3 接生 jiēshēng

delivery N 1 送交 sòngjiāo, 递交 dìjiāo 2 发表 fābiǎo 3 接生 jiēshēng, 分娩 fēnmiǎn

delta N 三角洲 sānjiǎozhōu

delude V 欺骗 qīpiàn, 哄骗 hǒngpiàn

deluge I N 1 大洪水 dàhóngshuǐ 2 大量涌来的东西 dàliàng yǒnglái de dōngxi II V 使…淹没 shǐ…yānmò

delusion N 错觉 cuòjué, 幻觉 huànjué

deluxe ADJ 豪华的 háohuá de, 优质的 yōuzhì de

delve V 探索 tànsuǒ, 钻研 zuānyán

demagogic ADJ 煽动的 shāndòng de, 蛊惑的 gǔhuò de

demand I N 1 要求 yāoqiú 2 需求 xūqiú market demand 市场需求 shìchǎng xūqiú II V 要求 yāoqiú

demanding ADJ 1 要求很高的 [+任务] yāoqiú hěn gāo de [+rènwu] 2 费力的 fèilì de 3 要求过高的 [+老板] yāoqiú guògāo de [+lǎobǎn], 苛求的 kēqiú de

demeaning ADJ 贬低的 biǎndǐ de, 侮辱的 wǔrǔ de

demeanor N 举止 jǔzhǐ, 风度 fēngdù

demented ADJ 疯狂的 fēngkuáng de, 变态的 biàntài de

dementia N 1 痴呆 chīdāi 2 精神错乱 jīngshén cuòluàn

demerit N 1 过失 guòshī, 过错 guòcuò 2 记过 jìguò

demise N 1 死亡 sǐwáng, 消亡 xiāowáng 2 终结 zhōngjié

demo N 1 样品 yàngpǐn 2 演示 yǎnshì

democracy N 1 民主 (制度) mínzhǔ (zhìdù) 2 民主国家 mínzhǔ guójiā

democratic ADJ 民主的 mínzhǔ de Democratic Party (美国) 民主党 (Měiguó) Mínzhǔdǎng

demographics N 人口统计 (数据) rénkǒu tǒngjì (shùjù)

demolish V 拆除 chāichú

demolition N 拆除 chāichú

demon N 1 魔鬼 móguǐ inner demon 心魔 xīnmó 2 高手 gāoshǒu, 技艺高超的人 jìyì gāochāo de rén

demonstrate V 1 显示 xiǎnshì 2 示范 shìfàn, 演示 yǎnshì

demonstrative ADJ 1 感情外露的 gǎnqíng wàilù de 2 示范的 [+教学] shìfàn de [+jiàoxué]

demonstrator N 1 示范者 shìfànzhě, 演示者 yǎnshìzhě 2 示威游行者 shìwēi yóuxíngzhě

demoralize V 使…泄气 shǐ…xièqì

demote V 将…降职 jiāng…jiàngzhí

demur V 静静的 xiánjìng de, 端庄的 duānzhuāng de

den N 1 (野生动物的) 窝 (yěshēng dòngwù de) wō, 洞穴 dòngxué 2 贼窝 zéiwō, 赌窟 dǔkū 3 密室 mìshì

denial N 1 否认 fǒurèn 2 拒绝给予 jùjué jǐyǔ

denigrate V 贬低 biǎndǐ

denim N 粗斜面布 cū xiémiàn bù

denominate V 定价 dìngjià

denomination N 1 面值 miànzhí 2 [宗教] 派别 [zōngjiào] pàibié

denounce V 指责 zhǐzé, 谴责 qiǎnzé

dense ADJ 1 浓密的 nóngmì de, 稠密的 chóumì de 2 密度大的 mìdù dà de 3 难

316

density N 密度 mìdù

dent I N 1 凹痕 āohén 2 减少 jiǎnshǎo, 减轻 jiǎnqīng II V 1 使…产生凹痕 shǐ…chǎnshēng āohén 2 损害 sǔnhài, 削弱 xuēruò
to dent one's image 损害形象 sǔnhài xíngxiàng

dentist N 牙科医生 yákē yīshēng

dentures N 假牙 jiǎyá [M. WD 副 fù]

denunciation N 谴责 qiǎnzé, 斥责 chìzé

deny V 1 否认 fǒurèn 2 拒绝 jùjué, 不给 bùgěi

deodorant N 除臭剂 chúchòujì

depart V 1 离开 líkāi, 离去 líqù 2 死亡 sǐwáng

department N 1 [政府+] 部门 [zhèngfǔ+] bùmén 2 [大学+] 系 [dàxué de+] xì
department store 百货商店 bǎihuò shāngdiàn

departure N 1 离开 líkāi, 离去 líqù 2 启程 qǐchéng, 上路 shànglù 3 背离 bèilí

depend V 1 依靠 yīkào 2 得看 děikàn
It/That depends. 看情况 kàn qíngkuàng

dependable ADJ 可靠的 kěkào de

dependent I ADJ 依赖于 yīlàiyú, 有赖于 yǒulàiyú
a dependent child 要抚养的孩子 yào fǔyǎng de háizi II N 家属 jiāshǔ
army dependents 军人家属 jūnrén jiāshǔ, 军属 jūnshǔ

depict V 描写 miáoxiě, 描绘 miáohuì

deplete V 减少 jiǎnshǎo, 损耗 sǔnhào

deplorable ADJ 极坏的 jí huài de, 应受谴责的 yīng shòu qiǎnzé de

deplore V 1 强烈批评 qiángliè pīpíng 2 深感惋惜 shēngǎn wǎnxī

deploy V 部署 bùshǔ

deport V 驱逐出境 qūzhú chūjìng

deposit I N 1 首期付款 shǒuqī fùkuǎn, 定金 dìngjīn 2 预付租金 yùfù zūjīn, 押金 yājīn 3 [银行+] 存款 [yínháng+] cúnkuǎn 4 矿藏 kuàngcáng II V 1 把…放在 bǎ…fàng zài 2 存入 [+银行] cún rù [+yínháng] 3 沉淀 chéndiàn

depot N 1 库存处 kùcún chù, 仓库 cāngkù 2（小）车站（xiǎo）chēzhàn

depraved ADJ 道德彻底败坏的 dàodé chèdǐ bàihuài de, 腐败透顶的 fǔbài tòudǐng de

depreciate V 1 [货币+] 贬值 [+huòbì+] biǎnzhí 2 贬低 [+价值] biǎndī [+jiàzhí]

depressed ADJ 忧郁 yōuyù, 感到忧郁 gǎndào yōuyù

depressing ADJ 令人忧愁的 lìng rén yōuchóu de

depression N 1 忧郁（症）yōuyù (zhèng) 2 经济萧条 jīngjì xiāotiáo (qī)
the Depression（三十年代）经济大萧条 (sānshí niándài) jīngjì Dàxiāotiáo 3 低气压 dīqìyā 4 低洼（地）dīwā (dì)

deprive V 剥夺 bōduó

deprived ADJ 贫困的 pínkùn de, 穷苦的 qióngkǔ de

depth N 深度 shēndù

deputy N 副 fù, 副手 fùshǒu

derail V 1 [火车+] 出轨 [huǒchē+] chūguǐ 2 破坏 [+计划] pòhuài [+jìhuà]

deranged ADJ 精神错乱的 jīngshén cuòluàn de

derelict ADJ 1 破败的 [+建筑物] pòbài de [+jiànzhù wù], 废弃的 fèiqì de 2 玩忽职守的 [+官员] wánhū zhíshǒu de [+guānyuán], 渎职的 dúzhí de

derision N 嘲笑 cháoxiào

derivation N 起源 qǐyuán, 出处 chūchù

derivative¹ N 1 派生物 pàishēngwù, [语言] 派生词 [yǔyán] pàishēngcí 2 [化学] 提取物 [huàxué] tíqǔwù 3 [金融] 衍生投资 [jīnróng] yǎnshēng tóuzī

derivative² ADJ 非独创的 fēi dúchuàng de, 模仿的 mófǎng de

derive V 1 获取 huòqǔ, 得到 dédào 2 起源于 qǐyuán yú

dermatitis N 皮肤炎 pífūyán

dermatology N 皮肤病学 pífūbìngxué

derogatory ADJ 侮辱的 wǔrǔ de, 贬低的 biǎndī de

derrick N 1 油井架 yóujǐngjià, 钻塔 zuàntǎ 2（货轮）吊杆起重机 (huò lún) diàogān qǐzhòngjī

descend V 下降 xiàjiàng, 下落 xiàluò

to descend from 是…的后代 shì…de hòudài

descendant N 后代 hòudài, 后裔 hòuyì

descent N 1 下降 xiàjiàng, 下落 xiàluò 2 下坡路 xiàpōlù 3 出身 chūshēn, 血统 xuètǒng

describe V 描写 miáoxiě, 描绘 miáohuì

description N 描写 miáoxiě, 描绘 miáohuì

descriptive ADJ 描写的 miáoxiě de, 描绘的 miáohuì de

desecrate V 亵渎 xièdú, 污辱 wūrǔ

desecration N 亵渎 xièdú

desensitize V 使…变得不敏感 shǐ…biàn de bù mǐngǎn, 使…习惯 shǐ…xíguàn

desert I N 沙漠 shāmò [M. WD 片 piàn] II V 离开 líkāi, 抛弃 pāoqì

deserve V 值得 zhíde

design N, V 设计 shèjì

designate V 指定 zhǐdìng, 指派 zhǐpài

designation N 指定 zhǐdìng, 指派 zhǐpài

designer N 设计师 shèjìshī II ADJ 特别设计的 tèbié shèjì de
designer drug 化合迷幻药 huàhé míhuànyào

desirable ADJ 可取的 kěqǔ de, 称心的 chènxīn de

desire I N 愿望 yuànwàng, 欲望 yùwàng II V 希望得到 xīwàng dédào, 欲求 yùqiú

desist V 停止 tíngzhǐ

desk N 1 办公桌 bàngōngzhuō, 写字台 xiězìtái [M. WD 只 zhǐ/张 zhāng] 2 工作台 gōngzuòtái, 服务台 fúwùtái
front desk [旅馆] 前台 [lǚguǎn] qiántái
information desk 问事处 wènshìchù

desktop N 1 桌面 zhuōmiàn 2 桌上型电脑 zhuōshàngxíng diànnǎo
desktop publishing 桌面出版 zhuōmiàn chūbǎn

desolate ADJ 荒凉的 huāngliáng de

despair I N 绝望 juéwàng II V 感到绝望 gǎndào juéwàng

desperate ADJ 1 不顾一切的 búgù yíqiè de, 拼命的 pīnmìng de 2 非常想要的 fēicháng xiǎngyào de

despicable ADJ 卑鄙的 bēibǐ de, 可鄙的 kěbǐ de

despise V 鄙视 bǐshì, 看不起 kànbuqǐ

despite PREP 尽管 jǐnguǎn

despondent ADJ 忧伤的 yōushāng de, 沮丧的 jǔsàng de

despot N 暴君 bàojūn

dessert N（饭后）甜食 (fànhòu) tiánshí, 甜点心 tiándiǎnxin

destabilize V 使…不稳定 shǐ…bùwěndìng

destination N 目的地 mùdìdì, 终点 zhōngdiǎn

destined ADJ（命中）注定的 (mìngzhōng) zhùdìng de

destiny N 命运 mìngyùn

destroy V 毁灭 huǐmiè, 破坏 pòhuài

destroyer N 驱逐舰 qūzhújiàn

destruction N 毁灭 huǐmiè, 破坏 pòhuài

destructive ADJ 破坏性的 pòhuàixìng de

detach V 拆开 chāikāi, 脱落 tuōluò

detached ADJ 超然的 chāorán de, 客观的 kèguān de

detachment N 1 超然 chāorán, 客观 kèguān 2 [军事] 小分队 [jūnshì] xiǎofēnduì

detail I N 细节 xìjié, 详情 xiángqíng
in detail 详细地 xiángxì de
II V 详细叙述 xiángxì xùshù
to detail sb to do sth 派遣某人去做某事 pàiqiǎn mǒurén qù zuò mǒushì

detailed ADJ 详细的 xiángxì de

detain V 1 拘留 jūliú, 扣留 kòuliú 2 阻留 zǔliú

detect V 察觉 chájué, 发现 fāxiàn

detective N 侦探 zhēntàn

detector N 探测器 tàncèqì
smoke detector 烟雾报警器 yānwù bàojǐng qì

detention N 1 拘留 jūliú, 扣留 kòuliú 2 [学校] 课后留校 [xuéxiào] kè hòu liúxiào

deter V 制止 zhìzhǐ, 威慑 wēishè

detergent N 洗衣粉 xǐyīfěn, 洗涤精 xǐdíjīng

deteriorate V 越来越坏 yuèláiyuè huài, 恶化 èhuà

determination N 1 决心 juéxīn 2 [官方] 决定 [guānfāng+] juédìng 3 [成份] 测定 [chéngfèn+] cèdìng

determine v 1 下决心 xià juéxīn, 决定 juédìng 2 确定 quèdìng

determiner N 限定词 xiàndìngcí

deterrent N 威慑力 wēishèlì, 威慑手段 wēishè shǒuduàn

detest v 憎恨 zēnghèn, 嫌恶 xiánwù

dethrone v 把…赶下台 bǎ…gǎnxiàtái, 推翻 tuīfān

detonate v 引爆 yǐnbào

detonator N 引爆装置 yǐnbàozhuāngzhì, 雷管 léiguǎn

detour v 绕道（而行）ràodào (ér xíng)

detox I N 戒酒治疗 jièjiǔ zhìliáo, 戒毒治疗 jièdú zhìliáo II v 戒酒治疗 jièjiǔ zhìliáo 戒毒治疗 jièdú zhìliáo

detoxification N 排毒 páidú

detract v 贬损 biǎnsǔn, 诋毁 dǐhuǐ

detriment N 伤害 shānghài

detrimental ADJ 有害的 yǒuhài de

devalue v 贬值 biǎnzhí

devastate v 1 使…极其伤心 shǐ…jíqí shāngxīn, 使…垮掉 shǐ…kuǎdiào 2 摧毁 [+城市] cuīhuǐ [+chéngshì], 毁掉 huǐdiào

devastating ADJ 1 让人极其伤心的 [+消息] ràng rén jíqí shāngxīn de [+xiāoxi] 2 毁灭性的 [+打击] huǐmièxìng de [+dǎjī]

devastation N 摧毁 cuīhuǐ, 摧残 cuīcán

develop N 1 发展 fāzhǎn, 开发 kāifā 2 发育 fāyù 3 开始出现 [+问题] kāishǐ chūxiàn [+wèntí] 4 冲印 [+底片] chōngyìn [+dǐpiàn]

developed ADJ 1 发达的 [+国家] fādá de [+guójiā] 2 更严重的 [+危机] gèng yánzhòng de [+wēijī]

developing ADJ 发展中的 fāzhǎnzhōng de

development N 发展 fāzhǎn, 开发 kāifā

a new housing development 新建住宅区 xīnjiàn zhùzháiqū

2 新情况 xīn qíngkuàng

deviate I v 偏离 piānlí II ADJ 变态的 biàntài de

deviation N 偏差 piānchā, 异常 yìcháng

device N 1 设备 shèbèi, 设施 shèshī 2 [测试+] 装置 [cèshì+] zhuāngzhì 3 [通讯+] 手段 [tōngxùn+] shǒuduàn, 方法 fāngfǎ

devil N 1 魔鬼 móguǐ 2 家伙 jiāhuo

lucky devil 幸运的家伙 xìngyùn de jiāhuo

3 调皮鬼 tiáopí guǐ

to play the devil's advocate 故意唱反调 gùyì chàng fǎndiào

devilish ADJ 1 恶毒的 èdú de, 坏透了的 huàitòule de 2 淘气的 táoqì de, 调皮的 tiáopí de

devious ADJ 欺诈的 qīzhà de, 不老实的 bù lǎoshí de

devise v 设计出 shèjìchū, 想出 xiǎngchū

devoid ADJ 完全没有的 wánquán méiyǒu de, 毫无的 háowú

devolve v 权力下放 quánlì xiàfàng

devote v 把…奉献给 bǎ…fèngxiàn gěi

to devote oneself to 献身于 xiànshēn yú

devoted ADJ 忠诚的 zhōngchéng de, 挚爱的 zhì'ài de

devotee N 爱好者 àihàozhě, 仰慕者 yǎngmùzhě

devotion N 1 忠诚 zhōngchéng, 挚爱 zhì'ài 2 献身 xiànshēn, 奉献 fèngxiàn

devour v 1 狼吞虎咽地吃 lángtūn hǔyàn de chī 2 贪婪地阅读 tānlán de yuèdú 3 吞噬 tūnshì, 耗尽 hàojìn

devout ADJ 虔诚的 qiánchéng de

dew N 露水 lùshuǐ [M. WD 滴 dī]

dexterous, dextrous ADJ 灵巧的 língqiǎo de, 敏捷的 mǐnjié de

diabetes N 糖尿病 tángniàobìng

diabetic I ADJ 糖尿病的 tángniàobìng de II N 糖尿病人 tángniàobìngrén

diabolical ADJ 恶魔似的 èmó shì de, 邪恶的 xié'è de

diagnose v 诊断 zhěnduàn

diagnosis N 诊断 zhěnduàn

diagonal I ADJ 1 斜的 xié de, 斜线的 xiéxiàn de 2 对角的 duìjiǎo de II N 斜线 xiéxiàn, 对角线 duìjiǎoxiàn

diagram N 图表 túbiǎo, 示意图 shìyìtú

dial I v 拨号 bō hào

dial tone 拨音号 bōyīnhào

II N 刻度盘 kèdùpán

dialect N 方言 fāngyán

dialogue, dialog N 对话 duìhuà

dialogue box 对话框 duìhuàkuàng

dialysis N（血液）透析 (xuèyè) tòuxī

diameter N 直径 zhíjìng

diamond N 1 钻石 [+戒指] zuànshí [+jièzhi] 2 菱形 [+瓷砖] língxíng [+cízhuān] 3 [纸牌] 方块牌 [zhǐpái+] fāngkuàipái

diaper N 尿布 niàobù [M. WD 块 kuài]

diaphragm N 横膈膜 hénggémó

diarrhea N 腹泻 fùxiè

diary N 日记 rìjì, 日记簿 rìjìbù

diatribe N 严厉谴责 yánlì qiǎnzé, 愤怒抨击 fènnù pēngjī

dice I N 1 骰子 shǎizi
to roll the dice 掷骰子 zhì shǎizi
2 小块食物 xiǎo kuài shíwù II v 把…食物切成小块 bǎ…shíwù qiēchéng xiǎo kuài

dicey ADJ 冒险的 màoxiǎn de, 不可靠的 bù kěkào de

dick N 1 鸡巴 jība 2 笨蛋 bèndàn

dictaphone N 口述录音机 kǒushù lùyīnjī

dictate v 1 口授 kǒushòu 2 强制规定 qiángzhì guīding

dictation N 1 口授 kǒushòu 2 [学校] 听写练习 [xuéxiào] tīngxiě liànxí

dictator N 独裁者 dúcáizhě

dictatorship N 独裁政府 dúcái zhèngfǔ, 专政 zhuānzhèng

diction N 用词 yòngcí, 措词 cuòcí

dictionary N 词典 cídiǎn [M. WD 本 běn], 字典 zìdiǎn [M. WD 本 běn]

did See do

didn't See do

die[1] v 1 死 sǐ, 去世 qùshì 2 [旧风俗+] 消失 [jiù fēngsú+] xiāoshī 3 [机器+] 停止运转 [jīqì+] tíngzhǐ yùnzhuǎn

die[2] N 1 金属模具 jīnshǔmó jù, 铸模 zhùmó 2 骰子 shǎizi

diesel N 柴油 cháiyóu
diesel engine 柴油发动机 cháiyóu fādòngjī, 柴油机 cháiyóují

diet I N 1 日常食品 rìcháng shípǐn 2（规定）食谱 (guīding) shípǔ
to be on diet 按规定食谱饮食 àn guīding shípǔ yǐnshí, 控制饮食 kòngzhì yǐnshí
II v 节食 jiéshí, 控制饮食 kòngzhì yǐnshí

differ v 不同 bùtóng

Tastes differ. 各人口味不同。Gè rén kǒuwèi bùtóng.

difference N 1 不同的地方 bùtóng de dìfang, 分歧 fēnqí 2 差别 chābié, 差异 chāyì
to make a difference 产生影响 chǎnshēng yǐngxiǎng, 起作用 qǐzuòyòng

different ADJ 不同 bùtóng

differentiate v 区别 qūbié, 辨别 biànbié

difficult ADJ 1 困难的 kùnnan de, 难的 nán de 2 难以对付的 [+人] nányǐ duìfu de [+rén]

difficulty N 困难 kùnnan, 难处 nánchu

diffuse v 1 分散 fēnsàn 2 减轻 jiǎnqīng, 减弱 jiǎnruò 3 使…扩散 shǐ…kuòsàn

dig v (PT & PP dug) 1 挖 wā, 挖掘 wājué
to dig one's own grave 自掘坟墓 zìjuéfénmù
2 搜寻 sōuxún, 搜集 sōují
to dig into ① 开始使用 kāishǐ shǐyòng ② 插入 chārù
to dig up 挖掘出 wājué chū, 发现 fāxiàn

digest I v 消化 xiāohuà II N 摘要 zhāiyào, 文摘 wénzhāi
Reader's Digest 读者文摘 Dúzhě Wénzhāi

digestion N 消化 xiāohuà

digestive ADJ 消化的 xiāohuà de

digit N 1（1 到 9）数字 (1 dào 9) shùzì 2 手指 shǒuzhǐ, 脚趾 jiǎozhǐ

digital I ADJ 数字的 shùzì de, 数码的 shùmǎ de
digital camera 数码照相机 shùmǎ zhàoxiàngjī

dignified ADJ 有尊严的 yǒuzūnyán de, 庄重的 zhuāngzhòng de

dignitary N 显贵 xiǎnguì [M. WD 位 wèi], 要人 yàorén [M. WD 位 wèi]

dignity N 尊严 zūnyán, 尊贵 zūnguì

digress v 离题 lítí, 跑题 pǎotí

digression N 离题 lítí, 跑题 pǎotí

dike N 堤坝 dībà, 坝 dī, 坝台 bà

dilapidated ADJ 破烂的 pòlàn de, 快倒塌的 kuài dǎotā de

dilapidation N 破烂的状态 pòlàn de zhuàngtài

dilate v 扩大 kuòdà, 扩张 kuòzhāng

dilemma N 两难境地 liǎngnán jìngdì

diligence N 勤奋 qínfèn

diligent ADJ 勤奋的 qínfèn de

dilute I v 1 稀释 xīshì, 冲淡 chōngdàn 2 使…削弱 shǐ… xuēruò II ADJ 稀释的 xīshì de

dilution N 稀释 xīshì

dim ADJ 昏暗的 hūn'àn de, 模糊的 móhu de

dime N 一角钱 yì jiǎo qián, 一毛钱 yì máo qián
dime store 廉价小商品店 liánjià xiǎoshāngpǐn diàn
a dime a dozen 多得不值钱 duō dé bù zhíqián

dimension N 1 [三个+] 维度 [sānge+] wéidù 2 [新的+] 方面 [xīn de+] fāngmiàn 3 (dimensions) 尺寸 chǐcùn

dimensional ADJ 维度的 wéi dù de
three-dimensional 三维的 sānwéi de, 立体的 lìtǐ de

diminish v 1 [人数+] 减少 [rénshù+] jiǎnshào, 减小 jiǎnxiǎo 2 削弱 [+重要性] xuēruò [+zhòngyàoxìng], 降低 jiàngdī

diminutive ADJ 个子很矮小的 gèzi hěn ǎixiǎo de

dimple N 酒窝 jiǔwō

dim sum N 中国点心 Zhōngguó diǎnxin

din N 嘈杂声 cáozáshēng, 喧闹声 xuānnàoshēng

dine v 进餐 jìncān, 吃饭 chīfàn
to dine out 外出用餐 wàichū yòngcān, 到饭店去吃饭 dào fàndiàn qù chīfàn

diner N 便宜的小饭馆 piányi de xiǎo fànguǎn [M. WD 家 jiā]

dingy ADJ 肮脏破旧的 āngzāng pòjiù de

dinner N 1 正餐 zhèngcān, 晚饭 wǎnfàn 2 宴会 yànhuì, 晚宴 wǎnyàn
dinner party 家宴 jiāyàn
dinner service [一套+] 西餐餐具 [yītào+] xīcān cānjù

dinnertime N 用餐时间 yòngcān shíjiān

dinosaur N 恐龙 kǒnglóng

dip I v 1 浸 jìn, 蘸 zhàn 2 下降 xiàjiàng, 降低 jiàngdī II N 1 调味酱 tiáowèi jiàng 2 (短时间的) 游泳 (duǎn shíjiān de) yóuyǒng 3 小量减少 xiǎoliàng jiǎnshǎo

diphtheria N 白喉 báihóu

diploma N 文凭 wénpíng, 毕业证书 bìyè zhèngshū [M. WD 张 zhāng/份 fèn]

diplomat N 外交官 wàijiāoguān

diplomatic ADJ 1 外交的 wàijiāo de 2 世故练达的 shìgù liàndá de, 讲究策略的 jiǎngjiu cèlüè de

dipstick N 油量计 yóuliángjì

dire ADJ 极其严重的 jíqí yánzhòng de, 极糟的 jí zāo de

direct I ADJ 1 直接的 zhíjiē de
direct current 直流电 zhíliúdiàn
direct deposit 直接存款付薪 zhíjiē cúnkuǎn fù xīn
2 坦率的 tǎnshuài de, 率直的 shuàizhí de II v 1 针对 zhēnduì 2 指挥 zhǐhuī, 指导 zhǐdǎo III ADV 直接 zhíjiē, 直接地 zhíjiē de

direction N 方向 fāngxiàng
directions 指路 zhǐ lù, 指明方向 zhǐmíng fāngxiàng
sense of direction 方向感 fāngxiàng-gǎn

directive N 指令 zhǐlìng, 指示 zhǐshì

director N 1 [公司] 董事 [gōngsī] dǒngshì 2 (电影) 导演 (diànyǐng) dǎoyǎn

directory N 1 姓名地址录 xìngmíng dìzhǐ lù 2 (计算机) 文档目录 (jìsuànjī) wéndàng mùlù

dirt N 1 灰尘 huīchén, 尘土 chéntǔ
dirt cheap 极其便宜 jíqí piányi
dirt road 泥路 nílù
2 丑闻 chǒuwén
to dig up dirt on sb 发掘某人的丑闻 fājué mǒurén de chǒuwén

dirty ADJ 1 肮脏 āngzāng 2 黄色的 huángsè de, 下流的 xiàliú de
a dirty trick 卑鄙花招 bēibǐ huāzhāo, 下流手段 xiàliú shǒuduàn

disability N 残疾 cánjí, 残障 cánzhàng

disable v 使 [±兵+] 残疾 shǐ [shìbīng+] cánjí, 使 [系统+] 无法使用 shǐ [xìtǒng+] wúfǎ shǐyòng

disabled ADJ 残疾的 cánjí de, 残障的 cánzhàng de

disadvantage N 不利条件 búlì tiáojiàn, 缺陷 quēxiàn

disadvantaged ADJ **1** 处于不利地位的 chǔ yú búlì dìwèi de **2** 社会下层的 shèhuì xiàcéng de, 弱势的 ruòshì de

disagree V 不同意 bù tóngyì

disagreeable ADJ 讨厌的 tǎoyàn de

disallow V 不允许 bù yǔnxǔ, 驳回 bóhuí

disappear V **1** 消失 xiāoshī **2** 失踪 shīzōng, 丢失 diūshī

disappearance N **1** 消失 xiāoshī **2** 失踪 shīzōng, 丢失 diūshī

disappoint V 使…失望 shǐ…shīwàng

disappointing ADJ 令人失望的 lìng rén shīwàng de

disapproval N 不赞成 bú zànchéng, 反对 fǎnduì

disapprove V 不赞成 bú zànchéng, 反对 fǎnduì

disarm V 解除武装 jiěchú wǔzhuāng

disarmament N 裁军 cáijūn

disarming ADJ 消除敌意的 xiāochú díyì de, 让人感到友好的 ràng rén gǎndào yǒuhǎo de

disarray N 混乱 hùnluàn

disaster N **1** 灾难 zāinàn, 灾害 zāihài **2** 彻底失败 chèdǐ shībài

disavow V 否认 fǒurèn

disband V 解体 jiětǐ, 解散 jiěsàn

disbelief N 不相信 bù xiāngxìn, 怀疑 huáiyí

disc See **disk**

discard I V **1** 扔掉 [+旧衣服] rēngdiào [+jiù yīfú] **2** 打出 [+扑克牌] dǎchū [+pūkèpái] II N **1** 扔掉的东西 rēngdiào de dōngxi, 废物 fèiwù **2** 打出的牌 dǎchū de pái, 废牌 fèi pái

discern V 觉察出 juécháchū, 辨明 biànmíng

discerning ADJ 有眼力的 yǒu yǎnlì de, 识别力很强的 shíbiélì hěn qiáng de

discharge I V 准许…离开 zhǔnxǔ…líkāi
to be discharged from a hospital (病人) 出院 (bìngrén) chūyuàn
to be discharged from the Army (军人) 退役 (jūnrén) tuìyì
2 排放 [+污水] páifàng [+wūshuǐ]
to discharge polluted water 排放污水 páifàng wūshuǐ

3 履行 [+职责] lǚxíng [+zhízé] II N **1** 准许离开 zhǔnxǔ líkāi **2** 排放 páifàng

disciplinarian N 严格执行纪律者 yángé zhíxíng jìlǜ zhě

discipline I N **1** 纪律 jìlǜ **2** 处分 chǔfèn, 处罚 chǔfá **3** 学科 xuékē
core disciplines 重点学科 zhòngdiǎn xuékē, 重点课程 zhòngdiǎn kèchéng
II V **1** 惩罚 chéngfá **2** 管教 guǎnjiào

disclaim V 正式否认 zhèngshì fǒurèn

disclaimer N 免责声明 miǎnzé shēngmíng

disclose V 透露 tòulù

disclosure N 透露 tòulù

disco N 迪斯科舞（厅）dísīkēwǔ (tīng)

discotheque N 迪斯科舞厅 dísīkēwǔ tīng

discolor V（使…）褪色／变色 (shǐ…) tuìsè/biànsè

discomfort N **1** 不舒服 bùshūfú, 不适 búshì **2** 使人不舒服的东西 shǐrén bùshūfú de dōngxī

disconcerting ADJ 令人心烦意乱的 lìng rén xīn fán yì luàn de, 令人窘迫的 lìng rén jiǒngpò de

disconnected ADJ 无关联的 wú guānlián de, 断开的 duànkāi de

discontent ADJ 不满足的 bù mǎnzú de, 不满意 bù mǎnyì

discontinue V 停止 tíngzhǐ, 中断 zhōngduàn

discord N 不和 bù hé, 不协调 bù xiétiáo

discount I N **1** 折扣 zhékòu **2** [商品+] 打折扣 [shāngpǐn+] dǎ zhékòu, 削价 xuējià **2** 不重视 [某一可能性+] búzhòngshì [+mǒu yì kěnéngxìng]

discourage V **1** 使…丧失信心 shǐ…sàngshī xìnxīn, 使…灰心 shǐ…huīxīn

discouraging ADJ 令人丧气的 lìngrén sàngqì de, 令人灰心的 lìngrén huīxīn de

discourse N **1** [严肃的+] 交谈 [yánsù de+] jiāotán, 讨论 tǎolùn **2** [关于国际法的+] 论述 [guānyú guójìfǎ de+] lùnshù **3** [学术的+] 话语 [xuéshù de+] huàyǔ

discourteous ADJ 不礼貌的 bù lǐmào de, 失礼的 shīlǐ de

discover V 发现 fāxiàn

discovery N 发现 fāxiàn

discredit I v 使…变得不可信 shǐ...biàn de bù kěxìn, 破坏…的信誉 pòhuài...de xìnyù II N 丧失信誉 sàngshī xìnyù

discreet ADJ 谨慎的 jǐnshèn de, 慎重的 shènzhòng de

discrepancy N 差异 chāyì, 不一致 bù yízhì

discretion N 谨慎 jǐnshèn, 慎重 shènzhòng

discriminate v 歧视 qíshì

discriminating ADJ 有识别能力的 yǒu shíbié nénglì de, 有鉴赏力的 yǒu jiànshǎnglì de

discrimination N 歧视 qíshì

discus N 铁饼 tiěbǐng
discus-throwing 掷铁饼（运动）zhì tiěbǐng (yùndòng)

discuss v 讨论 tǎolùn, 商讨 shāngtǎo

discussion N 讨论 tǎolùn, 商讨 shāngtǎo

disdainful ADJ 藐视的 miǎoshì de, 轻视的 qīngshì de

disease N 疾病 jíbìng [M. WD 种 zhǒng]

disembark v 下车 xià chē, 下飞机 xià fēijī, 下船 xià chuán

disenchanted ADJ 感到幻灭的 gǎndào huànmiè de, 失望的 shīwàng de

disenfranchised ADJ 被剥夺权力的 bèi bōduó quánlì de

disengage v 分离 fēnlí, 摆脱 bǎituō

disentangle v 分清 fēnqīng, 梳理 shūlǐ

disfavor N 不喜欢 bù xǐhuan, 反感 fǎngǎn

disfigure v 毁坏…的容貌 huǐhuài...de róngmào

disfigurement N 毁容 huǐróng

disgrace I N 耻辱 chǐrǔ II v 使…蒙受耻辱 shǐ...méngshòuchǐrǔ, 给…丢脸 gěi...diūliǎn

disgruntled ADJ 不满的 bùmǎn de, 恼火的 nǎohuǒ de

disguise v, N 伪装 wěizhuāng

disgust v 使…厌恶 shǐ...yànwù, 使…极为反感 shǐ...jíwéi fǎngǎn

disgusting ADJ 使人厌恶的 shǐ rén yànwù de

dish I N 1 菜盘 càipán, 盘子 pánzi
dish rack 碗碟架 wǎndiéjià
2 一盘菜 yì pán cài, 菜 cài 3 碟形天线

dié xíng tiānxiàn II v 1 (to dish out) 大量分发 dàliàng fēnfā
to dish out unwanted advice 随便提供别人不需要的建议 suíbiàn tígōng biérén bù xūyào de jiànyì
2 (to dish up) 上菜 shàngcài

disheartened ADJ 沮丧的 jǔsàng de, 灰心的 huīxīn de

disheartening ADJ 令人沮丧的 lìng rén jǔsàng de, 令人灰心的 lìng rén huīxīn de

disheveled ADJ 衣衫凌乱的 yīshān língluàn de, 衣冠不整的 yīguānbùzhěng de

dishonest ADJ 不诚实的 bù chéngshí de, 不老实的 bù lǎoshí de

dishonor I N 耻辱 chǐrǔ II v 使…蒙羞 shǐ...méngxiū, 使…丢脸 shǐ...diūliǎn

dishonorable ADJ 不光彩的 bù guāngcǎi de

dishwasher N 洗碗机 xǐwǎnjī

dishwashing detergent, liquid N 餐具洗涤剂 cānjù xǐdíjì

disillusionment N 幻灭 huànmiè, 醒悟 xǐngwù

disinclined ADJ 不愿意 bú yuànyì

disinfect v 给…消毒 gěi...xiāodú

disinfectant N 消毒 xiāodú

disinherit v 剥夺…的继承权 bōduó...de jìchéngquán

disintegrate v 使…分崩离析 shǐ...fēnbēng líxī, 使…瓦解 shǐ...wǎjiě

disintegration N 分崩离析 fēnbēng líxī, 瓦解 wǎjiě

disinterest N 无利益关系 wú lìyì guānxi, 无偏见 wú piānjiàn

disinterested ADJ 无利害关系的 wú lìhài guānxi de, 公正的 gōngzhèng de

disjointed ADJ 不连贯的 bù liánguàn de, 散乱的 sǎnluàn de

disk (disc) N 1 磁盘 cípán
disk drive 磁盘驱动器 cípán qūdòng qì
2 圆盘 yuánpán

diskette N [计算机+] 软盘 [jìsuànjī+] ruǎnpán

dislike v, N 不喜欢 bù xǐhuan, 讨厌 tǎoyàn

dislocate v 脱位 tuōwèi

dislodge v 把…移开 bǎ...yíkāi

disloyal ADJ 不忠诚的 bù zhōngchéng de, 不忠 bù zhōng

dismal ADJ 凄凉的 qīliáng de, 令人忧郁的 lìng rén yōuyù de

dismantle v 1 拆除 [+旧机器] chāichú [+jiù jīqì], 拆开 chāikāi 2 废除 [+旧制度] fèichú [+jiù zhìdù], 取消 qǔxiāo

dismay I N 1 惊恐 jīngkǒng 2 失望 shīwàng, 沮丧 jǔsàng II v 使…失望 shǐ...shīwàng, 使…担忧 shǐ...dānyōu

dismember v 肢解 zhījiě

dismiss v 1 解散 jiěsàn 2 解雇 jiěgù 3 不理会 bù lǐhuì, 不屑一顾 bú xiè yígù

dismissal N 1 解雇 jiěgù 2 不予理会 bùyǔ lǐhuì

dismissive ADJ 不予理会的 bùyǔ lǐhuì de

dismount v 1 下马 xià mǎ, 下车 xià chē 2 取下 qǔxià, 卸下 xièxià

disobedience N 不顺从 bú shùncóng, 不听话 bù tīnghuà

disobey v 不服从 bù fúcóng, 违抗 wéikàng

disorder N 1 混乱 hùnluàn
to throw ... into disorder 使…陷入混乱状态 shǐ...xiànrù hùnluàn zhuàngtài 2 (身体) 失调 (shēntǐ) shītiáo, 紊乱 wěnluàn, 病 bìng
mental disorder 精神病 jīngshénbìng 3 (社会) 动乱 (shèhuì) dòngluàn, 骚乱 sāoluàn

disorderly ADJ 破坏公共秩序的 pòhuài gōnggòng zhìxù de, 扰乱治安的 rǎoluàn zhì'ān de

disorganized ADJ 计划不周的 jìhuà bùzhōu de, 毫无计划的 háowú jìhuà de

disoriented ADJ 1 迷失方向的 míshī fāngxiàng de 2 头脑混乱的 tóunǎo hùnluàn de

disown v 与…断绝关系 yǔ...duànjué guānxi

disparage v 说某人的坏话 shuō mǒurén de huàihuà, 贬低 biǎndī

disparate ADJ 完全不同的 wánquán bùtóng de, 不相干的 bùxiānggān de

disparity N 不公平 bùgōngpíng, 差异 chāyì

dispassionate ADJ 客观冷静的 kèguān

lěngjìng de

dispatch I v 派遣 pàiqiǎn, 调遣 diàoqiǎn II v 派遣 pàiqiǎn, 调遣 diàoqiǎn 2 公文 gōngwén 3 [新闻+] 报道 [xīnwén+] bàodào

dispel v 驱散 qūsàn, 消除 xiāochú

dispensary N 配药处 pèiyàochù, 药房 yàofáng [M. WD 家 jiā]

dispense v 发放 fāfàng, 分发 fēnfā
to dispense medicine 配药 pèiyào
to dispense with 省掉 shěngdiào, 不需要 bù xūyào

dispersal N 驱散 qūsàn, 散开 sànkāi

disperse v 驱散 qūsàn, 散开 sànkāi

dispirited ADJ 灰心丧气的 huīxīn sàngqì de

displace v 1 移动 yídòng 2 撤…的职 chè...de zhí 3 取代 qǔdài

displacement N 1 移动 yídòng 2 撤职 chèzhí 3 取代 qǔdài

display I v 1 陈列 chénliè, 展出 zhǎnchū 2 显示 xiǎnshì II N 1 陈列 chénliè, 展出 zhǎnchū 2 显示 xiǎnshì, 炫耀 xuànyào

displease v 使…不高兴 shǐ...bù gāoxīng, 使…不满意 shǐ...bù mǎnyì

displeasure N 不悦 búyuè, 不满 bùmǎn

disposable ADJ 1 一次性的 yícìxìng de 2 可支配的 kě zhīpèi de
disposable income 可支配收入 kězhīpèi shōurù

disposal N 处置 chǔzhì, 处理 chǔlǐ
at sb's disposal 供某人使用 gōng mǒurén shǐyòng

dispose v 处置 chǔzhì, 处理 chǔlǐ

disposition N 1 [快乐的+] 性情 [kuàilè de+] xìngqíng, 性格 xìnggé 2 处置 [+个人财产] chǔzhì [+gèrén cáichǎn], 出让 chūràng 3 部署 [+军队] bùshǔ [+jūnduì] 4 倾向 [+妥协] qīngxiàng [+tuǒxié], 意向 yìxiàng

dispossess v 剥夺 [+财产] bōduó [+cáichǎn]

disproportionate ADJ 不成比例的 bù chéng bǐlì de, 不相称的 bùxiāngchèn de

disprove v 证明…是虚假的 zhèngmíng...shì xūjiǎ de, 反驳 fǎnbó

dispute I N 争端 zhēngduān, 争议

zhēngyì II v 1 对…提出异议 duì…tíchū yìyì 2 与…争论 yǔ…zhēnglùn

disqualify v 取消…的资格 qǔxiāo…de zīge

disregard I v 不顾 búgù，忽视 hūshì II N 无视 wúshì，忽视 hūshì

disrepair N 失修 shīxiū，破旧 pòjiù

disreputable ADJ 名声不好的 míngshēng bùhǎo de，声名狼藉的 shēngmíng lángjí de

disrespect N 不尊重 bù zūnzhòng，轻慢无礼 qīngmàn wúlǐ

disrespectful ADJ 不尊重的 bù zūnzhòng de，轻慢无礼的 qīngmàn wúlǐ de

disrupt v 1 扰乱 rǎoluàn 2 中断 zhōngduàn

disruption N 1 扰乱 rǎoluàn 2 中断 zhōngduàn

disruptive ADJ 扰乱的 rǎoluàn de，捣乱的 dǎoluàn de

dissatisfaction N 不满意 bù mǎnyì，不满 bùmǎn

dissatisfied ADJ 感到不满意 gǎndào bù mǎnyì

dissect v 解剖 jiěpōu

disseminate v 散布 sànbù，传播 chuánbō

dissemination N 散布 sànbù，传播 chuánbō

dissension N 争执 zhēngzhí，意见不一 yìjiàn bùyī

dissent I N 异议 yìyì II v 持有异议 chíyǒu yìyì

dissertation N（博士）论文 (bóshì) lùnwén [M. WD 篇 piān]

disservice N 损害 sǔnhài，帮倒忙 bāngdàománg

dissident I ADJ 持不同政见的 chí bùtóng zhèngjiàn de II N 持不同政见者 chí bùtóng zhèngjiànzhě

dissimilar ADJ 很不相同的 hěn bù xiāngtóng de

dissipate v 消散 xiāosàn，消失 xiāoshī

dissociate v 开 fēnkāi，分离 fēnlí
　to dissociate oneself from 断绝与…的关系 duànjué yǔ…de guānxi

dissolute ADJ 放荡的 fàngdàng de

dissolution N [婚约的+] 解除 [hūnyuē de+] jiěchú，终结 zhōngjié

dissolve v 1 [固体+] 溶解 [gùtǐ+] róngjiě 2 解除 [+婚约] jiěchú [+hūnyuē]

dissuade v 劝阻 quànzǔ

distance N 距离 jùlí
　long-distance runner 长跑运动员 chángpǎo yùndòngyuán

distant ADJ 1 远距离的 yuǎnjùlí de，遥远 yáoyuǎn 2 疏远的 shūyuǎn de，冷淡 lěngdàn

distaste N 厌恶 yànwù，反感 fǎngǎn

distend v 使…膨胀 shǐ…péngzhàng，使…肿胀 shǐ…zhǒngzhàng

distill v 1 蒸馏 zhēngliú 2 提炼 tíliàn

distillery N 酿酒厂 niàngjiǔchǎng，酿酒者 niàngjiǔ zhě

distinct ADJ 明显的 míngxiǎn de，清清楚楚的 qīngqīng chǔchǔ de

distinction N 1 区别 qūbié 2 殊荣 shūróng，荣誉 róngyù

distinctive ADJ 与众不同的 yǔ zhòng bùtóng de，特别的 tèbié de

distinguish v 区别 qūbié，分别 fēnbié

distinguished ADJ 杰出的 jiéchū de，卓越的 zhuóyuè de

distort v 1 歪曲 [+事实] wāiqū [+shìshí]，扭曲 niǔqū 2 使 [+形象] 失真 shǐ [+xíngxiàng+] shīzhēn

distortion N 1 歪曲 wāiqū，扭曲 niǔqū 2 变形 biànxíng

distract v 1 使…分心 shǐ…fēnxīn 2 使…心烦意乱 shǐ…xīn fán yì luàn

distracted ADJ 心烦意乱的 xīn fán yì luàn de，心神不定的 xīnshén búdìng de

distress I N 1（精神上的）痛苦 (jīngshén shàng de) tòngkǔ 2 贫困 pínkùn，困苦 kùnkǔ II v 使…痛苦 shǐ… tòngkǔ，使…不安 shǐ…bù'ān
　a distress signal 求救信号 qiújiù xìnhào

distressed ADJ 极其忧愁的 jíqí yōulǜ de，十分苦恼的 shífēn kǔnǎo de

distribute v 分配 fēnpèi

distributor N 1 分销商 fēnxiāoshāng 2 配电器 pèidiàn qì

district N 区 qū
　shopping district 购物区 gòuwùqū
　district attorney 地方检察官 dìfang jiǎncháguān

distrust N, V 不信任 bú xìnrèn, 猜疑 cāiyí

disturb V 1 打扰 dǎrǎo, 干扰 gānrǎo
a "Do Not Disturb" sign "请勿打扰" 的牌子 "qǐngwù dǎrǎo" de páizi
2 使…焦虑 shǐ…jiāolǜ, 使…烦恼 shǐ…fánnǎo
mentally disturbed 精神上不正常 jīngshén shàng bùzhèngcháng

disturbance N 1 干扰 [+日常生活] gānrǎo [+rìcháng shēnghuó], 扰乱 rǎoluàn
2 [种族+] 骚乱 [zhǒngzú+] sāoluàn, 动乱 dòngluàn

ditch I N 沟渠 gōu qú
drainage ditch 排水沟 páishuǐ gōu
II V 1 开沟渠 kāi gōuqú 2 丢弃 diūqì, 抛弃 pāoqì

ditto N 同上 tóngshàng, 同前 tóngqián
I say ditto. (Ditto.) 我也一样。 Wǒ yěyíyàng. 我也是。 Wǒ yěshì.

diva N 歌剧女主角 gējù nǚzhǔjué, 女歌唱家 nǚ gēchàngjiā

dive I V (PT **dived, dove**; PP **dived**) 1 跳水 tiàoshuǐ 2 潜水 qiánshuǐ 3 [飞机+] 俯冲 [fēijī+] fǔchōng II N 1 [股票+] 大幅度下降 [gǔpiào+] dàfúdù xiàjiàng 2 [飞机+] 俯冲 [fēijī+] fǔchōng 3 [守门员+] 扑过去 [shǒuményuán+] pūguòqù

dived See dive

diver N 潜水员 qiánshuǐyuán

diverge V 1 [意见+] 出现分歧 [yìjiàn+] chūxiàn fēnqí 2 [道路+] 分岔 [dàolù+] fēnchà, 分开 fēnkāi

divergent ADJ 分歧很大的 fēnqí hěn dà de, 很不相同的 hěn bù xiāngtóng de

diverse ADJ 多样化的 duōyànghuà de, 各种各样的 gèzhǒng gèyàng de

diversion N 1 消遣 xiāoqiǎn, 娱乐 yúlè 2 转移 zhuǎnyí, 转向 zhuǎnxiàng 3 转移注意力的事物 zhuǎnyí zhùyìlì de shìwù

diversity N 多样性 duōyàngxìng, 多元状态 duōyuán zhuàngtài

divert V 转移 zhuǎnyí, 转向 zhuǎnxiàng

divide V 1 把…分为 bǎ…fēnwéi, 划分 huàfēn 2 除, 除以 chú yǐ 3 分配 fēnpèi

dividend N 股息 gǔxī, 红利 hónglì

divider N [公路+] 中间隔离带 [gōnglù+] zhōngjiān gélídài 2 [档案+] 分隔卡 [dàng'àn+] fēngé kǎ

divine I ADJ 1 上帝的 Shàngdì de, 神圣的 shénshèng de
divine right 神授之权 shén shòu zhī quán
2 极好的 jíhǎo de, 极妙的 jí miào de

diving N 潜水 qiánshuǐ
diving board 跳水板 tiàoshuǐbǎn
diving suit 潜水服 qiánshuǐ fú

divisible ADJ 1 可分的 kě fēn de 2 可除尽的 kě chújìn de

division N 1 分开 fēnkāi, 划分 huàfēn
division of labor 分工 fēngōng
2 除, 除法 chúfǎ 3 部门 bùmén 4 (体育) 级 (tǐyù) jí, 级别 jíbié 5 (军队) 师 (jūnduì) shī
air-borne division 空降师 kōngjiàng shī

divorce V, N 1 离婚 líhūn
divorce settlement 离婚协议 líhūn xiéyì
to file for divorce 提出离婚 tíchū líhūn
2 分开 fēnkāi, 分离 fēnlí

divorcee N 离婚女子 líhūn nǚzǐ

divulge V 泄露 xièlòu, 透露 tòulù

DIY (= do-it-yourself) ABBREV 自己动手做的 zìjǐ dòngshǒu zuò de

dizzy ADJ 头晕 tóuyūn, 眩晕 xuànyùn

DJ (= disc jockey) ABBREV 电台唱片节目主持人 diàntái chàngpiàn jiémù zhǔchírén, 舞厅唱片播放员 wǔtīng chàngpiàn bōfàng yuán

do [NEG **do not** ABBREV **don't**; 3rd person: **does** NEG **does not** ABBREV **doesn't**. PAST NEG **did** NEG **did not** ABBREV **didn't**] (PT **did**; PP **done**) V 1 做 zuò, 干 gàn 2 行 xíng, 可以 kěyǐ
to do away with ① 摆脱 bǎituō ② 干掉 [+人] gàndiào [+rén], 杀死 shāsǐ
to do a favor 做好事 zuò hǎoshì, 帮忙 bāngmáng
to do a lot for 有利 yǒulì
to do well by sb 善待某人 shàndài mǒurén
to do up ① 系上 [+纽扣] jìshang [+niǔkòu], 扣上 kòushang ② 装修 [+房屋] zhuāngxiū [+fángwū]

to do without 没有…也行 méiyǒu… yěxíng

to have nothing to do with 与…无关 yǔ…wúguān

to have something to do with 与…有关 yǔ…yǒuguān

docile ADJ 温顺的 wēnshùn de, 驯服的 xùnfú de

dock I N 1 码头 mǎtou, 船坞 chuánwù 2 [法庭+] 被告席 [fǎtíng+] bèigàoxí II V 1 进码头 jìn mǎtou 2 扣 [+工资] kòu [+gōngzī]

docket I N 1 诉讼摘录 sùsòng zhāilù 2 议事日程 yìshì rìchéng 3 单据 dānjù

doctor N 1 医生 yīshēng 2 博士 bóshì (= Dr.)
Doctor of Philosophy (Ph.D.) 博士 bóshì

doctrine N 信条 xìntiáo, 主义 zhǔyì

docudrama N 文献影片 wénxiàn yǐngpiàn, 文献片 wénxiànpiàn

document I N 1 文件 wénjiàn 2 (计算机) 文件 / 文档 (jìsuànjī) wénjiàn/wéndàng II V 1 记录 jìlù 2 [事实+] 证明 [shìshí+] zhèngmíng

documentary N 纪录片 jìlùpiàn

documentation N 1 证明文件 zhèngmíng wénjiàn 2 搜集提供证明文件 sōují tígōng zhèngmíng wénjiàn

dodge I V 1 躲开 duǒkāi, 避开 bìkāi II N 1 逃避 táobì 2 托词 tuōcí, 脱身伎俩 tuōshēn jìliǎng

doe N 母鹿 mǔ lù, 母兔 mǔ tù

does See do

doesn't See do

dog I N 1 狗 gǒu [M. WD 只 zhī/条 tiáo] 2 低劣的东西 dīliè de dōngxi, 蹩脚货 biéjiǎohuò
dog-eat-dog 你死我活的 nǐ sǐ wǒ huó de
to be dog-tired 累得要死 lèi deyàosǐ II V 追随 zhuīsuí, 跟踪 gēnzōng

dog-eared ADJ (书 / 文件) 折角的 (shū/wénjiàn) zhéjiǎo de, 卷边的 juǎnbiān de

dogged ADJ 顽强的 wánqiáng de, 不屈不挠的 bùqū bùnáo de

doggy bag N 剩菜袋 shèngcàidài

dogmatic ADJ 自以为是的 zì yǐwéi shì de, 武断的 wǔduàn de

do-gooder N (多管闲事的) 慈善家 (duōguǎn xiánshì de) císhànjiā

doing N 做的事 zuò de shì
to be sb's own doing 自己干的坏事 zìjǐ gàn de huàishì
to take some doing 得花些功夫 děi huā xiē gōngfu

doldrums N 1 [经济+] 萧条 [jīngjì+] xiāotiáo, 低潮 dīcháo
in the doldrums [经济+] 处在停滞状态 [jīngjì+] chǔzài tíngzhì zhuàngtài 2 情绪低落 qíngxù dīluò

dole I V (to dole out) 少量地发放 shǎoliàng de fāfàng II N 救济金 jiùjì jīn
on the dole 领取救济金 lǐngqǔ jiùjìjīn

doleful ADJ 愁苦的 chóukǔ de, 哀伤的 āishāng de

doll I N 1 洋娃娃 yángwáwa, 玩偶 wán'ǒu II V (to doll up) 打扮得花枝招展 dǎban dé huāzhī zhāo zhǎn

dollar N 美元 Měiyuán, 元 yuán
Australian dollar 澳元 Àoyuán

dolphin N 海豚 hǎitún [M. WD 条 tiáo]

domain N 领域 lǐngyù, 领地 lǐngdì

dome N 圆屋顶 yuánwūdǐng, 穹顶 qióngdǐng

domestic ADJ 1 国内的 guónèi de 2 家庭内的 jiātíng nèi de

domesticated ADJ 家养的 jiāyǎng de

dominant ADJ 占优势的 zhàn yōushì de, 主要的 zhǔyào de

dominate V 支配 zhīpèi, 主导 zhǔdǎo

domineering ADJ 专横的 zhuānhèng de, 霸道的 bàdào de

dominion N 统治 (权) tǒngzhì (quán) 2 自治领 Zìzhìlǐng

domino N 多米诺骨牌 duōmǐnuògǔpái
dominoes 多米诺骨牌游戏 duōmǐnuògǔpái yóuxì

donate V 捐赠 juānzèng, 赠送 zèngsòng

donation N 捐赠 juānzèng

done I See do II ADJ 1 做好了 zuòhǎo le 2 煮好了 zhǔ hǎole
It's a done deal. 生米已经煮成熟饭。 Shēngmǐ yǐjīng zhǔ chéngshú fàn. 木已成舟。 Mù yǐ chéng zhōu.

donkey N 驴 (子) lǘ (zi) [M. WD 头 tóu]

donkey work 单调乏味的苦差事 dāndiào fáwèi de kǔchāishì

donor N 捐赠者 juānzèngzhě, 捐献者 juānxiànzhě

don't See do

doodle v 乱涂乱写 luàn tú luànxiě

doom I N 1 毁灭 huǐmiè, 失败 shībài 2 (doom and gloom) 一片阴暗 yípiàn yīn'àn, 绝望 juéwàng II v 注定 [+失败／灭亡] zhùdìng [+shībài/mièwáng]
to doom to failure 注定失败 zhùdìng shībài

doomsday N 世界末日 shìjiè mòrì

door N 门 mén [m. wo 扇 shàn/道 dào]
door to door 挨门挨户 āiménāihù
next door 隔壁 gébì

doorman N 门卫 ménwèi

doormat N 1 蹭鞋垫 cèngxiédiàn [m. wo 块 kuài] 2 任人欺负的人 rènrén qīfu de rén, 逆来顺受的人 nìlái shùnshòu de rén

doorstep N 门前台阶 mén qián tái jiē

doorway N 出入口 chūrùkǒu

dope I N 1 大麻 dàmá, 毒品 dúpǐn 2 傻瓜 shǎguā 3 内幕消息 nèimù xiāoxi II v 1 [运动员+] 服用兴奋剂 [yùndòng-yuán+] fúyòng xīngfènjì 2 服用麻醉剂 fúyòng mázuìjì

dork N 傻瓜 shǎguā

dormant ADJ 1 休眠的 [+火山] xiūmián de [+huǒshān], 冬眠的 [+灰熊] dōngmián de [+huī xióng] 2 暂时不用的 [+账户] zànshí bùyòng de [+zhànghù]

dormitory, dorm N [学生+] 宿舍 [xuésheng+] sùshè

DOS (= Disk Operating System) ABBREV 磁盘操作系统 cípán cāozuò xìtǒng

dosage N（药物的）剂量（yàowù de) jìliàng, 服用量 fúyòng liáng
recommended dosage（医生）嘱咐的剂量（yīshēng）zhǔfu de jìliàng

dose N 剂量 jìliàng
a lethal dose of sedatives 致命的镇静药剂量 zhìmìng de zhènjìngyào jìliàng 2 一次剂量 yícì jìliàng, 一剂 yí jì
a dose of antibiotics 一剂抗菌素 yí jì kàngjūnsù
3 一回 yìhuí, 一点 yìdiǎn

a dose of reality 一点现实感 yìdiǎn xiànshígǎn
II v 给 [+病人] 服药 gěi [+bìngrén] fú yào

dot I N 小点儿 xiǎo diǎnr II v 加上点儿 jiāshang diǎnr
dot the i's and cross the t's 在字母 "i" 上加点儿，在 "t" 上加横线 zài zìmǔ "i" shang jiādiǎnr, zài "t" shang jiā héngxiàn, 注意细节 zhùyì xìjié
dotted line 虚线 xūxiàn

dot-com ADJ 与⋯网上公司有关的 yǔ... wǎngshàng gōngsī yǒuguān de

dote v 溺爱 nì'ài, 宠爱 chǒng'ài

double I ADJ 1 加倍的 jiābèi de
double date 两对男女同时约会 liǎng duì nánnǚ tóngshí yuēhuì
double vision 叠影 diéyǐng, 复视 fù shì
double whammy 双重打击 shuāng-chóng dǎjī, 祸不单行 huò bù dān xíng 2 双人的 shuāngrén de, 双重的 shuāngchóng de
double standard 双重标准 shuāngchóng biāozhǔn
II v 加倍 jiābèi III N 1 两倍 liǎngbèi, 双份 shuāngfèn 2 替身演员 tìshēnyǎnyuán
IV ADV 双重 shuāng bèi
to see double 看到叠影 kàndào diéyǐng

double-check v 一再检查 yízài jiǎnchá, 复查 fùchá

double-park v 并排停放 bìngpái tíngfàng

double-spaced ADJ 双倍行距的 shuāng bèi hángjù de

double-talk N 含糊其辞的话 hánhu qí cí dehuà

double-time I N 双倍工资 shuāng bèi gōngzī II ADV 以加倍的速度 yǐ jiābèi de sùdù, 尽可能快 jìnkěnéng kuài

doubly ADV 加倍地 jiābèi de

doubt I N 怀疑 huáiyí
reasonable doubt 合理疑点 hélǐ yídiǎn
without doubt 毫无疑问 háowú yíwèn
II v 怀疑 huáiyí, 不相信 bù xiāngxìn

doubtful ADJ 大有疑问的 dàyǒu yíwèn de, 不确定的 bú quèdìng de

doubtless ADV 无疑地 wúyí de

dough N 1 生面团 shēngmiàn tuán 2 钱 qián

doughnut, donut N 炸面圈 zhámiàn-quān, 多福饼 duōfúbǐng

dour ADJ 1 脸色阴郁的 liǎnsè yīnyù de, 毫无笑意的 háowú xiàoyì de 2 严厉的 yánlì de

douse V 1 泼水 pōshuǐ, 浇水 jiāoshuǐ 2 把…浸入水中 bǎ...jìnrù shuǐ zhōng 3 灭火 mièhuǒ

dove I N 1 鸽子 gēzi 2 鸽派人物 gēpài rénwù II V See **dive**

dowdy ADJ (女子穿着) 不时髦的 (nǚzǐ chuānzhuó) bùshí máo de, 过时的 guòshíde, 土气的 tǔqìde

down I ADV 下 xià, 下面 xiàmiàn
  down payment 首期付款 shǒuqī fùkuǎn, 定金 dìngjīn
  II PREP 向下 xiàngxià III V 1 喝下 [+一大杯啤酒] hēxià [+yí dà bēi píjiǔ], 吞下 [+三个汉堡包] tūnxià [+sānge hànbǎo-bāo] 2 击败 [+球队] jībài [+qiúduì], 打倒 dǎdǎo IV N 羽绒 yǔróng, 绒毛 róngmáo

down-and-out ADJ 穷愁潦倒的 qióng-chóu liǎodào de, 穷困的 qióngkùn de

downcast ADJ 垂头丧气的 chuítóu sàngqì de, 沮丧的 jǔsàng de

downfall N 垮台 kuǎtái, 破产 pòchǎn

downgrade V 1 降职 jiàng zhí 2 减弱 jiǎnruò, 贬低 biǎndī

downhill I ADV 向山下 xiàng shān xià
  to go downhill 走下坡路 zǒu xiàpōlù, 每况愈下 měi kuàng yù xià
  II ADJ 下坡的 xiàpō de
  to be all downhill 从此一帆风顺 cóngcǐ yìfān fēng shùn

download V 下载 xiàzài

downplay V 把…看得不重要 bǎ...kàn dé bú zhòngyào

downpour N 倾盆大雨 qīngpén dàyǔ

downright ADV 十足的 shízú de, 完全的 wánquán de

downside N 不利方面 búlì fāngmiàn

downsize V 精简裁员 jīngjiǎn cáiyuán

Down's syndrome N 唐氏综合征 tángshì zōnghézhēng

downstairs I ADV (在) 楼下 (zài) lóuxià
  II ADJ 楼下的 lóuxià de

downstate ADJ, ADV [州的+] 南部地区 [zhōu de+] nánbù dìqū

downtime N 停机期间 tíngjī qījiān

down-to-earth ADJ 脚踏实地的 jiǎo tà shídí de, 实实在在的 shíshí zàizài de

downtown I N 市中心 shìzhōngxīn II ADJ, ADV 市中心的／地 shìzhōngxīn de

downtrodden ADJ 被践踏的 bèi jiàntà de, 受压迫的 shòuyāpò de

downturn N [经济+] 下滑期 [jīngjì+] xiàhuáqī, 衰退期 shuāituìqī

downward(s) ADV 向下 xiàngxià, 朝下 cháoxià I ADJ 向下的 xiàngxià de

dowry N 嫁妆 jiàzhuang [M. WD 份 fèn]

doze V 打瞌睡 dǎ kēshuì
  to doze off (不知不觉) 打盹 (bùzhī bùjué) dǎdǔn

dozen N 一打 yì dá, 十二 (个) shí'èr (ge)
  baker's dozen 一打加一个 yìdá jiā yíge, 十三个 shísān ge
  dozens of 几十 jǐshí, 好多 hǎoduō

Dr. (= Doctor) ABBREV 博士 bóshì, 医生 yīshēng

drab ADJ 1 单调乏味的 dāndiào fáwèi de 2 暗淡的 àndàn de

draconian ADJ 严厉的 yánlì de, 严酷的 yánkù de

draft I N 1 草案 cǎo'àn 2 征兵制 zhēng-bīngzhì
  draft dodger 逃避兵役者 táobì bīngyì zhě
  3 选拔 (运动员) xuǎnbá (yùndòngyuán)
  draft pick 选拔进职业队的运动员 xuǎnbá jìn zhíyè duì de yùndòngyuán
  4 冷风 lěngfēng 5 汇票 huìpiào II ADJ 起草 qǐcǎo 2 征召 (入伍) zhēngzhāo (rùwǔ) 3 选拔 xuǎnbá, 挑选 tiāoxuǎn

draft beer N 散装啤酒 sǎnzhuāng píjiǔ

drafty ADJ 透风的 tòufēng de

drag I V 1 拖 tuō, 拉 lā, 拽 zhuài II N 1 乏味的人 (或事) fáwèi de rén (huò shì) 2 累赘 léizhuì

dragon N 龙 lóng [M. WD 条 tiáo]

dragonfly N 蜻蜓 qīngtíng

drain I V 1 排水 páishuǐ 2 使…精疲力尽 shǐ...jīngpí lìjìn 3 喝完 hē wán 4 N 下水道 xiàshuǐdào, 下水管 xiàshuǐguǎn to be a drain on 对…消耗很大 duì… xiāohào hěn dà

down the drain 浪费掉 làngfèi diào, 一无收获 yìwú shōuhuò

drainage N 1 排水 páishuǐ 2 排水系统 páishuǐ xìtǒng

drained ADJ 精疲力尽的 jīngpí lìjìn de

drama N 戏剧 xìjù
drama class 戏剧课 xìjù kè
drama group 戏剧小组 xìjù xiǎozǔ

dramatic ADJ 1 戏剧的 xìjù de 2 戏剧性的 xìjùxìng de, 惊人的 jīngrén de

dramatize V 把…改变成戏剧 bǎ…gǎibiànchéng xìjù

drank See **drink**

drape V 披挂 pīguà, 披盖 pīgài

drapery N 1 厚窗帘 hòu chuānglián [M. WD 块 kuài] 2 打褶的布料 dǎzhě de bùliào

drapes N 厚窗帘 hòu chuānglián

drastic ADJ 激烈的 jīliè de, 严厉的 yánlì de

draw I V (PT **drew**; PP **drawn**) 1 画 huà
to draw a line in the sand 警告 jǐnggào 2 拉 lā, 拔 bá 3 吸引 [+注意力] xīyǐn [+zhùyìlì] 4 领取 [+救济金] lǐngqǔ [+jiùjìjīn] 5 抽签 chōuqiān II N 1 平局 píngjú 2 抽奖 chōujiǎng 3 具有吸引力的人（或地方）jùyǒu xīyǐnlì de (huò dìfang)

drawback N 缺点 quēdiǎn

drawbridge N 吊桥 diàoqiáo

drawer N 抽屉 chōutì

drawing N 铅笔画 qiānbǐhuà, 素描 sùmiáo
drawing board 制图板 zhìtúbǎn

drawl I V 拖长声调慢吞吞地说 tuōcháng shēngdiào màntūntūn de shuō II N 拖长声调慢吞吞说话 tuōcháng shēngdiào màntūntūn shuōhuà

drawn[1] ADJ 苍白憔悴的 cāngbái qiáocuì de

drawn[2] V See **draw**

dread N, V 惧怕 jùpà, 担忧 dānyōu

dreadful ADJ 可怕的 kěpà de, 令人担忧的 lìng rén dānyōu de

dream I N 1 梦 mèng, 梦境 mèngjìng 2 梦想 mèngxiǎng, 理想 lǐxiǎng
a dream house 理想的住宅 lǐxiǎng de zhùzhái

a dream come true 梦想成真 mèngxiǎng chéngzhēn
II V (PT & PP **dreamed**, **dreamt**) 做梦 zuòmèng

dreamed, **dreamt** See **dream**

dreamer N 空想家 kōngxiǎngjiā

dreamy ADJ 1 如梦的 [+感觉] rú mèng de [+gǎnjué], 梦幻的 mènghuàn de 2 爱幻想的 [+小女孩] ài huànxiǎng de [+xiǎonǚhái]

dreary ADJ 1 乏味的 [+讲座] fáwèi de [+jiǎngzuò] 2 沉闷的 [+气氛] chénmèn de [+qìfēn], 阴沉的 [+天气] yīnchén de [+tiānqì]

dredge V 挖掘 wājué, 疏浚 shūjùn

dregs N 渣滓 zhāzǐ

drench V 使…湿透 shǐ…shītòu

dress I N 女装 nǚzhuāng [M. WD 套 tào], 连衫裙 liánshānqún [M. WD 件 jiàn]
II V 1 穿衣服 chuān yīfú
to dress down ① 穿得比平时随便 chuān dé bǐ píng shí suíbiàn ② 训斥 xùnchì
to dress up 打扮 dǎbàn
2 包扎 [+伤口] bāozā [+shāngkǒu] 3 给 [+蔬菜] 加调料 gěi [+ shūcài] jiā tiáoliào III ADJ 1 正式场合穿的 zhèngshì chǎnghé chuān de 2 服装的 fúzhuāng de
dress code 服装要求 fúzhuāng yāoqiú

dressing N 1 穿衣 chuān yī 2 包扎用品 bāozā yòngpǐn, 敷料 fūliào 3 调料 tiáoliào
dressing gown 晨衣 chén yī
dressing room [剧院+] 化妆室 [jùyuàn+] huàzhuāngshì, [体育场+] 更衣室 [tǐyùchǎng+] gēngyīshì

dressy ADJ 时髦的 shímáo de, 漂亮的 piàoliang de

drew See **draw**

drib V 滴 dī, 点滴 diǎndī
in dribs and drabs 点点滴滴地 diǎndiǎn dīdīdī de, 零星地 língxīng de

dribble V 1 流（口水）liú (kǒushuǐ), 淌（口水）tǎng (kǒushuǐ) 2 运（球）yùn (qiú)

drift I N 1 漂流 piāoliú, 流动 liúdòng 2 雪堆 xuě duī, 沙堆 shā duī II V 1 漂流 piāoliú, 流动 liúdòng

to drift apart [人和人+] 渐渐疏远 [rén hé rén+] jiànjiàn shūyuǎn

drifter N 漂泊者 piāobózhě, 流浪者 liúlàngzhě

drill I N 1 钻孔机 zuānkǒngjī 2 操练 cāoliàn 3 演习 yǎnxí
fire drill 消防演习 xiāofángyǎnxí
II V 1 钻孔 zuānkǒng 2 训练 xùnliàn, 操练 cāoliàn

drink I N 1 饮料 yǐnliào
cold drink 冷饮 lěngyǐn
2 喝酒 hējiǔ, 酗酒 xùjiǔ II V (PT drank; PP drunk) 1 喝 hē 2 喝酒 hējiǔ, 酗酒 xùjiǔ

drinking problem N 酗酒问题 xùjiǔ wèntí

drip I V 滴水, 滴下 dī xià II N 1 滴水, 滴水声 dīshuǐ shēng 2 静脉滴注器 jìngmài dīzhùqì
drip-feed 静脉滴注 jìngmài dī zhù

drip-dry ADJ 滴干 dī gān

drive I V (PT drove; PP driven) 1 驾驶 jiàshǐ, 开车 kāichē 2 用车送 yòngchē sòng 3 赶赶, 驱赶 qūgǎn II N 1 开车 kāichē, 乘车 chéngchē
to drive ... crazy/nuts 逼得...发疯 bīdé...fāfēng, 逼得...受不了 bī dé...shòubuliǎo
2 本能要求 běnnéng yāoqiú
sex drive 性本能 xìng běnnéng, 性欲 xìngyù
3 运动 yùndòng
membership drive 发展新会员运动 fāzhǎn xīnhuì yuán yùndòng
4 干劲 gànjìn, 魄力 pòlì 5 (计算机) 驱动器 (jìsuànjī) qūdòngqì

drivel N 胡说八道 húshuō bādào

driven¹ See drink

driven² ADJ 有进取心的 yǒu jìnqǔxīn de

driver N 驾驶员 jiàshǐyuán, 司机 sījī
driver's license 驾驶执照 jiàshǐ zhízhào

driveway N (私人) 车道 (sīrén) chēdào

drizzle I N 细雨 xìyǔ, 毛毛雨 máomáoyǔ II V 下细雨 xiàxì yǔ, 下毛毛雨 xià máomaoyǔ

droll ADJ 滑稽可笑的 gǔjī kěxiào de, 古里古怪的 gǔ lǐ gǔguài de

drone I V 发出嗡嗡声 fāchū wēngwēng-shēng II N 1 嗡嗡声 wēngwēngshēng 2 工蜂 gōngfēng, 雄蜂 xióngfēng 3 无线电遥控设备 wúxiàndiàn yáokòng shèbèi, 无人驾驶飞机 wúrén jiàshǐ fēijī

drool I V 流口水 liú kǒushuǐ II N 口水 kǒushuǐ

droop V 低垂 dīchuí, 下垂 xiàchuí

drop I V 1 落下 luòxià 2 下车 xiàchē 3 下降 xiàjiàng 4 无意中／突然说出 wúyìzhōng/túrán shuōchū
to drop a bomb 突然说出惊人消息 túrán shuōchū jīngrén xiāoxi
5 将...除名 jiāng...chúmíng, 开除 kāichú
to drop anchor 抛锚 pāomáo
to drop by/in 顺道拜访 shùndào bàifǎng
to drop dead 突然死亡 huran shiwang II N 1 水滴 shuǐdī
a drop in the bucket 杯水车薪 bēishuǐ chēxīn
eye/ear/nose drops 眼／耳朵／鼻药水 yǎn/ěrduo/bí yàoshuǐ
2 下降 xiàjiàng 3 空投 kōng tóu
air drops of relief supplies 空投救济物资 kōng tóu jiùjì wùzī

dropout N 中途辍学的人 zhōngtú chuòxué de rén

dropper N 滴管 dīguǎn

droppings N [鸟+] 屎 [niǎo+] shǐ, [动物+] 粪便 [dòngwù+] fènbiàn

drought N 干旱 gānhàn, 旱灾 hànzāi

drove¹ V See drive

drove² N 1 一群牲畜 yìqún shēngchù 2 一大群人 yí dà qún rén

drown V 1 淹死 yānsǐ 2 浸泡 jìnpào

drowsy ADJ 昏昏欲睡的 hūnhūn yùshuì de

drudge I N 做繁重无聊工作的人 zuò fánzhòng wúliáo gōngzuò de rén II V 做繁重无聊的工作 zuò fánzhòng wúliáo de gōngzuò

drudgery N 繁重无聊的工作 fánzhòng wúliáo de gōngzuò, 苦工 kǔgōng

drug I N 1 毒品 dúpǐn
drug addict 吸毒者 xīdúzhě
drug dealing/trafficking 贩毒 fàndú
drug rehabilitation 吸毒康复 xīdú kāngfù, 戒毒 jiè dú

hard drugs 剧毒品 jùdúpǐn
to do drugs 吸毒 xīdú
2 药 yào，药品 yàopǐn **II** v **1**（用药）麻醉 (yòngyào) mázuì **2** 投放麻醉药 tóufàng mázuìyào
drugstore N **1** 杂货店 záhuòdiàn [M. WD 家 jiā] **2** 药店 yàodiàn [M. WD 家 jiā]
drum I N **1** 鼓 gǔ [M. WD 面 miàn] **2** 大油桶 dà yóutǒng **II** v [击+] 鼓 [jī+] gǔ
drummer N 鼓手 gǔshǒu
drumstick N **1** 鸡腿 jītuǐ [M. WD 条 tiáo] **2** 鼓槌 gǔchuí [M. WD 根 gēn]
drunk I v See drink **II** ADJ 喝醉 hēzuì
drunk driving, drink driving 酒后驾车 jiǔhòu jiàchē
III v 醉鬼 zuìguǐ，酒鬼 jiǔguǐ
drunkard N 醉鬼 zuìguǐ，酒鬼 jiǔguǐ
drunken ADJ 喝醉酒的 hēzuì jiǔ de
dry I ADJ **1** 干 gān，干燥 gānzào
dry clean 干洗 gānxǐ
dry goods ① 干货 gānhuò ② 纺织品 fǎngzhīpǐn
2 干 [+葡萄酒] gān [+pútaojiǔ] **3** 乏味的 [+课程] fáwèi de [+kèchéng] **II** v 使…变干 shǐ…biàn gān，晒干 shàigān
dryer, drier N 烘干机 hōnggānjī
dual ADJ 双重的 shuāngchóng de
dual nationality 双重国籍 shuāngchóng guójí
dub v **1** 给…起绰号 gěi…qǐ chuòhào **2** [给电影+] 配音 [gěi diànyǐng+] pèiyīn
dubious ADJ 可疑的 kěyí de，不可靠的 bùkěkào de
duck I N 鸭子 yāzi [M. WD 只 zhī] **II** v 低下头躲避 [打过来的球] dīxià tóu duǒbì [+dǎguòlái de qiú]，弯腰躲避 wānyāo duǒbì，闪开 shǎnkāi
duckling N 小鸭子 xiǎo yāzi [M. WD 只 zhī]
duct N 管道 guǎndào
dud ADJ 废物 fèiwù
dude N 男人 nánren
dude ranch 度假牧场 dùjià mùchǎng
due I ADJ **1** 到期的 dàoqī de
due date ① 预产期 yùchǎnqī ② 最后期限 zuìhòu qīxiàn
2 应付的 yìngfu de
due process, due process of law 合法

的诉讼程序 héfǎ de sùsòng chéngxù
due to 由于 yóuyú
II N 应有的权益 yīngyǒu de quányì
dues 会员费 huìyuánfèi
duel N **1** [体育运动+] 激烈的竞争 [tǐyù yùndòng+] jīliè de jìngzhēng **2** 唇枪舌剑的争论 chúnqiāng shéjiàn de zhēnglùn
duet N 二重唱 èrchóngchàng，二重奏 èrchóngzòu
dug See dig
dugout N **1** [棒球场边的+] 休息棚 [bàngqiú chǎng biān dí de +] xiūxipéng **2** 独木舟 dúmùzhōu [M. WD 只 zhī]
dull ADJ **1** 沉闷的 [+电影] chénmèn de [+diànyǐng] **2** 愚笨的 [+孩子] yúbèn de [+háizi] **3** 钝的 [+刀] dùn de [+dāo] **4** 隐隐的 [+疼痛] yǐnyǐn de [+téngtòng]
duly ADV 恰当地 qiàdàng de，应当地 yīngdāng de
dumb I ADJ **1** 愚蠢的 yúchǔn de **2** 哑巴的 yǎba de **II** v 把…搞得过于简单 bǎ…gǎode guòyú jiǎndǎn
dumbbell N 哑铃 yǎlíng
dumbfounded ADJ 惊讶得不知所措 jīngyà dé bù zhī suǒ cuò，惊讶极了 jīngyà jíle
dummy I N **1** 笨蛋 bèndàn **2** 人体模型 réntǐ móxíng **3** 仿制样品 fǎngzhì yàngpǐn **II** ADJ 仿真的 fǎngzhēn de，假的 jiǎde
dump v **1** 丢弃 [+垃圾] diūdiào [+lājī]，丢弃 [+男朋友] diūqì [+nánpéngyou] **2** 倾销 [+商品] qīngxiāo [+shāngpǐn]，倾倒 qīngdǎo **3** [电脑+] 转存 [+文件] [diànnǎo+] zhuǎncún [+wénjiàn]
dumpster N 装垃圾的大铁桶 zhuāng lājī de dà tiětǒng
dunce N 愚笨的人 yúbèn de rén
dune N 沙丘 shāqiū
dung N 牛粪 niúfèn，[动物的+] 粪便 [dòngwù de+] fènbiàn
dungeon N 地牢 dìláo
dunk v **1** 把 [+食物] 浸一下 bǎ [+shíwù] jìn yíxià **2** [篮球+] 扣篮 [lánqiú+] kòulán
duo N 两人表演 liǎng rénbiǎo yǎn
dupe I v 欺骗 qīpiàn，哄骗 hǒngpiàn

duplex N 二连式住宅 èrliánshì zhùzhái

duplicate I N 复制品 fùzhìpǐn, 副本 fùběn
duplicate of a key 配制的钥匙 pèizhì de yàoshi
in duplicate 一设两份 yí shè liǎngfèn
II v 复制 fùzhì

duplicity N 欺诈 qīzhà

durable ADJ 耐用的 nàiyòng de

duration N 持续时间 chíxù shíjiān

duress N 胁迫 xiépò, 威逼 wēibī

during PREP 在…期间 zài…qījiān

dusk N 黄昏时分 huánghūn shífen
from dawn till dusk 从早到晚 cóng zǎo dào wǎn

dust I N 灰尘 huīchén II v 1 擦去灰尘 cā qù huīchén 2 在…上撒 [+粉状物] zài… shàng sǎ [+fěnzhuàngwù]

duster N 掸子 dǎnzi, 抹布 mābù

dusty ADJ 满是灰尘的 mǎn shì huīchén de

Dutch I N 1 荷兰语 Hèlányǔ 2 荷兰人 Hèlánrén II ADJ 荷兰的 hèlán de
to go Dutch 各付各的帐 gè fù gè de zhàng, 平摊费用 píng tān fèiyòng

dutiful ADJ 尽职的 jìnzhí de, 顺从的 shùncóng de

duty N 1 责任 zérèn, 义务 yìwù
sense of duty 责任感 zérèngǎn
garbage duty (日常) 倒垃圾的工作 (rìcháng) dào lájī de gōngzuò 2 税 shuì
customs duty 关税 guānshuì

duty-free ADJ 免税的 miǎnshuì

DVD (= digital video disk) ABBREV 数字视频光盘, 数字视频光盘 shùzì shìpín guāngpán, DVD

dwarf I N 1 小矮人 xiǎo'ǎirén, 侏儒 zhūrú II v 使…显得微小 shǐ…xiǎnde wēixiǎo

dwell (PT & PP dwelled, dwelt) v 居住 jūzhù
to dwell on (sth) 老是想到 lǎoshì xiǎngdào, 说个没完 shuō gè méiwán

dwelled, dwelt See dwell

dweller N 居住在…的人 / 动物 jūzhù zài…de rén/dòngwù

dwindle v 越来越少 yuèláiyuè shǎo, 越来越小 yuèláiyuè xiǎo

dye I N 染料 rǎnliào II v 染 rǎn

dynamic ADJ 精力充沛的 jīnglì chōngpèi de, 生气勃勃的 shēngqì bóbó de

dynamics N 动力学 dònglìxué, 力学 lìxué

dynamite I N 炸药 zhàyào II v (用炸药) 炸毁 (yòng zhàyào) zhàhuǐ

dynamo N 1 直流电机 zhíliú fādiànjī 2 精力充沛的人 jīnglì chōngpèi de rén 3 强大的动力 qiángdà de dònglì

dynasty N 朝代 cháodài, 王朝 wángcháo

dysentery N 痢疾 lìji

dysfunctional ADJ 1 违法正常规范的 wéifǎ zhèngcháng guīfàn de 2 有功能障碍的 yǒu gōngnéng zhàng'ài de

dyslexia N 诵读困难症 sòngdú kùnnan zhēng, 诵读困难 sòngdú kùnnan

E

each ADJ, PRON 各 gè, 每 měi
each other 彼此 bǐcǐ, 互相 hùxiāng

eager ADJ 热切 rèqiè, 热衷 rèzhōng

eagle N 鹰 yīng, 老鹰 lǎoyīng

eagle-eyed ADJ 目光锐利的 mùguāng ruìlì de

ear¹ N 1 耳 ěr, 耳朵 ěrduo 2 听觉 tīngjué, 听力 tīnglì
to be all ears 全神贯注地听 quánshén guànzhù de tīng
to be put out on one's ears 被迫离开 bèipò líkāi
to go in one ear and out the other 一只耳朵进, 一只耳朵出 yì zhī ěrduo jìn, yì zhī ěrduǒ chū, 只当耳边风 zhǐdàng ěrbiānfēng

ear² N [麦+] 穗 [mài+] suì

eardrum N 耳膜 ěrmó

early I ADJ 1 很早的 hěn zǎo de
The early bird catches the worm. 早起的鸟儿吃到虫。(→捷足先登。) Zǎoqǐ de niǎor chīdao chóng. (→Jiézú xiāndēng.) 2 初期 chūqī II ADV 1 早 zǎo 2 早期 zǎoqī, 初期 chūqī

earmark I v 指定…作为专门款项 zhǐdìng…zuòwéi zhuānmén kuǎnxiàng II N 特征 tèzhēng, 标记 biāojì

earn v 1 挣钱 zhèngqián, 赚钱 zhuànqián
earned income 劳动收入 láodòng shōurù, 工资 gōngzī
to earn one's keep 做工换取食宿 zuògōng huànqǔ shísù
2 获得 huòdé, 赢得 yíngdé

earnest I ADJ 认真的 rènzhēn de II N 严肃 认真 yánsù rènzhēn
in earnest 认真地 rènzhēn de

earnings N 工资 gōngzī, 薪水 xīnshui

earphones N 耳机 ěrjī [M. WD 副 fù]

earplugs N 耳塞 ěrsāi

earring N 耳环 ěrhuán [M. WD 副 fù]

earshot N 可听见的距离 kě tīngjiàn de jùlí
within earshot 在听得到的范围 zài tīngdé dào de fànwéi
out of earshot 在听不到的范围 zài tīngbùdào de fànwéi

earth N 1 地球 dìqiú 2 泥土 nítǔ
what on earth 到底 dàodǐ, 究竟 jiūjìng
3 世界 shìjiè 4 大地 dàdì, 地面 dìmiàn
to come down to earth 回到现实 huídào xiànshí

earthly ADJ 世俗的 shìsú de, 尘世的 chénshì de
no earthly reason 毫无理由 háowú lǐyóu

earthquake N 地震 dìzhèn

earth-shattering ADJ 惊天动地的 jīngtiān dòngdì de

earthworm N 蚯蚓 qiūyǐn [M. WD 条 tiáo]

earthy ADJ 1 自然的 zìrán de, 朴实的 pǔshí de 2 泥土的 nítǔ de

ease I N 1 （工作）容易 (gōngzuò) róngyì
ease of use 使用方便 shǐyòng fāngbiàn
2 （生活）安逸 (shēnghuó) ānyì, 舒适 shūshì
at ease 不拘无束 wújū wúshù, 轻松自在 qīngsōng zìzài
3 （军事口令）稍息 (jūnshì kǒulìng) shāoxī II v 减轻 [+工作负担] jiǎnqīng [+gōngzuò fùdān], 缓和 [+紧张局势] huǎnhé [+jǐnzhāng júshì]

easel N 画架 huàjià

easily ADV 1 容易地 róngyì de, 不费力地 bú fèilì de 2 明显地 míngxiǎn de, 没有疑问 méiyǒu yíwèn

east I N 东 dōng, 东面 dōngmiàn II ADJ 东 dōng, 东面 dōngmiàn III ADV 朝东 cháodōng, 向东 xiàngdōng
the East 东方 dōngfāng
the Middle East 中东 Zhōngdōng

eastbound ADJ 向东的 xiàng dōng de

Easter N 复活节 Fùhuójié
Easter egg 复活节彩蛋 Fùhuójié cǎidàn

eastern ADJ 东面的 dōngmiàn de, 东方的 dōngfāngde

eastward ADJ 朝东面的 cháo dōngmiàn de

easy I ADJ 1 容易 róngyì
Easier said than done. 说说容易做起来难。Shuōshuo róngyì zuòqǐlái nán.
to take it easy 别着急, 慢慢来。Bié zháojí, mànmàn lái.
easy money 很容易赚的钱 hěn róngyì zhuàn de qián, 来得容易的钱 láide róngyì de qián
2 轻松的 qīngsōng de, 方便的 fāngbiàn de
I'm easy. 我随便。Wǒ suíbiàn。都可以。Dōu kěyǐ。
II ADV 放松 fàngsōng

easygoing ADJ 随和的 suíhe de, 心平气和的 xīnpíngqìhé de

eat (PT **ate**; PP **eaten**) v 吃 chī, 吃饭 chīfàn
to eat one's heart out 嫉妒 jídu, 难过 nánguò
to eat one's word 承认说错了话 chéngrèn shuōcuò le huà

eaten See **eat**

eaves N 屋檐 wūyán

eavesdrop v 偷听 tōutīng, 窃听 qiètīng

ebb N 退潮 tuìcháo
ebb and flow 起伏 qǐfú, 涨落 zhǎngluò
to ebb away 衰退 shuāituì, 逐渐减少 zhújiàn jiǎnshǎo

e-book N 电子书（籍）diànzǐ shū (jí)

ebullience N 欣喜 xīnxǐ

e-business N 电子商务 diànzǐ shāngwù

eccentric I ADJ 怪诞的 guàidàn de II N 怪诞的人 guàidàn de rén, 怪人 guàirén

echo I N 1 回声 huíshēng, 回音 huíyīn 2 （意见／感情的）共鸣 (yìjiàn/gǎnqíng de) gòngmíng II v 1 发出回声 fāchū huíshēng, 回响 huíxiǎng **2** 附和 fùhè, 重复 chóngfù

eclipse I N 日食 rìshí, 月食 yuèshí **II** V 遮蔽 [+日光或月光] zhēbì [+rìguāng huò yuèguāng] **2** 胜过 shèngguò

ecological ADJ 生态的 shēngtài de

ecology N 生态（学）shēngtài (xué)

e-commerce N 电子商务 diànzǐ shāngwù, 电子商业 diànzǐ shāngyè

economic ADJ 经济的 jīngjì de

economical ADJ 节省的 jiéshěng de, 节俭的 jiéjiǎn de

economics N **1** 经济学 jīngjìxué **2** 经济意义 jīngjì yìyì, 经济因素 jīngjì yīnsù

economist N 经济学家 jīngjìxuéjiā

economize V 节省 jiéshěng

economy I N **1** 经济 jīngjì

   market economy 市场经济 shìchǎng jīngjì

   service-based economy 以服务行业为基础的经济 yǐ fúwù hángyè wéi jīchǔ de jīngjì

2 节省 jiéshěng, 节约 jiéyuē **II** ADJ 便宜的 piányí de, 经济的 jīngjì de

   economy pack 经济包 jīngjìbāo

ecosystem N 生态系统 shēngtài xìtǒng

ecstasy N 狂喜 kuángxǐ **2** 摇头丸 yáotóuwán

eczema N 湿疹 shīzhěn

eddy I N 漩涡 xuánwō **II** V 起漩涡 qǐ xuánwō

edge I N 边 biān, 边缘 biānyuán **2** 优势 yōushì, 竞争力 jìngzhēnglì

   to gain a competitive edge 获得竞争优势 huòdé jìngzhēng yōushì

II V 加边 jiā biān **2** 慢慢移动 mànmàn yídòng **3** 渐渐发展 jiànjiàn fāzhǎn

edgy ADJ 紧张不安的 jǐnzhāng bù'ān de

edible ADJ 可以食用的 kěyǐ shíyòng de

edict N 法令 fǎlìng [M. WD 条 tiáo]

edification N 启示 qǐshì

edifice N 宏伟的建筑物 hóngwěi de jiànzhùwù, 大楼 dàlóu

edify V 教诲 jiàohuì, 开导 kāidǎo

edit V 编辑 biānjí

edition N **1** 版本 bǎnběn **2** 一集 yì jí, 一期 yìqī

first edition (of a book)（一本书的）第一版 (yì běn shū de) dìyībǎn

editor N 编辑 biānjí

editorial N 社论 shèlùn [M. WD 篇 piān]

educate V 教育 jiàoyù, 训练 xùnliàn

educated ADJ 受过教育的 shòuguo jiàoyù de, 有知识的 yǒu zhīshi de

education N 教育 jiàoyù

educational ADJ 教育的 jiàoyù de, 有教育意义的 yǒu jiàoyù yìyì de

edutainment N 教育娱乐电影／电视节目 jiàoyù yúlè diànyǐng/diànshì jiémù

eel N 鳝 mán, 鳗鱼 mányú [M. WD 条 tiáo]

eerie ADJ 怪异而恐怖的 guàiyì ér kǒngbù de

effect I N 效果 xiàoguǒ, 作用 zuòyòng

   side effect（药品的）副作用 (yàopǐn de) fùzuòyòng

II V 引起 yǐnqǐ, 造成 zàochéng

   to effect immediate change 立即引起变化 lìjí yǐnqǐ biànhuà

effective ADJ 有效的 yǒuxiào de

   to be/become effective 生效 shēngxiào

effects N 私人物品 sīrén wùpǐn

effeminate ADJ 女人气的 nǚrénqì de, 娘娘腔的 niángniangqiāng de

effervescent ADJ 冒气泡的 mào qìpào de

efficiency N 效率 xiàolǜ

efficient ADJ 高效率的 gāoxiàolǜ de

effigy N 模拟像 mónǐ xiàng

effluent N 污水 wūshuǐ, 废液 fèiyè

effort N 努力 nǔlì, 气力 qìlì **2** 费力 fèilì, 痛苦的事 tòngkǔ de shì

effortless ADJ 不费力的 bú fèilì de

effusive ADJ（过于）热情的 (guòyú) rèqíng de, 热情奔放的 rèqíng bēnfàng de

e.g. (= for example) ABBREV 例如 lìrú

egg I N **1** 蛋 dàn, 鸡蛋 jīdàn **2** 卵 luǎn

   egg cell 卵细胞 luǎnxìbāo

II V 怂恿 sǒngyǒng, 鼓动 gǔdòng

eggplant N 茄子 qiézi

eggshell N 蛋壳 dànké

ego N 自我 zìwǒ

   an ego trip 自我表现的行为 zìwǒ biǎoxiàn de xíngwéi

   to have a big ego 自以为很了不起 zì yǐwéi hěn liǎobuqǐ

egotistical ADJ 自高自大的 zìgāo zìdà de, 自负的 zìfù de

egregious ADJ 极坏的 jí huài de, 令人震惊的 lìng rén zhènjīng de

eight NUM 八 bā, 8

eighteen NUM 十八 shíbā, 18

eighteenth NUM 第十八 dì shíbā

eighth NUM 第八 dì bā

either I ADJ (of two) 任何一个 rènhé yí ge, 两个都 liǎng ge dōu II PRON (of two) 任何一个 rènhé yí ge III ADV 也（不）yě (bù) either … or … …或者… …huòzhě…, 不是…就是… bú shì…jiùshì…

ejaculate V 射精 shèjīng

eject V 弹出 dàn chū, 推出 tuīchū

eke V (to eke out) 勉强维持（生计）miǎnqiǎng wéichí (shēngjì)

elaborate I ADJ 精心制作的 jīngxīn zhìzuò de, 精心设计的 jīngxīn shèjì de II V 详细说明 xiángxì shuōmíng

elapse V (时间) 过去 (shíjiān) guòqù, 流逝 liúshì

elastic I ADJ 1 有弹性的 yǒu tánxìng de 2 有伸缩性的 [+计划] yǒu shēnsuōxìng de [+jìhuà] II N 橡皮圈 xiàngpíquān, 松紧带 sōngjǐndài

elasticity N 弹性 tánxìng

elated ADJ 欣喜的 xīnxǐ de

elation N 欣喜 xīnxǐ

elbow I N 1 肘 zhǒu, 肘部 zhǒu bù 2 衣服的肘部 yīfu de zhǒu bù II V 用肘挤开 yòng zhǒu jǐ kāi

elder I ADJ 年长的 niánzhǎng de elder brother 哥哥 gēge elder sister 姐姐 jiějie II N 长者 zhǎngzhě, 长辈 zhǎngbèi

elderly ADJ 年老的 lǎonián de, 上了年纪的 shàngle niánjì de elderly man/gentleman 老先生 lǎoxiānsheng elderly woman/lady 老太太 lǎotàitai

elect I V 1 选举 [+国会议员] xuǎnjǔ [+guóhuì yìyuán] president-elect 当选总统 dāngxuǎn zǒngtǒng 2 选择 xuǎnzé II ADJ 当选了的 dāngxuǎnle de

election N 选举 xuǎnjǔ

elective I N 选修课 xuǎnxiūkè [M. WD 门 mén] II ADJ 1 选举产生的 [+代表] xuǎnshēng de [+dàibiǎo] 2 选择性的 [+治疗] xuǎnzéxìng de [+zhìliáo], 非必需的 [+课程] fēi bìxū de [+kèchéng]

electoral ADJ 与选举有关的 yǔ xuǎnjǔ yǒuguān de electoral college 总统选举团 zǒngtǒng xuǎnjǔ tuán

electorate N 全体选民 quántǐ xuǎnmín

electric ADJ 1 电（器）的 diàn(qì) de electric chair 电椅 diànyǐ 2 激动人心的 jīdòng rénxīn de

electrical See **electric** ADJ 1

electrician N 电工 diàngōng

electricity N 1 电 diàn 2 极其激动的情绪 jíqí jīdòng de qíngxù, 激情 jīqíng

electrify V 1 使 [+铁路系统] 电气化 shǐ [+tiělù xìtǒng] diànqìhuà, 供电 gōngdiàn 2 使 [+听众] 万分激动 shǐ [+tīngzhòng] wànfēn jīdòng

electrocute V 1 触电身亡 chùdiàn shēnwáng 2 用电刑处死 yòng diànxíng chǔsǐ

electrode N 电极 diànjí

electron N 电子 diànzǐ

electronic ADJ 电子的 diànzǐ de, 用电子操作的 yòng diànzǐ cāozuò de electronic funds transfer 电子资金转账 diànzǐ zījīn zhuǎnzhàng

electronics N 1 [学习+] 电子学 [xuéxí+] diànzǐxué 2 [发展+] 电子工业 [fāzhǎn+] diànzǐ gōngyè 3 [购买+] 电子设备 [gòumǎi+] diànzǐ shèbèi

elegance N 优雅 yōuyǎ, 高雅 gāoyǎ

elegant ADJ 优雅的 yōuyǎ de, 高雅的 gāoyǎ de

element N 1 元素 yuánsù [M. WD 种 zhǒng] 2 因素 yīnsù, 成份 chéngfèn to be in one's element 适得其所 shì dé qí suǒ the elements 恶劣天气 èliè tiānqì

elementary ADJ 1 初级的 chūjí de elementary school 小学 xiǎoxué 2 基本的 jīběn de an elementary right 基本的权利 jīběn de quánlì

elephant N 象 xiàng, 大象 dàxiàng

elevate v 使…上升 shǐ…shàngshēng, 提升 tíshēng

elevated ADJ **1** 高出地面的 gāochū dìmiàn de

an elevated highway 高架公路 gāojià gōnglù

2 偏高的 piāngāo de

elevator N 电梯 diàntī [M. WD 部 bù], 升降机 shēngjiàngjī [M. WD 部 bù]

eleven NUM 十一 shíyī, 11

eleventh NUM 第十一 dì shíyī

at the eleventh hour 最后一刻 zuìhòu yīkè

elf N 小精灵 xiǎojīnglíng

elicit v 引出 yǐnchū, 套出 tàochū

to elicit a response 得到回应 dédào huíyìng

eligible ADJ **1** 有资格的 yǒu zīgé de **2** 合适的 [+婚姻对象] héshì de [+hūnyīn duìxiàng]

eliminate v **1** 消除 [+分歧] xiāochú [+fēnqí], 消灭 xiāomiè **2** 淘汰 [+选手] táotài [+xuǎnshǒu]

elite I N 精英 jīngyīng II ADJ 精锐的 jīngruì de, 杰出的 jiéchū de

elite troops 精锐部队 jīngruì bùduì

elixir N 灵丹妙药 língdān miàoyào

elk N 驼鹿 tuólù, 麋 mí

ellipse N 椭圆 tuǒyuán

ellipsis N **1** 省略 shěnglüè **2** 省略号 shěnglüèhào (…)

elongate v 使…变得瘦长 shǐ…biàn de shòucháng, 拉长 lācháng

elongated ADJ 瘦长的 shòucháng de

elope v 私奔 sībēn

eloquent ADJ 雄辩的 xióngbiàn de, 口才极好的 kǒucái jíhǎo de

else ADV 别的 biéde, 其他的 qítā de

elsewhere ADV 别的地方 biéde dìfang, 其他地方 qítā dìfang

elucidate v 阐明 chǎnmíng, 解释清楚 jiěshì qīngchu

elude v 逃避 táobì, 躲避 duǒbì

elusive ADJ **1** 很难捕捉的 [+猎物] hěn nán bǔzhuō de [+lièwù] **2** 难以说清的 [+词义] nányǐ shuōqīng de [+cíyì]

emaciated ADJ 消瘦的 xiāoshòu de, 憔悴的 qiáocuì de

email, e-mail I N 电子邮件 diànzǐ yóujiàn, 伊妹儿 yī mèir

e-mail address 电子邮件地址 diànzǐ yóujiàn dìzhǐ

II v 给…发电子邮件 gěi…fā diànzi yóujiàn

emanate v 来自 láizì, 发自 fāzì

emancipate v 解放 jiěfàng

embalm v 做防腐处理 zuò fángfǔ chǔlǐ

embankment N 堤岸 dī'àn, 堤围 dīwéi

embargo N, v 禁运 jìnyùn

embark v **1** 上飞机 shàng fēijī, 上船 shàng chuán **2** 出发 chūfā, 启程 qǐchéng

to embark on sth 开始做某事 kāishǐ zuò mǒushì

embarrass v 使…难堪 shǐ … nánkān, 使…难为情 shǐ…nánwéiqíng

embassy N 大使馆 dàshǐguǎn

the American embassy in Beijing 美国驻北京大使馆 Měiguó zhù Běijīng dàshǐguǎn

embattled ADJ **1** 被（敌人）包围的 bèi (dírén) bāowéi de **2** 困难重重的 kùnnan chóngchóng de

embed v **1** 插入 chārù **2** 深植 shēn zhí

embellish v **1** 装饰 zhuāngshì, 修饰 xiūshì **2** 给 [+故事] 添枝加叶 gěi [gùshi+] tiān zhī jiā yè

ember N 余烬 yújìn

embezzle v 贪污 tānwū, 侵吞 qīntūn

embittered ADJ 怨恨的 yuànhèn de, 怨愤的 yuànfèn de

emblem N 标志 biāozhì, 象征 xiàngzhēng

embodiment N 化身 huàshēn, 体现 tǐxiàn

emboss v 用浮雕图案装饰 yòng fúdiāo tú'àn zhuāngshì

embrace v **1** 拥抱 yōngbào [+朋友] [+péngyou] **2** 采纳 [+建议] cǎinà [+jiànyì], 接受 jiēshòu

embroider v **1** 绣 xiù, 刺绣 cìxiù **2** 给 [+故事] 添油加醋 gěi [+gùshi] tiān yóu jiā cù

embroiled ADJ 被卷入 bèi juǎnrù

embryo N 胚胎 pēitāi

embryonic ADJ 处于萌芽阶段的 chǔyú méngyá jiēduàn de, 刚起步的 gāng qǐbù de

emcee (ABBREV **mc**) N 司仪 sīyí

emerald N 翡翠 fěicuì, 绿宝石 lǜbǎoshí

emerge V 显露 xiǎnlù, 出现 chūxiàn

emergency N 紧急情况 jǐnjí qíngkuàng
  emergency landing 紧急降落 jǐnjí jiàngluò
  emergency room (ER) 急救室 jíjiùshì, 急诊室 jízhěnshì
  emergency services 紧急应变部门 jǐnjí yìngbiàn bùmén

emeritus ADJ 荣誉的 róngyù de
  professor emeritus 荣誉退休教授 róngyù tuìxiū jiàoshòu

emigrant N（移居外国的）移民 (yíjū wàiguó de) yímín

emigrate V（向外）移民 (xiàngwài) yímín

eminent ADJ 著名的 zhùmíng de, 杰出的 jiéchū de

emirate N（阿拉伯）酋长国 (Ālābó) qiúzhǎngguó

emission N 排气 páiqì, 排放物 páifàng wù

emit V 发出 fāchū

e-money N 电子货币 diànzǐ huòbì

emoticon N 表情符号 biǎoqíng fúhào

emotion N 感情 gǎnqíng

emotional ADJ **1** 感情的 gǎnqíng de
  emotional quotient (EQ) 情商 qíngshāng
  2 情绪激动的 [+球赛观众] qíngxù jīdòng de [+qiúsài guānzhòng], 感情用事的 gǎnqíng yòngshì de

empathize V 有同感 yǒu tónggǎn

empathy N 同感 tónggǎn

emperor N 皇帝 huángdì [M. WD 位 wéi]

emphasis N **1** 重点 zhòngdiǎn **2** 重要性 zhòngyàoxìng
  to give/place emphasis on 重视 zhòngshì, 强调 qiángdiào

emphasize V 强调 qiángdiào

empire N 帝国 dìguó

empirical ADJ 经验的 jīngyàn de, 实验的 shíyàn de

employ V **1** 雇用 gùyòng, 聘用 pìnyòng **2** 使用 shǐyòng

employee N 雇员 gùyuán

employer N 雇主 gùzhǔ

employment N **1** 就业 jiùyè **2** 使用 shǐyòng

emporium N 大百货商场 dà bǎihuò shāngchǎng

empower V 给…权力 gěi...quánlì, 使…有权 shǐ...yǒuquán

empress N 女皇 nǚhuáng [M. WD 位 wéi], 皇后 Huánghòu [M. WD 位 wéi]

emptiness N **1** 空虚（的感觉）kōngxū (de gǎnjué) **2** 空旷 kōngkuàng

empty ADJ **1** 空 kōng, 空的 kōng de **2** 空洞的 kōngdòng de, 空虚的 kōngxū de

empty-handed ADJ 两手空空的 liǎngshǒu kōngkōng de, 一无所获的 yīwú suǒ huò de

emulate V **1** 仿效 fǎngxiào, 模仿 mófǎng **2** 仿真 fǎngzhēn

enable V 使…能够 shǐ...nénggòu

enact V 制定 [+法规] zhìdìng [+fǎguī]

enamel N **1** 搪瓷 tángcí **2** 珐琅质 fàlángzhì

enamored ADJ 迷恋 míliàn, 喜爱 xǐʼài

encase V 包住 bāozhù

enchanted ADJ **1** 被施了魔法的 [+镜子] bèi shī le mófǎ de [+jìngzi] **2** 陶醉的 [+情人] táozuì de [+qíngrén]

enchanting ADJ 令人陶醉的 lìng rén táozuì de

encircle V 围绕 wéirào, 环绕 huánrào

enclave N 聚居地 jùjūdì

enclose V **1** 附上 fùshàng **2** 围住 wéizhù

enclosure N **1** 围场 wéichǎng, 圈地 quāndì **2**（信中）附件 (xìnzhōng) fùjiàn

encompass V **1** 包括 bāokuò, 包含 bāohán **2** 围绕 wéirào, 围住 wéizhù

encore I N 加演的节目 jiā yǎn de jiémù II INTERJ 再来一个 zài lái yí gè

encounter I V（意外）遇到 (yìwài) yùdào II N 相遇 xiāngyù, 遭遇 zāoyù
  a close encounter 近距离遭遇 jìnjùlí zāoyù

encourage V 鼓励 gǔlì, 支持 zhīchí

encroach V 侵占 qīnzhàn, 蚕食 cánshí

encrusted ADJ 覆盖着硬壳的 fùgài qiáng yìngké de

encrypt V 给 [+计算机] 加密 gěi [+jìsuànjī] jiāmì

encumbrance N 阻碍 zǔ'ài, 妨碍 fáng'ài

encyclopedia N 百科全书 bǎikē quánshū

end I N 1 尽头 jìntóu
end zone 球门区 qiúménqū
2 结局 jiéjú, 结束 jiéshù 3 目的 mùdì
to make ends meet 收支相抵 shōuzhī xiāngdǐ
II V 结束 jiéshù
All's well that ends well. 结果好才是一切都好。Jiéguǒ hǎo cái shì yíqiè dōu hǎo.

endanger V 使…处于危险 shǐ…chǔyú wēixiǎn, 危及 wēijí
an endangered species 濒危物种 bīnwēi wùzhǒng

endear V 使…受欢迎 shǐ…shòu huānyíng

endearment N 示爱的言行 shì ài de yánxíng
a term of endearment 爱称 àichēng

endeavor I N 努力 nǔlì, 行动 xíngdòng
human endeavor 人类活动 rénlèi huódòng
II V 努力 nǔlì

endemic ADJ 地方性的 [+疾病] dìfāngxìng de [+jíbìng]

ending N 结局 jiéjú, 结尾 jiéwěi

endless ADJ 没完没了的 méiwán méiliǎo de, 无休止的 wú xiūzhǐ de

endorse V 1 赞同 [+行动计划] zàntóng [+xíngdòng jìhuà], 支持 zhīchí 2 背书 [+支票] bèishū [+zhīpiào] 3 为 [+产品] 代言 wèi [+chǎnpǐn] dàiyán

endowment N 1 捐助 juānzhù, 捐助物 juānzhùwù 2 [音乐+] 天赋 [yīnyuè+] tiānfù

endurance N 忍耐力 rěnnàilì, 耐力 nàilì

endure V 1 忍耐 rěnnài, 忍受 rěn shòu 2 持续（下去）chíxù (xiàqù)

enduring ADJ 持久的 chíjiǔ de

enemy N 敌人 dírén
arch enemy 头号敌人 tóuhào dírén, 大敌 dàdí

energetic ADJ 精力充沛的 jīnglì chōngpèi de

energy N 1 精力 jīnglì, 活力 huólì 2 能 néng, 能量 néngliàng
solar/atomic energy 太阳 / 原子能 tàiyáng/yuánzǐnéng

enforce V（强制）执行 (qiángzhì) zhíxíng, 实施 shíshī

engage V 1 聘用 pìnyòng 2 吸引 [+兴趣] xīyǐn [+xìnqu] 3 与 [+敌军] 交战 yǔ [+díjūn] jiāozhàn

engaged ADJ 1 订了婚的 dìngle hūn de 2（电话）占线 (diànhuà) zhànxiàn

engagement N 1 订婚 dìnghūn
engagement ring 订婚戒指 dìnghūn jièzhǐ
2 约会 yuēhuì
a previous engagement 已经订好的约会 yǐjīng dìnghǎode yuēhuì
3（军队）交战 (jūnduì) jiāozhàn

engender V 引起 yǐnqǐ, 导致 dǎozhì

engine N 1 引擎 yǐnqíng, 发动机 fādòngjī 2 机车 jīchē
fire engine 消防车 xiāofángchē

engineer N 1 工程师 gōngchéngshī
civil/electronics/software engineer 土木 / 电子 / 软件工程师 tǔmù/diànzǐ/ruǎnjiàn gōngchéngshī
2 轮机员 lúnjīyuán, 火车司机 huǒchē sījī

engineering N 工程 gōngchéng, 工程师行业 gōngchéngshī hángyè
hydraulic engineering 水利工程 shuǐlì gōngchéng

English I N 1 英语 Yīngyǔ 2 英格兰人 Yīnggélánrén, 英国人 Yīngguórén
American English 美式英语 Měishì Yīngyǔ
British English 英式英语 Yīngshì Yīngyǔ
II ADJ 1 英格兰的 Yīnggélán de, 英国的 Yīngguó de 2 英语的 Yīngyǔ de

engrave V 雕刻 diāokè
be engraved on one's mind 铭刻在脑中 míngkè zài nǎo zhōng

engraving N 版画 bǎnhuà

engrossed ADJ 全神贯注的 quánshén guànzhù de

engulf V 吞没 tūnmò

enhance V 提高 tígāo, 改进 gǎijìn

enigma N 神秘的人 / 事物 shénmì de rén/shìwù

enjoy V 1 喜爱 xǐ'ài 2 享受 xiǎngshòu
to enjoy oneself 开心 kāixīn, 过得很愉快 guòde hěn yúkuài

enjoyable ADJ 愉快的 yúkuài de, 开心的 kāixīn de

enlarge V 放大 fàngdà, 增大 zēngdà

enlargement N 1 放大 fàngdà, 增大 zēngdà 2 放大的照片 fàngdà de zhàopiàn

enlighten V 启迪 qǐdí, 开导 kāidǎo

enlightened ADJ 开明的 kāimíng de, 明智的 míngzhì de

enlist V 1 请求（帮助）qǐngqiú (bāngzhù) 2 参加（军队）cānjiā (jūnduì)

enliven V 使…生动有趣 shǐ…shēngdòng yǒuqù

en masse ADV 全体 quántǐ, 整体 zhěngtǐ

enmity N 敌意 díyì, 仇恨 chóuhèn

enormity N 1 艰巨性 jiānjù xìng 2 严重性 yánzhòngxìng

enormous ADJ 巨大的 jùdà de

enough I PRON 足够 zúgòu II ADV 足够 zúgòu, 够 gòu

enrage V 使…大怒 shǐ…dà nù, 激怒 jīnù

enraged ADJ 激怒的 jīnù de, 大怒的 dà nù de

enrich V 1 使 [+文化生活] 丰富 shǐ [+wénhuà shēnghuó] fēngfù 2 强化 qiánghuà 3 使…富裕 shǐ…fùyù

enroll V 招收 [+学生] zhāoshōu [+xuésheng]

enrollment N 入学 rùxué, 注册 zhùcè

en route ADV 在路上 zài lùshang, 沿途 yántú

ensemble N 1 小乐队 xiǎo yuèduì 2 成套的东西 chéngtào de dōngxi

enshrine V 珍藏 zhēncáng, 铭记 míngjì

ensign N 1（美国）海军少尉 (Měiguó) hǎijūn shàowèi 2 舰旗 jiàn qí

enslave V 奴役 núyì

ensue V（接着）发生 (jiēzhe) fāshēng

ensure V 确保 quèbǎo, 担保 dānbǎo

entail V 需要 xūyào

entanglement N 卷入 juǎnrù, 纠纷 jiūfēn

enter V 1 进入 jìnrù 2 加入 jiārù, 参加 cānjiā 3（在计算机里）输入 [+信息] (zài jìsuànjī lǐ) shūrù [+xìnxī]

enterprise N 1 企业 qǐyè [M. WD 家 jiā] 2 开创精神 kāichuàng jīngshén, 创业能力 chuàngyè nénglì

enterprising ADJ 富有创业精神的 fùyǒu chuàngyè jīngshén de

entertain V 1 使…高兴 shǐ…gāoxìng 2 招待 zhāodài 3 抱有（想法）bàoyǒu (xiǎngfǎ)

entertainment N 1 娱乐 yúlè, 文娱节目 wényú jiémù 2 招待 zhāodài

entertainment center 娱乐中心 yúlè zhōngxīn

entertainment cost 招待费 zhāodàifèi

enthrall V 使…入迷 shǐ…rùmí, 迷住 mízhù

enthralling ADJ 使人入迷的 shǐrén rùmí de, 非常有趣的 fēicháng yǒuqù de

enthuse V 热情高涨 rèqíng gāozhǎng

enthusiasm N 1 热情 rèqíng 2 极大的兴趣 jídà de xìngqu

enthusiastic ADJ 热情的 rèqíng de

entice V 诱惑 yòuhuò, 引诱 yǐnyòu

enticing ADJ 有诱惑力的 yǒu yòuhuòlì de, 迷人的 mírén de

entire ADJ 全部的 quánbù de, 整个 zhěnggè

entirety N 全部 quánbù, 整个 zhěnggè

entitle V 1 使…有权 shǐ…yǒuquán 2 给…题名 gěi…tímíng

entitled ADJ 1 有权利的 yǒuquánlì de 2 书（电影, 戏）名叫 shū (diànyǐng, xì) míng jiào

entity N 实体 shítǐ

entomology N 昆虫学 kūnchóngxué

entourage N 随行人员 suíxíng rényuán

entrails N 内脏 nèizàng, 肠子 chángzi

entrance N 1 入口 rùkǒu 2 进入 jìnrù

entranced ADJ 着迷的 zháomí de

entrant N 参赛者 cānsàizhě

entrap V 使…陷入圈套 shǐ…xiànrùquāntào, 诱骗 yòupiàn

entreat V 恳求 kěnqiú

entrée N 1 主菜 zhǔcài 2 进入权 jìnrù quán, 进入许可 jìnrù xǔkě

entrenched ADJ 根深蒂固的 gēnshēn dìgù de, 不可动摇的 bùkě dòngyáo de

entrepreneur N 企业家 qǐyèjiā

entrust V 委托 wěituō

entry N 1 进入 jìnrù

No Unauthorized Entry 非公莫入 fēigōng mòrù

2 入口 rùkǒu, 进入通道 jìnrù tōngdào
3（词典）词条 (cídiǎn) cí tiáo, 条目
tiáomù **4** 参赛作品 cānsài zuòpǐn

entwined ADJ 交错在一起的 jiāocuò zài
yìqǐ de, 密切有关的 mìqiè yǒuguān de

enumerate V 列举 lièjǔ

enunciate V 清晰地发音吐字 qīngxī de
fāyīn tǔzì

envelop V 包住 bāozhù, 裹住 guǒ zhù

envelope N 信封 xìnfēng
stamped addressed envelope 贴好邮
票写好地址的回信信封 tiēhǎo yóupiào
xiěhǎo dìzhǐ de huíxìn xìnfēng

enviable ADJ 叫人羡慕的 jiào rén xiànmù
de

envious ADJ 羡慕的 xiànmù de, 妒忌的
dùjì de

environment N 环境 huánjìng
natural environment 自然环境 zìrán
huánjìng
pollution of the environment 环境污
染 huánjìng wūrǎn

environmental ADJ 环境的 huánjìng de

environs N 周围 zhōuwéi

envisage V 展望 zhǎnwàng, 想像 xiǎngxiàng

envision V 设想 shèxiǎng, 想像 xiǎngxiàng

envoy N 使者 shǐzhě [M. WD 位 wéi], 外交
官 wàijiāoguān [M. WD 位 wéi]

envy I V 羡慕 xiànmù, 嫉妒 jídù II N 1 羡
慕 xiànmù, 嫉妒 jídù 2 被人羡慕的东西
bèi rén xiànmù de dōngxi
the envy of the world 人人都羡慕
的东西／事物 rénrén dōu xiànmù de
dōngxi/shìwù

enzyme N 酶 méi

ephemeral ADJ 短暂的 duǎnzàn de, 瞬息
的 shùnxī de

epic I N 史诗 shǐshī, 史诗般的电影（或
小说）shǐshī bān de diànyǐng (huò
xiǎoshuō) II ADJ 1 史诗的 shǐshī de 2 英
雄的 yīngxióng de, 宏伟的 hóngwěi de

epicenter N（地震）中心 (dìzhèn)
zhōngxīn, 震中 zhènzhōng

epidemic N 流行病 liúxíngbìng, 传染病
chuánrǎnbìng [M. WD 种 zhǒng]

epilepsy N 癫痫 diānxián, 羊痫疯
yángxiánfēng

epilogue N 1 结尾 jiéwěi, 终场 zhōngchǎng 2 结束语 jiéshùyǔ

episode N 1（连续剧）一集 (liánxùjù) yì
jí 2 一段经历 yíduàn jīnglì

epistle N 书信 shūxìn, 信 xìn

epitaph N 墓志铭 mùzhìmíng

epithet N 1 [污辱性的+] 描写词语
[wūrǔxìng de+] miáoxiě cíyǔ 2 绰号
chuòhào, 别名 biémíng

epitomize V 成为…的典范 chéngwéi...de
diǎnfàn, 象征 xiàngzhēng

epoch N 时代 shídài, 纪元 jìyuán

EQ (= emotional quotient) ABBREV 情绪智
商 qíngxù zhìshāng, 情商 qíngshāng

equal I ADJ 1 平等 píngděng 2 等于 děngyú
equal sign 等号 děnghào (=)
II V 等于 děngyú

equality N 平等 píngděng

equalize V 使…平等 shǐ...píngděng, 使…
相等 shǐ...xiāngděng

equally ADV 平等地 píngděng de, 相同地
xiāngtóng de

equanimity N 镇静 zhènjìng, 镇定
zhèndìng

equate V 平等看待 píngděng kàndài

equation N 等式 děngshì

equator N 赤道 chìdào

equestrian ADJ 骑马的 qímǎ de, 马术的
mǎshù de

equilateral ADJ 等边的 děngbiān de

equilibrium N 均衡 jūnhéng, 平衡
pínghéng

equine ADJ 马的 mǎ de

equinox N 春分 chūnfēn, 秋分 qiūfēn, 昼
夜平分时 zhòuyè píngfēn shí

equip V 装备 zhuāngbèi, 配备 pèibèi
well-equipped 设施齐全的 shèshī
qíquán de, 装备良好的 zhuāngbèi
liánghǎo de

equipment N 设备 shèbèi, 装备 zhuāngbèi

equitable ADJ 公平的 gōngpíng de, 公正
的 gōngzhèng de

equity N 1 公平 gōngpíng, 公正 gōngzhèng 2 [房产的+] 财产净值 [fángchǎn
de+] cáichǎn jìngzhí

equivalent I ADJ 等值的 děngzhí de, 相等的 xiāngděng de **II** N 等价物 děngjiàwù, 对应物 duìyìngwù

equivocal ADJ 含糊的 hánhu de, 模棱两可的 móléng liǎngkě de

era N 时代 shídài, 年代 niándài

eradicate V 根除 gēnchú, 彻底消灭 chèdǐ xiāomiè

erase V 消除 xiāochú, 抹去 mǒqù

eraser N **1** 橡皮 xiàngpí [M. WD 块 kuài] **2** 黑板擦 hēibǎn cā [M. WD 块 kuài]

erect I ADJ 笔直的 bǐzhí de, 垂直的 chuízhí de **II** V 建立 [+纪念碑] jiànlì [+jìniànbēi], 建造 jiànzào

erection N **1** 建立 jiànlì, 建造 jiànzào **2** [阴茎+] 勃起 (yīnjīng+) bóqí

erode V **1** 侵蚀 [+土壤] qīnshí [+tǔrǎng] **2** 削弱 [+权力] xuēruò [+quánlì]

erosion N **1** [土壤受到+] 侵蚀 [tǔrǎng shòudào+] qīnshí **2** [权力的+] 削弱 [quánlì de+] xuēruò

erotic ADJ 色情的 sèqíng de, 性的 xìng de

err V 犯错误 fàn cuòwù

to err on the side of caution 宁可犯错，也要谨慎。Nìngkě fàncuò, yě yào jǐnshèn.

To err is human, to forgive divine. 犯错是人，宽恕是神。Fàncuò shì rén, kuānshù shì shén.

errand N 差事 chāishi, 跑腿儿 pǎotuǐr

to send sb on an errand 派某人去办一件事 pài mǒurén qù bàn yí jiàn shì

errata N 勘误表 kānwùbiǎo

erratic ADJ 不稳定的 bùwěndìng de, 不可捉摸的 bùkě zhuōmō de

erroneous ADJ 错误的 cuòwù de

error N **1** 错误 cuòwù **2** 谬误 miùwù

erupt V（火山）爆发 (huǒshān) bàofā

escalate V **1** 升级 shēngjí **2** 升高 shēng-gāo

escalator N 自动扶梯 zìdòng fútī [M. WD 部 bù]

escapade N **1** 刺激行为 cìjī xíngwéi **2** 越轨行为 yuèguǐ xíngwéi

escape I V **1** 逃离 táolí, 逃避 táobì

to escape one's attention 逃避某人的注意 táobì mǒurén de zhùyì

2 记不起 [+某人的姓名] jì bùqǐ [+mǒurén de xìngmíng] **II** N 逃离 táolí, 逃避 táobì

eschew V 回避 huíbì, 躲避 duǒbì

escort I V **1** 押送 [+犯人] yāsòng [+fàn-rén], 护送 hùsòng **2** 为 [+旅游者] 导游陪同 wéi [+lǚyóuzhě] dǎoyóu péitóng **II** N 护卫者 hùwèizhě **2** 妓女 jìnǚ

male escort 男妓 nánjì

Eskimo N 爱斯基摩人 Àisījīmórén

esophagus N 食管 shíguǎn

esoteric ADJ 深奥的 shēn'ào de

especially ADV 特别 tèbié, 尤其 yóuqí

espionage N 间谍活动 jiàndié huódòng

espresso N 蒸馏咖啡 zhēngliú kāfēi

essay N 文章 wénzhāng, 论说文 lùnshuōwén, 散文 sǎnwén

essence N **1** 要素 yàosù, 本质 běnzhì

Time is of the essence. 时间是至关重要的。Shíjiān shì zhìguān zhòngyào de. **2** 精油 jīngyóu, 精 jīng

vanilla essence 香草精 xiāngcǎojīng

essential I ADJ 必不可少的 bì bùkěshǎo de, 必要的 bìyào de **II** N 必需品 bìxūpǐn

the essentials 要点 yàodiǎn

establish V 成立 chénglì, 建立 jiànlì

establishment N **1** 成立 chénglì, 建立 jiànlì **2** 机构 jīgòu, 组织 zǔzhī

estate N **1** 地产 dìchǎn, 房地产 fángdìchǎn **2** 遗产 yíchǎn

estate tax 遗产税 yíchǎnshuì

esteem N, V 尊重 zūnzhòng, 尊敬 zūnjìng

to hold sb in esteem 对某人很尊敬 duì mǒurén hěn zūnjìng

estimate V, N 估计 gūjì

estimation N 估计 gūjì

in sb's estimation 根据某人的估计 gēnjù mǒurén de gūjì

estranged ADJ **1** 分居的（夫妻）fēnjū de (fūqī) **2** 不再联系的（亲友）búzài liánxì de (qīnyǒu)

estrogen N 雌激素 cíjīsù

estuary N 河流入海口 héliú rǔhǎikǒu, 河口 hékǒu

etc (= etcetera) ABBREV 等等 děngděng

etch V 蚀刻 shíkè

eternal ADJ 永恒的 yǒnghéng de, 永远的 yǒngyuǎn de

eternity N 1 永恒 yǒnghéng, 永远 yǒngyuǎn 2 来生 láishēng, 来世 láishì

ether N（乙）醚（yǐ）mí

ethereal ADJ 飘逸的 piāoyì de, 超凡的 chāofán de

ethic N 伦理 lúnlǐ, 道德体系 dàodé tǐxì

ethical ADJ 伦理的 lúnlǐ de

ethics N 1 道德规范 dàodé guīfàn 2 伦理学 lúnlǐxué

ethnic ADJ 种族的 zhǒngzú de, 民族的 mínzú de
ethnic minority 少数民族群体 shǎoshù mínzú qúntǐ
an ethnic slur 侮辱少数民族的诽谤 wūrǔ shǎoshù mínzú de fěibàng

ethos N 精神特质 jīngshén tèzhì

etiquette N 礼仪 lǐyí

etymology N 词源 cíyuán, 词源学 cíyuánxué

EU (= the European Union) ABBREV 欧洲联盟 Ōuzhōu Liánméng

eulogy N 颂词 sòngcí [M. WD 篇 piān]

eunuch N 太监 tàijiàn

euphemism N 委婉语 wěiwǎnyǔ

euphoria N 异常兴奋 yìcháng xīngfèn, 无名欣喜 wúmíng xīnxǐ

euro N 欧元 Ōuyuán

Europe N 欧洲 Ōuzhōu

European I ADJ 欧洲的 Ōuzhōu de II N 欧洲人 Ōuzhōurén

euthanasia N 安乐死 ānlèsǐ

evacuate V 撤离 chè lí

evade V 回避 huíbì, 避开 bìkāi

evaluate V 评估 pínggū, 评价 píngjià

evangelist N 福音传道者 fúyīn chuándàozhě

evaporate V 1 [气体+] 挥发 [qìtǐ+] huīfā, 蒸发 zhēngfā 2 [人+] 消失 [rén+] xiāoshī

evasion N 回避 huíbì, 避开 bìkāi

evasive ADJ 推脱的 tuītuō de, 回避的 huíbì de

eve N 前一天 qián yìtiān, 前夜 qiányè

even 1 ADJ 平的 píng de, 平坦的 píngtǎn de 2 平衡的 pínghéng de, 均恒的 jūnhéng de
even number 偶数 ǒushù
II ADV 甚至 shènzhì III V 1 使…平坦 shǐ...píngtǎn 2 使…平衡 shǐ...pínghéng

to even out 使…相等 shǐ...xiāngděng

evening N 1 晚上 wǎnshang, 傍晚 bàngwǎn
evening dress, evening wear 夜礼服 yèlǐfú

evenly ADV 均匀地 jūnyún de

event N 1 事件 shìjiàn
in any event 不管怎样 bùguǎn zěnyàng
in the event of 万一 wànyī
2 活动 huódòng 3（体育）项目（tǐyù）xiàngmù

eventful ADJ 发生很多事情的 fāshēng hěn duō shìqing de, 多事之秋 duōshì zhī qiū

eventual ADJ 最终的 zuìzhōng de

eventuality N 可能发生的事情 kěnéng fāshēng de shìqing, 可能产生的恶果 kěnéng chǎnshēng de èguǒ

ever ADV 1 一直 yìzhí 2 在任何时候 zài rènhé shíhou

evergreen I ADJ 常青的 chángqīng de, 常绿的 chánglǜ de II N 常青树 chángqīngshù [M. WD 棵 kē]

everlasting ADJ 永恒的 yǒnghéng de, 永久的 yǒng jiǔ de

every ADJ 每 měi, 每个 měi ge

everybody (= everyone)

everyday ADJ 每天的 měitiān de, 日常的 rìcháng de

everyone PRON 每个人 měige rén, 人人 rénrén, 大家 dàjiā

everything PRON 每件事 měi jiàn shì, 一切 yíqiè

everywhere ADV 每个地方 měi ge dìfang, 到处 dàochù

evict V（依法）驱逐（yīfǎ）qūzhú, 赶出 gǎnchū

evidence N 1 证据 zhèngjù 2 证词 zhèngcí

evident ADJ 明显的 míngxiǎn de

evil I N 邪恶 xié'è
the lesser of two evils 两害相比较轻者 liǎng hài xiāngbǐ jiào qīng zhě
II ADJ 邪恶的 xié'è de 2 恶魔的 èmó de, 恶魔似的 èmó shìde
evil spirit 恶鬼 èguǐ

evocative ADJ 唤起 huànqǐ, 引起 yǐnqǐ

evolution N 进化（论）jìnhuà (lùn)

evolutionary ADJ 1 进化（论）的 jìnhuà (lùn) de 2 演变的 yǎnbiàn de

evolve V 逐步演变 zhúbù yǎnbiàn

ewe N 母羊 mǔyáng [M. WD 头 tóu]

exacerbate V 使…恶化 shǐ...èhuà

exact ADJ 确切的 quèqiè de, 精确的 jīngquè de

exactly ADV 1 完全地 wánquán de, 精确地 jīngquè de 2 正是 zhèngshì 3 正是这样 zhèng shì zhèyàng, 确实如此 quèshí rúcǐ

exaggerate V 夸大 kuādà, 夸张 kuāzhāng

exaggerated ADV 夸大的 kuādà de, 夸张的 kuāzhāng de

exalt V 赞扬 zànyáng, 歌颂 gēsòng

examination N 1 检查 jiǎnchá [M. WD 次 cì], 检验 jiǎnyàn [M. WD 次 cì] 2 考试 kǎoshì [M. WD 次 cì/场 cháng]

examine V 检查 jiǎnchá, 检验 jiǎnyàn

example N 1 例子 lìzi
for example 例如 lìrú
2 榜样 bǎngyàng, 范例 fànlì

exasperating ADJ 让人恼怒的 ràng rén nǎonù de

excavate V 发掘 fājué, 挖掘 wājué

exceed V 超出 chāochū, 超过 chāoguò

exceedingly ADV 极其 jíqí, 非常 fēicháng

excel V 1 优于 yōuyú, 胜过 shèngguò 2 擅长 shàncháng

excellence N 卓越 zhuóyuè, 优秀 yōuxiù

except I PREP 1 除了 chúle, 除了…以外 chúle...yǐwài 2 只是 zhǐ shì II V 除去 chúqù, 除掉 chúdiào

exception N 例外 lìwà

exceptional ADJ 1 杰出的 jiéchū de, 出类拔萃的 chūlèi bácuì de 2 例外的 lìwài de, 特殊的 tèshū de

excerpt N 摘录 zhāilù, 节录 jiélù

excess I N 过分 guòfèn, 过量 guòliàng
in excess of 超过 chāoguò
II ADJ 多余的 duōyú de, 额外的 éwài de
excess baggage 超重行李 chāozhòng xínglǐ

excesses N 过激行为 guòjī xíngwéi, (不必要的) 暴力 (bú bìyào de) bàolì

exchange I N 1 交换 jiāohuàn, 兑换 duìhuàn

exchange rate 兑换率 duìhuànlǜ
2 交易所 jiāoyìsuǒ
New York Stock Exchange (NYSE) 纽约证券交易所 Niǔyuē zhèngquàn jiāoyìsuǒ
II V 交换 jiāohuàn

excise I N （特种）消费税 (tèzhǒng) xiāofèishuì, 国内货物税 guónèi huòwùshuì II V 除去 chúqù, 切除 qiēchú

excited ADJ 激动 jīdòng, 兴奋的 xīngfèn de

exciting ADJ 令人激动地 lìng rén jīdòng de

exclaim V 叫喊 jiàohǎn, 呼叫 hūjiào

exclamation N 叫喊声 jiàohǎn shēng, 呼叫声 hūjiàoshēng

exclude V 1 不包括 bù bāokuò 2 排除 [+可能性] páichú [+kěnéngxìng]

excluding PREP 不包括 bù bāokuò, 除了 chúle

exclusive ADJ 1 独家的 [+采访] dújiā de [+cǎifǎng], 专门的 zhuānmén de 2 难以进入的 [+俱乐部] nányǐ jìnrù de [+jùlèbù] 3 昂贵的 [+餐厅] ángguì de [+cāntīng]

excommunicate V 开除 [+出教会] kāichú [+chū jiàohuì], 逐出教门 zhúchū jiàomén

excrement N 粪便 fènbiàn

excrete V 排泄 páixiè

excruciating ADJ 剧烈疼痛的 jùliè téngtòng de, 疼痛的难以忍受的 téngtòng de nányǐ rěnshòu de

excursion N 短途旅游 duǎntú lǚyóu

excuse I V 1 原谅 yuánliàng
Excuse me 对不起 duìbùqǐ
2 为…辩解 wèi...biànjiě II N 理由 lǐyóu, 借口 jièkǒu

execute V 1 执行 zhíxíng, 实施 shíshī 2 处以死刑 chù yǐ sǐxíng, 处死 chǔsǐ

execution N 1 执行 zhíxíng, 实施 shíshī 2 处死 chǔsǐ

executive I N 高级管理人员 gāojí guǎnlǐ rényuán
the Executive （政府）行政部门 (zhèngfǔ) xíngzhèng bùmén
II ADJ 执行的 zhíxíng de

executor N 遗嘱执行人 yízhǔ zhíxíngrén

exemplary ADJ 可以作为好榜样的 kěyǐ zuòwéi hǎo bǎngyàng de, 楷模的 kǎimó de

exemplify V 是…的典型例子 shì…de diǎnxíng lìzi

exempt I ADJ 被免除的 bèi miǎnchú de
exempt from taxation 免于缴税 miǎnyú jiǎoshuì
II V 免除 miǎnchú

exercise I N 1 (体育)锻炼 (tǐyù) duànliàn 2 体操 tǐcāo, 健身操 jiànshēncāo 3 练习 liànxí 4 活动 huódòng
a futile exercise 没有效果的活动 méiyǒu xiàoguǒ de huódòng, 徒劳之举 túláo zhī jǔ
5 (军事)演习 (jūnshì) yǎnxí
a joint naval exercise 联合海军演习 liánhé hǎijūn yǎnxí
II V 1 (体育)锻炼 (tǐyù) duànliàn 2 运用 [+权力] yùnyòng [+quánlì], 行使 xíngshǐ

exert V 施加 shījiā
to exert oneself 努力 nǔlì, 卖力 màilì

exertion N 1 运用 yùnyòng 2 用力 yònglì, 努力 nǔlì

exhale V 呼气 hūqì

exhaust I V 使…精疲力尽 shǐ…jīngpí lìjìn 2 用尽 yòngjìn II N 1 (汽车)废气 (qìchē) fèiqì 2 排气管 páiqìguǎn, 排气系统 páiqì xìtǒng

exhaustion N 1 精疲力尽 jīngpí lìjìn 2 耗尽 hàojìn, 用完 yòngwán

exhibit I V 1 展览 zhǎnlǎn, 展示 zhǎnshì 2 显示 xiǎnshì, 展示 zhǎnshì II N 1 展览品 zhǎnlǎnpǐn [M. WD 件 jiàn] 2 (法庭上的)证物 (fǎtíng shàng de) zhèngwù [M. WD 件 jiàn]

exhibition N 展览 zhǎnlǎn, 展览会 zhǎnlǎnhuì
to make an exhibition of oneself 出洋相 chūyángxiàng, 出丑 chūchǒu

exhilarated ADJ 兴高采烈的 xìnggāo cǎiliè de

exhilarating ADJ 让人极其兴奋的 ràng rén jíqí xīngfèn de

exhort V 恳请 kěnqǐng, 劝告 quàngào

exhortation N 规劝 guīquàn, 劝谕 quànyù

exhume V 掘出 (尸体) juéchū (shītǐ)

exile I V 流放 liúfàng, 放逐 fàngzhú II N 1 流放 liúfàng, 流亡 liúwáng 2 流放者 liúfàngzhě
a political exile 政治流放者 zhèngzhì liúfàngzhě
in exile 流放中 liúfàng zhōng

exist V 存在 cúnzài, 有 yǒu

existence N 1 存在 cúnzài 2 生存 shēngcún

exit I N 1 出口 chūkǒu, 出口处 chūkǒuchù 2 离去 líqù, 退场 tuìchǎng
to make a hasty exit 匆忙离去 cōngmáng líqù
II V 1 离开 líkāi 2 退出 tuìchū

exodus N (大批人)离开 (dàpī rén) líkāi

exonerate V 免除 (指控) miǎnchú (zhǐkòng)

exorbitant ADJ [价格+] 过高的 [jiàgé+] guògāo de, 昂贵的 ángguì de

exorcise V 忘却 wàngquè, 忘掉 wàngdiào 2 驱除 qūchú, 消除 xiāochú

exotic ADJ 异国情调的 yìguó qíngdiào de, 异国的 yìguó de

expand V 变大 biàn dà, 扩张 kuòzhāng

expansive ADJ 1 广阔的 [+麦田] guǎngkuò de [+màitián] 2 扩张的 [+野心] kuòzhāng de [+yěxīn] 3 开朗健谈的 [+朋友] kāilǎng jiàntán de [+péngyou]

expatriate N 居住在外国的人 jūzhù zài wàiguó de rén, 侨民 qiáomín

expect V 1 期待 qīdài, 指望 zhǐwàng 2 [女子+] 怀孕 [nǚzǐ+] huáiyùn

expectant ADJ 1 期待的 qīdài de, 期望的 qīwàng de 2 怀孕的 huáiyùn de
an expectant mother 快要当母亲的人 kuàiyào dāng mǔqīn de rén, 孕妇 yùnfù

expectation N 期待 qīdài, 期望 qīwàng
contrary to expectation 出乎意料 chūhū yìliào

expediency N 不讲原则只求效果的做法 bù jiǎng yuánzé zhǐ qiú xiàoguǒ de zuòfǎ, 权宜之计 quányí zhī jì

expedient ADJ 权宜之计的 quányí zhī jì de, 应急的 yìngjí de

expedite V 加快 jiākuài, 促进 cùjìn

expedition N 探险 (队) tànxiǎn (duì), 考察 (队) kǎochá (duì)

expel v 1 驱逐 qūzhú, 开除 kāichú 2 排出 [+气体] páichū [+qìtǐ]

expend v 花费 huāfèi

expendable ADJ 可有可无的 kěyǒu kěwú de, 不必保留的 búbì bǎoliú de

expenditure N 花费 huāfèi, 费用 fèiyòng

expense N 费用 fèiyòng [M. WD 笔 bǐ], 花费 huāfèi
at the expense of 以…为代价 yǐ...wéi dàijià

expensive ADJ 昂贵的 ángguì de

experience I N 1 经历 jīnglì 2 经验 jīngyàn
Experience is the better teacher. 经验是最好的老师。Jīngyàn shì zuì hǎo de lǎoshī.
II v 经历 jīnglì, 体验 tǐyàn

experiment I N 1 实验 shíyàn [M. WD 项 xiàng/次 cì], 试验 shìyàn [M. WD 项 xiàng/次 cì] II v 实验 shíyàn, 试验 shìyàn

expert I N 专家 zhuānjiā [M. WD 位 wéi], 行家 hángjiā [M. WD 位 wéi] II ADJ 专家的 zhuānjiā de, 内行的 nèiháng de
expert advice 专家意见 zhuānjiā yìjiàn

expertise N 专业知识 zhuānyè zhīshi

expiration N 过期失效 guòqī shīxiào
expiration date 失效日期 shīxiào rìqī

expire v 过期 guòqī, 到期 dàoqī

explain v 1 解释 jiěshì 2 说明 shuōmíng, 给出原因 gěichū yuányīn

explanation N 解释 jiěshì

explanatory ADJ 解释的 jiěshì de, 说明的 shuōmíng de

expletive N 骂人的话 màrén dehuà [M. WD 句 jù], 粗话 cūhuà [M. WD 句 jù]

explicable ADJ 容易理解的 róngyì lǐjiě de

explicit ADJ 1 清楚的 qīngchu de, 直截了当的 zhíjiéliǎodàng de 2（色情描写）露骨的 (sèqíng miáoxiě) lùgǔ de

explode v 爆炸 bàozhà

exploit¹ N 英勇行为 yīngyǒng xíngwéi, 壮举 zhuàngjǔ

exploit² v 1 剥削 [+雇员] bōxuē [+gùyuán] 2 利用 [+资源] lìyòng [+zīyuán], 开发 kāifā

exploitation N 剥削 bōxuē
exploitation of child labor 剥削童工 bōxuē tónggōng

2 利用 lìyòng

explore v 1 探索 tànsuǒ 2 仔细研究 zǐxì yánjiū, 考察 kǎochá

explorer N 探险者 tànxiǎnzhě, 探险家 tànxiǎnjiā

explosion N 1 爆炸 bàozhà [M. WD 次 cì] 2 急剧增长 jíjù zēngzhǎng
population explosion 人口急剧增长 rénkǒu jíjù zēngzhǎng, 人口爆炸 rénkǒu bàozhà

explosive I ADJ 1 会爆炸的 huì bàozhà de 2 爆炸性的 bàozhàxìng de II N 炸药 zhàyào

exponent N 倡导者 chàngdǎozhě, 拥护者 yōnghùzhě

export I v 出口 chūkǒu II N 出口（商品）chūkǒu (shāngpǐn)

expose v 1 暴露 bàolù 2 揭露 jiēlù

exposed ADJ 暴露在外的 bàolù zàiwài de

exposition N 1 详细讲解 xiángxì jiǎngjiě 2 展览会 zhǎnlǎnhuì, 博览会 bólǎnhuì

exposure N 1 暴露 bàolù 2 揭露 jiēlù 3 曝光（量）bàoguāng (liáng)
exposure meter（摄影用）曝光表 (shèyǐng yòng) bàoguāngbiǎo

express¹ v 表示 biǎoshì, 表达 biǎodá
to express oneself 表达自己的意思 / 观点 biǎodá zìjǐ de yìsi/guāndiǎn

express² I ADJ 快速的 kuàisù de, 高速的 gāosù de
Express Mail Delivery Service (EMD) 特快专递 tèkuài zhuān dì
II N 1 特快邮递 tèkuài yóudì 2 特快火车 tèkuài huǒchē [M. WD 列 liè]

expression N 1 表达法 biǎodáfǎ, 习惯用语 xíguàn yòngyǔ 2 表情 biǎoqíng 3 表达意见 / 感情 biǎodá yìjiàn/gǎnqíng

expressive ADJ 富于表现力的 fùyú biǎoxiànlì de, 充满感情的 chōngmǎn gǎnqíng de

expressly ADV 1 明确地 míngquè de 2 特意地 tèyì de

expressway N 快速干道 kuàisù gàndào

expulsion N 1 开除 kāichú, 驱逐 qūzhú 2 排出 páichū

exquisite ADJ 精美的 jīngměi de, 精致的 jīngzhì de

extend v 1 伸 shēn, 伸展 shēnzhǎn 2 延长 yáncháng
extended family 扩大式家庭 kuòdà shì jiātíng, 大家庭 dàjiātíng
3 提供 [+帮助] tígōng [+bāngzhù]

extension N 1 （电话）分机 (diànhuà) fēnjī, （电话）分机号码 (diànhuà) fēnjī hàomǎ 2 延期 yánqī 3 扩展 kuòzhǎn, 扩大 kuòdà
extension cord 电线延长线 diànxiàn yánchángxiàn
4 （大学）附设部 (dàxué) fùshèbù

extensive ADJ 1 广泛的 guǎngfàn de 2 大范围的 dà fànwéi de, 广大的 guǎngdà de

extent N 1 程度 chéngdù
to a certain/some extent 在一定程度上 zài yídìng chéngdùshang
2 范围 fànwéi

exterior I ADJ 外面的 wàimiàn de, 外部来的 wàibù láide II N 外部 wàibù, 外面 wàimiàn

external ADJ 外部的 wàibù de
(of medicine) for external use 外用药 wàiyòngyào

extinct ADJ 1 灭绝的 mièjué de, 灭种的 mièzhǒng de 2 熄灭了的 xīmièle de

extinction N 灭绝 mièjué, 灭种 mièzhǒng
on the brink of extinction 频临灭绝 pínlín mièjué
2 熄灭 xīmiè, 消灭 xiāomiè

extinguish v 灭灭 mièmiè, 消灭 xiāomiè

extol v 高度赞扬 gāodù zànyáng

extort v 敲诈勒索 qiāozhà lèsuǒ

extortion N 敲诈勒索 qiāozhà lèsuǒ

extra I ADJ 附加的 fùjiā de II ADV 特别 tèbié, 非常 fēicháng III N 1 外加的东西（如付款）wàijiā de dōngxi (rú fùkuǎn) 2 （报纸）号外 (bàozhǐ) hàowài 3 （电影）临时演员 (diànyǐng) línshí yǎnyuán

extract I v 拔出 báchū, 取出 qǔchū 2 提炼 tíliàn, 采榨 cǎijué 3 设法取得 shèfǎ qǔdé II N 1 提炼物 tíliànwù, 浓缩物 nóngsuōwù 2 摘录 zhāilù, 选段 xuǎnduàn [M. WD 段 duàn/篇 piān]

extraction N 1 提炼 tíliàn 2 血统 xuètǒng, 出身 chūshēn

extracurricular ADJ 课外的 kèwài de

extracurricular activities 课外活动 kèwài huódòng

extradite v 引渡 yǐndù

extraneous ADJ 不相关的 bù xiāngguān de, 无足轻重的 wúzú qīngzhòng de

extraordinary ADJ 1 非凡的 fēifán de, 极其出色的 jíqí chūsè de 2 很特别的 hěn tèbié de

extraterrestrial I ADJ 外星的 wàixīng de II N 外星生物 wàixīng shēngwù, 外星人 wàixīngrén

extravagant ADJ 奢侈豪华的 shēchǐ háohuá de, 挥霍无度的 huī huò wúdù de

extreme I ADJ 1 极端的 jíduān de, 极其 jíqí 2 极限的 jíxiàn de, 尽头的 jìntóu de II N 极端 jíduān

extremely ADV 极其 jíqí

extremities N 四肢 sìzhī, 手脚 shǒujiǎo

extricate v 解救 jiějiù

extrovert N 性格外向的人 xìnggé wàixiàng de rén

exuberance N 朝气 zhāoqì, 活力 huólì

exuberant ADJ 朝气蓬勃的 zhāoqì péngbó de, 精力旺盛的 jīnglì wàngshèng de

exude v 表现出 biǎoxiànchū 2 渗透出 shèntòuchū

exult v 欢欣鼓舞 huānxīn gǔwǔ

eye N 1 眼睛 yǎnjing 2 眼力 yǎnlì, 眼光 yǎnguāng
to have an eye for sth 对某事物有鉴赏能力 duì mǒu shìwù yǒu jiànshǎng nénglì
an eye for an eye, a tooth for a tooth 以眼还眼，以牙还牙 yǐ yǎn huán yǎn, yǐ yá huán yá

eyebrow N 眉毛 méimao [M. WD 条 tiáo]
to raise one's eyebrows 表示惊讶／反对 biǎoshì jīngyà/fǎnduì

eye-catching ADJ 醒目 xǐngmù, 令人注目 lìng rén zhùmù de

eye-opener N 使人大开眼界的事 shǐ rén dà kāi yǎnjiè de shì

eyeshadow N 眼影 yǎnyǐng

eyesight N 视力 shìlì

eyesore N 刺眼的东西 cìyǎn de dōngxi, 难看的事物 nánkàn de shìwù

eyewitness N 目击者 mùjīzhě

F

fable N 寓言（故事）yùyán (gùshi)

fabric N 布料 bùliào [M. WD 块 kuài]，织品 zhīpǐn [M. WD 件 jiàn]

fabricate V **1** 编造 [+故事] biānzào [+gùshi]，捏造 niēzào **2** 制造 [+部件] zhìzào [+bùjiàn]

fabulous ADJ **1** 极好的 jíhǎo de，好得不得了 hǎo dé bùdéliǎo **2** 巨大的 jùdà de，大得惊人的 dà dé jīngrén de

façade N **1** 表面 biǎomiàn，外表 wàibiǎo **2**（建筑物的）正面 (jiànzhùwù de) zhèngmiàn

face N **1** 脸 liǎn，面孔 miànkǒng **2** 表面 biǎomiàn
  face value 表面价值 biǎomiàn jiàzhí
  to lose face 丢脸 diūliǎn，丢面子 diū miànzi
  to pull a long face 拉长脸 lācháng liǎn，一脸不高兴的表情 yì liǎn bù gāoxìng de biǎoqíng
  II V **1** 面临 [+挑战] miànlín [+ tiǎozhàn]，面对 miànduì **2** 正视 [+现实] zhèngshì [+xiànshí]
  to face the music 接受批评 jiēshòu pīpíng
  to face up to 勇敢正视 [+困难的处境] yǒnggǎn zhèngshì [+kùnnan de chǔjìng]

Facebook N（网络通信）脸谱 (wǎngluò tōngxìn) liǎnpǔ

faceless ADJ 不受重视的 bú shòu zhòngshì de，没有趣味的 méiyǒu qùwèi de

facelift N **1** 面部拉皮手术 miànbù lāpí shǒushù **2** [建筑物+] 翻新 [jiànzhùwù+] fānxīn

facet N **1** 方面 fāngmiàn **2**（宝石的）琢面 (bǎoshí de) zhuómiàn

facial **I** ADJ 脸部的 liǎnbù de **II** N 面部美容 miànbù měiróng

facile ADJ **1** 肤浅的 fūqiǎn de，浅薄的 qiǎnbó de **2** 过于容易的 guòyú róngyì de **3** 未经认真考虑的 wèijīng rènzhēn kǎolǜ de，随便的 suíbiàn de

facilitate V 使…容易 shǐ…róngyì，便于 biànyú

facility N **1** 设施 shèshī **2** 才能 cáinéng

facsimile N **1** [文件+] 复制品 [wénjiàn+] fùzhìpǐn，[名画+] 摹本 [míng huà+] móběn **2** 传真 chuánzhēn

fact N 事实 shìshí
  a fact of life 现实 xiànshí
  the facts of life 性知识 xìng zhīshi
  in fact, as a matter of fact 事实上 shìshíshang

faction N 派别 pàibié，派系 pàixì

factor N 因素 yīnsù

factory N 工厂 gōngchǎng [M. WD 家 jiā/座 zuò]

factual ADJ 事实的 shìshí de，基于事实的 jīyú shìshí de

faculty N **1** 全体教师 quántǐ jiàoshī，师资 shīzī **2** 天生的能力 tiānshēng de nénglì
  the mental faculty 大脑功能 dànǎo gōngnéng，思维能力 sīwéi nénglì

fad N 短暂的时髦 duǎnzàn de shímáo，一时的风尚 yìshí de fēngshàng

fade V **1** [记忆+] 逐渐消失 [jìyì+] zhújiàn xiāoshī **2** [颜色+] 褪色 [yánsè+] tuìsè

Fahrenheit (ABBREV F) N 华氏温度 huáshì wēndù
  45° F 华氏42度 huáshì sìshìèr dù

fail **I** V **1** [努力+] 失败 [nǔlì+] shībài **2** 没有能 méiyǒu néng，未能 wèi néng **3** [考试+] 不及格 [kǎoshì+] bùjígé **4** [刹车+] 失灵 [shāchē+] shīlíng **5** [机器／人体器官+] 出毛病 [jīqì/réntǐ qìguān+] chūmáobing，失灵 shīlíng **6** [生意+] 倒闭 [shēngyì+] dǎobì **7** 使 [+人] 失望 shǐ [+rén] shīwàng **II** N (without fail) 必定 bìdìng，一定 yídìng

failing **I** N 缺点 quēdiǎn，弱点 ruòdiǎn **II** PREP 如果不行 rúguǒ bùxíng

failsafe ADJ **1** 配有安全保障装置的 pèiyǒu ānquán bǎozhàng zhuāngzhì de **2** 万无一失的 wànwú-yìshī de

failure N **1** 失败 shībài，倒闭 dǎobì **2** 没有能 méiyǒu néng **3** [考试+] 不及格 [kǎoshì+] bùjígé **4** 失灵 shīlíng **5** 失败者 shībàizhě

faint **I** ADJ 微弱的 wēiruò de **II** V 晕倒 yūndǎo **III** N 昏厥 hūnjué

fair **I** ADJ **1** 公正的 gōngzhèng de **2** 中等水平的 zhōngděng shuǐpíng de **3** 金黄

的（头发）jīnhuáng de (tóufa), 白皙的（肤色）báixī de (fūsè) **4** 晴朗的（天气）qínglǎng de (tiānqì) **II** ADV 公正地 gōngzhèng de, 公平地 gōngping de

fair and square 正大光明地 zhèngdà guāngmíng de

play fair 公平办事 gōngping bànshì

III N **1** 集市 jíshì **2** 交易会 jiāoyìhuì

job fair 职业招聘会 zhíyè zhāopìnhuì

trade fair 商品交易会 shāngpǐn jiāoyìhuì

3 博览会 bólǎnhuì

book fair 图书博览会 túshū bólǎnhuì

fairground N 露天游乐场 lùtiān yóulèchǎng, 露天集市 lùtiān jíshì

fairly ADV **1** 公正地 gōngzhèng de **2** 相当地 xiāngdāng de, 还不错 hái búcuò

fairy N 小仙子 xiǎoxiānzǐ, 小精灵 xiǎojīnglíng

fairy tale 童话 tónghuà, 童话故事 tónghuà gùshi

faith N **1** 极其信任 jíqí xìnrèn **2** 信仰 xìnyǎng **3** 宗教 zōngjiào

faithful ADJ **1** 忠诚的 zhōngchéng de **2** 准确可靠的 [+翻译] zhǔnquè kěkào de [+ fānyì]

faithless ADJ 不守信义的 bù shǒu xìnyì de, 不可依赖的 bùkě yīlài de

fake I N **1** 假货 jiǎhuò **2** 假冒者 jiǎmàozhě **II** ADJ 伪造的 wěizào de, 假冒的 jiǎmào de

a fake artwork 假冒艺术品 jiǎmào yìshùpǐn

III V 假装 jiǎzhuāng, 伪装 wěizhuāng

to fake one's signature 伪造某人的签名 wěizào mǒurén de qiānmíng

falcon N 猎鹰 lièyīng [M. WD 只 zhī]

fall¹ I N **1** 跌倒 diēdǎo, 摔倒 shuāidǎo **2** 下降 xiàjiàng, 下跌 xiàdiē

fall guy 替罪羊 tìzuìyáng

3 降雨量 jiàngyǔliàng **II** V (PT fell; PP fallen) **1** 跌倒 diēdǎo, 摔倒 shuāidǎo **2** 下降 xiàjiàng, 落下 luòxia

to fall short (of) 缺少 quēshǎo, 缺乏 quēfá

to fall through 未能成功 wèi néng chénggōng, 失败 shībài

fall² N 秋季 qiūjì, 秋天 qiūtian

fallacy N 谬论 miùlùn, 错误的看法 cuòwù de kànfa

fallen V See **fall¹**

fallible ADJ 会出错的 huì chūcuò de, 难免犯错误的 nánmiǎn fàn cuòwù de

fallout N **1** [核爆炸后的+] 放射性尘埃 [hébàozhà hòu de+] fàngshèxìng chén'āi **2** [金融危机的+] 不良后果 [jīnróng wēijī de+] bùliáng hòuguǒ

fallow ADJ **1** 休耕的 [+土地] xiūgēng de [+tǔdì] **2** 休闲的 [+人] xiūxián de [+rén]

falls N 瀑布 pùbù [M. WD 条 tiáo]

false ADJ **1** 错误的 cuòwù de

a false step 失足 shīzú, 出错 chūcuò **2** 假的 jiǎ de, 虚假的 xūjiǎ de

under false pretenses 以欺诈手段 yǐ qīzhà shǒuduàn

3 虚伪的 xūwěi de

false alarm 一场虚惊 yì cháng xūjīng

falsehood N 谎言 huǎngyán

falsify V 伪造 wěizào, 篡改 cuàngǎi

falter V **1** [勇气+] 变弱 [yǒngqì+] biàn ruò **2** [经济+] 衰退 [jīngjì+] shuāituì **3** 支支吾吾地说 zhīzhī wūwū de shuō

fame N 名气 míngqì, 名声 míngshēng

famed ADJ 有名的 yǒumíng de

familiar ADJ **1** 熟悉的 shúxi de, 精通的 jīngtōng de

to be familiar with 对…熟悉 duì… shúxi

2 随便的 suíbiàn de, 亲切的 qīnqiè de

familiarity N **1** 熟悉 shúxī, 精通 jīngtōng **2** 亲切 qīnqiè

family N **1** 家 jiā, 家庭 jiātíng

family tree 家谱图 jiāpǔtú

single-parent family 单亲家庭 dānqīn jiātíng

2 年幼的子女 niányòu de zǐnǚ, 孩子 háizi

family planning 计划生育 jìhuà shēngyù

3 亲人 qīnrén, 家人 jiārén

immediate family 直系亲属 zhíxì qīnzú

4 （动物／植物）科 (dòngwù/zhíwù) kē, （语言）语族 (yǔyán) yǔzú

famine N 饥荒 jīhuang

famished ADJ 饥饿的 jī'è de

famous ADJ 有名的 yǒumíng de, 著名的 zhùmíng de
to be famous for 因…而出名 yīn…ér chūmíng

fan¹ I N 1 扇子 shànzi [M. WD 把 bǎ] II V 扇 shàn, 扇动 shāndòng
to fan out 呈扇形散开 chéng shànxíng sànkāi

fan² N 热情崇拜者 rèqíng chóngbàizhě, …迷 …mí, 粉丝 fěnsī
fan club 追星俱乐部 zhuī xīng jùlèbù, 影迷会 yǐngmí huì
football fan 足球迷 zúqiúmí

fanatic N 狂热分子 kuángrè fènzi

fanciful ADJ 1 花哨的 [+装饰] huāshao de [+zhuāngshì] 2 空想的 [+念头] kōngxiǎng de [+niàntou]

fancy I ADJ 1 豪华的 [+汽车] háohuá de [+qìchē], 新潮的 xīncháo de 2 优质的 [+乳制品] yōuzhì de [+rǔzhìpǐn] 3 高难度的 [+舞蹈动作] gāonándù de [+wǔdǎo dòngzuò] II N 1 喜爱 xǐ'ài
to take a fancy to sb 喜欢上某人 xǐhuan shàng mǒurén
2 想象力 xiǎngxiànglì
a flight of fancy 幻想 huànxiǎng
III V 1 以为 yǐwéi, 错认为 cuò rènwéi
to fancy oneself 自以为 zì yǐwéi, 自认为是 zì rènwéi shì
2 喜爱 xǐ'ài

fanfare N 1 嘹亮的小号声 liáoliàng de xiǎohào shēng 2 大张声势 dà zhāng shēngshì

fang N（动物）尖牙 (dòngwù) jiānyá

fantasize V 幻想 huànxiǎng

fantastic ADJ 1 好极了 hǎo jí le, 太妙了 tài miào le 2 荒诞的 huāngdàn de, 古怪的 gǔguài de

FAQ (= frequently asked questions) AB-BREV 常问问题 chángwèn wèntí

far I ADV 1 远 yuǎn, 遥远 yáoyuǎn 2 比比…得多 yuǎn bǐ…de duō II ADJ 远 yuǎn, 遥远 yáoyuǎn
to be a far cry from 相差很远 xiāngchà hěn yuǎn
so far 到目前为止 dào mùqián wéizhǐ

faraway ADJ 遥远的 yáoyuǎn de

farce N 闹剧 nàojù

fare¹ N 1 [飞机、火车和长途汽车+] 票价 [fēijī、huǒchē hé chángtú qìchē+] piàojià 2 出租汽车乘客 chūzū qìchē chéngkè 3 膳食 shànshí, 食物 shíwù

fare² V 进展 jìnzhǎn
to fare well/badly 情况很好 / 很坏 qíngkuàng hěn hǎo/hěn huài

farewell N 告别 gàobié
farewell party 告别聚会 gàobié jùhuì, 告别宴会 gàobié yànhuì

far-fetched ADJ 牵强附会的 qiānqiǎng-fùhuì de

farm I N 农场 nóngchǎng II V 经营农场 jīngyíng nóngchǎng, 务农 wùnóng

farmer N 农场主 nóngchǎngzhǔ

farmhand N 农场工人 nóngchǎng gōngrén

farmyard N 农家院落 nóngjiā yuànluo

far-off ADJ 偏远的 piānyuǎn de

far-out ADJ 远离的 yuǎnlí de

far-reaching ADJ 深远的 shēnyuǎn de

far-sighted ADJ 目光远大的 mùguāngyuǎndà de

fart V 放屁 fàngpì

fascinating ADJ 让人着迷的 ràng rén zháomí de

fascination N 1 着迷 zháomí, 迷恋 míliàn 2 极大的吸引力 jídà de xīyǐnlì

fascist I N 法西斯分子 fǎxīsī fènzi II ADJ 法西斯的 fǎxīsī de

fashion I N 1 流行式样 liúxíng shìyàng, 风尚 fēngshàng 2 时装 shízhuāng
fashion show 时装表演 shízhuāng biǎoyǎn
II V 1 制作 zhìzuò 2 塑造 sùzào, 形成 xíngchéng

fashionable ADJ 流行的 liúxíng de, 时髦的 shímáo de

fast¹ I ADJ 快 kuài, 迅速 xùnsù
fast food 快餐 kuàicān
II ADV 1 快 kuài, 迅速 xùnsù
to fast forward 快进 kuài jìn
2 紧紧地 jǐnjǐn de
Not so fast! 慢点! Màn diǎn! 仔细点! Zǐxì diǎn!

fast asleep 熟睡 shúshuì

fast² I v 禁食 jìnshí, 斋戒 zhāijiè II n 禁食
（期）(qī), 斋戒 zhāijiè

fasten v 系上 [+安全带] jìshang [+ānquán
dài], 关紧（门／窗）guānjǐn (mén/
chuāng)

to fasten one's attention on sth 把注
意力集中在某事上 bǎ zhùyìlì jízhōng zài
mǒushì

fastener, fastening n 扣件 kòujiàn, 扣紧
物 kòujǐn wù

fastidious ADJ 过分讲究的 guòfènjiǎngjiū
de, 挑剔的 tiāoti de

fat I ADJ 胖 pàng

fat farm 减肥营 jiǎnféiyíng

II n 脂肪 zhīfáng, 肥肉 féiròu

fatal ADJ 1 致命的 [+错误] zhìmìng de
[+cuòwù] 2 毁灭性的 [+打击] huǐmièxìng
de [+dǎjī], 灾难性的 zāinànxìng de

fatalistic ADJ 宿命论的 sùmìnglùn de

fatality n 死亡（事件）sǐwáng (shìjiàn)

fate n 命运 mìngyùn

father n 1 父亲 fùqīn

father-in-law 岳父 yuèfù (wife's
father), 公公 gōnggong (husband's
father)

2 …之父 …zhī fù, 开创者 kāichuàngzhě
the father of one's country 国父
guófù

3（天主教）神父 (Tiānzhǔjiào) shénfu

father figure 父亲般的人物 fùqīn bān
de rénwù,（崇敬的）长者 (chóngjìng
de) zhǎngzhě

fatherly ADJ 父亲（般）的 fùqīn (bān) de

Father's Day n 父亲节 fùqīnjié

fathom v 彻底了解 chèdǐ liǎojiě, 完全看清
楚 wánquán kàn qīngchǔ

fatigue n 疲劳 píláo, 疲倦 píjuàn

fatten v 使…长肥 shǐ…zhǎng féi, 喂肥
wèiféi

fatty ADJ 高脂肪的 gāo zhīfáng de 2 肥
胖的 féipàng de

fatuous ADJ 愚昧的 yúmèi de, 昏庸的
hūnyōng de

faucet n 水龙头 shuǐlóngtóu, 开关龙
头 kāiguānzhě

fault n 1 过错 guòcuò 2 缺点 quēdiǎn

to find fault with 挑剔毛病 tiāoti
máobìng

3（地表的）断层 (dìbiǎo de) duàncéng

faulty ADJ 有毛病的 yǒu máobìng de
2 有缺点的 yǒu quēdiǎn de

fauna n 动物（群）dòngwù (qún)

favor n 1 善意的行为 shànyì de xíngwéi
2 赞成 zànchéng, 支持 zhīchí

in favor of 赞成 zànchéng, 同意 tóngyì

to find favor with sb 受到某人的喜爱
shòudào mǒurén de xǐ'ài

to curry favor with 奉承讨好 fèngcheng
tǎohǎo, 拍马屁 pāi mǎpì

II v 1 赞同 [+计划] zàntóng [+jìhuà], 支
持 zhīchí 2 偏爱 [+人] piān'ài [+rén]

the most favored nation 最惠国（待
遇）zuìhuìguó (dàiyù)

favorable ADJ 1 有利的 yǒulì de 2 优惠的
yōuhuì de 3 给人好印象的 gěi rén hǎo
yìnxiàng de

to make a favorable impression 给人
留下好印象 gěi rén liúxià hǎo yìnxiàng

favorite I ADJ 最喜爱的 zuì xǐ'ài de II n
1 最喜爱的人（或东西）zuì xǐ'ài de rén
(huò dōngxi), 宠儿 chǒng'ér 2 最有希望
获胜的人 zuì yǒu xīwàng huòshèng
de rén

fawn¹ v 巴结 bājie, 讨好 tǎohǎo

fawn² n 1 幼鹿 yòu lù [M. WD 头 tóu] 2 浅
黄褐色 qiǎnhuáng hèsè

fax I n (= fascimile) ABBREV 传真 chuánzhēn,
电传 diànchuán II v 电传 diànchuán
fax machine 传真机 chuánzhēnjī

faze v 使…窘迫 shǐ…jiǒngpò, 使…感到困
扰 shǐ…gǎndào kùnrǎo

FBI (= the Federal Bureau of Investigation) ABBREV （美国）联邦调查局
(Měiguó) Liánbāng Diàocájú

fear I v 1 怕 pà, 惧怕 jùpà, 恐怕 kǒngpà
2 担忧 dānyōu II n 怕 pà, 惧怕 jùpà

fearful ADJ 担心的 dānxīn de, 惧怕的
jùpà de

fearless ADJ 无畏的 wúwèi de, 无所惧怕
的 wú suǒ jùpà de

feasibility n 可行 kěxíng, 可行性 kěxíngxìng
feasibility study/report 可行性研究／
报告 kěxíngxìng yánjiū/bàogào

351

feasible ADJ 可行的 kěxíng de, 办得到的 bàndédào de

feast I N 宴会 yànhuì, 盛宴 shèngyàn II V 大吃大喝 dàchī dàhē, 尽情饱餐 jìnqíng bǎocān
to feast one's eye on 欣赏 [+美景／美色] xīnshǎng [+měijǐng/měisè]

feat N 事迹 shìjì

feather I N 羽毛 yǔmáo [M. WD 根 gēn]
Birds of a feather flock together. 物以类聚，人以群分。Wù yǐ lèi jù, rén yǐ qún fēn.
II V 长羽毛 zhǎng yǔmáo
to feather one's nest（通过不正当手段）致富（tōngguò bú zhèngdāng shǒuduàn）zhìfù, 敛财 liǎncái

feathery ADJ 羽毛状的 yǔmáozhuàng de

feature I N 1 特征 tèzhēng 2 容貌 róngmào 3（报纸杂志）特写报道 (bàozhǐ zázhì) tèxiě bàodào,（电视）特别报道 (diànshì) tèbié bàodào 4 故事片（电影）gùshìpiàn (diànyǐng) II V 1 由…主演 yóu…zhǔyǎn
a blockbuster movie featuring Kate Winslet 一部由凯特·温斯莱主演的大片 yí bù yóu Kǎitè·Wēnsīlái zhǔyǎn de dàpiàn
2 成为…的特色 chéngwéi…de tèsè 3 特别推介（商品）tèbié tuījiè (shāngpǐn)

February N 二月 èryuè

feces N 粪便 fènbiàn

fed V See fall

federal ADJ 联邦政府的 liánbāng zhèngfǔ de, 联邦的 liánbāng de

federation N 联盟 liánméng, 联合会 liánhéhuì

fed up ADJ 厌烦的 yànfán de, 受够了的 shòu gòu le de

fee N 费 fèi, 费用 fèiyòng
annual fee 年费 niánfèi
legal fee 律师费 lǜshīfèi

feeble ADJ 微弱的 wēiruò de, 菲薄的 fěibó de

feeble-minded ADJ 思维不清的 sīwéi bùqīng de, 弱智的 ruòzhì de

feed I V (PT & PP **fed**) 喂 wèi II N 1（动物）饲料 (dòngwù) sìliào

chicken feed 鸡饲料 jī sìliào
2 燃料输送管 ránliào shūsòng guǎn, 进料管 jìnliào guǎn

feedback N 反馈 fǎnkuì

feeding N 喂奶 wèinǎi

feel I V (PT & PP **felt**) 1 感觉 gǎnjué 2 感到 gǎndào 3 摸 mō, 抚摸 fǔmō
to feel like 觉得 juéde, 感到 gǎndào
II N 感觉 gǎnjué, 感受 gǎnshòu
to get a feel for sth 对某事有感受 duì mǒushì yǒu gǎnshòu, 对某事有所了解 duì mǒushì yǒusuǒ liǎojiě
to get the feel of sth 适应某事物 shìyìng mǒushìwù

feeler N 1 试探 shìtàn 2 [昆虫的+] 触须 [kūnchóng de+] chùxū, 触角 chùjiǎo
to put out feelers 进行试探 jìnxíng shìtàn

feeling N 1 感情 gǎnqíng 2 感觉 gǎnjué
to hurt sb's feelings 伤害感情 shānghài gǎnqíng
to put one's feelings into words 用语言表达感情 yòngyǔ yán biǎodá gǎnqíng
3 预感 yùgǎn
to have a feeling that ... 有…的预感 yǒu…de yùgǎn

feign V 假装 jiǎzhuāng, 装出 zhuāngchū

feint V（拳击）佯攻 (quánjī) yánggōng, 虚晃一拳 xū huǎng yì quán

feisty ADJ 1 精力充沛的 jīnglì chōngpèi de 2 勇于争辩的 yǒngyú zhēngbiàn de, 好斗的 hào dòu de

feline ADJ 猫科的 māo kē de, 猫的 māo de II N 猫科动物 māo kē dòngwù, 猫 māo [M. WD 只 zhī]

fell[1] v See fall[1]

fell[2] v 砍伐（树木）kǎnfá (shùmù)

fellow N 1 人 rén, 男人 nánrén 2 研究生奖学金获得者 yánjiūshēng jiǎngxuéjīn huòdézhě, 学者 xuézhě 3 [学会的+] 会员 [xuéhuì de+] huìyuán

fellowship N 1 研究生奖学金 yánjiūshēng jiǎngxuéjīn 2（基督教）团契 (Jīdūjiào) tuánqì 3 友情 yǒuqíng

felon N 重罪犯 zhòngzuì fàn

felony N 重罪 zhòngzuì

felt[1] V See feel II N 毛毡 máozhān

felt tip pen 毡头笔 zhān tóu bǐ

female I ADJ 1（动物/鸟类）雌的（dòngwù/niǎolèi）cí de, 母的 mǔ de **2**（人）女的（rén）nǚ de, 女性的 nǚxìng de **II N 1** 女人 nǚrén, 女子 nǚzǐ **2** 雌性动物 cíxìng dòngwù, 母动物 mǔ dòngwù

feminine ADJ 女性的 nǚxìng de

feminist N 女权主义者 nǚquánzhǔyì zhě

fence I N 栅栏 zhàlan, 篱笆 líba
Good fences make good neighbors. 栅栏牢，邻居好。Zhàlan láo, línjū hǎo. **II v 1** 用栅栏（篱笆）围起来 yòng zhàlan (líba) wéi qǐlái **2** 击剑 jījiàn

fencing N 击剑（运动）jījiàn (yùndòng)

fend v 抵挡 dǐdǎng
to fend for oneself 独立谋生 dúlì móushēng, 照料自己 zhàoliào zìjǐ

fender N 挡泥板 dǎngníbǎn, 翼板 yì bǎn

ferment I v 发酵 fājiào **II N** 骚动 sāodòng, 动乱 dòngluàn

fern N 蕨类植物 juélèizhíwù

ferocious ADJ 凶猛的 xiōngměng de, 狂暴的 kuángbào de

ferret I v 搜查找出 sōuchá zhǎochū **II N** 雪貂 xuě diāo [M. WD 只 zhī]

ferry I N 渡轮 dùlún [M. WD 艘 sōu] **II v**（用渡轮、直升飞机等）运送 (yòng dùlún, zhíshēng fēijī děng) yùnsòng, 摆渡 bǎidù

fertile ADJ 1 肥沃的 [+土地] féiwò de [+tǔdì] **2** 能生育的 [+妇女] néng shēngyù de [+fùnǚ] **3** 丰富的 [+想象力] fēngfù de [+xiǎngxiànglì]

fertilizer N 肥料 féiliào

fervent ADJ 强烈的 qiángliè de, 真诚的 zhēnchéng de

fervor N 激情 jīqíng, 热情 rèqíng

fester v 1 [关系+] 越来越糟 [guānxi +] yuèláiyuè zāo, 恶化 èhuà **2** [伤口+] 溃烂 [shāngkǒu+] kuìlàn **3** [垃圾+] 腐烂发臭 [lājī+] fǔlàn fāchòu

festival N 节 jié, 节日 jiérì

festive ADJ 喜庆的 xǐqìng de, 节日的 jiérì de

fetal ADJ 胎儿的 tāi'ér de
a fetal position 胎儿的姿势 tāi'ér de zìshì, 胎位 tāiwèi

fetch v 1 拿来 nálái, 接来 jiēlái **2** 卖到 màidào

fete I v 致敬 zhìjìng **II N** 庆祝活动 qìngzhù huódòng

fetid ADJ 恶臭的 èchòu de

fetish N 迷恋 míliàn, 恋物癖 liànwùpǐ
foot fetish 恋脚癖 liànjiǎopǐ

fetter v 束缚 shùfù

fetters N 束缚 shùfù, 桎梏 zhìgù

fetus N 胎儿 tāi'ér, 胚胎 pēitāi

feud N 长期的纠纷 chángqī de jiūfēn, 怨仇 yuànchóu

feudal ADJ 封建（制度）的 fēngjiàn (zhìdù) de

fever N 1 发烧 fāshāo **2** 狂热 kuángrè, 极度兴奋 jídù xīngfèn

feverish ADJ 1 发烧的 fāshāo de **2** 极度兴奋的 jídù xīngfèn de

few I ADJ 很少 hěn shǎo, 不多 bù duō **II PRON** 一些 yìxiē, 不多 bù duō
a few 有些 yǒuxiē

fiancé N 未婚夫 wèihūnfū

fiancée N 未婚妻 wèihūnqī

fiasco N 惨败 cǎnbài, 大败 dàbài

fiat N 法令 fǎlìng, 命令 mìnglìng

fib I N 无关紧要的谎言 wúguān jǐnyào de huǎngyán, 小谎话 xiǎo huǎnghuà **II v** 撒小谎 sā xiǎo huǎng

fiber N 纤维 xiānwéi
fiber optics 光纤通讯 guāngxiāntōngxùn

fiberglass N 纤维玻璃 xiānwéi bōli

fibrous ADJ 多纤维的 duō xiānwéi de

fickle ADJ 经常变化的 jīngcháng biànhuà de, 变化无常的 biànhuàwúcháng de

fiction N 小说 xiǎoshuō [M. WD 本 běn], 虚构作品 xūgòu zuòpǐn [M. WD 本 běn]

fictional ADJ 小说的 xiǎoshuō de

fictitious ADJ 虚构的 xūgòu de

fiddle I v 1 [手指+] 拨弄 [shǒuzhǐ+] bōnòng **2** 拉小提琴 lā xiǎotíqín **II N** 小提琴 xiǎotíqín [M. WD 把 bǎ]

fidelity N 1 [夫妻+] 忠贞 [fūqī zhījiān+] zhōngzhēn, 忠诚 zhōngchéng **2** [音响设备+] 保真（度）[yīnxiǎng shèbèi+] bǎozhēn (dù)

fidget v 手脚不停地动 shǒujiǎo bùtíngde dòng, 坐立不安 zuòlì bù'ān

field I N 1 田 tián, 农田 nóngtián [M. WD 片 piàn] 2 场地 chǎngdì [M. WD 块 kuài]
field day ① 体育活动日 tǐyù huódòng rì ② 大显身手的时机 dàxiǎn shēnshǒu de shíjī
football field 足球场 zúqiúchǎng
field event 田赛项目 tiánsài xiàngmù
field test 现场试验 xiànchǎng shìyàn
field trip（学生）实地考察 (xuésheng) shídì kǎochá
magnetic field 磁场 cíchǎng
II v 1 回答（难题）huídá (nántí) 2 接球 jiē qiú

fielder N（棒球）守场员 (bàngqiú) shǒuchǎngyuán

fieldwork N 实地考察 shídì kǎochá, 野外调查 yěwài diàochá

fiend N 恶魔 èmó
dope fiend 吸毒者 xīdúzhě
sex fiend 色情狂 sèqíngkuáng

fiendish ADJ 恶魔似的 èmó shìde, 极其可怕的 jíqí kěpà de

fierce ADJ 1 凶猛 xiōngměng 2 激烈 jīliè

fiery ADJ 1 燃烧的 ránshāo de, 着火的 zháohuǒ de 2 火辣辣的 huǒlàlà de, 火热的 huǒrè de 3 激情燃烧的 jīqíng ránshāo de

fiesta N 节日 jiérì, 喜庆日 xǐqìngrì 2 宗教节日 zōngjiào jiérì

fifteen NUM 十五 shíwǔ, 15

fifth NUM 第五 dì wǔ

fifty NUM 五十 wǔshí, 50

fifty-fifty I ADJ 平分的 píngfēn de, 一半一半的 yíbàn yíbàn de II ADV 一半对一半 yíbàn duì yíbàn, 对半 duìbàn

fig N 无花果 wúhuāguǒ

fight I v (PT & PP **fought**) 1 战斗 zhàndòu 2 打架 dǎjià, 争吵 zhēngchǎo 3 奋斗 fèndòu II N 1 打架 dǎjià 2 吵架 chǎojià, 争吵 zhēngchǎo

fighter N [自由+] 斗士 [zìyóu+] dòushì 2 [职业+] 拳击手 [zhíyè+] quánjīshǒu 3 [空军+] 战斗机 [kōngjūn+] zhàndòujī

figment N 凭空想象出来的事物 píngkōng xiǎngxiàng chūlái de shìwù
a figment of one's imagination 凭空想象出来的事物 píngkōng xiǎngxiàng

figure I N 1 身材 shēncái 2 数字 shùzì 3 人物 rénwù, 人士 rénshì II v 1 崭露头角 zhǎnlù tóujiǎo 2 计算 jìsuàn

figurehead N 有名无实的领袖 yǒu míng wú shí de lǐngxiù

figure of speech N 比喻 bǐyù

filch v 小偷小摸 xiǎotōu xiǎomō

file I N 1 档案 dàng'àn 2 档案计算机 dàng'àn (jìsuànjī), 文件 wénjiàn
back-up file 储备文件 chǔbèi wénjiàn
3 锉刀 cuòdāo
nail file 指甲刀 zhǐjiǎdāo
II v 1 正式立案 zhèngshì lì'àn
to file a divorce 正式提出离婚 zhèngshì tíchū líhūn
2 (to file away) 把…存档 bǎ...cúndàng
3 锉（平）cuò (píng)

filet, fillet N（去骨的）肉片 / 鱼片 (qù gǔ de) ròupiàn/yúpiàn

filigree N 金银丝饰品 jīnyínsī shìpǐn

filing v 存档 cúndàng, 归档 guīdàng

fill v 1 装满 zhuāngmǎn, 倒满 dàomǎn
to fill out a form 填表 tiánbiǎo
II N 充分 chōngfèn, 足够 zúgòu
to eat one's fill 吃得饱饱的 chī dé bǎo-bǎo de, 吃得心满意足 chī dé xīnmǎn yìzú

filling I N 1 [补牙的] 填料 [bǔ yá de+] tiánliào, 填补物 tiánbǔ wù 2 [食品+] 馅心 [shípǐn+] xiàn xīn, 馅 xiàn II ADJ 使人吃得饱饱的 shǐ rén chī dé bǎobǎo de

filly N 小母马 xiǎo mǔmǎ [M. WD 匹 pǐ]

film I N 1 胶卷 jiāojuǎn [M. WD 卷 juǎn] 2 电影 diànyǐng [M. WD 部 bù] 3 薄膜 bómó, 薄层 báo céng II v 拍摄 pāishè

filmmaker N 电影导演 diànyǐng dǎoyǎn, 电影制片人 diànyǐng zhìpiànrén

filmstrip N 幻灯片 huàndēngpiàn

filter I N 1 过滤器 guòlǜqì, 漏斗 lòudǒu 2（照相机）滤色镜 (zhàoxiàngjī) lǜsèjìng II v 过滤 guòlǜ

filth N 脏东西 zàng dōngxi, 污秽 wūhuì

filthy ADJ 极其肮脏 jíqí āngzāng, 污秽不堪 wūhuìbùkān

fin N 鱼鳍 yúqí 2（飞机）垂直尾翼 (fēijī) chuízhí wěiyì

shark's fin soup 鱼翅汤 yúchìtāng

final I ADJ 最终的 zuìzhōng de, 最后 的 zuìhòu de **II** N **1** 期终考试 qīzhōng kǎoshì, 大考 dàkǎo **2** 决赛 juésài

finale N [歌剧+] 最后一幕 [gējù+] zuìhòu yímù, [交响乐+] 终曲 [jiāoxiǎngyuè+] zhōngqǔ

finalist N 决赛选手 juésài xuǎnshǒu

finalize V 最后定下 zuìhòu dìngxià, 确定 quèdìng

finally ADV 终于 zhōngyú, 最终 zuìzhōng

finance I N **1** 财务 cáiwù, 财政 cáizhèng
corporate finance 公司财政 gōngsī cáizhèng
2 金融 jīnróng
finance company 金融公司 jīnróng gōngsī, 信贷公司 xìndài gōngsī
3 款项 kuǎnxiàng, 钱 qián **II** V 为…提供 资金 wéi…tígōng zījīn, 出资 chūzī

finances N **1** [公司+] 资金 [gōngsī+] zījīn **2** 财务管理 cáiwù guǎnlǐ

financial ADJ 财务的 cáiwù de
financial aid 助学金 zhùxuéjīn, 助学贷 款 zhùxué dàikuǎn [M. WD 份 fèn/笔 bǐ]

finch N 雀科鸟类 què kē niǎolèi, 雀 què

find I V (PT & PP found) **1** 找到 zhǎodao **2** 发现 fāxiàn
to find out 发现 fāxiàn
3 觉得 juéde **II** N 被发现的东西 bèi fāxiàn de dōngxi
an archeological find 考古发现 kǎogǔ fāxiàn, 出土文物 chū tǔ wénwù

finding N **1** 调查（研究）结果 diàochá (yánjiū) jiéguǒ **2** 发现 fāxiàn

fine¹ ADJ **1** 美好的 měihǎo de, 极好的 jíhǎo de **2** 晴朗的 [+天气] qínglǎng de [+tiānqì] **3** 健康的 [+身体] jiànkāng de [+shēntǐ], 身体好的 shēntǐ hǎo de **4** 细 微的 xìwēi de
a fine line 极细微的差别 jí xìwēi de chābié
not to put too fine a point on 说得不 客气一点 shuó de bú kèqi yìdiǎn

fine² I V 对…罚款 duì…fákuǎn
to be fined for speeding 因超速驾车而 被罚款 yīn chāosù jiàchē ér bèi fákuǎn **II** N 罚款 fákuǎn, 罚金 fájīn

finesse I N 技巧 jìqiǎo **II** V 巧妙而略 带欺骗性地处理 qiǎomiào ér lüè dài qīpiànxìng de chǔlǐ

finger I N 手指 shǒuzhǐ
index finger 食指 shízhǐ
middle finger 中指 zhōngzhǐ
ring finger 无名指 wúmíngzhǐ
small finger 小指 xiǎozhǐ
II V 用手指触摸 yòng shǒuzhǐ chùmō

fingernail N 指甲 zhǐjia

fingerprint N 指纹 zhǐwén

fingertip N 指尖 zhǐjiān
to have sth at one's fingertips 随时可 供使用 suíshí kěgōng shǐyòng

finicky ADJ 爱挑剔的 ài tiāoti de

finish I V **1** 结束 jiéshù **2** 完成 wánchéng, …完…wán **3** 获得名次 huòdé míngcì **II** N **1** 结果 jiéguǒ **2** 光洁度 guāngjiédù
finish line 终点线 zhōngdiǎnxiàn

finite ADJ 有限制的 yǒuxiàn zhì de, 有限 的 yǒuxiàn de

fir N 冷杉 lěngshān [M. WD 棵 kē]

fire I N **1** 火 huǒ
to catch fire 着火 zháohuǒ
2 火灾 huǒzāi [M. WD 场 cháng]
fire alarm 火警报警器 huǒjǐng bàojǐngqì
fire department 消防队 xiāofángduì
fire drill 防火演习 fánghuǒ yǎnxí
fire fighter 消防员 xiāofángyuán
fire hydrant 消防龙头 xiāofánglóngtóu
to open fire 开枪 kāiqiāng
II V **1** 开枪 kāiqiāng **2** 解雇 jiěgù **3** 使… 激动 shǐ…jīdòng, 激励 jīlì

firearm N 枪支 qiāngzhī

firebrand N 煽动暴乱者 shāndòng bàoluàn zhě

firecracker N 爆竹 bàozhú, 鞭炮 biānpào

firefly N 萤火虫 yínghuǒchóng [M. WD 只 zhī]

fireplace N 壁炉 bìlú

fireproof ADJ 防火的 fánghuǒ de, 耐火 的 nàihuǒ de

firewall N 防火墙 fánghuǒqiáng

fireworks N 焰火 yànhuǒ

firing line N 火线 huǒxiàn, 前线 qiánxiàn
to be on the firing line 处在受到攻击

的地位 chǔzài shòudào gōngjī de dìwèi,
首当其冲 shǒudāngqíchōng

firing squad N 行刑队 xíngxíngduì

firm I ADJ 1 坚固的 jiāngù de, 结实的
jiēshi de 2 坚定的 jiāndìng de **II** N 商
行 shānghángh [M. WD 家 jiā], 事务所
shìwùsuǒ, 公司 gōngsī [M. WD 家 jiā]
law firm 法律事务所 fǎlǜ shìwùsuǒ

first I PRON, ADJ 第一 dìyī, 最早 zuìzǎo
first aid 急救 jíjiù
first class 头等舱 tóuděngcāng, 第一类
邮件 dìyī lèi yóujiàn
first lady 第一夫人 dìyī fūrén, 总统夫人
zǒngtǒng fūrén
first name 名字 míngzì, 名 míng
first person 第一人称 dìyī rénchēng
first things first 重要的事先做 zhòngyào
de shì xiān zuò
love at first sight 一见钟情 yíjiàn
zhōngqíng
II ADV 第一 dìyī, 首先 shǒuxiān
at first 起先 qǐ xiān, 刚开始 gāng kāishǐ
first of all 首先 shǒuxiān

firsthand ADJ, ADV 第一手 dìyīshǒu

firstly ADV 第一 dìyī, 首先 shǒuxiān

fiscal ADJ 财政的 cáizhèng de
fiscal year 财务年度 cáiwù niándù, 会计
年度 kuàijì niándù

fish I N 鱼 yú [M. WD 条 tiáo] **II** V 捕鱼
bǔyú, 钓鱼 diàoyú

fisherman N 钓鱼者 diàoyúzhě, 渔民
yúmín

fishery N 渔场 yúchǎng

fishing N 钓鱼 diàoyú, 捕鱼 bǔyú
fishing rod 钓鱼竿 diàoyúgān

fishy ADJ 1 鱼腥气的 yú xīngqì de 2 可疑
的 kěyí de

fission N（原子）裂变 (yuánzǐ) lièbiàn

fissure N 裂缝 lièfèng

fist N 拳头 quántou, 拳 quán

fit I ADJ 1 合适 héshì 2 健康 jiànkāng,
身体好 shēntǐ hǎo **II** V 1 （PT & PP fit,
fitted）合身 héshēn 2 适合 [+心意]
shìhé [+xīnyì] 3 安装 [+家具] ānzhuāng
[+jiājù], 组装 zǔzhuāng **III** N 1 发脾气
fāpíqì
to throw a fit 大发脾气 dàfā píqì

2 （病或强烈感情）发作 (bìng huò
qiángliè gǎnqíng) fāzuò
fits of laughter 一阵阵大笑 yí zhèn
zhèn dàxiào
3 (a good fit) 适合 shìhé

fitful ADJ 一阵阵的 yízhèn zhèn de

fitness N 健康 jiànkāng, 身体好 shēntǐ
hǎo

fitting I ADJ 合适的 héshì de, 恰当的
qiàdàng de **II** N 1 试穿 shìchuān
fitting room 试衣间 shìyījiān
2 装置 zhuāngzhì

five NUM 五 wǔ, 5

fix I V 1 修理 xiūlǐ 2 准备 zhǔnbèi
to fix a meal 准备一顿饭 zhǔnbèi yídùn
fàn, 做饭 zuòfàn
3 确定 quèdìng 4 操纵 [+比赛] cāozòng
[+bǐsài] **II** N 1 困境 kùnjìng
to be in a fix 处于困境 chǔyú kùnjìng
2 毒品 dúpǐn, 上瘾的东西 shàngyǐn de
dōngxi 3 受到非法操纵的事 shòudào
fēifǎ cāozòng de shì

fixation N 过分的兴趣 guòfèn de xìngqu,
偏爱 piān'ài

fixed ADJ 固定的 gùdìng de
to have fixed ideas 抱有固执的想法
bàoyǒu gùzhí de xiǎngfǎ

fixture N 1 固定装置 gùdìng zhuāngzhì
2 一直在的东西／节目 yīzhí zài de
dōngxi/jiémù, 不会离去的东西 bú huì
líqù de dōngxi

fizz N [饮料的+] 泡沫 [yǐnliào de+] pàomò

fizzle V 最终失败 zuìzhōng shībài

fjord N 峡湾 xiáwān

flab N 松弛的赘肉 sōngchí de zhuìròu

flabbergasted ADJ 大吃一惊的 dàchī-
yìjīng de

flabby ADJ 1 松弛的（肌肉）sōngchí de (jīròu)
2 无力的（争辩）wúlì de (zhēngbiàn)

flaccid ADJ 软弱的 ruǎnruò de, 松软的
sōngruǎn de

flag I N 旗 qí, 旗子 qízi **II** V 1 标出 [+重要
部分] biāo chū [+zhòngyào bùfen], 标
志 biāozhì 2 [经济+] 变得疲软 [+jīngjì]
biàn de píruǎn 3 (to flag down) 招手要
[+出租汽车] 停下 zhāoshǒu yào [+chūzū
qìchē] tíng xià

flagpole N 旗杆 qígān [M. WD 根 gēn]

flagship N 旗舰 qíjiàn 2 标志性／最佳产品 biāozhìxìng/zuìjiā chǎnpǐn

flagstone N 石板 shíbǎn

flail V 挥动 [+手臂或腿] huīdòng [+shǒubì huò tuǐ]

flair N 天赋 tiānfù, 天分 tiānfèn

flak N 强烈的批评 qiángliè de pīpíng

flake I N 1 小薄片 xiǎo báopiàn 2 健忘而古怪的人 jiànwàng ér gǔguài de rén II V 1 碎成小片 suì chéng xiǎopiàn 2 剥落 bōluò

flamboyant ADJ 1 炫耀的 xuànyào de, 卖弄的 màinong de 2（色彩）艳丽的 (sècǎi) yànlì de

flame I N 1 火焰 huǒ, 火焰 huǒyàn 2 欲火 yùhuǒ, 情欲 qíngyù
old flame 往日情人 wǎngrì qíngrén
II V 变成火红色 biànchéng huǒhóngsè

flaming ADJ 1 熊熊燃烧的 [+大火] xióngxióng ránshāo de [+dàhuǒ] 2 火红的 [+落日] huǒhóng de [+luòrì], 光亮的 guāngliàng de

flamingo N 火烈鸟 huǒlièniǎo

flammable ADJ 易燃的 yìrán de

flank I N 侧翼 cèyì, 侧面 cèmiàn II V 在…的侧翼 zài…de cèyì
to be flanked by 两边有 liǎngbiān yǒu, 两边是 liǎngbiān shì

flap I V 1 [鸟+] 拍动 [+翅膀] [niǎo+] pāidòng [+chìbǎng] 2 [旗+] 呼啦啦地拍动 [qí+] hūlālā de pāi dòng II N 1（信封）封盖口 (xìnfēng) fēng gài kǒu 2 激动不安 jīdòng bù'ān, 慌乱 huāngluàn

flare I V [火+] 突然烧旺 [huǒ+] tūrán shāo wàng
to flare up 突然大怒 tūrán dà nù, 突然狂暴起来 tūrán kuángbào qǐlái
II N 闪光信号 shǎnguāng xìnhào, 闪光灯 shǎnguāngdēng

flare-up N 突然爆发 tūrán bàofā

flash I V 1 闪光 shǎnguāng 2 迅速传送 [+消息] xùnsù chuánsòng [+xiāoxi] 3 [汽车+] 飞驰 [qìchē+] fēichí II N 闪光 shǎnguāng [M. WD 道 dào]

flashback N 1 倒叙 dàoxù 2 往事突然重现 wǎngshì tūrán chóngxiàn

flashcard N 识图卡 shítúkǎ, 识字卡 shízìkǎ

flasher N 露阴狂 lùyīnkuáng

flashlight N 电筒 diàntǒng, 手电筒 shǒudiàntǒng

flask N 1 扁酒瓶 biǎn jiǔpíng 2 烧瓶 shāopíng

flat I ADJ 1 平坦 píngtǎn 2 没有气的 [+轮胎／球等] méiyǒu qì de [+lúntāi/qiú děng] 3 走了气的 [+饮料] zǒu le qì de [+yǐnliào] 4 偏低的 [+音乐] piāndī de [+yīnyuè] 5 萧条的 [+经济] xiāotiáo de [+jīngjì], 不景气的 bùjǐngqì de 6 固定的 [+价格] gùdìng de [+jiàgé] 7（音乐）降半音 (yīnyuè) jiàng bànyīn
E flat 降 E 调 jiàng E tiáo
II N 1 漏气的轮胎 lòuqì de lúntāi, 瘪胎 biě tāi 2 降半音符号 jiàng bànyīn fúhào (♩) III ADV 1 平坦地 píngtǎn de 2 (to fall flat) [笑话+] 不好笑 [xiàohua+] bùhǎo xiào, 完全失败 wánquán shībài

flatten V 把…弄平 bǎ…nòng píng

flatter V 1 恭维 gōngwéi, 讨好 tǎohǎo 2 胜过 [+真人] shèngguò [+zhēnrén]

flattery N 恭维 gōngwéi, 奉承 fèngcheng

flatulence N [胃肠+] 气涨的 [wèicháng+] qì zhǎng de

flaunt V 炫耀 xuànyào, 夸耀 kuāyào

flavor I N 1 [冰淇淋+] 味道 [bīngqílín de+] wèidao, 味 wèi 2 [地中海的+] 风味 [Dìzhōnghǎi de+] fēngwèi, 情调 qíngdiào II V 对…加味 duì…jiā wèi

flavoring N 调味品 tiáowèipǐn

flaw N 缺陷 quēxiàn, 缺点 quēdiǎn

flawed ADJ 有缺陷的 yǒu quēxiàn de, 错误的 cuòwù de

flawless ADJ 没有缺点的 méiyǒu quēdiǎn de, 无瑕的 wúxiá de, 完美的 wánměi de

flax N 亚麻 yàmá

flea N 跳蚤 tiàozǎo [M. WD 只 zhī]
flea collar 驱蚤项圈 qū zǎo xiàngquān
flea market 旧货市场 jiùhuò shìchǎng

fleck N 斑点 bāndiǎn

fled V See flee

fledgling I ADJ 新生的 xīnshēng de II N（刚学飞的）小鸟 (gāng xué fēi de) xiǎoniǎo

flee (PT & PP **fled**) v 逃走 táozǒu, 逃掉 táodiào

fleece I N 羊毛 yángmáo, 羊皮 yángpí II v 向 [+用户] 过多收费 xiàng [+yònghù] guòduō shōufèi, 榨取 zhàqǔ

fleet N 舰队 jiànduì, 船队 chuánduì, (汽）车队 (qì) chēduì

fleeting ADJ 极其短暂的 jíqí duǎnzàn de

flesh I N 肉 ròu
one's own flesh and blood 亲骨肉 qīngǔròu, 亲人 qīnrén
II v 使…长肉 shǐ...zhǎngròu
to flesh out 使…更生动 shǐ...gèng shēngdòng, 使…更丰富 shǐ...gèng fēngfù

fleshy ADJ 肉体的 ròutǐ de, 肉欲的 ròuyù de

flew v See fly[1]

flex v 收紧 (肌肉) shōujǐn (jīròu)
to flex one's muscle 展示实力 zhǎnshì shílì

flexibility N 灵活性 línghuóxìng

flexible ADJ 1 灵活的 [+安排] línghuó de [+ānpái], 有弹性的 yǒu tánxìng de 2 易弯曲的 yì wānqū de, 柔软的 róuruǎn de

flextime N 弹性工作时间 tánxìng gōngzuò shíjiān

flick I v 弹去 tán qù, 弹 tán II N 1 弹 tán 2 动作片 dòngzuò piàn

flicker I v 1 [火+] 闪烁 [huǒ+] shǎnshuò 2 [表情+] 闪现 [biǎoqíng+] shǎnxiàn II N 闪烁 shǎnshuò

flier, flyer N 1 广告纸 guǎnggàozhǐ 2 飞行员 fēixíngyuán

flight N 1 飞行 fēixíng 2 航班 hángbān
night flight 夜间飞行 yèjiān fēixíng
non-stop flight 直航 zhíháng
3 一段楼梯 yí duàn lóutī 4 逃跑 táopǎo

flighty ADJ 反复无常的 fǎnfù wúcháng de, 见异思迁的 jiàn yì sī qiān de

filmsy ADJ 1 轻薄的 [+衣服] qīngbáo de [+yīfú] 2 不牢固的 [房屋／设备+] bù láogù de [fángwū/shèbèi+], 简陋 jiǎnlòu de 3 不可靠的 [论点+] bùkěkào de [lùndiǎn+]

flinch v 1 退缩 tuìsuō 2 回避 huíbì

fling I v (PT & PP **flung**) 抛 [+球] pāo [+qiú], 扔 rēng

to fling oneself 扑 pū, 冲 chōng
II N 一时的放纵 yìshí de fàngzòng, 一段风流情 yí duàn fēngliúqíng

flint N 火石 huǒshí [M. WD 块 kuài]

flip I v 1 翻转 fānzhuǎn, 翻过来 fānguolái 2 旋转 xuánzhuǎn
to flip out 突然大发脾气 tūrán dàfā píqí
to flip a coin 抛硬币（来决定）pāo yìngbì (lái juédìng)
II N 筋斗 jīndǒu, 空翻 kōngfān
a backward flip 后空翻 hòukōngfān
(decided by) a flip of the coin 由抛硬币来决定 yóu pāo yìngbì lái juédìng
III ADJ 轻率的 qīngshuài de

flippant ADJ 轻率的 qīngshuài de, 轻佻的 qīngtiāo de

flipper N （游泳用）鸭脚板 (yóuyǒng yòng) yājiǎobǎn

flirt I v 调情 tiáoqíng
to flirt with (danger) 轻率地对待 qīngshuài de duìdài
II N 调情者 tiáoqíngzhě

flirtation N 1 调情 tiáoqíng 2 一时的兴趣 yìshí de xìngqu

flirtatious ADJ 爱调情的 ài tiáoqíng de

float I v 1 漂浮 piāofú 2 飘飘 piāopiāo 3 提出（建议）tíchū (jiànyì) 4 浮动（货币）fúdòng (huòbì) II N 1 花车 huāchē 2 备用零钱 bèiyòng língqián

flock I N 一群鸟 yì qún niǎo, 一群羊 yì qún yáng II v 成群结队地前往 chéngqún jiéduì de qiánwǎng

flog v 1 鞭打 biāndǎ, 棒打 bàngdǎ 2 出售 chūshòu, 卖 mài

flogging N 鞭打 biāndǎ, 棒打 bàngdǎ

flood I v 淹没 yānmò II N 洪水 hóngshuǐ, 水灾 shuǐzāi

floodgate N 防洪闸 fánghóng zhá

floodlight N 泛光灯 fànguāngdēng, 探照灯 tànzhàodēng [M. WD 台 tái]

floor I N 1 地板 dìbǎn
floor lamp 落地台灯 luòdì táidēng
2 （楼房）层 (lóufáng) céng, 楼层 lóu céng
floor plan 楼层平面图 lóucéng píngmiàntú
to take the floor （在重要会议上）开始发言 (zài zhòngyào huìyì shàng) kāishǐ

358

fāyán,（在舞会上）率先跳舞 (zài wǔhuì shàng) shuàixiān tiàowǔ

floorboard N 木地板 mù dìbǎn

flop I v 1 猛然坐下 / 躺下 / 倒下 měngrán zuòxià/tǎngxià/dǎoxià 2 彻底失败 chèdǐ shībài, 砸锅 záguō 3 [鸟 / 鱼+] 扑腾 [niǎo/yú+] pūténg II N 1 重重落下 chóngchóng luòxià, 重摔 zhòng shuāi 2 失败 shībài, 砸锅 záguō

floppy ADJ 松软垂下的 sōngruǎn chuíxià de

floppy disk, floppy N 软盘 ruǎnpán

flora N 植物（群）zhíwù (qún)

floral ADJ 用花装饰的 yòng huā zhuāngshì de, 花的 huā de

florist N 花店店主 huādiàn diànzhǔ

floss I N 洁牙线 jiéyáxiàn [M. WD 根 gēn] II v 使用洁牙线 shǐyòng jiéyáxiàn

flotation N 1 漂浮 piāofú
    flotation ring 救生圈 jiùshēngquān
    2 首次发行 shǒucì fāxíng

flotilla N 小舰队 xiǎo jiànduì, 小船队 xiǎochuán duì

flotsam N 1 （水面上）漂浮垃圾 (shuǐmiàn shàng) piāofú lājī 2 废物 fèiwù

flounder¹ v 1 遇到大困难 yùdào dà kùnnan 2 艰难地行走 jiānnán de xíngzǒu

flounder² N 鲆鱼 píng yú [M. WD 条 tiáo], 鲆鱼肉 píngyúròu

flour N 面粉 miànfěn

flourish I v 1 兴旺繁荣 xīngwàng fánróng II N 华丽的词藻 huálì de cízǎo, 不必要的装饰 bú bìyào de zhuāngshì
    with a flourish 用夸张的动作 yòng kuāzhāng de dòngzuò

flout v 公然无视 gōngrán wúshì, 违背 wéibèi

flow v, N 流 liú, 流动 liúdòng
    to go with the flow 随大流 suí dàliú, 随遇而安 suí yù ér ān
    to go against the flow 反潮流 fǎn cháoliú
    flow chart 流程图 liúchéngtú

flower I N 花 huā, 花儿 huār II v 开花 kāihuā

flowery ADJ 1 用花装饰的 [+图案] yòng huā zhuāngshì de [+tú'àn] 2 华丽

的 [+文体] huálì de [+wéntǐ], 花哨的 huāshao de

flown v See fly¹

flu (= influenza) N 流感 liúgǎn, 流行性感冒 liúxíngxìng gǎnmào

fluctuate v 上下波动的 shàngxià bōdòng de, 波动的 bōdòng de

fluency N 流利 liúlì

fluent ADJ 流利的 liúlì de

fluff I N 蓬松毛 péngsōng máo, 线团 xiàntuán II v 1 把…拍松 bǎ…pāi sōng 2 起毛球 qǐ máoqiú

fluffy ADJ 毛茸茸的 máoróngróng de

fluid I N 流体 liútǐ, 流质 liúzhì
    fluid ounce 液盎司 yè àngsī
    II ADJ 1 流动的 liúdòng de 2 优雅流畅的 [+演奏] yōuyǎ liúchàng de [+yǎnzòu]

fluids N 体液 tǐyè

fluke N 侥幸 jiǎoxìng

flung v See fling

flunk v 不及格 bù jígé, 没有通过 méiyǒu tōngguò

flunky, flunkey N 1 勤杂工 qínzágōng 2 马屁精 mǎpìjīng

fluorescent ADJ 荧光的 yíngguāng de
    fluorescent light 日光灯 rìguāngdēng

fluoride N 氟化物 fúhuàwù

flurry N 一阵忙乱 yí zhèn mángluàn, 慌乱 huāngluàn

flush I v 1 水冲 shuǐ chōng, 冲洗 chōngxǐ 2 [脸+] 发红 [liǎn+] fāhóng II N 1 水冲 shuǐ chōng, 冲洗 chōngxǐ 2 一阵（情绪）yízhèn (qíngxù)
    a flush of pride 一阵自豪感 yízhèn zìháogǎn
    III ADV 齐平地 qí píngde

flushed ADJ 脸红的 liǎnhóng de
    flushed with excitement 激动得脸色通红 jīdòng dé liǎnsè tōnghóng

flustered ADJ 紧张慌乱的 jǐnzhāng huāngluàn de

flute N 长笛 chángdí, 笛 dí

flutter I v 1 拍打 [+翅膀] pāi dǎ [+chìbǎng] 2 [旗+] 飘动 [qí+] piāodòng 3 [心+] 快速跳动 [xīn+] kuàisù tiàodòng II N 拍打 pāidǎ, 飘动 piāodòng

flux N 流动 liúdòng

in a flux 不断变化中 búduàn biànhuà zhōng

fly¹ v (PT **flew**; PP **flown**) **1** 飞 fēi, 飞翔 fēixiáng **2** 飞 fēi, 飞行 fēixíng **3** 驾驶飞机 jiàshǐ fēijī

fly² N **1** (PL **flies**) 苍蝇 cāngying **2** (裤子) 拉锁盖 lāsuǒ gài, 拉链 lāliàn

fly-by-night ADJ 靠不住的 kàobúzhù de, 长不了的 chángbùliǎo de

flying I N 乘飞机 chéngfēijī, 飞行 fēixíng II ADJ 能飞的 néng fēi de
  flying saucer 飞碟 fēidié
  to get off to a flying start 有良好的开端 yǒu liánghǎo de kāiduān, 打响第一炮 dǎxiǎng dìyī pào

flyswatter N 苍蝇拍 cāngying pāi

foal N 马驹 mǎjū, 幼马 yòu mǎ

foam I N 泡沫 pàomò [M. WD 块 kuài]
  foam rubber 海绵橡胶 hǎimián xiàngjiāo
  II V 起泡沫 qǐ pàomò

fob V (to fob sth off) 用欺骗手段把某物处理掉 yòng qīpiàn shǒuduàn bǎ mǒuwù chǔlǐdiào

focal point N 焦点 jiāodiǎn, 重点 zhòngdiǎn

focus I N **1** 重点 zhòngdiǎn **2** 焦点 jiāodiǎn, 焦距 jiāojù II V 把重点放在 bǎ zhòngdiǎn fàng zài
  out of focus 焦距不对 jiāojù bú duì, 模糊 móhu

fodder N **1** 饲料 sìliào **2** 素材 sùcái

foe N 仇敌 chóudí, 敌人 dírén

fog I N 雾 wù II V 蒙上水汽 méng shàng shuǐqì

fogbound ADJ 因大雾而受阻的 yīn dà wù ér shòuzǔ de

fogey, fogy N 守旧的人 shǒujiù de rén, 老顽固 lǎowángu

foggy ADJ 多雾的 duō wù de, 有雾的 yǒu wù de

foil I N **1** 铂纸 bózhǐ, 锡纸 xīzhǐ **2** 陪衬物 péichènwù, 陪衬 péichèn II V 挫败 cuòbài

foist V 把…强加于 bǎ…qiángjiā yú
  to foist sth on sb 把某物强加给某人 bǎ mǒuwù qiángjiā gěi mǒurén

fold I V **1** 折叠 zhédié

folding bed 折叠床 zhédiéchuáng
  to fold one's arms 交叉双臂 jiāochā shuāngbì
2 [公司+] 倒闭 [gōngsī+] dǎobì II N 折叠的部分 zhédié de bùfen, 褶 zhě

folder N 文件夹 wénjiàn jiā

foliage N 树叶 shùyè, 叶子 yèzi

folk N 民间的 mínjiān de
  folk music 民间音乐 mínjiān yīnyuè
  folk remedy 民间疗法 mínjiān liáofǎ

folklore N 民俗学 mínsúxué, 民俗 mínsú

folks N 人们 rénmen
  country folks 乡下人 xiāngxiàrén
  townsfolks 城里人 chénglǐrén
2 (one's folks) 父母 fùmǔ, 家里人 jiālǐrén

follow V **1** 跟着 gēnzhe, 跟随 gēnsuí **2** 接着发生 jiēzhe fāshēng **3** 遵循 zūnxún **4** 留意 [+形势的发展] liúyì [+xíngshì de fāzhǎn], 关注 guānzhù **5** 领会 [+别人的话] lǐnghuì [+biérén dehuà], 听懂 tīngdǒng

follower N 追随者 zhuīsuízhě, 支持者 zhīchízhě

following I ADJ 下一个 xià yí ge, 下列 xiàliè II N (一群) 追随者 (yìqún) zhuī-suízhě, (一群) 支持者 (yìqún) zhīchízhě
  the following 下列 xiàliè
III PREP 在…以后 zài...yǐhòu, 由于 yóuyú

follow-up I ADJ 后续的 hòuxù de II N 后续行动 hòuxù xíngdòng, 随访 suífǎng

folly N 荒唐事 huāngtángshì, 蠢事 chǔnshì

fond ADJ **1** 喜爱的 xǐ'ài de **2** 痴心的 chīxīn de
  a fond hope 痴心妄想 chīxīn wàngxiǎng

fondle V 爱抚 àifǔ, 抚弄 fǔnòng

fondly ADV 深情地 shēnqíng de
  to fondly believe 天真地以为 tiānzhēn de yǐwéi

font N 字形 zìxíng, 字体 zìtǐ

food N 食物 shíwù, 食品 shípǐn
  food bank 食品救济站 shípǐn jiùjìzhàn
  food poisoning 食物中毒 shíwù zhòngdú
  baby food 婴儿食品 yīng'ér shípǐn

health food 保健食品 bǎojiàn shípǐn

food for thought 需要认真考虑的事 xūyào rènzhēn kǎolǜ de shì

fool I N 傻瓜 shǎguā，笨蛋 bèndàn II v 欺骗 qīpiàn，哄骗 hǒngpiàn

foolhardy ADJ 鲁莽而又愚蠢的 lǔmǎng ér yòu yúchǔn de，傻大胆 shǎ dàdàn

foolish ADJ 傻的 shǎ de，愚蠢的 yúchǔn de

foolproof ADJ 万无一失的 wànwúyìshī de，不会出毛病的 bú huì chūmáobìng de

foot I N 足 zú，脚 jiǎo [M. WD 只 zhī]

foot locker 床脚柜 chuángjiǎoguì

II v (to foot the bill) 付款 fùkuǎn，付账 fùzhàng

footage N 镜头 jìngtóu，一组镜头 yìzǔ jìngtóu

football N 1（美国）橄榄球（Měiguó）gǎnlǎnqiú，美式足球 Měishì zúqiú 2 足球 zúqiú

footfall N 脚步声 jiǎobùshēng

foothill N 山麓 shānlù，小山 xiǎo shān

foothold N 立足点 lìzúdiǎn，稳固的地位 wěngù de dìwèi

footing N 1 状况 zhuàngkuàng，基础 jīchǔ

on an equal footing 以平等的地位 yǐ píngděng de dìwèi

2 站稳 zhànwěn

to lose one's footing 没有站稳 méiyǒu zhànwěn，站不稳 zhàn bùwěn

footloose ADJ 无牵无挂的 wúqiān wúguà de，随心所欲的 suí xīn suǒ yù de

footloose and fancy-free 无牵无挂的 wúqiān wúguà de，随心所欲的 suí xīn suǒ yù de

footnote N 脚注 jiǎozhù

footpath N 小路 xiǎolù [M. WD 条 tiáo]

footprint N 脚印 jiǎoyìn，足迹 zújì

footstep N 脚步声 jiǎobùshēng，脚印 jiǎoyìn

footwear N 鞋类 xié lèi

footwork N 1 [拳击手的+] 步法 [quánjīshǒu de+] bùfǎ 2 [外交+] 手腕 [wàijiāo+] shǒuwàn

for I PREP 1 为 wéi，为了 wèile 2 花（钱）huā (qián)，以…为代价 yǐ...wéi dàijià

for all I know 我真的不知道 wǒ zhēnde bù zhīdào

for now 目前 mùqián，暂时 zànshí

for rent 招租 zhāozū

3 支持 zhīchí II CONJ 因为 yīnwèi，由于 yóuyú

forage v 搜索 sōusuǒ，寻找 xúnzhǎo

foray N 1 短暂的尝试 duǎnzàn de chángshì 2 突袭 tūxí

forbade, forbid v See **forbid**

forbear (PT **forbore**; PP **forborne**) v 忍耐 rěnnài

forbearance N 忍耐宽容 rěnnài kuānróng，自制 zìzhì

forbid (PT **forbade, forbid**; PP **forbidden**) v 禁止 jìnzhǐ

forbidden I ADJ 被禁止的 bèi jìnzhǐ de

forbidden fruit 禁果 jìnguǒ

II v See **forbid**

forbore, forborne v See **forbear**

force I N 力 lì，力量 lìliang

(armed) forces 武装力量 wǔzhuāng lìliang，军队 jūnduì

II v 强迫 qiǎngpò

forced ADJ 1 强迫的 [+纪律] qiǎngpò de [+jìlǜ] 2 勉强的 [+笑] miǎnqiǎng de [+xiào]

forcefed v See **forcefeed**

forcefeed (PT & PP **forcefed**) v 强迫…进食 qiǎngpò...jìnshí，强喂 qiáng wèi

forceful ADJ 有说服力的 yǒu shuōfúlì de

forceps N 钳子 qiánzi，镊子 nièzi

forcibly ADV 强行地 qiángxíng de

ford N 浅滩 qiǎntān，渡口 dùkǒu

fore I N 前面 qiánmian

to come to the fore 开始显著 kāishǐ xiǎnzhe，开始变得重要 kāishǐ biànde zhòngyào

II ADJ 前部的 qiánbù de

forearm N 前臂 qiánbì

forebear N 祖先 zǔxiān，祖宗 zǔzōng

foreboding N 不祥的预感 bùxiáng de yùgǎn

forecast I v (PT & PP **forecast**) 预报 yùbào 预兆 yùzhào II N 预报 yùbào

foreclose v [银行+] 收回房产 [yínháng+] shōuhuí fángchǎn

foreclosure N（银行）收回房产 (yín-háng+) shōuhuí fángchǎn
forefathers N 前辈 qiánbèi, 祖先 zǔxiān
forefinger N 食指 shízhǐ
forefront N 前列 qiánliè, 前沿 qiányán
foreground N 1（相片或图画+）近景 [xiàngpiàn huò túhuà+] jìnjǐng 2 重要地位 zhòngyào dìwèi
forehead N 额 é, 前额 qián é
foreign ADJ 外国的 wàiguó de
　foreign exchange 外汇 wàihuì
　foreign policy 外交政策 wàijiāo zhèngcè
　foreign trade 对外贸易 duìwài màoyì
　to be foreign to sb 对某人来说很陌生的 duì mǒurén láishuō hěn mòshēng de
foreleg N（动物）前腿 (dòngwù) qiántuǐ [M. WD 条 tiáo]
foreman N 工头 gōngtóu, 工长 gōngzhǎng
foremost ADJ 1 首要的 shǒuyào de, 最重要的 zuì zhòngyào de
　first and foremost 首先 shǒuxiān
　2 最杰出的 [+科学家] zuì jiéchū de [+kēxuéjiā], 屈指首一的 qūzhǐ shǒu yī de
forensic ADJ 法庭的 fǎtíng de, 法医的 fǎyī de
　forensic medicine 法医（学）fǎyī (xué)
forerunner N 先驱 xiānqū, 前身 qiánshēn
foresaw V See **foresee**
foresee (PT **foresaw**; PP **foreseen**) V 预知 yùzhī
foreseeable ADJ 在可见的未来 zài kějiàn de wèilái, 可以预见的 kěyǐ yùjiàn de
foreseen V See **foresee**
foreshadow V 预示 yùshì
foresight N 先见之明 xiānjiàn zhī míng, 远见 yuǎnjiàn
forest N 森林 sēnlín [M. WD 片 piàn]
　forest ranger 林警 lín jǐng, 管林人 guǎnlínrén
forestall V 预先阻止 yùxiān zǔzhǐ
forestry N（森）林学 (sēn) línxué, 林业 línyè
foretaste N 预兆 yùzhào, 预示 yùshì
foretell (PT & PP **foretold**) V 预言 yùyán
forethought N 事先的考虑 shìxiān de kǎolǜ, 筹划 chóuhuà
foretold V See **foretell**

forever ADV 永远 yǒngyuǎn, 很长时间 hěn cháng shíjiān
forewarn V 事先警告 shìxiān jǐnggào, 预警 yùjǐng
foreword N 前言 qiányán
forfeit I V 丧失 sàngshī, 失去 shīqù II N（作为惩罚）丧失的东西 (zuòwéi chéngfá) sàngshī de dōngxi, 没收物 mòshōu wù
forgave V See **forgive**
forge I V 1 伪造 [+文件] wěizào [+wénjiàn] 2 建立 [+关系] jiànlì [+guānxi] 3 锻造 [+剑] duànzào [+jiàn] II N 1 锻铁炉 duàntiělú, 锻造车间 duànzào chējiān 2 铁匠铺 tiějiàngpù
forger N 伪造者 wěizàozhě
forgery N 1 伪造罪 wěizàozuì, 伪造 wěizào 2 伪造品（伪造文件、赝品画、伪币等）wěizàopǐn (wěizào wénjiàn, yíng pǐnhuà, wěibì děng)
forget (PT **forgot**; PP **forgotten**) V 忘记 wàngjì
forgetful ADJ 健忘的 jiànwàng de, 记性很差的 jìxing hěn chà de
forgive (PT **forgave**; PP **forgiven**) V 原谅 yuánliàng, 宽恕 kuānshù
　to forgive and forget 宽恕并且遗忘（→不念旧恶）kuānshù bìngqiě yíwàng (→bú niàn jiù'è)
forgiven V See **forgive**
forgiving ADJ 1 宽容的 [+人] kuānróng de [+rén] 2 容许出错的 róngxǔ chūcuò de
forgo [also **forego**] (PT **forwent**; PP **forgone**) V 放弃 fàngqì
forgone V See **forgo**
forgot, forgotten V See **forget**
fork I N 1 叉 chā [M. WD 把 bǎ], 叉子 chāzi 2 岔路 chàlù, 岔口 chàkǒu II V 1 用叉子 yòng chāzi 2 分岔 fēn chà 3 (to fork over/out/up) 付出（钱）fùchū (qian)
forklift N 叉车 chāchē, 铲车 chǎnchē
forlorn ADJ 孤独凄凉的 gūdú qīliáng de
form I N 1 形式 xíngshì, 状态 zhuàngtài 2 表格 biǎogé [M. WD 张 zhāng/份 fèn] 3 [运动员的+] 竞技状态 [yùndòngyuán de+] jìngjì zhuàngtài II V 形成 xíngchéng, 组成 zǔchéng

formal I ADJ 1 正式 zhèngshì 2 正规 zhèngguī **II** N 1 正式的 [+邀请] zhèngshì de [+yāoqǐng] 2 正规的 [+教育] zhèngguī de [+jiàoyù]

formality N 1（必办的）手续 (bì bàn de) shǒuxù 2 [婚礼上的+] 礼节 [hūnlǐ shàng de+] lǐjié

format I N 格式 géshi, 样式 yàngshì **II** v 把…格式化 bǎ…géshi huà

formation N 1 形成 xíngchéng, 组成 zǔchéng 2 [士兵的+] 列队 [shìbīng de+] lièduì

formative ADJ 促使形成的 cùshǐ xíngchéng de

formative years 人格形成的时期 réngé xíngchéng de shíqī

former I ADJ 以前的 yǐqián de, 前 qián **II** N 前者 qiánzhě

formidable ADJ 令人生畏的 lìng rén shēng wèi de, 很厉害的 hěn lìhai de

formula N 1 方案 fāng'àn 2 方程式 fāngchéngshì, 公式 gōngshì 3 配方 pèifāng

formulate v 1 制定 [+计划、规则等] zhìdìng [+jìhuà, guīzé děng] 2 配制 [化工产品] pèizhì [+huàgōng chǎnpǐn] 3 清晰表达 [+想法] qīngxī biǎodá [+xiǎngfǎ]

fornicate v 通奸 tōngjiān

forsake (PT **forsook**; PP **forsaken**) v 放弃 fàngqì, 遗弃 fàngqì

forswear (PT **forswore**; PP **forsworn**) v 发誓放弃 fāshì fàngqì

fort N 要塞 yàosài, 堡垒 bǎolěi

forte N 专长 zhuāncháng, 强项 qiángxiàng

forth ADV 向前 xiàngqián

forthcoming ADJ 1 即将来到的 [+事件] jíjiāng láidào de [+shìjiàn] 2 愿意提供的 yuànyì tígōng de

forthright ADJ 坦率的 tǎnshuài de, 直言不讳的 zhíyán búhuì de

fortification N 加强 jiāqiáng

fortifications 防御工事 fángyù gōngshì

fortify v 1 设防于 shèfáng yú 2 加强 jiāqiáng, 激励 jīlì 3 强化 [食品] qiánghuà (shípǐn)

fortnight N 两个星期 liǎng gè xīngqī, 双周 shuāng zhōu

fortress N 堡垒 bǎolěi, 要塞 yàosài

fortunate ADJ 幸运的 xìngyùn de

fortune N 1 一大笔钱 yí dàbǐ qián, 财富 cáifù

to make a fortune 赚一大笔钱 zhuàn yí dàbǐ qián, 发财 fācái

2 运气 yùnqì, 命运 mìngyùn

fortune teller 算命的人 suànmìng de rén, 算命先生 suànmìng xiānsheng

to tell one's fortunes 算命 suànmìng

forty NUM 四十 sìshí, 40

forum N 论坛 lùntán

forward I [also **forwards**] ADV 向前 xiàngqián **II** ADJ 1 向前的 xiàngqián de, 在前部的 zàiqián bù de 2 预先的 yùxiān de, 前瞻性的 qiánzhānxìng de **III** v 转交 zhuǎnjiāo, 转寄 zhuǎnjì **IV** N 前锋 qiánfēng

forwent v See **forgo**

fossil N 化石 huàshí

fossil fuel 矿物燃料 kuàngwù ránliào

foster I v 1 促进 cùjìn, 助长 zhùzhǎng 2 照管（孩子）zhàoguǎn (háizi) **II** ADJ 收养的 shōuyǎng de, 寄养的jìyǎng de

fought v See **fight**

foul I v 1 犯规 fànguī 2 污染 wūrǎn, 弄脏 nòngzāng

to foul up 把…搞得一团糟 bǎ…gǎode yìtuánzāo

II N（体育比赛）犯规 (tǐyù bǐsài) fànguī

III ADJ 1 又脏又臭的 [+气味] yòu zàng yòu chòu de [+qìwèi] 2 肮脏的 [+空气] āngzāng de [+kōngqì] 3 恶劣的 [+天气] èliè de [+tiānqì]

foul language 粗话 cūhuà, 脏话 zānghuà

foul play 违法行为 wéifǎ xíngwéi

in a foul mood 心情很坏 xīnqíng hěn huài

found¹ v See **find**

found² (PT & PP **founded**) v 建立 jiànlì, 创建 chuàngjiàn

foundation N 1 基础 jīchǔ 2 基金会 jījīn huì 3 地基 dìjī, 房基 fángjī

founder¹ N 创立人 chuànglìrén, 创办者 chuàngbànzhě

founder² v 1 [船只+] 沉没 [chuánzhǐ+] chénmò 2 [生意+] 垮掉 [shēngyì+] kuǎdiào

founding father N 创始人 chuàngshǐrén

foundry N 铸造车间 zhùzào chējiān, 铸造厂 zhùzàochǎng

fountain N 喷泉 pēnquán, 喷泉池 pēnquánchí
  fountain pen 自来水笔 zìláishuǐbǐ, 钢笔 gāngbǐ

four NUM 四 sì, 4

fourteen NUM 十四 shísì, 14

fourteenth NUM 第十四 dì shísì

fourth NUM 第四 dì sì

(the) Fourth of July N 美国独立纪念日 Měiguó dúlì jìniànrì

fowl N 家禽 jiāqín

fox N 狐狸 húli [M. WD 只 zhī]

foyer N 休息厅 xiūxitīng, 大堂 dàtáng

fracas N 喧闹的斗殴 xuānnào de dòu'ōu

fraction I N 1 极小的部分 jíxiǎo de bùfen, 非常少 fēicháng shǎo 2 小于一的数目 xiǎoyú yí de shùmù, 分数 (如 ¼, ⅜) fēnshù (rú ¼, ⅜)

fractional ADJ 1 少量的 shǎoliàng de 2 小数的 xiǎoshù de

fracture I V 1 [骨+] 断裂 [gǔ+] duànliè 2 [组织+] 出现裂痕 [zǔzhī+] chūxiàn lièhén II N 1 骨折 gǔzhé 2 裂缝 lièfèng

fragile ADJ 1 易碎的 [+花瓶] yì suì de [+huāpíng], 易损坏的 yì sǔnhuài de
  Fragile! Handle With Care. 易碎物品，小心轻放。Yì suì wùpǐn, xiǎoxīnqīngfàng. 2 虚弱的 [+身体] xūruò de [+shēntǐ], 脆弱的 cuìruò de

fragment I N 1 [玻璃／金属+] 碎片 [bōli/jīnshǔ] suìpiàn 2 [谈话的+] 片断 [tánhuà de+] piànduàn

fragmentary ADJ 1 碎片的 suìpiàn de 2 片断的 piànduàn de

fragrance N 香味 xiāngwèi, 香气 xiāngqì, 芬芳 fēnfāng

fragrant ADJ 香的 xiāng de, 芬芳的 fēnfāng de

frail ADJ 柔弱的 róuruò de

frailty N 柔弱 róuruò, 弱点 ruòdiǎn

frame I N 1 镜框 jìngkuàng 2 框架 kuàngjià
  frame of mind 思想状况 sīxiǎng zhuàngkuàng
  II V 1 给 [+一幅画] 装框 gěi [+yìfú huà]

zhuāng kuàng 2 陷害 [+无辜者] xiànhài [+wúgūzhě] 3 仔细考虑 [+答复] zǐxì kǎolǜ [+dáfù]

frames N 眼镜框 yǎnjìngkuàng

frame-up N 阴谋陷害 yīnmóu xiànhài, 陷害 xiànhài

framework N 1 框架 kuàngjià 2 [法律的+] 体系 [fǎlǜ de+] tǐxì

franchise N 1 特许经营 tèxǔ jīngyíng 2 特许经营店 tèxǔ jīngyíngdiàn, 专卖店 zhuānmàidiàn [M. WD 家 jiā]

frank¹ ADJ 坦率的 tǎnshuài de, 坦诚的 tǎnchéng de

frank² V （在信封上）加盖 "邮资已付" (zài xìnfēng shàng) jiāgài "yóuzī yǐfù"

frantic ADJ 1 惊恐的 jīngkǒng de, 情绪失控的 qíngxù shīkòng de 2 紧张纷乱的 jǐnzhāng fēnluàn de

fraternal ADJ 兄弟般的 xiōngdìbān de, 亲如手足的 qīn rú shǒuzú de

fraternity N 1 男生联谊会 nánshēng liányìhuì 2 情谊 qíngyì, 博爱 bó'ài

fraud N 1 诈骗 zhàpiàn, 欺骗 qīpiàn 2 骗子 piànzi

fraudulent ADJ 欺诈的 qīzhà de, 舞弊的 wǔbì de

fraught ADJ 充满的 chōngmǎn de
  fraught with problems 问题成堆的 wèntí chéngduī de

fray V 1 磨损 mósǔn, 磨破 mópò 2 [神经+] 紧张 [shénjīng+] jǐnzhāng
  frayed nerves 紧张的神经 jǐnzhāng de shénjīng

freak I N 1 怪人 guàirén, 怪物 guàiwu 2 狂热爱好者 kuángrè àihàozhě
  control freak 喜欢控制别人的人 xǐhuan kòngzhì biéren de rén, 支配欲极强的人 zhīpèiyù jíqiáng de rén
  II V 突然大怒 tūrán dà nù, 突然失态 tūrán shī tài III ADJ 奇怪的 qíguài de, 离奇的 líqí de
  a freak accident 离奇的事故 líqí de shìgù

freckle N 雀斑 quèbān

free I ADJ 1 自由的 zìyóude
  free thinker 思想自由的人 sīxiǎng zìyóu de rén
  free throw 罚球 fáqiú

free will 自由意志 zìyóu yìzhì
2 免费的 miǎnfèi de **3** 有空的 yǒukòng de **II** v **1** 释放 shìfàng **2** 解救 jiějiù **III** ADV 免费地 miǎnfèi de
feel free 随意 suíyì

freebie N 免费小礼品 miǎnfèi xiǎo lǐpǐn

freedom N **1** 自由 zìyóu **2** 免受 miǎnshòu
freedom from fear 免受恐惧 miǎnshòu kǒngjù

free-for-all N **1** 七嘴八舌的争吵 qīzuǐ bāshé de zhēngchǎo **2** 混战 hùnzhàn

freehand ADJ 徒手画的 túshǒu huà de

freelance I ADJ 自由职业的 zìyóu zhíyède
freelance translator 个体翻译工作者 gètǐ fānyì gōngzuòzhě
II v 从事自由职业 cóngshì zìyóu zhíyè

freeload v 吃白食 chī báishí, 白吃白拿 bái chī bái ná

freely ADV 自由自在地 zìyóu zìzài de, 自如地 zìrú de

freeway N 高速公路 gāosù gōnglù

freeze I v (PT **froze**; PP **frozen**) **1** 冻结 dòngjié, 结冰 jiébīng **2** 极冷 jí lěng
II N **1** 冻结 dòngjié **2** 寒流 hánliú

freeze-dried ADJ 快速冷冻干燥的 kuàisù lěngdòng gānzào de

freezer N 冷藏箱 lěngcángxiāng

freezing N 冰点 bīngdiǎn
freezing point 冰点 bīngdiǎn
below/above freezing point 零度以下／以上 língdù yìxià/ yìshàng

freight N 货物 huòwù
freight train（火车）货车（huǒchē）huòchē
II v 运输 yùnshū

freighter N 货轮 huòlún [M. WD 艘 sōu]

French I ADJ **1** 法国的 Fǎguó de
French toast 法式炸面包片 Fǎshì zhá miànbāopiàn
2 法国人的 Fǎguórén de **II** N **1** 法语 Fǎyǔ **2** 法国人 Fǎguórén

frenetic ADJ 疯狂的 fēngkuáng de, 狂乱的 kuángluàn de

frenzied ADJ 狂热的 kuángrè de

frenzy N 狂热 kuángrè

frequency N **1** 频率 pínlǜ **2** 发生的次数 fāshēng de cìshù

frequent ADJ 频繁的 pínfán de
frequent flier 经常乘坐飞机的旅客 jīngcháng chéngzuò fēijī de lǚkè

fresh ADJ **1** 新的 [+东西] xīn de [+dōngxi]
2 新鲜的 [+水果] xīnxian de [+de shuǐguǒ]
3 冷冷的 [+风] lěnglěng de [+fēng]
4 精神饱满的 [+人] jīngshen bǎomǎn de [+rén]
to make a fresh start 从新开始 cóng xīn kāishǐ

freshen v 使…干净清新 shǐ…gānjìng qīngxīn

freshman N（高中或大学）一年级学生 (gāozhōng huò dàxué) yìniánjí xuésheng

freshwater ADJ 淡水 dànshuǐ

fret v 烦恼 fánnǎo, 发愁 fāchóu

fretful ADJ 烦躁的 fánzào de, 发牢骚的 fāláosāo de

friction N 摩擦 mócā, 倾轧 qīngyá

Friday N 星期五 xīngqīwǔ, 周五 zhōuwǔ

fridge N 冰箱 bīngxiāng [M. WD 台 tái]

friend N 朋友 péngyou
A friend in need is a friend indeed. 患难见真交。Huànnàn jiàn zhēn jiāo.
to make friends (with)（和…）交朋友 (hé…) jiāo péngyou

friendly ADJ 友好的 yǒuhǎo de
user-friendly 方便使用者的 fāngbiàn shǐyòngzhě de

friendship N 友谊 yǒuyì

fries N (French fries) 炸薯条 zhá shǔtiáo, 炸土豆条 zhá tǔdòutiáo

fright N 惊吓 jīngxià

frighten v 惊吓 jīngxià, 使害怕 shǐ hàipà

frightening ADJ 可怕的 kěpà de

frigid ADJ **1** 冷淡的 lěngdàn de **2**（女子）性冷淡的 (nǚzǐ) xìng lěngdàn de **3** 严寒的 yánhán de

frill N **1** 不必要的额外物品 bú bìyào de éwài wùpǐn **2** 饰边 shìbiān

fringe N **1** 边缘 biānyuán, 边缘组织 biānyuán zǔzhī **2** 流苏 liúsū, 缘饰 yuánshì
fringe benefit 附加福利 fùjiā fúlì, 额外津贴 éwài jīntiē

Frisbee N 飞盘 fēipán, 飞碟 fēidié

frisk v **1** 对 [+旅客] 搜身 duì [+lǚkè]

sōushēn, 安全检查 ānquán jiǎnchá
2 [小狗+] 欢蹦乱跳 [xiǎo gǒu+]
huānbèngluàntiào

fritter I N 油炸馅饼 yóuzhá xiànbǐng
II v 浪费 làngfèi, 挥霍 huīhuò

fritz N 故障 gùzhàng

frivolity N 轻浮 qīngfú, 轻佻 qīngtiāo

frivolous ADJ 极不严肃的 jí bù yánsù de,
轻率的 qīngshuài de

fro ADV 向后 xiànghòu
to and fro 来来回回的 láilái huíhuí de

frog N 蛙 wā [M. WD 只 zhī], 青蛙 qīngwā
[M. WD 只 zhī]

frolic I v 欢快地玩耍 huānkuài de
wánshuǎ II N 嬉闹 xīnào

from PREP 1 从 cóng 2 是⋯人 shì⋯rén,
来自 láizì
from now on 从现在开始 cóng xiànzài
kāishǐ
3 离⋯lí⋯, 距⋯jù⋯.

front I ADJ 前面的 qiánmian de, 前方的
qiánfāng de II N 前面 qiánmian, 正面
zhèngmiàn
in front of 在⋯前面 zài⋯qiánmian
2 外表 wàibiǎo, 装出来的样子
zhuāngchū láide yàngzi
to put on a brave front 装出勇敢的样
子 zhuāngchū yǒnggǎn de yàngzi
3 领域 lǐngyù, 活动 huódòng

frontier N 前沿 qiányán, 前线 qiánxiàn

frontrunner N 领先者 lǐngxiān zhě

frost I N 1 霜 shuāng 2 冰冻的天气 bīng-
dòng de tiānqì, 严寒 yánhán II v 1 结霜
jié shuāng 2 撒上糖霜 sā shàng
tángshuāng

frostbite N 冻伤 dòngshāng

froth I N 1 沫 mò, 白沫 báimò 2 空谈 kōng-
tán, 美好的空想 měihǎo de kōngxiǎng
II v 起泡沫 qǐpàomò, 冒白沫 mào
báimò
to be frothing at the mouth 气得发昏
qì dé fāhūn

frothy ADJ 1 泡沫多的 pàomò duō de 2 空
洞的 kōngdòng de, 肤浅的 fūqiǎn de

frown v 皱眉头 zhòu méitou
to frown upon 对⋯很不赞成 duì⋯hěn
bú zànchéng

froze v See freeze

frozen I ADJ 1 冷冻的 lěngdòng de 2 [人
+] 冷极了 [rén+] lěng jíle, 冻坏了 dòng
huài le II v See freeze

frugal ADJ 节俭的 jiéjiǎn de

fruit N 1 水果 shuǐguǒ 2 成果 chéngguǒ
fruit tree 果树 guǒshù
to bear fruit 结果 jiéguǒ

fruitcake N 水果蛋糕 shuǐguǒ dàngāo

fruitful ADJ 富有成果的 fùyǒu chéngguǒ
de

fruitless ADJ 没有结果的 méiyǒu jiéguǒ
de, 无效的 wúxiào de

fruity ADJ 有水果味的 yǒu shuǐguǒ wèi de

frustrate v 1 使⋯恼怒 shǐ⋯nǎonù 2 挫败
cuòbài, 阻挠 zǔnáo

frustrated ADJ 气恼的 qìnǎo de, 沮丧的
jǔsàng de

fry v (油) 煎 (yóu) jiān, 炸 zhá, 炒 chǎo
to deep-fry 油炸 yóuzhá
to shallow-fry 炒 chǎo

fry-pan, frying pan N 平底煎锅 píngdǐ
jiānguō

fuck v 性交 xìngjiāo
Fuck off! 滚你的蛋! Gǔn nǐde dàn!

fudge N 乳脂软糖 rǔzhī ruǎntáng

fuel N 燃料 ránliào II v 1 加燃料 jiā
ránliào 2 刺激 cìjī, 促进 cùjìn

fugitive N 逃犯 táofàn, 逃亡者 táowángzhě

fulfill v 1 实现 shíxiàn, 达到 dádào 2 满足
mǎnzú
to fulfill oneself 实现自己的潜能 shíxiàn zìjǐ de qiánnéng, 充分发挥自己的才
能 chōngfèn fāhuī zìjǐ de cáinéng

fulfilling ADJ 给人成就感的 gěi rén chéng-
jiùgǎn de, 使人满意的 shǐ rén mǎnyì de

full I ADJ 1 满的 mǎn de, 充满的
chōngmǎn de
full house [电影院+] 客满
[diànyǐngyuàn+] kèmǎn
full moon 满月 mǎnyuè
2 饱了 bǎo le, 吃饱了 chībǎo le
on a full stomach 刚吃饱 gāng chībǎo le
3 整整的 zhěngzhěng de, 全部的
quánbù de
full speed 全速 quánsù
II ADV 正好 zhènghǎo, 直接地 zhíjié de

to know full well 完全明白 wánquán míngbai

III N (in full) 全部地 quánbù de, 一点不少的 yìdiǎn bùshǎo de

full-blown ADJ 充分发展了的 chōngfèn fāzhǎn le de, 成熟的 chéngshú de

full-fledged ADJ **1** 羽毛长好的 [+鸟] yǔmáo zhǎnghǎo de [+niǎo] **2** 经过全面训练的 [+教师] jīngguò quánmiàn xùnliàn de [+jiàoshī], 成熟的 chéngshú de

full-grown ADJ 发育成熟的 fāyù chéngshú de

full-length ADJ **1** 全身的 [+肖像] quánshēn de [+xiàoxiàng] **2** 不经节缩的 [+文章] bù jīngjiésuō de [+wénzhāng]

full-scale ADJ 全面的 quánmiàn de, 最大限度的 zuìdà xiàndù de

full-time ADJ 全日的 quánrì de

fumble I v **1** 摸索 mōsuo, 乱摸 luànmō **2** 接球不稳 jiēqiú bùwěn, 失球 shī qiú **II** N 失球 shī qiú

fume v [一言不发地+] 生气 [yìyán bù fā de+] shēngqì, 怒火中烧 nùhuǒ zhōng shāo

fumes N 难闻的气味 nánwén de qìwèi

fumigate v 烟熏 yānxūn

fun I N 乐趣 lèqù, 欢乐 huānlè

for fun 取乐 qǔlè

to make fun of 嘲笑 cháoxiào

II ADJ **1** 好玩的 hǎowán de, 让人快乐的 ràng rén kuàilè de **2** 好玩儿的 hǎowánr de, 逗笑的 dòuxiào de

function I N **1** 功能 gōngnéng **2** 函数 hánshù **II** v 起作用 qǐ zuòyòng, 运转 yùnzhuǎn

function key（计算机）功能键 (jìsuànjī) gōngnéngjiàn

functional ADJ **1** 实用的 shíyòng de **2** 正常运转的 zhèngcháng yùnzhuǎn de

fund I N **1** 专款 zhuānkuǎn **2** 资金 zījīn, 钱 qián **II** v 拨款 bō kuǎn, 资助 zīzhù

fundamental I ADJ **1** 基本的 jīběn de, 根本的 gēnběn de **II** N 基本原理 jīběn yuánlǐ

funding N 拨款 bō kuǎn, 出资 chūzī **2** 专款 zhuānkuǎn

fund-raising ADJ 募款 mù kuǎn, 筹款 chóu kuǎn

funeral N 葬礼 zànglǐ

funeral home 殡仪馆 bìnyíguǎn

funky ADJ **1** 时髦的 shímáo de, 有趣的 yǒuqù de **2** 臭烘烘的 chòuhōnghōng de, 脏兮兮的 zàngxīxī de

funnel I N [水+] 漏斗 lòudǒu, 烟囱 yāncōng **II** v [水+] 流经漏斗 [shuǐ+] liú jīng lòudǒu [qián+] huìjí [qián]

funny ADJ **1** 好笑的 hǎoxiào de, 可笑的 kěxiào de **2** 奇怪的 qíguài de

fur N 毛皮 máopí

furious ADJ **1** 狂怒的 kuángnù de **2** 强烈的 [+攻击] qiángliè de [+gōngjī]

furl v 卷起 juǎnqǐ, 折起 zhéqǐ

furlong N 休假 xiūjià

furnace N 熔炉 rónglú, 火炉 huǒlú

furnish v 为…配备家具 wéi…pèi bèi jiājù **2** 提供 tígōng

furniture N 家具 jiājù

furor, furore N 公众的愤怒 gōngzhòng de fènnù

furrow I N **1** 犁沟 lígōu [M. WD 道 dào] **2** 皱纹 zhòuwén [M. WD 道 dào] **II** v **1** 开沟槽 kāi gōucáo **2** 起皱纹 qǐ zhòuwén

furry ADJ 毛茸茸的 máoróngróng de

further I ADV **1** 进一步 jìnyíbù **2** 更远地 gèng yuǎn de **3** 而且 érqiě **II** ADJ 进一步的 jìnyíbù de **III** v 促进 cùjìn, 推进 tuījìn

furthermore ADV 而且 érqiě, 不仅 bù jǐn rúcǐ

furthest ADJ, ADV 最远的 / 地 zuì yuǎn de

furtive ADJ 偷偷的 tōutōu de, 鬼鬼祟祟的 guǐguǐ suìsuì de

fury N 狂怒 kuángnù, 暴怒 bàonù

fuse I N **1** [电表+] 保险丝 [diànbiǎo+] bǎoxiǎnsī **2** [炸弹的+] 定时引信 [zhàdàn de+] dìngshí yǐnxìn

to have a short fuse 容易发火 róngyì fāhuǒ, 脾气急躁 píqi jízào

II v **1** 熔合 rónghé **2** 使…结合 shǐ…jiéhé

fuse-box N 保险丝盒 bǎoxiǎnsīhé

fusion N 熔合 rónghé, 融合 rónghé

fusion jazz 融合爵士乐 rónghé juéshìyuè

fuss I N 不必要的激动 bú biyào de jīdòng, 无事生非 wúshì shēngfēi

to kick up a fuss 因为小事而大吵大闹 yīnwèi xiǎoshì ér dàchǎo dànào

to make a fuss over 过分注意 guòfèn zhùyì, 过分照顾 guòfèn zhàogù **II** v **1** 局促不安 júcù bù'ān **2** 过分讲究 guòfèn jiǎngjiū

to fuss over 过分地照料 guòfèn de zhào liào

fussy ADJ 过分讲究的 guòfèn jiǎngjiū de, 挑剔的 tiāoti de

futile ADJ 无用的 wúyòng de

futility N 徒劳 túláo

future I N **1** 将来 jiānglái, 未来 wèilái **2** 前途 qiántú **II** ADJ 将来的 jiānglái de, 未来的 wèilái de

fuzzy ADJ **1** 模糊的 móhu de **2** 不清楚的 bùqīngchu de

fuzzy logic 模糊逻辑 móhu luóji

FYI (= for your information) ABBREV 仅供参考 jǐn gōng cānkǎo

G

gab v 喋喋不休 diédié bùxiū, 闲扯 xiánchě

gadget N 小玩意儿 xiǎowányir

gaffe N 说错话 shuōcuò huà, 失言 shīyán

gag¹ I v **1** 作呕 zuò'ǒu, 想吐 xiǎng tǔ **2** 用布塞住嘴 yòng bù sāizhù zuǐ **3** 不让 [+人] 说话 bú ràng [+rén] shuōhuà, 压制言论自由 yāzhì yánlùn zìyóu **II** N 塞住嘴的布 sāizhù zuǐ de bù

gag² N 笑话 xiàohua

gaggle N 一群鹅 yì qún é

gaiety N 欢乐 huānlè

gaily ADV 色彩鲜艳的 sècǎi xiānyàn de

gain I v **1** 获得 huòdé, 赢得 yíngdé **2** 增加 zēngjiā

to gain on 渐渐赶上 jiànjiàn gǎnshàng **II** N **1** 增进 zēngjìn, 增加 zēngjiā

One man's gain is another man's loss. 有人得，便有人失。Yǒurén dé, biàn yǒurén shī.

2 获利 huòlì, 收益 shōuyì

gait N 步伐 bùfá

gal N 女孩 nǚhái

gala N 盛会 shènghuì, 欢庆 huānqìng

galaxy N 星系 xīngxì

gale N 大风 dàfēng, 八级大风 bā jí dàfēng

gall N 厚脸皮 hòu liǎnpí

to have the gall to ... 竟然有脸把… jìngrán yǒu liǎnpí...

gallant ADJ **1** 英勇的 yīngyǒng de **2**（对女子）献殷勤的 (duì nǚzǐ) xiàn yīnqín de

gall bladder N 胆囊 dǎnnáng

gallery N **1** 画廊 huàláng **2** 美术馆 měishùguǎn

art gallery 艺术馆 yìshùguǎn

3 楼座 lóuzuò

galley N 船上的厨房 chuánshàng de chúfáng

gallivant v 游逛 yóuguàng

gallon N 加仑 jiālún

gallop I v [马+] 飞奔 [mǎ+] fēibēn **II** N [马的+] 飞奔 [mǎ de+] fēibēn

gallows N 绞刑架 jiǎoxíngjià

galore ADJ 大量的 dàliàng de

gambit N 策略 cèlüè, 手段 shǒuduàn

gamble I v 赌博 dǔbó, 冒险 màoxiǎn **II** N 赌博 dǔbó, 冒险（的做法）màoxiǎn (de zuòfǎ)

to take a gamble 冒一下险 mào yíxià xiǎn

gambler N 赌徒 dǔtú

game I N

game plan（体育比赛）策略 (tǐyù bǐsài) cèlüè

game show（电视）有奖比赛节目 (diànshì) yǒu jiǎng bǐsài jiémù

to play games 玩花招 wán huāzhāo

2（球赛）局 (qiúsài) jú, 盘 pán **3** 猎物 lièwù

games N 运动会 yùndònghuì

the Olympic Games 奥林匹克运动会 Àolínpǐkè Yùndònghuì

gamut N 所有的 suǒyǒu de, 全部的 quánbù de

gander N 公鹅 gōng é

gang I N 帮 bāng, 帮派 bāngpài **II** v 结帮结伙 jié bāng jié huǒ

to gang up on 合伙对付 héhuǒ duìfu

gangling ADJ 又高又瘦动作笨拙的 yòu gāo yòu shòu dòngzuò bènzhuō de

gangplank N 跳板 tiàobǎn, 步桥 bùqiáo

gangrene N 坏疽 huàijū

gangster N 犯罪团伙成员 fànzuì tuánhuǒ chéngyuán, 匪徒 fěitú

gangway N 大跳板 dà tiàobǎn, 大步桥 dà bùqiáo

gap N 1 空隙 kòngxì, 间隔 jiàngé 2 差距 chājù, 差别 chābié

gape V 目瞪口呆地看 mùdèng kǒudāi de kàn

gaping ADJ 张开的 zhāngkāi de, 敞开的 chǎngkāi de

garage N 1 车库 chēkù [M. WD 间 jiān] garage sale 旧物大甩卖 jiùwù dàshuǎimài 2 修车行 xiū chē háng [M. WD 家 jiā]

garb N 服装 fúzhuāng, 制服 zhìfú [M. WD 件 jiàn/套 tào]

garbage N 1 垃圾 lājī garbage disposal 厨房垃圾处理机 chúfáng lājī chǔlǐjī garbage truck 垃圾车 lājīchē 2 废话 fèihuà, 愚蠢的念头 yúchǔn de niàntou

garden N 1 花园 huāyuán 2 菜园 càiyuán garden center 花木商店 huāmù shāngdiàn

gardener N 园艺工人 yuányì gōngrén, 花匠 huājiàng

gardens N 植物园 zhíwùyuán botanical gardens 植物园 zhíwùyuán

gargantuan ADJ 巨大的 jùdà de, 特大的 tèdà de

gargle V 漱口 shùkǒu, 漱喉 shù hóu to gargle with salt water 用盐水漱口 yòng yánshuǐ shùkǒu

gargoyle N 滴水嘴 dīshuǐzuǐ

garish ADJ 过于艳丽的 guòyú yànlì de

garland N 花环 huāhuán

garlic N 大蒜 dàsuàn a clove of garlic 一个蒜瓣 yí ge suànbàn

garment N 服装 fúzhuāng [M. WD 件 jiàn/套 tào]

garnish I V 给…加上配菜 gěi…jiāshàng pèicài II N 配菜 pèicài, 装饰菜 zhuāngshìcài

garrison N 卫戍部队 wèishù bùduì

garrulous ADJ 说个不完的 shuō gè bù wán de, 絮絮叨叨的 xùxu dāodāo de

garter N 吊带 diàodài garter snake 束带蛇 shùdài shé

gas I N 1 (gasoline) 汽油 qìyóu gas guzzler 耗油厉害的车 hàoyóu lìhai de chē, 油老虎 yóu lǎohǔ gas station 加油站 jiāyóuzhàn 2 气体 qìtǐ 3 煤气 méiqì gas mask 防毒面具 fángdú miànjù gas stove 煤气灶 méiqì zào II V 用毒气杀死 yòng dúqì shā sǐ, 毒死 dúsǐ

gash N 又深又长的切口 yòu shēn yòu cháng de qièkǒu, 伤口 shāngkǒu

gasoline N 汽油 qìyóu

gasp I V (大口) 喘气 (dà kǒu) chuǎnqì to gasp for air 呼吸急促 hūxī jícù II N 喘气 chuǎnqì, 深呼吸 shēn hūxī

gassy ADJ [肠胃+] 胀气的 [chángwèi+] zhàngqì de

gastric ADJ 胃的 wèi de gastric ulcer 胃溃疡 wèikuìyáng

gastronomic ADJ 美食的 měishí de a gastronomic tour 美食之旅 měishí zhī lǚ

gasworks N 煤气厂 méiqìchǎng

gate N 大门 dàmén

gatecrasher N 不请自来的人 bù qǐng zì lái de rén

gateway N 出入口 chūrùkǒu, 入门 rùmén

gather V 1 聚集 jùjí, 集合 jíhé 2 收集 shōují to gather up 收拾起 shōushiqǐ

gathering N 集会 jíhuì

gaudy ADJ 俗丽的 súlì de, 花哨的 huāshao de

gauge I N 测量仪器 cèliáng yíqì, 表 biǎo tire-pressure gauge (汽车) 轮胎气压表 (qìchē) lúntāi qìyābiǎo II V 1 测量 cèliáng 2 估计 gūjì, 判定 pàndìng to gauge public opinions 对社会舆论作出估计 duì shèhuì yúlùn zuòchū gūjì

gaunt ADJ 憔悴的 qiáocuì de, 瘦削的 shòuxuē de

gauntlet N 夹道鞭刑 jiādào biānxíng to run the gauntlet 受到攻击 shòudào gōngjī, 经受困难 jīngshòu kùnnan to throw down the gauntlet 挑战 tiǎozhàn

gauze N 纱布 shābù

gave V See give

gawk V 呆呆地看 dāidāide kàn, 傻傻 shǎ kàn

gawky ADJ 笨手笨脚的 bènshǒu bènjiǎo de

gay I ADJ 1 同性恋的 tóngxìngliàn de 2 快活的 kuàihuo de II N 男同性恋者 nán tóngxìngliànzhě

gaze V, N 凝视 níngshì, 注视 zhùshì

gazebo N 凉亭 liángtíng [M. WD 座 zuò]

gazelle N 瞪羚 dènglíng [M. WD 只 zhī/头 tóu]

gazette N 1 报纸 bàozhǐ [M. WD 张 zhāng/份 fèn] 2 杂志 zázhì [M. WD 本 běn]

gear I N 1 (汽车) 排挡 (qìchē) páidǎng to change gears 换挡 huàn dǎng 2 设备 shèbèi, 工具 gōngjù II V 调整 tiáozhěng to be geared to 使适合 shǐ shìhé to be geared up 准备好 zhǔnbèi hǎo

gearbox N 变速箱 biànsùxiāng

gearshift N 换挡杆 huàndǎnggǎn

geek N 怪人 guàirén, 怪家伙 guài jiāhuo

geese N See goose

geezer N 老头子 lǎotóuzi

geisha N 日本艺妓 Rìběn yìjì

gel I N 冻胶 dòngjiāo hair gel 发胶 fàjiāo II V 涂发胶 tú fàjiāo

gelatin N 骨胶 gǔjiāo

gem N 宝石 bǎoshí [M. WD 颗 kē/粒 lì/块 kuài]

gender N 性别 xìngbié

gene N 基因 jīyīn

genealogy N 家谱 jiāpǔ, 家谱图 jiāpǔtú

general ADJ 1 大致的 dàzhì de in general 一般来说 yì bān láishuō 2 普遍的 pǔbiàn de general store 杂货店 záhuòdiàn the general public 公众 gōngzhòng 3 总 zǒng a general election 大选 dàxuǎn II N 将军 jiāngjūn [M. WD 位 wéi]

generalization N 概括 gàikuò, 归纳 guīnà

to make sweeping generalizations 笼统地概括 lǒngtǒng de gàikuò

generalize V 1 概括分类 gàikuò fēnlèi 2 笼统地表达 lǒngtǒng de biǎodá

generally ADV 1 普遍地 pǔbiàn de 2 一般 (地) 来说 yì bān (de) láishuō

generate V 产生 chǎnshēng, 引起 yǐnqǐ

generation N 1 代 dài, 世代 shìdài generation gap 代沟 dàigōu 2 产生 chǎnshēng

generator N 发电机 fādiànjī

generic ADJ 1 没有注册商标的 [+商品] méiyǒu zhùcè shāngbiāo de [+shāngpǐn] 2 通用的 [+称呼] tōngyòng de [+chēnghu], 泛指的 fànzhǐ de

generous ADJ 慷慨 kāngkǎi, 大方 dàfang

genesis N 起源 qǐyuán, 开端 kāiduān Genesis (圣经) 创世纪 (Shèngjīng) chuàngshìjì

genetic ADJ 基因的 jīyīn de genetic engineering 基因工程 jīyīn gōngchéng genetic fingerprint 基因图谱 jīyīn túpǔ, 遗传指纹 yíchuán zhǐwén

genetics N 遗传学 yíchuánxué

genial ADJ 和蔼可亲的 hé'ǎi kěqīn de

genie N 妖怪 yāoguài

genital ADJ 生殖器的 shēngzhíqì de

genitals N 外生殖器 wàishēngzhíqì

genius N 天才 (人物) tiāncái (rénwù), 天赋 tiānfù a stroke of genius 天才之举 tiāncái zhī jǔ

genocide N 种族灭绝 zhǒngzú mièjué

genome N 基因组 jīyīnzǔ human genome 人类基因组 rénlèi jīyīnzǔ

genre N (文学艺术的) 种类 (wénxué yìshù de) zhǒnglèi, 类型 lèixíng

genteel ADJ 1 彬彬有礼的 bīnbīn yǒulǐ de 2 雅致的 yǎzhì de

gentile N (对犹太人而言的) 异教徒 (duì Yóutàirén éryán de) yìjiàotú, 非犹太人 fēi Yóutàirén

gentle ADJ 温和 wēnhé, 温柔 wēnróu

gentleman N 1 先生 xiānsheng 2 君子 jūnzǐ, 绅士 shēnshì

gently ADV 温和地 wēnhé de, 轻柔地 qīngróu de

gentry N 上流社会人士 shàngliú shèhuì rénshì

genuine ADJ 真诚的 zhēnchéng de, 真正的 zhēnzhèng de

genus N (生物) 属 (shēngwù) shǔ

geographical ADJ 地理的 dìlǐ de

geography N 1 地理 (学) dìlǐ (xué)
economic geography 经济地理学 jīngjì dìlǐxué
physical geography 自然地理学 zìrán dìlǐxué
2 地理情况 dìlǐ qíngkuàng

geologist N 地质学家 dìzhìxuéjiā

geometric ADJ 几何学的 jǐhéxué de

geometry N 几何 (学) jǐhé (xué)

geriatrics N 老年医学 lǎoniányīxué

germ N 细菌 xìjūn

German I ADJ 德国的 Déguó de
German shepherd 德国牧羊犬 Déguó mùyáng quǎn
II N 1 德国人 Déguórén 2 德语 Déyǔ

germinate V 1 发芽 fāyá, 使…发芽 shǐ…fāyá 2 开始产生 kāishǐ chǎnshēng, 萌发 méngfā

gestation N 1 怀孕 (期) huáiyùn (qī) 2 [新技术的+] 形成 [xīn jìshù de+] xíngchéng, 形成期 xíngchéng qī

gesticulate V 做手势 zuò shǒushì

gesture I N 1 [表示欢迎的+] 手势 [biǎoshì huānyíng de+] shǒushì 2 [友好的+] 姿势 [yǒuhǎo de+] zīshì, 表示 biǎoshì II V 打手势 dǎ shǒushì

get (PT got; PP gotten) V 1 得到 dédào, 买到 mǎidào 2 变得 biàndé 3 到达 dàodá 4 使得 shǐde, 让 ràng
to get across 把意思表达清楚 bǎ yìsi biǎodá qīngchu
to get along with 相处 xiāngchǔ
to get away with 不受惩罚 bú shòu chéngfá
to get by 勉强维持 miǎnqiáng wéichí
to get the phone/door 接电话 / 开门 jiē diànhuà/kāi mén

getaway N 1 [周末+] 旅游 [zhōumò+] lǚyóu 2 逃跑 táopǎo

a getaway car [犯罪分子+] 准备逃跑的汽车 [fànzuì fènzǐ+] zhǔnbèi táopǎo de qìchē

get-together N 联欢 liánhuān, 联欢会 liánhuānhuì

geyser N 间隙喷泉 jiànxì pēnquán

ghastly ADJ 极其糟糕的 jíqí zāogāo de, 极其可怕的 jíqí kěpà de

ghetto N 贫民区 pínmínqū, 贫民窟 pínmínkū

ghost N 鬼 guǐ, 鬼魂 guǐhún
ghost writer 代笔人 dàibǐrén

ghoul N 食尸鬼 shíshīguǐ

giant I N 1 巨人 jùrén 2 [工业界+] 重要人物 [gōngyèjiè+] zhòngyào rénwù, 巨头 jùtóu, [流行音乐+] 巨星 [liúxíng yīnyuè+] jùxīng II ADJ 巨大的 jùdà de, 特大的 tèdà de

gibberish N 胡言乱语 húyán luànyǔ

giblets N (家禽) 内脏 (jiāqín) nèizàng

giddy ADJ 1 快活的 kuàihuo de, 开心得忘乎所以的 kāixīn dé wàng hū suǒyǐ de
to be giddy with successes 因成功而冲昏头脑 yīn chénggōng ér chōnghūn tóunǎo
2 眩晕的 xuànyùn de

gift N 1 礼物 lǐwù [M. WD 件 jiàn/份 fèn]
gift certificate 购物礼券 gòuwù lǐquàn
gift wrap 礼品包装纸 lǐpǐn bāozhuāngzhǐ
2 天生的才能 tiānshēng de cáinéng

gifted ADJ 天才的 tiāncái de
a special class for gifted children 天才儿童特别班 tiāncái értóng tèbiébān

gig N 演奏会 yǎnzòu huì, (音乐) 演出 (yīnyuè) yǎnchū

gigabyte N 千兆字节 qiānzhào zìjié

gigantic ADJ 巨大的 jùdà de

giggle V 咯咯地笑 gēgē de xiào, 傻乎乎地笑 shǎhūhū de xiào

gild V 给…镀金 gěi…dùjīn
to gild the lily 画蛇添足 huà shé tiān zú

gill N 鱼鳃 yúsāi

gilt I ADJ 镀金的 dùjīn de
gilt-edged 金边的 jīnbiān de
II N 1 镀金层 dùjīncéng 2 金边股票 jīnbiān gǔpiào

gimmick N 花招 huāzhāo
  advertising gimmicks 广告花招 guǎnggào huāzhāo
gin N 杜松子酒 Dùsōngzǐjiǔ
ginger N 姜 jiāng, 生姜 shēngjiāng
  ginger ale 姜味汽水 jiāng wèi qìshuǐ
gingerbread N 姜饼 jiāngbǐng
giraffe N 长颈鹿 chángjǐnglù
girder N 大梁 dàliáng
girdle N 紧身褡 jǐnshēn dā
girl N 1 女孩 nǚhái
  girlfriend 女朋友 nǚpéngyou
  Girl Scouts 女童子军 nǚ tóngzǐjūn
  2 女儿 nǚ'ér
girth N 围长 wéicháng, (人的) 腰围 (rén de) yāowéi
gist N 主要内容 zhǔyào nèiróng, 要点 yàodiǎn
give (PT **gave**; PP **given**) V 1 给 gěi, 给与 jǐyǔ 2 举行 jǔxíng
  to give away 赠送 zèngsòng
  to give up 放弃 fàngqì
giveaway I N 1 赠送 zèngsòng, 捐赠 juānzèng
  holiday giveaway 假日捐赠 jiàrì juānzèng
  2 赠送的东西 zèngsòng de dōngxi, 赠品 zèngpǐn II ADJ 等于是送的 děngyú shì sòng de, 极其便宜的 jíqí piányi de
given I V See give II ADJ 任何特定的 rènhé tèdìng de
  at any given time 在任何 (特定的) 时间 zàirèn hé (tèdìng de) shíjiān
  III PREP 考虑到 kǎolùdào IV N 基本事实 jīběn shìshí, 肯定的事实 kěndìng de shìshí
  given name 名字 míngzì
glacial ADJ 1 冰川的 bīngchuān de, 冰的 bīng de 2 冷冰冰的 (表情) lěngbīngbīng de (biǎoqíng)
glacier N 冰川 bīngchuān
glad ADJ 高兴 gāoxìng
gladiator N 角斗士 juédòushì
gladly ADV 1 高兴地 gāoxìngde 2 乐意地 lèyì de
glamor N 迷人的诱惑 mírén de yòuhuò, 魅力 mèilì
  glamor girl 时髦迷人的姑娘 shímáo

mírén de gūniang, 时尚女郎 shíshàng nǚláng
glamorous ADJ 迷人的 mírén de, 有诱惑力的 yǒu yòuhuòlì de
glance V, N 看一下 kàn yíxià, 看一眼 kàn yìyǎn
gland N 腺 xiàn
  sweat gland 汗腺 hànxiàn
glare V 1 愤怒地注视 fènnù de zhùshì 2 [玻璃窗+] 发出强光 [bōlichuāng+] fāchū qiáng guāng
glaring ADJ 1 怒视的 nùshì de 2 刺眼的 [+阳光] cìyǎn de [+yángguāng] 3 明显的 [+错误] míngxiǎn de [+cuòwù]
glass N 1 玻璃杯 bōli bēi 2 玻璃 bōli
glass ceiling N 无形的限制 wúxíng de xiànzhì
glasses N 眼镜 yǎnjìng [M. WD 副 fù]
  sunglasses 太阳眼镜 tàiyáng yǎnjìng
glassware N 玻璃器皿 bōli qìmǐn
glassy ADJ 光亮的 guānglòng de, 光滑的 guānghuá de
glaze I V 1 [目光+] 呆滞 [mùguāng+] dāizhì 2 上釉 shàngyòu II N 釉 yòu
gleam I N 1 闪光 shǎnguāng 2 闪现 shǎnxiàn II V 1 [玻璃+] 闪光 [bōli+] shǎnguāng 2 闪现 [+表情] shǎnxiàn [+biǎoqíng]
glean V 搜集 sōují
glee N 欣喜 xīnxǐ, 兴奋 xīngfèn
glen N 峡谷 xiágǔ, 幽谷 yōugǔ
glib ADJ 1 油嘴滑舌的 [+节目主持人] yóuzuǐ huáshé de [+jiémù zhǔchírén] 2 草率的 [+结论] cǎoshuài de [+jiélùn]
glide V 滑行 huáxíng
glider N 滑翔机 huáxiángjī [M. WD 架 jià]
glimmer I N 微光 wēiguāng
  a glimmer of hope 一线希望 yí xiàn xīwàng
  II V 发出微光 fāchū wēiguāng
glimpse I N 一眼 yìyǎn, 一瞥 yìpiē 2 短暂的经历 duǎnzàn de jīnglì II V 1 瞥见 piējiàn 2 突然领悟 tūrán lǐngwù, 顿悟 dùnwù
glint I V 闪闪发光 shǎnshǎn fāguāng, 闪烁 shǎnshuò II N 闪光 shǎnguāng
glisten V 闪闪发光 shǎnshǎn fāguāng, 闪闪发亮 shǎnshǎn fāliàng

glitch N 故障 gùzhàng, 差错 chācuò
computer glitch 电脑故障 diànnǎo gùzhàng

glitter I v 闪光 shǎnguāng, 闪烁 shǎnshuò II N 1 闪光 shǎnguāng, 闪烁 shǎnshuò 2 诱惑（力）yòuhuò (lì)

gloat v 得意洋洋 déyì yángyáng
to gloat over sb's misfortune 因别人的不幸而得意 yīn biéren de búxìng ér déyì, 幸灾乐祸 xìngzāi lèhuò

global ADJ 全球的 quán dìqiú de, 世界范围的 shìjièfànwéide
global warming 全球变暖 quánqiú biànnuǎn

globe N 1 地球 dìqiú
from every corner of the globe 世界各地的 shìjiè gèdì de 2 地球仪 dìqiúyí

globule N 水滴 shuǐdī, 水珠 shuǐzhū

gloom N 1 幽暗 yōu'àn, 昏暗 hūn'àn 2 忧伤 yōushāng

gloomy ADJ 1 阴暗的 [+房间] yīn'àn de [+fángjiān] 2 悲观的 bēiguān de

glorify v 1 赞美 [+上帝] zànměi [+Shàngdì] 2 颂扬 [+冒险精神] sòngyáng [+màoxiǎn jīngshén], 吹捧 chuīpěng

glorious ADJ 光荣的 guāngróng de, 荣耀的 róngyào de, 辉煌的 huīhuáng de

glory N 光荣 guāngróng, 荣耀 róngyào, 辉煌 huīhuáng
one's former glory 昔日的辉煌 xīrì de huīhuáng

gloss I N 1 [银器+] 光泽 [yínqì+] guāngzé, 光亮 guāngliàng 2 [古诗+] 注释 [gǔshī+] zhùshì, 注解 zhùjiě II v 加注释 jiāzhù shì

glossary N 词汇表 cíhuìbiǎo, 难词表 náncíbiǎo

glossy ADJ 有光泽的 yǒuguāng zé de
glossy paper 上光纸 shàngguāng zhǐ

glove N 手套 shǒutào [M. WD 只 zhī/副 fù]
glove compartment（汽车）贮藏柜 (qìchē) zhùcáng guì

glow v 1 发出光亮 fāchū guāngliàng
to glow with happiness 因幸福而容光焕发 yīn xìngfú ér róngguāng huànfā 2 [脸部+] 发热 [liǎn bù+] fārè N 1 光亮 guāngliàng, 发热 fārè 2 脸上（健

康）的光泽 liǎnshàng (jiànkāng) de guāngzé 3（美好的）感觉 (měihǎo de) gǎnjué
a glow of pride 自豪的感觉 zìháo de gǎnjué

glower v 怒目而视 nùmù ér shì, 怒视 nùshì

glowing ADJ 热烈赞扬的 rèliè zànyáng de, 好话连篇的 hǎohuà liánpiān de

glue I N 胶 jiāo, 胶水 jiāoshuǐ II v 粘贴 zhān tiē, 胶合 jiāohé

glum ADJ 闷闷不乐的 mènmèn bú lè de, 沉闷的 chénmèn de

glut N 供应过剩 gōngyìng guòshèng

glutton N 嘴馋的人 zuǐchán de rén, 馋嘴鬼 chánzuǐguǐ

GM (= genetically modified) ABBREV 转基因 zhuǎnjīyīn
GM food 转基因食物 zhuǎnjīyīn shíwù

gnarled ADJ 1 多瘤多节的 [+树] duō liú duōjié de [+shù], 扭曲的 niǔqū de 2 粗糙的 [+手] cūzào de [+shǒu]

gnash v 咬牙 yǎoyá
to gnash one's teeth 咬牙切齿 yǎo yá qiē chǐ

gnat N 叮人的小虫 dīng rén de xiǎo chóng [M. WD 只 zhī]

gnaw v 1 啃 kěn, 咬 yǎo 2 折磨 zhémo, 使…精神痛苦 shǐ…jīngshen tòngkǔ

gnawing ADJ 折磨人的 zhémo rén de, 令人痛苦的 lìng rén tòngkǔ de

GNP (= Gross National Product) ABBREV 国民生产总值 guómín shēngchǎn zǒngzhí

go I v (PT went; PP gone) 1 去 qù, 到…去 dào…qù 2 离去 líqu, 离开 líkāi
Go away! 走开! zǒukāi
to go back 回到 huídao
to go on ① 继续 jìxù ② 发生 fāshēng
to go out 出去玩 chūqu wán
to go shopping/camping/swimming 去购物／去野营／去游泳 qù gòuwù/qù yěyíng/qù yóuyǒng
II N 尝试 chángshì
to make a go of sth 试图 shìtú, 使 [+生意] 成功 shǐ [+shēng yì] chénggōng

goad v 驱使 qūshǐ, 激励 jīlì

go-ahead I N 准许 zhǔnxǔ, 许可 xǔkě
to give sb the go-ahead 给予准许 jǐyǔ
zhǔnxǔ
II ADJ 领先的 lǐngxiān de
a go-ahead touchdown 使球队领先的
触地得分 shǐ qiúduì lǐngxiān de chù dì
défēn

goal N 1 目标 mùbiāo 2 球门 qiúmén
to score a goal 踢（打）进一球 tī (dǎ)
jìn yì qiú

goalkeeper N 守门员 shǒuményuán

goalpost N 球门柱 qiúménzhù

goat N 山羊 shānyáng

goatee N （山羊）胡子 (shānyáng) húzi

gobble V 狼吞虎咽 lángtūn hǔyàn

gobbledygook N 冗长难懂又无聊的文
字 rǒngcháng nándǒng yòu wúliáo de
wénzì, 官样文章 guānyàng wénzhāng

go-between N 中间人 zhōngjiānrén

goblet N 高脚杯 gāojiǎobēi [M. WD 只 zhǐ]

goblin N 调皮的小妖精 tiáopí de
xiǎoyāojīng

go-cart N 单座赛车 dān zuò sàichē

God N 上帝 Shàngdì, 老天 Lǎotiān
God helps those who help themselves. 天助自助者。 Tiān zhù zì zhù
zhě.

god N 神 shén, 神仙 shénxian

godchild N 教子 jiàozǐ, 教女 jiàonǚ

goddammit INTERJ 该死 gāisǐ, 他妈的
tāmāde

goddamn ADJ 该死的 gāisǐ de

goddess N 女神 nǚshén [M. WD 位 wéi]

godfather N 教父 jiàofù

god-fearing ADJ 敬畏上帝的 jìngwèi
Shàngdì de

godless ADJ 不敬上帝的 bùjìng Shàngdì
de, 不信神的 bú xìn shén de

godlike ADJ 神圣的 shénshèng de, 如同
神明的 rútóng shénmíng de

godly ADJ 虔诚的 qiánchéng de

godmother N 教母 jiàomǔ

godparent N 教父 jiàofù, 教母 jiàomǔ

godsend N 飞来的好运 fēiláide hǎoyùn,
意外的惊喜 yìwài de jīngxǐ

go-getter N 有进取心的人 yǒu jìnqǔxīn
de rén

goggle-eyed ADJ 瞪大眼睛的 dèng dà
yǎnjīng de, 极其惊讶的 jíqí jīngyà de

goggles N 防风眼镜 fángfēng yǎnjìng, 护
目镜 hùmùjìng [M. WD 副 fù]

going I N 1 离去 líqù 2 进展 jìnzhǎn
rough going 进展艰难 jìnzhǎn jiānnán
II ADJ 通行的 tōngxíng de
going rate 通行的价格 tōngxíng de
jiàgé, 时价 shíjià

gold I N 金（子）jīn (zi), 黄金 huángjīn
All that glitters is not gold. 闪光的不
都是金子。 Shǎnguāng de bù dōu shì
jīnzi.
II ADJ 1 金子的 jīnzi de
gold digger 靠色相骗取钱财的女人 kào
sèxiāng piànqǔ qiáncái de nǚrén
gold standard 金本位 jīnběnwèi
2 金黄色的 jīn huáng sè de

golden ADJ 1 金子的 jīnzi de, 金色的 jīnsè
de 2 极好的 jíhǎo de, 宝贵的 bǎoguì de
a golden handshake 优厚的退休金
yōuhòu de tuìxiūjīn, 一大笔离职费 yí
dàbǐ lízhí fèi
a golden opportunity 非常难得的机会
fēicháng nándé de jīhuì

goldfish N 金鱼 jīnyú [M. WD 条 tiáo]

goldmine N 1 金矿 jīnkuàng [M. WD 座
zuò] 2 财源 cáiyuán, 宝库 bǎokù

golf N 高尔夫球 gāo'ěrfūqiú
golf course 高尔夫球场
gāo'ěrfūqiúchǎng

gondola N 1 [意大利威尼斯的+] 平底船
[Yìdàlì Wēinísī de+] píngdǐchuán 2 [风
景点+]（电）缆车 [fēngjǐng diǎn+]
diànlǎnchē, 缆车 lǎnchē

gone V See go

goner N 快完蛋的人 kuài wándàn de rén

gong N 锣 luó [M. WD 面 miàn]

gonorrhea N 淋病 lìnbìng

good I ADJ 1 好的 hǎo de, 优良的
yōuliáng de 2 守规矩的 shǒu guījǔ de,
乖的 guāi de 3 愉快的 yúkuài de
Have a good holiday! 祝你假期愉
快! Zhù nǐ jiàqī yúkuài!
4 有益健康的 yǒuyì jiànkāng de
to be good for sb 对某人的健康有益
duì mǒurén jiànkāng yǒuyì

II N 1 好处 hǎochu, 利益 lìyì 2 善 shàn, 道德 dàodé

to do good 有好处 yǒu hǎochù

be good at 擅长于 shàncháng yú, 善于 shànyú

as good as 跟…一样 gēn...yíyàng

for good 永远 yǒngyuǎn

good morning 早上好 zǎoshang hǎo

good afternoon 下午好 xiàwǔ hǎo

good evening 晚上好 wǎnshang hǎo

good night 晚安 wǎn'ān

goodbye 再见 zàijiàn

good-for-nothing N 一无用处的人 yìwú yòngchu de rén, 懒人 lǎn rén

good-humored ADJ 快活友好的 kuàihuo yǒuhǎo de

good-looking ADJ 好看的 [+人] hǎokàn de [+rén], 漂亮的 piàoliang de

good-natured ADJ 性情温和的 xìngqíng wēnhé de

goodness N 1 善 shàn, 善良 shànliáng 2 食物中最有营养的部分 shíwù zhōng zuì yǒu yíngyǎng de bùfen

goods N 货物 huòwù, 商品 shāngpǐn

dry goods 纺织品 fǎngzhī pǐn

electrical goods 电器用品 diànqì yòngpǐn

goodwill N 善意 shànyì, 友善 yǒushàn

goody, goodie N 好吃的东西 hǎochī de dōngxi

goof I v 1 出错 chūcuò, 搞错 gǎocuò II N 愚蠢的错误 yúchǔn de cuòwù

goofy ADJ 傻乎乎的 shǎhūhū de

Google N [搜索引擎] 谷歌 [sōusuǒyǐnqíng] Gǔgē

goon N 1 打手 dǎshou, 暴徒 bàotú 2 傻瓜 shǎguā, 蠢货 chǔnhuò

goose (PL **geese**) N 鹅 é [M. WD 只 zhī]

wild goose 大雁 dàyàn

goose-bumps N 鸡皮疙瘩 jīpí gēda

gorge I N 峡谷 xiágǔ II v 狼吞虎咽 lángtūn hǔyàn

to gorge oneself on sth 狼吞虎咽地吃某物 lángtūn hǔyàn de chī mǒuwù

gorgeous ADJ 极好的 jíhǎo de, 好极了的 hǎo jíle de

gorilla N 大猩猩 dàxīngxing

gory ADJ 暴力的 bàolì de

gosh INTERJ 啊呀 āyā

gosling N 小鹅 xiǎo é

gospel N 1 (圣经) 福音 (Shèngjīng) Fúyīn 2 信条 xìntiáo 3 福音音乐 Fúyīn yīnyuè

gospel truth 绝对真实的事 juéduì zhēnshí de shì

gossip I N 1 流言蜚语 liúyán fēiyǔ, 道听途说的话 dàotīng túshuō de huà 2 喜欢谈论别人私生活的人 xǐhuan tánlùn biérén sīshēnghuó de rén

gossip mill 制造流言蜚语的人 zhìzào liúyán fēiyǔ de rén

II v 说别人的闲话 shuō biérén de xiánhuà, 传播流言蜚语 chuánbō liúyán fēiyǔ

got v See get

gotcha INTERJ 1 抓住了 zhuāzhù le 2 我赢了 wǒ yíng le

gotten v See get

gouge v 凿 (孔) záo (kǒng)

gourd N 葫芦 húlu

gourmet I N 美食家 měishíjiā II ADJ 美食的 měishí de

a gourmet restaurant 美食餐厅 měishí cāntīng, 高级饭店 gāojí fàndiàn

gout N 痛风 (病) tòngfēng (bìng)

govern v 1 治理 zhìlǐ, 管辖 guǎnxiá 2 控制 kòngzhì, 支配 zhīpèi

government N 1 政府 zhèngfǔ 2 治理 zhìlǐ

governor N 1 (美国) 州长 (Měiguó) Zhōuzhǎng 2 总督 Zǒngdū

gown N 1 女夜礼服 nǚ yèlǐfú 2 (医院 / 实验室) 白大褂 (yīyuàn/shíyànshì) báidàguà

GP (= general practitioner) ABBREV 普通医生 pǔtōng yīshēng, 全科医生 quánkē yīshēng

GPS (= global positioning system) ABBREV 1 全球定位系统 quánqiú dìngwèi xìtǒng 2 导航器 dǎohángqì

grab v, N 抓住 zhuāzhu

to grab a chance 抓住机会 zhuāzhù jīhuì

to be up for grabs 大家都可以争取 dàjiā dōu kěyǐ zhēngqǔ

grace N 1 优雅 yōuyǎ 2 宽限 kuānxiàn

grace period 宽限期 kuānxiànqī **3** 感恩祷告 gǎn'ēn dǎogào

to have the grace to 有…的气量 yǒu…de qìliàng, 有…的雅量 yǒu…de yǎliàng

graceful ADJ **1** 优雅的 yōuyǎ de, 优美的 yōuměi de **2** 得体的 détǐ de, 礼貌的 lǐmào de

gracious ADJ **1** 仁慈的 réncí de, 和善的 héshàn de **2** 奢华的（生活）shēhuá de (shēnghuó)

gradation N 渐变 jiànbiàn, 层次 céngcì, 等级 děngjí

grade I N **1** 年级 niánjí

    grade school 小学 xiǎoxué

2 等级 děngjí **3** 分数 fēnshù II V 评分 píngfēn

gradient N 坡度 pōdù, 倾斜度 qīngxié dù

gradual ADJ 逐渐 zhújiàn, 渐渐 jiànjiàn

gradually ADV 逐渐地 zhújiàn de, 渐渐地 jiànjiàn de

graduate I N 毕业生 bìyèshēng II V 毕业 bìyè III ADJ 研究生的 yánjiūshēng de

    graduate school 研究生院 yánjiūshēng yuàn

    graduate student 研究生 yánjiūshēng

graduation N **1** 毕业 bìyè **2** 毕业典礼 bìyè diǎnlǐ

graffiti N 乱涂乱画 luàn tú luàn huà, 涂鸦 túyā

graft I N **1** 以权谋私 yǐ quán móu sī, 贪污 tānwū **2**（枝条）移接 (zhītiáo) jiàjiē **3**（皮肤）移植 (pífū) yízhí II V **1** 嫁接 [+枝条] jiàjiē [+zhītiáo] **2** 移植 [+皮肤] yízhí [+pífū]

grain N **1** 谷物 gǔwù, 粮食 liángshi **2**（木头）纹理 (mùtou) wénlǐ **3** 颗粒 kēlì

    a grain of truth 一点道理 yìdiǎn dàoli

gram N 克 kè

grammar N **1** 语法 yǔfǎ **2** 语法书 yǔfǎ shū [M. WD 本 běn]

grand ADJ **1** 雄伟的 xióngwěi de **2** 宏大的 hóngdà de

    grand jury 大陪审团 dàpéishěntuán

    grand prix 国际汽车大赛 guójì qìchē dàsài

    grand slam（棒球）全垒打 (bàngqiú) quánlěidǎ, (牌桥) 大满贯 (qiáopái) dà mǎnguàn

grandchild See **granddaughter, grandson**

granddad N 爷爷 yéye (paternal grandpa), 外公 wàigōng (maternal grandpa)

granddaughter N 孙女 sūnnǚ (one's son's daughter), 外孙女 wàisūnnǚ (one's daughter's daughter)

grandeur N 宏伟壮丽 hóngwěi zhuànglì

grandfather N 祖父 zǔfù (paternal grandfather), 外祖父 wàizǔfù (maternal grandfather)

    grandfather clock 落地式自鸣钟 luòdìshì zìmíngzhōng

grandma N 奶奶 nǎinai (paternal grandma), 姥姥 lǎolao (maternal grandma)

grandmother N 祖母 zǔmǔ (paternal grandmother), 外祖母 wàizǔmǔ (maternal grandmother)

grandpa N See **grandad**

grandparent N 祖父母 zǔfùmǔ (paternal grandparents), 外祖父母 wàizǔfùmǔ (maternal grandparents)

grandson N 孙子 sūnzi (one's son's son), 外孙 wàisūn (one's daughter's son)

grandstand N 大看台 dà kàntái

granite N 花岗岩 huāgǎngyán [M. WD 块 kuài]

granny N See **grandma**

grant I V **1** 同意 tóngyì, 准许 zhǔnxǔ **2** 承认 [+事实] chéngrèn [+shìshí] II N 拨款 bō kuǎn, 经费 jīngfèi

    to take for granted 想当然 xiǎngdāngrán

granulated ADJ 砂状的 shā zhuàng de

granule N 小颗粒 xiǎo kēlì

    instant coffee granules 速溶咖啡精 sùróng kāfēijīng

grape N 葡萄 pútao [M. WD 颗 kē/串 chuàn]

grapefruit N 西柚 xīyòu, 葡萄柚 pútáoyòu

grapevine N 葡萄（藤）pútao (téng)

    to hear about sth on the grapevine 从传闻中听到 cóng chuánwén zhōng tīngdào, 听到小道新闻 tīngdào xiǎodào xīnwén

graph N 图表 túbiǎo [M. WD 张 zhāng]

bar graph 条形图 tiáoxíngtú

pie graph 饼形分析图 bǐngxíng fēnxītú

graphic I ADJ 1 绘图的 huìtú de, 印刷的 yìnshuā de 2 详细的 [+报导] xiángxì de [+bàodǎo] 3 色情下流的 [+描述] sèqíng xiàliú de [+miáoshù]

graphic design 图像设计 túxiàng shèjì II N (graphics) 图表 túbiǎo [M. WD 张 zhāng], 图像 túxiàng [M. WD 张 zhāng]

grapple V 1 扭打 niǔdǎ 2 努力对付 [+困境] nǔlì duìfu [+kùnjìng], 设法解决 [+难题] shèfǎ jiějué [+nántí]

grasp I V 1 抓牢 zhuā láo, 抓紧 zhuājǐn 2 完全理解 [+一个概念] wánquán lǐjiě [+yí ge gàiniàn] II N 1 理解 [+能力] lǐjiě [+nénglì] 2 达到 dádào, 到手 dàoshǒu

grass N 草 cǎo [M. WD 颗 kē], 青草 qīngcǎo

grass roots 草根阶层 cǎogēn jiēcéng, 基层 jīcéng

The grass is always greener on the other side. 别人的情况总是比自己好。Biéren de qíngkuàng zǒngshì bǐ zìjǐ hǎo. 家花哪有野花香。Jiāhuā nǎyǒu yěhuā xiāng. 外国的月亮比较圆。Wàiguó de yuèliàng bǐjiào yuán.

grasshopper N 蚱蜢 zhàměng [M. WD 只 zhǐ], 蝗虫 huángchóng [M. WD 只 zhǐ]

grassland N 草原 cǎoyuán

grate I V 磨碎 mósuì, 发出刺耳的声音 fāchū cì'ěr de shēngyīn II N 铁栅 tiězhà

grateful ADJ 感谢 gǎnxiè, 感恩 gǎn'ēn

grater N 磨碎器 mósuì qì

gratification N 满足 mǎnzú

instant gratification 立即满足 lìjí mǎnzú

gratis ADJ, ADV 免费的 miǎnfèi de, 免费 miǎnfèi

gratitude N 感激 (之情) gǎnjī (zhī qíng), 谢意 xièyì

gratuity N 小费 xiǎofèi

grave[1] N 墓 mù, 坟墓 fénmù, 墓 fén

grave[2] ADJ 严重的 yánzhòng de

gravel N 碎石子 suì shízi

gravelly ADJ 1 碎石子的 suì shízi de 2 低哑的 [+声音] dīyǎ de [+shēngyīn]

graveside N 坟墓边 fénmù biān

gravestone N 墓碑 mùbēi [M. WD 块 kuài]

graveyard N 墓地 mùdì

gravitation N 引力 yǐnlì

gravity N 地心引力 dìxīn yǐnlì, 重力 zhònglì

gravy N 肉汁 ròu zhī

gray I ADJ 灰色的 huīsè de II N 灰色 huīsè

gray matter 大脑 dànǎo, 智力 zhìlì

graze V 1 [动物+] 吃草 [dòngwù+] chī cǎo, 放牧 fàngmù 2 擦破 cāpò, 擦伤 cāshāng

grease I N 1 油脂 yóuzhī 2 润滑油 rùnhuáyóu II V 给…涂上油 gěi…tú shàngyóu

to grease sb's palm 向某人行贿 xiàng mǒurén xínghuì

greasy ADJ 1 油脂很多的 yóuzhī hěn duō de 2 油腻腻的 yóunìnì de

a greasy spoon 破旧肮脏的小饭馆 pòjiù āngzāng de xiǎo fànguǎn

great ADJ 1 大的 dà de 2 极好的 jíhǎo de 3 伟大 wěidà

a great many 很多 hěn duō

greatly ADV 非常 fēicháng, 大大的 dàdà de

greed N 贪心 tānxīn, 贪婪 tānlán

greedy ADJ 1 贪吃 tānchī, 嘴馋 zuǐchán 2 贪心的 tānxīn de

Greek I ADJ 希腊的 Xīlà de II N 1 希腊人 Xīlàrén 2 希腊语 Xīlàyǔ

It's all Greek to me. 我对此一窍不通。Wǒ duì cǐ yíqiào bùtōng.

green I ADJ 1 绿色的 lǜsè de 2 环境 (保护) 的 huánjìng (bǎohù) 3 年轻而没有经验的 niánqīng ér méiyǒu jingyan de 4 (脸色) 苍白的 (liǎnsè) cāngbái de II N 1 绿 (色) lǜ (sè)

green card 绿卡 lǜkǎ 2 草地 cǎodì, 草场 cǎochǎng

bowling green 草地滚木球场 cǎodì gǔnmùqiúchǎng

greenback N 美元 Měiyuán

greenhouse N 温室 wēnshì

greenhouse effect 温室效应 wēnshì xiàoyìng

greet V 1 问好 wènhǎo, 打招呼 dǎ zhāohu 2 欢迎 huānyíng

greeting N 1 问候 wènhòu, 问好 wènhǎo 2 祝贺 zhùhè

greeting card (祝) 贺卡 (zhù) hè kǎ

gregarious ADJ 合群的 héqún de, 喜爱交际的 xǐ'ài jiāojì de

grenade N 手榴弹 shǒuliúdàn

grew V See grow

greyhound N 1 灰狗 huīgǒu 2 (美国) 灰狗长途汽车 (Měiguó) huīgǒu chángtú qìchē

grid N 1 电力网 diànlìwǎng 2 方格图案 fānggé tú'àn 3 (地图) 坐标方格 (dìtú) zuòbiāo fānggé

griddle N 平底锅 píngdǐguō

gridiron N 1 橄榄球球场 gǎnlǎnqiú qiúchǎng 2 烤架 kǎojià

gridlock N 1 僵局 jiāngjú, (工作) 停顿 (gōngzuò) tíngdùn 2 交通堵塞 jiāotōng dǔsè

grief N 悲伤 bēishāng, 悲哀 bēi'āi

grievance N 委屈 wěiqu, 抱怨 bàoyuàn

grieve V 使…非常难过 shǐ...fēicháng nánguò, 使…感到悲痛 shǐ...gǎndào bēitòng

grill I V 烤烤, 烧烤 shāokǎo II N 1 烧烤架 shāokǎojià 2 烧烤餐厅 shāokǎo cāntīng

grim ADJ 1 令人担忧的 [+前景] lìng rén dānyōu de [+qiánjǐng] 2 严肃的 [+法官] yánsù de [+fǎguān] 3 严峻的 yánjùn de

grimace I V 1 (开玩笑) 扮鬼脸 (kāiwánxiào) bàn guǐliǎn 2 (因疼痛 / 厌恶) 扭曲了脸 (yīn téngtòng/yànwù) niǔqūle liǎn

grime N (一层) 油腻 (yìcéng) yóunì

grimy ADJ 油腻的 yóunì de

grin I V 咧开嘴笑 liě kāi zuǐ xiào
to grin and bear it 苦笑忍受 kǔxiào rěnshòu
II N 咧开嘴笑 liě kāi zuǐ xiào

grind I V (PT & PP ground) 1 碾碎 [+咖啡豆] niǎnsuì [+kāfēi dòu] 2 绞碎 [+肉] jiǎo suì [+ròu] 3 磨 [+刀] mó [+dāo] II N 苦工 kǔgōng

grinder N 碾磨机 niǎnmójī

grinding ADJ 折磨人的 zhémó rén de
grinding poverty 折磨人的贫穷 zhémó rén de pínqióng

grindstone N 磨刀石 módáoshí

grip I N 紧握 jǐnwò 2 牢牢控制 láoláo kòngzhì

to get to grips with 真正懂得并且能应付 zhēnzhèng dǒngde bìngqiě néng yìngfù

3 控制 (力) kòngzhì (lì)
to lose one's grip 失去控制 shīqù kòngzhì

4 理解力 lǐjiělì 5 夹子 jiāzi II V 1 紧紧地握住 jǐnjǐn de wòzhù 2 引起…注意 yǐnqǐ...zhùyì

gripe I V 发牢骚 fā láosāo, 抱怨 bàoyuàn II N 牢骚 láosāo, 抱怨的小事 bàoyuàn de xiǎoshì

grisly ADJ 恐怖的 kǒngbù de

gristle N (肉) 软骨 (ròu) ruǎngǔ

grit I N 1 沙砾 shālì 2 决心和勇气 juéxīn hé yǒngqì II V 磨轧 móyà
to grit one's teeth 咬紧牙关 yǎojǐn yáguān

groan V 痛苦呻吟 tòngkǔ shēnyín

grocery store N 食品杂货店 shípǐn záhuò diàn

groggy ADJ 1 [头脑+] 昏昏沉沉的 [tóunǎo+] hūnchénchén de 2 [四肢+] 无力的 [sìzhī+] wúlì de

groin N 腹股沟 fùgǔgōu

groom I V 1 穿戴打扮 chuāndài dǎban
a well-groomed young man 穿戴打扮得整整齐齐的年轻人 chuāndài dǎban dé zhěngzhěng qíqí de niánqīngrén
2 [动物+] 梳理皮毛 [dòngwù+] shūlǐ pímáo 3 培养 [+接班人] péiyǎng [+jiēbānrén] II N 1 新郎 xīnláng 2 马夫 mǎfū

groove N 1 凹槽 āocáo [M. WD 道 dào]
2 正常状态 zhèngcháng zhuàngtài
to get back in the groove 重新进入正常状态 chóngxīn jìnrù zhèngcháng zhuàngtài

groovy ADJ 时髦的 shímáo de, 流行的 liúxíng de

grope V [在黑暗中+] 摸索 [zài hēi'àn zhōng+] mōsuo

gross I ADJ 1 总的 zǒngde
gross national product 国民生产总值 guómín shēngchǎn zǒngzhí
gross weight 毛重 máozhòng
2 恶心的 ěxīn de 3 恶劣的 èliè de, 极坏

的 jí huài de **II** v **1** 总利润 zǒng lìrùn **2** 税前工资 shuì qián gōngzī

grotesque ADJ 怪诞的 guàidàn de, 荒唐 的 huāngtang de

grotto N 石窟 shíkū

grouch N 牢骚不断的人 láosāo búduàn de rén, 愤愤不平的人 fènfèn bùpíng de rén

grouchy ADJ (因为疲劳) 心情很糟 (yīnwéi píláo) xīnqíng hěn zāo

ground¹ I N **1** 地 dì, 地面 dìmiàn
   ground crew (机场) 地勤人员 (jīchǎng) dìqín rényuán
   sports ground 体育场 tǐyù chǎng, 操场 cāo chǎng
   to gain ground 取得优势 qǔdé yōushì, 渐渐取胜 jiànjiàn qǔshèng
   to stand one's ground 坚持立场 jiānchí lìchǎng, 坚持己见 jiānchí jǐjiàn **2** 意见 yìjiàn, 立场 lìchǎng
   to give ground (in an argument) (在争论中) 让步 (zài zhēnglùn zhōng) ràngbù **II** v **1** (飞机) 停止飞行 (fēijī) tíngzhǐ fēixíng **2** 不准 (小孩) 做喜欢做的事 bùzhǔn (xiǎohái) zuò xǐhuan zuò de shì

ground² I v See grind **II** ADJ 碾碎的 niǎnsuì de, 磨细的 mó xì de
   ground beef 牛肉馅 niúròubīng

groundless ADJ 没有根据的 méiyǒu gēnjù de

ground rule N 基本规则 jīběn guīzé [M. WD 条 tiáo]

groundwork N 基础 jīchǔ

group I N **1** 组 zǔ, 小组 xiǎozǔ **2** 群 qún
   group therapy 集体心理治疗 jítǐ xīnlǐ zhìliáo **3** 集团 jítuán **II** v **1** 聚集成一组 jùjí chéng yīzǔ **2** 分组 fēnzǔ

grouping N 同类人／事 tónglèi rén/shì

grouse N, v 抱怨 bàoyuàn

grove N 小树林 xiǎoshù lín

grovel v 卑躬屈膝 bēigōng qūxī, 点头哈腰 diǎn tóu hā yāo

grow (PT grew; PP grown) v **1** 增长 zēngzhǎng **2** 生长 shēngzhǎng
   Grow up! 快快长大！ (→ 别这么幼稚！) Kuàikuài zhǎng dà! (→ Bié zhème yòuzhì!)

3 变得 biànde

grower N 种植者 zhòngzhízhě, 种植公司 zhòngzhí gōngsī [M. WD 家 jiā]

growl v **1** 怒气冲冲地说话 nùqì chōng-chōng de shuōhuà **2** [狗+] 低声吼叫 [gǒu+] dīshēng hǒujiào

grown v See grow

grown-up I N 成人 chéngrén **II** ADJ 成年 的 chéngnián de, 成熟的 chéngshú de

growth N **1** 增长 zēngzhǎng **2** 生长 shēngzhǎng **3** 肿瘤 zhǒngliú, 赘生物 zhuìshēngwù

grub N **1** 食物 shíwù **2** 蛆 qū

grubby ADJ **1** 肮脏的 [+衣服] āngzāng de [+yīfu], 不干净的 bùgān jìng de **2** 卑鄙 的 bēibǐ de

grudge I N 怨恨 yuànhèn
   to bear a grudge against sb 对某人有 怨恨 duì mǒurén yǒu yuànhèn
   to hold grudges 记住怨恨 jìzhù yuàn-hèn, 记仇 jìchóu **II** v 勉强 [+做] miǎnqiǎng [+zuò]

grudging ADJ 勉强的 miǎnqiǎng de

gruel N 燕麦粥 yànmài zhōu, 麦片粥 màipiànzhōu

grueling ADJ 令人精疲力竭的 lìng rén jīngpí lìjié de

gruesome ADJ 恐怖的 kǒngbù de, 可怕 的 kěpà de

gruff ADJ 生硬的 shēngyìng de, 不耐烦的 bùnàifán de

grumble v 发牢骚 fāláosāo

grumpy ADJ 脾气不好又爱发牢骚的 píqi bù hǎo yòu àifā láosāo de

grunt I v **1** [猪+] 咕噜咕噜叫 [zhū+] gūlū gūlū jiào **2** 嘟哝 dūnong, 嘟哝地说 dūnong de shuō **II** N 嘟哝 dūnong, 嘟哝 声 dūnong shēng

guarantee I v **1** 保证 bǎozhèng, 担 保 dānbǎo **2** 保修 bǎoxiū **II** N **1** 保证 bǎozhèng **2** 保修单 bǎoxiū dān **3** 担保 dānbǎo
   loan guarantee 贷款担保 dàikuǎn dānbǎo

guarantor N 担保人 dānbǎorén

guard I N **1** 保安 (人员) bǎo'ān (rén-yuán) **2** (篮球、橄榄球) 后卫 (lánqiú, gǎnlǎnqiú) hòuwèi **II** v **1** 保卫 bǎowèi, 守护 shǒuhù **2**（体育）防守 (tǐyù) fángshǒu

guarded ADJ 谨慎的 jǐnshèn de, 提防的 dīfang de

guardian N **1** 监护人 jiānhùrén **2** 保卫者 bǎowèizhě

guardian angel 守护天使 shǒuhù tiānshǐ

guardianship N 监护人身份 jiānhùrén shēnfen

guardrail N 护栏 hùlán

guerrilla N 游击队员 yóujíduìyuán

guerrilla warfare 游击战 yóujízhàn

guess I v **1** 猜 cāi, 猜想 cāixiǎng **2** 认为 rènwéi, 想 xiǎng **II** N 猜想 cāixiǎng, 猜测 cāicè

anybody's guess 谁都不知道 shéi dōu bù zhīdào

guesswork N 猜测 cāicè

guest N **1** 客人 kèren, 宾客 bīnkè **2** 特邀演员 tèyāo yǎnyuán **3** 房客 fángkè

guff N 胡说八道 húshuō bādào

guffaw N, v 哈哈大笑 hāha dàxiào

guidance N 引导 yǐndǎo, 指导 zhǐdǎo

guidance counselor 咨询顾问 zīxún gùwèn, 辅导员 fǔdǎoyuán

guide I N **1** 向导 xiàngdǎo **2** 指南 zhǐnán [M. WD 本 běn] **3** 手册 shǒucè, 指南 zhǐnán **II** v **1** 引导 yǐndǎo **2** 指导 zhǐdǎo

guidebook N 旅行手册 lǚxíng shǒucè

guidelines N 指导方针 zhǐdǎo fāngzhēn

guild N 同业公会 tóngyègōnghuì, 行会 hánghuì

guile N 诡计 guǐjì, 欺骗 qīpiàn

by guile and skill 连蒙带骗 lián méng dài piàn

guillotine N 断头台 duàntóutái

guilt N **1** 有罪 yǒuzuì, 犯罪 fànzuì **2** 内疚 nèijiū, 羞愧 xiūkuì

guilt-ridden ADJ 有负罪感的 yǒu fùzuìgǎn de, 内疚的 nèijiū de

guilty ADJ 有罪的 yǒuzuì de

guinea pig N **1** 豚鼠 túnshǔ **2** 当试验品的人 dāng shìyànpǐn de rén

guise N 伪装 wěizhuāng, 外表 wàibiǎo

guitar N 吉他 jítā [M. WD 把 bǎ]

gulf N **1** 海湾 hǎiwān

the Persian Gulf 波斯湾 Bōsī wān

2 重大分歧 zhòngdà fēnqí, 鸿沟 hónggōu

gull N 海鸥 hǎiʼōu [M. WD 只 zhī/头 tóu]

gullible ADJ 容易受骗的 róngyì shòupiàn de, 轻信的 qīngxìn de

gully N 冲沟 chōnggōu, 隘谷 àigǔ

gulp I v **1** 很快地吞下 hěn kuài de tūnxià **2** 大口吸气 dà kǒu xīqì **II** N 吞咽 tūnyàn

gum I N **1** 口香糖 kǒuxiāngtáng

chewing gum 口香糖 kǒuxiāngtáng

2 牙龈 yáyín, 牙床 yáchuáng

bleeding gum 牙龈出血 yáyín chūxuè

3 树胶 shùjiāo **II** v（用树胶）粘合 (yòng shùjiāo) zhānhé

gumption N 魄力 pòlì, 精明 jīngmíng

gun I N **1** 枪 qiāng, 炮 pào [M. WD 支 zhī], 炮 páo [M. WD 门 mén] **2** 喷射器 pēnshèqì **II** v 加速 jiāsù, 猛踩油门 měng cǎi yóumén

gunboat N 炮舰 pàojiàn [M. WD 艘 sōu]

gunfire N 炮火 pàohuǒ

gung-ho ADJ 非常热切的 fēicháng rèqiè de, 狂热的 kuángrè de

gunman N 持枪歹徒 chíqiāng dǎitú

gunner N 炮手 pàoshǒu

gunpoint N 枪口 qiāngkǒu

at gunpoint 在枪口威逼下 zài qiāngkǒu wēibī xià

gunpowder N 火药 huǒyào

gunshot N **1**（枪炮）射击 (qiāngpào) shèjī **2** 枪炮声 qiāngpàoshēng

gurgle I v [水+] 潺潺地流 [shuǐ+] chánchán de liú **II** N 潺潺流水声 chánchán liúshuǐshēng

gush I v **1** 大量喷出 dàliàng pēn chū, 涌出 yǒngchu **2** 滔滔不绝地说 tāotāo bùjué de shuō **II** N 大量喷出的液体 dàliàng pēnchū de yètǐ

gusher N **1** 喷油井 pēnyóujǐng [M. WD 口 kǒu] **2** 滔滔不绝地说话的人 tāotāo bùjué de shuōhuà de rén

gust I N 一阵狂风 yízhèn kuángfēng, 一阵大雪 yízhèn dàxuě **II** v [风+] 劲吹 [fēng+] jìngchuī

gusto N 热情 rèqíng

with gusto 兴致勃勃地 xìngzhìbóbó de

gut ADJ 直觉的 zhíjué de, 本能的 běnnéng de
gut feeling 强烈的直觉 qiángliè de zhíjué
gut reaction 本能的反应 běnnéng de fǎnyìng

guts I N 1 内脏 nèizàng, 肠胃 chángwèi
a pain in one's guts 肚子痛 dùzi tòng
2 勇气 yǒngqì
to have guts (to do sth) 有勇气做某事 yǒu yǒngqì (zuò mǒushì)
II v 彻底烧毁 chèdǐ shāohuǐ

gutter N 1 (路边) 排水沟 (lùbiān) páishuǐgōu [M. WD 条 tiáo] 2 (屋檐) 雨水槽 (wūyán) yǔshuǐcáo [M. WD 条 tiáo]

guttural ADJ 发自喉中的 fāzì hóuzhòng de, 低沉的 dīchén de

guy N (青年) 男人 (qīngnián) nánren
you guys 大家 dàjiā, 各位 gèwèi

guzzle v 1 大吃大喝 dàchī dàhē, 狂饮 kuángyǐn 2 大量耗油 dàliàng hàoyóu

gym N 健身房 jiànshēnfáng [M. WD 座 zuò], 体育馆 tǐyùguǎn [M. WD 座 zuò]

gymnasium N See gym

gymnast N 体操运动员 tǐcāo yùndòng-yuán

gymnastics N 体操 (运动) tǐcāo (yùndòng)

gynecologist N 妇科医生 fùkē yīshēng

gypsy N 吉卜赛人 Jípǔsàirén

gyrate v 快速旋转 kuàisù xuánzhuǎn

gyroscope, gyro N 回转仪 huízhuǎnyí

H

habit N 1 习惯 xíguàn 2 坏习惯 huài xíguàn, 毒瘾 dúyǐn
to break the habit 戒掉坏习惯 jiè diào huài xíguàn, 戒掉毒瘾 jiè diào dúyǐn

habitable ADJ 可以住人的 kěyǐ zhù rén de, 适于居住的 shìyú jūzhù de

habitat N 栖息地 qīxīdì, 居住地 jūzhùdì

habitation N 居住 jūzhù

habitual ADJ 习惯 (性) 的 xíguàn (xìng) de

hack[1] v 1 乱砍 luàn kǎn, 乱劈 luàn pī

2 非法侵入 [+他人的计算机系统] fēi fǎ qīnrù [+tārén de jìsuànjī xìtǒng]

hack[2] N 1 低级文人 dījí wénrén, 雇佣文人 gùyōng wénrén 2 老马 lǎo mǎ 3 出租车 chūzūchē, 出租车司机 chūzūchē sījī

hacker N 黑客 hēikè, 电脑迷 diànnǎo mí

hacksaw N 钢锯 gāngjù

had v See have

hag N 丑陋的老太婆 chǒulòu de lǎotàipó, 母夜叉 mǔyèchā

haggard ADJ (面容) 憔悴的 (miànróng) qiáocuì de

haggle v 争吵 zhēngchǎo, 讨价还价 tǎojià huánjià
to haggle over prices 讨价还价 tǎojià huánjià

ha INTERJ 哈哈 hāhā

hail[1] v 1 大声招呼 dàshēng zhāohu, 叫 jiào 2 赞扬 zànyáng, 称赞 chēngzàn

hail[2] I N 冰雹 bīngbáo II v 下冰雹 xià bīngbáo

hailstone N 雹 (子) báo (zi)

hailstorm N 雹暴 báobào

hair N 1 毛 máo [M. WD 根 gēn], 毛发 máofà [M. WD 根 gēn] 2 头发 tóufa
to split hair 吹毛求疵 chuī máo qiú cī

haircut N 理发 lǐfà

hairdresser N 理发师 lǐfàshī

hairline N 发际线 fàjì xiàn

hair-raising ADJ 使人发毛耸立的 shǐrén fàmáo sǒnglì de, 万分惊险的 wànfēn jīngxiǎn de

hairstyle N 发型 fàxíng

hairy ADJ 多毛的 duō máo de, 毛茸茸的 máoróngróng de

halcyon ADJ 美好的 měihǎo de
halcyon years 太平盛世 tàipíng shèng-shì

hale ADJ 老当益壮的 lǎodāng yìzhuàng de

half I NUM 半 bàn, 一半 yí bàn
half time 半场休息 bàn chǎng xiūxi
II N 半 bàn, 一半 yí bàn
half-and-half 一半一半的 yíbàn yíbàn de, 稀奶油 xīnǎiyóu
III ADV 部分 bùfen, 一半 yí bàn IV ADJ 一半 yíbàn

half-baked ADJ 不成熟的 bù chéngshú de

half-brother N 同父／异母兄弟 tóng fù/yì mǔ xiōngdì

half-hearted ADJ 半心半意的 bànxīnbànyì de

half-mast N 降半旗 jiàngbànqí
to fly at half-mast 降半旗 jiàngbànqí

half-sister N 同父／异母姐妹 tóng fù/yì mǔ jiěmèi

half-time N（球类比赛）中场休息 (qiúlèi bǐsài) zhōngchǎng xiūxi

half-truth N 半真半假的鬼话 bànzhēn bànjiǎ de guǐhuà

halfway ADV 半路 bànlù，中间 zhōngjiān

hall N 1 走廊 zǒuláng，过道 guòdào 2 大厅 dàtīng，堂 táng 3（大学生）宿舍楼 (dàxuéshēng) sùshè lóu

hallelujah INTERJ 哈利路亚 Hālìlùyà，赞美上帝 zànměi Shàngdì，感谢上帝 gǎnxiè Shàngdì

hallmark N 特征 tèzhēng，标志 biāozhì
to bear the hallmark of sth 带有某事物的特征 dàiyǒu mǒushìwù de tèzhēng

hallowed ADJ 神圣的 shénshèng de

Halloween N 万圣节（十月三十一日夜晚）Wànshèngjié (shíyuè sānshíyī rì yèwǎn)

hallucination N 幻觉／幻视／幻听 huànjué/huànshì/huàntīng

hallway N 门厅 méntīng，走廊 zǒuláng

halo N 光轮 guānglún，光圈 guāngquān

halt v, N 停止 tíngzhǐ

halting ADJ 断断续续的 duànduàn xùxù de，犹犹豫豫的 yóuyóu yùyù de

halve v 1 把…一分为二 bǎ…yìfēn wéi èr，对半分 duìbàn fēn 2 把…减半 bǎ… jiǎnbàn

ham I N 1 火腿 huǒtuǐ 2 表演过火的演员 biǎoyǎn guòhuǒ de yǎnyuán 3 业余无线电爱好者 yèyú wúxiàndiàn àihàozhě
ham radio 业余无线电台 yèyú wúxiàndiàntái
II v 表演过火 biǎoyǎn guòhuǒ，夸张地表演 kuāzhāng de biǎoyǎn

hamburger N 1 汉堡牛肉饼 hànbǎo niúròubǐng，汉堡包 hànbǎobāo 2 碎牛肉 suìniúròu

hamlet N 小村庄 xiǎo cūnzhuāng，小村子 xiǎo cūnzi

hammer I N 锤子 chuízi，榔头 lángtou [M. WD 把 bǎ] II v 反复敲打 fǎnfù qiāodǎ

hammock N 吊床 diàochuáng

hamper I v 阻碍 zǔ'ài，妨碍 fáng'ài II N 大篮子 dà lánzi
picnic hamper 野餐食品篮 yěcān shípǐn lán

hamster N 金仓鼠 jīn cāngshǔ

hamstring[1] N 腘绳肌腱 guóshéng jījiàn

hamstring[2] (PT & PP **hamstrung**) v 使…受挫 shǐ…shòucuò，阻扰 zǔrǎo

hamstrung v See **hamstring**[2]

hand I N 1 手 shǒu
hand luggage 手提行李 shǒutí xínglǐ
on the one hand … on the other hand 一方面…另一方面 yì fāngmian… lìng yì fāngmiàn
by hand 手工的 shǒugōng de
to shake hands with 和…握手 hé… wòshǒu
2 帮助 bāngzhu 3（钟）指针 (zhōng) zhǐzhēn 4 手上的牌 shǒushang de pái
II v 交 jiāo，递 dì

handbag N 手提包 shǒutíbāo，坤包 kūnbāo

handbook N 手册 shǒucè，指南 zhǐnán

handcuff I N 手铐 shǒukào II v 给…戴上手铐 gěi…dàishàng shǒukào

handful N 一把 yì bǎ

handicap N 不利条件 búlì tiáojiàn，障碍 zhàng'ài

handicapped ADJ 有生理缺陷的 yǒu shēnglǐ quēxiàn de，残障的 cánzhàng de
the handicapped 残障人士 cánzhàng rénshì

handiwork N 1 所做的事 suǒ zuò de shì 2 手工 shǒugōng，手工艺品 shǒugōngyìpǐn

handkerchief N 手帕 shǒupà

handle I N 把 bǎ，柄 bǐng，把手 bǎshǒu II v 1 拿 ná，抓 zhuā，摆弄 bǎinòng
Handle with care. 小心轻放。Xiǎoxīn qīng fàng.
2 管理 guǎnlǐ，控制 kòngzhì 3 处理 chǔlǐ，对付 duìfu

handler N **1** 搬运工 bānyùn gōng **2**（动物）驯练员 (dòngwù) xùnliànyuán

handmade ADJ 手工制作的 shǒugōng zhìzuò de

hand-me-down N（从哥哥姐姐那里传下来的）旧衣服 (cóng gēge jiějie nàli chuánxiàlai de) jiù yīfú

handout N **1** 救济款 jiùjìkuǎn，救济物资 jiùjì wùzī [M. WD 批 pī] **2** 讲义 jiǎngyì，材料 cáiliào [M. WD 份 fèn]

handpicked ADJ 精心挑选的 jīngxīn tiāoxuǎn de，亲自挑选的 qīnzì tiāoxuǎn de

handshake N 握手 wòshǒu

hands off INTERJ 别碰 bié pèng

handsome ADJ **1** 英俊的 [+男子] yīngjùn de [+nánzǐ] **2** 健美的 [+女子] jiànměi de [+nǚzǐ] **3** 出手大方的 [+礼物、捐助] chūshǒu dàfāng de [+lǐwù, juānzhù]，慷慨的 kāngkǎi de

hands-on ADJ 实际操作的 shíjì cāozuò de，(计算机) 上机的 (jìsuànjī) shàngjī de
hands-on computer training 计算机操作训练 jìsuànjī cāozuò xùnliàn

handstand N 双手倒立 shuāngshǒu dàolì

hands up INTERJ 举起手来 jǔqǐ shǒulái

handwriting N **1** 书写 shūxiě，手写 shǒuxiě **2** 书法 shūfǎ

handy ADJ **1** 方便的 fāngbiàn de **2** 在手边的 zài shǒubiān de **3** 手巧的 shǒuqiǎo de

handyman N 手巧的人 shǒuqiǎo de rén，善于做零星修理的人 shànyú zuò língxīng xiūlǐ de rén

hang¹ (PT & PP **hung**) V 挂 guà，悬挂 xuánguà
to hang in there 坚持下去 jiānchí xiàqù，挺住 tǐng zhù
to hang on 等一会 děng yíhuì
to hang up 挂断（电话）guàduàn (diànhuà)

hang² V (PT & PP **hanged**) **1** 吊死 diàosǐ **2** 处以绞刑 chǔyǐjiǎoxíng

hangar N 飞机库 fēijīkù [M. WD 座 zuò]

hanger N 衣架 yījià

hang glider N 悬挂式滑翔机 xuánguàshì huáxiángjī [M. WD 架 jià]

hanging N 绞刑 jiǎoxíng

hangman N 字母猜字游戏 zìmǔ cāizì yóuxì

hangout N 常去的地方 cháng qù de dìfang，聚集地 jùjí dì

hangover N 酗酒后第二天感到不适 xùjiǔ hòu dì'èrtiān gǎndào bùshì，宿醉 sùzuì
a hangover from sth 遗留的问题 yíliú de wèntí，后遗症 hòuyízhèng

hangup N 烦恼 fánnǎo，焦虑 jiāolǜ，心理障碍 xīnlǐ zhàng'ài

hanker V 渴望 kěwàng，追求 zhuīqiú

hankie, hanky See handkerchief

haphazard ADJ 杂乱无章的 záluàn wúzhāng de，毫无计划的 háowú jìhuà de

hapless ADJ 倒霉的 dǎoméi de

happen V **1** 发生 fāshēng **2** 碰巧 pèngqiǎo

happening I ADJ 时髦的 shímáo de，流行的 liúxíng de II N 发生的事情 fāshēng de shìqíng

happily ADV **1** 幸福地 xìngfú de **2** 高兴地 gāoxìng de **3** 幸运地 xìngyùn de，幸好 xìnghǎo

happiness N 幸福 xìngfú，快乐 kuàilè

happy ADJ **1** 幸福的 xìngfú de **2** 高兴的 gāoxìng de **3** 满意的 mǎnyì de
Happy birthday to you! 祝你生日快乐! Zhù nǐ shēngrì kuàilè!
Happy New Year! 新年快乐! Xīnnián kuàilè! 新年好! Xīnniánhǎo!

happy-go-lucky ADJ 乐天知命的 lè tiān zhī mìng de，无忧无虑的 wúyōu wúlǜ de

harangue V **1** 做长篇演说 zuò chángpiān yǎnshuō **2** 滔滔不绝地训斥 tāotāo bùjué de xùnchì

harass V 骚扰 sāorǎo

harbor N 港 gǎng，港湾 gǎngwān

hard I ADJ **1** 硬 yìng，坚硬 jiānyìng
hard hat 安全帽 ānquánmào **2** 艰难的 jiānnán de **3** 苛刻的 kēkè de
to be hard on 对…很苛刻 duì…hěn kēkè II ADV **1** 努力地 nǔlì de **2** 艰难地 jiānnán de **3** 严重地 yánzhòng de

hard-and-fast ADJ 固定不变的 gùdìng búbiàn de
hard and fast rules 严格的规定 yángé de guīdìng

hardball N (to play hardball) 采取强硬手段 cǎiqǔ qiángyìng shǒuduàn

hard-boiled ADJ 1 [蛋+] 煮得老的 [dàn+] zhǔ dé lǎo de 2 不露声色的 bú lù shēngsè de, 精明老练的 jīngmíng lǎoliàn de

hard cash N 现钞 xiànchāo, 现金 xiànjīn

hard copy N 打印文本 dǎyìn wénběn

hardcore ADJ 1 顽固不化的 wángù búhuà de 2 露骨的 lùgǔ de
hardcore pornography 赤裸裸的色情作品 chìluǒluǒ de sèqíng zuòpǐn

hard currency N 硬通货 yìngtōnghuò

hard disk, hard disk drive N（计算机）硬盘 yìngpán

harden V 1（使…）变硬 (shǐ)…biàn yìng 2（使）…更强硬 (shǐ)…gèng qiángyìng 3 使…冷酷无情 shǐ…lěngkù wúqíng

hard-headed ADJ 1 心肠很硬的 xīncháng hěn yìng de, 没有同情心的 méiyǒu tóngqíngxīn de 2 讲究实际的 jiǎngjiu shíjì de, 头脑清醒的 tóunǎo qīngxǐng de

hardline ADJ 强硬路线的 qiángyìng lùxiàn de

hardly ADV 1 刚刚 gānggāng, 仅仅 jǐnjǐn 2 几乎不 jīhū bù 3 一点也不 yìdiǎn yě bù, 根本不 gēnběn bù

hard-nosed ADJ 无动于衷的 wúdòng yú zhōng de, 不妥协的 bù tuǒxié de

hard of hearing 听觉不好的 tīngjué bùhǎo de, 有听力障碍的 yǒu tīnglì zhàng'ài de

hard-pressed ADJ 困难重重的 kùnnan chóngchóng de, 窘迫的 jiǒngpò de

hardship N 艰难 jiānnan, 苦难 kǔnàn

hard-up ADJ 缺钱的 quē qián de, 钱很紧的 qián hěn jǐn de

hardware N 1（计算机）硬件 (jìsuànjī) yìngjiàn 2 机器设备 jīqì shèbèi 3 军事装备 jūnshì zhuāngbèi 4 五金制品 wǔjīn zhìpǐn

hard-working ADJ 努力工作的 nǔlì gōngzuò de, 勤奋的 qínfèn de

hardy ADJ 能吃苦耐劳的 néng chīkǔ nàiláo de, 坚强的 jiānqiáng de

hare N 野兔 yětù [M. WD 只 zhī]

harebrained ADJ 轻率浮躁的 qīngshuài fúzào de, 愚蠢的 yúchǔn de

harelip N 兔唇 tùchún

harem N 1（伊斯兰国家）妻妾 (Yīsīlán guójiā) qīqiè 2 后宫 hòugōng

hark V 仔细听 zǐxì tīng, 倾听 qīngtīng
to hark back to 使人（回）想起 shǐrén (huí) xiǎng qǐ

harlot N 妓女 jìnǚ, 婊子 biǎozi

harm I N 坏处 huàichu, 损害 sǔnhài
No harm done. 没关系。Méiguānxi.
II V 损害 sǔnhài, 伤害 shānghài

harmful ADJ 有害的 yǒuhài de

harmless ADJ 1 无害的 [+动物] wúhài de [+dòngwù] 2 无恶意的 [+玩笑] wú èyì de [+wánxiào]

harmonica N 口琴 [M. WD 把 zhī]

harmony N 1 和谐 héxié, 融洽 róngqià 2（音乐）和声 (yīnyuè) héshēng

harness I N 1（马的）挽具 (mǎ de) wǎnjù, 马具 mǎjù 2（人的）保险带 (rén de) bǎoxiǎndài II V 治理利用 zhìlǐ lìyòng

harp I N 竖琴 shùqín II V (to harp on) 唠唠叨叨地说 láoláo dāodāo de shuō, 没完没了地说 méiwán méiliǎo de shuō

harpsichord N 拨弦古钢琴 bōxián-gǔgāngqín

harrowing ADJ 令人难受的 lìng rén nánshòu de, 令人痛苦的 lìng rén tòngkǔ de

harsh ADJ 1 苛刻的 kēkè de, 严厉的 yánlì de 2 严苛的 yánkǔ de, 严酷的 yánkù de

harvest I N 1 收获 shōuhuò 2 收获量 shōuhuòliàng, 收成 shōucheng
to reap a bumper harvest 获得丰收 huòdé fēngshōu
II V 收获 shōuhuò

has V See have

hash N 1 肉末土豆泥 ròumò tǔdòuní 2 大麻毒品 dàmá dúpǐn

hasn't See have

hassle I N 1 麻烦 máfan II V 一再打扰 yízài dǎrǎo, 骚扰 sāorǎo

haste N 匆忙 cōngmáng
More haste, less speed. 越是匆忙越是慢。(→欲速则不达。) Yuè shì cōngmáng yuè shì màn. (→Yù sù zé bù dá.)

hasten V 加快 jiākuài, 加速 jiāsù

hasty ADJ 仓促的 cāngcù de, 匆忙的 cōngmáng de

hat N 帽子 màozi [M. WD 顶 dǐng]
hats off to sb 向某人致敬 xiàng mǒurén zhìjìng

hatch I v 1 [蛋+] 孵化 [dàn+] fūhuà 2 策划出 [+计划、秘密] cèhuà chū [+jìhuà, mìmì] II N (船、飞机) 舱口，舱门 (chuan, fēijī) cāngkǒu, cāng mén

hatchback N 两舱门式汽车 liǎng cāngmén shì qìchē [M. WD 辆 liàng]

hatchet N (短柄) 小斧头 (duǎn bǐng) xiǎo fǔtou [M. WD 把 bǎ]

hate I v 1 非常不喜欢 fēicháng bù xǐhuan, 讨厌 tǎoyàn 2 (憎) 恨 (zèng) hèn II N 仇恨 chóuhèn

hateful ADJ 1 充满仇恨的 chōngmǎn chóuhèn de 2 可憎的 kězēng de, 讨厌的 tǎoyàn de

hatred N 恨 hèn, 仇恨 chóuhèn

haughty ADJ 傲慢的 àomàn de, 目中无人的 mùzhōng wú rén de

haul I v 搬运 bānyùn, 拉 lā, 拖 tuō
to haul off 强绑 yìng tuō, 抓捕 zhuābǔ II N 1 时期 shíqī, 距离 jùlí
long haul 长途 chángtú, 很长的距离 hěn cháng de jùlí
over the long/short haul 长 / 短期 cháng/duǎnqī
2 大量赃物 dàliàng zāngwù, 大量走私物品 dàliàng zǒusī wùpǐn

haunches N 后腿 hòutuǐ

haunt I v 1 [鬼魂+] 出没 [guǐhún+] chūmò 2 [烦人的事+] 纠缠 [fánrén de shì+] jiūchán, 烦扰 fánrǎo II N 经常去的地方 jīngcháng qù de dìfang

haunted ADJ 有鬼的 yǒuguǐ de, 闹鬼的 nàoguǐ de

have [NEG **have not** ABBREV **haven't**; 3rd person: **has**; NEG **has not** ABBREV **hasn't**] (PT & PP **had**) I v 1 有 yǒu, 拥有 yōngyǒu
to have time 有空 yǒu kòng, 有时间 yǒu shíjiān
2 有 yǒu, 具有 jùyǒu 3 吃 chī, 喝 hē 4 生病 shēngbìng
to have a bad cold 感冒 gǎnmào II AUX v 得 děi, 必须 bìxū
to have (got) to 得 děi, 不得不 bùdébù

had better 最好 zuìhǎo, 还是 háishi

haven N 安全地带 ānquán dìdài, 避难所 bìnànsuǒ

haven't See have

have to, has to v 得 děi, 必须 bìxū

havoc N 巨大的破坏 jùdà de pòhuài, 浩劫 hàojié

hawk N 1 鹰 yīng [M. WD 只 zhī], 老鹰 lǎoyīng [M. WD 只 zhī] 2 鹰派人物 yīngpài rénwù, 强硬派 qiángyìngpài

hawker N（叫卖的）小贩 (jiàomài de) xiǎofàn

hay N 干草 gāncǎo, 牧草 mùcǎo
Make hay while the sun shines. 趁天晴的时候, 打晒干草。(→趁热打铁。) Chèn tiān qíng de shíhou, dǎ shài gāncǎo. (→Chèn rè dǎ tiě.)
hay fever 枯草热 kūcǎorè, 花粉病 huāfěnbìng

haystack N 干草堆 gāncǎoduī

hazard I N 危险 wēixiǎn, 隐患 yǐnhuàn
hazard lights（汽车）危险警示灯 (qìchē) wēixiǎn jǐngshì dēng
occupational hazard 职业危险 zhíyè wēixiǎn
II v 猜测 cāicè

hazardous ADJ 危险的 de wēixiǎn de

haze N 烟雾 yānwù, 雾气 wùqì

hazel I N 榛树 zhēn shù [M. WD 棵 kē]
II ADJ 淡褐色的 dànhèsè de

hazelnut N 榛子 zhēnzi [M. WD 颗 kē]

hazy ADJ 1 雾蒙蒙的 [+天空] wù méng-méng de [+tiānkōng] 2 模糊的 [+印象] móhu de [+yìnxiàng]

H-bomb N 氢弹 qīngdàn [M. WD 枚 méi]

he PRON 他 tā

head I N 1 头 tóu, 头部 tóubù
head count 数人头 shù réntóu
2 领导人 lǐngdǎorén, 长 zhǎng, 头头 tóutou
head of state 国家元首 guójiā yuánshǒu
3 头脑 tóunǎo, 智力 zhìlì
to use one's head 动脑子 dòng nǎozi II v 1 带领 dàilǐng, 率领 shuàilǐng 2 朝···行进 cháo...xíngjìn 3 用头顶球 yòngtóu dǐng qiú

385

headache N 头疼 tóuténg, 头痛 tóutòng

headfirst ADV 1 头朝前地 tóu cháoqián de 2 轻率地 qīngshuài de, 鲁莽地 lǔmǎng de

headgear N 帽子 màozi, 头饰 tóushì

headhunter N 1 割取敌人头颅作为战利品的部落 gē qǔ dírén tóulú zuòwéi zhànlìpǐn de bùluò 2 物色人才的人 wùsè réncái de rén

heading N 标题 biāotí

headland N 海岬 hǎijiǎ

headlight N (汽车) 前灯 (qìchē) qiándēng, 车头灯 chētóudēng

headline N 1 (报纸的) 标题 (bàozhǐ de) biāotí [M. WD 条 tiáo] 2 (社会上的) 热门话题 (shèhuìshang de) rèmén huàtí
  to make the headline 成为热门话题 chéngwéi rèmén huàtí
  3 新闻提要 xīnwén tíyào

headlong ADV 1 头朝前地 tóu cháoqián de 2 轻率地 qīngshuài de
  to rush headlong into 轻率地 [+做某事] qīngshuài de [+zuò mǒushì]

headmaster, headmistress N (私立学校) 校长 (sīlì xuéxiào) xiàozhǎng

head-on ADV 迎面 yíngmiàn
  to meet head-on 迎面相撞 yíngmiàn xiāngzhuàng

head-phones N 耳机 ěrjī [M. WD 副 fù]

headquarters N 1 (军队) 司令部 (jūnduì) sīlìngbù 2 (公司) 总部 (gōngsī) zǒngbù

headstrong ADJ 固执的 gùzhí de, 任性的 rènxìng de

head-to-head ADJ, ADV 直接 (的／地) [+竞争] zhíjiē (de) [+jìngzhēng], 正面 (的／地) zhèngmiàn (de)

headway N 进展 jìnzhǎn
  to make headway 取得进展 qǔdé jìnzhǎn

headwind N 顶头风 dǐngtóu fēng, 顶风 dǐngfēng

heal V 愈合 yùhé, 治愈 zhìyù

health N 健康 (情况) jiànkāng (qíngkuàng)
  health care 保健 bǎojiàn
  health club 保健俱乐部 bǎojiàn jùlèbù

healthy ADJ 1 健康的 jiànkāng de 2 对健康有利的 duì jiànkāng yǒulì de

heap I N 堆 duī II V 堆积 duījī, 堆放 duīfàng

hear (PT & PP **heard**) V 1 听 tīng, 听到 tīngdao
  hard of hearing See **hard**
  to hear from sb 得到关于某人的消息 dédào guānyú mǒurén de xiāoxi, 收到某人的来信／电邮 shōudào mǒurén de láixìn/diànyóu
  to hear of 听说 tīngshuō
  2 [法庭+] 审理 [fǎtíng+] shěnlǐ
  to hear a case 审理一件案子 shěnlǐ yí jiàn ànzi

heard V See **hear**

hearing N 听觉 tīngjué, 听力 tīnglì 2 证会 tīngzhènghuì
  hearing aid 助听器 zhùtīngqì
  hearing impaired 有听力障碍的 yǒu tīnglì zhàng'ài de

hearsay N 传闻 chuánwén, 道听途说 dàotīng túshuō

hearse N 灵车 língchē [M. WD 辆 liàng]

heart N 1 心 xīn, 心脏 xīnzàng 2 心 xīn, 心地 xīndì, 心情 xīnqíng
  heart attack 心脏病发作 xīnzàngbìng fāzuò
  heart disease 心脏病 xīnzàngbìng

heartache N 痛心 tòngxīn, 极其悲痛 jíqí bēitòng

heartbeat N 心跳 xīntiào

heartbroken ADJ 心碎的 xīnsuì de, 极其悲痛的 jíqí bēitòng de

heartburn N 胃炎热 wèiyánrè, 烧心 shāoxīn

heartfelt ADJ 衷心的 zhōngxīn de

hearth N 壁炉边 bìlú biān

heartily ADV 1 开怀地 [+大笑] kāihuái de [+dàxiào] 2 完全地 [+同意] wánquán de [tóngyì]

heartland N 心脏地区 xīnzàng dìqū, 腹地 fùdì

heartless ADJ 没有心肝的 méiyǒu xīngān de, 残酷的 cánkù de

heartrending ADJ 让人极其同情的 ràng rén jíqí tóngqíng de, 让人心酸的 ràng rén xīn suān de

heartstrings N 心弦 xīnxián, 内心深处 nèixīn shēnchù

to pull at sb's heartstrings 触动心弦 chùdòng xīnxián, 深深打动人心 shēnshēn dǎdòng rénxīn

heart-throb N 年轻人迷恋的明星 niánqīngrén míliàn de míngxīng

heartwarming ADJ 暖心人的 nuǎn rénxīn zhī

hearty ADJ 1 热情友好的 [+欢迎] rèqíng yǒuhǎo de [huānyíng] 2 丰盛的 [+晚餐] fēngshèng de [+wǎncān]

heat I N 1 热 rè, 热量 rèliàng 2 高温天气 gāowēn tiānqì

heat wave 高温期 gāowēnqī, 热浪 rèlàng

II v 变暖 biàn nuǎn, 变热 biàn rè

to heat up 热一下 rè yíxià

heated ADJ 1 加热的 [+游泳池] jiārè de [+yóuyǒngchí] 2 有暖气的 [+房间] yǒu nuǎnqì de [+fángjiān] 3 激烈的 [+争论] jīliè de [+zhēnglùn]

heated swimming-pool 温水游泳池 wēnshuǐ yóuyǒngchí

heater N 加热器 jiārèqì, 暖气 nuǎnqì

heathen I N 异教徒 yìjiàotú

heave I v (PT & PP **heaved, hove**) 1 用力拉 yònglì lā, 用力高举 yònglì gāojǔ 2 剧烈起伏 jùliè qǐfú 3 呕吐 ǒutù

to heave a sigh of relief 放心地舒了一口气 fàngxīn de shū le yì kǒu qì

II v 1 用力拉 yònglì lā, 用力高举 yònglì gāojǔ 2 呕吐 ǒutù

heaven N 1 天堂 tiāntáng, 老天爷 lǎotiānyé 2 极好的情况 jí hǎo de qíngkuàng, 美好乐园 měihǎo lèyuán

Good Heavens! 老天爷呐! Lǎotiānyé a!

heavily ADV 1 大量地 dàliàng de [+hēshuǐ] 2 重重地 zhòngzhòng de [+chuǎnxī]

heavy ADJ 1 重的 zhòng, 沉重 chénzhòng

heavy industry 重工业 zhònggōngyè

2 很大的 hěn dà de, 很多的 hěn duō de 3 繁忙的 fánmáng de, 忙碌的 mánglù de

a heavy day at the office 办公室里繁忙的一天 bàngōngshì lǐ fánmáng de yìtiān 4 难消化的食物 nán xiāohuà de shíwù

heavy-duty ADJ 1 耐用的 [+材料] nàiyòng de [+cáiliào] 2 重型的 [+机器] zhòngxíng de [+jīqì] 3 认认真真的 [+谈话] rèn rènzhēn zhēnde [+tánhuà]

heavy-handed ADJ 粗暴的 cūbào de, 高压的 gāo yā de

heavyweight N 1 (体育) 重量级选手 (tǐyù) zhòngliàngjí xuǎnshǒu 2 重量级人物 zhòngliàngjí rénwù

Hebrew N 1 希伯来人 Xībóláirén 2 希伯来语 Xībóláiyǔ

heckle v (在公众集会上) 打断 [+发言] (zài gōngzhòng jíhuì shàng) dǎduàn [+fāyán], 呛声 qiāngshēng

hectare N 公顷 (10,000平方公尺) gōngqǐng (10,000 píngfāng gōngchǐ)

hectic ADJ 忙乱的 mánluàn de

hedge I N 1 树篱 shùlí 2 预防措施 yùfáng cuòshī II v 1 回避 [+问题] huíbì [+wèntí] 2 预防 [+风险] yùfáng [+fēngxiǎn]

to hedge one's bets 多边下 (赌) 注 duō chù xià (dǔ) zhù, 脚踩两条船 jiǎo cǎi liǎng tiáo chuan

heed I v 听取 tīng, 听取 tīngqǔ II N 注意 zhùyì, 考虑 kǎolǜ

to take heed of, to pay heed to 认真听 考虑 rènzhēn kǎolǜ

heedless ADJ 不注意 búzhùyì, 掉以轻心 diàoyǐqīngxīn

heel N 1 脚跟 jiǎogēn 2 鞋后跟 xié hòugēn

hefty ADJ 1 大块头的 [+人] dàkuàitóu de [+rén] 2 巨额的 [+金钱] jù'é de [+jīnqián] 3 很高的 [+价钱] hěn gāo de [+jiàqian]

height N 高度 gāodù

heighten v 增加 zēngjiā, 增强 zēngqiáng

heights N 高地 gāodì [M. WD 块 kuài]

heinous ADJ 1 极其邪恶的 jíqí xié'è de 2 糟透了的 zāotòu le de

heir N 财产继承人 cáichǎn jìchéngrén

heiress N 女财产继承人 nǚ cáichǎn jìchéngrén

heirloom N 传家宝 chuánjiābǎo [M. WD 件 jiàn]

heist N 抢劫 (商店或银行) qiǎngjié (shāngdiàn huò yínháng)

held v See hold

helicopter N 直升飞机 zhíshēng fēijī [M. WD 架 jià]

helium (He) N 氦 hài

hell N 1 地狱 dìyù 2 极坏的情况 jí huài de qíngkuàng
　to raise hell 大声吵闹 dàshēng chǎonào

hello INTERJ 1 你好 nǐhǎo
　to say hello 问好 wènhǎo
　2 (打电话时) 喂 (dǎ diànhuà shí) wèi

helm N 舵 duò, 舵柄 duòbǐng

helmet N 头盔 tóukuī [M. WD 顶 dǐng], 安全帽 ānquánmào [M. WD 顶 dǐng]

help I v 帮 bāng, 帮助 bāngzhu, 帮忙 bāngmáng
　can't help (doing) 忍不住 rěnbuzhù, 禁不住 jīnbuzhù
II N 1 帮助 bāngzhu 2 佣人 yōngrén, 帮手 bāngshǒu

helper N 帮手 bāngshǒu, 助手 zhùshǒu

helpful ADJ 有帮助的 yǒubāngzhu de

helping¹ N 一份 (食品／菜) yí fèn (shípǐn/cài)

helping² ADJ 帮助的 bāngzhù de
　a helping hand 帮助 bāngzhù, 援助 yuánzhù

helpless ADJ 1 无助的 wúzhù de, 束手无策的 shùshǒu wú cè de 2 情不自禁的 qíng bú zìjīn de

hem I N (衣服) 边 (yīfu) biān, 折边 zhé biān II v 缝边 féng biān

hemisphere N 半球 bànqiú
　the northern hemisphere 北半球 Běibànqiú

hemline N (衣服的) 下摆 (yīfu de) xiàbǎi

hemlock N 毒芹 dú qín

hemoglobin N 血红蛋白 xuèhóng dànbái

hemophilia N 血友病 xuèyǒubìng

hemorrhoids N 痔 zhì, 痔疮 zhì chuāng

hemp N 大麻 dàmá

hen N 母鸡 mǔjī [M. WD 只 zhī]

hence ADV 因而 yīn'ér, 因此 yīncǐ

henceforth, henceforward ADV 从今以后 cóngjīn yǐhòu, 从此以后 cóngcǐ yǐhòu

henchman N 亲信 qīnxìn, 喽啰 lóuluo

hepatitis N 肝炎 gānyán

her I ADJ 她的 tāde II PRON 她 tā

herald v 预示 yùshì

herb N 1 (调味) 香草 (tiáowèi) xiāngcǎo 2 药草 yàocǎo

herbivore N 食草类动物 shícǎo lèi dòngwù

herd I N 一群 [+牛] yìqún [+niú] II v 把 [+人群] 集中在一起 bǎ [+rénqún] jízhōng zài yìqǐ

here ADV 这里 zhèlǐ, 这儿 zhèr

hereabouts ADV 附近 fùjìn

hereafter ADV 今后 jīnhòu
　the hereafter 来世 láishì

hereby ADV 特此 tècǐ, 兹 zī

hereditary ADJ 遗传的 yíchuán de

heredity N 遗传 yíchuán

herein ADV 在此处 zài cǐchù, 在此情况下 zài cǐ qíngkuàng xià

heresy N 异教 yìjiào, 邪说 xiéshuō

heretic N 异教徒 yìjiàotú

herewith ADV 附上 fùshàng, 随函附上 suí hán fùshàng

heritage N 1 遗产 yíchǎn 2 传统 chuántǒng

hermit N 隐士 yǐnshì, 遁世者 dùnshìzhě

hernia N 疝 shàn, 疝气 shànqì

hero N 1 英雄 yīngxióng, 勇士 yǒngshì
　a national hero 民族英雄 mínzú yīngxióng
　2 (电影／小说) 男主角 (diànyǐng/xiǎoshuō) nán zhǔjué, 男主人公 nán zhǔréngōng

heroic ADJ 英雄的 yīngxióng de, 英勇的 yīngyǒng de

heroin N 海洛因 hǎiluòyīn

heroine N 女英雄 nǚyīngxióng [M. WD 位 wèi], 女勇士 nǚ yǒngshì [M. WD 位 wèi]

heron N 鹭鸶 lù sī [M. WD 只 zhī]

herpes N 疱疹 pàozhěn

herring N 鲱鱼 fēiyú [M. WD 条 tiáo]
　a red herring 转移他人注意力的小事 zhuǎnyí tārén zhùyìlì de xiǎoshì

hers PRON 她的 tāde

herself PRON 她自己 tā zìjǐ, 她亲自 tā qīnzì

hesitant ADJ 犹豫的 yóuyù de, 举棋不定的 jǔqí bùdìng de

hesitate v 犹豫 yóuyù, 拿不定主意 ná bùdìng zhǔyì

hesitation N 犹豫 yóuyù, 迟疑 chíyí

heterogeneous ADJ 混杂的 hùnzá de

heterosexual I ADJ 异性恋的 yìxìngliàn de II N 异性恋者 yìxìngliànzhě

hew V (PT **hewed**; PP **hewed**, **hewn**) 砍 kǎn, 劈 pī

hexagonal ADJ 六角形的 liùjiǎoxíng de, 六边形的 liùbiānxíng de

hey INTERJ 喂 wèi, 嘿 hēi

heyday N 全盛时期 quánshèng shíqī

hi INTERJ 你好 nǐ hǎo

hibernation N 冬眠 dōngmián

hiccup, hiccough I N 1 呃逆 ènì, 打嗝 dǎ gé 2 小问题 xiǎo wèntí II V 打呃 dǎ'è, 打嗝 dǎ gé

hick N 乡巴佬 xiāngbalǎo

hickey N 吻痕 wěnhén

hid V See **hide**¹

hidden I V See **hide**¹ II ADJ 隐藏的 yǐncáng de

hide¹ (PT **hid**; PP **hidden**) V 1 隐蔽 yǐnbì, 隐藏 yǐncáng 2 躲 duǒ, 躲藏 duǒcáng
hide and seek 捉迷藏游戏 zhuōmícáng yóuxì

hide² N（动物）皮（dòngwù）pí

hideaway N 躲藏地 duǒcángdì

hideous ADJ 难看极了 nánkàn jíle, 丑陋 不堪 chǒulòu bùkān

hideout N 躲藏地 duǒcángdì, 藏匿 cángnì

hiding N 1 躲藏 duǒcáng, 藏匿 cángnì
to go into hiding 躲藏起来 duǒcáng qǐ lái, 藏匿 cángnì
2 痛打 tòngdǎ
to give sb a hiding 痛打某人 tòngdǎ mǒurén, 把某人痛打一顿 bǎ mǒurén tòngdǎ yídùn

hierarchy N 等级 děngjí, 等级制度 děngjí zhìdù

hi-fi (= high fidelity) ABBREV 高保真 [+音 响设备] gāobǎozhēn [+yīnxiǎng shèbèi]

high I ADJ 1 高 gāo 2 高层的 gāocéng de, 重要的 zhòngyào de 3 中期的 zhōngqī de, 最重要的时期 zuì zhòngyào de shíqī 4（吸毒后）极度兴奋的 (xīdú hòu) jídù xīngfèn de
high school 中学 zhōngxué
junior high school 初级中学 chūjí zhōngxué, 初中 chūzhōng

senior high school 高级中学 gāojí-zhōngxué, 高中 gāozhōng
II N 高 gāo
to look/search high and low 到处寻找 dàochù xúnzhǎo
III N 1 最高点 zuìgāodiǎn 2（吸毒后 的）极度兴奋 (xīdú hòu de) jídù xīngfèn

highbrow ADJ（趣味）高雅的 (qùwèi) gāoyǎ de, 修养很高的 xiūyǎng hěn gāo de

high-class ADJ 高档的 gāodàng de, 优质 的 yōuzhì de

higher education N 高等教育 gāoděng jiàoyù

high-handed ADJ 专横的 zhuānhèng de, 盛气凌人的 shèngqì líng rén de

high-heel ADJ 高跟鞋 gāogēnxié

high jump N 跳高（运动）tiàogāo (yùndòng)

highlands N 高原 gāoyuán

high-level ADJ 高层的 gāocéng de

highlight I V 1 使…突出 shǐ...tūchū 2（在 计算机上）突出显示 (zài jìsuànjī shàng) tūchū xiǎnshì, 标示 biāoshì II N 1 最重 要的部份 zuì zhòngyào de bùfen 2（照 片上的）强光部分 (zhàopiàn shàng de) qiáng guāng bùfen

highlighter N 亮光笔 liàngguāngbǐ

highly ADV 1 高度地 gāodù de 2 极其 jíqí
to speak highly of 称赞 chēngzàn

Highness N 殿下 Diànxià

high-pitched ADJ 高音的 gāoyīn de, 尖声 的 jiānshēng de

high-powered ADJ 1 大功率的 [+卡车] dàgōnglǜ de [+kǎchē] 2 实力雄厚的 [+ 公司] shílì xiónghòu de [+gōngsī]

high-pressure ADJ 高气压的 gāoqìyā de, 高压的 gāoyā de

high-profile ADJ（故意）引人注目 的 (gùyì) yǐn rén zhùmù de, 高调的 gāodiào de

high-rise N 高层建筑 gāocéng jiànzhù, 高 楼 gāolóu [M. WD 幢 zhuàng]

high-spirited ADJ 活泼的 huópo de, 生气 勃勃的 shēngqì bóbó de

high-strung ADJ 易激动的 yì jīdòng de, 敏感的 mǐngǎn de

high-tech ADJ 高科技的 gāokējì de
high tide N 高潮 gāocháo
highway N 公路 gōnglù
hijack V 1 劫持 [+飞机／船] jiéchí [+fēijī/chuán] 2 把持 [+组织] bǎchí [+zǔzhī]
hike I N 1 徒步旅行 túbù lǚxíng, 远足 yuǎnzú
　on a long hike in the hills 在山间长途徒步旅行 zài shān jiān chángtú túbù lǚxíng
　2 [价格+] 大幅度上升 [jiàgé+] dàfúdù shàng shēng
　a hike in food prices 食品价格大幅度上升 shípǐn jiàgé dàfúdù shàngshēng
II V 1 徒步旅行 túbù lǚxíng, 远足 yuǎnzú 2 [价格+] 大幅度上升 [jiàgé+] dàfúdù shàng shēng
hilarious ADJ 极好笑的 jí hǎoxiào de, 极搞笑的 jí gǎoxiào de
hilarity N 欢笑 huānxiào
hill N （小）山 (xiǎo) shān
hillside N 山坡 shānpō
hilly ADJ 多山（丘）的 duōshān (qiū) de
hilt N 刀把 dāobǎ
　to the hilt 最大极限 zuìdà jíxiàn
him PRON 他 tā
himself PRON 他自己 tā zìjǐ, 他亲自 tā qīnzì
　by himself 他自己一个人 tā zìjǐ yí ge rén
hind ADJ 后面的 hòumian de
　the hind leg （动物）后腿 (dòngwù) hòutuǐ
hinder V 阻挡 zǔdǎng
Hindi N 印地语 Yìndìyǔ
hindrance N 妨碍 fáng'ài
　without let or hindrance 毫无障碍的 háowú zhàng'ài de, 畅通无阻的 chàngtōng wúzǔ de
hindsight N 后见之明 hòu jiàn zhī míng, 事后聪明 shìhòu cōngming
　with the benefit of hindsight 依靠后见之明 yīkào hòu jiàn zhī míng
Hindu N 印度教教徒 Yìndùjiào jiàotú
Hinduism N 印度教 Yìndùjiào
hinge I N 铰链 jiǎoliàn II V (to hinge on/upon) 取决于 qǔjuéyú
hint I N 1 暗示 ànshì, 提示 tíshì 2 一点儿

yìdiǎnr, 细微 xìwēi II V 暗示 ànshì, 提示 tíshì
hinterland N 内地 nèidì, 偏远地区 piānyuǎn dìqū
hip[1] N 臀部 túnbù
hip[2] ADJ 赶时髦的 gǎnshímáo de
hippie, hippy N 嬉皮士 xīpíshì
hippopotamus, hippo N 河马 hémǎ
hire I V 1 雇用 gùyòng, 聘任 pìnrèn 2 租用 zūyòng, 租赁 zūlìn II N 出租 chūzū, 租用 zūyòng
　a sex-for-hire business 色情服务公司 sèqíng fúwù gōngsī
his ADJ, PRON 他的 tāde
Hispanic I ADJ 西班牙语或葡萄牙语国家的 Xībānyáyǔ huò Pútáoyáyǔ guójiā de, 拉丁美洲的 Lādīngměizhōu de II N 拉丁美洲人 Lādīngměizhōurén
hiss I V 1 发出嘶嘶声 fāchū sī sī shēng 2 发嘘声反对 fā xū shēng fǎnduì II N 嘶嘶声 sīsīshēng
historian N 历史学家 lìshǐ xuéjiā, 研究历史的人 yánjiū lìshǐ de rén
historical ADJ 历史的 lìshǐ de
history N 1 历史 lìshǐ
　to make history 创造历史 chuàngzào lìshǐ
　2 发展史 fāzhǎnshǐ
hit I V (PT & PP hit) 1 打 dǎ 2 碰 pèng, 撞 zhuàng II N 1 打击 dǎjī 2 走红的人／事 zǒuhóng de rén/shì, 成功 chénggōng
hit-and-run ADJ 1 肇事后逃逸 zhàoshì hòu táoyì 2 打了就跑的 dǎ le jiù pǎo de
hitch[1] V 搭顺风车 dā shùnfēng chē
　to hitch a ride 搭一段顺风车 dā yí duàn shùnfēng chē
hitch[2] N 故障 gùzhàng
　without a hitch 顺利地 shùnlì de
hitchhike V See **hitch**[1]
hither and thither ADV 这里那里 zhèli nàli, 到处 dàochù
hitherto ADV 迄今 qìjīn, 至今 zhìjīn
hit man N 职业杀手 zhíyè shāshǒu
HIV (= human immunodeficiency virus) ABBREV 艾滋病病毒 àizībìng bìngdú
　HIV positive 艾滋病病毒检测呈阳性 àizībìng bìngdú jiǎncè chéng yángxìng

hive N 蜂巢 fēngcháo, 蜂房 fēngfáng

hoard I v 储藏 chǔcáng, 囤积 túnjī II N 储藏物资 chǔcáng wùzī, 囤积物资 túnjī wùzī

a secret hoard of treasure 秘密的宝物储藏 mìmì de bǎowù chǔcáng

hoarse ADJ 哑 yǎ, 嘶哑 sīyǎ

to shout oneself hoarse 大声喊叫得嗓子嘶哑 dàshēng hǎnjiào dé sǎngzi sīyǎ

hoax I N 骗局 piànjú

to play a hoax 设置骗局 shèzhì piànjú

II v 欺骗 qīpiàn, 作弄 zuònòng

hobble v 一瘸一拐地走 yì liú yì guǎi de zǒu, 跛行 bǒxíng

hobby N 嗜好 shìhào, (业余) 爱好 (yèyú) àihào

hobnob v 与比自己地位高的人亲密交谈 yǔ bǐ zìjǐ dìwèi gāo de rén qīnmì jiāotán, 高攀 gāopān

hobo N 流浪汉 liúlànghàn

hock I N 债 zhài, 债务 zhàiwù

in hock ① 负债 fùzhài ② 被典当 bèi diǎndàng, 被抵押 bèi dǐyā

II v 典当 diǎndàng, 抵押 dǐyā

hockey N 冰球 (运动) bīngqiú (yùndòng)

hoe N 锄头 chútou [M. WD 把 bǎ]

hog N 猪 zhū [M. WD 头 tóu] 2 贪吃的人 tānchī de rén, 贪婪的人 tānlán de rén II v 独占 dúzhàn, 不分享 bù fēnxiǎng

hoist I v 升起 shēngqǐ, 吊起 diào qǐ II N 起重机 qǐzhòngjī

hold I v (PT & PP **held**) 1 拿 ná, 握 wò 2 抱 bào, 抱住 bàozhu 3 扶 fú, 扶持 fúzhù 4 可容纳 kě róngnà 5 举行 jǔxíng 6 担任 dānrèn

to hold on 等等 děngděng, 等一等 děngyīděng

II N 拿住 názhu, 抓住 zhuāzhu

to get hold of 得到 dédào, 弄到 nòng-dao

holder N 1 (信用卡／护照) 持有人 (xìn-yòngkǎ/hùzhào) chíyǒurén 2 容器 róngqì

holding N 拥有的财产 yōngyǒu de cáichǎn

holding company 控股公司 kònggǔ gōngsī

holdup N 持枪抢劫 chíqiāng qiǎngjié

hole I N 1 洞 dòng 2 (野兽的) 洞穴 (yěshòu de) dòngxué 3 (高尔夫球) 球洞 (gāo'ěrfūqiú) qiú dòng II v 1 打 (高尔夫球) 入洞 dǎ (gāo'ěrfūqiú) rù dòng 2 (to hole up) 躲藏 duǒcáng, 藏匿 cángnì

holiday N 假日 jiàrì, 假期 jiàqī

holiday season 年末假日期间 niánmò jiàrì qījiān

summer holiday 暑假 shǔjià

winter holiday 寒假 hánjià

holiness N 神圣 shénshèng

holistic ADJ 整体的 zhěngtǐ de

holistic medicine 整体医学 zhěngtǐ yīxué

holler V, N 大叫大嚷 dàjiào dàrǎng

hollow I ADJ 1 空心的 kōngxīn de 2 空洞的 kōngdòng de II N 小山谷 xiǎo shāngǔ

holly N 冬青树 dōngqīng shù

Hollywood N 好莱坞 Hǎoláiwù, 美国电影业 Měiguó diànyǐngyè

holocaust N 大屠杀 dà túshā

hologram N 全息图 quánxītú

holster N 手枪皮套 shǒuqiāng pítào

holy ADJ 神的 shén de, 神圣的 shénshèng de

Holy Bible 圣经 Shèngjīng

homage N 崇敬 chóngjìng, 敬意 jìngyì

home I N 1 家 jiā, 家庭 jiātíng, 家宅 jiāzhái

Home, sweet home. 家，甜蜜的家。Jiā, tiánmì de jiā.

home town 家乡 jiāxiāng

to feel at home 感到在家一样 gǎndào zài jiā yíyàng

to make yourself at home 别客气，请随意。Biékèqi, qǐng suíyì.

2 国内 guónèi 3 (养老) 院 (yǎnglǎo) yuàn

children's home 孤儿院 gū'éryuàn, 儿童福利院 értóng fúlìyuàn

II ADV 在家 zài jiā III ADJ 家里的 jiālide, 家用的 jiāyòng de

home cooking 家常饭菜 jiācháng fàncài

IV v (to home in on) 对准 duìzhǔn

homecoming N 返乡 fǎnxiāng

homecoming dance 校友返校日舞会 xiàoyǒu fǎnxiàorì wǔhuì, 校友日 Xiàoyǒu rì

homeland N 国土 guótǔ, 祖国 zǔguó

homeless ADJ 无家可归的 wú jiā kě guī de

the homeless 无家可归者 wújiākěguīzhě

homely ADJ 1 相貌平平的 [+人] xiàngmào píngpíng de [+rén] 2 简单的 [+饭菜] jiǎndàn de [+fàncài]

homemade ADJ 家里做的 jiāli zuò de, 自制的 zìzhì de

homemaker N 家庭主妇 jiātíng zhǔfù

homeopathy N 顺势疗法 shùnshì liáofǎ

homepage N（网址）主页（wǎngzhǐ）zhǔyè

homer N（棒球）本垒打（bàngqiú）běnlěidǎ

home run N（棒球）本垒打（bàngqiú）běnlěidǎ

homesick ADJ 想家的 xiǎngjiā de, 思乡的 sīxiāng de

homestead N 农庄 nóngzhuāng, 庄园 zhuāngyuán

homework N 家庭作业 jiātíng zuòyè, 功课 gōngkè

homey ADJ 象家里一样的 xiàng jiāli yíyàng de, 舒适自在的 shūshì zìzài de

homicide N 1 杀人的 shārén de, 谋杀的 móushā de 2（警察局）凶杀科 (jǐngchájú) xiōngshākē

homogeneous ADJ 同一的 tóngyī de

homonym N 同音同形异义词 tóngyīn tóngxíng yìyìcí

homophone N 同音异义词 tóngyīn yìyìcí

homosexual I ADJ 同性恋的 tóngxìngliàn de II N 同性恋者 tóngxìngliànzhě

homosexuality N 同性恋 tóngxìngliàn

honcho N 头儿 tóur, 负责人 fùzérén

hone V 磨练 móliàn, 提高 [+能力] tígāo [+nénglì]

honest ADJ 诚实的 chéngshí de, 老实的 lǎoshi de

honestly ADV 1 诚实地 chéngshí de, 老实地 lǎoshi de 2 实在 shízài, 确实 quèshí

honesty N 诚实 chéngshí, 老实 lǎoshi

honey N 1 蜜 mì, 蜂蜜 fēngmì 2 亲爱的 qīn'ài de, 心肝宝贝儿 xīngān bǎobèir

honeycomb N 蜂巢 fēngcháo, 蜂窝 fēngwō

honeymoon N 蜜月 mìyuè

honk I V 按（汽车）喇叭 àn (qìchē) lǎba II N（汽车）喇叭声 (qìchē) lǎbashēng

honor I N 1 光荣 guāngróng, 荣幸 róngxìng 2 荣誉 róngyù 3 高尚品德 gāoshàng pǐndé

Your Honor 法官大人 fǎguān dàrén II V 1 向…致敬 xiàng...zhìjìng 2 兑现 duìxiàn, 实现 shíxiàn

in honor of 为 wèi, 为了 wèile

honorable ADJ 品德高尚的 pǐndé gāoshàng de, 值得尊敬的 zhíde zūnjìng de

honorary ADJ 1 荣誉的 róngyù de

an honorary citizen 荣誉公民 róngyù gōngmín

2 名誉的 míngyù de

honorary doctorate 名誉博士学位 míngyù bóshì xuéwèi

honors N 大学荣誉学位课程 dàxué róngyù xuéwèi kèchéng

to graduate with honors 以优等成绩毕业 yǐ yōuděng chéngjì bìyè

hood N 1 风帽 fēngmào 2（汽车）发动机罩盖 (qìchē) fādòngjī zhàogài

hooded ADJ 带风帽的 dài fēngmào de

hoodlum N 恶棍 ègu)n, 坏小子 huàixiǎozi

hoodwink V 哄骗 hǒngpiàn

hoof (PL **hoofs/hooves**) N 蹄（子）tí (zi)

hook I N 钩子 gōuzi

coat hook 衣钩 yīgōu

II V 钩住 gōu zhu

hooked ADJ 1 钩状的 gōu zhuàng de

2 成瘾的 chéngyǐn de

be hooked on computer games 对电脑游戏上瘾 duì diànnǎo yóuxì shàngyǐn, 着迷于电脑游戏 zháomí yú diànnǎo yóuxì

hooker N 妓女 jìnǚ

hooky N 逃学 táoxué

hooligan N 流氓 liúmáng, 恶棍 èguòn

hoop N 圈 quān, 环 huán

hoops N 篮球运动 lánqiú yùndòng

to shoot hoops 打篮球 dǎ lánqiú

hooray INTERJ 好啊 hǎo a, 太好了 tài hǎo le

hoot I N 嘘声 xūshēng, 嘲笑 cháoxiào
II v 发出嘘声 fāchū xūshēng, 嘲笑 cháoxiào

hop v, N 蹦 bèng, 蹦跳 bèngtiào
a hop, skip and a jump 极短的距离 jí duǎn de jùlí, 很近 hěn jìn

hope I v 希望 xīwàng **II** N **1** 希望 xīwàng **2** 寄予希望的人／事 jìyǔ xīwàng de rén/shì

hopeful ADJ 有希望的 yǒu xīwàng de

hopefully ADV **1** 如果一切顺利 rúguǒ yíqiè shùnlì, 很有可能 hěn yǒu kěnéng **2** 充满希望的 chōngmǎn xīwàng de

hopeless ADJ **1** 没有希望的 méiyǒu xīwàng de, 无救的 wú jiù de
a hopeless case 无药可救的病人 wú yào kě jiù de bìngrén, 毫无办法的情况 háowú bànfǎ de qíngkuàng **2** 糟透了 zāotòule

hopelessly ADV **1** 毫无办法 háowú bànfǎ, 处于绝境 chǔyú juéjìng **2** 不能自拔的 bù néng zì bá de

horde N 一大群 [+旅游者] yí dà qún [+lǚyóuzhě]

horizon N 地平线 dìpíngxiàn

horizons N 视野 shìyě, 范围 fànwéi
to open new horizons 开拓新天地 kāituò xīn tiāndì

horizontal ADJ 水平的 shuǐpíng de, 横向的 héngxiàng de

hormone N 荷尔蒙 hé'ěrméng, 激素 jīsù
growth hormone 生长激素 shēngzhǎng jīsù

horn N **1** 喇叭 lǎba **2** (动物的) 角 (dòngwù de) jiǎo

hornet N 大黄蜂 dàhuángfēng

horoscope N 星相算命 xīngxiàng suànmìng

horrendous ADJ 骇人的 hài rén de, 可怕的 kěpà de

horrible ADJ **1** 可怕的 kěpà de **2** 糟透了的 zāo tòule de, 极讨厌的 jí tǎoyàn de

horrid ADJ 极其糟糕的 jíqí zāogāo de

horrified ADJ 深感恐惧的 shēngǎn kǒngjù de

horrifying ADJ 极其恐怖的 jíqí kǒngbù de, 可怕极了 kěpà jíle

horror I N **1** 恐怖 kǒngbù **2** 恐怖的事 kǒngbù de shì
to one's horror 使某人大为恐慌 shǐ mǒurén dàwéi kǒnghuāng

hors d'oeuvre N 开胃菜 kāiwèicài, 开胃小吃 kāiwèi xiǎochī

horse N 马 mǎ [M. WD 匹 pǐ]

horseback N 马背 mǎbèi
horseback riding 骑马 qímǎ

horseplay N 打闹 dǎnào

horsepower N 马力 mǎlì

horticulture N 园艺 (学) yuányì (xué)

hose I N 水管 shuǐguǎn **2** 连裤袜 liánkùwà [M. WD 双 shuāng] **II** v **1** (用水管) 冲 (yòng shuǐguǎn) chōng **2** 欺骗 qīpiàn

hosiery N 袜类 wà lèi

hospice N 临终医院 línzhōng yīyuàn, 安养院 ānyǎng yuàn

hospitable ADJ **1** 好客的 [+人] hàokè de [+rén] **2** 适宜的 [+条件] shìyí de [+tiáojiàn]

hospital N 医院 yīyuàn
to be admitted to the hospital 住进医院 zhù jìn yīyuàn, 住院 zhùyuàn
to be discharged from the hospital 出院 chūyuàn

hospitality N 好客 hàokè
hospitality industry 旅馆服务业 lǚguǎn fúwùyè

hospitalize v 住医院 zhùyīyuàn, 住院 zhùyuàn

host¹ I N (F **hostess**) **1** 主人／女主人 zhǔrén/nǚzhǔrén **2** (电视) 节目主持人 (diànshì) jiémù zhǔchírén **3** (活动) 东道主 (huódòng) dōngdàozhǔ, (国际活动) 东道国 (guójì huódòng) dōngdàoguó **II** v **1** 主持 zhǔchí **2** 举办 jǔbàn

host² N (a host of) 许多 xǔduō

hostage N 人质 rénzhì
to hold sb hostage 把某人扣作人质 bǎ mǒurén kòu zuò rénzhì

hostel N 旅舍 lǚshè
Youth Hostel 青年旅舍 qīngnián lǚshè

hostile ADJ 敌对的 díduì de, 抱有敌意的 bàoyǒu díyì de
a hostile takeover 恶意接管 èyì jiēguǎn

hostility N 敌意 díyì
hot ADJ **1** 热 rè
  hot dog 热狗 règǒu, 长香肠 cháng xiāngcháng
  hot plate 平板电炉 píngbǎn diànlú
  hot potato 棘手的问题 jíshǒu de wèntí
  hot seat 困难的处境 kùnnan de chǔjìng
  2 辣的（食物）là de (shíwù) **3** 暴躁的 bàozao de
  a hot temper 暴躁的脾气 bàozao de píqi
  4 色情的 sèqíng de
hotcake N 煎饼 jiānbǐng
  to sell like hotcakes 非常畅销 fēicháng chàngxiāo
hotel N 旅馆 lǚguǎn, 酒店 jiǔdiàn
hotheaded ADJ 头脑发热的 tóunǎo fārè de, 性急冲动的 xìngjí chōngdòng de
hotline N 热线 rèxiàn
hotshot N 自信的成功者 zìxìn de chénggōngzhě
hotspot N（电脑网页）热点 (diànnǎo wǎngyè) rèdiǎn
hot-tempered ADJ 脾气暴躁的 píqi bàozao de
hot-water bottle N 热水袋 rèshuǐ dài
hot-wire V 强行起动（汽车）qiángxíng qǐdòng (qìchē)
hound I V 骚扰 sāorǎo, 追住不放 zhuī zhù bù fàng II N 狗 gǒu, 猎狗 liègǒu
hour N 小时 xiǎoshí, 钟头 zhōngtóu
  opening hours（商店/银行）营业时间 (shāngdiàn/yínháng) yíngyè shíjiān,（图书馆/博物馆）开放时间 (túshūguǎn/bówùguǎn) kāifàng shíjiān
  visiting hours（医院）探病时间 (yīyuàn) tànbìng shíjiān
  after hours 下班后 xiàbān hòu
hourglass N 沙漏 shālòu
  an hourglass figure 细腰身材 xìyāo shēncái
hourly ADJ, ADV **1** 每一小时的 měi yī xiǎoshí de **2** 按小时计算的 àn xiǎoshí jìsuàn de
house I N **1** 住宅 zhùzhái, 房子 fángzi
  the White House 白宫 Báigōng
  house arrest 软禁 ruǎnjìn
  2 议院 yìyuàn

  the House（美国）众议院 (Měiguó) Zhòngyìyuàn
  3 公司 gōng sī
  publishing house 出版社 chūbǎnshè
  4 剧院 jùyuàn
  opera house 歌剧院 gējùyuàn
II V 为…提供住房 wéi…tígōng zhùfáng
housebound ADJ 只能待在家里的 zhǐ néng dài zài jiālide
housebroken ADJ（宠物）不在屋内便溺的 (chǒngwù) búzài wūnèi biànnào de
household N 家庭 jiātíng, 户儿 hù
  head of a household 户主 hùzhǔ
housekeeper N **1** 管家 guǎnjiā **2** [旅馆+] 清洁工 [lǚguǎn de+] qīngjiégōng
housekeeping N 家务管理 jiāwù guǎnlǐ
House of Representatives N（美国）众议院 (Měiguó) Zhòngyìyuàn
houseplant N 室内盆栽植物 shìnèi pénzāi zhíwù
house-sitter N 看管房屋的人 kānguǎn fángwū de rén
housewarming N 庆祝乔迁的聚会 qìngzhù qiáoqiān de jùhuì
housewife N 家庭主妇 jiātíng zhǔfù
housework N 家务事 jiāwùshì
housing N 住房 zhùfáng
  public housing 政府为低收入家庭提供的住房 zhèngfǔ wéi dī shōurù jiātíng tígōng de zhùfáng, 公房 gōngfáng
hover V 盘旋 pánxuán
hovercraft N 气垫船 qìdiànchuán
how ADV **1** 怎样 zěnyàng, 怎么样 zěnmeyàng **2** 多少 duō, 多么 duōme
howdy INTERJ 你好 nǐhǎo
however I ADV **1** 不管怎么样 bùguǎn zěnmeyàng, 无论如何 wúlùn rúhé **2** 然而 rán'ér, 但是 dànshì II CONJ 不管怎么样 bùguǎn zěnmeyàng, 无论如何 wúlùn rúhé
howl V **1** [动物+] 嚎叫 [dòngwù+] háojiào **2** 叫叫 hǒujiào,[人+] 象动物一样嚎叫 [rén+] xiàng dòngwù yíyàng háojiào
  to howl with laughter 狂笑 kuángxiào
HQ (= headquarters) ABBREV（军队）司令部 (jūnduì) sīlìngbù,（公司）总部 (gōngsī) zǒngbù

HR (= human resources) ABBREV 人力资源（管理）rénlìzīyuán (guǎnlǐ), 人事（管理）rénshì (guǎnlǐ)

HTML (= Hypertext Markup Language) ABBREV（计算机）超文本标记语言 (jìsuànjī) chāowénběn biāojì yǔyán

hub N 中心 zhōngxīn, 枢纽 shūniǔ
from hub to tire 从头到尾 cóng tóu dào wěi, 完全地 wánquán de

huddle I v 挤作一团 jǐ zuò yì tuán
to huddle around 围着 wéizhe
II N 挤在一起的人 jǐ zài yìqǐ de rén

hue N 色调 sèdiào, 色度 sèdù

huff I v 气喘吁吁 qìchuǎn xūxū II N 气吁吁 qì xūxū
in a huff 怒气冲冲 nùqì chōngchōng

hug v, N 拥抱 yōngbào

huge ADJ 巨大的 jùdà de, 极大的 jídà de

hulk N 废弃的飞机／轮船／火车 fèiqì de fēijī/lúnchuán/huǒchē

hull N 1 船体 chuántǐ 2 壳体 gǔké, 豆荚 dòujiá

hum I v 1 哼 [+歌／曲子] hēng [+gē/qǔzi] 2 活跃 huóyuè, 忙碌 mánglù II N 1 哼歌声 hēnggēshēng 2 嗡嗡声 wēngwēngshēng

human I ADJ 人（类）的 rén(lèi) de
To err is human; to forgive, divine. 犯错误是人性, 饶恕错误是神性。Fàn cuòwù shì rénxìng, ráoshù cuòwù shì shénxìng.
human race 人类 rénlèi
human rights 人权 rénquán
II N 人 rén
human nature 人性 rénxìng, 人的本性 rén de běnxìng

humane ADJ 人道的 réndào de, 仁慈的 réncí de

humanist N 人本主义者 rénběn zhǔyìzhě, 人文主义者 rénwén zhǔyìzhě

humanitarian I ADJ 人道主义的 réndào zhǔyì de II N 人道主义者 réndào zhǔyìzhě

humanities N 人文学科 rénwén xuékē

humanity N 1 人类 rénlèi 2 博爱 bó'ài, 仁慈 réncí

mankind N 人类 rénlèi

humanly ADV 人的 rén de
humanly possible 尽最大努力 jìn zuì dà nǔlì

humble I ADJ 1 谦恭的 qiāngōng de, 谦虚的 qiānxū de 2 卑微的 [+出身] bēiwēi de [+chūshēn] II v 使…谦 shǐ...bēiqiān

humdrum ADJ 单调乏味的 dāndiào fáwèi de

humid ADJ 潮湿的 cháoshī de, 湿气很重的 shīqì hěn zhòng de

humidifier N 增湿器 zēngshī qì

humidity N 湿度 shīdù

humiliate v 羞辱 xiūrǔ, 使…丢脸 shǐ...diūliǎn, 使…蒙羞 shǐ...méngxiū

humiliation N 羞辱 xiūrǔ

humility N 谦虚 qiānxū, 谦恭 qiāngōng

humor N 幽默 yōumò, 诙谐 huīxié
sense of humor 幽默感 yōumògǎn

humorous ADJ 幽默的 yōumò de

hump N 1 圆形隆起物 yuánxíng lóngqǐ wù 2 驼峰 tuófēng

hunch N 预感 yùgǎn II v 弓起 [+背] gōng qǐ [+bèi]

hunchback N 驼背的人 tuóbèi de rén, 驼背 tuóbèi

hundred NUM 百 bǎi, 一百 yì bǎi

hundredweight N 美担（= 100磅/45.36公斤）měidàn (= 100 bàng/45.36 gōng jīn)

hung v See hang[1]
hung jury 未能取得一致意见的陪审团 wèi néng qǔdé yízhì yìjiàn de péishěntuán
hung up 担忧的 dānyōu de

hunger I N 1 饥饿 jī'è
hunger strike 绝食 juéshí
2 渴求 kěqiú
hunger for knowledge 对知识的渴求 duì zhīshi de kěqiú
II v (to hunger for) 渴求 kěqiú
to hunger for recognition 渴求获得他人的认可 kěqiú huòdé tārén de rènkě

hungry ADJ 饿 è, 饥饿的 jī'è de

hunk N 身材魁梧的人 shēncái kuíwú de rén, 性感的男子 xìnggǎn de nánzǐ

hunt I v 1 打猎 dǎliè 2 寻找 xúnzhǎo, 搜索 sōusuǒ II N 寻找 xúnzhǎo

hunter N 猎人 lièrén

hunting N 打猎 dǎliè、猎取 lièqǔ
bargain hunting 寻找便宜货 xúnzhǎo
piányihuò

hurdle I N 1 [法律+] 障碍 [fǎlǜ+] zhàng'ài
2 [赛跑的+] 拦架 [sàipǎo de+] lánjià II V
跨越 kuàyuè [+lánjià]

hurl V 投掷 tóuzhì、扔 rēng

hurricane N 飓风 jùfēng

hurried ADJ 匆忙的 cōngmáng de

hurry I V 1 匆忙地做 cōngmáng de zuò
2 催促 cuīcù II N 匆忙 cōngmáng
Hurry up! 快! Kuài!

hurt I V (PT & PP hurt) 1 伤害 shānghài
2 感到疼痛 gǎndao téngtòng II N（感
情）伤害（gǎnqíng）shānghài

hurtful ADJ 伤害人的 shānghài rén de、使
人痛苦的 shǐrén tòngkǔ de

hurtle V 猛冲 měngchōng

husband N 丈夫 zhàngfu

hush I V 使…安静 shǐ…ānjìng
to hush up 保密 bǎomì、秘而不宣 mì ér
bù xuān
II N（重大事件前的）沉默（zhòngdà
shìjiàn qián de）chénmò

hush-hush ADJ 秘密的 mìmì de

husk N（谷物）外皮（gǔwù）wàipí、壳 ké

husky I ADJ 1 [嗓子+] 沙哑的 [sǎngzi+]
shǎyǎ de 2 高大健壮的 [+男子] gāodà
jiànzhuàng de [+nánzǐ] II N 爱斯基摩犬
Àisījīmó quǎn

hustle I V 乱推 luàn tuī、混乱 hùnluàn
II N 忙碌 mánglù
hustle and bustle 忙碌喧闹 mánglù
xuānnào

hustler N 妓女 jìnǚ

hut N 小棚屋 xiǎo péngwū [M. WD 间 jiān]

hutch N 兔笼 tù lóng

hybrid N 1 杂交品种 zájiāo pǐnzhǒng、杂
种 zázhǒng 2 混合物 hùnhéwù
hybrid car 油电两用车 yóu diàn
liǎngyòng chē

hydrant N 消防笼头 xiāofáng lóngtou、消
防栓 xiāofáng shuān

hydraulics N 水压系统 shuǐyā xìtǒng

hydroelectric ADJ 水力发电的 shuǐlì
fādiàn de

hydrogen (H) N 氢（气）qīng (qì)

hydrogen bomb N **H-bomb**

hydroplane V 水上飞机 shuǐshàng fēijī

hyena N 鬣狗 lièɡǒu [M. WD 只 zhī]

hygiene N（个人）卫生（gèrén）
wèishēng

hygienic ADJ（个人）卫生的（gèrén）
wèishēng de

hymn N 赞美诗 zànměishī、颂歌 sònggē

hype N, V [媒体的+] 大肆炒作 [méitǐ de+]
dàsì chǎozuò

hyper ADJ 过于兴奋的 guòyú xīngfèn
de、非常激动的 fēicháng jīdòng de
II SUFFIX 过分的 guòfèn de、过度的
guòdù de

hyperactive ADJ 过于活跃的 [+儿童]
guòyú huóyuè de [+értóng]、多动的
duōdòng de

hyperlink N 超链接 chāo liànjiē

hypersensitive ADJ 过敏的 guòmǐn de

hypertension N 高血压 gāoxuèyā

hyphen N 连接符 liánjiēfú (-)

hyphenated ADJ（用连接号）连接起来的
（yòng liánjiēhào）liánjiē qǐlái de

hypnosis N 催眠（状态）cuīmián
(zhuàngtài)

hypnotic ADJ 催眠的 cuīmián de

hypnotism N 催眠状态 cuīmián
zhuàngtài

hypnotize V 对…催眠术 duì…cuīmiánshù

hypochondriac N 过分担心健康的人
guòfèn dānxīn jiànkāng de rén、无病呻
吟者 wú bìng shēnyínzhě

hypocrisy N 伪善 wěishàn

hypocrite N 伪善者 wěishànzhě、伪君子
wěijūnzǐ

hypodermic ADJ 皮下注射针头 pí xià
zhùshè zhēntóu

hypothermia N 体温过低 tǐwēn guò dī、
寒冷 hánlěng

hypothesis N 假设 jiǎshè

hypothetical ADJ 假设的 jiǎshè de

hysterectomy N 子宫切除术 zǐgōng
qiēchúshù

hysteria N 1 狂热 kuángrè、狂热情绪
kuángrè qíngxù 2 歇斯底里 xiēsīdǐlǐ、癔
病 yìbìng

hysterical ADJ 狂热的 kuángrè de，歇斯底里的 xiēsīdǐlǐ de

hysterics N 歇斯底里 xiēsīdǐlǐ

to go into hysterics 控制不了感情 kòngzhì bùliǎo gǎnqíng，歇斯底里发作 xiēsīdǐlǐ fāzuò

I

I PRON 我 wǒ

ice N 冰 bīng

ice cream 冰淇淋 bīngqílín
ice cube 冰块 bīngkuài
ice hockey 冰球（运动）bīngqiú (yùndòng)

iceberg N 冰山 bīngshān

the tip of the iceberg ① 冰山的一角 bīngshān de yìjiǎo ② 大问题的一小部分 dà wèntí de yì xiǎo bùfen

ice skate I V 溜冰 liūbīng II N 溜冰鞋 liūbīng xié [M. WD 只 zhī/双 shuāng]

icicle N 冰柱 bīngzhù，冰凌 bīnglíng

icing N 糖霜 tángshuāng

icon N 1 崇拜的偶像 chóngbài de ǒuxiàng 2（计算机的）图标（jìsuànjī de）túbiāo

icy ADJ 1 冰冷的 bīnglěng de 2 结冰的 jiébīng de 3 冷淡的 [+态度] lěngdàn de [+tàidu]，极不友好的 jí bùyǒuhǎo de

ID I (= identity, identification) ABBREV 1 个人身份 gèrén shēnfen 2 身份证明 shēnfenzhèng míng

ID card, identity card 身份证 shēnfenzhèng

II V 辨认 [+罪犯] biànrèn [+zuìfàn]

idea N 1 主意 zhǔyi 2 认识 rènshi 3 想法 xiǎngfǎ

I don't have the slightest idea who did it. 我一点儿也不知道是谁干的。Wǒ yìdiǎnr yě bù zhīdào shì shéi gàn de.

ideal I N 理想 lǐxiǎng II ADJ 理想的 lǐxiǎng de，最合适的 zuì héshì de

idealistic ADJ 理想主义的 lǐxiǎngzhǔyì de

identical ADJ 完全相同的 wánquán xiāngtóng de，同一的 tóngyī de

identifiable ADJ 可以识别的 kěyǐ shíbié de，可以辨认的 kěyǐ biànrèn de

identification N 1 辨认 biànrèn，识别 shíbié 2 身份（证明）shēnfen (zhèng-míng)

identity N 1 身份 shēnfen 2 个性 gèxìng，（自身的）特征（zìshēn de）tèzhēng

identity crisis 失去自身特征的危险 shīqù zìshēn tèzhēng de wēixiǎn 3 同一性 tóngyīxìng

ideology N 意识形态 yìshíxíngtài

idiocy N 极度愚蠢的 jídù yúchǔn de

idiom N 1 成语 chéngyǔ 2 习惯用语 xíguàn yòngyǔ

idiomatic ADJ 1 地道的 [+中文] dìdao de [+Zhōngwén] 2 成语的 chéngyǔ de，习惯用语的 xíguàn yòngyǔ de

idiosyncrasy N 特性 tèxìng

idiot N 白痴 báichī，大笨蛋 dà bèndàn

idiotic ADJ 极其愚蠢的 jíqí yúchǔn de，白痴一样的 báichī yíyàng de

idle I ADJ 1 闲置不用的 [+设备] xiánzhì búyòng de [+shèbèi] 2 没有意义的 [+话] méiyǒu yìyì de [+huà] 3 懒惰的 lǎnduò de，闲散的 xiánsǎn de

the idle rich 富贵闲人 fùguì xiánrén

II V 1 使 [+设备] 闲置 shǐ [+shèbèi] xián zhì 2 [发动机+] 空转 [fādòngjī+] kōngzhuàn

idol N 偶像 ǒuxiàng

idolatry N 偶像崇拜 ǒuxiàng chóngbài，过分崇拜 guòfèn chóngbài

idolize V 极为崇拜 jíwéi chóngbài

idyllic ADJ 恬静宜人的 tiánjìng yírén de

if I CONJ 1 如果 rúguǒ，要是 yàoshi 2 是否 shìfǒu，是不是 shìbushì，会不会 huì bù huì

even if 即使 jíshǐ

only if 只有 zhǐyǒu，只要 zhǐyào
if I were you 要是我是你的话 yàoshi wǒ shì nǐ de huà

II N 可能 kěnéng，可能性 kěnéngxìng

igloo N（爱斯基摩人）圆顶小屋（Àisījīmórén）yuándǐng xiǎo wū

ignite V 1 点燃 [+炸药] diǎnrán [+zhàyào] 2 激发 [+热情] jīfā [+rèqíng]

ignition N（汽车）点火装置（qìchē）diǎnhuǒ zhuāngzhì，点火开关 diǎnhuǒ kāiguān ignition key（汽车）启动钥匙 (qìchē) qǐdòng yàoshi

ignoble ADJ 卑鄙的 bēibǐ de, 不光彩的 bù guāngcǎi de

ignominious ADJ 极不光彩的 jí bù guāngcǎi de, 耻辱的 chǐrǔ de

ignorance N 无知 wúzhī

ignore v 不理睬 bù lǐcǎi

ill I ADJ 1 生病 shēngbìng 2 坏的 huài de, 有害的 yǒuhài de

ill effects 有害效果 yǒuhài xiàoguǒ, 不良反应 bùliáng fǎnyìng

3 (ill at ease) 不自在 bú zìzài, 紧张的 jǐnzhāng de II ADV 不好地 bù hǎo de III N 伤害 shānghài, 厄运 èyùn

ill-advised ADJ 不明智的 bùmíngzhì de

illegal I ADJ 非法的 fēifǎ de, 违法的 wéifǎ de II N 非法移民 fēifǎ yímín, 非法滞留者 fēifǎ zhìliúzhě

illegible ADJ 难以辨认的 [+字迹] nányǐ biànrèn de [+zìjì]

illegitimate ADJ 1 私生的 sī shēng de, 非婚生的 fēi hūn shēng de

an illegitimate child 私生子 sīshēngzǐ 2 非法的 fēifǎ de

ill-equipped ADJ 装备不良的 zhuāngbèi bù liáng de, 没有很好准备的 méiyǒu hěn hǎo zhǔnbèi de

ill-fated ADJ 倒霉的 dǎoméi de, 注定失败的 zhùdìng shībài de

illicit ADJ 1 违法的 wéifǎ de 2 社会不容的 shèhuì bù róng de

illiteracy N 不识字 bù shízì, 文盲 wénmáng

ill-mannered ADJ 不礼貌的 bù lǐmào de, 粗鲁的 cūlǔ de

illness N 病 bìng

illogical ADJ 不合逻辑的 bù hé luójí de, 不合道理的 bùhé dàolǐ de

ill-treat v 虐待 nüèdài

illuminate v 1 照亮 [+房间] zhàoliàng [+fángjiān] 2 阐明 [+道理] chǎnmíng [+dàolǐ]

illumination N 照亮 zhàoliàng, 阐明 chǎnmíng

illusion N 幻觉 huànjué, 幻想 huànxiǎng
optical illusion 视错觉 shìcuòjué

illusory ADJ 虚构的 xūgòu de, 虚假的 xūjiǎ de

illustrate v 1 举例子解释 jǔ lìzi jiěshì, 举例子说明 jǔ lìzi shuōmíng 2 画插图 huà chātú

illustration N 1 图示 túshì, 图解 tújiě 2 插图 chātú 3 说明 shuōmíng

illustrious ADJ 杰出的 jiéchū de, 著名的 zhùmíng de

image N 1 形象 xíngxiàng 2 印象 yìnxiàng, 图像 túxiàng

imaginary ADJ 想像的 xiǎngxiàng de

imagination N 想像力 xiǎngxiànglì

imaginative ADJ 想像力丰富的 xiǎngxiànglì fēngfù de

imagine v 1 想像 xiǎngxiàng 2 设想 shèxiǎng

imbalance N 不平衡 bù pínghéng

imbecile I N 笨人 bènrén, 蠢货 chǔnhuò II ADJ 愚蠢透顶的 yúchǔn tòudǐng de

imbibe v 喝 [+酒] hē [+jiǔ]

imbue v 使…充满 shǐ…chōngmǎn

imitate v 1 模仿 mófǎng, 仿效 fǎngxiào 2 模拟 mónǐ

imitation I N 1 模仿 mófǎng, 仿效 fǎngxiào 2 仿制品 fǎngzhìpǐn, 伪造品 wěizàopǐn II ADJ 仿造的 fǎngzào de, 人造的 rénzào de

imitation leather 人造（皮）革 rénzào (pí) gé

immaculate ADJ 1 完美的 wánměi de, 无瑕可击的 wúxiá kějī de 2 十分清洁整齐的 shífēn qīngjié zhěngqí de

immaterial ADJ 1 无关紧要的 wúguān jǐnyào de 2 非实体的 fēi shítǐ de

immature ADJ 1 不成熟的 bù chéngshú de 2 未充分发育的 wéi chōngfèn fāyù de

immaturity N 不成熟 bù chéngshú, 发育不全 fāyù bù quán

immediate ADJ 1 立即的 lìjí de, 即刻的 jíkè de 2 当前的 dāngqián de, 目前的 mùqián de 3 直接的 zhíjiē de
the immediate future 最近 zuìjìn

immediately ADV 立即 lìjí, 即刻 jíkè

immense ADJ 巨大的 jùdà de, 宏大的 hóngdà de

immerse v 浸没 jìnmò, 沉浸 chénjìn
to immerse oneself in 潜心于 qiánxīn
yú

immersion N 1 [黄豆] 沉浸 [huángdòu+]
chénjìn 2 专注 [+政治活动] zhuānzhù
[+zhèngzhì huódòng] 3 沉浸式外语教
学法 chénjìnshì wàiyǔ jiàoxuéfǎ

immigration N 移民（问题）yímín (wèntí)

imminent ADJ 即刻会发生的 jíkè huì
fāshēng de

immobile ADJ 固定的 gùdìng de, 动弹不
得的 dòngtanbùdé de

immoral ADJ 不道德的 bú dàodé de

immortal I ADJ 1 不会死的 bú huì sǐ de,
长生不老的 chángshēngbùlǎo de 2 不
朽的 [+功绩] bùxiǔ de [+gōngjì] II N 长
生不老者 chángshēngbùlǎozhě, 仙人
xiānrén

immovable ADJ 1 不能移动的 bùnéng
yídòng de, 固定的 gùdìng de 2 不可动
摇的 bùkě dòngyáo de, 十分坚定的 shífēn
jiāndìng de

immune ADJ 1 有免疫力的 yǒu miǎnyìlì
de 2 不受影响的 bú shòu yǐngxiǎng de
immune system 免疫系统 miǎnyì
xìtǒng

immunity N 免疫 miǎnyì, 免疫性
miǎnyìxìng

immutable ADJ 不能改变的 bùnéng
gǎibiàn de, 永恒的 yǒnghéng de

imp N 1 小鬼 xiǎoguǐ 2 小淘气 xiǎo táoqì

impact I N 1 影响 yǐngxiǎng 2 冲击
chōngjī, 撞击 zhuàngjī II v 产生（重
大）影响 chǎnshēng (zhòngdà)
yǐngxiǎng

impaired ADJ 受损的 shòusǔn de

impale v 刺穿 cìchuān

impart v 1 传授 chuánshòu 2 给予 jǐyǔ,
赋予 fùyǔ

impartial ADJ 不偏不倚的 bùpiān bùyǐ
de, 公正的 gōngzhèng de

impassable ADJ 不能通过的 bùnéng
tōngguò de

impasse N 僵局 jiāngjú

impassive ADJ 冷淡的 lěngdàn de

impatience N 没有耐心的 méiyǒu nàixīn,
不耐烦 búnàifán

impatient ADJ 没有耐心的 méiyǒu nàixīn
de, 不耐烦的 búnàifán de

impeach v 弹劾 tánhé, 控告 kònggào

impeachment N 弹劾 tánhé, 控告
kònggào

impeccable ADJ 无瑕可击的 wúxiákějī
de, 完美的 wánměi de

impede v 妨碍 fáng'ài, 迟缓 chíhuǎn

impediment N 1 残疾 cánjí 2 妨碍
fáng'ài

impel v 促使 cùshǐ, 驱使 qūshǐ

impending ADJ 即将发生的 jíjiāng
fāshēng de, 即将来临的 jí jiāng láilín de

impenetrable ADJ 1 不能进入的 bùnéng
jìnrù de 2 不能理解的 [+文章] bù néng
lǐjiě de [+wénzhāng], 费解的 fèijiě de

imperative I ADJ 绝对必须的 juéduì bìyào
de, 紧迫的 jǐnpò de II N 1 当务之急
dāngwù zhī jí 2（语法）祈使语气 (yǔfǎ)
qíshǐ yǔqì

imperfect I ADJ 不完美的 bù wánměi de
II N（语法）未完成时态 (yǔfǎ) wèi
wánchéng shítài

imperfection N 不完美性 bù wánměi xìng

imperial ADJ 帝国的 dìguó de, 皇帝的
huángdì de

imperil v 使…陷于危险境地 shǐ…xiànyú
wēixiǎn jìngde

impersonal ADJ 1 无人情味的 wúrén
qíngwèi de, 冷漠的 lěngmò de 2 (语法)
无人称的 (yǔfǎ) wúrénchēng de

impersonator N 1 冒充者 [+行骗]
màochōngzhě [+xíngpiàn] 2 [滑稽+] 模
仿者 [gǔjī+] mófǎngzhě

impertinent ADJ 没有礼貌的 méiyǒu
lǐmào de, 粗鲁的 cūlǔ de

impervious ADJ 1 不能渗透的 [+材料]
bùnéng shèntòu de [+cáiliào] 2 [对批
评+] 无动于衷的 [duì pīpíng+] wúdòng
yú zhōng de

impetuous ADJ 冲动的 chōngdòng de

impetus N 1 动力 dònglì, 冲力 chōnglì
2 推动 tuīdòng, 促进 cùjìn

impinge on v 影响到 yǐngxiǎng dào

impish ADJ 顽皮的 wánpí de

implacable ADJ 难以满足的 nányǐ mǎnzú
de, 难以平息的 nányǐ píngxī de

implant I v 移植 yízhí, 注入 zhùrù II N（手术）植入物(shǒushù) zhírùwù

implement I v 执行 zhíxíng, 实施 shíshí II N 工具 gōngjù, 用具 yòngjù

implicate v 使…受牵连 shǐ…shòu qiānlián

implication N 1 含义 hányì, 暗示 ànshì 2 牵连 qiānlián

implicit ADJ 1 隐含的 yǐnhán de, 暗指的 ànzhǐ de 2 (implicit trust) 绝对信任 juéduì xìnrèn

implore v 恳求 kěnqiú, 哀求 āiqiú

imply v 意味着 yìwèizhe, 暗示 ànshì

impolite ADJ 不礼貌的 bù lǐmào de

import I v 进口 jìnkǒu II N 进口货 jìnkǒuhuò import duty 进口税 jìnkǒushuì

importance N 重要性 zhòngyàoxing to attach importance to 重视 zhòngshì

important ADJ 重要的 zhòngyào de

impose v 强加 qiángjiā to impose tax [政府+] 征税 [zhèngfǔ+] zhēngshuì

imposing ADJ 壮观的 zhuàngguān de, 宏伟的 hóngwěi de

impossible ADJ 1 不可能的 bù kěnéng de 2 极难对付的 jínán duìfù de

imposter N 冒充的人 màochōng de rén, 冒牌货 màopáihuò

impotence N 1 阳痿 yángwěi 2 无能为力 wú néng wéilì de

impotent ADJ 1 无性交能力的 wú xìngjiāo nénglì de, 阳痿的 yángwěi de 2 无能为力的 wú néng wéilì de

impound v 扣押 kòuyā, 扣留 kòuliú

impoverished ADJ 非常贫困的 fēicháng pínkùn de

impractical ADJ 1 不恰当的 bú qiàdàng de 2 不会应付实际问题的 [+人] bú huì yìngfu shíjì wèntí de [+rén]

imprecise ADJ 不精确 bù jīngquè

imprecision N 不精确（性）bù jīngquè (xìng)

impregnable ADJ 1 无法攻克的 [+堡垒] wúfǎ gōngkè de [+bǎolěi] 2 无懈可击的 [+论点] wúxiè kějī de [+lùndiǎn]

impress v 1 给人好印象 gěi rén hǎo yìnxiàng, 使人敬佩 shǐ rén jìngpèi 2 使…牢记 shǐ…láojì

to impress the urgency of environmental protection on the public 使公众牢记环境保护的迫切性 shǐ gōngzhòng láojì huánjìng bǎohù de pòqièxìng 3 压印 yā yìn, 盖印 gài yìn

impression N 1 印象 yìnxiàng to make an impression on 给人印象 gěi rén yìnxiàng 2 印记 yìnjì, 印痕 yìnhén

impressive ADJ 给人良好印象的 gěi rén liánghǎo yìnxiàng de

imprint I N 印证 yìnzhèng II v 在…加印 zài…jiā yìn

imprison v 监禁 jiānjìn, 把…投进监狱 bǎ…tóu jìn jiānyù

imprisonment N 监禁 jiānjìn

improbable ADJ 1 不大可能的 [+事件] búdà kěnéng de [+shìjiàn] 2 出人意料的 [+搭档] chūrén yìliào de [+dādàng], 不可思议的 bùkěsīyì de

impromptu I ADJ 即兴的 [+表演] jíxīng de [+biǎoyǎn], 即席的 [+演说] jíxí de [+yǎnshuō] II ADV 即兴 jíxīng, 即席 jíxí

improper ADJ 不妥当 bù tuǒdāng, 不合适 bù héshì

impropriety N 不妥 bù tuǒ, 不合适 bù héshì

improve v 改善 gǎishàn, 改进 gǎijìn

improvise v 现编 xiàn biān, 临时凑出 línshí còuchū

impudence N 冒失 màoshi, 厚颜 hòuyán

impulse N 1 冲动 chōngdòng impulse buying 一时冲动下的购买 yìshí chōngdòng xià de gòumǎi 2 电脉冲 diànmàichōng, 神经冲动 shénjīng chōngdòng

impulsive ADJ 冲动的 chōngdòng de

impunity N (with impunity) 不受惩罚 bú shòu chéngfá

impure ADJ 不纯的 bù chún de

impurity N 1 不纯 bùchún 2 杂质 zázhí

in I PREP 1 在…里 zài…lǐ 2 在…之内 zài…zhīnèi, 在…期间 zài…qījiān 3 在…以后 zài…yǐhòu 4 在…方面 zài…fāngmiàn II ADV 1 进入 jìnrù, 入 rù 2 在 [+家 / 办公室] zài [+jiā/bàngōngshì]

inability N 不能 bù néng, 无力 wú lì

inaccessible ADJ **1** 难达到的 nán dádào de **2** 得不到的 dé búdào de, 买不起的 mǎibuqǐ de

inaccurate ADJ 不准确 bù zhǔnquè

inaction N 无行动 wú xíngdòng, 无所作为 wú suǒ zuòwéi

inadequate ADJ 不足的 bù zú de, 欠缺的 qiànquē de

inadmissible ADJ（法律）不可接受的（fǎlǜ）bùkě jiēshòu de

inadvertent ADJ 因疏忽而造成的 yīn shūhu ér zàochéng de, 粗心大意的 cūxīn dàyì de

inadvisable ADJ 不明智的 bù míngzhì de, 不可取的 bùkě qǔ de

inane ADJ 极其愚蠢的 jíqí yúchǔn de, 无聊的 wúliáo de

inanimate ADJ 无生命的 wú shēngmìng de

inappropriate ADJ 不合适的 bù héshì de, 不恰当的 bù qiàdàng de

inarticulate ADJ 不能表达自己的 bùnéng biǎodá zìjǐ de, 说不清楚的 shuō bùqīngchu de

inasmuch as CONJ 由于 yóuyú, 因为 yīnwèi

inaudible ADJ 听不见的 tīngbújiàn de

inaugural ADJ **1** 就职的 jiùzhí de
an inaugural speech 就职演说 jiùzhí yǎnshuō
2 首次的 shǒucì de
inaugural show 首次演出 shǒucì yǎnchū

inaugurate V **1** [为州长+] 举行就职典礼 [wéi Zhōuzhǎng+] jǔxíng jiùzhí diǎnlǐ **2** [为大楼+] 举行落成典礼 [wéi dàlóu+] jǔxíng luòchéngdiǎnlǐ

inauspicious ADJ 不吉利的 bù jílì de, 不详的 bùxiáng de

in-between ADJ 介于两者之间的 jièyú liǎngzhě zhījiān de

inborn ADJ 天生的 [+能力] tiānshēng de [+nénglì]

inbred ADJ **1** 天生的 tiānshēng de **2** 近亲繁殖的 jìnqīn fánzhí de

incalculable ADJ 数不清的 shǔbuqīng de, 无法估量的 wúfǎ gūliang de

incandescence N 炽热 chìrè, 白炽 báichì

incantation N 咒语 zhòuyǔ

incapable ADJ 不能（的）bùnéng (de), 不会（的）bú huì (de)

incapacitate V **1** 使 [+人] 失去能力 shǐ [+rén] shīqù nénglì **2** 使 [+系统] 不能正常运转 shǐ [+xìtǒng] bùnéng zhèngcháng yùnzhuǎn

incarcerate V 监禁 jiānjìn, 幽禁 yōujìn

incarnation N 化身 huàshēn, 体现 tǐxiàn
the Incarnation 上帝化身为基督 Shàngdì huàshēn wéi Jīdū

incendiary ADJ **1** 燃烧的 [+炸弹] ránshāo de [+zhàdàn] **2** 极具煽动性的 [+演说] jí jù shāndòngxìng de [+yǎnshuō]

incense¹ N 香 xiāng, 焚香 fénxiāng

incense² V 激怒 jīnù

incentive N 激励 jīlì, 鼓励 gǔlì

inception N 开创 kāichuàng

incessant ADJ 不停的 bù tíng de, 没完没了的 méiwán méiliǎo de

incest N 乱伦 luànlún

inch I N 英寸 yīngcùn
inch by inch 慢慢地 mànmàn de, 一点一点地 yìdiǎn yìdiǎn de
II V 慢慢地移动 mànmàn de yídòng

incidence N 发生率 fāshēnglǜ

incident N 事件 shìjiàn

incidental ADJ **1** 偶然的 ǒurán de **2** 次要的 cìyào de, 附带的 fùdài de
incidental fees 杂费 záfèi

incinerate V 烧毁 shāohuǐ

incinerator N 焚化炉 fénhuàlú

incipient ADJ 刚开始的 gāng kāishǐ de

incise V 刻（上）kè (shàng)

incision N **1** 切入 qiērù, 切开 qiēkāi **2** 切口 qiēkǒu

incisive ADJ 切中要害的 qièzhòng yàohài de, 直截了当的 zhíjiéliǎodàng de

incisor N 门齿 ménchǐ, 门牙 ményá

incite V 煽动 shāndòng, 鼓动 gǔdòng

inclination N **1** [妥协的+] 意向 [tuǒxié de+] yìxiàng **2** [逃避灾害的+] 倾向 [táobì zāihài de+] qīngxiàng **3** 斜坡 xiépō

incline I V **1**（使…）倾向于 [+反抗]（shǐ…）qīngxiàng yú [+fǎnkàng] **2**（使…）倾斜（shǐ…）qīngxié II N 斜坡 xiépō

include v 包括 bāokuò
including PREP 包括 bāokuò
inclusion N 包括 bāokuò, 包含 bāohán
incoherent ADJ 没有条理的 méiyǒu tiáolǐ de, 杂乱无章的 záluàn wúzhāng de
income N 收入 shōurù
   income tax 收入税 shōurùshuì
incoming ADJ 1 进来的 [+电子邮件] jìnlai de [+diànzǐ yóujiàn] 2 新当选的 [+国会议员] xīn dāngxuǎn de [+Guóhuì Yìyuán]
incommunicado ADJ, ADV 不得与外界联系 bùde yǔ wàijiè liánxì
incomparable ADJ 无可比拟的 wúkě bǐnǐ de
incompatible [ADJ 1 不兼容的 [+软件] bù jiānróng de [+ruǎnjiàn] 2 不相容的 [+言论] bù xiāngróng de [+yánlùn] 3 合不来的 [+姐妹] hébùlái de [+jiěmèi]
incompetent ADJ 不能胜任的 bùnéng shèngrèn de, 不称职的 bú chènzhí de
incomplete ADJ 不完整的 bù wánzhěng de, 不完全的 bù wánquán de
incomprehensible ADJ 不可理解的 bùkě lǐjiě de
inconceivable ADJ 不能想象的 bùnéng xiǎngxiàng de, 不可思议的 bùkě sīyì de
inconclusive ADJ 非结论性的 fēi jiélùnxìng de, 无结论的 wú jiélùn de
incongruous ADJ 不协调的 bù xiétiáo de
inconsequential ADJ 不重要的 bú zhòngyào de
inconsiderate ADJ 不为他人考虑的 bú wèi tārén kǎolǜ de
inconsistency N 自相矛盾 zìxiāng máodùn, 前后不一 qiánhòu bùyī
inconsistent ADJ 前后不一的 qiánhòu bùyī de, 自相矛盾的 zìxiāng máodùn de
inconsolable ADJ 悲伤得无法安慰的 bēishāng de wúfǎ ānwèi de
inconspicuous ADJ 不显眼的 bù xiǎnyǎn de
incontinence N（大小便）失禁 (dàxiǎobiàn) shījìn
incontrovertible ADJ 无可否认的 wúkě fǒurèn de
inconvenience I N 不便之处 búbiàn zhīchù, 麻烦 máfan **II** v 带来不便 dàilái búbiàn, 造成麻烦 zàochéng máfan
inconvenient ADJ 不方便的 bù fāngbiàn de, 麻烦的 máfan de
incorporate v 吸收 xīshōu, 包容 bāoróng
incorporated (ABBREV **Inc**) ADJ 股份有限公司 gǔfèn yǒuxiàn gōngsī
incorrect ADJ 不正确的 bú zhèngquè de, 错误的 cuòwù de
incorrigible ADJ 不可救药的 bù kě jiùyào de
incorruptible ADJ 刚正清廉的 gāngzhèng qīnglián de
increase I v 增长 zēngzhǎng, 增加 zēngjiā **II** N 增加 zēngjiā, 增长 zēngzhǎng
incredible ADJ（令人）难以置信的 (lìng rén) nányǐ zhìxìn de
incredulous ADJ 不相信的 bù xiāngxìn de, 怀疑的 huáiyí de
increment N 增长 zēngzhǎng
incremental ADJ 逐步增长的 zhúbù zēngzhǎng de
incriminate v 显示 [+嫌疑犯] 有罪 xiǎnshì [+xiányífàn] yǒuzuì, 牵连 qiānlián
incubator N 1 孵化器 fūhuàqì 2（早产）婴儿保育箱 (zǎochǎn) yīng'ér bǎoyùxiāng
inculcate v 反复灌输 fǎnfù guànshū, 一再教诲 yízài jiàohuì
incumbent I ADJ 现任的 xiànrèn de **II** N 现任者 xiànrènzhě
incur v 引起 yǐnqǐ, 导致 dǎozhì
incurable ADJ 无法治愈的 wúfǎ zhìyù de, 不可医治的 bùkě yīzhì de
incursion N 突袭 tūxí, 侵犯 qīnfàn
indebted ADJ [对朋友的帮助+] 十分感激的 [duì péngyou de bāngzhù+] shífēn gǎnjī de
indecent ADJ 1 下流的 [+言语] xiàliú de [+yányǔ] 2 离谱的 [+价格] lípǔ de [+jiàgé], 完全不能接受的 wánquán bùnéng jiēshòu de
indecision N 犹豫（不决）yóuyù (bù jué)
indecisive ADJ 1 犹豫（不决）的 yóuyù (bù jué) de 2 结果不明确 jiéguǒ bù míngquè de
indeed ADV 确实 quèshí, 的确 díquè

indefensible ADJ 不可原谅的 bùkě yuánliàng de, 无法辩解的 wúfǎ biànjiě de

indefinable ADJ 难以名状的 nányǐ míngzhuàng de, 难以解释的 nányǐ jiěshì de

indefinite ADJ 不确定的 bú quèdìng de, 不定的 bú dìng de

indelible ADJ 不可磨灭的 bù kě mómiè de

indelicate ADJ 不文雅的 bù wényǎ de, 粗鲁的 cūlǔ de

indemnity N 1 (损失) 保障 (sǔnshī) bǎozhàng 2 赔偿金 péichángjīn, 赔款 péikuǎn

indent V 缩格 (书写) suō gé (shūxiě)

indentation N 1 (行首) 空格 (hángshǒu) kònggé 2 凹口 āokǒu

independence N 独立 dúlì
Independence Day (Fourth of July) (美国) 独立日 (七月四日) (Měiguó) dúlì rì (qīyuè sìrì)

independent ADJ 独立的 dúlì de, 不需帮助 bù xū bāngzhù de

in-depth ADJ 深入的 shēnrù de

indescribable ADJ 难以形容的 nányǐ xíngróng de, 难以描绘的 nányǐ miáohuì de

indestructible ADJ 不可摧毁的 bùkě cuīhuǐ de

indeterminate ADJ 不确定的 bú quèdìng de

index I N (PL **indices**) 1 (图书) 索引 (túshū) suǒyǐn 2 (股票) 指数 (gǔpiào) zhǐshù 3 标指 biāozhǐ
index card 索引卡片 suǒyǐn kǎpiàn
index finger 食指 shízhǐ
II V 编索引 biān suǒyǐn

Indian I ADJ 1 印度的 Yìndù de
Indian Ocean 印度洋 Yìndùyáng
2 印第安人的 Yìndì'ānrén de II N 1 印度人 Yìndùrén 2 印第安人 Yìndì'ānrén
American Indian 美洲印第安人 Měizhōu Yìndì'ānrén

indicate V 1 显示 xiǎnshì, 指示 zhǐshì 2 表示 biǎoshì, 示意 shìyì

indication N 显示 xiǎnshì, 表示 biǎoshì

indicator N 1 指示 zhǐshì, 指示器 zhǐshìqì 2 指针 zhǐzhēn

indices N See **index**

indict V 控告 kònggào, 起诉 qǐsù
to be indicted for a crime 被控犯罪 bèikòng fànzuì

indictment N 控告 kònggào, 起诉 qǐsù
under indictment 受到起诉 shòudào qǐsù

indifference N 漠不关心 mò bù guānxīn, 无所谓 wúsuǒwèi

indifferent ADJ 漠不关心的 mò bù guānxīn de, 无所谓的 wúsuǒwèi de

indigenous ADJ 土生土长的 tǔshēng tǔzhǎng de, 土著的 tǔzhù de

indigestible ADJ 1 难消化的 [+食物] nán xiāohuà de [+shíwù] 2 难以理解的 [+数据] nányǐ lǐjiě de [+shùjù]

indigestion N 消化不良 xiāohuà bùliáng

indignant ADJ 愤慨的 fènkǎi de, 气愤的 qìfèn de

indignity N 侮辱 wǔrǔ, 轻侮 qīngwǔ

indirect ADJ 间接的 jiànjiē de
indirect object 间接宾语 jiànjiē bīnyǔ

indiscreet ADJ 不谨慎的 bù jǐnshèn de, 言行失检的 yánxíng shī jiǎn de

indiscretion N 不谨慎 bù jǐnshèn, 言行失检 yánxíng shī jiǎn

indiscriminate ADJ 不加区别的 bù jiā qūbié de, 不分青红皂白的 bù fēn qīng hóng zào bái de

indispensable ADJ 不可缺少的 bùkě quēshǎo de, 必需的 bìxū de

indisputable ADJ 不容置疑的 bùróng zhìyí de, 完全正确的 wánquán zhèngquè de

indistinct ADJ 模糊不清的 móhu bùqīng de

individual I ADJ 个别的 gèbié de, 个人的 gèrén de II N 个人 gèrén

individualist N 按照个人意愿行事的人 ànzhào gèrén yìyuàn xíngshì de rén, 特立独行的人 tèlì dúxíng de rén

individually ADV 个别地 gèbié de, 一个一个地 yígeyíge de

indivisible ADJ 不可分割的 bùkě fēn'gē de

indoctrinate V 向…灌输思想 xiàng… guànshū sīxiǎng

indolence N 懒惰 lǎnduò

indomitable ADJ 不屈不挠的 bù qū bù náo de

indoor ADJ 室内的 shìnèi de

indoors ADV 室内 shìnèi, 房子里 fángzi lǐ

induce v 1 劝诱 quànyòu, 诱导 yòudǎo 2 [药物+] 诱发 [yàowù+] yòufā, 引产 yǐnchǎn

inducement N 劝诱 quànyòu, 诱导 yòudǎo

induct v 1 使…就职 shǐ…jiùzhí 2 吸纳…为会员 xīnà…wéi huìyuán

induction N 1 就职 jiùzhí 2 归纳法 guīnàfǎ

indulge v 1 让…尽情享受 ràng…jìnqíng xiǎngshòu 2 满足 [+欲望] mǎnzú [+yùwàng], 放纵 fàngzòng

indulgence N 1 纵容 zòngróng 2 嗜好 shìhào, 迷恋(的事物) míliàn (de shìwù)

industrial ADJ 工业的 gōngyè de
   industrial accident 工伤事故 gōngshāng shìgù
   industrial action 罢工 bàgōng, 怠工 dàigōng

industrialist N 工业家 gōngyèjiā, 企业家 qǐyèjiā [M. WD 位 wèi]

industrialization N 工业化 gōngyèhuà

industrious ADJ 勤劳的 qínláo de

industry N 1 工业 gōngyè 2 行业 hángyè, 产业 chǎnyè

inedible ADJ 不可食用的 bùkě shíyòng de

ineffective ADJ 无效果的 wú xiàoguǒ de

ineffectual ADJ 无能的 wú néng de, 没有效果的 méiyǒu xiàoguǒ de

inefficient ADJ 效率低下的 xiàolǜ dīxiàde

inelegant ADJ 不雅致的 bù yǎzhì de, 不雅的 bù yǎ de

ineligible ADJ 无资格的 wú zīge de

inept ADJ 没有技能的 méiyǒu jìnéng de, 笨拙的 bènzhuō de

ineptitude N 没有技能(的状态)méiyǒu jìnéng (de zhuàngtài)

inequality N 不平等 bù píngděng

inequity N 不公正 bù gōngzhèng, 不公平(现象)bùgōngpíng (xiànxiàng)

inert ADJ 1 惰性的 [+气体] duòxìng de [+qìtǐ] 2 迟缓的 [+行动] chíhuǎn de [+xíngdòng]

inertia N 惰性 duòxìng, 惯性 guànxìng

inescapable ADJ 不可避免的 bùkě bìmiǎn de

inessential ADJ 非必需的 fēi bìxū de, 可有可无的 kěyǒu kěwú de

inestimable ADJ (多得)难以估计的 (duō dé) nányí gūjì de

inevitable ADJ 不可避免的 bùkě bìmiǎn de, 必然的 bìrán de

inexact ADJ 不精确的 bù jīngquè de

inexcusable ADJ 不可原谅的 bùkě yuánliàng de

inexhaustible ADJ 取之不尽的 qǔ zhī bú jìn de, 无穷无尽的 wúqióng wújìn de

inexorable ADJ 不可阻挡的 bùkě zǔdǎng de, 无法停止的 wúfǎ tíngzhǐ de

inexpensive ADJ 不贵的 bú guì de, 便宜的 piányi de

inexperienced ADJ 没有经验的 méiyǒu jīngyàn de, 缺乏经验的 quēfá jīngyàn de

inexplicable ADJ 无法解释的 wúfǎ jiěshì de

inextricable ADJ 不可分割的 bùkě fēngē de, 密不可分的 mìbùkěfēn de

infallible ADJ 不犯错的 bú fàncuò de, 永远正确的 yǒngyuǎn zhèngquè de

infamous ADJ 臭名昭彰的 chòumíng zhāozhāng de

infancy N 1 婴儿期 yīng'érqī 2 初期 chūqī, 早期 zǎoqī

infant N 婴儿 yīng'ér, 幼儿 yòu'ér

infantile ADJ 1 婴幼儿的 yīngyòu'ér de 2 幼稚的 yòuzhì de

infantry N 步兵部队 bùbīng bùduì

infatuation N 痴迷 chīmí, 迷恋 míliàn

infect v 1 传染 chuánrǎn, 感染 gǎnrǎn 2 影响 [+别人的情绪] yǐngxiǎng [+biéren de qíngxù]

infectious ADJ 传染的 chuánrǎn de, 感染的 gǎnrǎn de

infer v 推断 tuīduàn, 推定 tuīdìng

inference N 推断 tuīduàn, 推论 tuīlùn

inferior I ADJ 次等的 cìděng de, 低劣的 dīliè de II N 下属 xiàshǔ, 部下 bùxià

inferno N 1 炼狱 liànyù, 地狱 dìyù 2 猛烈燃烧的大火 měngliè ránshāo de dàhuǒ

infertility N 1 不育症 búyùzhèng 2 (土地)贫瘠 (tǔdì) pínjí

infest V [昆虫／老鼠+] 成群 [kūnchóng/lǎoshǔ+] chéngqún

infidel N 异教徒 yìjiàotú

infidelity N 通奸 tōngjiān, (夫妻) 不贞 (fūqī) bùzhēn

infield N （棒球场）内场 (bàngqiúchǎng) nèichǎng

infighting N 内讧 nèihòng, 窝里斗 wōlǐdòu

infiltrate V 渗透 shèntòu, 打入 [+内部] dǎrù [+nèibù]

infiltrator N 渗透者 shèntòuzhě

infinite ADJ 无限止的 wú xiànzhǐ de, 无限的 wú xiàn de

infinitive N 动词不定式 dòngcí búdìngshì, 动词的原形 dòngcí de yuánxíng

infirm ADJ 体弱多病的 tǐruò duōbìng de, 年老体弱的 niánlǎo tǐruò de

infirmary N 医务室 yīwùshì, 医院 yīyuàn

infirmity N 1 体弱多病 tǐruò duōbìng 2 疾病 jíbìng

inflamed ADJ 发炎的 fāyán de, 红肿的 hóngzhǒng de

inflammable ADJ 1 易燃的 [+材料] yìrán de [+cáiliào] 2 易怒的 [+人] yì nù de [+rén]

inflammation N 1 发炎 fāyán 2 炎症 yánzhèng

inflatable ADJ 充气的 chōngqì de

inflate V 1 给…充气 gěi…chōngqì 2 使 [+人] 自高自大 shǐ [+rén] zìgāo zìdà 3 使 [+价格] 上升 shǐ [+jiàgé] shàngshēng

inflated ADJ 1 充了气的 [+救生衣] chōngle qì de [+jiùshēngyī] 2 过高的 [+价格] guògāo de [+jiàgé], 通货膨胀的 tōnghuò péngzhàng de 3 夸大的 [+数据] kuādà de [+shùjù], 言过其实的 yán guò qí shí de

inflation N 通货膨胀 tōnghuò péngzhàng

inflationary ADJ 引起通货膨胀的 yǐnqǐ tōnghuò péngzhàng de

inflexible ADJ 不灵活的 bùlínghuó de, 不可更改的 bùkě gēnggǎi de

inflict V 使…遭受 shǐ…zāoshòu

influence N, V 影响 yǐngxiǎng

influential ADJ 有影响力的 yǒu yǐngxiǎnglì de

influenza (= flu) N 流行性感冒 liúxíngxìng gǎnmào, 流感 liúgǎn

influx N 大量涌入 dàliàng yǒngrù

infomercial N 商品信息专题电视片 shāngpǐn xìnxī zhuāntí diànshìpiàn

inform V 1 通知 tōngzhī 2 (to inform on sb) 告发 gàofā, 举报 jǔbào

informal ADJ 非正式的 fēi zhèngshì de, 随和友好的 suíhé yǒuhǎo de

informant N 提供信息的人 tígōng xìnxī de rén, 告密者 gàomìzhě

information N 信息 xìnxī, 情报 qíngbào

information retrieval（计算机）信息检索 (jìsuànjī) xìnxī jiǎnsuǒ

information superhighway 信息高速公路 xìnxī gāosù gōnglù

information technology (IT) 信息技术 xìnxī jìshù

informative ADJ 提供大量信息的 tígōng dàliàng xìnxī de, 内容丰富的 nèiróng fēngfù de

informed ADJ 1 见多识广的 [+人] jiàn duō shí guǎng de [+rén]

well-informed 消息灵通的 xiāoxi língtōng de

2 有根据的 [+决定／选择] yǒu gēnjù de [+juédìng/xuǎnzé]

infrared ADJ 红外线的 hóngwàixiàn de

an infrared camera 红外线照相机 hóngwàixiàn zhàoxiàngjī

infrastructure N 基础设施 jīchǔ shèshī, 基础结构 jīchǔ jiégòu

infrequent ADJ 不是经常的 bú shì jīngcháng de, 不常见的 bù chángjiàn de

infringe V 违反 wéifǎn, 侵犯 qīnfàn

infuriate V 使…大怒 shǐ…dà nù, 激怒 jīnù

infuriating ADJ 让人极为愤怒的 ràng rén jíwéi fènnù de

infuse V 1 向 [+儿童] 灌输思想 xiàng [+értóng] guànshū sīxiǎng 2 冲泡 [+茶叶] chōngpào [+cháyè], 泡茶 pào chá

infusion N 1 灌输思想 guànshū sīxiǎng 2 冲泡茶叶 chōngpào cháyè, 泡茶 pàochá

ingenuity N 发明才能 fāmíng cáinéng, 心灵手巧 xīnlíng shǒuqiǎo

ingest V 摄取 [+食物] shèqǔ [+shíwù]

ingot N (金／银) 锭 (jīn/yín) dìng

ingrained ADJ 根深蒂固的 gēnshēn dìgù de, 顽固的 wángù de

ingratiate V 讨好 tǎohǎo
to ingratiate oneself with 讨好 tǎohǎo, 取得⋯欢心 qǔdé⋯huānxīn

ingratitude N 忘恩负义 wàng ēn fù yì, 不知领情 bùzhī lǐngqíng

ingredient N (食品／药品的) 成份 (shípǐn/yàopǐn de) chéngfèn [M. WD 种 zhǒng]

inhabit V 居住 jūzhù

inhabitant N 居民 jūmín, 居住者 jūzhùzhě

inhaler N 吸入器 xīrùqì

inherent ADJ 内在的 nèi zài de, 与生俱来的 yǔ shēng jù lái de

inherit V 继承 jìchéng

inheritance N 遗产 yíchǎn

inhibit V 抑制 yìzhì, 制约 zhìyuē

inhospitable ADJ 不适合居住的 bú shìhé jūzhù de, 恶劣的 èliè de

in-house ADJ, ADV 内部的 nèibù de
an in-house magazine [公司+] 内部杂志 [gōngsī+] nèibù zázhì

inhuman ADJ 无人性的 wú rénxìng de

inhumane ADJ 不人道的 bù réndào de, 残忍的 cánrěn de

inimitable ADJ 无可仿效的 wúkě fǎngxiào de, 无与伦比的 wú yǔ lúnbǐ de

initial I ADJ 起初的 qǐchū de, 开始的 kāishǐ de II N 名字的首字母 míngzì de shǒu zìmǔ III V 签上姓名的首字母 qiānshang xìngmíng de shǒu zìmǔ

initiate V 1 开始 kāishǐ, 发动 fādòng 2 吸收 [+新会员] xīshōu [+xīnhuì yuán]

initiative N 1 行动 xíngdòng 2 主动性 zhǔdòngxìng, 积极性 jījíxìng

inject V 1 注射 [+针剂] zhùshè [+zhēnjì] 2 投入 [+资金] tóurù [+zījīn]

injunction N (法院的) 禁令 (fǎyuàn de) jìnlìng

injure V 损伤 sǔnshāng, 伤害 shānghài

injury N 损伤 sǔnshāng, 伤害 shānghài

injustice N 不公正 (行为／待遇) bù gōngzhèng (xíngwéi/dàiyù)

ink N 墨 mò, 油墨 yóumò, 墨水 mòshuǐ

ink cartridge 油墨盒 yóumòhé

inkling N 模糊的想法 móhu de xiǎngfǎ
to have no Inkling 一点也不知道 yìdiǎn yě bù zhīdào, 毫无所知 háowú suǒzhī

inlaid ADJ 镶嵌着⋯的 xiāngqiànzhe...de

inland I ADJ 内陆的 nèilù de II ADV 在内陆 zài nèilù

in-laws N 姻亲 yīnqīn
brother-in-law 内兄 (内弟) nèixiōng (nèidì) (wife's elder/younger brother), 大伯子 (小叔子) dàbázi (xiǎoshūzi) (husband's elder/younger brother), 姐夫 (妹夫) jiěfū (mèifū) (elder/younger sister's husband), 连襟 liánjīn (wife's sister's husband)
father-in-law 岳父 yuèfù (wife's father), 公公 gōnggong (husband's father)
mother-in-law 岳母 yuèmǔ (wife's mother), 婆婆 pópo (husband's mother)
sister-in-law 嫂子 sǎozi (elder brother's wife), 弟媳 dìxí (younger brother's wife), 姑子 gūzi (husband's sister), 姨子 yízi (wife's sister), 妯娌 zhóuli (husband's brother's wife)

inlet N 小海湾 xiǎo hǎiwān

inmate N 1 (监狱) 囚犯 (jiānyù) qiúfàn 2 (医院) 病人 (yīyuàn) bìngrén

inn N 小旅店 xiǎo lǚdiàn [M. WD 家 jiā]

innate ADJ 天生的 tiānshēng de, 固有的 gùyǒu de

inner ADJ 里面的 lǐmiàn de, 内部的 nèibù de
inner ear 内耳 nèi'ěr
inner circle 核心集团 héxīn jítuán, 小圈子 xiǎoquānzi
inner city (一般穷人居住的) 市中心 (yìbān qióngrén jūzhù de) shìzhōngxīn, 旧城区 jiù chéngqū

innermost ADJ 内心深处 nèixīn shēnchù

innocence N 1 清白无辜 qīngbái wúgū 2 (儿童的) 天真无邪 (értóng de) tiānzhēn wúxié

innocent ADJ 1 清白无辜的 qīngbái wúgū de 2 天真无邪的 tiānzhēn wúxié de

innocuous ADJ 没有危险的 méiyǒu wēixiǎn de, 没有恶意的 méiyǒu èyì de, 无害的 wúhài de

innovate V 革新 géxīn, 创新 chuàngxīn

innovative ADJ 创新的 chuàngxīn de

innovator N 革新者 géxīnzhě, 创新者 chuàngxīnzhě

innuendo N 影射 yǐngshè, 暗示 ànshì

innumerable ADJ 无数的 wúshù de

inoculate V 给...接种 (疫苗) gěi...jiēzhòng (yìmiáo), 不合时宜 bùhé shíyí de

inoffensive ADJ 不触犯人的 bú chùfàn rén de, 不得罪人的 bù dézuì rén de

inopportune ADJ 不合适的 bù héshì de

inordinate ADJ 过度的 guòdù de, 极度 jídù de

inorganic ADJ 无机的 wújī de

inpatient N 住院病人 zhùyuàn bìngrén

input I N 1 (输入计算机的) 信息 (shūrù jìsuànjī de) xìnxī 2 (资金 / 建议的) 投入 (zījīn/jiànyì de) tóurù II V (PT & PP **input**) 输入 [+信息] shūrù [+xìnxī]

inquest N 询问 xúnwèn, 审讯 shěnxùn

inquire V 询问 xúnwèn, 查询 cháxún

inquiring ADJ 1 追根究底的 zhuī gēn jiū dǐ de 2 有疑问的 yǒu yíwèn de

inquiry N 询问 xúnwèn, 查询 cháxún

inquisitive ADJ 爱追根究底的 ài zhuī gēn jiū dǐ de, 好奇的 hàoqí de

inroads N 突然袭击 tūrán xíjī
to make inroads 侵占 qīnzhàn, 消耗 xiāohào

ins and outs N 详情细节 xiángqíng xìjié

insane ADJ 精神错乱的 de jīngshén cuòluàn de, 发疯的 fāfēng de

insanity N 1 精神错乱 jīngshén cuòluàn 2 愚蠢至极 (的行为) yúchǔn zhìjí (de xíngwéi)

insatiable ADJ 不满足的 bù mǎnzú de, 贪得无厌的 tāndé wúyàn de

inscribe V 雕刻 diāokè, 题字 tízì

inscrutable ADJ 不可理解的 bùkě lǐjiě de, 神秘的 shénmì de

insect N 昆虫 kūnchóng, 虫子 chóngzi

insecticide N 灭虫剂 mièchóngjì

insecure ADJ 1 无安全感的 [+职业] wú ānquángǎn de [+zhíyè] 2 缺乏自信的 [+人] quēfá zìxìn de [+rén]

insecurity N 1 无安全感 wú ānquángǎn 2 缺乏自信 quēfá zìxìn

inseminate V 使 [+动物] 受精 shǐ [+dòngwù] shòujīng, 使 [+人] 怀孕 shǐ [+rén] huáiyùn

insensible ADJ 1 (insensible of) 没有意识到的 méiyǒu yìshídào de 2 (insensible to) 对...没有感觉 duì...méiyǒu gǎnjué

insensitive ADJ 不敏感的 bù mǐngǎn de, 麻木的 mámù de

inseparable ADJ 形影不离的 [+朋友] xíngyǐng bùlí de [+péngyou], 亲密无间的 qīnmì wújiàn de

insert I V 插入 chārù, 加进 jiājìn II N 1 插页广告 chāyè guǎnggào 2 插入物 chārùwù

inset N 附图 fùtú, 附加资料 fùjiā zīliào

inside I PREP 在...里面 zài...lǐmian II ADV 里面 lǐmian, 在里面 zài lǐmian III N 里面 lǐmian IV ADJ 里面的 lǐmian de, 内部的 nèibù de

insider N 内部人 nèibùrén, 圈内人 quānnèirén
insider trading 内线交易 nèixiàn jiāoyì

insidious ADJ 暗藏的 àncáng de, 暗中为害的 ànzhōng wéi hài de

insight N 1 洞察力 dòngchálì, 眼光 yǎnguāng 2 顿悟 dùnwù

insignificance N 无重大意义 wú zhòngdà yìyì, 无足轻重 wúzú qīngzhòng

insincere ADJ 不诚恳的 bù chéngkěn de, 虚伪的 xūwěi de

insinuate V 暗示 ànshì

insipid ADJ 淡而无味的 dàn ér wúwèi de, 无味的 wúwèi de

insist V 坚持 jiānchí, 一定要 yídìng yào

insistence N 坚持 jiānchí

insistent ADJ 坚持的 jiānchí de

insolent ADJ 傲慢无礼的 àomàn wúlǐ de

insoluble ADJ 1 无法解决的 [+难题] wúfǎ jiějué de [+nántí] 2 不溶解 [+于水] 的 bùróngjiě [+yú shuǐ] de

insolvency N 无还债能力 wú huánzhài nénglì, 破产 pòchǎn

insolvent ADJ 无还债能力的 wú huánzhài nénglì de, 破产的 pòchǎn de

insomnia N 失眠 (症) shīmián (zhèng)

inspect V 1 仔细检查 zǐxì jiǎnchá 2 视察 [+分公司] shìchá [+fēngōngsī]

inspection N 1 仔细检查 zǐxì jiǎnchá 2 视察 shìchá

inspector N 视察员 shìcháyuán, 巡视员 xúnshìyuán

inspiration N 灵感 línggǎn, 启示 qǐshì

inspirational ADJ 给人启示的 gěi rén qǐshì de, 鼓舞人心的 gǔwǔ rénxīn de

inspire V 鼓舞 gǔwǔ, 激励 jīlì

instability N 不稳定 bù wěndìng

install V 1 安装 ānzhuāng 2 任命 rènmìng, 使…就职 shǐ…jiùzhí

installation N 1 安装 ānzhuāng 2 装置 zhuāngzhì, 设备 shèbèi 3 [军事+] 设施 [jūnshì+] shèshī

installment N 1 分期付款（额）fēnqī fùkuǎn (é) 2 [电视连续剧+] 集 [diànshì liánxùjù+] jí

instance N 事例 shìlì, 例子 lìzi
   for instance 例如 lìrú, 比如 bǐrú

instant I ADJ 立即的 lìjí de, 即刻的 jíkè de
   instant coffee 速溶咖啡 sùróng kāfēi
   instant noodle 速泡面 sùpàomiàn
   II N 片刻 piànkè
   in an instant 一下子 yíxiàzi, 顷刻之间 qǐngkè zhī jiān

instantaneous ADJ 即将的 jíjiāng de, 立即的 lìjí de

instead ADV 代替 dàitì
   instead of 而不是 ér bùshì

instigate V 煽动 shāndòng, 挑动 tiǎodòng

instigation N 煽动 shāndòng, 挑动 tiǎodòng

instigator N 煽动者 shāndòngzhě, 煽风点火的人 shānfēng diǎnhuǒ de rén

instill V 长期灌输 chángqī guànshū

instinct N 本能 běnnéng, 天性 tiānxìng

institute N 院 yuàn, 学院 xuéyuàn, 研究院 yánjiūyuàn
   research institute 科学研究院 kēxué yánjiū yuàn
   II V 制定 zhìdìng, 开创 kāichuàng

institution N 1 机构 jīgòu
   an institution of higher education 高等院校 gāoděng yuànxiào, 大学 dàxué 2 制度 zhìdù, 规章制度 guīzhāng zhìdù

institutionalized ADJ 1 把…送进精神病院 / 养老院 bǎ…sòngjìn jīngshén

bìngyuàn/yǎnglǎoyuàn 2 把…制度化 bǎ…zhìdùhuà

instruct V 1 指令 zhǐlìng, 指示 zhǐshì 2 教 jiāo, 传授 chuánshòu

instruction N 1 指令 zhǐlìng, 指示 zhǐshì
   instruction manual 使用 / 维修手册 shǐyòng/wéixiū shǒucè 2 教 jiāo, 教授 jiāoshòu

instructor N 教员 jiàoyuán [M. WD 位 wèi], 教练 jiàoliàn, 指导者 zhǐdǎozhě

instrument N 1 器具 qìjù, 器械 qìxiè
   instrument panel 仪表板 yíbiǎobǎn 2 乐器 yuèqì

insubordinate ADJ 不服从的 bù fúcóng de, 不听话的 bù tīnghuà de

insubordination N 拒不服从（的行为）jù bùfúcóng (de xíngwéi), 违抗命令 wéikàng mìnglìng

insubstantial ADJ 1 证据不足的 [+论点] zhèngjù bùzú de [+lùndiǎn] 2 虚幻的 xūhuàn de

insufferable ADJ 难以忍受的 nányǐ rěnshòu de

insufficient ADJ 不足的 bùzú de, 不够的 búgòu de

insular ADJ 1 岛屿的 dǎoyǔ de 2 闭塞不守的 bìsè bǎoshǒu de

insulate V 使…绝缘 / 隔热 / 隔音 shǐ…juéyuán/gérè/géyīn

insulin N 胰岛素 yídǎosù

insult N, V 侮辱 wǔrǔ

insurance N 1 保险 bǎoxiǎn 2 保险业 bǎoxiǎn yè
   contents insurance 家庭财产保险 jiātíng cáichǎn bǎoxiǎn
   health insurance 医疗保险 yīliáo bǎoxiǎn
   house insurance 房产保险 fángchǎn bǎoxiǎn

insure V 1 投保 tóubǎo 2 确保 quèbǎo

insurgent N 起义者 qǐyìzhě, 叛乱分子 pànluàn fènzǐ

insurmountable ADJ 不可逾越的 bùkě yúyuè de, 不可克服的 bùkě kèfú de

insurrection N 起义 qǐyì, 暴动 bàodòng

intact ADJ 未被损伤的 wèi bèi sǔnshāng de, 完美无缺的 wánměi wúquē de

intake N 吸入（量）xīrù (liáng)

intangible ADJ 1 难以捉摸的 [+气氛] nányǐ zhuōmo de [+qìfen] 2 无形的 [+价值] wúxíng de [+jiàzhí]

integer N 整数 zhěngshù

integrate V 1 使…结合 shǐ...jiéhé 2 使…融合 shǐ...rónghé

integrated ADJ 综合的 zōnghéde, 协调的 xiétiáo de

integrity N 1 诚信 chéngxìn, 正直 zhèngzhí
moral integrity 高尚的道德 gāoshàng de dàodé
2 完整 wánzhěng
territorial integrity（国家）领土完整 (guójiā) lǐngtǔ wánzhěng

intelligence N 1 智力 zhìlì
intelligence quotient (IQ) 智商 zhìshāng
artificial intelligence 人工智能 réngōng zhìnéng
2 情报 qíngbào, 谍报 diébào
the Central Intelligence Agency (CIA)（美国）中央情报局 (Měiguó) Zhōngyāng Qíngbàojú

intelligent ADJ 智力很高的 zhìlì hěn gāo de, 聪明的 cōngmíng de
intelligent life 智能生命 zhìnéng shēngmìng
intelligent terminal（计算机）智能终端 (jìsuànjī) zhìnéng zhōngduān

intend V 打算 dǎsuàn, 意图 yìtú

intense ADJ 1 强烈的 qiángliè de, 剧烈的 jùliè de 2 过于认真的 [+人] guòyú rènzhēn de [+rén]

intensify V 加强 jiāqiáng, 加剧 jiājù

intensity N 强度 qiángdù

intensive ADJ 深入的 shēnrù de, 彻底的 chèdǐ de

intent I N 目的意图 mùdì yìtú
for all intents and purposes 实际上 shíjìshàng
agreement of intent 意向书 yìxiàngshū
II ADJ (intent on (doing sth)) 决意（做某事）juéyì (zuòmǒushì)

intention N 打算 dǎsuàn, 意图 yìtú

intentional ADJ 故意的 gùyì de

intently ADV 全神贯注地 quánshén guànzhù de

inter V 埋葬 máizàng

interact V 互相起作用 hùxiāng qǐ zuòyòng, 互动 hùdòng

interaction N 互相影响 hùxiāng yǐngxiǎng, 互动 hùdòng

interactive ADJ 1 互相起作用的 hùxiāng qǐ zuòyòng de, 互相影响的 hùxiāng yǐngxiǎng de 2（人和计算机）互动的 (rén hé jìsuànjī) hùdòng de

intercede V 代为请求 dàiwéi qǐngqiú, 为…说情 wéi...shuōqíng

intercept V 拦截 lánjié, 截住 jiézhù

intercession N 求情 qiúqíng, 说情 shuōqíng

interchange I N 1 交换 jiāohuàn, 互换 hùhuàn 2（公路上的）立体交叉道 (gōnglù shàng de) lìtǐ jiāochādào II V 互换 hùhuàn, 互相替换 hùxiāng tìhuan

intercom N 内部通讯系统 nèibù tōngxùn xìtǒng, 对讲系统 duìjiǎng xìtǒng

intercontinental ADJ 洲际的 zhōujì de, 跨洲的 kuà zhōu de

intercourse N 1 性交 xìngjiāo 2 [感情的+] 沟通 [gǎnqíng de+] gōutōng, 交流 jiāoliú

interdependence N 相互依赖 xiānghù yīlài

interest N 1 兴趣 xìngqu 2 利益 lìyì, 好处 hǎochu 3 利息 lìxī

interested ADJ 1 对…感兴趣 duì...gǎn xìngqu 2 有关系的 yǒu guānxi de
an interested party（利益）相关的一方 (lìyì) xiāngguān de yìfāng

interesting ADJ 有趣 yǒuqù, 有意思 yǒu yìsi

interface N 1（计算机）接口 (jìsuànjī) jiēkǒu, 接口程序 jiēkǒu chéngxù 2 相互影响 xiānghù yǐngxiǎng

interfere V 干涉 gānshè, 干预 gānyù

interim I ADJ 临时的 línshí de II N (in the interim) 在此期间 zài cǐ qíjiān

interior I N 1 内部 nèibù, 里面 lǐmian 2 室内 shìnèi II ADJ 内部的 nèibù de
interior design 室内装饰 shìnèi zhuāngshì

interjection N 1 插话 chāhuà 2 感叹词 gǎntàncí

interlock V 使…连锁 shǐ…liánsuǒ, 使…连接 shǐ…liánjiē

interloper N 擅自闯入者 shànzì chuǎngrù zhě, 不速之客 búsù zhī kè

interlude N 插曲 chāqǔ, 间歇 jiànxiē

intermarriage N 通婚 tōnghūn

intermediary I N 1 调解人 tiáojiěrén, 中间人 zhōngjiānrén 2 代表 dàibiǎo, 代理人 dàilǐrén II ADJ 1 中间的 zhōngjiān de 2 调解人的 tiáojiěrénde, 中间人的 zhōngjiānrén de

intermediate ADJ 中等的 zhōngděng de, 中间的 zhōngjiān de

interminable ADJ 冗长乏味的 rǒngcháng fáwèi de

intermission N 幕间休息 mùjiān xiūxi

intermittent ADJ 断断续续的 duànduàn xùxù de, 间歇的 jiànxiē de

intern[1] N 实习医生 shíxí yīshēng, 实习人员 shíxí rényuán

intern[2] V 拘留 jūliú, 关押 guānyā

internal ADJ 1 内部 nèibù 2 国内 guónèi
  internal medicine 内科 nèikē, 内科医学 nèikē yīxué
  Internal Revenue Service (IRS) 税务局 shuìwùjú

international ADJ 国际的 guójì de

Internet N 互联网 hùliánwǎng, 英特网 yīngtèwǎng
  Internet service provider (ISP) 互联网服务提供者 hùliánwǎng fúwù tígōng zhě
  Internet café 网吧 wǎngbā
  Internet chat room 聊天室 liáotiānshì

internship N 实习（期间）shíxí (qījiān)

interpersonal ADJ 人际的 rénjì de

interplanetary ADJ 星球之间的 xīngqiú zhījiān de, 球际的 qiú jì de

interplay N 相互作用 xiānghù zuòyòng

interpose V（使…）插入 (shǐ…) chārù

interpret V 1 翻译 fānyì, 当口译 dāng kǒuyì 2 解释 jiěshì

interracial ADJ 种族之间的 zhǒngzú zhījiān de

interrogate V 审讯 shěnxùn, 询问 xúnwèn

interrupt V 打断 dǎduàn

intersect V 相交 xiāngjiāo, 交叉 jiāochā

intersection N 交叉口 jiāochākǒu, 交点 jiāodiǎn

intersperse V 散布 sànbù, 点缀 diǎnzhui

interstate I ADJ（美国）州际（的）(Měiguó) zhōujì (de) II N（美国）州际公路 (Měiguó) zhōujì gōnglù

intertwined ADJ 1 缠绕在一起的 chánrào zài yìqǐ de 2 紧密相关的 jǐnmì xiāngguān de

interval N 间歇 jiànxiē
  at regular intervals 定期 dìngqī

intervene V 1 介入 jièrù, 干预 gānyù 2 阻扰 zǔrǎo, 阻碍 zǔ'ài

intervention N 介入 jièrù, 干预 gānyù

interview N, V 1 采访 cǎifǎng 2 面试 miànshì, 面谈 miàntán
  job interview 求职面试 qiúzhí miànshì

interviewee N 1 被采访者 bèi cǎifǎngzhě 2 接受面试的人 jiēshòu miànshì de rén

interviewer N 采访者 cǎifǎngzhě 2 主持面试者 zhǔchí miànshì zhě

interweave V (PT **interwove**; PP **interwoven**) 交织（在一起）jiāozhī (zài yìqǐ)

intestinal ADJ 肠道的 chángdào de, 肠内的 cháng nèi de

intestine N 肠 cháng, 肠道 chángdào
  large intestine 大肠 dàcháng
  small intestine 小肠 xiǎocháng

intimacy N 1 亲密 qīnmì 2 性行为 xìng xíngwéi
  intimacies 亲昵的言语行为 qīnnì de yányu xíngwéi

intimate ADJ 1 亲密的 qīnmì de 2 私人的 sīrén de, 隐私的 yǐnsī de
  be intimate with sb 和某人发生性关系 hé mǒurén fāshēng xìng guānxi

intimidate V 恫吓 dònghè, 威胁 wēixié

into PREP 进入 jìnrù, 到里面 dào lǐmian

intolerable ADJ 无法忍受的 wúfǎ rěnshòu de, 无法容忍的 wúfǎ róngrěn de

intolerant ADJ 1 不能包容的 bùnéng bāoróng de, 心胸狭窄的 xīnxiōng xiázhǎi de 2 不能忍受的 bùnéng rěnróng, 过敏的 guòmǐn de
  lactose intolerant 对乳制品过敏的 duì rǔzhìpǐn guòmǐn de

intonation N 语调 yǔdiào

intoxicated ADJ 1 喝醉酒的 hēzuì jiǔ de 2 陶醉 táozuì, 冲昏头脑的 chōnghūn tóunǎo de

intoxication N 醉酒 zuìjiǔ

intractable ADJ 难解决的 nán jiějué de, 棘手的 jíshǒu de

intramural ADJ 校内的 xiào nèi de

intransigent ADJ 不让步的 bú ràngbù de, 不讲理的 bù jiǎnglǐ de

intravenous ADJ 静脉内的 jìngmài nèi de
intravenous drug 静脉注射的药物 jìngmài zhùshè de yàowù

intrepid ADJ 勇敢的 yǒnggǎn de, 无畏的 wúwèi de

intricacy N 复杂 fùzá
intricacies 复杂的细节 fùzá de xìjié

intricate ADJ 错综复杂的 cuòzōng fùzá de

intrigue I v 1 引起…的兴趣／好奇心 yǐnqǐ…de xìngqu/hàoqíxīn 2 策划阴谋 cèhuà yīnmóu II N 阴谋 yīnmóu, 密谋 mìmóu

intriguing ADJ 引人入胜的 yǐn rén rù shèng de

intrinsic ADJ 固有的 gùyǒu de, 内在的 nèizài de

introduce v 1 介绍 jièshào 2 引进 yǐnjìn 3 引导 yǐndǎo, 让…首次接触 ràng…shǒucì jiēchù

introduction N 1 介绍 jièshào 2 引进 yǐnjìn 3 引论 yǐnlùn, 入门 rùmén

introductory ADJ 入门的 rùmén de, 引言的 yǐnyán de
an introductory essay 引言 yǐnyán

introspection N 反省 fǎnxǐng

introspective ADJ 反省的 fǎnxǐng de

introvert N 性格内向的人 xìnggé nèixiàng de rén

introverted ADJ 性格内向的 xìnggé nèixiàng de, 不爱交际的 bú ài jiāojì de

intrude v 侵扰 qīnrǎo, 侵入 qīnrù

intruder N 入侵者 rùqīnzhě

intrusive ADJ 侵扰的 qīnrǎo de, 扰乱的 dǎorǎo de

intuition N 直觉 zhíjué

intuitive ADJ 直觉的 zhíjué de

inundate v 淹没 yānmò, 泛滥 fànlàn

be inundated with [+letters] 收到大量 [+来信] shōudào dàliàng [+láixìn]

invade v 侵入 qīnrù, 侵略 qīnlüè

invader N 入侵者 rùqīnzhě, 侵略者 qīnlüèzhě

invalid I ADJ 1 无效的 [+合同] wúxiào de [+hétong] 2 站不住脚的 [+理由] zhànbuzhù jiǎo de [+lǐyóu] II N (慢性) 病人 (mànxìng) bìngrén

invalidate v 1 使 [+身份证] 无效 shǐ [+shēnfenzhèng] wúxiào 2 证明 [+论点] 是错误的 zhèngmíng [+lùndiǎn] shì cuòwù de

invaluable ADJ 无价的 wújià de, 极其宝贵的 jíqí bǎoguì de

invariable ADJ 不变的 búbiàn de, 一直的 yìzhí de

invasion N 侵入 qīnrù, 侵略 qīnlüè

invent v 1 发明 fāmíng 2 编造 [+谎言] biānzào [+huǎngyán], 捏造 niēzào

invention 1 发明 (物) fāmíng (wù) 2 编造 biānzào, 捏造 niēzào

inventor N 发明者 fāmíngzhě

inventory N 清单 qīngdān, 详细目录 xiángxì mùlù
to take inventory 列出清单 lièchū qīngdān, 盘点 (存货) pándiǎn (cúnhuò)

inverse N, ADJ 相反 (的) xiāngfǎn de
in inverse proportion to 与…成反比例 yǔ…chéng fǎnbǐlì

invert v 使…倒置 shǐ…dàozhì

invest v 1 (商业) 投资 (shāngyè) tóuzī 2 投入 [+时间／金钱] tóurù [+shíjiān/jīnqián]

investigate v 调查 diàochá

investment v 投资 tóuzī

inveterate ADJ 根深蒂固的 gēnshēn dìgù de, 难改的 nán gǎi de

invigorate v 使…生气勃勃 shǐ…shēngqì bóbó, 使…精力充沛 shǐ…jīnglì chōngpèi

invincible ADJ 不可战胜的 bùkě zhànshèng de, 不可征服的 bùkě zhēngfú de

invisible ADJ 看不见的 kànbujiàn de, 隐形的 yǐnxíng de

invitation N 1 邀请 yāoqǐng 2 请帖 qǐngtiě, 请柬 qǐngjiǎn

invite I v **1** 邀请 yāoqǐng **2** 招致 [+批评] zhāozhì [+pīpíng], 引起 yǐnqǐ II N 邀请 yāoqǐng

invoice I N 发货／工作清单 fāhuò/gōngzuò qīngdān II v 发出发货／工作清单 fāchū fāhuò/gōngzuò qīngdān

invoke v 诉诸 [+法律] zhūsù [+fǎlǜ], 实施 shíshī

involuntary ADJ 不受意识控制的 bú shòu yìshí kòngzhì de, 不自觉的 bú zìjué de

involve v **1** 涉及 shèjí **2** 需要 xūyào

involvement N 涉及 shèjí, 牵连 qiānlián

inward ADJ **1** 内心的 nèixīn de **2** 向内的 xiàng nèi de

iodine (I) N 碘 diǎn

ion N 离子 lízǐ

IOU (= I owe you) ABBREV 借条 jiètiáo [M. wD 张 zhāng]

IQ ABBREV See **intelligence**

irascible ADJ 脾气暴躁的 píqí bàozao de, 脾气很坏的 píqí hěn huài de

irate ADJ 极为愤怒的 jíwéi fènnù de

iridescent ADJ 变色的 biànsè de, 彩虹色的 cǎihóngsè de

Irish I ADJ 爱尔兰的 Àiěrlán de II N **1** 爱尔兰人 Àiěrlánrén **2** 爱尔兰语 Àiěrlányǔ

irk v 使…恼怒 shǐ...nǎonù, 使…气恼 shǐ...qìnǎo

iron I N **1** 铁 tiě **2** 熨斗 yùndǒu
ironing board 熨衣板 yùnyībǎn
Strike while the iron is hot. 趁热打铁。Chèn rè dǎ tiě.
II ADJ 铁的 tiě de III v 熨烫 [+衣服] yùntàng [+yīfu]

ironic ADJ 有讽刺意味的 yǒu fěngcì yìwèi de

irony N 讽刺 fěngcì

irrational ADJ 不合理的 bù hélǐ de

irreconcilable ADJ 不可调和的 bùkě tiáohé de, 不相容的 bù xiāngróng de

irrefutable ADJ 无可辩驳的 wúkě biànbó de

irregular ADJ **1** 不规则的 bù guīzé de **2** 不定时的 bú dìngshí de
irregular heart beats 心率不齐 xīnlǜ bù qí

irregularity N **1** 不规则 bùguīzé **2** 违规行为 wéiguī xíngwéi, 违规 wéiguī

irrelevance N 不相关 bù xiāngguān, 无关 wúguān

irrelevant ADJ 不相关的 bù xiāngguān de, 无关的 wúguān de

irreparable ADJ 无法弥补的 wúfǎ míbǔ de

irreplaceable ADJ 不可代替的 bùkě dàitì de, 独一无二的 dúyī wú'èr de

irreproachable ADJ 无可指责的 wúkě zhǐzé de, 没有过失的 méiyǒu guòshī de

irresistible ADJ 无法抗拒的 wúfǎ kàngjù de

irrespective of PREP 不管 bùguǎn, 不顾 búgù

irresponsible ADJ 不负责任的 bú fù zérèn de, 没有责任心的 méiyǒu zérènxīn de

irreverent ADJ 不尊敬的 bù zūnjìng de, 不谦恭的 bù qiāngōng de

irreversible ADJ 不可逆转的 bùkě nìzhuǎn de, 不可挽回的 bùkě wǎnhuí de

irrevocable ADJ 不可更改的 bùkě gēnggǎi de, 不可取消的 bùkě qǔxiāo de

irrigation N 灌溉 guàngài

irritable ADJ **1** 易怒的 [+老人] yì nù de [+lǎorén] **2** 疼痛的 [+伤口] téngtòng de [+shāngkǒu]

irritant N **1** 让人恼火的事 ràng rén nǎohuǒ de shì **2** 刺激物 cìjīwù

irritate v **1** 使 [+人] 恼怒 shǐ [+rén] nǎonù **2** 使 [+伤口] 发炎 shǐ [+shāngkǒu] fāyán **3** 使…疼痛 shǐ...téngtòng

irritation N **1** 恼火 nǎohuǒ, 恼怒 nǎonù **2** 让人恼火的事 ràng rén nǎohuǒ de shì **3** 疼痛 téngtòng, 发炎 fāyán

IRS ABBREV See **internal**

is See **be**

Islam N 伊斯兰 Yīsīlán, 伊斯兰教 Yīsīlánjiào

island N 岛 dǎo

islander N 岛上的居民 dǎo shàng de jūmín, 岛民 dǎomín

isle N 岛 dǎo

isolate v **1** 隔离 [+病人] gélí [+bìngrén] **2** 分离 [+物质] fēnlí [+wùzhì] **3** 孤立 [+敌人] gūlì [+dírén]

isolated ADJ 1 孤立的 gūlì de 2 孤零零的 gūlínglíng de
an isolated incident 孤立的事件 gūlì de shìjiàn
an isolated island（大洋中）一个孤零零的小岛（dàyáng zhōng）yí ge gūlínglíng de xiǎodǎo

isolation N 隔离 gélí
isolation ward 隔离病房 gélíbìngfáng

ISP ABBREV See **Internet**

issue I N 1 有争论的问题 yǒu zhēnglùn de wèntí, 问题 wèntí 2（杂志）期（zázhì）qī
to take issue with 不同意 bù tóngyì, 有争议 yǒu zhēngyì
II v 1 发表 [+声明] fābiǎo [+shēngmíng] 2 发行 [+邮票] fāxíng [+yóupiào] 3 分发 [+枪支] fēnfā [+qiāngzhī]

IT ABBREV See **information**

it PRON 它 tā

Italian I ADJ 意大利的 Yìdàlì de II N 1 意大利语 Yìdàlìyǔ 2 意大利人 Yìdàlìrén

italics N 斜体字 xiétǐzì

itch I v 痒 yǎng, 发痒 fāyǎng II N 1 痒 yǎng, 发痒 fāyǎng 2 渴望 kěwàng

item N 1 项目 xiàngmù, 条目 tiáomù 2 一条新闻 yì tiáo xīnwén

itemize v 一项一项地记下 yí xiàng yí xiàng de jìxià, 分项记载 fēnxiàng jìzǎi

itinerant ADJ 流动的 liúdòng de
itinerant circus 流动马戏团 liúdòng mǎxìtuán

itinerary N 旅行日程表 lǚxíng rìchéngbiǎo
to plan an itinerary 计划旅行日程 jìhuà lǚxíng rìchéng

its ADJ 它的 tā de

itself PRON 它自己 tā zìjǐ

IV (= intravenous) ABBREV 静脉滴注 jìngmài dī zhù

ivory N 1 象牙 xiàngyá
ivory tower 象牙塔 xiàngyá tǎ 2 象牙色 xiàngyá sè

ivy N 常青藤 chángqīng téng

J

jab I v 1 刺 cì, 猛击 měngjī 2 打针 dǎzhēn, 注射 zhùshè II N 批评（的话）pīpíng (de huà), 责备（的话）zébèi (de huà)
to take a jab at 抨击 pēngjī

jack I N 1 起重器 qǐzhòng qì, 千斤顶 qiānjīndǐng 2（纸牌）杰克牌 (zhǐpái) jiékè pái, J 牌 J pái II v (to jack up)（用起重器）顶起 [+重物] (yòng qǐzhòngqì) dǐng qǐ [+zhòngwù]

jackal N 豺 chái, 胡狼 húláng

jackass N 讨厌的蠢货 tǎoyàn de chǔnhuò

jacket N 1 上衣 shàngyī [M. WD 件 jiàn], 夹克衫 jiākèshān [M. WD 件 jiàn] 2 封面 hùfēng, 书套 shūtào 3 保护罩 bǎohùzhào

jack-knife I N 折刀 zhédāo [M. WD 把 bǎ] II v 弯曲 wānqū

jack-of-all-trades N 博而不精的人 bó ér bù jīng de rén, 万事通 wànshìtōng

jackpot N 一大笔钱 yí dà bǐ qián
to hit the jackpot ① 赢得大奖 yíngdé dàjiǎng, 中头彩 zhòng tóucǎi ②（突然）交上好运 (tūrán) jiāo shàng hǎoyùn

jade N 玉 yù, 碧玉 bìyù, 翡翠 fěicuì

jaded ADJ 厌倦的 yànjuàn de, 没有激情的 méiyǒu jīqíng de

jagged ADJ 锯齿状 jùchǐzhuàng

jaguar N 美洲豹 Měizhōubào

jail I N 1 监狱 jiānyù 2 看守所 kānshǒusuǒ II v 监禁 jiānjìn

jailor, jailer N 监狱看守 jiānyù kānshǒu

jam I N 1 果酱 guǒjiàng 2 交通堵塞 jiāotōng dǔsè II v 1 [车辆+] 堵塞 [chēliàng+] dǔsè 2 把…塞进 bǎ...sāijìn
to jam on the brakes 猛踩刹车 měng cǎi shāchē

jamboree N 1 童子军大会 tóngzǐjūn dàhuì 2 喧闹的大会 xuānnào de dàhuì

jammed ADJ 1 挤满 [+人] 的 jǐmǎn [+rén] de 2 塞满 [+东西] 的 sāimǎn [+dōngxi] de 3 卡住的 [+锁] qiǎzhù de [+suǒ]

jam-packed ADJ 1 挤满 [+人] 的 jǐmǎn [+rén] de

[+rén] de 2 塞满 [+东西] 的 sāimǎn [+dōngxi] de

jangle I v（使金属）发出丁零当啷声 (shǐ jīnshǔ) fāchū dīnglíng dāngláng shēng II N 刺耳的金属当啷声 cì'ěr de jīnshǔ dānglāngshēng

janitor N（照管房屋的）工人 (zhàoguǎn fángwū de) gōngrén, 工友 gōngyǒu
school janitor 校工 xiàogōng

January N 一月 yīyuè

Japanese I ADJ 日本的 Rìběn de II N 1 日语 Rìyǔ 2 日本人 Rìběnrén

jar N 广口瓶 guǎngkǒupíng, 罐子 guànzi II v 1 使…烦乱 shǐ…fánluàn 2 碰伤 pèngshāng

jargon N 行话 hánghuà, 专门术语 zhuānmén shùyǔ

jaundice N 黄疸病 huángdǎnbìng

jaundiced ADJ 1 患黄疸病的 huàn huángdǎnbìng de 2 有偏见的 yǒu piānjiàn de

jaunt N 短途旅游 duǎntú lǚyóu

javelin N 标枪 biāoqiāng
javelin 掷标枪（运动）zhì biāoqiāng (yùndòng), 标枪投掷（运动）biāoqiāng tóuzhì (yùndòng)

jaw N 1 颌 gé, 上下颌 shàng xià gé 2 下巴 xiàba

jaws N 1（猛兽的）嘴 (měngshòu de) zuǐ 2 钳口 qiánkǒu
jaws of death 生死关头 shēngsǐ guāntóu

jaywalking N 乱穿马路 luàn chuān mǎlù

jazz N 爵士（音）乐 juéshì (yīn) yuè

jazzy ADJ 1 鲜艳的 xiānyàn de 2 爵士风格的 juéshì fēnggé de

jealous ADJ 妒嫉的 dùjì de

jealousy N 妒嫉（的行为）dùjì (de xíngwéi)

jeans N 牛仔裤 niúzǎikù [M. WD 条 tiáo]

jeep N 吉普车 jípǔchē [M. WD 辆 liàng]

jeer I v 嘲笑 cháoxiào, 哄笑 hōngxiào II N 嘲笑 cháoxiào

jeez INTERJ 哎呀 āiyā

jelly N 果酱 guǒjiàng, 果冻 guǒdòng

jellyfish N 海蜇 hǎizhé, 水母 shuǐmǔ

jeopardize v 使…陷入危险地 shǐ…xiànrù wēixiǎn jìngdì

jeopardy N 危险（的境地）wēixiǎn (de jìngdì)

in jeopardy 处于险境 chǔyú xiǎnjìng

jerk[1] I v 猛地一动 měng de yídòng II N 猛拉 měng lā

jerk[2] N 蠢人 chǔnrén, 鲁莽的人 lǔmǎng de rén

jerky[1] ADJ 忽动忽停的 hūdòng hūtíng de, 晃动的 huàngdòng de

jerky[2] ADJ 熏肉条 xūnròutiáo, 肉干 ròugān

jersey N 1 运动衫 yùndòngshān 2 针织弹力衫 zhēnzhī tánlì shān [M. WD 件 jiàn]

jest I N 笑话 xiàohua, 俏皮话 qiàopíhuà
in jest 开玩笑地 kāiwánxiào de
II v 说笑话 shuō xiàohua, 开玩笑 kāi wánxiào

jester N（宫廷）小丑 (gōngtíng) xiǎochǒu, 弄臣 nòngchén

Jesus (Jesus Christ) N 耶稣（基督）Yēsū (Jīdū)

jet I N 1 喷气式飞机 pēnqìshì fēijī [M. WD 架 jià]
jet engine 喷气发动机 pēnqì fādòngjī
jet lag 时差反应 shíchā fǎnyìng
jet stream 高空急流 gāokōng jíliú
2 喷射流 pēnshèliú 3 黑玉 hēi yù II v 1 乘喷气式飞机 chéng pēnqìshì fēijī 2 喷射 pēnshè

jetty N 1 小码头 xiǎo mǎtou 2 防波堤 fángbōdī

Jew N 犹太人 Yóutàirén

jewel N 珠宝 zhūbǎo, 宝石 bǎoshí
jewel box 首饰盒 shǒushíhé

jeweler N 珠宝商 zhūbǎoshāng

jeweler's 珠宝商店 zhūbǎo shāngdiàn, 首饰店 shǒushidiàn

jewelry N 珠宝 zhūbǎo, 首饰 shǒushi

Jewish ADJ 犹太人的 Yóutàirén de, 犹太的 Yóutài de

jibe[1] N, v 挖苦 wāku, 嘲弄 cháonòng

jibe[2] v 相一致 xiāng yízhì, 符合 fúhé

jig N 吉格舞（曲）jí gé wǔ (qū)

jiggle v（使…）快速移动 (shǐ…) kuàisù yídòng

jigsaw puzzle N 拼图（玩具）pīn tú (wánjù)

jilt v 突然抛弃情人 tūrán pāoqì qíngrén, 突然断交 tūrán duànjiāo

jingle I v（使…）发出叮当的声响 (shǐ…)

fāchū dīngdāng de shēngxiǎng **II** N **1** 叮
当声 dīngdāng shēng **2** 短歌 duǎn gē

jinx N 不详的人 bùxiángde rén, 不详的
事 bùxiángde shì **2** 倒霉的时期 dǎoméi
de shíqī

jitters N 紧张不安 jǐnzhāng bù'ān, 焦
虑 jiāolǜ

jittery ADJ 紧张不安的 jǐnzhāng bù'ān de,
焦虑的 jiāolǜ de

jive I N 摇摆舞 yáobǎiwǔ **II** V 跳摇摆舞
tiào yáobǎiwǔ

job N **1** 职业 zhíyè, 工作 gōngzuò
job description 工作职责范围 gōngzuò
zhízé fànwéi
job security 工作保障 gōngzuò
bǎozhàng
2 职责 zhízé, 任务 rènwù
to do a good job 做得好 zuò de hǎo
an insider job 内部作案 nèibù zuò'àn,
监守自盗 jiānshǒu zì dào

jobless ADJ 没有工作的 méiyǒu gōngzuò
de, 失业的 shīyè de

jockey I N 赛马骑师 sàimǎ qíshī **II** V **1** [赛
马骑师+] 骑马 [sàimǎ qíshī+] qímǎ **2** 激
烈争夺 [+职位] jīliè zhēngduó [+zhíwèi]

jocular ADJ 爱说笑的 ài shuōxiào de

jog I V **1** 慢长跑 màn chángpǎo, 跑步
pǎobù **2** 轻碰 qīngpèng, 轻推 qīng tuī
to jog sb's memory 唤起某人的记忆
huànqǐ mǒurén de jìyì
II N **1** 慢长跑 màn chángpǎo, 慢跑
mànpǎo **2** 轻碰 qīngpèng, 轻推 qīng tuī

jogging N 健身慢跑 jiànshēn mànpǎo

john N **1** 厕所 cèsuǒ **2** 嫖客 piáokè

join V **1** 参加 cānjiā **2** 跟⋯一起 gēn...yìqǐ
3 连接 liánjiē, 结合 jiéhé

joint I ADJ 联合的 liánhé de, 联名的
liánmíng de
joint bank account 联名银行账户
liánmíng yínháng zhànghù
II N **1** 关节 guānjié **2** 结合部 jiéhébù,
连接处 liánjiēchù **3** (含有大麻的) 香
烟 (hányǒu dàmá de) xiāngyān **4** 酒吧
jiǔbā, 饭店 fàndiàn

jointly ADV 联合地 liánhé de

joint venture N 合资企业 hézī qǐyè

joke I N 笑话 xiàohua, 玩笑 wánxiào

to play a practical joke 搞恶作剧 gǎo
èzuòjù
II V 说笑话 shuō xiàohua

joker N **1** 小丑 xiǎochǒu **2** (纸牌) 百搭牌
(zhǐpái) bǎidā pái [M. WD 张 zhāng]

jokingly ADV 开玩笑地 kāi wánxiào de, 不
是一本正经地 bú shì yìběnzhèngjīng de

jolly ADJ 高兴的 gāoxìng de, 快活的
kuàihuo de

jolt I N (突然的) 震动 (tūrán de)
zhèndòng **II** V 使⋯震动 shǐ...zhèndòng

jostle V 推挤 tuǐjǐ, 拥挤 yōngjǐ

jot V (草草) 记下 (cǎocǎo) jìxià

journal N **1** 报刊 bàokān, 期刊 qīkān **2** 日
志 rìzhì, 日记 rìjì

journalism N 新闻事业 xīnwén shìyè, 新
闻工作 xīnwén gōngzuò

journalist N (新闻) 记者 (xīnwén) jìzhě

journey I N (长途) 旅行 (chángtú)
lǚxíng **II** V 旅行 lǚxíng

jovial ADJ 快活友善的 kuàihuo yǒushàn
de, 快快乐乐的 kuàikuài lèlè de

jowls N 下颌 xiàgé

joy N **1** 极大的快乐 jídà de kuàilè, 欢愉
huānyú **2** 欢愉的事 huānyú de shì

joyful ADJ 快乐的 kuàilè de, 令人欢愉的
lìng rén huānyú de

joyous ADJ 欢乐的 huānlè de

joystick N (电脑游戏 / 飞机) 操纵杆
(diànnǎo yóuxì/fēijī) cāozònggǎn

jubilant ADJ 兴高采烈的 xìnggāo cǎiliè
de, 狂欢的 kuánghuān de

jubilee N (25 / 50) 周年纪念日
(èrshíwǔ/wǔshí) zhōunián jìniàn rì

Judaism N 犹太教 Yóutàijiào, 犹太文化
Yóutài wénhuà

Judas N 犹大 Yóudà, 叛徒 pàntú

judge I N **1** 法官 fǎguān [M. WD 位 wèi]
2 裁判 cáipàn [M. WD 位 wèi] **3** (对某
事有/没有) 判断能力的人 (duì mǒushì
yǒu/méiyǒu) pànduàn nénglì de rén
a good judge of character 能识人的人
néng shí rén de rén
II V **1** 判断 pànduàn **2** 审判 [+案件]
shěnpàn [+ànjiàn], 审理 shěnlǐ

judgment N **1** 判断 (力) pànduàn (lì)
poor judgment 判断错误 pànduàn cuòwù

2 判决 pànjué

judicial ADJ 法庭的 fǎtíng de
　judicial branch 司法部门的 sīfǎ bùmén de

judicious ADJ 审慎的 shěnshèn de, 明智的 míngzhì de

judo N 柔道 róudào

jug N (水) 壶 (shuǐ) hú

juggle I v **1** 杂耍 záshuǎ **2** 应付 [+很多工作] yìngfu [+hěn duō gōngzuò] **3** 玩弄 [+数字] wánnòng [+shùzì]

juggler N 杂耍演员 záshuǎ yǎnyuán

jugular N 颈静脉 jǐngjìngmài
　to go for the jugular 激烈攻击 jīliè gōngjī

juice I N **1** 果汁 guǒzhī, 菜汁 càizhī **2** 肉汁 ròuzhī II v 榨 (果汁) zhà (guǒzhī)

July N 七月 qīyuè

jumble I N 杂乱的一堆 záluàn de yìduī II v 使…杂乱 shǐ…záluàn

jumbo ADJ 特大 (号) 的 tèdà (hào) de
　jumbo jet 巨型喷气式客机 jùxíng pēnqìshì kèjī

jump I v **1** 跳 tiào, 跳跃 tiàoyuè **2** 猛增 měngzēng, 暴涨 bàozhǎng
　jump rope 跳绳 tiàoshéng

jumper N **1** 无袖连衣裙 wú xiù liányīqún **2** (篮球) 跳投 (lánqiú) tiàotóu
　jumper cable 启动连线 qǐdòng liánxiàn

jump-start v **1** (用启动连线) 发动 [+汽车] (yòng qǐdòng liánxiàn) fādòng [+qìchē] **2** 帮助启动 [+项目] bāngzhù qǐdòng [+xiàngmù], 推动 tuīdòng

jumpsuit N 女式连衫裤 nǚshì liánshānkù

jumpy ADJ 心惊肉跳的 xīn jīng ròu tiào de

junction N 交叉 (口) jiāochā (kǒu)

juncture N (特定) 时刻 (tèdìng) shíkè, 当口 dāngkǒu

June N 六月 liùyuè

jungle N 丛林 cónglín

junior I ADJ 地位较低的 dìwèi jiào dī de
　junior college 两年制专科学院 liǎngniánzhì zhuānkē xuéyuàn
　junior high school 初级中学 chūjí zhōngxué, 初中 chūzhōng
　II N **1** (中学／大学) 三年级学生 (zhōngxué/dàxué) sānniánjí xuésheng

be two/three years one's junior 比某人小两／三岁 bǐ mǒurén xiǎo liǎng/sān suì
　2 年纪较小的人 niánjì jiàoxiǎo de rén

junk I N **1** 垃圾货 lājīhuò, 无用的旧东西 wúyòng de jiù dōngxī
　junk food 垃圾食品 lājī shípǐn
　junk mail 垃圾邮件 lājī yóujiàn
　2 中国式帆船 Zhōngguóshì fānchuán II v 废弃 fèiqì

junta N 军政府 jūnzhèngfǔ

jurisdiction N 管辖 (权) guǎnxiá (quán), 司法 (权) sīfǎ (quán)

juror N 陪审团成员 péishěntuán chéngyuán

jury N 陪审团 péishěntuán
　The jury is still out. 还没有定论。Hái méiyǒu dìnglùn.
　member of the jury 陪审员 péishěnyuán
　2 (比赛) 评判委员会 (bǐsài) píngpàn wěiyuánhuì

just¹ ADV **1** 正是 zhèng shì
　just then 正在那时 zhèngzài nàshí
　2 正要 zhèng yào, 刚要 gāng yào **3** 仅仅 jǐnjǐn, 只是 zhǐ shì **4** 刚才 gāngcái, 刚刚 gānggāng

just² ADJ 公正的 gōngzhèng de

justice N **1** 公正 gōngzhèng, 正义 zhèngyì **2** 司法 sīfǎ **3** 法官 fǎguān [M. WD 位 wèi]
　Justice of the Peace 太平绅士 tàipíng shēnshì

justification N (正当) 理由 (zhèngdàng) lǐyóu

justify v 证明…有理由 zhèngmíng…yǒu lǐyóu, 证明…合理 zhèngmíng…hélǐ

jut v 突出 tūchū, 伸出 shēnchū

juvenile I ADJ **1** 青少年的 qīngshàonián de
　juvenile delinquent 青少年罪犯 qīngshàonián zuìfàn
　2 幼稚的 yòuzhì de, 不成熟的 bù chéngshú de II N 青少年 qīngshàonián

juxtaposition N (把不同的东西) 并列 (bǎ bùtóng de dōngxi) bìngliè

K

kabob, kebab N 烤肉串 kǎoròuchuàn

kaleidoscope N **1** 万花筒 wànhuātǒng **2** 千变万化 qiānbiàn wànhuà, 多姿多彩 duōzī duōcǎi

kangaroo N 袋鼠 dàishǔ

karaoke N 卡拉OK kǎlā OK

karat [British **carat**] N 开 kāi, K 22 karat 22开（黄金）22 kāi (huángjīn), 22 K（黄金）22 K (huángjīn)

karate N 空手道 kōngshǒudào

kayak N 小艇 xiǎotǐng [M. WD 艘 sōu]

keel I N (to stay on an even keel) 保持平稳 bǎochí píngwěn II V (to keel over) 翻倒 fāndǎo, 倒下 dǎoxià

keen ADJ **1** 热切的 rèqiè de, 非常希望的 fēicháng xīwàng de **2** 敏捷的 [+头脑] mǐnjié de [+tóunǎo] **3** 敏锐的 [+眼力] mǐnruì de [+yǎnlì]

keenly ADV 敏锐地 mǐnruì de, 强烈地 qiángliè de

keep I V (PT & PP **kept**) **1** 保有 bǎoyǒu, 留下 liúxia
to keep a diary 记日记 jì rìjì
to keep one's promise 实现诺言 shíxiàn nuòyán
2 留住 liúzhù, 保留 bǎoliú **3** 一直 yìzhí, 老是 lǎoshi
to keep ... from doing ... 不让…做… búràng...zuò...
to keep up with 跟上 gēnshang
Keep Out! 不准入内! Bùzhǔn rùnèi!
to keep fit 保持健康 bǎochí jiànkāng
II N 生活费 shēnghuófèi
to earn one's keep 养活自己 yǎnghuo zìjǐ, 谋生 móushēng

keeper N **1** （动物）饲养员 (dòngwù) sìyǎngyuán **2** （财产）管理者 (cáichǎn) guǎnlǐzhě

keg N 大（啤酒）圆桶 dà (píjiǔ) yuántǒng

kennel N **1** 狗窝 gǒuwō **2** 养狗场 yǎnggǒucháng

kept See **keep**

kernel N **1** 果仁 guǒ rén, 果核 guǒhé **2** 要点 yàodiǎn

kernel of truth 主要事实 zhǔyào shìshí, 要点 yàodiǎn

kerosene N 煤油 méiyóu

ketchup N 番茄酱 fānqiéjiàng

kettle N 水壶 shuǐhú

key I N **1** 钥匙 yàoshi
spare key 备用钥匙 bèiyòng yàoshi
skeleton key 万能钥匙 wànnéng yàoshi
2 键 jiàn **3** 关键 guānjiàn **4**（练习题／考题的）答案 (liànxítí/kǎotí de) dá'an
II ADJ 关键的 guānjiàn de, 至关重要的 zhìguān zhòngyào de III V **1** (to key in) 把 [+信息] 输入电脑 bǎ [+xìnxī] shūrù diànnǎo **2** (to key a car) 用钥匙划伤车 yòng yàoshi huáshāng chē

keyboard N 键盘 jiànpán
keyboard skill 打字技术 dǎzì jìshù

keyhole N 锁眼 suǒyǎn

keynote ADJ 主旨的 zhǔzhǐ de, 主题的 zhǔtí de
keynote speech 主题发言 zhǔtí fāyán, 主要发言 zhǔyào fāyán

kg (= kilogram) ABBREV See **kilogram**

khaki N **1** 卡其黄 kǎqí huáng **2** 卡其布 kǎqíbù

khakis N 卡其布裤子 kǎqíbù kùzi

kick V, N 踢 tī
to kick in [药物+] 开始生效 [yàowù+] kāishǐ shēngxiào
to kick off 开球 kāiqiú, [球赛+] 开始 [qiúsài+] kāishǐ
kick boxing 跆拳道 táiquándào
to get a kick out of sth 从某事得到乐趣 cóng mǒushì dédào lèqù

kickback N 回扣 huíkòu

kickoff N 开球 kāiqiú, 比赛开始 bǐsài kāishǐ

kick-start I N **1** 脚踏启动器 jiǎotà qǐdòngqì **2** 启动 qǐdòng, 促进 cùjìn II V **1** 发动 [+摩托车] fādòng [+mótuōchē] **2** 启动 [+经济] qǐdòng [+jīngjì], 刺激 cìjī

kid I N **1** 小孩子 xiǎo háizi **2** 小山羊 xiǎo shānyáng II V 哄骗 hōngpiàn, 开玩笑 kāi wánxiào, 说着玩 shuōzhe wán
just kidding 只是开个玩笑 zhǐ shì kāi gè wánxiào
III ADJ 幼小的 yòuxiǎo de

one's kid brother/sister 小弟弟 / 小妹妹 xiǎodìdi/xiǎomèimei

kidnap I v 绑架 bǎngjià II N 绑架 bǎngjià

kidnapper N 绑匪 bǎngfěi, 绑架的罪犯 bǎngjià de zuìfàn

kidney N 肾（脏）shèn (zàng)
kidney bean 四季豆 sìjìdòu, 芸豆 yúndòu

kill v 1 杀死 shāsǐ
to kill time 消磨时间 xiāomó shíjiān
to kill two birds with one stone 一石二鸟 yì shí èr niǎo, 一箭双雕 yíjiàn shuāngdiāo, 一举两得 yì jǔ liǎng dé
2 终止 [+疼痛] zhōngzhǐ [+téngtòng] 3 对 [+人] 极为生气 duì [+rén] jíwéi shēngqì II N 1 捕杀 bǔshā 2 被捕杀的动物 bèibǔ shā de dòngwù

killer N 杀手 shāshǒu
killer whale 杀人鲸 shārénjīng, 虎鲸 hǔjīng, 逆戟鲸 nìjǐ jīng
II ADJ 好得要命的 hǎo de yàomìng de, 极好的 jíhǎo de

killing N 1 谋杀 móushā
to make a killing 一下子赚大钱 yíxiàzi zhuàn dàqián
II ADJ 要命的
a killing workload 要人命的工作量 yào rénmìng de gōngzuòliàng, 累死人的工作量 lèisǐ rén de gōngzuòliàng

kiln N 窑 yáo

kilobyte N 千字节 qiān zìjié

kilogram N 公斤 gōngjīn, 千克 qiānkè

kilometer N 公里 gōnglǐ, 千米 qiānmǐ

kilowatt N 千瓦 qiānwǎ

kin N 家人 jiārén, 亲属 qīnshǔ
next of kin（最亲近的）亲属 (zuì qīnjìn de) qīnshǔ

kind I N 种 zhǒng, 种类 zhǒnglèi II ADJ 好心的 hǎoxīn de, 和蔼的 hé'ǎi de
kind of 有点儿 yǒudiǎnr

kindergarten N 幼儿园 yòu'éryuán

kind-hearted ADJ 好心的 hǎoxīn de, 仁慈的 réncí de

kindle v 1 点燃 diǎnrán 2 激起 jīqǐ

kindly ADV 1 好心地 hǎoxīn de, 仁慈地 réncí de
to put it kindly 往好里说 wǎng hǎo lǐ shuō

2 请 qǐng, 能不能 néngbunéng

kindness N 好意 hǎoyì, 仁慈 réncí

kindred I N 亲属（关系）qīnshǔ (guānxi) II ADJ 同样的 tóngyàng de
kindred spirit 心投意合的人 xīn tóu yìhé de rén

kinfolk N 家人 jiārén, 亲属 qīnshǔ

king N 1 国王 guówáng 2（纸牌）老 K 牌 (zhǐpái) lǎo K pái

kingdom N 1 王国 wángguó
the United Kingdom of Great Britain and Northern Ireland 大不列颠及北爱尔兰联合王国 Dàbùlièdiān jí Běi Ài'ěrlán Liánhé Wángguó
the Kingdom of God 天国 Tiānguó
2 界 jiè
the animal kingdom 动物界 dòngwùjiè

kingfisher N 翠鸟 cuìniǎo

kinky ADJ 变态的 biàntài de

kiosk N 小商亭 xiǎo shāngtíng

kiss v, N 吻 wěn, 亲吻 qīnwěn
to kiss sb's ass 拍马屁 pāi mǎpì
to kiss sth goodbye 失去获得某事的机会 shīqùhuòdé mǒushì de jīhuì
the kiss of death 死亡之吻 sǐwáng zhī wěn, 带来灾难的事 dàilái zāinàn de shì

kit N 成套工具 chéngtào gōngjù
repair kit 修理用的成套工具 xiūlǐ yòng de chéngtào gōngjù

kitchen N 厨房 chúfáng

kite N 风筝 fēngzheng

kitten N 小猫 xiǎomāo

kiwi N 1 几维鸟 jǐ wéi niǎo, 鹬鸵鸟 yùtuó niǎo 2 新西兰人 Xīnxīlánrén
kiwi fruit 猕猴桃 míhóutáo

kleptomaniac N 有偷窃癖的人 yǒu tōuqièpǐ de rén, 偷窃狂 tōuqiè kuáng

km ABBREV See kilometer

knack N 天生的本领 tiānshēng de běnlíng

knapsack N 大背包 dà bēibāo

knead v 揉 [+面团] róu [+miàntuán], 揉捏 [+背部] róu niē [+bèibù]

knee N 膝 xī, 膝盖 xīgài
to bring sb to his/her knees 使某人屈服 shǐ mǒurén qūfú
on one's knees 跪着 guìzhe

knee-cap N 膝盖骨 xīgàigǔ

kneel v (PT & PP **knelt, kneeled**) 跪 guì, 跪下 guìxia

knelt See **kneel**

knew See **know**

knickers N 灯笼裤 dēnglongkù [M. WD 条 tiáo]

knick-knack N 小摆设 xiǎobǎishè

knife I N (PL **knives**) 刀 dāo [M. WD 把 bǎ]
carving knife 切肉刀 qièròudāo
paper knife 裁纸刀 cáizhǐdāo
II v 用刀扎 yòng dāo zhā

knight I N 1（古代欧洲）骑士 (gǔdài Ōuzhōu) qíshì 2（英国）爵士 (Yīngguó) juéshì II v 封…为骑士 fēng…wéi juéshì

knighthood N 爵士头衔 juéshì tóuxián

knit I v (PT & PP **knit, knitted**) 1 编结 biānjié 2 紧密地结合 jǐnmì de jiéhé II N 编结（品／装）biānjié (pǐn/ fúzhuāng)

knob N 球形把手 qiúxíng bǎshǒu

knobby ADJ 似球形把手的 sì qiúxíng bǎshǒu de

knock I v 1 敲（打）qiāo (dǎ)
to knock down 碰倒 pèngdǎo, 打到 dǎdào
to knock off 下班 xiàbān
2 批评 pīpíng II N 1 敲击声 qiāojī shēng
2 倒霉的事 dǎoméi de shì
to have a few hard knocks in one's life 生活中遇到一些倒霉事 shēnghuó zhōng yùdào yìxiē dǎoméi shì

knocker N 门环 ménhuán

knockout N 1 击倒 jī dǎo 2 极具魅力的人 jí jù mèilì de rén
knockout pills 麻醉药 mázuìyi, 蒙汗药 ménghànyào
knockout punch 把对手打倒在地的一拳 bǎ duìshǒu dǎdào zài dì de yì quán

knoll N 小土丘 xiǎo tǔqiū

knot I N 1（绳）结 (shéng) jié 2 紧张（感）jǐnzhāng (gǎn)
to feel the knots in one's stomach 感到非常紧张 gǎndào fēicháng jǐnzhāng, 心揪得紧紧地 xīn jiū dé jǐnjǐn de II v 把…打成结 bǎ…dǎchéng jié, 打结 dǎ jié

know v (PT **knew**; PP **known**) 1 知道

zhīdào 2 认识 rènshi, 结识 jiéshí 3 精通 jīngtōng, 熟悉 shúxī II N 知晓 zhīxiǎo
in the know 知晓内情 zhīxiǎo nèiqíng

know-how N 知识 zhīshi, 技术 jìshù

knowingly ADV 1 心照不宣地 xīnzhào bù xuān de 2 故意地 gùyìde, 明知故犯地 míngzhī gùfàn de

knowledge N 1 知识 zhīshi 2 知道 zhīdào, 理解 lǐjiě
to the best of my knowledge 就我所知 jiù wǒ suǒ zhī
3 学问 xuéwèn

knowledgeable ADJ 知识丰富的 zhīshí fēngfù de

known¹ v See **know**

known² ADJ 大家知道的 dàjiā zhīdào de, 知名的 zhīmíng de

knuckle I N 指节 zhǐjié II v (to knuckle under) 屈服 qūfú, 认输 rènshū

koala (bear) n（澳洲）树袋熊 (Àozhōu) shùdàixióng

Koran N 古兰经 Gǔlánjīng, 可兰经 Kělánjīng

Korean I ADJ 韩国的 Hánguó de, 朝鲜的 Cháoxiān de II N 1 韩语 Hányǔ, 朝鲜语 Cháoxiānyǔ 2 韩国人 Hánguórén, 朝鲜人 Cháoxiānrén

kosher ADJ 符合犹太教规定的 fúhé Yóutàijiào guīdìng de

kowtow v 1 磕头 kētóu, 叩头 kòutóu
2 卑躬屈膝 bēigōng qūxī, 唯命是从 wéi mìng shì cóng

Kremlin N（俄国）克里姆林宫 (Éguó) Kèlǐmǔlíngōng, 俄国政府 Éguó zhèngfǔ

kudos N 威望 wēiwàng, 荣誉 róngyù

kung fu（中国）功夫 (Zhōngguó) gōngfu

L

label I N 标签 biāoqiān, 标记 biāojì II v 加标记 jiā biāojì, 加标签 jiā biāoqiān

labor I N 1 劳动 láodòng 2 劳工 láogōng, 工人 gōngrén
labor camp 劳改营 láogǎiyíng
Labor Day 劳动节 Láodòngjié

manual/physical labor 体力劳动 tǐlì láodòng

skilled labor 技术工人 jìshù gōngrén

3 分娩（期）fēnmiǎn (qī) **II v** 劳动 láodòng, 劳作 láozuò

laboratory N 实验室 shíyànshì

laborer N 体力劳动者 tǐlì láodòngzhě

laborious ADJ 缓慢而吃力的 huǎnmàn ér chīlì de

labyrinth N 迷宫 mígōng, 曲径 qūjìng

lace I N 1 网眼织物 wǎngyǎn zhīwù **2** 鞋带 xiédài **II v** 用带子束紧 yòng dàizi shùjǐn

to lace up 系上 jìshang

laceration N 划破 huápò, 撕裂 sīliè

lack I v 缺乏 quēfá **II N** 缺乏 quēfá, 短缺 duǎnquē

lacking ADJ 缺乏 quēfá

lackluster ADJ 平平淡淡的 píngpíng dàndàn de, 毫不吸引人的 háo bù xīyǐnrén de

laconic ADJ 精炼的 jīngliàn de, 简洁的 jiǎnjié de

lacquerware N 漆器 qīqì

lacy ADJ 网眼织物的 wǎngyǎn zhīwù de

lad N 小伙子 xiǎohuǒzi, 男孩 nánhái

ladder N 1 梯子 tīzi **2** 阶梯 jiētī

the corporate ladder 公司的阶梯 gōngsī de jiētī

laden ADJ 满载的 mǎnzài de, 装满的 zhuāngmǎn de

ladies' room N 女厕所 nǚcèsuǒ

ladle N 长柄勺 chángbǐngsháo [**M. WD** 把 bǎ], 勺资 sháozi

lady (PL ladies) N 1 女士 nǚshì, 小姐 xiǎojiě

First Lady 总统夫人 zǒngtǒng fūrén

2 女子 nǚzǐ, 女人 nǚrén

lag I v 落后 luòhòu

to lag behind 落后于 luòhòu yu, 比…落后 bǐ...luòhòu

II N 间歇 jiànxiē

jet lag 飞行时差综合症 fēixíng shíchā zōnghézhēng, 时差反应 shíchāfǎnyìng

lager N 淡啤酒 dàn píjiǔ

lagoon N 泻湖 xièhú, 环礁湖 huánjiāo hú

laid See **lay**[1]

laidback ADJ 悠闲自在的 yōuxián zìzài de

lain See **lie**[1]

lair N 1 藏身地 cángshēndì **2** 兽穴 shòuxué

laissez-faire N 自由放任的经济政策 zìyóu fàngrèn de jīngjì zhèngcè, 不干预主义 bù gānyù zhǔyì

lake N 湖 hú, 湖泊 húpō

lakeside N 湖畔 húpàn, 湖滨 húbīn

lama N 喇嘛 Lǎma,（藏传佛教的）僧侣 (cángchuán Fójiào de) sēnglǚ

lamb N 1 羊肉 yángròu **2** 小羊 xiǎo yáng, 羊羔 yánggāo

roast lamb 烤羊肉 kǎo yángròu

lambing season 羊羔出生的季节 yánggāo chūshēng de jìjié

lame ADJ 1 跛的 bǒ de, 瘸的 qué de

a lame duck 跛足鸭 bǒzúyā, 任期将满的总统 rènqī jiāng mǎn de zǒngtǒng

2 处于困境的 [+人] chǔyú kùnjìng de [+rén]

a lame duck president 任期将满（无所作为）的总统 rènqī jiāng mǎn (wú suǒ zuòwéi) de zǒngtǒng

lament I v 1 悲痛 bēitòng, 哀悼 āidào **2** 抱怨 baoyuan **II N** 挽歌 wǎngē [**M. WD** 首 shǒu/曲 qū], 哀乐 āiyuè

laminate v 层压板 céngyābǎn

laminated ADJ 塑料薄膜覆盖的 sùliào bómó fùgài de, 烫塑的 tàng sù de

lamp N 灯 dēng

desk/table lamp 台灯 táidēng

street lamp 街灯 jiēdēng

lampoon v 讽刺 fěngcì, 挖苦 wāku

lampshade N 灯罩 dēngzhào

lance N 长矛 cháng máo

land I N 1 土地 tǔdì

land of milk and honey 乳蜜之乡 rǔmì zhī xiāng, 鱼米之乡 yúmǐ zhī xiāng

2 国土 guotu, 国家 guojia **II v 1** [飞机+] 着陆 [fēijī+] zhuólù **2** [军队+] 登陆 [jūnduì+] dēnglù

landfill N 垃圾场 lājī chǎng

landing N 1（飞机）着陆 (fēijī) zhuólù,（船）登陆 (chuán) dēnglù **2** 楼梯平台 lóutī píngtái

landing gear（着陆）起落架 (zhuólù) qǐluòjià

landing pad 直升飞机起落场 zhíshēng fēijī qǐluò chǎng

landing strip 简易跑道 jiǎnyì pǎodào

landlady N 女房东 nǚ fángdōng

landlocked ADJ 内陆的 nèilù de, 无海岸线的 wú hǎi'ànxiàn de

landlord ADJ 房东 fángdōng

landmark N 地标 dìbiāo

landowner N 土地拥有者 tǔdì yōngyǒuzhě, 地主 dìzhǔ

landscape I N 风景 fēngjǐng, 色景 jǐngsè II V 对…进行景观美化 duì…jìnxíng jǐngguān měihuà

landslide N 1 山崩 shānbēng, 塌方 tāfāng 2 (选举) 压倒性胜利 (xuǎnjǔ) yādǎoxìng shènglì

lane N 1 巷 xiàng, 小街 xiǎo jiē [M. WD 条 tiáo] 2 车道 chēdào

the fast lane 快车道 kuàichēdào

language N 1 语言 yǔyán

foreign language 外国语 wàiguóyǔ, 外语 wàiyǔ

strong language 强硬的语言 qiángyìng de yǔyán

language student/teacher 语言学生／老师 yǔyán xuésheng/lǎoshī

2 计算机语言 jìsuànjī yǔyán

a programming language 程序语言 chéngxù yǔyán

3 粗话 cūhuà, 骂人话 màrénhuà

languid ADJ 懒洋洋的 lǎnyāngyāng de, 慢吞吞的 màntūntūn de

lanky ADJ 又高又瘦的 yòu gāo yòu shòu de

lantern N 灯笼 dēnglong

lap¹ N 1 腿 tuǐ, 胸 xī 2 (跑道的) 一圈 (pǎodào de) yìquān

in the lap of luxury 养尊处优 yǎngzūn chǔyōu

lap² V 轻轻拍打 qīngqīng pāida

to lap up (动物) 舔饮 (dòngwù) tiǎn yǐn

lapel N 翻领 fānlǐng

lapse I N 1 疏忽 shūhu, 失误 shīwù

memory lapse 暂时失忆 zànshí shī yì 2 (时间) 流逝 (shíjiān) liúshì 3 (一时的) 下降 (yìshí de) xiàjiàng II V 1 保

险+] 终止 [bǎoxiǎn+] zhōngzhǐ, 失效 shīxiào 2 渐渐结束 jiànjiàn jiéshù

laptop N 笔记本电脑 bǐjìběn diànnǎo [M. WD 台 tái], 膝上电脑 xīshang diànnǎo

larceny N 偷窃罪 tōuqièzuì, 盗窃罪 dàoqièzuì

large ADJ 1 大 dà 2 (身材) 高大的 (shēncái) gāodà de

be at large 在逃 zàitáo, 未被抓到 wèi bèi zhuā dào

largely ADV 主要地 zhǔyào de

large-scale ADJ 大规模的 dàguīmó de

lark N 1 云雀 yúnquè [M. WD 只 zhī] 2 玩乐 wánlè

for a lark 为了玩乐 wèile wánlè, 为了消遣 wèile xiāoqiǎn

larva N 幼虫 yòuchóng

laryngitis N 喉炎 hóuyán

lascivious ADJ 好色的 hàosè de, 淫荡的 yíndàng de

laser N 激光 (器) jīguāng (qì)

laser printer 激光打印机 jīguāng dǎyìnjī

lash I V 1 鞭打 [+犯人] biāndǎ [+fànrén] 2 捆绑 [+行李] kǔnbǎng [+xíngli] 3 抨击 [+政客] pēngjī [+zhèngkè]

to lash out 猛烈抨击 měngliè pēngjī II N 鞭子 biānzi [M. WD 条 tiáo]

lasso I N 套索 tàosuǒ II V 用套索套捕 (牛马) yòng tàosuǒ tào bǔ (niúmǎ)

last I ADJ 1 最后的 zuìhòu de

last name 姓 xìng

2 上一个 shàng yí ge 3 最不合适的 zuì bù héshì de, 最不可能的 zuì bù kěnéng de II ADV 最后 zuìhòu III V 1 持续 chíxù 2 (够用) [qián+] gòuyòng IV N 1 最后一个 zuìhòu yí ge 2 (at long last) 终于 zhōngyú, 总算 zǒngsuàn

last-ditch ADJ 最后的 zuìhòu de

a last-ditch effect 最后的努力 zuìhòu de nǔlì

lasting ADJ 持久的 chíjiǔ de, 耐久的 nàijiǔ de

lastly ADV 最后 zuìhòu

latch I N 门闩 ménshuān, 窗闩 chuāng shuān II V (用门闩／窗闩) 闩上 (yòng ménshuān/chuāng shuān) shuānshang

late I ADJ **1** 迟到 chídào **2** 晚 wǎn **3** 已故的 yǐ gù de
his late grandfather 他已故的祖父 tā yǐ gù de zǔfù
II ADV 比通常晚 bǐ tōngcháng wǎn
Better late than never. 迟做比不做好。Chí zuò bǐ bú zuò hǎo. 晚来比不来好。Wǎnlái bǐ bùlái hǎo.

lately ADV 最近 zuìjìn, 近来 jìnlái
latent ADJ 潜在的 qiánzài de
later I ADV 后来 hòulái, 以后 yǐhòu II ADJ 较晚的 jiào wǎn de, 以后的 yǐhòu de
lateral ADJ 侧面的 cèmiàn de, 侧的 cè de
latest ADJ 最后的 zuìhòu de, 最新的 zuì xīn de
at the latest 最迟 zuì chí, 最晚 zuì wǎn
latex N 胶乳 jiāorǔ
lather I N 肥皂泡沫 féizào pàomò II V **1** 起泡沫 qǐ pàomò **2** 用皂沫涂 yòng zào mò tú
Latin I ADJ 拉丁国家的 Lādīng guójiā de, 拉丁的 Lādīng de
Latin America 拉丁美洲 Lādīng Měizhōu
II N **1** 拉丁语 Lādīngyǔ **2** 拉丁美洲人 Lādīng Měizhōu rén
latitude N 纬度 wěidù
latrine N 户外厕所 hùwài cèsuǒ
latter I N 后者 hòuzhě II ADJ **1** 后者的 hòuzhě de **2** 后期的 hòuqī de, 末期的 mòqī de
lattice N 格子图案／结构 gézi tú'àn/jiégòu
laudable ADJ 值得赞美的 zhíde zànměi de
laugh I V 大笑 dàxiào
to laugh at 取笑 qǔxiào
II N 笑（声）xiào (shēng)
to get a laugh out of sth 从做某事得到很多乐趣 cóng zuò mǒushì dédào hěn duō lèqù
laughing stock N 笑柄 xiàobǐng
laughter N **1** 笑 xiào, 大笑 dàxiào **2** 笑声 xiàoshēng
launch I V **1** 发动 [+运动] fādòng [+yùndòng] **2** 发射 [+航天飞机] fāshè [+hángtiān fēijī] **3** 投入 [+市场] tóurù [+shìchǎng] **4** 发行 [+新书] fāxíng [+xīnshū] II N **1** 发射 fāshè, 发出 fāchū
launch pad 发射场 fāshèchǎng

2 汽艇 qìtǐng
launder V **1** 洗（黑）钱 xǐ (hēi) qián **2** 洗熨（衣服）xǐ yùn (yīfu)
laundry N **1** 洗衣房 xǐyīfáng, 洗衣店 xǐyīdiàn **2** 要洗的衣服 yào xǐ de yīfu, 洗好的衣服 xǐ hǎo de yīfu
laureate N 奖章获得者 jiǎngzhāng huòdézhě [M. WD 位 wèi]
Nobel laureate 诺贝尔奖获得者 Nuòbèi'ěr jiǎng huòdézhě
lava N 岩浆 yánjiāng
lavatory N 厕所 cèsuǒ, 洗手间 xǐshǒujiān
lavish I ADJ 铺张的 pūzhāng de, 豪华的 háohuá de II V 过分慷慨地给予 guòfèn kāngkǎi de gěiyú
to lavish praise on sb 对某人大加赞扬 duì mǒurén dà jiā zànyáng
law N **1** 法律 fǎlǜ, 法规 fǎguī
law and order 法律和秩序 fǎlǜ hé zhìxù, 法治 fǎzhì
to break the law 犯法 fànfǎ
2 法学 fǎxué, 法律业务 fǎlǜ yèwù
law firm 法律事务所 fǎlǜ shìwùsuǒ
3 规律 fǎlǜ, 法则 fǎzé
law of the jungle 丛林法则 cónglín fǎzé, 弱肉强食的法则 ruòròu qiángshí de fǎzé
4（体育）规则 (tǐyù) guīzé
law-abiding ADJ 奉守法律的 fèng shǒu fǎlǜ de, 守法的 shǒufǎ de
lawful ADJ 合法的 héfǎ de
lawless ADJ 不守法的 bù shǒufǎ de
lawn N 草坪 cǎopíng, 草地 cǎodì
lawn tennis 草地网球（运动）cǎodì wǎngqiú (yùndòng)
lawsuit N 法律案件 fǎlǜ ànjiàn, 诉讼 sùsòng
lawyer N 律师 lǜshī
criminal lawyer 刑事律师 xíngshì lǜshī
lax ADJ 松懈的 sōngxiè de, 马虎的 mǎhu de
laxative N 通便药 tōngbiàn yào, 泻药 xièyào
lay[1] (PT & PP **laid**) V **1** 放 fàng, 放置 fàngzhì **2** 铺 pū, 铺设 pūshè **3** 产卵 chǎnluǎn, 下蛋 xiàdàn
to lay off 解雇 jiěgù

lay² ADJ **1** 不担任神职的 bù dānrèn shénzhí de, 世俗的 shìsú de **2** 非专业的 fēi zhuānyè de, 外行的 wàiháng de

lay³ V See **lie¹**

layer N 层 céng II V 把…堆成层 bǎ…duī chéng céng

layman N 外行 wàiháng, 门外汉 ménwàihàn

lay-off N 解雇 jiěgù

layout N **1** 版面设计 bǎnmiànshèjì, 版式 bǎnshì **2** [花园的+] 布局 [huāyuán de+] bùjú

layover N 中途停留 zhōngtútíngliú

layperson N 普通信徒 pǔtōng xìntú, 门外汉 ménwàihàn

lazy ADJ **1** 懒惰 lǎnduò **2** 使人懒洋洋的 shǐrén lǎnyāngyāng de **3** 慢吞吞的 màntūntūn de

lead¹ I V (PT & PP **led**) **1** 带领 dàilǐng
to lead to 导致 dǎozhì, 造成 zàochéng **2** 领导 lǐngdǎo **3** 领先 lǐngxiān **4** 生活 shēnghuó, 过 guò **5** 使 shǐ, 导致 dǎozhì **6** 通向 tōngxiàng, 通达 tōngdá II N 领先 lǐngxiān, 领先地位 lǐngxiān dìwèi
to follow sb's lead 仿效某人 fǎngxiào mǒurén **2** 线索 xiànsuǒ **3** (电影) 主角 (diànyǐng) zhǔjué

lead² (Pb) N 铅 qiān, 铅笔芯 qiānbǐxīn
a lead foot 喜欢开快车的人 xǐhuan kāi kuàichē de rén

leader N 领袖 lǐngxiù [M. WD 位 wèi], 领导人 lǐngdǎorén [M. WD 位 wèi]

leadership N 领导（地位）lǐngdǎo (dìwèi)

leading ADJ 主要的 zhǔyào de
a leading question 诱导性问题 yòudǎoxìng wèntí
leading role 主角 zhǔjué

leaf I N (PL **leaves**) **1** 叶子 yèzi **2** （一）页（纸）yè (shǐ) II V (to leaf through) 翻阅 [+书] fānyuè [+shū]

leaflet N 传单 chuándān

leafy ADJ **1** 绿树成荫的 [+住宅区] lǜ shù chéngyìn de [+zhùzháiqū] **2** 多叶的 [+蔬菜] duōyè de [+shūcài]

league N 联盟 liánméng, 联合会 liánhéhuì

leak I N 漏洞 lòudòng, 裂缝 lièfèng II V **1** 漏 lòu **2** 泄露 [+秘密] xièlòu [+mìmì]
to leak out [消息+] 泄漏出去 [xiāoxi+] xièlòu chūqu

leakage N **1** 漏出 lòuchū, 渗出 shènchū **2** 泄漏 xièlòu, 泄露 xièlòu

lean¹ V (PT & PP **leaned, leant**) 靠 kào, 前（后）倾 qián (hòu) qīng

lean² ADJ **1** 瘦 shòu, 瘦而健康 shòu ér jiànkāng **2** 瘦 [+肉] shòu [+ròu], 脂肪少的 zhīfáng hěn shǎo de

leap I V (PT & PP **leaped, leapt**) 跳 tiào, 跳跃 tiàoyuè
to leap at 抓住 [+机会] zhuāzhù [+jīhuì] II N 跳跃 tiàoyuè
by leaps and bounds 突飞猛进 tūfēi měngjìn

leap year N 闰年 rùnnián

learn V (PT & PP **learned/learnt**) **1** 学习 xuéxí, 学会 xuéhuì **2** 获悉 huòxī, 听说 tīngshuō **3** 记住 jìzhu
to learn one's lesson 记住教训 jìzhu jiàoxun, 吸取教训 xīqǔ jiàoxun

learned I V See **learn** II ADJ 有学问的 yǒu xuéwèn de, 博学的 bóxué de

learning N **1** 学问 xuéwèn, 知识 zhīshi
a man of learning 一位很有学问的人 yíwèi hěn yǒu xuéwèn de rén **2** 学习 xuéxí
learning disability 学习障碍 xuéxí zhàng'ài

lease I N 租约 zūyuē, 租契 zūqì
a one-year lease on an apartment 为期一年的公寓租约 wéiqī yìnián de gōngyù zūyuē II V **1** 出租 chūzū **2** 租用 zūyòng

leash N 绳子 shéngzi [M. WD 条 tiáo]
(dog) on a leash（狗）用绳子牵住 (gǒu) yòng shéngzi qiān zhù

least ADV, ADJ 最少（的）zuì shǎo (de), 最小（的）zuì xiǎo (de)
at least 至少 zhìshǎo

leather N 皮（革）pí (gé)

leave I V (PT & PP **left**) **1** 离开 líkāi **2** 留下 liúxià
to leave sb alone 不打搅某人 bù dǎjiǎo mǒurén

to leave sth alone 不动某物 bú dòng mǒu wù
II 假 jià, 假期 jiàqī
leave of absence 获准休假 huòzhǔn xiūjià
maternity leave 产假 chǎnjià
sick leave 病假 bìngjià

leaven N 1 酵母 jiàomǔ 2 使事物变得有趣的小事 shǐ shìwù biàn de yǒuqù de xiǎoshì **II** v 使…变得有趣 shǐ…biàn de yǒuqù

lecherous ADJ 好色的 hàosè de

lectern N 斜面讲桌 xiémiàn jiǎngzhuō

lecture I N 讲座 jiǎngzuò, 讲课 jiǎngkè **II** v 1 讲课 jiǎngkè, 做讲座 zuò jiǎngzuò 2 教训 jiàoxun

lecturer N 讲师 jiǎngshī
a senior lecturer 高级讲师 gāojí jiǎngshī

led See **lead**¹

ledger N 分类帐 fēnlèizhàng, 账本 zhàngběn

leech N 蚂蟥 mǎhuáng [M. WD 条 tiáo]

leek N 韭葱 jiǔcōng

leer I v 色迷迷地看 sèmímí de kàn **II** N 色迷迷的眼神 sèmímí de yǎnshén

leeway N 自由行事的余地 zìyóu xíngshì de yúdì

left¹ I N 左 zuǒ, 左边 zuǒbiān
left field 左外场 zuǒ wàichǎng
II ADJ, ADV 左的 zuǒ de, 左边 zuǒbiān
the left 左派 zuǒpài

left² See **leave**

left-handed ADJ 用左手的 yòng zuǒshǒu de, 左撇子的 zuǒpiězi de

leftovers N 剩菜 shèngcài

leftwing ADJ 左翼 zuǒyì

leg N 1 腿 tuǐ, 大腿 dàtuǐ 2 一段（旅程）yí duàn (lǚchéng)

legacy N 1 遗留下来的情况 yíliú xiàlái de qíngkuàng 2 遗产 yíchǎn

legal ADJ 1 法律的 fǎlǜ de 2 合法的 héfǎ de

legality N 合法（性）héfǎ (xìng)

legend N 1 传说 chuánshuō, 传奇 chuánqí 2 传奇性人物 chuánqí xìng rénwù 3（图片）说明 (túpiàn) shuōmíng, 图例 túlì

legendary ADJ 1 传奇的 chuánqí de 2 著名的 zhùmíng de, 大名鼎鼎的 dàmíng dǐngdǐng de

leggings N 绑腿 bǎngtuǐ [M. WD 条 tiáo]

leggy ADJ 腿长的 tuǐ cháng de

legible ADJ 可以认读的 kěyǐ rèn dú de

legion N 一大批人 yí dàpī rén, 很多人 hěn duō rén

legislate v 制定法律 zhìdìng fǎlǜ, 立法 lìfǎ

legislation N 立法 lìfǎ

legislature N 立法机构 lìfǎ jīgòu

legitimacy N 合法（性）héfǎ (xìng)

legitimate ADJ 1 合法的 héfǎ de 2 正当的 zhèngdàng de
a legitimate reason 正当的理由 zhèngdàng de lǐyóu
a legitimate child 合法婚姻所生的子女 héfǎ hūnyīn suǒ shēngde zǐnǔ, 婚生子 hūn shēngzǐ

leisure N 休闲 xiūxián
at one's leisure 有空时 yǒukòng shí

leisurely I ADJ 从容的 cóngróng de, 悠闲的 yōuxián de **II** ADV 从容地 cóngróng de, 悠闲地 yōuxián de

lemon N 柠檬 níngméng

lemonade N 柠檬汽水 níngméng qìshuǐ

lend (PT & PP **lent**) v 借给 jiè gěi, 借出 jiè chū

length N 1 长度 chángdù 2 时间（长度）shíjiān (chángdù)
at length ① 长时间地 chángshíjiān de ② 最终 zuìzhōng, 最后 zuìhòu

lengthy ADJ 1 冗长的 [+报告] rǒngcháng de [+bàogào], 过于详细的 guòyú xiángxì de 2 漫长的 [+等待] màncháng de [+děngdài]

lenient ADJ 宽大的 kuāndà de, 仁慈的 réncí de

lens N 1（照相机）镜头 (zhàoxiàngjī) jìngtóu [M. WD 片 piàn] 2（眼镜）镜片 (yǎnjìng) jìngpiàn [M. WD 片 piàn]
contact lens 隐形眼镜 yǐnxíng yǎnjìng

lent v See **lend**

leopard N 豹 bào [M. WD 只 zhī/头 tóu]

leper N 麻风病人 máfēng bìngrén

lesbian N, ADJ 女同性恋者 nǔ tóngxìngliànzhě

less I PRON, ADJ 较少的 jiào shǎo de, 较小的 jiào xiǎo de, 不那么 bú nàme **II** ADV 较少 jiào shǎo, 不那么 bú nàme

lessee N 承租人 chéngzū rén, 租户 zūhù

lessen V 使…减少 shǐ…jiǎnshǎo

lesser ADJ 次要的 cìyào de, 较小的 jiào xiǎo de

lesson N **1** 课 kè, 课程 kèchéng **2** 教训 jiàoxun
to learn a lesson See **learn**
to teach sb a lesson See **teach**

lest CONJ 以免 yǐmiǎn, 免得 miǎnde
Lest We Forget. 永志不忘。Yǒng zhì bú wàng.

let V (PT & PP let) 让 ràng, 允许 yǔnxǔ
to let go (of) 放开 fàngkāi, 放掉 fàngdiao
let alone 更不用说 gèng bú yòng shuō

letdown N 失望 shīwàng, 令人失望的事 lìng rén shīwàng de shì

lethal ADJ 致命的 zhìmìng de

lethargic ADJ 无精打采的 wújīng dǎcǎi de, 懒洋洋的 lǎnyāngyāng de

letter N **1** 信 xìn **2** 字母 zìmǔ
to the letter 不折不扣地 bù zhé bú kòu de, 精确地 jīngquè de

lettuce N 生菜 shēngcài, 莴苣 wōjù

letup N 减弱 jiǎnruò, 松懈 sōngxiè

leukemia N 白血病 báixuèbìng

levee N 防洪堤 fánghóngtí

level I ADJ 平的 píng de, 平坦的 píngtǎn de **II** N **1** 水平线 shuǐpíngxiàn **2** 水平 shuǐpíng
basic/beginner's level 初级水平 chūjí shuǐpíng
advanced level 高级水平 gāojí shuǐpíng
III V **1** 把 [+地面] 弄平 bǎ [+dìmiàn] nòng píng, 使…平坦 shǐ…píngtǎn **2** 推倒 [+房屋] tuīdǎo [+fángwū]
to level accusation (提出) 指控 (tíchū) zhǐkòng

leveler N 使人人平等的事 shǐ rénrén píngděng de shì
Death is the great leveler. 死亡，让人人平等。Sǐwáng, ràng rénrén píngděng. (→ 人无论贵贱，都不免一死。Rén

wúlùn guìjiàn, dōu bùmiǎn yì sǐ.)

lever N **1** 杠杆 gànggǎn, 操纵杆 cāozòngg gǎn **2** 手段 shǒuduàn **II** V (用杠杆) 撬动 (yòng gànggǎn) qiàodòng

leverage N **1** 杠杆作用 gànggǎn zuòyòng **2** 影响 yǐngxiǎng, 力量 lìliang **3** 借贷经营 jièdài jīngyíng **II** V 借贷经营 jièdài jīngyíng

levitation N 漂浮空中 piāofú kōngzhōng

levity N 轻松 qīngsōng, 活跃 huóyuè

levy I V 征税 zhēngshuì **II** N 税 (款) shuì (kuǎn), 征 (款) zhēng (kuǎn)

lewd ADJ 好色的 hàosè de, 淫荡的 yíndàng de

liability N **1** 责任 zérèn, 义务 yìwù **2** 累赘 léizhuì, 不利因素 búlì yīnsù **3** (liabilities) 债务 zhàiwù, 负债 fùzhài

liable ADJ **1** 很可能会 [+犯错误] hěn kěnéng huì [+fàn cuòwù], 很容易遭受 [+攻击] hěn róngyì zāoshòu [+gōngjī] **2** 应负责的 yìng fùzé de
liable for taxes 应缴税的 yìng jiǎoshuì de

liaise V 联络 liánluò, 联系 liánxì

liaison N **1** 联络 liánluò
liaison officer 联络官 liánluòguān **2** (男女之间) 私通 (nánnǚ zhījiān) sītōng

liar N 说谎的人 shuōhuǎng de rén
You liar! 你这个坏蛋说谎! Nǐ zhè ge huàidàn shuōhuǎng!

libel I N 诽谤 fěibàng
libel suit 诽谤诉讼 fěibàng sùsòng **II** V 诽谤 fěibàng, 说…的坏话 shuō…de huàihuà

liberal I ADJ 宽容的 kuānróng de, 开明的 kāimíng de
liberal arts 文科 wénkē **II** N 宽容大度的人 kuānróng dàdù de rén, 自由派 zìyóu pài

liberalize V **1** 使…自由化 shǐ…zìyóuhuà **2** 放宽 fàngkuān

liberate V 解放 jiěfàng, 解救 jiějiù

liberation N 解放 jiěfàng, 解救 jiějiù

liberty N 自由 zìyóu, 自由权 zìyóuquán

libido N 性欲 xìngyù

librarian N 图书馆馆长 túshūguǎn

425

guǎnzhǎng, 图书馆馆管理人员 túshūguǎn guǎnlǐ rényuán
library N 图书馆 túshūguǎn, 图书室 túshūshì
lice See **louse**
license I N 执照 zhízhào, 许可证 xǔkězhèng
driver's license 汽车驾驶执照 / 证 qìchē jiàshǐ zhízhào/zhèng
gun license 持枪许可证 chíqiāng xǔkězhèng
license plate 汽车执照牌 qìchēzhízhàopái
II v 许可 xǔkě, 准许 zhǔnxǔ
lick I v 1 舔 tiǎn
to lick one's lips 舔唇 tiǎn chún, 热切期望 rèqiè qīwàng
2 打败 dǎbài II N 1 舔 tiǎn 2 少量 shǎoliàng
licking N 1 痛打 tòngdǎ 2 失败 shībài, 失利 shīlì
lid N 盖 (子) gài (zi)
lie[1] I v (PT **lay**, PP **lain**) 1 躺 tǎng
to lie down 躺下 tǎngxia
to lie low 躲藏 duǒcáng, 隐蔽起来 yǐnbì qǐlái
2 在于 zàiyú 3 位于 wèiyú
lie[2] I v 说谎 shuōhuǎng II N 谎言 huǎngyán
lie detector 测谎器 cèhuǎngqì
lien N 扣押权 kòuyāquán
lieu N (in lieu of) 代替 dàitì
lieutenant N (陆军 / 海军陆战队) 中尉 (lùjūn/hǎijūn lùzhànduì) zhōngwèi, （海军 / 空军）上尉 (hǎijūn/kōngjūn) shàngwèi
life (PL **lives**) N 生命 shēngmìng
life buoy 救生圈 jiùshēngquān
life insurance 人寿保险 rénshòu bǎoxiǎn
life support system 生命维持器械 shēngmìng wéichí qìxiè
2 生活 shēnghuó 3 一生 yìshēng, 寿命 shòumìng
life expectancy 平均寿命 píngjūn shòumìng
early life （人生的）早期 (rénshēng de) zǎoqī, 早年 zǎonián

all one's life 终生 zhōngshēng, 终身 zhōngshēn
4 无期徒刑 wúqī túxíng, 终身监禁 zhōngshēn jiānjìn
life sentence 无期徒刑 wúqī túxíng, 终身禁监 zhōngshēn jìnjiān
lifeboat N 救生艇 jiùshēngtǐng
lifeguard N 救生员 jiùshēngyuán
lifeless ADJ 1 死的 sǐde 2 无生气的 wú shēngqì de, 无活力的 wú huólì de, 无生命的 wú shēngmìng de
lifelike ADJ 生动逼真的 shēngdòng bīzhēn de, 栩栩如生的 xǔxǔ rú shēng de
lifeline N 生命线 shēngmìngxiàn, 命脉 mìngmài
lifelong ADJ 终生的 zhōngshēng de
lifesaver N 救星 jiùxīng
lifestyle N 生活方式 shēnghuó fāngshi
life-threatening ADJ 危及生命的 wēijí shēngmìng de
lifetime N 一生 yìshēng, 终生 zhōng-shēng
lift I v 1 抬起 táiqǐ, 举起 jǔqǐ 2 提高 [+水平] tígāo [+shuǐpíng], 增加 zēngjiā
to lift one's spirits 提高某人的情绪 tígāo mǒurén de qíngxù
3 解除 jiěchú [+禁令] [+jìnlìng], 撤销 chèxiāo II N 1 升降机 shēngjiàngjī [M. WD 台 tái] 2 (to give sb a lift) 让人搭便车 ràng mǒurén dābiàn chē, 使某人精神振作 shǐ mǒurén jīngshén zhènzuò
ligament N 韧带 rèndài
light[1] I N 1 光 guāng, 光线 guāngxiàn
light year 光年 guāngnián
2 灯光 dēngguāng 3 灯 dēng, 电灯 diàndēng [M. WD 盏 zhǎn]
light bulb 灯泡 dēngpào, 电灯泡 diàn dēngpào
II v (PT & PP **lit**, **lighted**) 1 点燃 diǎnrán 2 照亮 zhàoliàng
light[2] ADJ 1 轻的 qīng de
light-fingered ① 有偷窃习惯的 yǒu tōuqiè xíguàn de ② （弹奏乐器）手指灵巧的 (tánzòu yuèqì) shǒuzhǐ língqiǎo de
2 （衣服）轻便的 qīngbiàn de, 薄的 bó de 3 淡颜色的 dàn yánsè de

light brown eyes 浅棕色的眼睛 qiǎn zōngsè de yǎnjing

lighter N 打火机 dǎhuǒjī

light-headed ADJ **1** 晕眩的 yūnxuàn de **2** 头脑不清的 tóunǎo bù qīng de, 步履不稳的 bùlǚ bù wěn de

light-hearted ADJ 轻松愉快的 qīngsōng yúkuài de, 无忧无虑的 wúyōu wúlǜ de

lighthouse N 灯塔 dēngtǎ [M. WD 座 zuò]

lighting N 照明 (灯) zhàomíng (dēng)

lightning I N 闪电 shǎndiàn [M. WD 道 dào] II ADJ 闪电般的 shǎndiàn bān de at lightning speed 以闪电般的速度 yǐ shǎndiàn bān de sùdù

lightweight I N **1** (体育) 轻量级 (tǐyù) qīngliàngjí **2** 没有分量的人 méiyǒu fènliàng de rén, 微不足道的人 wēi bù zú dào de rén II ADJ **1** 轻便的 [+机器] qīngbiàn de [+jīqì] **2** 轻薄的 [+衣服] qīngbó de [+yīfu] **3** 浅薄的 [+书籍] qiǎnbó de [+shūjí]

likable ADJ 惹人喜爱的 rě rén xǐ'ài de

like[1] I V **1** 喜欢 xǐhuan **2** 喜好 xǐhào would like 想要 xiǎngyào II N **1** 喜欢的事 xǐhuan de shì sb's likes and dislikes 某人喜欢和不喜欢的事 mǒurén xǐhuan hé bù xǐhuan de shì **2** 像…的事 xiàng…de shì … and the like 以及诸如此类的事 yǐjí zhū rú cǐlèi de shì the likes of sb 像某人这种人 xiàng mǒurén zhè zhǒng rén

like[2] I PREP 像…一样 xiàng…yíyàng II CONJ 就像 jiù xiàng like I said 就像我说过的（那样）jiù xiàng wǒ shuō guò de (nà yàng)

like[3] ADJ 相似的 xiāngsì de, 相像的 xiāngxiàng de

likelihood N 可能（性）kěnéng (xìng) in all likelihood 极有可能 jí yǒu kěnéng

likely I ADJ 很可能的 hěn kěnéng de II ADV 很可能 hěn kěnéng

likeness N **1** 相像 xiāngxiàng, 相似 xiāngsì **2** 画像 huàxiàng [M. WD 幅 fú], 片片 zhàopiàn [M. WD 张 zhāng]

likewise ADV 同样地 tóngyàng de

liking N 喜欢 xǐhuan, 爱好 àihào to take a liking to sb 喜欢上某人 xǐhuan shang mǒurén

lilt N 抑扬顿挫的声音 yìyáng dùncuò de shēngyīn

lily N 百合花 bǎihéhuā

limb N **1** (树) 主干 (shù) zhǔgàn **2** (四) 肢 (sì) zhī, 臂 bì be out on a limb 处于孤立无援的境地 chǔyú gūlì wúyuán de jìngdì

limbo N (be in limbo) 处于不确定的状态 chǔyú bú quèdìng de zhuàngtài

lime N **1** 石灰 shíhuī **2** 酸橙树 suānchéng shù [M. WD 棵 kē]

limelight N 公众关注的中心 gōngzhòng guānzhù de zhōngxīn to seek the limelight 爱出风头 ài chū fēngtou

limit I N **1** 限度 xiàndù within limits 在合理的范围内 zài hélǐ de fànwéinèi speed limit 最高车速 zuì gāo chēsù **2** 边缘 biānyuán off limit 不准入内 bù zhǔn rù nèi II V 限制 xiànzhì

limitation N 限制 xiànzhì

limited ADJ **1** 有限的 yǒuxiàn de **2** 受到限制的 shòudào xiànzhì de

limousine N 大型豪华轿车 dàxíng háohuá jiàochē [M. WD 辆 liàng]

limp I ADJ 软绵绵的 ruǎnmiánmián de, 无力的 wúlì de II V 一瘸一拐地走 yì qué yì guǎi de zǒu III N 一瘸一拐地走 yìqué yìguǎi de zǒu, 跛行 bǒxíng

linchpin, lynchpin N 关键人物 guānjiàn rénwù, 关键的事 guānjiàn de shì

line I N **1** 线 xiàn **2** 排队 páiduì **3** 皱纹 zhòuwén **4** 电话线 diànhuàxiàn online 联网 liánwǎng, 上网 shàngwǎng **5** 态度 tàidu, 立场 lìchǎng to take a hard line on sth 对某事采取强硬立场 duì mǒushì cǎiqǔ qiángyìng lìchǎng **6** (书页上的) 行 (shūyè shàng de) háng II V 排成一行 pái chéng yì háng finish line 终点线 zhōngdiǎnxiàn

lineage N 1 行数 xíng shù 2 血统 xuè-tǒng, 家系 jiāxì

linear ADJ 1 线条的 xiàntiáo de 2 线性的 xiànxìng de
linear thinking 线性思维 xiànxìng sīwéi
3 长度的 chángdù de
linear measurements 长度测量 chángdù cèliáng

lined ADJ 1 印有线条的 [+纸] yìn yǒu xiàntiáo de [+zhǐ] 2 有衬里的 [+上衣] yǒu chènlǐ de [+shàngyī]

linen N 家用纺织品 (床单、台布、内衣等) jiāyòng fǎngzhīpǐn (chuángdān, táibù, nèiyī děng)

liner[1] N 客轮 kèlún [M. WD 艘 sōu]
cruise liner 游轮 yóulún

liner[2] N 衬里 chènlǐ, 衬垫 chèndiàn
liner notes (激光唱盘) 说明文字 (jīguāng chàngpán) shuōmíng wénzì

linesman N 1 (橄榄球) 锋线球员 (gǎnlǎnqiú) fēngxiàn qiúyuán 2 (铁路) 养路工 (tiělù) yǎnglùgōng

line-up N 1 (球类比赛) 运动员阵容 (qiúlèi bǐsài) yùndòngyuán zhènróng 2 (演出) 全体演员 (yǎnchū) quántǐ yǎnyuán 3 (电视) 一系列节目 (diànshì) yíxìliè jiémù

linger V [人+] 逗留不离去 [rén+] dòuliú bù líqù, [事+] 持续 [shì+] chíxù

lingerie N (女子) 内衣裤 (nǚzǐ) nèiyīkù

lingo N 隐语 yǐnyǔ, 行话 hánghuà

linguist N 1 语言学家 yǔyánxuéjiā 2 通晓多国语言的人 tōngxiǎo duōguó yǔyán de rén

linguistics N 语言学 yǔyánxué

liniment N 涂剂 túx́i, 搽剂 chájì

lining N (衣服) 衬里 (yīfu) chènlǐ

link I V 1 连接 liánjiē 2 与…有关义… yǒuguān II N 1 关系 guānxi, 联系 liánxi
to link up 连接 (电脑) liánjiē (diànnǎo) 2 (计算机) 链接 (jìsuànjī) liànjiē 3 环节 huánjié
a weak link (in sth) (某事中的) 薄弱环节 (mǒushì zhòngde) bóruò huánjié

linkage N 1 连接系列 liánjiē xìliè 2 关联原则 guānlián yuánzé

lint N 棉绒 miánróng

lion N (F **lioness**) 狮子 shīzi
the lion's share 最大的份额 zuì dà de fèn'é

lip N 嘴唇 zuǐchún
lip gloss 亮彩唇膏 liàng cǎi chúngāo
lip synch 假唱 jiǎ chàng
to keep one's lips sealed 守口如瓶 shǒu kǒu rú píng
to pay lip service 只说好话没有行动 zhǐ shuō hǎohuà méiyǒu xíngdòng, 口惠而实不至 kǒu huì ér shí bù zhì

lip-read V 唇读 chúndú, 观察对方的唇形 (来猜测语意) guānchá duìfāng de chún xíng (lái cāicè yǔyì)

lipstick N 唇膏 chúngāo, 口红 kǒuhóng

liqueur N 利口酒 lìkǒu jiǔ

liquid N 液体 yètǐ II ADJ 1 液体的 yètǐ de 2 很容易变成现金的 hěn róngyì biànchéng xiànjīn de
liquid assets 流动资金 liúdòng zījīn

liquidate V 停业清理 tíngyè qīnglǐ, 清算 (破产企业) qīngsuàn (pòchǎn qǐyè)

liquor N 烈性酒 lièxìng jiǔ
liquor store 酒店 jiǔdiàn

list I N 1 单子 dānzi [M. WD 份 fèn/张 zhāng], 清单 qīngdān 2 目录 mùlù
list price (厂商的) 定价 (chǎngshāng de) dìngjià
shopping list 购物单 gòuwùdān
II V 列出 lièchū

listen V 1 听 tīng 2 (你) 听着 (nǐ) tīngzhe
to listen in 偷听 tōutīng
to listen up 注意听 zhùyì tīng

listener N 听者 tīngzhě, 听众 tīngzhòng

listing N (清单上的) 一项 (qīngdān shàng de) yí xiàng
listings 活动内容时间表 huódòng nèiróng shíjiānbiǎo

listless ADJ 无精打采的 wújīng dǎcǎi de, 懒洋洋的 lǎnyāngyāng de

lit See **light**[1]

lite ADJ 低度的 dī dù de, 低脂肪的 dī zhīfáng de
lite beer 淡啤酒 dàn píjiǔ

liter N 公升 gōngshēng

literal ADJ 字面上的 zìmiàn shàng de, 逐字的 zhúzì de

a literal translation 逐字的翻译 zhúzì de fānyì

literally ADV **1** 按照字面 ànzhào zìmiàn **2** 确实 quèshí, 简直 jiǎnzhí

to take … literally 照字面理解 zhào zìmiàn lǐjiě

literate ADJ 能读会写的 néng dú huì xiě de, 识字的 shízì de

literature N **1** 文学 wénxué **2** 文献资料 wénxiàn zīliào

medical literature 医学文献 yīxué wénxiàn

lithe ADJ 柔软灵活的 róuruǎn línghuó de

litigation N 诉讼 sùsòng

litmus test 1 试金石 shìjīnshí, 检验 jiǎnyàn **2** 石蕊测试 shíruǐ cèshì

litter¹ **I** N 垃圾 lājī

litter bag 垃圾袋 lājīdài

II V 乱扔垃圾 luànrēng lājī

litter² N 一窝（幼兽）yìwō (yòu shòu)

a litter of puppies 一窝小狗 yìwō xiǎogǒu

litterbug N 乱扔垃圾的人 luànrēng lājī de rén

little I ADJ **1** 小 xiǎo **2** 年幼的 niányòu de, 小 xiǎo **3** 不多的 bù duō de, 很少的 hěn shǎo de **II** ADV 稍许一点儿 shāoxǔ yìdiǎnr

a little while 一会儿 yíhuìr

little by little 一点一点地 yì diǎnr yìdiǎnr de

live I V **1** 活 huó, 生活 shēnghuó

to live and let live 自己活，也让别人活。Zìjǐ huó, yě ràng biéren huó. **2** 居住 jūzhù, 住 zhù

to live together 同居 tóngjū

II ADJ **1** 现场 xiànchǎng **2** 活着的 huózhāo de

an experiment on live animals 活体动物实验 huótǐ dòngwù shíyàn

livelihood N 生计 shēngjì

lively ADJ 活跃的 huóyuè de, 活泼的 huópo de

liven V（使…）活跃起来 (shǐ…) huóyuè qǐlái,（使…）更有趣 (shǐ…) gèng yǒuqù

liver N 肝（脏）gān (zàng)

lives N, PL See **life**

livestock N 牲畜 shēngchù, 家畜 jiāchù

livid ADJ **1** 气得脸色铁青的 qì dé liǎnsè tiěqīng de, 大怒的 dà nù de **2** 铅灰色的 qiān huīsè de

living I ADJ **1** 活的 huó de

the living 活着的人 huózhe de rén, 生者 shēngzhě

2 在使用的 zài shǐyòng de

living room 起居室 qǐjushì, 客厅 kètīng

living standard 生活水平 shēnghuó shuǐpíng

II N 生计 shēngjì

to make a living 谋生 móushēng

lizard N 蜥蜴 xīyì [M. WD 只 zhī]

load I N **1** 一大批 yí dà pī, 大量 dàliàng **2**（一车）运载物 (yì chē) yùnzàiwù

a truck/boat/coach load of 一卡车 / 一船 / 一旅游车 yì kǎchē/yì chuán/yì lǚyóuchē

3（沉重的）负担 (chénzhòng de) fùdàn **4** 附加费 fù jiāfèi **II** V **1** 装载 zhuāngzài **2** 给（枪）上子弹 gěi (qiāng) shàng zǐdàn

loaded ADJ **1** 装着货物的 [+卡车] zhuāngzhe huòwù de [+kǎchē] **2** 有子弹的 [+枪] zhuāngyǒu zǐdàn de [+qiāng] **3**（棒球）满垒的 (bàngqiú) mǎnlěi de **4** 话中有话的 [+问题] huà zhōng yǒu huà de [+wèntí]

a loaded question 别有用心的 biéyǒu yòngxīn de wèntí

5 富有的 fùyǒu de, 有钱的 yǒuqián de

loaf¹ (PL **loaves**) N 大面包 dà miànbāo

loaf² V 游手好闲 yóu shǒu hào xián, 虚度光阴 xūdù guāngyīn

loan I N **1** 借出物 jièchūwù **2** 借款 jièkuǎn, 笔 bǐ, 贷款 dàikuǎn

loan shark N 放高利贷者 fàng gāolìdài zhě

II V 借出 jièchū

on loan 借来的 jièlái de

loanword N 外来语 wàiláiyǔ, 借译词 jièyìcí

loath ADJ 厌恶 yànwù, 不愿意 bú yuànyì

loathing N 厌恶 yànwù, 强烈的反感 qiángliè de fǎngǎn

loaves See **loaf**[1]

lobby I N 1 大厅 dàtīng, 大堂 dàtáng
2 (美国国会的) 游说团 (Měiguó Guóhuì de) yóushuìtuán
a powerful environmental lobby 强大的环保游说团 qiángdà de huánbǎo yóushuìtuán
II V (美国政治) 游说 (Měiguó zhèngzhì) yóushuì

lobe N 1 耳垂 ěrchuí 2 (脑) 叶 (nǎo) yè, (肺) 叶 (fèi) yè

lobster N 龙虾 lóngxiā [M. WD 只 zhī]

local I ADJ 1 本地的 běndì de, 本地的 běndì de 2 局部的 júbù de II N 当地人 dāngdì rén

locality N 地区 dìqū

locally ADV 在当地 zài dāngdì, 在本地 zài běndì

locate V 1 找到 zhǎodao 2 设在 shè zài
to be located in/at 位于 wèi yú, 坐落在 zuòluò zài

location N 位置 wèizhi

lock I N 1 锁 suǒ
combination lock 号码锁 hàomǎsuǒ
2 水闸 shuǐzhá, 船闸 chuánzhá
lock, stock and barrel 全部 quánbù
3 一绺 (头发) yì liǔ (tóufa) II V 锁 suǒ, 锁上 suǒshàng
to lock sb up 把某人监禁起来 bǎ mǒurén jiānjìn qǐlái, 把某人关起来 bǎ mǒurén guān qǐlái

locker N 存放柜 cúnfàngguì
locker room 衣物间 yīwùjiān, 更衣室 gēngyīshì

locket N 盒式项链坠物 héshì xiàngliàn zhuìwù

locksmith N 锁匠 suǒjiang, 修锁工人 xiū suǒ gōngrén

locomotive N 火车头 huǒchētóu, 机车 jīchē [M. WD 台 tái]

locust N 蝗虫 huángchóng

lodge I V 1 租住 zū zhù, 寄宿 jìsù 2 供…寄宿 gōng…jìsù 3 卡在 qiǎ zài, 卡住 qiǎ zhù 4 提出 [+抗议] tíchū [+kàngyì] II N 1 小屋 xiǎo wū 2 地方分会 dìfang fēnhuì

lodging N 住宿的地方 zhùsù de dìfang, 寄宿处 jìsùchù

loft N 阁楼 gélóu

lofty ADJ 1 崇高的 [+理想] chónggāo de [+lǐxiǎng] 2 高傲的 [+人] gāo'ào de [+rén], 傲慢的 àomàn de

log I N 1 木材 mùcái, 木块 mùkuài
log cabin 原木小屋 yuánmù xiǎowū
2 飞行日记 fēixíng rìjì, 航海日记 hánghǎi rìjì II V 1 砍伐 (树木) kǎnfá (shùmù) 2 正式记录 zhèngshì jìlù 3 工作了 (若干时间) gōngzuò le (ruògān shíjiān)
to log in/on (计算机) 进入系统 (jìsuànjī) jìnrù xìtǒng
to log out/off (计算机) 退出系统 (jìsuànjī) tuìchū xìtǒng

loggerheads N (at loggerheads with sb) 与某人不和 yǔ mǒurén bùhé, 同某人争吵 tóng mǒurén zhēngchǎo

logging N 伐木 (业) fámù (yè)

logic N 逻辑 (学) luóji (xué)

logistics N 组织安排工作 zǔzhī ānpái gōngzuò, 后勤 (工作) hòuqín (gōngzuò)

logo N 标志 biāozhì, 标识 biāoshì

loincloth N 腰布 yāobù [M. WD 块 kuài]

loiter V 游荡 yóudàng, 闲逛 xiánguàng

loll V 懒洋洋地坐 / 躺 lǎnyāngyāng de zuò/tǎng

lollipop N 棒糖 bàngtáng [M. WD 根 gēn/块 kuài]

lone ADJ 孤独的 gūdú de, 仅有的 jǐnyǒu de

lonely ADJ 1 寂寞的 jìmò de, 孤独的 gūdú de 2 荒无人烟的 huāng wú rényān de

lonesome ADJ 孤独的 gūdú de, 孤寂的 gūjì de

long[1] I ADJ 长 cháng
long jump 跳远 (运动) tiàoyuǎn (yùndòng)
long shot 可能性不大的事 kěnéngxìng bùdà de shì, 玄乎的事 xuánhu de shì II ADV 长时间 cháng shíjiān
long before/after 在…很久以前 / 以后 zài…hěn jiǔ yǐqián/yǐhòu
for long 很久 hěn jiǔ
as long as 只要 zhǐ yào

long[2] V 渴望 kěwàng, 盼望 pànwang
a longed-for reunion 盼望已久的团聚 pànwang yǐjiǔ de tuánjù

long-distance ADJ 长途的 chángtú de
long-distance call 长途电话 chángtú diànhuà

longevity N 长寿 chángshòu

longhand N 普通手写 pǔtōng shǒuxiě

longing N 渴望 kěwàng
a longing for friendship 对友谊的渴望 duì yǒuyì de kěwàng

longitude N 径度 jìngdù
longitude 30° east 东经30度 dōngjīng sānshí dù

long-lasting ADJ 1 长久的 chángjiǔ de, 耐用的 nàiyòng de 2 纵向的 zòngxiàng de, 经度的 jīngdù de

long-lived ADJ 长期存在的 chángqī cúnzài de, 长寿的 chángshòu de

long-lost ADJ 丢失很久的 diūshī hěn jiǔ de, 久未见面的 jiǔwèi jiànmiàn de

long-range ADJ 1 远程的 yuǎnchéng de, 远距离的 yuǎnjùlí de 2 长期的 chángqī de

long-running ADJ 持续很长时间的 chíxù hěn chángshíjiān de

long-standing ADJ 长期（存在）的 chángqī (cúnzài) de

long-suffering ADJ 长期忍受的 chángqī rěnshòu de

long-term ADJ 长期的 chángqī de

long-winded ADJ 絮絮叨叨的 xùxù dāodao de

look I v 1 看 kàn, 瞧 qiáo
to look after 照顾 zhàogu, 照料 zhàoliào
to look down upon 看不起 kànbuqǐ
to look forward to 期待 qīdài, 盼 pàn 2 寻找 xúnzhǎo 3 看上去 kànshangqu II N 1 看 kàn 2 表情 biǎoqíng

lookout N 岗哨 gǎngshào, 了望台 liàowàngtái
to be on the lookout for 监视 jiānshì

loom I v 1 隐隐出现 yǐnyǐn chūxiàn 2 临近 línjìn II N 织布机 zhībùjī [M. WD 架 jià]

loony ADJ 怪异的 guàiyì de, 愚蠢的 yúchǔn de

loop I N 1 环形 huánxíng 2 圈 quān, 环 huán

to be out of the loop 圈外人 quānwàirén
II v 把…绕成圈 bǎ…ràochéng quān

loophole N 漏洞 lòudòng, 空子 kòngzi

loose ADJ 1 松 sōng, 松开 sōngkāi 2 宽松的（衣服）kuānsōng de (yīfu) 3 不精确的 bù jīngquè de, 粗略的 cūlüè
a loose translation 粗略的译文 cūlüè de yìwén

loosen v（使…）变松 (shǐ…) biàn sōng, 松开 sōngkāi

loot I v 1 抢劫 qiǎngjié, 掠夺 lüèduó II N 1 赃物 zāngwù 2 战利品 zhànlìpǐn 3 钱财 qiáncái

lopsided ADJ 歪斜的 wāixié de, 倾斜的 qīngxié de

Lord N 上帝 Shàngdì, 耶稣 Yēsū

lord N 1（英国）贵族 (Yīngguó) guìzú 2 主人 zhǔrén

lose (PT & PP lost) v 1 丢失 [+钱包] diūshī [+qiánbāo], 失去 [+工作] shīqù [+gōngzuò]
to lose one's way 迷路 mílù
to lose heart 丧失信心 sàngshī xìnxīn 2 输 [+比赛] shū [+bǐsài]

loss N 1 丧失 sàngshī 2 损失 sǔnshī 3（商业）亏损 (shāngyè) kuīsǔn

lost N I ADJ 1 丢失的 [+宠物] diūshī de [+chǒngwù] 2 迷路的 [+旅行者] mílù de [+lǚxíngzhě] 3 浪费掉的 [+时间] làngfèi diào de [+shíjiān] II v See lose

lot I PRON, ADJ 1 (a lot of, lots of) 很多 hěn duō, 许多 xǔduō 2 很多 hěn duō
to have a lot on one's plate 有很多事情要处理 yǒu hěn duō shìqing yào chǔlǐ, 有很多难题要解决 yǒu hěn duō nántí yào jiějué
II ADV 多 duō, 得多 dé duō III N 1 一块地 yí kuài dì 2 一块空地 yí kuài kòngdì 3 命运 mìngyùn, 运气 yùnqì
to draw lots 抽签 chōuqiān
to throw in your lot with sb 与某人共命运 yǔ mǒurén gòng mìngyùn 3 一批人 yìpī rén, 一群人 yìqún rén

lotion N 护肤液 hùfūyè 2 药液 yàoyè

lottery N 彩票 cǎipiào, 乐透 lètòu

loud ADJ 1 响 xiǎng, 大声 dàshēng 2 色彩

过分鲜艳的 sècǎi guòfèn xiānyàn de,
刺眼的 cìyǎn de

loudspeaker N 扩音器 kuòyīnqì, 扬声器 yángshēngqì

lounge I N （旅馆）休息室 (lǚguǎn) xiūxìshì, （机场）候机大厅 (jīchǎng) hòujī dàtīng
lounge chair 躺椅 tǎngyǐ
II v 懒洋洋地坐 lǎnyāngyāng de zuò, 懒洋洋地站 ǎnyāngyāng de zhàn

louse I N (PL **lice**) 虱子 shīzi II v (to louse up) 把…弄糟 bǎ…nòngzāo

lousy ADJ 糟透了的 zāotòule de

lovable ADJ 让人喜爱的 ràng rén xǐ'ài de, 可爱的 kě'ài de

love I v 1 喜爱 xǐ'ài 2 爱 ài, 心爱 xīn'ài II N 1 爱 ài 2 爱情 àiqíng
love affair 恋爱关系 liàn'ài guānxi
love seat 双人小沙发 shuāngrén xiǎo shāfā

lovely ADJ 1 可爱的 kě'ài de 2 美妙的 měimiào de, 极好的 jíhǎo de

lover N 1 情人 qíngrén 2 爱好者 àihàozhě

lovesick ADJ 害相思病的 hài xiāngsībìng de

low ADJ 1 低 dī 2 低下的 dīxià de

lowbrow ADJ 低俗的 dīsú de, 庸俗的 yōngsú de

lowdown[1] N 最重要的信息 zuì zhòngyào de xìnxī

lowdown[2] ADJ 卑劣的 bēiliè de, 低下的 dīxià de

low-end ADJ 低档的 dīdàng de, 廉价的 liánjià de

lower I v 降低 jiàngdī II ADJ 较低的 jiào dī de

lowfat ADJ 低脂肪的 dī zhīfáng de

low-key ADJ 低调的 dīdiào de

lowly ADJ 低微的 dīwēi de, 低下的 dīxià de

lowlying ADJ 高出海面不多的 gāochū hǎimiàn bù duō de

loyal ADJ 忠诚的 zhōngchéng de

loyalty N 忠诚 zhōngchéng, 忠心 zhōngxīn

lozenge N 糖锭 tángdìng
cough lozenge 止咳糖 zhǐkétáng

lubricant N 滑润剂 huárùnjì

lubricate v 给…加润滑剂 gěi…jiā rùnhuájì

lucid ADJ 1 神志清楚的 shénzhì qīngchu de 2 表达清楚的 biǎodá qīngchu de

luck N 运气 yùnqi, 运道 yùndào
Good luck! 祝您好运! Zhù nín hǎo yùn!
Just my luck! 都怪我运气不好! Dōu guài wǒ yùnqi bù hǎo!

lucky ADJ 幸运的 xìngyùn de

lucrative ADJ 赚大钱的 zhuàn dàqián de, 利润丰厚的 lìrùn fēnghòu de

ludicrous ADJ 可笑的 kěxiào de, 荒唐的 huāngtang de

lug v 艰难地拖 jiānnán de tuō

luggage N 行李 xínglì [M. WD 件 jiàn]

lukewarm ADJ 1 温吞的 [+水] wēntun de [+shuǐ] 2 冷淡的 [+态度] lěngdàn de [+tàidu]

lull I v 使…平静下来 shǐ…píngjìng xiàlai II N 间歇 jiànxiē

lullaby N 摇篮曲 yáolánqǔ, 催眠曲 cuīmiánqǔ

lumbago N 腰肌劳损 yāojī láosǔn, 腰痛 yāotòng

lumber I N 木材 mùcái II v 1 伐木制成木材 fámù zhìchéng mùcái 2 缓慢笨拙地移动 huǎnmàn bènzhuō de yídòng

luminous ADJ 1 发光的 fā guāng de 2 色彩亮丽的 sècǎi liànglì de

lump I N 块 kuài, 肿块 zhǒng kuài
lump sum 一次性付款 yícìxìng fùkuǎn
to have a lump in one's throat 感到哽咽 gǎndào gěngyè
II v 把…混在一起 bǎ…hùn zài yìqǐ

lumpy ADJ 有团块的 yǒu tuánkuài de, 疙疙瘩瘩的 gēgedada de

lunacy N 疯狂 fēngkuáng, 精神错乱 jīngshén cuòluàn

lunar ADJ 月（亮）的 yuè (liàng) de

lunatic I ADJ 精神错乱的 jīngshén cuòluàn de, 疯的 fēng de II N 精神病患者 jīngshénbìng huànzhě, 疯子 fēngzi

lunch I N 午餐 wǔcān, 午饭 wǔfàn II v 午饭吃 chī wǔfàn, 进午餐 jìn wǔcān

lung N 肺 fèi
lung function 肺功能 fèi gōngnéng

lunge v, N 猛冲 měngchōng, 猛扑 měngpū

lurch¹ v 跌跌撞撞 diēdiē zhuàngzhuàng

lurch² N 1 晃动 huàngdòng 2 踉跄 liàngqiàng

to leave sb in the lurch 使某人处于困境而不顾 shǐ mǒurén chǔyú kùnjìng ér bú gù

lure v 引诱 yǐnyòu, 诱惑 yòuhuò

lurid ADJ 骇人听闻的 hàirén tīngwén de, 充满性和暴力的 chōngmǎn xìng hé bàolì de

lurk v 潜伏 qiánfú

luscious N 美味的 měiwèi de

lush ADJ 茂盛的 màoshèng de

lust I N 强烈的性欲 qiángliè de xìngyù II v 1 强烈渴求发生性关系 qiángliè kěqiú fāshēng xìng guānxi de 2 热烈追求 rèliè zhuīqiú, 恋恋 tānliàn

luster N 光彩 guāngcǎi, 光耀 guāngyào

lusty ADJ 健壮的 jiànzhuàng de, 精力充沛的 jīnglì chōngpèi de

luxurious ADJ 奢侈的 shēchǐ de, 豪华的 háohuá de

luxury N 1 奢侈 shēchǐ, 豪华 háohuá 2 奢侈品 shēchǐpǐn

luxury hotel 豪华旅馆 háohuá lǚguǎn

lymph N 淋巴 línbā

lymphoma N 淋巴肿瘤 línbā zhǒngliú

lynch v 用私刑处死 yòng sīxíng chǔsǐ

lyric I N 抒情诗 shūqíngshī [M. WD 首 shǒu] II ADJ 抒情的 [+歌声] shūqíng de [+gēshēng]

lyricist N 歌词作者 gēcí zuòzhě

M

M.A. (= Master of Arts) ABBREV 文学硕士（学位）wénxué shuòshì (xuéwèi)

ma N 妈 mā, 妈妈 māma

macabre ADJ 与死亡有关的 yǔ sǐwáng yǒuguān de, 恐怖的 kǒngbù de

machete N 大砍刀 dà kǎndāo

machine I N 机器 jīqì [M. WD 台 tái] machine gun 机关枪 jīguānqiāng sewing machine 缝纫机 féngrènjī washing machine 洗衣机 xǐyījī II v 用机器加工 yòng jīqì jiāgōng

machinery N 器械 qìxiè, 机器 jīqì

machinist N 机器操作工 jīqì cāozuògōng

macho ADJ 有男子汉气概的 yǒu nánzǐhàn qìgài de, 有阳刚气的 yǒu yánggāng qì de

mackerel N 鲭鱼 qīng yú [M. WD 条 tiáo]

mad ADJ 1 发疯 fāfēng 2 十分生气 shífēn shēngqì, 气得要命 qìde yàoming 3 极其愚蠢 jíqí yúchǔn

like mad 极快地 jí kuài de, 拼命地 pīnmìng de

mad cow disease 疯牛病 fēngniúbìng

madam, ma'am N 太太 tàitai, 夫人 fūrén

maddening ADJ 让人极为恼火的 ràng rén jíwéi nǎohuǒ de

made See make

madhouse N 很多人闹哄哄的地方 hěn duō rén nàohōnghōng de dìfang, 疯人院 fēngrényuàn

madly ADV 发疯似地 fāfēng shìde

be madly in love with sb 发疯似地爱上某人 fāfēng sì de zhuàng mǒurén, 爱某人爱得要命 ài mǒurén ài deyàoming

madman N 狂人 kuángrén, 疯子 fēngzi

madness N 精神错乱 jīngshén cuòluàn, 疯狂 fēngkuáng

Madonna N 圣母玛丽亚 Shèngmǔ Mǎlìyà

maelstrom N 混乱的局面 hùnluàn de júmiàn, 大动乱 dà dòngluàn

maestro N（音乐）大师（yīnyuè）dàshī

mafia N 黑手党 hēishǒudǎng

magazine N 1 杂志 zázhì, 期刊 qīkān 2 子弹夹 zǐdànjiā, 弹盒 dànhé 3 弹药库 dànyàokù, 军火库 jūnhuǒkù 4 胶卷盒 jiāojuǎnhé

maggot N 蛆 qū [M. WD 条 tiáo]

magic I N 魔术 móshù, 戏法 xìfǎ

to work like magic 取得神奇的效果 qǔdé shénqí de xiàoguǒ

II ADJ 魔术的 móshù de, 有魔力的 yǒu mólì de

a magic number 一个神奇的数字 yí ge shénqí de shùzì

magic touch 神奇本领 shénqí běnlǐng

magical ADJ 1 有魔力的 yǒu mólì de 2 奇异的 qíyì de, 迷人的 mírén de

magician N 魔术师 móshùshī, 变戏法的人 biànxìfǎ de rén

magistrate N 地方法官 dìfang fǎguān

magnanimous ADJ 宽宏大量的 kuānhóng dàliàng de

magnate N 巨头 jùtóu, 大亨 dàhēng

magnet N **1** 磁铁 cítiě [M. WD 块 kuài], 磁石 císhí [M. WD 块 kuài] **2** 特别有吸引力的人／地方 tèbié yǒu xīyǐnlì de rén/dìfang

magnetic ADJ 磁性的 cíxìng de

magnetism N **1** 磁性 cíxìng **2** 魅力 mèilì

magnification N 放大（率）fàngdà (lù)

magnificent ADJ 宏伟壮丽的 hóngwěi zhuànglì de, 宏大的 hóngdà de

magnify V 放大 fàng dà
a magnifying glass 放大镜 fàngdàjìng

magnitude N **1** 重大 zhòngdà **2** [地震+]度 [dìzhèn+] dù
an earthquake of magnitude six 六级地震 liù jí dìzhèn

magpie N 喜鹊 xǐque [M. WD 只 zhī]

mahjong, mahjongg N 麻将（牌）májiàng (pái)
to play mahjong 打麻将 dǎ májiàng

maid N 女佣人 nǚ yōngrén, 清洁女工 qīngjié nǚgōng

maiden N 少女 shàonǚ
maiden name 女子婚前的姓 nǚzǐ hūnqián de xìng

mail I N **1** 邮件 yóujiàn **2** 邮政 yóuzhèng II V 邮寄 yóujì
mail order 邮购 yóugòu

mailbox N 信箱 xìnxiāng, 邮箱 yóuxiāng

mailing list N **1** 邮寄名单 yóujì míngdān **2**（计算机）邮件列表 (jìsuànjī) yóujiàn lièbiǎo

mailman N 邮递员 yóudìyuán

maim V 使…残废 shǐ...cánfèi

main ADJ 主要的 zhǔyào de
main course 主菜 zhǔcài
the main thing 最重要的事 zuì zhòngyào de shì

mainframe N（大型计算机）主机 (dàxíng jìsuànjī) zhǔjī

mainland N 大陆 dàlù, 本土 běntǔ

mainly ADV 主要（地）zhǔyào (de), 大部分（地）dàbùfen (de)

mainstay N 支柱 zhīzhù, 骨干 gǔgàn

mainstream N, ADJ 主流（的）zhǔliú (de)

maintain V **1** 保养 bǎoyǎng, 维修 wéixiū **2** 保持 bǎochí, 维持 wéichí

maintenance N **1** 维修 wéixiū, 保养 bǎoyǎng **2** 保持 bǎochí, 维持 wéichí

majestic ADJ 雄伟的 xióngwěi de, 庄严的 zhuāngyán de

majesty N 雄伟 xióngwěi, 庄严 zhuāngyán
Your Majesty 国王陛下 guówáng bìxià, 皇帝陛下 huángdì bìxià

major I ADJ 重要的 zhòngyào de, 主要的 zhǔyào de II N **1** 大学主修科目 dàxué zhǔxiū kēmù **2** 主修某专业的学生 zhǔxiū mǒu zhuānyè de xuésheng **3**（军队）少校 (jūn duì) shàoxiào III V 主修 zhǔxiū

majority N 多数 duōshù
the overwhelming majority 绝大多数 juédà duōshù
the silent majority 沉默的大多数 chénmò de dàduōshù

make I V (PT & PP **made**) **1** 做 zuò, 制造 zhìzào
be made of 是…做的 shì...zuò de
Made in China 中国制造 Zhōngguó zhìzào
2 使 shǐ, 让 ràng, 使得 shǐde **3** 挣（钱）zhèng (qián) **4** 成为 chéngwéi
to make the bed 铺床 pūchuáng
to make out 弄清 nòngqīng
to make up 构成 gòuchéng
to make ends meet 收支相抵 shōuzhī xiāngdǐ
II N 牌子 páizi, 品牌 pǐnpái

make-believe ADJ 虚假的 xūjiǎ de, 假的 jiǎ de

maker N 制造商 zhìzàoshāng, 生产厂 shēngchǎnchǎng

makeshift ADJ 临时的 línshí de

makeup N 化妆品 huàzhuāngpǐn, 化妆用品 huàzhuāng yòngpǐn

making N 制造 zhìzào, 制作 zhì zuò
(a tragedy) of one's own making 自己一手造成的（悲剧）zìjǐ yīshǒu zàochéng de (bēijù)

makings N 要素 yàosù, 素质 sùzhì
to have the makings of an entrepre-

neur 具备企业家的素质 jùbèi qǐyèjiā de sùzhì

malady N **1** 疾病 jíbìng **2** 弊端 bìduān, 通病 tōngbìng

the malady of the welfare state（社会）福利制度的弊端 (shèhuì) fúlì zhìdù de bìduān

malaise N **1** 烦躁不安的情绪 fánzào bù'ān de qíngxù **2** 心神不定 xīnshén búdìng

malaria N 疟疾 nüèjí

male I ADJ **1** 雄（性）的 xióng (xìng) de **2** 男性的 nánxìng de II N 雄性动物 xióngxìng dòngwù, 男人 nánren

male chauvinist 大男子主义 dànánzǐ zhǔyì

malevolent ADJ 恶意的 èyì de

malformation N 畸形（的器官）jīxíng (de qìguān)

malfunction I N 故障 gùzhàng, 失灵 shīlíng II V 不能正常运转 bùnéng zhèngcháng yùnzhuǎn

malicious ADJ 恶意的 èyì de, 恶毒的 èdú de

malign I V 诽谤 fěibàng, 中伤 zhòngshāng II ADJ 有害的 yǒuhài de

malignant ADJ **1** 恶性的 èxìng de

a malignant tumor 恶性肿瘤 èxìng zhǒngliú

2 恶意的 èyì de, 邪恶的 xié'è de

mall N 购物中心 gòuwù zhōngxīn

malleable ADJ **1** 可锻造的 [+金属] kě duànzào de [+jīnshǔ] **2** 易受影响的 [+人] yì shòu yǐngxiǎng de [+rén]

mallet N **1** 木槌 mùchuí [M. WD 根 gēn] **2** 长柄球棍 chángbǐng qiúgùn

malnourished ADJ 营养不良的 yíngyǎng bùliáng de

malnutrition N 营养不良 yíngyǎng bùliáng

malpractice N 玩忽职守 wánhū zhíshǒu

malt N **1** 麦芽 màiyá **2** 麦乳精（饮料）màirǔjīng (yǐnliào)

mama N 妈妈 māma

mammal N 哺乳动物 bǔrǔ dòngwù

mammogram N 乳房X光照片 rǔfáng X guāng zhàopiàn

mammoth ADJ 巨大的 jùdà de

man I N (PL **men**) **1** 男人 nánren, 男子

nánzǐ **2** 人 rén, 人类 rénlèi II V 使用 shǐyòng, 操纵 cāozòng

manacle N 镣铐 liàokào, 手铐 shǒukào, 脚镣 jiǎoliáo

manage v I **1** 设法 shèfǎ, 做成 zuòchéng **2** 经营 jīngyíng **3** 管理 guǎnlǐ

management N **1** 管理 guǎnlǐ, 经营 jīngyíng

database management 数据库管理 shùjùkù guǎnlǐ

system management 系统管理 xìtǒng guǎnlǐ

2 管理人员 guǎnlǐ rényuán, 资方 zīfāng

manager N 经理 jīnglǐ

Mandarin N（中国）普通话 (Zhōngguó) Pǔtōnghuà, 国语 guóyǔ, 华语 Huáyǔ

mandate I N **1** 授权 shòuquán **2** 托管权 tuōguǎnquán, 受托管的国家 shòutuōguǎn de guójiā **3** 训令 xùnlìng II V **1** 指示 zhǐshì, 指令 zhǐlìng **2** 授权 shòuquán, 委任 wěirèn

mandatory ADJ 法定的 fǎdìng de, 强制性的 qiángzhìxìng de

mane N 鬃毛 zōngmáo

maneuver I N **1** 熟练的动作 shúliàn de dòngzuò **2** 花招 huāzhāo, 巧计 qiǎojì II V 熟练地操作 shúliàn de cāozuò, 巧妙地移动 qiǎomiào de yídòng

room to maneuver 回旋的余地 huíxuán de yúdì

joint maneuvers 联合军事演习 liánhé jūnshì yǎnxí

manger N（牲畜）食槽 (shēngchù) shícáo

mangle v **1** 伤害 shānghài **2** 弄糟 nòngzāo, 糟蹋 zāota

mango N 芒果（树）mángguǒ (shù)

mangrove N 红树 hóngshù [M. WD 棵 kē]

manhandle v 粗暴地推 [+人] cūbào de tuī [+rén], 粗暴地对待 cūbào de duìdài

manhole N 检修孔 jiǎnxiūkǒng, 进入孔 jìnrénkǒng

manhood N **1** 男子气概 nánzǐ qìgài **2**（男子）成年 (nánzǐ) chéngnián

manhunt N 搜捕 sōubǔ, 追捕 zhuībǔ

mania N **1** 狂热 kuángrè **2** 躁狂症 zàokuángzhèng

maniac N 疯子 fēngzi, 迷 mí

computer maniac 电脑迷 diànnǎomí, 电脑发烧友 diànnǎo fāshāoyǒu

manic ADJ 焦躁的 jiāozào de, 十分激动的 shífēn jīdòng de

manicure N, V 修指甲 xiū zhǐjia

manifest I V 表现 biǎoxiàn, 表露 biǎolù II ADJ 明显的 míngxiǎn de, 显著的 xiǎnzhe de

manifestation N 明显迹象 míngxiǎn jìxiàng

manifold I ADJ 多方面的 duōfāngmiàn de, 各种各样的 gèzhǒng gèyàng de II N（发动机的）歧管（fādòngjī de）qíguǎn

manipulate V 1 操纵 cāozòng, 影响 yǐngxiǎng 2 处理 [+国家] chǔlǐ [+guójiā]

manipulative ADJ 1 善于操纵他人的 shànyú cāozòng tārén de 2 推拿正骨法的 tuīná zhènggǔfǎ de

mankind N 人类 rénlèi

manly ADJ 有男子汉气概的 yǒu nánzǐhàn qìgài de, 阳刚气的 yánggāngqì de

man-made ADJ 人造的 rénzào de, 人工的 réngōng de

mannequin, manikin N 人体模型 réntǐ móxíng, 橱窗模特儿 chúchuāng mótèr

manner N 1 方式 fāngshì, 方法 fāngfǎ 2 态度 tàidu, 仪态 yítài

mannerism N（言谈举止的）习惯性动作（yántán jǔzhǐ de）xíguànxìng dòngzuò, 习性 xíxìng

manners N 礼貌 lǐmào

manor N 庄园大宅 zhuāngyuán dàzhái

manpower N 劳动力 láodònglì, 人力 rénlì

mansion N 大宅 dàzhái, 大厦 dàshà

manslaughter N 过失杀人 guòshī shārén

mantel, mantelpiece N 壁炉架 bìlújià

mantle N 1 披风 pīfēng, 斗篷 dǒupéng
to inherit sb's mantle 继承某人的衣钵 jìchéng mǒurén de yībō
2 一层 yìcéng
a mantle of snow 一层积雪 yìcéng jīxuě

mantra N 1 一再重复的名言 yízài chóngfù de míngyán 2 祷文 dǎowén

manual I ADJ 体力的 tǐlì de, 手工的 shǒugōng de II N 使用说明 shǐyòng shuōmíng, 使用手册 shǐyòng shǒucè

manual labor 体力劳动 tǐlì láodòng, 体力活 tǐlìhuó

manufacture I V 制造 zhìzào II N 1 制造 zhìzào 2 制造品 zhìzàopǐn, 产品 chǎnpǐn
manufacturing industry 制造业 zhìzàoyè

manufacturing N 制造业 zhìzàoyè

manure N 粪肥 fènféi

manuscript N 手稿 shǒugǎo, 原稿 yuángǎo

many ADJ 很多 hěn duō, 许多 xǔduō

map I N 地图 dìtú II V 1 绘制地图 huìzhì dìtú 2 策划 cèhuà, 筹划 chóuhuà

maple N 枫树 fēngshù [M. WD 棵 kē]

mar V 损坏 sǔnhuài, 把…弄脏 bǎ… nòngzāng

marathon N 马拉松赛跑 mǎlāsōng sàipǎo

marauding ADJ 侵扰的 qīnrǎo de, 四处抢杀的 sìchù qiǎng shā de

marble N 1 大理石 dàlǐshí 2 弹子 dànzi, 玻璃弹子 bōli dànzi
game of marbles 弹子游戏 dànzi yóuxì

March N 三月 sānyuè

march I V 齐步行进 qíbù xíngjìn, 行军 xíngjūn
marching band 军乐队 jūnyuèduì
II N 1 [军队+] 行军 [jūn duì+] xíngjūn 2 示威游行 shìwēi yóuxíng 3 进行曲 jìnxíngqǔ

mare N 母马 mǔ mǎ [M. WD 匹 pǐ]

margarine N 人造黄油 rénzào huángyóu

margin N 1 页边空白的 yèbiān kòngbái de 2 差数 chāshù
by a wide margin 以很大的差数 yǐ hěn dà de chāshù
3 利润 lìrùn
pre-tax margin 税前利润 shuì qián lìrùn
4 边缘 biānyuán
to live on the margins of society 生活在社会边缘 shēnghuó zài shèhuì biānyuán

marginal ADJ 1 极小的 jíxiǎo de, 可以忽略不计的 kěyǐ hūlüè bújì de 2 边缘的 biānyuán de

marijuana N 大麻（烟）dàmá（yān）

marina N 1 小港湾 xiǎo gǎngwān 2 游艇停泊港 yóutǐng tíngbógǎng

marinade N 混合调味酱 hùnhé tiáowèijiāng

marinate V 把 [+鱼] 浸在调味酱里 bǎ [+yú] jìn zài tiáowèijiàng lǐ

marine ADJ 1 海洋的 hǎiyáng de 2 海运的 hǎiyùn de

marital ADJ 婚姻的 hūnyīn de
marital status 婚姻状况 hūnyīn zhuàngkuàng

maritime ADJ 海事的 hǎishì de, 船舶的 chuánbó de

mark I N 1 痕迹 hénjì, 污斑 wūbān 2 记号 jìhào
punctuation mark 标点符号 biāodiǎn fúhào
3（学生的）分数 (xuésheng de) fēnshù
II V 1 做记号 zuò jìhào, 写着 xiězhe
to mark down 降低价格 jiàngdī jiàgé
to mark up 提高价格 tígāo jiàgé
2 纪念 jìniàn

markdown N 减价 jiǎnjià

marker N 1 标志 biāozhì 2 记号笔 jìhàobǐ

market I N 市场 shìchǎng
market price 市场价格 shìchǎng jiàgé, 时价 shíjià
market share 市场占有率 shìchǎng zhànyǒulǜ
buyer's market 买方市场 mǎifāng shìchǎng
seller's market 卖方市场 màifāng shìchǎng
II V 推销 tuīxiāo

marketable ADJ 有销路的 yǒu xiāolù de, 符合市场需求的 fúhé shìchǎng xūqiú de

marketing N 营销 yíngxiāo, 推销 tuīxiāo

marketplace N 1 商业销售活动 shāngyè xiāoshòu huódòng 2（露天）市场 (lùtiān) shìchǎng

marking N 1 识别标志 shíbié biāozhì 2 斑点 bāndiǎn

marksman N 神枪手 shénqiāngshǒu

markup N 提价幅度 tíjià fúdù

marmalade N 柑橘果酱 gānjú guǒjiàng

maroon V 将…遗弃在荒野 jiāng…yíqì zài huāngyě

marquee N 大帐篷 dà zhàngpéng

marriage N 婚姻 hūnyīn

marrow N 1 骨髓 gǔsuǐ
bone marrow transplant 骨髓移植 gǔsuǐ yízhí
2 最深处 zuì shēnchù, 骨子里 gǔzilǐ
to know sb to the marrow 透彻地了解某人 tòuchè de liǎojiě mǒurén

marry V 1 结婚 jiéhūn 2 为…主持婚礼 wéi…zhǔchí hūnlǐ

Mars N 火星 huǒxīng

marsh N 沼泽地 zhǎozédì

marshal N 1（美国）联邦政府执法官 (Měiguó) liánbāng zhèngfǔ zhífǎguān 2（美国）消防局长 (Měiguó) xiāofáng júzhǎng 3（游行）总指挥 (yóuxíng) zǒngzhǐhuī 4（军队）元帅 (jūnduì) yuánshuài
grand marshal 大司仪 dà sīyí

marshmallow N 棉花糖 miánhuātáng

marsupial N 有袋动物 yǒudài dòngwù

martial ADJ 军事的 jūnshì de, 打斗的 dǎdòu de
martial arts 武术 wǔshù, 功夫 gōngfu
martial law 军事管制 jūnshì guǎnzhì, 戒严 jièyán

martyr I N 烈士 lièshì, 殉道者 xùndàozhě II ADJ (be martyred) 成为烈士 chéngwéi lièshì, 成为殉道者 chéngwéi xùndàozhě

martyrdom N 殉道 xùndào

marvel I N 奇迹 qíjì II V 对…感到惊讶 duì…gǎndào jīngyà, 惊叹 jīngtàn

marvelous ADJ 绝妙的 juémiào de, 极好的 jí hǎo de

Marxism N 马克思主义 Mǎkèsī zhǔyì

mascot N 吉祥物 jíxiángwù

masculine ADJ 男性的 nánxìng de, 有男性特征的 yǒu nánxìng tèzhēngde

masculinity N 男性特征 nánxìng tèzhēng, 阳刚气 yánggāngqì

mash I V 把…捣烂 bǎ…dǎolàn
mashed patato 土豆泥 tǔdòuní
II N 糊状物 húzhuàngwù

mask I N 1 面具 miànjù, 假面具 jiǎ miànjù 2 面罩 miànzhào, 口罩 kǒuzhào II V 掩饰 yǎnshì, 掩盖 yǎngài

masked ADJ 蒙面的 méngmiàn de

mason N 砖石匠 zhuānwǎjiàng

masquerade I N 1 假面舞会 jiǎmiàn

437

wǔhuì 2 伪装 wěizhuāng II v 伪装
wěizhuāng, 假装 jiǎzhuāng

mass I N 1 大量 dàliàng, 大批 dàpī
the masses 群众 qúnzhòng
2 质量 zhìliàng II ADJ 大量的 dàliàng de
mass media 大众传播媒介 dàzhòng
chuánbō méijiè
mass murderer 谋杀多人的凶手
móushā duō rén de xiōngshǒu
mass production 大量生产 dàliàng
shēngchǎn, 大规模生产 dàguīmó
shēngchǎn
III v 集中 jízhōng

Mass N （天主教）弥撒 (Tiānzhǔjiào)
mísa, 弥撒曲 mísaqǔ

massacre I N 大屠杀 dà túshā II v 屠
杀 túshā

massage I N 按摩 ànmó, 推拿 tuīná
massage parlor 按摩院 ànmóyuàn, 妓
院 jìyuàn
II v 给…按摩 / 推拿 gěi…ànmó/tuīná

massive ADJ 1 又大又重的 [+大门] yòu
dà yòu zhòng de [+dàmén], 厚重的
hòuzhòng de 2 巨大的 jùdà de

mass-produce v 大批量生产 dà pīliàng
shēngchǎn

mast N 桅杆 wéigān [M. WD 根 gēn]

master I N 1 主人 zhǔrén
master of ceremonies 司仪 sīyí
2 大师 dàshī 3 硕士 shuòshì
master's degree, master's 硕士学位
shuòshì xuéwèi
II v 精通 jīngtōng III ADJ 1 技艺精湛的
jìyì jīngzhàn de
master chef 技艺精湛的大厨师 jìyì
jīngzhàn de dàchúshī
2 原始的 yuánshǐ de, 最重要的 zuì
zhòngyào de
master key 万能钥匙 wànnéng yàoshi

mastermind I N 出谋划策者 chūmóu
huàcè zhě, 幕后策划者 mùhòu cèhuà
zhě II v 出谋划策 chūmóu huàcè

masterpiece N 杰作 jiézuò, 名作 míng-
zuò [M. WD 部 bù/幅 fú]

mastery N 1 精通 jīngtōng, 掌握 zhǎngwò
2 控制（权）kòngzhì (quán)

masturbate v 手淫 shǒuyín, 自慰 zìwèi

mat N 席子 xízi [M. WD 张 zhāng], 垫子
diànzi [M. WD 块 kuài]

matador N 斗牛士 dòuniúshì

match¹ I N 1 火柴 huǒchái

match² I N 1 比赛 bǐsài 2 相配的东西
xiāngpèi de dōngxi
a perfect match 完全相配的人 wánquán xiāngpèi de rén, 天作之合 tiānzuò
zhī hé
3 对手 duìshǒu
to be no match for sb 不是某人的对手
bú shì mǒurén de duìshǒu
II v 相配 xiāngpèi

matchbox N 火柴盒 huǒcháihé

matching ADJ 相配的 xiāngpèi de

matchless ADJ 无与伦比的 wú yǔ lúnbǐ
de, 举世无双的 jǔshì wúshuāng de

match-maker N 媒人 méirén

mate I N 1 伙伴 huǒbàn 2 （动物）交配对
象 (dòngwù) jiāopèi duìxiàng II v
（动物）交配 (dòngwù) jiāopèi

material I N 1 布料 bùliào, 料子 liàozi 2 材
料 cáiliào
raw materials 原材料 yuáncáiliào
II ADJ 1 物质上的 wùzhì shàng de
material comforts 物质享受 wùzhì
xiǎngshòu
2 （法律上）至关重要的 (fǎlǜshàng)
zhìguān zhòngyào de
material evidence 重要证据 zhòngyào
zhèngjù

materialistic ADJ 实利主义的 shílì zhǔyì
de

maternal ADJ 1 母亲的 mǔqin de, 母
性的 mǔxìng de 2 母亲方面的 mǔqin
fāngmiàn de
maternal grandmother 外祖母
wàizǔmǔ

maternity ADJ 孕妇的 yùnfù de
maternity leave 产假 chǎnjià
maternity ward 产科病房 chǎnkē
bìngfáng

math N 数学 shùxué

mathematician N 数学家 shùxuéjiā

mathematics N 数学 shùxué

matinee N 下午场 xiàwǔcháng, 日间演出
rìjiān yǎnchū

matriarch N 女家长 nǚ jiāzhǎng, 女族长 nǚ zúzhǎng [M. WD 位 wèi]

matriarchal ADJ 女子统治的 nǚzǐ tǒngzhì de, 母系的 mǔxì de
a matriarchal society 母系社会 mǔxì shèhuì

matriculation N 注册入学 zhùcè rùxué

matrimony N 婚姻 hūnyīn

matron N 1 中年已婚的妇女 zhōngnián yǐhūn de fùnǚ 2 女总管 nǚ zǒngguǎn

matronly ADJ 中年妇女的 zhōngnián fùnǚ de, 发福的 fāfú de

matte, matt ADJ 无光泽的 wú guāngzé de

matted ADJ 缠结在一起的 chánjié zài yìqǐ de

matter I N 1 事情 shìqíng, 事件 shìjiàn 2 问题 wèntí 3 情况 qíngkuàng 4 物质 wùzhí II v 重要 zhòngyào, 有关系 yǒu guānxi
It doesn't matter. 没有关系。Méiyǒu guānxi.

matter-of-fact ADJ 就事论事的 jiùshì lùnshì de, 不动感情的 búdòng gǎnqíng de

mattress N 床垫 chuángdiàn

mature I ADJ 1 成熟的 chéngshú de 2 到期的 [+存款] dàoqī de [+cúnkuǎn] II v 1 （人）成熟 (biàn de) chéngshú 2 （存款+）到期 [cúnkuǎn+] dàoqī

maturity N 1 成熟 chéngshú 2 到期 dàoqī

maudlin ADJ 1 哭哭啼啼的 [+人] kūkū títí de [+rén] 2 伤感而可笑的 [+歌曲] shānggǎn ér kěxiào de [+gēqǔ]

maul v 撕破皮肉 sīpò pí'ròu, 伤害 shānghài

mausoleum N 陵墓 língmù

mauve N, ADJ 淡紫色（的）dànzǐsè (de)

maverick N 独立思考的人 dúlì sīkǎo de rén, 自行其事的人 zìxíng qí shì de rén

max I N 最大限度 zuì dà xiàndù II v (to max out) 用得精光 yòng dé jīngguāng

maxim N 格言 géyán

maximize v 把…增加到最大限度 bǎ… zēngjiā dào zuì dà xiàndù

maximum N 1 最大量 zuì dà liáng 2 ADJ 最大的 zuì dà de, 最多的 zuì duō de

May N 五月 wǔyuè

May [NEG **may not**] MODAL V (PT **might**) 1 可能 kěnéng 2 可以 kěyǐ

maybe ADV 或许 huòxǔ, 大概 dàgài

May Day N (五一) 劳动节 (Wǔyī) Láodòngjié

mayonnaise N 蛋黄酱 dànhuángjiàng

mayor N 市长 shìzhǎng [M. WD 位 wèi]

maze N 迷宫 mígōng

MC (= Master of Ceremonies) ABBREV 司仪 sīyí

M.D. (= Doctor of Medicine) ABBREV 医学博士 yīxué bóshì

me PRON 我 wǒ

meadow N 草地 cǎodì, 牧场 mùchǎng

meager ADJ 极少的 jí shǎo de, 微薄的 wēibó de

meal N 1 （一顿）饭 (yí dùn) fàn 2 （谷物的）粗磨粉 (gǔwù de) cū mòfěn

mealtime N 吃饭时间 chīfàn shíjiān, 开饭时间 kāifàn shíjiān

mealy-mouthed ADJ （说话）转弯抹角的 (shuōhuà) zhuǎnwān mòjiǎo de

mean¹ (PT & PP **meant**) v 1 意思是 yìsi shì 2 有意 yǒuyì 3 意味着 yìwèizhe

mean² ADJ 1 卑鄙的 bēibǐ de 2 刻薄的 kèbó de, 小气的 xiǎoqi de
a no mean player 一个出色的运动员 yí ge chūsè de yùndòngyuán

mean³ N (the mean) 平均数 píngjūnshù

meander v 1 [河水+] 弯弯曲曲地流 [héshuǐ+] wānwān qūqū de liú 2 [人+] 荡来荡去 [rén+] dànglái dàngqù 3 [谈话+] 东拉西扯 [tánhuà+] dōnglā xīchě

meaning N 1 意思 yìsi 2 意义 yìyì

meaningful ADJ 有意义的 yǒu yìyì de, 有意思的 yǒu yìsi de

meaningless ADJ 毫无意义的 háowú yìyì de, 没有价值的 méiyǒu jiàzhí de

means N 1 手段 shǒuduàn, 方法 fāngfǎ
by all means 当然 dāngrán
by no means 一点都不 yìdiǎn dōu bù
2 收入 shōurù, 财产 cáichǎn
to live beyond one's means 花费超过收入 huāfèi chāoguò shōurù, 透支 tòuzhī

meant See **mean¹**

meantime N (in the meantime) 与此同时 yǔ cǐ tóngshí

meanwhile ADV 同时 tóngshí

measles N 麻疹 mázhěn

German measles 风疹 fēngzhěn

measly ADJ 少得可怜的 shǎo dé kělián de

measure I N 1 措施 cuòshī

half measures（效果不佳的）折中办法 (xiàoguǒ bùjiā de) zhézhōng bànfǎ, 将就措施 jiāngjiu cuòshī

2 量具 liángjù, 量器 liáng qì

tape measure（钢）卷尺 (gāng) juǎnchǐ, 软尺 ruǎnchǐ

in large/some measure 在很大／某种程度上 zài hěn dà/mǒuzhǒng chéngdù shàng

II V 量 liáng, 测量 cèliáng

measurement N 1 度量 dùliàng 2 长度 chángdù, 宽度 kuāndù

the metric system of measurement 公制度量衡 gōngzhì dùliànghéng

meat N（食用的）肉 (shíyòng de) ròu

meatball N 肉丸 ròu wán

meaty ADJ 1 肉很多的 ròu hěn duō de 2 重大的 zhòngdà de

Mecca N 1（沙特阿拉伯）麦加 (Shādì Ālābó) Màijiā 2 朝圣地 cháoshèngdì, 众人向往的地方 zhòngrén xiàngwǎng de difang

mechanic N 汽车修理工 qìchē xiūlǐgōng, 机械工 jīxiè gōng

mechanical ADJ 1 机械（方面）的 jīxiè (fāngmiàn) de, 机械操纵的 jīxiè cāozòng de

mechanical failure 机械故障 jīxiè gùzhàng

2 机械的 [+回答] jīxiè de [+huídá], 不加思索的 bù jiā sīsuǒ de

mechanism N 1 机械装置 jīxiè zhuāngzhì 2 机制 jīzhì, 机构 jīgòu

survival mechanism 求生手段 qiúshēng shǒuduàn

medal N 奖牌 jiǎngpái, 奖章 jiǎngzhāng

gold medal 金牌 jīnpái

medalist N 奖牌获得者 jiǎngpái huòdézhě

medallion N 圆形挂饰 yuánxíng guàshì

meddle V 干预 gānyù, 管闲事 guǎn xiánshì

media N（新闻）媒体 (xīnwén) méitǐ

mass media 大众媒体 dàzhòng méitǐ

median I N 1（道路）中间安全带 (dàolù) zhōngjiān ānquándài 2（统计）中位数 (tǒngjì) zhōngwèishù II ADJ 中间的 zhōngjiān de, 中位的 zhōngwèi de

the median price 中位价 zhōngwèijià

mediate V 调解 tiáojiě, 调停 tiáotíng

mediation N 调解 tiáojiě, 调停 tiáotíng

mediator N 调解员 tiáojiě yuán

medical ADJ 1 医学的 yīxué de, 医疗的 yīliáo de

medical certificate 疾病证明 jíbìng zhèngmíng

medical school 医学院 yīxuéyuàn

medical checkup 体格检查 tǐgé jiǎnchá

2 内科的 nèikē de

medication N 药物 yàowù

medicine N 1 药 yào, 医药 yīyào

Good medicine tastes bitter. 良药苦口。Liángyào kǔkǒu。

2 医学 yīxué, 医药 yīyào

medieval ADJ 中世纪的 Zhōngshìjì de

mediocre ADJ 平庸的 píngyōng de, 一般的 yìbān de

meditate V 沉思 chénsī, 打坐 dǎzuò

meditation N 沉思 chénsī, 打坐 dǎzuò

Mediterranean ADJ 地中海的 Dìzhōnghǎi de

the Mediterranean 地中海 Dìzhōnghǎi

medium I ADJ 中等的 zhōngděng de, 中号的 zhōnghào de

medium rare 半熟的 bàn shóu de

II N 1 传播媒介 chuánbō méijiè 2 方法 fāngfǎ, 手段 shǒuduàn

medium-size(d) ADJ 中号的 zhōnghào de

medley N 1（音乐）组合曲 (yīnyuè) zǔhéqǔ, 组曲 zǔqǔ 2（游泳）混合接力赛 (yóuyǒng) hùnhé jiēlìsài 3（食品）大拼盘 (shípǐn) dà pīnpán

meek ADJ 温顺的 wēnshùn de

meet I V (PT & PP **met**) 1 会见 huìjiàn, 见面 jiànmiàn 2 接 jiē, 迎接 yíngjiē 3 满足 [+需要] mǎnzú [+xūyào], 符合 [+要求] fúhé [+yāoqiú] II N（运动）会 (yùndòng) huì

meeting N 会议, 会议 huìyì
meeting house 聚会所 jùhuìsuǒ

mega ADJ 百万倍 bǎiwànbèi

megabyte N（计算机）兆字节 (jìsuànjī) zhàozìjié

megalomania N 妄自尊大 wàngzì zūn dà

megaphone N 喇叭筒 lǎbatǒng

megastore N 超大型商店 chāo dàxíng shāngdiàn

megaton N 百万吨（级）bǎiwàndūn (jí)

melancholy I ADJ 忧郁的 yōuyù de II N 忧郁症 yōuyùzhèng

melee N 混乱局面 hùnluàn júmiàn

mellow I ADJ 1 温和平静的 [+心情] wēnhé píngjìng de [+xīnqíng] 2 友善随和的 [+人] yǒushàn suíhe de [+rén] 3 圆润悦耳的 [+声音] yuánrùn yuè'ěr de [+shēngyīn] 4 醇和的 [+酒] chúnhé de [+jiǔ] II v 1 使…变得温和平静 shǐ…biàn de wēnhé píngjìng 2 使 [+颜色] 变得柔和 shǐ [+yánsè] biàn de róuhe

melodious ADJ 悦耳动听的 yuè'ěr dòngtīng de

melodrama N 1 情节剧 qíngjiéjù [M. WD 出 chū/部 bù] 2 戏剧化的局面 xìjùhuà de júmiàn

melody N 1 主旋律 zhǔxuánlǜ, 主调 zhǔdiào 2 曲调 qǔdiào

melon N 瓜 guā

melt v 融化 rónghuà

meltdown N 崩溃 bēngkuì, 彻底瘫痪 chèdǐ tānhuàn
financial meltdown 金融崩溃 jīnróng bēngkuì

melting point N 熔点 róngdiǎn

melting pot N（民族）大熔炉 (mínzú) dàrónglú

member N 成员 chéngyuán, 会员 huìyuán
life member 终身会员 zhōngshēn huìyuán

membership N 1 会员资格 huìyuán zīgé 2 全体会员 quántǐ huìyuán
membership fee 会员费 huìyuánfèi

membrane N（薄）膜 (bó) mó, 膜状物 mózhuàngwù

memento N 纪念品 jìniànpǐn

memo, memorandum N 公务便条 gōngwù biàntiáo, 备忘录 bèiwànglù

memoirs N 回忆录 huíyìlù [M. WD 本 běn]

memorabilia N（与某人或某事物有关的）收藏纪念品 (yǔ mǒurén huò mǒu shìwù yǒuguān de) shōucáng jìniànpǐn

memorable ADJ 值得纪念的 zhíde jìniàn de, 难忘的 nánwàng de

memorial I ADJ 悼念的 dàoniàn de, 纪念（死者）的 jìniàn (sǐzhě) de
memorial service 追悼仪式 zhuīdào yíshì
II N 纪念碑 jìniànbēi
Memorial Day 阵亡将士纪念日 zhèn-wáng jiàngshì jìniànrì

memorize v 记住 jìzhu

memory N 记忆力 jìyìlì 2 记忆 jìyì
in memory of 纪念 jìniàn

men See **man**

menace N 1 威胁 wēixié, 恫吓 dònghè 2 危险人物 wēixiǎn rénwù

menagerie N 1 一批野生动物 yīpī yěshēng dòngwù 2 一帮形形色色的人 yìbāng xíngxíng sèsè de rén

mend v 1 缝补 féngbǔ, 修补 xiūbǔ
to mend one's ways 改过自新 gǎiguò zìxīn
to mend fences 恢复良好关系 huīfù liánghǎo guānxi, 消释前嫌 xiāoshì qiánxián
2 [骨头+] 愈合 [gǔtou+] yùhé

menial ADJ 不需要技能的 bù xūyào jìnéng de, 枯燥的 kūzào de
a menial job 低档工作 dīdàng gōngzuò, 粗活 cūhuó

menopause N（女子）更年期 (nǚzǐ) gēngniánqī, 绝经 juéjīng

menstrual ADJ 月经的 yuèjīng de
menstrual period 月经期 yuèjīng qī

menstruate v [妇女+] 来月经 [fùnǚ+] lái yuèjīng, 行经 xíngjīng

mental ADJ 1 精神的 jīngshén de, 智力的 zhìlì de 2 精神病的 jīngshénbìng de
mental health 精神医学 jīngshén yīxué
mental hospital 精神病院 jīngshén bìngyuàn

mentality N 心态 xīntài

mentally handicapped ADJ 有智力缺陷的 yǒu zhìlì quēxiàn de, 弱智的 ruòzhì de

mention I v 提到 tídào II N 提及 tíjí

mentor N 导师 dǎoshī [M. WD 位 wèi]

menu N 菜单 càidān, 菜谱 càipǔ

meow N 猫叫声 māo jiàoshēng

mercenary I N 雇佣兵 gùyōngbīng II ADJ 只是为钱的 zhǐ shì wéi qián de, 唯利是图的 wéi lì shì tú de

merchandise N 商品 shāngpǐn, 货物 huòwù

merchant I N 商人 shāngrén, 批发商 pīfāshāng II ADJ 商业的 shāngyè de

mercifully ADV 幸运地 xìngyùn de, 幸亏 xìngkuī

mercury (Hg) N 汞 gǒng, 水银 shuǐyín

mercy N 仁慈 réncí, 宽恕 kuānshù
   at the mercy of sb 听任某人摆布 tīngrèn mǒurén bǎibù
   a mercy mission 救援任务 jiùyuán rènwu

mercy-killing N 安乐死 ānlèsǐ

mere ADJ 只不过 zhǐbúguò, 仅仅 jǐnjǐn

merely ADV 仅仅 jǐnjǐn, 只不过 zhǐbúguò

merge v 1 合并 hébìng, 融合 rónghé 2 [车辆+] 会合 [chēliàng+] huìhé

merger N [公司+] 合并 [gōngsī+] hébìng

merit I N 优点 yōudiǎn, 长处 chángchù II v 值得 zhíde, 应得 yīngdé

meritocracy N 精英管理／统治 jīngyīng guǎnlǐ/tǒngzhì

mermaid N 美人鱼 měirényú

merry ADJ 快乐的 kuàilè de
   Merry Christmas! 圣诞快乐！Shèngdàn kuàilè!

merry-go-round N 旋转木马 xuánzhuǎn mùmǎ

mesh I N 1 网状物 wǎngzhuàng wù 2 混合物 hùnhéwù II v 把…相配 bǎ… xiāngpèi

mesmerize v 迷住 mízhù

mess¹ I N 1 脏乱的状态 zāngluàn de zhuàngtài 2 一团糟 yì tuán zāo II v 1 (to mess around) 鬼混 guǐhùn 2 (to mess up) 弄槽 nòngzāo

mess² N 军人食堂 jūnrén shítáng
   mess hall 军人食堂 jūnrén shítáng

message N 1 信息 xìnxī, 口信 kǒuxìn, 短信 duǎnxìn
   to get the message 得到了信息 dédaole xìnxī, 明白了意思 míngbaile yìsi 2 启示 qǐshì, 主题 zhǔtí

messenger N 信使 xìnshǐ, 传递信息的人 chuándì xìnxī de rén

messiah N 1 救世主 Jiùshìzhǔ, 救星 jiùxīng 2 （基督教）耶稣基督 (Jīdūjiào) Yēsū Jīdū 3 （犹太教）弥赛亚 (Yóutàijiào) Mísàiyà

Messrs. See **Mr.**

messy ADJ 1 脏乱 zāngluàn 2 极其复杂麻烦 jíqí fùzá máfan

met See **meet**

metabolism N 新陈代谢 xīn chén dài xiè

metal N 1 金属 jīnshǔ
   metal detector 金属探测器 jīnshǔ tàncèqì
   precious metal 贵金属 guìjīnshǔ 2 重金属摇滚乐 zhòngjīnshǔ yáogǔnyuè

metallic ADJ 金属（般）的 jīnshǔ (bān) de

metamorphosis N （彻底的）变化 (chèdǐ de) biànhuà

metaphor N 比喻 bǐyù, 隐喻 yǐnyù

mete v (to mete out) 给予 [+惩罚] jǐyǔ [+chéngfá]

meteor N 流星 liúxīng [M. WD 颗 kē]

meteoric ADJ 1 流星（似）的 liúxīng (sì) de 2 突发而迅速的 tūfā ér xùnsù de

meteorology N 气象学 qìxiàngxué

meter N 1 公尺 gōngchǐ, 米 mǐ 2 仪表 yíbiǎo
   electricity meter 电表 diànbiǎo
   gas meter 煤气表 méiqìbiǎo
   parking meter 停车计时表 tíngchē jìshíbiǎo
   water meter 水表 shuǐbiǎo

methane N 甲烷 jiǎwán, 沼气 zhǎoqì

method N 1 方法 fāngfǎ 2 条理 tiáolǐ, 秩序 zhìxù

methodical ADJ 有条理的 yǒu tiáolǐ de, 井井有条的 jǐngjǐng yǒutiáo de

Methodist N 遁道宗信徒 dùndàozōng xìntú

meticulous ADJ 注意细节的 zhùyì xìjié de, 十分谨慎的 shífēn jǐnshèn de

metric ADJ 公制的 gōngzhì de, 十进制的 shíjìnzhì de
　metric system 公制 gōngzhì, 十进制 shíjìnzhì

metro N 地下铁路系统 dìxià tiělù xìtǒng

metropolis N 大城市 dà chéngshì, 大都会 dà dūhuì

metropolitan ADJ 大城市的 dà chéngshì de, 大都会的 dà dūhuì de

mettle N 勇气 yǒngqì, 毅力 yìlì

Mexican I ADJ 墨西哥的 Mòxīgēde
　II N 1 墨西哥语 Mòxīgēyǔ 2 墨西哥人 Mòxīgērén

mezzanine N 1 夹层楼 jiācénglóu, 夹楼 jiālóu 2 (剧院) 底层楼厅的前面几排 (jùyuàn) dǐcéng lóu tīng de qiánmian jǐ pái

mice See **mouse**

microbe N 微生物 wēishēngwù

microbiology N 微生物学 wēishēngwùxué

microchip N 微晶片 wēijīngpiàn, 微芯片 wēixìnpiàn [M. WD 块 kuài]

microcomputer N 微型电脑 wēixíng diànnǎo, 微机 wēijī

microfiche N 微缩胶片 wēisuō jiāopiàn

microfilm N 微缩胶卷 wēisuō jiāojuǎn

microorganism N 微生物 wēishēngwù

microphone (ABBREV **mike**) N 扩音器 kuòyīnqì, 麦克风 màikèfēng

microprocessor N (计算机) 微处理器 (jìsuànjī) wēichǔlǐqì

microscopic ADJ 微小的 wēixiǎo de, 显微镜的 xiǎnwēijìng de

midair N 空中 kōngzhōng

midday N 中午 zhōngwǔ, 午间 wǔjiān

middle I N 中间 zhōngjiān, 中部 zhōngbù
　II ADJ 中间的 zhōngjiān de
　Middle Ages 中世纪 (年代) Zhōngshìjì (niándài)
　Middle America ① (美国) 中部地区 (Měiguó) zhōngbù dìqū ② 美国中产阶级 Měiguó zhōngchǎnjiējí
　middle class 中产阶级 zhōngchǎn jiējí
　Middle East 中东 (地区) Zhōngdōng (dìqū)
　middle school (美国) 初级中学 (Měiguó) chūjí zhōngxué, 初中 chūzhōng

middle-aged N 中年 zhōngnián

middleman N 中间人 zhōngjiānrén, 中间商 zhōngjiānshāng

midget N 矮人 ǎirén, 矮子 ǎizi

midlife crisis N 中年危机 zhōngnián wēijī

midnight N 午夜 wǔyè, 半夜 bànyè

midriff N 腹部 fùbù

midst N (in the midst) 在…中间 zài... zhōngjiān

midterm N 1 期中考试 qīzhōng kǎoshì 2 (官员任职的) 中期 (guānyuán rènzhí de) zhōngqī

midway ADJ, ADV 中途 (的) zhōngtú (de)

midweek ADJ, ADV 在一周中 zài yìzhōu zhōng

midwife N 助产士 zhùchǎnshì, 接生员 jiēshēngyuán

miffed ADJ 有点恼火的 yǒudiǎn nǎohuǒ de

might[1] [NEG **might not**] MODAL V 1 可能 kěnéng, 或许 huòxǔ 2 可以 kěyǐ 3 不妨 bùfāng
　might as well 还是 háishi, 还不如 hái bùrú

might[2] N 威力 wēilì, 力量 lìliang
　Might is right. 强权即公理。 Qiángquán jí gōnglǐ.

mighty ADJ 1 极其强大的 jíqí qiángdà de 2 巨大的 jùdà de, 庞大的 pángdà de

migraine N 偏头痛 piāntóutòng

migrant N 1 (经济) 移民 (jīngjì) yímín 2 候鸟 hòuniǎo, 迁徙动物 qiānxǐ dòngwù

migratory ADJ 移居的 yíjū de, 迁都的 qiāndū de

mike See **microphone**

mild ADJ 1 温和的 wēnhé de, 轻微的 qīngwēi de 2 淡的 (味道) dàn de (wèidao)

mildew N 霉 (菌) méi (jùn)

mile N 英里 yīnglǐ

mileage N 1 行车里程 xíngchē lǐchéng 2 利益 lìyì, 好处 hǎochu

milestone N 里程碑 lǐchéngbēi [M. WD 块 kuài]

milieu N 生活环境 shēnghuó huánjìng
militant I ADJ 激进的 jījìn de II N 战斗人员 zhàndòurényuán
military I ADJ 军事的 jūnshì de II N 军队 jūnduì
milk I N 1 奶 nǎi 2 牛奶 niúnǎi
　　milkman 送牛奶的工人 sòng niúnǎi de gōngrén
　　milk shake 泡沫牛奶 pàomò niúnǎi, 奶昔 nǎixī
　　3 乳液 rǔyè II V 1 挤奶 jǐ'nǎi 2 榨取 zhàqǔ
milky ADJ 1 多奶的 duō nǎi de 2 乳白色的 rǔbáisè de
Milky Way N 银河 Yínhé
mill N 1（工）厂（gōng）chǎng 2 磨粉机 mòfěnjī
　　steel mill 钢铁厂 gāngtiěchǎng
　　II V 1 将 [+谷物] 磨碎 jiāng [+gǔwù] mósuì 2 (to mill around) 来回乱转 láihuí luàn zhuǎn
millennium N（一）千年（yì）qiānnián
millet N 小米 xiǎomǐ [M. WD 颗/粒 lì]
milligram N 毫克 háokè
milliliter N 毫升 háoshēng
millimeter N 毫米 háomǐ
millinery N 帽类 màolèi
million NUM 百万 bǎiwàn
　　millions 数百万的 shù bǎiwàn de, 很多的 hěn duō de
millionaire N 百万富翁 bǎiwàn fùwēng
mime I N 1 哑剧 yǎjù 2 做手势（来表达意思）zuò shǒushì (lái biǎodá yìsi) II V 演哑剧 yǎn yǎjù
mimic I V 模仿（他人）mófǎng (tārén) II N 滑稽模仿表演 gǔjī mófǎng biǎoyǎn
mince V 1 把 [+食物] 剁碎 bǎ [+shíwù] duòsuì 2 吞吞吐吐地说话 tūntūn tǔtǔ de shuōhuà
　　not to mince one's words 直截了当地说 zhíjié liǎodàng de shuō
mind I N 1 头脑 tóunǎo, 心智 xīnzhì 2 心思 xīnsi, 主意 zhǔyi
　　to change one's mind 改变主意 gǎibiàn zhǔyi
　　to make up one's mind 打定主意 dǎdìng zhǔyi, 决定 juédìng

　　II V 1 在意 zàiyì 2 注意 zhùyì, 留神 liúshén 3 照看 zhàokān, 管理 guǎnlǐ
mindful ADJ 留意的 liúyì de, 记住的 jìzhu de
mindless ADJ 1 不动脑子的 búdòng nǎozi de 2 没有脑子的 méiyǒu nǎozi de, 愚笨的 yúbèn de
mine[1] PRON 我的 wǒ de
mine[2] I N 1 矿 kuàng
　　coal mine 煤矿 méikuàng
　　gold mine 金矿 jīnkuàng
　　II V 开矿 kāikuàng, 采矿 cǎikuàng
minefield N 布雷区 bùléiqū
miner N 矿工 kuànggōng
mineral N 矿物质 kuàngwùzhì
　　mineral water 矿泉水 kuàngquánshuǐ
minesweeper N 扫雷艇 sǎoléitǐng
mingle V 混合 (shǐ...) hùnhé
mini ADJ 小型的 xiǎoxíng de
miniature I ADJ 微型的 wēixíng de
　　miniature golf 小型高尔夫球场 xiǎoxíng gāo'ěrfū qiúchǎng
　　II N 1 微型复制品 wēixíng fùzhìpǐn 2 袖珍画像 xiùzhēn huàxiàng
minimal ADJ 极小的 jí xiǎo de, 极少的 jí shǎo de
minimize V 把…降低到最小限度 bǎ... jiàngdī dào zuì xiǎo xiàndù
minimum I N 最小量 zuì xiǎo liáng, 最低限度 zuì dī xiàndù II ADJ 最小 zuì xiǎo, 最少 zuì shǎo
　　minimum wage 最低工资 zuì dī gōngzī
mining N 采矿（业）cǎikuàng (yè)
miniskirt N 超短裙 chāoduǎnqún
minister I N 1 部长 bùzhǎng 2 牧师 mùshi II V 1 当牧师 dāng mùshi 2 (to minister to) 帮助 bāngzhù
ministry N 1（政府）部 (zhèngfǔ) bù 2 牧师的职责 mùshì de zhízé
minivan N 小型客车 xiǎoxíng kèchē, 面包车 miànbāochē [M. WD 辆 liàng]
mink N 水貂（皮）shuǐdiāo (pí)
minor I ADJ 次要的 cìyào de, 不很重要的 bú hěn zhòngyào de II N 未成年人 wèi chéngniánrén III V 副修 fùxiū
minority N 少数 shǎoshù
minstrel N 歌手 gēshǒu

mint¹ I v 1 创造（新词）chuàngzào (xīncí) **2** 授予学位 shòuyǔ xuéwèi
a newly minted graduate 一位新获得学位的大学毕业生 yíwèi xīn huòdé xuéwèi de dàxué bìyèshēng
II N 铸币厂 zhùbìchǎng [M. WD 座 zuò]
to make a mint 赚一大笔钱 zhuàn yí dà bǐ qián
III ADJ (in mint condition) 崭新的 zhǎnxīn de

mint² N 薄荷 bòhe, 薄荷糖 bòhetáng

minus I v PREP 1 减去 jiǎnqù **2** 少了 shǎole, 缺少 quēshǎo **II N 1** 减号 jiǎnhào, 负号 fùhào
minus sign 减号 jiǎnhào, 负号 fùhào (−)
2 缺点 quēdiǎn **III ADJ 1** 零下 língxià
minus 10° 零下十度 língxià shí dù (−10°)
2（学校分数）减 (xuéxiào fēnshù) jiǎn
B minus 减 B jiǎn (B−)

minuscule ADJ 极其微小的 jíqí wēixiǎo de

minute¹ N 分 fēn, 分钟 fēnzhōng
at the last minute 最后一刻 zuì hòu yí kè
at any minute 随时 suíshí, 马上 mǎshàng

minute² ADJ 极小的 jíxiǎo de, 微小的 wēixiǎo de

minutes N（会议）记录 (huìyì) jìlù
to keep minutes 做（会议）记录 zuò (huìyì) jìlù

miracle N 奇迹 qíjì

miraculous ADJ 奇迹般的 qíjì bān de, 神奇的 shénqí de

mirage N 海市蜃楼 hǎishì shènlóu

mire N 1 泥潭 nítán **2** 困境 kùnjìng

mirror N 镜子 jìngzi
mirror image ① 非常相像的事物 fēicháng xiāngxiàng de shìwù ② 完全相反的事物 wánquán xiāngfǎn de shìwù
rearview mirror 后视镜 hòushì jìng
II v 与…完全一样 yǔ...wánquán yíyàng

mirth N 欢乐 huānlè

misadventure N 灾祸 zāihuò, 不幸 búxìng

misapprehension N 误会 wùhuì, 误解 wùjiě

misappropriate v 挪用 nuóyòng, 盗用 dàoyòng

misbehave v 行为不端 xíngwéi bùduān, 做坏事 zuò huàishì

miscalculate v 1 误算 [+开支] wù suàn [+kāizhī] **2** 错误估计 [+形势] cuòwù gūjì [+xíngshì], 错误判断 cuòwù pànduàn

miscarriage N 流产 liúchǎn, 小产 xiǎochǎn

miscellaneous ADJ 各种各样的 gèzhǒng gèyàng de, 混杂的 hùnzá de
miscellaneous expenses 杂费 záfèi

mischief N 调皮捣乱 tiáopí dǎoluàn

mischievous ADJ 调皮捣乱的 tiáopí dǎoluàn de

misconception N 错误想法 cuòwù xiǎngfǎ, 误解 wùjiě

misconduct N 行为不端 xíngwéi bùduān

misconstrue v 误解 wùjiě

misdeed N 错误行为 cuòwù xíngwéi, 违法行为 wéifǎ xíngwéi

misdirect v 1 错误地使用 cuòwù de shǐyòng **2** 把…送错地方 bǎ...sòngcuò dìfang

miser N 守财奴 shǒucáinú, 小气鬼 xiǎoqiguǐ

miserable ADJ 悲惨的 bēicǎn de

miserly ADJ 1 吝啬 lìnsè, 小气的 xiǎoqi de **2** 少得可怜的 shǎo dé kělián de

misery N 苦难 kǔnàn, 痛苦 tòngkǔ

misfit N 不适应环境的人 bú shìyìng huánjìng de rén

misfortune N 不幸 búxìng

misgiving N 疑虑 yílǜ, 担忧 dānyōu

misguided ADJ 事与愿违的 shì yǔ yuàn wéi de, 帮倒忙的 bāngdàománg de

mishandle v 对…处理不当 duì...chǔlǐ búdàng

mishap N 小过失 xiǎo guòshī, 小事故 xiǎo shìgù

misinform v 向…提供错误信息 xiàng... tígōng cuòwù xìnxī

misinterpret v 曲解 qūjiě, 误解 wùjiě

misjudge v 错误判断 cuòwù pànduàn, 误判 wùpàn

mislaid See mislay

mislay (PT & PP mislaid) v 忘记把 [钥匙+] 放在哪里 wàngjì bǎ [yàoshi+] fàng zài nǎli

mislead (PT & PP misled) v 误导 wùdǎo

mismanage V 管理不善 guǎnlǐ búshàn, 错误处置 cuòwù chǔzhì

mismanagement N 管理不善 guǎnlǐ bú shàn, 处置失当 chǔzhì shīdàng

mismatch N 错误的搭配 cuòwù de dāpèi

misnomer N 错误的名称 cuòwù de míngchēng

misogyny N 对女性的憎恨 duì nǚxìng de zēnghèn, 厌女症 yànnǚzhēng

misplace V 错放 cuò fàng

misplaced ADJ 错给的 cuò gěi de, 不应该给予的 bù yīnggāi jǐyǔ de

misprint N 印刷错误 yìnshuā cuòwù

misquote V 错误地使用 cuòwù de shǐyòng, 错误地引述 cuòwù de yǐnshù

misread (PT & PP **misread**) V 1 错误地判断 cuòwù de pánduàn 2 读错 dú cuò

misrepresent V (故意) 错误地描述 (gùyì) cuòwù de miáoshù

miss[1] I V 1 错过 cuòguò 2 想念 xiǎngniàn, 怀念 huáiniàn II N 失误 shīwù
A miss is as good as a mile. 因小失误失败, 终究也是失败。Yīn xiǎo shīwù shībài, zhōngjiū yě shì shībài.

miss[2] N 小姐 xiǎojiě

misshapen ADJ 畸形的 jīxíng de, 变形的 biànxíng de

missile N 导弹 dǎodàn [M. WD 枚 méi]

missing ADJ 1 失踪的 shīzōng de 2 丢失的 diūshī de, 找不到的 zhǎobudào de
a missing document 一份丢失的文件 yí fèn diūshī de wénjiàn
3 缺少的 quēshǎo de, 漏掉的 lòudiào de
missing link 缺少的一环 quēshǎo de yì huán

mission N 1 使命 shǐmìng 2 代表团 dàibiǎotuán 3 传教 chuánjiào, 布道 bùdào

missionary N 传教士 chuánjiàoshì

misspell V (PT & PP **misspelled, misspelt**) 拼错 pīn cuò

misspend (PT & PP **misspent**) V 使用不当 shǐyòng búdàng, 滥用 lànyòng

misspent V See **misspend**

misstep N 失误 shīwù, 失策 shīcè

mist I N 雾气 wùqì, 水蒸气 shuǐzhēngqì II V 蒙上雾气 méng shàng wùqì

mistake I N 错误 cuòwù, 过失 guòshī

II V (PT **mistook**; PP **mistaken**) 1 误会 wùhuì, 误解 wùjiě 2 把…误认为 bǎ… wùrènwéi

mistaken I V See **mistake** II ADJ 弄错的 nòngcuò de

mister See **Mr.**

mistletoe N 槲寄生 hújìshēng

mistook See **mistake**

mistreat V 虐待 nüèdài

mistress N 1 情妇 qíngfù 2 女主人 nǚzhǔrén

mistrial N 无效审判 wúxiào shěnpàn

mistrust V 不信任 bú xìnrèn

misty ADJ 有雾的 yǒu wù de, 多雾的 duō wù de

misunderstand V 误解 wùjiě, 误会 wùhuì

misuse I V 1 用错 yòngcuò 2 滥用 [+公款] lànyòng [+gōngkuǎn] II N 1 错用 cuòyòng 2 滥用 lànyòng

mite[1] N 螨 mǎn, 螨虫 mǎnchóng

mite[2] N (a mite of) 有点儿 yǒudiǎnr

mitigate V 减少 jiǎnshǎo, 减轻 jiǎnqīng

mitt N 防护手套 fánghù shǒutào
boxing mitt 拳击手套 quánjī shǒutào

mitten N 连指手套 lián zhǐ shǒutào

mix I V 1 混合 hùnhé 2 和 [+不很熟的人] 交往 hé [+bù hěn shú de rén] jiāowǎng
to mix up 弄提 nòng hùn, 混淆 hùnxiáo II N 混合 (物) hùnhé (wù)

mixed ADJ 混合的 hùnhé de
mixed marriage 异族通婚 yìzú tōnghūn, 异教通婚 yìjiào tōnghūn

mixture N 混合物 hùnhéwù

moan I V 1 呻吟 shēnyín 2 抱怨 bàoyuàn II N 1 呻吟 (声) shēnyín (shēng) 2 怨声 yuàn shēng

moat N 护城河 hùchénghé

mob I N (一群) 暴民 (yìqún) bàomín II V 围住 wéizhù

mobile ADJ 移动的 yídòng de, 流动的 liúdòng de
mobile home 流动住房 liúdòng zhùfáng
mobile phone 移动电话 yídòng diànhuà, 手机 shǒujī

mobility N 流动性 liúdòngxìng
upward mobility 提升 (社会) 地位 tíshēng (shèhuì) dìwèi

mobster N 犯罪集团成员 fànzuì jítuán chéngyuán, 暴徒 bàotú

mock I v 嘲笑 cháoxiào, 嘲弄 cháonòng II ADJ 1 模拟的 mónǐ de
a mock trial 模拟审判 mónǐ shěnpàn
2 装出来的 zhuāngchūlái de, 假装的 jiǎzhuāng de
mock indignation 装作愤怒的样子 zhuāngzuò fènnù de yàngzi

mockery N 1 无用的东西 wúyòng de dōngxi
to make a mockery of 使…变得无用 shǐ...biàn de wúyòng
2 嘲弄 cháonòng

mode N 方式 fāngshì, 模式 móshì

model I N 1 模特儿 mótèr 2 模型 móxíng 3 型号 xínghào 4 榜样 bǎngyàng II ADJ 1 模范的 mófàn de, 楷模的 kǎimó de
a model student 模范学生 mófàn xuésheng
2 模型（的）móxíng (de)
model train 火车模型 huǒchē móxíng III v 1 当模特儿 dāng mótèr 2 以…为榜样 yǐ...wéi bǎngyàng III ADJ
be modeled on sth 仿照某物 fǎngzhào mǒuwù

modem N 调制调解器 tiáozhì tiáojiěqì

moderate I ADJ 适度的 shìdù de, 不偏激的 bù piānjī de II v 1 主持 [+辩论会] zhǔchí [+biànlùnhuì] 2 调解 [+争执] tiáojiě [+zhēngzhí] 3 使 [+观点] 缓和 shǐ [+guāndiǎn] huǎnhé III N 温和派（人士）wēnhépài (rénshì)

moderation N 1 缓和 huǎnhé 2 节制 jiézhì, 不过分 bú guòfēn
in moderation 适度地 shìdù de, 有节制地 yǒu jiézhì de

modern ADJ 1 现代的 xiàndài de 2 现代化的 xiàndàihuà de 3 新式的 xīnshì de, 时髦的 shímáo de

modernization N 现代化 xiàndàihuà

modest ADJ 1 谦虚的 qiānxū de 2 朴素的 pǔsù de, 不起眼的 bù qǐyǎn de

modesty N 谦虚 qiānxū

modification N 修改 xiūgǎi, 调节 tiáo jié

modify v 修改 xiūgǎi, 调节 tiáojié

modular ADJ 模块化的 mókuàihuà de

module N 1 单元 dānyuán, 部件 bùjiàn 2（计算机软件）模块 (jìsuànjī ruǎnjiàn) mókuài 3（宇宙飞船）分离舱 (yǔzhòu fēichuán) fēnlícāng

mohair N 马海毛绒 mǎhǎimáoróng

Mohammed N 穆罕默德（伊斯兰教领袖）Mùhǎnmòdé (Yīsīlánjiào lǐngxiù)

moist ADJ 湿润的 shīrùn de, 潮湿的 cháoshī de

moisten v 使…湿润 shǐ...shīrùn

moisture N 湿气 shīqì, 水汽 shuǐqì

moisturizer N 润肤膏 rùnfūgāo

molar N 臼齿 jiùchǐ, 磨牙 móyá

molasses N 糖浆 tángjiāng

mold¹ N 1 模具 mújù, 模式 móshì
to break the mold 打破模式 dǎpò móshì
2 类型 lèixíng, 气质 qìzhì
the mold of a typical businessman 典型商人的气质 diǎnxíng shāngrén de qìzhì
3 霉（菌）méi (jùn)

mold² v 1 用模具制作 [+蛋糕] yòng mújù zhìzuò [+dàngāo] 2 塑造 [+青年人] sùzào [+qīngniánrén]

molder v 腐烂 fǔlàn, 烂掉 làndiào

moldy ADJ 发霉的 fāméi de

mole N 1（色素）痣 (sèsù) zhì 2 内奸 nèijiān, 奸细 jiānxì 3 鼹鼠 yǎnshǔ

molecule N 分子 fènzǐ

molest v（性）骚扰 (xìng) sāorǎo, 猥亵 wěixiè

mollify v 安抚 ānfǔ, 平息怒气 píngxī nùqì

molt v [动物+] 蜕皮 [dòngwù+] tuìpí, [鸟+] 换羽 [niǎo+] huànyǔ

molten ADJ 熔化的 rónghuà de

mom N 妈妈 māma

moment N 1 片刻 piànkè, 一会儿 yíhuìr 2 那时 nàshí, 正在那时 zhèngzài nàshí 3 时机 shíjī
for the moment 暂时 zànshí

momentary ADJ 一时的 yìshí de, 片刻的 piànkè de

momentous ADJ 重大的 zhòngdà de, 重要的 zhòngyào de

momentum N 势头 shìtóu, 动力 dònglì

mommy N 妈咪 māmī

monarch N 君主 jūnzhǔ, 国王／女王 guówáng/nǚwáng

monarchy N 君主政体 jūnzhǔ zhèngtǐ

monastery N 修道院 xiūdàoyuàn [M. WD 座 zuò], 寺院 sìyuàn [M. WD 座 zuò]

Monday N 星期一 xīngqīyī, 周一 zhōuyī

monetary ADJ 货币的 huòbì de, 金融的 jīnróng de

money N 钱 qián, 金钱 jīnqián
Money makes the world turn. 有钱能使鬼推磨。Yǒu qián néng shǐ guǐ tuī mò.
(→ If you have money you can make the devil push your mill stone.)
money order 汇票 huìpiào, 汇款单 huìkuǎndān

mongrel N 杂种狗 zázhǒng gǒu

monitor I N 1 (机算计) 显示器 (jīsuànjì) xiǎnshìqì [M. WD 台 tái] 2 (安全) 监视器 (ānquán) jiānshìqì, 监护器 jiānhùqì 3 (学校) 班长 (xuéxiào) bānzhǎng, 级长 jízhǎng II V 1 监视 jiānshì, 监听 jiāntīng

monk N 修道士 xiūdào shì, 僧侣 sēnglǚ
Buddhist monk 和尚 héshang

monkey N 猴（子）hóu (zi)

mono N 1 单声道音响系统 dān shēng dào yīnxiǎng xìtǒng 2 腺热 xiàn rè

monochrome ADJ 单色的 dānsè de, 黑白的 hēibái de

monogamy N 一夫一妻制 yìfūyīqīzhì

monogram N 字母组合图案 zìmǔ zǔ hé tú'àn

monolithic ADJ 1 宏伟的 [+大楼] hóngwěi de [+dàlóu] 2 庞大的 [+组织] pángdà de [+zǔzhī]

monologue N 独白 dúbái [M. WD 篇 piān]

monopolize V 垄断 lǒngduàn, 独占 dúzhàn

monopoly N 1 垄断（权）lǒngduàn (quán) 2 垄断企业 lǒngduàn qǐyè

monorail N 单轨铁道 dānguǐ tiědào

monosyllable N 单音节 dān yīnjié

monotonous ADJ 单调的 dāndiào de, 乏味的 fáwèi de

monsoon N 雨季 yǔjì

monster N 巨大的怪物 jùdà de guàiwu, 魔鬼 móguǐ

monstrosity N 巨大丑陋的东西 jùdà chǒulòu de dōngxi

montage N 剪辑 jiǎnjí, 蒙太奇 Méngtàiqí

month N 月 yuè, 月份 yuèfèn

monthly I ADJ 每月的 měiyuè de, 每月一次的 měi yuè yícì de II ADV 每月 měi yuè III N 月刊 yuèkān

monument N 纪念碑 jìniànbēi

monumental ADJ 1 伟大的 wěidà de, 不朽的 bùxiǔ dé 2 巨大的 jùdà de

moo N 牛呻声 niú mōu shēng, 哞 mōu

mooch V 乞讨 qǐtǎo, 讨 tǎo

mood N 1 情绪 qíngxu, 心情 xīnqíng
in no mood to do sth 不想做某事 bù xiǎng zuò mǒushì
2 不好的心情 bù hǎo de xīnqíng
to be in a mood 心情不好 xīnqíng bù hǎo, 暗暗生气 àn'àn shēngqì

moody ADJ 情绪多变的 qíngxù duōbiàn de, 喜怒无常的 xǐnù wúcháng de

moon N 1 月亮 yuè, 月亮 yuèliang 2 月球 yuèqiú

moonlighter N 从事第二职业的人 cóngshì dì'èr zhíyè de rén

moor¹ V 停泊 tíngbó

moor² N 荒野 huāngyě

mooring N 1 停泊地 tíngbódì 2 系泊用具 xìbó yòngjù

moose N (PL **moose**) 麋 mí, 驼鹿 tuólù

moot ADJ 1 没有结论的 méiyǒu jiélùn de
a moot point 还有争议的事 háiyǒu zhēngyì de shì
2 不会再发生的 búhuì zài fāshēng de, 不再重要的 búzài zhòngyào de

mop I N 1 拖把 tuōbǎ 2 蓬乱的头发 péngluàn de tóufa II V (用拖把) 拖地板 (yòng tuōbǎ) tuō dìbǎn

mope V 闷闷不乐 mènmèn búlè

moped N 机动自行车 jīdòng zìxíngchē

moral I ADJ 1 道德的 dàodé de 2 有道德的 yǒu dàodé de II N 教育意义 jiàoyù yìyì, 寓意 yùyì

morale N 士气 shìqì, 斗志 dòuzhì

morality N 道德（观）dàodé (guān), 道德水准 dàodé shuǐzhǔn

moralize V 说教 shuōjiào, 训导 xùndào

morals N 道德（准则）dàodé (zhǔnzé)

loose morals 低下的道德准则 dīxià de dàodé zhǔnzé, 放荡的品行 fàngdàng de pǐnxíng

morass N 1 困境 kùnjìng 2 沼泽（地）zhǎozé (di)

moratorium N 暂停 zàntíng

morbid ADJ 1 病态的 bìngtài de, 不健康的 bú jiànkāng de 2 疾病的 jíbìng de

more I ADJ 更多的 gèngduō de, 比较多的 bǐjiào duō de II PRON 更多的（东西）gèngduō de (dōngxi) III ADV 更 gèng, 比较 bǐjiào

more and more 越来越（多）yuèláiyuè (duō)

not any more 不再 búzài

moreover ADV 而且 érqiě, 此外 cǐwài

morgue N 停尸房 tíng shī fáng, 太平间 tàipíngjiān

morning N 1 上午 shàngwǔ (from 6.00 a.m. to 12 noon) 2 早上 zǎoshang (from 6.00 a.m.–8.00 a.m.)

morning glory 牵牛花 qiānniúhuā

moron N 白痴 báichī, 蠢货 chǔnhuò

morose ADJ 阴郁的 yīnyù de, 闷闷不乐的 mènmèn bú lè de

morph V 变形 biànxíng, 改变 gǎibiàn

morphine N 吗啡 mǎfēi

Morse code N 莫尔斯密码 Mò'ěrsī mìmǎ

morsel N 一点儿食物 yìdiǎnr shíwù

mortal I ADJ 1 不会长生不老的 bú huì chángshēngbùlǎo de, 会死亡的 huì sǐwáng de 2 致命的 [+打击] zhìmìng de [+dǎjī]

mortal sin 弥天大罪 mítiān dàzuì

3 极度的 [+恐惧] jídù de [+kǒngjù] II N 凡人 fánrén, 普通人 pǔtōngrén

mortality N 1 死亡率 sǐwánglǜ 2 终有一死 zhōng yǒu yì sǐ

mortar N 1 迫击炮 pǎijīpào [M. WD 门 mén] 2 砂浆 shā jiāng 3 研钵 yánbō, 臼 jiù

mortarboard N 学位帽 xuéwèimào

mortgage I N 抵押贷款 dǐyā huòkuǎn, 按揭 ànjiē II V 抵押 dǐyā

mortician N 丧葬承办人 sāngzàng chéngbàn rén, 殡仪馆工作人员 bìnyíguǎn gōngzuò rényuán

mortify V 使…难堪 shǐ…nánkān

mortuary N 停尸房 tíngshīfáng, 太平间 tàipíngjiān

mosaic N 马赛克 mǎsàikè, 镶嵌图案 xiāngqiàn tú'àn

Moslem N See Muslim

mosque N 清真寺 qīngzhēnsì

mosquito N 蚊子 wénzi [M. WD 只 zhī]

moss N 苔藓 táixiǎn

mossy ADJ 有苔藓的 yǒu táixiǎn de

most I ADJ 大多数 dàduōshù II PRON 大多数 dàduōshù III ADV 最 zuì

most of all 最重要的 zuì zhòngyào de

mostly ADV 大部分 dàbùfen, 通常 tōngcháng

motel N 汽车旅馆 qìchē lǚguǎn

moth N 飞蛾 fēié [M. WD 只 zhī]

mothball N 樟脑丸 zhāngnǎowán

mother I N 1 母亲 mǔqin, 妈妈 māma

Mother Earth 大地母亲 dàdì mǔqin

teenage mother 少女母亲 shàonǚ mǔqin

2 起源 qǐyuán, 根源 gēnyuán

Necessity is mother of invention. 需要是发明之母。Xūyào shì fāmíng zhī mǔ.

3 范例 fànlì, 最好／最坏的事例 zuì hǎo／zuì huài de shìlì

the mother of battles 最激烈的战斗 zuì jīliè de zhàndòu

II V 像母亲一样照管 [+他人] xiàng mǔqin yíyàng zhàoguǎn [+tārén]

motherboard N（计算机）主板 (jìsuànjī) zhǔbǎn

mother-in-law N 岳母 yuèmǔ (one's wife's mother), 婆婆 pópo (one's husband's mother)

Mother's Day N 母亲节 Mǔqinjié

motif N 1 主题 zhǔtí 2 图案 tú'àn

motion I N 1 运动 yùndòng, 移动 yídòng

motion picture 电影 diànyǐng

to go through the motion 装样子 zhuāng zhuāng yàngzi

2 动议 dòngyì, 提议 tíyì II V 做手势 zuò shǒushì, 示意 shìyì

motionless ADJ 不动的 búdòng de, 静止的 jìngzhǐ de

motivate V 激励 jīlì, 激发 jīfā

motivated ADJ 有动机的 yǒu dòngjī de

motivation N 动机 dòngjī, 原因 yuányīn

motive N 动机 dòngjī, 原因 yuányīn

motley ADJ 形形色色的 xíngxíng sèsè de

motor I N 发动机 fādòngjī, 马达 mǎdá
II ADJ 机动车辆的 jīdòng chēliàng de
motor home 旅宿汽车 lǚsù qìchē, 房车
fáng chē
motor vehicle 机动车辆 jīdòng chēliàng

motorbike N 摩托车 mótuōchē

motorcade N 车队 chēduì

motorcycle N（大型）摩托车 (dàxíng)
mótuōchē [M. WD 辆 liàng]

motorist N 开汽车的人 kāi qìchē de rén,
驾车人 jiàchē rén

mottled ADJ 杂色的 zásè de, 斑驳的
bānbó de

motto N 座右铭 zuòyòumíng, 格言 géyán

mound N 1 土堆 tǔduī, 土丘 tǔqiū 2 堆
duī

mount¹ V 1 骑上 qíshang, 跨上 kuàshang
2 增长 zēngzhǎng, 上升 shàngshēng 3
裱贴 [+图画] biǎotiē [+túhuà]

mount² N 山 shān, 峰 fēng

mountain N 1 山 shān, 山岳 shānyuè
to make a mountain out of a mole-
hill 小题大做 xiǎo tí dà zuò
mountain bike 山地车 shāndìchē
2 (mountains of) 大量的 dàliàng de, 一
大堆的 yídàduī de

mountaineering N 登山（运动）
dēngshān (yùndòng)

mountainous ADJ 多山的 duōshān de

mountainside N 山坡 shānpō

mountaintop N 山顶 shāndǐng

mourn V 哀悼 āidào

mourner N 参加葬礼者 cānjiā zànglǐ zhě

mourning N 1 哀悼 āidào, 悲痛 bēitòng
2 丧服 sāngfú [M. WD 件 jiàn]

mouse (PL **mice**) N 1（老）鼠 (lǎo) shǔ
2 (also PL **mouses**)（计算机）鼠标
(jìsuànjī) shǔbiāo
Mickey Mouse 米老鼠 Mǐlǎoshǔ

mousse N 奶油冻 nǎiyóudòng

mousy ADJ 1 安静害羞的 [+女孩] ānjìng
hàixiū de [+nǚhái] 2 灰褐色的 huīhèsè
de

mouth I N 1 嘴 zuǐ, 嘴巴 zuǐba 2 口状物
kǒu zhuàng wù
mouth of a river 河口 hékǒu, 入海口
rùhǎikǒu
II V 1 不出声地说 bù chūshēng de shuō
2 言不由衷地说 [+动听的话] yán bù
yóuzhōng de shuō [+dòngtīng de
hǎohuà]

mouthful N 1 一口（食物／饮料）yìkǒu
(shíwù/yǐnliào) 2 满口 mǎnkǒu 3 长而拗
口的词 cháng ér àokǒu de cí

mouthpiece N 1 代言人 dàiyánrén, 喉
舌 hóushé 2（电话）送话口 (diànhuà)
sònghuàkǒu 3（乐器）吹口 (yuèqì)
chuīkǒu

mouthwash N 漱口药水 shùkǒu yàoshuǐ

mouth-watering ADJ 令人馋言欲滴
的 lìng rén chányán yù dī de, 诱人的
yòurén de

movable ADJ 活动的 huódòng de

move I V 1 动 dòng, 移动 yídòng 2 迁移
qiānyí, 搬家 bānjiā 3 感动 gǎndòng
4（会议上）提出动议 (huìyìshang) tíchū
dòngyì, 提议 tíyì II N 1 动 dòng, 移动
yídòng 2 迁移 qiānyí, 搬家 bānjiā 3 行
动 xíngdòng

movement N 1 动 dòng, 动静 dòngjìng
2 运动 yùndòng

mover N 1 搬运工人 bānyùn gōngrén
2 有势力的人 yǒu shìlì de rén
a mover and shaker 权势人物 quánshì
rénwù

movie N 电影 diànyǐng
movie star 电影明星 diànyǐng míngxīng

movies N 电影院 diànyǐngyuàn [M. WD 座
zuò/家 jiā]

moving ADJ 1 感动人的 gǎndòng rén de,
感人至深的 gǎnrén zhì shēn de 2 移动
的 yídòng de

mow (PT **mowed**; PP **mown, mowed**) V
割草 gē cǎo

mower N 割草机 gēcǎojī [M. WD 台 tái]

Mr. (= mister PL **Messrs**) ABBREV 先生
xiānsheng

Mrs. (= missis/missus) ABBREV 太太 tàitai

Ms. N 女士 nǚshì

much I ADJ 很多 hěn duō II PRON 很多

hěn duō III ADV 很 hěn，非常 fēicháng

how much ① 多么地 duōme de ② 多少钱 duōshao qián，多少 duōshao

too much 太多 tài duō

muck N 污物 wūwù，污秽 wūhuì

mucous ADJ 粘液的 niányède

mucus N 粘液 niányè

mud N (烂) 泥 (làn) ní

muddle I V (to muddle along) 混日子 hùnrìzi，得且过 dé guò qiě guò II N 混乱 hùnluàn

muddy I ADJ 1 沾泥的 zhānní de 2 泥泞的 níníng de II V 使…沾上污泥 shǐ…zhān-shang wūní

mudslide N 泥石流 níshíliú

muff V 把…弄错 bǎ…nòngcuò

muffin N 小面包圈 xiǎo miànbāoquān，小甜饼 xiǎo tiánbǐng

muffle V 1 使 [+声音] 减弱 shǐ [+shēng-yīn] jiǎnruò 2 把…包起来 bǎ…bāo qǐlái，裹住 guǒzhù

muffler N 1 消音器 xiāoyīnqì 2 厚围巾 hòu wéijīn

mug¹ N 大杯子 dà bēizi，茶缸 chágāng

mug² V (行凶) 抢劫 (xíngxiōng) qiǎngjié

mugger N (行凶) 抢劫犯 (xíngxiōng) qiǎngjiéfàn

mugshot N (罪犯的) 面部照片 (zuìfàn de) miànbù zhàopiàn

mulch I N 腐叶 fǔ yè II V 用腐叶覆盖 yòng fǔ yè fùgài

mule N 骡子 luózi [M. WD 头 tóu]

as stubborn as a mule 顽固的人 wángù de rén，固执的人 gùzhí de rén 2 被雇用来夹带毒品的人 bèi gùyòng lái jiādài dúpǐn de rén，毒品走私犯 dúpǐn zǒusī fàn

mull V 1 在 [+葡萄酒] 内放糖和香料后加热 zài [+pútaojiǔ] nèi fàng táng hé xiāngliào hòu jiārè 2 (to mull over) 反复思考 [+问题] fǎnfù sīkǎo [+wèntí]

multicolored ADJ 有不同色彩的 yǒu bùtóng sècǎi de

multicultural ADJ 多元文化的 duōyuán wénhuà de

multilateral ADJ 多方的 duōfāng de，多边的 duōbiān de，多国的 duōguó de

multilateral negotiation 多边谈判 duōbiān tánpàn

multimedia N, ADJ 多媒体（的）duōméitǐ (de)

multinational I ADJ 跨国的 kuàguó de，多国的 duōguó de

multinational manufacturer 跨国制造商 kuàguó zhìzàoshāng II N 跨国公司 kuàguó gōngsī

multiple¹ ADJ 多个的 duōge de，多种的 duōzhǒng de

multiple choice 选择题 xuǎnzétí

multiple² N 倍数 bèishù

multiplex N 多放映厅电影院 duō fàng-yìngtīng diànyǐngyuàn [M. WD 座 zuò]

multiplication N 乘法（运算）chéngfǎ (yùnsuàn)

multiracial ADJ 多种族的 duōzhǒngzú de

multitude N 大量 dàliàng，大批 dàpī

the multitude 大众 dàzhòng，民众 mínzhòng

mum N (mum's the word) 别讲给人家听 bié jiǎng gěi rénjiā tīng II ADJ 沉默的 chénmò de

to keep mum 守口如瓶 shǒu kǒu rú píng

mumble V 含糊地说 hánhu de shuō

mummy N 木乃伊 mùnǎiyī [M. WD 具 jù]

mumps N 腮腺炎 sāixiànyán

munch V（用力）嚼（yònglì）jiáo

munchies N 零食 língshí，小吃 xiǎochī

mundane ADJ 平淡乏味的 píngdàn fáwèi de，平凡无奇的 píngfán wú qí de

municipal ADJ 市（政府）的 shì (zhèngfǔ) de

munitions N 军火 jūnhuǒ，军需品 jūnxūpǐn

mural N 壁画 bìhuà [M. WD 幅 fú]

murder I N 谋杀 móushā，谋杀案 móushā'àn II V 谋杀 móushā

murderous ADJ 可能杀人的 kěnéng shārén de，凶残的 xiōngcán de

murky ADJ 1 见不到底的 [+水] jiànbúdào dǐ de [+shuǐ] 2 复杂难懂的 [+问题] fùzá nándǒng de [+wèntí]

murmur I V 1 轻柔低语 qīngróu dīyǔ II N 1 低语声 dīyǔ shēng 2（心脏）杂

音 (xīnzàng) záyīn **3** 悄悄抱怨 qiāoqiāo bàoyuàn

a murmur of opposition 轻轻的反对声 qīngqīng de fǎnduìshēng

without a murmur 毫无怨言 háowú yuànyán

muscle N 肌肉 jīròu

muscular ADJ 肌肉发达的 jīròu fādá de

muse V 默默思考 mòmò sīkǎo

museum N 博物馆 bówùguǎn

mush N 烂糊状的东西 lànhú zhuàng de dōngxi

mushroom N 蘑菇 mógu

mushy ADJ **1** 软乎乎的 [+香蕉] ruǎn hū hū de [+xiāngjiāo] **2** 过于多情的 guòyú duōqíng de

music N 音乐 yīnyuè, 乐曲 yuèqǔ

to face the music 受责备 shòu zébèi

musical I ADJ **1** 音乐的 yīnyuè de **2** 有音乐天赋的 yǒu yīnyuè tiānfù de II N 音乐喜剧 yīnyuè xǐjù

musing N 沉思 chénsī, 思索 sīsuǒ

musk N 麝香 shèxiāng

Muslim N, ADJ 穆斯林（的）Mùsīlín (de), 伊斯兰教信徒（的）Yīsīlán jiào xìntú (de)

muss V 弄乱 nòngluàn

mussel N 贻贝 yíbèi, 壳菜 qiàocài, 淡菜 dàncài

must I [NEG must not ABBREV mustn't] MODAL V **1** 必须 bìxū **2** 一定 yídìng, 想必 xiǎngbì II N 必不可少的东西 bì bùkě shǎo de dōngxi, 必须做的事 bìxū zuò de shì

mustache N 小胡子 xiǎo húzi

mustang N 小野马 xiǎo yěmǎ

mustard N 芥末（酱）jièmo (jiàng)

muster V 召集 zhàojí, 集合 jíhé

to muster up courage 鼓足勇气 gǔzú yǒngqì

musty ADJ 发霉的 fāméi de, 发出霉味的 fāchū méi wèi de

mutation N（动植物）变异 (dòngzhíwù) biànyì

mute I ADJ **1** 不会说话的 bú huì shuōhuà de, 哑的 yǎ de **2** 不说话的 bù shuō huà de, 默不作声的 mòbù zuòshēng de II N 哑巴 yǎba III V 使 [+声音] 减弱 shǐ [+shēngyīn] jiǎnruo, 使 [+声音] 消失

shǐ [+shēngyīn] xiāoshì

mutilate V 使…伤残 shǐ…shāngcán, 肢解 zhījiě

mutilation N 使人伤残的 shǐrén shāngcán de, 肢解 zhījiě

mutinous ADJ 反叛的 fǎnpàn de, 拼命的 pīnmìng de

mutiny N 反叛 fǎnpàn, 兵变 bīngbiàn

mutt N 杂种狗 zázhǒng gǒu

mutter I V 嘀咕 dígu, 咕哝 gūnong II N 嘀咕声 dígushēng

mutton N 羊肉 yángròu

mutual ADJ 相互的 xiānghù de, 彼此的 bǐcǐ de, 共同的 gòngtóng de

mutual fund 单位投资 dānwèi tóuzī, 共同基金 gòngtóng jījīn

muzzle I N **1**（动物的）口鼻部 (dòngwù de) kǒubíbù **2**（狗的）口套 (gǒu de) kǒutào **3**（枪）口 (qiāng) kǒu,（炮）口 (páo) kǒu II V **1** 不让…说话 búràng…shuōhuà **2** 给狗戴口套 gěi gǒu dài kǒutào

my ADJ 我的 wǒde

myopic ADJ **1** 近视的 jìnshi de **2** 目光短浅的 mùguāng duǎnqiǎn de

myriad I N (a myriad of) 无数的 wúshù de II ADJ 无数的 wúshù de

myself PRON 我自己 wǒ zìjǐ

mysterious ADJ 神秘的 shénmì de, 不可思议的 bùkě sīyì de

mystery N 神秘的事物 shénmì de shìwù, 无法解释的事 wúfǎ jiěshì de shì

mystic, mystical ADJ 神秘（主义）的 shénmì (zhǔyì) de

mystic N 神秘主义者 shénmì zhǔyì zhě

mysticism N 神秘主义 shénmì zhǔyì

myth N **1** 神话（故事）shénhuà (gùshi) **2** 无根据的说法 wú gēnjù de shuōfa

mythology N 神话（学）shénhuà (xué)

N

nab V 当场抓获 dāngchǎng zhuāhuò

nag I V **1** 不停地指责／抱怨 bùtíngde zhǐzé/bàoyuàn, 唠叨 láodao **2** 困扰 kùnrǎo II N **1** 爱唠叨的人 ài láodao de rén **2**（老）马 (lǎo) mǎ

nagging ADJ 不断困扰人的 búduàn kùnrǎo rén de, 烦人的 fánrén de

nail I N 1 钉 dīng, 钉子 dīngzi 2 指甲 zhǐjia, 趾甲 zhǐjiǎ
nail polish 指甲油 zhǐjiayóu
II v 1 用钉子钉住 yòng dīngzi dìngzhù 2 抓住 zhuā zhù, 逮住 dài zhù
to nail sb/sth down 最终确定 zuìzhōng quèdìng, 终于获得 zhōngyú huòdé

nailbrush N 指甲刷 zhǐjiashuā

naive ADJ 天真的 tiānzhēn de, 幼稚的 yòuzhì de

naked ADJ 裸体的 luǒtǐ de
the naked eye 肉眼 ròuyǎn
naked truth 明显的事实 míngxiǎn de shìshí

name I N 1 名字 míngzi, 姓名 xìngmíng
name tag 姓名牌 xìngmíngpái
2 名称 míngchēng 3 名声 míngshēng, 声誉 shēngyù
in the name of 以…的名义 yǐ...de míngyì
the name of the game 最重要的东西 zuì zhòngyào de dōngxi
II v 1 取名 qǔmíng, 命名 mìngmíng 2 说出名字 shuōchū míngzi
to name your price 出个价 chū gè jià, 你说要多少钱 nǐ shuō yào duōshaoqián

nameless ADJ 1 不便提及的 búbiàn tíjí de 2 无名的 wúmíng de, 未名的 wèi míng de 3 不知其名的 bùzhī qí míng de

namely ADV 也就是说 yě jiù shì shuō, 即 jí

namesake N 同名的人 tóngmíng de rén

nanny N 保姆 bǎomǔ

nano technology N 纳米技术 nàmǐjìshù

nap I N（白天）小睡（báitiān）xiǎoshuì
II v 在（白天）小睡 zài（báitiān）xiǎoshuì

nape N 颈背 jǐngbèi, 后颈 hòujǐng

napkin N 1 餐巾 cānjīn [M. WD 块 kuài] 2 餐巾纸 cānjīnzhǐ [M. WD 张 zhāng]

narcissism N 自恋 zì liàn, 自我欣赏 zìwǒ xīnshǎng

narcotic I N 麻醉剂 mázuìjì II ADJ 1 麻醉剂的 mázuìjì de 2 毒品的 dúpǐn de
narcotic addiction 毒瘾 dúyǐn

narrate v 叙述 xùshù, 讲述 jiǎngshù

narration N 叙述 xùshù, 解说 jiěshuō

narrative N 故事 gùshi, 叙事 xùshì

narrator N 叙述者 xùshùzhě, 解说人 jiěshuōrén

narrow I ADJ 1 窄 zhǎi, 狭窄 xiázhǎi 2 心胸狭小的 xīnxiōng xiáxiǎo de, 狭隘的 xiá'ài de 3 微弱的 wēiruò de, 有限的 yǒuxiàn de
a narrow majority 微弱多数 wēiruò duōshù
II v（使…）变窄（shǐ…）biàn zhǎi
to narrow down 缩小范围 suōxiǎo fànwéi, 缩小差距 suōxiǎo chājù

narrow-minded ADJ（思想）不开放的（sīxiǎng）bù kāifàng de, 保守的 bǎoshǒu de

nasal ADJ 1 鼻（子）的 bí (zi) de 2 鼻音的 bíyīn de

nasty ADJ 1 让人厌恶的 ràng rén yànwù de 2 恶劣的 èliè de

nation N 1 国家 guójiā 2 民族 mínzú
the Chinese nation 中华民族 Zhōnghuá Mínzú

national I ADJ 1 国家的 guójiā de, 民族的 mínzú de 2 国有的 guóyǒu de, 国立的 guólì de
national anthem 国歌 guógē
national monument 国家保护单位 guójiā bǎohù dānwèi
national park 国家公园 guójiā gōngyuán
II N 国民 guómín, 公民 gōngmín
Chinese national 一名中国公民 yì míng Zhōngguó gōngmín

nationalism N 民族主义 mínzú zhǔyì

nationalist I ADJ 民族主义的 mínzú zhǔyì de II N 民族主义者 mínzú zhǔyìzhě

nationality N 国籍 guójí
American nationality 美国国籍 Měiguó guójí
dual nationality 双重国籍 shuāngchóng guójí

nationwide ADJ 全国范围（的）quánguó fànwéi (de), 全国性的 quánguó xìng de

native I ADJ 1 出生地的 chūshēngdì de 2 当地的 dāngdì de, 土生的 tǔshēng de
II N 1 本国人 běnguó rén

a Native American 美国印第安人 Měiguó Yìndì'ān rén

2 当地土生的动／植物 dāngdì tǔshēng de dòng/zhíwù

Nativity, nativity N 耶稣降生 Yēsū jiàngshēng

a Nativity play 叙述耶稣降生的短剧 xùshù Yēsū jiàngshēng de duǎn jù

NATO (= North Atlantic Treaty Organization) ABBREV 北大西洋公约组织 Běidàxīyáng Gōngyuē zǔzhī

natural I ADJ **1** 自然的 zìrán de, 天然的 tiānrán de

natural gas 天然气 tiānránqì

natural resources 自然资源 zìrán zīyuán

natural selection 自然淘汰 zìrántáotài, 天择 tiānzé

2 本能的 běnnéng de, 本性的 běnxìng de **3** 天生的 tiānshēng de II N 天生具有某种才能的人 tiānshēng jùyǒu mǒuzhǒng cáinéng de rén, 天才 tiāncái

naturalist N 博物学家 bówùxuéjiā

naturalization N 归化 guīhuà

naturally ADV **1** 自然地 zìrán de **2** 天生（地）tiānshēng (de) **3** 大大方方地 dàdà fāngfāng de

nature N **1** 大自然 dà zìrán **2** 本性 běnxìng, 天性 tiānxìng

nature reserve 自然保留地 zìrán bǎoliúdì

naught N 零 líng

to come to naught 毫无结果 háo wú jiéguǒ, 泡汤 pàotāng

naughty ADJ 调皮捣蛋的（小孩）tiáopí dǎodàn de (xiǎohái)

nauseous ADJ 想呕吐的 xiǎng ǒutù de, 感到恶心的 gǎndào èxīn de

nauseating ADJ 让人呕吐的 ràng rén ǒutù de, 令人作呕的 lìngrén zuò'ǒu de

nautical ADJ 船舶的 chuánbó de, 航海的 hánghǎi de

nautical mile 海哩 hǎi li

naval ADJ 海军的 hǎi jūn de

nave N（教堂的）中堂 (jiàotáng de) zhōngtáng

navel N 肚脐 dùqí

navigable ADJ 可通航的 kě tōngháng de

navigate V **1** 航行 hángxíng, 导航 dǎoháng **2** 找对方向 zhǎo duì fāngxiàng

navigation N 航行（学）hángxíng (xué), 航海术 hánghǎi shù, 航空（术）hángkōng (shù)

navigator N 领航员 lǐnghángyuán

navy N 海军 hǎijūn

navy blue 海军蓝 hǎijūn lán

near I ADJ **1** 近的 jìn de, 不远的 bùyuǎn de

in the near future 在不久的将来 zài bùjiǔ de jiānglái

2 近似 jìnsì, 相似 xiāngsì II ADV 近 jìn III PREP 离…近 lí…jìn IV V 接近 jiējìn, 靠近 kàojìn

nearby ADJ 附近的 fùjìn de

nearly ADV 很接近地 hěn jiējìn de, 几乎 jīhū

nearsighted ADJ 近视的 jìnshì de

neat ADJ **1** 整齐的 zhěngqí de **2** 爱整洁的 ài zhěngjié de **3** 挺好的 tǐng hǎo de **4**（不加冰／水的）纯酒 (bù jiā bīng/shuǐ de) chúnjiǔ

necessarily ADV 必然（地）bìrán (de)

not necessarily 不一定 bù yídìng, 未必 wèibì

necessary ADJ **1** 必需的 bìxū de **2** 有必要的 yǒu bìyào de

necessitate V 使…成为必需 shǐ…chéngwéi bìxū

necessity N 必要的东西 bìyào de dōngxi

neck I N **1** 颈 jǐng, 头颈 tóujǐng

neck and neck 不相上下 bù xiāng shàng xià

2 瓶颈 píngjǐng II V 拥抱亲吻 yōngbào qīnwěn, 热吻 rèwěn

necklace N 项链 xiàngliàn

necktie N 领带 lǐngdài [M. WD 条 tiáo/根 gēn]

nectar N **1** 浓果汁 nóng guǒzhī **2** 花蜜 huāmì

nectarine N **1** 油桃 yóutáo **2** 油桃树 yóutáo shù [M. WD 棵 kē]

née ADJ（女子的）婚前姓 (nǔzǐ de) hūnqián xìng

need I V 需要 xūyào, 有必要 yǒu bìyào II N 需要 xūyào

A friend in need is a friend indeed. 困难中的朋友才是真正的朋友 (→ 患难见真交。) Kùnnàn zhòng de péngyou cái shì zhēnzhèng de péngyou (→ Huànnàn jiàn zhēn jiāo. *Adversity shows up a true friend.*)

needs 基本需要 jīběn xūyào

needle I N 针 zhēn, 指针 zhǐzhēn, 注射针 zhùshèzhēn **II** V 刺激 cìjī, 激怒 jīnù

needless ADJ 不必要的 búbìyào de
needless to say 不用说 búyòng shuō, 当然 dāngrán

needy ADJ 贫困的 pínkùn de, 缺食少衣的 quē shí shǎo yī de

negate V **1** 否定 fǒudìng, 否认 fǒurèn **2** 取消 [+决定] qǔxiāo [+juédìng]

negative ADJ **1** 消极的 xiāojí de **2** 否定的 fǒudìng de **3** (化验) 阴性的 (huàyàn) yīnxìng de

neglect I V 忽略 hūlüè, 不重视 bú zhòngshì II N 忽略 hūlüè, 忽略 hūlüè
neglect of duty 玩忽职守 wánhū zhíshǒu

neglectful ADJ 疏忽 (大意) 的 shūhu (dàyì) de

negligee, negligé N (女式) 薄料内衣 (nǚ shì) báoliào nèiyī

negligence N 疏忽大意 shūhu dàyì, 玩忽职守 wánhū zhíshǒu

negligible ADJ 可忽视的 kě hūshì de, 微不足道的 wēi bùzú dào de

negotiable ADJ **1** 可谈判的 kě tánpàn de, 可协商的 kě xiéshāng de **2** 可通行的 kě tōngxíng de

negotiate V 谈判 tánpàn

Negro N 黑人 hēirén

neigh I V (马) 嘶 (mǎ) sī **II** N 马嘶声 mǎsīshēng

neighbor N **1** 邻居 línjū **2** 旁边的人 pángbiān de rén

neighborly ADJ (邻居之间) 友好的 (línjū zhījiān) yǒuhǎo de, 睦邻的 mùlín de

neither I PRON (两／二者) 都不 (liǎng/èrzhě) dōu bù **II** ADV 也不 yě bù
neither ... nor 既不…也不 jì bù...yě bù, …和…都不 ...hé...dōu bù

neon (Ne) N 氖 nǎi

neon light 霓虹灯 níhóngdēng

nephew N 侄子 zhízi (brother's son), 外甥 wàisheng (sister's son)

nepotism N 裙带关系 qúndài guānxi

nerd N 书呆子 shūdāizi
computer nerd 电脑迷 diànnǎo mí

nerve N **1** 胆量 dǎnliàng, 勇气 yǒngqì **2** (厚) 脸皮 (hòu) liǎnpí **3** 神经 shénjīng

nerve-racking ADJ 让人心烦 (意乱) 的 ràng rén xīnfán (yì luàn) de

nerves N 焦虑紧张 jiāolǜ jǐnzhāng

nervous ADJ 紧张 jǐnzhāng, 不自在 bú zìzài
a nervous breakdown 精神崩溃 jīngshén bēngkuì
the nervous system 神经系统 shénjīng xìtǒng

nest I N **1** 鸟巢 niǎocháo, 鸟窝 niǎowō **2** (小动物的) 窝 (xiǎo dòngwù de) wō, 穴 xué
nest egg 积蓄 jīxù
II V 筑巢 zhù cháo

nestle V 偎依 wēiyī

nestling N 幼鸟 yòuniǎo, 雏鸟 chúniǎo

net¹ N 网 wǎng

net² I V **1** 净赚 [+一大笔钱] jìngzhuàn [+yídàbǐ qián] **2** 获得 huòdé, 获取 huòqǔ **II** ADJ 净的 jìng de
net income 净收入 jìngshōurù
net result 最终结果 zuìzhōng jiéguǒ
net weight 净重 jìngzhòng

netting N 网 wǎng, 网状物 wǎngzhuàng wù

nettle I N 荨麻 qiánmá **II** V 惹恼 rěnǎo

network I N **1** 系统 xìtǒng, 网 wǎng **2** (计算机) 网络 (jìsuànjī) wǎngluò **II** V **1** 使 [+计算机] 联网 shǐ [+jìsuànjī] liánwǎng **2** 联络的 liánluò de, 接触 jiēchù

neurology N 神经 (病) 学 shénjīng (bìng) xué

neurotic I N 神经官能症 (患者) shénjīng guānnéngzhèng (huànzhě) **II** ADJ 神经质的 shénjīngzhì de, 神经过敏的 shénjīng guòmǐn de

neuter I V 阉割 [+雄性动物] yāngē [+xióngxìng dòngwù] **II** ADJ **1** 中性的 zhōngxìng de **2** 无生殖器的 wú shēngzhíqì de [+动物]

neutral ADJ **1** 中立的 [+国家] zhōnglì de [+guójiā] **2** 素淡的 [+颜色] sùdàn de [+yánsè] **3** 中性的 [+词语] zhōngxìng de [+cíyǔ]

neutralize v **1** 使… [+国家] 中立 shǐ… [+guójiā] zhōnglì **2** 使 [+毒药] 无效 shǐ [+dúyào] wúxiào

never ADV 从不 cóng bù, 永远不 yǒngyuǎn bù

nevertheless ADV 尽管如此 jǐnguǎn rúcǐ, 然而 rán'ér

new ADJ **1** 新 xīn, 新的 xīn de
New Age 新时代 xīnshídài
New Year 新年 xīnnián
New Year's Day 元旦 Yuándàn
New Year's Eve 除夕 chúxī
2 不熟悉的 bùshú xī de

newborn I N 新生儿 xīnshēng'ér II ADJ 新生的 xīnshēng de

newcomer N 新来的人 xīnlái de rén, 新手 xīnshǒu

newfangled ADJ 新花样的 xīn huāyàng de

newly ADV 新近（地）xīnjìn (de)

newlyweds N 新婚夫妇 xīnhūn fūfù

news N **1** 消息 xiāoxi
No news is good news. 没有消息就是好消息。Méiyǒu xiāoxi jiù shì hǎo xiāoxi.
2 新闻 xīnwén **3** 新闻节目 xīnwén jiémù
news agency 新闻通讯社 xīnwéntōngxùn shè
news bulletin 新闻简讯 xīnwén jiǎnxùn

newscaster N （电视）新闻播报员 (diànshì) xīnwén bōbàoyuán

newsletter N 简讯 jiǎnxùn

newspaper N 报 bào, 报纸 bàozhǐ

newsstand N 报摊 bàotān, 卖报摊 mài bàotān

New Testament N （圣经）新约全书 (Shèngjīng) Xīnyuē quán shū

next I ADJ **1** 下 xià, 下一个 xià yí ge
next door 隔壁 gébì
next week 下星期 xià xīngqī, 下周 xià zhōu
next month 下个月 xià ge yuè
next time 下次 xià cì, 下一次 xià yí cì
next year 明年 míngnián

2 隔壁的 [+房间] gébì de [+fángjiān] II ADV 接着 jiēzhe, 接下来 jiēxiàlái III PRON 下一个 xià yí ge
next of kin 最近的亲属 zuìjìn de qīnshǔ

nib N 笔尖 bǐjiān

nibble I v 一点一点地吃 yìdiǎn yìdiǎn de chī, 啃 kěn II N 一小口 yì xiǎokǒu

nice ADJ **1** 好 hǎo, 令人愉快的 lìng rén yúkuài de **2** 友好 yǒuhǎo, 和善 héshàn **3** 正派的 zhèngpài de

nice-looking ADJ 好看的 hǎokàn de, 漂亮的 piàoliang de

nicely ADV 很好地 hěnhǎo de, 让人满意地 ràng rén mǎnyì de

nicety N **1** 细节 xìjié
legal niceties 法律细节 fǎlǜ xìjié
2 细微的区别 xìwēi de qūbié

niche N **1** 特定的市场 tèdìng de shìchǎng **2** 正好合适的工作 zhènghǎo héshì de gōngzuò **3** 壁龛 bìkān

nick [1] N (in the nick of time) 正在这当口 zhèngzài zhè dāngkǒu

nick [2] I N 小切口 xiǎo qiēkǒu II v 留下小切口 liúxia xiǎo qiēkǒu

nickel-and-dime ADJ 小规模的 xiǎoguīmó de, 小打小闹的 xiǎo dǎ xiǎo nào de

nickname N 绰号 chuòhào, 外号 wàihào

nicotine N 尼古丁 nígǔdīng

niece N 侄女 zhínǚ (brother's daughter), 外甥女 wàishengnǚ (sister's daughter)

night N 夜 yè, 夜晚 yèwǎn
night and day, day and night 日日夜夜 rìrì yèyè
night club 夜总会 yèzǒnghuì
night owl 喜欢熬夜的人 xǐhuan áoyè de rén, 夜猫子 yèmāozi
night school 夜校 yèxiào

nightgown N 睡袍 shuìpáo

nightfall N 天黑时分 tiānhēi shífen, 傍晚 bàngwǎn

nightlife N 夜生活 yèshēnghuó, 夜间娱乐 yèjiān yúlè

nightly ADJ, ADV 每晚（的）měi wǎn (de), 每夜（的）měi yè (de)

nightmare N **1** 恶梦 èmèng **2** 极其可怕的经历 jíqí kěpà de jīnglì

nightstand, night table N 床头柜 chuángtóuguì

nil N 无 wú, 零 líng
virtually nil 几乎为零 jīhū wéi líng

nimble ADJ 敏捷的 mǐnjié de, 灵敏的 língmǐn de

nine NUM 九 jiǔ, 9

nineteen NUM 十九 shíjiǔ, 19

nineteenth NUM 第十九 dì shíjiǔ

ninety NUM 九十 jiǔshí, 90

ninth NUM 第九 dìjiǔ

nip I v 1 啃咬 (轻轻地) qīngqīng de) kěn yǎo 2 掐断 [+花朵] qiāduàn [+huāduǒ]
to nip sth in the bud 消灭在萌芽状态 xiāomiè zài méngyá zhuàngtài
3 冻伤 dòngshāng II N (轻) 咬 (轻) yǎo, (轻) 啃 (qīng) kěn
nip and tuck 两种可能性都有 liǎng zhǒng kěnéngxìng dōu yǒu, 胜负难分 shèngfù nánfēn

nipple N 1 乳头 rǔtóu 2 橡皮奶嘴 xiàngpí nǎizuǐ

nitpicking ADJ 过分挑剔的 guòfèn tiāoti de, 鸡蛋里挑骨头 jīdàn lǐ tiāo gútou

nitrogen (N) N 氮 dàn

nitty-gritty N 实质性部份 shízhìxìng bùfen

nitwit N 笨人 bènrén

no I ADV 不 bù, 不是 bú shì, 没有 méiyou
no good 没有好处 méiyou hǎochu
no more/less than 不多于 / 少于 bùduō yú/shǎoyú
II ADJ 没有 méiyou
in no time 马上 mǎshàng
III N 拒绝 jùjué, 不 bù

nobility N 贵族 (阶级) guìzú (jiējí)

noble I ADJ 1 高尚的 gāoshàng de 2 贵族的 guìzú de II N 贵族 guìzú

nobody I PRON 没有人 méiyou rén II N 无足轻重的人 wúzú qīngzhòng de rén, 小人物 xiǎorénwù

no-brainer N 不用动脑筋的事 búyòng dòng nǎo jìng de shì, 十分简单的事 shífēn jiǎndān de shì

nocturnal ADJ 夜间 (活动) 的 yèjiān (huódòng) de

nod v 1 点头 diǎntóu 2 (to nod off) 打瞌睡 dǎkēshuì

node N 1 (计算机系统的) 终端计算机 (jìsuànjī xìtǒng de) zhōngduān jìsuànjī 2 交点 jiāodiǎn
lymph node 淋巴结 línbājié

no-fault ADJ 不考虑是谁造成过失的 bùkǎolǜ shì shéi zàochéng guòshī de
a no-fault divorce 无过失离婚 wú guòshī líhūn

noise N 噪音 zàoyīn

noiselessly ADV 无声无息地 wúshēng wúxí de, 静悄悄地 jìngqiāoqiāo de

noisy ADJ 吵闹的 chǎonào de, 嘈杂的 cáozá de

nomad N 1 游牧者 yóumùzhě 2 经常搬家 / 换工作的人 jīngcháng bānjiā/huàngōng zuò de rén, 经到处旅行的人 jīngcháng dàochù lǚxíng de rén

nomadic ADJ 游牧 (部落) 的 yóumù (bùluò) de

nominal ADJ 1 名义上的 míngyìshàng de 2 名词 (性) 的 míngcí (xìng) de
a nominal phrase 名词 (性) 词组 míngcí (xìng) cízǔ
3 象征性的 xiàngzhēngxìng de, 极少的 jí shǎo de
a nominal fee 象征性收费 xiàngzhēngxìng shōufèi

nominate v 1 提名 tímíng 2 任命 rènmìng

nomination N 1 提名 tímíng 2 任命 rènmìng

nominee N 被提名者 bèi tímíng zhě

nonaggression N 互不侵犯的 wúbù qīn fàn de

nonalcoholic ADJ 不含酒精的 bù hán jiǔjīng de

nonchalant ADJ 毫不在意的 háobù zàiyì de, 若无其事的 ruòwú qí shì de

noncombatant N 非战斗人员 fēi zhàndòu rényuán

noncommittal ADJ 不做承诺的 bú zuò chéngnuò de, 不明确表态的 bù míngquè biǎotài de

non-dairy ADJ 不含奶的 bù hán nǎi de

nondescript ADJ 难以描绘的 nányí miáohuì de, 平淡无奇的 píngdàn wúqí de

none I PRON 一个也没有 yí ge yě méiyou

none other than 正是 zhèng shì, 恰恰是 qiàqià shì

II ADV 一点也没有 yìdiǎn yě méiyǒu

none the better 一点也没有更好 yìdiǎn yě méiyǒu gèng hǎo

nonentity N 无名之辈 wúmíng zhī bèi

nonetheless ADV 尽管如此 jǐnguǎn rúcǐ, 然而 rán'ér, 但是 dànshì

nonexistent ADJ 不存在的 bù cúnzài de

nonfat ADJ 不含脂肪的 bù hán zhīfáng de, 脱脂的 tuōzhī de

nonfiction N 非小说类书籍 fēi xiǎoshuō lèi shūjí

nonintervention N 不干涉 bù gānshè

non-negotiable ADJ **1** 没有商量余地的 [+安排] méiyǒu shāngliang yúdi de [+ānpái] **2** 不可转让的 [+支票] bùkě zhuǎnràng de [+zhīpiào]

no-no N 不准干的事 bùzhǔn gàn de shì, 不许可的事 bù xǔkě de shì

no-nonsense ADJ 务实的 wùshí de, 实用的 shíyòng de

nonpayment N 无力支付 wúlì zhīfù

nonplussed ADJ 惊奇得无以对答的 jīngqí de wúyǐ duìdá de, 不知所措的 bù zhī suǒ cuò de

nonprofit ADJ 非盈利（性）的 fēi yínglì (xìng) de

non-refundable ADJ 不可退款的 bùkě tuìkuǎn de

non-renewable ADJ 不可再生的 bùkě zàishēng de

non-resident N 非本国／本地居民 fēi běnguó/běndì jūmín

nonsense N **1** 胡说 húshuō, 荒唐念头 huāngtáng niàntou **2** 胡闹 húnào, 胡非为 húzuò fēiwéi

nonstandard ADJ 不标准的 bù biāozhǔn de

nonstick ADJ 不沾食物的 bù zhān shíwù de

nonstop ADJ, ADV 不停顿（的）bù tíng-dùn (de), 直达的 zhídá de

nonverbal ADJ 不用言语表达的 bú yòng yányǔ biǎodá de

nonviolence N 非暴力行为 fēibàolì xíngwéi

noodle N 面 miàn

noodle soup 汤面 tāngmiàn

fried noodle 炒面 chǎomiàn

nook N（房间的）角落（fángjiān de) jiǎoluò

noon N 正午 zhèngwǔ, 中午 zhōngwǔ

no one PRON 没有人 méiyǒu rén

noose N 绳套 shéngtào, 绞索 jiǎosuǒ

nope ADV 不 bù, 不是 bú shì

nor ADV 也不 yě bù

norm N 规范 guīfàn, 标准 biāozhǔn

normal I ADJ 正常的 zhèngcháng de

II N 正常水平 zhèngcháng shuǐpíng

normality N 正常状态 zhèngcháng zhuàngtài

normally ADV 正常 zhèngcháng, 正常地 zhèngcháng de

north I N 北 běi, 北面 běimiàn II ADJ 北面的 běimiàn de, 朝北的 cháo běi de North American ① 北美洲的 Běiměi zhōu de ② 北美洲人 Běiměi zhōu rén the North Pole 北极 Běijí

III ADJ（朝）北（cháo）běi

northbound ADJ 往北的 wǎng běi de, 北行的 běi xíng de

northeast I N **1** 东北（方向）dōngběi (fāngxiàng) **2** 东北（地区）dōngběi (dìqū) II ADJ **1** 在东北（地区）的 zài dōngběi (dìqū) de **2** 来自东北（地区的）láizì dōngběi (dìqū de) III ADV 朝东北（方向）cháo dōngběi (fāngxiàng)

northerly ADJ 在北部的 zài běibù de, 朝北部的 cháo běibù de the northerly 北面吹来的风 běimiàn chuī láide fēng, 北风 běifēng

northern ADJ 北方的 běifāng de the northern hemisphere 北半球 Běi bànqiú

northerner N 北方人 Běifāngrén

Northern Lights N 北极光 Běijíguāng

northward ADJ, ADV 往北（的）wǎng běi (de)

northwest I N **1** 西北（方向）xīběi (fāngxiàng) **2** 西北（地区）xīběi (dìqū) II ADJ **1** 在西北（地区）的 zài xīběi (dìqū) de **2** 来自西北（地区）的 láizì xīběi (dìqū) de III ADV 朝西北（方向）cháo xīběi (fāngxiàng)

nose I N 鼻子 bízi
to have a runny nose 流鼻涕 liú bíti
nose job 鼻子整形（手术）bízi zhěngxíng (shǒushù)
II V (to nose around) 四处查看 sìchù chákàn, (to nose forward) [车辆+] 缓慢前行 [chēliàng+] huǎnmàn qiánxíng

nosebleed N 鼻出血 bíchūxuè

nosedive I N 1 （飞机）俯冲 (fēijī) fǔchōng 2 （股票）猛跌 (gǔpiào) měngdiē
II V 1 [飞机+] 突然俯冲 [fēijī+] tūrán fǔchōng 2 （股票）猛跌 (gǔpiào) měngdiē

nostalgia N 怀旧（情绪）huáijiù (qíngxù)

nostril N 鼻孔 bíkǒng

nosy, nosey ADJ 爱打听别人隐私的 ài dǎtīng biéren yǐnsī de

not ADV 不 bù
not at all 一点也不 yì diǎn yě bù, 根本不 gēnběn bù
not only … but also 不但…而且… búdàn…érqiě…

notable I ADJ 值得注意的 zhíde zhùyì de, 显著的 xiǎnzhe de II N 著名人物 zhùmíng rénwù, 名人 míngrén

notation N 1 （一套）符号 (yítào) fúhào 2 标志法 biāozhìfǎ

notch I N 1 （V字形）切口 (V zìxíng) qièkǒu, 凹口 āo kǒu 2 等级 děngjí II V 1 刻 （V字形）切口 kè (V zìxíng) qièkǒu 2 (to notch up) 赢得 [+胜利] yíngdé [+shènglì]

note I N 1 笔记 bǐjì
to take notes 纪录 jìlù
to make a mental note of 记在心里 jì zài xīnlí
2 便条 biàntiáo 3 注解 zhùjiě 4 纸币 zhǐbì, 钞票 chāopiào 5 音调 yīndiào, 音符 yīnfú
a high/low note 高／低音 gāo/dīyīn
II V 1 注意 zhùyì 2 指出 zhǐchū

notebook N 笔记（本）bǐjì (běn) [M. WD 本 běn]

notepaper N 便条纸 biàntiáo zhǐ [M. WD 张 zhāng], 信纸 xìnzhǐ [M. WD 张 zhāng]

noteworthy ADJ 值得注意的 zhíde zhùyì de

nothing PRON 没有什么 méiyǒu shénme,

没有什么东西 méiyǒu shénme dōngxi
nothing but 只不过 zhǐbuguò, 仅仅是 jǐnjǐn shì
nothing less than 完全是 wánquán shì
to have nothing to lose 不会有损失 bú huì yǒu sǔnshī

notice I N 1 布告 bùgào, 通知 tōngzhī
2 (to give notice) 提出离职／辞职 tíchū lízhí/cízhí II V 注意到 zhùyìdao
to take no notice of 不理会 bù lǐhuì

noticeable ADJ 看得到的 kàndédào de, 显著的 xiǎnzhe de

notification N 通知 tōngzhī

notify V 通知 tōngzhī

notion N 概念 gàiniàn, 观念 guānniàn

notorious ADJ 臭名远扬的 chòumíng yuǎn yáng de, 有坏名声的 yǒu huài míngshēng de

notwithstanding PREP 尽管 jǐnguǎn

nougat N 牛轧糖 niúgáitáng

noun N 名词 míngcí

nourish V 1 给…营养 gěi…yíngyǎng, 滋养 zīyǎng 2 怀有 [+感情] huáiyǒu [+gǎnqíng]

nourishment N 营养 yíngyǎng

novel I N 小说 xiǎoshuō

novel² ADJ 新的 xīn de, 新奇的 xīnqí de

novelist N 小说家 xiǎoshuōjiā, 小说作者 xiǎoshuō zuòzhě

novelty N 1 新奇 xīnqí 2 新鲜玩意儿 xīnxian wányìr

November N 十一月 shíyīyuè

novice N 新手 xīnshǒu, 初学者 chūxuézhě

now I ADV 1 现在 xiànzài 2 立刻 lìkè, 马上 mǎshàng
by now 到（到）现在 (dào) xiànzài
from now on 从现在起 cóng xiànzài qǐ
right now 马上 mǎshàng, 就是现在 jiùshì xiànzài
II CONJ (now that) 既然 jìrán

nowadays ADV 现今 xiànjīn, 如今 rújīn

nowhere ADV 没有（什么）地方 méiyǒu (shénme) dìfang, 无处 wúchù
to get nowhere 毫无进展 háowú jìnzhǎn

nozzle N 喷嘴 pēnzuǐ

nuance N 细微差异 xìwēi chāyì

nuclear ADJ 原子核的 yuánzǐhé de, 核子的 hézǐ de
　nuclear family 核心家庭 héxīn jiātíng
　nuclear power 核电 hédiàn
　nuclear reaction 核反应 héfǎnyìng
　nuclear weapon 核武器 hé wǔqì

nucleus N 1 核子 hézǐ 2 细胞核 xìbāohé 3 核心（人物）héxīn (rénwù)

nude I ADJ 裸体的 luǒtǐ de II N 裸体画 luǒtǐhuà, 人体雕塑 réntǐ diāosù

nudge V 1 用（肘）轻推 yòng (zhǒu) qīng tuī
　to nudge one's way in 往前挤 wǎngqián jǐ
　2 劝说 quànshuō, 鼓励 gǔlì

nudist I N 裸体主义者 luǒtǐ zhǔyìzhě II ADJ 裸体的 luǒtǐde
　nudist camp 裸体营 luǒtǐyíng, 天体营 tiāntǐyíng

nugget N 1 小（天然）金块 xiǎo (tiānrán) jīnkuài 2（食物）小块 (shíwù) xiǎo kuài 3 有重大价值的东西 yǒu zhòngdà jiàzhí de dōngxi
　a nugget of information 有重大价值的信息 yǒu zhòngdà jiàzhí de xìnxī

nuisance N 讨厌鬼 tǎoyànguǐ, 讨厌的事 tǎoyàn de shì
　to make a nuisance of oneself 做令人讨厌的事 zuò lìng rén tǎoyàn de shì

nuke I N 核武器 hé wǔqì II V 用核武器攻击 yòng hé wǔqì gōngjī

null ADJ 无效的 wúxiào de
　null and void 无效的 wúxiào de

nullify V 宣布…（在法律上）无效 xuānbù…(zài fǎlǜshàng) wúxiào

numb I ADJ 麻木的 mámù de, 失去感觉的 shīqù gǎnjué de II V 使…失去感觉 shǐ…mámù, 使…失去感觉 shǐ…shīqù gǎnjué

number I N 1 数字 shùzì 2 数目 shùmù, 号码 hàomǎ
　number crunching 做数字工作 zuò shùzì gōngzuò, 运算 yùnsuàn
　3 数量 shùliàng
　number one 第一 dìyī, 最好的 zuìhǎo de II V 给…编号 gěi…biānhào
　to number the pages 编页码 biān yèmǎ
　2 总共 zǒnggòng, 共计 gòngjì

The days are numbered. 不会很久了。Bú huì hěn jiǔ le. 快完蛋了。Kuài wándàn le.

numeral N 数词 shùcí

numerical ADJ 数字上的 shùzì shàng de, 数量上的 shùliàng shàng de

numerous ADJ 众多的 zhòngduō de, 数量很多的 shùliàng hěn duō de

nun N 修女 xiūnǚ
　Buddhist nun 尼姑 nígū

nuptial ADJ 婚姻的 hūnyīn de, 婚礼的 hūnlǐ de
　nuptial vows 婚姻誓言 hūnyīn shìyán
　pre-nuptial agreement 婚前契约 hūnqián qìyuē

nuptials N 婚礼 hūnlǐ

nurse I N 护士 hùshi II V 1 护理 [+病人] hùlǐ [+bìngrén] 2 给 [+婴儿] 喂奶 gěi [+yīng'ér] wèinǎi 3 心中充满 [+仇恨] xīnzhōng chōngmǎn [+chóuhèn]

nursery N 1 托儿所 tuō'érsuǒ
　nursery rhyme 童谣 tóngyáo, 儿歌 érgē
　2 苗圃 miáopǔ

nurture V, N 培育 péiyù, 培养 péiyǎng

nut N 1 坚果 jiānguǒ, 干果 gānguǒ 2 螺母 luómǔ, 螺帽 luómào 3 怪人 guàirén
　soccer nut 足球迷 zúqiúmí
　a hard nut to crack 棘手的问题 jíshǒu de wèntí
　a tough nut 难对付的人 nán duìfu de rén

nutrient N 营养 yíngyǎng, 滋养 zīyǎng

nutrition N 营养 yíngyǎng

nutritious ADJ 营养丰富的 yíngyǎng fēngfù de

nuts ADJ 发疯的 fāfēng de, 发狂的 fākuáng de
　to go nuts 气得发疯 qìde fāfēng

nutshell N (in a nutshell) 用一句话来说 yòng yí jù huà láishuō, 一言以蔽之 yì yán yǐ bì zhī

nutty ADJ 1 古怪的 gǔguài de, 发疯的 fāfēng de 2 有坚果味的 yǒu jiānguǒ wèi de

nuzzle V（用鼻子）触碰 (yòng bízi) chùpèng

nylon N 尼龙 nílóng

nylons N 尼龙长袜 nílóng chángwà, 连裤袜 liánkùwà

nymph N 仙女 xiānnǚ

nymphomania N（女子）性欲旺盛 (nǚzǐ) xìngyù wàngshèng

O

oaf N（男）傻瓜 (nán) shǎguā, 笨蛋 bèndàn

oak N 1 橡树 xiàngshù [M. WD 棵 kē] 2 橡木 xiàng mù

oar N 桨 jiāng

oasis N 绿洲 lǜzhōu

oath N 1 誓言 shìyán
to take/swear an oath 宣誓 xuānshì
to take the oath of office 宣誓就职 xuānshì jiùzhí
2 咒骂 zhòumà, 诅咒 zǔzhòu

oats N 燕麦 yànmài
to sow wild oats（年轻时）生活放荡 (niánqīng shí) shēnghuó fàngdàng

obedience N 服从 fúcóng, 顺从 shùncóng

obedient ADJ 顺从的 shùncóng de, 听话的 tīnghuà de

obese ADJ（过度）肥胖的 (guòdù) féipàng de

obey V 服从 fúcóng

obituary N 讣告 fùgào [M. WD 份 fèn]

object I N 1 物体 wùtǐ, 东西 dōngxi
Unidentified Flying Object (UFO) 不明飞行物 bù míng fēixíngwù
2 目的 mùdì, 目标 mùbiāo 3（语法）宾语 (yǔfǎ) bīnyǔ **II** V 反对 fǎnduì

objection N 反对 fǎnduì, 厌恶 yànwù

objectionable ADJ 令人厌恶的 lìng rén yànwù de

objective I N 目标 mùbiāo, 目的 mùdì
II ADJ 客观的 kèguān de, 真实的 zhēnshí de

obligation N 义务 yìwù, 职责 zhízé

obligatory ADJ 必须做的 bìxū zuò de, 强制性的 qiángzhìxìng de

oblige V 1 迫使 pòshǐ 2 应请求（做）yìng qǐngqiú (zuò)

to feel obliged to do sth 感到有义务做某事 gǎndào yǒu yìwù zuò mǒushì
much obliged 非常感谢 fēicháng gǎnxiè

obliging ADJ 乐意助人的 lèyì zhù rén de

oblique ADJ 1 间接的 jiànjiē de 2 斜的 xié de, 倾斜的 qīngxié de

oblivious ADJ 未注意到的 wèi zhùyì dào de, 未察觉的 wèi chájué de

oblong ADJ, N 长方形（的）chángfāng-xíng (de), 椭圆形（的）tuǒyuánxíng (de)

obnoxious ADJ 讨厌的 tǎoyàn de, 极坏的 jí huài de

obscene ADJ 淫秽的 yínhuì de, 下流的 xiàliú de

obscenity N 淫秽／下流（的语言／行为）yínhuì/xiàliú (de yǔyán/xíngwéi)

obscure I ADJ 1 不出名的 bù chūmíng de, 不为人知的 bù wéi rén zhī de 2 难以理解的 nányǐ lǐjiě de, 晦涩的 huìsè de **II** V 使…难以理解 shǐ…nányǐ lǐjiě, 混淆 hùnxiáo

observance N 1 遵守 zūnshǒu, 奉行 fèngxíng 2 庆祝 qìngzhù

observant ADJ 观察能力很强的 guānchá nénglì hěn qiáng de

observation N 1 观察 guānchá 2 言论 yánlùn, 评论 pínglùn

observatory N 天文台 tiānwéntái, 气象台 qìxiàngtái [M. WD 座 zuò]

observe V 1 观察 guānchá, 注意到 zhùyìdao 2 纪念 [+节日] jìniàn [+jiérì], 庆祝 qìngzhù

obsessed ADJ 老是想着的 lǎoshi xiǎngzhe de, 痴迷 chīmí

obsession N 着迷 zháomí, 强迫性思维 qiǎngpòxìng sīwéi

obsolescence N 过时 guòshí, 废弃 fèiqì

obsolete ADJ 过时的 guòshí de, 废弃的 fèiqì de

obstacle N 障碍（物）zhàng'ài (wù)

obstetrics N 产科（学）chǎnkē (xué)

obstinacy N 固执 gùzhí, 顽固 wángù

obstinate ADJ 固执的 gùzhí de, 顽固的 wángù de

obstruct V 1 阻隔 zǔ'ài, 妨碍 fáng'ài 2 堵塞 [+交通] dǔsè [+jiāotōng]

obstruction N 1 堵塞（物）dǔsè (wù), 梗塞 gěngsè 2 扰乱 zǔrǎo

obtain V 获得 huòdé, 取得 qǔdé

obtainable ADJ 能得到的 néng dédào de

obtrude V 强行闯入 qiángxíng chuǎngrù

obtuse ADJ 1 愚笨的 yúbèn de 2（数学）钝角 (shùxué) dùnjiǎo
an obtuse triangle 钝角三角形 dùnjiǎo sānjiǎoxíng

obverse N 对立面 duìlìmiàn, 相反的事物 xiāngfǎn de shìwù

obvious ADJ 明显的 míngxiǎn de

obviously ADV 明显（地）míngxiǎn (de)

occasion N 1 场合 chǎnghé, 时刻 shíkè 2 特殊的事件 tèshū de shìjiàn, 喜庆的场合 xǐqìng de chǎnghé

occasionally ADV 偶然地 ǒurán de, 有时候 yǒushíhòu

occult I N 神秘行为 shénmì xíngwéi, 魔法 mófǎ II ADJ 神秘的 shénmì de, 奥秘的 àomì de

occupancy N 占用（期）zhànyòng (qī), 占有（期）zhànyǒu (qī)

occupation N 1 占领 zhànlǐng, 占据 zhànjù 2 职业 zhíyè

occupational ADJ 职业的 zhíyè de
occupational therapy 职业治疗 zhíyè zhìliáo

occupy V 1 占据 zhànjù, 占用 zhànyòng 2（军事）占领 (jūnshì) zhànlǐng

occur V 1 发生 fāshēng 2 想到 xiǎngdao, 想起 xiǎngqǐ

occurrence N 发生（的事）fāshēng (de shì), 出现 chūxiàn

ocean N 洋 yáng, 海洋 hǎiyáng

oceanography N 海洋学 hǎiyángxué

o'clock ADV 点钟 diǎnzhōng, 点 diǎn

octagon N 八角形 bājiǎoxíng, 八边形 bābiānxíng

October N 十月 shíyuè

octopus N 章鱼 zhāngyú

odd ADJ 1 古怪的 gǔguài de, 奇特的 qítè de
an odd ball 举止古怪的人 jǔzhǐ qíguài de rén
the odd man out 与众不同的人 yǔ zhòng bù tóng de rén
2 奇数的 jīshù de 3 偶尔的 ǒu'ěr de, 零

星的 língxīng de 4 多一点 duō yìdiǎn
20-odd 二十多个 èrshí duō gè

oddity N 1 古怪（的人）gǔguài (de rén) 2 奇特（的事）qítè (de shì)

oddly ADV 奇怪地 qíguài de, 古怪地 gǔguài de

oddments N 零头 língtóu, 碎屑 suìxiè

odds N 可能（性）kěnéng (xìng)
against all odds 尽管困难重重 jǐnguǎn kùnnan chóngchóng
odds and ends 零星杂物 língxīng záwù

odious ADJ 丑恶的 chǒu'è de, 可憎的 kězēng de

odometer N（汽车）里程计 (qìchē) lǐchéng jì

odor N 气味 qìwèi

odorless ADJ 无气味的 wú qìwèi de

odyssey N 漫长艰难的旅程 màncháng jiānnán de lǚchéng

of PREP 1 …的 ...de 2 来自 láizì
a sage of the East 一位来自东方的圣贤 yíwèi láizì dōngfāng de shèngxián

off I ADV 1 取消 qǔxiāo 2 除掉 chúdiao, 减去 jiǎnqu 3 离儿, 离去 líqù II PREP 1 离去 líqù 2 附近 fùjìn

offbeat ADJ 不寻常的 bùxúncháng de, 不落俗套的 búluò sútào de

offcolor ADJ 下流的 xiàliú de, 黄色的 huángsè de

offend V 冒犯 màofàn, 触怒 chùnù

offender N 违法者 wéifǎzhě, 罪犯 zuìfàn
first-time offender 初犯（罪犯）chūfàn (zuìfàn)

offense N 1 违法行为 wéifǎ xíngwéi, 犯法 fànfǎ 2 伤害 shānghài, 伤害感情 shānghài gǎnqíng
No offense. 请不要见怪。Qǐng bú yào jiànguài.

offensive ADJ 冒犯的 màofàn de, 很不礼貌的 hěn bù lǐmào de

offer I V 1 提供 tígōng 2 出价 chūjià, 报价 bàojià 3 表示愿意提供 biǎoshì yuànyì tígōng II N 1（提供帮助的）建议 (tígōng bāngzhu de) jiànyì 2 出价 chūjià

offering N 1 赠品 zèngpǐn, 献金 xiànjīn 2 提供的东西 tígōng de dōngxi

offhand ADJ, ADV 不假思索的 bù jiǎ

sīsuǒ de, 脱口而出的 tuōkǒu ér chū de **2** 漫不经心的 màn bù jīngxīn de

office N **1** 办公室 bàngōng shì, 办公大楼 bàngōng dàlóu **2** 办事处 bànshì chù
office building 办公大楼 bàngōng dàlóu, 写字楼 xiězì lóu

officer N **1** 军官 jūnguān **2** 警官 jǐngguān **3**（政府）官员 (zhèngfǔ) guānyuán **4**（公司）高级职员 (gōngsī) gāojí zhíyuán

official I ADJ 官方的 guānfāng de, 正式的 zhèngshì de II N 官员 guānyuán

officiate V 行使正式的职责 xíngshǐ zhèngshì de zhízé

offline ADV（计算机）不联网地 (jìsuàn jī) bùliánwǎng de, 脱机（地）tuōjī (de)
to work offline 脱机工作 tuōjī gōngzuò

offpeak ADJ 非高峰（时间）的 fēi gāofēng (shíjiān) de
offpeak hours 非高峰时间 fēi gāofēng shíjiān

offset（PT & PP offset）V **1** 补偿 bǔcháng, 弥补 míbǔ **2** 衬托 chèntuō

offshoot N 分支 fēnzhī

offshore ADJ, ADV **1** 在近海的 zài jìnhǎi de **2** 境外的 jìngwài de, 海外的 hǎiwài de
offshore investment 海外投资 hǎiwài tóuzī

offspring N 子孙后代 zǐsūn hòudài

off-the-record ADJ 不公开发表的 bù gōngkāi fābiǎo de, 私下的 sīxia de

often ADV 经常 jīngcháng, 常常 chángcháng

ogle V（色迷迷地）盯着看 (sèmímí de) dīngzhe kàn

ogre N 吃人妖魔 chīrén yāomó

ohm N 欧姆 Ōumǔ

oil I N **1** 油 yóu **2** 石油 shíyóu
oil slick 浮油 fúyóu
oil well 油井 yóujǐng
olive oil 橄榄油 gǎnlǎnyóu
deep sea fish oil 深海鱼油 shēnhǎiyúyóu
II v 加润滑油 jiā huárùnyóu, 上油 shàng yóu

oily ADJ 含油的 [+鱼] hán yóu de [+yú], 油质的 [+头发] yóuzhì de [+tóufa], 油滑的 [+人] yóuhuá de [+rén]

ointment N 油膏 yóugāo, 软膏 ruǎngāo

OK I ADJ, ADV **1** 好 hǎo, 不错 búcuò **2** 行 xíng, 可以 kěyǐ II v 同意 tóngyì, 批准 pīzhǔn III INTERJ 好吧 hǎo ba

old ADJ **1** 老 lǎo, 上了年纪的 shàngle niánjì de
old age 老年（时期）lǎonián (shíqī)
old timer 老资格的人 lǎozīgé de rén, 老前辈 lǎoqiánbèi
2 旧 jiù **3** 熟悉的 shúxī de, 有深交的 yǒu shēnjiāo de
old boy network（男）校友关系网 (nán) xiàoyǒu guānxiwǎng
old friend 老朋友 lǎopéngyou

old-fashioned ADJ 老式的 lǎoshì de, 守旧的 shǒujiù de

oldie N **1** 名人 míngrén **2** 旧物 jiùwù

Old Testament N（圣经）旧约书 (Shèngjīng) Jiùyuēshū

olive N 橄榄 gǎnlǎn [M. WD 颗 kē]
to offer an olive branch 表示和解 biǎoshì héjiě

Olympic Games N 奥林匹克运动会 Àolínpǐkè Yùndònghuì

omelet, omelette N 煎蛋卷 jiāndànjuǎn

omen N 预兆 yùzhào, 兆头 zhàotou

ominous ADJ 不吉利的 bù jílì de, 不详的 bùxiáng de

omission N 省略（的东西）shěnglüè (de dōngxi), 遗漏 yílòu

omit v 省略 shěnglüè, 排除 páichú

omnipotent ADJ 全能的 quánnéng de

omniscience N 全知 quánzhī

omnivorous ADJ 杂食的 [+动物] zá shí de [+dòngwù]

on I PREP **1** 在…上 zài...shang **2** 在 zài **3** 关于 guānyú II ADV **1** 继续 jìxù, …下去 ...xiaqu **2** 穿着 chuānzhe, 戴着 dàizhe **3** 接通 jiētōng
to turn/switch on 开（灯，电视机，etc.）kāi (dēng, diànshìjī, etc.)
to get on 乘 chéng

once I ADV **1** 一次 yí cì
once more 再一次 zài yí cì, 又一次 yòu yí cì
at once ① 马上 mǎshàng ② 同时 tóng-shí

once in a while 偶尔 ǒu'ěr
2 曾经 céngjīng
once upon the time 从前 cóngqián
II CONJ 一旦 yīdàn, 一旦 yídàn

once-over N 大致一看 dàzhì yīkàn
to give sb/sth the once-over 对某人／某事粗略地打量一下 duì mǒurén/mǒushì cūlüè de dǎliang yíxià

oncoming ADJ 迎面而来的 yíngmiàn érlái de

one I NUM **1** 一 yī II PRON 一个 yí ge
one by one 一个接着一个 yí ge jiēzhe yíge
one another 相互 xiānghù, 彼此 bǐcǐ

one-of-a-kind ADJ 独一无二的 dúyī wú èr de

onerous ADJ 繁重的（工作）fánzhòng de (gōngzuò), 艰巨的（任务）jiānjù de (rènwu)

oneself PRON 自己 zìjǐ, 自身 zìshēn

one-sided ADJ 片面的 piànmiàn de, 不公正的 bù gōngzhèng de

onetime ADJ **1** 从前的 cóngqián de **2** 一次性的 yícìxìng de, 只发生一次的 zhǐ fāshēng yící de

one-to-one ADJ **1** 一对一的 [+讨论] yīduìyī de [+tǎolùn] **2** 一比一的 [+兑换率] yībǐyī de [+duìhuànlǜ]

one-way ADJ 单（方）向的 dān (fāng) xiàng de
a one-way street 单行（街）道 dānxíng (jiē) dào

ongoing ADJ 持续的 chíxù de

onion N 洋葱 yángcōng

online ADJ, ADV 联网的 liánwǎng de, 联线的 liánxiàn de

onlooker N 旁观者 pángguānzhě

only I ADV 只 zhǐ, 只有 zhǐyǒu, 只是 zhǐ shì
II ADJ 唯一的 wéiyī de
an only child 独生子女 dúshēng zǐnǚ
III CONJ 只是 zhǐ shì, 但是 dànshì

onrush N 向前猛冲 xiàngqián měngchōng

onset N 开始 kāishǐ

onto PREP 到…上 dào...shang, 在…上 zài...shang

onus N 责任 zérèn

onward ADV, ADJ 向前（方）的／地 xiàngqián (fāng) de

oops INTERJ 啊呀 āyā

ooze I V 慢慢流出 mànmàn liúchū, 渗出 shènchū II N **1** 慢慢流动 mànmàn liúdòng **2** 淤泥 yūní

opal N 蛋白石 dànbáishí, 澳宝 àobǎo

opaque ADJ **1** 不透明的 [+玻璃] bú tòumíng de [+bōli] **2** 难懂的 [+文字] nándǒng de [+wénzì]

open I ADJ **1** 开（着）的 kāi (zhe) de, 打开的 dǎkāi de **2** 营业中的 yíngyè zhōng de **3** 开放的 kāifàng de
open house 开放日 kāifàngrì
an open plan 公开计划 gōngkāi jìhuà
4 公开的 gōngkāi de
an open secret 公开的秘密 gōngkāi de mìmì
5 还没有结论的 hái méiyǒu jiélùn de, 还没有决定的 hái méiyǒu juédìng de
to keep an open mind 不匆忙下结论 bù cōngmáng xià jiélùn
II V **1** 开 kāi, 打开 dǎkāi **2** 开始营业 kāishǐ yíngyè, 开门 kāimén **3** 开放 kāifàng
to open fire 开火 kāihuǒ

open-air ADJ 露天的 lùtiān de

open-and-shut case N 很容易解决的问题 hěn róngyì jiějué de wèntí

open-ended ADJ **1** 无限期的 wúxiànqī de **2** 无明确答案的 [+问题] wú míngquè dá'àn de [+wèntí]

opener N **1** 开启器 [瓶／罐子的] 工具 kāiqǐ [píng/guànzi de] gōngjù **2** （体育比赛）开局 (tǐyù bǐsài) kāijú
for openers 首先 shǒuxiān

opening I N **1** [新店+] 开张 [xīndiàn+] kāizhāng **2** [新公司+] 开业 [xīn gōngsī+] kāiyè **3** [职位的+] 空缺 [zhíwèi de+] kòngquē **4** 通道 tōngdào **5** 孔 kǒng, 洞 dòng II ADJ 首次的 shǒucì de

open-minded ADJ 思想开放的 sīxiǎng kāifàng de

openness N **1** 坦诚 tǎn chéng **2** 开明 kāimíng, 思想（开通）sīxiǎng (kāitōng)

opera N 歌剧 gējù
Peking opera 京剧 Jīngjù, 京戏 Jīngxì

operate V **1** 操纵 cāozòng, 操作 cāozuò

464

2 运行 yùnxíng, 运转 yùnzhuǎn **3** 动手术 dòng shǒushù

operation N **1** 手术 shǒushù [M. WD 次 cì] **2** 行动 xíngdòng **3** 运转 yùnzhuǎn

operative I ADJ **1** 起作用的 qǐ zuòyòng de **2** 关键的 guānjiàn de
the operative word 最重要的词 zuì zhòngyào de cí
II N **1** 特工 tègōng, 间谍 jiàndié **2** 操作工 cāozuògōng, 技工 jìgōng

operator N 操作工 cāozuògōng, 操作员 cāozuòyuán, (电话)接线员 (diànhuà) jiēxiànyuán
computer operator 电脑操作员 diànnǎo cāozuòyuán
sewing-machine operator 缝纫机操作工 féngrènjī cāozuògōng

ophthalmology N 眼科(学) yǎnkē (xué)

opinion N **1** 意见 yìjiàn, 看法 kànfǎ **2** 舆论 yúlùn, 公众看法 gōngzhòng kànfǎ
public opinion 舆论 yúlùn, 民意 mínyì
to have a high/low opinion of 对…评价很高／不高 duì…píngjià hěn gāo/bù gāo

opium N 鸦片 yāpiàn

opponent N 反对者 fǎnduìzhě, 对手 duìshǒu

opportune ADJ **1** 合适的 [+时刻] héshì de [+shíkè] **2** 及时的 [+行动] jíshí de [+xíngdòng]

opportunist N (不讲原则的)机会主义者 (bù jiǎng yuánzé de) jīhuìzhǔyìzhě

opportunity N 机会 jīhuì
Opportunity knocks at the door only once. 机不可失, 时不再来。Jī bù kě shī, shí bú zài lái. (→ The opportunity shouldn't be missed and this occasion will not come again.)

oppose V **1** 反对 fǎnduì **2** 对抗 duìkàng

opposite I ADJ 相对的 xiāngduì de, 对面的 duìmiàn de II N 相反的事物 xiāngfǎn de shìwù III PREP, ADV 在…对面的 zài…duìmiàn de

opposition N **1** 反对 fǎnduì **2** (体育比赛)竞争对手 (tǐyù bǐsài) jìngzhēng duìshǒu **3** (the Opposition)反对党 fǎnduìdǎng

oppress V **1** 压迫 yāpò **2** 使…感到压抑 shǐ…gǎndào yāyì

oppressed ADJ **1** 受压迫的 shòu yāpò de **2** 受压抑的 shòu yāyì de

oppressive ADJ **1** 暴虐的 [+统治] bàonüè de [+tǒngzhì], 不公平的 bùgōngpíng de **2** 压抑的 [+气氛] yāyì de [+qìfēn] **3** 闷热的 [+天气] mēnrè de [+tiānqì]

opt V 选择 xuǎnzé
to opt out 决定(不做某事)juédìng (bú zuò mǒushì), 逃避 táobì

optic ADJ 眼睛的 yǎnjing de, 视觉的 shìjué de

optical ADJ **1** 光学的 guāngxué de
optical fiber 光学纤维 guāngxué xiānwéi **2** 视觉的 shìjué de
optical illusion 视错觉 shì cuòjué

optician N 眼镜(制造)商 yǎnjìng (zhìzào) shāng

optimism N 乐观主义 lèguān zhǔyì

optimistic ADJ 乐观的 lèguān de

optimize V 使…最优化 shǐ…zuì yōuhuà, 使…最有效 shǐ…zuì yǒuxiào

optimum ADJ 最优的 zuì yōu de, 最佳的 zuì jiā de
an optimum condition 最佳条件 zuì jiā tiáojiàn

option N 选择 xuǎnzé, 选择权 xuǎnzéquán

optional ADJ 可选择的 kě xuǎnzé de, 非强迫的 fēi qiǎngpò de

optometrist N 验光师 yànguāngshī

opulence N 豪华 háohuá, 奢侈 shēchǐ

or CONJ **1** 或者 huòzhě **2** 还是 háishi **3**(要)不然 (yào) bùrán, 否则 fǒuzé

oral I ADJ **1** 口头的 kǒutóu de **2** 口腔的 kǒuqiāng de
oral examination 口试 kǒushì
oral contraceptive 口服避孕药 kǒufú bìyùnyào
II N 口试 kǒushì

orange N **1** 橙子 chéngzi, 橘子 júzi
orange juice 橘子汁 júzizhī **2** 橙黄色 chénghuángsè, 橘红色 júhóngsè

orang-utang N 红毛猩猩 hóngmáo xīngxing [M. WD 只 zhī]

orator N 演说家 yǎnshuō jiā

oratory N 1 演说技巧 yǎnshuō jìqiǎo 2 雄辩的口才 xióngbiàn de kǒucái

orbit I N 1 轨道 guǐdào 2 范围 fànwéi
II v 环绕 [+轨道] 运行 huánrào [+guǐdào] yùnxíng

orchard N 果园 guǒyuán

orchestra N 管弦乐队 (guǎnxián) yuèduì
symphony orchestra 交响乐队 jiāoxiǎng yuèduì

orchid N 兰花 lánhuā [M. WD 株 zhū/朵 duǒ]

ordain v 任命…为牧师 rènmìng…wéi mùshi, 授予…神职 shòuyǔ…shénzhí

ordeal N 痛苦经历 tòngkǔ jīnglì, 艰难过程 jiānnán guòchéng

order I N 1 顺序 shùnxù 2 秩序 zhìxù
law and order 法律与秩序 fǎlǜ yǔ zhìxù
3 订单 dìngdān, 订货单 dìnghuò 4 命令 mìnglìng II v 1 点菜 diǎn cài 2 订购 dìnggòu 3 命令 mìnglìng, 嘱咐 zhǔfù
in order to 为了 wèile

orderly I ADJ 有条理的 yǒu tiáolǐ de, 守秩序的 shǒu zhìxù de II N (医院) 勤杂工 (yīyuàn) qínzágōng

ordinal I ADJ 顺序的 shùnxù de
ordinal number 序数 (词) xùshù (cí)
II N 序数 xùshù

ordinance N 法令 fǎlìng, 法规 fǎguī

ordinarily ADV 通常 (来说) tōngcháng (láishuō)

ordinary ADJ 普通的 pǔtōng de, 平常的 píngcháng de

ore N 矿石 kuàngshí

organ N 1 器官 qìguān 2 风琴 fēngqín

organic ADJ 1 有机的 yǒujī de, 生物的 shēngwù de
organic vegetables 有机蔬菜 yǒujī shūcài
2 (人体) 器官的 (réntǐ) qìguān de

organism N 有机体 yǒujītǐ, 生物 shēngwù

organization N 组织 zǔzhī
non-governmental organization (NGO) 非政府组织 fēizhèngfǔ zǔzhī

organize v 组织 zǔzhī, 安排 ānpái

organized ADJ 1 有组织的 yǒu zǔzhī de
organized crime 有组织犯罪 yǒu zǔzhī fànzuì, 集团犯罪 jítuán fànzuì

2 (时间) 安排得很好的 (shíjiān) ānpái de hěn hǎode, 有条有理的 yǒutiáo yǒulǐ de

organizer N 组织者 zǔzhīzhě

orgasm N 性高潮 xìng gāocháo

orgy N 纵欲狂欢 zòngyù kuánghuān

orient v 定 (方) 位 dìng (fāng) wèi
to be oriented towards 将…作为主要目的 jiāng…zuòwéi zhǔyào mùdì

Orient N 东方 dōngfāng

orientation N 1 目标 mùbiāo, 目的 mùdì 2 倾向 qīngxiàng 3 (让新来者) 熟悉情况 (ràng xīnláizhě) shúxī qíngkuàng
orientation week (大学) 新生入学周 (dàxué) xīnshēng rùxué zhōu

origin N 1 起源 qǐyuán, 来历 láilì
country of origin (产品) 原产国 (chǎnpǐn) yuánchǎn guó
2 出身 chūshēn, (家庭) 背景 (jiātíng) bèijǐng

original ADJ 1 原始的 yuánshǐ de, 最初的 zuìchū de 2 新颖的 xīnyǐng de, 有创见的 yǒu chuàngjiàn de

originality N 独创 (性) dúchuàng (xìng), 创造力 chuàngzàolì

ornament I N 装饰物 zhuāngshì wù
II v 点缀 diǎnzhuì

ornate ADJ 装饰华丽的 zhuāngshì huálì de, 装饰过分的 zhuāngshì guòfèn de

ornithologist N 鸟类学家 niǎolèixuéjiā

orphan I N 孤儿 gū'ér II v (be orphaned) 成为孤儿 chéngwéi gū'ér

orphanage N 孤儿院 gū'éryuàn

orthodox ADJ 正统的 zhèngtǒng de

orthopedics N 矫形外科 jiǎoxíng wàikē

oscillate v 1 来回摆动 láihuí bǎidòng, 振荡 zhèndàng 2 反复改变 fǎnfù gǎibiàn

ostentatious ADJ 讲究排场的 jiǎngjiu páichǎng de, 铺张的 pūzhāng de

ostracize v 排斥 páichì, 抵制 dǐzhì

ostrich N 鸵鸟 tuóniǎo [M. WD 只 zhī]

other I ADJ 其他的 qítā de, 另外的 lìngwài de
the other day 不久前一天 bù jiǔ qián yì tiān
every other day/week/year, etc. 每隔一天／一星期／一年 měi gé yì tiān/yì

xīngqī/yì nián, 每两天／两周／两年一次
měi liǎng tiān/liǎng zhōu/liǎng nián yí
cì

in other words 也就是说 yě jiù shì
shuō, 换句话说 huàn jù huà shuō
II PRON 另一个 lìng yí ge

otherwise I CONJ 不然 bùrán, 否则 fǒuzé
II ADV 不同 bù tóng, 不同地 bù tóng de

otter N 水獭 shuǐtǎ [M. WD 只 zhī]

ouch INTERJ 哎哟 āiyō, 疼啊 téng a

ought to [NEG **ought not to**] MODAL V 应
该 yīnggāi, 该 gāi

ounce N 盎司 àngsī, (英) 两 (yīng) liǎng
(= 28.35 克 kè)

our PRON 我们的 wǒmen de

ours PRON 我们的 wǒmen de

ourselves PRON (我们) 自己 (wǒmen)
zìjǐ

oust V 把…赶走 bǎ…gǎnzǒu

out ADV **1** 外面 wàimian, 不在 (家／办公
室) búzài (jiā/bàngōngshì)

Get out! 出去! 滚出去! Chūqu!
Gǔnchūqu!

2 有差错的 yǒu chācuò de **3** 不可能 bù
kěnéng

outage N 断供期 duàngòngqī

power outage 停电期间 tíngdiànqījiān

outbreak N 爆发 bàofā, 突发 tūfā

epidemic outbreak 流行病突发 liúxíngbìng tūfā

outburst N 突然大发脾气 tūrán dàfā píqi,
(强烈情绪的) 爆发 (qiángliè qíngxù
de) bàofā

outcast N 被遗弃的人 bèi yíqì de rén

outcome N 结果 jiéguǒ

outdated ADJ 过时的 guòshí de, 老式的
lǎoshì de

outdoors ADV 户外 hùwài

outer ADJ 外面的 wàimiàn de, 远离中心的
yuǎnlí zhōngxīn de

outer space 外层空间 wàicéng
kōngjiān

outgoing ADJ 外向的 wàixiàng de, 开朗
的 kāilǎng de

outing N 远足 yuǎnzú, 短途旅行 duǎntú
lǚxíng

outlet N **1** 电源插座 diànyuán chāzuò

2 零售商店 língshòushāng diàn, 经销点
jīngxiāo diǎn **3** 通风口 tōngfēngkǒu, 排
水道 páishuǐdào **4** 发泄 (强烈感情) 的
方法 fāxiè (qiángliè gǎnqíng) de fāngfǎ

outline I N **1** 提纲 tígāng **2** 轮廓 lúnkuò,
外形 wàixíng **II** V 扼要说明 èyào
shuōmíng

outlive V 活得比…长 huó dé bǐ…cháng

to outlive one's usefulness 不再有
用 búzài yǒuyòng, 失去功效 shīqù
gōngxiào

outlying ADJ 边远的 biānyuǎn de, 外围
的 wàiwéi de

out of PREP **1** 从…里出来 cóng…lǐ chūlái
2 用完 yòngwán **3** 出于 chūyú

out of curiosity 出于好奇心 chū yú
hàoqí xīn

out of bounds ① (球类运动) 球出界
(qiúlèiyùndòng) qiú chūjiè ② 不准入内
bùzhǔn rùnèi

out of touch 脱离现实 tuōlí xiànshí,
不了解现实情况 bùliǎojiě xiànshí
qíngkuàng

out of work 失业 shīyè

outpatient N 门诊病人 ménzhěn bìngrén

outperform V 做得比…好 zuòde bǐ…
hǎo, 胜过 shèngguò

outpost N 边缘军事哨所 biānyuán
jūnshì shàosuǒ, 边缘贸易点 biānyuán
màoyìdiǎn

outpouring N **1** 大量涌现 dàliàng
yǒngxiàn **2** 强烈感情的表达 qiángliè
gǎnqíng de biǎodá

output N (出) 产量 (chū) chǎnliàng

outrage I N 震怒 zhènnù, 极大的愤慨 jídà
de fènkǎi **II** V 使…震怒 shǐ…zhènnù

outrageous ADJ **1** 令人震怒的 [+行为]
lìngrén zhènnù de [+xíngwéi] **2** 极不合
理的 [+价格] jí bùhélǐ de [+jiàgé], 离谱
的 lípǔ de

outreach N 扩大服务 kuòdà fúwù

outright I ADJ **1** 彻底的 chèdǐ de **2** 毫不
掩饰的 háobù yǎnshì de **II** ADV **1** 彻底地
chèdǐ de **2** 不掩饰地 bù yǎnshì de **3** 立
刻 lìkè, 立即 lìjí

outrun V 跑得比…快 pǎo de bǐ…kuài, 超
过 chāoguò

outset N 开头 kāitóu, 开始 kāishǐ

outshine V 使…黯然失色 shǐ…ànrán shīsè, 优于 yōuyú

outside I ADV （在）外面 (zài) wàimiàn II ADJ 外面的 wàimiàn de, 室外的 shìwài de III PREP 在…外面 zài…màimian IV N 外面 wàimian

outsider N （局）外人 (jú) wàirén

outskirts N 远郊 yuǎnjiāo, 郊区 jiāoqū

outsmart V 比…精明 bǐ…jīngmíng

outsourcing N 将工作外包 jiāng gōngzuò wàibāo, 从外部采购（部件）cóng wàibù cǎigòu (bùjiàn)

outspoken ADJ 直言不讳的 zhíyán búhuì de, 坦率的 tǎnshuài de

outstanding ADJ 杰出的 jiéchū de, 出色的 chūsè de

outstretched ADJ 张开的 zhāngkāi de, 伸展的 shēnzhǎn de

outstrip V 在数量上超过 zài shùliàng shàng chāoguò, 多于 duōyú

outward ADJ 向外（的／地）xiàngwài (de), 外面（的／地）wàimiàn (de)

outweight V 超过 chāoguò

outwit V 智胜 zhì shèng

oval ADJ 椭圆形 tuǒyuánxíng

ovary N 卵巢 luǎncháo

ovation N （热烈）鼓掌 (rèliè) gǔzhǎng

oven N 烘箱 hōngxiāng, 烤炉 kǎolú

over I ADV 1 倒下 dǎoxià
to fall over 摔倒 shuāidǎo, 倒下 dǎoxià
2 在 zài, 到 dào
over there 在那里 zài nàli
3 翻转 fānzhuǎn
to turn over 翻过来 fānguòlái
II ADV 结束 jiéshù, 完了 wánle III PREP 1 在…上方 zài…shàngfāng 2 覆盖在… fùgài zài… 3 在…之上 zài…zhīshàng, 超过 chāoguò

overall I ADJ 一切的 yíqiè de II ADV 总之 zǒngzhī, 总共 zǒnggòng

overalls N 背带工装裤 bēidài gōngzhuāngkù [M. WD 条 tiáo]

overbearing ADJ 专横 zhuānhèng

overboard ADV (to fall overboard)（从船上）掉入水中 (cóng chuánshàng) diào rù shuǐ zhōng

to go overboard 做得太过分 zuòde tài guòfèn

overburdened ADJ 负担过重的 fùdān guòzhòng de

overcast ADJ （天空）多云的 (tiānkōng) duōyún de

overcharge V 多收…的钱 duō shōu… de qián, 要价太高 yàojià tàigāo 2 使… 充电过度 shǐ…chōngdiàn guòdù

overcoat N 大衣 dàyī [M. WD 件 jiàn]

overcome V 1 克服 [+障碍] kèfú [+zhàng'ài] 2 使…失去知觉 shǐ…shīqù zhījué

overcrowded ADJ 太拥挤 tài yōngjǐ, 人太多 rén tài duō

overdo V 做得过火 zuòde guòhuǒ, 做得过份 zuòde guòfèn

overdose I N 1 药物过量 yàowù guòliàng, 过量服用 guòliàng fúyòng 2 过量 guòliàng, 过分喜爱 guòfèn xǐ'ài II V 用药过量 yòngyào guòliàng

overdraft N 透支（额）tòuzhī (é)

overdraw V（存款账户）透支 (cúnkuǎn zhànghù) tòuzhī

overdue ADJ 1 过期不付的 [+借款] guòqī búfù de [+jièkuǎn] 2 过期不还的 [+图书] guòqī bù huán de [+túshū] 3 过期不交的 [+作业] guòqī bù jiāo de [+zuòyè]

overeat V 吃得过多 chī dé guòduō

overestimate V 过高估计 guògāo gūjì

overextend V (to overextend oneself) 消费超过财力 xiāofèi guòguò cáilì, 超前消费 chāoqián xiāofèi

overflow I V 溢出 yìchū, 漫过 mànguò II N 1 泛滥 fànlàn, 溢流 yìliú 2 溢流管 yìliú guǎn [M. WD 条 tiáo] 3 无法容纳的人（或物）wúfǎ róngnà de rén (huò wù)

overgrown ADJ 长满 zhǎngmǎn

overhang V 悬在…上方 xuán zài… shàngfāng

overhaul V 1 彻底检修 [+洪水系统] chèdǐ jiǎnxiū [+gōngshuǐ xìtǒng] 2 对 [+税收制度] 全面改革 duì [+shuìshōu zhìdù] quánmiàn gǎigé

overhead[1] ADJ, ADV 在头顶（的／地）zài tóudǐng (de), 在空中（的／地）zài kōngzhōng (de) overhead projector（高射）投影仪 (gāo shè) tóuyǐngyí

overhead² N **1** 行政管理费用 xíngzhèng guǎnlǐfèi yòng, 管理成本 guǎnlǐ chéngběn **2** 透明胶片 tòumíng jiāopiàn

overhear V 无意中听到 wúyìzhōng tīngdào

overjoyed ADJ 非常高兴的 fēicháng gāoxìng de

overland ADJ, ADV 经陆路（的／地）jīng lùlù (de)

overlap I V **1** 部份重叠 bùfèn chóngdié II N 重叠（的部份）chóngdié (de bùfen)

overload I V **1** 使 [+卡车] 超重装载 shǐ [+kǎchē] chāozhòng zhuāngzài **2** 使 [+电器设备] 超负荷 shǐ [+diànqì shèbèi] chāofùhè II N **1** 超重装载 chāozhòng zhuāngzài **2**（电器设备）超负荷 (diànqì shèbèi) chāofùhé

overlook V **1** 俯瞰 fǔkàn, 俯视 fǔshì **2** 忽视 hūshì, 忽略 hūlüè **3** 不计较 bújì jiào, 原谅 yuánliàng

overly ADV（太）过于 (tài) guòyú
not overly 不太 bútài

overnight I ADJ 在一夜间 zài yíyè jiān
an overnight flight 整夜飞行 zhěngyè fēixíng
an overnight success 一举成功 yìjǔ chénggōng
II ADV（一）夜间 (yí) yèjiān

overpass N 天桥 tiānqiáo [M. WD 座 zuò], 立交桥 lìjiāoqiáo [M. WD 座 zuò]

overpopulation N 人口过多 rénkǒu guòduō

overpowering ADJ 不可抗拒的 bùkě kàngjù de, 强烈的 qiángliè de

overpriced ADJ 定价太高的 dìngjià tàigāo de

overreact V 对…反应过度 duì...fǎnyìng guòdù

override V **1** 推翻 [+以前的决定] tuīfān [+yǐqián de juédìng] **2** 改变 [+自动程序] gǎibiàn [+zìdòng chéngxù] **3** 比…更重要 bǐ...gèng zhòngyào

overrule V 否决 fǒujué, 推翻 tuīfān
Objection overruled. 反对无效。Fǎnduì wúxiào.

overrun¹ V **1** [植物+] 蔓延 [zhíwù+] mànyán **2** [河水+] 溢出 [héshuǐ+] yìchū, 泛滥 fànlàn

overrun² N 超支 chāozhī

overseas ADJ, ADV 海外的 hǎiwài de, 国外的 guówài de

oversee V 监督 jiāndū, 监管 jiānguǎn

overshadow V **1** 给…蒙上阴影 gěi... méng shàng yīnyǐng **2** 使…相形见绌 shǐ...xiāngxíng jiànchù

overshoot V **1** 错过 [+目的地] cuòguò [+mùdìdì] **2** 超出 [+预算] chāochū [+yùsuàn]

oversight N 疏忽 shūhu, 失误 shīwù

oversimplification N 过分简单（化）guòfèn jiǎndān (huà)

oversleep V 睡过头 shuìguòtóu

overstate V 夸大 kuādà, 夸张 kuāzhāng

overtake V **1** 领先 lǐngxiān, 超过 chāoguò **2** 突然降临 tūrán jiànglín

overthrow V 推翻 tuīfān, 打倒 dǎdǎo

overtime N **1** 加班时间 jiābān shíjiān **2** 加班费 jiābānfèi **3**（体育比赛）加时 (tǐyù bǐsài) jiā shí

overture N **1** 序曲 xùqǔ **2** 主动表示（友好）zhǔdòng biǎoshì (yǒuhǎo)
to make overtures to sb 向某人示好 xiàng mǒurén shìhǎo

overturn V 推翻 tuīfān, 否决 fǒujué

overview N 概况 gàikuàng, 概述 gàishù

overweight ADJ（体重）超重 (tǐzhòng) chāozhòng

overwhelming ADJ **1** 压倒的 yādào de **2** 不可抗拒的 bùkě kàngjù de
an overwhelming majority 压倒多数 yādào duōshù, 绝对多数 juéduì duōshù

overwork V（使…）工作过度 (shǐ...) gōngzuò guòdù

overwrought ADJ 神经非常紧张的 shénjīng fēicháng jǐnzhāng de, 极其焦虑的 jíqí jiāolǜ de

owe V **1** 欠 qiàn
to owe sb a favor 欠某人人情 qiàn mǒurén rénqíng
2（应该）把…归功于 (yīnggāi) bǎ... guīgōng yú

owing to PREP 由于 yóuyú

owl N 猫头鹰 māotóuyīng [M. WD 只 zhī]
own I V 拥有 yōngyǒu II ADJ, PRON 自己的 zìjǐ de
owner N 物主 wùzhǔ, 业主 yèzhǔ
ox N 公牛 gōngniú [M. WD 头 tóu]
oxygen N 氧气 yǎngqì
oyster N 牡蛎 mǔlì, 生蚝 shēng háo
ozone N 臭氧 chòuyǎng
ozone layer 臭氧层 chòuyǎngcéng

P

pace I N 1 速度 sùdù
to speed up the pace 加快速度 jiākuài sùdù
2 (一)步 (yí) bù
to step a pace 走一步 zǒu yíbù
II V 1 慢步走 mànbù zǒu, 踱步 duó bù
to pace the floor 在房间里走来走去 zài fángjiān lǐ zǒulái zǒuqù, 在房间里踱步 zài fángjiān lǐ duóbù
2 为…定速 wéi…dìngsù
Pacific Ocean N 太平洋 Tàipíngyáng
pacifier N 1 镇静剂 zhènjìngjì 2 橡皮奶嘴 xiàngpí nǎizuǐ
pacify V 1 使…平静（下来）shǐ…píngjìng (xiàlai) 2 平定 píngdìng
pack I N 1 包 bāo, 盒 hé, 副 fù 2 群 qún
a pack of cigarettes 一包香烟 yì bāo xiāngyān
a pack of gum 一盒口香糖 yì hé kǒuxiāngtáng
a pack of wolves 一群狼 yì qún láng
II V 1 把…装进 [+箱子] bǎ…zhuāngjìn [+xiāngzi] 2 把…包装好 bǎ…bāozhuāng hǎo 3 [人+] 挤进 [+rén] jǐjìn
to pack up ① 收拾行李 shōushi xíngli ② 停止工作 tíngzhǐ gōngzuò, 收工 shōugōng
to pack one's bags 卷铺盖走人 juǎn pūgai zǒurén
package I N 1 包裹 bāoguǒ 2 套 tào
package deal 一揽子交易 yì lǎn zi jiāoyì
package tour 配套旅游 pèitào lǚyóu
II V 1 把 [+东西] 打包 bǎ [+dōngxi]

dǎbāo 2 对 [+人] 进行包装 duì [+rén] jìnxíng bāozhuāng
packer N 打包工 dǎbāo gōng
packet N 1 一小包 yì xiǎobāo, 一小袋 yì xiǎo dài 2 (计算机) 信息包 (jìsuànjī) xìnxībāo
pad I N 1 拍纸簿 pāizhǐbù [M. WD 本 běn]
note pad 记事本 jìshìběn
2 护垫 hùdiàn [M. WD 块 kuài]
knee pad 护膝 hùxī
3 (妇女用的) 卫生巾 (fùnǚ yòng de) wèishēngjīn 4 (导弹) 发射台 (dǎodàn) fāshètái 5 (直升飞机) 停机坪 (zhíshēng fēijī) tíngjīpíng 6 (动物的) 爪垫 (dòngwù de) zhuǎdiàn II V 1 (用软物) 填塞 (yòng ruǎn wù) tiánsāi 2 虚报 [+费用] xūbào [+fèiyòng] 3 放轻脚步走 fàngqīng jiǎobù zǒu
padding N 1 垫衬材料 diàn chèn cáiliào 2 (书中) 凑篇幅的内容 (shū zhōng) còu piānfu de nèiróng
paddle I N 短浆 duǎnjiāng [M. WD 把 bǎ] II V 用浆划 yòng jiāng huà
paddy, rice paddy N 水稻田 shuǐdào tián [M. WD 块 kuài]
padlock I N 挂锁 guàsuǒ II V (用挂锁) 锁上 (yòng guàsuǒ) suǒshàng
pagan N, ADJ 异教 (徒) yìjiào (tú)
page I N 页 yè II V 1 (用扩音器) 唤人 (yòng kuòyīnqì) huàn rén 2 翻页 fān yè
to page through 很快地翻阅 hěn kuài de fānyuè
pageant N 1 盛装游行 shèngzhuāng yóuxíng 2 (选美) 表演 (xuǎn měi) biǎoyǎn
pager N 寻呼机 xúnhūjī
pagoda N (宝) 塔 (bǎo) tǎ
paid See pay
pail N 提桶 títǒng
pain N 疼痛 téngtòng, 痛苦 tòngkǔ
to be a pain (in the neck) 极其讨厌 jíqí tǎoyàn
pained ADJ (感情) 受到伤害的 de, (感到) 痛苦的 (gǎndào) tòngkǔ de
painful ADJ 1 疼痛的 téngtòng de 2 (令人) 痛苦的 [+事] (lìngrén) tòngkǔ de [+shì]

a painful decision（令人）痛苦的决定 (lìng rén) tòngkǔ de juédìng

painkiller N 止痛药 zhǐtòngyào

pains N 尽力（去做某事）jìnlì（qù zuò mǒushì）

painstaking ADJ 仔细的 zǐxì de, 精心的 jīngxīn de

paint I N 漆 qī, 油漆 yóuqī
paint thinner 油漆稀释液 yóuqī xīshì yè
II v 漆 qī, 油漆 yóuqī 2（用油彩）画 (yòng yóucǎi) huà, 绘画 huìhuà
Wet paint. 油漆未干。Yóuqī wèi gān.

painter N 1 画家 huàjiā 2 油漆工 yóuqīgōng

painting N 绘画作品 huìhuà zuòpǐn, （图）画 (tú) huà

pair I N 双 shuāng, 副 fù, 对 duì
a pair of gloves 一副手套 yí fù shǒutào
a pair of scissors 一把剪刀 yì bǎ jiǎndāo
a pair of spectacles 一副眼镜 yí fù yǎnjìng
a pair of pants 一条裤子 yì tiáokùzi
a pair of dancers 一对舞伴 yí duì wǔbàn
II v 和某人配成一对 he mǒurén pèichéng yíduì

pajamas N 睡衣睡裤 shuìyī shuìkù

pal N 好朋友 hǎo péngyou

palace N 1 王宫 wánggōng, 皇宫 huánggōng, 宫殿 gōngdiàn 2（像王宫一样的）豪华大宅（xiàng wánggōng yíyàng de）háohuá dàzhái

palate N 味觉 wèijué

palatial ADJ 象宫殿似的 xiàng gōngdiàn sìde, 豪华的 háohuá de

pale ADJ 1 苍白的 cāngbái de 2 浅淡的 qiǎndàn de II v 使…相形失色 shǐ… xiāngxíngshīsè

palette N 调色板 tiáosèbǎn [M. WD 块 kuài]

palimony N 分居赔偿金 fēnjū péichángjīn

pall I N 1（一层）烟幕 (yìcéng) yānmù
to cast a pall over sth 给某事蒙上阴影 gěi mǒushì méng shàng yīnyǐng
2 棺罩 guān zhào II v 渐渐失去吸引力 jiànjiàn shīqù xīyǐnlì

pallbearer N 抬棺者 tái guān zhě, 护柩者 hù jiù zhě

pallet N 货板 huòbǎn, 托盘 tuōpán

pallid ADJ 苍白的 cāngbái de, 无血色的 wú xuèsè de

pallor N 苍白 cāngbái

palm I N 1 手掌 shǒuzhǎng, 手心 shǒuxīn
palm top 掌上电脑 zhǎngshàng diànnǎo
to read sb's palm 看手相 kàn shǒuxiàng
2 (palm tree) 棕榈树 zōnglúshù [M. WD 棵 kē]
II v (to palm sth off) 哄骗人接受假货 hǒngpiàn rén jiēshòu jiǎhuò

Palm Sunday N（基督教）棕榈主日 (Jīdūjiào) zōnglú zhǔrì

palpable ADJ 可以感觉到的 kěyǐ gǎnjué dào de, 明显的 míngxiǎn de

palpitations N 心悸 xīnjì, 心动过速 xīndòng guòsù, 心律不齐 xīnlǜ bù qí

paltry ADJ 太少的 tài shǎo de, 微不足道的 wēi bùzú dào de

pamper v 娇惯 jiāoguàn, 娇养 jiāoyǎng

pamphlet N 小册子 xiǎocèzi

pan I N 1 锅 guō, 平底锅 píngdǐguō
broiler pan 烤盘 kǎo pán
roasting pan 烤盘 kǎo pán
saucepan 长柄锅 chángbǐng guō
2 浅盘 qiǎnpán, 淘金盘 táojīn pán
II v 1 严厉批评 [+电影] yánlì pīpíng [+diànyǐng] 2 [摄像机+] 摇动拍摄 [shèyǐngjī+] yáodòng pāishè 3（金等）淘 (jīn děng) táo
to pan out [事件+] 进展 [shìjiàn+] jìnzhǎn

panacea N 万灵药 wànlíngyào

panache N 潇洒自如 xiāosǎ zìrú

pancreas N 胰（腺）yí (xiàn)

panda N 熊猫 xióngmāo
giant panda 大熊猫 dàxióngmāo

pandemic N（广泛流传的）流行病 (guǎngfàn liúchuán de) liúxíngbìng

pandemonium N 大混乱 dà hùnluàn

pander v 迎合 yínghé, 讨好 tǎohǎo

pane N（窗子）玻璃 (chuāngzi) bōli

panel[1] N 专家小组 zhuānjiā xiǎozǔ, 委员会 wěiyuánhuì

panel² I N 1 护墙板 hù qiáng bǎn, 镶板 xiāngbǎn [M. WD 块 kuài] 2 仪表板 yíbiǎobǎn, 操纵台 cāozòng tái II V 铺设护墙板 pūshè hùqiángbǎn

room paneled with walnut wood 铺设桃木护墙板的房间 pūshè táomù hùqiángbǎn de fángjiān

panelist N 专家小组成员 zhuānjiā xiǎozǔ chéngyuán

pang N 剧痛 jùtòng

panhandler N 乞丐 qǐgài, 叫花子 jiàohuāzi

panic I N 惊慌 jīnghuāng, 惊恐 jīngkǒng
panic-stricken 惊慌失措的 jīnghuāng shīcuò de
II V (使⋯) 惊慌 (shǐ...) jīnghuāng

panic-stricken ADJ 惊慌失措的 jīnghuāng shīcuò de

panoramic ADJ 全景的 quánjǐng de

pant V 气喘 qìchuǎn

panther N 黑豹 hēibào [M. WD 只 zhī]

panties N (女子) 内裤 (nǚzǐ) nèikù

pantomime N 哑剧 yǎjù [M. WD 出 chū]

pantry N 食物储藏室 shíwù chǔcángshì

pants N 裤子 kùzi

pantsuit N (女式) 裤套装 (nǚ shì) kù tàozhuāng [M. WD 套 tào]

pantyhose N (女式) 连裤袜 (nǚ shì) liánkùwà [M. WD 双 shuāng]

papa N 爸爸 bàba

papacy N 教皇的职权 Jiàohuáng de zhíquán

paper I N 1 纸 zhǐ
paper clip 回形针 huíxíngzhēn
2 报纸 bàozhǐ 3 (学校课程) 文章 (xuéxiào kèchéng) wénzhāng 4 论文 lùnwén 5 证件 zhèngjiàn, 文件 wénjiàn
II V 用纸糊 yòng zhǐ hú
to paper over a problem 掩盖问题 yǎngài wèntí

paperback N 简装本 jiǎnzhuāng běn

paperweight N 镇纸 zhènzhǐ

paperwork N 文书工作 wénshū gōngzuò

par N 1 水平 shuǐpíng, 标准 biāozhǔn
below par ① 在 (一般) 水平之下 zài (yìbān) shuǐpíng zhī xià ② 身体欠佳 shēntǐ qiànjiā

on a par with 与⋯水平相同 yǔ... shuǐpíng xiāngtóng
2 (高尔夫球) 标准杆数 (gāo'ěrfūqiú) biāozhǔn gǎn shù

parable N 寓言故事 yùyán gùshi

parachute I N 降落伞 jiàngluò sǎn
II V 1 [军人+] 跳伞 [jūnrén+] tiàosǎn 2 空投 [+救济物资] kōngtóu [+jiùjì wùzī]

parade N 庆祝游行 qìngzhù yóuxíng
New York's Village Halloween Parade 纽约万圣节大游行 Niǔyuē wàn shèng jié dà yóuxíng

paradise N 天堂 tiāntáng, 乐园 lèyuán

paradox N 1 似乎自相矛盾的情况 sìhu zìxiāng máodùn de qíngkuàng 2 是非而是的隽语 shìfēi ér shì de juànyǔ

paraffin N 石蜡 shílà

paragon N (完美的) 典范 (wánměi de) diǎnfàn

paragraph N (文章中的) 段 (wénzhāng zhòngde) duàn, 段落 duànluò

parakeet N 长尾小鹦鹉 cháng wěi xiǎo yīngwǔ [M. WD 只 zhī]

paralegal N 律师助手 lǜshī zhùshǒu

parallel I N 1 平行线 píngxíng xiàn 2 相同的人或情况 xiāngtóng de rén huò qíngkuàng II ADJ 1 平行的 píngxíng de 2 相同的 xiāngtóng de III V 与⋯相似 yǔ...xiāngsì

paralysis N 瘫痪 tānhuàn

paralytic I ADJ 瘫痪的 tānhuàn de II N 瘫痪病人 tānhuàn bìngrén

paramedic N 辅助医务人员 fǔzhù yīwù rényuán, 护理人员 hùlǐ rényuán

paramilitary I ADJ 准军事的 zhǔn jūnshì de II N 准军事人员 zhǔn jūnshì rényuán

paramount ADJ 最重要的 zuì zhòngyào de, 高于一切的 gāoyú yíqiè de

paranoid ADJ 1 多疑的 duōyí de, 疑神疑鬼的 yíshén yíguǐ de 2 偏执狂的 piānzhíkuáng de

paraphernalia N 随身物品 suíshēn wùpǐn

paraphrase I V 对⋯释义 duì...shìyì, 改述 gǎi shù II N 释义 shìyì, 改述 gǎi shù

paraplegic N 半身不遂者 bànshēn bùsuí zhě

partition

parasite N 寄生虫 jìshēngchóng
parasitic ADJ 寄生的 jìshēng de
paratrooper N 空降部队 kōngjiàng bùduì, 伞兵 sǎnbīng
parcel I N 1 邮包 yóubāo, 包裹 bāoguǒ 2 一块（土地）yí kuài (tǔdì)
parcel post（美国）包裹邮递系统 (Měiguó) bāoguǒ yóudì xìtǒng
II v (to parcel out) 把…分成小部份 bǎ... fēnchéng xiǎo bùfen
parched ADJ 极其干旱的 jíqí gānhàn de, 干枯的 gānkū de
parchment N 羊皮纸 yángpízhǐ [M. WD 张 zhāng]
pardon I v 1 宽恕 kuānshù, 原谅 yuánliàng 2 赦免 shèmiǎn [+犯人] [+fànrén]
pardon me 对不起 duìbuqǐ
Pardon? 请再说一遍。Qǐng zàishuō yí biàn.
II N 赦免令 shèmiǎnlìng
pare v 1 削减 xuējiǎn, 减少 jiǎnshǎo 2 削皮 xiāopí
parent N 父亲或母亲 fùqin huò mǔqin
parental ADJ 父母的 fùmǔ de
parental guidance 父母的指导 fùmǔ de zhǐdǎo
parenthesis N 圆括号 yuánkuòhào [( )]
parenthood N 父母的身份 fùmǔ de shēnfen
parish N（基督教）教区 (Jīdūjiào) jiàoqū
parishioner N 教区居民 jiàoqū jūmín
parity N（报酬）相同 (bàochou) xiāngtóng, 同等 tóngděng
park I N 1 公园 gōngyuán 2（天然）公园 (tiānrán) gōngyuán
national park 国家公园 guójiā gōngyuán
amusement park 娱乐场场 yúlè cháng, 乐园 lèyuán
car park 停车场 tíngchē chǎng
II v 1 停车 tíngchē
park and ride 换车通勤 huànchē tōngqín
2 放置 tíngfàng
parka N（带帽的）风雪大衣 (dài mào de) fēngxuě dàyī
parking N 停车 tíngchē

parking ticket 违章停车罚款 wéizhāng tíngchē fákuǎn
parking lot 停车场 tíngchēchǎng
parkway N 林荫大道 línyìn dàdào
parliament N 国会 Guóhuì
parlor N 商店 shāngdiàn
dental parlor 牙科诊所 yákē zhěnsuǒ
funeral parlor 殡仪馆 bìnyíguǎn
icecream parlor 冰淇凌店 bīngqilín diàn
parody I N（滑稽）模仿 (huájī) mófǎng II v（滑稽地）模仿 [huájīde+] mófǎng
parole I N 假释 jiǎshì II v 准许假释 zhǔnxǔ jiǎshì
parquet N 镶木地板 xiāngmù dìbǎn
parrot N 鹦鹉 yīngwǔ [M. WD 只 zhī]
parsley N 西芹 xīqín
parsnip N 欧洲萝卜 Ōuzhōu luóbo
part I N 1 部分 bùfen 2 零件 língjiàn 3 角色 juésè
to play a part (in) 扮演角色 bànyǎn juésè, 起到作用 qǐdao zuòyòng
to take part (in) 参加 cānjiā
II v 1（使）…分开 (shǐ)...fēnkāi 2 [与朋友+] 分手 [yǔ péngyou+] fēnshǒu
partial I ADJ 部分的 bùfen de
be partial to 偏袒 piāntǎn, 偏爱 piān'ài
participant N 参加者 cānjiāzhě, 参与者 cānyùzhě
participate v 参加 cānjiā, 参与 cānyù
participation N 参加 cānjiā, 参与 cānyù
particle N 1 微粒 wēilì 2（原子中的）粒子 (yuánzǐ zhòng de) lìzi
particular I ADJ 特别的 tèbié de, 特殊的 tèshū de II N (in particular) 特别（地）tèbié (de), 尤其 yóuqí
particularly ADV 特别 tèbié
particulars N 细节 xìjié, 详情 xiángqíng
parting I N 分离 fēnlí, 离别 líbié II ADJ 临别（时）的 línbié (shí) de
parting shot 临别时的攻击 línbié shí de gōngjī
partisan ADJ 热烈支持某一党派的 rèliè zhīchí mǒu yì dǎngpài de
partition I N 1（国家的）分裂 (guójiā de) fēnliè 2 隔墙 géqiáng II v 分割 fēngē, 分开 fēnkāi

partly ADV 部分 bùfen, 部分地 bùfen de

partner N 1 合伙人 héhuǒrén 2 搭档 dādàng 3 性伴侣 xìng bànlǚ, 配偶 pèi'ǒu 4 舞伴 wǔbàn

partnership N 合伙（关系）héhuǒ (guānxi), 合作（关系）hézuò (guānxi)

part-time ADJ 兼职（的／地）jiānzhí (de), 部分时间的 bùfen shíjiān de

partway ADV 1（在）途中（zài）túzhōng 2 一段时间后 yí duàn shíjiān hòu

party I N 1 派对 pàiduì, 聚会 jùhuì, 社交聚会 shèjiāo jùhuì

birthday party 生日庆祝会 shēngrì qìngzhù huì

garden party 游园会 yóuyuán huì

2（政）党（zhèng）dǎng 3 小组 xiǎozǔ II V 尽情吃喝玩乐 jìnqíng chīhē wánlè

pass I V 1 通过 tōngguò, 经过 jīngguò 2 经过 zǒuguo 3 传承, 递, 传递 chuándì 4 去世 guòqù 5 通过 [+考试] tōngguò [+kǎoshì],（考试）及格 (kǎoshì) jígé

to pass away 去世 qùshì

to pass out 昏厥 hūnjué, 晕倒 yūndǎo II N 1 传承, 传递 chuándì 2 通行证 tōngxíng zhèng 3（考试）及格 (kǎoshì) jígé 4 山口 shānkǒu

passable ADJ 过得去的 guòdequ de, 还可以的 hái kěyǐ de

passage N 1 通道 tōngdào 2 通过 tōngguò 3（书／乐曲）一段 (shū/yuèqǔ) yí duàn 4（时间的）流逝 (shíjiān de) liúshì

passageway N（狭窄的）通道 (xiázhǎi de) tōngdào [M. WD 条 tiáo]

passbook N（银行）存折 (yínháng) cúnzhé [M. WD 本 běn]

passé ADJ 过时的 guòshí de, 老式的 lǎoshì de

passenger N 乘客 chéngkè

passenger seat（汽车）驾驶员旁边的座位 (qìchē) jiàshǐyuán pángbiān de zuòwèi

passerby N 过路人 guòlùrén

passing I ADJ 1 经过的 [+车辆] jīngguò de [+chēliàng] 2 一时的 [+兴趣] yìshí de [+xìngqù] II N 1 终止 zhōngzhǐ, 消失 xiāoshī

passing of time 时间的流逝 shíjiān de liúshì

2 去世 qùshì, 过世 guòshì 3 (in passing) 顺便提到 shùnbiàn tídào

passion N 激情 jīqíng, 热爱 rè'ài

passionate ADJ 感情强烈的 gǎnqíng qiángliè de, 充满激情的 chōngmǎn jīqíng de

passive I ADJ 被动的 bèidòng de

passive smoking 被动抽烟 bèidòng chōuyān

II N 被动式 bèidòngshì

passport N 护照 hùzhào

password N 口令 kǒulìng, 通行字 tōngxíng zì

past I ADJ 过去的 guòqù de II N 过去 guòqù III PREP 1 晚于 wǎn yú, 在… 以后 zài...yǐhòu 2 远于 yuǎn yú, 过了… guòle... 3 经过 jīngguò 4 (past caring) 不在乎 búzàihu

paste I N 1 浆糊 jiànghu, 糨糊 jiànghu 2 糊状物 húzhuàng wù 3 [鱼+] 酱 [yú+] jiàng II V 1（用糨糊）粘帖 (yòng jiànghu) zhān tiē 2（计算机）粘帖 (jìsuànjī) zhān tiē

pastel I N 1 彩色粉笔 cǎisè fěnbǐ, 蜡笔 làbǐ 2 彩色粉笔画 cǎisè fěnbǐhuà II ADJ 浅 [+颜色] qiǎn [+yánsè], 淡 dàn

pasteurize V 灭菌 mièjūn, 消毒 xiāodú

pastime N 消遣 xiāoqiǎn, 娱乐 yúlè

pastor N 牧师 mùshī

pastry N 1 油酥面团 yóu sū miàntuán 2 油酥点心 yóu sū diǎnxin [M. WD 块 kuài/件 jiàn]

pasture N 牧场 mùchǎng

pasty ADJ 苍白的 cāngbái de II N（肉等的）馅饼 (ròu děng de) xiànbǐng

pat I V 轻轻地拍 qīngqīng de pāi

to pat sb on the back 赞扬某人 zànyáng mǒurén

II N 1 轻拍 qīng pāi 2（黄油等）小块 (huángyóu děng) xiǎokuài

a pat on the back 赞扬 zànyáng

III ADJ 脱口而出的 [+回答] tuōkǒu ér chū de [+huídá]

patch I N 1（衣服上的）补丁 (yīfu shàng de) bǔdīng 2（计算机）程序补

474

丁 (jìsuànjī) chéngxù bǔdìng **3** 膏药 gāoyao **4** 小块土地 xiǎo kuài tǔdì **IV 1** 缝补 [+衣服] féngbǔ [+yīfu] **2** (to patch up) 修补 [+关系] xiūbǔ [+guānxi], 解决 分歧 jiějué [+fēnqí]

patchy ADJ **1** 局部零星的 [+阵雨] júbù língxīng de [+zhènyǔ] **2** 零碎的 [+知识] língsuì de [+zhīshi]

patent I N 专利（权）zhuānlì (quán) II V 取得专利（权）qǔdé zhuānlì (quán) III ADJ 明显的 míngxiǎn de
a patent lie 明显的谎言 míngxiǎn de huǎngyán

patently ADV 显然地 xiǎnrán de

paternal ADJ **1** 父亲的 fùqin de **2** 父权的 fùquán de

paternity N 父亲的身份 fùqin de shēnfen
paternity leave 陪产假 péi chǎnjià

path N 小路 xiǎolù, 道路 dàolù

pathetic ADJ **1** 可怜的 kělián de **2** 没用的 méiyòng de

pathological ADJ **1** 病态的 bìngtài de, 无法控制的 wúfǎ kòngzhì de
a pathological liar 无法不撒谎的人 wúfǎ bù sāhuǎng de rén, 说谎成性的人 shuōhuǎng chéngxìng de rén **2** 病理（学）的 bìnglǐ (xué) de

pathology N 病理（学）bìnglǐ (xué)

pathos N 引起怜悯的因素 yǐnqǐ liánmǐn de yīnsù, 感伤力 gǎnshāng lì

pathway N 途径 tújìng

patience N 耐心 nàixīn, 忍耐心 rěn nài xīn

patient I ADJ 耐心的 nàixīn de II N 病人 bìngrén

patio N 露天平台 lùtiān píngtái

patriarch N（男）家长 (nán) jiāzhǎng, 族长 zúzhǎng, 受尊敬的长者 shòu zūnjìng de zhǎngzhě

patriarchal ADJ 父权制的 fùquánzhì de

patricide N 弑父（罪）shì fù (zuì), 杀父罪 shā fù zuì

patriot N 爱国者 àiguózhě

patriotic ADJ 爱国（主义）的 àiguó (zhǔyì) de

patriotism N 爱国主义 àiguózhǔyì

patrol I N **1** 巡逻 xúnluó, 巡查 xúnchá

2 巡逻兵 xúnluó bīng, 巡逻队 xúnluóduì II V 巡逻 xúnluó, 巡查 xúnchá

patrolman N 巡警 xúnjǐng, 巡逻（保安）人员 xúnluó (bǎo'ān) rényuán

patron N **1** 赞助人 zànzhùrén, 资助人 zīzhù rén **2** 顾客 gùkè

patronage N **1** 赞助 zànzhù, 资助 zīzhù **2** 任命权 rènmìng quán

patronize V **1** 以高人一筹的姿态对待 [+人] yǐ gāorén yì chóu de zītài duìdài [+rén] **2** 光顾 [+饭店] guānggù [+fàndiàn]

patter N **1** 急速的轻拍声 jísù de qīng pāi shēng, 啪嗒啪嗒声 pādā pādā shēng **2** 顺口溜 shùnkǒuliū

pattern N **1** 图案 tú'àn, 花样 huāyàng **2** 模式 móshì, 方式 fāngshì II V 模仿 mófǎng, 仿效 fǎngxiào

patty N 肉饼 ròubǐng [M. WD 块 kuài]

paucity N 贫乏 pínfá, 贫困 pínkùn

paunch N（男人的）大肚子 (nánren de) dàdùzi, 啤酒桶肚子 píjiǔtǒng dùzi

pauper N 贫民 pínmín, 穷人 qióngrén

pause N, V 暂停 zàntíng, 停顿 tíngdùn

pave V 铺（路）pū (lù)
to pave the way for sb/sth 为某人／某事铺设道路 wéi mǒurén/mǒushì pūshè dàolù, 为某事做准备 wéi mǒushì zhǔnbèi

pavement N **1** 铺好的路面 pū hǎode lùmiàn **2** 人行道 rénxíngdào

pavilion N **1** 展览馆 zhǎnlǎnguǎn **2** 亭子 tíngzi

paw I N（动物的）爪子 (dòngwù de) zhuǎzi II V **1** 用爪子抓 yòng zhuǎzi zhuā **2** 对 [+青年女子] 动手动脚 duì [+qīngnián nǚzǐ] dòngshǒu dòngjiǎo

pawn I N **1**（象棋）兵 (xiàngqí) bīng, 卒 zú **2**（被利用的）棋子 (bèi lìyòng de) qízǐ II V 典当 diǎndàng, 抵押 dǐyā

pawnshop N 当铺 dàngpù

pay I V (PT & PP paid) 付 [+钱] fù [+qián], 付钱（给某人）fùqián (gěi mǒurén)
to pay attention to 注意 zhùyì, 关注 guānzhù
to pay back 还（债）huán (zhài)
to pay for 受惩罚 shòu chéngfá

to pay off ① 还清（债）huánqīng (zhài) ② 获得成功 huòdé chénggōng, 产生利润 chǎnshēng lìrùn II N 工资 gōngzī, 报酬 bàochou

payable ADJ 应付的 yìngfu de (a check) payable to sb 应付给某人（的支票）yìngfu gěi mǒurén (de zhīpiào)

paycheck N 工资支票 gōngzī zhīpiào, 薪酬 xīnchóu

payday N 发薪日 fāxīnrì

payload N （有效）载重量 (yǒuxiào) zàizhòngliàng

payment N 付款 fùkuǎn

payoff N 得益 déyì, 收益 shōuyì

payroll N 发薪员工名单 fāxīn yuángōng míngdān

be on the payroll (of a company) 是（一家公司的）雇员 shì (yì jiā gōngsī de) gùyuán

pay-TV N 收费电视（频道）shōufèi diànshì (píndào)

PC (= personal computer) ABBREV 个人电脑 gèrén diànnǎo [M. WD 台 tái]

pea N 豌豆 wāndòu [M. WD 粒 lì]

peace N 1 和平 hépíng 2 安静 ānjìng, 宁静 níngjìng

to make peace with sb 和某人和解 hé mǒurén héjiě

peaceable ADJ 温和的 wēnhé de, 不爱争吵的 bú àizhēng chǎo de

Peace Corps N （美国）和平队 (Měiguó) Hépíngduì

peaceful ADJ 1 和平的 hépíng de 2 安静的 ānjìng de, 宁静的 níngjìng de

peacekeeping forces N （联合国）维持和平部队 (Liánhéguó) wéichí hépíng bùduì

peacetime N 和平时期 hépíng shíqī

peach N 桃树 táoshù, 桃子 táozi

peacock N 孔雀 kǒngquè [M. WD 只 zhī]

peak I N 顶峰 dǐngfēng, 最高点 zuìgāodiǎn II V 达到顶峰 dádào dǐngfēng III ADJ 最高的 zuìgāo de

peal N 响亮的声音 xiǎngliàng de shēngyīn

a peal of thunder 一阵雷声 yízhèn léishēng

peals of laughter 一阵阵笑声 yízhèn zhèn xiàoshēng

peanut N 花生（米）huāshēng (mǐ) [M. WD 颗 kē]

peanut butter 花生酱 huāshēngjiàng

peanuts N 很少的钱 hěn shǎo de qián

pear N 梨树 líshù [M. WD 棵 kē], 梨 lí

pearl N 珍珠 zhēnzhū

pearl necklace 一串珍珠项链 yíchuàn zhēnzhū xiàngliàn

2 珍珠色 zhēnzhū sè

peasant N 农民 nóngmín

peat N 泥炭 nítàn, 泥灰 níhuī

pebble N 卵石 luǎnshí, 小圆石 xiǎo yuánshí

peck I V [鸟+] 啄 [niǎo+] zhuó 2 [情人+] 轻吻 [qíngrén+] qīng wěn II N 1 （鸟）啄 (niǎo) zhuó 2 轻吻 qīng wěn

pecking order N （社群中的）等级 (shèqún zhōng de) děngjí

peculiar ADJ 怪异的 guàiyì de, 奇特的 qítè de

peculiarity N 1 独特（性）dútè (xìng) 2 奇异的东西 qíyì de dōngxi

pedal I N 踏板 tàbǎn II V 踩踏板 cǎi tàbǎn

peddle V 兜售 dōushòu

pedestal N 基座 jīzuò

to place sb on a pedestal 偶像崇拜某人 ǒuxiàng chóngbài mǒurén

pedestrian I N 行人 xíngrén, 步行者 bùxíngzhě II ADJ 1 行人的 xíngrén de

pedestrian crossing 行人横道线 xíngrénhéngdào xiàn

2 平淡无奇的 píngdàn wúqí de

pediatrician N 儿科医生 érkēyīshēng

pedicure N 修脚 xiūjiǎo

pedigree N 血统 xuètǒng, 谱系 pǔxì II ADJ 纯种的 chúnzhǒng de

pee V, N 撒尿 sāniào, 小便 xiǎobiàn

peek I V 偷看 tōukàn II N 偷看（一眼）tōukàn (yìyǎn)

peel I V 削／剥 (水果+) xiāo/bō [+shuǐguǒ] pí, [油漆+] 剥落 [yóuqī+] bōluò II N 果皮 guǒpí

peep N, V 偷看 tōukàn, 窥视 kuīshì

peephole N 窥视孔 kuīshìkǒng

peeping Tom N 喜欢偷看的人 xǐhuan tōukàn de rén, 窥视狂 kuīshìkuáng

peer[1] N 1 同龄（或地位）相同的人 tónglíng (huò dìwèi) xiāngtóng de rén, 同龄人 tónglíngrén, 同事 tóngshì, 同伴 tóngbàn

peer pressure 同辈人的压力 tóngbèi rén de yālì

2（英国）贵族（Yīngguó）guìzú

peer[2] V 盯着看 dīngzhe kàn, 凝视 níngshì

peerless ADJ 无与伦比的 wú yǔ lúnbǐ de

peeve N 令人恼火的事 lìngrén nǎohuǒ de shì

peg N 1 挂衣钩 guàyīgōu 2（小提琴）弦轴 (xiǎotíqín) xiánzhóu II V 把…固定在（某一水平）bǎ…gùdìng zài (mǒu yì shuǐpíng)

pejorative ADJ 贬义的 biǎnyì de, 贬损的 biǎnsǔn de

Pekingese, Pekinese N 哈巴狗 hǎbāgǒu

pelican N 鹈鹕 tíhú [M. WD 只 zhī]

pellet N 小硬球 xiǎo yìngqiú

pelt I V 连续投掷 liánxù tóuzhì, 扔 rēng II N 兽皮 shòupí [M. WD 张 zhāng]

pelvis N 骨盆 gǔpén

pen[1] I N 笔 bǐ

The pen is mightier than the sword. 文事胜武功。Wénshì shèng wǔgōng.

pen name 笔名 bǐmíng
pen pal 笔友 bǐyǒu

II V（用笔）写 (yòngbǐ) xiě

pen[2] N（关养畜的）栏／圈 (guān yǎngjiā chū de) lán/quān

penal ADJ 刑罚的 xíng zuì de

penal code 刑法典 xíngfǎ diǎn

penalize V 惩罚 chéngfá, 处罚 chǔfá

penalty N 惩罚 chéngfá, 处罚 chǔfá

penance N 自我惩罚 zìwǒ chéngfá, 忏悔 chànhuǐ

pencil N 铅笔 qiānbǐ

pencil drawing 铅笔画 qiānbǐ huà

pendant N 挂件 guà jiàn, 垂饰 chuí shì

pending I PREP 当…时 dāng…shí, 直到 zhídào II ADJ 未定的 wèidìng de 2 即将发生的 jíjiāng fāshēng de

pendulum N 钟摆 zhōngbǎi

penetrate V 1 进入 jìnrù, 打进 dǎjìn 2 穿透 chuāntòu, 渗透 shèntòu

penetrating ADJ 1 有深度的 [+见解] yǒu

shēndù de [+jiànjiě], 有洞察力的 yǒu dòngchálì de 2 刺耳的 [+尖叫] cì'ěr de [+jiānjiào]

penguin N 企鹅 qǐ'é [M. WD 只 zhī/头 tóu]

penicillin N 青霉素 qīngméisù, 盘尼西林 pánníxīlín

peninsula N 半岛 bàndǎo

penis N 阴茎 yīnjīng

penitence N 忏悔 chànhuǐ, 悔过 huǐguò

penitentiary N 监狱 jiānyù

penknife N 小折刀 xiǎozhédāo

pennant N 三角旗 sānjiǎoqí

penniless ADJ 身无分文的 shēn wúfēn wén de, 一贫如洗的 yìpín rú xǐ de

penny N（英国／加拿大）一分钱 (Yīngguó/Jiānádà) yì fēn qián

pension[1] N 养老金 yǎnglǎo jīn, 退休金 tuìxiū jīn

pension fund 退休基金 tuìxiū jījīn

pension[2] N（法国的）旅舍 (Fǎguó de) lǚshè

pensioner N 领取养老金的人 lǐngqǔ yǎnglǎojīn de rén, 老年人 lǎoniánrén

pensive ADJ 忧伤的 yōushāng de

pentagon N 五边形 wǔbiānxíng

Pentecostal I ADJ 五旬节派教会的 wǔxúnjiépài jiàohuì de 2 Pentecostal churches 五旬节派教会 wǔxúnjiépài jiàohuì

II N 五旬节派教会教友 wǔxúnjiépài jiàohuì jiàoyǒu

penthouse N 楼顶公寓 lóudǐng gōngyù

pent-up ADJ 郁结的 yùjié de

penury N 贫穷 pínqióng, 贫困 pínkùn

peon N 劳工 láogōng, 苦工 kǔgōng

people I N 人 rén, 人们 rénmen

the people 人民 rénmín

II V (be peopled with) 充满 chōng mǎn, 挤满 jǐmǎn

(the) People' Republic of China (PRC) 中华人民共和国 Zhōnghuá Rénmín Gònghéguó

pep I V 使…充满活力 shǐ…chōngmǎn huólì II N 活力 huólì, 精力 jīnglì

pep talk 鼓动士气的讲话 gǔdòng shìqì de jiǎnghuà, 打气的讲话 dǎqì de jiǎnghuà

pepper I N 胡椒粉 hújiāofěn, 辣椒粉 làjiāofěn II V 1 撒胡椒粉 sā hújiāofěn 2 使 [+讲话] 有趣 shǐ [+jiǎnghuà] yǒuqù

peppermint N 薄荷 bòhe

Pepsi N 百事可乐 Bǎishì Kělè

per PREP 每每

per capita ADJ, ADV 人均（的）rénjūn (de)

perceive V 1 察觉 chájué, 注意到 zhùyìdào 2 认为 rènwéi

percent (%) ADJ 百分之… bǎifēnzhī...

percentage N 百分比 bǎifēnbǐ

perceptible ADJ 可以察觉到的 kěyǐ chájué dào de

perception N 1 察觉 chájué 2 认为 rènwéi

perch I N 1（鸟）栖息处（niǎo）qīxī chù 2（观看的）高处（guānkàn de）gāo chù II V 1 [鸟+] 栖息 [niǎo+] qīxī 2 (be perched on) 位于 wèiyú

percussion N 1 打击乐器 dǎjīyuèqì 2 撞击声 zhuàngjī shēng

peremptory ADJ 专横的 zhuānhèng de, 霸道的 bàdào de

perennial I ADJ 长期的 chángqī de, 多年的 duōnián de II N 多年生植物 duōniánshēng zhíwù

perfect I ADJ 完美的 wánměi de, 尽善尽美的 jìnshàn jìnměi de
Practice makes perfect. 熟能生巧。Shú néng shēng qiǎo. (→ Long experience produces skill.)
II V 使…完美 shǐ...wánměi

perfection N 完美 wánměi, 完善 wánshàn

perfectionist N 完美主义者 wánměizhǔyìzhě

perfectly ADV 完美地 wánměi de, 完全 wánquán, 十分 shífēn

perform V 1 表演 biǎoyǎn, 演出 yǎnchū 2 做 zuò, 履行 lǚxíng

performance N 1 演出 yǎnchū, 表演 biǎoyǎn 2（工作）表现（gōngzuò）biǎoxiàn

performer N 表演者 biǎoyǎnzhě, 演出者 yǎnchūzhě

perfume I N 香水 xiāngshuǐ II V 使…充满香气 shǐ...chōngmǎn xiāngqì

perfunctory ADJ 敷衍（了事）fūyǎn (liǎoshì) de, 草率的 cǎoshuài de

perhaps ADV 或许 huòxǔ, 大概 dàgài

perilous ADJ 危险的 wēixiǎn de, 险要的 xiǎnyào de

perimeter N 四周 sìzhōu, 周围 zhōuwéi

period I N 1 一段时间 yí duàn shíjiān, 时期 shíqī 2（在学校）一节课（zài xuéxiào）yì jié kè, 一堂课 yì táng kè 3 句号 jùhào 4 月经 yuèjīng II ADJ 特定历史时期的 tèdìng lìshǐ shíqī de
a period piece 历史戏剧／电影

periodic, periodical ADJ 定期的 dìngqī de

periodical N 期刊 qīkān, 杂志 zázhì

peripheral I ADJ 1 边缘的 biānyuán de, 外围的 wàiwéi de 2 次要的 cìyào de II N（计算机）外围设备（jìsuànjī）wàiwéi shèbèi

periphery N 边缘 biānyuán

periscope N 潜望镜 qiánwàngjìng [M. WD 台 tái]

perish V 1 死亡 sǐwáng 2 消亡 xiāowáng 3 [水果+] 腐烂 [shuǐguǒ+] fǔlàn

perishable ADJ [食物+] 易腐烂的 [shíwù+] yì fǔlàn de

perjure V 作伪证 zuò wěizhèng

perjury N 伪证（罪）wěizhèng (zuì)

perk I N 特殊福利 tèshū fúlì, 特权 tèquán II V 振作（起来）zhènzuò (qǐlái)

perky ADJ 自信而快活的 zìxìn ér kuàihuo de, 生气勃勃的 shēngqì bóbó de

permanent ADJ 永久的 yǒngjiǔ de, 持久的 chíjiǔ de

permeate V 充满 chōngmǎn, 弥漫 mímàn

permissible ADJ 允许的 yǔnxǔ de, 许可的 xǔkě de

permission N 许可 xǔkě, 准许 zhǔnxǔ

permissive ADJ 放纵的 fàngzòng de, 宽容的 kuānróng de

permit I V 允许 yǔnxǔ, 准许 zhǔnxǔ II N 许可（证）xǔkě (zhèng)

permutation N 排列 páiliè, 组合 zǔhé

pernicious ADJ 恶毒的 èdú de, 极有害的 jí yǒuhài de

perpendicular ADJ 垂直的 chuízhí de, 直立的 zhílì de

perpetrate v 犯（罪）fàn (zuì), 做（错事）zuò (cuò shì)

perpetrator N 犯罪者 fànzuìzhě, 作恶者 zuò'èzhě

perpetual ADJ 永恒的 yǒnghéng de, 持续不变的 chíxù búbiàn de

perpetuate v 使 [+坏事] 永远存在下去 shǐ [+huàishì] yǒngyuǎn cúnzài xiàqu

perplexity N 困惑 kùnhuò, 茫然 mángrán

perquisite N See perk I (N)

per se ADV 本身 běnshēn, 就其本身而言 jiù qí běnshēn éryán

persecute v 迫害 pòhài

persecution N 迫害 pòhài

  persecution complex 受迫害妄想症 shòupò hài wàngxiǎng zhēng

perseverance N 坚韧（精神）jiānrèn (jīngshén)

persevere v 锲而不舍 qiè ér bù shě, 坚持不懈 jiānchí bú xiè

persist v 1 坚持 jiānchí, 执意 zhíyì 2 [坏天气+] 持续 [huài tiānqì+] chíxù

persistent ADJ 1 坚持的 jiānchí de, 执意的 zhíyì de 2 持续的 [+大雨] chíxù de [+dàyǔ]

person N 人 rén

  in person 亲自 qīnzì

personal ADJ 1 个人的 gèrén de, 私人的 sīrén de

  personal belongings 个人物件 gèrén wùjiàn, 私人财物 sīrén cáiwù

  personal hygiene 个人卫生 gèrén wèishēng

  personal organizer 掌上电脑 zhǎngshàng diànnǎo

  personal trainer 私人健身教练 sīrén jiànshēn jiàoliàn

  2 人身攻击的 rénshēn gōngjī de, 批评个人的 pīpíng gèrénde

personality N 1 个性 gèxìng, 性格 xìnggé 2 [电视+] 名人 [diànshì+] míngrén

personalize v 印上姓名 yìn shàng xìngmíng 2 个性化 gèxìng huà

personally ADV 就个人而言 jiù gèrén éryán

personnel N 1 全体员工 quántí yuángōng 2 人事部门 rénshì bùmén

perspective N 1 [看问题的+] 视角 [kàn wèntí de+] shìjiǎo, 观点 guāndiǎn

  to keep ... in perspective 正确认识 zhèngquè rènshi

  2 透视画法 tòushì huàfǎ

perspiration N 汗水 hànshuǐ

perspire v 出汗 chūhàn, 流汗 liúhàn

persuade v 1 说服 shuōfú, 劝服 quànfú 2 使…相信 shǐ...xiāngxìn

persuasion N 说服 shuōfú, 劝服 quànfú

pert ADJ 1 活泼可爱的 [+女孩] huópo kě'ài de [+nǚhái] 2 调皮的 [+回答] tiáopí de [+huídá]

pertain v 与…直接有关 yǔ...zhíjiē yǒuguān

pertinent ADJ 直接有关的 zhíjiē yǒuguān de

perturbed ADJ 感到不安的 gǎndào bù'ān de, 烦恼的 fánnǎo de

peruse v 阅读 yuèdú

pervade v 弥漫 mímàn, 遍及 biànjí

pervasive ADJ 普遍的 pǔbiàn de, 无处不在的 wúchù búzài de

perverse ADJ 不合常理的 bùhé chánglǐ de, 乖张的 guāizhāng de

pervert I v 使…变坏 shǐ...biànhuài, 破坏 pòhuài II N 性变态者 xìng biàntàizhě

pesky ADJ 令人讨厌的 lìngrén tǎoyàn de

pessimism N 悲观主义 bēiguānzhǔyì

pessimistic ADJ 悲观（主义）的 bēiguān (zhǔyì) de

pest N 有害动物 yǒuhài dòngwù, 害虫 hàichóng, 害鸟 hàiniǎo

pester v 不断烦扰 búduàn fánrǎo, 纠缠 jiūchán

pesticide N 灭虫剂 miè chóng jì

pet I N 宠物 chǒngwù

  pet name 小名 xiǎomíng, 昵称 nìchēng

  pet store 宠物商店 chǒngwù shāngdiàn II v 抚弄 fǔnòng, 摸 [+宠物] mō [+chǒngwù] III ADJ 特别喜爱的 tèbié xǐ'ài de

petal N 花瓣 huābàn [M. WD 片 piàn]

petite ADJ 娇小的 jiāoxiǎo de

petition I v 请愿 qǐngyuàn, 请求 qǐngqiú II N 请愿（书）qǐngyuàn (shū)

petrified ADJ 惊呆了的 jīng dāi le de, 吓呆的 xiàdāi de

  petrified wood 石化木 shíhuà mù

petrochemical N 石（油）化（学）shí (yóu) huà (xué)

petroleum N 石油 shíyóu

petty ADJ 琐碎的 suǒsuì de, 小的 xiǎode
petty cash 小额现金 xiǎo'é xiànjīn
petty crime 轻罪 qīngzuì

petulant ADJ 随意发脾气的 suíyì fāpíqi de, 任性暴躁的 rènxìng bàozao de

pew N（教堂）长木椅（jiàotáng）cháng mù yǐ [M. WD 排 pái/张 zhāng]

PG (= parental guidance) ADJ 在家长指导下观看（的电影）zài jiā zhǎng zhǐdǎo xià guānkàn (de diànyǐng)

phallus N 男性生殖器 nánxìng shēngzhíqì, 阴茎 yīnjīng

phantom N 1 幽灵 yōulíng, 鬼魂 guǐhún 2 幻影 huànyǐng

pharmaceutical ADJ 制药（工业）zhìyào (gōngyè)

pharmacology N 药理学 yàolǐxué

pharmacy N 药店 yàodiàn, 药房 yàofáng

Pharoah N 法老（古埃及统治者）Fǎlǎo (gǔ Āijí tǒngzhìzhě)

phase I N 阶段 jiēduàn, 时期 shíqī II v (to phase in) 逐步实行 zhúbù shíxíng
to phase out 逐步停止 zhúbù tíngzhǐ

Ph.D. N 博士（学位）bóshì (xuéwèi)

pheasant N 雉 zhì, 野鸡 yějī

phenomenal ADJ 非凡的 fēifán de, 不同寻常的 bùtóng xúncháng de

phenomenon N 1 现象 xiànxiàng 2 奇迹 qíjì, 奇人 qírén

philandering N, ADJ 玩弄女性 wánnòng nǚxìng, 风流放荡 fēngliú fàngdàng

philanthropist N 慈善家 císhànjiā

philistine N 不懂文学艺术的人 bùdǒng wénxué yìshù de rén, 没有教养的人 méiyǒu jiàoyǎng de rén

philosophical ADJ 1 哲学的 zhéxué de 2 想得开的 xiǎng dé kāi de, 豁达的 huòdá de

phlegm N 痰 tán

phlegmatic ADJ 不会激动的 bú huì jīdòng de, 冷漠的 lěngmò de

phobia N 恐惧 kǒngjù

phoenix N 凤凰 fènghuáng [M. WD 只 zhī]

phone I N 电话（机）diànhuà (jī)
phone booth（共用）电话亭 (gòngyòng) diànhuàtíng

phone number 电话号码 diànhuà hàomǎ
to be on the phone 在打电话 zàidǎ diànhuà
II v 打电话 dǎ diànhuà

phonetics N 语音学 yǔyīnxué

phon(e)y I ADJ 1 假冒 [+产品] 的 jiǎmào [+chǎnpǐn] de 2 假装的 [+友好] jiǎzhuāng de [+yǒuhǎo], 虚伪的 xūwěi de II N 伪造品 wěizàopǐn, 虚假的东西 xūjiǎ de dōngxi

phosphorus (P) N 磷 lín

photo N 照片 zhàopiàn, 象片 xiàng piàn
photo finish ① 摄影定胜负 shèyǐng dìng shèngfù ② 难分胜负的比赛 nánfēn shèngfù de bǐsài

photocopier N 复印机 fùyìnjī

photocopy N 复印件 fùyìnjiàn, 影印 yǐngyìn II v 复印 fùyìn, 影印 yǐngyìn

photogenic ADJ 上镜（头）的 shàng jìng (tóu) de, 上相的 shàngxiàng de

photograph N 照片 zhàopiàn

photographer N 摄影师 shèyǐngshī, 摄影家 shèyǐng jiā

photography N 摄影（术）shèyǐng (shù)

photosynthesis N 光合作用 guānghé zuòyòng

phrase I N 1 短语 duǎnyǔ, 词组 cízǔ 2 警句 jǐngjù, 隽语 juànyǔ II v（用词语）表达 (yòngcí yǔ) biǎodá

phrasing N 1 措词 cuòcí, 选词 xuǎn cí 2 乐句划分 yuèjù huàfēn

physical I ADJ 1 身体的 shēntǐ de 2 物质的 wùzhì de
physical education (PE) 体育 tǐyù
physical therapy 物理疗法 wùlǐliáofǎ, 理疗 lǐliáo
II N 体格检查 tǐgé jiǎnchá

physician N（内科）医生 (nèikē) yīshēng

physicist N 物理学家 wùlǐxuéjiā [M. WD 位 wèi]

physics N 物理（学）wùlǐ (xué)

physiology N 1 生理学 shēnglǐxué 2 生理（机能）shēnglǐ (jīnéng)

physiotherapy N 物理疗法 wùlǐliáofǎ, 理疗 lǐliáo

physique N 体格 tǐgé

pi (π) N 圆周率 yuánzhōulǜ (= 3.1416)

pianist N 钢琴演奏者 gāngqín yǎnzòu-zhě, 钢琴家 gāngqínjiā [M. WD 位 wèi]

piano N 钢琴 gāngqín [M. WD 架 jià]

pick I V 1 挑选 tiāoxuǎn 2 采 cǎi, 采集 cǎijí 3 挖 wā, 剔 tī
to pick one's nose 挖鼻孔 wā bíkǒng
to pick up ① (使) 站起来 (shǐ) zhànqǐlai ② 拣起来 jiǎnqǐlai, 收拾起 shōushiqǐ ③ 好转 hǎozhuǎn ④ (开汽车) 接人 (kāi qìchē) jiē rén ⑤ 结识 jiéshí, 搭上 dāshang
to pick on 找…的岔子 zhǎo…de chàzi
II N 1 挑选 tiāoxuǎn 2 最好的 zuìhǎo de, 精华 jīnghuá

pickax N 镐 gǎo, 鹤嘴锄 hèzuǐchú

picket I N 1 抗议者 kàngyìzhě 2 (罢工) 纠察队 (bàgōng) jiūcháduì
picket line 纠察线 jiūcháxiàn
II V 1 抗议示威 kàngyì shìwēi 2 [罢工工人+] 设置纠察队 [bàgōng gōngrén+] shèzhì jiūcháduì

pickle I N 1 酸黄瓜 suānhuángguā 2 腌菜 yāncài II V 腌制 [+黄瓜] yānzhì [+huángguā]

pickpocket N 扒手 páshǒu, 贼 zéi
Beware of pickpockets. 谨防扒手。Jǐnfáng páshǒu.

pickup I N 1 敞篷小货车 chǎngpéng xiǎo huòchē [M. WD 辆 liàng] 2 增加 zēngjiā, 提高 tígāo 3 提取的时间 tíqǔ de shíjiān II ADJ 临时拼凑的 [+游戏／比赛] línshí pīncòu de [+yóuxì/bǐsài]

picnic I N 1 野餐 yěcān 2 轻松愉快的事 qīngsōng yúkuài de shì II V 举行野餐 jǔxíng yěcān

pictorial I ADJ 有图片的 yǒu túpiàn de II N 画报 huàbào [M. WD 本 běn]

picture N 1 画 huà, 图画 túhuà
picture book 图画书 túhuà shū 2 照片 zhàopiàn [M. WD 张 zhāng] 3 情景 qíngjǐng 4 [电视+] 图像 [diànshì+] túxiàng

pie N 馅饼 xiànbǐng [M. WD 块 kuài]
as easy as pie 极容易 jí róngyì
pie in the sky 空中楼阁 kōngzhōng lóugé

pot pie 菜肉馅饼 cài ròuxiànbǐng

piece I N 1 块 kuài, 份 fèn, 片 piàn 2 件 jiàn, 条 tiáo
a piece of advice 一个忠告 yí ge zhōnggào
a piece of information 一条信息 yì tiáo xìnxī
a piece of news 一条新闻 yì tiáo xīnwén
to smash/tear to pieces 砸／撕得粉碎 zá/sīde fěnsuì
to be a piece of cake 容易极了 róngyì jíle, 轻而易举 qīng ér yì jǔ
II V (to piece together) [把细节+] 拼合起来 [bǎxì jié+] pīnhé qǐlai

piecemeal ADJ, ADV 一步一步（的）yíbù yíbù (de), 逐步（的）zhúbù (de)

piecework N 计件工作 jìjiàn gōngzuò

pie chart N 圆形统计图 yuánxíng tǒngjìtú

pier N 1 (突堤) 码头 (tū dī) mǎtou 2 桥墩 qiáodūn

pierce V 刺穿 cì chuān
pierced ears 耳朵穿孔的 ěrduo chuānkǒng de

piercing ADJ 1 刺耳的 [+声音] cì'ěr de [+shēngyīn], 尖利的 jiānlì de 2 锐利的 [+眼光] ruìlì de [+yǎnguāng]

piety N 虔诚的 qiánchéng de

pig I N 1 猪 zhū 2 贪吃的人 tānchī de rén, 肮脏的人 āngzāng de rén II V (to pig out) 大吃（大喝）dà chī (dà hē)

pigeon N 鸽子 gēzi [M. WD 只 zhī]

pigeonhole I N 信件格 xìnjiàn gé, 文件格 wénjiàn gé II V 把 [人+] 不公平地归类 bǎ [rén+] bùgōngpíng de guīlèi

piggy N 小猪 xiǎo zhū [M. WD 头 tóu]
piggy bank 储蓄罐 chǔxù guàn

piggyback ride N 骑在别人背上 qí zài biéren bēishang

piglet N 小猪 xiǎo zhū, 猪崽 zhūzǎi

pigment N 1 (天然) 色素 (tiānrán) sèsù 2 颜料 yánliào

pigpen, pigsty N 1 猪圈 zhūjuàn, 猪栏 zhūlán 2 极其肮脏凌乱的地方 jíqí āngzāng língluàn de dìfang

pigtail N 发辫 fàbiàn, 辫子 biànzi

pike N 1 收费高速公路 shōufèi gāosù gōnglù 2 狗鱼 gǒuyú 3 长矛 chángmáo

pile I N 1（一大）堆 (yí dà) duī 2 大量 dàliàng, 许多 xǔduō 3 桩（子）zhuāng (zi) II V 堆起来 duīqǐlai

piles See **hemorrhoids**

pile-up N 多车相撞（事故）duō chē xiāngzhuàng (shìgù)

pilfer V 偷窃 [+不太值钱的东西] tōuqiè [+bútài zhíqián de dōngxi], 小偷小摸 xiǎotōu xiǎomō

pilgrim N 朝圣者 cháoshèngzhě

pilgrimage N 朝圣 cháoshèng

piling N 房柱 fáng zhù [M. WD 根 gēn],（桥）墩 (qiáo) dūn

pill N 药片 yàopiàn [M. WD 片 piàn], the pill 口服避孕药 kǒufú bìyùnyào

pillar N 房柱 fángzhù [M. WD 根 gēn], 柱子 zhùzi [M. WD 根 gēn]

pillion N 摩托车后座 mótuōchē hòuzuò, to ride pillion 骑在摩托车后座 qí zài mótuōchē hòuzuò

pillow N 枕头 zhěntou, pillow case 枕头套 zhěntoutào

pilot I N 1（飞机）驾驶员 (fēijī) jiàshǐyuán, 飞行员 fēixíng yuán 2 领港员 lǐnggǎngyuán II V 驾驶（飞机）jiàshǐ (fēijī) III ADJ 试验性的 shìyànxìng de, 试点的 shìdiǎn de, pilot project 试验项目 shìyàn xiàngmù, pilot light ①（煤气灶）常燃火苗 (méiqìzào) cháng ránhuǒ miáo ②（显示通电的）指示灯 (xiǎnshì tōngdiàn de) zhǐshìdēng

pimp N 拉皮条的男子 lāpítiáo de nánzǐ

pimple N 粉刺 fěncì

PIN (= personal identity number) ABBREV 个人密码 gèrén mìmǎ

pin I N 1 大头针 dàtóuzhēn, 别针 biézhēn, safety pin 安全别针 ānquán biézhēn, 别针 biézhēn, 2 饰针 shìzhēn, rolling pin 擀面杖 gǎnmiàn zhàng, 3（保龄球）球柱 (bǎolíngqiú) qiúzhù II V 把…固定住 bǎ…gùdìng zhù, to pin down 使…明确表态 shǐ…míngquè biǎotài, 使…详细说明 shǐ…xiángxì shuōmíng 2 (to pin one's hope on sb/sth) 把希望

寄托在某人／某事上 bǎ xīwàng jìtuō zài mǒurén/mǒushì shàng

pincer N 螯 áo

pincers N 钳子 qiánzi [M. WD 把 bǎ]

pinch I V 1 掐 qiā, 拧 nǐng, 夹 jiā 2 偷 tōu, 顺手牵羊 shùnshǒu qiān yáng II N 掐 qiā, 拧 nǐng, 夹 jiā, pinch of salt 一撮盐 yì cuō yán, to take sth with a pinch of salt 对（某事）心存怀疑 duì (mǒushì) xīn cún huáiyí

pine[1] N 松树 sōngshù [M. WD 棵 kē], pine needle 松针 sōngzhēn

pine[2] V (to pine for sb) 苦苦思念某人 kǔkǔ sīniàn mǒurén

pineapple N 菠萝 bōluó, 凤梨 fènglí

ping N 砰的一声 pēng de yì shēng

ping-pong N 乒乓球（运动）pīngpāngqiú (yùndòng)

pinion V 剪去 [+鸟的] 飞羽 jiǎn qù [+niǎo de] fēiyǔ

pink I ADJ 粉红的 fěnhóng de, 淡红的 dànhóng de, 浅红的 qiǎnhóng de II N 粉红 fěnhóng, 淡红 dànhóng, 浅红 qiǎnhóng, pink slip ① 汽车所有权证明 qìchē suǒyǒuquán zhèngmíng ② 解雇通知书 jiěgù tōngzhīshū

pinnacle N 1 顶点 dǐngdiǎn, 顶峰 dǐngfēng 2（教堂）顶尖 (jiàotáng de) dǐngjiān

pinpoint I N 极小的点 jíxiǎo de diǎn, with pinpoint accuracy 极其精确 jíqí jīngquè II V 精确地说出 jīngquè de shuōchū

pinprick N（用针刺出来的）小孔 (yòng zhēncì chūlái de) xiǎokǒng

pinstriped ADJ 有细条纹的 yǒu xì tiáowén de, a pinstriped suit 一套条纹西服 yítào tiáowén xīfú

pint N 品脱 pǐntuō (= 0.4732 liter)

pinup N 性感美女图 xìnggǎn měinǚtú

pioneer I N 先锋 xiānfēng, 先驱 xiānqū II V 开创 kāichuàng, 当先驱 dāngxiān qū

pious ADJ 虔诚的 qiánchéng de

pip N 1 [苹果的+] 籽 [píngguǒ de+] zǐ, 种子 zhǒngzi 2（骰子的）点 (tóuzi de) diǎn

pipe I N 1 管道 guǎndào 2 烟斗 yāndǒu
  pipe dream 白日梦 báirìmèng
  sewer pipe 污水管 wūshuǐ guǎn
  II v 1 用管道运输 yòng guǎndàoyùnshū
  2 吹奏（管乐器）chuīzòu (guǎnyuèqì)

pipeline N 管道 guǎndào
  in the pipeline [计划+] 正在进行中
  [jìhuà+] zhèngzài jìnxíngzhōng

piping I N 管道系统 guǎndào xìtǒng
  II ADV (piping hot) 非常烫的 fēicháng
  tàng de

piquant ADJ 1 辛辣开胃的 [+食物] xīnlà
  kāiwèi de [+shíwù] 2 有趣的 [+故事]
  yǒuqù de [+gùshi], 激动人心的 jīdòng
  rénxīn de

pique I v 1 激起 [+好奇心] jīqǐ [+hàoqí-
  xīn] 2 使…生气 shǐ…shēngqì II N 激怒
  jīnù
  in a fit of pique 一怒之下 yí nù zhīxià

piracy N 1 海盗（行为）hǎidào (xíngwéi)
  2（出版物）非法翻印 (chūbǎnwù) fēifǎ
  fānyìn,（电子产品）非法复制 (diànzǐ
  chǎnpǐn) fēifǎ fùzhì, 盗版 dàobǎn

pirate I N 1 盗版者 dàobǎn zhě, 偷盗版
  权的人 tōudào bǎnquán de rén 2 海
  盗 hǎidào II v 盗版 dàobǎn, 偷盗版权
  tōudào bǎnquán
  pirated edition 盗版本 dàobǎn běn

piss v, N 撒尿 sānniào

pissed, pissed off ADJ 恼火的 nǎohuǒ
  de, 失望的 shīwàng de

pistol N 手枪 shǒuqiāng [M. WD 把 bǎ]

piston N 活塞 huósāi

pit N 1 坑 kēng, 大坑 dà kēng 2 矿井
  kuàngjǐng 3 麻点 mádiǎn 4（水果）硬
  核（水果）yìng hé
  cherry pit 樱桃核 yīngtáo hé

pitch I v 1（棒球）当投手 (bàngqiú)
  dāng tóushǒu 2 定调 dìngdiào, 定音
  dìngyīn 3 (to pitch a tent) 搭帐篷 dā
  zhàngpéng II N 1（棒球）投球 (bàngqiú) tóuqiú 2 音调 yīndiào 3 沥青 lìqīng
  pitch black 漆黑 qīhēi

pitcher N 1（茶）壶 (chá) hú 2（棒球）
  投手 (bàngqiú) tóushǒu

piteous ADJ 让人怜悯的 ràng rén liánmǐn
  de

pitfall N 陷阱 xiànjǐng, 隐患 yǐnhuàn

pitiful ADJ 1 可怜的 kělián de 2 很糟糕的
  hěn zāogāo de, 整糟的 biéjiǎo de

pitiless ADJ 没有怜悯心的 méiyǒu liánmǐn
  xīn de, 冷酷的 lěngkù de

pit-stop N（赛车中的）停车加油维修
  时间 (sàichē zhòngde) tíngchē jiāyóu
  wéixiū shíjiān
  to make a pit-stop（长途驾车旅行
  中）中途停车休息 (chángtú jiàchē
  lǚxíngzhōng) zhōngtú tíngchē xiūxi

pittance N 少得可怜的钱 shǎo dé kělián
  de qián

pity I N 1 怜悯 liánmǐn, 可怜 kělián 2 可
  惜 kěxī, 遗憾 yíhàn II v 怜悯 liánmǐn, 同
  情 tóngqíng

pivot N 1 支点 zhīdiǎn, 支轴 zhī zhóu
  2 关键（人物或事情）guānjiàn (rénwù
  huò shiqing), 中心 zhōngxīn II v（在支
  轴上）移动 (zài zhī zhóu shàng) yídòng

pixie N 小妖怪 xiǎo yāoguài, 小精灵 xiǎo
  jīnglíng

pizza N 比萨饼 bǐsà bǐng, 意大利馅饼
  Yìdàlì xiànbǐng
  Pizza Hut 必胜客 Bìshèngkè, 比萨饼店
  bǐsà bǐngdiàn

placard N 1 标语牌 biāoyǔpái, 广告牌
  guǎnggàopái [M. WD 块 kuài] 2 布告
  bùgào, 招贴 zhāotiē [M. WD 张 zhāng]

placate v 使…平息 shǐ…píngxí, 安抚 ānfǔ

place I N 1 地方 dìfang 2 地位 dìwèi, 身份
  shēnfen 3 场合 chǎnghé 4 位子 wèizi
  II v 1 把…放在 bǎ…fàng zài, 使…处于
  shǐ…chǔyú 2 确定价格／年代 quèdìng
  jiàgé/niándài
  to place a call 打电话 dǎ diànhuà
  to place an order 下订单 xià dìngdān

placebo N 1（做药物试验用的）无效对照
  剂 (zuò yàowù shìyànyòng de) wúxiào
  duìzhàojì 2 安慰剂 ānwèijì

placement N 1 安置 ānzhì 2 放置 fàngzhì, 布置 bùzhì

placenta N 胎盘 tāipán

placid ADJ 平静的 píngjìng de, 宁静的
  níngjìng de

plagiarism N 剽窃（行为）piāoqiè (xíngwéi), 抄袭（行为）chāoxí (xíngwéi)

plague I N 1 瘟疫 wēnyì 2 鼠疫 shǔyì 3 祸害 huòhai, 麻烦 máfan II V 困扰 kùnrǎo, 烦扰 fánrǎo

plaid N（布料的）彩格图案 (bùliào de) cǎi gé tú'àn

plain I ADJ 1 明白的 míngbai de, 明显的 míngxiǎn de 2 简单的 jiǎndān de, 朴素的 pǔsù de 3 坦率的 [+话] tǎnshuài de [+huà]
plain truth 坦率的事实 tǎnshuài de shìshí, 老实话 lǎoshi huà
II N 平原 píngyuán

plainclothes ADJ 穿便衣的 [+警察] chuān biànyī de [+jǐngchá]

plainly ADV 1 清楚地 qīngchu de, 明显地 míngxiǎn de 2 坦率地 [+说话] tǎnshuài de [+shuōhuà] 3 朴素地 [+穿衣] pǔsù de [+chuān yī]

plaintiff N 原告 yuángào, 起诉人 qǐsùrén

plaintive ADJ 哀伤的 āishāng de

plan I N 1 计划 jìhuà, 规划 guīhuà 2 平面图 píngmiàntú 3 示意图 shìyìtú II V 计划 jìhuà, 订计划 dìng jìhuà

plane I N 1 飞机 fēijī 2 平面 píngmiàn 3 刨子 bàozi II ADJ 平面的 píngmiàn de III V 用刨子刨平 yòng bàozi bàopíng

planet N 行星 xíngxīng

planetarium N 天文馆 tiānwénguǎn [M. WD 座 zuò], 太空馆 tàikōng guǎn

plank N 厚木板 hòu mùbǎn [M. WD 块 kuài/条 tiáo]

planner N 规划者 guīhuàzhě, 策划者 cèhuàzhě

planning N 计划 jìhuà, 规划 guīhuà
family planning 计划生育 jìhuà shēngyù

plant I N 1 植物 zhíwù, 作物 zuòwù 2 花 huā, 花草 huācǎo 3 厂 chǎng, 工厂设备 gōngchǎng shèbèi 4 栽赃物 zāizàng wù 5 间谍 jiàndié II V 1 种 zhǒng, 种植 zhòngzhí 2 安插 [+间谍] ānchā [+jiàndié]

plantation N 庄园 zhuāngyuán 2 种植园 zhòngzhíyuán

planter N 种植者 zhòngzhí zhě 2 种植机 zhòngzhí jī 3 花盆 huāpén

plaque N 1（金属或石料的）饰板 (jīnshǔ huò shíliào de) shì bǎn 2 牙斑 yá bān

plasma N 1 血浆 xuèjiāng 2 等离子体 děnglí zǐtǐ

plaster N 1 灰泥 huīní 2 熟石膏 shúshígāo
plaster cast 石膏绷带 shígāo bēngdài, 石膏夹 shígāo jiā
3 橡皮膏 xiàngpígāo II V 1 抹石灰 mǒ shíhuī 2 在…上厚厚地涂抹 zài…shàng hòu hòu de túmǒ

plastic I N 1 塑料 sùliào
plastic surgery 整容外科 zhěngróng wàikē, 整容手术 zhěngróng shǒushù
II ADJ 做作的 [+笑容] zuòzuò de [+xiàoróng], 不自然的 bú zìrán de

plate N 1 盘子 pánzi, 碟子 diézi 2（镀金／银的）金属 (dùjīn/yín de) jīnshǔ, 镀金／银的器皿 dùjīn/yín de qìmǐn 3 假牙 jiǎyá, 牙齿校正器 yáchǐ jiàozhèngqì

plateau N 1 高原 gāoyuán 2 稳定时期 wěndìng shíqī

plated ADJ 镀 [+金银] 的 dù [+jīn/yín] de

platelet N 血小板 xuèxiǎobǎn

platform N 1 讲台 jiǎngtái, 舞台 wǔtái 2（火车站）站台 (huǒchēzhàn) zhàntái, 月台 yuètái 3（钻井）平台 (zuànjǐng) píngtái 4（政党）纲领 (zhèngdǎng) gānglǐng

plating N 金属镀层 jīnshǔ dùcéng

platinum (Pt) N 铂 bó, 白金 báijīn

platonic ADJ 柏拉图式的 Bólātú shì de, 纯精神恋爱的 chún jīngshén liàn'ài de

platoon N（军队）排 (jūnduì) pái

platter N 大盘子 dà pánzi
seafood platter 海鲜大拼盘 hǎixiān dà pīnpán

platypus N 鸭嘴兽 yāzuǐshòu

plaudits N 赞扬 zànyáng, 颂扬 sòngyáng

plausible ADJ 似有道理的 sìyǒu dàolǐ de, 可信的 kě xìn de

play I V 1 玩 wán, 玩耍 wánshuǎ 2 比赛 bǐsài 3 打（球）dǎ (qiú), 下（棋）xià (qí) 4 演奏 yǎnzòu, 弹 dàn, 拉 lā 5 演戏 yǎnxì, 表演 biǎoyǎn II N 1 游戏 yóuxì
All work and no play makes Jack a dull boy. 整天工作不会玩，使杰克呆头呆脑。Zhěngtiān gōngzuò bú huì wán, shǐ Jiékè dāitóu dāinǎo.
2 戏剧 xìjù, 剧本 jùběn

to play a part/role ① 扮演…的角色 bànyǎn…de juésè ② 起…的作用 qǐ…de zuòyòng

to play a trick/jokes on 恶作剧 èzuòjù play on words 双关语 shuāngguānyǔ

playboy N 花花公子 huāhuā gōngzi

play-by-play N (play-by-play commentary)（体育）比赛实况报导 (tǐyù) bǐsài shíkuàng bàodǎo

a play-by-play man（体育）比赛实况播音员 (tǐyù) bǐsài shíkuàng bōyīnyuán

player N 1 球员 qiúyuán, 选手球员 xuǎnshǒu qiúyuán, 选手 xuǎnshǒu 2（事件）参与者 (shìjiàn) cānyùzhě 3（乐器）演奏者 (yuèqì) yǎnzòuzhě 4 (a CD player) 激光唱机 jīguāngchàngjī

playful ADJ 开玩笑的 kāiwánxiào de, 轻快的 qīngkuài de

playground N 操场 cāochǎng, 游戏场 yóuxìchǎng

playmate N 1 玩伴 wán bàn, 游戏伙伴 yóuxì huǒbàn 2 性玩乐伙伴 xìng wánlè huǒbàn

playoff N 总决赛 zǒng juésài

playroom N 游戏室 yóuxì shì

plaything N 1 玩具 wánjù 2 玩物 wánwù, 玩弄的对象 wànnòng de duìxiàng

playwright N 剧作家 jùzuòjiā

plaza N 1 广场 guǎngchǎng, 市场 shìchǎng 2 购物区 gòuwù qū

plea N 1 恳求 kěnqiú, 请求 qǐngqiú 2（法庭上）申诉 (fǎtíng shàng) shēnsù

plea-bargain N 辩诉交易 biànsù jiāoyì, 认罪求情 rènzuì qiúqíng

plead (PT & PP **pled/pleaded**) v 1 恳求 kěnqiú, 央求 yāngqiú 2 争辩 zhēngbiàn, 解释 jiěshì 3 (to plead guilty/ not guilty)（法庭上）承认／不承认有罪 (fǎtíng shàng) chéngrèn/bùchéngrèn yǒuzuì

pleasant ADJ（使人）愉快的 (shǐrén) yúkuài de, 可心的 kěxīn de

pleasantry N 客套话 kètàohuà, 寒暄 hánxuān

please I INTERJ 请 qǐng II v 使…愉快 shǐ…yúkuài, 使…满意 shǐ…mǎnyì

pleased ADJ 愉快的 yúkuài de, 满意的 mǎnyì de

pleasurable ADJ 愉快的 yúkuài de

pleasure N 1 愉快 yúkuài, 满足 mǎnzú 2 乐事 lèshì 3 令人愉快的事 lìng rén yúkuài de shì, 乐事 lèshì

pleat I N 褶（子）zhě (zi) II v 打褶（子）dǎzhě (zi)

pleated ADJ 有褶的 yǒu zhě de

pled See plead

pledge I N 1 誓言 shìyán, 保证 bǎozhèng a pledge of love 爱情誓约 àiqíng shìyuē

2 抵押品 dǐyāpǐn II v 1 发誓 fāshì, 保证 bǎozhèng 2 宣誓加入 xuānshì jiārù

plentiful ADJ 丰富的 fēngfù de, 富饶的 fùráo de

plenty I PRON 充裕 chōngyù, 绰绰有余 chuòchuò yǒuyú II ADV 绰绰有余 chuòchuò yǒuyú

plethora N (a plethora of) 过多的 guòduō de, 许多 xǔduō

pliable, pliant ADJ 1 柔韧的 [+材料] róurèn de [+cáiliào], 柔软的 róuruǎn de 2 柔顺的 [+人] róushùn de [+rén], 易受影响的 yì shòu yǐngxiǎng de

pliers N 钳子 qiánzi [M. WD 把 bǎ]

plight N 困境 kùnjìng, 悲惨的境地 bēicǎn de jìngde

plod v 1 缓慢而沉重地走 huǎnmàn ér chénzhòng de zǒu 2 做辛苦而单调的工作 zuò xīnkǔ ér dāndiào de gōngzuò

plodding ADJ 缓慢的 huǎnmàn de, 艰难的 jiānnán de

plop I v 1 扑通一声落下 pūtōng yì shēng luòxià 2 随便地扔 suíbiàn de rēng II N 扑通声 pūtōng shēng

plot¹ I N 1 情节 qíngjié The plot thickens. 情况变得复杂起来。Qíngkuàng biàn de fùzá qǐlái. 2 阴谋 yīnmóu, 秘密计划 mìmì jìhuà II v 密谋 mìmóu, 策划 cèhuà

plot² I N（小块）土地 (xiǎo kuài) tǔdì II v 标绘出…的位置 biāohuì chū…de wèizhì

plow, plough I N 犁 lí [M. WD 把 bǎ] II v 1 犁 [+地] lí [+dì], 耕 [+地] gēng [+dì] 2 用雪犁清除雪 yòng xuělí qīngchú xuě

to plow on 继续努力 jìxù nǔlì

ploy N 计谋 jìmóu, 手段 shǒuduàn

pluck I v 1 拔 [+鸡毛] bá [+jīmáo] 2 弹 [+琴弦] dàn [+qínxián] 3 拉 lā 4 采 [+花] cǎi [+huā] II N 勇气 yǒngqì, 胆量 dǎnliàng

plug I N 1 插头 chātóu
to pull the plug 中断（资助）zhōngduàn (zīzhù)
2（浴缸）塞子 (yùgāng) sāizi 3（汽车）火花塞 (qìchē) huǒhuāsāi II v 1 堵塞 dǔsè 2 填补 tiánbǔ 3 插入插头 chārù chātóu, 接通电源 jiētōng diàn yuán

plum N (plum tree) 李（子）树 lǐ (zi) shù [M. WD 棵 kē]

plumber N 水暖工 shuǐnuǎngōng, 管子工 guǎnzigōng

plumbing N 1 水暖管道（设备）shuǐnuǎn guǎndào (shèbèi) 2 水暖工的工作 shuǐnuǎngōng de gōngzuò

plume N 1（鲜艳的长）羽毛 (xiānyàn de cháng) yǔmáo 2 一缕 [+烟雾] yì lǚ [+yānwù]

plummet v 急剧跌落 jíjù diēluò

plump I ADJ 胖乎乎的 pànghūhū de, 丰满的 fēngmǎn de II v 使…胖起来 shǐ... pàng qǐlái 2 把 [+枕头] 拍得松软 bǎ [+zhěntou] pāi de sōngruǎn

plunder I v 掠夺 lüèduó, 抢劫 qiǎngjié II N 1 掠夺 lüèduó, 抢劫 qiǎngjié 2 战利品 zhànlìpǐn

plunge I v 1 突然冲下 tūrán chōng xià, 突然撞 tūrán zhuàng II N 冲 chōng, 暴跌 bàodiē
to take the plunge 决定冒险 juédìng màoxiǎn

plunk v 乱扔 luànrēng
to plunk down 花很多钱 huā hěn duō qián

plural N, ADJ 复数 fùshù

plus I PREP 加 jiā II CONJ 再加上 zài jiāshang, 而且 érqiě III ADJ 多于 duōyú (school grades) A/B/C plus A/B/C 加（A+/B+/C+）A/B/C jiā (A+ / B+ / C+)
plus sign 加号 jiāhào (+)
IV N 有利因素 yǒulì yīnsù, 优点 yōudiǎn
pluses and minuses 有利和不利因素 yǒulì hé búlì yīnsù, 利弊 lìbì

plush ADJ 豪华舒适的 háohuá shūshì de

ply I N 1（胶合板）层 (jiāohébǎn) céng, （卫生纸）层 (wèishēngzhǐ) céng, 绳（股）绳 (gǔ) 2 两层卫生纸 liǎngcéng wèishēngzhǐ II v [船+] 定期航行 [chuán+] dìngqī hángxíng
to ply one's trade 从事自己的行当 cóngshì zìjǐ de hángdang

plywood N 胶白板 jiāo báibǎn

pneumatic ADJ 用压缩空气推动的 yòng yāsuōkōngqì tuīdòng de

pneumonia N 肺炎 fèiyán

poach v 1 偷猎 [+大象] tōu liè [+dàxiàng] 2 挖走 [+球员] wā zǒu [+qiúyuán] 3 煮 [+鸡蛋] zhǔ [+jīdàn]

poacher N 偷猎者 tōu lièzhě

pocket I N 1 口袋 kǒudài
pocket change 零钱 língqián
pocket money 零花钱 línghuāqián
2 财力 cáilì, 收益 shōuyì
out of one's own pocket 自掏腰包 zì tāo yāobāo
3 小片地区 xiǎopiàn dìqū
pockets of shower 小片地区有阵雨 xiǎopiàn dìqū yǒu zhènyǔ
II v 1 放进口袋 fàngjìn kǒudài 2 侵吞 qīntūn

pocketbook N 小笔记本 xiǎo bǐjìběn

pockmark N 麻点 mádiǎn

pod N 豆荚 dòujiá

podiatrist N 足病医生 zúbìng yīshēng

podium N（讲）台 (jiǎng) tái,（演出）台 (yǎnchū) tái

poem N 诗 shī [M. WD 首 shǒu], 诗歌 shīgē [M. WD 首 shǒu]

poet N 诗人 shīrén

poetic ADJ 诗歌的 shīgē de, 有诗意的 yǒu shīyì de
poetic justice 应得的惩罚 yīngdé de chéngfá, 恶有恶报 è rén bì yǒu èbào

poetry N 诗歌 shīgē

poignant ADJ 令人哀伤的 lìngrén āishāng de, 令人惋惜的 lìngrén wǎnxī de

point I N 1 点 diǎn
point of view 看法 kànfa, 视角 shìjiǎo
up to a point 在一定程度上 zài yídìng chéngdùshang

to make a point of 特地 tèdì, 很重视 hěn zhòngshì

2 要点 yàodiǎn, 关键 guānjiàn
point man 重要骨干 zhòngyào gǔgàn, 负责人 fùzérén

3 道理 dàolǐ, 价值 jiàzhí **4** 时刻 shíkè **5** (小数) 点 (xiǎoshù)diǎn **6** (比赛得) 分(bǐsài dé) fēn **II** v 指 zhǐ, 对 duì
to point out 指出 zhǐchū

pointblank ADV **1** 近距离 [+射击] jìnjùlí [+shèjí] **2** 直截了当地 [+拒绝] zhíjiéliǎodàng de [+jùjué], 断然 duànrán

pointed ADJ **1** 尖的 [+指甲] jiān de [+zhǐjia] **2** 锐利的 [+批评] ruìlì de [+pīpíng], 尖刻的 jiānkè de

pointer N **1** 指示棒 zhǐshì bàng **2** (仪器的) 指针 (yíqì de) zhǐzhēn **3** (计算机) 鼠标箭头 (jìsuànjī) shǔbiāo jiàntóu **4** 指示猎犬 zhǐshì lièquǎn [M. WD 只 zhǐ/条 tiáo]

pointless ADJ 没有意义的 méiyǒu yìyì de

poise **I** N 沉着 chénzhuó, 自信 zìxìn **II** v 使…平衡 shǐ…pínghéng

poised ADJ **1** 作好准备的 zuò hǎo zhǔnbèi de **2** 沉着自信的 chénzhuó zìxìn de

poison **I** N 毒 dú, 毒药 dúyào
One man's meat is another man's poison. 一个人的肉食是另一个人毒药。(→ 各人的口味爱好不同。) Yí ge rén de ròushí shì lìng yí ge rén dúyào. (→ Gèrén de kǒuwèi àihào bù tóng.)
II v 放毒 fàngdú

poisoning **I** N **1** 中毒 zhòngdú
food poisoning 食物中毒 shíwù zhòngdú
2 投毒 tóudú

poisonous ADJ 有毒的 yǒudú de

poke **I** v 伸入 [+头] shēnrù [+tóu], 插入 chārù **2** 刺入 cìrù, 戳进 chuōjìn
to poke fun at 取笑 qǔxiào
to poke one's nose into sth 多管闲事 duōguǎn xiánshì
II v 戳 chuō, 捅 tǒng
to take a poke at sb 打某人一拳 dǎ mǒurén yìquán, 批评某人 pīpíng mǒurén

poker N **1** 拨火棒 bōhuǒ bàng [M. WD 根 gēn] **2** 打 [+扑克牌] dǎ [+pūkèpái]

polar ADJ 北极的 Běijí de, 南极的 Nánjí de
polar bear 北极熊 Běijíxióng

Polaroid N **1** 一次成象照相机 yícì chéng-xiàng zhàoxiàngjī [M. WD 台 tái] **2** 一次成象图片 yícì chéngxiàng túpiàn [M. WD 张 zhāng]

Pole N 波兰人 Bōlánrén

pole N **1** 杆 gǎn, 杆子 gānzi [M. WD 根 gēn], 竿 gān [M. WD 根 gēn]
fishing pole 鱼竿 yúgān
2 极 jí, 南极 Nánjí, 北极 Běijí
the North Pole 北极 Běijí
the South Pole 南极 Nánjí
3 电极 diànjí, 磁极 cíjí
be poles apart 截然相反 jiérán xiāngfǎn, 完全不同 wánquán bùtóng

police **I** N 警察 jǐngchá, 警方 jǐngfāng
police department 警察局 jǐngchájú
police force 警察部队 jǐngchá bùduì
police state 警察国家 jǐngchá guójiā
II v 监督 jiāndū, 监察 jiānchá

policeman (woman) N 警察 jǐngchá, 男 (女) 警察 nán (nǚ) jǐngchá

policy N **1** 政策 zhèngcè **2** 保险单 bǎoxiǎn dān, 保险 bǎoxiǎn

polio N 小儿麻痹症 xiǎo'ér mábìzhèng

Polish **I** ADJ 波兰的 Bōlán de, 波兰人的 Bōlánrén de, 波兰语的 Bōlányǔ de **II** N 波兰语 Bōlányǔ

polish v **1** 擦亮 [+银器] cāliàng [+yínqì], 磨光 [+地板] móguāng [+dìbǎn] **2** 修改 [+文章] xiūgǎi [+wénzhāng], 润色 rùnsè
to polish up ① 擦亮 cāliàng ② (进修) 提高 (jìnxiū) tígāo

polished ADJ **1** 擦亮的 cāliàng de, 磨光的 móguāng de **2** 优美的 yōuměi de, 文雅的 wényǎ de

polite ADJ 有礼貌的 yǒulǐmào de

political ADJ 政治的 zhèngzhì de
political prisoner 政治犯 zhèngzhìfàn

politician N 政客 zhèngkè, 政治领袖 zhèngzhì lǐngxiù

politics N **1** 政治 zhèngzhì **2** 权术 quánshù, 勾心斗角 gōuxīn dòujiǎo **3** 政治学 zhèngzhìxué

polka N 波尔卡舞曲 Bō'ěrkǎwǔ qū [M. WD 首 shǒu]

poll I N 1 民意调查 mínyì diàochá, 民意测验 mínyì cèyàn 2 选举 xuǎnjǔ II v 对…进行民意调查 duì...jìnxíng mínyì diàochá

pollen N 花粉 huāfěn

　pollen count 花粉量 huāfěn liáng

pollinate v 给 [+果树] 授花粉 gěi [+guǒshù] shòu huāfěn

polling station N 投票站 tóupiàozhàn

pollster N 民意调查者 mínyì diàocházhě

pollutant N 污染物 wūrǎnwù

pollute v 污染 wūrǎn, 弄脏 nòngzāng

pollution N 污染 wūrǎn

polo N 马球（运动）mǎqiú (yùndòng)

　polo shirt 马球衫 mǎqiúshān

polyester N 涤纶 dílún

polygamous ADJ 一夫多妻的 yìfūduōqī de

polygamy N 一夫多妻制 yìfūduōqī zhì

polygon N 多边形 duōbiānxíng, 多角形 duōjiǎoxíng

polygraph N 测谎器 cèhuǎngqì [M. WD 台 tái]

polytechnic N 综合性理工学院 zōnghéxìng lǐgōng xuéyuàn, 工艺专科学校 gōngyì zhuānkē xuéxiào

polyunsaturated fat N 不饱和脂肪 bù bǎohé zhīfáng

pomegranate N 石榴 shíliu

pomp N 盛大的仪式 shèngdà de yíshì, 盛典 shèngdiǎn

pompom N 小绒球 xiǎo róngqiú

pompous ADJ 自命不凡的 zìmìng bùfán de, 爱摆架子的 ài bǎi jiàzi de

poncho N 披风 pīfēng, 斗篷 dǒupéng

pond N 池塘 chítáng

ponder v 郑重考虑 zhèngzhòng kǎolǜ, 深思 shēnsī

ponderous ADJ 1 笨拙的 [+行动] bènzhuō de [+xíngdòng] 2 严肃而乏味的 [+说教] yánsù ér fáwèi de [+shuōjiào]

pontiff N（天主教）教皇 (Tiānzhǔjiào) Jiàohuáng

pony N 小种马 xiǎo zhǒngmǎ

ponytail N 马尾辫 mǎwěi biàn

pooch N 狗 gǒu [M. WD 只 zhī/条 tiáo]

poodle N 长毛狗 [M. WD 只 zhī/条 tiáo]

pooh-pooh v 嗤之以鼻 chī zhī yǐ bí

pool I N 1 池 chí, 水池 shuǐ chí 2 游泳池 yóuyǒng chí 3 台球 táiqiú

　pool table 台球桌 táiqiú zhuō

　to play pool 打台球 dǎ táiqiú

4 公用物 gōngyòng wù 5 备用人员 bèiyòng rényuán II v 集中使用 jízhōng shǐyòng

poop I N 大便 dàbiàn II v 拉大便 lādà biàn

poor ADJ 1 穷 qióng, 贫穷 pínqióng 2 不好的 bù hǎo de 3 差的 chà de, 蹩脚的 biéjiǎo de

　to be in poor health 身体不好 shēntǐ bù hǎo

　the poor 穷人 qióngrén

poorly ADV 很差（地）hěn chà (de)

pop¹ I v 1 发出噼啪的声音 fāchū pīpā de shēngyīn 2 爆 [+玉米花] bào [+yùmǐhuā] 3 蹦出 bèng chū 4 很快地来（或去）hěn kuài de lái (huò qù) II N 1 噼啪声 pīpā shēng 2 汽水 qìshuǐ, 啤酒 píjiǔ

pop² N 流行音乐 liúxíng yīnyuè

　pop concert 流行音乐会 liúxíng yīnyuè huì

pop³ N 爸爸 bàba

popcorn N 爆玉米花 bào yùmǐhuā

Pope N（天主教）教皇 (Tiānzhǔjiào) Jiàohuáng [M. WD 位 wèi]

poplar N 杨树 yángshù [M. WD 棵 kē]

poppy N 罂粟 yīngsù

popular ADJ 1 很受欢迎的 hěn shòu huānyíng de 2 流行的 liúxíng de 3 大众的 dàzhòng de

popularity N 1 流行 liúxíng 2 受欢迎 shòu huānyíng

popularize v 使…流行 shǐ...liúxíng, 使…普及 shǐ...pǔjí

popularly ADV 大众（地）dàzhòng (de)

　popularly priced 定价适中 dìngjià shìzhōng

populate v (be populated by) 居住着 jūzhùzhe

　densely populated 人口稠密的 [+地区] rénkǒu chóumì de [+dìqū]

population N 1 人口 rénkǒu 2（动物的）数量 (dòngwù de) shùliàng

porcelain N 瓷器 cíqì
an expensive porcelain dinner set 一套昂贵的瓷器餐具 yítào ángguì de cíqì cānjù

porch N 门廊 ménláng

porcupine N 豪猪 háozhū

pore¹ N 毛孔 máokǒng

pore² v (to pore over) 长时间仔细阅读 chángshíjiān zǐxì yuèdú

pork N 猪肉 zhūròu

pornography N 色情作品 sèqíng zuòpǐn, 黄色电影／杂志 huángsèdiànyǐng/zázhì

porous ADJ 多孔的 duōkǒng de, 水能渗透的 shuǐnéng shèntòu de

porridge N (燕麦) 粥 (yànmài) zhōu

port N 1 港 gǎng, 港口 gǎngkǒu 2 (计算机) 插口 (jisuànjī) chākǒu 3 (船舶／飞机) 左舷 (chuánbó/fēijī) zuǒxián 4 (葡萄牙) 波尔图葡萄酒 (Pútaoyá) bō ěr tú pútaojiǔ

portable I ADJ 1 手提式的 shǒutíshì de, 便携式的 biànxiéshì de
a portable toilet 流动厕所 liúdòng cèsuǒ 2 (计算机) 可兼容 (程序) (jisuànjī) kě jiānróng [+chéngxù] II N 手提式电器 shǒutíshì diànqì

portal N 1 (互联网) 门户网站 (hùliánwǎng) ménhù wǎngzhàn 2 大门 dàmén

portent N 预兆 yùzhào, 迹象 jìxiàng

porter N 1 (行李) 搬运工 (xíngli) bānyùn gōng 2 (大楼) 修理工 (dàlóu) xiūlǐ gōng, 清洁工 qīngjiégōng 3 (旅馆) 守门人 (lǚguǎn) shǒumén rén

portfolio N 1 公事包 gōngshìbāo 2 (个人) 投资组合 (gèrén) tóuzī zǔhé
investment portfolio 投资组合 tóuzī zǔhé 3 (政府高级官员的) 职责范围 (zhèngfǔ gāojí guānyuán de) zhízé fànwéi

porthole N (飞机／船) 舷窗 (fēijī/chuán) xiánchuāng

portion I N 1 (一) 部分 (yí) bùfen 2 一份 (食物) yí fèn (shíwù)
double portion of chips 两份炸土豆条 liǎngfèn zhátǔdòutiáo
II v (to portion out) 把…分成几份 bǎ… fēnchéng jǐ fèn, 分 fēn

portly ADJ 胖的 pàng de, 发福的 fāfú de

portrait N 肖像 xiàoxiàng [M. WD 幅 fú]

portray v 1 描绘 miáohuì, 描述 miáoshù 2 扮演 (角色) bànyǎn [+juésè]

Portuguese I ADJ 葡萄牙的 Pútaoyá de, 葡萄牙人的 Pútaoyárén de, 葡萄牙语 Pútaoyáyǔ II N 1 葡萄牙语 Pútaoyáyǔ 2 葡萄牙人 Pútaoyárén

pose I v 1 摆姿势 (拍照或画象) bǎi zīshì (pāizhào huò huàxiàng)
to pose as 冒充 màochōng 2 引起 (问题) yǐnqǐ [+wèntí], 导致 dǎozhì II N 1 姿势 zīshì 2 装腔作势的举止 zhuāngqiāng zuòshì de jǔzhǐ

posh ADJ 高档的 gāodàng de, 豪华的 háohuá de

position N 1 位置 wèizhì 2 姿势 zīshì 3 地位 dìwèi 4 职务 zhíwù 5 立场 lìchǎng

positive ADJ 1 肯定的 kěndìng de, 无疑的 wúyí de 2 积极的 jījí de 3 阳性的 yángxìng de

positively ADV 1 确实 (地) quèshí (de), 无疑 (地) wúyí (de) 2 积极地 jījí de, 正面地 zhèngmiàn de, 肯定地 kěndìng de

posse N (a posse of) 一群 yìqún, 一大帮 yí dàbāng

possess v 1 有 yǒu, 持有 chíyǒu, 拥有 yōngyǒu 2 控制 kòngzhì, 支配 zhīpèi

possession N 1 拥有 yōngyǒu, 持有 chíyǒu 2 财产 cáichǎn

possessive I ADJ 1 占有欲很强的 zhànyǒu yù hěn qiáng de 2 (语法) 所有格的 (yǔfǎ) suǒyǒugé de II N 所有格 (形式) suǒyǒugé (xíngshì)

possibility N 1 可能性 kěnéng xìng 2 可能的事 kěnéng de shì

possible ADJ 可能的 kěnéng de

possum N 负鼠 fùshǔ, 袋貂 dàidiāo

post I N 1 柱子 zhùzi 2 要职 yàozhí, 重要的位置 zhòngyào de wèizhì 3 (British) 邮件 yóujiàn
post office 邮政局 yóuzhèngjú
post office box 邮箱 yóuxiāng, 信箱 xìnxiāng
II v 贴公告 tiē gōnggào, 通告 tōnggào
Post no bills. 请勿张贴。 Qǐn gwù zhāngtiēt.

postage N 邮资 yóuzī

postal ADJ 邮政的 yóuzhèng de
　postal service 邮政 yóuzhèng

postcard N 明信片 míngxìnpiàn

postdate V（在支票上）写比实际晚的日期 (zài zhīpiào shàng) xiě bǐ shíjì wǎn de rìqī

postdoctoral ADJ 博士后的 bóshìhòu de

poster N 海报 hǎibào, 广告画 guǎnggàohuà

posterior N 臀部 túnbù, 屁股 pìgu

posterity N 子孙后代 zǐsūn hòudài

postgraduate I ADJ 研究生的 yánjiū-shēng de, 硕士（或博士）的 shuòshì (huò bóshì) de II N 硕士（或博士）研究生 shuòshì (huò bóshì) yánjiūshēng

posthumous ADJ 死后发生的 sǐhòu fāshēng de
　a posthumous son 遗腹子 yífùzǐ

Post-it N 便条粘贴纸 biàntiáo zhāntiē zhǐ [M. WD 张 zhāng]

postman N 邮递员 yóudìyuán

postmark N 邮戳 yóuchuō

postmaster N 邮政局长 yóuzhèngjú-zhǎng

postmortem N 1 尸体检验 shītǐ jiǎnyàn 2（对失败的）事后检讨 (duì shībài de) shìhòu jiǎntǎo

postnatal ADJ 产后的 chǎnhòu de, 分娩的 fēnmiǎn de
　postnatal depression 产后忧郁（症）chǎnhòu yōuyù (zhēng)

postpone V 把…延期 bǎ...yánqī, 推迟 tuīchí

postponement N 延期 yánqī

postscript (ABBREV P.S.) N 附笔 fùbǐ, 又及 yòují

postulate V, N 假定 jiǎdìng, 假设 jiǎshè

posture N 1 仪态 yítài 2 立场 lìchǎng, 姿态 zītài

pot I N 1 锅 guō, 壶 hú
　coffee pot 咖啡壶 kāfēi hú
　tea pot 茶壶 chá hú
　2 花盆 huāpén 3 大麻 dàmá II V 把植物移植到花盆里 bǎ zhíwù yízhí dào huāpén lǐ

potato N 土豆 tǔdòu, 马铃薯 mǎlíngshǔ

potato chip N（炸）土豆片 (zhá) tǔdòupiàn

potbelly N 大肚子 dàdùzi, 啤酒桶肚子 píjiǔtǒng dùzi

potent ADJ 1 有效的 [+药] yǒuxiào de [+yào] 2 强有力的 [+武器] qiángyǒulì de [+wǔqì] 3 有性能力的 [+男子] yǒu xìngnénglì de [+nánzǐ]

potential I ADJ 潜在的 qiánzài de II N 潜力 qiánlì

potentially ADV 潜在地 qiánzài de, 可能 kěnéng

pothead N 吸大麻的人 xī dàmá de rén

potholder N 防烫厚布垫 fáng tàng hòu bù diàn [M. WD 块 kuài]

pothole N（路面）凹坑 (lùmiàn) āokēng

potion N 药水 yàoshuǐ
　love potion 春药 chūnyào, 发情药水 fāqíng yào shuǐ

potluck (potluck dinner/lunch) N 自带菜肴的聚餐 zì dài càiyáo de jùcān, 百乐餐 bǎi lè cān

potpourri N 1 百花香 bǎihuāxiāng 2（音乐或文学）集锦 (yīnyuè huò wénxué) jíjǐn

pottery N 陶器 táoqì

potty N（小孩用的）便盆 (xiǎohái yòng de) biànpén

pouch N 小袋（子）xiǎo dài (zi)

poultry N 家禽 jiāqín

pounce V 突然猛扑 tūrán měngpū, 突然袭击 tūrán xíjī

pound I N 1 磅 bàng 2（英）镑 (Yīng) bàng (£) II V 1 连续猛击 liánxù měngjī 2 [心脏+] 剧烈跳动 [xīnzàng+] jùliè tiàodòng

pour V 1 倒 dǎo, 倾倒 qīngdǎo 2 下倾盆大雨 xià qīngpén dàyǔ
　It never rains but it pours. 要么不下雨，一下下就大雨倾盆。(→ 祸不单行。) Yàome bù xiàyǔ, yí xià jiù dàyǔ qīngpén. (→ Huò bù dān xíng. *Misfortunes never come singly.*)

poverty N 贫穷 pínqióng
　the poverty line 贫困线 pínkùnxiàn

poverty-stricken ADJ 极其贫穷的 jíqí pínqióng de

P.O.W (= prisoner of war) ABBREV 战俘 zhànfú

P.O.W. camp 战俘营 zhànfúyíng

powder I N 粉末 fěnmò

powder room （女用）卫生间 (nǚ yòng) wèishēngjiān

II v 给 [+皮肤] 涂粉 gěi [+pífū] túfěn

power N 1 权力 quánlì, 力量 lìliang

power base 权力基础 quánlìjīchǔ

power of attorney （法律）代理权 (fǎlù) dàilǐ quán

2 政治权力 zhèngzhì quánlì, 政权 zhèngquán **3** 电力 diànlì

power tool 电动工具 diàndònggōngjù

powerboat N 摩托赛艇 mótuō sàitǐng [M. WD 艘 sōu]

powerful ADJ 1 强有力的 qiángyǒulì de **2** 权力大的 quánlì dà de, 强大的 qiángdà de

powerless ADJ 无权的 wúquán de, 无势力的 wú shìlì de

practicable ADJ 行得通的 xíngdetōng de, 可行的 kěxíng de

practical ADJ 1 实践的 shíjiàn de, 实际的 shíjì de **2** 实用的 shíyòng de **3** 讲究实际的 jiǎngjiu shíjì de

practical joke 恶作剧 èzuòjù

practicality N 1 可行性 kěxíngxìng **2** 实际（情况）shíjì (qíngkuàng)

practice I N 1 实践 shíjiàn, 实际 shíjì **2** 练习 liànxí **4** （医生）诊所 (yīshēng) zhěnsuǒ, （律师）事务所 (lùshī) shìwùsuǒ **II** v (British **practise**) 1 练习 liànxí **2** 执业 zhíyè, 当医生 dāng yīshēng, 当律师 dāng lùshī

practicing ADJ 1 开业的 kāiyè de

practicing lawyer 开业律师 kāiyè lùshī **2** 遵循教义的 [+宗教徒] zūnxún jiàoyì de [+zōngjiàotú]

practitioner N 开业者 kāiyè zhě, 从业者 cóngyèzhě

medical practitioner 开业医生 kāiyè yīshēng **2** 实践者 shíjiànzhě

pragmatic ADJ 讲究实用的 jiǎngjiu shíyòng de, 务实的 wùshí de

prairie N 草原 cǎoyuán

prairie dog 草原犬鼠 cǎoyuán quǎnshǔ

praise V, N 表扬 biǎoyáng, 赞扬 zànyáng

praiseworthy ADJ 值得赞扬的 zhíde zànyáng de

prance v 昂首阔步 ángshǒu kuòbù

prank N 恶作剧 èzuòjù

prankster N 恶作剧者 èzuòjùzhě

prattle N 絮絮叨叨地说 xùxu dāodāo de shuō

prawn N 大虾 dàxiā [M. WD 只 zhī]

pray v 祈祷 qídǎo, 祷告 dǎogào

prayer N 祈祷 qídǎo, 祷告 dǎogào

preach v 1 布道 bùdào, 宣扬 xuānyáng **2** 说教 shuōjiào

preacher N 讲道者 jiǎngdàozhě, 说教的人 shuōjiào de rén

preamble N 前言 qiányán, 序言 xùyán

prearranged ADJ 预先安排好的 yùxiān ānpái hǎo de

precarious ADJ 不稳定的 bùwěndìng de, 有危险的 yǒu wēixiǎn de

precaution N 预防（措施）yùfáng (cuòshī)

precautionary ADJ 预防（性）的 yùfáng (xìng) de

precede v 在…前发生 zài...qián fāshēng

precedent N 先例 xiānlì, 判例 pànlì

to set a precedent 开创先例 kāichuàng xiānlì

precept N 准则 zhǔnzé

precinct N 1 分区 fēnqū **2** 警察分局 jǐngchá fēnjú **3** 周围地区 zhōuwéi dìqū

precious I ADJ 珍贵的 zhēnguì de

precious metal 贵金属 guìjīnshǔ

precious stone 宝石 bǎoshí

II ADV (precious little) 非常少 fēicháng shǎo

precipice N 悬崖 xuányá

precipitate I v 迅速导致 xùnsù dǎozhì, 加速 jiāsù **II** ADJ 仓促的 cāngcù de, 贸然的 màorán de **III** N 沉淀物 chéndiànwù

precipitation N 1 降雨（或雪）jiàngyǔ (huò xuě), 降雨（或雪）量 jiàngyǔ (huò xuě) liáng **2** 沉淀 chéndiàn **3** 仓促 cāngcù

précis N 摘要 zhāiyào

precise ADJ 精确的 jīngquè de, 精密的 jīngmì de

precisely ADV 1 精确地 jīngquè de 2 恰好 qiàhǎo, 正巧是 zhèngqiǎo shì

preclude V 使…不能 shǐ…bùnéng, 防 止 fángzhǐ

precocious ADJ 早熟的 zǎoshú de, 智力 超常的 zhìlì chāocháng de

preconceived ADJ 预先形成的 yùxiān xíngchéng de

preconception N 先入为主的偏见 xiān rù wéi zhǔ de piānjiàn

precondition N 先决条件 xiānjué tiáo-jiàn, 前提 qiántí

precursor N 前身 qiánshēn

predate V 先于…发生 xiānyú…fāshēng

predator N 1 捕食其他动物的动物 bǔshí qítā dòngwù de dòngwù 2 掠夺者 lüè-duózhě, 损人利己的人 sǔnrén lìjǐ de rén

predecessor N 前任 qiánrèn, 前辈 qiánbèi

predestined ADJ 命中注定（的） mìngzhōng zhùdìng (de)

predetermined ADJ 预先确定（的） yùxiān quèdìng (de)

predicament N 困境 kùnjìng

predicate N（语法）谓语 (yǔfǎ) wèiyǔ

predict V 预言 yùyán, 预测 yùcè

prediction N 预言 yùyán, 预测 yùcè

predilection N 偏爱 piān'ài

predisposed ADJ 1 有…倾向的 yǒu…qīngxiàng de 2 易患 [+高血压] 的 yìhuàn [+gāoxuèyā] de

predominance N 优势 yōushì

predominantly ADV 绝大多数（地） juédà duōshù (de)

predominate V 占主要地位 zhàn zhǔyào dìwèi

preeminent ADJ 卓越的 zhuóyuè de, 杰 出的 jiéchū de

preempt V 先发制人以阻止 [+敌人的进 攻] xiānfāzhìrén yǐ zǔzhǐ [+dírén de jìngōng]

preen V [鸟+] 整理羽毛 [niǎo +] zhěnglǐ yǔmáo

to preen oneself [人+] 精心打扮 [rén+] jīngxīn dǎban

pre-existing ADJ 早先就存在的 zǎoxiān jiù cúnzài de

prefabricated ADJ 预制的 yùzhì de

preface I N 序言 xùyán, 前言 qiányán
II V 以…作为开始 yǐ…zuòwéi kāishǐ

prefer V 更喜欢 gèngxǐhuan, 比较喜欢 bǐjiào xǐhuan

preferable ADJ 更可取的 gèng kěqǔ de, 更好 gènghǎo

preferably ADV 更可取（地）gèng kěqǔ (de), 最好 zuìhǎo

preference N 偏爱 piān'ài
in preference to sth 不要某事 búyào mǒu shì

prefix N 前缀 qiánzhuì

pregnancy N 怀孕（期）huáiyùn (qī)

pregnant ADJ 1 怀孕的 huáiyùn de 2 富 有含义的 fùyǒu hányì de, 意味深长的 yìwèi shēncháng de
a pregnant pause 意味深长的停顿 yìwèi shēncháng de tíngdùn

preheat V 预热 yùrè

prehistoric ADJ 史前的 shǐqián de

prejudge V 过早判断 guòzǎo pànduàn

prejudice I N 偏见 piānjiàn, 成见 chéngjiàn II V 使…有偏见 shǐ…yǒu piānjiàn, 使…有成见 shǐ…yǒu chéngjiàn

preliminary I ADJ 初步的 chūbù de, 起始 的 qǐshǐ de II N (preliminaries) 初步行 动 chūbù xíngdòng, 筹备工作 chóubèi gōngzuò

prelude N（戏剧）序幕 (xìjù) xùmù, （音乐）序曲 (yīnyuè) xùqǔ

premarital ADJ 婚前的 hūnqián de
premarital sex 婚前性行为 hūnqián xìng xíngwéi

premature ADJ 过早的 guòzǎo de, 不成 熟的 bùchéngshú de
premature death 早逝 zǎoshì, [儿童+] 夭折 [értóng+] yāozhé, [中年人+] 英年 早逝 [zhōngniánrén+] yīngnián zǎoshì

premeditated ADJ 预谋的 yùmóu de

premenstrual ADJ 月经前的 yuèjīng qián de

premier I N 总理 zǒnglǐ II ADJ 最好的 zuìhǎo de, 首要的 shǒuyào de

première N（电影）首映 (diànyǐng) shǒu-yìng,（戏剧）首演 (xìjù) shǒuyǎn,（电视 连续剧）首播 (diànshì liánxùjù) shǒubō

premise N 前提 qiántí

premises N 房屋连土地 fángwū lián tǔdì, 场所 chǎngsuǒ

premium N 1 保险费 bǎoxiǎnfèi 2 优质汽油 yōuzhì qìyóu
at a premium 紧缺 jǐnquē
to place a premium on sth 高度重视某事 gāodù zhòngshì mǒushì

premonition N 预感 yùgǎn

prenatal ADJ 产前的 chǎnqián de, 孕期的 yùnqī de

preoccupied ADJ 全神贯注的 quánshén guànzhù de, 入神的 rùshén de

preordained ADJ 命中注定的 mìngzhōng zhùdìng de

prepaid ADJ 预付的 yùfù de
prepaid envelope 邮资已付的信封 yóuzīyǐfù de xìnfēng

preparation N 准备 zhǔnbèi
to make preparations for 准备 zhǔnbèi, 为…作准备 wèi...zuò zhǔnbèi

preparatory ADJ 预备的 yùbèi de, 准备的 zhǔnbèi de
preparatory school (prep school) 私立预备学校 sīlì yùbèi xuéxiào

prepare V 准备 zhǔnbèi

prepared ADJ 1 有准备的 yǒu zhǔnbèi de, 做好准备的 zuò hǎo zhǔnbèi de
be prepared for the worst 做最坏打算 zuò zuì huài dǎsuan
2 愿意的 yuànyì de

preponderance N 优势 yōushì, 多数 duōshù

preposition N 介词 jiècí, 前置词 qiánzhìcí

preposterous ADJ 荒诞的 huāngdàn de, 完全不合理的 wánquán bùhélǐ de

preppy ADJ 私立学校学生的 sīlì xuéxiào xuéshēng de

preregister V 预先登记 yùxiān dēngjì, 预先注册 yùxiān zhùcè

prerequisite N 先决条件 xiānjué tiáojiàn, 必need条件 bìbèi tiáojiàn

prerogative N 特权 tèquán

presage V 预示 yùshì, 预告 yùgào

Presbyterian N 长老会教徒 Zhǎnglǎohuì jiàotú

preschool N 学前班 xué qián bān, 幼儿园 yòu'éryuán

prescribe V 1 [医生+] 嘱咐（使用）开处方 [yīshēng+] zhǔfù (shǐyòng) kāi chǔfāng 2 规定 guīdìng, 指定 zhǐdìng

prescription N 处方 chǔfāng [M. WD 份 fèn/张 zhāng], 药方 yàofāng [M. WD 份 fèn/张 zhāng]

prescriptive ADJ 规定的 guīdìng de, 指定的 zhǐdìng de

presence N 1 在场 zàichǎng, 出席 chūxí 2 风采气势 fēngcǎi qìshì

present[1] ADJ 1 在场的 zàichǎng de, 出席的 chūxí de 2 目前的 mùqián de, 现在的 xiànzài de II N 现在 xiànzài, 目前 mùqián

present[2] I N 礼物 lǐwù, 礼品 lǐpǐn II V 1 给予 [+礼物] jǐyǔ [+lǐwù], 赠与 zèngyǔ 2 提出 [+论文] tíchū [+lùnwén], 宣布 xuānbù 3 上演 [+戏剧] shàngyǎn [+xìjù], 演出 yǎnchū

presentable ADJ 拿得出手的 nádéchūshǒu de, 体面的 tǐmian de

presentation N 1 报告 bàogào, 陈述 chénshù
to give a presentation on the new project 介绍新产品 jièshào xīnchǎnpǐn 2 授予 shòuyǔ, 颁发 bānfā
presentation ceremony 授奖仪式 shòujiǎng yíshì
3 (a presentation copy) 赠阅本 zèngyuèběn

present-day ADJ 今日的 jīnrì de, 现今的 xiànjīn de

presently ADV 立即 lìjí, 即刻 jíkè

preservation N 保护 bǎohù, 维护 wéihù

preservative N 防腐剂 fángfǔjì

preserve I V 保护 bǎohù, 保护 bǎohù II N 1 自然保护区 zìrán bǎohùqū 2 独占的地盘 dúzhàn de dìpán 3 果酱 guǒjiàng

preside V 主持 zhǔchí, 负责 fùzé

presidency N 总统的职位 zǒngtǒng de zhíwèi, 大学校长的职位 dàxué xiàozhǎng de zhíwèi

president N 总统 zǒngtǒng, 大学校长 dàxué xiàozhǎng, 主席 zhǔxí
president of a bank 银行行长 yínháng hángzhǎng
president of a club 俱乐部主任 jùlèbù zhǔrèn

president of a company 公司董事长 gōngsī dǒngshìzhǎng

president-elect N 当选总统 dāngxuǎn zǒngtǒng

presidential ADJ 总统的 zǒngtǒng de
presidential suite（旅馆的）总统套房 (lǚguǎn de) zǒngtǒng tàofáng

press I N 1 新闻界 xīnwén jiè
press agent 新闻代理人 xīnwén dàilǐrén
press conference 记者招待会 jìzhě zhāodàihuì
press release 新闻稿 xīnwéngǎo
2 出版社 chūbǎnshè II v 1 按 àn 2 熨烫 [+衬衫] yùn tàng [+chènshān], 烫平 tàngpíng 3 压平 yāpíng, 压碎 yāsuì 4 催促 cuīcù, 力劝 lìquàn 5 (to press charges) 提出诉讼 tíchū sùsòng

pressed ADJ (be pressed for time/money) 时间／资金紧张 shíjiān/zījīn jǐnzhāng

pressing ADJ 紧迫的 jǐnpò de

pressure I N 1 压力 yālì 2（大）气压 (dà) qìyā
pressure cooker 压力锅 yālì guō
II v 对…施加压力 duì…shījiā yālì

pressure group N 压力集团 yālì jítuán

pressurized ADJ 加压的 jiāyā de, 增压的 zēngyā de

prestige N 威望 wēiwàng, 声望 shēngwàng

prestigious ADJ 有声望的 yǒushēng wàng de, 威望很高的 wēiwàng hěn gāo de

presume v 猜想 cāixiǎng, 认为 rènwéi, 推测 tuīcè

presumptuous ADJ 自以为是的 zì yǐwéi shì de, 冒失的 màoshi de

presuppose v 预先假设 yùxiān jiǎshè, 预设 yùshè

pretend I v 假装 jiǎzhuāng II ADJ 假装的 jiǎzhuāng de, 假想的 jiǎxiǎng de

pretense N 假装 jiǎzhuāng, 伪称 wěichēng
under false pretense 以虚假的借口 yǐ xūjiǎ de jièkǒu
under the pretense of 以…为借口 yǐ…wéi jièkǒu, 借口 jièkǒu

pretentious ADJ 装腔作势的 zhuāngqiāng zuòshì de, 矫饰的 jiǎoshì de

pretext N 借口 jièkǒu, 托词 tuōcí
under the pretext that 以…为借口 yǐ…wéi jièkǒu

pretty I ADJ 漂亮的 piàoliang de, 可爱的 kě'ài de II ADV 相当 xiāngdāng

prevail v 1 占优势 zhàn yōushì, 占上风 zhàn shàngfēng 2 盛行 shèngxíng, 流行 liúxíng

prevailing ADJ 流行的 liúxíng de, 普遍的 pǔbiàn de

prevalence N 流行的程度 liúxíng de chéngdù

prevent v 防止 fángzhǐ, 阻止 zǔzhǐ

prevention N 防止 fángzhǐ, 阻止 zǔzhǐ
Prevention is better than cure. 预防胜于治疗。Yùfáng shèngyú zhìliáo.

preventive ADJ 预防（性）的 yùfáng (xìng) de, 防备的 fángbèi de

preview N（电影）预映 (diànyǐng) yùyìng,（戏剧）预演 (xìjù) yùyǎn

previous ADJ 前一个 qián yí ge, 上一个 shàng yí ge

previously ADV 以前 yǐqián, 先前 xiānqián

prewar ADJ, ADV 战前（的）zhànqián (de)

prey I N 被捕食的动物 bèi bǔshí de dòngwù, 猎物 lièwù
beast of prey 食肉猛兽 shí ròu měngshòu
to fall prey to 成为…的牺牲品 chéngwéi…de xīshēngpǐn
II v (to prey on) 伤害 shānghài

price I N 1 价格 jiàgé, 价钱 jiàqian 2 代价 dàijià
the asking price 要价 yàojià
at any price 不惜代价 bù xī dàijià
II v 给…定价 / 标价 gěi…dìngjià/biāojià

priceless ADJ 无价的 wújià de, 价值极高的 jiàzhí jí gāo de

pricey, pricy ADJ（价格）昂贵的 (jiàgé) ángguì de

prick I v 1（刺）破 (cì) pò,（扎）穿 (zhā) chuān 2 刺痛 cìtòng
to prick up one's ears 竖起耳朵听 shùqǐ ěrduo tīng
II N 1 刺孔 cìkǒng 2 刺痛 cìtòng

prickle I N 1 皮刺 pí cì 2 刺痛（感）cìtòng (gǎn) II v 刺痛 cìtòng

prickly ADJ **1** 多刺的 [+玫瑰] duō cì de [+méigui] **2** 引起刺痛的 yǐnqǐ cìtòng de **3** 棘手的 [+事] jíshǒu de [+shì]

pride N 骄傲 jiāo'ào, 自傲 zì'ào

priest N 神甫 shénfu, 教士 jiàoshì

prim ADJ 古板的 gǔbǎn de, 一本正经的 yì běn zhèngjīng de

prima donna N **1** 首席女歌唱家 shǒuxí nǚ gēchàngjiā **2** 妄自尊大的人 wàng zì zūn dà de rén

primal ADJ 原始的 yuánshǐ de, 基本的 jīběn de

primarily ADV 主要地 zhǔyào de

primary ADJ **1** 首要的 shǒuyào de, 第一的 dìyī de **2** 最初的 zuìchū de, 基本的 jīběn de
primary care 基础保健 jīchǔ bǎojiàn
primary color 原色 yuánsè, 基色 jīsè

prime I ADJ 最重要的 zhòngyào de, 最好的 zuìhǎo de
prime number 质数 zhìshù
prime time 黄金时段 huángjīn shíduàn II N 盛年 shèngnián, 鼎盛年华 dǐng-shèng niánhuá III V (to be primed) 准备好 zhǔnbèi hǎo, 做好准备 zuòhǎo zhǔnbèi

primer N **1** 底漆 dǐqī **2** 入门指南（书）rùmén zhǐnán (shū)

primeval ADJ **1** 太初的 tàichū de, 太古的 tàigǔ de **2** 远古的 yuǎngǔ de, 原始的 yuánshǐ de

primitive ADJ 原始的 yuánshǐ de

primp V 梳妆打扮 shūzhuāngdǎbàn

primrose N **1** 报春花 bàochūnhuā [M. WD 朵 duǒ] **2** 淡黄色 dànhuángsè

prince N 王子 wángzǐ, 亲王 qīnwáng

princely ADJ **1** 王子的 wángzǐ de, 亲王的 qīnwáng de **2** 慷慨的 kāngkǎi de, 大度的 dàdù de
a princely sum 一笔巨款 yìbǐ jùkuǎn

princess N 公主 gōngzhǔ, 王妃 wángfēi

principal I ADJ 主要的 zhǔyào de II N **1** 校长 xiàozhǎng, 院长 yuànzhǎng **2** 本金 běnjīn, 资本 zīběn

principality N 公国 gōngguó

principally ADV 主要地 zhǔyào de

principle N **1** 原则 yuánzé **2** 原理 yuánlǐ

principled ADJ 有原则的 yǒu yuánzé de, 坚持原则的 jiānchí yuánzé de

print I V **1** 印 yìn, 印刷 yìnshuā
to print money 大量印发钞票 dàliàng yìnfā chāopiào
2 用印刷体书写 yòngyìn shuā tǐ shūxiě II N **1** 印刷字体 yìnshuā zìtǐ
the fine print 小号印刷体 xiǎohào yìnshuātǐ, 文件的细节 wénjiàn de xìjié
in print [书+] 买得到 [shū+] mǎidedào
out of print 绝版（书）juébǎn (shū), 买不到的书 mǎibudào de shū
2 印刷品 yìnshuāpǐn
printed matter （邮寄的）印刷品 (yóujì de) yìnshuāpǐn
3 (印出来的)照片 (yìnchū láide) zhàopiàn, 电影拷贝 diànyǐng kǎobèi
4 印记 yìnjì, 印痕 yìnhén

printer N **1** （计算机）打印机 (jìsuànjī) dǎyìnjī [M. WD 台 tái] **2** 印刷工人 yìnshuāgōngrén

printout N （计算机）打印出来的材料 (jìsuànjī) dǎyìn chūlái de cáiliào [M. WD 份 fèn]

prior ADJ 事先的 shìxiān de, 以前的 yǐqián de
prior to sth 在某事之前 zài mǒushì zhī qián

prioritize V 确定…先后顺序 quèdìng… xiānhòu shùnxù

priority N **1** 最重要的事 zuìzhòngyào de shì, 首先要做的事 shǒuxiān yào zuò de shì
to get one's priorities right 按照轻重缓急办事 ànzhào qīng zhòng huǎn jí bànshì
to give priority to 把…作为重点 bǎ… zuòwéi zhòngdiǎn, 优先办理 yōuxiān bànlǐ
2 优先（权）yōuxiān (quán)
to have priority over 享有优先权 xiǎngyǒu yōuxiānquán

prism N 棱镜 léngjìng

prison N 监狱 jiānyù [M. WD 座 zuò]

prisoner N 犯人 fànrén, 囚犯 qiúfàn
prisoner of conscience 政治犯 zhèng-zhìfàn, 良心犯 liángxīn fàn

pristine ADJ 崭新的 zhǎnxīn de, 一尘不染的 yì chén bù rǎn de

privacy N 隐私（权）yǐnsī (quán)

private I ADJ 1 私人的 sīrén de
private investigator 私家侦探 sījiā zhēntàn
private parts 生殖器 shēngzhíqì, 私处 sīchù
2 私立的 sīlì de, 私营的 sīyíng de
private enterprise 私营企业制 sīyíng qǐyè zhì
II N (in private) 私下（地）sīxia (de), 秘密地 mìmì de

privilege N 特权 tèquán, 特殊的荣幸 tèshū de róngxìng

privy I ADJ (privy to) 了解 [+内情] de liǎojiě [+nèiqíng] de II N 厕所 cèsuǒ

prize I N 奖 jiǎng, 奖赏 jiǎngshǎng, 奖品 jiǎngpǐn II V 十分珍视 shífēn zhēnshì, 高度重视 gāodù zhòngshì III ADJ 优等的 yōuděng de, 获奖的 huòjiǎng de

prizefight N 职业拳击赛 zhíyè quánjī sài

pro N 专业人员 zhuānyè rényuán, 职业运动员 zhíyè yùndòngyuán
to go pro 成为职业运动员 chéngwéi zhíyè yùndòngyuán

probability N 1 可能性 kěnéngxìng
in all probability 极有可能 jí yǒu kěnéng
2 概率 gàilǜ

probable ADJ 很可能的 hěn kěnéng de

probably ADV 很有可能（地）hěn yǒu kěnéng de

probation N 1（罪犯）缓刑 (zuìfàn) huǎnxíng 2（雇员）试用期 (gùyuán) shìyòngqī 3（雇员）留任察用期 (gùyuán) liúrèn chá yòng qī
probation officer 缓刑监督官 huǎnxíng jiāndū guān

probe I V 调查 diàochá II N 1（彻底）调查 (chèdǐ) diàochá 2 航天探测器 hángtiān tàncèqì

problem N 1 难题 nántí, 困难 kùnnan 2 问题 wèntí 3 题目 tímù
No problem. ① 没问题。Méi wèntí.
② 没什么 méishénme

problematic ADJ 有很多难题的 yǒu hěn

duō nántí de, 很难对付的 hěn nán duìfu de

procedure N 1 程序 chéngxù, 步骤 bùzhòu 2（特殊的）外科手术 (tèshū de) wàikē shǒushù

proceed V 1（继续）进行 (jìxù) jìnxíng, 进行下去 jìnxíng xiàqu 2 行进 xíngjìn, 前进 qiánjìn

proceedings N 1 [刑事+] 诉讼 [xíngshì+] sùsòng 2 会议记录 huìyì jìlù

proceeds N 收入 shōurù, 收益 shōuyì

process I N 1 过程 guòchéng 2 工艺流程 gōngyìliúchéng II V 1 加工 [+食品] jiāgōng [+shípǐn] 2 处理 [+数据] chǔlǐ [+shùjù]

procession N 1 游行队伍 yóuxíng duìwǔ, 车队 chēduì 2 一系列（事件）yíxìliè (shìjiàn)

processor N（计算机）信息处理器 (jìsuànjī) xìnxī chǔlǐqì

proclamation N 公告 gōnggào, 宣言 xuānyán

procrastinate V 耽搁 dāngě, 拖延 tuōyán

procreation N 生育（后代）shēngyù (hòudài)

procure V 获取 huòqǔ, 采购 cǎigòu

procurement N 获取 huòqǔ, 采购 cǎigòu

prod V 1 激励 jīlì, 促使 cùshǐ 2 戳 chuō, 捅 tǒng

prodigal I ADJ 挥霍浪费的 huīhuòlàngfèi de II N 挥霍浪费的人 huīhuòlàngfèi de rén

prodigy N 奇才 qícái, 神童 shéntóng

produce I V 1 生产 shēngchǎn 2 出产 chūchǎn 3 出示 [+文件] chūshì [+wénjiàn] 4 制作电影／电视节目 zhìzuò diànyǐng/diànshì jiémù II N 蔬菜水果 shūcài shuǐguǒ, 农产品 nóngchǎnpǐn

producer N 1 生产者 shēngchǎnzhě, 制造厂商 zhìzào chǎng shāng 2（电影／电视／广播）制片人 (diànyǐng/diànshì/guǎngbō) zhìpiànrén

product N 1 产品 chǎnpǐn, 制品 zhìpǐn 2 结果 jiéguǒ, 产物 chǎnwù 3（数学）乘积 (shùxué) chéngjī

production N 1 生产 shēngchǎn 2 电影作品 diànyǐng zuòpǐn, 戏剧作品 xìjù zuòpǐn

productive ADJ 1 多产的 duō chǎn de

2 富有成效的 fùyǒuchéngxiào de 3 生产性 [+设备] 的 shēngchǎnxìng [+shèbèi] de

profane ADJ 1 亵渎（神灵）的 xièdú (shénlíng) de 2 下流的 [+语言] xiàliú de [+yǔyán]

profanity N 亵渎的语言 xièdú de yǔyán, 下流话 xiàliúhuà

profess V 1 自称 zìchēng, 谎称 huǎngchēng 2 公开表明 gōngkāi biǎomíng

profession N 1 专业 zhuānyè, 职业 zhíyè 2 [所有的+] 专业人士 [suǒyǒu de+] zhuānyè rénshì 3 公开表白 gōngkāi biǎobái

professional I ADJ 专业的 zhuānyè de II N 专业人士 zhuānyè rénshì

professionalism N 专业精神 zhuānyè jīngshén, 精益求精的态度 jīng yì qiú jīng de tàidu

professor N 教授 jiàoshòu, 大学教师 dàxué jiàoshī

proffer V（正式）提出 [+道歉] (zhèngshì) tíchū [+dàoqiàn]

proficiency N 精通 jīngtōng, 熟练 shúliàn
proficiency in Chinese 中文水平 Zhōngwén shuǐpíng, 精通中文 jīngtōng Zhōngwén

proficient ADJ 精通的 jīngtōng de, 熟练的 shúliàn de
be proficient in a language 精通一门言语 jīngtōng yìmén yǔyán

profile N 1（人头部的）侧面 (réntóu bù de) cèmiàn 2（人物）简介 (rénwù) jiǎnjiè
to keep a high/low profile 保持高／低姿态 bǎochí gāo/dī zītài

profit I N 1 利润 lìrùn
profit margin 利润率 lìrùnlǜ
profit sharing 分享利润 fēnxiǎng lìrùn, 分红制 fēnhóngzhì
gross profit 毛利 máolì
net profit 净利润 jìng lìrùn, 纯利润 chún lìrùn
2 利益 lìyì, 好处 hǎochu II V 1 对…有益／利 duì…yǒuyì/lì 2 获利 huòlì

profitable ADJ 可获利的 kě huò lì de, 盈利的 yínglì de

profiteering N 牟取非法暴利（的行为）móuqǔ fēifǎ bàolì (de xíngwéi)

profound ADJ 1 深刻的 shēnkè de, 深远的 shēnyuǎn de 2 知识渊博的 zhīshi yuānbó de

profuse ADJ 大量的 dàliàng de, 极其丰富的 jíqí fēngfù de

progeny N 后代 hòudài 2 后续的事 hòuxù de shì

prognosis N 预后 yùhòu, 预测 yùcè

program N 1（电视／演出）节目 (diànshì/yǎnchū) jiémù 2（电脑）程序 (diànnǎo) chéngxù 3 课程 kèchéng 4 方案 fāng'àn, 计划 jìhuà

programmer N（计算机）程序编写员 (jìsuànjī) chéngxù biānxiěyuán

progress I N 1 进步 jìnbù 2 进展 jìnzhǎn II V 1 [工作+] 进展 [gōngzuò+] jìnzhǎn 2 [人+] 缓慢行进 [rén+] huǎnmàn xíngjìn

progression N 1 进展 jìnzhǎn 2 移动 yídòng, 行进 xíngjìn

progressive I ADJ 进步的 jìnbù de II N 进步人士 jìnbùrénshì [M. WD 位 wèi]

prohibit V 禁止 jìnzhǐ

prohibitive ADJ 1 禁止（性）的 jìnzhǐ (xìng) de 2 高得负担不起的 [+价格] gāo de fùdān bùqǐ de [+jiàgé]

project I N 1 项目 xiàngmù 2 课题 kètí, 作业 zuòyè II V 1 预计 yùjì, 推测 tuīcè 2 放映 [电影] fàngyìng (diànyǐng) 3 作投影图 zuò tóuyǐngtú

projection N 1 预测 yùcè, 推断 tuīduàn 2 凹出物 āo chū wù 3 投影 tóuyǐng, 投射 tóushè

projector N 幻灯机 huàndēngjī, 电影放映机 diànyǐng fàngyìngjī

proletariat N 无产阶级 wúchǎnjiējí

proliferate V 扩散 kuòsàn

proliferation N 扩散 kuòsàn
a prohibition on the proliferation of nuclear weapons 禁止核武器扩散 jìnzhǐ héwǔqì kuòsàn

prolific ADJ 多产的 [+作家] duō chǎn de [+zuòjiā]

prologue N（戏剧）序幕 (xìjù) xùmù,（叙事诗）序诗 (xùshìshī) xù shī,（书）序言 (shū) xùyán

prolong V 延长 yáncháng, 拉长 lācháng

prolonged ADJ 持续很久的 chíxù hěn jiǔ de, 长时间的 chángshíjiān de

prom N（高中生的）学年舞会（gāo-zhōngsheng de）xuénián wǔhuì, 嘉年华会 jiānián huáhuì

senior prom（中学生）毕业舞会（zhōngxuésheng）bìyè wǔhuì

promenade N 海滨散步道 hǎibīn sànbù dào

prominence N 1 突出 tūchū, 显著 xiǎnzhe 2 杰出 jiéchū

to gain prominence 开始闻名 kāishǐ wénmíng

prominent ADJ 1 显著的 xiǎnzhe de 2 杰出的 jiéchū de

promiscuous ADJ 淫乱的 yínluàn de, 滥交的 lànjiāo de

promise V, N 承诺 chéngnuò, 答应 dāying

promising ADJ 大有前途的 dàyǒu qiántú de, 大有希望的 dàyǒu xīwàng de

promo N 广告短片 guǎnggào duǎnpiàn

promontory N 海角 hǎijiǎo

promote V 1 促进 cùjìn 2 促销 cùxiāo 3 提升 tíshēng, 晋升 jìnshēng

promoter N [绿色生活方式+] 倡导者 [lǜsè shēnghuó fāngshì+] chàngdǎozhě 2 [音乐会+] 主办者 [yīnyuèhuì+] zhǔbànzhě

promotion N 1 提升 tíshēng, 晋升 jìnshēng 2 促进 cùjìn 3 促销 cùxiāo, 推销 tuīxiāo

prompt¹ ADJ 及时的 jíshí de, 迅速的 xùnsù de

prompt² I V 促使 cùshǐ, 引起 yǐnqǐ II N 1 （计算机）提示（jìsuànjī）tíshì 2 （给演员的）提词（gěi yǎnyuán de）tící

prone ADJ 倾向于…的 qīngxiàng yú...de, 容易…的 róngyì...de

prone to accidents 容易发生事故的 róngyì fāshēng shìgù de

pronoun N（语法）代词（yǔfǎ）dàicí

pronounce V 1 发音 fāyīn 2 宣告 xuāngào

pronouncement N 公告 gōnggào, 声明 shēngmíng

pronto ADV 马上 mǎshàng, 立刻 lìkè

pronunciation N 发音 fāyīn

proof¹ N 证明 zhèngmíng, 证据 zhèngjù

proof² ADJ 能抵挡…的 néng dǐdǎng...de, 防…的 fáng...de

bulletproof 防弹的 fángdàn de

earthquake-proof 抗地震的 kàng dìzhèn de

proofread V 校对 jiàoduì

prop I V 支撑 zhīchēng, 支持 zhīchí II N 1 支撑物 zhīchēng wù 2 小道具 xiǎo dàojù

propaganda N 宣传 xuānchuán

propagate V 1 繁殖 [+植物] fánzhí [+zhíwù] 2 传播 [+信仰] chuánbō [+xìnyǎng]

propel V 推进 tuījìn, 推动 tuīdòng

propeller N 螺旋桨 luóxuánjiǎng, 推进器 tuījìnqì

propensity N 习性 xíxìng, 倾向（性）qīngxiàng（xìng）

proper ADJ 1 适当的 shìdàng de, 恰当的 qiàdàng de 2 符合礼仪的 fúhé lǐyí de, 正派的 zhèngpài de

properly ADV 适当地 shìdàng de

property N 1 财产 cáichǎn [M. WD 笔 bǐ] 2 房地产 fángdìchǎn, 产业 chǎnyè

intellectual property 知识产权 zhīshi chǎnquán

stolen property 赃物 zāngwù

3 性质 xìngzhì, 特性 tèxìng

prophecy N（宗教的）预言（zōngjiào de）yùyán

prophet N 1 （宗教的）先知（zōngjiào de）xiānzhī 2 （新观念的）倡导者（xīn guānniàn de）chàngdǎozhě

proponent N 支持者 zhīchízhě, 提倡者 tíchàngzhě

proportion N 1 比例 bǐlì 2 部分 bùfen

in proportion to sth 按照与某物的比例 ànzhào yǔ mǒu wù de bǐlì

proportional ADJ 成比例的 chéngbǐlì de

proposal N 1 提议 tíyì 2 求婚 qiúhūn

propose V 1 提议 tíyì 2 求婚 qiúhūn 3 打算 dǎsuan

proposition I N 1 观点 guāndiǎn, 见解 jiànjiě 2 [商业+] 提议 [shāngyè+] tíyì, 建议 jiànyì II V 提出发生性关系 tíchū fāshēng xìng guānxi

proprietary ADJ 1 专卖的 [+产品]

zhuānmài de [+chǎnpǐn] **2** 属于自己的 [+感觉] shǔyú zìjǐ de [+gǎnjué]

proprietary information （公司）内部 信息 (gōngsī) nèibù xìnxī

proprietor N 拥有者 yōngyǒuzhě, 老板 lǎobǎn

propriety N 得体的行为 détǐ de xíngwéi, 规范（的言行）guīfàn (de yánxíng)

propulsion N 推进力 tuījìnlì, 推进器 tuījìnqì

pro rata ADJ 按比例计算的 [+报酬] àn bǐlì jìsuàn de [+bàochou]

prose N 散文 sǎnwén [M. WD 篇 piān] prose poem 散文诗 sǎnwénshī

prosecute V 起诉 qǐsù, 检控 jiǎnkòng

prosecution N **1** 起诉 qǐsù, 检控 jiǎnkòng **2** 检控方 jiǎnkòng fāng, 原告（律师）yuángào (lǜshī)

proselytize V 说服 shuōfú [+人] 入教 shuōfú [+rén] rùjiào

prospect I N **1** 前景 qiánjǐng in prospect 可能即将发生 kěnéng jíjiāng fāshēng **2** 会成功的人 huì chénggōng de rén II V 勘探 kāntàn, 勘察 kānchá

prospective ADJ 可能的 kěnéng de, 预期的 yùqī de

prospectus N **1** [简况+] 小册子 [jiǎnkuàng+] xiǎocèzi **2** [投资+] 计划书 [tóuzī+] jìhuà shū

prosper V 兴旺 xīngwàng, 成功 chénggōng

prosperity N 兴旺 xīngwàng, 繁荣 fánróng

prosthesis N 假肢 jiǎzhī, 假牙 jiǎyá

prostitute I N 妓女 jìnǚ II V 出卖 [+自己的才能] chūmài [+zìjǐ de cáinéng], 滥用 lànyòng to prostitute oneself 卖淫 màiyín, 出卖自己 chūmài zìjǐ

prostrate I ADJ 俯卧的 fǔwò de, 卧倒在地的 wòdǎo zài dì de, [被悲伤+] 压垮的 [bèi bēishāng+] yā kuǎ de, 一蹶不振的 yì jué bú zhèn de II V (to prostrate oneself) 拜倒 bàidǎo be prostrate 一蹶不振 yì jué bú zhèn, 压垮的 yā kuǎ de

protagonist N **1** [电影+] 主要人物

[电影+] zhǔyào rénwù, 主角 zhǔjué **2** 提倡者 tíchàngzhě, 支持者 zhīchízhě

protect V 保护 bǎohù, 保卫 bǎowèi

protection N 保护 bǎohù, 保卫 bǎowèi

protective ADJ 保护（性）的 bǎohù (xìng) de protective custody 保护性拘留 bǎohùxìng jūliú

protégé N 被保护人 bèi bǎohùrén, 门生 ménshēng

protein N 蛋白质 dànbáizhì

protest V, N 抗议 kàngyì

Protestant I ADJ （基督教）新教的 (Jīdūjiào) Xīnjiào de II N （基督教）新教徒 (Jīdūjiào) Xīnjiàotú

protocol N **1** 礼仪 lǐyí **2** 协议 xiéyì, 协定 xiédìng

proton N 质子 zhìzǐ

prototype N 原型 yuánxíng, 典范 diǎnfàn

protractor N 量角器 liángjiǎoqì

protruding ADJ 凸出的 tūchū de

proud ADJ 骄傲的 jiāo'ào de, 自傲的 zì'ào de

prove V (PT **proved**; PP **proved**, **proven**) 证明 zhèngmíng

proven ADJ 被证实的 bèi zhèngshí de

proverb N 谚语 yànyǔ

proverbial ADJ 大名鼎鼎的 dàmíng dǐngdǐng de the proverbial sth 常言中的 cháng yánzhōng de

provide V 提供 tígōng, 供给 gòngjǐ to provide for 养活 yǎnghuo

provided (that) CONJ 如果 rúguǒ, 假设 jiǎshè

providence N 天意 tiānyì, 天命 tiānmìng

provider N 供应者 gòngyīngzhě

providing CONJ 如果 rúguǒ, 假设 jiǎshè

province N **1** [中国的+] 省 [Zhōngguó de+] shěng Sichuan Province of China 中国四川省 Zhōngguó Sìchuānshěng **2** [知识的+] 领域 [zhīshi de+] lǐngyù, 范围 fànwéi

provincial I ADJ **1** 省的 shěng de, 行政的 xíngzhèng de the provincial government of Sichuan

四川省政府 Sìchuānshěng zhèngfǔ
2 狭隘的 xiá'ài de, 守旧的 shǒujiù de
II N 外省人 wàishěngrén, 来自小地方的
人 láizì xiǎo dìfang de rén
provision N 1 提供 tígōng, 供应 gòngyìng
2 条款 tiáokuǎn, 规定 guīdìng
provisions N 粮食 liángshi, 食物 shíwù
proviso N 附加条件 fùjiā tiáojiàn, 前提
qiántí
provocative ADJ 1 挑衅（性）的 tiǎoxìn
(xìng) de 2 十分性感的 shífēn xìnggǎn
de, 挑逗性的 tiǎodòu xìng de
provoke V 激怒 jīnù, 激起 jīqǐ
provost N（大学）教务长 (dàxué)
jiàowùzhǎng
prow N 船头 chuántóu
prowess N 高超的技艺 gāochāo de jìyì
prowl I V 来回行走 láihuí xíngzǒu, 巡
逻 xúnluó **II** N (on the prowl) 四处寻觅
sìchù xúnmì, 流窜 liúcuàn
proximity N 邻近 línjìn, 靠近 kàojìn
proxy N 代理人 dàilǐrén
    proxy vote 委托投票 wěituō tóupiào
    by proxy 委托他人代理 wěituō tārén dàilǐ
prudent ADJ 慎重的 shènzhòng de, 理性
的 lǐxìng de
prudish ADJ（在性方面）一本正经的
(zài xìng fāngmiàn) yìběnzhèngjīng
(de)
prune¹ V (to prune back) 1 修剪 [+树枝]
xiūjiǎn [+shùzhī] 2 剪除 jiǎnchú, 除
去 chúqù
prune² N 西梅干 xī méi gān
prurient ADJ 好色的 hàosè de, 淫荡的
yíndàng de
pry V 1 撬开 qiàokāi 2 打听 [+别人的隐私]
dǎtīng [+biéren de yǐnsī]
    prying eyes 窥视者 kuīshìzhě
psalm N 圣歌 shènggē [M. WD 首 shǒu],
赞美诗 zànměishī [M. WD 首 shǒu]
pseudonym N 笔名 bǐmíng
psyche N 心灵 xīnlíng, 灵魂 línghún
psychedelic ADJ 引起迷幻的 [+药物] yǐn
qǐ míhuàn de [+yàowù]
psychiatry N 精神病学 jīngshénbìngxué
psychic I ADJ 通灵的 tōnglíng de, 超自然
的 chāo zìrán de

psychic prediction 通灵预言 tōnglíng
yùyán
II N 通灵的人 tōnglíng de rén, 有特异功
能的人 yǒu tèyì gōngnéng de rén
psycho N 精神病人 jīngshénbìngrén, 变态
人格者 biàntài réngé zhě
psychoanalysis N 精神分析（治疗法）
jīngshén fēnxī (zhìliáofǎ)
psychoanalyze V 对…进行精神分析
duì…jìnxíng jīngshén fēnxī, 用精神分析
法治疗 yòng jīngshén fēnxīfǎ zhìliáo
psychological ADJ 心理学的 xīnlíxué de,
心理上的 xīnlǐ shàng de
psychology N 心理（学）xīnlǐ (xué)
psychopath N 精神病患者 jīngshénbìng
huànzhě, 严重精神变态者 yánzhòng
jīngshén biàntàizhě
psychosis N 精神病 jīngshénbìng
psychotic I ADJ 精神病的 jīngshénbìng de
II N 精神病患者 jīngshénbìng huànzhě
pub N 酒吧 jiǔbā
puberty N 青春期 qīngchūnqī
pubescent ADJ 处于青春期的 chǔyú
qīngchūnqī de
pubic ADJ 阴部的 yīnbù de
    pubic hair 阴毛 yīnmáo
public I N 公众 gōngzhòng, 大众 dàzhòng
    in public 在公众场合 zài gōngzhòng
chǎnghé
II ADJ 1 公共的 gōnggòng de, 公用的
gōngyòng de
    public access 公众进入权 gōngzhòng
jìnrù quán
    public address (PA) system 扩音系统
kuòyīn xìtǒng
    public assistance 政府补助 zhèngfǔ
bǔzhù
    public housing 政府住房 zhèngfǔ
zhùfáng
    public relations 公共关系 gōnggòng
guānxì, 公关 gōngguān
    public school 公立学校 gōnglì xuéxiào,
（英国）私立学校 (Yīngguó) sīlì xuéxiào
2 公开的 gōngkāi de
    to go public 公开 gōngkāi, 公布于众
gōngbù yú zhòng

publication N 1 出版 chūbǎn 2 出版物 chūbǎn wù, 书刊报章 shūkān bàozhāng

publicity N 公共关注 gōnggòng guānzhù, 宣传 xuānchuán
good/bad publicity 有利的 / 不利的宣传 yǒulì de/búlì de xuānchuán
publicity campaign 宣传活动 xuānchuán huódòng

publicize V 传播 chuánbō, 公开 gōngkāi

publicly ADV 公开 gōngkāi

publish V 出版 chūbǎn

publisher N 出版人 chūbǎnrén, 出版商 chūbǎnshāng, 出版公司 chūbǎn gōngsī

publishing N 出版事业 chūbǎn shìyè, 出版界 chūbǎnjiè

puck N 冰球 bīngqiú

pucker V 撅起嘴 juē qǐ zuǐ

pudding N 布丁 bùdīng, 甜食 tiánshí

puddle N 水坑 shuǐkēng, 小水潭 xiǎoshuǐ tán

pudgy ADJ 肥胖的 féipàng de

puerile ADJ 傻乎乎的 shǎhūhū de, 孩子气的 háiziqì de

puff I V 1 (吸烟时) 喷烟 (xīyān shí) pēn yān 2 [烟囱+] 冒烟 [yāncōng+] màoyān 3 喘粗气 chuǎn cū qì II N 吸 (烟) xī (yān)

puffy ADJ [眼睛+] 肿大的 [yǎnjing+] zhǒngdà de

puke I V 呕吐 ǒutù II N 呕吐物 ǒutù wù

pull I V 1 拉 lā 2 拖 tuō, 牵 qiān 3 拔 bá
to pull one's leg 戏弄 xìnòng, 对…说假话 duì…shuō jiǎhuà
to pull one's weight 尽力, 做好本份工作 jìnlì, zuòhǎo běnfèn gōngzuò
to pull over [汽车+] 停在路边 [qìchē+] tíng zài lùbiān
II N 1 拉 lā, 拖 tuō, 牵 qiān 2 拉绳 lā shéng 3 吸引力 xīyǐnlì

pulley N 滑轮 huálún

pullout N 1 撤离 chèlí 2 插页 chāyè

pullover N 套头毛衣 tàotóu máoyī

pulmonary ADJ 肺的 fèi de

pulp I N 1 果肉 guǒròu 2 纸浆 zhǐjiāng II V 把…捣成浆 bǎ…dǎo chéng jiāng III ADJ 低俗的 dīsú de
pulp fiction 低俗小说 dīsú xiǎoshuō

pulpit N (教堂中的) 讲坛 (jiàotáng zhòng de) jiǎngtán, 布道坛 bùdàotán

pulsate V 有规律的振动 yǒuguīlǜ de zhèndòng

pulse I N 1 脉搏 màibó 2 [光波+] 脉冲 [guāngbō+] màichōng 3 [社会+] 动向 [shèhuì+] dòngxiàng, 走向 zǒuxiàng 4 (音乐) 拍子 (yīnyuè) pāizi, 节奏 jiézòu II V 1 (心脏+) 搏动 [xīnzàng+] bódòng 2 [机器+] 振动 [jīqì+] zhèndòng

pulverize V 把…磨成粉末 bǎ…mó chéng fěnmò

puma N 美洲狮 měizhōushī [M. WD 只 zhī/头 tóu]

pumice N 浮石 fúshí [M. WD 块 kuài]

pummel V [拳头+] 连续捶打 [quántou+] liánxù chuídǎ

pump I N 1 抽水机 chōushuǐ jī, 泵 bèng 2 打气筒 dǎqì tǒng II V 1 抽水 chōushuǐ 2 打气 dǎqì

pumpkin N 南瓜 nánguā [M. WD 只 zhī]

pun N 双关语 shuāngguānyǔ, 一语双关 yìyǔ shuāngguān

punch[1] I V 1 用拳猛击 yòng quán měngjī 2 按 [+键] àn [+jiàn] 3 打洞 dǎdòng
to punch in/out (上班 / 下班) 打卡 (shàngbān/xiàbān) dǎkǎ
II N 1 (用拳) 猛击 (yòng quán) měngjī 2 穿孔机 chuānkǒngjī

punch[2] N 潘趣酒 pānqùjiǔ, 混合饮料 hùnhé yǐnliào

punching bag N (拳击练习用的) 吊袋 (quánjī liànxí yòng de) diào dài

punch line N 抛出笑料的妙语 pāochū xiàoliào de miàoyǔ

punctuate V 1 加标点符号 jiā biāodiǎn fúhào 2 (be punctuated by) 不时被打断 bùshí bèi dǎdan

punctuation N 标点符号 (用法) biāodiǎn fúhào (yòngfǎ)
punctuation mark 标点符号 biāodiǎn fúhào

puncture I N (轮胎的) 穿孔 (lúntāi de) chuānkǒng II V 扎穿 [+轮胎] zhā chuān [+lúntāi]

pundit N 权威 quánwēi, 专家 zhuānjiā

pungent ADJ 1 刺鼻的 [+气味] cìbí de

[+qìwèi] **2** 辛辣的 [+文章] xīnlà de [+wénzhāng]

punish V 罚 fá, 惩罚 chéngfá

punishable ADJ 会受到惩罚的 huì shòudào chéngfá de, 应受到惩罚的 yìng shòudào chéngfá de

punishable by/with life imprisonment 会被判终身监禁 huì shòudào zhōngshēn jiānjìn

punishment N 惩罚 chéngfá, 处罚 chǔfá

punitive ADJ 惩罚（性）的 chéngfá (xìng) de

punk N 朋克 péng kè, 小流氓 xiǎo liúmáng

punk rock 朋克摇滚乐 péng kè yáogǔnyuè

punt I N **1** 悬空长球 xuánkōng cháng qiú **2** 方头平底船 fāngtóu píngdǐchuán [M. WD 艘 sōu] II V **1** 踢悬空长球 tī xuánkōng cháng qiú **2** 乘方头平底船 chéng fāngtóu píngdǐchuán

puny ADJ **1** 瘦小的 [+孩子] shòuxiǎo de [+háizi] **2** 微薄的 [+利润] wēibó de [+lìrùn]

pup N 小狗 xiǎogǒu [M. WD 只 zhī]

pupil[1] N 小学生 xiǎo xuésheng

pupil[2] N 瞳孔 tóngkǒng

puppet N **1** 木偶 mù'ǒu **2** 傀儡 kuǐlěi

puppeteer N 玩木偶的人 wán mù'ǒu de rén, 木偶艺人 mù'ǒu yìrén

puppy N 小狗 xiǎogǒu [M. WD 只 zhī]

puppy love 少男少女的恋情 shàonán shàonǚ de liànqíng, 早恋 zǎoliàn

purchase I V 购买 gòumǎi II N 购买的物品 gòumǎi dào de wùpǐn

pure ADJ 纯的 chún de, 纯净的 chúnjìng de

puree N [番茄+] 酱 [fānqié+] jiàng, 糊糊 hú hú

purgatory N 炼狱 liànyù, 遭受极大苦难的地方 zāoshòu jídà kǔnàn de dìfang

purge I V 清洗 [+政敌] qīngxǐ [+zhèngdí], 清除 qīngchú II N 清洗（行动）qīngxǐ (xíngdòng)

purification N 净化 jìnghuà

purify V 使…纯净 shǐ…chúnjìng, 净化 jìnghuà

purity N 纯洁（度）chúnjié (dù), 纯度 chúndù

purple I N 紫色 zǐsè II ADJ 紫色的 zǐsè de

purport I V 据说 jùshuō, 声称 shēngchēng II N 大意 dàyì

purpose N 目的 mùdì

on purpose 故意（地）gùyì (de)

to no purpose 毫无成果 háowú chéngguǒ

accidentally on purpose 明明是故意却装作无意 míngmíng shì gùyì què zhuāngzuò wúyì

purposeful ADJ **1** 有明确目的的 yǒu míngquè mùdì de **2** 坚定的 jiāndìng de, 果断的 guǒduàn de

purposely ADV 故意（地）gùyì (de)

purr I V **1** [猫+] 发出呼噜声 [māo+] fāchū hūlushēng **2** [人+] 轻柔地说 [rén+] qīngróu de shuō II N 轻柔的说话声 qīngróu de shuōhuàshēng

purse I N **1**（女用）钱包 (nǚ yòng) qiánbāo, 手提包 shǒutíbāo **2** 资金 zījīn

public purse 政府资金 zhèngfǔ zījīn

to control the purse string 控制财权 kòngzhì cáiquán, 掌管钱财 zhǎngguǎn qiáncái

II V (to purse one's lips) 撅起嘴巴 juē qǐ zuǐba

purser N（客轮的）事务长 (kèlún de) shìwùzhǎng

pursue V **1** 追求 [+财富] zhuīqiú [+cáifù] **2** 追赶 [+小偷] zhuīgǎn [+xiǎotōu] **3** 从事 cóngshì, 继续 jìxù

purvey V 供应 [+商品] gōngyìng [+shāngpǐn], 提供 [+信息] tígōng [+xìnxī]

pus N 脓 nóng

push I V **1** 推 tuī **2** 按 àn **3** 推动 tuīdòng, 逼迫 bīpò **4** 贩卖 fànmài

to push around 摆布 bǎibù

to push on 继续前进 jìxù qiánjìn

to push up 提高价格 tígāo jiàgé

II N **1** 推 tuī **2** 试图 shìtú

pusher N 毒品贩子 dúpǐn fànzi

pushover N 很容易被说服的人 hěn róngyì bèi shuōfú de rén, 容易被影响的人 róngyì bèi yǐngxiǎng de rén

push-up N 俯卧撑 fǔwòchēng

pushy ADJ 咄咄逼人的 duōduō bīrén de

pussycat N 猫咪 māomī [M. WD 只 zhī]

2 温和的好人 wēnhé de hǎorén

put V (PT & PPT **put**) **1** 放 fàng, 放置 fàngzhì **2** 写, 写下 xiěxia **3** 表达 biǎodá **4** 使 shǐ

to put aside 储蓄 chǔxù

to put away 放回去 fàng huíqu

to put down 羞辱 xiūrǔ

to put on ① 穿上 [+衣服／鞋子] chuānshang [+yīfu/xiézi] ② 增加 [+体重] zēngjiā [+tǐzhòng] ③ 放 [+音乐] fàng [+yīnyuè]

(to feel) put out 感到有点恼火 gǎndào yǒudiǎn nǎohuǒ

putrefy V 腐烂 fǔlàn

putrid ADJ 腐臭的 fǔchòu de

putt V 轻轻地打 [+高尔夫球] qīngqīngde dǎ [+gāo'ěrfūqiú], 推 [+高尔夫球] tuī [+gāo'ěrfūqiú]

putty N 油灰 yóuhuī

put upon ADJ (to feel put upon) 感到被人占了便宜 gǎndào bèi rénzhànle piányi

puzzle I N **1** 智力游戏 zhìlì yóuxì

crossword puzzle 纵横填字游戏 zònghéng tiánzìyóuxì

2 不可理解的事 bùkě lǐjiě de shì II V 使...困惑 shǐ...kùnhuò, 把...弄糊涂 bǎ...nònghú tú **2** 苦思冥想 kǔsī míngxiǎng

pygmy N 非常矮小的人 fēicháng ǎixiǎo de rén, 侏儒 zhūrú

pylon N **1** 高压电线架 gāoyādiàn xiàn jià **2** 圆锥形路障 yuánzhuī xíng lùzhàng

pyramid N 金字塔 jīnzìtǎ, 金字塔形物 jīnzìtǎxíng wù

pyre N 火葬柴堆 huǒzàng chái duī

python N（大）蟒蛇（dà）mǎngshé

Q

quack[1] I V [鸭子+] 嘎嘎叫 [yāzi+] gāgā jiào II N [鸭子+] 嘎嘎叫声 [yāzi+] gāgā jiàoshēng

quack[2] N 冒牌医生 màopáiyīshēng, 庸医 yōngyī

quadrangle N 四边形 sìbiānxíng, 四角形 sìjiǎoxíng

quadrant N 四分之一圆 sì fēn zhī yī yuán

quadrilateral N 四边形 sìbiānxíng

quadriplegic N 四肢瘫痪者 sìzhī tānhuàn zhě II ADJ 四肢瘫痪的 sìzhī tānhuàn de

quadruped N 四足动物 sìzú dòngwù

quadruple I V 增加到四倍 zēngjiā dào sìbèi, 增加三倍 zēngjiā sānbèi, 翻两番 fān liǎng fān II ADJ 四倍的 sìbèi de

quadruplet N 四胞胎之一 sìbāotāi zhī yī

quagmire N **1** 泥潭 nítán **2**（难以脱身的）困境 (nán yǐ tuōshēn de) kùnjìng

quail[1] N 鹌鹑 ānchún [M. WD 只 zhī]

quail[2] V 发抖 fādǒu, 害怕 hàipà

quaint ADJ 古色古香的 gǔsè gǔxiāng de, 奇特的 qítè de

quake I V **1** [人+] 颤抖 [rén+] chàndǒu, 哆嗦 duōsuo **2** [大地+] 震动 [dàdì+] zhèndòng II N 地震 dìzhèn

qualification N 资格 zīgé, 资格证明 zīgé zhèngmíng

qualify V 获得资格 huòdé zīgé

qualitative ADJ 质量（上）的 zhìliàng (shàng) de, 性质的 xìngzhì de

qualitiative analysis 定性分析 dìngxìng fēnxī

quality I N **1** 品质 pǐnzhì **2** 质量 zhìliàng II ADJ 优质的 yōuzhì de, 高质量的 gāo zhìliàng de

quality control 质量管理 zhìliàng guǎnlǐ

quality time 宝贵时光 bǎoguì shíguāng

qualm N 疑虑 yílǜ, 不安 bù'ān

quandary N（不知所措的）困境 (bù zhī suǒ cuò de) kùnjìng

quantify V 用数字测定 yòng shùzì cèdìng, 量化 liànghuà

quantitative ADJ 数量（上）的 shùliàng (shàng) de

quantitative analysis 定量分析 dìngliàng fēnxī

quantity N 数量 shùliàng

in quantity 大量 dàliàng, 大批 dàpī

quantum N 量子 liàngzǐ

quantum leap 突飞猛进 tūfēi měngjìn, 飞跃 fēiyuè

quarantine I N 隔离检疫（期）gélí jiǎnyì (qī) II V 对...隔离检疫 duì...gélí jiǎnyì

quark N 夸克 kuākè

quarrel N, V 争吵 zhēngchǎo, 吵架 chǎojià

quarrelsome ADJ 爱争吵的 ài zhēngchǎo de

quarry I N 1 采石场 cǎishíchǎng 2 猎场 lièchǎng II v 采石 cǎishí

quart N 夸脱 kuātuō (= 0.9463 liter)

quarter I N 1 四分之一 sì fēn zhī yī 2 一刻钟 yí kè zhōng 3 季度 jìdù 4（大学的）学季 (dàxué de) xué jì 5 25分的硬币 èrshíwǔ fēn de yìngbì II ADJ 四分之一的 sì fēn zhī yī de

quarterfinal N 四分之一决赛 sì fēn zhī yī juésài

quarterly I ADJ, ADV 一年四次的 yìnián sìcì de, 季度的 jìdù de II N 季刊（杂志）jìkān (zázhì)

quarters N 居住的地方 jūzhù de dìfang, 住处 zhùchù
servants' quarters 佣人睡房 yōngrén shuìfáng

quartet N 四重唱（小组）sìchóngchàng (xiǎozǔ), 四重奏（乐队）sìchóngzòu (yuèduì)
string quartet 弦乐四重奏乐队 xiányuè sìchóngzòu yuèduì

quartz N 石英 shíyīng

quash v 1 平息 [+骚乱] píngxī [+sāoluàn], 镇压 zhènyā 2 撤销 [+上诉] chèxiāo [+shàngsù], 废除 fèichú

quaver I v 1 颤抖 chàndǒu 2 用颤抖的声音说 yòng chàndǒu de shēngyīn shuō II N 颤抖 chàndǒu, 颤音 chànyīn

quay N 码头 mǎtou

queasy ADJ（感到）恶心的 (gǎndào) èxīn de, 想呕吐 xiǎng ǒutù

queen N 女王 nǚwáng, 王后 wánghòu
queen bee 蜂后 fēng hòu

queer I ADJ 1 怪怪的 guài guài de, 奇怪的 qíguài de 2 同性恋的 tóngxìngliàn de, 双性恋的 shuāngxìngliàn de, 变性恋的 biànxìng liàn de II N 同性恋者 tóngxìngliànzhě

quell v 镇压 zhènyā, 平息 píngxī

quench v (to quench one's thirst) 解渴 jiěkě, (to quench a fire) 灭火 mièhuǒ

querulous ADJ 爱发牢骚的 ài fāláoshào de, 老是抱怨的 lǎoshì bàoyuàn de

query I N 疑问 yíwèn, 问题 wèntí II v 1 提出疑问 tíchū yíwèn 2 询问 xúnwèn

quest N, V 追求 zhuīqiú, 探求 tànqiú

question I N 1 问题 wèntí
question mark 问号 wènhào (?)
2 考题 kǎotí
without question 肯定无疑 kěndìng wúyí
out of the question 绝对不可能 juéduì bù kěnéng
(It's a) good question! 问得好！我也不知道。Wènde hǎo! Wǒ yě bù zhīdào.
II v 1 [警察+] 审问 [jǐngchá+] shěnwèn 2 怀疑 huáiyí, 质疑 zhìyí

questionable ADJ 1 有问题的 [+结论] yǒu wèntí de [+jiélùn], 不能确定的 bùnéng quèdìng de 2 不诚实的 [+交易] bù chéngshí de [+jiāoyì]

questionnaire N 问卷 wènjuàn, 调查表 diàochábiǎo [M. WD 份 fèn]

queue I N 1（计算机）队列 (jìsuànjī) duìliè
print queue 打印队列 dǎyìn duìliè
2 排队 páiduì II v 排队 páiduì

quibble I v（为小事）争吵 (wéi xiǎoshì) zhēngchǎo II N 有一点不满意 yǒu yìdiǎn bù mǎnyì

quick I ADJ 1 快的 kuài de, 迅速的 xùnsù de 2 聪明的 cōngming de, 灵活的 línghuó de
quick study 学得很快的聪明人 xué dehěn kuài de cōngmíngrén
3 性急的 jíxìng de II ADV 快快（地）kuài kuài (de), 迅速（地）xùnsù (de)

quicken v（使…）加快 (shǐ...) jiā kuài

quickly ADV 快 kuài, 迅速 xùnsù

quicksand N 流沙 liúshā

quick-tempered ADJ 脾气急躁的 píqì jízào, 性急的 xìngjí de

quick-witted ADJ 敏捷的 mínjié de, 对答如流的 duìdá rú liú de

quid pro quo N 交换（物）jiāohuàn (wù)

quiet I ADJ 1 安静的 ānjìng de 2 清淡的 qīngdàn de II N 平静 píngjìng

quill N 羽毛管 yǔmáo guǎn
quill pen 羽毛笔 yǔmáo bǐ

quilt N 被子 bèizi [M. WD 条 tiáo]

patchwork quilt 百衲被 bǎinà bèi

quinine N 奎宁 kuíníng, 金鸡纳霜 jīnjīnàshuāng

quintessential ADJ 典型的 diǎnxíng de, 典范的 diǎnfàn de

quintet N 五重唱（小组）wǔchóngchàng (xiǎozǔ), 五重奏（乐队）wǔchóngzòu (yuèduì)

quintuplet N 五胞胎之一 wǔbāotāi zhī yī

quip I v 说俏皮话 shuō qiàopihuà II N 俏皮话 qiàopihuà

quirk N 1 古怪的行为 gǔguài de xíngwéi, 怪癖 guàipǐ 2 奇怪的巧事 qíguài de qiǎoshì, 奇合 qíhé

quit v (PT & PP quit) 1 辞去 [+工作] cíqù [+gōngzuò], 离开 líkāi 2 停止 [+抽烟] tíngzhǐ [+chōuyān], 不再 búzài

quite ADV 相当 xiāngdāng
not quite 不完全 bù wánquán, 不十分 bù shífēn

quits ADJ 停止（做某事）tíngzhǐ (zuò mǒu shì), 结束 jiéshù

quitter N 打退堂鼓的人 dǎ tuìtánggǔ de rén, 半途而废的人 bàntú ér fèi de rén

quiver N 微微发抖 wēiwēi fādǒu, 颤抖 chàndǒu

quiz I N 小测验 xiǎo cèyàn II v 1 查问 cháwèn 2 给 [+学生] 做小测验 gěi [+xuéshēng] zuò xiǎocèyàn

quorum N（会议的）法定人数 (huìyì de) fǎdìng rénshù

quota N 配额 pèi'é, 定量 dìngliàng

quotable ADJ 值得引用的 zhíde yǐnyòng de

quotation N 1 引言 yǐnyán 2 报价 bàojià
quotation marks 引号 yǐnhào（" "）

quote I v 1 引用…的话 yǐnyòng…de huà 2 报价 bàojià II N 引言 yǐnyán

quotient N（数学）商（数）(shùxué) shāng (shù)
intelligence quotient (IQ) 智商 zhìshāng

Quran N See Koran

qwerty ADJ (a qwerty keyboard) 标准键盘 biāozhǔn jiànpán

R

rabbi N（犹太教的）教士 (Yóutàijiào de) jiàoshì, 拉比 lābǐ

rabbit N 兔（子）tù (zi) [M. WD 只 zhī]

rabble N（一群）暴民 (yìqún) bàomín, （一帮）痞子 (yìbāng) pǐzi

rabies N 狂犬病 kuángquǎn bìng

raccoon N 浣熊 huànxióng [M. WD 头 tóu]

race¹ N（跑步、游泳等）比赛 (pǎobù、yóuyǒng děng) bǐsài II v 1 参加 [+赛车] 比赛 cānjiā [+sàichē] bǐsài 2 飞快地奔跑 fēikuài de bēnpǎo

race² N 种族 zhǒngzú
race relations 种族关系 zhǒngzú guānxi

race-course, racetrack N 赛道 sàidào

racial ADJ 种族的 zhǒngzú de
racial discrimination 种族歧视 zhǒngzú qíshì

racism N 种族主义 zhǒngzú zhǔyì

racist I ADJ 种族主义的 zhǒngzúzhǔyì de II N 种族分子 zhǒngzú fènzi

rack I N 架子 jiàzi
dish rack 盘碟架 pándié jià
luggage rack 行李架 xínglijià
wine rack 酒瓶架 jiǔ píng jià
II v (to rack one's brains) 绞尽脑汁 jiǎojìn nǎozhī

racket N 1 吵闹 chǎonào 2 非法勾当 fēifǎ gòudang 3 球拍 qiúpāi

racketeering N 非法勾当（如敲诈，勒索，诈骗）fēifǎ gòudang (rú qiāozhà, lèsuǒ, zhàpiàn)

racquet N 球拍 qiúpāi

racy ADJ 带有性挑逗的 dàiyǒu xìng tiǎodòu de, 有趣味的 yǒuqù wèi de

radar N 雷达 léidá

radial ADJ 辐射状的 fúshè zhuàng de
radiant tire 辐射状轮胎 fúshè zhuàng lúntāi

radiant ADJ 1 喜气洋洋的 xǐqì yángyáng de, 容光焕发的 róngguāng huànfā de 2 光辉的 guānghuī de, 灿烂的 cànlàn de

radiate v 1 发射出 [+光辉] fāshè chū [+guānghuī] 2 显示出 xiǎnshì chū

radiation N 辐射 fúshè

radiation sickness 放射病 fàngshèbìng
radiator N 1 （汽车的）散热器 (qìchē de) sànrèqì 2 （房屋的）暖气装置 (fángwū de) nuǎnqì zhuāngzhì
radical I ADJ 1 根本的 [+改变] gēnběn de [+gǎibiàn]，彻底的 chèdǐ de 2 激进的 [+政治主张] jījìn de [+zhèngzhì zhǔzhāng]，极端的 jíduān de 3 激进分子 jījìn fènzi
radio I N 1 收音机 shōuyīnjī，无线电 wúxiàndiàn 2 无线电收发设备 wúxiàndiàn shōufā shèbèi 3 广播事业 guǎngbō shìyè II v 用无线电发送信息 yòng wúxiàndiàn fāsòng xìnxī
radioactive ADJ 有放射性的 [+材料] yǒu fāshè xìng de [+cáiliào]
radiology N 放射（医）学 fàngshè (yī) xué
radiotherapy N 放射治疗 fàngshèzhìliáo
radish N 小萝卜 xiǎoluóbo
radius N （园的）半径 (yuán de) bànjìng
raffle I N 抽奖 chōujiǎng II v (to raffle off) 以…为奖品 yǐ...wéi jiǎngpǐn
raft N 木筏 mùfá，橡皮筏 xiàngpífá
rafter N 1 乘筏的人 chéng fá de rén 2 椽子 chuánzi
rafting N 漂流（运动）piāoliú (yùndòng)
rag I N 1 抹布 mābù 2 （低质量的）报纸 (dī zhìliàng de) bàozhǐ，小报 xiǎobào 3 See **ragtime**
rag doll 布娃娃 bùwáwa
II v (to rag on) 戏弄 xìnòng
ragbag N (a ragbag of sth) 杂乱无章的东西 záluàn wúzhāng de dōngxi，七零八碎的事物 qīlíng bāsuì de shìwù
rage I N 大怒 dà nù
to fly into a rage 突然大发脾气 tūrán dà fā píqi
II v 1 激烈地进行 jīliè de jìnxíng 2 对…大发脾气 duì...dà fā píqi
ragged, raggedy ADJ 1 破烂的 [+衣服] pòlàn de [+yīfu]，衣衫褴褛的 yīshān lánlǚ de 2 不完美的 [+表演] bù wánměi de [+biǎoyǎn]
ragtime N 雷格泰姆（音乐/舞蹈）léigétàimǔ (yīnyuè/wǔdǎo)
raid I v 1 袭击 xíjī，突袭 tūxí 2 [警察+] 突袭搜捕 [jǐngchá+] tūxí sōubǔ II N 1 袭击

xíjī，突袭 tūxí 2 （警察）突袭搜捕 (jǐngchá) tūxí sōubǔ 3 挪用 [+资金] nuóyòng [+zījīn]
rail[1] N 1 栏杆 lángān，扶手 fúshou 2 铁轨 tiěguǐ
by rail 乘火车（旅行）chénghuǒchē (lǚxíng)
rail[2] v 声讨 shēngtǎo
railing N 栏杆 lángān，扶手 fúshou
railroad N 铁路 tiělù，铁道 tiědào
rain I N 雨 yǔ，雨水 yǔshuǐ II v 下雨 xiàyǔ
rain forest 雨林 yǔlín
rainbow N 虹 hóng，彩虹 cǎihóng
rain check N 1 近期兑现的优惠券 jìnqī duìxiàn de yōuhuì quàn 2 （体育）近期比赛入场券 (tǐyù) jìnqī bǐsài rùchǎngquàn 张 zhāng]
to take a rain check 改日再做某事 gǎirì zài zuò mǒu shì
raincoat N 雨衣 yǔyī [M. WD 件 jiàn]
raindrop N 雨点 yǔdiǎn
rainfall N 降雨量 jiàngyǔliàng
rainstorm N 暴雨 bàoyǔ
rainwater N 雨水 yǔshuǐ
rainy ADJ 多雨的 duō yǔ de，经常下雨的 jīngcháng xiàyǔ de
to save for a rainy day 存钱以备不时之需 cúnqián yǐbèi bùshízhīxū
raise I v 1 举起 jǔqǐ，升起 shēngqǐ，抬起 táiqǐ 2 提高 tígāo 3 饲养 sìyǎng 4 提出 [+问题] tíchū [+wèntí] II N 加薪 jiā xīn
to raise hell/Cain 大吵大闹 dà chǎo dà nào
rake I N 耙子 pázi [M. WD 把 bǎ] II v 用耙子耙 yòng pázi bà
to rake leaves 把落叶耙在一起 bǎ luòyè bà zài yìqǐ
rally I N 1 大型 [+抗议] 集会 dàxíng [+kàngyì] jíhuì 2 汽车拉力赛 qìchē lālìsài 3 [股票+] 反弹 [gǔpiào+] fǎntán，重新振作 chóngxīn zhènzuò II v 1 集合 jíhé 2 重新振作 chóngxīn zhènzuò，反弹 fǎntán
RAM (= Random Access Memory) ABBREV （计算机）随机存取存储器 (jìsuànjī) suíjī cúnqǔ cúnchǔqì
ram I v 猛撞 měngzhuàng II N 公羊 gōngyáng [M. WD 头 tóu]

506

Ramadan N（伊斯兰教）斋月 (Yīsīlánjiào) zhāiyuè

ramble V, N **1** 漫步 mànbù, 闲逛 xiánguàng **2** 漫谈 màntán, 没有边际的说很多话 méiyǒu biānjì de shuō hěn duō huà

rambling ADJ **1** 漫无边际的 [+文章] màn wú biānjì de [+wénzhāng] **2** 杂乱无章的 [+建筑] záluàn wúzhāng de [+jiànzhù]

ramification N 意料不到的后果 yìliào búdào de hòuguǒ

ramp N（出入高速公路的）坡道 (chūrù gāosù gōnglù de) pōdào

rampage V, N 横冲直撞 héngchōng zhízhuàng

to go on a rampage 骚乱 sāoluàn, 闹事 nàoshì

rampant ADJ 猖獗的 chāngjué de, 失控的 shīkòng de

ramshackle ADJ 破烂的 pòlàn de

ran See **run**

ranch N 大牧场 dà mùchǎng, 大农场 dà nóngchǎng

ranch house 牧场式住房 mùchǎngshì zhùfáng

rancher N 牧场主 mùchǎng zhǔ, 农场主 nóngchǎng zhǔ

rancid ADJ 变味的 [+黄油] biànwèi de [+huángyóu], 不新鲜的 bù xīnxian de

rancor N 怨恨 yuànhèn, 深仇 shēn chóu

random I ADJ 随意的 suíyì de, 任意的 rènyì de

random sample 随机抽样 suíjī chōuyàng II N (at random) 随机（地）suíjī (de), 任意（地）rènyì (de)

rang See **ring**

range I N **1** 系列 xìliè **2** 范围 fànwéi **3** 幅度 fúdù **4** 距离 jùlí II V **1** 范围在…和…之间 fànwéi zài...hé...zhījiān **2** 涉及 shèjí **3** 排列 páiliè

ranger N **1** 护林员 hùlínyuán, 管理员 guǎnlǐyuán **2** 巡逻骑警 xúnluó qíjǐng

rank I N **1** 级别 jíbié, 军阶 jūnjiē **2** 社会阶层 shèhuì jiēcéng, 身份 shēnfen II V 分成等级 fēnchéng děngjí, 排名 páimíng III ADJ **1** 十足的 shízú de, 完全的 wánquán de **2** 难闻的 nánwén de

rank and file N 普通成员 pǔtōng chéngyuán

ranking I N 排名 páimíng, 名次 míngcì II ADJ 级别最高的 jíbiézuìgāo de, 高级的 [+官员] gāojí de [+guānyuán]

rankle V 使…十分恼火 shǐ...shífēn nǎohuǒ

ransack V **1** 彻底搜查 chèdǐ sōuchá **2** 洗劫 xǐjié

ransom I N（绑架）赎金 (bǎngjià) shújīn II V 付赎金救人 fù shújīn jiù rén

rant V 怒气冲冲地叫嚷 nùqì chōngchōng de jiàorǎng

rap I N **1** 轻敲 qīngqiāo **2** 指控 zhǐkòng drunk driving rap 酒后驾车的指控 jiǔhòu jiàchē de zhǐkòng **3**（音乐）说唱乐 (yīnyuè) shuōchàngyuè II V **1** 轻敲 qīngqiāo

to rap sb on the knuckles 轻轻地批评某人 qīngqīng de pīpíng mǒurén **2** 气愤地指责 qìfèn de zhǐzé **3** 念出说唱乐的歌词 niàn chū shuōchàng yuè de gēcí

rape V, N 强奸 qiángjiān, 强暴 qiángbào date rape 约会强奸 yuēhuì qiángjiān

rapid ADJ 迅速的 xùnsù de rapid heartbeats 心动过速 xīndòng guòsù

rapids N 激流 jīliú

rapport N 融洽关系 róngqià guānxi to establish a rapport with sb 与某人建立融洽关系 yǔ mǒurén jiànlì róngqià guānxi

rapt ADJ 出神的 chūshén de, 全神贯注的 quánshén guànzhù de with rapt attention 全神贯注地 quánshén guànzhù de

rapture N 狂喜 kuángxǐ

rare ADJ **1** 稀有的 xīyǒu de, 难得的 nándé de **2** 半熟的 bàn shóu de

rarely ADV 很少（发生）hěn shǎo (fāshēng)

raring ADJ 急切的 jíqiè de, 渴望的 kěwàng de

rarity N **1** 珍贵的东西 zhēnguì de dōngxi, 稀有的宝物 xīyǒu de bǎowù **2** 不常发生的事 bù cháng fāshēng de shì

rascal N 恶棍 èqùn, 无赖 wúlài

rash I ADJ 急躁的 jízào de, 草率的 cǎoshuài de **II** N 皮疹 pízhěn
to break out in a rash 起疹子 qǐ zhěnzi, 发出疹子 fāchū zhěnzi

rasp I v 发出刺耳的声音 fāchū cìěr de shēngyīn **II** N 1 粗哑刺耳的声音 cūyǎ cìěr de shēngyīn 2 粗锉刀 cūcuòdāo

rat I N (老)鼠 (lǎo) shǔ [M. WD 只 zhī]
rat race 无休止的竞争 wú xiūzhǐ de jìngzhēng, 相互倾轧 xiānghù qīngyà **II** v (背信弃义地)告密 (bèixìn qìyì de) gàomì

rate N 1 率 lǜ, 比率 bǐlǜ 2 费用 fèiyòng, 价格 jiàgé 3 速度 sùdù
first-rate 一等 yì děng, 第一流 dìyī liú
at any rate 不管怎么说 bùguǎn zěnme shuō, 无论如何 wú lùn rú hé

rather ADV 相当 xiāngdāng
rather than 不 bù, 不是 bú shì
would rather 宁愿 nìngyuàn

ratification N 正式签署 zhèngshì qiānshǔ, 批准 pīzhǔn

ratify v 正式签署 [+条约] zhèngshì qiānshǔ [+tiáoyuē], 批准 pīzhǔn

rating N 1 等级 děngjí, 率 lǜ 2 (电影的)级别 (diànyǐng de) jíbié
approval rating 支持率 zhīchílǜ
credit rating 信用等级 xìnyòng děngjí

ratings N (电影/电视)收视率 (diànyǐng/diànshì) shōushìlǜ

ratio N 比 (例) bǐ (lì), 比率 bǐlǜ

ration N 配给(量) pèijǐ (liáng) **II** v 定量供应 dìngliàng gōngyìng, 实行配给 shíxíng pèijǐ

rationale N 原因 yuányīn, 依据 yījù

rationalize v 1 合理的解释 hélǐ de jiěshì 2 合理化 hélǐhuà

rations N (每日的)口粮配给 (měirì de) kǒuliáng pèijǐ

rattle I v 1 使…咯咯震动 shǐ…gēgē zhèndòng 2 使…神经紧张 shǐ…shénjīng jǐnzhāng **II** N 1 咯咯的声音 gēgē de shēngyīn 2 拨浪鼓(玩具) bōlànggǔ (wánjù)

rattlesnake N 响尾蛇 xiǎngwěishé

raucous ADJ 1 噪杂的 [+人群] zàozá de [+rénqún] 2 沙哑的 [+声音] shāyǎ de [+shēngyīn]

raunchy ADJ 色情的 sèqíng de, 下流的 xiàliú de

ravage v 严重摧毁 yánzhòng cuīhuǐ, 毁坏 huǐhuài

rave I v 胡言乱语 húyán luànyǔ
to rave about 赞赏 zànshǎng
to rant and rave 大叫大嚷 dàjiào dàrǎng, 大骂 dàmà **II** ADJ 赞扬的 zànyáng de
rave review 热烈好评 rèliè hǎopíng **III** v 狂欢聚会 kuánghuān jùhuì

raven N 渡鸦 dùyā [M. WD 只 zhī]

ravenous ADJ 极饿的 jí'è de, 饿的 è de

ravine N 深谷 shēngǔ, 峡谷 xiágǔ

raving ADJ 胡言乱语的 húyán luànyǔ de
raving success 巨大成功 jùdà chénggōng

ravish v 1 使…陶醉 shǐ…táozuì 2 强奸 qiángjiān

ravishing ADJ 令人心醉的 lìngrén xīnzuì de, 十分美丽的 shífēn měilì de

raw ADJ 1 生的 [+食物] shēng de [+shíwù]
raw materials 原材料 yuán cáiliào 2 不成熟的 [+人] bùchéngshú de [+rén], 没有经验的 méiyǒu jīngyàn de
a raw recruit 新兵 xīnbīng 3 阴冷的 [+天气] yīnlěng de [+tiānqì]

ray N 光线 guāngxiàn
a ray of hope 一线希望 yí xiàn xīwàng

rayon N 人造丝 rénzàosī

raze v 把…夷为平地 bǎ…yí wéi píngdì

razor N 剃刀 tìdāo, 剃须刀 tì hú dāo

razz v 嘲笑 cháoxiào

re PREP 关于 guānyú

reach I v 1 到达 dàodá 2 够得着 gòudezháo 3 伸手拿 shēnshǒu ná 4 和…联系 hé…liánxì **II** N 1 河段 héduàn
the upper/lower reaches (of a river) (河流)上游/下游 (héliú) shàngyóu/xiàyóu
2 可能得到 kěnéng dédào
out of/beyond (one's) reach ① 在手伸不到的地方 zài shǒu shēnbudào de dìfang ② 买不起 mǎibuqǐ
within (one's) reach ① 在手伸得到的地方 zài shǒu shēndedào de dìfang, 在可以达到的地方 zài kěyǐ dádào de dìfang ② 买得起 mǎideqǐ

react v 反应 fǎnyìng
to react against 反对 fǎnduì, 反抗 fǎnkàng

reaction N 1 反应 fǎnyìng, 反响 fǎnxiǎng 2 药物反应 yàowù fǎnyìng, 生理反应 shēnglǐ fǎnyìng

reactionary I ADJ 反动的 fǎndòng de II N 反动派 fǎndòngpài, 反动份子 fǎndòng fènzi

reactive ADJ 反应(性的)fǎnyìng (xìng) de

reactor N (核)反应堆 (hé) fǎnyìngduī

read (PT & PP **read**) v 1 读 dú, 阅读 yuèdú, 看得懂 kàndedǒng 2 读到 dúdào, 看到 kàndào
to read between the lines 仔细读(找出言外之意)zǐxì dú (zhǎochū yán wài zhī yì)

readable ADJ (读起来)有趣的 (dú qǐlái) yǒuqù de, 易读的 yì dú de

readership N 读者(群)dúzhě (qún)

readily ADV 1 容易地 róngyì de 2 乐意地 lèyì de

readiness N 1 愿意 yuànyì, 情愿 qíngyuàn 2 准备好 zhǔnbèi hǎo, 准备就绪 zhǔnbèi jiùxù

reading N 1 阅读 yuèdú 2 阅读材料 yuèdú cáiliào 3 理解 lǐjiě, 解释 jiěshì

readjust v 重新适应 chóngxīn shìyìng, 调整适应 tiáozhěng shìyìng

read-only memory See **ROM**

readout N (计算机)信息读出 (jìsuànjī) xìnxī dú chū

ready ADJ 准备好 zhǔnbèihǎo
(Get) ready, (get) set, go! 各就各位, 预备, 起! Gè jiù gè wèi, yùbèi, qǐ!

ready-made ADJ 现成的 xiànchéng de

ready-to-wear 现成的(服装)xiàn-chéng de (fúzhuāng)

real I ADJ 真正的 zhēnzhèng de, 真实的 zhēnshí de II ADV 确实 quèshí, 实在 shízài

real estate N 房地产 fángdìchǎn
real estate agency 房地产公司 fángdìchǎn gōngsī
real estate agent 房地产经纪人 fángdìchǎn jīngjìrén

realistic ADJ 现实(主义)的 xiànshí (zhǔyì) de, 讲究实际的 jiǎngjiu shíjì de

reality N 现实 xiànshí, 真实情况 zhēnshí qíngkuàng
reality show 写实节目 xiěshí jiémù, 真人秀 zhēnrén xiù

realization N 1 意识 yìshi, 领悟 lǐngwù 2 实现 shíxiàn, 达到 dádào

realize v 1 意识到 yìshidao, 了解 liǎojiě 2 实现 shíxiàn

really ADV 真正地 zhēnzhèng de, 真地 zhēn de
not really 不太 bú tài

realm N 领域 lǐngyù, 范围 fànwéi

real-time ADJ (计算机)即时处理的 (jìsuànjī) jíshí chǔlǐ de

realtor N 房地产经纪人 fángdìchǎn jīngjìrén

ream N 1 令 lìng (= 500 张纸 zhāngzhǐ) 2 大量(文字材料)dàliàng (wénzì cáiliào)

reap v 获得 huòdé
You reap what you sow. 种瓜得瓜, 种豆得豆。Zhòng guā dé guā, zhòng dòu dé dòu.

rear¹ I N 1 后面 hòumian, 背面 bèimiàn
to bring up the rear 处在最后的地位 chǔzài zuìhòu de dìwèi
2 臀部 túnbù II ADJ 后面的 hòumian de
rear door 后门 hòumén

rear² v 1 养育 [+孩子] yǎngyù [+háizi], 抚养 fǔyǎng 2 饲养 [+家畜] sìyǎng [+jiā-chù] 3 [动物+] 用后腿直立 [dòngwù+] yòng hòutuǐ zhílì 4 (to rear its ugly head) [丑闻+] 出现 [chǒuwén+] chūxiàn, 冒头 màotóu

rearrange v 重新安排 chóngxīn ānpái

reason I N 1 原因 yuányīn, 理由 lǐyóu 2 理性 lǐxìng, 道理 dàolǐ II v 1 思考 sīkǎo 2 推论 tuīlùn

reasonable ADJ 1 讲道理的 jiǎng dàolǐ de 2 符合情理的 fúhé qínglǐ de

reasonably ADV 1 相当(地)xiāngdāng (de) 2 合情合理(地)héqíng hélǐ (de), 按照情理 ànzhào qínglǐ
reasonably priced 价格合理的 jiàgé hélǐ de

reasoning N 1 推理 tuīlǐ 2 道理 dàolǐ

reassure v 使…放心 shǐ...fàngxīn, 消除疑虑 xiāochú yílǜ

reassuring ADJ 让人放心的 ràng rén fàngxīn de, 安慰的 ānwèi de

rebate N（部分）退款 (bùfen) tuìkuǎn, 回扣 huíkòu

rebel I N 造反者 zàofǎnzhě, 反叛 fǎnpàn II V 造反 zàofǎn, 反叛 fǎnpàn

rebellion N 叛乱 pànluàn

rebellious ADJ 反抗的 fǎnkàng de, 反叛的 fǎnpàn de

rebirth N 1 重生 chóngshēng, 再生 zàishēng 2 复兴 fùxīng

reboot V 重新启动（计算机）chóngxīn qǐdòng (jìsuànjī)

rebound I V 1 [球+] 弹回 [qiú+] tánhuí 2 [价格+] 回升 [jiàgé+] huíshēng, 反弹 fǎntán II N（on the rebound）1 [球+] 在弹回 [qiú+] zài tánhuí 2 [事情+] 正有起色 [shìqíng+] zhèng yǒuqǐsè

on the rebound 因失恋而情绪低落时 yīn shīliàn ér qíngxù dīluò shí

rebuff V 回绝 huíjué, 拒绝 jùjué

rebuild V 重建 chóngjiàn, 恢复 huīfù

rebuke I V 指责 zhǐzé, 斥责 chìzé II N 指责 zhǐzé

rebut V 驳斥 bóchì, 反驳 fǎnbó

recalcitrant ADJ 不听话的 [+小孩] bù tīnghuà de [+xiǎohái], 难管的 nán guǎn de

recall I V 1 想起 xiǎngqǐ 2 回想 huíxiǎng, 回忆 huíyì 3 [制造厂商+] 回收 [+产品] [zhìzào chǎngshāng+] shōuhuí [+chǎnpǐn] 4 召回 [+大使] zhàohuí [+dàshǐ] 5（在计算机上）重新调出信息 (zài jìsuànjī shàng) chóngxīn tiáo chū xìnxī II N 1 记忆（力）jìyì (lì) 2（对官员的）罢免 (duì guānyuán de) bàmiǎn 3（商品）收回令 (shāngpǐn) shōuhuílìng

recant V 公开宣布放弃 [+以前的观点] gōngkāi xuānbù fàngqì [+yǐqián de guāndiǎn]

recap, recapitulate N 重新说一下内容简要 chóngxīn shuō yíxià nèiróng jiǎnyào, 复习 fùxí

recapture V 1 重新抓获 [+逃犯] chóngxīn zhuāhuò [+táofàn] 2 再现 [+历史时期] zàixiàn [+lìshǐ shíqí]

recede V 1 渐渐消失 jiànjiàn xiāoshī 2 [洪水+] 退去 [hóngshuǐ+] tuìqù

receipt N 收据 shōujù, 收条 shōutiáo

receive V 1 收到 shōudao 2 得到 dédao, 受到 shòudao

receiver N 1（电话）听筒 (diànhuà) tīngtǒng 2 破产企业管理人 pòchǎn qǐyè guǎnlǐ rén 3 买卖赃物者 mǎimai zāngwùzhě 4（电子信号）接收机 (diànzǐ xìnhào) jiēshōujī 5（橄榄球）接球手 (gǎnlǎnqiú) jiēqiúshǒu

receivership N 破产管理 pòchǎn guǎnlǐ

recent ADJ 近来的 jìnlái de

receptacle N 容器 róngqì

reception N 1 招待会 zhāodàihuì, 宴会 yànhuì

wedding reception 婚宴 hūn yàn

2 接待 jiēdài, 欢迎 huānyíng

reception desk（旅馆的）接待处 (lǚguǎn de) jiēdài chù, 登记台 dēngjì tái 3（电视机的）收视质量 (diànshìjī de) shōushì zhìliàng,（收音机的）接收性能 (shōuyīnjī de) jiēshōu xìngnéng

poor reception（电视）收视质量很差 (diànshì) shōushì zhìliàng hěn chà

receptionist N 接待员 jiēdài yuán

recess N 中途休息时间 zhōngtú xiūxi shíjiān, 休会 xiūhuì

recession N（经济）衰退（期）(jīngjì) shuāituì (qī)

recharge V 1 给 [+电池] 充电 gěi [+diànchí] chōngdiàn 2 使…恢复精力 shǐ...huīfù jīnglì

recipe N 烹饪法 pēngrèn fǎ, 菜谱 càipǔ

recipient N 领受者 lǐngshòu zhě, 得奖人 déjiǎngrén

reciprocate V 报答 bàodá, 给以回报 gěiyǐ huíbào

recital N（音乐）演奏会 (yīnyuè) yǎnzòu huì,（诗歌）朗诵会 (shīgē) lǎngsòng huì

recite V 朗诵 lǎngsòng, 背诵 bèisòng

reckless ADJ 不考虑后果的 bù kǎolǜ hòuguǒ de, 鲁莽的 lǔmǎng de

reckon V 1 估计 gūjì 2 看作 kànzuò, 认为 rènwéi

to reckon with 认真对付 rènzhēn duìfu

reckoning N 1 估计 gūjì, 估算 gūsuàn 2（a day of reckoning）算总帐的日子

suàn zǒngzhàng de rìzi, 报应的那一天 bàoyìng de nà yì tiān

reclaim v 1 回收 [+有用材料] huíshōu [+yǒuyòng cáiliào] 2 收回 [+部分税款] shōuhuí [+bùfen shuìkuǎn] 3 开垦 [+土地] kāikěn [+tǔdì]

recline v 躺 tǎng

recluse N 隐居者 yǐnjūzhě, 隐士 yǐnshì

recognition N 1 认出 rènchū 2 认识到 rènshidào, 接受 jiēshòu 3 承认 chéngrèn 4 表彰 biǎozhāng, 赞扬 zànyáng

recognize v 1 认出 rènchū, 辨认出 biànrènchū 2 认识到 rènshidao 3 承认 chéngrèn, 公认 gōngrèn 4 表彰 biǎozhāng, 赞扬 zànyáng

recoil I v 1 （因厌恶）退避 (yīn yànwù) tuìbì 2 [枪炮+] 反冲 [qiāngpào+] fǎnchōng II N 反冲 fǎnchōng, 后座力 hòuzuòlì

recollect v 努力回想 nǔlì huíxiǎng, 记起 jìqǐ

recollection N 1 想起 xiǎngqǐ 2 记忆 jìyì, 回忆 huíyì

recommend v 1 推荐 tuījiàn, 介绍 jièshào 2 建议 jiànyì

recommendation N 1 推荐 tuījiàn, 介绍 jièshào 2 （正式）建议 (zhèngshì) jiànyì, 意见 yìjiàn

recompense N, v 补偿 bǔcháng, 赔偿 péicháng

reconcile v 使…重归于好 shǐ…chóng guīyú hǎo, 调和 tiáohé

reconciliation N 重归于好 chóng guīyú hǎo, 调和 tiáohé, 和解 héjiě
spirit of reconciliation 和解的精神 héjiě de jīngshén

reconnaissance N 侦察 zhēnchá
reconnaissance aircraft 侦察机 zhēnchájī

reconnoiter v 侦察 zhēnchá

reconsider v 重新考虑 chóngxīn kǎolǜ

reconstitute v 重组 chóngzǔ, 重建 chóngjiàn

reconstruct v 1 再现 [+某一事件] zàixiàn [+mǒuyī shìjiàn] 2 重建 chóngjiàn

reconstruction I N 1 重建 chóngjiàn 2 重现 chóngxiàn 3 修复手术 xiūfù shǒushù

record I N 1 记录 jìlù 2 最高记录 zuìgāo jìlù 3 唱片 chàngpiàn [M. WD 张 zhāng]
record player 唱机 chàngjī
III v 记录下来 jìlùxiàlai
off the record 不得发表的 bù dé fābiǎo de

recorder N 录音机 lùyīnjī [M. WD 台 tái], 摄录机 shèxiàngjī

recording N 录音 lùyīn, 录象 lùxiàng

recount v 叙述 xùshù, 描述 miáoshù

re-count N 重新计算选票 chóngxīn jìsuàn xuǎnpiào

recoup v 偿还 chánghuán, 补偿 bǔcháng

recourse N 求助（的对象）qiúzhù (de duìxiàng)
without recourse to sth 得不到某事物的帮助 dé búdào mǒushìwù de bāngzhù

recover v 1 康复 kāngfù 2 恢复 huīfù 3 找回 zhǎohuí

recovery N 1 恢复健康 huīfù jiànkāng, 康复 kāngfù 2 [经济+] 复苏 [jīngjì+] fùsū 3 重新获得 chóngxīn huòdé, [失物的+] 复得 [shīwù de+] fùdé

recreate v 重建 chóngjiàn, 重演 chóngyǎn

recreation N 消遣 xiāoqiǎn, 娱乐 yúlè

recruit I v 吸收新成员 xīshōu xīn chéng-yuán, 招募 zhāomù II N 新成员 xīn chéngyuán, 新兵 xīn bīng

rectal ADJ 直肠的 zhícháng de

rectangle N 长方形 chángfāngxíng, 矩形 jǔxíng

rectify v 纠正 jiūzhèng, 矫正 jiǎozhèng

rector N 1 （基督教）教区长 (Jīdūjiào) jiàoqūzhǎng 2 学院院长 xuéyuàn yuànzhǎng

rectum N 直肠 zhícháng

recuperate v [病人+] 康复 [bìngrén+] kāngfù, 复原 fùyuán

recur v 复发 fùfā, 重现 chóngxiàn

recyclable ADJ 可回收利用的 kě huíshōu lìyòng de

recycle v 回收利用 huíshōu lìyòng

red N, ADJ 红（的）hóng (de), 红色（的）hóngsè (de)
red carpet 红地毯 hóng dìtǎn,（对贵

511

宾的）容重接待 (duì guìbīn de) róng-zhòng jiēdài
Red Cross 红十字 Hóng shízì
red meat 牛羊肉 niúyángròu

red-blooded ADJ 血气方刚的 xuèqì fāng gāng de

redden V (使…)变红 (shǐ…) biàn hóng

redeem V 1 补救 bǔjiù, 补偿 bǔcháng
to redeem oneself 挽回声誉 wǎnhuí shēngyù
a redeeming feature 可以起弥补作用的特点 kěyǐ qǐ míbǔ zuòyòng de tèdiǎn 2 赎回 [+抵押物] shúhuí [+dǐyāwù]

redemption I N 1 补救 bǔjiù, 挽救 wǎnjiù
to be past redemption 不可挽回的 bùkě wǎnhuí de, 不可救药的 bù kě jiùyào de 2 兑换（现款）duìhuàn (xiànkuǎn)

redevelop V 重新开放 chóngxīn kāifā, 重建 chóngjiàn

redevelopment N 重新开放 chóngxīn kāifā, 重建 chóngjiàn

red-eye N 夜间航班 yèjiān hángbān

red-handed ADJ (to catch sb red-handed) 当场抓获某人 dāngchǎng zhuāhuò mǒurén

red-herring N 转移注意力的事情 zhuǎnyí zhùyìlì de shìqíng

redhot ADJ 1 炽热的 [+金属] chìrè de [+jīnshǔ] 2 火热的 [+爱情] huǒrè de [+àiqíng] 3 令人万分激动的 [+故事] lìng rén wànfēn jīdòng de [+gùshi]

redirect V 使…改变方向 shǐ…gǎibiàn fāngxiàng

red-light district N 红灯区 hóngdēngqū

redo V 重做 zhòng zuò

redouble V (to redouble one's efforts) 加倍努力 jiābèi nǔlì

redress I V 1 修正 xiūzhèng, 纠正 jiūzhèng II N 赔偿 péicháng

reduce V 减少 jiǎnshǎo, 降低 jiàngdī

redundancy N 1 多余（的东西）duōyú (de dōngxi) 2 解雇（员工）jiěgù (yuángōng)
redundancy compensation 解雇补偿 jiěgù bǔcháng
redundancy notice 解雇通知 jiěgù tōngzhī

redundant ADJ 1 多余的 duōyú de, 重复的 chóngfù de 2 被解雇的 bèi jiěgù de, 失业的 shīyè de

reed N 芦苇 lúwěi

re-educate V 再教育 zài jiàoyù, 重新教育 chóngxīn jiàoyù

reef N 礁（石）jiāo (shí)

reek I V 发出臭味 fāchū chòuwèi II N 臭味 chòuwèi

reel I N 一卷（线）yí juàn (xiàn)，一盘（电影片）yìpán (diànyǐngpiàn) II V 1 摇摇晃晃地走 yáoyán huǎnghuǎng de zǒu 2 慌乱 huāngluàn，眩晕 xuànyūn

reelection N 重新选举 chóngxīn xuǎnjǔ

re-enact V 重演 chóngyǎn, 再现 zàixiàn

reentry N 再次进入 zàicì jìnrù, 重返 chóngfǎn

refer V 1 指 zhǐ, 针对 zhēnduì 2 提到 tídao 3 查阅 cháyuè 4 转交 zhuǎnjiāo

referee N 1 (体育比赛) 裁判（员）(tǐyù bǐsài) cáipàn (yuán) 2 (学术论文) 审阅人 (xuéshù lùnwén) shěnyuè rén 3 (纠纷) 调停人 (jiūfēn) tiáotíngrén

reference N 1 提到 tídao 2 注文，附注 zhù wén, fùzhù 3 证明 zhèngmíng，介绍信 jièshào xìn 4 参考 cānkǎo
reference book 参考书 cānkǎo shū
reference library 参考书图书馆 cānkǎoshū túshūguǎn

referendum N 全民投票 quánmín tóupiào, 公民直接投票 gōngmín zhíjiē tóupiào

refill[1] V 1 再注满 zài zhù mǎn 2 再斟满一杯 zài zhēnmǎn yìbēi

refill[2] N 新添制 xīn tiān zhì
refill for a ballpoint pen 圆珠笔笔芯 yuánzhūbǐ bǐxīn

refinance V 重新安排财务／债务 chóngxīn ānpái cáiwù/zhàiwù

refine V 1 提炼 [+石油] tíliàn [+shíyóu] 2 逐步改进 zhúbù gǎijìn

refined ADJ 1 提炼过的 tíliàn guò de, 精炼的 jīngliàn de 2 高雅的 [+古典音乐爱好者] gāoyǎ de [+gǔdiǎn yīnyuè àihàozhě] 3 [精确的+] 测量方法 [jīngquè de+] cèliáng fāngfǎ

refinery N 提炼厂 tíliàn chǎng

oil refinery 炼油厂 liànyóuchǎng

refinish v 再抛光 [+家具] zài pāoguāng [+jiājù]

reflect v 1 反映 fǎnyìng 2 思考 sīkǎo 3 反射 fǎnshè

reflection N 1 倒影 dàoyǐng
one's reflection in the mirror 镜子里的自己 jìngzi lǐ de zìjǐ
2 思考 sīkǎo
upon reflection 经过思考 jīngguò sīkǎo
3 反映 fǎnyìng
reflection of sb's intelligence 反映出某人的智力 fǎnyìng chū mǒurén de zhìlì
4 反射 fǎnshè
light reflection 光线的反射 guāngxiàn de fǎnshè

reflective ADJ 1 沉思的 chénsī de 2 反光的 fǎnguāng de

reflector N 1 反光板 fǎnguāng bǎn 2 反射镜 fǎnshèjìng

reflex N（生理）反射（shēnglǐ）fǎnshè
reflex action 反射动作 fǎnshè dòngzuò，本能反应 běnnéng fǎnyìng

reform v, N 改革 gǎigé，改进 gǎijìn
reform school 少年管教所 shàonián guǎnjiàosuǒ

refrain[1] v 克制 kèzhì，抑制 yìzhì
to refrain from laughing 克制住不笑 kèzhì zhù bú xiào，忍住不笑 rěnzhù bú xiào

refrain[2] N 1 副歌 fùgē 2 一再重复的话 yízài chóngfù de huà

refresh v 使…恢复精力 shǐ…huīfù jīnglì
to refresh one's memory 唤起记忆 huànqǐ jìyì
2 更新 [+计算机信息] gēngxīn [+jìsuànjī xìnxī]

refresher course N 进修课程 jìnxiū kèchéng [M. WD 门 mén]

refreshing ADJ 清新的 qīngxīn de，提神的 tíshén de

refreshments N 点心饮料 diǎnxīn yǐnliào

refrigerator N 冰箱 bīngxiāng，电冰箱 diàn bīngxiāng

refuel v 给…加燃料 gěi…jiā ránliào 2 使 [+感情] 更强烈 shǐ [+gǎnqíng] gèng qiángliè，重新点燃 chóngxīn diǎnrán

refuge N 避难所 bìnànsuǒ，庇护所 bìhùsuǒ

refugee N 难民 nànmín

refund I N 退款 tuìkuǎn [M. WD 笔 bǐ]
II v 退款 tuìkuǎn，退票 tuìpiào

refurbishment N 翻修 fānxiū

refusal N 拒绝 jùjué

refuse[1] v 拒绝 jùjué

refuse[2] N 废物 fèiwù，垃圾 lājī

refute v 驳斥 bóchì，反驳 fǎnbó

regain v 收回 shōuhuí，恢复 huīfù

regal ADJ 帝王般的 dìwáng bān de

regalia N（典礼时的）盛装（diǎnlǐ shí de）shèngzhuāng

regard I v 把…看作 bǎ…kànzuo
II N 1 尊重 zūnzhòng 2 关心 guānxīn，关注 guānzhù
in this/that regard 关于这 / 那方面 guānyú zhè/nà fāngmiàn
with regard to 关于 guānyú

regarding PREP 关于 guānyú

regardless ADV 不管 bùguǎn，不顾 bùgù

regards N 问候 wènhòu，致意 zhìyì

regenerate v 再生 zàishēng，恢复 huīfù

regent N 摄政者 shèzhèngzhě
prince regent 摄政王 Shèzhèngwáng

regime N 政权 zhèngquán，政府 zhèngfǔ

regiment N（军队）团（jūnduì）tuán
regiment commander 团长 tuánzhǎng

region N 地区 dìqū，区域 qūyù

regional ADJ 地区的 dìqū de，区域性的 qūyùxìng de

register I v 1 注册 zhùcè 2 登记 dēngjì
II N 登记簿 dēngjì bù
cash register 收银机 shōuyínjī

registered mail N 保价信 bǎojiàxìn [M. WD 封 fēng]

registrar N（大学）教务长（dàxué）jiàowùzhǎng

registration N 1（大学）注册（dàxué）zhùcè 2 登记 dēngjì
voter registration 选民登记 xuǎnmín dēngjì
3 机动车登记证 jīdòngchē dēngjìzhèng

registry N 1 登记 dēngjì，注册 zhùcè
bridal registry 新婚礼品单 xīnhūn lǐpǐn dān

2 登记处 dēngjìchù

regress v 倒退 dàotuì, 退化 tuìhuà

regret N, v 懊悔 àohuǐ, 遗憾 yíhàn

regretful ADJ 懊悔的 àohuǐ de, 遗憾的 yíhàn de

regrettable ADJ 让人懊悔的 ràng rén àohuǐ de, 令人遗憾的 lìngrén yíhàn de

regroup v 重新编组 chóngxīn biānzǔ, 重组 chóngzǔ

regular I ADJ 1 正常的 zhèngcháng de 2 常规的 chángguī de 3 有规则的 yǒu guīzé de, 整齐的 zhěngqí de II N 1 常客 chángkè, 老主顾 lǎozhǔgù 2 正规兵 zhèngguī bīng

regulate v 1 [通过规章来+] 管理 [tōngguò guīzhāng lái+] guǎnlǐ, 控制 kòngzhì 2 调整 [+机器] tiáozhěng [+jīqì], 校准 jiàozhǔn

regulation N 1 规章 guīzhāng, 规定 guīdìng, 条例 tiáolì
safety regulations 安全条例 ānquán tiáolì
2 管理 guǎnlǐ, 控制 kòngzhì
financial regulation 金融管理 jīnróng guǎnlǐ

regurgitate v 1 吐出已吞咽的食物 tùchū yǐ tūnyàn de shíwù, 回翻 huí fān 2 不加思索地重复 [+别人的话] bù jiā sīsuǒ de chóngfù [+biérende huà]

rehab N (吸毒者的) 康复治疗 (xīdúzhě de) kāngfù zhìliáo
rehab center 康复中心 kāngfù zhōngxīn, 戒毒所 jièdúsuǒ

rehabilitate v 1 使…恢复正常生活 shǐ… huīfù zhèngcháng shēnghuó 2 恢复…的名誉 huīfù…de míngyù, 平反 píngfǎn

rehash I v 用新方式重复 [+旧内容] yòng xīn fāngshì chóngfù (jiù nèiróng) II N 新瓶装旧酒 xīnpíng zhuāng jiùjiǔ

rehearsal N 排练 páiliàn, 排演 páiyǎn
dress rehearsal 彩排 cǎipái

rehearse v 排练 páiliàn, 排演 páiyǎn

reign I N 统治 (时期) tǒngzhì (shíqī)
reign of terror 恐怖统治 kǒngbùtǒngzhì
II v 1 统治 [+一个王国] tǒngzhì [+yí ge wángguó] 2 占支配地位 zhàn zhīpèi dìwèi

reimburse v 付还 fùhuán, 偿还 chánghuán
to reimburse sb for travel expenses 给某人报销旅差费 gěi mǒurén bàoxiāo lǚchāifèi

rein I N 缰绳 jiāngshéng [M. WD 条 tiáo]
to give sb free rein 给某人行动的自由 jǐyǔ mǒurén xíngdòng de zìyóu
II v (to rein in) 加强管理／控制 jiāqiáng guǎnlǐ/kòngzhì

reincarnation N 再生 zàishēng, 转世 zhuǎnshì

reindeer N 驯鹿 xùnlù [M. WD 头 tóu]

reinforcement N 加强 jiāqiáng, 增强 zēngqiáng

reinforcements N 增援部队 zēngyuánbùduì

reinstate v 使…恢复原职 shǐ…huīfù yuánzhí 2 恢复（原来的）制度／规章 huīfù (yuánlái de) zhìdù/guīzhāng

reinvent v（在现有基础上）重新制定 (zài xiànyǒu jīchǔ shàng) chóngxīn zhìdìng
to reinvent oneself 改变自我 gǎibiàn zìwǒ, 改头换面 gǎitóu huànmiàn
to reinvent the wheel 做别人早已做过的事 zuò biéren zǎoyǐ zuò guò de shì, 浪费精力 làngfèi jīnglì

reissue v 重新发行 chóngxīn fāxíng, 重印 chóngyìn II N 重新发行的唱片 chóngxīn fāxíng de chàngpiàn, 重印的书刊 chóngyìn de shūkān

reiterate N 反复地讲 fǎnfù de jiǎng, 重申 chóngshēn

reject I v 1 拒绝 jùjué, 不赞同 bú zàntóng 2 拒绝接受 jùjué jiēshòu, 丢弃 diūqì II N 退货 tuìhuò, 残次产品 cáncì chǎnpǐn

rejoice v 欢欣 huānxīn, 欣喜 xīnxǐ

rejoin v 1 重新加入 [+组织] chóngxīn jiārù [+zǔzhī], 重返 chóngfǎn 2 回答 huídá

rejoinder N 巧妙地回答 qiǎomiào de huídá

rejuvenate v 1 使 [+人] 变得年轻 shǐ [+rén] biàn de niánqīng, 使…恢复活力 shǐ…huīfù huólì 2 重振 [+地区] chóngzhèn [+dìqū]

rekindle v 重新激起 [+兴趣] chóngxīn jīqǐ [+xìngqu]

relapse N（旧病／坏习惯）复发

(jiùbìng/huài xíguàn) fùfā, 故态复萌 gùtàifùméng

relate v **1** 联系起来 liánxìqǐlai **2** 理解 lǐjiě **3** 讲述 jiǎngshù

related ADJ **1** 与…有关的 yǔ…yǒuguān de **2** 与…是亲戚 yǔ…shì qīnqi

relation N **1** 关系 guānxi **2** 亲戚 qīnqi

relationship N **1** 关系 guānxi **2** 情人关系 qíngrén guānxi, 夫妻关系 fūqī guānxi

relative I ADJ 相对的 xiāngduì de II N 亲戚 qīnqi

relatively ADV 相对（地）xiāngduì (de), 比较（地）bǐjiào (de)

relatively speaking 相对来说 xiāngduì láishuō

relax v 放松 fàngsōng

relaxation N **1** 松弛 sōngchí

relaxation therapy 松弛疗法 sōngchí liáofǎ

2 休闲 xiūxián, 消遣 xiāoqiǎn

relay I v 传达 chuándá, 传递 chuándì II N **1** 接力赛跑 jiēlìsàipǎo **2** 转播设备 zhuǎnbō shèbèi

release I v **1** 释放 shìfàng **2** 放开 fàngkai **3** 发行 [+电影] fāxíng [+diànyǐng] II N 释放 shìfàng

relegate v 贬低 biǎndī

to relegate sb to 把某人降低到… bǎ mǒurén jiàngdī dào…

relent v 变得温和 / 宽容 biàn de wēnhé/kuānróng, 不再坚持 búzài jiānchí

relentless ADJ 无情的 wúqíng de, 严厉的 yánlì de

relevance N 关系 guānxi

reliable ADJ 可靠的 kěkào de, 可依赖的 kě yīlài de

reliance N 依赖 yīlài, 依靠 yīkào

relic N 遗迹 yíjì, 遗物 yíwù

relief¹ N **1** 不再担忧 bú zài dānyōu **2** 解痛 jiětòng, 救济物资 jiùjì wùzī

relief² N 浮雕 fúdiāo

relief map 地势图 dìshìtú, 地形图 dìxíngtú

relieve v **1** 减轻 jiǎnqīng **2** 替换 tìhuan

to relieve oneself 大小便 dàxiǎobiàn

to relieve sb of duties/a post 解除某人的职务 / 职位 jiěchú mǒurén de zhíwù/zhíwèi

religion N 宗教 zōngjiào

religious ADJ **1** 宗教的 zōngjiào de **2** 相信宗教的 xiāngxìn zōngjiào de, 虔诚的 qiánchéng de

relinquish v 放弃 fàngqì, 交出 jiāochū

relish I v **1** 享受 xiǎngshòu, 真心喜欢 zhēnxīn xǐhuan **2** 调味品 tiáowèipǐn **2** 享受 xiǎngshòu, 喜欢 xǐhuan

relive v 重温 chóngwēn, 回忆 huíyì

relocate v 重新安置 chóngxīn ānzhì, 迁移 qiānyí

reluctance N 不情愿 bùqíngyuàn, 勉强 miǎnqiǎng

reluctant ADJ 不情愿 bù qíngyuàn, 勉强 miǎnqiǎng

rely v **1** 依靠 yīkào, 依赖 yīlài **2** 信赖 xìnlài, 信任 xìnrèn

remain v **1** 仍然是 réngrán shì, 还是 hái shì **2** 仍然存在 réngrán cúnzài, 还在 hái zài **3** 留下 liúxia, 剩下 shèngxia

remainder N 剩余部份 shèngyú bùfen, 余数 yúshù

remaining ADJ 剩下的 shèngxia de, 留下的 liúxia de

remains N **1** 遗址废墟 yízhǐ fèixū **2** 遗体 yítǐ

Roman remains 罗马时代的遗址 Luómǎ shídài de yízhǐ

remark I N [一句+] 话 [yí jù+] huà, 评论 pínglùn II v 说 shuō, 评论 pínglùn

remarkable ADJ 不寻常的 bù xúncháng de, 了不起的 liǎobuqǐ de

remarry v 再婚 zàihūn, 再娶 zàiqǔ, 再嫁 zàijià

remedial ADJ **1** 补救的 bǔjiù de, 治疗的 zhìliáo de

remedial action 补救措施 bǔjiù cuòshī

2 补习的 bǔxí de

remedial English class 英文补习班 Yīngwén bǔxíbān

remedy I N **1** 补救办法 bǔjiù bànfǎ **2** 药物 yàowù, 治疗 zhìliáo

herbal remedy 草药治疗 cǎoyào zhìliáo

II v 补救 bǔjiù, 改善 gǎishàn

remember v **1** 记住 jìzhu, 记得 jìde **2** 悼念 [+死者] dàoniàn [+sǐzhě], 纪念 jìniàn **3** 给…送礼物 gěi…sònglǐ wù

remind v 提醒 tíxǐng, 使…想起 shǐ…xiǎngqǐ

reminder N 1 提醒（物）tíxǐng (wù)
a friendly reminder 友好的提醒 yǒuhǎo de tíxǐng
2 让人回忆过去的东西 ràng rén huíyì guòqù de dōngxi
a reminder of her high school days 让她回想起中学时代的东西 ràng tā huíxiǎng qǐ zhōngxué shídài de dōngxi

reminisce v 缅怀往事 miǎnhuái wǎngshì, 追忆往事 zhuīyì wǎngshì

remiss ADJ 玩忽职守的 wánhū zhíshǒu de, 失误的 shīwù de

remission N 1 减轻（时期）jiǎnqīng (shíqī), 缓解（期）huǎnjiě (qī) 2 减免刑期 jiǎnmiǎn xíngqī

remit v 汇款 huìkuǎn

remittance N 汇款（额）huìkuǎn (é)

remnant N 剩余物 shèngyú wù, 残余 cányú

remodel v 整修 zhěngxiū, 重新塑造 chóngxīn sùzào

remonstrate v 抗议 kàngyì

remorse N 悔恨 huǐhèn, 深深的内疚 shēnshēn de nèijiù

remorseful ADJ 悔恨的 huǐhèn de, 极其内疚的 jíqí nèijiù de

remote ADJ 1 遥远的 yáoyuǎn de
remote control 遥控器 yáokòng qì
2 冷淡的 lěngdàn de, 漠不关心的 mò bù guānxīn de 3 微小的 wēixiǎo de
remote chance 微小的机会 wēixiǎo de jīhuì

remove v 1 拿掉 nádiao, 移开 yíkāi 2 排除 páichú 3 免职 miǎnzhí

remuneration N 酬金 chóujīn

renal ADJ 肾脏的 shènzàng de

rename v 重新命名 chóngxīn mìngmíng, 更名 gēngmíng

render v 1 使…成为 shǐ…chéngwéi
to render sth obsolete 使某物过时 shǐ mǒuwù guòshí
2 给予 jǐyǔ, 提供 tígōng
services rendered 提供的服务 tígōng de fúwù

rendezvous I N 1 相会 xiānghuì, 约会 yuēhuì 2 约会地点 yuēhuì dìdiǎn II v 相会 xiānghuì, 会合 huìhé

rendition N 1 表演 biǎoyǎn, 演奏 yǎnzòu 2 翻译 fānyì, 译文 yìwén

renegade I N 叛徒 pàntú, 变节者 biànjiézhě II ADJ 变节的 biànjié de, 背叛的 bèipàn de

renege v 违背 wéibèi
to renege on a promise 违背诺言 wéibèi nuòyán

renew v 1 延长 yáncháng, 延期 yánqī
to renew a book（从图书馆）续借图书 (cóng túshūguǎn) xùjiè túshū
2 恢复 [+关系] huīfù [+guānxì]

renewable ADJ 1 可再生的 kě zàishēng de 2 可延期的 kě yánqī de, 可延续的 kě yánxù de

renewal N 延长 yáncháng, 延期 yánqī

renounce v（正式）放弃 (zhèngshì) fàngqì, 抛弃 pāoqì

renovate v 修复 xiūfù, 装修 zhuāngxiū

renovation N 修复 xiūfù, 装修 zhuāngxiū

renowned ADJ 著名的 zhùmíng de, 有名望的 yǒu míngwàng de

rent I v 1 租借 zūjiè, 租用 zūyòng 2 出租 chūzū II N 租金 zūjīn, 房租 fángzū

rental I N 1 租借（物）zūjiè (wù), 租赁（物）zūlìn (wù) 2 租金 zūjīn II ADJ 供出租的 gōngchūzū de, 租来的 zū láide

renunciation N（正式）放弃 (zhèngshì) fàngqì, 抛弃 pāoqì

reorder v 1 重新订购 chóngxīn dìnggòu 2 重新安排 chóngxīn ānpái
to reorder one's priorities 重新安排轻重缓急 chóngxīn ānpái qīngzhònghuǎnjí

reorganize v 改组 gǎizǔ, 改编 gǎibiān

repair I v 1 修 xiū, 修理 xiūlǐ II N 1 修理 xiūlǐ, 修缮 xiūshàn 2 (in good repair) [房屋+] 情况良好 [fángwū+] qíngkuàng liánghǎo

reparation N 赔偿 péicháng, 赔款 péikuǎn

repatriate v 遣送…回国 qiǎnsòng…huíguó, 遣返 qiǎnfǎn

repay v 付还 fùhuán, 偿还 chánghuán 2 报答 bàodá

repayment N 1 付还 fùhuán, 偿还 chánghuán 2 还款（额）huánkuǎn (é) 3 报答 bàodá

repeal v 废除 fèichú, 取消 qǔxiāo

repeat I v 1 重复 chóngfù
to repeat oneself 重复自己说过的话 chóngfù zìjǐ shuō guò dehuà
2 重播 [+电视节目] chóngbō [+diànshì jiémù] II N 1 重现的事 chóngxiàn de shì 2 重播的（电视）节目 chóngbō de (diànshì) jiémù
repeat customer 回头客 huítóukè

repeated ADJ 反复的 fǎnfù de, 再三的 zàisān de

repeatedly ADV 反复地 fǎnfù de

repel v 1 使…厌恶 shǐ…yànwù, 使…强烈反感 shǐ…qiángliè fǎngǎn 2 驱除 qūchú, 驱走 qūzǒu

repellent I N 除虫剂 chúchóngjì
mosquito repellent 驱蚊剂 qūwénjì
II ADJ 令人厌恶的 lìngrén yànwù de, 令人反感的 lìng rén fǎngǎn de

repent v 忏悔 chànhuǐ, 懊悔 àohuǐ

repentant ADJ 忏悔的 chànhuǐ de, 懊悔的 àohuǐ de

repercussion N 反响 fǎnxiǎng, 持续的影响 chíxù de yǐngxiǎng

repertoire N 1（剧团／演员的）全部剧目 (jùtuán/yǎnyuán de) quánbù jùmù 2（某人的）全部技能 (mǒurén de) quánbù jìnéng

repetitious ADJ（一再）重复的 (yízài) chóngfù de

repetitive ADJ 重复的 chóngfù de

rephrase v 重新措词 chóngxīn cuòcí, 换个说法 huàn gè shuōfa

replace v 1 替代 tìdài, 替换 tìhuan 2 放回 fànghuí

replacement N 接替 jiētì, 替代（物）tìdài (wù)
kneel replacement 膝部置换手术 xībù zhìhuàn shǒushù

replay v, N 1 重播 [+电视节目] chóngbō [+diànshì jiémù] 2 重新比赛 chóngxīn bǐsài

replenish v 再装满 zài zhuāngmǎn, 补充 bǔchōng

replete ADJ 充足的 chōngzú de, 充裕的 chōngyù de

replica N 复制品 fùzhìpǐn

replicate v 复制 fùzhì, 重做 zhòngzuò

reply I v 回答 huídá, 回复 huífù II N 回答 huídá, 答复 dáfù

report I N 报告 bàogào
report card（学生）成绩报告单 (xuésheng) chéngjì bàogàodān
II v 报告 bàogào

reporter N 记者 jìzhě

repose N, v 1 休息 xiūxi 2 安置 ānzhì

repository N 1 仓库 cāngkù 2 知识渊博的人／书 zhīshi yuānbó de rén/shū

repossess v 收回 shōuhuí

reprehensible ADJ 应受谴责的 yìng shòu qiānzé de

represent v 1 代表 dàibiǎo 2 象征 xiàngzhēng, 是…的象征 shì…de xiàngzhēng

representative I N 代表 dàibiǎo II ADJ 有代表性的 yǒu dàibiǎoxìng de

repress v 1 抑制 [+感情／冲动] yìzhì [+gǎnqíng/chōngdòng], 克制 kèzhì 2 镇压 [+抗议者] zhènyā [+kàngyìzhě]

reprieve N 1 缓解 huǎnjiě, 缓刑 huǎnxíng 2 死刑撤销令 sǐxíng chèxiāo lìng

reprimand v, N 谴责 qiānzé, 斥责 chìzé

reprint I v 重印 chóngyìn, 再版 zàibǎn II N 重印本 chóngyìn shū

reprisal N 报复（行动）bàofu (xíngdòng)

reprise N, v 重演 chóngyǎn, 重奏 chóngzòu

reproach N, v 责备 zébèi, 责怪 zéguài
beyond reproach 无可非议 wúkě fēiyì, 完全 wánquán

reproduce v 1 [生物+] 繁殖 [shēngwù+] fánzhí 2 复制 [+艺术品] fùzhì [+yìshùpǐn]

reproduction N 1 繁殖 fánzhí, 生殖 shēngzhí 2 复制（品）fùzhì (pǐn)
reproduction furniture 仿古家具 fǎnggǔ jiājù

reproductive ADJ 繁殖的 fánzhí de, 生殖的 shēngzhí de

reprove v 责备 zébèi, 指责 zhǐzé

reptile N 爬行动物 páxíng dòngwù

republic N 共和国 gònghéguó

republican I ADJ（美国）支持共和党的 (Měiguó) zhīchí Gònghédǎng de II N 1（美国）共和党支持者 (Měiguó)

Gònghédǎng zhīchízhě **2** 共和（国／政体）的 gònghé (guó/zhèngtǐ) de

repudiation N **1** 驳斥 bóchì **2** 拒绝（接受）jùjué (jiēshòu)

repugnant ADJ 强烈反感的 qiángliè fǎngǎn de, 极其厌恶的 jíqí yànwù de

repulse V **1** 使…强烈反感 shǐ…qiángliè fǎngǎn, 使…极其厌恶 shǐ…jíqí yànwù **2** 击退 jītuì, 打退 dǎtuì

repulsion N **1** 强烈反感 qiángliè fǎngǎn, 厌恶 yànwù **2** 排斥（力）páichì (lì)

repulsive ADJ 令人强烈反感的 lìngrén qiángliè fǎngǎn de, 令人厌恶的 lìng rén yànwù de

reputable ADJ 声誉良好的 shēngyù liánghǎo de, 有信誉的 yǒu xìnyù de

reputation N 名声 míngshēng, 名望 míngwàng

repute N 名声 míngshēng, 名望 míngwàng

request I N 请求 qǐngqiú, 要求 yāoqiú II V 请 qǐng, 请求 qǐngqiú

requiem N 安魂弥撒 ānhún mísa **2** 安魂曲 ānhún qū

require V **1** 需要 xūyào **2** 要求 yāoqiú

requirement N **1** 必需的事物 bìxū de shìwù **2** 规定的条件 guīdìng de tiáojiàn

requisite I ADJ 必要的 bìyào de, 必需的 bìxū de II N 必需的事物 bìxū de shìwù

reroute V 改变路线 gǎibiàn lùxiàn

rerun I N 重演的电影 chóngyǎn de diànyǐng, 重播的电视／广播节目 chóngbō de diànshì/guǎngbō jiémù II V 重演 [+电影] chóngyǎn [+diànyǐng], 重播 [+电视／广播节目] chóngbō [+diànshì/guǎngbō jiémù]

rescind V 废除 fèichú, 取消 qǔxiāo

rescue V, N 救援 jiùyuán, 营救 yíngjiù rescue team 救援队 jiùyuán duì, 营救人员 yíngjiù rényuán

research I V 研究 yánjiū, 调查 diàochá II N 研究 yánjiū research and development (R & D) 研究和开发 yánjiū he kāifā

resemblance N （外表的）相似 (wàibiǎo de) xiāngsì, 相像 xiāngxiàng to bear a resemblance to sb 长的很像某人 zhǎng de hěn xiàng mǒurén

resent V 怨恨 yuànhèn, 愤愤不平 fènfèn bùpíng

resentful ADJ 怨恨的 yuànhèn de, 十分不满的 shífèn bùmǎn de

reservation N **1** 保留 bǎoliú, 预订 yùdìng to make a reservation 预订 [+机票／旅馆房间] yùdìng [+jīpiào/lǚguǎn fángjiān] **2** 疑问 yíwèn to express reservation 表示怀疑 biǎoshì huáiyí

reserve I V 保留 bǎoliú, 预订 yùdìng to reserve the right (to do sth) 保留（做某事的）权利 bǎoliú (zuò mǒushì de) quánlì II N **1** 储备（金）chǔbèi (jīn) in reserve 备用 bèiyòng **2** 拘谨寡言 jūjǐn guǎyán to drop one's reserve 不再矜持 búzài jīnchí **3** （野生动物）保护区 (yěshēng dòngwù) bǎohùqū **4** 后备部队 hòubèibùduì

reserved ADJ 预订的 yùdìng de **2** 矜持的 jīnchí de, 拘谨寡言的 jūjǐn guǎyán de

reservoir N **1** 水库 shuǐkù **2** 储藏 chǔcáng vast reservoir of information on the Internet 互联网上大量的信息 hùliánwǎng shàng dàliàng díxìn xī

reshuffle N, V 调整 tiáozhěng, 改组 gǎizǔ

reside V 居住 jūzhù

residence N **1** 居住 jūzhù permanent residence 永久居住（权）yǒngjiǔ jūzhù (quán) **2** 寓所 yùsuǒ [M. WD 座 zuò] private residence 私人住宅 sīrén zhùzhái, 私寓 sīyù

residency N **1** （医生）住院实习（期）(yīshēng) zhùyuàn shíxí (qī) **2** 永久居住权 yǒngjiǔ jūzhù quán

resident I N **1** 居民 jūmín **2** 住院（实习）医生 zhùyuàn (shíxí) yīshēng II ADJ 居住的 jūzhù de resident artist in a university 大学常驻艺术家 dàxué chángzhù yìshùjiā

residential ADJ 住宅区的 zhùzháiqū de a leafy residential area 树木成荫的住宅区 shùmù chéngyìn de zhùzháiqū

residue N 残留（物）cánliú (wù), 剩余
（物）shèngyú (wù)

resign V 1 辞职 cízhí 2 (to resign oneself
to sth) 无可奈何地接受某事 wúkě nàihé
de jiēshòu mǒushì

resignation N 1 辞职 cízhí 2 顺从
shùncóng, 无可奈何地接受 wúkě nàihé
de jiēshòu

resigned ADJ 1 无可奈何的 wúkě
nàihé de 2 屈从的 qūcóng de, 顺从的
shùncóng de

resilience N 复苏的能力 fùsū de nénglì,
弹性 tánxìng

resin N（合成）树脂 (héchéng) shùzhī

resist V 1 抵抗 [+攻击] dǐkàng [+gōngjī],
抵制 dǐzhì 2 忍住 [+冲动] rěnzhù
[+chōngdòng], 顶住 dǐngzhù
to resist temptation 顶住诱惑 dǐngzhù
yòuhuò

resistance N 1 抵抗 dǐkàng, 抗拒 kàngjù
2（身体的）抵抗力 (shēntǐ de) dǐkànglì

resolute ADJ 坚决的 jiānjué de, 坚定的
jiāndìng de

resolution N 1 决议 juéyì
U.N. resolution 联合国的一项决议
Liánhéguó de yí xiàng juéyì
2 决定 juédìng, 决心 juéxīn
New Year's Resolutions 新年决心
xīnnián juéxīn
3 解决（办法）jiějué (bànfǎ)

resolve I V 1 决定 juédìng, 下决心 xià
juéxīn 2 解决 [+难题] jiějué [+nántí]
II N 决心 juéxīn
unyielding resolve 不可动摇的决心
bùkě dòngyáo de juéxīn

resonance N 1 嘹亮 liáoliàng, 洪亮 hóngliàng 2 共鸣 gòngmíng 3 共振 gòngzhèn

resonate V 1 回荡 huídàng 2 产生共鸣 /
共振 chǎnshēng gòngmíng/gòngzhèn

resort¹ I N 手段 shǒuduàn
the last resort 最后一招 zuìhòu yìzhāo
II V 求助于 qiúzhù yú, 诉诸 sùzhū
to resort to law 求助于法律 qiúzhù yú
fǎlǜ, 诉诸法律 sùzhū fǎlǜ

resort² N 度假地 dùjiàdì
summer resort 避暑地 bìshǔdì

resound V 回荡 huídàng, 回响 huíxiǎng

resounding ADJ 极响亮的 jí xiǎngliàng
de, 洪亮的 hóngliàng de

resource N 1 资源 zīyuán
natural resources 自然资源 zìrán zīyuán
2 资料 zīliào, 信息资源 xìnxī zīyuán

resourceful ADJ 办法很多的 bànfǎ hěn
duō de, 足智多谋的 zúzhì duōmóu de

respect I N 1 尊敬 zūnjìng
to pay last respects 向死者告别 xiàng
sǐzhě gàobié
2 尊重 zūnzhòng 3 方面 fāngmiàn
II V 1 尊敬 zūnjìng 2 尊重 zūnzhòng

respectable ADJ 1 体面的 [+外表] tǐmian
de [+wàibiǎo] 2 正派的 [+行为] zhèngpài de [+xíngwéi] 3 还过得去的 [+成绩]
hái guòdeqù de [+chéngjì]

respectful ADJ 恭敬的 gōngjìng de, 彬彬
有礼的 bīnbīn yǒulǐ de

respective ADJ 各自的 gèzì de

respiration N 呼吸 hūxī

respirator N 人工呼吸器 réngōng hūxīqì

respite N 暂停 zàntíng, 暂缓 zànhuǎn

resplendent ADJ 华丽的 huálì de, 辉煌的
huīhuáng de

respond V 1 反应 fǎnyìng 2 回答 huídá,
答复 dáfù

response N 反应 fǎnyìng

responsibility N 1 责任 zérèn 2 职责
zhízé

responsible ADJ 1 负有责任的 fùyǒu
zérèn de 2 有责任心的 yǒu zérènxīn de
3 负责的 fùzé de
to hold ... responsible 要…负责任
yào...fù zérèn

responsive ADJ 1 反应快的 fǎnyìng kuài
de, 机敏的 jīmǐn de
be responsive to treatment 容易治疗
的 róngyì zhìliáo de
2 同情的 tóngqíng de, 响应的 xiǎngyìng
de

rest¹ N 剩下的东西 shèngxia de dōngxi,
其余 qíyú

rest² I N 休息 xiūxi
rest home 疗养所 liáoyǎngsuǒ
II V 1 休息 xiūxi
rest assured 放心 fàngxīn
2 [死者+] 长眠 [sǐzhě+] chángmián

Rest in Peace (RIP) 安息 ānxī
3 (to rest upon) 依赖于 yīlàiyú, 依据 yījù
restate v 重申 chóngshēn, 换一种方式说 huàn yìzhǒng fāngshì shuō

restaurant N 饭店 fàndiàn [M. WD 家 jiā], 餐馆 cānguǎn [M. WD 家 jiā]

restful ADJ 使人心情平静的 shǐrén xīnqíng píngjìng de, 悠闲的 yōuxián de

restitution N 赔偿 péicháng

restive ADJ 不安宁的 bù ānníng de, 难控制的 nán kòngzhì de

restless ADJ 烦躁的 fánzào de, 静不下来的 jìng bú xià lái de

restoration N **1** 恢复 huīfù **2** 修复 xiūfù

restore v **1** 恢复 [+信心] huīfù [+xìnxīn], 回复 huífù **2** 修复 [+家具] xiūfù [+jiājù]

restrain v **1** 克制 kèzhì, 控制 kòngzhì **2** 制服 [+罪犯] zhìfú [+zuìfàn]

restraint N **1** 克制 kèzhì, 抑制 yìzhì **2** 限制 xiànzhì, 约束 yuēshù

restrict v 限制 xiànzhì

restricted ADJ **1** 受限制的 shòu xiànzhì de **2** 内部的 nèibù de, 不准外传的 bù zhǔn wàichuán de
restricted document 内部文件 nèibù wénjiàn

restriction N 限制 xiànzhì
to impose restrictions 加以限制 jiāyǐ xiànzhì

restrictive ADJ 限制（性）的 xiànzhì (xìng) de

restroom N 洗手间 xǐshǒujiān

restructure v 改组 gǎizǔ, 调整 [+组织] tiáozhěng [+zǔzhī]

result I N **1** 结果 jiéguǒ
as a result of 由于 yóuyú
2 效果 xiàoguǒ, 成果 chéngguǒ **3** 成绩 chéngjì, 业绩 yèjì II v 发生 fāshēng
to result from 起因于 qǐyīn yú, 是由于 shì yóuyú
to result in 造成了 zàochéng le

resultant ADJ 因而发生的 yīn'ér fāshēng de, 作为后果的 zuòwéi hòuguǒ de

resume v 重新开始 chóngxīn kāishǐ, 继续 jìxù
to resume one's position 恢复原职 huīfù yuánzhí

résumé N 个人简历 gèrén jiǎnlì, 履历 lǚlì

resurface v **1** 重新出现 chóngxīn chūxiàn, 重现 chóngxiàn **2** 重铺路面 chóng pūlù miàn

resurgence N 重新流行 chóngxīn liúxíng, 死灰复燃 sǐhuī fùrán

resurrection N 复活 fùhuó, 恢复 huīfù

resuscitate v 抢救 qiǎngjiù,（使…）恢复呼吸 (shǐ...) huīfù hūxī
Do not resuscitate. 不要抢救。 Búyào qiǎngjiù.

resuscitation N 抢救 qiǎngjiù

retail I N 零售 língshòu
a chain of retail stores 零售连锁店 língshòu liánsuǒdiàn
II ADV 以零售价（格）yǐ língshòujià (gé)
III v 零售 língshòu, 零卖 língmài

retailer N 零售商 língshòushāng, 零售（商）店 língshòu (shāng) diàn

retain v **1** 保留 bǎoliú **2** 记住 jìzhu **3** 付定金聘请 [+律师] fùdìng jīn pìnqǐng [+lǜshī]

retake v 收复 shōufù, 夺回 duóhuí

retaliate v 报复 bàofù, 反击 fǎnjī

retard I v 使…迟缓 shǐ...chíhuǎn, 阻碍 zǔ'ài II N 笨蛋 bèndàn

retarded ADJ 智力发展迟缓的 zhìlì fāzhǎn chíhuǎn de, 弱智的 ruòzhì de

retch v 恶心 èxīn, 作呕 zuò'ǒu

retention N 保留 bǎoliú, 留住 liúzhù

rethink v 重新考虑 chóngxīn kǎolǜ, 反思 fǎnsī

reticence N 沉默寡言 chénmò guǎyán

retina N 视网膜 shìwǎngmó

retinue N（一大批）随从 (yí dàpī) suícóng, 随行人员 suíxíng rényuán

retire v **1** 退休 tuìxiū **2** 退出（体坛）tuì chū (tǐtán)

retiree N 退休者 tuìxiūzhě

retirement N 退休 tuìxiū, 退休生活 tuìxiū shēnghuó
retirement home（退休）老人福利院 (tuìxiū) lǎorén fúlìyuàn

retort v, N 反驳 fǎnbó, 回嘴 huízuǐ

retract v **1** 正式收回 [+说过的话] zhèngshì shōuhuí [+shuōguòde huà] **2** 缩回 suōhuí

retraction N 正式收回 zhèngshì shōuhuí, 撤回 chèhuí

retread N 翻新的轮胎 fānxīn de lúntāi **2** 翻版 fānbǎn

retreat I v **1** [军队+] 撤退 [jūnduì+] chètuì **2** [撤回+] 承诺 [chèhuí+] chéngnuò **3** 往后退 wǎnghòu tuì II N **1** (军队) 撤退 (jūnduì) chètuì **2** (承诺的) 撤回 (chéngnuò de) chèhuí **3** 后退 hòutuì **4** 休养地 xiūyǎng dì

retrial N 重新审理 chóngxīn shěnlǐ, 重审 chóngshěn

retribution N 惩罚 chéngfá, 报应 bàoyìng

retrieve v **1** 收回 shōuhuí, 找到 zhǎodào **2** (计算机) 检索 (jìsuànjī) jiǎnsuǒ

retroactive ADJ 有追溯效力的 yǒu zhuīsù xiàolì de

retrospective ADJ 回顾的 huígù de

retry v 重新审理 [+案件] chóngxīn shěnlǐ [+ànjiàn], 重审 chóngshěn

return I v **1** 回 huí, 返回 fǎnhuí **2** 还 huán, 归还 guīhuán **3** 报复 huíbào, 报答 bàodá II N **1** 返回 fǎnhuí **2** 归还 guīhuán **3** 恢复 huīfù **4** 往返票 wǎngfǎn piào **5** (投资的) 回报 (tóuzī de) huíbào, 利润 lìrùn

returnable ADJ **1** 必须归回的 [+文件] bìxū guīhuí de [+wénjiàn] **2** 可以收回的 [+瓶子] kěyǐ shōuhuí de [+píngzi]

reunion N **1** 团聚 tuánjù **2** (校友) 聚会 (xiàoyǒu) jùhuì

reunite v (使⋯) 再联合 (shǐ⋯) zài liánhé, (使⋯) 重聚 (shǐ⋯) chóngjù **be reunited with sb** 与某人团聚 yǔ mǒurén tuánjù

rev I N 旋转一周 xuánzhuàn yìzhōu, 一转 yì zhuǎn II v (to rev up) 加快转速 jiākuài zhuǎnsù

revaluation N **1** (货币) 升值 (huòbì) shēngzhí **2** 重新估价 chóngxīn gūjià

revalue v **1** 使 [+货币] 升值 shǐ [+huòbì] shēngzhí **2** 重新估价 chóngxīn gūjià

revamp v 更新 gēngxīn, 修改 xiūgǎi

reveal v **1** 显露 xiǎnlù, 露出来 lòuchulai **2** 透露 tòulù, 揭露 jiēlù

revealing ADJ **1** 揭露性的 [+书／文章] jiēlùxìng de [+shū/wénzhāng] **2** 暴露的 [+衣服] bàolù de [+yīfu]

revel v **1** 狂欢 kuánghuān **2** (to revel in) 陶醉于 táozuì yú

revelation N **1** 揭露 jiēlù **2** 揭露出来的事 jiēlù chūlái de shì **3** (上帝的) 启示 (Shàngdì de) qǐshì

revelry N 狂欢 kuánghuān, 寻欢作乐 xúnhuān zuòlè

revenge N **1** 报仇 bàochóu, 复仇 fùchóu II v (为⋯) 报仇 (wéi⋯) bàochóu **be revenged on sb** 向某人报仇 xiàng mǒurén bàochóu **to revenge sb** 为某人报仇 wéi mǒurén bàochóu

revenue N 收入 shōurù

reverberate v 回响 huíxiǎng, 回荡 huídàng

revere v 尊敬 zūnjìng, 崇敬 chóngjìng

reverence N 尊敬 zūnjìng, 崇敬 chóngjìng

Reverend N 牧师 mùshi

reverie N 幻想 huànxiǎng, 梦想 mèngxiǎng

reversal N 倒转 dàozhuǎn, 逆转 nìzhuǎn **reversal of fortune** 时运倒转 shíyùn dàozhuǎn, 交恶运 jiāo èyùn

reverse I v **1** [汽车+] 倒退 [qìchē+] dàotuì **2** 颠倒 [+顺序] diāndǎo [+shùnxù] **3** 取消 [+原判] qǔxiāo [+yuánpàn] **to reverse a ruling** 取消裁决 qǔxiāo cáijué II N **1** [硬币的+] 背面 [yìngbì de+] bèimiàn **2** [工作中的+] 挫折 [gōngzuò zhòngde+] cuòzhé, 恶运 èyùn **3** (汽车的) 倒车挡 (qìchē de) dàochēdǎng **to put the car into reverse** 把车挂上倒车挡 bǎchē guàshang dàochēdǎng III ADJ 背面的 bèimiàn de, 反面的 fǎnmiàn de **reverse discrimination** 逆向歧视 nìxiàng qíshì

revert v 回复 [+到以前的情况] huífù [+dào yǐqián de qíngkuàng]

review I N **1** 复查 fùchá, 检查 jiǎnchá **2** 评论 pínglùn II v **1** 复查 fùchá, 检查 jiǎnchá **2** 写评论 xiě pínglùn **3** 复习功课 fùxí gōngkè

reviewer N 评论家 pínglùnjiā

revile v 辱骂 rǔmà, 谩骂 mànmà

revise v 1 修订 xiūdìng, 改正 gǎizhèng
2 复习（功课）fùxí (gōngkè)

revision N 修订 xiūdìng, 修正 xiūzhèng

revitalize v 使…重获新活力 shǐ...zhòng huò huólì, 使…新生 shǐ...xīnshēng

revival N 复兴 fùxīng, 再生 zàishēng

revive v 1（使…）苏醒（shǐ...）sūxíng
2 再次流行 zàicì liúxíng, 恢复 huīfù

revoke v 吊销 [+执照] diàoxiāo [+zhízhào], 废除 fèichú

revolt N, v 反叛 fǎnpàn, 起义 qǐyì

revolting ADJ 令人厌恶的 lìngrén yànwù de, 令人作呕的 lìngrén zuò'ǒu de

revolution N 1 革命 gémìng 2 重大变革 zhòngdà biàngé, 重大突变 zhòngdà tūbiàn 3 旋转一周 [太阳，行星+] xuánzhuǎn yìzhōu [tàiyáng, xíngxīng+]

revolve v 1（使…）旋转（shǐ...）xuánzhuǎn 2 (to revolve around) 围绕 wéirào

revolver N 左轮手枪 zuǒlúnshǒuqiāng

revue N（时事讽刺）歌舞表演 (shíshì fěngcì) gēwǔ biǎoyǎn

revulsion N 厌恶 yànwù, 憎恨 zēnghèn

reward I N 报偿 bàocháng, 报酬 bàochou [M. WD 份 fèn] II v 报偿 bàocháng, 报酬 bàochou, 奖赏 jiǎngshǎng

rewind (PT & PP **rewound**) v 倒回 dǎo huí

rewire v 更换路线 gēnghuàn lùxiàn

reword v 换个说法 huàn gè shuōfa

rework v 改编 gǎibiān

rewrite v 重写 zhòng xiě, 改写 gǎixiě

rhapsody N 1 狂想曲 kuángxiǎngqǔ [M. WD 首 shǒu] 2 赞美 zànměi

rhetorical ADJ 修辞的 xiūcí de
a rhetorical question 修辞性疑问句 xiūcíxìng yíwènjù

rheumatic ADJ 风湿病的 fēngshībìngde
rheumatic fever 风湿热 fēngshīrè

rheumatism N 风湿病 fēngshībìng

rhinoceros N 犀牛 xīniú [M. WD 头 tóu]

rhubarb N 大黄 dàihuáng

rhyme I N 1 韵 yùn, 韵脚 yùnjiǎo 2 同韵词 tóngyùncí II v 押韵 yāyùn

rhythm N 节奏 jiézòu

rib I N 1 肋骨 lèigǔ

rib cage 胸腔 xiōngqiāng
2 肋条肉 lèitiáo ròu [M. WD 块 kuài] II v 跟…开玩笑 gēn...kāi wánxiào

ribald ADJ 粗俗的 cūsú de, 下流的 xiàliú de

ribbon N 丝带 sīdài [M. WD 条 tiáo], 缎带 duàndài [M. WD 条 tiáo]

rice N 1 米饭 mǐfàn 2 米 mǐ, 稻米 dàomǐ
rice paddy（水）稻田 (shuǐ) dào tián

rich ADJ 1 富裕 fùyù, 富有的 fùyòu de 2 富有 fùyòu, 有丰富的 yǒu fēngfù de

riches N 财富 cáifù

richly ADV 1 富贵地 fùguì de, 华丽地 huálì de
richly flavored 味道浓郁的 wèidao nóngyù de
2 大量地 dàliàng de

rickets N 佝偻病 gōulóubìng

rickety ADJ 1 快要散架的 [+椅子] kuàiyào sǎnjià de [+yǐzi] 2 摇摇晃晃的 yáoyáo huǎnghuǎng de

rickshaw N 人力车 rénlìchē, 黄包车 huángbāochē

rid v (PT & PP **rid**) 摆脱 bǎituō
to get rid of 摆脱 bǎituō, 清除 qīngchú

riddance N (good riddance) 终于滚蛋了 zhōngyú gǔndàn le, 走得好 zǒu de hǎo

riddle N 1 谜（语）mí (yǔ) 2 奥秘 àomì

riddled ADJ 1 充满…的 chōngmǎn...de 2 到处是小洞的 dàochù shì xiǎodòng de

ride I v (PT **rode**; PP **ridden**) 1 骑 [+马 / 自行车] qí [+mǎ/zìxíngchē] 2 乘坐 [+火车] chéngzuò [+huǒchē] II N 乘 [+汽车 / 火车 / 摩托车] chéng [+qìchē/huǒchē/mótuōchē]
to take sb for a ride 欺骗某人 qīpiàn mǒurén

ridge N 山脊 shānjǐ

ridicule N, v 嘲笑 cháoxiào, 取笑 qǔxiào

ridiculous ADJ 可笑的 kěxiào de, 荒唐的 huāngtáng de

rife ADJ 流行的 liúxíng de, 普遍存在的 pǔbiàn cúnzài de

rifle¹ N 枪 qiāng, 步枪 bùqiāng

rifle² v 翻遍 [+抽屉] fān biàn [+chōutì]

rift N 1 裂缝 lièfèng 2 分裂 fēnliè, 分歧 fēnqí

rig I V **1** 操纵 [+选举] cāozòng [+xuǎnjǔ]
2 给 (船) 配备绳索帆具 gěi (chuan)
pèibèi shéngsuǒ fānjù II N (石油) 钻井
架 (shíyóu) zuān jǐngjià
rigging N 帆缆 fānlǎn, 帆具 fānjù

right I ADJ **1** 正确的 zhèngquè de, 对的 duì
de **2** 恰当的 qiàdàng de, 适当的 shìdàng
de **3** 右面的 yòumiàn de
right field (棒球) 右外场 (bàngqiú)
yòu wàichǎng
II ADV **1** 就 jiù, 正 zhèng **2** 正确地
zhèngquè de, 对 duì **3** 右面 yòumiàn
III N **1** 正确 zhèngquè, 正当 zhèngdàng
2 权利 quánlì **3** 右 yòu, 右面 yòumiàn
IV V (to right a wrong) 纠正错误
jiūzhèng cuòwù

righteous ADJ 正义的 zhèngyì de
righteous anger 义愤 yìfèn

righteousness N 正义 zhèngyì

rightful N 合法的 héfǎ de, 公正的
gōngzhèng de
a rightful owner 合法主人 héfǎ zhǔrén

right-hand ADJ 右边的 yòubian de, 右侧
的 yòucè de

rightly ADV 正确地 zhèngquè de, 有道理
的 yǒudào lǐ de

rights N 特许使用权 tèxǔ shǐyòngquán
property rights (法定) 房产使用权
(fǎdìng) fángchǎn shǐyòngquán

right-wing N, ADJ (政治) 右翼 (的)
(zhèngzhì) yòuyì (de)

rigid ADJ **1** 严格的 [+方法] yángé de
[+fāngfǎ] **2** 僵硬的 [+观点] jiāngyìng de
[+guāndiǎn]

rigidity N 严格 yángé, 僵硬 jiāngyìng

rigor N 严谨 yánjǐn

rigorous ADJ 严谨的 yánjǐn de, 严格的
yángé de

rile V 激怒 jīnù

rim I N 边缘 biānyuán II V 环绕 huánrào

rind N (水果的) 厚皮 (shuǐguǒ de) hòu
pí

ring[1] N **1** 戒指 jièzhi
ring finger 无名指 wúmíngzhǐ
2 环 huán, 圆圈 yuánquān
key ring 钥匙环 yàoshihuán
3 拳击／摔跤台 quánjī/shuāijiāo tái

to retire from the ring 退出拳击运动
tuìchū quánjī yùndòng
4 犯罪团伙 fànzuì tuánhuǒ

ring[2] I N **1** 铃声 língshēng
to have a familiar ring 听起来耳熟
tīngqilai ershú
2 语气 yǔqì
to have a ring of truth 听起来像真的
tīngqilai xiàng zhēnde
II V (PT rang; PP rung) **1** 按电铃 àn
diànlíng, 打铃 dǎlíng **2** [铃+] 响 [líng+]
xiǎng
to ring a bell 听起来耳熟 tīngqilai ershú

ringleader N (匪帮) 头目 (fěibāng)
tóumù

ringside N 台边区 tái biānqū
ringside seat 台边区前排座位 tái biān
qū qiánpáizuòwèi

ringworm N (头) 癣 (tóu) xuǎn

rink N 溜冰场 liūbīngchǎng, 旱冰场
hànbīngchǎng

rinse I V 冲洗 chōngxǐ II N **1** 冲洗 chōngxǐ
2 染发剂 rǎnfà jì

riot I N **1** 骚乱 sāoluàn, 暴乱 bàoluàn
riot police 防暴警察 fángbào jǐngchá
a riot of color 色彩绚丽 sècǎi xuànlì
II V 骚乱 sāoluàn, 闹事 nàoshì

RIP (= "Rest in Peace") ABBREV 安息 ānxī

rip I V 撕裂 sīliè
to rip into 不公平的猛烈抨击
bùgōngpíng de měngliè pēngjī
to rip sb off 欺诈 qīzhà, 多收钱 duō
shōuqián
II N 裂缝 lièfèng, 裂口 lièkǒu

ripe ADJ 成熟的 chéngshú de

ripen V (使…) 成熟 (shǐ…) chéngshú

ripoff N **1** 要价不合理的商品 yàojià bù
hélǐ de shāngpǐn, 宰人的东西 zǎirén de
dōngxi **2** (音像) 盗版 (yīnxiàng) dàobǎn

ripple I V 泛起微波 fàn qǐ wēibō II N 微波
细浪 wēibō xì làng
a ripple of laughter 一阵笑声 yízhèn
xiàoshēng
ripple effect 连锁反应 liánsuǒ fǎnyìng

rise I V (PT rose; PP risen) **1** 上涨 shàngzhǎng, 增加 zēngjiā **2** [太阳+] 升起 [tài-
yáng+] shēngqǐ **3** [社会地位+] 上升

[shèhuì dìwèi+] shàngshēng 4 起床 qǐchuáng
to rise to one's feet 站起来 zhànqǐlai
II N 增加 zēngjiā
to give rise to 引起 yǐnqǐ
risk I N 1 风险 fēngxiǎn
risk-free 没有风险的 méiyǒu fēngxiǎn de
to run the risk of ... 冒…的险 mào…de xiǎn
to take a risk 冒险 màoxiǎn
II V 冒险 màoxiǎn
riskiness N 冒险（性）màoxiǎn (xìng), 冒险的程度 màoxiǎn de chéngdù
risky ADJ 冒险的 màoxiǎn de
risqué ADJ 粗俗的 cūsú de, 色情的 sèqíng de
rite N 仪式 yíshì, 礼仪 lǐyí
ritual I N 1 仪式 yíshì, 礼仪 lǐyí, 惯例 guànlì, 老程式 lǎo chéngshì II ADJ 仪式的 yíshì de, 礼仪的 lǐyí de
rival I N （竞争）对手 (jìngzhēng) duì-shǒu II V 可与…相匹敌 kě yǔ…xiāng pǐdí, 与…旗鼓相当 yǔ…qígǔxiāngdāng
rivalry N 竞争 jìngzhēng, 争斗 zhēngdòu
gang rivalry 帮派争斗 bāngpài zhēngdòu
river N 河 hé, 江 jiāng
riverbed N 河床 héchuáng
riverside N 河边 hébiān
rivet I N 铆钉 mǎodīng [M. WD 枚 méi]
II V 1 用铆钉固定 yòng mǎodīng gùdìng 2 吸引 [+注意] xīyǐn [+zhùyì]
roach N 1 (= cockroach) 蟑螂 zhāngláng 2 （大麻烟的）烟蒂 (dàmáyān de) yāndì
road N 道路 dàolù [M. WD 条 tiáo], 公路 gōnglù [M. WD 条 tiáo]
main road 主要街道 zhǔyào jiēdào
side/back road 小路 xiǎolù
road test 道路试车 dàolù shìchē
roadblock N 路障 lùzhàng
roadkill N 公路上被压死的动物 gōnglù shàng bèi yā sǐde dòngwù
roadside N 路边 lùbiān, 路旁 lùpáng
roadway N 车行道 chēxíngdào
roadworthy ADJ 可以行驶的 kěyǐ xíngshǐ de, 可以上路的 kěyǐ shànglù de
roam V 漫步 mànbù, 闲逛 xiánguàng

roaming N 漫游 mànyóu
roar V, N （动物）吼叫 [dòngwù+] hǒujiào, 咆哮 páoxiào
roast I V 烤 kǎo, 烘 hōng II N 1 烤肉 kǎoròu 2 露天烧烤聚会 lùtiān shāokǎo jùhuì III ADJ 烤好的 kǎo hǎode
roast beef 烤牛肉 kǎoniúròu
rob V 抢 qiǎng, 抢劫 qiǎngjié
robber N 强盗 qiángdào, 抢劫犯 qiǎngjié fàn
robbery N 抢劫 qiǎngjié
robe N 1 [法官的+] 长袍 [fǎguān de+] chángpáo 2 睡袍 shuìpáo [M. WD 件 jiàn]
robot N 机器人 jīqì rén
robotics N 机器人制造及运用研究 jīqìrén zhìzào jí yùnyòng yánjiū, 机器人学 jīqìrénxué
robust ADJ 1 健壮的 [+人] jiànzhuàng de [+rén] 2 健全的 [+组织] jiànquán de [+zǔzhī] 3 坚固的 [+房屋] jiāngù de [+fángwū]
rock¹ N 石头 shítou [M. WD 块 kuài], 岩石 yánshí
rock² I V 1 摇动 yáodòng
The hand that rocks the cradle rules the world. 摇动摇篮的手统治世界。 Yáodòng yáolán de shǒu tǒngzhì shìjiè.
2 剧烈震动 jùliè zhèndòng II N 摇滚音乐 yáogǔn yīnyuè
rock 'n' roll 摇滚乐 yáogǔnyuè
rock bottom I N 谷底 gǔdǐ II ADJ 最低的 zuìdī de
rock bottom prices 最低价 zuìdījià, 跳楼价 tiàolóu jià
to hit rock bottom 达到最坏的境况 dádào zuì huài de jìngkuàng, 陷入谷底 xiànrù gǔdǐ
rocker N 1 摇椅 yáoyǐ [M. WD 把 bǎ] 2 摇滚乐手 yáogǔnyuè shǒu [M. WD 名 míng]
rocket I N 火箭 huǒjiàn
rocket scientist 火箭专家 huǒjiàn zhuānjiā, 极其聪明博学的人 jíqí cōngming bóxué de rén
II V 迅速上升 xùnsù shàngshēng, 猛增 měngzēng

rocky ADJ **1** 多岩石的 duō yánshí de **2** 困难重重的 kùnnan chóngchóng de

rod N 杆 gǎn, 棍 gùn

rodent N 啮齿动物 nièchǐ dòngwù, 老鼠 lǎoshu, 松鼠 sōngshǔ

rodeo N 牛仔竞技表演 niúzǎi jìngjì biǎoyǎn

roe N 鱼籽 yúzǐ

rogue[1] ADJ 不守规矩的 bù shǒu guīju de, 制造麻烦的 zhìzào máfan de

rogue[2] N 恶棍 ègùn, 坏蛋 huàidàn

roguish ADJ 淘气的 táoqì de, 调皮的 tiáopí de

role N **1** 作用 zuòyòng **2** 角色 juésè
　leading role 主要人物 zhǔyào rénwù, 主角 zhǔjué
　a role model 榜样 bǎngyàng, 楷模 kǎimó

role-play N 角色扮演 juésè bànyǎn

roll I V **1** 滚 gǔn, 滚动 gǔndòng **2** 转动 zhuàndòng **3** 卷起 juǎnqǐ **4** 轧平 yàpíng II N **1** 卷 juàn **2** 名单 míngdān
　roll call 点名 diǎnmíng
　3 小圆面包 xiǎo yuán miànbāo

roller N **1** 滚筒 gǔntǒng **2** 卷发夹 juǎnfà jiā

roller coaster N 过山车 guòshānchē, 云霄飞车 yúnxiāo fēi chē

roller skate I N 旱冰鞋 hànbīngxié II V 溜旱冰 liū hànbīng

rollicking ADJ 热闹的 rènao de, 喧闹的 xuānnào de

rolling ADJ 连绵起伏的 liánmiánqǐfú de

rolling-pin N 擀面棍 gǎnmiàn gùn

roly-poly ADJ 圆圆胖胖的 yuányuán pàngpàng de

ROM (= Read-Only Memory) ABBREV （计算机）只读存储器 (jìsuànjī) zhǐ dú cúnchǔ qì

Roman Catholic N 罗马天主教会 Luómǎ Tiānzhǔ jiàohuì

romantic I ADJ 浪漫的 làngmàn de II N **1** 浪漫的人 làngmàn de rén, 爱幻想的人 ài huànxiǎng de rén **2** 浪漫主义者 làngmànzhǔyìzhě

romp I V 追赶打闹 zhuī pǎo dǎnào II N 嬉闹 xīnào, 玩耍 wánshuǎ

roof I N 屋顶 wūdǐng, 车顶 chēdǐng
　a roof over one's head 栖身之地 qīshēn zhī dì
　under one roof 住在同一所房子 zhù zài tóng yì suǒ fángzi
II V 盖屋顶 gài wūdǐng
　tile-roofed 瓦屋顶 wǎwū dǐng

roofing N 盖层面材料 gàicéng miàn cáiliào

roofrack N （汽车）车顶（行李）架 (qìchē) chēdǐng (xíngli) jià

rooftop N 屋顶 wūdǐng

rookie N 新队员 xīn duìyuán, 新人 xīnrén

room I N **1** 房间 fángjiān **2** 空间 kōngjiān **3** 余地 yúdì
　room and board 供应住宿和膳食 gōngyìng zhùsù hé shànshí
　room service 客房（用餐）服务 kèfáng (yòngcān) fúwù
　to room with sb 和某人同住一室 hé mǒurén tóng zhù yí shì

roommate N 室友 shìyǒu

roost I N （鸟的）栖息处 (niǎo de) qīxī chù, 鸟窝 niǎowō, 鸟巢 niǎocháo II V [鸟+] 栖息 [niǎo+] qīxī
　has come home to roost 来报应 láibào yìng

rooster N 公鸡 gōngjī, 雄鸡 xióngjī [M. WD 只 zhī]

root I N **1** 根 gēn, 根子 gēnzi **2** （家族的）根 (jiāzú de) gēn, 老根 lǎo gēn
　root beer 根汁汽水 gēn zhī qìshuǐ
　3 根源 gēnyuán II V [植物+] 生根 [zhíwù+] shēnggēn

rootless ADJ 无根的 wú gēn de, 无归属感的 wú guīshǔ gǎn de

rope I N 绳 shéng, 绳子 shéngzi, 绳索 shéngsuǒ II V 用绳子捆绑 yòng shéngzi kǔnbǎng

rosary N 念珠 niànzhū

rose[1] N **1** 玫瑰 méiguì, 玫瑰花 méiguihuā **2** 粉红色 fěnhóngsè

rose[2] V See **rise**

roster N 名单 míngdān, 值勤表 zhíqín biǎo
　duty roster 值勤表 zhíqín biǎo, 值日表 zhírìbiǎo

rostrum N 讲台 jiǎngtái

rosy ADJ 1 玫瑰色的 méiguīsè de, 粉红色的 fěnhóngsè de 2 美好的 měihǎo de, 充满希望的 chōngmǎn xīwàng de

rot I v 烂 làn, 腐烂 fǔlàn II N 1 腐烂（的过程）fǔlàn (de guòchéng) 2（制度的）腐败 (zhìdù de) fǔbài

rotary ADJ 旋转的 xuánzhuǎn de

rotate v 1（使⋯）旋转 (shǐ...) xuán-zhuǎn,（使⋯）转动 (shǐ...) zhuàndòng 2 轮换 lúnhuàn, 轮流 lúnliú

rotation N 1 选转 xuánzhuǎn 2 轮换 lúnhuàn

rote N 死记硬背 sǐjì yìngbèi

rote learning 死记硬背的学习方法 sǐjì yìngbèi de xuéxí fāngfǎ

rotor N 转动件 zhuàndòng jiàn, 转子 zhuànzǐ

rotten ADJ 1 腐烂的 fǔlàn de, 变质的 biànzhì de 2 糟透的 zāotòu de

rotund ADJ 圆胖的 yuán pàng de

rotunda N 圆形建筑物 yuánxíng jiànzhù wù

rouge N 胭脂 yānzhi

rough I ADJ 1 高低不平的 gāodī bù píng de 2 粗暴的 cūbào de 3 粗略的 cūlüè de II v (to rough it out) 过艰苦的生活 guò jiānkǔ de shēnghuó, (rough sb up) 殴打某人 ōudǎ mǒurén III N 1（高尔夫球场的）深草区 (gāo'ěrfū qiúchǎng de) shēn cǎo qū 2 草图 cǎotú, 略图 lüètú

to take the rough with the smooth 既能享受也能吃苦 jì néng xiǎngshòu yě néng chīkǔ, 能伸能屈 néng shēn néng qū IV ADV 粗野（地）cūyě (de)

roughage N（食物中的）粗纤维 (shíwù zhòngde) cūxiānwéi

rough-and-tumble ADJ（很多人）残酷竞争的 (hěn duō rén) cánkù jìngzhēng de

roughhouse v 打闹 dǎnào, 殴斗 ōudòu

roughly ADV 大致上 dàzhìshàng, 大约 dàyuē

roughshod ADJ (to run roughshod over sth) 粗暴对待某事物 cūbào duìdài mǒushìwù

roulette N 轮盘赌 lúnpándǔ

round I ADJ 1 圆的 yuán de 2 整数的 zhěngshù de 3 来回的 láihuí de, 往返的 wǎngfǎn de II N 1 一系列（事件）yíxìliè (shìjiàn)

the next round of talks 下一轮会谈 xià yì lún huìtán

2（比赛的）一轮 (bǐsài de) yìlún, 一局 yìjú, 一场 yìchǎng 3 巡访 xún fǎng, （医生的）定期出诊 (yīshēng de) dìngqī chūzhěn

a mailman's rounds 邮递员的定时递信 yóudìyuán de dìngqī dìxìn

4 一发（子弹）yìfā (zǐdàn), 一次（射击）yícì (shèjī) III v 环绕 huánrào

to round sb up 聚拢 jùlǒng

IV ADV 旋转（地）xuánzhuǎn (de)

round about 大约 dàyuē

V PREP 围绕 wéirào

roundabout ADJ 拐弯抹角的 guǎiwān mǒjiǎo de

round-the-clock ADJ 日夜的 rìyè de, 二十四小时的 èrshísì xiǎoshí de

round-trip ADJ 往返的 wǎngfǎn de

rouse v 1 唤醒 huànxǐng 2 振奋 zhènfèn, 激励 jīlì 3 引起⋯的兴趣 yǐnqǐ...de xìngqu

rousing ADJ 激励人的 jīlì rén de

rout v, N 彻底击败 chèdǐ jībài, 溃败 kuìbài

route I N 1 路线 lùxiàn 2 航线 hángxiàn, 行车路线 xíngchē lùxiàn

bus route 公共汽车路线 gōnggòng qìchē lùxiàn

3 [做事的+] 方法 [zuòshì de+] fāngfǎ 4 公路 gōnglù

route 68 68号公路 68 hào gōnglù

II v 按特定路线传送 àn tèdìng lùxiàn chuánsòng

routine I N 常规 chángguī, 例行公事 lìxíng gōngshì

daily routine 每天的例行公事 měitiān de lìxíng gōngshì

II ADJ 惯例的 guànlì de, 例行的 lìxíng de

roving ADJ (a roving reporter) 巡回（记者）xúnhuí (jìzhě)

row¹ N 排 pái II v 划华 huá, 划船 huáchuán

in a row 连续 liánxù

row² N, V（大声）吵架 (dàshēng) chǎojià

rowboat N 划艇 huátǐng [M. wp 艘 sōu]

rowdy ADJ 吵吵闹闹的 chǎochǎo nàonào de, 粗野的 cūyě de

royal N, ADJ 王室（的）wáng shì (de), 皇家（的）huángjiā (de)

royalty N 1 版税 bǎnshuì, 稿费 gǎofèi
a royalty of 7% for each copy sold 每出售一本得稿费7% měi chūshòu yìběn dé gǎofèi 7%
2 王室成员 wángshì chéngyuán, 皇族成员 huángzú chéngyuán

RSVP (= Repondez s'il vous plaît) ABBREV 敬请赐复 jìngqǐng cì fù

rub I v 擦 cā, 摩擦 mócā
to rub sb the wrong way 惹怒某人 rěnù mǒurén
to rub salt into a wound 雪上加霜 xuě shàng jiā shuāng
II N 擦 cā, 摩擦 mócā
the rub 问题 wèntí, 难题 nántí

rubber N 橡皮 xiàngpí
rubber band 橡皮筋 xiàngpíjīn

rubbery ADJ 橡皮似的 xiàngpí shìde

rubbish I N 1 胡说八道 húshuō bādào, 废话 fèihuà **2** 垃圾 lājī II v 把…说得一无所是 bǎ...shuó de yīwú suǒ shì

rubble N 瓦砾 wǎlì

rubdown N 1 按摩 ànmó **2** 擦平 mópíng

ruby N 红宝石 hóngbǎoshí [M. WD 颗 kē]

rudder N（方向）舵 (fāngxiàng) duò

ruddy ADJ（脸色+）红润的 [liǎnsè+] hóngrùn de, 气色很好的 qìsè hěn hǎo de

rude ADJ 粗鲁的 cūlǔ de, 无礼的 wúlǐ de
a rude awakening 突然发觉 tūrán fājué

rudimentary ADJ 基本的 jīběn de, 初浅的 chūqiǎn de

rudiments N 基础（部份）jīchǔ (bùfen)

rue v 后悔 hòuhuǐ, 懊悔 àohuǐ

ruffle I v 把…弄乱 bǎ...nòngluàn
to ruffle sb's feathers 使别人不快 shǐ biérén bùkuài
II N（衣服的）褶边 (yīfu de) zhě biān

rug N 小地毯 xiǎo dìtǎn [M. WD 块 kuài]

rugby N（英式）橄榄球 (Yīngshì) gǎnlǎnqiú

rugged ADJ 1 高低不平的 [+地形] gāodī bùpíng de [+dìxíng], 崎岖的 qíqū de

2 坚固的 [+汽车] jiāngù de [+qìchē], 结实的 jiēshí de **3** 粗犷的 [+容貌] cūguǎng de [+róngmào] **4** 自信的 [+人] zìxìn de [+rén]
rugged individualism 自信而粗犷的个人主义 zìxìn ér cūguǎng de gèrénzhǔyì

ruin I v 1 毁灭 huǐmiè, 毁坏 huǐhuài **2** 使…破产 shǐ... pòchǎn II N 毁坏 huǐhuài
ruins 废墟 fèixū

rule I N 1 规则 guīzé **2** 统治 tǒngzhì, 执政 zhízhèng II v 1 统治 tǒngzhì, 执政 zhízhèng **2**（法庭+）裁决 [fǎtíng+] cáijué
as a rule 通常 tōngcháng

ruler N 1 统治者 tǒngzhìzhě **2** 尺 chǐ

ruling I N（法庭的）裁决 (fǎtíng de) cáijué, 裁定 cáidìng II ADJ 执政的 zhízhèng de

rum N 朗姆酒 Lǎngmǔjiǔ

rumble I v 1 发出隆隆声 fāchū hōnglōng shēng **2** [肚子饿得+] 咕咕叫 [dùzi è dé+] gūgū jiào II N 隆隆声 hōnglōng shēng

ruminate v 1 长时间沉思 chángshíjiān chénsī **2** [动物的+] 反刍 [dòngwù de+] fǎnchú

rummage v 翻找 fānzhǎo
rummage sale 旧物义卖 jiùwù yìmài

rumor N 谣传 yáochuán, 谣言 yáoyán

rump N 臀部 túnbù

rumple v 把…弄皱 bǎ...nòng zhòu

run I v (PT ran; PP run) **1** 跑 pǎo, 奔跑 bēnpǎo **2** 管理 guǎnlǐ **3** 行驰 xíngchí **4** 运行 yùnxíng **5** 流 liú, 流淌 liútǎng **6** 竞选 jìngxuǎn
to run across/into 遇见 yùjiàn
to run after ① 追 zhuī ② 追求 zhuīqiú
to run out of 用完 yòngwán
to run through 快快检查 kuàikuài jiǎnchá
II N 1 跑步 pǎobù
to do sth on the run 边跑边做事 biān pǎo biān zuòshì, 急急匆匆 jíjí cōngcōng
to be on the run 东藏西躲 dōngcángxīduǒ
2 竞选 jìngxuǎn **3** 挤兑（银行）jǐduì (yínxíng), 抛售（货币）pāoshòu (huòbì) **4**（棒球比赛）一分 (bàngqiú bǐsài) yìfēn

runaway I N 离家出走的儿童 líjiā chūzǒu de értóng **II** ADJ **1** 离家出走的 líjiā chūzǒu de **2** 失控的 [+车辆] shīkòng de [+chēliàng]
a runaway success 迅速的成功 xùnsù de chénggōng

run-down[1] ADJ **1** 破旧的 [+房屋] pòjiù de [+fángwū] **2** 虚弱的 [+人] xūruò de [+rén]

run-down[2] N 简报 jiǎnbào, 要点 yàodiǎn

rung[1] See ring (v)

rung[2] N **1** (梯子的) 横档 (tīzi de) héngdàng **2** (社会) 等级 (shèhuì) děngjí, 地位 dìwèi

run-in N 争吵 zhēngchǎo

runner N **1** 参加赛跑的人 cānjiā sàipǎo de rén **2** 雪橇滑板 xuěqiāo huábǎn **3** (a drug runner) 走私毒品的人 zǒusī dúpǐn de rén

runner-up N 亚军 yàjūn, 第二名 dìèrmíng

running N **1** 跑步 pǎobù, 赛跑 sàipǎo
running commentary 现场实况报道 xiànchǎng shíkuàng bàodào
running mate 竞选伙伴 jìngxuǎnhuǒbàn
running water 自来水 zìláishuǐ
in running order (机器) 运行正常 (jīqì) yùnxíng zhèngcháng **2** 经营 jīngyíng, 管理 guǎnlǐ

runny ADJ 流鼻涕眼泪的 liú bítì yǎnlèi de

run-of-the-mill ADJ 极普通的 jí pǔtōng de, 很一般的 hěn yìbān de

run-up N (跳高时的) 助跑 (tiàogāo shí de) zhùpǎo
the run-up to sth 某事件的前奏 mǒu shìjiàn de qiánzòu

runway N (机场) 跑道 (jīchǎng) pǎodào

rupture I V **1** 破裂 pòliè **II** V (使…) 破裂 (shǐ...) pòliè

rural ADJ 农村的 nóngcūn de

ruse N 诡计 guǐjì

rush I V **1** 匆匆来去 cōngcōng láiqù **2** 催促 cuīcù **II** N **1** 匆忙 cōngmáng, 赶紧 gǎnjǐn **2** 繁忙时期 fánmáng shíqī
the Christmas rush 圣诞节前的购物忙季 Shèngdànjié qián de gòuwù mángjì
rush hour (交通) 高峰时间 (jiāotōng) gāofēng shíjiān

Russian I ADJ 俄国的 Éguóde, 俄国人的 Éguórén de, 俄语的 Éyǔ de **II** N **1** 俄国人 Éguórén **2** 俄语 Éyǔ

rust I N **1** 铁锈 tiěxiù **2** (植物的) 锈病 (zhíwù de) xiùbìng **II** V (使…) 生锈 (shǐ...) shēngxiù

rustle I V (使…) 沙沙作响 (shǐ...) shāshā zuòxiǎng **II** N 沙沙声 shāshā shēng

rustproof ADJ 防锈的 fángxiù de

rusty ADJ **1** 生锈的 shēngxiù de **2** 荒废的 huāngfèi de, 生疏的 shēngshū de

rut N 车辙 chēzhé
be stuck in a rut 刻板而乏味地生活 kèbǎn ér fáwèi de shēnghuó, 没有新意 méiyǒu xīnyì

ruthless ADJ 无情的 wúqíng de, 冷酷的 lěngkù de

rye N 裸麦 luǒmài

S

Sabbath N 安息日 Ānxīrì

sabbatical N (大学教师) 学术休假 (dàxué jiàoshī) xuéshù xiūjià

saber N **1** 佩剑 pèijiàn [M. WD 把 bǎ], 花剑 huājiàn **2** 军刀 jūndāo, 马刀 mǎdāo

sable N **1** 貂皮 diāopí [M. WD 张 zhāng] **2** 貂 diāo [M. WD 只 zhī]

saccharine ADJ **1** 过分甜蜜的 guòfèn tiánmì de **2** 自作多情的 zìzuò duōqíng de, 肉麻的 ròumá de

sabotage V, N (蓄意) 破坏 (xùyì) pòhuài

sac N (动植物的) 囊 (dòngzhíwù de) nāng

saccharine ADJ **1** 过分甜蜜的 guòfèn tiánmì de **2** 自作多情的 zìzuò duōqíng de, 肉麻的 ròumá de

sachet N 香袋 xiāngdài

sack[1] N **1** 大厚纸袋 dà hòu zhǐdài **2** 麻袋 mádài [M. WD 只 zhī], 粗衣袋 cū yīdài

sack[2] V **1** (橄榄球) 擒抱 [+四分卫] (gǎnlǎnqiú) qín bào [+sì fēn wèi] **2** 解雇 [+工人] jiěgù [+gōngrén] **3** [军队+] 洗劫 [jūnduì+] xǐjié **4** (to sack out) 上床睡觉 shàngchuáng shuìjiào

sacrament N (基督教) 圣餐 (Jīdūjiào) Shèngcān, 圣事 Shèngshì

sacred ADJ **1** 神圣的 shénshèng de **2** 神的 shén de, 宗教的 zōngjiào de sacred cow 神圣的信条 shénshèngde xìntiáo

sacrifice I v 牺牲 [+自己的利益] xīshēng [+zìjǐ de lìyì], 放弃 fàngqì **II** N 牺牲 xīshēn

the ultimate supreme sacrifice 牺牲自己的生命 xīshēng zìjǐ de shēngmìng, 捐躯 juānqū

sacrilege N 1 亵渎神明（的行为）xièdú shénmíng (de xíngwéi) 2 不敬（行为）bújìng (xíngwéi)

sad ADJ 悲哀的 bēi'āi de, 难过的 nánguò de, 伤心的 shāngxīn de

saddle I N 1 马鞍 mǎ'ān 2（自行车／摩托车）车座 (zìxíngchē/mótuōchē) chēzuò **II** v 装马鞍 zhuāng mǎ'ān

saddlebag N 1（马）鞍囊 (mǎ) ānnáng 2（自行车／摩托车车座后的）工具袋 (zìxíngchē/mótuōchē chēzuò hòu de) gōngjùdài, 挂包 guàbāo

sadly ADV 1 伤心地 shāngxīn de 2 很可惜 hěn kěxī, 说来伤心 shuōlái shāngxīn

safari N 非洲野外观兽旅行 Fēizhōu yěwài guān shòu lǚxíng

safe I ADJ 安全的 ānquán de, 保险的 bǎoxiǎn de

to be on the safe side 为了安全（起见）wèile ānquán (qǐjiàn)

safe sex 安全性交 ānquánxìng jiāo **II** N 保险箱 bǎoxiǎnxiāng, 保险柜 bǎoxiǎnguì

safe-deposit box N（银行）保险箱 (yínháng) bǎoxiǎn xiāng

safeguard I N 保护（性）措施 bǎohù (xìng) cuòshī, 安全措施 ānquán cuòshī **II** v 保护 bǎohù, 保卫 bǎowèi

safekeeping N 妥善保管 tuǒshàn bǎoguǎn

for safekeeping 以便妥善保管 yǐbiàn tuǒshàn bǎoguǎn

safety N 安全 ānquán

Safety first. 安全第一。Ānquán dìyī.
safety belt 安全带 ānquándài
safety valve 安全阀 ānquánfá

sag v 1 [肌肉+] 下垂 [jīròu+] xiàchuí, 下陷 xiàxiàn 2 [价格+] 下跌 [jiàgé+] xiàdiē, 下降 xiàjiàng

saga N 长篇家族史 chángpiān jiāzú shǐ

sage I N 圣人 shèngrén, 哲人 zhérén **II** ADJ 贤明的 xiánmíng de, 明智的 míngzhì de

said I v See say **II** ADJ 上述的 shàngshù de

sail I N 1 帆 fān [M. WD 张 zhāng] 2 起航 qǐháng **II** v 航行 hángxíng

sailboat N 帆船 fānchuán [M. WD 艘 sōu]

sailing N 1 帆船运动 fānchuán yùndòng 2 启程时间 qǐchéng shíjiān, 航班 hángbān

smooth sailing 一帆风顺 yì fān fēng shùn

sailor N 水手 shuǐshǒu, 海员 hǎiyuán

saint N 1 圣人 shèngrén 2 道德高尚的人 dàodé gāoshàng de rén, 仁慈的人 réncí de rén, 大好人 dà hǎorén

sake N (for the sake of sb/sth) 为了某人／某事 wèile mǒurén/mǒushì

salable, saleable ADJ 可以出售的 kěyǐ chūshòu de

salad N 凉拌菜沙律 liángbàncài shālù, 色拉 sèlā

salad bar 凉拌菜自助柜 liángbàncài zìzhùguì
salad dressing 凉拌菜调味酱 liáng-bàncài tiáowèi jiàng

salary N 工资 gōngzī, 薪水 xīnshui

sale N 1 卖 mài, 出售 chūshòu 2 减价出售 jiǎnjià chūshòu

clearance sale 清仓大拍卖 qīngcāng dà pāimài
on sale ① 在出售 zài chūshòu, 在上市 zài shàngshì ② 在减价出售 zài jiǎnjià chūshòu

sales N 销售额量 xiāoshòu'é liàng

sales representative 销售代表 xiāoshòu dàibiǎo
sales slip (receipt) 购物发票 gòuwù fāpiào
sales tax 销售税 xiāoshòushuì

salesperson N 推销员 tuīxiāoyuán, 售货员 shòuhuòyuán

salient ADJ 显著的 xiǎnzhe de, 明显的 míngxiǎn de

saline I ADJ（含）盐的 (hán) yán de **II** N 生理盐水 shēnglǐ yánshuǐ

saliva N 口水 kǒushuǐ, 唾沫 tuòmo

salivate V 流口水 liú kǒushuǐ, 垂涎 (三尺) chuíxián (sānchǐ)

sallow ADJ 灰黄色的 huīhuáng sè de

salmon N 鲑鱼 guīyú [M. WD 条 tiáo], 大马哈鱼 dàmǎhǎyú [M. WD 条 tiáo]

salon N 院 yuàn, 厅 tīng, 店 diàn
beauty salon 美容厅 měiróngtīng
bridal salon 婚纱店 hūnshādiàn

saloon N 1 客厅 kètīng 2 酒吧 jiǔbā

salt N 盐 yán
salt shaker 盐瓶 yánpíng
the salt of the earth 平凡而诚实的好人 píngfán ér chéngshí de hǎorén, 社会中坚力量 shèhuì zhōngjiān lìliàng
to take sth with a pinch of salt 不完全相信某事 bù wánquán xiāngxìn mǒushì

saltwater N 海水 hǎishuǐ, 咸水 xiánshuǐ

salty ADJ 1 咸 (的) xián (de) 2 粗俗的 cūsú de

salutation N 称呼 (语) chēnghu (yǔ)

salute I V 1 向…敬礼 xiàng…jìnglǐ, 行军礼 xíngjūn lǐ 2 赞扬 zànyáng II N 敬礼 jìnglǐ, 致敬 zhìjìng

salvage I V 1 抢救 qiǎngjiù 2 挽救 wǎnjiù, 挽回 wǎnhuí II N 1 抢救 qiǎngjiù, 救援 jiùyuán 2 抢救出来的东西 qiǎngjiù chūlái de dōngxi

salvation N (基督教) 拯救 (Jīdūjiào) zhěngjiù, 挽救 wǎnjiù
Salvation Army (基督教) 救世军 (Jīdūjiào) Jiùshìjūn

salve I N 1 宽慰 kuānwèi, 缓解 huǎnjiě 2 (解痛) 软膏 (jiětòng) ruǎngāo II V (to salve one's conscience) 使良心得到宽慰 shǐ liángxīn dédào kuānwèi

salvo N (大炮) 齐放 (dàpào) qífàng

Samaritan N 助人为乐者 zhù rén wéi lè zhě

same I ADJ 相同的 xiāngtóng de, 同样的 tóngyàng de
at the same time 同时 tóngshí
same difference 都一样 dōu yíyàng
II PRON 同样的人／物 tóngyàng de rén/wù

sample I N 样品 yàngpǐn II V 试 shì, 试用 shìyòng

random sample 抽样 chōuyàng

sampling N 抽样调查 chōuyàng diàochá

samurai N (古代日本的) 武士 (gǔdài Rìběn de) wǔshì

sanatorium, sanitorium N 疗养院 liáoyǎngyuàn

sanctify V 1 使…神圣化 shǐ…shénshèng huà 2 认可 rènkě

sanction I N (sanctions) 批准 pīzhǔn, 认可 rènkě
to break sanctions 打破制裁 dǎpò zhìcái
to impose sanctions on 对…实施制裁 duì…shíshí zhìcái
to lift sanctions 取消制裁 qǔxiāo zhìcái
II V 1 制裁 zhìcái 2 批准 pīzhǔn, 许可 xǔkě

sanctity N 神圣 (性) shénshèng (xìng)

sanctuary N 1 避难所 bìnànsuǒ, 庇护所 bìhùsuǒ
to give sanctuary to 提供避难 (所) tígōng bìnàn (suǒ)
to seek sanctuary 寻求庇护 xúnqiú bìhù
2 (动物) 保护区 (dòngwù) bǎohùqū
wildlife sanctuary 野生动物保护区 yěshēng dòngwù bǎohùqū

sand I N 沙 shā
sand dune 沙丘 shāqiū
II V 磨光 móguāng

sandal N 凉鞋 liángxié [M. WD 双 shuāng]

sandbag I N 沙包 shābāo, 沙袋 shādài
II V 用沙包堵 yòng shābāo dǔ

sandbank N 沙坝 shābà

sandbox N 沙箱 shāxiāng, 沙坑 shākēng

sandcastle N (在海滩堆成的) 沙堡 (zài hǎitān duī chéng de) shābǎo

sandpaper I N 1 砂纸 shāzhǐ, 沙皮纸 shāpí zhǐ II V 用砂纸打磨 yòng shāzhǐ dǎmó

sandstone N 砂岩 shāyán

sandstorm N 沙 (尘) 暴 shā (chén) bào

sandwich I N 1 夹心面包 jiāxīn miànbāo, 三明治 sānmíngzhì
club sandwich 大三明治 dà sānmíngzhì
II V (be sandwiched between) 被夹在…中间 bèi jiā zài…zhōngjiān

sandy ADJ 1 被沙覆盖的 bèi shā fùgài de 2 浅黄色的 qiǎnhuángsè de

sane ADJ 头脑清醒的 tóunǎo qīngxǐng de, 明智的 míngzhì de

sang See sing

sanguine ADJ 乐观的 lèguān de, 充满自信的 chōngmǎn zìxìn de

sanitary ADJ (清洁) 卫生的 (qīngjié) wèishēng de, 有利健康的 yǒulì jiànkāng de

sanitary napkin 卫生巾 wèishēngjīn

sanitation N 公共卫生 gōnggòng wèishēng

sanitation worker 垃圾工 lājī gōng

sanity N 明智 míngzhì, 理智 lǐzhì

sank See sink

Santa Claus N 圣诞老人 Shèngdàn Lǎorén

sap I N (植物的) 液 (zhíwù de) yè, 汁 zhī II v 使…伤元气 shǐ…shāng yuánqì, 消耗 xiāohào

sapling N 幼树 yòushù [M. WD 棵 kē]

sapphire N 蓝宝石 lánbǎoshí

sappy ADJ 1 多液的 [+植物] duō yè de [+zhíwù] 2 多情善傻乎乎的 duōqíng de shǎhūhū de

sarcastic ADJ 挖苦的 wākǔ de, 刻薄讽刺的 kèbó fěngcì de

sardine N (罐头) 沙丁鱼 (guàntou) shādīngyú

be packed like sardines 拥挤不堪 yōngjǐ bùkān

sardonic ADJ 嘲讽的 cháofěng de

sari N (印度女子穿的) 莎丽服 (Yìndù nǚzǐ chuān de) shālìfú [M. WD 件 jiàn]

sash N 1 宽腰带 kuān yāodài [M. WD 条 tiáo] 2 绶带 shòudài [M. WD 条 tiáo]

sass N, V 对…粗言无理 duì…cūlì wúlí

sassy ADJ 粗鲁无礼的 cūlì wúlí de

sat See sit

Satan N 魔鬼 móguǐ, 撒旦 Sādàn

satanic ADJ 1 崇拜魔鬼的 chóngbài móguǐ de 2 恶魔般的 èmó bān de, 邪恶的 xié'è de

satellite N 卫星 wèixīng

satellite dish 卫星电视碟形天线 wèixīng diànshì diéxíng tiānxīng

satellite television 卫星电视 wèixīng diànshì, 卫视 wèi shì

satin N 缎 (子) duàn (zi)

satire N 讽刺 (作品) fěngcì (zuòpǐn)

satirist N 讽刺作家 fěngcì zuòjiā

satisfaction N 满意 mǎnyì

satisfactory ADJ 令人满意的 lìngrén mǎnyì de

satisfied ADJ (感到) 满意的 (gǎndào) mǎnyìde

a satisfied customer 满意的顾客 mǎnyì de gùkè

satisfy v 1 使…满意 shǐ…mǎnyì 2 使…满足 shǐ…mǎnzú

satisfying ADJ 令人满意的 lìngrén mǎnyì de

saturate v 1 (使…) 浸湿 (shǐ…) jìnshī 2 (使…) 充满 (shǐ…) chōngmǎn, 饱和 bǎohé

saturated ADJ 1 浸透了的 jìntòu le de 2 饱和的 bǎohé de

saturated fat 饱和脂肪 bǎohézhīfáng

saturation N 1 浸透 jìntòu 2 饱和 bǎohé

saturation advertising 密集广告 mìjí guǎnggào

Saturday N 星期六 xīngqīliù

sauce N 酱 jiàng, 调味汁 tiáowèizhī, 沙士 shāshì

tomato sauce 番茄酱 fānqiéjiàng

saucepan N (有柄) 平底锅 (yǒu bǐng) píngdǐguō

saucer N 茶托 chátuō, 茶碟 chádié

saucy ADJ 色情的 sèqíng de, 无礼的 wúlǐ de, 有趣的 yǒuqù de

sauna N 1 蒸气浴 zhēngqìyù, 桑那浴 sāngnàyù 2 蒸气浴室 zhēngqì yùshì, 桑那浴室 sāngnà yùshì

saunter N, V 慢慢踱步 mànmàn duóbù, 慢慢地走 mànmàn de zǒu

sausage N 香肠 xiāngcháng

sauté v 快炒 [+素菜] kuài chǎo [+sùcài]

savage I ADJ 野蛮的 yěmán de II N 野蛮人 yěmánrén

save I v 1 (拯) 救 (zhěng) jiù 2 存 (钱) cún (qián), 储蓄 chǔxù 3 省 shěng, 节省 jiéshěng

A penny saved is a penny earned. 省

下一分钱，就是多赚一分钱。Shěngxia yì fēn qián, jiù shì duō zhuàn yì fēn qián. **4** (电脑) 存盘 (diànnǎo) cún pán, 储存 chǔcún

to save face 保全面子 bǎoquán miànzi **II** N (守门员) 救球 (shǒuményuán) jiù qiú **III** PREP 除了 chúle

savings N **1** 储蓄 chǔxù, 存款 cúnkuǎn **2** 省下的钱 shěngxia de qián

savings account 储蓄账户 chǔxù zhànghù

savings bank 储蓄银行 chǔxù yínháng

savior N 救世主 Jiùshìzhǔ, 救星 jiùxīng

savor N **1** 好味道 hǎo wèidao **2** [生活的+] 乐趣 [shēnghuó+] de lèqù

savory I ADJ 美味的 měiwèi de, 鲜美的 xiānměi de **II** N 香薄荷 xiāng bòhe

savvy I N (丰富的) 知识 (fēngfù de) zhīshi **II** ADJ 知识丰富的 zhīshífēngfù de

saw¹ V See **see**

saw² N 锯 (子) jù (zi) [M. WD 把 bǎ] **II** V (PT **sawed**, PP **sawn**, **sawed**) (用锯子) 锯 (yòng jùzi) jù

sawdust N (锯) 木屑 (jù) mù xiè

sawmill N 锯木厂 jùmùchǎng

saxophone N 萨克斯管 sàkèsīguǎn

say I V (PT & PP **said**) **1** 说 shuō

they say 据说 jùshuō

that is to say 也就是说 yě jiù shì shuō

having said that 尽管如此 jǐnguǎn rúcǐ, 不过 búguò

2 说明 shuōmíng, 表达 biǎodá **II** N 说话的权利 shuōhuà de quánlì, 发言权 fāyánquán

saying N 俗话 súhuà [M. WD 句 jù]

scab N 破坏罢工的人 pòhuài bàgōng de rén, 工贼 gōngzéi **2** (伤) 痂 (shāng) jiā

scads N 大量 dàliàng, 大批 dàpī

scaffold N **1** 脚手架 jiǎoshǒujià **2** 升降吊架 shēngjiàng diàojià, 吊篮 diào lán **3** 绞刑架 jiǎoxíng jià

scald I V **1** 烫伤 tàngshāng **2** 把…加热到接近沸点 bǎ...jiārè dào jiējìn fèidiǎn **II** N 烫伤 tàngshāng

scale¹ N **1** 规模 guīmó **2** 级别 jíbié, 等级 děngjí **II** V (to scale sth back/down) 缩小某事的规模 suōxiǎo mǒushì de guīmó

scale² N (鱼) 鳞 (yú) lín **II** V 刮鱼鳞 guāyúlín

scale³ V 攀登 (山峰) pāndēng (shānfēng)

scales N 秤 chèng

scallop N 扇贝 shànbèi

scalp I N 头皮 tóupí **II** V 倒卖 dǎomài

scalpel N 手术刀 shǒushùdāo [M. WD 把 bǎ], 解剖刀 jiě bàodāo [M. WD 把 bǎ]

scaly ADJ 有鳞的 yǒu lín de

scam N 骗局 piànjú, 诈骗 (行为) zhàpiàn (xíngwéi)

scamper V 跳跳蹦蹦 tiào tiào bèng bèng

scan I V **1** 浏览 [+报纸标题] liúlǎn [+bàozhǐ biāotí] **2** 迅速地查找 xùnsù de cházhǎo **3** [用扫描器+] 扫描 [yòng sǎomiáoqì+] sǎomiáo **II** N 扫描检查 sǎomiáo jiǎnchá

ultrasound scan 超声波扫描 (检查) chāoshēngbō sǎomiáo (jiǎnchá)

scandal N 丑闻 chǒuwén

scanner N 扫描装置 sǎomiáo zhuāngzhì [M. WD 台 tái], 扫描仪 sǎomiáo yí

scant ADJ 不足的 bùzú de, 少量的 shǎoliàng de

scapegoat N 替罪羊 tìzuìyáng

scar N 伤疤 shāngbā, 疤痕 bāhén **II** V (be scarred with) 留下…的伤疤 liúxià...de shāngbā

scarce ADJ 稀有的 xīyǒu de, 缺乏的 quēfá de

scarcity N 短缺 duǎnquē, 不足 bùzú

scare I V 惊吓 jīngxià **II** N 惊吓 jīngxià

scarecrow N 稻草人 dàocǎorén

scarf N 围巾 wéijīn [M. WD 条 tiáo], 头巾 tóujīn [M. WD 条 tiáo]

scarlet ADJ, N 猩红色 xīnghóngsè, 绯红色 fēihóng sè

scary ADJ 吓人的 xiàrén de, 恐怖的 kǒngbù de

scathing ADJ 极其严厉的 jíqí yánlì de, 尖刻的 jiānkè de

scatter V **1** 散开 sànkāi **2** 撒 sā

scatterbrained ADJ 心不在焉的 xīnbúzàiyān de, 疏忽的 shūhu de

scavenge V **1** [动物+] 吃剩的动物吃剩的东西 [dòngwù+] chī biéde dòngwù chī shèng de dōngxi, 吃腐肉 chī fǔròu

2 [人+] 在垃圾中寻食 [rén+] zài lājī zhōng xún shí

scenario N **1** 可能发生的情况 kěnéng fāshēng de qíngkuàng

the worst scenario 最坏的情况 zuì huài de qíngkuàng

2（电影）脚本 (diànyǐng) jiǎoběn

scene N **1**（戏剧的）场 (xìjù de) chǎng, 场景 chǎngjǐng **2** 景色 jǐngsè **3** 现场 xiànchǎng **4** (to make a scene) 大吵大闹 dà chǎo dà nào, 大发脾气 dà fā píqi

behind the scenes 幕后 mùhòu

scenery N **1** 自然景色 zìrán jǐngsè **2**（舞台）布景 (wǔtái) bùjǐng

scenic ADJ 景色优美的 jǐngsè yōuměi de

scent N **1** 气味 qìwèi, 气息 qìxī

to throw sb off the scent 使某人失去线索 shǐ mǒurén shīqù xiànsuǒ

2 香味 xiāngwèi, 芳香 fāngxiāng

II v **1** 散布香味 sànbù xiāngwèi **2** [动物+] 嗅出 (dòngwù+) xiù chū

scepter N （国王／女王的）权杖 (guówáng/nǚwáng de) quánzhàng

schedule I N **1**（火车／汽车）时刻表 (huǒchē/qìchē) shíkèbiǎo **2**（工作）日程表 (gōngzuò) rìchéng biǎo

ahead of schedule 提前 tíqián

II v 安排在（某一时间）ānpái zài (mǒu yìshíjiān)

scheduled flight 定期航班 dìngqī hángbān

scheme I N **1** 方案 fāng'àn, 计划 jìhuà **2** 诡计 guǐjì, 阴谋 yīnmóu **II** v 策划 cèhuà, 阴谋 yīnmóu

schizophrenia N 精神分裂症 jīngshén fēnlièzhèng

scholar N 学者 xuézhě [M. WD 位 wèi]

scholarly ADJ 学术的 xuéshù de

scholarship N **1** 奖学金 jiǎngxuéjīn [M. WD 笔 bǐ] **2** 学术研究 xuéshù yánjiū, 学问 xuéwèn

scholastic ADJ 教学的 jiàoxué de, 学术的 xuéshù de

school N **1**［中、小+] 学校 [zhōng, xiǎo+] xuéxiào

elementary school/primary school 小学 xiǎoxué

high school 中学 zhōngxué

after school 课外 kèwài

to be in school 在学校（上课）zài xuéxiào

2［大学+] 院、系 [dàxué+] yuàn、xì

graduate school 研究生院 yánjiūshēng yuàn

3（鱼）群 qún **II** v 训练 xùnliàn, 教育 jiàoyù

schooner N **1** 双桅帆船 shuāng wéi fānchuán **2** 大啤酒杯 dà píjiǔ bēi

science N **1** 科学 kēxué

science fiction See **sci-fi**

pure science 纯科学 chún kēxué

social science 社会科学 shèhuì kēxué

2 自然科学 zìrán kēxué, 理科 lǐkē

science park 科学园区 kēxué yuánqū, 新科技开发区 xīn kējì kāifāqū

scientific ADJ 科学的 kēxué de

scientist N 科学家 kēxuéjiā, 科学工作者 kēxué gōngzuòzhě

sci-fi (= science fiction) ABBREV 科学幻想小说 kēxué huànxiǎng xiǎoshuō

scintillating ADJ 闪烁发光的 shǎnshuò fāguāng de

scissors N 剪刀 jiǎndāo

scoff v 嘲笑 cháoxiào

scold v 训斥 xùnchì, 斥责 chìzé

scone N 司康烤饼 sī kāng kǎobǐng

scoop I N **1**（冰淇淋）勺 (bīngqílín) sháo, 球形勺 qiúxíng sháo **2** 独家抢先报导 dújiā qiǎngxiān bàodǎo **II** v **1** 用勺铲起 yòng sháo chǎn qǐ **2** 抢先报导 qiǎngxiān bàodǎo

scooter N **1** 小型摩托车 xiǎoxíng mótuō chē **2** 踏板车 tàbǎn chē

scope N **1** 范围 fànwéi

to extend the scope of 扩大…的范围 kuòdà…de fànwéi

2（发挥才能的）机会 (fāhuī cáinéng de) jīhuì

scope for creativity 发挥创造性的机会 fāhuī chuàngzàoxìng de jīhuì

II v (to scope out) 了解 liǎojiě, 查明 chámíng

scorch I v **1**（使…）烤焦 (shǐ…) kǎojiāo **2** 烫伤 [+人] tàngshāng [+rén] **II** N 烤焦 kǎojiāo, 枯萎 kūwěi

scorching ADJ 太阳火辣辣的 tàiyáng huǒlàlà de, 极热的 jí rè de

score I N 1 比分 bǐfēn, 得分 défēn
 to keep score 记分 jìfēn
 to settle a score 报仇 bàochóu, 算旧账 suàn jiùzhàng
 2 分数 fēnshù 3 乐谱 yuèpǔ 4 二十 èrshí
 scores of 许多 xǔduō, 大量 dàliàng
II v 1 得分 défēn
 to score ponts 得分 défēn, 赢得好感 yíngdé hǎogǎn
 2 获得成功 huòdé chénggōng

scorer N 1（体育比赛的）记分员 (tǐyù bǐsài de) jìfēnyuán 2 得分的运动员 défēn de yùndòngyuán

scorn N, V 鄙视 bǐshì, 蔑视 mièshì

scorpion N 蝎子 xiēzi

Scot N 苏格兰人 Sūgélán rén

Scotch N（苏格兰）威士忌酒 (Sūgélán) wēishìjì jiǔ

scotch V 制止 zhìzhǐ, 阻止 zǔzhǐ

scot-free ADV (to get off scot-free) 逃脱惩罚 táotuō chéngfá

Scotland N 苏格兰 Sūgélán

Scottish ADJ 苏格兰的 Sūgélán de, 苏格兰人的 Sūgélán rén de

scoundrel N 恶棍 ègùn, 无赖 wúlài

scour V 1 擦亮 [+餐具] cāliàng [+cānjù] 2 彻底搜查 [+地方] chèdǐ sōuchá [+dìfang]

scourge I N 大祸害 dàhuòhài, 灾星 zāixīng II v 使...遭受巨大灾难 shǐ...zāoshòu jùdà zāinàn

scout I N 侦察兵 zhēnchábīng 2 童子军 tóngzǐjūn
 talent scout 物色新秀者 wùsè xīnxiù zhě
II v 1 侦察 zhēnchá
 to scout for 物色新秀 wùsè xīnxiù
 2 寻找 xúnzhǎo

scowl I N 愤怒的表情 fènnù de biǎoqíng II v 愤怒地看 fènnù de kàn, 怒视 nùshì

Scrabble N 纵横拼字游戏 zònghéng pīnzì yóuxì

scrabble V 翻找 fānzhǎo

scraggly ADJ 凌乱的 língluàn de, 散乱的 sànluàn de

scram V 逃离 táo lí, 跑开 pǎokāi

scramble I v 1 争夺 zhēngduó, 争抢 zhēngqiǎng
 to scramble for front seats 争夺前排的座位 zhēngduó qiánpái de zuòwèi
 2 仓促行动 cāngcù xíngdòng
 to scramble to safety 仓促逃离到安全地带 cāngcù táolí dào ānquán dìdài
 scrambled egg 炒蛋 chǎodàn
 3（美式橄榄球）持球抢跑 (Měishì gǎnlǎnqiú) chí qiú qiǎng pǎo
II N 1 争夺 zhēngduó 2 乱忙 luànmáng

scrap I N 1 废料 fèiliào, 废品 fèipǐn
 scrap metal 金属废料 jīnshǔ fèiliào
 2 吃剩的食物 chī shèng de shíwù
 table scraps 剩菜 shèngcài
 3 小纸片 xiǎo zhǐpiàn, 碎布片 suìbù piàn
II v 1 把...当废料处理 bǎ...dāng fèiliào chǔlǐ 2 放弃 fàngqì 3 争吵 zhēngchǎo

scrapbook N 剪贴簿 jiǎntiēbù

scrape I v 1 刮 guā
 to scrape sth away 把某物刮掉 bǎ mǒuwù guādiào
 to scrape sth clean 把某物刮干净 bǎ mǒuwù guā gānjìng
 2 摩擦 mócā, 擦伤 cāshāng
 to scrape by 勉强度日 miǎnqiǎng dùrì
 to scrape through 勉强通过 miǎnqiǎng tōngguò
 3 [金属+] 发出刮擦声 [jīnshǔ+] fāchū guācāshēng II N 1 擦伤 cāshāng 2 困境 kùnjìng

scrappy ADJ 敢作敢为的 gǎn zuò gǎn wèi de

scratch I v 1 搔 [+皮肤] sāo [+pífū]
 to scratch the surface 触及（问题的）表面 (wèntí de) biǎomiàn
 to scratch one's head 大伤脑筋 dà shāng nǎojīn
 2 [猫+] 抓 [māo+] zhuā, 划伤 huá shāng II N 1 刮擦 guāchā, 划痕 huáhén
 from scratch 从零开始 cóng líng kāishǐ

scratchy ADJ 1 扎人的 zhārén de 2 低沉沙哑的 [+嗓音] dīchén shāyǎ de [+sǎngyīn] 3 疼痛的 [+喉咙] téngtòng de [+hóulóng]

scrawl I v 1 潦草地写 liáocǎo de xiě II N 潦草写成的东西 liáocǎo xiě chéng de dōngxi, 潦草的笔迹 liáocǎo de bǐjì

scrawny ADJ 瘦弱的 shòuruò de
scream I V 尖叫 jiānjiào, 大声呼喊 dàshēng hūhǎn II N 尖叫声 jiānjiào shēng
screech I V [车轮+] 发出刺耳声 [chēlún+] fāchū cì'ěr shēng,
to screech to a halt [汽车+] 突然刹车停下 [qìchē+] tūrán shāchē tíng xià
II N（车轮的）刺耳声 (chēlún de) cì'ěr shēng
screen I N 1 屏幕 píngmù
screen saver（计算机）屏幕保护程序 (jìsuànjī) píngmù bǎohù chéngxù
2 纱窗 shāchuāng 3 屏风 píngfēng II V 1 检查 jiǎnchá, 审查 shěnchá
to be screened for breast cancer 作乳房癌检查 zuò rǔfáng ái jiǎnchá
2 隐蔽 yǐnbì, 遮蔽 zhēbì
screenplay N（电影／电视）剧本 (diànyǐng/diànshì) jùběn
screenwriter N（电影／电视）剧本作者 (diànyǐng/diànshì) jùběn zuòzhě
screw I N 螺丝钉 luósī dīng
to have a screw loose 头脑出了问题 tóunǎo chūle wèntí, 有点儿怪 yǒudiǎnr guài, 古怪 gǔguài
II V 1 用螺丝钉钉上 yòng luósī dīng dìngshang 2 拧上 nǐngshang, 拧紧 nǐngjǐn
to screw up 搞糟 gǎozāo
screwball N 古怪的人 gǔguài de rén
screwball comedy 荒诞喜剧 huāngdàn xǐjù
screw-driver N 螺丝刀 luósīdāo
screwed up ADJ 1 弄糟的 [+计划] nòngzāo de [+jìhuà] 2 焦躁的 [+人] jiāozào de [+rén]
scribble I V 1 潦草的写 liǎocǎo de xiě 2 乱涂乱画 luàn tú luàn huà II N 乱涂乱写 luàn tú luànxiě
script I N 1 演讲稿 yǎnjiǎnggǎo 2 电影剧本 diànyǐng jùběn 3 笔迹 bǐjì, 手迹 shǒujì
to read from a script 照稿念 zhào gǎozi niàn
II V 1 写 [+演讲稿／剧本] xiě [+yǎnjiǎnggǎo/jùběn] 2 精心策划 jīngxīn cèhuà
scripted ADJ 1 预先写好的 [+演讲] yùxiān

xiě hǎo de [+yǎnjiǎng], 照稿宣读的 zhào gǎo xuāndú de 2 刻意安排的 [+事件] kèyì ānpái de [+shìjiàn]
scripture N 1 基督教圣经 Jīdūjiào Shèngjīng 2（宗教）经文 (zōngjiào) jīngwén, 圣书 shèngshū
scroll I N 纸卷 zhǐ juàn, 卷轴 juànzhóu II V（在计算机显示器上）上下滚动 (zài jìsuànjī xiǎnshìqì shàng) shàngxià gǔndòng
scrooge N 守财奴 shǒucáinú, 吝啬鬼 lìnsèguǐ
scrotum N 阴囊 yīnnáng
scrub[1] V, N 擦洗 cāxǐ, 刷洗 shuāxǐ
scrub[2] N 矮树丛 ǎishùcóng, 灌木丛 guànmù cóng
scruffy ADJ 邋遢的 lāta de, 肮脏的 āngzāng de
scrumptious ADJ 美味的 měiwèi de
scrunch V 把…揉成一团 bǎ...róu chéng yì tuán
scruple N 顾忌 gùjì, 顾虑 gùlǜ
scrupulous ADJ 1 诚实公正的 chéngshí gōngzhèng de, 讲良心道德的 jiǎng liángxīn dàodé de 2 细微认真的 xìwēi rènzhēn de, 一丝不苟的 yìsī bùgǒu de
scrutinize V 仔细检查 zǐxì jiǎnchá, 细查 xìchá
scuba-diving N 斯库巴潜泳 sīkùbā qiányǒng
scuff V 使…磨损 shǐ...mósǔn
scuffle V, N 扭打 niǔdǎ
sculptor N 雕塑家 diāosùjiā, 雕刻家 diāokèjiā
sculpture I N 雕塑 diāosù, 雕塑作品 diāosù zuòpǐn II V 雕塑 diāosù
scum N 1 浮渣 fúzhā 2 人渣 rén zhā, 人类渣滓 rénlèi zhāzǐ
scumbag N 人渣 rén zhā, 人类渣滓 rénlèi zhāzǐ
scurry N, V 小步急跑 xiǎobù jí pǎo
scurvy N 坏血病 huàixuèbìng
scuttle V 1 破坏 pòhuài, 力阻 lìzǔ 2 小步疾行 xiǎobù jíxíng
scythe N 长柄大镰刀 cháng bǐng dàliándāo
sea N（大）海 (dà) hǎi

sea level 海平面 hǎi píng miàn

sea plane 海上飞机 hǎi shàng fēijī

seabed N 海床 hǎichuáng, 海底 hǎidǐ

seafood N 海鲜 hǎixiān

seagull N 海鸥 hǎi'ōu [M. WD 只 zhī]

seahorse N 海马 hǎimǎ [M. WD 只 zhī]

seal¹ N 海豹 hǎibào [M. WD 头 tóu]

seal² V 封闭 fēngbì
to seal a deal 确保达成交易 quèbǎo dáchéng jiāoyì

seal³ N 印章 yìnzhāng, 图章 túzhāng

sealed ADJ 1 密封的 [+信封] mìfēng de [+xìnfēng] 2 保密的 [+文件] bǎomì de [+wénjiàn]

sealion N 海狮 hǎishī [M. WD 头 tóu]

seam N 1 缝 fèng, 线缝 xiànfèng 2 (煤) 矿层 (méi)kuàng céng

seaman N 海员 hǎiyuán

seamless ADJ 1 无缝的 wú féng de 2 连贯的 liánguàn de

seamstress N 女裁缝 nǚ cáifeng, 女缝纫工 nǚ féngrèngōng

seamy ADJ 丑陋的 chǒulòu de
the seamy side 阴暗面 yīn'ànmiàn

sear V 烧焦 shāojiāo, 烧烤 shāokǎo

search N, V 寻找 xúnzhǎo, 搜索 sōusuǒ
search and rescue 搜索营救 sōusuǒ yíngjiù
search engine 搜索引擎 sōusuǒ yǐnqíng
search party 搜索队 sōusuǒ duì
Search me! 我不知道! Wǒ bù zhīdào!

searching ADJ 探究的 tànjiū de
searching inquiry 彻底的调查 chèdǐ de diàochá

searchlight N 探照灯 tànzhàodēng

searing ADJ 1 灼热的 [+天气] zhuórè de [+tiānqì], 炽热的 chìrè de 2 严苛的 [+语言] yánkè de [+yǔyán]

seashell N 海贝壳 hǎibèiké

seashore N 海岸 hǎi'àn, 海滩 hǎitān

seasick ADJ 晕船的 yùnchuán de

seaside ADJ 海边的 hǎibiān de, 海滨的 hǎibīn de

season¹ N 1 季节 jìjié 2 时令 shílíng 3 时期 shíqī
season ticket 季票 jìpiào

season² V 给 [+食物] 加调料 gěi [+shíwù] jiā tiáoliào

seasonal ADJ 季节性的 jìjiéxìng de

seasoned ADJ 1 有经验的 [+水手] yǒu jīngyàn de [+shuǐshǒu] 2 调好味的 [+食物] tiáo hǎo wèi de [+shíwù]

seasoning N 调味品 tiáowèipǐn

seat I N 1 座位 zuòwèi
aisle seat 靠过道的座位 kào guòdào de zuòwèi
passenger seat 副驾驶员座位 fùjiàshǐyuán zuòwèi, 驾驶员旁边的座位 jiàshǐyuán pángbiān de zuòwèi
window seat 靠窗口的座位 kào chuāngkǒu de zuòwèi
2 席位 xíwèi
a seat on the committee 委员会中的一个席位 wěiyuánhuì zhòng de yí ge xíwèi, 委员会成员 wěiyuánhuì chéngyuán
II V 1 坐 zuò 2 坐得下 zuòdexia

seaweed N 海草 hǎicǎo, 海藻 hǎizǎo

secession N 退出 [+某组织] tuìchū [+mǒu zǔzhī], 脱离 [+某国而独立] tuōlí [+mǒu guó ér dúlì]

secluded ADJ 僻静的 pìjìng de, 僻远的 pìyuǎn de

seclusion N 隐居 yǐnjū

second¹ I ADJ 1 第二 dì'èr
second base (棒球的) 二垒 (bàngqiú de) èr lěi
second nature 第二天性 dì'èrtiān xìng
second person 第二人称 dì èr rénchēng
second sight 预见 (力) yùjiàn (lì)
2 另一个 lìng yí ge, 再一次 zàiyícì
second chance/opinion 再一次机会 zàiyícì jīhuì, 另一种意见 lìngyì zhǒng yìjiàn
II ADV 第二 dì'èr, 其次 qícì III V 附议 fùyì, 支持 zhīchí

second² N 1 秒 miǎo 2 片刻 piànkè
in a second 极快地 jí kuài de, 瞬间 shùnjiān

secondary ADJ 1 第二位的 dì'èr wèi de, 次要的 cìyào de
secondary school 中等学校 zhōngděng xuéxiào, 中学 zhōngxué

2 继发性的 jìfāxìng de
secondary infection 继发性感染 jì fā xìnggǎn rǎn
second-class ADJ 二等的 èrděng de
second-class citizen 二等公民 èrděng gōngmín
second-guess V **1** 事后批评 shìhòu pīpíng **2** 猜测 cāicè，预测 yùcè
secondhand I N 二手货 èrshǒu huò，旧货 jiù huò II ADJ 二手的 èrshǒu de
secondhand store 旧货店 jiùhuòdiàn
secondly ADV 第二 dìèr，其次 qící
second-rate ADJ 次等的 cìděng de
seconds N **1** 第二份（饭菜）dì èr fèn (fàncài) **2** 次品（服装）cìpǐn (fúzhuāng)
secrecy N 保密 bǎomì
secret I N 秘密 mìmì
to keep a secret 保守秘密 bǎoshǒu mìmì
II ADJ 秘密（的）mìmì (de)，隐蔽的 yǐnbì de
secret service 特工处 tègōng chù，特工部门 tègōng bùmén
to keep sth secret from sb 对某人隐瞒某事 duì mǒurén yǐnmán mǒushì
secretarial ADJ 秘书的 mìshū de
secretariat N 秘书处 mìshūchù
the U.N. Secretariat 联合国秘书处 Liánhéguó Mìshūchù
secretary N **1** 秘书 mìshu **2**（美国）部长 bùzhǎng
(U.S.) Secretary of State（美国）国务卿（美国）Guówùqīng
secrete V 分泌 fēnmì
secretion N 分泌 fēnmì
secretive ADJ 严守秘密的 yánshǒu mìmì de，守口如瓶的 shǒu kǒu rú píng de
sect N 派别 pàibié，（宗教）教派（zōngjiào）jiàopài
sectarian ADJ 教派（之间）的 jiàopài (zhījiān) de
sectarian conflict 教派（之间）冲突 jiàopài (zhījiān de) chōngtū
section N **1** 部分 bùfen，段 duàn **2** 部门 bùmén **3**（报纸）栏目（bàozhǐ）lánmù
sector N 部门 bùmén，领域 lǐngyù
secular ADJ 世俗的 shìsú de，非宗教的 fēi zōngjiào de

secure I ADJ **1** 安全的 ānquán de，没有风险的 méiyǒu fēngxiǎn de **2** 牢固的 láogù de，绝对安全的 juéduì ānquán de II V **1** 固定住 gùdìngzhu **2** 获得 huòdé，得到 dédào **3** 保护 bǎohù，使…免于攻击 shǐ…miǎnyú gōngjī
security N **1** 安全 ānquán **2** 保障 bǎozhàng **3** 抵押品 dǐyā pǐn
security check 安（全）检（查）ān (quán) jiǎn (chá)
security forces 保安部队 bǎo'ān bùduì，安全部队 ānquán bùduì
social security 社会保障 shèhuì bǎozhàng
sedan N 小轿车 xiǎojiàochē
sedate ADJ 庄重的 zhuāngzhòng de，严肃的 yánsù de
sedated ADJ 服用了镇静剂的 fúyòngle zhènjìngjì de
sedative N 镇静剂 zhènjìngjì
sedentary ADJ **1** 坐着的 zuòzhe de，很少活动的 hěn shǎo huódòng de **2** 定居的 dìngjū de，不迁移的 bù qiānyí de
sedentary population 固定人口 gùdìng rénkǒu
sediment N 沉淀（物）chéndiàn (wù)
sedimentary ADJ 沉积的 chénjī de
seditious ADJ 煽动推翻政府的 shāndòng tuīfān zhèngfǔ de
seduce V 勾引 gōuyǐn，引诱 yǐnyòu
seduction N 勾引 gōuyǐn，引诱 yǐnyòu
seductive ADJ（性感）诱人的 (xìnggǎn) yòurén de，富有性感诱惑力的 fùyǒu xìnggǎn yòuhuòlì de
see (PT **saw**; PP **seen**) V **1** 看到 kàndao **2** 理解 lǐjiě，明白 míngbai
Oh, I see. 啊，我明白了。A, wǒ míngbai le.
I don't see why not. 没有什么不以。Méiyǒu shénme bù kěyǐ.
3 看望 kànwàng **4** 会面 huìmiàn **5** 想 xiǎng
seed N **1**（植物的）种子（zhíwù de）zhǒng-zi **2**（水果/蔬菜）籽（shuǐguǒ/shūcài de）zǐ **3**（体育比赛）种子选手（tǐyù bǐsài）zhǒngzǐ xuǎnshǒu，种子队 zhǒngzǐduì
seedless ADJ 无籽的 wú zǐ de

a seedless watermelon 无籽西瓜 wú zǐ xīguā

seedling N 幼苗 yòumiáo, 秧苗 yāngmiáo

seedy ADJ 肮脏下流的 āngzāng xiàliú de

seek V (PT & PP **sought**) 谋求 móuqiú, 寻求 xúnqiú

　to seek one's fortune 离家寻求成功和财富 líjiā xúnqiú chénggōng hé cáifù

seem V 看来 kànlai, 似乎 sìhū

seeming ADJ 表面上的 biǎomiànshàng de, 似乎…的 sìhū…de

seen See **see**

seep V 渗漏 shènlòu

seepage N 渗漏 shènlòu

seesaw I N 跷跷板 qiāoqiāobǎn II V 时上时下（地动）shí shàng shíxià (de dòng)

seethe V 1 发怒火中烧 fānù, 怒火中烧 nùhuǒzhōngshāo

　to seethe with jealousy 妒火中烧 dùhuǒ zhōngshāo, 因妒嫉而愤怒 yīn dùjí ér fènnù **2** 到处都是 dàochù dōu shì

　to seethe with ants 到处都是蚂蚁 dàochù dōu shì mǎyǐ, 满是蚂蚁 mǎn shì mǎyǐ

see-through ADJ 透明的 tòumíng de

segment N 1 部分 bùfen 2 线段 xiànduàn 3 片 piàn, 节 jié

segmented ADJ 分段的 fēnduàn de, 分节的 fēnjié de

segregate V 分离 fēnlí, 隔离 gélí

segregation N 分离 fēnlí, 隔离 gélí

seismic ADJ 地震的 dìzhèn de

seismograph N 地震仪 dìzhènyí

seismology N 地震学 dìzhènxué

seize V 1 一把抓住 yì bǎ zhuāzhu, 紧紧抓住 jǐnjǐn zhuāzhu, 夺过 duóguo 2 扣押 kòuyā, 没收 mòshōu

seizure N 1 没收 mòshōu

　drug seizure 没收毒品 mòshōu dúpǐn **2**（疾病的）突然发作 (jíbìng de) tūrán fāzuò, 昏厥 hūnjué

seldom ADV 不常常 bù chángcháng, 很少 hěn shǎo

select I V 选择 xuǎnzé, 选拔 xuǎnbá II ADJ 1 精心挑选出来的 jīngxīn tiāoxuǎn chūlai de 2 少数人专用的 shǎoshùrén zhuānyòng de

selection N 1 选择 xuǎnzé, 选拔 xuǎnbá 2 挑选出来的人或物 tiāoxuǎn chūlai de rén huò wù

selective ADJ 1 有选择的 [+记忆] yǒu xuǎnzé de [+jìyì] 2 认真挑选的 [+顾客] rènzhēn tiāoxuǎn de [+gùkè]

self N 自我 zìwǒ, 自己 zìjǐ

self-absorbed ADJ 自顾自的 zìgùzìde

self-appointed ADJ 自封的 zìfēng de, 自以为是…的 zì yǐwéi shì…de

self-assurance N 十足的自信 shízú de zìxìn

self-centered ADJ 自我中心的 zìwǒ zhōngxīn de

self-confident ADJ 自信的 zìxìn de

self-conscious ADJ 怕羞的 pà xiū de, 不自然的 bú zìrán de

self-control N 自我控制 zì wǒ kòngzhì, 自制力 zìzhìlì

self-defeating ADJ 效果适得其反的 xiàoguǒ shì dé qí fǎn de

self-defense N 自卫 zìwèi

self-denial N 克己苦行 kèjǐ kǔxíng, 自我牺牲 zìwǒ xīshēng

self-destructive ADJ 自我毁灭的 zìwǒ huǐmiè de

self-discipline N 自我约束 zìwǒ yuēshù, 自律 zìlǜ

self-employed ADJ 拥有自己的生意的 yōngyǒu zìjǐ de shēngyì de, 个体经营的 gètǐ jīngyíng de

self-esteem N 自尊（心）zìzūn (xīn)

self-evident ADJ 显而易见的 xiǎn'éryìjiàn de, 不言而喻的 bùyán'éryù de

self-explanatory ADJ 无需解释的 wúxū jiěshì je

self-fulfilling prophecy N 自我应验的预言 zìwǒ yìngyàn de yùyán, 咒语成真 zhòuyǔ chéng zhēn

self-help N 自助 zìzhù, 自救 zìjiù

self-image N 自我形象 zìwǒ xíngxiàng

self-important ADJ 妄自尊大 wàng zì zūn dà, 自负的 zìfù de

self-improvement N 自我改进 zìwǒ gǎijìn

self-indulgence N 放纵 fàngzòng

self-inflicted ADJ 自作自受的 zìzuò zìshòu de

self-interest N 自我利益 zìwǒ lìyì, 自私自利 zìsī zìlì
be motivated by pure self-interest 纯粹出于自私自利的动机 chúncuì chūyú zìsī zìlì de dòngjī

selfish ADJ 自私的 zìsī de

selfless ADJ 无私的 wúsī de

self-made ADJ 白手起家而成功的 báishǒu qǐjiā ér chénggōng de
self-made millionaire 白手起家的百万富翁 báishǒu qǐjiā de bǎiwàn fùwēng

self-pity N 自怜 zì lián
tears of self-pity 自怜的眼泪 zì lián de yǎnlèi

self-portrait N 自画像 zìhuàxiàng

self-possessed ADJ 镇定的 zhèndìng de

self-preservation N 自我保护 zìwǒ bǎohù

self-reliance N 自力更生 zìlì gēngshēng

self-respect N 自尊 zìzūn
to keep one's self-respect 保持自尊 bǎozhí zìzūn

self-respecting ADJ 有自尊心的 yǒu zìzūnxīn de

self-restraint N 自我克制 zìwǒ kèzhì de

self-sacrifice N 自我牺牲 zìwǒ xīshēng

self-seeking ADJ 追逐私利的 zhuīzhú sīlì de

self-service ADJ 自助式的 zìzhù shì de

self-serving ADJ 只为谋私利的 zhǐ wèi móu sīlì de

self-styled ADJ 自封的 zìfēng de

self-sufficiency N 自给自足 zìjǐ zìzú

self-supporting ADJ 自食其力的 zìshí qílì de

sell V (PT & PP **sold**) **1** 卖 mài, 出售 chūshòu **2** 销售 xiāoshòu **3** 兜售 dōushòu, 推销 tuīxiāo

selling point N 卖点 màidiǎn

sellout N **1** 门票售完的比赛／演出 ménpiào shòu wán de bǐsài/yǎnchū **2** 背信弃义者 bèixìn qìyì zhě, 叛徒 pàntú

semantic ADJ 语义（上）的 yǔyì (shàng) de, 词义（上）的 cíyì (shàng) de

semblance N 相似的情况／事物 xiāngsì de qíngkuàng/shìwù

semen N 精液 jīngyè

semester N 学期 xuéqī

semicircle N 半圆 bànyuán

semicolon N 分号 fēnhào

semiconductor N 半导体 bàndǎotǐ

semifinal N 半决赛 bànjuésài

seminal ADJ 开创性的 kāichuàngxìng de, 对后来者有巨大影响的 duì hòuláizhě yǒu jùdà yǐngxiǎng de

seminar N 讨论课 tǎolùnkè, 研讨会 yántǎohuì

seminary N 神学院 shénxuéyuàn

semiprecious ADJ 次贵重的 [+宝石] cì guìzhòng de [+bǎoshí]

Semitic ADJ **1** 闪米特人的 Shǎnmǐtèrén de, 闪米特语的Shǎnmǐtèyǔ de **2** 犹太人的 Yóutàirén de

senate N **1** 参议院 cānyìyuàn **2** （某些大学的）校董会 (mǒuxiē dàxué de) xiàodǒnghuì

senator N 参议员 cānyìyuán

send (PT & PP **sent**) V **1** 寄 jì, 发 fā **2** 送 sòng **3** 派 pài, 派遣 pàiqiǎn
to send for 要求…来 yāoqiú…lái, 请 qǐng

senile ADJ 年老糊涂的 niánlǎo hútu de

senior I ADJ **1** 年长的 niánzhǎng de
senior citizen 老年人 lǎoniánrén, 长者 zhǎngzhě
2 资深的 zīshēn de II N 高中毕业班学生 gāozhōng bìyèbān xuésheng

seniority N 高年资 gāonián zī, 资历 zīlì

sensation N **1** 感觉 gǎnjué **2** 轰动 hōngdòng

sensational ADJ **1** 引起轰动的 [+消息] yǐnqǐ hōngdòng de [+xiāoxi], 耸人听闻的 sǒngrén tīngwén de **2** 令人激动的 [+演出] lìngrén jīdòng de [+yǎnchū]

sensationalize V 把 [+一条新闻] 渲染得耸人听闻 bǎ [+yì tiáo xīnwén] xuànrǎn dé sǒngrén tīngwén

sense I N **1** 感觉 gǎnjué
sense of humor/guilt 幽默感／负罪感 yōumògǎn/fùzuìgǎn
2 理解力jiělì, 领悟 lǐngwù **3** 词义 cíyì, 意义 yìyì II V 感觉到 gǎnjuédào
to make sense 有道理 yǒudàolǐ

539

in a sense 在一定意义上 zài yídìng yìyìshang

senseless ADJ 1 无知觉的 wú zhījué de 2 没有意义的 méiyǒu yìyì de

senses N 理智 lǐzhì

sensibility N 感觉 gǎnjué, 感受（力）gǎnshòu (lì)

sensible ADJ 明白事理的 míngbai shìlǐ de, 懂事的 dǒngshì de

sensitive ADJ 1 敏感的 mǐngǎn de 2 能理解的 néng lǐjiě de, 体贴的 tǐtiē de 3 需小心处理的 xū xiǎoxīn chǔlǐ de, 机密的 jīmì de
commercially sensitive 商业机密的 shāngyè jīmì de
4 对…很灵敏的 duì…hěn língmǐn de
light-sensitive 对光敏感的 duìguāng mǐngǎn de

sensor N 传感器 chuánggǎnqì

sensory ADJ 感官的 gǎnguān de

sensual ADJ 肉欲的 ròuyù de, 性感的 xìnggǎn de

sensuous ADJ 给感官快感的 gěi gǎnguān kuàigǎn de, 赏心悦目的 shǎngxīn yuèmù de

sent See send

sentence I N 1 句子 jùzi 2 判决 pànjué II V 判决 pànjué, 判处 pànchǔ

sentiment N 意见 yìjiàn, 态度 tàidu
public sentiment 公众的情绪 gōngzhòng de qíngxù

sentimental ADJ 1 自作多情的 zìzuò duōqíng de, 多愁善感 duōchóu shàngǎn 2 感情上的 gǎnqíng shàng de
sentimental value 感情价值 gǎnqíng jiàzhí

sentry N 哨兵 shàobīng, 卫兵 wèibīng

separate I ADJ 1 分开的 fēnkāi de 2 不相关的 bù xiāngguān de II V 1 分开 fēnkāi, 分离 fēnlí
to separate the men from the boys 把强者和弱者区分开来 bǎ qiángzhě hé ruòzhě qūfēn kāilái, 把勇敢者和胆怯者区分开来 bǎ yǒnggǎnzhě hé dǎnqièzhě qūfēn kāilái
to separate the sheep from the goats 区分好人和坏人 qūfēn hǎorén hé huàirén

2 [夫妻+] 分居 [fūqī] fēnjū

separation N 1 分开 fēnkāi 2 分居 fēnjū

September N 九月 jiǔyuè

sequel N 续集 xùjí, 后续 hòuxù

sequence N 顺序 shùnxù

sequential ADJ 顺序的 shùnxù de, 连续的 liánxù de

sequin N 闪光塑料小圆片 shǎnguāng sùliào xiǎo yuánpiàn [M. WD 片 piàn]

serenade I N 小夜曲 xiǎoyèqǔ II V 对…唱／奏小夜曲 duì…chàng/zòu xiǎoyèqǔ

serendipity N 发现珍奇事物的天生本领 fāxiàn zhēnqí shìwù de tiānshēng běnlǐng

serene ADJ 安详的 ānxiáng de, 安宁的 ānníng de

sergeant N 军士 jūnshì, 巡佐 xúnzuǒ

serial I ADJ 1 一系列的 yíxìliè de
serial killer 系列杀人犯 xìliè shārénfàn, 连环杀手 liánhuán shāshǒu
2 （按）顺序（安排）的 (àn) shùnxù (ānpái) de
serial number 顺序编号 shùnxù biānhào
II N 电视连续剧 diànshì liánxùjù, 报刊连载小说 bàokān liánzǎi xiǎoshuō

series N 1 一系列 yíxìliè 2 连续剧 liánxùjù

serious ADJ 1 严重的 yánzhòng de, 重大的 zhòngdà de 2 严肃的 yánsù de 3 认真的 rènzhēn de

seriously ADV 1 严重（地）yánzhòng (de) 2 严肃（地）yánsù (de) 3 严格（地）yángé (de)
to take sb seriously 把某人当作值得尊重的人 bǎ mǒurén dāngzuò zhíde zūnzhòng de rén
4 认真（地）rènzhēn de

sermon N （基督教的）布道 (Jīdūjiào de) bùdào, 讲道 jiǎngdào

serpent N （大）蛇 (dà) shé [M. WD 条 tiáo]

serrated ADJ 有锯齿的 yǒu jùchǐ de

serum N 免疫血清 miǎnyì xuèqīng

servant N 佣人 yōngrén, 仆人 púrén

serve I V 1 为…服务 wéi…fúwù, 接待 jiēdài 2 服役 fúyì, 当兵 dāngbīng 3 提供食品 tígōng shípǐn 4 用作 yòngzuo 5 发球 fā qiú

it serves ... right 活该 huógāi
II v（网球／排球）发球 (wǎngqiú/páiqiú) fāqiú

server N **1**（计算机）服务器 (jìsuànjī) fúwù qì **2** 发球者 fāqiú zhě **3**（饭店）服务员 (fàndiàn) fúwùyuán，侍者 shìzhě

service I N **1** 服务 fúwù

service charge 服务费 fúwùfèi，小费 xiǎofèi

service station（汽车）加油站 (qìchē) jiāyóuzhàn

service industry 服务业 fúwùyè，第三产业 dìsān chǎnyè

2 任职 rènzhí **3** 宗教仪式 zōngjiào yíshì **4** 效力 xiàolì **II** v **1** 维修 wéixiū，保养 bǎoyǎng **2** 支付利息 zhīfù lìxī

public services 公用事业 gōngyòng shìyè

serviceable ADJ **1** 可以使用的 [+设备] kěyǐ shǐyòng de [+shèbèi] **2** 还可以的 [+食物] hái kěyǐ de [+shíwù]

services N (the services) 军队 jūnduì，武装部队 wǔzhuāng bùduì

servile ADJ 完全屈从的 wánquán qūcóng de，奴颜婢膝的 núyánbìxī de

serving N 一份食物 yí fèn shíwù

five servings of fruit and vegetable every day 每天五份水果蔬菜 měitiān wǔ fèn shuǐguǒ shūcài

session N **1**（一段）时间 (yí duàn) shíjiān **2** 开庭 kāitíng **3** 学期 xuéqī

to be in session 正在开会 zhèngzài kāihuì，正在开庭 zhèngzài kāitíng

set I v (PT & PP **set**) **1** 摆 bǎi，摆放 bǎifàng **2** 调 tiáo，调整 tiáozhěng **3** 建立 jiànlì，创造 chuàngzào

to set an example 树立榜样 shùlì bǎngyàng

4（日）落 (rì) luò

to set aside 省下 shěngxia，留下 liúxia

to set up ① 成立 chénglì ② 准备好使用 zhǔnbèihǎo shǐyòng，安装 ānzhuāng ③ 竖立 shùlì

II N **1** 一套 yí tào，一付 yí fù **2** 电视机 diànshìjī，收音机 shōuyīnjī **3**（电影／电视）拍摄场 (diànyǐng/diànshì) pāishèchǎng，戏剧布景 (xìjù) bùjǐng **4**（球

赛）一盘 (qiúsài) yìpán **5** 一组（乐曲）yìzǔ (yuèqǔ)

setback N 挫折 cuòzhé

setter N **1** 蹲伏猎犬 dūnfú lièquǎn **2** 制定者 zhìdìngzhě

example-setter 树立榜样的人 shùlì bǎngyàng de rén

setting N **1** 环境 huánjìng **2** 背景 bèijǐng **3** 定位档 dìngwèidàng

settle v **1** 定居 dìngjū **2** 安顿 āndùn **3** 解决 [+争端] jiějué [+zhēngduān]

to settle out of court 法庭外和解 fǎtíng wài héjiě

4 偿还 chánghuán，结清 jiéqīng

settled ADJ **1** 不可能改变的 bùkěnéng gǎibiàn de **2** 安定的 [+生活] āndìngde [+shēnghuó]，舒适的 shūshì de

settlement N **1**（和解）协议 (héjiě+) xiéyì **2** 结账 jiézhàng，偿还 chánghuán **3** 定居 dìngjū

settler N 定居者 dìngjūzhě，移民 yímín

set-up N **1** 安排 ānpái，布局 bùjú **2**（计算机系统的）调试 (jìsuànjī xìtǒng de) tiáoshì，装配 zhuāngpèi **3** 全套设备 quántào shèbèi **4** 圈套 quāntào，陷阱 xiànjǐng

seven NUM 七 qī, 7

seventeen NUM 十七 shíqī, 17

seventh NUM 第七 dìqī

seventy NUM 七十 qīshí, 70

sever v **1** 切断 qiēduàn

a severed finger 断指 duàn zhǐ

2 断绝 [+关系] duànjué [+guānxi]

several I ADJ 几个 jǐ ge，一些 yìxiē
II PRON 几个 jǐ ge，一些 yìxiē

severance pay N 解雇费 jiěgù fèi，离职金 lízhí jīn

severe ADJ **1** 严厉的 yánlì de **2** 剧烈的 jùliè de

sew (PT **sewed**; PP **sewn**) v 缝 féng，缝纫 féngrèn

sewage N（下水道的）污水 (xiàshuǐdào de) wūshuǐ

sewer N 下水道 xiàshuǐdào，阴沟 yīngōu

sewn See **sew**

sex N **1** 性别 xìngbié **2** 性行为 xìng xíngwéi，性交 xìngjiāo

541

sex education 性教育 xìng jiàoyù
opposite sex 异性 yìxìng

sexist ADJ 性别歧视的 xìngbié qíshì de, 歧视妇女的 qíshì fùnǚ de

sex symbol N 性感偶像 xìnggǎn ǒuxiàng

sexual ADJ 1 性别的 xìngbié de 2 性交的 xìngjiāo de

sexual assault 性侵犯 xìng qīnfàn, 强奸 qiángjiān

sexual harassment 性骚扰 xìng sāorǎo

sexual transmitted diseases (STDs) 性传播疾病 xìng chuánbō jíbìng

sexuality N 性欲 xìngyù, 性行为 xìng xíngwéi

sexy ADJ 性感的 xìnggǎn de, 引起性欲的 yǐnqǐ xìngyù de

shabby ADJ 1 破旧的 [+城区] pòjiù de [+chéngqū], 寒酸的 [+衣服] hánsuān de [+yīfu] 2 不公平的 [+对待] bù gōngping de [+duìdài]

shack I N 简陋的小屋 jiǎnlòu de xiǎo wū, 棚屋 péngwū [M. WD 间 jiān] II V (to shack up with sb) 与某人同居 yǔ mǒurén tóngjū

shackle I N 1 镣铐 liàokào [M. WD 副 fù] 2 枷锁 jiāsuǒ, 桎梏 zhìgù
the shackle of the family 家庭的桎梏 jiātíng de zhìgù
II V 1 给...带上镣铐 gěi...dàishang liàokào 2 束缚 shùfù

shade I N 1 荫 yìn, 背阴 bèiyīn 2 (色彩的) 浓淡 (sècǎi de) nóngdàn
a warm shade 暖色 nuǎnsè
3 细微差别 xìwēi chābié
shades of opinions 各种不同意见 gèzhǒng bùtóng yìjiàn
4 灯罩 dēngzhào II V 为...遮阳 wéi...zhēyáng

shades N 百叶窗 bǎiyèchuāng, 遮阳窗帘 zhēyáng chuānglián

shadow I N 影子 yǐngzi, 阴影 yīnyǐng
beyond/without a shadow of doubt 毫无疑问 háowú yíwèn
II V 跟踪 gēnzōng, 盯梢 dīngshāo

shady ADJ 1 遮阴的 zhēyáng de, 背阴的 bèiyīn de 2 不正当的 búzhèngdāng de, 可疑的 kěyí de

a shady deal 一项可疑的交易 yí xiàng kěyí de jiāoyì

shaft N 1 竖井 shùjǐng
elevator shaft 电梯竖井 diàntī shùjǐng
2 (a shaft of sunshine) 一道阳光 yídào yángguāng

shaggy ADJ (毛发) 又长又乱的 (máofà) yòu cháng yòu luàn de

shake I V (PT **shook**; PP **shaken**) 1 摇动 yáodòng
to shake one's fist 挥动拳头 huīdòng quántou
to shake one's head 摇头 yáotóu
2 [人+] 发抖 [rén+] fādǒu, 打颤 dǎchàn
3 动摇 [+信心] dòngyáo [+xìnxīn] II N 1 摇动 yáodòng, 摇晃 yáohuang 2 泡沫牛奶 pàomò niúnǎi, 奶昔 nǎixī

shaken See **shake**

shakeup N 改组 gǎizǔ
a major shakeup of the company 公司的大改组 gōngsī de dà gǎizǔ

shaky ADJ 1 摇晃的 [+椅子] yáohuang de [+yǐzi] 2 不牢靠的 [+知识] bù láokào de [+zhīshi] 3 颤抖的 [+声音] chàndǒu de [+shēngyīn]

shall MODAL V (PT **should**) 1 必须 bìxū, 应当 yīngdāng 2 一定会 yídìng huì 3 要不要 yàobuyào
Shall I ...? 要不要我...? Yàobuyào wǒ...?
We shall see. 我们再看看吧。 Wǒmen zài kàn kàn ba.

shallot N 青葱 qīngcōng [M. WD 根 gēn]

shallow ADJ 1 浅 qiǎn 2 肤浅 fūqiǎn

sham I N 1 虚假 xūjiǎ 2 骗局 piànjú, 假象 jiǎxiàng 3 假冒者 jiǎmào zhě II ADJ 虚假的 xūjiǎ de
a sham marriage 虚假的婚姻 xūjiǎ hūnyīn, 假结婚 jiǎ jiéhūn

shambles N (in a shambles) 彻底失败 chèdǐ shībài, 一团糟 yìtuánzāo

shame I N 1 羞耻 xiūchǐ, 耻辱 chǐrǔ 2 可惜 kěxí
Shame on you! 你真丢脸! Nǐ zhēn diūliǎn!
II V 使...感到羞愧 shǐ...gǎndào xiūkuì

shamefaced ADJ 面有愧色的 miànyǒukuìsè de, 羞愧的 xiūkuì de

shameful ADJ 可耻的 [+行为] kěchǐ de [+xíngwéi]

shameless ADJ 无耻的 [+人] wúchǐ de [+rén]

shampoo I N 洗发精 xǐfà jīng, 香波 xiāngbō II V (用洗发精) 洗头发 (yòng xǐfàjīng) xǐtóufa

shantytown N 棚户区 pénghùqū, 贫民区 pínmínqū

shape I N 1 形状 xíngzhuàng 2 状态 zhuàngtài, 情况 qíngkuàng
in shape 身体健康 shēntǐ jiànkāng
II V 形成 xíngchéng 2 使…成形 shǐ... chéngxíng

share I V 1 分享 fēnxiǎng, 合用 héyòng 2 共有 gòngyǒu II N 1 个人的份儿 gèrén de fènr 2 股 gǔ, 股份 gǔfèn [M. WD 份 fèn]

shark N 鲨鱼 shāyú [M. WD 条 tiáo]

sharp ADJ 1 锐利的 [+刀子] ruìlì de [+dāozi], 锋利的 fēnglì de 2 尖锐的 [+批评] jiānruì de [+pīpíng] 3 急剧的 [+上升] jíjù de [+shàngshēng] 4 敏锐的 [+头脑] mǐnruì de [+tóunǎo]
as sharp as a tack 头脑机敏 tóunǎo jīmǐn
5 剧烈的 [+疼痛] jùliè de [+téngtòng]
sharp pain 剧痛 jùtòng

sharpen V 1 使 [+刀子] 锋利 shǐ [+dāozi] fēnglì 2 使 [+照片] 清晰 shǐ [+zhàopiàn] qīngxī

sharpener N 磨刀器 módāo qì, 卷笔刀 juǎnbǐdāo

shatter V 1 使 [+玻璃] 粉碎 shǐ [+bōli] fěnsuì 2 使 [+希望] 破灭 shǐ [+xīwàng] pòmiè

shatterproof ADJ 防碎的 fángsuì de

shave V, N 刮胡子 guā húzi, 剃须 tìxū
a close shave 侥幸脱险 jiǎoxìng tuōxiǎn

shaver N (电动) 剃刀 (diàndòng) tìdāo

shawl N 披肩大围巾 pījiān dà wéijīn

she PRON 她 tā

sheaf (PL **sheaves**) N (一) 叠 (纸) (yì) dié (zhǐ)

shear (PT **sheared**; PP **shorn**) V 1 给羊剪毛 gěi yáng jiǎnmáo, 剪羊毛 jiǎnyángmáo

2 剪断 jiǎnduàn, 砍掉 kǎndiào

shears N 园艺大剪刀 yuányì dà jiǎndāo

sheath N 1 (刀) 套 (dāo) tào, (剑) 鞘 (jiàn) qiào 2 (女子) 紧身衣 (nǚzǐ) jǐnshēnyī [M. WD 件 jiàn]

shed¹ N 小库房 xiǎo kùfáng, 工具房 gōngjùfáng [M. WD 间 jiān]

shed² V (PT & PP **shed**) 1 摆脱 bǎituō, 去掉 qùdiào
to shed hairs 掉毛 diào máo
2 流出 liúchū
to shed blood 流血 liú xiè
to shed tears 流泪 liú lèi
3 [灯+] 发光 [dēng+] fāguāng

sheen N 一层光泽 yì céng guāngzé

sheep (PL **sheep**) N 羊 yáng [M. WD 只 zhī/头 tóu], 绵羊 miányáng
a flock of sheep 一群羊 yì qún yáng
sheep dog 牧羊犬 mùyángquǎn

sheepish ADJ 窘困的 jiǒngkùn de, 腼腆的 miǎntian de

sheer ADJ 1 十足的 shízú de, 纯粹的 chúncuì de
sheer folly 纯粹是愚蠢 chúncuì shì yúchǔn
sheer luck 完全是运气 wánquán shì yùnqì
2 陡峭的 [+悬崖] dǒuqiào de [+xuányá]
3 极薄的 jí báo de, 几乎透明的 jīhū tòumíng de

sheet N 1 床单 chuángdān 2 一张 yì zhāng

sheik(h) N (阿拉伯) 酋长 (Ālābó) qiúzhǎng, 王子 wángzǐ

shelf (PL **shelves**) N 搁板 gēbǎn, 搁架 gējià

shell N 1 壳 ké, 外壳 wàiké, 甲 jiǎ 2 贝壳 bèiké 3 子弹 zǐdàn, 炮弹 pàodàn

shellfish N 贝类 (动物) bèilèi (dòngwù)

shelter I N 1 遮蔽 zhēbì 2 遮蔽所 zhēbì suǒ, 避难的地方 bìnàn de dìfang
II V 1 遮蔽 zhēbì, 挡住 dǎngzhu 2 窝藏 wōcáng

sheltered ADJ 1 避开风雨的 bìkāi fēngyǔ de 2 备受庇护的 bèishòu bìhù de

shelve V 1 搁置 [+计划] gēzhì [+jìhuà] 2 将 [+商品] 放在货架上 jiāng [+shāngpǐn] fàng zài huò jià shàng

shepherd I N 牧羊人 mùyángrén **II** v 带领 [+一群人] dàilǐng [+yìqún rén]

sheriff N（美国）民选的县治安官 (Měiguó) mínxuǎn de xiàn zhì'ānguān

shh INTERJ 嘘 xū

shield N 盾 dùn, 盾牌 dùnpái

shift I N **1** 变化 biànhuà **2**（早／晚+）班 [zǎo/wǎn+] bān

day shift 白天班 báitiān bān, 日班 rìbān

night shift 夜班 yèbān

II v **1** 变化 biànhuà **2** 转移 zhuǎnyí, 转换 zhuǎnhuàn

to shift the responsibility 转嫁责任 zhuǎnjià zérèn

shifty ADJ 狡猾的 [+人] jiǎohuá de [+rén]，贼眼溜溜的 zéiyǎn liūliū de

shimmer N 闪闪发微光 shǎnshǎn fā wēiguāng

shin N 肋部 lèibù, 小腿 xiǎotuǐ

shine I v (PT & PP shone) **1** 照（耀）zhào (yào) **2** 照射 zhàoshè **3** (PT & PP shined) 擦亮 cāliàng **II** N **1** 光泽 guāngzé, 光亮 guāngliàng **2** 擦亮 cāliàng

shingle N **1** 木瓦 mù wǎ, 墙面板 qiángmiàn bǎn **2**（海滩上的）卵石 (hǎitān shàng de) luǎnshí

shingles N 带状疱疹 dàizhuàng pàozhěn

shining ADJ 光辉的 guānghuī de, 杰出的 jiéchū de

shining example 光辉榜样 guānghuī bǎngyàng

shiny ADJ 光滑发亮的 guānghuá fāliàng de

ship I N 船 chuán, 舰 艇 jiàn tǐng **II** v 运送 yùnsòng, 发出 fāchū

shipload N（船舶）运载量／载人数 (chuánbó) yùnzàiliàng/zàirén shù

a shipload of grain 一船的谷物 yì chuán de gǔwù

shipment N **1** 一批货物 yì pī huòwù **2** 运送 yùnsòng

illegal shipment of weapons 非法运送武器 fēifǎ yùnsòng wǔqì

shipwreck I N **1** 船只失事 chuánzhī shīshì, 海难 hǎinàn **2** 失事船只 shīshì chuánzhī [M. WD 艘 sōu] **II** v [船+] 沉没 [chuán+] chénmò

shipyard N 造船厂 zàochuán chǎng

shirk v 逃避 [+责任] táobì [+zérèn]

shirt N 衬衫 chènshān

shirtsleeves N 衬衫袖子 chènshān xiùzi

in shirtsleeves 只穿衬衫 zhǐ chuān chènshān

shit N **1** 粪便 fènbiàn, 大便 dàbiàn

Oh, shit! 啊呀，坏了！Āyā, huàile!

2 呸，放屁！Pēi, fàngpì!

to feel like shit 感到很不舒服 gǎndào hěn bù shūfú, 感到浑身不对劲 gǎndào húnshēn búduìjìn

shiver N, v 发抖 fādǒu

to shiver with cold 冷得发抖 lěng de fādǒu

shoal N **1** 一大群鱼 yí dà qún yú **2** 浅滩 qiǎntān

shock I N **1** 震惊 zhènjīng **2** 震动 zhèndòng, 冲击 chōngjī

shock absorber 减震器 jiǎnzhènqì

shock wave 冲击波 chōngjībō, 强烈反应 qiángliè fǎnyìng

3 休克 xiūkè

shock therapy 休克疗法 xiūkè liáofǎ

II v 震惊 zhènjīng

cultural shock 文化冲击 wénhuà chōngjī

shocking ADJ 令人震惊的 lìngrén zhènjīng de

shod v **1** See shoe **II** v **2** 穿着…鞋子的 chuānzhuó…xiézi de

shoddy ADJ **1** 粗制滥造的 [+商品] cūzhì lànzào de [+shāngpǐn], 劣质的 lièzhì de **2** 不公正的 bù gōngzhèng de

shoe I N 鞋 xié, 鞋子 xiézi

ballet shoes 芭蕾舞鞋 bālěiwǔxié

walking shoes 步行鞋 bùxíngxié

If the shoe fits, (wear it.) 如果说得对，就接受吧。Rúguǒ shuōde duì, jiù jiēshòu ba.

II v (PT & PP shod) 给（马）钉铁蹄 gěi (mǎ) dīng tiětí

shoehorn N 鞋拔 xiébá

shoestring N 鞋带 xiédài

a shoestring budget 微薄的预算 wēibó de yùsuàn

on a shoestring 精打细算 jīngdǎ xìsuàn

shone See shine

shoo I INTERJ 嘘 xū **II** v (to shoo sb away) 把某人赶走 bǎ mǒurén gǎnzǒu

shook See **shake**

shook-up ADJ 心烦意乱的 xīn fán yì luàn de

shoot¹ I v (PT & PP **shot**) **1** 开枪 kāiqiāng, 射击 shèjī

to shoot on sight 见人就开枪 jiàn rén jiù kāiqiāng

2 拍摄（照片/电影/电视片）pāishè (zhàopiàn/diànyǐng/diànshì piàn) **3** 投 [+篮] tóu [+lán], 射 [+门] shè [+mén]

to shoot the breeze 聊天 liáotiān, 侃大山 kǎn dàshān

to shoot your mouth off 到处乱说 dàochù luànshuō

II N **1**（照片/电影/电视片）拍摄 (zhàopiàn/diànyǐng/diànshì piàn) pāishè **2** 打猎 dǎliè

shoot² N 芽 yá, 苗 miáo

shooting star N 流星 liúxīng

shop I N **1** 店 diàn [M. WD 家 jiā], 店铺 diànpù [M. WD 家 jiā] **2** 工场 gōngchǎng [M. WD 间 jiān], 车间 chējiān **3** 工艺课 gōngyìkè, 手工课 shǒugōngkè **II** v 购物 gòuwù, 买东西 mǎi dōngxi

shoplift v 偷窃商品 tōuqiè shāngpǐn

shoplifting N 商店货物扒窃 shāngdiàn huòwù páqiè

shopping N 购物 gòuwù

shipping cart 购物推车 gòuwù tuīchē

shopping mall 购物中心 gòuwù zhōngxīn, 商场 shāngchǎng

shopping spree 尽情采购 jìnqíng cǎigòu

to go shopping 上街买东西 shàngjiē mǎi dōngxi, 上街采购 shàngjiē cǎigòu

shore I N 岸边 ànbiān, 海岸 hǎi'àn, 湖畔 húpàn **II** v (to shore up) 支撑 zhīchēng

shorn See **shear**

short I ADJ **1** 短 duǎn

short circuit 短路 duǎnlù

short cut 近路 jìnlù, 捷径 jiéjìng

short wave 短波 duǎnbō

2 矮 ǎi, 矮小 ǎixiǎo **3** 不够 bú gòu, 缺乏 quēfá

in short supply 很缺乏 hěn quēfá

to be short with 对…很粗暴无礼 duì… hěn cūbào wúlǐ, 简慢 jiǎnmàn

II v 使 [+电器] 短路 shǐ [+diànqì] duǎnlù

III N (in short) 简单地说 jiǎndān de shuō **IV** ADV **1** (short of) 除非 chúfēi, 要不是 yàobùshì **2** (to stop short of) 差一点 chàyìdiǎn, 险些 xiǎnxiē **3** (to cut short) 突然中断 tūrán zhōngduàn, 打断 dǎduàn

shortage N 短缺 duǎnquē

short-change v 少给找头 shǎo gěi zhǎotou, 欺诈 qīzhà

shortcoming N 缺点 quēdiǎn

shorten v 缩短 suōduǎn

shortfall N 差额 chā'é, 不足之数 bùzú zhī shù

shorthand N 速记（法）sùjì (fǎ)

shorthanded ADJ 人手不够的 rénshǒu búgòu de

shortlist v 准备决选名单 zhǔnbèi juéxuǎn míngdān

be shortlisted 进入决赛 jìnrù juésài

short-lived ADJ 短暂的 duǎnzàn de

shortly ADV **1** 不久 bù jiǔ **2** 不耐烦地 bú nàifán de

short-range ADJ **1** 短程的 duǎnchéng de **2** 短期的 duǎnqī de, 近期的 jìnqī de

a short-range plan 近期计划 jìnqī jìhuà

shorts N 短裤 duǎnkù [M. WD 条 tiáo]

short-sighted ADJ **1** 近视的 [+眼睛] jìnshì de [+yǎnjing] **2** 短视的 [+政策] duǎnshì de [+zhèngcè]

short-term ADJ 短期的 duǎnqī de

short-term lease 短期租赁 duǎnqī zūlìn

shot I v See **shoot II** N **1** 射击 shèjī **2** 注射 zhùshè **3** 镜头 jìngtóu

shot in the arm 兴奋剂 xīngfènjì, 令人鼓舞的事 lìngrén gǔwǔ de shì

shotgun N 猎枪 lièqiāng

shotgun wedding（因女方已怀孕）不得不举行的婚礼（yīn nǚfāng yǐ huáiyùn）bùdebù jǔxíng de hūnlǐ, 奉子成婚 fèng zi chénghūn

should [NEG **should not** ABBREV **shouldn't**] MODAL v **1** 应该 yīnggāi **2** 可能 kěnéng

shoulder I N 肩膀 jiānbǎng

shoulder bag 挎包 kuàbāo, 肩背包 jiānbēi bāo

to shrug one's shoulder 耸肩膀 sǒng jiānbǎng

II v 承担 [+责任] chéngdān [+zérèn]

shout v, N 喊 hǎn, 喊叫 hǎnjiào

to shout at 对…嚷嚷 duì…rāngrang

shove N, v 推 tuī

push and shove 你推我挤 nǐtuīwǒjǐ

shovel I N 铁锹 tiěqiāo, 铲子 chǎnzi [M. WD 把 bǎ] II v 用铲子铲起 yòng chǎnzi chǎn qǐ

show I v (PT showed; PP shown) 1 显示 xiǎnshì 2 给…看 gěi…kàn 3 放 fàng, 放映 fàngyìng II N 1 演出 yǎnchū 2 节目 jiémù 3 展览 zhǎnlǎn

to be on show 展览中 zhǎnlǎn zhōng, 展出中 zhǎnchū zhōng

4 表面的样子 biǎomiàn de yàngzi

show business 演艺界 yǎnyìjiè

to show … around 带领…参观 dàilíng…cānguān

to show off 显示 xiǎnshì, 卖弄 màinong

to show up 来 lái, 出席 chūxí

showcase I N [新产品+] 展示 [xīnchǎnpǐn+] zhǎnshì, 陈列 chénliè II v 展示 [+新产品] zhǎnshì [+xīn chǎnpǐn]

showdown N 摊牌 tānpái, 决战 juézhàn

shower I N 1 阵雨 zhènyǔ 2 淋浴 (间) línyù (jiān) 3 (baby shower) 产前送礼会 chǎnqián sònglǐ huì, (bridal shower) 结婚送礼会 jiéhūn sònglǐ huì II v 1 洗淋浴 xǐ línyù 2 洒落 sǎluò 3 大量地给 dàliàng de gěi

to shower sb with praise 对某人赞扬有加 duì mǒurén zànyáng yǒu jiā

showgirl N 歌舞女演员 gēwǔ nǚyǎnyuán

showing N 1 (电影) 放映 (diànyǐng) fàngyìng

a private showing 内部放映 nèibù fàngyìng

2 (艺术品) 展览 (yìshùpǐn) zhǎnlǎn 3 表现 biǎoxiàn

a disappointing showing 令人失望的表现 lìngrén shīwàng de biǎoxiàn

showmanship N 表演技巧 biǎoyǎn jìqiǎo 2 (政客) 作秀 (zhèngkè) zuòxiù

shown See show

show-off N 喜欢卖弄自己的人 xǐhuan màinong zìjǐ de rén

showpiece N 公开展示的东西 gōngkāi zhǎnshì de dōngxi, 样板 yàngbǎn

showtime N 开演时间 kāiyǎn shíjiān

It's showtime! 演出现在开始了! Yǎnchū xiànzài kāishǐ le!

shrank See shrink

shrapnel N 弹片 dànpiàn [M. WD 片 piàn]

shred I N 细条 xìtiao, 碎片 suìpiàn

to tear sth to shreds 把某物撕成碎片 bǎ mǒuwù sī chéng suìpiàn

II v 1 把 [+文件] 切碎 bǎ [+wénjiàn] qiēsuì 2 把 [+食物] 切成碎片 bǎ [+shíwù] qiēchéng suìpiàn

shredder N 碎纸机 suìzhǐjī

shrewd ADJ 精明的 jīngmíng de, 判断正确的 pànduàn zhèngquè de

shriek N, v 尖叫 jiānjiào, 尖声喊叫 jiānshēng hǎnjiào

a shriek of terror 恐怖的尖叫声 kǒngbù de jiānjiào shēng

shrill ADJ 尖叫的 jiānjiào de

shrimp N 小虾 xiǎoxiā

shrine N 圣坛 shèng tán, 圣地 shèngdì

shrink¹ (PT shrank; PP shrunk) v 缩小 suōxiǎo, 缩小 suōxiǎo

to shrink from 逃避 táobì

shrink² 精神病医生 jīngshénbìng yīshēng

shrivel, shrivel up v (使…) 收缩 (shǐ…) shōusuō, (使…) 干瘪 (shǐ…) gānbiě

shroud I N 1 覆盖 (物) fùgài (wù), 遮蔽 (物) zhēbì (wù)

in a shroud of secrecy 在完全秘密之中 zài wánquán mìmì zhī zhōng

2 (包) 尸布 (bāo) shī bù II v 覆盖 fùgài, 遮蔽 zhēbì

shrub N 灌木 guànmù [M. WD 棵 kē]

shrug I v 耸肩 sǒngjiān

to shrug off 不予重视 bùyǔ zhòngshì, 不加理会 bù jiā lǐhuì

II N 耸肩 sǒngjiān

shrunk See shrink

shrunken ADJ 干瘪的 gānbiě de

shudder v 发抖 fādǒu, 颤抖 chàndǒu

shuffle I v 1 拖着脚走 tuōzhe jiǎo zǒu,

蹒跚 pánshān **2** 洗牌 xǐpái **3** 调动 [+人员] diàodòng [+rényuán] **II** N **1** 拖着脚走路 tuōzhe jiǎo zǒulù, 蹒跚 pánshān **2** 洗牌 xǐpái **3** （人员）调动 (rényuán) diàodòng

shun v 躲避 duǒbì, 躲开 duǒkāi

shunt I v **1** 使 [电/血液+] 分流 shǐ [diàn/xuèyè] fēnliú **2** 把 [+人] 转移到 bǎ [+rén] zhuǎnyí dào **II** N 旁路 pánglù, 旁通道 pángtōng dào

shush v 示意保持安静 shìyì bǎochí ānjìng, 叫人别作声 jiào rén bié zuòshēng

shut v (PT & PP **shut**) 关上 guānshang
to shut down 关门 guānmén, 停止营业（生产）tíngzhǐ yíngyè (shēngchǎn)
to shut up 闭嘴 bìzuǐ
II 关好的 guānhǎo de

shutdown N 关闭 guānbì, 停业 tíngyè

shutter N **1** （照相机）快门 (zhàoxiàngjī) kuàimén **2** 百叶窗 bǎiyèchuāng

shuttle I N **1** 来回往返的汽车／飞机 láihuí wǎngfǎn de qìchē/fēijī **2** （织布机）梭子 (zhībùjī) suōzi
shuttle diplomacy 穿梭外交 chuānsuō wàijiāo
II v 穿梭往返 chuānsuō wǎngfǎn

shuttle-cock N 羽毛球 yǔmáoqiú

shy I ADJ **1** 害羞的 hàixiū de **2** (shy of sth) 没有达到 méiyǒu dádào **II** v (to shy away from) 避开 bìkāi, 回避 huíbì

sibling N 兄弟姐妹 xiōngdì jiěmèi
sibling rivalry 兄弟姐妹之间的竞争 xiōngdì jiěmèi zhījiān de jìngzhēng

sick I ADJ **1** 病了 bìng le, 生病了 shēngbìng le
sick leave 病假 bìngjià
sick pay 病假工资 bìngjià gōngzī
2 恶心 ěxīn, 呕吐 ǒutù **3** 厌倦 yànjuàn
to make ... sick 叫…感到厌恶 jiào...gǎndào yànwù, 叫…感到愤慨 jiào...gǎndào fènkǎi
II N (the sick) 病人 bìngrén

sicken v **1** 使…厌恶 shǐ...yànwù **2** （使…）生病 (shǐ...) shēngbìng

sickening ADJ 令人厌恶的 lìng rén yànwù de, 令人作呕的 lìng rén zuò'ǒu de

sickle N 镰刀 liándāo [M. WD 把 bǎ]

sickly ADJ **1** 体弱多病的 [+人] tǐruò duōbìng de [+rén] **2** 难闻的 [+气味] nánwén de [+qìwèi]

sickness N 病 bìng, 疾病 jíbìng

side I N **1** 部分 bùfen, 部、部 bù **2** 身边 shēnbiān, 身旁 shēnpáng **3** 面 miàn, 侧面 cèmiàn **4** 边 biān **5** 一方 yì fāng **II** ADJ 旁边的 pángbiān de, 侧面的 cèmiàn de
a side street 小巷 xiǎoxiàng, 小路 xiǎolù
side dish 配菜 pèicài
side effect 副作用 fù zuòyòng
side order 另点的小菜 lìng diǎn de xiǎocài
III v (to side against) 站在…的对立面 zhàn zài...de duìlìmiàn
to side with 站在…的一面 zhàn zài...de yímiàn, 支持 zhīchí

sideboard N 餐具柜 cānjù guì

sideburns N 脸腮胡子 liǎnsāi húzi

sidekick N 助手 zhùshǒu

sideline I N 副业 fùyè
on the sideline 旁观 pángguān, 采取观望态度 cǎiqǔ guānwàng tàidu
II v 不让 [+运动员] 参加比赛 búràng [+yùndòngyuán] cānjiā bǐsài

sidelong ADJ (a sidelong glance) 斜着眼睛看 xiézhe yǎnjing kàn, 偷看 tōukàn

sideshow N **1** 主场外的游乐节目 zhǔchǎng wài de yóulè jiémù **2** 次要事件 cìyào shìjiàn

sidestep v 避开 bìkāi, 回避 huíbì

sidetrack v **1** 使…离题 shǐ...lítí **2** 拖延 tuōyán

sidewalk N 人行道 rénxíngdào [M. WD 条 tiáo]

sideways ADV 向一边（地）xiàng yìbiān (de)

sidle v 悄悄走近 qiāoqiāo zǒujìn

siege N 包围 bāowéi, 围困 wéikùn
to be under siege ① 被包围 bèibāo wéi ② 受到围攻 shòudào wéigōng

siesta N 午睡 wǔshuì

sieve I N （筛）子 (shāi) zi, 漏勺 lòusháo **II** v （用筛子）筛 (yòng shāizi) shāi

sift v **1** 筛 [+面粉] shāi [+miànfěn], 过滤 guòlǜ **2** 详细检查 xiángxì jiǎnchá

sigh I v 叹气 tànqì, 舒了口气 shū le kǒuqì II N 叹气 tànqì

sight N 1 视觉 shìjué 2 看到 kàndao 3 景象 jǐngxiàng
out of sight, out of mind 不看见，不想到。(→ 眼不见，心不烦。) Bú kànjiàn, bù xiǎng dào. (→ Yǎn bú jiàn, xīn bù fán.)

sighted ADJ 有视力的 yǒu shìlì de, 能看见的 néng kànjian de

sighting N 看到 kàndao, 目击 mùjī
sightings of the fugitive 多次看到逃犯 duōcì kàndào táofàn

sightread v 随看随奏 [+乐曲] suí kàn suí zòu [+yuèqǔ], 随看随唱 [+歌曲] suí kàn suí chàng [+gēqǔ]

sightseeing N 观光 guānguāng, 游览 yóulǎn

sign I N 1 符号 fúhào 2 标志 biāozhì 3 招牌 zhāopái 4 手势 shǒushì 5 迹象 jìxiàng II v 1 签字 qiānzì 2 打手势 dǎ shǒushì, 示意 shìyì
to sign for 签收 qiānshōu
to sign up ① 聘用 pìnyòng ② 报名参加 bàomíng cānjiā

signal I N 信号 xìnhào 2 标志 biāozhì II v 1 打手势示意 dǎ shǒushì shìyì 2 明确表示 míngquè biǎoshì III ADJ (a signal success) 巨大的成功 jùdà de chénggōng

signatory N 签署者 qiānshǔzhě, 签约国 qiānyuē guó

signature I N 1 签字 qiānzì, 签名 qiānmíng
an illegible signature 无法辨认的签名 wúfǎ biànrèn de qiānmíng
to collect signatures 收集签名 shōují qiānmíng
2 特征 tèzhēng, 标志 biāozhì II ADJ 标志性的 biāozhìxìng de, 特有的 tèyǒu de

significance N 意义 yìyì

significant ADJ 有重大意义的 yǒu zhòngdà yìyì de
significant other 最重要的那位（丈夫／妻子，男朋友／女朋友）zuì zhòng-yàode nà wèi (zhàngfu/qīzi, nánpéng-you/nǚpéngyou)

signify v 标志 biāozhì, 意味 yìwèi

signing N 签字 qiānzì, 签署 qiānshǔ
signing ceremony 签字仪式 qiānzì yíshì

signpost N 路标 lùbiāo, 指示牌 zhǐshì pái

silence N 1 寂静 jìjìng 2 沉默 chénmò
Speech is silver, and silence is golden 言语是银，沉默是金。Yányǔ shì yín, chénmò shì jīn.

silencer N 消声器 xiāoshēngqì

silent ADJ 1 寂静的 jìjìng de 2 沉默的 chénmò de, 一言不发的 yì yán bù fā de
(the) silent majority 沉默的大多数 chénmò de dàduōshù
silent partner 不参与经营的合伙人 bù cānyù jīngyíng de héhuǒrén

silhouette I N 侧面影像 cèmiàn yǐngxiàng, 黑色轮廓画象 hēisè lúnkuò huàxiàng II v 现出黑色轮廓 xiànchū hēisè lúnkuò

silk N 丝绸 sīchóu, 绸缎 chóuduàn

silkworm N 蚕 cán

silky ADJ 丝绸般的 sīchóu bān de, 光泽柔滑的 guāngzé róuhuá de

sill N 窗台 chuāngtái

silly ADJ 愚蠢的 yúchǔn de, 傻的 shǎ de

silt I N 淤泥 yūní, 泥沙 níshā II v (to silt up) 淤塞 yūsè

silver I N 1 银 yín, 银器 yínqì 2 银（白）色 yín (bái) sè II ADJ 银制的 yínzhì de, 银质的 yínzhì de
silver anniversary 银婚（纪念日）yínhūn (jìniànrì), 结婚二十五周年 jiéhūn èrshíwǔ zhōunián
silver medal 银牌 yínpái

silver-plated ADJ 镀银的 dùyín de

silversmith N 银匠 yínjiàng

silverware N 银器 yínqì

similar ADJ 相似的 xiāngshì de

similarity N 相似 xiāngsì, 相似性 xiāngsì xìng

simile N 明喻 míngyù

simmer I v 1（用文火）慢慢煮 (yòng wénhuǒ) mànmàn zhǔ, 炖 dùn 2（冲突）渐渐激化 (chōngtū) jiànjiàn jīhuà II N（用文火）慢慢煮 (yòng wénhuǒ) mànmàn zhǔ, 炖 dùn

simper v 傻笑 shǎxiào

simple ADJ 1 简单的 jiǎndān de 2 简朴的 jiǎnpú de

simple fracture 单纯性骨折 dānchún xìng gǔzhé

simple interest 单利 dānlì

simple-minded ADJ 头脑简单的 tóunǎo jiǎndān de

simplicity N 简单容易 jiǎndān róngyì

simplify V 简化 jiǎnhuà

simplified (Chinese) character 简体字 jiǎntǐzì

simply ADV 1 仅仅 jǐnjǐn, 只是 zhǐ shì 2 简直 jiǎnzhí 3 简单地 jiǎndān de 4 简朴地 jiǎnpǔ de

simulate V 模拟 mónǐ, 模仿 mófǎng

simulation N 模拟 mónǐ, 模仿 mófǎng

simulation exercise 模拟练习 mónǐ liànxí

simultaneous ADJ 同时（发生）tóngshí (fāshēng)

simultaneous interpreter 同声传译译员 tóngshēng chuányì yìyuán

sin N 罪 zuì, 罪孽 zuìniè 为 违犯教规 wéifàn jiàoguī, 犯罪 fànzuì

since I CONJ 1 自从 zìcóng 2 因为 yīnwèi, 由于 yóuyú II PREP 自从 zìcóng III ADV 自从那以后 zìcóng nà yǐhòu, 后来 hòulái

sincere ADJ 真诚的 zhēnchéng de

sincerely ADV 真诚地 zhēnchéng de

Sincerely Yours 您真诚的 nín zhēnchéng de, 你的 nǐde

sincerity N 真诚 zhēnchéng, 诚挚 chéngzhì

in all sincerity 十分真诚地 shífēn zhēnchéng de

sinewy ADJ 肌肉发达的 jīròu fādá de

sinful ADJ 有罪（过）的 yǒuzuì (guò) de, 极不应该的 jí bù yīnggāi de

sing (PT sang; PP sung) V 唱 chàng, 唱歌 chànggē

to sing sb's praises 高度赞扬某人 gāodù zànyáng mǒurén

Singapore N 新加坡 Xīnjiāpō

singe V 烧焦 shāojiāo

singer N 歌手 gēshǒu, 歌唱家 gēchàngjiā

pop singer 流行歌手 liúxíng gēshǒu

single I ADJ 1 一 yī, 唯一的 wéiyī de 2 单人的 dānrén de

single file 一路纵排 yílù zòng pái, 单行 dānxíng

3 单身（的）dānshēn (de) II V (to single out) 挑选出 tiāoxuǎn chū

single-breasted ADJ 单排纽扣的（上衣）dānpái niǔkòu de (shàngyī)

single-handed ADJ 单枪匹马的 dānqiāng pǐmǎ de, 独自一人的 dúzì yìrén de

single-minded ADJ 一心一意 yì xīn yí yì

singles N 1 单身汉 dānshēnhàn, 未婚女子 wèihūn nǚzǐ 2 单打比赛 dāndǎbǐsài

singly ADV 单个地 dān gè de, 一个一个地 yí ge yí ge de

singsong N 反复起伏的语调 fǎnfù qǐfú de yǔdiào

singular I ADJ 1 （语法）单数的 (yǔfǎ) dānshù de 2 唯一的 wéiyī de, 独一的 dúyī de 3 异常的 [+才能] yìcháng de [+cáinéng], 非凡的 fēifán de II N （语法）单数 (yǔfǎ) dānshù

sinister ADJ 邪恶的 xié'è de, 阴险的 yīnxiǎn de

sink[1] (PT sank; PP sunk) V 1 [石头+] 下沉 [shítou+] xiàchén 2 [价格+] 下降 [jiàgé+] xiàjiàng, 减少 jiǎnshǎo

to sink into despair 陷入绝望之中 xiànrù juéwàng zhīzhōng

to sink or swim 沉浮 chénfú, 自找生路 zìzhǎo shēnglù

3 挖 [+井] wā [+jǐng]

sink[2] 洗脸盆 xǐliǎnpén, 洗涤池 xǐdí chí

sinner N 有罪过的人 yǒu zuìguò de rén, 罪人 zuìrén

sinus N 鼻窦 bídòu

sip I V 小口喝 xiǎokǒu hē, 啜 chuò, 抿 mǐn II N 一小口 [+酒] yì xiǎokǒu [+jiǔ]

siphon I N 虹吸管 hóngxīguǎn II V 1 用虹吸管吸出 yòng hóngxīguǎn xīchū 2 （非法）抽调 [+资金] (fēifǎ) chōudiào [+zījīn]

sir N 先生 xiānsheng

siren N 气笛 qìdīng, 警报器 jǐngbàoqì

air-raid siren 空袭警报 kōngxí jǐngbào

sissy N 女孩子气的男孩 nǚháizi qì de nánhái, 娘娘腔的男孩 niángniangqiāng de nánhái

sister N 1 姐姐 jiějie, 妹妹 mèimei, 姐妹 jiěmèi

sister city 姐妹城市 jiěmèi chéngshì

2 修女 xiūnǚ

sisterhood N **1** 姐妹情谊 jiěmèi qíngyì **2** 妇女宗教团契 fùnǚ zōngjiào tuánqì

sister-in-law N 嫂嫂 sǎosao (elder brother's wife), 弟妹 dìmèi (younger brother's wife), 小姨 xiǎoyí (wife's sister), 小姑 xiǎogū (husband's sister)

sit (PT & PP sat) V **1** 坐 zuò
to sit back 放松休息 fàngsōng xiūxi
to sit up and take notice 开始关注 kāishǐ guānzhù, 警觉起来 jǐngjué qǐlái
2 [国会+] 开会 [guóhuì+] kāihuì
to sit on 是委员会成员 shì wěiyuánhuì chéngyuán

sit-down ADJ 有服务员侍候的 [+餐馆] yǒufú wùyuán shìhòu de [+cānguǎn], 非自助餐的 fēi zìzhùcān de

site I N 地方 dìfang, 地点 dìdiǎn
on site 在现场 zài xiànchǎng
camp site 露营地 lùyíngdì
construction/building site 建筑工地 jiànzhù gōngdì, 工地 gōngdì
II V (be sited) 位于 wèiyú

sit-in N 静坐示威 jìngzuò shìwēi

sitter N (babysitter)（替人照看孩子的）保姆 (tìrén zhàokàn háizi de) bǎomǔ

sitting N **1**（分批用餐的）一批 (fēnpī yòngcān de) yìpī **2** (in one sitting) 一口气 yìkǒuqì
a sitting duck 容易击中的目标 róngyì jīzhòng de mùbiāo

situation N **1** 形势 xíngshì **2** 处境 hǔjìng, 状况 zhuàngkuàng

situation comedy (ABBREV sitcom) N 情景喜剧 qíngjǐng xǐjù

sit-up N 仰卧起坐 yǎng wò qǐ zuò

six NUM 六 liù, 6

six-pack N 六罐／瓶装 liù guàn/píng zhuāng, 半打瓶 bàndǎ píng

sixteen NUM 十六 shíliù, 16

sixth NUM 第六 dìliù

sixty NUM 六十 liùshí, 60

sizable ADJ 相当大／多的 xiāngdāng dà/duō de

size N **1** 大小 dàxiǎo, 体积 tǐjī, 分量 fènliàng **2** 多少 duōshǎo, 数目 shùmù **3** 尺码 chǐmǎ

sizzle I V [在煎锅里+] 发出嘶嘶声 [zài jiānguō lǐ] fā chū sīsī shēng II N 嘶嘶声 sīsī shēng

skate I V 溜冰 liūbīng II N (ice skate) 滑冰鞋 huábīng xié [M. WD 双 shuāng], 溜冰鞋 liūbīng xié [M. WD 双 shuāng]
roller skate 旱冰鞋 hànbīng xié

skateboard N 滑板 huábǎn

skeleton N **1** 骨架 gǔjià, 骨骼 gǔgé
skeleton key 万能钥匙 wànnéng yàoshi
skeleton service 最基本的服务 zuì jīběn de fúwù
skeleton staff 必不可少的工作人员 bì bùkěshǎo de gōngzuò rényuán

skeptic N 怀疑论者 huáiyílùnzhě

skeptical ADJ 持怀疑态度的 chí huáiyí tàidù de, 不相信的 bù xiāngxìn de

sketch I N **1** 素描 sùmiáo, 速写 sùxiě **2** 滑稽短剧 gǔjī duǎnjù [M. WD 出 chū] II V 画速写 huà sùxiě, 画素描 huà sùmiáo

sketchy ADJ 粗略的 cūlüè de

skew V 歪曲的 wāiqū de, 曲解 qūjiě

skewer I N 烤肉叉 kǎoròuchā [M. WD 把 bǎ] II V（用烤肉叉）把 [+食物] 串起来 (yòng kǎoròuchā) bǎ [+shíwù] chuàn-qǐlái

ski I V 滑雪 huáxuě II N 滑雪板 huáxuě bǎn [M. WD 副 fù]

skid I V [汽车+] 滑向一边 [qìchē+] huá xiàng yìbiān, 打滑 dǎhuá II N（车辆）打滑 (chēliàng) dǎhuá
skid marks（汽车）打滑痕迹 (qìchē) dǎhuá hénjì

skies N 天空 tiānkōng

skill N 技能 jìnéng, 技巧 jìqiǎo

skilled ADJ 有技巧的 yǒu jìqiǎo de
skilled worker 技术工人 jìshù gōngrén

skillet N 长柄平底煎锅 chángbǐng píngdǐ jiānguō

skillful ADJ 高技能的 gāo jìnéng de, 有技巧的 yǒu jìqiǎo de, 熟练的 shúliàn de

skim V **1** 从液体表面撇去浮物 cóng yètǐ biǎomiàn piē qù fúwù **2** 浏览 [+报纸标题] liúlǎn [+bàozhǐ biāotí]
skim milk 脱脂牛奶 tuōzhǐ niúnǎi

skimpy ADJ **1** 太短的 [+裙子] tài duǎn de [+qúnzi], 过于暴露的 guòyú bàolù de

2 过分节省的 guòfèn jiéshěng de

skin I N **1** 皮肤 pífū **2** [动物／水果+] 皮 [dòngwù／shuǐguǒ+] pí

to be skin and bone 皮包骨 pí bāo gǔ, 骨瘦如柴 gǔ shòu rú chái

to have thick skin 脸皮厚 liǎnpí hòu

II v 剥去…的皮 bāoqù...de pí, 去皮 qùpí

skin-deep ADJ 肤浅的 fūqiǎn de

skinny ADJ 瘦得皮包骨头的 shòu dé pí bāo gútou de

skinny dipping 裸（体）（游）泳 luǒ (tǐ) (yóu) yǒng

skin-tight ADJ 紧身的 jǐnshēn de

skip I v **1** 轻快蹦跳 qīngkuài dé tiào, 蹦跳 bèngtiào

to skip rope 跳绳 tiàoshéng

2 匆匆离开 cōngcōng líkāi

to skip town 逃离出城 táolí chūchéng

3 不做 bú zuò, 跳过 tiàoguò

to skip breakfast 不吃早饭 bù chī zǎo fàn

II v 轻跳 qīng tiào, 蹦跳 bèngtiào

skipper I N **1** 船长 chuánzhǎng [M. WD 位 wèi] **2** 运动队长 yùndòngduì duìzhǎng **II** v 当船长／运动队长 dāng chuánzhǎng／yùndòngduì duìzhǎng

skirmish N 小规模冲突 xiǎoguīmó chōngtū

skirt I N 裙子 qúnzi **II** v **1** 沿着…边缘行走 yánzhe...biānyuán xíngzǒu **2** 绕过 [+敏感话题] ràoguò [+mǐngǎn huàtí]

skit N 滑稽短剧 gǔjì duǎnjù, 讽刺短文 fěngcì duǎnwén

skittish ADJ **1** [马+] 容易受惊的 [mǎ+] róngyì shòujīng de **2** [人+] 小心翼翼的 [rén+] xiǎoxīn yìyì de

skulk v 躲躲闪闪 duǒduǒ shǎnshǎn, 鬼鬼祟祟 guǐguǐ suìsuì

skull N 头颅 tóulú

skullcap N（牧师／犹太男子戴的）圆便帽 (mùshi／Yóutài nánzǐ dài de) yuán biànmào

skunk N 臭鼬 chòuyòu [M. WD 只 zhī], 黄鼠狼 huángshǔláng [M. WD 只 zhī]

sky（PL **skies**）N 天空 tiānkōng

skydiving N 跳伞（运动）tiàosǎn (yùndòng)

sky-high ADJ 极高的 [+价格] jí gāo de [+jiàgé]

skylight N 天窗 tiānchuāng [M. WD 扇 shàn]

skyline N（空中）轮廓线 (kōngzhōng) lúnkuòxiàn

skyrocket v 猛升 měng shēng, 剧增 jùzēng

skyscraper N 摩天大楼 mótiān dàlóu

slab N 厚板 hòubǎn, 平板 píngbǎn

a slab of beef 一大块牛肉 yí dà kuài niúròu

slack I ADJ **1** [生意+] 清淡的 [shēngyì+] qīngdàn de, 萧条的 xiāotiáo de **2** [纪律+] 松懈的 [jìlǜ+] sōngxiè de, 马虎的 mǎhu de **3** [绳子+] 松的 [shéngzi+] sōng de **II** N **1** 多余的资金／能力 duōyú de zījīn／nénglì **2** 松弛（部份）sōngchí (bùfen)

to take up the slack 接替 jiētì, 补足 bǔzú

III v 松劲 sōngjìn, 松懈 sōngxiè

slacken, slacken off v（使…）放慢／变弱 (shǐ...) fàng màn／biàn ruò

slacks N 便装裤 biànzhuāng kù [M. WD 条 tiáo]

slag N 炉渣 lúzhā [M. WD 块 kuài], 矿渣 kuàngzhā [M. WD 块 kuài]

slain See **slay**

slake v 满足 mǎnzú

to slake your thirst 解渴 jiěkě

to slake a desire 满足欲望 mǎnzú yùwàng

slam I v **1** 使劲关门 shǐjìn guānmén **2** 砰地放下 pēng de fàngxià

to slam on the brakes 猛踩刹车 měng cǎi shāchē

II N 碰的一声 pèng de yì shēng

slander N, v 诽谤 fěibàng, 诋毁 dǐhuǐ

slang N 俚语 lǐyǔ

slant I v 倾斜 qīngxié, 斜穿 xiéchuān **II** N **1** 斜面 xiémiàn, 斜线 xiéxiàn **2** 有偏向性的观点 yǒupiān xiàngxìng de guāndiǎn

slap I v **1** 用巴掌打 yòng bāzhang dǎ, 掴 [+耳光] guāi [+ěrguāng]

to slap sb on the back 赞扬恭贺某人 zànyáng gōnghè mǒurén

to slap sb on the face 打某人一巴掌 dǎ mǒurén yì bāzhǎng, 掴耳光 guāi ěrguāng

II N 一巴掌 yì bāzhǎng,（一记）耳光 (yí jì) ěrguāng

slapdash ADJ 草率仓促的 [+工作] cǎoshuài cāngcù de [+gōngzuò]

slash I v 1 猛砍 měngkǎn 2 大幅度削减 dàfúdù xuējiǎn II N 1 猛砍 měngkǎn 2 斜线号 xiéxiànhào (/)

slat N 薄板条 báobǎntiáo

slate¹ N 1 板岩 bǎnyán [M. WD 块 kuài], 板石 bǎnshí [M. WD 块 kuài]

a clean slate 清白的历史 qīng bái de lìshǐ, 无不良记录 wúbù liáng jìlù

2 候选人名单 hòuxuǎnrén míngdān

slate² v 预定 yùdìng, 预计 yùjì

slather v 给 [+面包] 涂上厚厚的一层 [+花生酱] gěi [+miànbāo] túshàng hòuhòude yìcéng [huāshēngjiàng]

slaughter v, N 屠宰 túzǎi, 屠杀 túshā

slaughterhouse N 屠宰场 túzǎichǎng

slave I N 1 奴隶 núlì 2 完全受摆布的人 wánquán shòu bǎibù de rén II v 苦干 kǔ gān, 拼命工作 pīnmìng gōngzuò

slave driver 奴隶监工 núlì jiāngōng, 驱使别人拼命工作的人 qūshǐ biéren pīnmìng gōngzuò de rén

slavery N 奴役 núyì

slay (PT **slew**; PP **slain**) v 杀死 shāsǐ, 谋杀 móushā

sleazy ADJ 低级庸俗的 dījí yōngsú de

sled N 雪橇 xuěqiāo

sledge hammer N 大锤 dàchuí

sleek ADJ 1 线条流畅优美的 [+轿车] xiàntiáo liúchàng yōuměi de [+jiàochē] 2 光滑的 [+毛皮] guānghuá de [+máopí]

sleep I v (PT & PP **slept**) 睡 shuì, 睡觉 shuìjiào

to sleep around 乱搞性关系 luàn gǎo xìng guānxi

to sleep over 在别人家过夜 zài biéren jiā guò yè

to lose sleep over … 因为…而睡不着 觉 yīnwèi…ér shuìbuzháo jiào

II N 睡眠 shuìmián

sleep deprivation 睡眠不足 shuìmián bùzú, 缺乏睡眠 quēfá shuìmián

sleeper N 1 (a heavy/light sleeper) 睡得很 深／很浅的人 shuì dehěn shēn/hěn qiǎn de rén 2 火车卧铺车厢 huǒchē wòpù chēxiāng 3 儿童睡衣 értóng shuìyī

sleepless ADJ 不眠的 bù mián de, 睡不着 觉的 shuì bù zháo jiào de

sleepless night 不眠之夜 bùmián zhīyè

sleepwalking N 梦游 mèngyóu

sleepy ADJ 瞌睡的 kēshuì de, 困倦的 kùnjuàn de

sleepyhead N 想睡觉的人 xiǎng shuìjiào de rén, 瞌睡虫 kēshuìchóng

sleet N 雨夹雪 yǔjiāxuě [M. WD 场 cháng]

sleeve N 衣袖 yīxiù, 袖子 xiùzi

sleeveless ADJ 无袖的 wú xiù de

sleigh N 雪橇 xuěqiāo

slender ADJ 苗条的 miáotiao de, 纤细的 xiānxì de

slept See **sleep**

sleuth N 侦探 zhēntàn

slew¹ 1 See **slay** 2 [汽车+] 突然急转弯 [qìchē+] tūrán jí zhuǎnwān

slew² N 大量 dàliàng

slice I N 1 一（薄）片 yì (báo) piàn

a slice of lemon 一片柠檬 yípiàn níngméng

2 一部分 yí bùfen

a slice of life 生活的一个片断 shēnghuó de yí ge piànduàn

a slice of profits 利润的一部分 lìrùn de yí bùfen

II v 把…切成薄片 bǎ…qiēchéng bópiàn

slick I ADJ 1 油滑的 [+推销员] yóuhuá de [+tuīxiāoyuán] 2 华丽而无意义的 [+演员] huálì ér wúyìyì de [+yǎnchū]

II N 1 (路面／水面上的) 浮油 (lùmiàn/ shuǐmiàn shàng de) fúyóu 2 优质光纸印 刷的精美杂志 yōuzhì guāngzhǐ yìnshuā de jīngměi zázhì III v 用油把头发梳得 光滑发亮 yòng yóu bǎ tóufa shū dé guānghuá fāliàng

slid See **slide**

slide I v (PT & PP **slid**) 1 滑 huá 2 下滑 xiàhuá, 下降 xiàjiàng 3 越来越坏 yuèláiyuè huài, 每况愈下 měi kuàng yù xià

II N 1 滑梯 huátī 2 幻灯片 huàndēngpiàn [M. WD 张 zhāng/套 tào]

slide projector 幻灯机 huàndēngjī

3 下滑 xiàhuá, 下降 xiàjiàng 4 崩落 bēngluò

sliding door N 拉门 lāmén, 滑动门

huádòng mén [M. WD 道 dào]

slight I ADJ 轻微的 qīngwēi de, 微小的 wēixiǎo de 2 微不足道的 wēibùzúdào de, 轻视 qīngshì

slightly ADV 稍 shāo, 稍微 shāowēi

slim I ADJ 1 苗条的 miáotiao de, 修长的 xiūcháng de 2 微小的 wēixiǎo de
slim chance 微小的机会 wēixiǎo de jīhuì 3 薄的 [+本子] báo de [+běnzi] II V 使⋯减少 shǐ…jiǎnshǎo

slime N 黏液 niányè, 黏糊糊的东西 niánhūhude dōngxi

slimy ADJ 黏糊糊的 niánhūhude

sling I V (PT & PP **slung**) 投 tóu, 掷 zhì, 抛 pāo II N 吊带 diàodài, 吊索 diàosuǒ
slings and arrows 恶意攻击 èyìgōngjī

slingshot N 弹弓 dàngōng

slink (PT & PP **slunk**) V 悄悄溜走 qiāoqiāo liūzǒu

slip I V 1 滑滑 huá huá, 滑动 huádòng 2 溜走 liū zǒu, 偷偷走动 tōutōu zǒudòng 3 下降 xiàjiàng II N 1 一小张纸 yì xiǎo zhāng zhǐ 2 失误 shīwù
a slip of the pen 笔误 bǐwù
a slip of the tongue 口误 kǒuwù

slipknot N 活结 huójié

slipper N 拖鞋 tuōxié

slippery ADJ 1 滑的 huá de, 光滑的 guānghuá de 2 油滑的 yóuhuá de, 狡猾的 jiǎohuá de

slipshod ADJ 不认真的 bú rènzhēn de, 马虎的 mǎhu de

slip-up N 失误 shīwù, 疏忽 shūhu

slit I V (PT & PP **slit**) 切开 qiēkāi, 撕开 sīkāi II N 狭长的口子 xiácháng de kǒuzi, 裂缝 lièfèng

slither V 弯弯曲曲地滑动 wānwān qūqū de huádòng

sliver N 碎片 suìpiàn, 一小片 yì xiǎo piàn

slob N 懒惰而肮脏的人 lǎnduò ér āngzāng de rén, 粗鲁无礼的人 cūlǔ wúlǐ de rén

slobber V 流口水 liú kǒushuǐ

slog I V 1 艰难地走 jiānnán de zǒu 2 辛苦地工作 xīnkǔ de gōngzuò II N 漫长而艰巨的事 màncháng ér jiānjù de shì

slogan N 标语 biāoyǔ, 口号 kǒuhào

slop I V [水+] 晃荡溢出 [shuǐ+] huàngdang yìchū II N 泔脚 gānjiǎo

slope I N 斜面 xiémiàn, 山坡 shānpō II V 倾斜 qīngxié

sloppy ADJ 马虎的 mǎhu de, 草率的 cǎoshuài de

slosh V 使 [+液体] 晃荡 shǐ [+yètǐ] huàngdang

sloshed ADJ 喝醉的 hēzuì de

slot I N 1 狭缝 xiáfèng, 投物口 tóu wù kǒu 2 固定时间 gùdìng shíjiān, 固定位置 gùdìng wèizhì
parking slot 停车位 tíngchēwèi II V 把⋯插入狭缝 bǎ…chārù xiáfèng

sloth N 1 树懒 shùlǎn 2 懒惰 lǎnduò

slouch I V 无精打采地坐 / 站 / 走 wújīng dǎcǎi de zuò/zhàn/zǒu II N 无精打采 wújīng dǎcǎi
be no slouch at sth 善于做某事 shànyú zuò mǒushì

slough[1] N 泥沼 nízhǎo, 泥潭 nítán

slough[2] V (to slough off) 1 脱皮 tuōpí 2 摆脱 [+不好的名声] bǎituō [+bùhǎo de míngshēng]

slovenly ADJ 不整洁的 bùzhěng jié de, 邋遢的 lāta de

slow I ADJ 1 慢 màn, 缓慢 huǎnmàn
the slow lane 慢车道 mànchē dào 2 愚笨的 [+人] yúbèn de [+rén]
be slow on the uptake 领会很慢的 lǐnghuì hěn màn de, 迟钝的 chídùn de 3 清淡的 [+生意] qīngdàn de [+shēngyì] II V 减慢 jiǎnmàn III ADV 慢慢（地） mànmàn (de)

slowdown N 1 放慢 fàngmàn
a slowdown in social life 社交活动放慢 shèjiāohuódòng fàngmàn 2（工人）怠工 (gōngrén) dàigōng

slowly ADV 慢慢 mànmàn, 慢慢地 mànmān de

sludge N 污泥 wūní, 污物 wūwù

slug I N 1 鼻涕虫 bítìchóng [M. WD 条 tiáo], 蛞蝓 kuòyú [M. WD 条 tiáo] 2 少量（烈性酒）shǎoliàng (lièxìngjiǔ) II V 用拳头打 yòng quántou dǎ
to slug it out 狠狠地打架 hěnhěn de dǎjià, 拼个输赢 pīn gè shūyíng

sluggish ADJ 缓慢的 huǎnmàn de, 无力的 wúlì de

sluice I N 水闸 shuǐzhá, 水门 shuǐmén

ll v 冲洗 chōngxǐ

slum l n 贫民窟 pínmínkū ll v 过苦日子 guò kǔrìzi

slumber l n 深睡 shēn shuì, 睡眠 shuìmián ll v 睡得很深 shuì dehěn shēn, 睡觉 shuìjiào

slump l v [价格+] 暴跌 [jiàgé+] bàodiē, 急剧下降 jíjù xiàjiàng 2 [人+] 突然倒下 [rén+] tūrán dǎoxià ll n 1 暴跌 bàodiē, 猛降 měng jiàng 2 衰落 shuāiluò, 衰退 shuāituì

slung See **sling**

slunk See **slink**

slur l v 1 含糊不清地说话 hánhu bùqīng de shuōhuà 2 污蔑 wūmiè, 诋毁 dǐhuǐ ll n 污蔑 wūmiè, 诋毁 dǐhuǐ

     racist slur 种族主义的诋毁 zhǒngzúzhǔyì de dǐhuǐ

slurp v 咕嘟咕嘟地喝 gūdū gūdū de hē

slush n 1 半融的雪 bàn róng de xuě, 雪水 xuěshuǐ 2 (加碎冰的) 冷饮 (jiā suì bīng de) lěngyǐn

     slush fund 行贿资金 xínghuì zījīn

slut n 浪荡女人 làngdàng nǔrén, 荡妇 dàngfù

sly ADJ 狡猾的 jiǎohuá de, 滑头的 huátóu de

smack l v 1 (用手掌) 拍打 (yòng shǒuzhǎng) pāida 2 有点…的味道 yǒudiǎn…de wèidao ll n 1 拍打 pāida 2 (to give sb a smack on the lip) 给某人一个响吻 gěi mǒurén yí ge xiǎng wěn

small l ADJ 1 小 (的) xiǎo (de)

     small change 零钱 língqián

     small claims court 小额索赔法庭 xiǎo'é suǒpéi fǎtíng

     small fry 小人物 xiǎorénwù

     small matter 小事 xiǎoshì, 不重要的事 bú zhòngyào de shì

     small talk 闲聊 xiánliáo, 寒暄 hánxuān

2 年幼的 niányòu de 3 少量的 shǎoliàng de

     a small fortune 一大笔钱 yí dà bǐ qián

ll n (the small of the back) 腰 yāo, 腰部 yāobù

smallpox n 天花 tiānhuā

small-scale ADJ 小规模的 xiǎoguīmó de, 小型的 xiǎoxíng de

small-time ADJ 不重要的 bú zhòngyào de

     small-time conman 小骗子 xiǎo piànzi

smart[1] ADJ 1 聪明的 cōngming de, 敏捷的 mǐnjié de

     the smart money [投资+] 高明人士 [tóuzī+] gāomíngrénshì

2 耍小聪明的 shuǎ xiǎocōngming de

     smart aleck 自作聪明的人 zìzuò cōngming de rén, 喜欢耍嘴皮子的人 xǐhuan shuǎ zuǐpízi de rén

smart[2] v 感到难过 gǎndào nánguò

smash l v 1 打破 [+玻璃] dǎpò [+bōli], 打碎 dǎsuì 2 打破 [+体育记录] dǎpò [+tǐyù jìlù] 3 [汽车+] 猛撞 [qìchē+] měngzhuàng 4 捣毁 [+犯罪集团] dǎohuǐ [+fànzuì jítuán] 5 [网球] 扣球 (wǎngqiú) kòuqiú, 杀球 shāqiú ll n 1 破碎声 pòsuì shēng, 碰撞声 pèngzhuàng shēng 2 获得巨大成功的新书／新剧 huòdé jùdà chénggōng de xīnshū/xīnjù

     smash hit 大获成功的新书／新剧 dà huò chénggōng de xīnshū/xīnjù

smashed ADJ 1 喝得烂醉的 hē dé lànzuì de 2 (吸毒后) 药性发作的 (xīdú hòu) yàoxìng fāzuò de

smattering n 一点点 yìdiǎndiǎn

smear l v 1 涂抹 túmǒ 2 弄脏 nòngzāng 3 污蔑 wūmiè, 诽谤 fěibàng ll n 1 污斑 wū bān, 油迹 yóujì 2 污蔑 wūmiè, 诽谤 fěibàng

     smear campaign 诽谤活动 fěibàng huódòng

smell l n 1 气味 qìwèi 2 嗅觉 xiùjué ll v 1 闻 wén, 闻出 wénchū

     I smell a rat. 我闻到老鼠的气味。(→ 我觉得有可疑的地方。) Wǒ wéndao lǎoshǔ de qìwèi. (→ Wǒ juéde yǒu kěyí de dìfang.)

2 闻起来 wénqǐlai

smelly ADJ 臭的 chòu de, 发出臭味的 fāchū chòuwèi de

smelt v 冶炼 róngliàn, 提炼 tíliàn

smidgen n 一点点 yìdiǎndiǎn

smile v, n 笑 xiào, 微笑 wēixiào

     to be all smiles 笑容满面 xiàoróng mǎnmiàn, 满面春风 mǎnmiàn chūnfēng

smirk N, V 不怀好意地笑 bù huái hǎoyì de xiào, 得意地笑 déyì de xiào

smith N 1 铁匠 tiějiang 2 工匠 gōngjiàng

smithereens N 碎片 suìpiàn

smitten ADJ (be smitten with sb) 对某人 一见钟情 duì mǒurén yíjiàn zhōngqíng, 深深爱上某人 shēnshēn àishang mǒurén

smock N 工作服 gōngzuòfú

smog N 烟雾 yānwù

smoke I N 烟 yān II V 1 吸烟 xī yān 2 冒 烟 màoyān

smoker N 吸烟者 xīyānzhě

smokescreen N 1 烟幕 yānmù 2 障眼法 zhàngyǎnfǎ, 伪装 wěizhuāng

smoky ADJ 烟雾弥漫的 yānwù mímàn de

smolder V 没有火焰地燃烧 méiyǒu huǒyàn de ránshāo, 焖烧 mèn shāo

smooch I V 亲密接吻 qīnmì jiēwěn II N 亲 密的接吻 qīnmì de jiēwěn

smooth I ADJ 1 平坦的 píngtǎn de, 光滑 的 guānghuá de 2 糊状物的 hú zhuàng de, 无颗粒的 wú kēlì de 3 圆滑的 yuánhuá de 4 顺利的 shùnlì de, 一帆风顺的 yì fān fēng shùn de II V 1 把…弄平 bǎ... nòng píng

to smooth the way 铺平道路 pūpíngdàolù

2 涂抹 [+油膏] túmǒ [+yóugāo]

smorgasbord N （品种丰富的）自助餐 (pǐnzhǒng fēngfù de) zìzhùcān

smother V 1 使…窒息 shǐ...zhìxī, 闷死 mènsi 2 覆盖 fùgài

SMS (= Short Message Service) ABBREV 短信服务 duǎnxìn fúwù

smudge I N 污斑 wūbān, 污渍 wūzì II V 把 …弄脏 bǎ...nòngzāng, 留下污渍 liúxia wū bān

smug ADJ 自鸣得意的 zìmíng déyì de, 自 我满意的 zìwǒ mǎnyì de

smuggle V 走私 zǒusī, 偷运 tōuyùn

smuggler N 走私者 zǒusīzhě

smut N 淫秽图书／画片 yínhuì túshū/ huàpiàn

snack N 点心 diǎnxin, 小吃 xiǎochī
snack bar 小吃店 xiǎochīdiàn, 点心铺 diǎnxin pū

snag I N 小故障 xiǎogù zhàng, 意外情况 yìwài qíngkuàng
to hit a snag 出了点故障 chū le diǎn gùzhàng
II V 1 钩破 gōu pò, 撕破 sīpò 2 抓住 zhuāzhù 3 引起注意 yǐnqǐ zhùyì

snail N 蜗牛 wōniú

snake N 蛇 shé [M. WD 条 tiáo]
snake oil 蛇油 shé yóu, （骗人的）万灵 良药 (piànrén de) wàn líng liángyào

snap I V 1 [树枝+] 啪的一声折断 [shùzhī+] pā de yì shēng shéduàn 2 [人+] 厉声地 说 [rén+] lìshēng de shuō 3 [人+] 精 神崩溃 [rén+] jīngshén bēngkuì 4 [狗 +] 猛咬 [gǒu+] měng yǎo 5 拍快照 pāi kuàizhào
to snap one's fingers 打响指 dǎxiǎng zhǐ
to snap out of it 别再伤心 bié zài shāngxīn, 振作起来 zhènzuòqǐlái
II N 1 （突然折断发出的）啪的一声 (tūrán shéduàn fāchū de) pā de yì shēng 2 轻而易举的事 qīng ér yìjǔ de shì III ADJ 仓促的 cāngcù de, 草率的 cǎoshuài de

snappy ADJ 1 时髦漂亮的 [+时装] shímáo piàoliang de [+shízhuāng] 2 活泼有趣的 [+语言] huópo yǒuqù de [+yǔyán]

snapshot N 快照 kuàizhào, 生活照 shēnghuó zhào

snare I N 1 （捕捉动物的）罗网 (bǔzhuō dòngwù de) luówǎng, 陷阱 xiànjǐng 2 （让人上当的）圈套 (ràng rén shàng-dàng de) quāntào II V 1 捕捉（动物） bǔzhuō (dòngwù) 2 诱（人）中圈套 yòu (rén) zhòng quāntào

snarl I V 1 [动物+] 呲牙咆哮 [dòngwù+] zī yá páoxiào 2 [人+] 愤怒地高叫 [rén+] fènnù de gāo jiào, 怒吼 nùhǒu 3 使 [+交 通] 堵塞 shǐ [+jiāotōng] dǔsè
to get snarled up 变得一团糟 biàn de yìtuánzāo

snatch I V 1 抢出 [+钱包] qiǎng zǒu [+qiánbāo], 夺走 duó zǒu 2 抓住 [+机会] zhuāzhù [+jīhuì] II N 片断 piànduàn
in snatches 断断续续地 duànduàn xùxù de

snazzy ADJ 漂亮的 piàoliang de, 光彩夺目的 guāngcǎi duómù de

sneak I V 1 偷偷地走 tōutōu de zǒu, 偷偷摸摸地行动 tōutōu mōmō de xíngdòng 2 偷运 [+毒品] tōuyùn [+dúpǐn]
to sneak a glance 偷偷地看一眼 tōutōu de kàn yìyǎn
II N 偷偷摸摸的人 tōutōu mōmō de rén
a sneak preview（电影）内部预映 (diànyǐng) nèibù yùyìng

sneakers N 胶底运动鞋 jiāo dǐ yùndòngxié

sneaking ADJ 暗暗的 àn'àn de
a sneaking suspicion 暗自怀疑 ànzì huáiyí

sneaky ADJ 偷偷摸摸的 tōutōu mōmō de

sneer V, N 冷笑 lěngxiào, 讥笑 jīxiào

sneeze V, N（打）喷嚏 (dǎ) pēntì

snicker N, V 暗自发笑 ànzì fāxiào, 暗笑 ànxiào

sniff N, V（出声地）闻 (chūshēng de) wén, 嗅 xiù
to sniff at 对…嗤之以鼻 duì…chī zhī yǐ bí, 不屑一顾 búxiè yígù

sniffle V 反复地抽鼻子 fǎnfù de chōu bízi

sniffles N 反复抽鼻子 fǎnfù chōu bízi
to have the sniffles 患轻感冒 huàn qīng gǎnmào

snip V, N 快速剪 kuàisù jiǎn, 剪断 jiǎnduàn

snipe V 1 打冷枪 dǎlěngqiāng, 狙击 jūjī 2 指责 zhǐzé, 攻击 gōngjī

sniper N 狙击手 jūjīshǒu

snippet N（音乐/消息）片断 (yīnyuè/xiāoxi) piànduàn

snitch V 1 告密 gàomì, 告发 gàofā 2 偷窃 tōuqiè, 小偷小摸 xiǎotōu xiǎomō

snob N 1 势利小人 shìlìxiǎorén
snob appeal（商品）对势利顾客的吸引力 (shāngpǐn) duì shìlì gùkè de xīyǐnlì 2 自命不凡的人 zìmìng bùfán de rén
wine snob 自以为很会品酒的人 zìyǐwéi hěn huì pǐn jiǔ de rén

snobbery N 势利 shìlì

snobbish, snobby ADJ 势利的 shìlì de

snooker N 斯诺克式台球 Sīnuòkè shì táiqiú

snoop N, V 打听 [+别人的隐私] dǎtīng [+biéren de] yǐnsī, 窥探 kuītàn

snooty ADJ 目中无人的 mùzhōng wúrén de, 妄自尊大的 wàng zì zūn dà de

snooze V, N 打盹 dǎ dǔn, 小睡 xiǎoshuì

snore V, N 打鼾 dǎ hān, 打呼噜 dǎ hūlu

snorkel I N 1（潜水）呼吸管 (qiánshuǐ) hūxī guǎn 2（潜水艇）通气管 (qiánshuǐtǐng) tōngqì guǎn II V 用呼吸管潜泳 yòng hūxī guǎn qiányǒng

snort V 哼鼻子 hēng bízi, 哼着鼻子说话 hēngzhe bízi shuōhuà
to snort at 对…嗤之以鼻 duì…chī zhī yǐ bí

snotty ADJ 自以为了不起的 zìyǐwéi liǎobuqǐ de

snout N（猪）鼻子 (zhū) bízi

snow I N 雪 xuě II V 下雪 xiàxuě

snowball I N 雪球 xuěqiú
snowball effect 滚雪球效应 gǔnxuěqiú xiàoyìng
II V（像滚雪球一样）迅猛增长/发展 (xiàng gǔnxuěqiú yíyàng) xùnměng zēngzhǎng/fāzhǎn

snowfall N 降雪 jiàngxuě, 降雪量 jiàngxuě liàng

snowman N 雪人 xuěrén

snowplow N 扫雪车 sǎoxuěchē

snowstorm N 暴风雪 bàofēngxuě

snow-white ADJ 雪白 xuěbái

snowy ADJ 1 下雪的 xiàxuě de, 多雪的 duō xuě de 2 雪白的 xuěbái de

snub V, N 冷落 lěngluò, 怠慢 dàimàn

snuff I V 1 掐灭 [+蜡烛] qiāmiè [+làzhú] 2 扼杀 èshā, 杀死 shāsǐ II N 鼻烟 bíyān

snug ADJ 1 温暖舒适的 [+家] wēnnuǎn shūshì de [+jiā] 2 安乐舒服的 [+人] ānlè shūfu de [+rén]

snuggle, snuggle up V 偎依 wēiyī, 蜷缩 quánsuō

so I ADV 1 这么 zhème, 那么 nàme, 如此 rúcǐ 2 这样 zhèyàng II CONJ 所以 suǒyǐ
so as to 以便于 yǐbiànyú, 这样 zhèyàng
so … as to 如此地…，以至于 rúcǐ de… yǐzhìyú
so that 以便于 yǐbiànyú, 这样 zhèyàng
so … that 如此地…，以至于 rúcǐ de…, 以至于 yǐzhìyú…，得之 de
… or so …左右 …zuǒyòu

soak N, V 浸 jìn, 浸透 jìntòu

so-and-so N 某某人 mǒumǒu rén, 某某事 mǒumǒu shì

soap N 肥皂 féizào [M. WD 块 kuài]
a bar of soap 一块肥皂 yí kuài féizào
soap opera 肥皂剧 féizàojù

soar V 1 急剧上升 jíjù shàngshēng 2 高飞 gāo fēi

S.O.B. (= son of a bitch) ABBREV 狗养的 gǒuyǎngde

sob N 哭泣 kūqì, 抽泣 chōuqì
sob story（骗人眼泪的）伤感故事 (piànrén yǎnlèi de) shānggǎn gùshi

sober I ADJ 1 清醒的 qīngxǐng de 2 严肃的 yánsù de, 朴素的 pǔsù de II V (to sober up) 使 [+醉酒者] 清醒过来 shǐ [+zuìjiǔ zhě] qīngxǐng guòlai

soccer N（英式）足球（Yīngshì）zúqiú

sociable ADJ 好交际的 hào jiāojì de, 喜欢与人交往的 xǐhuan yǔ rén jiāowǎng de

social ADJ 1 社会的 shèhuì de
social studies 社会科学课程 shèhuì kēxué kèchéng
social worker 社会福利工作者 shèhuì fúlì gōngzuòzhě, 社工 shègōng
2 社交的 shèjiāo de
social climber 试图向上爬的人 shìtú xiàngshàng pá de rén
social drinking 在交际场合饮酒 zài jiāojì chǎnghé yǐnjiǔ

socialism N 社会主义 shèhuìzhǔyì

socialite N 社交界名人 shèjiāojiè míngrén

society N 1 社会 shèhuì 2 社交界 shèjiāo jiè 3 社 shè, 协会 xiéhuì, 社团 shètuán

socioeconomic ADJ 社会经济的 shèhuì jīngjì de

sociologist N 社会学家 shèhuìxuéjiā

sociology N 社会学 shèhuìxué

sock[1] N 袜子 wàzi [M. WD 只 zhī, 双 shuāng], 短袜子 duǎn wàzi [M. WD 只 zhī, 双 shuāng]

sock[2] V 猛击 měngjī, 狠打 hěn dǎ

socket N 1（电源）插座 (diànyuán) chāzuò
floor socket 地面插座 dìmiàn chāzuò
headphone socket 耳机插座 ěrjī chāzuò

wall socket 墙上插座 qiáng shàng chāzuò
2 眼窝 yǎnwō

sod N 草皮 cǎopí

soda N 苏打 sūdá
soda pop 汽水 qìshuǐ
soda water 苏打水 sūdáshuǐ

sodden ADJ 湿淋淋的 shīlínlín de

sofa N 沙发 shāfā [M. WD 张 zhāng]

soft ADJ 1 柔软的 róuruǎn de 2 轻声的 qīngshēng de 3 软心肠的 ruǎn xīncháng de
soft touch 容易受骗上当的人 róngyì shòupiàn shàngdàng de rén, 软果子 ruǎnguǒzi

softball N 垒球 lěiqiú

soft-boiled ADJ 煮得半熟的 zhǔ dé bàn shóu de, 溏心的 tángxīn de

soften V 1 软化 ruǎnhuà 2 缓和 huǎnhé, 减少 jiǎnshǎo
to soften the impact 减弱冲击 jiǎnruò chōngjī

softhearted ADJ 软心肠的 ruǎn xīncháng de, 好心的 hǎoxīn de

soft-spoken ADJ 说话轻柔的 shuōhuà qīngróu de

software N 软件 ruǎnjiàn
anti-virus software 防（电脑）病毒软件 fáng (diànnǎo) bìngdú ruǎnjiàn

soggy ADJ 湿透的 shītòu de, 浸水的 jìnshuǐ de

soil I N 1 土壤 tǔrǎng, 泥土 nítǔ
one's native soil 某人的故土 mǒurén de gùtǔ
II V 弄脏 nòngzāng, 玷污 diànwū

sojourn N 短暂居住 duǎnzàn jūzhù, 暂住 zànzhù

solace N 慰藉 wèijí, 安慰 ānwèi

solar ADJ 太阳的 tàiyáng de
solar eclipse 日蚀 rìshí
solar panel 太阳能电池板 tàiyángnéng diànchí bǎn
solar system 太阳系 tàiyángxì

sold See **sell**

soldier I N 军人 jūnrén, 士兵 shìbīng
soldier of fortune 雇佣兵 gùyōngbīng
II V (to soldier on) 坚持下去 jiānchí xiàqu

sold-out ADJ 满座的 mǎnzuò de

sole¹ N 1 脚底 jiǎodǐ 2 鞋底 xiédǐ 3 鳎鱼 tǎyú [M. WD 条 tiáo]

sole² ADJ 唯一的 wéiyī de, 独有的 dúyǒu de

sole authorship 独享著作权 dúxiǎng zhùzuòquán

solely ADV 唯一地 wéiyī de, 独有地 dúyǒu de

solemn ADJ 严肃庄重的 yánsù zhuāngzhòng de

a solemn ceremony 庄重的仪式 zhuāngzhòng de yíshì

a solemn promise 严肃的承诺 yánsù de chéngnuò

solicit V 1 请求 [+募捐] qǐngqiú [+mùjuān], 征求 [+意见] zhēngqiú [+yìjiàn] 2 推销 [+商品] tuīxiāo [+shāngpǐn] 3 (妓女+) 拉客 [jìnǚ+] lākè

solicitor N 1 推销员 tuīxiāoyuán, 揽客 qiánkè 2 法务官 fǎwùguān 3 (英国) 初级律师 (Yīngguó) chūjí lǜshī

solicitor general (美国) 司法部副部长 (Měiguó) Sīfǎbù fùbùzhǎng

solicitous ADJ 关怀的 guānhuái de, 关心的 guānxīn de

solid I ADJ 1 固体的 gùtǐ de, 坚固的 jiāngù de 2 结实的 jiēshí de 3 牢靠的 láokào de, 可靠的 kěkào de II N 固体 gùtǐ

solidarity N 团结一致 tuánjié yízhì

solidify V 1 (使…) 变成固体 (shǐ…) biànchéng gùtǐ 2 巩固 gǒnggù, 加强 jiāqiáng

solids N 固体食物 gùtǐ shíwù

soliloquy N 独白 dúbái

solitaire N 1 独粒宝石 dúlì bǎoshí 2 单人纸牌游戏 dānrén zhǐpái yóuxì

solitary ADJ 单一的 dānyī de, 单独的 dāndú de

solitary confinement 单独监禁 dāndú jiānjìn, 禁闭 jìnbì

solitude N 孤独 gūdú, 单独 dāndú

in solitude 独自 (地) dúzì (de)

solo I ADJ, ADV 单人的 [+表演] dānrén de [+biǎoyǎn]

to play solo 做单人表演 zuò dānrén

biǎoyǎn, 单人飞行 dānrén fēixíng

II N 1 独奏曲 dúzòu qū, 独唱曲 dúchàng qū 2 独奏 dúzòu, 独唱 dúchàng, 单人 (飞行) 表演 dānrén (fēixíng) biǎoyǎn

violin solo 小提琴独奏 (曲) xiǎotíqín dúzòu (qū)

solo flight 单人飞行 dānrén fēixíng

soloist N 独奏者 dúzòu zhě, 独唱者 dúchàngzhě

solstice N (summer solstice) 夏至 xiàzhì, (winter solstice) 冬至 dōngzhì

soluble ADJ 1 可溶解的 [+固体] kěróngjiě de [+gùtǐ] 2 可解决的 [+问题] kě jiějué de [+wèntí]

solution N 1 解决 jiějué, 解决办法 jiějué bànfǎ 2 解答 jiědá, 答案 dá'àn 3 溶液 róngyè, 溶解 róngjiě

solve V 1 解决 jiějué 2 解答 jiědá

solvent N 溶剂 róngjì

somber ADJ 1 阴沉的 [+天空] yīnchén de [+tiānkōng] 2 严峻的 [+表情] yánjùn de [+biǎoqíng]

some I ADJ 有些 yǒuxiē, 一些 yìxiē II ADV 大约 dàyuē III PRON 一些 yìxiē

somebody See **someone**

someday ADV 总有一天 zǒng yǒu yìtiān, 有朝一日 yǒuzhāo yí rì

somehow ADV 1 总得 zǒngdé 2 不知怎么 搞的 bù zhī zěnme gǎo de, 不知怎样的 bùzhī zěnyàng de

someone, somebody PRON 有人 yǒurén, 某人 mǒurén

someone else 另一个人 lìng yí ge rén

someplace ADV 某个地方 mǒu gè dìfang

somersault I N 翻跟斗 fāngendou, 筋斗 jīndǒu II V 翻跟斗 fāngendou, 前 / 后滚翻 qián/hòu gǔnfān

something PRON 有东西 yǒu dōngxi, 有 事情 yǒu shìqing, 某物 mǒuwù, 某事 mǒushì

something like 就好像 jiù hǎoxiàng, 大 约 dàyuē

to have something to do with 和…有 关系 hé...yǒu guānxi

sometime I ADV 在某一个时候 zài mǒu yí ge shíhou

sometime before night 午夜前某个时

候 wǔyè qián mǒu gè shíhou
II ADJ 偶尔的 ǒu'ěr de

sometimes ADV 有时候 yǒushíhou

somewhat ADV 有点儿 yǒudiǎnr

somewhere ADV 什么地方 shénme
dìfang, 某地 mǒudì

son N 1 儿子 érzi
the Son 圣子 Shèngzǐ, 耶稣基督 Yēsū
Jīdū
2 孩子 háizi, 小伙子 xiǎohuǒzi

sonata N 奏鸣曲 zòumíngqǔ

song N 歌 gē, 歌曲 gēqǔ [M. WD 首 shǒu]

sonic ADJ 声音的 shēngyīn de, 声波的
shēngbō de
sonic boom 声震 shēng zhèn

son-in-law N 女婿 nǚxu

sonnet N 十四行诗 shísìhángshī

sonorous ADJ 洪亮的 [+声音] hóngliàng
de [+shēngyīn]

soon ADV 不久 bù jiǔ, 很快 hěn kuài
as soon as ... 一…就…, yī…jiù…

soot N 烟灰 yānhuī, 煤灰 méihuī

soothe V 使 [+某人] 平静 shǐ [+mǒurén]
píngjìng, 抚慰 fǔwèi

soothing ADJ 柔和平静的 róuhe píngjìng
de, 抚慰人心的 fǔwèi rénxīn de

sop V (to sop up) 抹干 mǒ gān, 吸干 xīgān

sophisticated ADJ 1 经历丰富的 [+人]
jīnglì fēngfù de [+rén], 老练的 lǎoliàn
de **2** 精密的 [+仪表] jīngmì de [+yíbiǎo],
尖端的 [+技术] jiānduān de [+jìshù]

sophomore N (高中或大学) 二年级
学生 (gāozhōng huò dàxué) èr niánjí
xuésheng

soporific ADJ 使人昏昏欲睡的 shǐrén
hūnhūn yùshuì de, 催眠的 cuīmián de

sopping ADJ 湿透的 shītòu de

soprano N 女高音（歌手）nǚgāoyīn
(gēshǒu)

sorbet N 冰糕 bīnggāo

sorcerer N 魔法师 mófǎ shī, 巫师 wūshī

sorcery N 巫术 wūshù, 魔法 mófǎ

sordid ADJ 1 肮脏的 [+地方] āngzāng de
[+dìfang] **2** 卑鄙的 [+行为] bēibǐ de
[+xíngwéi], 下流的 xiàliú de

sore I ADJ 酸痛 suāntòng II N 1 疤 bā **2** 伤
痛处 shāngtòng chù

sorely ADV 极其严重（地）jíqí yánzhòng
(de)

sorrow N 悲伤 bēishāng, 悲痛 bēitòng

sorry ADJ 1 对不起 duìbuqǐ **2** 难过 nánguò
3 遗憾 yíhàn **4** 惭愧 cánkuì

sort I N 1 (sort of) 有点儿 yǒudiǎnr **2** 种
（类）zhǒng (lèi) **3**（计算机操作）分类
(jìsuànjī cāozuò) fēnlèi, 排序 páixù II V
将…分类 jiāng…fēnlèi
to sort out 整理 zhěnglǐ
to sort through 查找 cházhǎo

SOS N 紧急求救信号 jǐnjí qiújiù xìnhào

so-so ADJ, ADV 一般性的 yìbānxìng de, 不
好也不坏 bùhǎo yě búhuài

soufflé N 蛋奶酥 dànnǎisū

sought See seek

sought-after ADJ 很受欢迎的 hěn shòu
huānyíng de, 吃香的 chīxiāng de

soul N 1 灵魂 línghún
soul mate 知己 zhījǐ, 心灵之交 xīnlíng
zhī jiāo
soul music 灵歌 línggē, 灵曲 língqǔ
2 人 rén **3** 精神 jīngshén, 特质 tèzhì

soulful ADJ 深情而伤感的 shēnqíng ér
shānggǎn de

soul-searching N 深刻反省 shēnkè
fǎnxǐng, 自我解剖 zìwǒ jiěpōu

sound I N 声音 shēngyīn
by the sound of it 听起来 tīngqilai, 看
来 kànlai
sound barrier 声障 shēngzhàng
sound effects 音响效果 yīnxiǎng xiàoguǒ
II V 听起来 tīngqilai, 似乎 sìhū
to sound sb out 探听某人的意见
tàntīng mǒurén de yìjiàn
Sounds good. 好啊 hǎo a
III ADJ 1 健全的 jiànquán de **2** 合理的
héllǐ de **IV** ADV (sound asleep) 睡得很熟
shuì dehěn shú

soundly ADV 1 深沉地 [+睡眠] shēnchén
de [+shuìmián] **2** 彻底地 [+打败] chèdǐ
de [+dǎbài]

soundproof ADJ 隔音的 géyīn de

soundtrack N 电影配乐 diànyǐng pèiyuè

soup N 汤 tāng, 羹 gēng
soup kitchen 救济穷人的流动厨房 jiùjì
qióngrén de liúdòng chúfáng

sour I ADJ **1** 酸 suān
sour cream 酸奶油 suān nǎiyóu
sour grapes 酸葡萄（心态）suān pútao (xīntài)
2 坏脾气的 huài píqi de **II** v 变坏 biàn huài

source N 来源 láiyuán
source code（计算机）源代码 (jìsuànjī) yuán dàimǎ

sourdough N 酵头 jiàotóu

south I N **1** 南面 nánmian **2** (the South) 南方 nánfāng **II** ADJ 南面的 nánmian de
South America 南美洲 Nán Měizhōu
the South Pole 南极 Nánjí
III ADV 在南面 zài nánmian
to go south 变坏 biànhuài, 恶化 èhuà

southbound ADJ 朝南的 cháonán de

southeast N 东南 dōngnán

southeastern ADJ 东南的 dōngnán de

southerly ADJ（在）南方的 (zài) nánfāng de
southerly wind 南风 nánfēng

southern ADJ 南的 nán de, 南部的 nánbù de
the southern hemisphere 南半球 nánbànqiú

southerner N 南方人 nánfāngrén, 南部人 nánbù rén

southward ADJ, ADV 向南（的）xiàng nán (de)

southwest N 西南 xīnán

southwestern ADJ 西南的 xīnán de

souvenir N 纪念品 jìniànpǐn

sovereign I ADJ 享有独立主权的 xiǎngyǒu dúlì zhǔquán de **II** N 君主 jūnzhǔ, 国王 guówáng, 女王 nǚwáng

sow¹ (PT sowed; PP sowed, sown) v 播（种）bō (zhǒng)
to sow one's wild oats（年轻时）放荡不羁 (niánqīng shí) fàngdàng bùjī, 到处拈花惹草 dàochù niānhuā rě cǎo

sow² N 母猪 mǔzhū [M. WD 头 tóu]

sown See sow¹

soy, soya N 黄豆 huángdòu [M. WD 粒 lì/颗 kē], 大豆 dàdòu [M. WD 粒 lì/颗 kē]
soy bean 黄豆 huángdòu, 大豆 dàdòu
soy sauce 酱油 jiàngyóu

spa N **1** 矿泉疗养地 kuàngquán liáoyǎngdì **2** 按摩浴缸 ànmó yùgāng **3** 水疗 shuǐliáo

space N **1** 空地 kòngdì, 地方 dìfang **3** 空间 kōngjiān

space-age ADJ 太空时代的 tàikōng shídài de, 高度现代化的 gāodù xiàndàihuà de
space-age laboratory 高度现代化的实验室 gāodù xiàndàihuà de shíyànshì

spacecraft/spaceship/space shuttle N 宇宙飞船 yǔzhòu fēichuán, 航天器 hángtiānqì

spaced-out ADJ 迷迷糊糊的 mími húhu de, 头脑不清楚的 tóunǎo bùqīngchu de

spacious ADJ 宽敞的 kuānchang de, 宽阔的 kuānkuò de

spade N **1**（纸牌/扑克牌）黑桃 (zhǐpái/pūkèpái) hēitáo **2** 锹 chǎn, 铲子 chǎnzi
Call a spade a spade. 是什么说什么。（→直言不讳。）Shì shénme jiù shuō shénme.（→ Zhíyán bú huì.）

spaghetti N（意大利）细面条 (Yìdàlì) xìmiàntiáo

span I N **1** 期间 qījiān **2** 持续时间 chíxù shíjiān
sb's life span 某人的寿命 mǒurén de shòumìng
attention span 注意力持续的时间 zhùyìlì chíxù de shíjiān
3 跨度 kuàdù, 全长 quáncháng **II** v **1**（大桥+）跨越 [dà qiáo+] kuàyuè **2**（事件+）持续 [shìjiàn+] chíxù

spangle N（服装的）金属饰片 (fúzhuāng de) jīnshǔ shìpiàn

Spanish I ADJ 西班牙的 Xībānyá de, 西班牙人的 Xībānyárén de, 西班牙语的 Xībānyáyǔ de **II** N **1** 西班牙人 Xībānyárén **2** 西班牙语 Xībānyáyǔ

spank v **1** 打（小孩）屁股 dǎ (xiǎohái) pìgu **2** 击败 jībài

spar v **1**（拳击手之间）练拳 (quánjīshǒu zhījiān) liànquán **2** 争论 zhēnglùn

spare I ADJ **1** 备用的 bèiyòng de
spare change 多余的硬币 duōyú de yìngbì
spare key 备用钥匙 bèiyòng yàoshi
2 空闲的 kòngxián de **II** v **1** 使…免受 shǐ…miǎnshòu

to spare sb the trouble 使某人免受麻烦 shǐ mǒurén miǎnshòu máfan

to spare sb's feelings 使某人免于难受 shǐ mǒurén miǎnyú nánshòu

2 不伤害 bù shānghài

Spare me. 饶了我吧。Ráo le wǒ ba.

3 不使用 bù shǐyòng, 节省 jiéshěng

to spare no expenses 不省省任何费用 bù jiéshěng rènhé fèiyòng, 不惜工本 bùxī gōngběn

III N 备用品 bèiyòngpǐn

sparingly ADV 节省地 jiéshěng de, 有节制地 yǒujié zhì de

spark I N **1** 火花 huǒhuā, 火星 huǒxīng

spark plug 火花塞 huǒhuāsāi

2 （麻烦的）起因 (máfan de) qǐyīn **3** 才智 cáizhì, 活力 huólì **II** V **1** 引起 [+麻烦] yǐnqǐ [+máfan], 导致 dǎozhì **2** 迸发火花 bèngfā huǒhuā

sparkle I V 闪闪发亮 shǎnshǎn fāliàng, 闪光 shǎnguāng **II** N **1** 闪亮 shǎnliàng, 闪光 shǎnguāng **2** 兴致 xìngzhì

sparrow N 麻雀 máquè [M. WD 只 zhī]

sparse ADJ 稀少的 xīshǎo de

sparsely ADV 稀少地 xīshǎo de

sparsely populated 人烟稀少的 rényān xīshǎo de

spartan ADJ 简朴的 jiǎnpǔ de, 清苦的 qīngkǔ de

spasm N 痉挛 jìngluán, 抽筋 chōujīn

a spasm of coughing 一阵猛烈的咳嗽 yízhèn měngliè de késou

spasmodic ADJ **1** 痉挛的 jìngluán de, 抽搐的 chōuchù de **2** 断断续续的 duàn-duàn xùxù de

spastic ADJ 极其笨拙的 jíqí bènzhuō de, 极易激动的 jí yì jīdòng de **II** N 患大脑麻痹的人 huàn dànǎo mábì de rén

spat[1] N 口角 kǒujué, 拌嘴 bànzuǐ

spat[2] V See **spit**

spate N (a spate of sth) 多起 [+事故] duō qǐ [+shìgù], 大量 dàliàng

a spate of H1N1 cases 多起猪流感病例 duōqǐ zhū liúgǎn bìnglì

spatter N, V 溅溅 jiàn, 洒 sǎ

spatula N 铲子 chǎnzi, 刮刀 guādāo

spawn I V **1** [鱼+] 大量产卵 [yú+] dàliàng

chǎnluǎn **2** 酿成 [+危机] niàngchéng [+wēijī] **II** N 成团的鱼卵 chéngtuán de yúluǎn

spay V 切除（动物的）卵巢 qiēchú (dòngwù de) luǎncháo

speak (PT **spoke**; PP **spoken**) V **1** 说 shuō **2** 说话 shuōhuà **3** 演讲 yǎnjiǎng, 演说 yǎnshuō

to speak out 公开发表议论 gōngkāi fābiǎo yìlùn, 公开抗议 gōngkāi kàngyì

to speak up 说得大声一点儿 shuō de dàshēng yìdiǎnr

speaker N **1** 演讲者 yǎnjiǎngzhě **2** 说某种语言的人 shuō mǒu zhǒng yǔyán de rén **3** 扬声器 yángshēngqì, 喇叭 lǎba

spear I N [M. WD 根 gēn/把 bǎ], 梭标 suō biāo **II** V **1** 用矛刺 yòng máo cì **2** 用叉子叉起 yòng chāzi chā qǐ

spearhead V 当...的先锋 dāng...de xiānfēng, 为...带头 wéi...dàitóu

special I ADJ 特别的 tèbié de, 特殊的 tèshū de

special education 特殊教育 tèshū jiàoyù

special effects 特技效果 tèjì xiàoguǒ **II** N **1** 特价 tèjià, 特别便宜的商品 tèbié piányi de shāngpǐn **2** 特别节目 tèbié jiémù

specialization N 专业分工 zhuānyè-fēngōng

specialize V 专门研究 [+中国经济] zhuānmén yánjiū [+Zhōngguó jīngjì], 专门从事 [体育用品销售] zhuānmén cóngshì [+tǐyù yòngpǐn xiāoshòu]

specialized ADJ 专门训练的 zhuānmén xùnliàn de, 专门的 zhuānmén de

specially ADV 专门地 zhuānmén de, 特地 tèdì

specialty N **1** 专业 zhuānyè, 专长 zhuāncháng **2** 特色菜 tèsècài, 特色食品 tèsè shípǐn

species N 种 zhǒng, 物种 wùzhǒng

specific ADJ 特定的 tèdìng de, 明确的 míngquè de

specific gravity 比重 bǐzhòng

specification N 规格说明 guīgé shuōmíng, 明细规则 míngxì guīzé

job specifications 职务详细说明 zhíwù xiángxì shuōmíng

technical specifications 技术指标说明 jìshù zhǐbiāo shuōmíng

specify v 详细说明 xiángxì shuōmíng, 明确规定 míngquè guīdìng

specimen N 抽样 chōuyàng, 样本 yàngběn

speck N 小斑点 xiǎo bāndiǎn, 污点 wūdiǎn

speckle N 小斑点 xiǎo bāndiǎn

spectacle N 1 景象 jǐngxiàng 2 不寻常的事 bùxúncháng de shì, 奇事 qíshì

to make a spectacle of yourself 丢人现眼 diūrén xiànyǎn, 出洋相 chūyángxiàng

spectacles N See glasses

spectacular I ADJ 壮观的 [+场面] zhuàngguān de [+chǎngmiàn], 宏伟的 hóngwěi de II N 壮观的场面 zhuàngguān de chǎngmiàn

spectator N 观众 guānzhòng, 观看者 guānkànzhě

spectator sport 观赏性体育项目 guānshǎng xìng tǐyù xiàngmù

spectrum N 1 光谱 guāngpǔ, 谱 pǔ 2 一系列 yíxìliè

a spectrum of opinion 一系列意见 yíxìliè yìjiàn

speculate v 1 推测 tuīcè, 思考 sīkǎo 2 做投机生意 zuò tóujī shēngyì

speculation N 1 推测 tuīcè 2（商业）投机 (shāngyè) tóujī

sped See **speed**

speech N 1 演说 yǎnshuō 2 说话的能力 shuōhuà de nénglì

freedom of speech 言论自由 yánlùn zìyóu

speechless ADJ 说不出话的 shuōbuchū huà de, 哑口无言的 yǎkǒu wúyán de

speechwriter N 演讲稿撰写人 yǎnjiǎnggǎo zhuànxiěrén

speed N 速度 sùdù

speed limit 最高限速 zuìgāo xiànsù

speed skating 速度滑冰 sùdù huábīng

II v (PT & PP sped) 1 快速行进 kuài sù xíngjìn 2 (to speed up) 使…加快速度 shǐ…jiākuài sùdù 3 超速驾驶 chāosù jiàshǐ

speedboat N 快艇 kuàitǐng

speedometer N（汽车的）速度表 (qìchē de) sùdùbiǎo

speedy ADJ 快速的 kuàisù de, 及时的 jíshí de

speedy recovery 早日康复 zǎorì kāngfù

spell[1] (PT & PP **spelled**, **spelt**) v 1 拼写 pīnxiě 2 造成 zàochéng

spell[2] N 1 一段（短暂的）时间 yí duàn (duǎnzàn de) shíjiān

a spell of unemployment 一段失业的时间 yí duàn shīyè de shíjiān

2 魔咒 mózhòu, 魔法 mófǎ

spellbound ADJ 入迷的 rùmí de, 被迷惑的 bèi míhuo de

spelling N 拼写 pīnxiě

spelling bee（单词）拼写比赛 (dāncí) pīnxiě bǐsài

spelt See **spell**

spend (PT & PP **spent**) v 花 huā [+钱／时间], 消耗 xiāohào

to spend the night with sb 与某人一起过夜 yǔ mǒurén yìqǐ guòyè, 与某人一夜情 yǔ mǒurén yíyèqíng

spending N 开支 kāizhī, 开销 kāixiao

spendthrift N 浪费金钱的人 làngfèi jīnqián de rén, 挥霍者 huīhuòzhě

spent I v See **spend** II ADJ 用过的 yòng guò de, 失效的 shīxiào de

to be a spent force 已丧失权力的 yǐ sàngshī quánlì de, 过气的 guòqì de

sperm N 精子 jīngzǐ

spew v 1 大量排出 [+有毒气体] dàliàng páichū [+yǒudú qìtǐ] 2 大肆宣扬 [+有害思想] dàsì xuānyáng [+yǒuhài sīxiǎng]

sphere N 1 球 qiú, 球体 qiútǐ 2 范围 fànwéi, 领域 lǐngyù

sphere of influence 势力范围 shìlì fànwéi

sphinx N（埃及）狮身人面像 (Āijí) shīshēn rénmiànxiàng

spice I N 香料 xiāngliào II v 给 [+食物] 添加香料 gěi [+shíwù] tiānjiā xiāngliào

spick-and-span ADJ 干干净净的 gāngān jìngjìng de, 一尘不染的 yì chén bù rǎn de

spicy ADJ 1 加了香料的 jiāle xiāngliào de

2 辣的 là de, 辣味的 làwèi de **3** 色情的 sèqíng de, 下流的 xiàliú de

spider N 蜘蛛 zhīzhū

spiffy ADJ 整洁漂亮的 [+服装] zhěngjié piàoliang de [+fúzhuāng]

spike I N（金属的）钉状物 (jīnshǔ de) dīng zhuàng wù, 尖铁 jiān tiě II V **1** 刺进 cì jìn, 插入 chārù **2** 大幅度上升 dàfúdù shàngshēng

to spike with 搀进 [+毒药 / 烈酒] chānjìn [+dúyào/lièjiǔ]

spikes N 钉鞋 dìngxié [M. WD 双 shuāng]

spill (PT & PP **spilled, spilt**) I V（使⋯）溢出 (shǐ...) yìchū,（使⋯）溅落 (shǐ...) jiànluò II N 溢出 yìchū

oil spill 石油泄漏 shíyóu xièlòu

spilt See spill

spin I V (PT & PP **spun**) **1** 旋转 xuánzhuǎn **2** 编造故事 biānzào gùshi

spin doctor 舆论导向专家 yúlùn dǎo-xiàng zhuānjiā, 公关顾问 gōngguān gùwèn

3 纺织 fǎngxiàn II N **1** 旋转 xuánzhuǎn, 旋球 xuán qiú **2** 兜风 dōufēng

to spin a tale/yarn 编造故事 biānzào gùshi

spinach N 菠菜 bōcài [M. WD 棵 kē]

spinal ADJ 脊椎的 jǐzhuī de, 脊髓的 jǐsuǐ de

spinal cord 脊髓 jǐsuǐ

spine N 脊椎 jǐzhuī, 脊柱 jǐzhù

spineless ADJ 没有骨气的 méiyǒu gǔqì de, 懦弱的 nuòruò de

spin-off N **1** 子公司 zǐgōngsī, 成立子公司 chénglì zǐgōngsī **2** 派生电视节目 pàishēng diànshì jiémù

spinster N 大龄未婚女子 dàlíng wèihūn nǚzǐ, 老处女 lǎochǔnǚ

spiral I N **1** 螺旋形 luóxuánxíng, 螺丝螺丝 luó-sī **2** 螺旋形过程 luóxuánxíng guòchéng

downward spiral 螺旋形下降 luó-xuánxíng xiàjiàng

II V 螺旋形上升 / 下降 luóxuánxíng shàngshēng/xiàjiàng

to spiral out of control 不断恶化以至于失去控制 búduàn èhuà yǐzhìyú shīqù kòngzhì

spire N [教堂+] 尖顶 [jiàotáng+] jiāndǐng, 塔顶 tǎdǐng

spirit N **1** 精神 jīngshén

team spirit 团队精神 tuánduì jīngshén

2 情绪 qíngxù

in high spirits 情绪很高 qíngxù hěn gāo

3 精灵 jīnglíng, 灵魂 línghún, 鬼魂 guǐhún

spirited ADJ 精神饱满的 jīngshén bǎomǎn de, 充满活力的 chōngmǎn huólì de

spiritual I ADJ 精神（上）的 jīngshén (shàng) de, 心灵的 xīnlíng de II N 灵歌 línggē

spit I N **1** 口水 kǒushuǐ, 唾液 tuòyè **2** 烤肉叉 kǎoròu chā [M. WD 把 bǎ] II V (PT & PP **spat**) 吐（掉）tǔ (diào)

to spit up blood 吐血 tǔ xiě

2 吐口水 tǔkǒu shuǐ, 吐痰 tǔtán

spite I N 恶意 èyì

in spite of 尽管 jǐnguǎn

II V 故意⋯使恼火 guyì... shǐ nǎohuǒ, 存心捉弄 cúnxīn zhuōnòng

spiteful ADJ 出于恶意的 chūyú èyì de, 存心捣乱的 cúnxīn dǎoluàn de

splash I N **1** 溅 jiàn, 泼 pō

to splash around 啪嗒啪嗒地趟水 pādā pādā de tàng shuǐ

II N（水的）溅泼声 (shuǐ de) jiàn pō shēng

to make a splash 引起公众的注意 yǐnqǐ gōngzhòng de zhùyì, 大出风头 dà chū fēngtou

splat N 啪嗒声 pādā shēng

splatter V（使⋯）溅满 (shǐ...) jiàn mǎn

a wall splattered with blood 溅满鲜血的墙 jiàn mǎn xiānxuè de qiáng

splendid ADJ **1** 出色的 [+成绩] chūsè de [+chéngjì], 极好的 jíhǎo de **2** 壮丽的 [+景色] zhuànglì de [+jǐngsè]

splendor N 壮丽 zhuànglì, 光辉 guānghuī

splint N（外科用）夹板 (wàikē yòng) jiābǎn

splinter I N（金属 / 木头）碎片 (jīnshǔ/mùtou) suìpiàn, 木刺 mùcì

splinter group 分裂出来的小派别 fēnliè chūlái de xiǎo pàibié

II v **1** 使 [+木头] 裂成碎片 shǐ [+mùtou] liè chéng suìpiàn **2** [团体+] 分裂 [tuántǐ+] fēnliè

split I v (PT & PP **split**) **1** 分开 fēnkāi, 分成 fēnchéng
to split a bill 分摊费用 fēntān fèiyòng **2** 裂开 lièkāi
to split sth three ways 把某物分成三份 bǎ mǒuwù fēnchéng sān fèn
to split up [夫妻+] 离婚 [fūqī+] líhūn, [朋友+] 断交 [péngyou+] duànjiāo
II N **1** 裂口 lièkǒu, 裂缝 lièfèng **2** (团体的) 分裂 (tuántǐ de) fēnliè, 分歧 fēnqí **3** 差别 chābié, 差异 chāyì **4** (a split second) 一刹那 yíchànà, 顷刻 qǐngkè **5** (split level) 错层式的 [+房间] cuòcéngshì de [+fángjiān]

splitting ADJ (splitting headache) 头痛欲裂的 tóutòng yù liè de

splurge N, v 任意挥霍 (金钱) rènyì huīhuò (jīnqián), 乱花钱 luànhuāqián

splutter v See **sputter**

spoil (PT & PP **spoiled**, **spoilt**) v **1** 弄坏 nònghuài, 毁掉 huǐdiao **2** 宠坏 chǒnghuài **3** [食物+] 变质 [shíwù+] biànzhì, 变坏 biànhuài

spoilsport N 破坏别人兴趣的人 pòhuài biéren xìngqu de rén, 扫兴者 sǎoxìngzhě

spoilt ADJ 宠坏的 [+小孩] chǒnghuài de [+xiǎohái], 惯坏的 guànhuài de
spoilt rotten 完全被宠坏了 wánquán bèi chǒnghuài le

spoke¹ v See **speak**

spoke² N (自行车) 轮轴 (zìxíngchē) lúnzhóu [M. WD 条 tiáo/根 gēn]

spoken¹ See **speak**

spoken² ADJ 口语的 kǒuyǔ de

spokesman N 发言人 fāyánrén

sponge I N 海绵 hǎimián
sponge cake 海绵 (状) 蛋糕 hǎimián (zhuàng) dàngāo, 松蛋糕 sōng dàngāo
II v **1** (用海绵或毛巾) 擦洗 (yòng hǎimián huò máojīn) cāxǐ **2** (to sponge on/off) 依赖 [+父母] 生活 yīlài [+fùmǔ] shēnghuó, 揩 [+朋友的] 油 kāi [+péngyou de] yóu

spongy ADJ 海绵似的 hǎimián shìde, 松软多孔的 sōngruǎn duōkǒng de

sponsor I N **1** (活动的) 赞助人 (huódòng de) zànzhùrén **2** (申请资格的) 担保人 (shēnqǐng zīge de) dānbǎorén, 保证人 bǎozhèngrén **3** (法案的) 提案人 (fǎ'àn de) tí'ànrén **II** v **1** 赞助 [+募捐活动] zànzhù [+mùjuān huódòng] **2** 为 [+某人] 做担保 wéi [+mǒurén] zuò dānbǎo **3** 提议 [+法案] tíyì [+fǎ'àn]

sponsorship N **1** 赞助 zànzhù **2** 担保 dānbǎo **3** 倡议 chàngyì

spontaneity N 自发 (性) zìfā (xìng)

spontaneous ADJ 自发的 zìfā de, 自动的 zìdòng de

spoof N 滑稽模仿 (作品) gǔjī mófǎng (zuòpǐn)

spooky ADJ 阴森吓人的 yīnsēn xiàrén de, 象有鬼的 xiàng yǒuguǐ de

spool N 卷轴 juànzhóu

spoon N 勺 sháo, 匙子 chízi
be born with a silver spoon in one's mouth 生在富贵人家 shēng zài fùguì rénjiā
II v (用勺子) 舀 (yòng sháozi) yǎo

spoonfeed See **spoonfeed**

spoonfeed (PT & PP **spoonfed**) v **1** 用匙子喂 [+婴儿] yòng chízi wèi [+yīng'ér] **2** 对 [+学生] 作填鸭式灌输 duì [+xuésheng] zuò tiányāshì guànshū

spoonful N 一匙 (糖) yì chí (táng)

sporadic ADJ 零星的 língxīng de, 断断续续的 duànduàn xùxù de

sport I N **1** 体育 tǐyù, 体育活动 tǐyù huódòng
sports center 体育运动中心 tǐyù yùndòng zhōngxīn
sports club 体育俱乐部 tǐyù jùlèbù
sports pages 体育版 tǐyù bǎn
2 娱乐 yúlè, 玩乐 wánlè
for sport 为了娱乐 wèile yúlè, 为了好玩 wèile hàowán
3 热情开朗的人 rèqíng kāilǎng de rén
a good sport 开得起玩笑的人 kāidéqǐ wánxiào de rén, 输得起的人 shūdéqǐ de rén
II v 炫耀 xuànyào, 卖弄 màinong

sporting ADJ（有关）体育运动的 (yǒuguān) tǐyù yùndòng de
sporting chance 相当大的机会 xiāngdāng dà de jīhuì，公平的机会 gōngpíng de jīhuì
sporting goods 体育用品 tǐyùyòngpǐn
sportsmanship N 体育道德 tǐyù dàodé，良好的体育风尚 liánghǎo de tǐyù fēngshàng
sportswear N 运动服装 yùndòngfú-zhuāng，休闲服装 xiūxiánfú zhuāng
sporty ADJ 漂亮花哨的 piàoliang huāshao de
spot I N 1 地点 dìdiǎn，地方 dìfang
on the spot 当场 dāngchǎng
spot check 抽样检查 chōuyàng jiǎnchá
2 斑点 bāndiǎn
A leopard never changes its spots. 豹不会改变斑点。Bào bú huì gǎibiàn bāndiǎn.（→ 本性难移。Běnxìng nán yí. *It is difficult to change one's nature.*）
II V 1 认出 rènchū，发现 fāxiàn 2 让 [+对方] ràng [+duìfāng] III ADJ 现货的 xiànhuò de，现付的 xiànfù de
spot sale 现货现金销售 xiànhuò xiànjīn xiāoshòu
spotless ADJ 一尘不染的 yì chén bù rǎn de
spotlight I N 1 聚光灯 jùguāngdēng 2（公众的）瞩目（gōngzhòng de）zhǔmù，高度的关注 gāodù de guānzhù II V 使…突出 shǐ…tūchū
spotty ADJ 1 有斑点的 yǒu bāndiǎn de 2 有好有坏的 yǒu hǎo yǒu huài de 3 时有时无的 shí yǒu shí wú de，断断续续的 duànduàn xùxù de
spouse N 配偶 pèi'ǒu
spout I N 1 喷管 pēnguǎn 2（茶壶）嘴 (cháhú) zuǐ 3 水柱 shuǐzhù II V 1 [液体+] 喷 pēn chū，喷涌 pēnyǒng 2 [人+] 滔滔不绝的说话 [rén+] tāotāo bùjué de shuōhuà，口若悬河 kǒu ruò xuánhé
sprain I V 扭伤 [+关节] niǔshāng [+guānjié] II N 扭伤 niǔshāng
sprang See **spring**[1]
sprawl I V 1 [人+] 伸开手脚躺／坐 [rén+]

shēnkāi shǒujiǎo tǎng/zuò 2 [植物+] 蔓生 [zhíwù+] mànshēng II N 1 伸开四肢的躺／坐姿势 shēnkāi sìzhī de tǎng/zuò zīshì 2 杂乱无章的房屋建筑 záluàn wúzhāng de fángwū jiànzhù
urban sprawl 杂乱无章的市镇扩展 záluàn wúzhāng de shìzhèn kuòzhǎn
spray I V 喷 pēn，喷洒 pēnsǎ II N 喷雾剂 pēnwù jì，喷雾液体 pēnwù yètǐ
spray gun 喷枪 pēnqiāng
body spray 香水喷雾 xiāngshuǐ pēnwù
hair spray 定发型喷雾 dìng fàxíng pēnwù
spread (PT & PP **spread**) V 1 铺开 pūkāi，摊开 tānkāi
to spread oneself thin 工作太多无法应付 gōngzuò tài duō wúfǎ yìngfù，摊子铺得太大 tānzi pū dé tàidà
to spread one's wings 开始独立生活 kāishǐ dúlì shēnghuó
2 传开 chuánkāi，传播 chuánbō 3 涂 tú
spree N 狂欢 kuánghuān，尽情作乐 jìnqíng zuòlè
buying/drinking/crime spree 大肆采购／狂饮／疯狂犯罪作案 dàsì cǎigòu/kuángyǐn/fēngkuáng fànzuì zuò'àn
sprig N 小树枝 xiǎo shùzhī [M. WD 根 gēn]
spring[1] I V (PT **sprang**; PP **sprung**) 跳跃 tiàoyuè
to spring a surprise 出其不意 chū qí bùyì
II N 弹簧 tánhuáng
spring[2] N 春天 chūntiān
spring[3] N 泉水 quánshuǐ，泉源 quán yuán
hot spring 温泉 wēnquán
springy ADJ 有弹性的 yǒu tánxìng de
sprinkle I V 1 洒 [+香水] sǎ [+xiāngshuǐ]，撒 [+花瓣] sā [+huābàn] 2 下小雨 xià xiǎoyǔ 3 以 [+俏皮话] 点缀 [+演讲] yǐ [+qiàopíhuà] diǎnzhuì [+yǎnjiǎng] II N 1（食物）碎屑 (shíwù) suìxiè 2 小雨 xiǎoyǔ
sprinkler N 洒水器 sǎshuǐqì
sprint I V 快速短跑 kuàisù duǎnpǎo，冲刺 chōngcì II N 短跑（比赛）duǎnpǎo (bǐsài)，冲刺 chōngcì
100-meter sprint 一百公尺短跑 yì bǎi gōngchǐ duǎnpǎo

sprout I v 1 [树+] 发芽 [shù+] fāyá 2 [突然+] 长出头发 [túrán+] zhǎng chū tóufa 3 [新城镇+] 大量涌现 [xīn chéngzhèn+] dàliàng yǒngxiàn II N 1 新芽 xīn yá, 嫩芽 nènyá 2 豆芽 dòuyá
bean sprout 豆芽 dòuyá

spruce v (to spruce up) 收拾整理 shōushi zhěnglǐ, 美化 měihuà

sprung See **spring**[1]

spry ADJ 充满活力的 [+老人] chōngmǎn huólì de [+lǎorén]

spud N 土豆 tǔdòu, 马铃薯 mǎlíngshǔ

spun See **spin**

spunky ADJ 胆大的 dǎndà de, 勇敢的 yǒnggǎn de

spur I N 1 马刺 mǎcì, 靴刺 xuēcì 2 刺激 cìjī, 激励 jīlì
on the spur of the moment 一时冲动之下 yì shí chōngdòng zhīxià
II v 刺激 cìjī, 促使 cùshǐ

spurious ADJ 1 虚假的 [+态度] xūjiǎ de [+tàidu], 虚伪的 xūwěi de 2 谬误的 [+论点] miùwù de [+lùndiǎn], 不能成立的 bùnéngchénglì de

spurn v (轻蔑地) 拒绝 (qīngmiè de) jùjué, 唾弃 tuòqì

spurt I v [火焰+] 喷出 [huǒyàn+] pēn chū, 迸发 bèngfā II N 喷出 pēnchū, 迸发 bèngfā

sputter v 1 [引擎+] 发出噼啪的声音 [yǐnqíng+] fāchū pī pā de shēngyīn 2 [人+] 结结巴巴地说 [rén+] jiējie bābā de shuō
to sputter along [工作+] 进行得很不顺利 [gōngzuò+] jìnxíng de hěn bú shùnlì

spy I N 间谍 jiàndié, 密探 mìtàn II v 1 从事间谍活动 cóngshì jiàndié huódòng 2 暗中监视 ànzhōng jiānshì

squabble v (因小事) 吵嘴 (yīn xiǎoshì) chǎozuǐ, 发生口角 fāshēng kǒujuǎ

squad N 1 (军队的) 班 (jūnduì de) bān, 小队 xiǎoduì 2 (警察的) 特别行动队 (jǐngchá de) tèbié xíngdòng duì
riot squad 防暴小组 fángbào xiǎozǔ 3 (体育) 运动队 (tǐyù) yùndòngduì
squad car 执勤警车 zhíqín jǐngchē

squadron N 1 飞行中队 fēixíng zhōngduì 2 (海军) 分遣舰队 (hǎijūn) fēnqiǎn jiànduì

squalid ADJ 1 肮脏的 [+地方] āngzāng de [+dìfang], 污秽的 wūhuì de 2 不道德的 [+行为] búdàodé de [+xíngwéi], 龌龊的 wòchuò de

squall N (一阵) 狂风 (yí zhèn) kuángfēng

squalor N 肮脏 āngzāng, 污秽 wūhuì

squander v 挥霍 huīhuò, 浪费 làngfèi

square I N 1 广场 guǎngchǎng 2 正方形 zhèngfāngxíng 3 平方 píngfāng II ADJ 1 正方形的 zhèngfāngxíng de 2 平方的 píngfāng de
square root 平方根 píngfānggēn
to eat a square meal 好好地吃一顿 hǎohǎo de chī yí dùn
to be back to square one 从头开始 cóng tóu kāishǐ
III v 自乘 zìchéng, 成为平方 chéngwéi píngfāng
to square the circle 做不可能做到的事 zuò bù kěnéng zuòdào de shì

squarely ADV 1 完全地 wánquán de, 毫不含糊地 háobù hánhu de 2 精确地 jīngquè de, 直接地 zhíjiē de

squash[1] N 1 壁球 bìqiú, 墙网球 qiáng wǎngqiú 2 南瓜 nánguā, 西葫芦 xīhúlu

squash[2] v 1 压扁 yābiǎn, 压碎 yāsuì 2 塞进 sāijìn, 挤乢 jǐ

squat I v 1 蹲 dūn
to squat down 蹲下来 dūnxià lái 2 擅自占用 [+旧房] shànzì zhànyòng [+jiùfáng]
II N 蹲 dūn III ADJ 矮胖的 ǎipàng de

squeak I v 发出尖厉短促的叫声 fāchū jiānlì duǎncù de jiàoshēng, 吱吱作响 zhīzhī zuòxiǎng II N 吱吱的响声 zhīzhī de xiǎngshēng

squeaky ADJ 吱吱作响的 zhīzhī zuòxiǎng de
squeaky clean ① 光洁的 guāngjié de ② 品行端正的 pǐnxíng duānzhèng de

squeal I v 1 发出长而尖锐的声响 fāchū cháng ér jiānruì de shēngxiǎng 2 (to squeal over sb) 举报某人 jǔbào mǒurén II N 长而尖锐的声响 cháng ér jiānruì de shēngxiǎng squeal of brakes 急刹车的声响 jíshāchē de shēngxiǎng

squeamish ADJ 容易感到恶心的 róngyì gǎndào èxīn de, 神经质的 shénjīngzhì de

squeeze I v 挤压, 挤压压 jǐyā
to squeeze sth out of sb 从某人口中逼出信息 cóng mǒurén kǒuzhōng bī chū xìnxī
II N 1 拥挤 yōngjǐ 2 （财务）困难 (cáiwù) kùnnan, 拮据 jiéjū
to put the squeeze on sb 逼迫某人 bīpò mǒurén
squeeze play 施加压力 shījiā yālì

squelch I v 1 吱吱咯咯作响 zhīzhī gēgē zuòxiǎng 2 消除 [+想法 / 说法] xiāochú [+xiǎngfǎ/shuōfǎ] II N 吱吱咯咯的声音 zhīzhī gēgē de shēngyīn

squid N 鱿鱼 yóuyú, 乌贼（鱼）wūzéi (yú)

squint I v 眯着眼睛看 mīzhe yǎnjing kàn II N 1 眯着眼睛 mīzhe yǎnjing 2 斜视（症）xiéshì (zhēng)

squirm I v 1 扭动（身体）niǔdòng (shēntǐ) 2 感到尴尬 gǎndào gāngà, 局促不安 júcù bù'ān II N 扭动（身体）niǔdòng (shēntǐ)

squirrel N 松鼠 sōngshǔ [M. WD 只 zhī]

squirt I v 喷射 pēnshè, 喷出 pēnchū, 射出 shèchū II N 喷射出来的东西 pēnshè chūlái de dōngxi

stab I v 用刀刺 [+人] yòng dāo cì [+rén], 捅 tǒng
to be stabbed to death 被刺身亡 bèicì shēnwáng
to stab sb in the back 背后说某人的坏话 bèihòu shuō mǒurén de huàihuà
II N（刀）刺（dāo）cì, 捅 tǒng
stab on the back 背后中伤 bèihòu zhòngshāng, 背叛 bèipàn

stabbing I N 利器伤人（罪）lìqì shāng rén (zuì) II ADJ 刀剧似的 [+疼痛] dāo gē shìde [+téngtòng], 一阵剧痛的 yí zhèn jùtòng de

stability N 稳定 wěndìng

stabilize v（使…）稳定 (shǐ...) wěndìng

stable¹ ADJ 1 稳定的 [+社会] wěndìng de [+shèhuì], 安定的 āndìng de 2 稳重

的 [+人] wěnzhòng de [+rén], 平静的 píngjìng de

stable² N 马厩 mǎjiù, 养马场 yǎngmǎchǎng

stack I N 1 一叠 yì dié, 一堆 yì duī
a stack of shoe boxes 一叠鞋盒 yì dié xié hé
2 高烟囱 gāo yāncōng 3 计算机临时资料存储 jìsuànjī línshí zīliào cúnchú
II N 堆放 duīfàng
to stack up 相比较 xiāng bǐjiào, 比高低 bǐ gāodī

stadium N 体育场 tǐyù chǎng, 运动场 yùndòngchǎng

staff¹ I N 职工 zhígōng, 雇员 gùyuán II N 配备员工 pèibèi yuángōng
fully staffed 员工配备齐全 yuángōng pèibèi qíquán
short staffed 员工配备不足 yuángōng pèibèi bù zú

staff² N 拐杖 guǎizhàng 2 五线谱 wǔxiànpǔ

stag N 成年雄鹿 chéngnián xióng lù
stag party 男人聚会 nánrén jùhuì

stage I N 1 阶段 jiēduàn 2 舞台 wǔtái
stage fright 怯场 qièchǎng, 临上场时的胆怯 lín shàngchǎng shí de dǎnqiè
to take the center stage 成为公众注意的焦点 chéngwéi gōngzhòng zhùyì de jiāodiǎn
II v 1 举行 jǔxíng, 举办 jǔbàn
to stage a comeback 复出 fùchū, 复辟 fùbì
2 上演 shàngyǎn

stagger I v 1 摇摇晃晃地走 yáoyáo huànghuàng de zǒu 2 使 [+人] 震惊 shǐ [+rén] zhènjīng II N 摇晃 yáohuang, 蹒跚 pánshān

staggering ADJ 令人震惊的 lìngrén zhènjīng de

staging N 演出 yǎnchū, 上演 shàngyǎn

stagnant ADJ 1 不流动的 [+水] bù liúdòng de [+shuǐ] 2 不发展的 bù fāzhǎn de, 停滞的 tíngzhì de

stagnate v 停滞 tíngzhì, 不发展 bù fāzhǎn

stagnation N 停滞 tíngzhì, 停顿 tíngdùn

staid ADJ 老派的 lǎopài de, 枯燥的 kūzào de

stain I N 1 污点 wūdiǎn, 污斑 wūbān II v 沾污 zhānwū, 弄脏 nòngzāng
stained glass 彩色玻璃 cǎisè bōli

stainless steel N 不锈钢 búxiùgāng

staircase, stairway N 楼梯 lóutī

stairs N 楼梯 lóutī

stake I N 1 尖桩 jiān zhuāng, 桩子 zhuāngzi 2 赌注 dǔzhù, 投资 tóuzī
to have a stake in 有股份的 yǒu gǔfèn de, 有利害关系 yǒu lìhài guānxi
II v 用 [+家产] 去赌博 yòng [+jiāchǎn] qù dǔbó, 拿 [+生命] 去冒险 ná [+shēngmìng] qù màoxiǎn
to stake a claim 声称拥有所有权 shēngchēng yōngyǒu suǒyǒuquán
to stake sth out 对某处进行监视 duì mǒuchù jìnxíng jiānshì

stakeholder N 1 股份持有人 gǔfèn chíyǒurén 2 利益相关者 lìyì xiāngguānzhě 3 (临时) 财产保管人 (línshí) cáichǎn bǎoguǎnrén

stale ADJ 1 不新鲜的 [+食物] bù xīnxian de [+shíwù] 2 乏味的 [+生活] fáwèi de [+shēnghuó]

stalemate N 1 僵局 jiāngjú, 僵持 jiāngchí 2 (象棋) 和棋 (xiàngqí) héqí

stalk¹ N (植物的) 茎 (zhíwù de) jīng, 杆 gǎn

stalk² v 跟踪的 gēnzōng, 纠缠骚扰 jiūchán sāorǎo

stalker N 跟踪者 gēnzōngzhě, 纠缠骚扰的人 jiūchán sāorǎo de rén

stall I N 1 摊摊 tāntān, 摊子 tānzi 2 (引擎) 停止运转 (yǐnqíng) tíngzhǐ yùnzhuǎn, 熄火 xīhuǒ 3 停滞 (状态) tíngzhì (zhuàngtài) II v 1 [飞机发动机+] 停止运转 [fēijī fādòngjī+] tíngzhǐ yùnzhuǎn, 熄火 xīhuǒ 2 停滞不前 tíngzhì bùqián, 停顿 tíngdùn 3 故意拖延 gùyì tuōyán
to stall for time 拖延时间 tuōyán shíjiān, 观望不前 guānwàng bù qián

stallion N 种马 zhǒngmǎ

stalwart ADJ 强壮的 qiángzhuàng de
stalwart supporter 忠实有力的支持者 zhōngshí yǒulì de zhīchízhě

stamina N 耐力 nàilì, 毅力 yìlì

stammer N, v 结结巴巴地说 jiējiēbābā de

shuō, 口吃 kǒuchī

stamp I N 1 邮票 yóupiào
commemorative stamp 纪念邮票 jìniàn yóupiào
2 印记 yìnjì II v 1 在…盖印 zài…gàiyìn 2 踩脚 duòjiǎo 3 踩 (脚) duò (jiǎo), 顿 (足) dùn (zú)

stampede I v 1 (人群+) 争先恐后地奔跑 [rénqún+] zhēngxiān kǒnghòu de bēnpǎo, 蜂拥 fēngyōng 2 [动物+] 奔逃 [dòngwù+] bēntáo II N 1 (动物的) 四处奔逃 (dòngwù de) sìchù bēntáo 2 (人群的) 奔跑 (rénqún de) bēnpǎo

stance N 立场 lìchǎng, 姿态 zītài
to adopt a neutral stance 采取中立的立场 cǎiqǔ zhōnglì de lìchǎng

stand I v (PT & PP **stood**) 1 站 zhàn, 站立 zhànlì 2 忍受 rěnshòu 3 经受 jīngshòu
to stand by ① 坚持 jiānchí ② 支持 zhīchí ③ 待命 dàimìng
to stand out 突出 tūchū
to stand up for 维护 wéihù
II N 1 架子 jiàzi
newspaper stand 报纸架 bàozhǐ jià
2 摊位 tānwèi, 售货摊 shòuhuò tān
exhibition stand 展示摊位 zhǎnshì tānwèi
3 立场 lìchǎng, 态度 tàidu
to take a stand against 明确表示反对 míngquè biǎoshì fǎnduì
4 (the stand) 证人席 zhèngrénxí

standard I N 1 标准 biāozhǔn 2 水准 shuǐzhǔn
standard of living 生活水准 shēnghuó shuǐzhǔn
3 手动档汽车 shǒudòngdàng qìchē 4 旗帜 qízhì II ADJ 1 标准的 biāozhǔn de 2 普通的 pǔtōng de, 正常的 zhèngcháng de

standard-bearer N 1 旗手 qíshǒu 2 领袖 lǐngxiù, 倡导人 chàngdǎorén

standardize v 使…标准化 shǐ…biāozhǔnhuà

standby N 1 备用品 bèiyòng pǐn 2 (乘客) 等候退票 (chéngkè) děnghòu tuìpiào
passenger on standby 等候退票的乘客 děnghòu tuìpiào de chéngkè
on standby 随时待命 suíshí dàimìng

stand-in N 替身 tìshēn, 替代者 tìdàizhě

standing I ADJ 长期有效的 chángqī yǒuxiào de, 常设的 chángshè de
standing order 长期订单 chángqī dìngdān
II N 地位 dìwèi, 等级 děngjí

standoff N（战斗中的）僵持局面（zhàndòu zhòngde）jiāngchí júmiàn

standout N（相貌／表现）突出的人（xiàngmào/biǎoxiàn）tūchū de rén

standpoint N 立足点 lìzúdiǎn, 立场 lìchǎng

standstill N 静止 jìngzhǐ, 停顿 tíngdùn
at a standstill 处于停顿状态 chǔyú tíngdùn zhuàngtài

standup ADJ 1 单人说笑表演 dānrén shuōxiào biǎoyǎn, 单口相声 dānkǒu xiàngsheng 2 竖立的 shùlì de

stank See **stink**

stanza N（诗的）节（shī de）jié

staple I N 1 订书钉 dìngshūdīng 2 主要食物 zhǔyào shíwù, 主食 zhǔshí 3 常用的人／事 chángjiàn de rén/shì II V 用订书钉钉住 yòng dìngshūdīng dìng zhù III ADJ 主要的 zhǔyào de, 最重要的 zuì zhòngyào de

stapler N 订书机 dìngshūjī

star I N 1 星 xīng
star sign 星座 xīngzuò
2 星级 xīngjí 3 明星 míngxīng II V 1 由… 主演 yóu...zhǔyǎn 2 主演 zhǔyǎn, 担任主角 dānrèn zhǔjué

starboard N（船的）右舷（chuán de）yòuxián, 右侧 yòucè

Starbucks N 星巴克咖啡馆 xīngbākè kāfēiguǎn

starch I N 1 淀粉 diànfěn 2 含淀粉的食物 hán diànfěn de shíwù 3 浆粉 jiāngfěn II V 用浆粉上浆 yòng jiāngfěn shàng jiāng

starchy ADJ 含有大量淀粉的 hányǒu dàliàng diànfěn de

stardom N（电影／体育）明星的地位（diànyǐng/tǐyù）míngxīng de dìwèi
to rise to stardom 成名 chéngmíng, 走红 zǒuhóng

stare I V 盯着看 dīngzhe kàn, 注视 zhùshì
to stare sb in the face ① 明摆在某人面前 míng bǎi zài mǒurén miànqián ②[灾难+]不可避免[zāinàn+] bùkě bìmiǎn
II N 盯视 dīngshì, 凝视 níngshì

starfish N 海星 hǎixīng

stark I ADJ 1 荒凉的 [+景色] huāngliáng de [+jǐngsè] 2 明显的 míngxiǎn de
in stark contrast 形成明显的对照 xíngchéng míngxiǎn de duìzhào
II ADV 完全地 wánquán de
stark naked 赤裸的 chìluǒ de, 一丝不挂的 yì sī bú guà de

starlet N 演配角的年轻女演员 yǎn pèijué de niánqīng nǚyǎnyuán, 二流女演员 èrliú nǚyǎnyuán

starlit ADJ 星光闪烁的 [+夜空] xīngguāng shǎnshuò de [+yèkōng]

starry ADJ 满天星斗的 de mǎntiān xīngdǒu de

start I V 1 开始 kāishǐ
to start a family 开始生儿育女 kāishǐ shēng'ér yùnǚ, 生第一个孩子 shēng dìyīgè háizi
to start from scratch 从头开始 cóngtóu kāishǐ, 零起点 líng qǐdiǎn
2 出发 chūfā 3 发动 fādòng 4 创建 chuàngjiàn II N 1 开始部分 kāishǐ bùfen 2 起点 qǐdiǎn, 起跑线 qǐpǎoxiàn
at the start 在起跑线上 zài qǐpǎoxiàn shàng
3 惊吓 jīngxià
to give sb a start 让某人吓一跳 ràng mǒurén xià yí tiào

starter N 1 起动装置 qǐdòng zhuāngzhì 2 第一道菜 dìyī dào cài 3 起跑发令员 qǐpǎo fālìngyuán 4（球队）首批上场队员（qiúduì）shǒupī shàngchǎng duìyuán
for starters 首先 shǒuxiān

startle V 惊吓 jīngxià, 吓…一跳 xià... yí tiào

start-up I ADJ 新创的 [+企业] xīnchuàng de [+qǐyè]
start-up budget 创业资金 chuàngyè zījīn
II N 新创办的小企业 xīn chuàngbàn de xiǎo qǐyè

starvation N 饥饿 jī'è

starve V 饿 è, 饿极了 è jíle

starved to death 饿死 èsǐ

stash I v 藏匿 cángnì, 隐藏 yǐncáng II N 隐藏的东西 yǐncáng de dōngxi

state I N 1 状态 zhuàngtài, 情况 qíng-kuàng 2 (美国) 州 (Měiguó) zhōu, (印度) 邦 (Yìndù) bāng

state university 州立大学 zhōulì dàxué

3 国家 guójiā

head of state 国家元首 guójiā yuánshǒu

State Department (美国) 国务院 (Měiguó) Guówùyuàn

Secretary of State (美国) 国务卿 (Měiguó)guówùqīng

II v 声明 shēngmíng, 发表声明 fābiǎo shēngmíng

stately ADJ 1 堂皇的 tánghuáng de, 宏大的 hóngdà de 2 庄严的 zhuāngyán de

statement N 声明 shēngmíng [M. WD 份 fèn]

financial statement 财务报表 cáiwù bàobiǎo

sworn statement 宣誓证词 xuānshì zhèngcí

state-of-the-art ADJ 最先进的 zuì xiān jìn de, 最高水平的 zuìgāo shuǐpíng de, 最新的 zuì xīn de

statesman N 政治家 zhèngzhìjiā

statesmanlike ADJ 1 政治家似的 zhèngzhìjiā shìde 2 有政治家风度的 yǒu zhèngzhìjiā fēngdù de

stateswoman N 女政治家 nǚ zhèngzhìjiā

static I ADJ 静止的 jìngzhǐ de, 不变的 búbiàn de II N 1 静电干扰 jìngdiàn gānrǎo 2 负面的议论 fùmiàn de yìlùn

station I N 1 站 zhàn, 车站 chēzhàn

station wagon 客货两用汽车 kèhuò liǎngyòng qìchē

police station 派出所 pàichūsuǒ, 警察局 jǐngchájú

2 无线电台 wúxiàndiàntái, 电视台 diànshìtái/频道 /píndào II v 部署 bùshǔ, 驻扎 zhùzhá

stationary ADJ 静止的 jìngzhǐ de, 不动的 bú dòng de

stationery N 1 文具 wénjù 2 信纸 xìnzhǐ [M. WD 张 zhāng]

statistician N 统计工作者 tǒngjì gōngzuòzhě, 统计学家 tǒngjìxuéjiā

statistics N 统计 (学) tǒngjì (xué)

statue N 雕像 diāoxiàng, 塑像 sùxiàng

the Statue of Liberty (纽约) 自由女神像 (Niǔyuē) zìyóu nǚshén xiàng

stature N 1 身材 shēncái 2 声望 shēngwàng, 地位 dìwèi

a scientist of international stature 一位有国际声望的科学家 yí wèi yǒu guójì shēngwàng de kēxuéjiā

status N 1 地位 dìwèi 2 状况 zhuàngkuàng

status quo 现状 xiànzhuàng

statute N 法令 fǎlìng, 法规 fǎguī

statute law 成文法 chéngwénfǎ

statutory ADJ (根据) 法令的 (gēnjù) fǎlìng de

statutory rape 法定强奸罪 fǎdìng qiángjiānzuì

staunch[1] ADJ 坚定忠实的 jiāndìng zhōngshí de

staunch[2], **stanch** v 止住 [+血] zhǐzhù [+xuè]

stave[1] (PT & PP **stove**, **staved**) v (to stave off) 避开 bìkāi, 阻挡 zǔdǎng

stave[2] N 五线谱 wǔxiànpǔ

stay I v 1 待 dài, 待在 dài zài

to stay put 留在原地 liú zài yuándì, 不动 bú dòng

to stay up 很晚还不睡 hěn wǎn hái bú shuì, 熬夜 áoyè

2 住 zhù, 住在 zhù zài 3 保持 bǎochí, 持续 chíxù II N 1 逗留 dòuliú, 停留 tíngliú 2 停止 tíngzhǐ, 推迟 tuīchí

steadfast ADJ 1 坚定的 jiāndìng de 2 忠诚的 zhōngchéng de

steady I ADJ 1 稳的 wěn de, 平稳的 píng-wěn de 2 稳重的 wěnzhòng de, 可靠的 kěkào de 3 均匀的 jūnyún de II v 1 (使…) 稳定 (shǐ...) wěndìng 2 (使…) 镇定 (shǐ...) zhèndìng

to steady one's nerves 使自己的心情平静下来 shǐ zìjǐ de xīnqíng píngjìng xiàlai

to steady oneself 站稳 zhànwěn

III ADV (to go steady with sb) 与某人确定恋爱关系 yǔ mǒurén quèdìng liàn'ài guānxi

steak N（牛）肉排 (niú) ròupái, 鱼排 yúpái

steal V (PT **stole**; PP **stolen**) 偷 tōu, 偷窃 tōuqiè
to steal a march on sb 抢在某人前面 qiǎng zài mǒurén miànqián
to steal the show 抢出风头 qiǎng chū fēngtou

stealth N 1 悄声秘密行动 qiǎoshēng mìmì xíngdòng 2 隐形系统 yǐnxíng xìtǒng
stealth aircraft 隐形飞机 yǐnxíng fēijī

stealthy ADJ 偷偷摸摸的 tōutōu mōmō de, 悄悄的 qiāoqiāo de

steam I N 蒸汽 zhēngqì
to blow off steam 发泄怒火 fāxiè nùhuǒ, 渲泄多余的精力 xuānxiè duōyú de jīnglì
to run out of steam 精疲力尽 jīngpí lìjìn
II V 1 蒸 [+食物] zhēng [+shíwù] 2 散发蒸汽 sànfā zhēngqì, 冒热气 mào rèqì

steamroller N 蒸汽压路机 zhēngqì yālùjī

steamy ADJ 1 充满水蒸汽的 [+更衣室] chōngmǎnshuǐ zhēngqì de [gēngyīshì] 2 色情的 sèqíng de

steel I N 钢 gāng, 钢材 gāngcái
steel wool 钢丝绒 gāngsīróng
II V (to steel oneself for) 坚强起来 jiānqiáng qǐlái

steely ADJ 钢铁般坚定的 gāngtiě bān jiāndìng de

steep I ADJ 陡 dǒu, 陡峭的 dǒuqiào de
II V 1 浸泡 jìnpào 2 (to be steeped in) 根植于（传统）gēnzhí yú (chuántǒng), 深陷在（争斗中）shēn xiàn zài (zhēngdòu zhōng)

steeple N（教堂）尖塔 (jiàotáng) jiān tǎ

steer V 1 驾驶 [+汽车] jiàshǐ [+qìchē] 2 引导 [+人] yǐndǎo [+rén]
to steer clear of sb/sth 避开某人／某事 bìkāi mǒurén/mǒushì
to steer a middle course 走中间道路 zǒu zhōngjiāndàolù

steering N（汽车／船舶的）操纵装置 (qìchē/chuánbó de) cāozòng zhuāngzhì
steering committee 程序委员会 chéngxù wěiyuánhuì

stellar ADJ 光彩夺目的 guāngcǎi duómù de, 出色的 chūsè de

stem I N 茎 jīng
stem cell 干细胞 gànxìbāo
II V 遏制 èzhì
to stem from 是由于 shì yóuyú, 起源于 qǐyuán yú

stench N 1 恶臭 èchòu 2 恶劣的社会风气 èliè de shèhuì fēngqì
stench of corruption 腐败的气息 fǔbài de qìxī

stenography N 速记（法）sùjì (fǎ)

step I N 1 脚步（声）jiǎobù (shēng) 2 一步 yí bù 3 台阶 táijiē II V 1 走 zǒu 2 踩 cǎi
to step on one's toes 惹怒 rěnù, 触犯 chùfàn
to step up 加强 jiāqiáng

stepbrother N 同父异母／同母异父的兄弟 tóng fù yì mǔ/tóng mǔ yì fù de xiōngdi

step-by-step ADJ 一步步（的）yíbù bù (de)

stepchild N 继子／继女 jìzǐ/jìnǚ

stepdaughter N 继女 jìnǚ

stepfather N 继父 jìfù

stepladder N 活梯 huótī

stepmother N 继母 jìmǔ

stepped-up ADJ 加快的 jiākuài de, 加强的 jiāqiáng de

stepping-stone N 1 垫脚石 diànjiǎoshí 2（事业发展中）阶梯 (shìyè fāzhǎnzhōng de) jiētī

stepsister N 同父异母／同母异父的姐妹 tóng fù yì mǔ/tóng mǔ yì fù de jiěmèi

stepson N 继子 jìzǐ

stereo N 立体声音响设备 lìtǐshēng yīnxiǎng shèbèi

stereotype I N 固定的模式 gùdìng de móshì, 老一套 lǎoyítào II V 1 把…模式化 bǎ...móshì huà 2 对…产生成见 duì...chǎnshēng chéngjiàn

sterile ADJ 1 无菌的 wújūn de, 消过毒的 xiāoguòdú de 2 不能生育／结果的 bùnéng shēngyù/jiéguǒ de

sterilize V 1 消毒 xiāodú, 灭菌 mièjūn 2 使…失去生殖能力 shǐ...shīqù shēngzhí nénglì, 对…做绝育手术 duì…zuòjué yù shǒushù

sterling N 优秀的, 极有价值的 yōuxiù de, jí yǒu jiàzhí de
sterling work 杰出的工作 jiéchū de gōngzuò

sterling silver N 标准纯银 biāozhǔn chúnyín

stern I ADJ 严厉的 yánlì de, 苛刻的 kēkè de II N 船尾 chuánwěi

steroid N 类固醇 lèigùchún

stethoscope N 听诊器 tīngzhěnqì

stew I V 炖 dùn, 煨 wēi, 焖 mèn
to stew in one's own juice 自作自受 zìzuò zìshòu
II N 炖菜 dùncài
be in a stew 焦急的 jiāojí de, 困惑的 kùnhuò de

steward N 1 (轮船 / 飞机上的) 男乘务员 (lúnchuán / fēijī shàng de) nán chéngwùyuán 2 (公共资产的) 守护人 (gōnggòng zīchǎn de) shǒuhùrén 3 伙食管理人 huǒshí guǎnlǐ rén

stick I V (PT & PP **stuck**) 1 粘 zhān, 粘住 zhānzhu 2 插入 chārù 3 卡住 qiǎzhu
to stick out 伸出 shēnchū
to stick to 坚持 jiānchí, 还是 hái shì
II N 1 小树枝 xiǎo shùzhī [M. WD 根 gēn] 2 棍 gùn [M. WD 根 gēn], 棒 bàng
walking stick 拐杖 guǎizhàng
3 条状物 tiáozhuàngwù
a stick of gum 一条口香糖 yìtiáo kǒuxiāngtáng

sticker N (粘帖) 标签 (zhāntiē) biāoqiān
sticker price 标 (签) 价 biāo (qiān) jià

stick-in-the-mud N 顽固守旧者 wángù shǒujiùzhě, 保守者 bǎoshǒuzhě

stickler N (a stickler for rules/details/protocols) 十分注重规则 / 细节 / 礼节的人 shífēn zhùzhòng guīzé/xìjié/lǐjié de rén

sticky ADJ 1 粘的 nián de 2 不愉快的 bù yúkuài de, 麻烦的 máfan de

stiff I ADJ 1 激烈的 jīliè de 2 硬 yìng, 坚硬的 jiānyìng de 3 不灵便的 bù língbiàn de, 疼痛的 téngtòng de
stiff drink 烈酒 lièjiǔ
II ADV 非常 fēicháng, 极其 jíqí
be bored stiff 厌烦得要死 yànfán de yàosǐ, 无聊得要命 wúliáo de yàomìng
III V 不付小费 bù fù xiǎofèi

stiffen V 1 使…变硬 shǐ…biàn yìng 2 突然生气 / 不友好 tūrán shēngqì/bùyǒuhǎo 3 (使…) 更严厉 / 强硬 (shǐ…) gèng yánlì/qiángyìng
to stiffen up [肌肉+] 僵硬 [jīròu+] jiāngyìng

stiff-necked ADJ 傲慢的 àomàn de, 倔强的 juéjiàng de

stifle V 1 使 [+人] 窒息 shǐ [+rén] zhìxī 2 抑制 yìzhì, 强忍住 qiáng rěnzhù

stigma N 羞耻 xiūchǐ, 丢脸的感觉 diūliǎn de gǎnjué

still[1] ADV 1 仍然 réngrán, 还是 hái shì 2 更加 gèngjiā

still[2] I ADJ 静止的 jìngzhǐ de
Still water run deep. 静水流深。Jìngshuǐ liú shēn.
still life 静物画 jìngwùhuà
II N 1 寂静 jìjìng 2 剧照 jùzhào 3 蒸馏器 zhēngliúqì

stillborn ADJ 1 死胎的 [+产儿] sǐtāi de [+chǎn'ér] 2 夭折的 [+计划] yāozhé de [+jìhuà]

stilted ADJ 生硬呆板的 shēngyìng dāibǎn de

stilts N 高跷 gāoqiāo [M. WD 付 fù]

stimulant N 兴奋剂 xīngfènjì

stimulating ADJ 使人振奋的 / 有精神的 shǐrén zhènfèn de/yǒu jīngshén de

stimulus N 刺激 (物) cìjī (wù), 促进 (因素) cùjìn (yīnsù)

sting V (PT & PP **stung**) 1 [蚊子+] 叮 [wénzi+] dīng, [蜜蜂+] 刺 [mìfēng+] cì 2 感到刺痛 gǎndao cìtòng II N 1 刺痛 cìtòng, 剧痛 jùtòng 2 圈套 quāntào
a sting operation (警察) 诱捕行动 (jǐngchá) yòubǔ xíngdòng

stinger N (昆虫的) 刺 (kūnchóng de) cì

stinginess N 小气 xiǎoqi, 吝啬 lìnsè

stingy ADJ 1 小气的 [+人] xiǎoqi de [+rén], 吝啬的 lìnsè de 2 极少的 [+食物] jí shǎo de [+shíwù]

stink I V (PT **stank**; PP **stunk**) 1 发臭 fā

chòu, 有臭味的 yǒu chòuwèi de 2 糟透
了 zāotòu le
to stink up the place 表现极差
biǎoxiàn jíchà
II N 恶臭 èchòu
to cause a stink 强烈抗议 qiángliè
kàngyì

stinker N 1 讨厌的人 tǎoyàn de rén
2 糟透的电影／书／比赛 zāotòu de
diànyǐng/shū/bǐsài

stinking ADJ 1 发出恶臭的 fāchū èchòu
de 2 糟透的 zāotòu de
stinking drunk 酩酊大醉 mǐngdǐng
dàzuì, 烂醉如泥 lànzuì rúní

stint I N 期限 qīxiàn, 任期 rènqī II v 限制
xiànzhì, 少量提供 shǎoliàng tígōng

stipend N（学生的）助学金 (xuésheng
de) zhùxuéjīn,（牧师的）生活费 (mùshi
de) shēnghuófèi, 薪金 xīnjīn

stipulate v 规定 guīdìng, 约定 yuēdìng

stipulation N 规定 guīdìng, 约定
yuēdìng 2 条款 tiáokuǎn

stir I v 1 搅拌 jiǎobàn 2 激发 [+感情] jīfā
[+gǎnqíng] 3 [风+] 吹动 [fēng+]
chuīdòng
to stir things up 挑起事端 tiǎoqǐ shìduān
II N 1 骚动 sāodòng, 激动 jīdòng 2 搅拌
jiǎobàn

stitch I N（缝）一针 (féng) yì zhēn II v 缝
féng, 缝合 fénghé
A stitch in time saves nine. 及时缝一
针，免得缝十针。(→ 小洞不补，大
洞吃苦。) Jíshí féng yì zhēn, miǎnde
féng shí zhēn. (→ Xiǎo dòng bù bǔ, dà
dòng chī kǔ. *If you don't mend a small
hole, you will suffer from a big hole.*)

stitches N (in stitches) 忍不住大笑
rěnbuzhù dàxiào

stock I N 1 存货 cúnhuò, 库存 kùcún
out of stock 没有现货 méiyǒu xiànhuò,
脱销 tuōxiāo
to take stock ① 盘点（货物）pán diǎn
(huòwù) ② 检讨 jiǎntǎo
2 股份 gǔfèn, 股票 gǔpiào
stock certificate 股权证 gǔquánzhèng
stock market 股票市场 gǔpiào
shìchǎng, 股市 gǔshì

3 汤汁 tāngzhī 4 牲畜 shēngchù II v 备
货 bèihuò, 储存 chǔcún
to stock up 备货 bèihuò

stockade N 栏 péng lán [M. WD 道 dào],
防御工事 fángyù gōngshì

stockbroker N 证券／股票经纪人
zhèngquàn/gǔpiào jīngjìrén

stockholder N 股票持有人 gǔpiào
chíyǒurén, 股东 gǔdōng

stocking N 长筒袜 chángtǒngwà

stockpile I N 贮存的大量物资／武器
zhùcún de dàliàng wùzī/wǔqì II v 贮存
zhùcún, 囤积 túnjī

stock-still ADV 一动不动地 yídòng bú
dòng de, 完全静止地 wánquán jìngzhǐ
de

stocky ADJ 身子矮而结实的 shēnzi ǎi ér
jiēshí de, 矮胖的 ǎipàng de

stockyard N 牲畜围栏 shēngchù wéilán

stoic, stoical ADJ 刻苦耐劳的 kèkǔnàiláo
de, 坚忍的 jiānrěn de

stoke v 1 给 [+炉子] 添加燃料 gěi [+lúzi]
tiānjiā ránliào 2 使 [+情绪] 加剧 shǐ
[+qíngxù] jiājù, 给 [+纠纷] 火上加油 gěi
[+jiūfēn] huǒshàng jiāyóu

stoked ADJ 非常兴奋的 fēicháng xīngfèn
de

stole See **steal**

stolen See **steal**

stolid ADJ 不激动的 bù jīdòng de, 无动于
衷的 wúdòng yú zhōng de

stomach I N 肚子 dùzi, 胃 wèi
to turn one's stomach 使人恶心 shǐrén
èxīn
II v 忍受 rěnshòu, 接受 jiēshòu

stomachache N 肚子痛 dùzi tòng, 胃痛
wèitòng

stomp v 重重地踩 zhòngzhòng de cǎi

stone I N 石（头）shí (tóu) [M. WD 块
kuài], 石块 shíkuài
precious stone 宝石 bǎoshí
a stone's throw 近在咫尺 jìn zài zhǐchǐ,
离得很近 líde hěnjìn
II v 向…扔石头 xiàng...rēng shítou

stoned ADJ（服毒后）极度兴奋 (fúdú
hòu) jídù xīngfèn

stonewall v 拒不回答 jù bù huídá

stoneware N 粗陶器 cū táoqì

stony ADJ 1 多石的 duō shí de 2 冷冰冰的 lěngbīngbīng de, 毫无同情心的 háowú tóngqíngxīn de

stood See **stand**

stool N 凳子 dèngzi

stoop I V 弯腰 wānyāo, 俯身 fǔshēn
to stoop to doing sth 道德堕落到做事 dàodé duòluò dào zuò mǒushì
a stooped old woman 驼背老太太 tuóbèi lǎotàitai
II N 驼背 tuóbèi
to walk with a stoop 驼着背走路 tuózhe bèi zǒulù

stop I V 1 停 tíng, 停住 tíngzhu 2 阻止 zǔzhǐ
to stop at nothing 不择手段 bù zé shǒuduàn
to stop short of doing sth 差一点做某事 chàyidiǎn zuò mǒushì
Stop the presses! 有惊人新闻! Yǒu jīngrén xīnwén!
to stop by 串门儿 chuànménr
II N 1 停止 tíngzhǐ
to put a stop on a check 通知银行不兑现支票 tōngzhī yínháng bú duìxiàn zhīpiào
2 停车站 tíngchēzhàn

stopgap N 临时替代的人 línshí tìdài de rén

stoplight N 红绿灯 hónglǜdēng, 交通灯 jiāotōngdēng

stopover N 中途停留 zhōngtútíngliú

stoppage N 停工 tínggōng, 罢工 bàgōng 2 停止 tíng zhǐ, 中止 zhōngzhǐ 3 堵塞物 dǔsèwù

stopper N 瓶塞 píngsāi

stopwatch N 秒表 miǎobiǎo

storage N 贮藏 zhùcáng, 储藏 chǔcáng
storage capacity（汽车行李箱）贮存空间 (qìchē xínglixiāng) zhùcún kōngjiān

store[1] N 店 diàn, 商店 shāngdiàn
department store 百货商店 bǎihuò shāngdiàn

store[2] I N 贮藏 zhùcáng, 储藏 chǔcáng
in store 快要发生 kuài yào fāshēng
II V 贮藏 zhùcáng, 储存 chǔcún

storehouse N 仓库 cāngkù [M. WD 座 zuò], 宝库 bǎokù [M. WD 座 zuò]

storehouse of information 信息宝库 xìnxī bǎokù

storekeeper N 店主 diànzhǔ

storeroom N 贮藏室 zhùcángshì

stork N 鹳 guàn [M. WD 只 zhī]

storm N 1 风暴 fēngbào, 暴风雨 bàofēngyǔ 2 风潮 fēngcháo, 浪潮 làngcháo
storm cloud ① 暴风云 bàofēngyún ② 凶兆 xiōngzhào
sand storm 沙（尘）暴 shā (chén) bào

stormy ADJ 1 暴风雨／雪的 bàofēngyǔ/xuě de 2 动荡的 dòngdàng de, 多风波的 duō fēngbō de

story[1] N 1 故事 gùshi
it's a long story 说来话长 shuō lái huà cháng
to make a long story short 长话短说 chánghuà duǎnshuō
2 新闻 xīnwén [M. WD 条 tiáo], 新闻报道 xīnwén bàodào [M. WD 条 tiáo]

story[2] N 层 céng, 层楼 cénglóu
a three-story (three-storied) house 一幢三层楼的房子 yí zhuàng sān céng lóu de fángzi

storyteller N 讲故事的人 jiǎng gùshi de rén, 说书人 shuōshū rén

stout I ADJ 1 粗壮的 cūzhuàng de, 结实的 jiēshi de 2 坚定勇敢的 jiāndìng yǒnggǎn de II N 烈性黑啤酒 lièxìng hēipíjiǔ

stove N 炉子 lúzi, 炉灶 lúzào

stowaway N 无票偷乘的人 wú piào tōu chéng de rén, 偷渡者 tōudùzhě

straddle V 1 骑坐 [+在自行车上] kuà zuò [+zài zìxíngchē shàng] 2 横跨 [+两地] héngkuà [+liǎng dì]

straggle V 1 [一队人+] 散乱地行进 [yí duì rén+] sànluàn de xíngjìn 2 [一个人+] 掉队 [yí gè rén+] diàoduì

straight I ADJ 1 直的 zhí de 2 正的 zhèng de, 端正的 duānzhèng de 3 连续的 liánxù de 4 正直的 zhèngzhí de, 诚实的 chéngshí de
straight shooter 正直的人 zhèngzhí de rén
to get straight A's 考试全部得"优" kǎoshì quánbù dé "A"

to keep a straight face 板着脸 bǎnzheliǎn

II ADV **1** 直接 zhíjiē, 马上 mǎshàng **2** 直截了当地 zhíjié liǎodàng de, 坦率地 tǎnshuài de

to think straight 有条理地思考 yǒu tiáolǐ de sīkǎo

III N **1** 异性恋者 yìxìngliànzhě **2** (the straight and narrow) 循规蹈矩的生活方式 xúnguī dǎojǔ de shēnghuó fāngshì

straighten V 把…弄直 bǎ...nòng zhí

to straighten sb out 使某人变好 shǐ mǒurén biàn hǎo

to straighten sth out 理清某事 lǐ qīng mǒushì

straightforward ADJ **1** 坦率地 tǎnshuài de, 坦诚的 tǎnchéng de **2** 简单明了的 jiǎndān míngliǎo de

strain¹ N **1** 拉力 lālì, 张力 zhānglì **2** 压力 yālì, 焦虑 jiāolǜ

under a lot of strain 承受很大压力 chéngshòu hěn dà yālì

3 负担 fùdān, 困难 kùnnan

to put a strain on sb 给某人带来负担 gěi mǒurén dàilái fùdān

4 品种 pǐnzhǒng, 类型 lèixíng

a new strain of virus 一种新病毒 yì zhǒng xīn bìngdú

strain² V **1** 竭力 jiélì [+去做某事 +qù zuò mǒushì], 全力以赴 quánlì yǐfù **2** 拉伤 lā shāng [+肌肉 +jīròu], 扭伤 niǔshāng **3** 使 [+关系] 紧张 shǐ [+guānxi] jǐnzhāng, 严重损伤 yánzhòng sǔnshāng

strained ADJ **1** 不自然的 [+气氛] bú zìrán de [+qìfen], 紧张的 jǐnzhāng de **2** 身心疲惫的 shēnxīn píbèi de

strainer N 过滤器 guòlǜqì

strait N **1** 海峡 hǎixiá

the Straits of Taiwan 台湾海峡 Táiwān hǎixiá

2 (in dire straits) 处于非常困难的境地 chǔyú fēicháng kùnnan de jìngdì

straitjacket N 约束 yuēshù, 限度 xiàndù

strand I N **1** 一股（绳／线）yì gǔ (shéng/xiàn) **2**（故事的）线索 (gùshi de) xiànsuǒ II V **1** 使 [+人] 滞留 shǐ

[+人] zhìliú **2** 使 [+人] 处于困境 shǐ [+人] chǔyú kùnjìng

stranded ADJ 被困（在）bèi kùn (zài), 滞留 zhìliú

strange ADJ **1** 奇怪 qíguài, 不寻常的 bù xúncháng de **2** 陌生（的）[+人] mòshēng (de) [+rén]

to feel strange 觉得不对劲 juéde bú duìjìn

stranger N 陌生人 mòshēng rén

strangle V **1** 勒死 lēisǐ, 绞死 jiǎosǐ **2** 严重阻碍 yánzhòng zǔ'ài

stranglehold N 有力的控制 yǒulì de kòngzhì

to break the stranglehold of sth 打破某事的束缚 dǎpò mǒushì de shùfù

strap I N 带（子）dài (zi) II V 用带子束住 yòng dàizi shù zhù, 捆扎 kǔnzā

strapped ADJ 没有多少钱的 méiyǒu duōshao qián de

stratagem N 计谋 jìmóu, 花招 huāzhāo

strategic ADJ 战略上（的）zhànlüè shàng (de), 策略上（的）cèlüè shàng (de)

strategice weapon 战略武器 zhānglüè wǔqì

strategy N **1** 策略 cèlüè **2** 战略（部署）zhànlüè (bùshǔ)

stratified ADJ 等级化的 [+社会] děngjíhuà de [+shèhuì]

stratum N **1**（社会）阶层 (shèhuì) jiēcéng **2** 岩层 yáncéng

straw N **1**（喝饮料的）吸管 (hē yǐnliào de) xīguǎn [M. WD 根 gēn] **2** 麦秆 màigǎn, 稻草 dàocǎo [M. WD 根 gēn]

straw hat 草帽 cǎomào

straw poll 非正式投票 fēi zhèngshì tóupiào, 民意测验 mínyì cèyàn

strawberry N 草莓 cǎoméi

stray I V 走入岔道 zǒu rù chàdào, 迷路 mílù **2** 偏离话题 piānlí huàtí II ADJ 迷路的 mílù de, 走失的 zǒushī de

a stray dog 流浪狗 liúlànggǒu

III N 走失的动物 zǒushī de dòngwù

streak I N **1** 条纹 tiáowén **2** 个性特征 gèxìng tèzhēng, 特色 tèsè

streak of adventurism 爱好冒险的个性特征 àihào màoxiǎn de gèxìng tèzhēng

3 一阵 yí zhèn, 一般时间 yì bān shíjiān
on a winning/losing streak 连续获胜／失败的时期 liánxù huòshèng/shībài de shíqī
II v 1 在…上加条纹 zài...shàng jiā tiáowén **2** 飞快地跑 fēikuài de pǎo

stream I N 小河 xiǎo hé, 溪流 xīliú
streams of consciousness 意识流 yìshíliú
II v 奔流 bēnliú, 流动 liúdòng

streamer N 彩色纸带 cǎisè zhǐdài

streamline v 使 [+企业] 效力更高 shǐ [+qǐyè] xiàolì gènggāo

street N 街 jiē, 街道 jiēdào [M. WD 条 tiáo]
street light 街灯 jiēdēng
street smarts 在城市社会底层生存的能力 zài chéngshì shèhuì dǐcéng shēngcún de nénglì
street value [毒品的+] 街头黑市价值 [dúpǐn de+] jiētóu hēishì jiàzhí

streetwise ADJ 善于在城市街头生存的 shànyú zài chéngshì jiētóu shēngcún de, 老于世故的 lǎoyú shìgù de

strength N 1 力（量）lì (liang) **2** 勇气 yǒngqì **3** 势力 shìlì **4** 强点 qiángdiǎn, 长处 chángchu

strengthen v 加强 jiāqiáng, 增强 zēngqiáng
to strengthen one's hand 增加某人的实力 zēngjiā mǒurén de shílì

strenuous ADJ 艰苦繁重的 jiānkǔ fánzhòng de **2** 强劲的 qiángjìn de

stress I N 1 忧虑 yōulǜ, 精神压力 jīngshén yālì **2** 强调 qiángdiào, 注重 zhùzhòng
to lay stress on sth 强调某事 qiángdiào mǒushì, 注重某事 zhùzhòng mǒushì
3 重力 zhònglì, 应力 yìnglì **4** 重音 zhòngyīn, 重读 chóngdú **II v 1** 强调 qiángdiào, 着重 zhuózhòng **2** 重读 zhòngdú

stressed ADJ 1 焦虑紧张的 jiāolǜ jǐnzhāng de **2** 受力的 [+金属] shòu lì de [+jīnshǔ] **3** 重读的 zhòngdú de

stressful ADJ 很紧张的 hěn jǐnzhāng de, 压力很大的 yālì hěn dà de

stretch v 1 拉长 lācháng, 撑大 chēngdà **2** 伸展 shēnzhǎn, 绵延 miányán **3** 伸懒腰 shēn lǎnyāo

stretcher N 担架 dānjià [M. WD 副 fù]

stricken ADJ 受到打击的 shòudào dǎjī de, 受灾的 [+地区] shòuzāi de [+dìqū], 受苦的 [+人] shòukǔ de [+rén]

strict ADJ 严格 yángé
a strict vegetarian 严格的素食（主义）者 yángé de sùshí (zhǔyì) zhě
in the strict sense 严格地说 yángé de shuō

strictly ADV 完全地 wánquán de, 确切地 quèqiè de

stride I v (PT **strode**) 大踏步走 dàtàbù zǒu **II N** 大步 dàbù, 阔步 kuòbù
to make great strides 取得巨大进步 qǔdé jùdà jìnbù

strident ADJ 1 坚定有力的 jiāndìng yǒulì de, 强烈的 qiángliè de **2** 刺耳的 cì'ěr de, 尖声的 jiān shēng de

strife N 争斗 zhēngdòu, 冲突 chōngtū

strike I v (PT & PP **struck**) **1** 打（击）dǎ (jī) **2** 罢工 bàgōng **3** 袭击 xíjī **4** 突然想起 tūrán xiǎngqǐ **5** 显得 xiǎnde
to strike a deal 达成交易 dáchéng jiāoyì
to strike up a conversation 开始交谈 kāishǐ jiāotán, 搭讪 dāshàn
II N 1 罢工 bàgōng
strike pay 罢工津贴 bàgōng jīntiē
to go on strike 参加罢工 cānjiā bàgōng, 举行罢工 jǔxíng bàgōng
2 军事打击 jūnshì dǎjī, 空袭 kōngxí
pre-emptive strike 先发制人的军事打击 xiān fā zhì rén de jūnshì dǎjī
3 (保龄球) 一击全中 (bǎolíngqiú) yì jī quán zhòng

strikebreaker N 破坏罢工者 pòhuài bàgōngzhě

striker N 罢工者 bàgōngzhě

striking ADJ 1 惊人的 jīngrén de, 显著的 xiǎnzhù de **2** 相貌出众的 [+人] xiàngmào chūzhòng de [+rén], 极具魅力的 jí jù mèilì de

string I N 1 线 xiàn **2** 一连串 yì liánchuàn, 一系列 yí xìliè **3** 附加条件 fùjiā tiáojiàn
no strings attached 不带任何附加条件 bú dài rènhé fùjiā tiáojiàn
4 (乐器的) 弦 (yuèqì de) xián
string instrument 弦乐器 xiányuèqì

II v (PT & PP **strung**) **1**（用线）串起来 (yòng xiàn) chuàn qǐlái **2** 悬挂起 xuánguàqǐ **3** 给乐器装弦 gěi yuèqì zhuāng xián

stringent ADJ 严格的 yángé de, 苛刻的 kēkè de

strings N（乐队）弦乐部 (yuèduì) xiányuèbù

stringy ADJ **1** 纤维多的 [+食物] xiānwéi duō de [+shíwù] **2** 极瘦的 jí shòu de

strip¹ v **1** 脱去 [+衣服] tuōqù [+yīfu] strip club 脱衣舞夜总会 tuōyīwǔ yèzǒnghuì to be stripped to the waist 光着上身的 guāngzhe shàngshēn de **2** 剥夺 [+权利] bōduó [+quánlì] **3** 剥掉 [+树皮] bōdiào [+shùpí]

strip² N **1** 一条 yìtiáo a strip of bacon 一条咸肉 yìtiáo xiánròu to cut sth into strips 把某物剪成长条 bǎ mǒuwù jiǎn chéng chángtiáo **2** 商业街 shāngyèjiē **3** 连环漫画 liánhuán mànhuà

stripe N 条纹 tiáowén，线条 xiàntiáo (people) of all stripes 各种各样的（人）gèzhǒng gèyàng de (rén)

striped ADJ 有彩色条纹的 yǒu cǎisè tiáowén de

stripper N 脱衣舞舞女 tuōyīwǔ wǔnǚ

striptease N 脱衣舞表演 tuōyīwǔ biǎoyǎn

strive (PT **strove**; PP **striven**) v 努力奋斗 nǔlì fèndòu

striven See **strive**

strode See **stride**

stroke I N **1** 中风 zhòngfēng，血管破裂 xuèguǎn pòliè **2**（体育运动的）击球 (tǐyù yùndòngde) **3**（写字）一笔 (xiě zì) yì bǐ，(画画)一画 (huà huà) yì huà **4**（钟）一响 (zhōng) yì xiǎng a stroke of luck 意外的好运 yìwài de hǎoyùn a stroke of genius 天才之作 tiāncái zhī zuò **II** v **1** 击球 jīqiú **2** 轻轻抚摸 qīngqīng fǔmō **3** 讨好 tǎohǎo

stroll N, v 散步 sànbù，闲逛 xiánguàng

stroller N 手推婴儿车 shǒutuī yīng'érchē

strong ADJ **1** 强有力的 qiáng yǒulì de，气力大的 qìlì dà de **2** 强大的 qiángdà de **3** 强烈的 qiángliè de **4** 浓的 nóng de

strong-arm ADJ 强制性的 qiángzhìxìng de a strong-arm method 强制的方法 qiángzhì de fāngfǎ

strongbox N 保险箱 bǎoxiǎnxiāng，保险柜 bǎoxiǎnguì

stronghold N 据点 jùdiǎn，大本营 dàběnyíng

strongly ADV 强烈地 qiángliè de

strong-willed ADJ 意志坚强的 yìzhì jiānqiáng de

strove See **strive**

struck See **strike**

structural ADJ 结构（性）的 jiégòu (xìng) de structural overproduction 结构性生产过剩 jiégòuxìng shēngchǎn guòshèng

structure I N **1** 结构 jiégòu **2** 条理（性）tiáolǐ (xìng) **II** v 组织安排 [+系统] zǔzhī ānpái [+xìtǒng] highly-structured 精心安排的 jīngxīn ānpái de

struggle I v **1** 尽力 jìnlì，努力 nǔlì **2** 搏斗 bódòu，打斗 dǎdòu **3** 作斗争 zuò dòuzhēng **II** N 奋斗 fèndòu

strum v 弹奏 [+吉他] tánzòu [+jítā]

strung See **string**

strung-out ADJ **1** 极度焦虑的 jídù jiāolǜ de **2** 有毒瘾的 yǒu dúyǐn de

strut I v 趾高气扬地走 zhǐgāo qìyáng de zǒu to strut one's stuff 卖弄自己 màinong zìjǐ，大显身手 dàxiǎn shēnshǒu **II** N **1** 趾高气扬的步伐 zhǐgāo qìyáng de bùfá **2** 支柱 zhīzhù [M. WD 根 gēn]，撑杆 chēnggǎn [M. WD 根 gēn]

stub I N **1** 香烟头 xiāngyāntóu，铅笔头 qiānbǐtóu **2** 支票存根 zhīpiào cúngēn **II** v (to stub ... out) 熄灭（烟头）xīmiè (yāntóu)

stubble N **1** 胡子茬儿 húzichár，短髭 duǎnzī **2** 残枝 cán zhī，茬 chá

stubborn ADJ **1** 顽固的 wángù de，固执

的 gùzhí de **2** 顽强的 [+抵抗] wánqiáng de [+dǐkàng]

stubby ADJ 粗短的 cūduǎn de

stuck I v See **stick** II ADJ 卡住了的 qiǎzhùle de, 动不了的 dòngbuliǎo de
to be stuck in traffic 遇到交通堵塞 yùdào jiāotōng dǔsè
to be stuck on sb 迷恋上某人 míliàn shàng mǒurén

stuck-up ADJ 自命不凡的 zìmìng bùfán de, 傲慢的 àomàn de

stud[1] N **1** 种马 zhǒngmǎ [M. WD 匹 pǐ], 种畜 zhǒngchù **2** 性感男子 xìnggǎn nánzǐ

stud[2] N 饰钉 shìdīng

studded ADJ 镶满…的 xiāng mǎn...de

student N 学生 xuésheng
student loan 助学贷款 zhùxué huòkuǎn
student teaching 教学实习 jiàoxué shíxí
student union 学生活动大楼 xuésheng huódòng dàlóu

studied ADJ 装模作样的 zhuāngmú zuòyàng de, 故意的 gùyì de

studies N 学科 xuékē
business studies 商科 shāngkē, 商业课程 shāngyè kèchéng
religious studies 宗教研究 zōngjiào yánjiū

studio N **1** 艺术家工作室 yìshùjiā gōngzuòshì **2** 照相馆 zhàoxiàngguǎn **3** 电影／电视制片厂 diànyǐng/diànshì zhìpiànchǎng
studio apartment 单间公寓 dān jiān gōngyù

studious ADJ **1** 勤奋好学的 [+学生] qínfèn hǎoxué de [+xuésheng] **2** 细致认真的 [+工作] rènzhēn de [+gōngzuò]

study I v **1** 学习 xuéxí **2** 研究 yánjiū **3** 仔细观察 zǐxì guānchá II N **1** 学习 xuéxí **2** 研究 yánjiū **3** 学科 xuékē **4** 书房 shūfáng, 研究室 yánjiūshì

stuff I N 东西 dōngxi II v 塞满 sāimǎn
to be stuffed 吃饱了 chībǎo le, 吃不下了 chībuxià le

stuffing N 馅 xiàn, 填料 tiánliào

stuffy ADJ **1** 空气不流通的 kōngqì bù liútōng de, 闷的 mèn de **2** 一本正经的 yìběn zhèngjīng de

stumble v **1** 绊脚 bànjiǎo **2** 绊跤 bànjiāo **3** 说错 shuōcuò, 结结巴巴地说 jiējie bābā de shuō
to stumble on 偶然碰到 ǒurán pèngdào

stumbling block N 绊脚石 bànjiǎoshí [M. WD 块 kuài], 障碍物 zhàng'àiwù

stump I N **1** 树桩 shùzhuāng, 树墩 shùdūn **2** 残余部分 cányú bùfen II v 把…难住 bǎ...nánzhù
to get sb stumped 难住某人 nánzhù mǒurén

stun v **1** 使…大吃一惊 shǐ...dàchīyìjīng **2** 使…失去知觉 shǐ...shīqù zhījué
stun gun 眩晕枪 xuànyùn qiāng

stung See **sting**

stunk See **stink**

stunning ADJ **1** 令人吃惊的 lìngrén chījīng de **2** 美得惊人的 měide jīngrén de, 极漂亮的 jí piàoliang de

stunt I N **1** （电影）特技动作 (diànyǐng) tèjì dòngzuò **2** （政治）花招 (zhèngzhì) huāzhāo
to pull a stunt 令人难堪的蠢事 lìngrén nánkān de chǔnshì
II v 抑制 yìzhì, 阻碍 zǔ'ài

stupefied ADJ 目瞪口呆的 mùdèng kǒudāi de

stupendous ADJ 巨大的 jùdà de, 了不起的 liǎobuqǐ de

stupid ADJ 愚蠢的 yúchǔn de

stupor N 昏迷的 hūnmí de, 不省人事的 bùxǐng rénshì de
to drink oneself to a stupor 喝得昏昏沉沉 hē dé hūnhūn chénchén

sturdy ADJ **1** 结实的 [+家具] jiēshi de [+jiājù], 坚固的 jiāngù de **2** 健壮的 [+人] jiànzhuàng de [+rén]

stutter v 结结巴巴地说 jiējiebābā de shuō, 口吃 kǒuchī

sty[1] N 猪圈 zhūjuàn

sty[2] N 麦粒肿 màilìzhǒng, 睑腺炎 jiǎnxiàn-yán

style I N **1** 风格 fēnggé **2** 款式 kuǎnshì, 式样 shìyàng II v 设计 [+发型] shèjì [+fàxíng]
to style oneself as 自称是 zìchēng shì, 以…自居 yǐ...zìjū

styling N（演奏／演说）风格 (yǎnzòu/ yǎnshuō) fēnggé

stylish ADJ 时髦的的 shímáo de, 漂亮的 piàoliang de

stylist N 发型师 fàxíngshī

stylistic ADJ 风格上的 fēnggé shàng de, 文体上的 wéntǐ shàng de

stylized ADJ 有独特风格的 yǒu dútè fēnggé de

stymie V 阻碍 zǔ'ài, 妨碍 fáng'ài

Styrofoam N（聚苯乙烯）泡沫塑料 (jùběnyǐxī) pàomò sùliào

suave ADJ 温文尔雅的 wēnwén ěryǎ de

subcommittee N（委员会下设的）小组 (wěiyuánhuì xiàshè de) xiǎozǔ

subconscious I N 潜意识 qiányìshí, 下意识 xiàyìshí II ADJ 潜意识的 qiányìshí de, 下意识的 xiàyìshí de

subcontinent N 次大陆 cìdàlù
the South Asian subcontinent 南亚次大陆 Nányà Cìdàlù

subculture N 亚文化（群）yà wénhuà (qún)

subdivide V 细分 xì fēn, 把…再分 bǎ… zàifēn

subdivision N 1 分支 fēnzhī 2（建造住宅的）一块土地 (jiànzào zhùzhái de) yí kuài tǔdì

subdue V 1 制服 zhìfú, 镇压 zhènyā 2 控制 kòngzhì, 抑制 yìzhì

subdued ADJ 1 稳重安静的 [+人] wěnzhòng ānjìng de [+rén] 2 沉闷的 [+气氛] chénmèn de [+qìfēn] 3 柔和的 [+灯光] róuhe de [+dēngguāng]

subject I N 1 题目 tímù, 主题 zhǔtí 2 课课 kè, 科目 kēmù 3（语法）主语 (yǔfǎ) zhǔyǔ 4 实验对象 shíyàn duìxiàng II ADJ (subject to) 1 受…约束 shòu… yuēshù 2 有待于… yǒudàiyú…
subject to change 可能改变 kěnéng gǎibiàn
subject to the law [人+] 受法律约束 [rén+] shòu fǎlǜ yuēshù
III V 使…遭受 shǐ…zāoshòu
to subject him to police investigation 使他受到警方调查 shǐ tā shòudào jǐngfāng diàochá

subjective ADJ 主观（上）的 zhǔguān (shàng) de

subjugate V 征服 zhēngfú, 降服 xiángfú

sublet V 转租 zhuǎnzū, 分租 fēnzū

sublime I ADJ 令人赞叹的 lìngrén zàntàn de, 至高无上的 zhìgāo wúshàng de II N 崇高 chónggāo, 至高无上 zhìgāo wúshàng

subliminal ADJ 潜意识的 qiányìshí de, 下意识的 xiàyìshí de

submarine N 潜水艇 qiánshuǐtǐng

submerged ADJ 在水面下的 zài shuǐmiàn xià de

submersion N 淹没 yānmò, 浸没 jìnmò

submission N 1 顺从 shùncóng, 屈从 qūcóng
to force sb to submission 强迫某人顺从 qiǎngpò mǒurén shùncóng 2 提交 tíjiāo, 呈送 chéngsòng

submissive ADJ 顺从的 shùncóng de, 屈从的 qūcóng de

submit V 1 呈送 [+文件] chéngsòng [+wénjiàn], 提交 tíjiāo 2 服从 [+规定] fúcóng [+guīdìng], 顺从 shùncóng

subordinate I V 使…从属于 shǐ… cóngshǔ yú
to subordinate the needs of the individual to those of the state 使个人需求从属于国家需求 shǐ gèrén xūqiú cóngshǔ yú guójiā xūqiú
II ADJ 从属的 cóngshǔ de, 次要的 cìyào de III N 下属 xiàshǔ, 下级 xiàjí, 部下 bùxià

subpoena I N 1（法庭上的）传票 (fǎtíng shàng de) chuánpiào II V [法庭+] 发出传票 [fǎtíng+] fāchū chuánpiào

subscribe V 1 订阅 [+报刊] dìngyuè [+bàokān] 2 [为某项服务+] 定期付款 [wéi mǒu xiàng fúwù+] dìngqī fùkuǎn 3 赞同 [+观点] zàntóng [+guāndiǎn]

subscriber N 订户 dìnghù

subscription N 订阅（费）dìngyuè (fèi), 用户费 yònghùfèi

subsequent ADJ 随后的 suíhòu de

subservient ADJ 恭顺的 gōngshùn de, 奉承的 fèngcheng de

subside V 1 逐渐减弱 zhújiàn jiǎnruò, 平

息 píngxī 2 [土地+] 下沉 [tǔdì+] xiàchén 3 [大水+] 退落 [dàshuǐ+] tuìluò

subsidiary N 子公司 zǐgōngsī **II** ADJ 附属的 fùshǔ de, 补充的 bǔchōng de

subsidize V 补贴 bǔtiē, 补助 bǔzhù

subsidy N 补贴 bǔtiē
government subsidy to agriculture 政府对农业的补贴 zhèngfǔ duì nóngyè de bǔtiē

subsist V 维持生存 wéichí shēngcún

subsistence N 1 维持生存 wéichí shēngcún 2 仅够活命的粮食／钱 jǐngòu huómìng de liángshí/qián
subsistence wage 仅够活命的工资 jǐn gòu huómìng de gōngzī

substance N 1 物质 wùzhì 2 实质内容 shízhì nèiróng
man of substance 有家产的人 yǒu jiāchǎn de rén, 富人 fùrén

substandard ADJ 低标准的 dī biāozhǔn de, 次等的 cìděng de

substantial ADJ 1 相当大的 xiāngdāng dà de, 可观的 kěguān de
substantial meal 丰盛的一餐 fēngshèng de yīcān
2 有权势的 yǒu quánshì de, 有影响的 yǒu yǐngxiǎng de

substantiate V 证实 zhèngshí, 证明 zhèngmíng

substitute I V 替代 tìdài II N 替代者 tìdàizhě, 代用品 dàiyòngpǐn
substitute teacher 代课老师 dàikè lǎoshī

subterfuge N 花招 huāzhāo, 诡计 guǐjì

subtitles N 1 (电影) 字幕 (diànyǐng) zìmù 2 (文章／书籍) 副标题 (wénzhāng/shūjí) fùbiāotí

subtle ADJ 微妙的 wēimiào de, 细微的 xìwēi de

subtract V 减 (去) jiǎn (qù), 扣除 kòuchú

suburb N 郊区 jiāoqū
the suburbs 郊区 jiāoqū, 城郊 chéngjiāo

suburban ADJ 郊区的 jiāoqū de

subversive I ADJ 颠覆性的 diānfùxìng de II N 颠覆分子 diānfù fènzi

subvert V 颠覆 diānfù

subway N 地铁 dìtiě [M. WD 条 tiáo], 地下铁路 dìxià tiělù [M. WD 条 tiáo]

succeed V 1 成功 chénggōng 2 继承 jìchéng

succeeding ADJ 随后的 suíhòu de, 接着的 jiēzhe de

success N 1 成功 chénggōng
I wish you success! 祝你成功！Zhù nǐ chénggōng!
2 成功人物 chénggōng rénwù, 成功的事 chénggōng de shì

successful ADJ 成功的 chénggōng de

succession N 1 连续 liánxù
in succession 接连 (地) jiēlián (de) 2 一连串 yìliánchuàn

successive ADJ 连续的 liánxù de, 接连的 jiēlián de

successor N 继承者 jìchéngzhě

succinct ADJ 简炼的 jiǎnliàn de, 简要的 jiǎnyào de

succor V 救济 jiùjì, 求助 qiúzhù

succulent ADJ 多汁水的 [+水果] duō zhīshuǐ de [+shuǐguǒ]

succumb V 屈服 qūfú, 屈从 qūcóng

such I ADJ 这样的 zhèyàng de, 如此的 rúcǐ de II PRON 这个 zhè ge
such as 就像 jiù xiàng, 比如 bǐrú
such-and-such 这样那样 zhèyàng nàyàng

suck N, V 吸 xī, 吮吸 shǔnxī
It sucks … …真不舒服 …zhēn bù shūfu

sucker N 1 容易上当的傻瓜 róngyì shàngdàng de shǎguā
to be a sucker to sth 偏爱某事物 piān'ài mǒushìwù
2 (动物的) 吸盘 (dòngwù de) xīpán

suckling N 1 乳儿 rǔ'ér 2 乳畜 rǔchù
suckling pig 乳猪 rǔzhū

suction N 吸 xī, 抽吸 chōuxī
suction pump 真空泵 zhēnkōngbèng

sudden ADJ 突然 tūrán
sudden death 加时加时决定胜负 jiā fēn jiā shí juédìng shèngfù

suddenly ADV 突然 tūrán

suds N 1 肥皂泡沫 féizàopào mò 2 啤酒 píjiǔ

sue v 控告 kònggào

suede N 绒面皮革 róngmiàn pígé, 软皮革 ruǎn pígé

suffer v 1 遭受 zāoshòu 2 患 [+病] huàn [+bìng] 3 变坏 biànhuài

suffice v 足够的 zúgòu de, 能满足的 néng mǎnzú de
suffice it to say 只要说…就(足)够了 zhǐyào shuō…jiù (zú) gòu le

sufficient ADJ 足够的 zúgòu de

suffix N 后缀 hòuzhuì

suffocate v 使 [+人] 窒息而死 shǐ [+rén] zhìxī ér sǐ, 闷死 mènsǐ

suffrage N 选举权 xuǎnjǔquán, 投票权 tóupiàoquán

sugar N 糖 táng, 食糖 shítáng

sugarcane N 甘蔗 gānzhe [M. WD 根 gēn]

sugarcoated ADJ 1 包有糖衣的 bāo yǒu tángyī de 2 美化的 měihuà de

suggest v 1 建议 jiànyì 2 暗示 ànshì

suggestion N 1 建议 jiànyì 2 暗示 ànshì

suggestive ADJ 暗示的 ànshì de
suggestive of sth 使人联想起某物 shǐrén liánxiǎng qǐ mǒuwù
2 性挑逗的 xìng tiǎodòu de

suicidal ADJ 有自杀倾向的 yǒu zìshā qīngxiàng de

suicide N 自杀 zìshā
to attempt suicide 试图自杀 shìtú zìshā, 自杀(未遂) zìshā (wèisuì)
to commit suicide 自杀(身亡) zìshā (shēnwáng)

suit[1] N 1 一套服装 yí tào fúzhuāng 2 同花色的纸牌 tóng huāsè de zhǐpái
a suit of hearts 一组红桃牌 yìzǔ hóngtáopái
3 (= lawsuit) 诉讼 sùsòng
to file suit against sb 对某人提出诉讼 duì mǒurén tíchū sùsòng

suit[2] v 适合 shìhé
Suit yourself. 随便你。Suíbiàn nǐ.

suitable ADJ 合适的 héshì de, 适宜的 shìyí de

suitcase N 手提箱 shǒutíxiāng, 皮箱 píxiāng

suite N 1 一套房间 yí tào fángjiān, 套房 tàofáng

bridal suite (旅馆)新婚套房 (lǚguǎn) xīnhūn tàofáng
2 一套家具 yí tào jiājù
bedroom suite 一套卧室家具 yí tào wòshì jiājù
3 (音乐)组曲 (yīnyuè) zǔqǔ

suitor N 求婚者 qiúhūnzhě, 求婚男子 qiúhūn nánzǐ

sulk v 生闷气 shēng mènqì

sulky ADJ 生闷气的 shēng mènqì de, 愠怒的 yùnnù de

sullen ADJ 面带怒容的 miàn dài nùróng de, 生气的 shēngqì de

sultan N 苏丹 Sūdān [M. WD 位 wèi]

sultry ADJ 1 闷热的 [+天气] mēnrè de [+tiānqì] 2 性感迷人的 [+女子] xìnggǎn mírén de [+nǚzǐ]

sum I N 1 一笔(钱)yì bǐ (qián) 2 总数 zǒngshù II v (to sum up) 总结 zǒngjié, 概括 gàikuò

summarize v 总结 zǒngjié

summary I N 总结 zǒngjié, 摘要 zhāiyào II ADJ 1 总结性(的)zǒngjié xìng (de), 概括(性)的 gàikuò (xìng) de 2 立即的 lìjí de
summary execution 立即处决 lìjí chǔjué

summer N 夏天 xiàtiān, 夏季 xiàjì
summer camp 夏令营 xiàlìngyíng
summer school 暑期班 shǔqībān

summertime N 夏天 xiàtiān, 夏令季节 xiàlìng jìjié

summon v 1 传唤 chuánhuàn
to summon the police 叫警察来 jiào jǐngchá lái, 报警 bàojǐng
2 鼓起 [勇气] gǔqǐ [+yǒngqì], 振作 [+精神] zhènzuò [+jīngshén]
to summon up courage 鼓足勇气 gǔzú yǒngqì

summons N (法庭的)传票 (fǎtíng de) chuánpiào

sumptuous ADJ 豪华的 háohuá de, 奢华的 shēhuá de

sun I N 太阳 tàiyáng II v 晒太阳 shài tàiyáng

sunbathing N 日光浴 rìguāngyù

sunblock N 防晒油／霜 fángshàiyóu/shuāng [M. WD 瓶 píng/盒 hé]

sunburn N 晒伤 shàishāng

sundae N 圣代冰淇淋 shèngdài bīngqílín

Sunday N 星期日 xīngqīrì, 星期天 xīngqītiān

sundown N 日落（时）rìluò (shí)

sundries N 杂物 záwù, 杂项 záxiàng

sundry ADJ 杂七杂八的 záqīzábā de, 各种各样的 gèzhǒng gèyàng de

sung See **sing**

sunglasses N 太阳眼镜 tàiyáng yǎnjìng, 遮阳镜 zhēyángjìng

sunk See **sink**¹

sunken ADJ **1** 沉没的 [+船只] chénmò de [+chuánzhī] **2** 凹陷的 [+双眼] āoxiàn de [+shuāngyǎn] **3** 低于周围的 dī yú zhōuwéi de
   a sunken living room 低于地面的客厅 dī yú dìmiàn de kètīng

sunlight N 日光 rìguāng

sunlit ADJ 阳光照耀的 yángguāng zhàoyào de

sunny ADJ 阳光充足的 yángguāng chōngzú de

sunrise N 日出（时分）rìchū (shífèn)

sunset N 日落（时分）rìluò (shífèn)

sunshine N 阳光 yángguāng, 日照 rìzhào

sunstroke N 中暑 zhòngshǔ

suntan N 太阳晒黑的皮肤 tàiyáng shàihēi de pífū

super ADJ 好极了 hǎo jíle

superb ADJ 好极了 hǎo jíle, 最好的 zuì hǎo de

supercilious ADJ 傲慢的 àomàn de, 目中无人的 mùzhōng wúrén de

superficial ADJ 表面（上）的 biǎomiàn (shàng) de, 肤浅的 fūqiǎn de

superfluous ADJ 多余的 duōyú de, 不必要的 bú bìyào de

superhighway N（超级）高速公路 (chāojí) gāosù gōnglù

superhuman ADJ 超过常人的 chāoguò chángrén de, 超人的 chāorén de

superintendent N **1** 主管人 zhǔguǎn rén, 总监 zǒngjiān
   superintendent of schools（美国）地区教育局长 (Měiguó) dìqū jiàoyùjú zhǎng

2（大楼）管理员 (dàlóu) guǎnlǐyuán

superior I ADJ 优越的 yōuyuè
   to act superior 摆出比别人优越的架子 bǎichū bǐ biéren yōuyuè de jiàzi
   to be superior to 比…优越 bǐ...yōuyuè
2 优质的 [+材料] yōuzhì de [+cáiliào], 高超的 gāochāo de **3** 上级的 shàngjí de II N 上级 shàngjí, 上司 shàngsi

superiority N 优越 yōuyuè, 优秀 yōuxiù
   sense of superiority 优越感 yōuyuègǎn

superlative I ADJ **1** 最好的 zuì hǎo de **2**（形容词／副词）最高级的 (xíngróngcí/fùcí) zuìgāojí de II N（形容词／副词）最高级形式 (xíngróngcí/fùcí) zuì gāojí xíngshì

supermarket N 超级市场 chāojí shìchǎng, 超市 chāoshì

supernatural I ADJ 超自然的 chāozìrán de II N 超自然事物／力量 chāozìrán shìwù/lìliang

superpower N 超级大国 chāojí dàguó

supersede V 替代 tìdài, 取代 qǔdài

supersonic ADJ 超音速的 chāoyīnsù de
   supersonic jet 超音速喷气式飞机 chāoyīnsù pēnqìshì fēijī

superstar N 超级明星 chāojí míngxīng

superstition N 迷信 míxìn

superstitious ADJ 迷信的 míxìn de

superstore N 超级商场 chāojí shāngchǎng

superstructure N **1**（建筑物）上部结构 (jiànzhùwù) shàngbù jiégòu **2**（社会）上层建筑 (shèhuì) shàngcéng jiànzhù

supervise V 监督指导 jiāndū zhǐdǎo

supervisor N **1**（大学研究生）导师 (dàxué yánjiūshēng) dǎoshī **2**（工程）监督 (gōngchéng) jiāndū

supper N 晚饭 wǎnfàn, 晚餐 wǎncān
   supper club 小型夜总会 xiǎoxíng yèzǒnghuì

supple ADJ 柔软的 róuruǎn de, 柔韧的 róurèn de

supplement I V 补充 bǔchōng, 增补 zēngbǔ II N 补充（物）bǔchōng (wù), 增补（物）zēngbǔ (wù)

supplementary ADJ 补充的 bǔchōng de, 增补的 zēngbǔ de

supplier N 供应商 gōngyìngshāng

supplies N 1 供应品 gōngyìngpǐn
medical supplies 医疗用品 yīliáo yòngpǐn
2 供应量 gōngyìngliáng

supply N, V 供给 gōngjǐ, 供应 gōngyìng
electricity supply 电力供应 diànlì
gōngyìng
supply and demand 供求（关系）
gōngqiú (guānxi)

support I V 1 支持 zhīchí 2 养活 yǎnghuo
3 维持 wéichí II N 1 支持 zhīchí 2 支撑物
zhīchēng wù

supportive ADJ 支持的 zhīchí de, 给予帮
助的 jǐyǔ bāngzhù de

suppose V 1 认为 rènwéi, 想 xiǎng 2 料想
liàoxiǎng, 预期 yùqí
be supposed to 应该 yīnggāi

supposedly ADV 据说 jùshuō, 一般认为
yì bān rènwéi

supposing CONJ 假设 jiǎshè, 假定 jiǎdìng

suppress V 1 抑制 [+发展] yìzhì
[+fāzhǎn], 阻止 zǔzhǐ 2 镇压 [+叛乱]
zhènyā [+pànluàn], 压制 yāzhì 3 封锁
[+信息] fēngsuǒ [+xìnxī]

supremacy N 最高地位 zuìgāo dìwèi
to challenge male supremacy 挑战男
性至上 tiǎozhàn nánxìng zhìshàng

supreme ADJ 最高的 zuìgāo de
Supreme Court 最高法院 zuìgāo
fǎyuàn

surcharge N 附加费 fùjiāfèi, 额外收费
éwài shōufèi
to levy a surcharge for excess
baggage 对超重行李收取附加费 duì
guòzhòng xínglǐ shōuqǔ fùjiāfèi

sure I ADJ 1 肯定 kěndìng 2 有把握 yǒu
bǎwò
a sure thing ① 当然 dāngrán ② 能有把
握的事 néng yǒu bǎwò de shì
to make sure (that) 确保 quèbǎo, 保证
bǎozhèng
II ADV 肯定（地）kěndìng (de), 当然
dāngrán
sure enough 果然 guǒrán, 果真
guǒzhēn

surefire ADJ 肯定能取得胜的 kěndìng néng
qǔshèng de

a surefire way 肯定能成功的办法
kěndìng néng chénggōng de bànfǎ

surely ADV 肯定地 kěndìng de, 无疑 wúyí

surf V 冲浪 chōnglàng 2 浏览 liúlǎn

surface I N 表面 biǎomiàn II V 浮出
表面 fúchū biǎomiàn, 突然出现 tūrán
chūxiàn

surfboard N 冲浪板 chōnglàngbǎn

surge I V 1 [水+] 汹涌而来 [shuǐ+]
xiōngyǒng érlái 2 [人群+] 蜂涌向前
[rénqún+] fēngyǒng ér qián 3 （感情）
涌起 (gǎnqíng) yǒngqǐ 4 （电流）浪涌
(diàn liú) làng yǒng II N 1 （水）汹涌
(shuǐ) xiōngyǒng 2 （人群）蜂拥 (rénqún) fēngyǒng 3 （感情）涌起 (gǎnqíng)
yǒngqǐ 4 电涌 diànyǒng

surgeon N 外科医生 wàikē yīshēng
brain sugeon 脑外科医生 nǎo wàikē
yīshēng
dental surgeon 口腔外科医生 kǒuqiāng
wàikē yīshēng

surgery N 1 外科（手术）wàikē (shǒushù)
plastic surgery 整形外科（手术）
zhěngxíng wàikē (shǒushù)
2 外科学 wàikēxué 3 手术室 shǒushùshì

surgical ADJ 1 外科手术的 wàikē shǒushù
de 2 外科手术式的 wàikē shǒushù shì
de, 精确的 jīngquè de

surly ADJ 脾气粗暴的 píqi cūbào de, 很不
友好的 hěn bù yǒuhǎo de

surmise V 推测 tuīcè, 猜测 cāicè

surmount V 克服 [障碍] kèfú [+zhàng'ài]

surname N 姓（氏）xìng (shì)

surpass V 超过 chāoguò, 超越 chāoyuè

surplus I N 剩余（额）shèngyú (é), 多余
（量）duōyú (liáng)
trade surplus 贸易顺差 màoyì shùnchā
II ADJ 剩余的 shèngyú de, 多余的 duōyú
de
surplus stock 多余的库存 duōyú de
kùcún

surprise I N 惊奇 jīngqí II V 使…惊奇
shǐ...jīngqí

surprising ADJ 令人（感到）惊奇的
lìngrén (gǎndào) jīngqí de

surreal ADJ 超现实的 chāoxiànshí de, 不
象真实的 bú xiàng zhēnshí de

surrender I v 1 投降 tóuxiáng 2 放弃 [+权利] fàngqì [+quánlì] II N 投降 tóuxiáng
unconditional surrender 无条件投降 wútiáojiàn tóuxiáng

surreptitious ADJ 秘密的 mìmì de

surreptitiously ADV 偷偷（地）tōutōu (de), 秘密地 mìmì de

surrogate I ADJ 替代的 tìdài de
surrogate mother 替不育者生育的妇女 tì búyùzhě shēngyù de fùnǚ, 替身母亲 tìshēn mǔqin
II N 1 替身 tìshēn 2 替身母亲 tìshēn mǔqin

surround v 围 wéi, 围住 wéizhu

surrounding ADJ 周围的 zhōuwéi de, 四周的 sìzhōu de

surroundings N 环境 huánjìng

surveillance N 1 监视 jiānshì
surveillance camera 监视摄像机 jiānshì shèxiàngjī
2（军事）侦察 (jūnshì) zhēnchá
surveillance mission 军事侦察任务 jūnshì zhēnchá rènwu
aerial surveillance 空中侦察 kōngzhōng zhēnchá

survey I v 1 调查 diàochá, 做（社会）调查 zuò (shèhuì) diàochá 2 概括论述 gàikuò lùnshù 3 勘测 kāncè 4 检查 jiǎnchá
II N 1（社会）调查 (shèhuì) diàochá
survey respondent 调查回音者 diàochá huíyīnzhě
doorstep survey 登门调查 dēngmén diàochá
2 勘测 kāncè 3 概论 gàilùn, 概述 gàishù
survey course 概论课 gàilùnkè

surveyor N（土地）测量员 (tǔdì) cèliángyuán, 勘测员 kāncèyuán

survival N 生存 shēngcún, 存活 cúnhuó
survival kit 救生包 jiùshēngbāo
survival of the fittest 适者生存 shìzhě shēngcún

survive v 1 幸存 xìngcún, 生存下来 shēngcún xialai
the only surviving member of the family 那个家庭中唯一还活着的成员 nàge jiātíng zhōng wéiyī hái huózhe de chéngyuán

2 活得比…长 huóde bǐ...cháng, 遗留下 yíliú xià

survivor N 1 幸存者 xìngcúnzhě, 生还者 shēnghuánzhě 2 善于在逆境中求存者 shànyú zài nìjìng zhōng qiúcúnzhě

susceptible ADJ 1 容易被感染的 róngyì bèi gǎnrǎn de, 容易生…病的 róngyì shēng…bìng de
be susceptible to depression 容易得忧郁症 róngyì dé yōuyùzhèng
2 容易受影响的 róngyì shòu yǐngxiǎng de
a highly susceptible girl 一个极易受影响的女孩 yí ge jí yì shòu yǐngxiǎng de nǚhái

suspect I v 疑心 yíxīn, 认为 rènwéi II N 嫌疑犯 xiányífàn III ADJ 可疑的 kěyí de, 不可信的 bùkě xìn de

suspend v 1 暂停 zàntíng 2 勒令停学 lèlìng tíng xué 3 悬挂 xuánguà, 吊 diào

suspenders N（裤子的）吊带 (kùzi de) diàodài [M. WD 副 fù]

suspense N（故事的）悬念 (gùshi de) xuánniàn
to keep sb in suspense 让人提心吊胆的 ràng rén tíxīn diàodǎn de

suspension N 1 暂停 zàntíng, 中止 zhōngzhǐ 2 停学 tíngxué, 暂时除名 zànshí chúmíng 3 悬架 xuán jià, 减震系统 jiǎnzhèn xìtǒng
suspension bridge 悬索桥 xuánsuǒqiáo

suspicion N 怀疑 huáiyí

suspicious ADJ 1 怀疑 huáiyí, 有疑心的 yǒu yíxīn de 2 使人怀疑的 shǐrén huáiyí de

sustain v 1 维持 [+生命] wéichí [+shēngmìng] 2 遭受 [+打击] zāoshòu [+dǎjī] 3 [法官+] 同意 [fǎguān+] tóngyì
objection sustained（法庭上）反对有效 (fǎtíng shàng) fǎnduì yǒuxiào

sustainable ADJ 能持续的 néng chíxù de, 能保持的 néng bǎochí de

sustenance N 食物 shíwù, 营养 yíngyǎng

svelte ADJ 身材修长的 shēncái xiūcháng de

swab I N 棉花球 miánhuaqiú, 药签 yàoqiān II v 清洗 qīngxǐ
to swab out 清洗伤口 qīngxǐ shāngkǒu

swagger I v（神气活现）大摇大摆地走

(shénqì huóxiàn) dàyáo dàbǎi de zǒu **II** N 神气活现的样子 shénqì huóxiàn de yàngzi, 狂妄自大 kuángwàng zìdà

swallow¹ I V 吞咽 [+食物] tūnyàn [+shíwù], 咽 yān
to swallow up 耗尽 hàojìn, 用完 yòngwán
2 压住 [+感情] yāzhù [+gǎnqíng]
to swallow one's pride 忍受屈辱 rěnshòu qūrǔ
II N 吞咽 tūnyàn

swallow² N 燕子 yànzi [M. WD 只 zhī]

swam See **swim**

swamp I N 沼泽（地）zhǎozé (dì) **II** V
1 淹没 yānmò **2** 使 [+人] 陷入 shǐ [+rén] xiànrù
to be swamped with problems 陷入难题之中 xiànrù nántí zhīzhōng

swan N 天鹅 tiān'é [M. WD 只 zhī]

swanky ADJ 十分时髦奢侈的 shífēn shímáo shēchǐ de

swap I V 交换 jiāohuàn, 交易 jiāoyì
to swap stories with sb 和某人相互讲述自己的经历 hé mǒurén xiānghù jiǎngshù zìjǐ de jīnglì
II N 交换 jiāohuàn, 交易 jiāoyì
swap meet 旧货交易市场 jiùhuò jiāoyì shìchǎng

swarm I V **1** [昆虫+] 成群 [kūnchóng+] chéngqún **2** [人群+] 蜂拥 [rénqún+] fēngyōng, 成群结队地移动 chéngqún jiéduì de yídòng **II** N 一群（昆虫／人）yìqún (kūnchóng/rén)

swarthy ADJ 皮肤黝黑的 pífū yǒuhēi de

swat V 重重地拍 zhòngzhòng de pāi, 重拍 zhòng pāi

swatch N 布样 bùyàng

SWAT (= Special Weapons and Tactics Team) ABBREV 特警队 tèjǐngduì

sway I V **1** （使…）摆动 (shǐ...) bǎidòng **2** 影响 yǐngxiǎng, 左右 zuǒyòu
be swayed by public opinions 受舆论的影响 shòu yúlùn de yǐngxiǎng
II N **1** 摆动 bǎidòng, 摇摆 yáobǎi **2** 影响（力）yǐngxiǎng (lì), 支配 zhīpèi

swear (PT **swore**; PP **sworn**) V **1** 骂脏话 mà zānghuà, 诅咒 zǔzhòu

to swear like a sailor 破口大骂 pòkǒu dàmà
2 宣誓 xuānshì, 保证 bǎozhèng
to swear sb to secrecy 要某人发誓保守秘密 yào mǒurén fāshì bǎoshǒu mìmì

sweat I N 汗 hàn, 汗水 hànshuǐ
no sweat 一点儿也不难 yìdiǎnr yě bù nán
II V **1** 出汗 chūhàn, 流汗 liúhàn **2** 努力工作 nǔlì gōngzuò **3** 焦虑 jiāolǜ, 担心 dānxīn
Don't sweat the small stuff. 别为小事操心。Bié wéi xiǎoshì cāoxīn.

sweater N 毛线衫 máoxiànshān, 套衫 tàoshān

sweatshirt N 棉毛衫 miánmáoshān, 运动衫 yùndòngshān [M. WD 件 jiàn]

sweaty ADJ **1** 汗水湿透的 [+衣衫] hànshuǐ shītòu de [+yīshān] **2** 使人出汗的 [+工作] shǐrén chūhàn de [+gōngzuò], 劳累的 láolèi de

sweep I V (PT & PP **swept**) **1** 扫, 打扫 [+房间] dǎsǎo [+fángjiān] **2** [风暴+] 扫过 [fēngbào+] sǎo guò, 掠过 lüèguò **3** [谣言+] 流行 [yáoyán+] liúxíng, 风行 fēngxíng **4** [政党+] 大获全胜 [zhèngdǎng+] dà huò quánshèng **II** N 扫动 sǎo dòng, 挥动 huīdòng
to make a sweep 大面积搜查 dàmiànjī sōuchá

sweeping ADJ **1** 范围广的 fànwéi guǎng de, 影响大的 yǐngxiǎng dà de
sweeping changes 影响深远的变化 yǐngxiǎng shēnyuǎn de biànhuà
2 笼统的 lǒngtǒng de
sweeping generalization 一概而论 yígài ér lùn

sweet ADJ **1** 甜 tián
to have a sweet tooth 喜欢吃甜食 xǐhuan chī tiánshí
2 香的 xiāng de, 芬香的 fēnxiāng de **3** 动听的 dòngtīng de, 悦耳的 yuè'ěr de **4** 温柔的 wēnróu de

sweeten V **1** （使…）变甜 (shǐ...) biàn tián **2** 使…更有吸引力 shǐ...gèng yǒu xīyǐnlì

sweetener N **1** 甜味调料 tián wèi tiáoliào

2 笼络人心的东西 lǒngluò rénxīn de dōngxi

sweetheart N 甜心 tiánxīn, 亲爱的 qīn'ài de, 情人 qíngrén

sweets N 糖果 tángguǒ

swell[1] I v (PT **swelled**; PP **swollen**, **swelled**) 肿 zhǒng, 红肿 hóngzhǒng

2 [河水+] 上涨 [héshuǐ+] shàngzhǎng **3** [数量+] 增大 [shùliàng+] zēngdà **4** 使…鼓起 shǐ...gǔqǐ

to swell with pride 得意洋洋 déyì yángyáng

II N **1** 浪涛 làngtāo, 浪涌 làngyǒng

heavy swells 大浪 dà làng

2 (音量) 增强 (yīnliàng) zēngqiáng

3 膨胀 péngzhàng

swell[2] ADJ 棒极了 bàng jíle

swelling N 肿块 zhǒngkuài, 肿胀 zhǒngzhàng

sweltering ADJ 酷热难忍的 kùrè nánrěn de

swept See **sweep**

swerve N, V 突然转向一边 tūrán zhuǎnxiàng yì biān

swift ADJ 迅速的 xùnsù de, 立刻的 lìkè de

swig I v 大口痛饮 dà kǒu tòngyǐn II N 大口饮 dà kǒu tòngyǐn

to take a few swigs 喝了几大口 hēle jǐ dà kǒu

swill I v 大口喝 dà kǒu hē, 痛饮 tòngyǐn II N 泔脚饲料 gānjiǎo sìliào

swim I v **1** (PT **swam**; PP **swum**) 游泳 yóuyǒng **2** (头脑) 发晕 (tóunǎo) fāyūn, 眩晕 xuànyùn II N 游泳 yóuyǒng

swindle I v 诈骗 zhàpiàn, 骗取 piànqǔ II N 诈骗 zhàpiàn, 骗局 piànjú

swindler N 诈骗犯 zhàpiànfàn, 骗子 piànzi

swine N **1** 猪 zhū [M. WD 头 tóu] **2** 令人讨厌的人 lìng rén tǎoyàn de rén, 混蛋 húndàn

swing I v (PT & PP **swung**) **1** (使…) 摆动 (shǐ...) bǎidòng, (使…) 摇摆 (shǐ...) yáobǎi **2** (使…) 旋转 (shǐ...) xuánzhuǎn, (使…) 拐弯 (shǐ...) guǎiwān **3** [想法+] 转变 [xiǎngfǎ+] zhuǎnbiàn II N **1** 秋千 qiūqiān **2** 挥动

huīdòng, 挥舞 huīwǔ **3** 转变 zhuǎnbiàn, 改变 gǎibiàn

to be in the swing of things 全力投入 quánlì tóurù

swinging ADJ 令人兴奋的 lìngrén xīngfèn de

the swinging 60s 自由放纵的（二十世纪）六十年代 zìyóu fàngzòng de (èrshí shìjì) liùshí niándài

swipe I v **1** 猛击 měngjī **2** 偷窃 tōuqiè **3** 刷 [+卡] shuā [+kǎ] II N **1** 猛烈抨击 měngliè pēngjī, 公开批评 gōngkāi pīpíng **2** 猛击 měngjī **3** (a swipe card) 刷卡 shuàn kǎ

swipe card deposits 刷卡存款 shuākǎ cúnkuǎn

Swiss I ADJ 瑞士的 Ruìshì de II N 瑞士人 Ruìshìrén

switch I v **1** 改改 gǎi, 改变 gǎibiàn **2** 交换位置 jiāohuàn wèizhi

to switch off 关 (灯 / 电视机 / 收音机) guān (dēng/diànshìjī/shōuyīnjī)

to switch on 开 (灯 / 电视机 / 收音机) kāi (dēng/diànshìjī/shōuyīnjī)

II N 开关 kāiguān

switchboard N 电话交换台 diànhuà jiāohuàntái

switchboard operator 交换台接线员 jiāohuàntái jiēxiànyuán

swivel I v 旋转 xuánzhuǎn II N 旋转 xuánzhuǎn

swivel chair 转椅 zhuànyǐ

swollen I v See **swell** II ADJ **1** 肿起来的 zhǒng qǐlái de **2** 上涨的 [+水] shàngzhǎng de [+shuǐ]

swoon V 欣喜若狂 xīnxǐ ruò kuáng

swoop N, V 向下猛冲 xiàngxià měngchōng

sword N 剑 jiàn, 刀 dāo

swordfish N 剑鱼 jiànyú [M. WD 条 tiáo]

sworn I v See **swear** II ADJ (sworn enemies) 死敌 sǐdí

sworn testimony 宣誓后作出的证词 xuānshì hòuzuò chū dízhèng cí

swum See **swim**

swung See **swing**

sycamore N 美国梧桐树 Měiguó wútóng shù, 悬铃木 xuánlíngmù

syllable N 音节 yīnjié

syllabus N 教学大纲 jiàoxué dàgāng

symbol N **1** 象征 xiàngzhēng, 标志 biāozhì **2** 符号 fúhào, 记号 jìhao

symbolic ADJ 象征性的 xiàngzhēngxìng de
a symbolic gesture 象征性姿态 xiàngzhēngxìng zītài

symbolism N 象征主义 xiàngzhēngzhǔyì

symbolize V 象征（着）xiàngzhēng (zhe), 是…的象征 shì…de xiàngzhēng

symmetri(cal) ADJ 对称的 duìchèn de

symmetry N 对称 duìchèn

sympathetic ADJ **1** 同情的 tóngqíng de **2** 赞同的 zàntóng de, 支持的 zhīchí de
to offer sb a sympathetic ear 同情地倾听某人诉说 tóngqíng de qīngtīng mǒurén sùshuō

sympathize V **1** （表白）同情 (biǎobái) tóngqíng, 怜悯 liánmǐn **2** 赞同 zàntóng, 支持 zhīchí

sympathy N 同情 tóngqíng, 同情心 tóngqíngxīn
to play on one's sympathy 利用某人的同情心 lìyòng mǒurén de tóngqíngxīn

symphony N 交响乐 jiāoxiǎngyuè
symphony orchestra 交响乐团 jiāoxiǎng yuètuán

symptom N **1** 症状 zhèngzhuàng **2** （严重问题的）征兆 (yánzhòng wèntí de) zhèngzhào

synagogue N 犹太教堂 Yóutài jiàotáng

sync N (in sync) 同步（的）tóngbù (de), 协调（的）xiétiáo (de)

synchronization N 同步（化）tóngbù (huà)

synchronize V 使…同步 shǐ…tóngbù
to synchronize the sound track with the picture 使（电影的）音响与画面同步 shǐ (diànyǐng de) yīnxiǎng yǔ huàmiàn tóngbù
synchronized swimming 花样游泳 huāyàng yóuyǒng

syndicate N 辛迪加 xīndíjiā, 大财团 dà cáituán
banking syndicate 银行集团 yínháng jítuán

syndrome N 综合症 zōnghézhēng

Down's Syndrome 唐氏综合症 táng shì zōnghézhèng

synonym N 同义词 tóngyìcí, 近义词 jìnyìcí

synonymous ADJ **1** 同义的 tóngyì de, 近义的 jìnyì de **2** 相同的 xiāngtóng de, 近似的 jìnsì de

synopsis N 提要 tíyào, 梗概 gěnggài

syntax N （语法学中的）句法 (yǔfǎxué zhòng de) jùfǎ, （计算机语言的）句法规则 (jìsuànjī yǔyán de) jùfǎ guīzé, 语法 yǔfǎ

synthesize V 合成 héchéng, 综合 zōnghé

synthesizer N 音响合成器 yīnxiǎng héchéngqì
speech synthesizer 言语合成器 yányǔ héchéngqì

synthetic ADJ 合成的 héchéng de, 人造的 rénzào de
synthetic material 合成材料 héchéng cáiliào

syphilis N 梅毒 méidú

syringe N **1** 注射器 zhùshèqì, 针筒 zhēntǒng **2** 洗涤器 xǐdíqì, 灌肠器 guànchángqì

syrup N 糖浆 tángjiāng

system N **1** 体系 tǐxì **2** 制度 zhìdù

systematic ADJ 系统的 xìtǒng de, 有条理的 yǒu tiáolǐ de

T

tab I N **1** 标签 biāoqiān, 布条 bùtiáo
to keep tabs on 密切注视 mìqiè zhùshì **2** 账单 zhàngdān [M. WD 份 fèn] **3** （计算机键盘）跳格键 (jìsuànjī jiànpán) tiàogéjiàn **4** （铁罐容器）拉环 (tiě guàn róngqì) lāhuán II V **1** （计算机）使用跳格键 (jìsuànjī) shǐyòng tiàogéjiàn **2** 选中 xuǎnzhòng, 选上 xuǎnshàng

tabby N 斑猫 bānmāo [M. WD 只 zhī]

tabernacle N 教堂 jiàotáng [M. WD 座 zuò], 礼拜堂 lǐbàitáng [M. WD 座 zuò]

table I N **1** 桌子 zhuōzi
dining table 餐桌 cānzhuō
to set the table （在餐桌上）摆上餐具

(zài cānzhuōshang) bǎishang cānjù **2** 表格 biǎogé
multiplication table 乘法表 chéngfǎbiǎo, 九九表 jiǔjiǔbiǎo
table of contents 目录 mùlù **II** v 搁置 gēzhì

tablecloth N 台布 táibù [M. WD 块 kuài], 桌布 zhuōbù [M. WD 块 kuài]

tablespoon N 大汤匙 dà tāngchí [M. WD 把 bǎ]

tablet N **1** 药片 yàopiàn **2** 石匾 shí biān, 金属匾 jīnshǔbiān
tablet PC 平板电脑 píngbǎn diànnǎo

tabloid N 通俗小报 tōngsú xiǎobào [M. WD 份 fèn]

taboo N 禁忌 jìnjì, 忌讳 jìhuì

tabulate v 把 [+数字] 用表格列出 bǎ [+shùzì] yòng biǎogé lièchū

tabulation N 制表格 zhìbiǎo gé

tacit ADJ 心照不宣的 xīnzhào bù xuān de, 有默契的 yǒu mòqì de
tacit agreement 默契 mòqì

taciturn ADJ 沉默寡言的 chénmò guǎyán de

tack¹ I N **1** 图钉 túdīng **2** 平头钉 píngtóudīng **3** 方法 fāngfǎ, 思路 sīlù **II** v 用图钉 / 平头钉把…钉住 yòng túdīng / píngtóudīng bǎ…dìngzhù

tack² I N **1** (帆船的) 航行方向 (fānchuán de) hángxíng fāngxiàng **2** (帆船) 改变航行方向 (fānchuán) gǎibiàn hángxíng fāngxiàng **II** v (帆船) 改变航行方向 [fānchuán+] gǎibiàn hángxíng fāngxiàng

tackle I v **1** 处理 chǔlǐ, 对付 duìfu **2** (橄榄球+) 阻挡 [gǎnlǎnqiú+] zǔdǎng, 抱截 bàojié **II** N **1** (橄榄球中的) 阻挡 (gǎnlǎnqiú zhòng de) zǔdǎng, 抱截 bàojié **2** 运动器具 yùndòng qìjù, 钓具 diàojù

tacky ADJ **1** 俗气的 súqi de, 不雅的 bù yǎ de **2** 有点粘糊糊的 yǒudiǎn niánhūhū de

tact N 机敏圆滑 jīmǐn yuánhuá, 待人的技巧 dàirén de jìqiǎo

tactful ADJ 讲究策略的 jiǎngjiu cèlüè de, 得体的 détǐ de

tactic N 手法 shǒufǎ, 策略 cèlüè

tactical ADJ **1** 策略 (上) 的 cèlüè (shàng) de **2** 战术 (性) 的 zhànshù (xìng) de

tactics N 战术谋略 zhànshù móulüè
delaying tactics 拖延战术 tuōyán zhànshù

tadpole N 蝌蚪 kēdǒu

tag¹ I N **1** 标签 biāoqiān
name tag 姓名标签 xingmíng biāoqiān
price tag 价格标签 jiàgé biāoqiān **2** (错误的) 称呼 (cuòwù de) chēnghu **3** (绳子 / 鞋带的) 金属包头 (shéngzi / xiédài de) jīnshǔ bāotóu **II** v **1** 给…贴上标签 gěi… tiēshang biāoqiān **2** 给 [+人] 取绰号 gěi [+rén] qǔ chuòhào, 把 [+人] 看成 bǎ [+rén] kànchéng
be tagged as a cheat 被看成是骗子 bèi kànchéng shì piànzi

tag² I v 抓人游戏 zhuārén yóuxì **II** v (在游戏中) 抓到 [+人] (zài yóuxì zhōng) zhuā dào [+rén]

tail I N **1** 尾巴 wěiba **2** 结尾部分 jiéwěi bùfen **II** v 跟踪 gēnzōng
to tail off 变小 / 变弱直至消失 biàn xiǎo / biàn ruò zhízhì xiāoshī

tailcoat N 燕尾服 yànwěifú

tailgate I v (驾车人+) 开车紧盯着前面的车 [jiàchērén+] kāichē jǐndīngzhe qiánmian de chē **II** N (汽车的) 后门 (qìchē de) hòumén

taillight N (汽车) 尾灯 (qìchē) wěidēng

tailor N 裁缝 cáiféng, 裁缝师傅 cáiféng shīfu

tailor-made ADJ **1** 裁缝特制的 [+服装] cáiféng tèzhì de [+fúzhuāng] **2** 量体定做的 liáng tǐ dìngzuò de, 正合适的 zhèng héshì de

tailspin N 失控状态 shīkòng zhuàngtài
to send … into a tailspin 使…陷入失控状态 shǐ…xiànrù shīkòng zhuàngtài

taint v **1** 沾污 [+名声] zhānwū [+míngshēng], 败坏 bàihuài
tainted money 不干净的钱 bù gānjìng de qián **2** 在食品中添加有毒物质 zài shípǐn zhōng tiānjiā yǒudú wùzhì
tainted milk powder (有) 毒奶粉 (yǒu) dú nǎifěn

Taiwan N 台湾 Táiwān

take I V 1（PT **took**; PP **taken**）1 带 dài, 送 sòng 2 拿 ná, 握 wò 3 带走 dàizǒu, 拿走 názǒu 4 花费 huāfèi 5 接受 jiēshòu, 领取 lǐngqǔ 6 承受 chéngshòu
to take after（跟父亲或母亲）很象 (gēn fùqin huò mǔqin) hěn xiàng
to take it for granted 认为理所当然 而不重视 rènwéi lǐ suǒ dāngrán ér bú zhòngshì, 不以为然 bù yǐ wéi rán
to take off（飞机）起飞 (fēijī) qǐfēi
to take ... out on 拿…出气 ná...chūqì
to take up 开始（工作、从事）kāishǐ (gōngzuò, cóngshì)
II N 1 营业额 yíngyè'é, 进帐 jìnzhàng 2 看法 kànfǎ, 观点 guāndiǎn 3 拍摄（电影／电视镜头）pāishè (diànyǐng/diànshì jìngtóu)

taken See **take**

takeoff N 1（飞机）起飞 (fēijī) qǐfēi, 升空 shēngkōng 2 滑稽模仿 huájī mófǎng

take-out N 外卖食品 wàimài shípǐn

takeover N（公司的）购股兼并 (gōngsī de) gòugǔ jiānbìng, 接管 jiēguǎn

talcum powder N 滑石粉 huáshífěn

tale N 1 故事 gùshi 2（可能是编造的）经历 (kěnéng shì biānzào de) jīnglì

talent N 1 特殊才能 tèshū cáinéng, 天才 tiāncái 2 有特殊才能的人 yǒu tèshū cáinéng de rén, 天才 tiāncái

talented ADJ 才能出众的 cáinéng chūzhòng de, 有天赋的 yǒu tiānfù de

talisman N 护身符 hùshēnfú, 辟邪物 bìxié wù

talk I V 1 谈话 tánhuà, 讲话 jiǎnghuà 2 谈论 tánlùn
to talk ... into 说服…做 shuōfú...zuò
to talk ... out of 说服…不做 shuōfú...bú zuò
to talk over 讨论 tǎolùn, 商量 shāngliang
II N 1 谈话 tánhuà
talk show（电视／广播的）访谈节目 (diànshì/guǎngbō de) fǎngtán jiémù 2 会谈 huìtán, 交谈 jiāotán 3 谣传 yáochuán

talkative ADJ 喜欢说话的 xǐhuan shuōhuà de, 多嘴的 duōzuǐ de

tall ADJ 高 gāo
a tall order 很难办到的事 hěn nán bàndào de shì

tally I N 1 账目 zhàngmù [M. WD 本 běn], 流水帐 liúshuǐzhàng [M. WD 本 běn] 2（体育比赛）记分 (tǐyù bǐsài) jìfēn
to keep a tally 记录 jìlù
II V 1 计算 [+得分／得票数] jìsuàn [+défēn/dépiàoshù] 2 与…一致 yǔ... yízhì, 相符合 xiāngfú hé

talon N（鸟的）利爪 (niǎo de) lìzhuǎ

tambourine N 铃鼓 línggǔ, 手鼓 shǒugǔ

tame I ADJ 驯服的 xùnfú de, 温顺的 wēnshùn de 2 平淡无味的 píngdàn wú wèi de II V 1 驯服 xùnfú, 驯化 xùnhuà 2 制服 zhìfú, 抑制 yìzhì

tamper V（to tamper with）瞎摆弄 xiā bǎinòng,（擅自）改动 (shànzì) gǎidòng

tampon N 月经棉塞 yuèjīng miánsāi

tan I ADJ 晒黑的 [+皮肤] shàihēi de [+pífū] 2 棕黄色的 zōnghuáng sè de II N 1 棕黄色（晒）zōng hè fùsè 2 棕黄色 zōnghuáng sè III V 晒黑 [+皮肤] shàihēi [+pífū]

tandem N 1 双人脚踏车 shuāngrén jiǎotàchē 2（两人）协同工作 (liǎng rén) xiétóng gōngzuò
in tandem with 同时 tóngshí, 同期 tóngqī

tang N 强烈的味道／气味 qiángliè de wèidao/qìwèi

tangent N（几何）切线 (jǐhé) qiēxiàn, 正切 zhèngqiē
to go off on a tangent 突然改变话题／做法 tūrán gǎibiàn huàtí/zuòfǎ

tangerine N 橘子 júzi, 红橘 hóngjú

tangible N 1 有形的 yǒuxíng de, 可触摸到的 kě chùmō dào de
tangible asset 有形资产 yǒuxíngzīchǎn 2 确实的 quèshí de
tangible proof 确实的证据 quèshí de zhèngjù

tangle I N 1 乱线团 luàn xiàntuán, 乱成一团的头发 luànchéng yì tuán de tóufa 2 纷乱 fēnluàn, 混乱 hùnluàn
to get into a tangle 搞得一团糟 gǎode yìtuánzāo

Ⅱ v 1 扭打 niǔdǎ, 打架 dǎjià 2（使…）乱成一团 (shǐ...) luànchéng yìtuán

tangled (up) ADJ 1 缠绕在一起的 [+电线] chánrào zài yìqǐ de [+diànxiàn] 2 纷乱复杂的 [+局势] fēnluàn fùzá de [+júshì]

tank N 1（水 / 油）箱 (shuǐ/yóu) xiāng 2 坦克（车）tǎnkè (chē) [M. WD 辆 liàng]

tanker N 油轮 yóulún [M. WD 艘 sōu], 油罐车 yóuguànchē [M. WD 辆 liàng]

tantalizing ADJ 诱人的 yòurén de, 逗引人的 dòuyǐn rén de

tantamount ADJ (be tantamount to) 相当于 xiāngdāngyú

tantrum N 突发脾气 tūfā píqi
to throw a tantrum [无缘无故地+] 大发脾气 [wúyuán wúgù de+] dà fā píqi

Taoism N 道家 Dàojiā, 道教 Dàojiào

tap[1] Ⅰ N 1（水）龙头 (shuǐ) lóngtóu
tap water 自来水 zìláishuǐ
on tap 取自酒桶的 [+啤酒] qǔzì jiǔtǒng de [+píjiǔ], 现成的 xiànchéng de 2 电话窃听器 diànhuà qiètīngqì Ⅱ v 1 窃听（电话）qiètīng (diànhuà) 2 从酒桶取酒 cóng jiǔtǒng qǔ jiǔ 3 利用 lìyòng, 开发 kāifā

tap[2] Ⅰ v 轻轻地敲击 qīngqīng de qiāojī
tap dancing 踢踏舞 tītàwǔ
Ⅱ N 轻踏 qīng tà, 轻拍 qīng pāi, 轻叩 qīng kòu

tape Ⅰ N 1 磁带 cídài, 录音带 lùyīndài, 录像带 lùxiàngdài [M. WD 盘 pán]
tape recorder 磁带录音机 cídài lùyīnjī 2 胶带 jiāodài
tape measure 卷尺 juǎnchǐ, 软尺 ruǎnchǐ
Ⅱ v 1 录音 lùyīn, 录像 lùxiàng
blank tape 空白磁带 kòngbái cídài
red tape 繁琐的公事程序 fánsuǒ de gōngshì chéngxù
2（用胶带）扎起来 (yòng jiāodài) zhā qǐlái

taper Ⅰ N 1 细长的蜡烛 xìcháng de làzhú [M. WD 根 gēn] Ⅱ v 1 渐渐变细 jiànjiàn biàn xì 2 渐渐终止 jiànjiàn zhōngzhǐ
tapering fingers 尖长的手指 jiān cháng de shǒuzhǐ

tapestry N 挂毯 guàtǎn [M. WD 块 kuài], 壁毯 bìtǎn [M. WD 块 kuài]

tar Ⅰ N 1 柏油 bǎiyóu, 沥青 lìqīng 2（烟草中的）焦油 (yāncǎo zhōngde) jiāoyóu Ⅱ v 用沥青铺路 yòng lìqīng pūlù

tardy ADJ 缓慢的 huǎnmàn de, 迟缓的 chíhuǎn de

target Ⅰ N 目标 mùbiāo 2 对象 duìxiàng 3 指标 zhǐbiāo Ⅱ v 以…为目标 yǐ...wéi mùbiāo

tariff N 1 关税 guānshuì 2 收费表 shōufèibiǎo 3 价目表 jiàmùbiǎo

tarmac N（机场）跑道 (jīchǎng) pǎodào

tarnish v 1 沾污 [+名誉] zhānwū [+míngyù], 使 [+名声] 蒙羞 shǐ [+míngshēng] méngxiū
tarnished honor 蒙上污点的荣耀 méngshàng wūdiǎn de róngyào 2 使 [+金属] 失去光泽 shǐ [+jīnshǔ] shīqù guāngzé

tarp, tarpaulin N 防水（帆）布 fángshuǐ (fān) bù

tart Ⅰ ADJ 1 微酸的 [+味道] wēi suān de [+wèidao] 2 尖刻的 [+回答] jiānkè de [+huídá] Ⅱ N 1 水果馅饼 shuǐguǒ xiànbǐng 2 荡妇 dàngfù

tartan N（苏格兰）格子花呢（图案）(Sūgélán) gézi huāní (tú'àn)

tartar N 牙垢 yágòu, 牙石 yáshí

task N 任务 rènwu
to take ... to task 指责 zhǐzé, 责备 zébèi

task force N 特遣部队 tèqiǎn bùduì, 特别行动队 tèbié xíngdòngduì

tassel N 流苏 liúsū, 缨璎 yīng

taste Ⅰ N 1 味道 wèidao 2 尝试 chángshì 3 口味 kǒuwèi Ⅱ v 1 尝出（味道）chángchū (wèidao) 2 有…的味道 yǒu...de wèidao
in good taste 得体 détǐ, 优雅 yōuyǎ
in bad taste 粗俗 cūsú

tasteful ADJ（品味）高雅的 (pǐnwèi) gāoyǎ de

tasteless ADJ 1 没有味道的 [+食物] méiyǒu wèidao de [+shíwù] 2 格调很低的 [+电视节目] gédiào hěn dī de [+diànshì jiémù], 无聊的 wúliáo de

tasty ADJ 美味可口的 měiwèi kěkǒu de

tattered ADJ 破烂的 [+衣服] pòlàn de [+yīfu]

tatters N 破烂衣服 pòlàn yīfu
in tatters ① [穿得+] 破烂烂烂 [chuān dé+] pòpòlànlàn ② 问题百出的 [+计划] wèntí bǎichū de [+jìhuà]

tattle V [小孩+] 向父母／老师告状 [xiǎohái+] xiàng fùmǔ/lǎoshī gàozhuàng, 打小报告 dǎ xiǎobàogào

tattletale N 打小报告的人 dǎ xiǎobàogào de rén, 搬弄是非者 bānnòngshìfēi zhě

tattoo[1] I N 纹身 wénshēn, 刺青 cìqīng
tattoo artist 纹身师 wénshēnshī
II V 刺花纹 cì huāwén, 纹身 wén shēn

tattoo[2] N 连续击鼓 liánxù jīgǔ, (英国) 军乐表演 (Yīngguó) jūnyuè biǎoyǎn

taught See teach

taunt N, V 嘲弄 cháonòng, 嘲笑 cháoxiào

taut ADJ 1 拉紧的 [+绳子] lājǐn de [+shéngzi], 绷紧的 bēngjǐn de 2 忧愁的 [+表情] yōuchóu de [+biǎoqíng]

tavern N 酒馆 jiǔguǎn [M. WD 家 jiā]

tawdry ADJ 1 不值钱的 [+货物] bù zhíqián de [+huòwù], 廉价的 liánjià de 2 无耻的 [+行为] wúchǐ de [+xíngwéi]

tawny ADJ 黄褐色的 huánghèsè de

tax I N 税 shuì, 税收 shuìshōu II V 1 征税 zhēngshuì, 收税 shōushuì 2 耗尽 hàojìn
tax break 减税优惠 jiǎn shuì yōuhuì
tax cut 减税 jiǎn shuì
tax dodge (合法或非法的) 避税 (héfǎ huò fēifǎ de) bì shuì
tax evasion (非法) 逃税 (fēifǎ) táo shuì
tax haven 避税天堂 bìshuì tiāntáng
tax return 报税单 bàoshuìdān

taxation N 税收 shuìshōu, 征税 zhēngshuì

tax-exempt ADJ 免税的 miǎnshuì de

taxi[1] N 出租汽车 chūzū qìchē
taxi stand 出租汽车候客地 chūzū qìchē hòukèdì

taxi[2] V [飞机+] 滑行 [fēijī+] huáxíng

taxidermy N 动物标本制作 (术) dòngwù biāoběn zhìzuò (shù)

taxiway N (跑道) 滑行道 (pǎodào) huáxíng dào

taxpayer N 纳税人 nàshuìrén

tea N 茶 chá
tea party 茶 (话) 会 chá (huà) huì
green tea 绿茶 lǜchá
jasmine tea 茉莉花茶 mòlì huāchá, 花茶 huāchá

teach (PT & PP **taught**) V 1 教 jiāo, 教会 jiāohuì 2 教训 jiàoxun
to teach ... a lesson 给…一个教训 gěi...yí ge jiàoxun

teaching N 教学 (工作) jiàoxué (gōngzuò)
student teaching 教学实习 jiàoxué shíxí

teak N 柚木 yóumù

team I N 1 队 duì, 团队 tuánduì
team player 善于与人合作者 shànyú yǔ rén hézuò zhě, 好伙伴 hǎo huǒbàn
team spirit 团队精神 tuánduì jīngshén 2 组 zǔ II V (to team up with) 与…结成一队 yǔ...jiéchéng yíduì, 与…合作 yǔ...hézuò

teammate N 队友 duìyǒu

teamwork N 合作 (精神) hézuò (jīngshén), 协作 (能力) xiézuò (nénglì)

tear[1] N 眼泪 yǎnlèi
in tears 在哭 zài kū
to burst into tears 放声大哭 fàngshēng dàkū
to shed tears 流泪 liúlèi

tear[2] I V (PT **tore**; PP **torn**) 撕 sī, 撕开 sīkai
can't tear oneself away 舍不得离开 shěbudé líkāi
II N [衣服上的+] 破洞 [yīfu shàng de+] pòdòng

tease I V 1 逗弄 dòunong, 取笑 qǔxiào 2 戏弄 xìnong, 惹怒 rěnù II N 1 逗弄 dòunong, 戏弄 xìnong 2 喜欢逗弄的人 xǐhuan dòunong de rén 3 性挑逗者 xìng tiǎodòu zhě, 风骚女人 fēngsāo nǚrén

teaspoon N 茶匙 cháchí [M. WD 把 bǎ], 小调羹 xiǎo tiáogēng [M. WD 把 bǎ]

teat N (动物的) 奶头 (dòngwù de) nǎitou

technical ADJ 1 技术的 jìshù de 2 很专业的 hěn zhuānyè de

technicality N 技术细节 jìshù xìjié, 程序细节 chéngxù xìjié

to release somebody on a technicality 出于程序细节的原因而释放某人 chūyú chéngxù xìjié de yuányīn ér shìfàng mǒurén

technically ADV **1** 从技术/程序细节上说 cóng jìshù/chéngxù xìjié shàng shuō **2** 技巧上的 jìqiǎo shàng de

technician N 技术员 jìshùyuán, 技师 jìshī computer technician 电脑技术员 diànnǎo jìshùyuán

technique N 技巧 jìqiǎo, 技能 jìnéng standard sales techniques 标准的销售技巧 biāozhǔn de xiāoshòu jìqiǎo

technologically ADV 从技术上说 chong jìshù shang shuō

technology N 技术 jìshù, 科技 kējì a sophisticated digital technology 尖端的数码技术 jiānduān de shùmǎ jìshù

tedious ADJ 冗长的 rǒngcháng de, 沉闷的 chénmèn de

tee N（高尔夫球）发球区域 (gāo'ěrfūqiú) fāqiú qūyù

tee shirt N See **T-shirt**

teem V 到处都是 dàochù dōu shì, 充满 chōngmǎn a pond teeming with fish 有很多鱼的池塘 yǒu hěnduō yú de chítáng

teen N See **teenager**

teenage ADJ 青少年的 qīngshàonián de teenage mother 少女母亲 shàonǚ mǔqin teenage problem 青少年问题 qīngshàonián wèntí

teenager N 青少年 qīngshàonián

teens N 青少年时期 qīng shàonián shíqī, 十几岁的年龄 shí jǐ suì de niánlíng

teeter V 站立不稳 zhànlì bùwěn, 摇摇欲坠 yáoyáo yù zhuì to be teetering on the brink of 处在…的边缘 chǔzài...de biānyuán

teethe V [婴儿+] 长乳牙 [yīng'ér+] zhǎng rǔyá

teetotaler N 不喝酒的人 bù hējiǔ de rén

telecommunications N 电信 diànxìn

teleconference N 电话会议 diànhuà huìyì

telegram N 电报 diànbào, 电文 diànwén

telegraph N（老式）电报 (lǎoshì) diànbào, 电报机 diànbàojī

telepathy N 心灵感应（术）xīnlíng gǎnyìng (shù), 遥感 yáogǎn

telephone I N 电话（机）diànhuà (jī) telephone directory/book 电话簿 diànhuà bù cordless telephone 无线电话 wúxiàn diànhuà international telephone call 国际长途电话 guójì chángtú diànhuà to make/return a telephone call 打/回电话 dǎ/huí diànhuà II V 打电话给 dǎ diànhuà gěi

telephoto lens N 长焦距镜头 chángjiāojù jìngtóu, 远摄镜头 yuǎnshè jìngtóu

telescope I N 望远镜 wàngyuǎnjìng II V **1**（象望远镜一样）伸缩 (xiàng wàngyuǎnjìng yíyàng) shēnsuō **2** 缩短 suōduǎn

televise V 在电视上播放 zài diànshìshàng bōfàng

television, TV I N 电视（机）diànshì (jī) television program 电视节目 diànshì jiémù digital television 数码电视 shùmǎ diànshì

telex N 打字电报 dǎzìdiànbào, 电传 diànchuán

tell (PT & PP **told**) V **1** 告诉 gàosu **2** 讲 jiǎng, 讲述 jiǎngshù **3** 吐露 tǔlù, 泄密 xièmì **4** 判断 pànduàn to tell ... from ... 分辨 fēnbiàn, 区分 qūfēn to tell off 责骂 zémà to tell the truth 说真的 shuō zhēn de

teller N 出纳（员）chūnà (yuán)

telltale ADJ 泄露秘密的 xièlòu mìmì de, 露馅的 lòu xiàn de

temp I N 临时雇员 línshí gùyuán, 临时工作 línshí gōngzuò II V 当临时雇员 dāng línshí gùyuán

temper I N **1** 坏脾气 huài píqi **2** 恶劣心情 èliè xīnqíng to have a hot temper 脾气暴躁 píqi bàozào

to keep one's temper 忍住不发脾气 rěnzhù bù fā píqì

to lose one's temper 发脾气 fā píqì

temperament N 气质 qìzhì, 性情 xìngqíng

sanguine temperament 热情乐观的气质 rèqíng lèguān de qìzhì

temperamental ADJ 1 喜怒无常的 [+人] xǐnù wúcháng de [+rén] 2 性能不稳定的 [+机器] xìngnéng bù wěndìng de [+jīqì]

temperance N 1 禁酒 jìnjiǔ, 戒酒 jièjiǔ 2 自己克制 zìjǐ kèzhì

temperate ADJ 1 有节制的 yǒu jiézhì de 2 温和的 wēnhé de

temperate climate 温带气候 wēndài qìhòu

temperature N 1 气温 qìwēn, 温度 wēndù

constant temperature 恒温 héngwēn 2 体温 tǐwēn, 温度 wēndù

to have a temperature 发烧 fāshāo

to take one's temperature 量体温 liáng tǐwēn

tempest N 暴风雨 bàofēngyǔ

a tempest in a teacup 茶壶里的风暴 cháhú lǐ de fēngbào, 小题大作 xiǎo tí dàzuò

tempestuous ADJ 1 暴风雨般的 [+时代] bàofēngyǔ bān de [+shídài] 2 风暴迭起的 [+关系] fēngbào diéqǐ de [+guānxi], 大起大落的 dàqǐ dàluò de

template N（计算机文件编写的）模板 (jìsuànjī wénjiàn biānxiě de) múbǎn

temple[1] N 庙（宇）miào (yǔ)

temple[2] N 太阳穴 tàiyángxué

temporary ADJ 暂时的 zànshí de, 临时的 línshí de

tempt V 引诱 yǐnyòu, 吸引 xīyǐn

to tempt fate 冒生命危险 mào shēngmìng wēixiǎn, 玩命 wánmìng

temptation N 1 诱惑 yòuhuò 2 有极大诱惑力的东西 yǒu jídà yòuhuòlì de dōngxi

to resist/succumb to the temptation 经受／经不起诱惑 jīngshòu/jīngbuqǐ yòuhuò

tempting ADJ 十分诱人的 shífēn yòurén de, 及吸引人的 jí xīyǐnrén de

ten NUM 十 shí, 10

the Ten Commandments 十诫 Shíjiè

tenant N 房客 fángkè, 租用人 zūyòngrén

tend V 1 倾向于 qīngxiàngyú, 往往 wǎngwǎng 2 照料 zhàoliào

tendency N 1 趋向 qūxiàng, 趋势 qūshì 2 习性 xíxìng, 倾向 qīngxiàng

suicidal tendency 自杀倾向 zìshā qīngxiàng

tender[1] ADJ 1 温柔的 [+态度] wēnróu de [+tàidu], 体贴的 tǐtiē de 2 嫩的 [+食物] nèn de [+shíwù] 3 疼痛的 [+身体] téngtòng de [+shēntǐ]

tender[2] N 提出 tíchū, 呈交 chéngjiāo

tenet N 基本信念 jīběn xìnniàn, 信条 xìntiáo

tennis N 网球运动 wǎngqiú yùndòng

tennis shoes 网球鞋 wǎngqiúxié

tenor N 男高音（歌手）nángāoyīn (gēshǒu)

tense I ADJ 1 紧张的 [+情绪] jǐnzhāng de [+qíngxù] 2 绷紧的 [+肌肉] bēngjǐn de [+jīròu], 僵直的 jiāngzhí de II V（使…）紧张 (shǐ...) jǐnzhāng,（使…）绷紧 (shǐ...) bēngjǐn

to be tensed up 极其紧张的 jíqí jǐnzhāng de

tension N 1 紧张（局势／心情）jǐnzhāng (júshì/xīnqíng) 2（肌肉）绷紧 (jīròu) bēngjǐn 3（绳子）拉紧 (shéngzi) lājǐn

tent N 帐篷 zhàngpeng

tentacle N 1（海洋动物的）触须 (hǎiyáng dòngwù de) chùxū, 触角 chùjiǎo 2 影响力 yǐngxiǎnglì

tentative ADJ 暂时的 zànshí de, 试探性的 shìtànxìng de

to make a tentative offer 提出试探性报价 tíchū shìtànxìng bàojià

tenth NUM 第十 dìshí

tenuous ADJ 不确定的 búquèdìng de

a tenuous relationship 脆弱的（人际）关系 cuìruò de (rénjì) guānxi

tenure N 1（教师）终身任职 (jiàoshī) zhōngshēn rènzhí 2（重要职位的）任期 (zhòngyào zhíwèi de) rènqī

tepid ADJ 冷漠的 lěngmò de, 不感兴趣的 bù gǎn xìngqù de

term I N **1** 术语 shùyǔ **2** 任期 rènqī
in the long/short term 长期／短期
chángqī/duǎnqī
3 (政府官员的) 任期 (zhèngfǔ
guānyuán de) rènqī **4** (犯人) 服刑期
限 (fànrén) fúxíng qīxiàn **5** (学校) 学期
(xuéxiào) xuéqī
term paper 学期论文 xuéqī lùnwén
II v 把…称作 bǎ…chēng zuò

terminal I N **1** 飞机候机大楼 fēijī hòujī
dàlóu, 公共汽车总站 gōnggòng qìchē
zǒngzhàn **2** (计算机) 终端 (jìsuànjī)
zhōngduān **II** ADJ **1** 不活的 bù huó de
terminal disease 绝症 juézhèng
2 越来越坏的 yuèláiyuè huài de, 没有希
望的 méiyǒu xīwàng de
terminal decline 最终的没落 zuìzhōng
de mòluò
3 终端的 zhōngduān de
terminal adaptor 终端适配器
zhōngduān shìpèiqì

terminate v 终止 zhōngzhǐ, 结束 jiéshù
termination N 终止 zhōngzhǐ, 结束 jiéshù
terminology N 术语 shùyǔ, 专门用语
zhuānmén yòngyǔ
terminus N (公共汽车／火车) 终
点站 (gōnggòng qìchē/huǒchē)
zhōngdiǎnzhàn
termite N 白蚁 báiyǐ
terms N 条款 tiáokuǎn
in terms of 在…方面 zài…fāngmian, 就
…而言 jiù…éryán
to be on good/bad terms with 和…关
系好／坏 hé…guānxi hǎo/huài
to come to terms with 接受现实
jiēshòu xiànshí
terrace N **1** 露天平台 lùtiān píngtái **2** 梯
田 tītián
terracotta N 赤陶 (土) chìtáo (tǔ)
terracotta warriors 兵马俑 bīngmǎyǒng
terrain N 地形 dìxíng, 地势 dìshì
terrestrial ADJ 地球的 dìqiú de, 陆栖的
lù qī de
terrible ADJ **1** 可怕的 kěpà de **2** 极其坏的
jíqí huài de, 糟透了的 zāotòu le de
terribly ADV 非常 fēicháng, 极其 jíqí
terrier N 小猎犬 xiǎo lièquǎn

terrific ADJ **1** 好极的 hǎo jí de, 棒极的
bàng jí de **2** 极大的 jídà de
terrify v 使 [+人] 恐惧 shǐ [+rén] kǒngjù
terrifying ADJ 令人恐惧的 lìngrén kǒngjù
de, 极其可怕的 jíqí kěpà de
territorial ADJ 领土的 lǐngtǔ de
territorial airspace 领空 lǐngkōng
territorial waters 领海 lǐnghǎi
territory N **1** 领土 lǐngtǔ **2** 领域 lǐngyù
unknown territory 未知的 (知识) 领域
wèizhī de (zhīshi) lǐngyù
3 地区 dìqū
sales territory 销售地区 xiāoshòu dìqū
terror N **1** 恐怖 kǒngbù **2** 恐怖活动
kǒngbù huódòng **3** 让人感到恐怖的人／
事 ràng rén gǎndào kǒngbù de rén/shì
terrorism N 恐怖主义 kǒngbù zhǔyì
terrorist N 恐怖分子 kǒngbùfènzǐ
terrorize v 恐吓 kǒnghè, 使 [+人] 恐怖 shǐ
[+rén] kǒngbù
terse ADJ 简短的 jiǎnduǎn de, 三言两语的
sānyán liǎngyǔ de
tertiary ADJ 第三级的 dì sān jí de
test I N **1** 测验 cèyàn [M. WD 次 cì] **2** 测试
cèshì [M. WD 次 cì]
test case (法律) 判例案件 (fǎlǜ) pànlì
ànjiàn
test drive (买车前的) 试车 (mǎi
chēqián de) shìchē
test pilot (新飞机) 试飞驾驶员 (xīn
fēijī) shìfēi jiàshǐyuán
test tube 试管 shìguǎn
3 考验 kǎoyàn [M. WD 次 cì] **II** v **1** 测试
cèshì **2** 考验 kǎoyàn
testament N (正式的) 证明 (zhèngshì
de) zhèngmíng
testicle N 睾丸 gāowán
testify v **1** (在法庭上) 作证 (zài fǎtíng
shàng) zuòzhèng **2** 证实 zhèngshí, 证明
zhèngmíng
testimonial N **1** 证明书 zhèngmíngshū,
推荐信 tuījiànxìn **2** 赞誉 zànyù, 表扬
biǎoyáng
testimony N **1** (法庭) 证词 (fǎtíng)
zhèngcí **2** 证明 zhèngmíng, 证据
zhèngjù
testy ADJ 烦躁不安的 fánzào bù'ān de

tetanus N 破伤风 pòshāngfēng
tether N 系绳 xì shéng, 系链 xì liàn
　at the end of one's tether 山穷水尽 shān qióng shuǐ jìn, 一筹莫展 yìchóu mòzhǎn

text I N 1 课文 kèwén [M. WD 篇 piān]
　2 文本 wénběn [M. WD 篇 piān] **3** 短信 duǎnxìn II v 发短信 fā duǎnxìn
textbook I N 课本 kèběn, 教科书 jiàokēshū II ADJ 规范的 guīfàn de, 典型 的 diǎnxíng de
　a textbook case 典型病例 diǎnxíng bìng-lì, 典型（法律）案例 diǎnxíng (fǎlǜ) ànlì
textile N 纺织品 fǎngzhīpǐn
　textile industry 纺织工业 fǎngzhī gōngyè
textual ADJ 文本的 wénběn de, 原文的 yuánwén de
　textual analysis 文本分析 wénběn fēnxī
texture N **1**（材料的）质地 (cáiliào de) zhìdì, 手感 shǒugǎn **2**（饮食的）口感 (yǐnshí de) kǒugǎn
textured ADJ **1** 质地粗糙的 [+衣料] zhìdì cūcāo de [+yīliào] **2** 结构丰富的 [+故事] jiégòu fēngfù de [+gùshi]
than CONJ 比 bǐ
thank v 谢 xiè, 感谢 gǎnxiè
thankful ADJ 很感谢 hěn gǎnxiè, 感激 的 gǎnjī de
thankless ADJ 出力不讨好的 chūlì bù tǎohǎo de
thanks I INTERJ 谢谢 xièxie II N 道谢的 话／做法 dàoxiè dehuà/zuòfǎ
　letter of thanks 感谢信 gǎnxièxìn
　thanks to 由于 yóuyú
Thanksgiving N 感恩节 Gǎn'ēn jié
that (PL **those**) I ADJ 那 nà II PRON 那, 那个 nà ge III CONJ (used to introduce a clause) IV ADV 那么 nàme
thatch N **1** 茅草 máocǎo **2** 茅草屋顶 máocǎo wūdǐng
thaw I v **1** [冰雪+] 融化 [bīngxuě+] rónghuà **2** [食品+] 解冻 [shípǐn+] jiědòng
　3 [态度+] 变得温和 [tàidu+] biàn de wēnhé II N **1** 冰雪融化（的时期） bīngxuě rónghuà (de shíqī) **2** [关系的+] 缓和 [guānxi de+] huǎnhé, 解冻 jiědòng

the ART 这 zhè, 那 nà
　the hottest day in a year 一年中最热的 一天 yìnián zhōng zuì rè de yìtiān
theater N **1** 戏剧（事业）xìjù (shìyè), 剧 作 jùzuò
　classic theater 古典戏剧 gǔdiǎn xìjù
　2 剧院 jùyuàn, 剧场 jùchǎng, 电影院 diànyǐngyuàn
theatergoer N 常上剧院的人 cháng shàng jùyuàn de rén, 戏迷 xìmí
theatrical ADJ **1** 戏剧的 xìjù de
　theatrical troupe 剧团 jùtuán
　2 剧院的 jùyuàn de **3** 戏剧性的 xìjùxìng de, 夸张的 kuāzhāng de
theft N 盗窃（罪）dàoqiè (zuì)
their ADJ, PRON 他们的 tāmen de, 她们的 tāmen de, 它们的 tāmen de
theirs PRON 他们的 tāmen de, 她们的 tāmen de, 它们的 tāmen de
them PRON 他们 tāmen, 她们 tāmen, 它 们 tāmen
theme N **1** 主题 zhǔtí
　theme park 主题乐园 zhǔtí lèyuán
　theme song 主题歌 zhǔtígē
　2 风格 fēnggé, 格调 gédiào **3**（音乐的） 主旋律 (yīnyuè de) zhǔxuánlǜ, 主调 zhǔdiào
themselves PRON 他们自己 tāmen zìjǐ, 她 们自己 tāmen zìjǐ, 它们自己 tāmen zìjǐ
　by themselves 独立地 dúzì de
　in themselves 就本身而言 jiù běnshēn éryán
then I ADV **1** 那时候 nà shíhou
　back then 往昔 wǎngxī
　then and only then 只有在那种情况这 zhǐyǒu zài nà zhǒng qíngkuàng xià
　2 然后 ránhòu II ADJ 那时的 nàshí de
　the then government 那时的政府 nàshí de zhèngfǔ
theologian N 神学家 shénxuéjiā, 神学研 究者 shénxué yánjiūzhě
theology N 神学 shénxué, 宗教信仰 zōngjiào xìnyǎng
theorem N（数学）定理 (shùxué) dìnglǐ
theoretical ADJ 理论（上）的 lǐlùn (shàng) de
theoretically ADV **1** 从理论上讲 cóng

lǐlùnshang jiǎng **2** 按道理讲 àn dàoli jiǎng

theory N **1** 理论 lǐlùn, 学说 xuéshuō

in theory 从理论上讲 cóng lǐlùnshang jiǎng

Darwin's theory of evolution 达尔文的进化论（学说）Dá'ěrwén de jìnhuàlùn (xuéshuō)

2 假设 jiǎshè, 推测 tuīcè

therapeutic ADJ **1** 治疗的 zhìliáo de **2** 使人镇静的 shǐrén zhènjìng de

therapy N **1**（治）疗法 (zhì) liáofǎ

alternative therapy 另类疗法 lìnglèi liáofǎ

2 心理治疗 xīnlǐ zhìliáo

relaxation therapy 放松疗法 fàngsōng liáofǎ

there I PRON (there + to be) 有 yǒu II ADV 那里 nàlǐ

thereabouts ADV 大约 dàyuē, 左右 zuǒyòu

thereafter ADV 从此以后 cóngcǐ yǐhòu, 此后 cǐhòu

thereby ADV 从而 cóng'ér, 因而 yīn'ér

therefore ADV 因此 yīncǐ, 所以 suǒyǐ

therein ADV 于此 yúcǐ, 缘此 yuán cǐ

thereupon ADV 随即 suíjí, 随后 suíhòu

thermal ADJ **1** 热 rè

thermal energy 热能 rènéng

2 保暖的 bǎonuǎn de, 保温的 bǎowēn de

thermal underwear 保暖内衣 bǎonuǎn nèiyī

thermometer N 温度计 wēndù jì, 体温计 tǐwēn jì

thermonuclear ADJ 热核的 rèhé de

thermostat N 恒温器 héngwēnqì

thesaurus N 分类词典 fēnlèi cídiǎn, 分类词汇大全 fēnlèi cíhuì dàquán [M. WD 本 běn]

these PRON, PL 这些 zhèxiē

they PRON, PL 他们 tāmen, 她们 tāmen, 它们 tāmen **2** 那些人 nàxiē rén, 人们 rénmen

they say 很多人说 hěn duō rén shuō, 据说 jùshuō

thick ADJ 厚 hòu **2** 粗 cū **3** 浓 nóng

thick soup 浓汤 nóngtāng

thicken V 使…变厚／粗／浓 shǐ…biàn hòu/cū/nóng

thicket N 灌木丛 guànmùcóng

thick-headed ADJ 非常愚笨的 fēicháng yúbèn de

thickness N 厚度 hòudù, 浓度 nóngdù

thickset ADJ 粗壮结实的 cūzhuàng jiēshi de

thick-skinned ADJ 厚脸皮的 hòuliǎnpí de, 经得起批评的 jīngdeqǐ pīpíng de

thief N 贼 zéi, 窃贼 qièzéi

thievery N 偷窃行为 tōuqiè xíngwéi

thigh N 大腿 dàtuǐ [M. WD 条 tiáo]

thimble N 顶针 dǐngzhēn, 针箍 zhēngū

thin I ADJ **1** 瘦 shòu **2** 薄 báo

thin crust pizza 薄底比萨饼 báo de bǐsàbǐng

3 细 xì **4** 稀 xī II V **1** [头发+] 变得稀少 [tóufa+] biàn de xīshǎo **2** [液体+] 稀释 [yètǐ+] xīshì

to thin the ranks 使（人员）减少 shǐ (rényuán) jiǎnshǎo

thing N **1** 东西 dōngxi **2** 事情 shìqing

not to know a thing about 一无所知 yì wú suǒ zhī

to do one's own thing 做自己喜欢做的事 zuò zìjǐ xǐhuan zuò de shì, 按照自己的意志办 ànzhào zìjǐ de yìzhì bàn

things N **1** 情况 qíngkuàng, 形势 xíngshì

all things considered 考虑到所有的情况 kǎolǜdào suǒyǒu de qíngkuàng

2 东西 dōngxi, 物品 wùpǐn

think I V **1** (PT & PP thought) 想 xiǎng

to think … over 慎重考虑 shènzhòng kǎolǜ

to think … up 想出 xiǎngchū

2 认为 rènwéi

to think poorly of 对…评价不高 duì…píngjià bù gāo

to think the world of 对…评价非常高 duì…píngjià fēicháng gāo

3 考虑 kǎolǜ II N 思考 sīkǎo, 考虑 kǎolǜ

thinking I N 想法 xiǎngfǎ, 态度 tàidu

to one's way of thinking 按照某人的想法 ànzhào mǒurén de xiǎngfǎ

II ADJ 有思想的 yǒu sīxiǎng de, 思考的 sīkǎo de

to put on one's thinking cap 开始思考 kāishǐ sīkǎo

thinly ADV 很薄地 hěn báo de, 稀疏地 xīshū de

thinly disguised 很容易看穿的 hěn róngyì kànchuān de

thinly staffed 人员短缺的 rényuán duǎnquē de

third NUM 第三 dìsān

third party [法律+] 第三方 [fǎlǜ+] dì sān fāng, 第三者 dìsānzhě

third person 第三人称 dìsān rénchēng

third rate 三流的 [+货色] sān liú de [+huòsè], 下等的 xiàděng de

thirst I N 1 (口) 渴 (kǒu) kě 2 渴望 kěwàng

a thirst for power 对权力的渴望 duì quánlì de kěwàng

II v (to thirst for/after) 渴望 kěwàng, 渴求 kěqiú

thirsty ADJ 口渴的 kǒukě de

thirsty for power 渴望权力 kěwàng quánlì

thirteen NUM 十三 shísān, 13

thirty NUM 三十 sānshí, 30

this (PL **these**) I ADJ 这 zhè II PRON 这 zhè, 这个 zhè ge

thongs N 人字凉鞋 rénzì liángxié

thorn N (植物的) 刺 (zhíwù de) cì

a thorn in one's side 肉中刺 ròuzhōngcì, 眼中钉 yǎnzhōngdīng

thorny ADJ 1 多刺的 [+植物] duō cì de [+zhíwù] 2 棘手的 [+问题] jíshǒu de [+wèntí]

thorough ADJ 1 彻底的 chèdǐ de, 全面的 quánmiàn de 2 仔细的 zǐxì de, 细致的 xìzhì de

thoroughbred N 纯种马 chúnzhǒngmǎ

thoroughfare N 大道 dàdào [M. WD 条 tiáo], 大路 dàlù [M. WD 条 tiáo]

thoroughly ADV 完全地 wánquán de, 彻底地 chèdǐ de

those ADJ, PRON, PL 那些 nàxiē

though I CONJ 虽然 suīrán II ADV 不过 búguò, 然而 rán'ér

as though 好像 hǎoxiàng, 似乎 sìhū

thought I v See **think** II N 1 想法 xiǎngfǎ, 看法 kànfǎ

just a thought 只是不成熟的想法 zhǐshì bù chéngshú de xiǎngfǎ

2 思考 sīkǎo

on second thought 经过重新考虑 jīngguò chóngxīn kǎolǜ

3 想到 xiǎngdao

thoughtful ADJ 1 周到的 zhōudao de, 体谅的 tǐliang de 2 沉思的 chénsī de, 深思的 shēnsī de

thoughtless ADJ 1 未经思考的 [+做法] wèijīng sīkǎo de [+zuòfǎ], 轻率的 qīngshuài de 2 不体谅他人的 [+人] bù tǐliang tārén de [+rén]

thousand NUM 千 qiān

thrash v 1 痛打 [+人] tòngdǎ [+rén] 2 打败 [+对手] dǎbài [+duìshǒu] 3 猛烈动作 měngliè dòngzuò

to thrash sth out 商讨某事并找出解决办法 shāngtǎo mǒushì bìng zhǎochū jiějué bànfǎ

thrashing N (一顿) 痛打 (yí dùn) tòngdǎ

thread I N 1 (细) 线 (xì) xiàn

sewing thread 缝衣线 féngyīxiàn

2 思路 sīlù, 头绪 tóuxù 3 一丝 yìsī, 一点点 yìdiǎn'r

thread of human decency 做人最起码的道德标准 zuòrén zuì qǐmǎ de dàodé biāozhǔn

II v 1 穿线 chuān xiàn 2 (用线) 把…串起来 (yòng xiàn) bǎ…chuàn qǐlái

threadbare ADJ 1 破旧的 [+衣服] pòjiù de [+yīfu] 2 陈旧的 [+借口] chénjiù de [+jièkǒu], 老掉牙的 lǎodiàoyá de

threat N 威胁 wēixié, 恐吓 kǒnghè

an empty threat 虚张声势的恐吓 xūzhāng shēngshì de kǒnghè

threaten v 1 威胁 wēixié 2 似乎会 sìhū huì

threatening ADJ 威胁 (性) 的 wēixié (xìng) de

three NUM 三 sān, 3

thresh v 打谷子 dǎgǔzi, 脱粒 tuōlì

threshold N 1 门槛 ménkǎn 2 下限 xiàxiàn

on the threshold of sth 处在某事物的开端 chǔzài mǒushìwù de kāiduān

to reach a critical threshold 达到关键的界限 dádào guānjiàn de jièxiàn

threw See **throw**

thrift N 节省 jiéshěng, 节俭 jiéjiǎn
thrift shop (慈善机构的）廉价旧货店 (císhàn jīgòu de) liánjià jiùhuòdiàn

thrifty ADJ 节省的 jiéshěng de, 节俭的 jiéjiǎn de

thrill I N 1（强烈的）激动 (qiángliè de) jīdòng, 狂喜 kuángxǐ 2 引起激动的事 yǐnqǐ jīdòng de shì II V 使 [+人] 极为激动 shǐ [+rén] jíwéi jīdòng, 使 [+人] 狂喜 shǐ [+rén] kuángxǐ

thrilled ADJ 深感激动的 shēngǎn jīdòng de, 极其兴奋的 jíqí xīngfèn de

thriller N 惊险电影／小说 jīngxiǎn diànyǐng/xiǎoshuō

thrive (PT **thrived**, **throve**; PP **thrived**, **thriven**) V 兴旺 xīngwàng, 茁壮成长 zhuózhuàng chéngzhǎng

throat N 喉咙 hóulóng, 嗓子 sǎngzi
to clear one's throat 清一下嗓子 qīng yíxià sǎngzi
to have a sore throat 嗓子疼 sǎngzi téng

throaty ADJ 声音沙哑的 shēngyīn shāyǎ de, 声音低沉的 shēngyīn dīchén de

throb I V 1 [心脏+] 跳动 [xīnzàng+] tiàodòng, 搏动 bódòng 2 [音乐+] 节奏强烈地振动 [yīnyuè+] jiézòu qiángliè de zhèndòng II N 跳动 tiàodòng, 振动 zhèndòng

throes N (in the throes of) 正处于困境之中 zhèng chǔyú kùnjìng zhīzhōng

throne N 1 王位 wángwèi, 皇位 huáng-wèi, 宝座 bǎozuò 2 王权 wángquán, 皇权 huángquán, 君权 jūnquán

throng I N 人群 rénqún II V [人群+] 聚集 [rénqún+] jùjí

throttle I V 1 掐死 qiāsǐ, 勒死 lēisǐ 2 扼杀 èshā, 压制 yāzhì II N （汽车）油门 (qìchē) yóumén, 节流阀 jiéliúfá
full throttle 全速地 quánsù de

through I PREP 1 通过 tōngguò 2 直到 zhídào 3 由于 yóuyú II ADJ 1 完了的 wán le, 用完了的 yòngwán le 2 恋爱关系结束了 liàn'ài guānxi jiéshù le, 吹了 chuī le

to read/think … through 从头到尾仔细地读 cóng tóu dào wěi zǐxì de dú, 想 xiǎng

throughout PREP 在…所有的地方／时候 zài...suǒyǒu de defang/shíhou

throw I V (PT **threw**; PP **thrown**) 1 扔 rēng, 投 tóu 2 猛力地推 měnglì de tuī 3 使…震惊 shǐ...zhènjīng
to throw caution to the wind 不顾一切风险 bùgù yíqiè fēngxiǎn
to throw a tantrum 大发脾气 dàfā píqi II N 投掷 tóuzhì, 距离 tóuzhí de jùlí
throw rug 小毯子 xiǎotǎnzi

throwaway ADJ 1 一次性的 [+商品] yícìxìng de [+shāngpǐn]
throwaway camera 一次性相机 yícìxìng xiàngjī
2 即兴的 jíxìng de, 不加考虑的 bù jiā kǎolǜ de
a throwaway comment 脱口而出的评语 tuōkǒu ér chū de píngyǔ

throwback N 复旧（现象）fùjiù (xiàn-xiàng), 返祖（现象）fǎnzǔ (xiànxiàng)

thrown See **throw**

thrust I V (PT & PP **thrust**) 1 猛推 měng tuī, 猛塞 měng sāi 2 刺 cì, 戳 chuō II N 1 猛推 měng tuī, 猛塞 měng sāi 2（发动机）推力 (fādòngjī de) tuīlì 3（讲话）要点 (jiǎnghuà de) yàodiǎn, 主旨 zhǔzhǐ

thud I N 重物碰击发出的声音 zhòngwù pèngjī fāchū de shēngyīn, 砰的一声 pēng de yì shēng II V 砰的一声碰击 pēng de yì shēng pèngjī

thug N 暴徒 bàotú

thumb N （大）拇指 (dà) mǔzhǐ
to give the thumbs up 称赞 chēngzàn

thumbdrive N 闪存棒 shǎncúnbàng

thumbnail I ADJ 简略的 [+描述] jiǎnlüè de [+miáoshù] II N 拇指甲 mǔzhǐjiǎ

thumbtack N 图钉 túdīng

thump I V 1 发出重击声 fāchū zhòngjī-shēng 2 心怦怦跳动 xīn pēngpēng tiàodòng II N 重击声 zhòngjīshēng

thunder N 1 雷 léi 2 轰隆声 hōnglōng shēng
a clap of thunder 一阵雷声 yí zhèn léishēng

thunderbolt N **1** 电闪雷鸣 diànshǎn léimíng **2** 晴天霹雳的事件 qíngtiān pīlì de shìjiàn

thunderous ADJ 雷鸣般的 léimíng bān de

thunderstorm N 雷雨 léiyǔ，雷电雨 léidiànyǔ

Thursday N 星期四 xīngqīsì，周四 zhōusì

thus ADV 因此 yīncǐ，结果是 jiéguǒ shì
thus far 到目前为止 dào mùqián wéi zhǐ，迄今为止 qì jīn wéi zhǐ

thwart V 阻扰 zǔrǎo，阻碍 zǔ'ài

thyroid, thyroid gland N 甲状腺 jiǎzhuàngxiàn

tic N（面部肌肉）抽搐 (miànbù jīròu) chōuchù

tick I N **1**（钟表的）滴答声 (zhōngbiǎo de) dīdāshēng **2**（股票价）微小变动 (gǔpiàojià) wēixiǎo biàndòng **3** 打勾的记号 dǎ gōu de jìhào (√) II V **1**［钟表+］滴答滴答响 [zhōngbiǎo+] dīdā dīdā xiǎng
to tick away [时间+] 一点一点过去 [shíjiān+] yìdiǎn yìdiǎn guòqù
What makes him tick? 是什么在左右他？Shì shénme zài zuǒyòu tā? 他是受什么影响的? Tā shì shòu shénme yǐngxiǎng de?
2 做打勾 (√) 的记号 zuò dǎ gōu de jìhào

ticket I N **1** 票（子）piào (zi) [M. WD 张 zhāng]，入场券 rùchǎngquàn [M. WD 张 zhāng]
ticket booth 售票亭 shòupiàotíng
ticket window 售票窗口 shòupiào chuāngkǒu
2（交通违章）罚款通知 (jiāotōng wéizhāng) fákuǎn tōngzhī [M. WD 张 zhāng]，罚单 fádān [M. WD 张 zhāng]
parking ticket 违章停车罚单 wéizhāng tíngchē fádān
speeding ticket 超速驾车罚单 chāosù jiàchē fádān
3 价格标签 jiàgé biāoqiān **4**（美国大选时）政党候选人名单 (Měiguó dàxuǎn shí) zhèngdǎng hòuxuǎnrén míngdān II V 给…罚单 gěi…fádān

tickle I V **1** 搔 [+人] 痒 sāo [+rén] yǎng **2** 使…开心 shǐ…kāixīn II N [嗓子+] 发痒 [sǎngzi+] fāyǎng

ticklish ADJ **1** 怕痒的 pàyǎng de **2** 需小心对待的 [+问题] xū xiǎoxīn duìdài de [+wèntí]

tidal ADJ 潮汐的 cháoxī de，潮水的 cháoshuǐ de
tidal wave 海啸 hǎixiào，浪潮 làngcháo

tidbit N 少量的精美食品 shǎoliàng de jīngměi shípǐn

tide I N **1** 潮 cháo，潮汛 cháoxùn **2**（社会）潮流 (shèhuì) cháoliú
to swim against the tide 逆潮流而动 nì cháoliú ér dòng
II V (to tide over) 渡过难关 dùguò nánguān

tidings N 消息 xiāoxi
great tidings 喜讯 xǐxùn

tidy ADJ 整齐的 zhěngqí de，整洁的 zhěngjié de
a tidy sum 一大笔钱 yí dà bǐ qián

tie I V **1** 系 xì，结 jié
to tie up ① 捆绑 kǔnbǎng ② 使停顿 shǐ tíngdùn，耽搁 dāngē ③ 非常繁忙 fēicháng fánmáng
2 打成平局 dǎchéng píngjú II N **1** 领带 lǐngdài **2** 平局 píngjú
to end in a tie 打成平局 dǎ chéng píngjú

tiebreaker N（平局以后的）决胜分/决胜局/决胜题 (píngjú yǐhòu de) juéshèng fēn/juéshèngjú/juéshèng tí

tier N **1** 一排（梯形座位）yì pái (tīxíng zuòwèi) **2** 层次 céngcì，等级 děngjí

tiff N 口角 kǒujué，小争吵 xiǎo zhēngchǎo

tiger N（老）虎 (lǎo) hǔ [M. WD 只 zhī]

tight I ADJ **1** 紧 jǐn **2** 严密 yánmì **3** 小气的 xiǎoqi de **4** 紧张的 jǐnzhāng de II ADV 紧紧地 jǐnjǐn de
hold tight 抓紧 zhuājǐn

tighten V **1**（使…）变紧 (shǐ…) biàn jǐn
to tighten one's belt 勒紧裤腰带 lēijǐn kùyāodài，紧缩开支 jǐnsuō kāizhī
to tighten a screw 拧紧螺钉 níngjǐn luódīng
2 加紧 jiājǐn，加强 jiāqiáng
to tighten one's hold on sth 加强

对某事的控制 jiāqiáng duì mǒushì de kòngzhì

tightrope N（杂技表演的）钢丝 (zájì biǎoyǎn de) gāngsī
to walk a tightrope 走钢丝 zǒugāngsī

tights N（女用）连裤袜 (nǚ yòng) liánkùwà [M. WD. 双 shuāng]

tightwad N 吝啬鬼 lìnsèguǐ, 小气鬼 xiǎoqìguǐ

tile I N 1（屋顶的）瓦（片）(wūdǐng de) wǎ (piàn) [M. WD 块 kuài] 2（铺地的）瓷砖 (pūdì de) cízhuān [M. WD 块 kuài] II v 铺设瓦片 pūshè wǎpiàn

till¹ CONJ, PREP See until

till² N 钱柜 qiánguì，钱箱 qiánxiāng

till³ v 耕 [+地] gēng [+dì]，种 [+田] zhǒng [+tián]

tilt I v（使…）倾斜 (shǐ...) qīngxié II N 1 倾斜 qīngxié，偏向 piānxiàng 2 (at full tilt) 全速地 quánsù de

timber N 木材 mùcái，原木 yuánmù

timberland N 林地 líndì，人造森林 rénzào sēnlín

timbre N 音色 yīnsè，音质 yīnzhì

time I N 1 时间 shíjiān
Time and tide wait for no man. 时不我待。 Shí bù wǒ dài.
time bomb 定时炸弹 dìngshí zhàdàn
time capsule 时代文物密封罐 shídài wénwù mìfēngguàn
time clock 考勤钟 kǎoqínzhōng
time limit 时限 shíxiàn，期限 qīxiàn
time off 休假 xiūjià，放假 fàngjià
time out（体育比赛中）暂停 (tǐyù bǐsài zhōng) zàntíng，（惩罚儿童的）禁闭时间 (chéngfá értóng de) jìnbì shíjiān
time zone 时区 shíqū
2 次 cì
at the same time 同时 tóngshí
for the time being 暂时 zànshí，目前 mùqián
in no time 马上 mǎshàng，很快 hěn kuài
on time 准时 zhǔnshí
to do time 在监狱服役 zài jiānyù fúyì，吃官司 chī guānsi
to have a good time 过得很愉快 guòde hěn yúkuài

time and a half 一点五倍工资 yīdiǎnwǔ bèi gōngzī
II v 1 安排…的时间 ānpái...de shíjiān 2 记录…的时间 jìlù...de shíjiān

time-consuming ADJ 花费很多时间的 huāfèi hěn duō shíjiān de，耗时的 hào shí de

time-honored ADJ 历史悠久的 lìshǐ yōujiǔ de，古老的 gǔlǎo de

time-keeper N（体育比赛的）计时员 (tǐyù bǐsài de) jìshíyuán

timeless ADJ 永远不会过时的 yǒngyuǎn bú huì guòshí de，万古常新的 wàngǔ cháng xīn de

timely ADJ 及时的 jíshí de，适时的 shìshí de

timer N 定时器 dìngshíqì
part-timer 兼职人员 jiānzhí rényuán
full-timer 全职人员 quánzhí rényuán

times PREP 乘以 chéngyǐ

timetable Same as **schedule** N

timid ADJ 胆小的 dǎnxiǎo de，胆怯的 dǎnqiè de

timidity N 胆怯 dǎnqiè

timing N 时间的选择 shíjiān de xuǎnzé
perfect timing 时间选择完美 shíjiān xuǎn dé wánměi

tin N 1 锡 xī 2 铁罐 tiěguàn，金属盒子 jīnshǔ hézi

tinder N 火绒 huǒróng，引火物 yǐnhuǒwù

tinge I N 1 淡淡的色彩 dàndàn de sècǎi 2 些微的感情 xiēwēi de gǎnqíng
tinge of regret 稍许有些悔意 shāoxǔ yǒuxiē huǐyì
II v 1 淡淡地着色 dàndàn de zhuó sè 2 使…稍带 [+感情] shǐ...shāo dài [+gǎnqíng]
a voice tinged with regret 稍带悔意的口吻 shāo dài huǐyì de kǒuwěn

tingle I v 1 感到刺痛 gǎndào cìtòng 2 感到兴奋 gǎndào xīngfèn II N 刺痛感 cìtòng gǎn

tinker v 马马虎虎地修理 mǎma hūhū de xiūlǐ，稍稍对付一下 shāoshāo duìfu yíxià

tinkle I v 发出叮当当声 fāchū dīngdāngshēng，叮当当当响 dīngdāng dīngdāng xiǎng II N 叮当声 dīngdāngshēng

tinsel N 1（装饰用的）闪光纸 (zhuāngshì yòng de) shǎnguāngzhǐ 2 花哨无用的东西 huāshao wúyòng de dōngxi

tint I N 1（淡）颜色 (dàn) yánsè 2 染发剂 rǎnfàjì II v 给 [+头发] 染色 gěi [+tóufa] rǎnsè

tiny ADJ 微小的 wēixiǎo de

tip¹ I N 小费 xiǎofèi II v 付小费 fù xiǎofèi

tip² I N 1 提示 tíshì 2 秘密情报 mìmì qíngbào II v 透露情报 tòulù qíngbào
to tip sb off sth 向某人通风报信 xiàng mǒurén tōngfēng bàoxìn

tip³ I N 1 顶端 dǐngduān
on the tip of one's tongue 就在嘴边（可是记不起）jiù zài zuǐbiān (kěshì jìbuqǐ)
II v（使…）倾斜 (shǐ...) qīngxié,（使…）倒下 (shǐ...) dǎoxià

tip-off N 1 提示 tíshì, 暗示 ànshì 2（警察的）告发 (jǐngchá de) gàofā, 通风报信 tōngfēng bàoxìn 3（篮球比赛）开球 (lánqiú bǐsài) kāiqiú

tipper N 给小费的人 gěi xiǎofèi de rén
a generous tipper 付小费很大方的人 fù xiǎofèi hěn dàfang de rén

tipster N 出卖情报的人 chūmài qíngbào de rén, 告密者 gàomìzhě

tipsy ADJ 稍微有点醉的 shāowēi yǒudiǎn zuì de

tiptoe I N 脚尖 jiǎojiān II v 踮着脚走 diànzhe jiǎo zǒu, 悄悄地走 qiāoqiāo de zǒu

tirade N 长篇抨击性讲话 chángpiān pēngjīxìng jiǎnghuà

tire, tyre N [汽车+] 轮胎 [qìchē+] lúntāi

tired ADJ 1 累 lèi, 疲倦的 píjuàn de 2 厌倦的 yànjuàn de

tireless ADJ（孜孜）不倦的 (zīzī) bújuàn de, 不知疲倦的 bù zhī píjuàn de

tiresome ADJ 烦人的 fánrén de, 令人厌烦的 lìngrén yànfán de

tiring ADJ 令人疲劳的 lìngrén píláo de, 令人疲倦的 lìngrén píjuàn de

tissue N 1（动／植物）组织 (dòng/zhíwù) zǔzhī
muscle tissue 肌肉组织 jīròuzǔzhī
2 纸巾 zhǐjīn, 面巾纸 miànjīnzhǐ [M. WD

张 zhāng] 3（包装）薄纸 (bāozhuāng) báozhǐ [M. WD 张 zhāng]

tit N（女人的）乳房 (nǚrén de) rǔfáng

titanic ADJ 力大无穷的 lìdà wúqióng de, 巨大的 jùdà de

tit-for-tat ADJ 针锋相对的 zhēnfēng xiāngduì de, 以牙还牙的 yǐ yá huán yá de

tithe N 什一税 shíyīshuì, 什一费 shíyīfèi

titillate v 使…兴奋的 shǐ...xīngfèn de,（性）挑逗 (xìng) tiǎodòu

title I N 1 书名 shūmíng, 题目 tímù
title page 书名页 shūmíngyè
title role 剧名角色 jùmíng juésè
2 称号 chēnghào, 头衔 tóuxián 3 所有权 suǒyǒuquán
title deed 产权证 chǎnquánzhèng, 房契 fángqì

titled ADJ 有贵族称号的 yǒu guìzú chēnghào de

titter v 窃笑 qièxiào, 傻笑 shǎxiào

tizzy N (in a tizzy) 心慌意乱的 xīn huāng yì luàn de

to¹ marker of verb infinitive

to² PREP 1 往 wǎng, 向 xiàng, 到 dào
to walk to town 走到城里 zǒudào chénglǐ
2（达）到 (dá) dào

toad N（癞）蛤蟆 (lài) háma [M. WD 只 zhī], 蟾蜍 chánchú [M. WD 只 zhī]

toady I N 马屁精 mǎpìjīng II v 拍马屁 pāi mǎpì, 奉承 fèngcheng

to and fro ADV 来来往往地 láilai wǎngwǎng de
to pace to and fro 走来走去 zǒulái zǒuqù

toast¹ I N 烤面包 kǎomiànbāo II v 烤 kǎo, 烘 hōng

toast² I N 祝酒 zhùjiǔ II v 为…举杯祝酒 wéi...jǔbēi zhùjiǔ

toaster N 烤面包器 kǎomiànbāoqì

tobacco N 烟草 yāncǎo, 烟叶 yānyè

tobacconist N 烟草商 yāncǎoshāng, 烟店老板 yāndiàn lǎobǎn

toboggan I N 平底木雪橇 píng dǐ mù xuěqiāo II v 坐平底木雪橇 zuò píng dǐ mù xuěqiāo

today N, ADV 今天 jīntiān

toddle v [幼儿+] 蹒跚学走路 [yòu'ér+] pánshān xué zǒulù

toddler N 刚学走路的小孩 gāng xué zǒulù de xiǎohái

toe N 脚趾 jiǎozhǐ

toehold N 立脚点 lìjiǎodiǎn
to get a toehold in sth 在某事中取得了立脚点 zài mǒushì zhōng qǔdé le lìjiǎodiǎn

toenail N 脚趾甲 jiǎozhǐjiǎ

toe-to-toe ADJ (to go toe-to-toe with sb) 与某人激烈对抗 yǔ mǒurén jīliè duìkàng

toffee N 太妃糖 tàifēitáng

tofu N 豆腐 dòufu

together I ADV 一起 yìqǐ, 一块儿 yíkuàir II ADJ 思路清晰的 sīlù qīngxī de, 有条有理的 yǒu tiáo yǒu lǐ de

toggle N (计算机) 切换键 (jìsuànjī) qiēhuànjiàn

toil I v 1 辛苦工作 xīnkǔ gōngzuò, 日夜劳作 rìyè láozuò 2 吃力地行走 chīlì de xíngzǒu II N 劳作 láozuò, 苦干 kǔgàn

toilet N 便缸 biàngāng, 厕所 cèsuǒ
to flush the toilet 冲洗马桶 chōngxǐ mǎtǒng
toilet paper 卫生纸 wèishēngzhǐ, 手纸 shǒuzhǐ [M. WD 张 zhāng]
toilet water 花露水 huālùshuǐ

toiletries N 梳洗用具 shūxǐ yòngjù

token I N 1 象征 xiàngzhēng, 标志 biāozhì 2 代币 dàibì
subway token 地铁代币 dìtiě dàibì
token of appreciation 感谢的象征 gǎnxiè de xiàngzhēng
II ADJ 象征性的 xiàngzhēngxìng de
a token compromise 象征性妥协 xiàngzhēngxìng tuǒxié

told See tell

tolerable ADJ 过得去 guòdequ, 尚可接受的 shàngkě jiēshòu de

tolerance N 宽容 kuānróng, 容忍 róngrěn
religious tolerance 宗教宽容 zōngjiào kuānróng, 容忍不同的宗教 róngrěn bùtóng de zōngjiào

tolerant ADJ 1 宽容的 kuānróng de, 容忍的 róngrěn de 2 能忍耐的 [+植物] néng rěnnài de [+zhíwù]

tolerate v 容忍 róngrěn, 容许 róngxǔ

toll[1] I N 1 伤亡人数 shāngwáng rénshù 2 道路使用费 dàolù shǐyòngfèi, 通行费 tōngxíngfèi
toll booth 道路收费处 dàolù shōufèichù, 公路收费处 gōnglù shōufèichù

toll[2] I N 钟声 zhōngshēng II v 敲 (丧) 钟 qiāo (sāngzhōng)

toll-bridge N 收费桥 shōufèiqiáo

toll-free ADJ 免费的 [+电话] miǎnfèi de [+diànhuà]

tomato N 番茄 fānqié, 西红柿 xīhóngshì
tomato sauce 番茄酱 fānqiéjiàng

tomb N 坟 fén, 坟墓 fénmù

tomboy N 假小子 jiǎxiǎozi, 野丫头 yěyātou

tombstone N 墓碑 mùbēi [M. WD 块 kuài]

tomcat N 公猫 gōng māo

tome N 大本厚书 dà běn hòu shū

tomfoolery N 愚蠢行为 yúchǔn xíngwéi

tomorrow N, ADV 明天 míngtiān

ton N 吨 dūn
tons of 大量的 dàliàng de

tone I N 1 语气 yǔqì, 腔调 qiāngdiào 2 主调 zhǔdiào, 调子 diàozi 3 色调 sèdiào, 色度 sèdù 4 电话信号 diànhuà xìnhào
an engaged tone 占线信号 zhànxiàn xìnhào
5 (肌肉) 结实程度 (jīròu) jiēshi chéngdù II v 使 [+肌肤] 健康 shǐ [+ jīfū] jiànkāng
to tone down ① 使颜色柔和 shǐ yánsè róuhé ② 使语气缓和 shǐ yǔqì huǎnhé

tone-deaf ADJ 不能辨别不同音的 bùnéng biànbié bùtóng yīn de

toner N 墨粉 mòfěn

tongs N 夹子 jiāzi, 镊子 nièzi

tongue I N 1 舌头 shétou
tongue twister 绕口令 ràokǒuling
2 语言 yǔyán
mother tongue 母语 mǔyǔ
a slip of the tongue 口误 kǒuwù

tongue-lashing N 破口大骂 pòkǒu dàmà, 狠狠训斥 hěnhěn xùnchì

tongue-tied ADJ 张口结舌的 zhāngkǒu jiéshé de, 说不出话的 shuōbuchū huà de

tonic I N 1 (滋) 补品 (zī) bǔpǐn, 强身剂 qiángshēnjì

tonic water 奎宁水 kuíníngshuǐ
2 有利于身心健康的事 yǒulì yú shēnxīn jiànkāng de shì **II** ADJ **1** 强身滋补的 qiángshēn zībǔ de **2** 有利的 yǒulì de
a tonic effect 很有利的效果 hěn yǒulì de xiàoguǒ

tonight N, ADV 今天晚上 jīntiān wǎnshang, 今天夜里 jīntiān yèlǐ

tonnage N **1** 总吨数 zǒngdūnshù **2**（船只的）吨位（chuánzhī de）dūnwèi

tonsil N 扁桃体 biǎntáotǐ, 扁桃腺 biǎntáoxiàn
to remove the tonsil 切除扁桃体 qiēchú biǎntáotǐ

too ADV **1** 也 yě **2** 太 tài

took See take

tool I N 工具 gōngjù
tool box 工具箱 gōngjùxiāng
tool shed 工具房 gōngjùfáng
II v (to tool up) 装备 zhuāngbèi

toot I v [+汽车喇叭] 按 [+qìchē lǎba]
to toot one's own horn 吹捧自己 chuīpěng zìjǐ, 自夸 zìkuā
II N 汽车喇叭声 qìchē lǎbashēng

tooth (PL **teeth**) N 牙齿 yáchǐ
to fight tooth and nail 尽极大努力 jìn jídà nǔlì
to have a sweet tooth 喜欢吃甜的东西 xǐhuan chī tián de dōngxi
to give teeth to … 使 [+规定] 有效力 shǐ [+guīdìng] yǒu xiàolì

toothache N 牙疼 yáténg, 牙痛 yátòng

toothbrush N 牙刷 yáshuā [M. WD 把 bǎ]

toothpaste N 牙膏 yágāo

toothpick N 牙签 yáqiān [M. WD 根 gēn]

top[1] I N **1** 顶 dǐng, 顶部 dǐngbù **2** [台+] 面 [tái+] miàn, [桌+] 面 [zhuō+] miàn **3** 最高地位 zuìgāo dìwèi, 顶峰 dǐngfēng
top dog 大人物 dàrénwù
4 [女子+] 上衣 [nǚzǐ+] shàngyī **II** ADJ 最高的 zuìgāo de, 顶级的 dǐngjí de **III** v 超过 chāoguò, 胜过 shèngguò
on top of ① 除了…以外 chúle…yǐwài ② 能对付 néng duìfu, 能控制 néng kòngzhì

top[2] N 陀螺 tuóluó

top-heavy ADJ **1** 上重下轻的 shàng

zhòng xià qīng de **2** 管理人员太多的 guǎnlǐ rényuán tài duō de, 将多兵少的 jiāng duō bīng shǎo de

topic N 话题 huàtí, 题目 tímù

topical ADJ 热门（话题）的 rèmén (huàtí) de

topless ADJ 不穿上衣的 [+女子] bù chuān shàngyī de [+nǚzǐ], 袒胸的 tǎnxiōng de

topmost ADJ 最上面的 zuì shàngmian de, 最高的 zuì gāo de

topnotch ADJ 第一流的 dìyīliú de, 最杰出的 zuì jiéchū de

topography N **1** 地貌（学）dìmào (xué), 地形 dìxíng **2**（国家的）概貌（guójiā de）gàimào, 概况 gàikuàng

topping N（加在食品上的）配料 (jiā zài shípǐnshàng de) pèiliào

topple v 推翻 tuīfān, 使…倒塌 shǐ…dǎotā

top-secret ADJ 绝密的 juémì de

topsy-turvy ADJ **1** 乱七八糟的 [+房间] luànqībāzāo de [+fángjiān], 凌乱不堪的 língluàn bùkān de **2** 有好有坏的 [+工作] yǒu hǎo yǒu huài de [+gōngzuò]

torch I N 火炬 huǒjù, 火把 huǒbǎ **II** v 点燃 diǎnrán

tore See tear[2]

torment I N 折磨 zhémo, 痛苦 tòngkǔ **II** v 折磨 zhémo, 使 [+人] 痛苦 shǐ [+rén] tòngkǔ

torn See tear[2]

tornado N 龙卷风 lóngjuǎnfēng
to be hit by a tornado 受到龙卷风的袭击 shòudào lóngjuǎnfēng de xíjī

torpedo I N 鱼雷 yúléi **II** v **1** 用鱼雷袭击 yòng yúléi xíjī **2** 破坏 pòhuài

torque N（发动机的）扭矩 (fādòngjī de) niǔjǔ

torrent N 激流 jīliú
a torrent of criticism 接连不断的抨击 jiēlián búduàn de pēngjī

torrid ADJ **1** 热烈的 [+情爱] rèliè de [+qíng'ài], 炽热的 zhìrè de **2** 灼热的 [+天气] zhuórè de [+tiānqì]

torso N 人体躯干 réntǐ qūgàn

tortilla N（墨西哥）薄玉米饼 (Mòxīgē) báo yùmǐbǐng [M. WD 片 piàn]

tortoise N（乌）龟 (wū) guī

tortuous ADJ 1 曲折的 qūzhé de, 弯弯曲曲的 wānwān qūqū de 2 错综复杂的 cuòzōng fùzá de

torture I N 酷刑 kùxíng, 刑讯 xíngxùn II v 1 对…施酷刑 duì…shī kùxíng
to torture sb to death 对某人实行酷刑致死 duì mǒurén shíxíng kùxíng zhìsǐ 2 折磨 zhémó

toss I v 1 扔 rēng, 掷 zhì
to toss out 扔掉 rēngdiào, 丢弃 diūqì 2 使…动荡 shǐ…dòngdàng
to toss and turn（在床上）翻来复去 (zài chuángshang) fānlái fùqù 3 掷硬币（以作决定）zhì yìngbì (yǐ zuò juédìng) II N (coin toss) 掷硬币以决定 zhì yìngbì yǐ juédìng

tot N 小娃娃 xiǎowáwá

total I ADJ 总的 zǒng de, 全部的 quánbù de II N 总数 zǒngshù III v 总数为 zǒngshù wéi, 共计 gòngjì

totality N 整体 zhěngtǐ, 全部 quánbù

totally ADV 完全 wánquán

tote bag N 大袋子 dà dàizi

totem N 图腾 túténg
totem pole 图腾柱 túténg zhù

totter v 1 摇摇晃晃 yáoyáo huànghuàng 2 摇摇欲坠 yáoyáo yù zhuì
to totter toward collapse 走向崩溃 zǒuxiàng bēngkuì

touch I v 1 触 chù, 接触 jiēchù 2 碰 pèng, 碰到 pèngdao 3 感动 gǎndòng
to touch on/upon 涉及 shèjí, 谈到 tándao
touch wood 老天保佑 lǎotiān bǎoyòu II N 1 碰 pèng, 触 chù, 接触 jiēchù
touch screen 触摸式显示屏 chùmō shì xiǎnshìpíng
to lose touch 失去联系 shīqù liánxi
to stay in touch 保持联系 bǎochí liánxi 2 手法 shǒufǎ, 风格 fēnggé 3 (a touch) 有点儿 yǒudiǎnr

touch-and-go ADJ 风险极大的 fēngxiǎn jídà de, 极其危险的 jíqí wēixiǎn de

touchdown N 1 （飞机）降落 (fēijī) jiàngluò 2 （橄榄球）触地得分 (gǎnlǎnqiú) chù dì dé fēn

touched ADJ 受感动的 shòu gǎndòng de, 感激的 gǎnji de

touchstone N 试金石 shìjīnshí, 检验标准 jiǎnyàn biāozhǔn

touchy ADJ 1 十分敏感的 [+人] shífēn mǐngǎn de [+rén] 2 微妙的 [+问题] wēimiào de [+wèntí]

tough I ADJ 1 坚韧的 [+材料] jiānrèn de [+cáiliào] 2 坚强的 [+人] jiānqiáng de [+rén], 耐劳的 nàiláo de 3 棘手的 [+问题] jíshǒu de [+wèntí], 困难的 kùnnán de
tough love 严厉的爱 yánlì de ài, 严格要求的真爱 yángé yāoqiú de zhēn ài II v (to tough it out) 渡过（难关）dùguò (nánguān), 挺过来 tǐngguòlai

toughen (up) v 使坚韧／坚强 shǐ jiānrèn/jiānqiáng

toupee N 假发 jiǎfà

tour I N 1 旅游 lǚyóu, 旅行 lǚxíng 2 参观 cānguān II v 旅游 lǚyóu, 旅行 lǚxíng
guided tour 有导游的旅游 yǒu dǎoyóu de lǚyóu
package tour 一揽子旅游 yìlǎnzi lǚyóu

tourism N 旅游业 lǚyóuyè

tourist I N 旅游者 lǚyóuzhě II ADJ 旅游（者／行业）的 lǚyóu (zhě/hángyè) de
tourist agency 旅游社 lǚyóushè
tourist class（飞机／轮船）经济舱 (fēijī/lúnchuán) jīngjìcāng
tourist trap 旅游者陷阱 lǚyóuzhě xiànjǐng

tournament N 锦标赛 jǐnbiāosài

tourniquet N 止血带 zhǐxuèdài

tousled ADJ 蓬乱的 [+头发] péngluàn de [+tóufa]

tout v 1 赞扬 zànyáng, 推崇 tuīchóng 2 推销 [+商品] tuīxiāo [+shāngpǐn], 兜售 dōushòu

tow v, N 拖 tuō, 牵引 qiānyǐn
tow truck 托运车 tuōyùn chē
in tow 紧跟在后面 jǐngēn zàihòu miàn

toward, towards PREP 1 朝着 cháozhe, 向着 xiàngzhe 2 对 duì, 对于 duìyú 3 接近 jiējìn

towaway zone N 禁止停车区（违章则拖走车）jìnzhǐ tíngchē qū (wéizhāng zé tuō zǒu chē)

towel I N 毛巾 máojīn

bath towel 浴巾 yùjīn

face towel 面巾 miànjīn

II v (to towel off/down) 用毛巾擦干 yòng máojīn cāgān

tower I N 1 高塔 gāo tǎ [M. WD 座 zuò]

observation tower 了望塔 liáowàngtǎ

TV tower 电视塔 diànshìtǎ

II v 高于 gāoyú

towering ADJ 1 高耸的 [+树] gāosǒng de [+shù] 2 杰出的 [+人物] jiéchū de [+rénwù]

town N 1 镇 zhèn, 小城 xiǎo chéng

town council 镇议会 zhèn yìhuì, 市议会 shì yìhuì

town hall 市政厅 shìzhèngtīng

2 闹市区 nàoshìqū

to go into town 到市区去 dào shìqū qù, 进城 jìn chéng

townhouse N 连栋房屋 liándòng fángwū, 排屋 pái wū

township N 镇 zhèn, 镇区 zhèn qū

townspeople, townsfolk N 城镇居民 chéngzhèn jūmín

toxic ADJ 有毒的 yǒudú de

toxic waste 有毒垃圾 yǒudú lājī

toxicity N 毒性 dúxìng

toxin N 毒素 dúsù

toy I N 玩具 wánjù, 小玩意儿 xiǎowányìr

II v (to toy with) 不很认真地考虑 bù hěn rènzhēn de kǎolǜ **III** ADJ 极小的 jíxiǎo de, 迷你型的 mínǐxíng de

trace I v 1 追踪 zhuīzōng 2 追寻…的根源 zhuīxún…de gēnyuán **II** N 1 踪迹 zōngjì

2 微量 wēiliàng

trace element 微量元素 wēiliàng yuánsù

tracer N 曳光弹 yèguāngdàn [M. WD 发 fā]

trachea N 气管 qìguǎn

track I N 1 轨迹 guǐjì, 轨道 guǐdào

track record 业绩记录 yèjì jìlù, 过去的表现 guòqù de biǎoxiàn

to keep/lose track of sth 保持／失去与某人的联系 bǎochí/shīqù yǔ mǒurén de liánxì

2 跑道 pǎodào, 径赛（长跑、短跑、等）jìngsài (chángpǎo、duǎnpǎo、děng)

track and field (events) 田径赛（项目）tiánjìngsài (xiàngmù)

3 小路 xiǎolù [M. WD 条 tiáo], 小道 xiǎodào **II** v 1 追踪 zhuīzōng, 跟踪 gēnzōng

to track sb down 追踪到某人 zhuīzōng dào mǒurén

2 记录 [+某人的表现] jìlù [+mǒurén de biǎoxiàn]

tract N 1（人体的）系统 (réntǐ de) xìtǒng

the digestive tract 消化系统 xiāohuàxìtǒng

2 一大片（土地）yí dàpiān (tǔdì) 3 [宣扬宗教的+] 小册子[xuānyáng zōngjiào de+] xiǎocèzi

traction N 1 附着摩擦力 fùzhuó mócālì 2 牵引（手）术 qiānyǐn (shǒu) shù

3（车辆）牵引力 (chēliàng) qiānyǐnlì

tractor N 拖拉机 tuōlājī, 拖车牵引车 tuōchē qiānyǐnchē [M. WD 辆 liàng]

trade I N 1 贸易 màoyì, 生意 shēngyì

trade deficit 贸易赤字 màoyì chìzì

trade fair 交易会 jiāoyìhuì

2 手艺 shǒuyì, 职业 zhíyè

to learn a trade 学一门手艺 xué yìmén shǒuyì

3 行业 hángyè

trade union 工会 gōnghuì

II v 1 从事贸易 cóngshì màoyì, 做买卖 zuò mǎimai 2 交换 jiāohuàn

trade-in N 作价贴换交易 zuòjià tiēhuàn jiāoyì

trademark N 商标 shāngbiāo

trade-off N 权衡得失 quánhéng déshī

trader N 商人 shāngrén, 经商者 jīngshāngzhě

tradition N 传统 chuántǒng, 惯例 guànlì

to break with tradition 打破惯例 dǎpò guànlì, 与传统决裂 yǔ chuántǒng juéliè

traditional ADJ 传统的 chuántǒng de

traffic I N 1 来往车辆 láiwǎng chēliàng, 交通 jiāotōng

traffic jam 交通堵塞 jiāotōng dǔsè

light/heavy traffic 很少／很多车辆 hěn shǎo/hěn duō chēliàng

2 交通运输 jiāotōng yùnshū

air traffic control 空中交通管制 kōng-

zhōng jiāotōng guǎnzhì
3 非法交易 fēifǎ jiāoyì **II** v 非法交易 fēifǎ
jiāoyì

trafficking N 非法贩卖 fēifǎ fànmài
arms trafficking 贩卖武器 fànmài wǔqì
drug trafficking 贩卖毒品 fànmài dúpǐn

tragedy I N 1 悲剧 bēijù 2 悲剧性事件
bēijùxìng shìjiàn, 惨剧 cǎnjù **3** 不幸
（事件）búxìng (shìjiàn)

tragic ADJ 悲剧性的 bēijùxìng de, 极其不
幸的 jíqí búxìng de

trail I v 1 跟在后面 gēn zài hòumiàn,
尾随 wěisuí, 跟踪 gēnzōng **2** 落后于
luòhòu yú
to trail off（声音）逐渐变小 (shēngyīn)
zhújiàn biàn xiǎo
II N 1 小路 xiǎolù, 小径 xiǎojìng **2** 足迹
zújì, 痕迹 hénjì
to be on the trail of 跟踪 gēnzōng

trailblazer N 开路先锋 kāilù xiānfēng, 创
始人 chuàngshǐrén

trailer N 1 挂车 guàchē [M. WD 辆 liàng],
拖车 tuōchē [M. WD 辆 liàng] **2**（拖在
汽车后的）活动房屋 (tuō zài qìchē hòu
de) huódòng fángwū **3**（电影）新片预
告 (diànyǐng) xīn piàn yùgào
trailer park 活动房车停车场 huódòng
fángchē tíngchēchǎng

train I N 1 火车 huǒchē, 列车 lièchē **2** 一
连串 yìliánchuàn, 一系列 yíxìliè
train of events 一系列事件 yíxìliè shìjiàn
one's train of thought 思路 sīlù
II v 1 训练 xùnliàn **2** 把 [+镜头] 对准 bǎ
[+jìngtóu] duìzhǔn, 把 [+枪口] 瞄准 bǎ
[+qiāngkǒu] miáozhǔn

trainee N 培训生 péixùnshēng, 实习生
shíxíshēng
teacher trainee 实习教师 shíxí jiàoshī

training N 训练 xùnliàn, 培训 péixùn

trait N 特征 tèzhēng, 品性 pǐnxìng
genetic trait 遗传特征 yíchuán tèzhēng
national trait 民族特性 mínzú tèxìng,
国民性 guómínxìng

traitor N 叛徒 pàntú, 卖国贼 màiguózéi

tram N 1 有轨电车 yǒuguǐ diànchē [M. WD
辆 liàng] **2**（上山）缆车 (shàngshān)
lǎnchē [M. WD 辆 liàng]

tramp I N 1 流浪汉 liúlànghàn, 游民
yóumín **2** 荡妇 dàngfù, 淫妇 yínfù **3** 沉
重的脚步声 chénzhòng de jiǎobùshēng
4 长途跋涉 chángtú báshè **II** v 脚步沉重
地走 jiǎobù chénzhòng de zǒu

trample v 1 践踏 jiàntà, 踩坏 cǎi huài
2 无视 [+他人的权利] wúshì [+tārén de
quánlì], 蔑视 mièshì

trampoline N 蹦床 bèngchuáng, 弹床 dàn
chuáng

trance N 恍惚（状态）huǎnghū (zhuàngtài)
in a trance 走神 zǒu shén, 发呆 fādāi

tranquil ADJ 宁静的 níngjìng de, 平静的
píngjìng de

tranquilizer N 镇静剂 zhènjìngjì, 安定药
āndìngyào

transact v 做生意 zuò shēngyì, 买卖
mǎimai

transaction N 1 交易 jiāoyì, 生意 shēngyì
online transaction 网上交易
wǎngshàng jiāoyì
2 办理 bànlǐ, 处理 chǔlǐ

transcend v 超越 chāoyuè, 超出 chāochū

transcontinental ADJ 横跨大陆的 héngkuà dàlù de
transcontinental railroad 横贯大陆的
铁路 héngguàn dàlù de tiělù

transcribe v 1 逐字记录 zhúzì jìlù **2** 用音
标记下 yòng yīnbiāo jìxià **3** 改编 [+乐曲]
gǎibiān [+yuèqǔ]

transcript N 1 文字记录 wénzì jìlù
2（大学）学生成绩单 (dàxué)
xuésheng chéngjìdān [M. WD 份 fèn]

transcription N 1 记录 jìlù, 标音 biāoyīn
2 抄本 chāoběn [M. WD 份 fèn], 副本
fùběn [M. WD 份 fèn]

transfer I v 1 转学 zhuǎnxué **2** 调动
diàodòng **3** 转账 zhuǎnzhàng, 转让
zhuǎnràng **II** N 1 调动 diàodòng **2** 转账
zhuǎnzhàng **3**（权力／财产的）转移
(quánlì/cáichǎn de) zhuǎnyí **4**（可移印
的）图案 (kě yíyìn de) tú'àn

transfixed ADJ 吓呆的 xiàdāi de, 惊呆的
jīngdāi de

transform v（使…）完全改变 (shǐ...)
wánquán gǎibiàn,（使…）变形 (shǐ...)
biànxíng

transfomation N 转变 zhuǎnbiàn, 改变 gǎibiàn

social transformation 社会变革 shèhuì biàngé

transfomer N 变压器 biànyāqì

transfusion N 1 输血 shūxuè 2 注入资金 zhùrù zījīn

transgress V 违反 [+道德标准] wéifǎn [+dàodé biāozhǔn], 违背 wéibèi

transient I ADJ 1 流动性的 [+人口] liúdòngxìng de [+rénkǒu] 2 短暂的 [+幸福] duǎnzàn de [+xìngfú] II N 流动人口 liúdòng rénkǒu, 旅馆住客 lǚguǎn zhùkè

transistor N 晶体管 jīngtǐguǎn

transistor radio 晶体管收音机 jīngtǐguǎn shōuyīnjī

transit N 运送 yùnsòng, 运输 yùnshū

transit camp 中转站 zhōngzhuǎnzhàn

transition N 过渡 guòdù, 转变 zhuǎnbiàn

peaceful transition 和平过渡 hépíng guòdù, 和平演变 hépíng yǎnbiàn

transitional ADJ 过渡的 guòdù de

transitional period 过渡阶段 guòdù jiēduàn

translate V 翻译 fānyì

to translate into 转化为 zhuǎnhuà wéi

translation N 1 翻译（作品）fānyì (zuòpǐn)

lost in translation [含义+] 在翻译过程中丢失 [hányì+] zài fānyì guòchéng zhōng diūshī

2 转化 zhuǎnhuà

translator N（翻）译者 (fān) yìzhě, 翻译家 fānyìjiā

translucent ADJ 半透明的 bàn tòumíng de

transmission N 1（汽车）传动装置 (qìchē) chuándòng zhuāngzhì, 变速器 biànsùqì

auto transmission 自动变速器 zìdòng biànsùqì, 自动排挡 zìdòng páidǎng

manual transmission 手动变速器 shǒudòng biànsùqì, 手动排挡 shǒudòng páidǎng

2（电视／电台）节目播放 (diànshì/diàntái) jiémù bōfàng 3（信号）播送 (xìnhào) bōsòng

transmit V 1 播送 bōsòng, 播放 bōfàng 2 传递 chuándì, 传播 chuánbō

transmitter N（电视／电台信号）发射机 (diànshì/diàntái xìnhào) fāshèjī

transparency N 1 幻灯片 huàndēngpiàn 2 透明（性）tòumíng (xìng)

transparent ADJ 1 透明的 tòumíng de 2 含义清晰的 hányì qīngxī de

transpire V [事件+] 发生 [shìjiàn+] fāshēng

it transpires that 透露出 tòulù chū, 人们得知 rénmen dézhī

transplant I V 移植 yízhí II N 1 移植 yízhí

heart transplant 心脏移植 xīnzàng yízhí

2 搬迁者 bānqiānzhě

transport V 运输 yùnshū, 运送 yùnsòng

transportation N 交通 jiāotōng, 交通运输 jiāotōng yùnshū

transpose V 调换 diàohuàn, 变换 biànhuàn

transsexual N 变性人 biànxìngrén

transvestite N 爱穿异性服装的人 ài chuān yìxìng fúzhuāng de rén

trap I N 1 捕动物的器具 bǔ dòngwù de qìjù 2 困境 kùnjìng II V 1 使…困在 shǐ…kùn zài 2 使…落入圈套 shǐ…luòrù quāntào, 诱骗 yòupiàn

trap door（天花板／地板的）活门 (tiānhuābǎn/dìbǎn de) huómén

trapeze N（杂技表演）高空秋千 (zájì biǎoyǎn) gāokōng qiūqiān

trapper N 设陷阱捕猎者 shè xiànjīng bǔlièzhě

trash I N 1 垃圾货 lājīhuò

trash can 垃圾桶 lājītǒng

to talk trash 说污辱性的话 shuō wūrǔxìng dehuà

2 一钱不值的东西／人 yì qián bù zhí de dōngxi/rén II V 1 把…说得一钱不值 bǎ… shuō de yì qián bù zhí, 抨击 pēngjī 2 损坏 sǔnhuài

trashy ADJ 垃圾般的 lājī bān de, 一钱不值的 yì qián bù zhí de

trauma N 痛苦经历 tòngkǔ jīnglì

emotional trauma 精神创伤 jīngshén chuāngshāng

traumatic ADJ 痛苦的 tòngkǔ de, 造成精神创伤的 zàochéng jīngshén chuāngshāng de
a traumatic experience 痛苦的经历 tòngkǔ de jīnglì

traumatize V 使⋯受到精神创伤 shǐ...shòudào jīngshén chuāngshāng, 使⋯痛苦 shǐ...tòngkǔ

travel I V 1 旅行 lǚxíng 2 传（递）chuán (dì) II N 旅行 lǚxíng
travel agency 旅行社 lǚxíngshè

traveler N 旅行者 lǚxíngzhě, 旅客 lǚkè
traveler's check 旅行支票 lǚxíng zhīpiào

traverse V 横越 héngyuè, 穿过 chuānguò

travesty N 嘲弄 cháonòng, 歪曲 wāiqū

trawl N 1 拖网 tuōwǎng [M. WD 张 zhāng] 2 搜寻 sōuxún, 查找 cházhǎo

trawler N 拖网渔轮 tuōwǎng yúlún

tray N 托盘 tuōpán

treacherous ADJ 1 阴险的 [+人] yīnxiǎn de [+rén], 背信弃义的 bèixìn qìyì de 2 (暗藏) 危险的 [+天气] (àncáng) wēixiǎn de [+tiānqì]

treachery N 背叛（行为）bèipàn (xíngwéi), 背信弃义 bèi xìn qì yì

tread (PT trod; PP trodden) I V 轻轻地踩踏 qīngqīng de cǎità
to tread carefully 做事十分小心 zuòshì shífēn xiǎoxīn, 言行谨慎 yánxíng jǐnshèn II N 1 轻轻的脚步（声）qīngqīng de jiǎobù (shēng) 2 轮胎花纹 lúntāi huāwén

treadmill N 1 踏步机 tàbùjī 2 单调枯燥的生活／工作 dāndiào kūzào de shēnghuó/gōngzuò

treason N 叛国罪 pànguózuì, 通敌罪 tōngdízuì
high treason 严重叛国罪 yánzhòng pànguózuì

treasure I N 1 珍宝 zhēnbǎo, 宝藏 bǎozàng
treasure house 宝库 bǎokù
family treasure 传家宝 chuánjiābǎo 2 珍贵的人 zhēnguì de rén II V 珍藏 zhēncáng, 珍惜 zhēnxī

treasurer N 财务主管 cáiwù zhǔguǎn, 司库 sīkù

treat I V 1 对待 duìdài 2 款待 kuǎndài, 请客 qǐngkè 3 治疗 zhìliáo II N 1 难得的好东西 nándé de hǎo dōngxi 2 请客 qǐngkè

treatable ADJ 可医治的 kě yīzhì de

treatise N 专题论文 zhuāntí lùnwén

treatment N 1 治疗 zhìliáo 2 对待 duìdài

treaty N 条约 tiáoyuē

treble¹ N (音乐的) 最高音部 (yīnyuè de) zuì gāo yīnbù

treble² V 成为三倍 chéngwéi sānbèi, 增加两倍 zēngjiā liǎngbèi

tree N 树（木）shù (mù), 乔木 qiáomù
not to see the wood for the trees 见树不见林 jiàn shù bú jiàn lín
treehouse 树上小屋 shù shàng xiǎo wū
tree surgery 树木修整（术）shùmù xiūzhěng(shù)

trek I V 长途艰苦跋涉 chángtú jiānkǔ báshè II N See **trekking**

trekking N 长途跋涉 chángtú báshè

trellis N 攀缘植物架 pānyuánzhíwùjià

tremble, V, N 发抖 fādǒu, 颤抖 chàndǒu

tremendous ADJ 巨大的 jùdà de, 非常的 fēicháng de

tremor N 1 (大地的) 轻微震动 (dàdì de) qīngwēi zhèndòng 2 (人体的) 颤抖 (réntǐ de) chàndǒu, 发抖 fādǒu

trench N 1 地沟 dìgōu, 壕沟 háogōu [M. WD 条 tiáo] 2 战壕 zhànháo [M. WD 条 tiáo]
trench coat 长雨衣 cháng yǔyī, 风衣 fēngyī

trenchant ADJ 尖刻的 jiānkè de, 直言不讳的 zhíyán búhuì de

trend N 趋势 qūshì, 走向 qūxiàng

trendsetter N 开创新潮流的人 kāichuàng xīn cháoliú de rén

trendy ADJ 新潮的 xīncháo de

trepidation N 恐惧不安 kǒngjùbù'ān

trespass V 非法进入 [+私人土地] fēifǎ jìnrù [+sīrén tǔdì]

trespassing N 非法进入私人土地 fēifǎ jìnrù sīrén tǔdì

trial N 1 审判 shěnpàn, 审理 shěnlǐ 2 试验 shìyàn 3 试用 shìyòng
trial and error 反复试验 fǎnfù shìyàn
trial run (办法) 试行 (bànfǎ) shìxíng,

（飞机）试航 (fēijī) shìháng,（汽车）试开 (qìchē) shìkāi

triangle N（三角（形）sānjiǎo (xíng)

tribe N 部落 bùluò

tribulation N 苦难 kǔnàn, 艰难 jiānnán

tribunal N 特别法庭 tèbié fǎtíng

tributary N 支流 zhīliú [M. WD 条 tiáo]

tribute N 颂词 sòngcí 2 礼品 lǐpǐn [M. WD 件 jiàn]
to pay last tribute to（向遗体）告别 (xiàng yítǐ) gàobié

triceps N（手臂上）三头肌 (shǒubì shàng) sāntóujī

trick I N 1 花招 huāzhāo
dirty trick 卑鄙伎俩 bēibǐ jìliǎng
to play tricks on 戏弄 xìnòng
2 诀窍 juéqiào
trick of the trade 行业的绝招 hángyè de juézhāo
3 戏法 xìfǎ, 魔术 móshù II V 欺骗 qīpiàn
trick or treat 不给好东西吃，就捣乱 bù gěi hǎo dōngxi chī, jiù dǎoluàn

trickery N 耍花招 shuǎ huāzhāo, 欺骗 qīpiàn

trickle I V 一滴一滴地流 yì dī yì dī de liú, 细流 xìliú II N 细流 xìliú

trickster N 骗子 piànzi

tricky ADJ 1 不容易对付的 bù róngyì duìfu de 2 诡计多端的 guǐjì duō duān de

tricycle N（小孩的）三轮自行车 (xiǎohái de) sānlún zìxíngchē

trident N 三叉戟 sānchājǐ

tried ADJ (tried and tested) 经过反复证明的 jīngguò fǎnfù zhèngmíng de

trifle I N 1 无价值的东西 wú jiàzhí de dōngxi, 小事 xiǎoshì
a trifle 有点儿 yǒudiǎnr
2 蛋糕甜食 dàngāo tiánshí II V (to trifle with) 小看 xiǎokàn, 轻慢 qīngmàn

trigger I N 1（枪）扳机 (qiāng) bānjī 2 引发（问题的）因素 yǐnfā (wèntí de) yīnsù, 导火线 dǎohuǒxiàn II V (to trigger off) 引发 yǐnfā, 引起 yǐnqǐ

trigonometry N（数学中的）三角（学）(shùxué zhōngde) sānjiǎo (xué)

trilateral ADJ 三边的 sān biān de, 三方的 sān fāng de

trillion NUM（一）万亿 (yí) wàn yì

trilogy N（小说／电影）三部曲 (xiǎoshuō/diànyǐng) sānbùqǔ

trim I V 1 修剪 [+胡子] xiūjiǎn [+húzi] 2 削减 [+预算] xuējiǎn [+yùsuàn] II ADJ 1 整洁的 [+小花园] zhěngjié de [+xiǎohuāyuán] 2 苗条的 [+女子] miáotiao de [+nǚzǐ], 修长的 xiūcháng de III N 1 修剪 xiūjiǎn 2 镶边（装饰）xiāngbiān (zhuāngshì)

trinket N 小饰品 xiǎo shìpǐn, 不值钱的小玩物 bùzhí qián de xiǎo wánwù

trio N 三重唱／奏 sānchóngchàng/zòu

trip I N 1 [短途+] 旅行 [duǎntú+] lǚxíng
business trip 出公差 chū gōngchāi
2（服毒品后的）幻觉 (fú dúpǐn hòu de) huànjué 3 绊倒 bàndǎo II V 1 绊倒 bàndǎo
to trip sb up ① 把某人绊倒 bǎ mǒurén bàndǎo ② 使某人犯错 shǐ mǒurén fàncuò
2 轻快的走路 qīngkuài de zǒulù

tripe N 牛／猪肚 niú/zhūdǔ

triple I ADJ 有三部分的 yǒu sān bù fēn de, 三个人的 sānge rén de
triple digits 三位数 sānwèishù
triple jump 三级跳（运动）sānjítiào (yùndòng)
triple play（棒球）三重杀 (bàngqiú) sānchóngshā
II V 使…成为三倍 shǐ...chéngwéi sānbèi, 使…增加两倍 shǐ...zēngjiā liǎngbèi

triplets N 三胞胎 sānbāotāi

triplicate N (in triplicate) 一设三份的 yí shè sān fèn de

tripod N 三脚架 sānjiǎojià

trite ADJ 老一套的 lǎoyítào de, 陈腐的 chénfǔ de

triumph I N 胜利 shènglì, 成就 chéngjiù, 成功 chénggōng
a triumph over adversary 战胜逆境取得的成功 zhànshèng nìjìng qǔdé de chénggōng
II V 战胜 zhànshèng, 获胜 huòshèng

triumphal ADJ 庆功的 qìng gōng de, 凯旋的 kǎixuán de
a triumphal parade 庆功大游行 qìng gōng dà yóuxíng

triumphant ADJ 胜利的 shènglì de, 成功的 chénggōng de

trivia N 琐碎的小事 suǒsuì de xiǎoshì, 细节 xìjié

trivial ADJ 微不足道的 wēi bù zú dào de, 不值一提的 bùzhí yì tí de

trod See **tread**

trodden See **tread**

troll N （北欧传说中的）妖精 (Běi'ōu chuán shuō zhōngde) yāojing

trolley N （有轨）电车 (yǒu guǐ) diànchē
trolley car 有轨电车 yǒuguǐ diànchē

trolleybus N 无轨电车 wúguǐ diànchē

trombone N 长号 chánghào

troop I N (troops) 部队 bùduì, 军队 jūnduì
troops deployment 调遣部队 diàoqiǎn bùduì
combat troops 战斗部队 zhàndòu bùduì
crack troops 精锐部队 jīngruì bùduì
regular troops 正规部队 zhèngguībùduì
II V 成群结队地走 chéngqún jiéduì de zǒu

trooper N （美国）州警察 (Měiguó) zhōu jǐngchá

trophy N 1 奖杯 jiǎngbēi, 奖牌 jiǎngpái
trophy cabinet 奖杯／奖牌陈列柜 jiǎngbēi/jiǎngpái chénlièguì
2 战利品 zhànlìpǐn

tropical ADJ 热带的 rèdài de

tropics N 热带（地区）rèdài (dìqū)

trot V 1 [马+] 小跑 [mǎ+] xiǎopǎo 2 [人+] 慢跑 [rén+] màn pǎo

trouble I N 1 麻烦 máfan, 烦恼 fánnǎo
2 病 bìng, 病痛 bìngtòng II V 麻烦 máfan
to be asking for trouble 自找麻烦 zì zhǎo máfan
to be in trouble 遇到麻烦 yùdao máfan

troubled ADJ 忧虑的 yōulǜ de, 担忧的 dānyōu de

troublemaker N 捣蛋鬼 dǎodàn guǐ, 捣蛋分子 dǎodàn fènzi

troubleshooting N 调解 tiáojiě, 解决难题 jiějué nántí

troublesome ADJ （引起）麻烦的 (yǐnqǐ) máfan de, 讨厌的 tǎoyàn de

trouble spot N 麻烦地带 máfan dìdài, 多事之地 duōshì zhī dì

trough N 1 食槽 shícáo, 水槽 shuǐcáo 2 山谷 shāngǔ, 浪谷 lànggǔ 3 低谷（期）dīgǔ (qī), 萧条期 xiāotiáoqī
from peak to trough 从高峰到低谷 cóng gāofēng dào dīgǔ

trounce V 以高分打败 yǐ gāofēn dǎbài

troupe N 歌舞团 gēwǔtuán, 剧团 jùtuán

trousers N 裤子 kùzi [M. WD 条 tiáo]

trout N 鳟鱼 zūnyú [M. WD 条 tiáo]

truancy N 逃学 táoxué

truant I ADJ 逃学的 táoxué de II N 逃学的学生 táoxué de xuésheng

truce N 停战（协定）tíngzhàn (xiédìng), 休战 xiūzhàn

truck I N 1 卡车 kǎchē [M. WD 辆 liàng]
truck driver 卡车司机 kǎchē sījī
baggage truck 垃圾车 lājīchē
delivery truck 送货车 sònghuòchē
pickup truck 敞篷小货车 chǎngpéng xiǎohuòchē
2 手推车 shǒutuīchē [M. WD 辆 liàng]
3 (have no truck with) 不与…来往不与…打交道 bù yǔ…láiwǎng, bù yǔ…dǎ jiāodao II V 用卡车装运 yòng kǎchē zhuāngyùn

trucking N 货车运输业 huòchē yùnshūyè

truckload N 一货车货物 yí huòchē huòwù, 货车装载量 (huòchē) zhuāngzàiliàng

truculent ADJ 好斗的 hǎo dǒu de, 易怒的 yì nù de

trudge I V 吃力地走 chīlì de zǒu, 艰难地走 jiānnán de zǒu II N 长途跋涉 chángtú báshè

true I ADJ 1 真的 zhēn de, 真实的 zhēnshí de 2 真诚的 zhēnchéng de
true to one's word 信守诺言 xìnshǒu nuòyán, 说到做到 shuōdào zuòdào
true to one's principle 忠实于原则 zhōngshí yú yuánzé, 遵循自己的原则 zūnxún zìjǐ de yuánzé
to come true 实现 shíxiàn
II N (out of true) 不正 bú zhèng, 不直 bù zhí

true-life ADJ 以事实为依据的 yǐ shìshí wéi yījù de, 真实的 zhēnshí de

truffle N 1 巧克力软糖 qiǎokèlì ruǎntáng [M. WD 块 kuài] 2 块菌 kuàijūn

truism N 不言自明的道理 bù yán zì míng de dàolì

truly ADV 1 真实地 zhēnshí de, 确实 quèshí 2 准确地 zhǔnquè de
really and truly 千真万确（地）qiānzhēn wànquè (de)

trump I N 1 王牌 wángpái, 将牌 jiàngpái II V 1 打出王牌 dǎchū wángpái 2 胜过 shèngguò

trumpet I N 1 喇叭 lǎba [M. WD 把 bǎ], 小号 xiǎohào [M. WD 把 bǎ] II V 自吹自擂 zìchuī zìléi de, 自我吹嘘 zìwǒ chuīxū

truncated ADJ 缩短了的 suōduǎnle de

trunk N 1 树干 shùgàn [M. WD 根 gēn] 2 大箱子 dà xiāngzi [M. WD 只 zhī] 3（人体）躯干 (réntǐ) qūgàn 4 大象鼻子 dàxiàng bízi, 象鼻 xiàngbí

trunks N (swimming trunks) 男式游泳裤 nánshì yóuyǒngkù [M. WD 条 tiáo]

trust I V 信任 xìnrèn II N 1 信任 xìnrèn 2 信托 xìntuō, 信托基金 xìntuō jījīn

trustee N 1 受托人 shòutuōrén 2 理事会成员 lǐshìhuì chéngyuán, 理事 lǐshì

trusting ADJ 容易信任别人的 róngyì xìnrèn biéren de, 轻信的 qīngxìn de

trustworthy ADJ 值得信赖的 zhíde xìnlài de, 可以信托的 kěyǐ xìntuō de

truth N 1 真相 zhēnxiàng, 真话 zhēnhuà 2 真理 zhēnlǐ
to tell the truth 说真的 shuō zhēn de

truthful ADJ 诚实的 chéngshí de, 说真话的 shuō zhēnhuà de

try I V 1 试 shì, 试图 shìtú 2 审问 shěnwèn II N 试 shì, 尝试 chángshì
to try ... on 试穿 shìchuān
to try ... out 测试 cèshì

tryout N 1（运动员的）选拔 (yùndòngyuán de) xuǎnbá 2（文艺节目）试演 (wényì jiémù) shìyǎn

Tsar N（俄国）沙皇 (Éguó) Shāhuáng

T-shirt N T恤衫 tīxùshān, 短袖运动衫 duǎnxiù yùndòngshān [M. WD 件 jiàn]

tub N 浴缸 yùgāng, 澡盆 zǎopén

tubby ADJ 矮胖的 ǎipàng de

tube N 管 guǎn, 管道 guǎndào
tube of toothpaste 一管牙膏 yì guǎn yágāo

test tube 试管 shìguǎn

tuberculosis N 结核病 jiéhébìng, 肺结核 fèijiéhé

tubing N 管道 guǎndào, 管子 guǎnzi

tubular ADJ 管状的 guǎnzhuàng de, 用管子制作的 yòng guǎnzǐ zhìzuò de

tuck I V 1 把 [+衣服] 塞进 bǎ [+yīfu] sāi jìn
to tuck one's shirt in 把衬衣下摆塞进去 bǎ chènyī xiàbǎi sāijìnqu
to tuck sb in 给某人披被子 gěi mǒurén yè bèizi
2 收藏 shōucáng, 藏起来 cángqǐlái II N 1（衣服的）缝褶 (yīfu de) féngzhe 2 小整容手术 xiǎo zhěngróng shǒushù
tummy tuck 腹部整平手术 fùbù zhěngpíng shǒushù

Tuesday N 星期二 xīngqī'èr, 周二 zhōu'èr

tug I V 拉 lā, 拖 tuō
to tug at one's heartstrings 触动某人的心 chùdòng mǒurén de xīn II N 1 猛拉 měng lā, 拖 tuō 2 感情上的触动 gǎnqíng shàng de chùdòng 3 (tugboat) 拖船 tuōchuán [M. WD 艘 sōu]

tug-of-war N 拔河（比赛）báhé (bǐsài)

tuition N 1 学费 xuéfèi 2 教学 jiàoxué

tumble I V 1 倒下 dǎoxià, 跌倒 diēdǎo 2 [价格+] 猛跌 [jiàgé+] měngdié II N（从高处）倒下 (cóng gāochù) dǎoxià, 跌倒 diēdǎo

tumbledown ADJ 摇摆欲坠的 yáobǎi yù zhuì de

tumbler N 无柄玻璃杯 wú bǐng bōlibēi

tummy N 肚子 dùzi

tumor N 肿瘤 zhǒngliú
benign tumor 良性肿瘤 liángxìng zhǒngliú
malignant tumor 恶性肿瘤 èxìng zhǒngliú

tumult N 1（一大群人的）混乱场面 (yídàqún rén de) hùnluàn chǎngmiàn 2 烦乱的情绪 fánluàn de qíngxù

tumultuous ADJ 极其混乱的 jíqí hùnluàn de, 乱哄哄的 luànhōnghōng de

tuna N 金枪鱼 jīnqiāngyú [M. WD 条 tiáo]

tundra N 冻土带 dòngtǔdài, 冻原 dòngyuán

tune I N 曲调 qǔdiào

out of tune 走调 zǒu diào

to change one's tune 改变言论 gǎibiàn yánlùn

II v 1 调音 tiáoyīn 2 调整 [+机器] tiáozhěng [+jīqì] 3 调整频道 tiáozhěng píndào

tuner N 1 (钢琴) 调音师 (gāngqín) tiáoyīnshī 2 (电视／收音机) 调谐器 (diànshìjī/shōuyīnjī) tiáoxiéqì

tune-up N (发动机的) 调试 (fādòngjī de) tiáoshì

tunic N 长袍 chángpáo [m. wo 件 jiàn]

tunnel N 1 隧道 suìdào [m. wo 条 tiáo] 2 地道 dìdao [m. wo 条 tiáo]

tunnel vision 管状视 guǎnzhuàngshì, 狭隘的眼光 xiá'ài de yǎnguāng

II v 挖掘隧道／地道 wājué suìdào/dìdao

turbine N 涡轮机 wōlúnjī [m. wo 台 tái]

turbulence N 1 强气流 qiángqìliú, 湍急水流 tuānjí shuǐliú 2 骚乱 sāoluàn, 骚动 sāodòng

turf N 1 (人工) 草皮 (réngōng) cǎopí 2 (自己的) 地盘 (zìjǐ de) dìpán

turf war [帮派间的+] 地盘争夺战 [bāngpài jiān de+] dìpán zhēngduózhàn

turgid ADJ 1 枯燥难懂的 kūzào nándǒng de 2 肿胀的 zhǒngzhàng de

turkey N 1 火鸡 huǒjī [m. wo 只 zhī] 2 失败的电影／剧作 shībài de diànyǐng/jùzuò

turmoil N 混乱 (状态) hùnluàn (zhuàngtài), 动乱 dòngluàn

turn I v 1 转身 zhuǎnshēn, 转向 zhuǎnxiàng 2 拐弯 guǎi, 打弯 dǎwān 3 变, 变为 biànwéi 4 翻 fān

to turn off 关掉 guāndiao, 关上 guānshang

to turn on 打开 dǎkāi

II N 1 轮到 lúndao 2 转动 zhuàndòng 3 转弯 zhuǎnwān

to do a good turn 帮助人 bāngzhu rén, 做好事 zuò hǎoshì

4 变化 biànhuà

to take a turn for the better/worse 好转／恶化 hǎozhuǎn/èhuà

turnabout N 一百八十度大转弯 yìbǎi bāshí dù dà zhuǎnwān, 彻底改变 chèdǐ gǎibiàn

turnaround N 好转 hǎozhuǎn, 脱离困境 tuōlí kùnjìng

turncoat N 叛徒 pàntú, 变节者 biànjiézhě

turning point N 转折点 zhuǎnzhédiǎn

turnip N 白萝卜 báiluóbo [m. wo 根 gēn]

turnkey ADJ 可立即使用的 [+计算机软件] kě lìjí shǐyòng de [+jìsuànjī ruǎnjiàn]

turnout N 出席人数 chūxí rénshù, 投票人数 tóupiào rénshù

a high/low voter turnout 选民投票人数多／少 xuǎnmín tóupiào rénshù duō/shǎo

turnover N 1 人员流动 (率) rényuán liúdòng (lǜ) 2 现金流动 xiànjīn liúdòng 3 小馅饼 xiǎo xiànbǐng [m. wo 块 kuài]

turnpike N 付费高速公路 fùfèi gāosù gōnglù [m. wo 条 tiáo]

turntable N 1 (唱机的) 唱盘 (chàngjī de) chàngpán 2 (微波炉的) 转盘 (wēibōlú de) zhuànpán

turpentine N 松节油 sōngjiéyóu

turquoise N 1 绿松石 lǜsōngshí 2 绿松石色 lǜsōngshísè, 绿蓝色 lǜlánsè

turtle N 海龟 hǎiguī [m. wo 只 zhī], 乌龟 wūguī

tusk N 象牙 xiàngyá, 獠牙 liáoyá

tussle N, v 扭打 niǔdǎ, 争斗 zhēngdòu

tutor N 1 私人教师 sīrén jiàoshī, 家庭教师 jiātíng jiàoshī **II** v 给…当私人教师 gěi… dāng sīrén jiàoshī, 辅导 fǔdǎo

tutorial I N 辅导课 fǔdǎokè **II** ADJ 辅导的 fǔdǎo de

tuxedo N 男式无尾礼服 nánshì wú wěi lǐfú

TV ABBREV See **television**

TV dinner N 电视便餐 diànshì biàncān

twang N 1 鼻音 bíyīn 2 拨 (琴) 弦的嗡嗡声 bō (qín) xián de wēngwēng shēng **II** v 1 用鼻音说话 yòng bíyīn shuōhuà 2 [琴弦+] 发出嗡嗡声 [qínxián+] fāchū wēngwēng shēng

tweak v 1 捏 [+鼻子] niē [+bízi] 2 对 [+句子] 作小修改 duì [+jùzi] zuò xiǎo xiūgǎi

tweed N 粗花呢 cūhuāní

tweezers N 镊子 nièzi [m. wo 副 fù]

twelfth NUM 第十二 dì shí'èr

twelve NUM 十二 shí'èr, 12

twenty NUM 二十 èrshí, 20

twenty-one NUM 二十一点（纸牌游戏）èrshí yī diǎn (zhǐpái yóuxì)

twice ADV 两次 liǎng cì, 两遍 liǎng biàn
Once bitten, twice shy. 一朝被蛇咬，三年怕井绳。Yì zhāo bèi shé yǎo, sān nián pà jǐngshéng. (→ *Once bitten by a snake, one fears a well rope for the next three years.*)
2 两倍 liǎng bèi

twiddle V 抚弄 fǔnòng, 把玩 bǎwán
to twiddle one's thumbs 互绕大拇指 hù rào dàmuzhǐ, 闲得无聊 xián dé wúliáo

twig N（小）树枝 (xiǎo) shùzhī [M. WD 根 gēn]

twilight N **1** 暮色 mùsè, 黄昏时分 huánghūn shífēn **2**（人生）晚年 (rénshēng) wǎnnián
twilight world 阴暗世界 yīn'àn shìjiè

twin I N 双胞胎中的一个 shuāngbāotāi zhōng de yí ge
fraternal twin 异卵双胞胎 yì luǎn shuāngbāotāi
identical twin 同卵双胞胎 tóng luǎn shuāngbāotāi
II ADJ 孪生的 luánshēng de
twin brother/sister 孪生兄弟／姐妹 luánshēng xiōngdì/jiěmèi
twin bed 双人床 shuāngrénchuáng

twine I N 双股线 shuānggǔxiàn **II** V 缠绕 chánrào, 盘绕 pánrào

twinge N 突然的刺痛 tūrán de cìtòng
a twinge of guilt 一阵内疚 yí zhèn nèijiù

twinkle V, N [灯光+] 闪烁 [dēngguāng+] shǎnshuò, 闪耀 shǎnyào

twirl N, V（使…）旋转／转动 (shǐ...) xuánzhuàn/zhuàndòng

twist I V **1** 扭（转）niǔ (zhuàn), 拧 nǐng
to twist one's ankle 扭伤脚踝 niǔshāng jiǎohuái
to twist one's arm 把某人的手臂反扭到背后 bǎ mǒurén de shǒubì fǎn niǔ dào bèihòu, 向某人施加压力 xiàng mǒurén shījiā yālì
to twist and turn [道路+] 弯弯曲曲 [dàolù+] wānwān qūqū
2 转动 [+瓶盖] zhuàndòng [+pínggài]

3 曲解 [+语言] qūjiě [+yǔyán] **II** N **1** 意外情况 yìwài qíngkuàng **2** 缠绕的形状 chánrào de xíngzhuàng **3** 扭摆舞 niǔbǎiwǔ **4** 扭（转）niǔ (zhuàn), 拧 nǐng

twisted ADJ **1** 扭曲的 niǔqū de **2** 反常的 fǎncháng de, 变态的 biàntài de

twister N 龙卷风 lóngjuǎnfēng

twitch N, V [肌肉+] 抽搐 [jīròu+] chōuchù, 抽动 chōudòng

twitter V, N [鸟+] 吱吱叫 [niǎo+] zhīzhījiào **2**（网络通讯）推特 (wǎngluò tōngxùn) tuītè

two NUM 二 èr, 两 liǎng
It takes two to tango. 要两个人才能跳探戈舞。Yào liǎng ge rén cái néng tiào tàngē wǔ. (→ *While a bowl produces no sound, two bowls may make a lot of noise.*)

two-bit ADJ 一钱不值的 yì qián bù zhí de, 微不足道的 wēi bù zú dào de

two-dimensional ADJ 二维的 èrwéi de, 平面的 píngmiàn de

two-faced ADJ 两面派的 liǎngmiànpài de, 两面三刀的 liǎngmiàn sāndāo de

two-piece ADJ 两件套的 [+服装] liǎng jiàn tào de [+fúzhuāng]

twosome N 一对搭档 yíduì dādàng

two-time V 偷情 tōuqíng

two-tone ADJ 双色的 [+服装／家具] shuāngsè de [+fúzhuāng/jiājù]

two-way ADJ 双向的 shuāngxiàng de
two-way trade 双向贸易 shuāngxiàng màoyì

tycoon N（工商）巨头 (gōngshāng) jùtóu

type I N **1** 类型 lèixíng
blood type 血型 xuèxíng
2 印刷字体 yìnshuā zìtǐ **3**（印刷用的）活字 (yìnshuā yòng de) huózì **II** V 用打字机／电脑打字 yòng dǎzìjī/diànnǎo dǎzì

typeface N（印刷用的）字体 (yìnshuā yòng de) zìtǐ

typewriter N 打字机 dǎzìjī [M. WD 台 tái/架 jià]

typewritten ADJ 用打字机打出来的 yòng dǎzìjī dǎchulai de

typhoid, typhoid fever N 伤寒 shānghán

typhoon N 台风 táifēng

typhus N 斑疹伤寒 bānzhěnshānghán

typical ADJ 1 典型的 diǎnxíng de 2 一贯如此的 yí guàn rúcǐ de

typically ADV 1 典型地 diǎnxíng de 2 一向 yíxiàng, 向来 xiànglái

typify V 是…的典型 shì…de diǎnxíng, 成为…的典型 chéngwéi…de diǎnxíng

typing N 打字（工作）dǎzì (gōngzuò)

typist N 打字员 dǎzìyuán

typo N 排列／打字错误 páiliè/dǎzì cuòwù

tyrannical ADJ 暴政的 bàozhèng de, 专横的 zhuānhèng de

tyranny N 1 暴政 bàozhèng, 专制统治 zhuānzhì tǒngzhì 2 专横 zhuānhèng, 暴虐 bàonüè

tyrant N 暴君 bàojūn

U

ubiquitous ADJ 到处都是的 dàochù dōu shì de, 无处不在的 wúchù bú zài de

udder N（母牛／母羊的）乳房 (mǔniú/mǔyáng de) rǔfáng

UFO (= Unidentified Flying Object) ABBREV 不明飞行物 bù míng fēixíng wù

ugh INTERJ 哎呀 āiyā

ugly ADJ 1 难看的 nánkàn de, 丑陋的 chǒulòu de 2 险恶的 xiǎn'è de

uh INTERJ 嗯 ng

UHF (= Ultra-High Frequency) ABBREV 超高频 chāogāopín

ulterior ADJ 隐秘 yǐnmì, 别有用心的 biè yǒu yòngxīn de
an ulterior motive 不可告人的动机 bùkě gàorén de dòngjī

ultimate I ADJ 1 最终的 [+目标] zuì zhōng de [+mùbiāo] 2 最大的 [+责任] zuì dà de [+zérèn] II N 极端 jíduān
the ultimate in bad taste 品味差到极点 pǐnwèi chàdào jídiǎn

ultimately ADV 最终 zuìzhōng, 终于 zhōngyú

ultimatum N 最后通牒 zuìhòu tōngdié [M. WD 份 fèn]

ultrasonic ADJ 超声波的 chāoshēngbō de

ultraviolet ADJ 紫外线的 zǐwàixiàn de

umbilical cord N 脐带 qídài

umbrage N (to take umbrage) 生气 shēngqì, 感到愤怒 gǎndào fènnù

umbrella N（雨）伞 (yǔ) sǎn [M. WD 把 bǎ]

umpire N 裁判（员）cáipàn (yuán)

umpteenth ADJ 第无数次的 dì wúshùcì de, 数不清的 shǔ bù qīng de

U.N. (= the United Nations) ABBREV 联合国 Liánhéguó

U.N.O. (= the United Nations Organization) ABBREV 联合国组织 Liánhéguó zǔzhī

unabashed ADJ 毫不掩饰的 háobù yǎnshì de, 公开宣扬的 gōngkāi xuānyáng de

unabated ADJ 不减弱的 bù jiǎnruò de, 保持势头的 bǎochí shìtóu de

unable ADJ 不能 bù néng

unabridged ADJ 未删节的 wèi shānjié de, 全文的 quánwén de

unacceptable ADJ 不可接受的 bù kě jiēshòu de, 不能容忍的 bùnéng róngrěn de

unaccountable ADJ 1 无法解释的 [+现象] wúfǎ jiěshì de [+xiànxiàng], 不能理解的 bù néng lǐjiě de 2 独断独行的 [+官员] dúduàn dúxíng de [+guānyuán]

unacknowledged ADJ 未受注意的 wèi shòu zhùyì de, 未被承认的 wèi bèi chéngrèn de

unadulterated ADJ 纯粹的 chúncuì de, 完全的 wánquán de

unaffected ADJ 1 不受影响的 bú shòu yǐngxiǎng de 2 不装腔作势的 bù zhuāngqiāng zuòshì de, 自然的 zìrán de

unaided ADJ 没有外来帮助的 méiyǒu wàilái bāngzhù de, 独立的 dúlì de

unanimous ADJ 一致的 yízhì de, 全体的 quántǐ de

unannounced ADJ 没有料想到的 méiyǒu liàoxiǎngdào de, 意外的 yìwài de

unanswered ADJ 未答复的 wèi dáfù de, 未回复的 wèi huífù de

unassuming ADJ 朴实无华的 pǔshí wúhuá de, 不摆架子的 bù bǎijiàzi de

unattached ADJ 1 没有（恋爱）对象的 [+青年] méiyǒu (liàn'ài) duìxiàng de [+qīngnián] 2 独立式的 [+车库] dúlì shì de [+chēkù]

unattended ADJ 无人照看的 wúrén zhàokàn de, 无人负责的 wúrén fùzé de

unauthorized ADJ 未经授权的 wèijīng shòuquán de, 未经批准的 wèijīng pīzhǔn de

unavailable ADJ 得不到的 débúdào de, 买不到的 mǎibúdào de

unavoidable ADJ 不可避免的 bùkě bìmiǎn de

unawares ADV 不知不觉地 bùzhī bùjué de, 无意中 wúyìzhōng
to catch sb unawares 让某人措手不及 ràng mǒurén cuòshǒu bù jí

unbalanced ADJ 1 不平衡的 bù pínghéng de
unbalanced budget 收支不平衡（的预算）shōuzhī bù pínghéng (de yùsuàn) 2 不公允的 [+论点] bù gōngyǔn de [+lùndiǎn] 3 错乱失常的 [+精神状态] cuòluàn shīcháng de [+jīngshén zhuàngtài]

unbearable ADJ 无法忍受的 wúfǎ rěnshòu de, 不可容忍的 bùkě róngrěn de

unblemished ADJ 清白的 qīngbái de, 无污点的 wú wūdiǎn de

unbounded ADJ 无边无际的 wúbiān wújì de, 无限的 wúxiàn de

uncalled-for ADJ 不适当的 bú shìdàng de, 不必要的 bú bìyào de

uncanny ADJ 不可思议的 bùkě sīyì de, 离奇的 líqí de

uncertain ADJ 不确定的 bú quèdìng de, 不能决定的 bùnéng juédìng de

unclaimed ADJ 无人认领的 wúrén rènlǐng de, 无人领取的 wúrén lǐngqǔ de
unclaimed luggage 无主行李 wúzhǔ xínglǐ

uncle N 伯父 bófù (father's elder brother), 叔父 shūfù (father's younger brother), 舅父 jiùfù (mother's brother), 姑父 gūfù (father's sister's husband), 姨夫 yífù (mother's sister's husband)

uncompromising ADJ 不妥协的 bù tuǒxié de, 不让步的 bú ràng bù de

unconditional ADJ 无条件的 wú tiáojiàn de
unconditional love 无条件的爱 wú tiáojiàn de ài

unconfirmed ADJ 未经证实的 wèijīng zhèngshí de

unconscionable ADJ 不讲良心的 bù jiǎng liángxīn de, 不道德的 bú dàodé de

unconstitutional ADJ 不符合宪法（精神）的 bù fúhé xiànfǎ (jīngshén) de, 违宪的 wéixiàn de

unconventional ADJ 非常规的 fēi chángguī de, 不合习俗的 bù hé xísú de

uncountable ADJ（语法）不可数的 (yǔfǎ) bùkěshù de
uncountable noun 不可数名词 bùkěshù míngcí

uncouth ADJ 没有教养的 méiyǒu jiàoyǎng de, 粗鲁的 cūlǔ de

uncover v 1 揭开… 盖子／覆盖物 jiēkāi…gàizi/fùgàiwù 2 发现 fāxiàn

uncut ADJ 未剪辑的 wèi jiǎnjí de, 未删节的 wèi shānjié de

undaunted ADJ 不退缩的 bú tuìsuō de, 大无畏的 dàwúwèi de

undecided ADJ 尚未决定的 shàngwèi juédìng de, 犹豫不决的 yóuyù bùjué de

undeniable ADJ 不可否认的 bùkě fǒurèn de

under I PREP 1 在…下面 zài…xiàmian, 到…下面 dào…xiàmian 2 少于 shǎoyú, 低于 dī yú 3 根据 [+法律] gēnjù [+fǎlǜ]
under construction/discussion 在建设／讨论之中 zài jiànshè/tǎolùn zhī zhōng
II ADV 下面 xiàmian, 以下 yǐxià

underachiever N 未充分发挥能力的者 wèi chōngfèn fāhuī nénglì zhě, 成绩不理想者 chéngjì bù lǐxiǎng zhě

underage ADJ 未成年的 wèi chéngnián de

undercharge v 对…少要价 duì…shǎo yàojià

underclass N 下层社会 xiàcéng shèhuì, 贫穷阶层 pínqióng jiēcéng

undercover ADJ 暗中进行的 ànzhōng jìnxíng de, 秘密的 mìmì de

to go undercover 暗中地 ànzhōng de, 暗暗地 àn'àn de

undercurrent N 潜伏的情绪 qiánfú de qíngxù, 隐患 yǐnhuàn

undercut V 1 削减 [+价格]（与同行竞争）xuējiǎn [+jiàgé]（yǔ tóngháng jìngzhēng）, 削价抢生意 xuējià qiǎng shēngyì 2 削弱 [+声誉] xuēruò [+shēngyù], 破坏 pòhuài

underdog N 竞争中处于劣势者 jìngzhēng zhōng chǔyú lièshì zhě, 被欺压者 bèiqīyāzhě

underestimate V 低估 dīgū

undergo V 经受 jīngshòu, 经历 jīnglì

undergraduate N 大学本科生 dàxué běnkēshēng

underground ADJ 1 在地下的 zài dìxià de underground cellar 地下酒窖 dìxià jiǔjiào 2 地下的 dìxia de
an underground terrorist organization 地下恐怖组织 dìxià kǒngbù zǔzhī

undergrowth N（大树下丛）灌木丛（dàshùxià de）guànmùcóng

underhanded ADJ 偷偷摸摸的 tōutōu mōmō de, 不光明正大的 bù guāngmíng zhèngdà de

underline V 1 在…下划线 zài...xià huàxiàn 2 突出 tūchū

underlying ADJ 根本的 gēnběn de, 基本的 jīběn de

undermine V 逐渐削弱 zhújiàn xuēruò, 损害 sǔnhài

underneath PREP, ADV 在…下面 zài...xiàmian

undernourished ADJ 营养不良的 yíngyǎng bùliáng de

underpants N 内裤 nèikù, 衬裤 chènkù

underpass N 地下通道 dìxià tōngdào

underpay V 付…过低的工资 fù...guòdī de gōngzī

underpin V 支持 zhīchí, 加固 jiāgù

underprivileged ADJ 贫困的 pínkùn de, 下层社会的 xiàcéng shèhuì de

underrated ADJ 被低估的 bèi dīgū de, 被看轻的 bèi kànqīng de

underscore V 强调 qiángdiào, 着重 zhuózhòng

underside N 底部 dǐbù, 下面 xiàmian

undersigned ADJ (the undersigned) 签名人 qiānmíngrén

undersized ADJ（尺寸）偏小的（chǐcùn）piān xiǎo de

understaffed ADJ 工作人员不足的 gōngzuò rényuán bù zú de, 人手不够的 rénshǒu bùgòu de

understand (PT & PP **understood**) V 1 理解 lǐjiě, 懂得 dǒngde 2 了解 liǎojiě, 知道 zhīdào

understandable ADJ 可以理解的 kěyǐ lǐjiě de

understanding I N 1 理解 lǐjiě, 理解力 lǐjiělì 2 体谅 tǐliàng, 谅解 liàngjiě
to come to an understanding 达成谅解 dáchéng liàngjiě
II ADJ 通情达理的 tōng qíng dá lǐ de

understated ADJ 不夸张的 bù kuāzhāng de, 有节制的 yǒu jiézhì de

understatement N 保守的说法 bǎoshǒu de shuōfa, 不夸张的说法 bù kuāzhāng de shuōfa

understood See **understand**

understudy N 预备演员 yùbèi yǎnyuán, 替身 tìshēn

undertake V 承担 chéngdān

undertaker N 丧葬承办人 sāngzàng chéngbànrén

undertaking N 重大任务 zhòngdà rènwu, 事业 shìyè

undertone N 1 潜在的感情 qiánzài de gǎnqíng, 隐含的意思 yǐnhán de yìsi 2 低声 dīshēng

underwater ADJ, ADV 水下（的）shuǐxià（de）

underwear N 内衣 nèiyī, 内裤 nèikù

underweight ADJ 重量不足的 zhòngliàng bù zú de, 体重不足的 tǐzhòng bù zú de

underworld N 1 黑社会 hēishèhuì 2 地狱 dìyù, 阴界 yīnjiè

underwrite V 1 负担…的费用 fùdān...de fèiyòng
to underwrite an environmental project 负担一个环保项目的费用 fùdān yíge huánbǎo xiàngmù de fèiyòng 2 为…保险 wèi...bǎoxiǎn

undesirable I ADJ 会造成损害的 huì zàochéng sǔnhài de, 不良的 bùliáng de **II** N (undesirables) 不良分子 bùliáng-fènzǐ

undeveloped ADJ 未开发的 wèi kāifā de, 不发达的 bù fādá de

undisclosed ADJ 不公开的 bù gōngkāi de, 秘密的 mìmì de

undisguised ADJ 公开的 gōngkāi de, 不加掩饰的 bù jiā yǎnshì de

undisturbed ADJ 不受干扰的 bù shòu gānrǎo de, 未改变的 wèi gǎibiàn de

undivided ADJ 未分割的 wèi fēngē de, 不分开的 bù fēnkāi de
undivided attention 全神贯注 quánshén guànzhù
undivided loyalty 忠心耿耿 zhōngxīn gěnggěng

undo V 1 解开 jiěkāi, 打开 dǎkāi 2 消除 xiāochú

undoing N (sb's undoing) 某人的垮台 / 失败 mǒurén de kuǎtái/shībài

undressed ADJ 不穿衣服的 bù chuān yīfú de, 裸体的 luǒtǐ de

undue ADJ 不应有的 bù yīngyǒu de, 过分的 guòfèn de

unduly ADV 过分地 guòfèn de, 不适当地 bú shìdāng de

undying ADJ 不灭的 bú miè de, 永恒的 yǒnghéng de

unearth V 1 挖掘 [+地下文物] wājué [+dìxià wénwù] 2 发现 [+真相] fāxiàn [+zhēnxiàng], 披露 pīlù

unearthly ADJ 奇异的 qíyì de, 不自然的 bú zìrán de

uneasy ADJ 1 忧虑不安的 yōulǜ bù'ān de 2 不安定的 bù'āndìng de, 不稳定的 bù wěndìng de
an uneasy truce 靠不住的休战 kàobuzhù de xiūzhàn

uneducated ADJ 未受教育的 wèi shòu jiàoyù de

unemployed ADJ 失业的 shīyè de

unemployment N 1 失业 shīyè
unemployment benefits 失业救济金 shīyè jiùjìjīn
2 失业救济金 shīyè jiùjì jīn

on unemployment 领取失业救济金 lǐngqǔ shīyè jiùjìjīn

unequal ADJ 1 不平等的 bù píngděng de 2 不胜任的 bú shèng rèn de
be unequal to the task 不能胜任这项任务 bùnéng shèngrèn zhè xiàng rènwu

unequivocal ADJ 明确的 míngquè de, 毫不含糊的 háobù hánhu de

unerring ADJ 不会出错的 bú huì chūcuò de, 永远正确的 yǒngyuǎn zhèngquè de

unethical ADJ 违反道德标准的 wéifǎn dàodé biāozhǔn de, 不道德的 bú dàodé de

uneven ADJ 1 不平坦的 [+道路] bù píngtǎn de [+dàolù] 2 水平不一的 shuǐpíng bùyī de, 有好有坏的 yǒu hǎo yǒu huài de
of uneven equality 质量有好有坏的 zhìliàng yǒu hǎo yǒu huài de

unexpected ADJ 没想到的 méi xiǎngdào de, 意外的 yìwài de
an unexpected visitor 意外的客人 yìwài de kèren, 不速之客 búsù zhī kè

unfailing ADJ 始终如一的 shǐzhōng rúyī de, 经久不衰的 jīngjiǔ bù shuāi de

unfair ADJ 不公平的 bù gōngpíng de, 不公正的 bù gōngzhèng de
unfair competition 不公平竞争 bù gōngpíng jìngzhēng

unfaithful ADJ 对 [+妻子] 不忠的人 duì [+qīzi] bù zhōng de rén, 有外遇的 yǒu wàiyù de

unfaltering ADJ 坚定不移的 jiāndìng búyí de

unfamiliar ADJ 不熟悉的 bù shúxī de, 陌生的 mòshēng de

unfasten V 解开 [+扣子] jiěkāi [+kòuzi]

unfavorable ADJ 1 不适宜的 bú shìyí de 2 不支持的 bù zhīchí de, 反对的 fǎnduì de

unfeeling ADJ 无情的 wúqíng de, 冷漠的 lěngmò de

unfinished ADJ 未完成的 wèi wánchéng de

unfit ADJ 1 不适合的 bú shìhé de
unfit for human inhabitation 不适合人

类居住的 bú shìhé rénlèi jūzhù de
2 身体不好的 shēntǐ bùhǎo de

unfold v [情节+] 展开 [qíngjié+] zhǎnkāi,
渐渐出现 jiànjiàn chūxiàn

unforeseen ADJ 未预料到的 wèi
yùliàodào de

unforgettable ADJ 忘不了的 wàngbuliǎo
de, 难忘的 nánwàng de

unfortunate ADJ **1** 倒霉的 dǎoméi de
2 不恰当的 bú qiàdàng de

unfortunately ADV 不幸 búxìng

unfounded ADJ 没有事实根据的 méiyǒu
shìshí gēnjù de, 编造的 biānzào de

unfurl v 打开 [+旗帜] dǎkāi [+qízhì], 扬起
[+风帆] yáng qǐ [+fēngfān]

ungainly ADJ 笨拙的 [+动机] bènzhuō de
[+dòngjī], 难看的 nánkàn de

unhappy ADJ **1** 不愉快的 bù yúkuài de
2 不满（意）的 bù mǎn (yì) de

unheard-of ADJ 前所未闻的 qiánsuǒ wèi
wén de, 空前的 kōngqián de

unholy ADJ **1** 不神圣的 bù shénshèng de
unholy alliance 邪恶同盟 xié'è tóngméng
2 不合理的 bù hélǐ de

UNICEF (= the United Nations International Children's Fund) ABBREV 联合国
儿童基金会 Liánhéguó értóng jījīnhuì

unicorn N 独角兽 dújiǎoshòu

unidentified ADJ 身份不明的 shēnfen
bùmíng de

uniform[1] N 制服 zhìfú

uniform[2] ADJ 一律的 yílǜ de, 一致的
yízhì de

unify v **1** （使…）统一（shǐ…）tǒngyī **2** 融
合 rónghé, 结合 jiéhé

unilateral ADJ 单方（面）的 dānfāng
(miàn) de

uninstall v 卸载 [+计算机软件] xièzài
[+jìsuànjī ruǎnjiàn]

uninsured ADJ 无保险的 wú bǎoxiǎn de

unintelligible ADJ 无法理解的 wúfǎ lǐjiě
de, 难懂的 nán dǒng de

uninterested ADJ 不感兴趣的 bù gǎn
xìngqù de, 没有兴趣的 méiyǒu xìngqu
de

union N **1** 工会 gōnghuì **2** 联合 liánhé

unique ADJ 独特的 dútè de, 独一无二的
dú yī wú èr de

unisex ADJ 不分男女的 bù fēn nánnǚ de,
男女皆宜的 nánnǚ jiē yí de

unison N (in unison) **1** 一致（地）yízhì
(de) **2** 齐声（地）qíshēng (de)

unit N **1** 单位 dānwèi **2** 单元 dānyuán **3** 部
件 bùjiàn **4** 小组 xiǎozǔ

unite v 联合 liánhé, 使…团结 shǐ…tuánjié
to be united in marriage 结成夫妻
jiéchéng fūqī, 结婚 jiéhūn

united ADJ 团结的 tuánjié de, 意见一致的
yìjiàn yízhì de

(the) United Kingdom (U.K.) N 联合王
国 Liánhé Wángguó, 英国 Yīngguó

(the) United States (U.S.) N 美国
Měiguó

unity N 团结 tuánjié, 统一 tǒngyī

universal ADJ 普遍的 pǔbiàn de, 全体的
quántǐ de
universal values 普世价值 pǔ shì jiàzhí

universe N 宇宙 yǔzhòu

university N 大学 dàxué

unjust ADJ 不公平的 bù gōngpíng de, 不
公正的 bù gōngzhèng de

unjustified ADJ 没有道理的 méiyǒu dàoli
de, 不合理的 bù hélǐ de

unkempt ADJ 凌乱的 [+头发] língluàn de
[+tóufa]

unknowingly ADV 不知道的 bù zhīdào
de, 不知情的 bù zhīqíng de

unknown ADJ 未知的 wèizhī de, 不知道的
bù zhīdào de
an unknown quantity 未知数 wèizhī-
shù, 让人捉摸不透的人 ràng rén zhuōmo bú tòu de rén

unleaded I ADJ 不含铅的 bù hán qiān de
II N 无铅汽油 wúqiānqìyóu

unleash v 释放 shìfàng, 发泄 fāxiè

unless CONJ 除非 chúfēi

unlike I PREP 不像 bú xiàng II ADJ 不相
像的 bù xiāngxiàng de, 不一样的 bù
yíyàng de

unlikely ADJ 不大可能（是真）的 bú dà
kěnéng (shì zhēn) de

unlisted ADJ 未登记的 wèi dēngjì de, 未
编入电话簿的 wèi biānrù diànhuàbù de

unload v **1** 卸（下）xiè (xia) **2** 推卸 [+责任] tuīxiè [+zérèn]，摆脱 bǎituō **3** 抛售 [+商品／股票] pāoshòu [+shāngpǐn/gǔpiào]

unlock v 开（锁）kāi (suǒ)

unloose v 松开 sōngkāi，解开 jiěkāi

unmarked ADJ 无标志的 wú biāozhì de
an unmarked police car 无标志的警车 wú biāozhì de jǐngchē

unmistakable ADJ 不会弄错的 bú huì nòngcuò de，显而易见的 xiǎn'éryìjiàn de

unmitigated ADJ 十足的 shízú de，完全的 wánquán de
unmitigated failure 完全彻底的失败 wánquán chèdǐ de shībài

unnamed ADJ 不知其名的 bùzhī qí míng de，不提姓名的 wèi tí xìngmíng de

unnerve v 使…丧失勇气 shǐ...sàngshī yǒngqì，使…忐忑不安的 shǐ...tǎntè bù'ān de

unobtrusive ADJ 不显眼的 bù xiǎnyǎn de，不引人注目的 bù yǐnrén zhùmù de

unoccupied ADJ 未被占用的 wèi bèi zhànyòng de，空着的 kòngzhe de

unpack v **1** 打开 [+行李] dǎkāi [+xínglǐ] **2** 对 [+电脑信息] 解包 duì [+diànnǎo xìnxī] jiě bāo

unpaid ADJ 未支付的 wèi zhīfù de

unpalatable ADJ **1** 吃不下去的 [+食物] chībuxiàqù de [+shíwù]，难吃的 nánchī de **2** 难以接受的 [+事实] nányǐ jiēshòu de [+shìshí]，讨厌的 tǎoyàn de

unplug v 拔去…的插头 bá qù...de chātóu

unprecedented ADJ 无先例的 wú xiānlì de，空前的 kōngqián de

unpredictable ADJ 不可预测的 bùkě yùcè de，捉摸不定的 zhuōmō bú dìng de

unprepossessing ADJ 不起眼的 bù qǐyǎn de，不引人注目的 bù yǐnrén zhùmù de

unpretentious ADJ 不装腔作势的 bù zhuāngqiāng zuòshì de，朴实的 pǔshí de

unprincipled ADJ 不讲原则的 bù jiǎng yuánzé de，肆无忌惮的 sìwú jìdàn de

unqualified ADJ 不合格的 bù hégé de

unquestionable ADJ 不成问题的 bùchéng wèntí de，毋庸置疑的 wúyōng zhìyí de

unravel v **1** 把…弄清楚 bǎ...nòngqīng-chǔ，解释清楚 jiěshì qīngchu **2** [关系+] 破裂 [guānxi+] pòliè，失败 shībài

unreadable ADJ **1** 读不下去的 dú bú xiàqu de，难读懂的 nán dú dǒng de **2** 字迹潦草的 zìjì liáocǎo de，难辨认的 nán biànrèn de

unrealistic ADJ 不现实的 bú xiànshí de，不切实际的 bú qiè shíjì de

unreasonable ADJ 不合理的 bù hélǐ de，不公平的 bù gōngpíng de

unrecoverable ADJ 无法回收的 wúfǎ huíshōu de，损失的 sǔnshī de

unrelated ADJ **1** 不相关的 bù xiāngguān de **2** 没有亲戚关系的 méiyǒu qīnqi guānxi de

unrelenting ADJ 不停歇的 bù tíngxiē de，持续的 chíxù de

unrequited ADJ (unrequited love) 单相思 dānxiāngsī，单恋 dānliàn

unreserved ADJ 毫无保留的 háowú bǎoliú de，完全的 wánquán de

unresponsive ADJ **1** 无反应的 wú fǎnyìng de
be unresponsive to medical treatment 医治无效 yīzhì wú xiào **2** 不作回应的 bú zuò huíyìng de，冷淡的 lěngdàn de

unrest N 不安定 bù'āndìng，动乱 dòngluàn

unrestrained ADJ 无拘束的 wú jūshù de，放纵的 fàngzòng de

unrivaled ADJ 无敌的 wúdí de，无与伦比的 wú yǔ lúnbǐ de

unruly ADJ 任性的 rènxìng de，不受管束的 bú shòu guǎnshù de

unsaid ADJ (better left unsaid) [有些话+] 最好不要说出来 [yǒuxiē huà+] zuìhǎo bú yào shuōchulai

unsavory ADJ 可厌的 kěyàn de，可憎的 kězēng de

unscathed ADJ 不受伤害的 bú shòu shānghài de

unscrew v 旋开 [+罐头盖] xuánkāi [+guàntóugài]，拧开 nǐngkāi

unscrupulous ADJ 不择手段的 bù zé shǒuduàn de，不讲道理的 bù jiǎng dàoli de

unseasonable ADV 不合时令 bù hé shílìng, 反常地 fǎncháng de

unseat V 使 [+人] 离职 / 下台 shǐ [+rén] lízhí/xiàtái

unseemly ADJ 不得体的 bù détǐ de, 不体面的 bù tǐmiàn de

unsettle V 使 [+人] 心绪不定 shǐ [+rén] xīnxù búdìng, 扰乱 [+人心] rǎoluàn [+rénxīn]

unsightly ADJ 不好看的 bù hǎokàn de, 难看的 nánkàn de

unskilled ADJ 非技术性的 fēi jìshùxìng de, 非熟练的 fēi shúliàn de

unsophisticated ADJ 1 不老练的 [+人] bù lǎoliàn de [+rén], 天真朴素的 tiānzhēn pǔsù de 2 不复杂的 [+工具] bú fùzá de [+gōngjù], 简单的 jiǎndān de

unspeakable ADJ 坏得无法形容的 huài dé wúfǎ xíngróng de, 说不出口的 shuōbuchū kǒu de

unspecified ADJ 未说明的 wèi shuōmíng de

unstoppable ADJ 不可阻挡的 bùkě zǔdǎng de, 一帆风顺的 yìfānfēngshùn de

unsung ADJ (unsung heroes) 默默无闻的英雄 mòmò wúwén de yīngxióng

unsustainable ADJ 不可持续的 bùkě chíxù de, 难以为继的 nányǐ wéijì de

unswerving ADJ 坚定不移的 jiāndìng búyí de

untapped ADJ 未开发利用的 wèi kāifā lìyòng de

untenable ADJ 难以维持的 nányǐ wéichí de, 难以继续的 nányǐ jìxù de

unthinkable ADJ 不可思议的 bùkě sīyì de, 难以置信的 nányǐ zhìxìn de

untie V 解开 [+结] jiěkāi [+jié]

until CONJ, PREP 直到 zhídào

untimely ADJ 不适时的 bú shìshí de
untimely death 过早死亡 guòzǎo sǐwáng

untiring ADJ 不知疲倦的 bùzhī píjuàn de, 坚持不懈的 jiānchí bú xiè de

untold ADJ 无数的 wúshù de, 无法估量的 wúfǎ gūliang de

untouchable ADJ 1 碰不得的 pèngbude de, 不可冒犯的 bùkě màofàn de 2 不可接触的 [+贱民] bùkě jiēchù de [+jiànmín]

untoward ADJ 异常的 yìcháng de, 意外的 yìwài de

unused[1] ADJ 未用过的 wèi yòngguo de

unused[2] ADJ 不习惯的 bù xíguàn de

unusual ADJ 不正常的 bú zhèngcháng de, 罕见的 hǎn jiàn de

unusually ADV 异常地 yìcháng de, 不同寻常地 bùtóng xúnchángde

unveil V 1 透露 tòulù, 宣布 xuānbù 2 揭幕 jiēmù

unwieldy ADJ 1 无法搬动的 [+大钢琴] wúfǎ bāndòng de [+dàgāngqín] 2 难以操作 / 控制的 [+系统] nányǐ cāozuò/kòngzhì de [+xìtǒng]

unwind V 放纵 fàngzòng, 松弛 sōngchí

unwittingly ADV 不知不觉(地) bùzhī bùjué (de), 无意中 wúyìzhòng

unwritten ADJ 不成文的 bùchéng wén de

unyielding ADJ 不屈从的 bù qūcóng de, 顽固的 wángù de

unzip V 1 拉开拉链 lākāi lāliàn 2 给(电脑文件)解压缩 gěi (diànnǎo wénjiàn) jiě yāsuō

up I ADV 1 向上 xiàng shàng, 起来 qǐlai 2 朝北面 cháo běimian, 在北面 zài běimian 3 朝 cháo, 向 xiàng 4 增加 zēngjiā 5 完 wán II ADJ 醒着 xǐngzhe III PREP 向上 xiàng shàng
up to ① 多达 duō dá ② 能胜任 néng shèngrèn
It's up to you 由你决定 yóu nǐ juédìng

up-and-coming ADJ 前途无量的 qiántú wúliàng de, 大有希望的 dàyǒu xīwàng de

upbeat ADJ 乐观的 lèguān de, 快乐的 kuàilè de

upbringing N [家庭+] 教养 [jiātíng+] jiàoyǎng

upcoming ADJ 即将来临的 jíjiāng láilín de

update V 更新 gēngxīn
to update sb on sth 为某人提供有关某事的最新信息 wéi mǒurén tígōng yǒuguān mǒushì de zuìxìn xìnxī

upend V 倒放 dàofàng, 颠倒 diāndǎo

upfront ADJ 1 坦率的 tǎnshuài de, 不吞吞吐吐的 bù tūntūn tǔtǔ de 2 (upfront fees) 马上要付的费用 mǎshàng yào fù de fèiyòng

upgrade V 升级 shēngjí, 升级换代 shēngjí huàndài

upheaval N 剧变 jùbiàn, 巨变 jùbiàn

uphill ADJ 1 上坡的 shàngpō de, 上山的 shàngshān de 2 艰难的 jiānnán de, 充满阻力的 chōngmǎn zǔlì de

uphold V 1 坚持 [+原则] jiānchí [+yuánzé], 维护 wéihù 2 维持 [+原来的决定] wéichí [+yuánlái de juédìng], 认可 rènkě

upholster V 为 [+椅子] 加上垫子／套子 wéi [+yǐzi] jiāshàng diànzi/tàozi

upkeep N 保养 bǎoyǎng, 维修 wéixiū

uplifting ADJ 令人情绪高涨的 lìngrén qíngxù gāozhǎng de

upon PREP 在…上 zài…shàng

upper ADJ 上面的 shàngmian de, 较高的 jiào gāo de
to gain the upper hand 占上风 zhàn shàngfēng, 处于有利地位 chǔyú yǒulì dìwèi
upper case 大写（字母）dàxiě (zìmǔ)
upper class 上层社会 shàngcéng shèhuì

uppermost ADJ 1 最高的 zuì gāo de 2 最重要的 zuì zhòngyào de
be uppermost in one's mind 某人心目中最重要的 mǒurén xīnmùzhōng zuì zhòngyào de

upright ADJ 1 笔直的 bǐzhí de, 挺直的 tǐngzhí de 2 正直的 zhèngzhí de

uprising N 起义 qǐyì, 暴动 bàodòng

upriver ADV 向上游 xiàng shàngyóu

uproar N 喧闹 xuānnào, 吵闹 chǎonào

uproot V 1 把 [+植物] 连根拔起 bǎ [+zhíwù] lián gēn bá qǐ 2 使 [+家庭] 迁居 shǐ [+jiātíng] qiānjú

upscale ADJ 高档的 gāodàng de, 高层次的 gāocéngcì de

upset I V (PT & PP upset) 1 打翻 [+一杯水] dǎfān [+yìbēi shuǐ] 2 打乱 [+计划] dǎluàn [+jìhuà] 3 使…心烦意乱 shǐ…xīn fán yì luàn, 不安 bù'ān II ADJ 1 心烦的 xīnfán de, 心情烦乱的 xīnqíng fánluàn de 2 不舒服的 bù shūfú de
to have an upset stomach 肚子痛 dùzi tòng, 肠胃不适 chángwèi búshì
III N 意外失败 yìwài shībài

upshot N 结果 jiéguǒ, 结局 jiéjú

upside down ADJ, ADV 上下颠倒（的）shàngxià diāndǎo (de), 翻转过来（的）fānzhuǎn guòlai (de)

upstage I V 抢…的风头 qiǎng…de fēngtou II ADV 朝着舞台后方 cháozhe wǔtái hòufāng

upstairs I ADV 在楼上 zài lóushang, 往楼上 wǎng lóushàng II ADJ 楼上的 lóushàng de
upstairs bedroom 楼上的卧室 lóushàng de wòshì

upstart N 暴发户 bàofāhù, 蹿红的 cuānhóng de

upstate ADJ（一个州的）北部地区 (yí ge zhōu de) běibù dìqū

upstream ADV 向上游 xiàng shàngyóu

upsurge N 急剧上升 jíjù shàngshēng, 剧增 jùzēng

upswing N 改进 gǎijìn, 起色 qǐsè

uptake N 1 领会 lǐnghuì, 理解 lǐjiě
slow/quick on the uptake 领会慢／快 lǐnghuì màn/kuài
2（养料的）摄取（yǎngliào de）shèqǔ

uptight ADJ 1 保守拘谨的 bǎoshǒu jūjǐn de 2 紧张不安的 jǐnzhāng bù'ān de, 愤怒的 fènnù de

up-to-date ADJ 最新的 zuì xīn de

upward ADJ, ADV 向上 xiàngshàng
upward to 超过 chāoguo

urban ADJ 城市的 chéngshì de, 市区的 shìqū de

urbane ADJ 温文尔雅的 wēnwén ěr yǎ de, 彬彬有礼的 bīnbīn yǒulǐ de

urchin N 小顽童 xiǎo wántóng

urge I V 催促 cuīcù, 促使 cùshǐ II N 冲动 chōngdòng
to repress sexual urges 抑制性冲动 yìzhì xìng chōngdòng

urgent ADJ 紧迫的 jǐnpò de, 紧急的 jǐnjí de

urinate V 小便 xiǎobiàn, 解手 jiěshǒu

urine N 尿 niào, 小便 xiǎobiàn

URL (= Uniform Resource Locator) ABBREV 因特网址 yīntèwǎngzhǐ

urn N 1（骨灰）瓮 (gǔhuī) wèng 2 大茶壶 dà cháhú

V

us PRON 我们 wǒmen

use V, N 1（使）用 (shǐ) yòng 2 消耗 xiāohào, 耗费 hàofèi

used ADJ 旧的 jiù de, 二手的 èrshǒu de

used to¹ MODAL V 过去 guòqu

used to² ADJ 习惯 xíguàn, 对…习惯 duì… xíguàn

useful ADJ 有用的 yǒuyòng de

useless ADJ 无用的 wúyòng de, 没有用的 méiyǒu yòng de

user N 使用者 shǐyòngzhě, 使用人 shǐyòngrén

user-friendly ADJ 容易使用的 róngyì shǐyòng de, 易操作的 yì cāozuò de

username N 使用人姓名 shǐyòngrén xìngmíng

usher I V 引领 yǐnlǐng, 引 yǐn, 领 lǐng II N [电影院+] 引座员 [diànyǐngyuàn+] yǐnzuòyuán, 引宾员 yǐnbīnyuán

usual ADJ 通常的 tōngcháng de

usually ADV 通常 tōngcháng, 平常 píngcháng

usurp V 篡夺 cuànduó,（非法）夺取 (fēifǎ) duóqǔ

utensil N 用具 yòngjù, 器皿 qìmǐn

uterus N 子宫 zǐgōng

utilities N 水电煤（气）服务 shuǐdiàn méi (qì) fúwù, 公共事业 gōnggòng shìyè

utilize V 利用 lìyòng

utmost ADJ 极端的 jíduān de

with utmost care 极其小心地 jíqí xiǎoxīn de

utopia N 乌托邦 Wūtuōbāng, 理想世界 lǐxiǎng shìjiè

utter I ADJ 完全的 wánquán de, 彻头彻尾的 chètóu chèwěi de

utter chaos 一片混乱 yípiàn hùnluàn

II V 说出 shuōchū, 讲 jiǎng

U-turn N 1 180度大转弯 yìbǎi bāshí dù dà zhuǎnwān 2 彻底改变 chèdǐ gǎibiàn

vacancy N 1 空缺的职位 kòngquē de zhíwèi 2（旅馆的）空房 (lǚguǎn de) kōngfáng

no vacancies 客满 kèmǎn

vacant ADJ 1 未占用的 [+房间] wèi zhànyòng de [+fángjiān], 空着的 kòngzhe de a vacant lot（城市里的）空地 (chéngshì lǐ de) kòngdì

2 空缺的 [+职位] kòngquē de [+zhíwèi]

3 茫然的 mángrán de, 若有所思的 ruò yǒu suǒsī de

vacate V 1 空出 [+房间] kòng chū [+fángjiān], 搬离 bānlí 2 离开 [+职位] líkāi [+zhíwèi]

vacation N 假期 jiàqī

vaccinate V 注射疫苗 zhùshè yìmiáo

vaccination N 疫苗接种 yìmiáo jiēzhòng vaccination against tetanus 预防破伤风的疫苗接种 yùfáng pòshāngfēng de yìmiáo jiēzhòng

vaccine N 疫苗 yìmiáo measles vaccine 麻疹疫苗 mázhěn yìmiáo

vacillate V 犹豫不决 yóuyù bùjué, 拿不定主意 nábúdìng zhǔyì

vacuum I N 1 真空 zhēnkōng 2（真空）吸尘器 (zhēnkōng) xīchénqì II V（用真空吸尘器）吸尘 (yòng zhēnkōng xīchénqì) xī chén vacuum cleaner 真空吸尘器 zhēnkōng xīchénqì

vagina N 阴道 yīndào

vagrant N 流浪汉 liúlànghàn, 游民 yóumín

vague ADJ 1 含糊的 hánhu de, 不清楚的 bù qīngchu de 2 模模糊糊的 mómó huhú de

vain ADJ 1 白费的 báifèi de, 无目的的 wú mùdì de

in vain 徒劳 túláo

2 自视过高的 zìshì guògāo de, 自负的 zìfù de

Valentine's Day N 情人节 qíngrénjié (February 14th)

valet N **1** 男佣人 nán yōngrén **2**（旅馆）男服务员 (lǚguǎn)
valet parking（旅馆）代客停车服务 (lǚguǎn) dàikè tíngchē fúwù

valiant ADJ 勇敢的 yǒnggǎn de, 英勇的 yīngyǒng de

valid ADJ **1** 有 [+法律] 效力的 yǒu [+fǎlǜ+] xiàolì de **2** 正当的 [+理由] zhèngdàng de [+lǐyóu], 合理的 hélǐ de

validate v **1** 使…生效 shǐ...shēngxiào **2** 证实 zhèngshí

validity N **1** 正当性 zhèngdàngxìng, 合理性 hélǐ xìng **2** 有效性 yǒuxiàoxìng

valley N 山谷 shāngǔ

valor N 勇气 yǒngqì, 英勇 yīngyǒng

valuable ADJ **1** 非常有价值的 fēicháng yǒu jiàzhí de, 贵重的 guìzhòng de **2** 宝贵的 bǎoguìde, 珍贵的 zhēnguì de

valuables N 贵重物品 guìzhòng wùpǐn

valuation N 估价 gūjià
market valuation 市场价值 shìchǎng jiàzhí, 市值 shì zhí

value I N 价值 jiàzhí
value-added tax 增值税 zēngzhíshuì
sentimental value 感情价值 gǎnqíng jiàzhí
II v **1** 珍视 zhēnshì **2** 估价 gūjià

values N 价值观（念）jiàzhí guān (niàn)

valve N **1** 阀 fá, 活门 huómén
safety valve 安全阀 ānquánfá
2（心脏）瓣膜 (xīnzàng) bànmó

vampire N 吸血鬼 xīxuèguǐ

van N **1** 小型货车 xiǎoxíng huòchē [M. WD 辆 liàng] **2** 小客车 xiǎokèchē, 面包车 miànbāochē [M. WD 辆 liàng]

vandalism N 破坏 pòhuài, 破坏行为 pòhuài xíngwéi

vandalize v 故意破坏 [+公共财物] gùyì pòhuài [+gōnggòng cáiwù]

vanguard N 先锋 xiānfēng, 前卫 qiánwèi

vanilla N 香草 xiāngcǎo, 香草味 xiāngcǎowèi
vanilla icecream 香草冰淇淋 xiāngcǎo bīngqílín

vanish v 消失 xiāoshī, 不见 bújiàn

vanity N 虚荣 xūróng, 虚荣心 xūróng xīn

vanquish v 征服 zhēngfú, 击败 jībài

vantage point N **1** 有利位置 yǒulì wèizhì **2** 立场 lìchǎng, 观点 guāndiǎn

vapor N（水）蒸汽 (shuǐ) zhēngqì

vaporize v（使…）蒸发 (shǐ...) zhēngfā, 汽化 qìhuà

variable I ADJ **1** 多变的 duōbiàn de **2** 情况不一样的 qíngkuàng bù yíyàng de, 变化的 biànhuà de II N **1** 可变因素 kěbiàn yīnsù **2**（数学）变量 (shùxué) biànliàng

variant ADJ, N 变体 biàntǐ, 变种 biànzhǒng

variation N 变化 biànhuà, 不同 bù tóng

varied ADJ 各种各样的 gèzhǒng gèyàng de, 形形色色的 xíngxíng sèsè de

variety N 品种 pǐnzhǒng
a variety of 各种 gè zhǒng, 种种 zhǒngzhǒng
variety show 综艺表演 zōngyì biǎoyǎn

various ADJ 不同的 bù tóng de

varnish I N 清漆 qīngqī, 亮光漆 zhàoguāngqī II v 涂上清漆 tú shàng qīngqī

vary v 不同 bù tóng, 变化 biànhuà

varying ADJ 不同的 bù tóng de, 有差异的 yǒu chāyì de

vase N 花瓶 huāpíng
Ming vase 中国明代的花瓶 Zhōngguó Míngdài de huāpíng

vasectomy N 输精管切除术 shūjīngguǎn qiēchúshù

vast ADJ 巨大的 jùdà de
vast majority 绝大多数 juédàduōshù

vastly ADJ 非常 fēicháng, 极其 jíqí

VAT (= value-added tax) ABBREV See value

vat N 大（水）缸 dà (shuǐ) gāng

vault[1] N **1**（银行）保险库 (yínháng) bǎoxiǎnkù **2**（地下）墓穴 (dìxia) mùxué [M. WD 座 zuò]

vault[2] v **1** 跳跃 tiàoyuè, 跳过 tiàoguò **2** 跃升 yuèshēng
pole vault 撑竿跳 chēnggāntiào

VCR (= video cassette recorder) ABBREV 录像机 lùxiàngjī

veal N 小牛肉 xiǎoniúròu

vegetable N 蔬菜 shūcài

vegetarian N 素食主义者 sùshízhǔyìzhě

vegetation N 植被 zhíbèi, 草木 cǎomù

vehement ADJ 强烈的 qiángliè de, 激烈的 jīliè de

vehicle N 1 车辆 chēliàng 2 媒介 méijiè, 表达工具 biǎodá gōngjù

veil I N 1 面纱 miànshā [M. WD 块 kuài]
bridal veil 新娘面纱 xīnniáng miànshā 2 烟幕 yānmù 3 (the veil)（伊斯兰国家妇女）戴面纱的制度 (Yīsīlánguójiā fùnǚ) dài miànshā de zhìdù II v 遮上面纱 zhēshàng miànshā

veiled ADJ 隐蔽的 yǐnbì de, 含蓄的 hánxù de
veiled threat 含蓄的威胁 hánxù de wēixié

vein N 1 [人体的+] 静脉 [réntǐ de+] jìngmài [M. WD 条 tiáo]
jugular vein 颈静脉 jǐng jìngmài 2 [叶子的+] 叶脉 [yèzi de+] yèmài 3 [石头的+] 纹路 [shítou de+] wénlù 4 矿脉 kuàngmài

velocity N 速度 sùdù

velvet N 天鹅绒 tiān'éróng, 丝绒 sīróng

vendetta N 1 报复 bàofu
personal/political vendetta 个人／政治报复 gèrén/zhèngzhì bàofu 2 世仇 shìchóu, 血仇 xuèchóu

vendor N 1（街头）小贩 (jiētóu) xiǎofàn 2 推销商 tuīxiāoshāng 3 卖主 màizhǔ

veneer N 1 贴板 tiēbǎn, 镶板 xiāngbǎn
walnut veneer 桃木镶板 táomù xiāngbǎn 2 假象 jiǎxiàng, 虚饰 xūshì
a veneer of kindness 和善的假象 héshàn de jiǎxiàng

venerable ADJ 德高望重的 dégāo wàngzhòng de, 深受尊敬的 shēnshòu zūnjìng de

venerate v 崇敬 chóngjìng, 敬重 jìngzhòng

Venetian blind N 百叶窗帘 bǎiyèchuānglián

vengeance N 报仇 bàochóu, 复仇 fùchóu
with a vengeance 变本加厉地 biànběn jiālì de, 过度地 guòdù de

vengeful ADJ 怀有复仇心的 huáiyǒu fùchóuxīn de, 报仇的 bàochóu de

venison N 鹿肉 lùròu

venom N 1 毒液 dúyè 2 极度憎恨 jídù zēnghèn

vent I N 1 通风孔 tōngfēngkǒng
to give vent to 发泄 [+怒火] fāxiè [+nùhuǒ]
II v 发泄 fāxiè, 发牢骚 fāláosāo
to vent one's spleen 发泄怒火 fāxiè nùhuǒ

ventilate v 1（使…）通风 (shǐ…) tōngfēng 2 发表 [+意见] fābiǎo [+yìjiàn]

ventilator N 1 通风装置 tōngfēngzhuāngzhì 2 人工呼吸机 réngōng hūxījī

ventriloquist N 口技表演者 kǒujì biǎoyǎnzhě, 口技演员 kǒujì yǎnyuán

venture I N 1 风险 fēngxiǎn, 冒险 màoxiǎn 2 风险投资 fēngxiǎn tóuzī, 商业投资 shāngyè tóuzī
venture capital 风险资本 fēngxiǎn zīběn
joint venture 合资企业 hézī qǐyè
II v 1 冒（风）险 mào (fēng) xiǎn 2 敢于 gǎnyú
Nothing ventured, nothing gained. 不入虎穴，焉得虎子? Bú rù hǔxué, yāndé hǔzǐ? (→ 不冒险进入虎穴，怎能抓到小老虎？ Bú màoxiǎn jìnrù hǔxué, zěn néng zhuā dào xiǎo lǎohǔ? If you don't venture into a tiger's den, how can you catch a tiger cub?)

venue N（举办）地点 (jǔbàn) dìdiǎn, 会址 huìzhǐ

veranda N 游廊 yóuláng [M. WD 条 tiáo], 走廊 zǒuláng [M. WD 条 tiáo]

verb N 动词 dòngcí

verbal ADJ 1 口头的 kǒutóu de
verbal agreement 口头协定 kǒutóu xiédìng 2 语言的 yǔyán de, 言词的 yáncí de
verbal skill 语言技能 yǔyán jìnéng

verbatim ADJ, ADV 逐字（的／地）zhúzì (de)
to quote sb verbatim 逐字引用某人的话 zhúzì yǐnyòng mǒurén de huà

verbose ADJ 话太多的 huà tài duō de, 啰嗦的 luōsuō de

verdict N（法庭）裁决 (fǎtíng) cáijué, 判决 pànjué
a guilty verdict 有罪裁定 yǒuzuì cáidìng

verge I N 边缘 biānyuán

on the verge of bankruptcy 濒于破财的边缘 bīnyú pòcái de biānyuán **II** v (to verge on) 接近 jiējìn, 几乎趋向 jīhū
to verge on the impossible 几乎不可能 jīhū bù kěnéng

verification N 核实 héshí, 证实 zhèngshí

verify v 核实 héshí, 证实 zhèngshí

veritable ADJ 真正的 zhēnzhèng de, 名副其实的 míngfù qíshí de

vermin N 害虫 hàichóng, 害兽 hàishòu **2** 害人精 hàirénjīng, 坏蛋 huàidàn

vernacular ADJ, N 本地语 běndìyǔ, 方言 fāngyán, 土话 tǔhuà

versatile ADJ **1** 多才多艺的 [+人] duōcái duōyì de [+rén], 多面手的 duōmiàn-shǒu de **2** 用途广泛的 [+工具] yòngtú-guǎngfàn de [+gōngjù], 万能的 wànnéng de

verse N **1** 诗 shī, 韵文 yùnwén **2** 一节 （歌词）yìjié (gēcí)

versed ADJ (be versed in) 精通 jīngtōng, 对…造诣很深 duì…zàoyì hěn shēn

version N **1** 版 bǎn **2** 说法 shuōfǎ .

versus PREP **1** （体育比赛／法律诉讼）…对… (tǐyù bǐsài/fǎlǜ sùsòng)…duì… **2** 与…相比 yǔ…xiāngbǐ, 与…相对 yǔ…xiāngduì

vertebra N 脊椎 jǐzhuī [M. WD 块 kuài], 椎骨 zhuīgǔ [M. WD 块 kuài]

vertical **I** ADJ 垂直的 chuízhí de **II** N 垂直线 chuízhíxiàn

vertigo N （登高而产生的）眩晕 (dēnggāo ér chǎnshēng de) xuànyùn, 头晕 tóuyūn

verve N 活力 huólì, 生机 shēngjī

very I ADV 非常 fēicháng **II** ADJ 正是 zhèng shì, 实在的 shízài de

vessel N **1** 航船 hángchuán, 艘 sōu **2** 容器 róngqì **3** 血管 xuèguǎn, 脉管 màiguǎn

vest N **1** 内衣背心 nèiyī bèixīn [M. WD 件 jiàn]
bulletproof vest 防弹背心 fángdàn bèixīn
2 马甲 mǎjiǎ [M. WD 件 jiàn]

vestige N 痕迹 hénjì, 遗迹 yíjī

vet I N **1** (= veterinarian) 兽医 shòuyī

2 (= veteran) 老兵 lǎobīng **II** v （政治）审查 (zhèngzhì) shěnchá
vetting procedure （政治）审查程序 (zhèngzhì) shěnchá chéngxù

veteran N 老兵 lǎobīng, 老手 lǎoshǒu

veterinarian N 兽医 shòuyī

veterinary ADJ 兽医的 shòuyī de
veterinary medicine 兽医（学）shòuyī (xué)

veto I v 否决 fǒujué, 反对 fǎnduì **II** N 否决 （权）fǒujué (quán)
veto power 否决权 fǒujuéquán

vex v 使…恼怒 shǐ…nǎonù

via PREP 经过 jīngguo

viability N 可行性 kěxíngxìng

viable ADJ **1** 切实可行的 qièshí kěxíng de **2** 能存活的 néng cúnhuó de

viaduct N 高架桥 gāojiàqiáo

vial N 小（药）瓶 xiǎo (yào) píng

vibe N 感觉 gǎnjué, 感应 gǎnyìng

vibrant ADJ **1** 令人兴奋的 lìngrén xīngfèn de, 充满活力的 chōngmǎn huólì de **2** 鲜艳明亮的 [+色彩] xiānyàn míngliàng de [+sècǎi]

vibrate v （使…）颤动 (shǐ…) chàndòng, （使…）震动 (shǐ…) zhèndòng

vibration N **1** 颤动 chàndòng, 震动 zhèndòng **2** 感应 gǎnyìng, 共鸣 gòngmíng
high-frequency vibration 高频振荡 gāopín zhèndàng

vicar N （教区）牧师 (jiàoqū) mùshi

vicarious ADJ 间接感受的 jiànjiē gǎnshòu de, 如同身临其境的 rútóng shēn lín qí jìng de

vice¹ I N **1** 犯罪（活动）fànzuì (huódòng), 邪恶（行为）xié'è (xíng-wéi)
vice squad 警察打击犯罪小组 jǐngchá dǎjī fànzuì xiǎozǔ
2 劣根性 liègēnxìng, （本性的）邪恶 (běnxìng de) xié'è

vice² ADJ 副 fù
vice president 副总统 fùzǒngtǒng, 副总裁 fùzǒngcái

vice versa ADV 反过来也是这样 fǎnguòlái yě shì zhèyàng, 反之亦然 fǎn zhī yì rán

vicinity N **1** 附近 fùjìn
in the vicinity of the school 学校附近 xuéxiào fùjìn
2 左右 zuǒyòu
in the vicinity of 7,000 years 七千年左右 qīqiān nián zuǒyòu

vicious ADJ 恶毒的 èdú de, 凶险的 xiōngxiǎn de
vicious circle 恶性循环 èxìng xúnhuán

victim N 受害人 shòuhài rén

victimize V 不公正地对待 bù gōngzhèng de duìdài, 迫害 pòhài

victor N 获胜者 huòshèngzhě, 胜利者 shènglìzhě
runaway victor 遥遥领先的获胜者 yáoyáo lǐng xiān de huòshèngzhě

victorious ADJ 获胜的 huòshèng de, 胜利的 shènglì de

victory N 胜利 shènglì, 赢 yíng

video I N 录像 lùxiàng
music video 音乐录像 yīnyuè lùxiàng
II ADJ 电视的 diànshì de, 视频的 shìpín de
video camera 摄像机 shèxiàngjī
video game 电子游戏 diànzǐ yóuxì

videotape I N 录像带 lùxiàngdài II V 把 [+电影] 录在录像带上 bǎ [+diànyǐng] lù zài lùxiàngdài shàng

vie V 竞争 jìngzhēng, 角逐 juézhú

view I N **1** 观点 guāndiǎn, 看法 kànfǎ **2** 景色 jǐngsè II V 考虑 kǎolǜ
in view of 由于 yóuyú, 考虑到 kǎolǜdao

viewer N 电视观众 diànshì guānzhòng, 电视观看者 diànshì guānkànzhě

vigil N **1** 守夜 shǒuyè, 陪夜 péi yè **2** (夜间) 静坐抗议 (yè jiān) jìngzuò kàngyì

vigilance N 警惕 (心) jǐngtì (xīn), 警戒 jǐngjiè

vigilant ADJ (保持) 警惕的 (bǎochí) jǐngtì de

vigor N 活力 huólì, 精力 jīnglì

vigorous ADJ 充满精力的 chōngmǎn jīnglì de, 精力充沛的 jīnglì chōngpèi de

vile ADJ 令人讨厌的 lìngrén tǎoyàn de, 坏透了的 huàitòule de

vilify V 污蔑 wūmiè, 中伤 zhòngshāng

villa N (乡间) 别墅 (xiāngjiān) biéshù

village N 村 cūn, 村庄 cūnzhuāng

villager N 村民 cūnmín

villain N **1** 坏人 huàirén, 罪犯 zuìfàn **2** (电影／小说中的) 反面人物 (diànyǐng/xiǎoshuō zhōngde) fǎnmiàn-rénwù, 反派角色 fǎnpài juésè

vindicate V 为…辩白 wéi...biànbái, 证明…清白 zhèngmíng...qīngbái

vindictive ADJ 有报复心的 yǒu bàofu xīn de, 怀恨在心的 huáihèn zài xīn de

vine N **1** 藤本植物 téngběn zhíwù **2** 葡萄 (藤) pútao (téng) [M. WD 棵 kē]

vinegar N 醋 cù

vineyard N 葡萄园 pútaoyuán

vintage I ADJ **1** 优质的 [+酒] yōuzhì de [+jiǔ]
vintage wine 特定年代出产的佳酿酒 tèdìng niándài chūchǎn de jiānniàngjiǔ
2 老式的 [+汽车] lǎoshì de [+qìchē], 珍藏的 zhēncáng de
vintage car 古董车 gǔdǒngchē, 珍藏老式车 zhēncáng lǎoshìchē
II N 酒的酿造年份 jiǔ de niàngzào nián-fèn

vinyl N 乙烯基 yǐxījī
vinyl flooring 乙烯基铺地材料 yǐxījī pūdì cáiliào

violate V **1** 违反 wéifǎn, 违背 wéibèi **2** 强奸 [+妇女] qiángjiān [+fùnǚ]

violation N **1** 违反 wéifǎn, 违背 wéibèi **2** 侵犯 qīnfàn, 侵害 qīnhài

violence N **1** 暴力 (行为) bàolì (xíngwéi)
domestic violence 家庭暴力 (行为) jiātíng bàolì (xíngwéi)
2 强大的破坏力量 qiángdà de pòhuàilì liáng

violent ADJ **1** 暴力的 bàolì de **2** 强烈的 qiángliè de
a violent earthquake 强地震 qiáng dìzhèn

violin N 小提琴 xiǎotíqín [M. WD 把 bǎ]

violinist N 小提琴手 xiǎotíqínshǒu

VIP (= very important person) ABBREV 大人物 dàrénwù, 贵宾 guìbīn

viper N 小毒蛇 xiǎo dúshé [M. WD 条 tiáo]

viral ADJ 病毒 (性) 的 bìngdú (xing) de, 病毒引起的 bìngdú yǐnqǐ de

virgin N **1** 处女 chǔnǚ, 贞女 zhēnnǚ **2** 未开发的 wèi kāifā de virgin land 未开发的处女地 wèi kāifā de chǔnǚdì

virginity N 处女状态 chǔnǚ zhuàngtài, 童真 tóngzhēn

virile ADJ 充满阳刚气的 chōngmǎn yánggāngqì de, 有男子气概的 yǒu nánzǐ qìgài de

virtual ADJ 1 爱交际的 ài jiāojì de, 事实上的 shìshíshang de 2（电脑中）虚拟的 (diànnǎo zhōng) xūnǐ de, 非真实世界的 fēi zhēnshí shìjiè de

virtual reality 虚拟现实 xūnǐ xiànshí

virtually ADV 1 实质上 shízhìshàng, 实际上 shíjìshàng 2 几乎 jīhū, 差不多 chàbuduō 3 虚拟地 xūnǐ de

virtue N 1 美德 měidé 2 优点 yōudiǎn, 优越性 yōuyuèxìng

by virtue of sth 凭借 píngjiè, 由于 yóuyú to make a virtue of necessity 很愿意地做不得不做的事 hěn yuànyì de zuò bùdebù zuò de shì

virtuoso N（音乐）名家 (yīnyuè) míngjiā, 高手 gāoshǒu

virtuous ADJ（品德）高尚的 (pǐndé) gāoshàng de, 善良的 shànliáng de

virulent ADJ 1 剧毒的 jùdú de, 迅速致死的 xùnsù zhìsǐ de 2 刻毒的 kèdú de, 恶毒的 èdú de

virus N 病毒 bìngdú

visa N 签证 qiānzhèng

entry visa 入境签证 rùjìng qiānzhèng exit visa 离境签证 líjìng qiānzhèng student's visa 学生签证 xuésheng qiānzhèng

transit visa 过境签证 guòjìng qiānzhèng

visage N 脸庞 liǎn, 面容 miànróng

vis-à-vis PREP 与…相比 yǔ...xiāngbǐ

vise N 老虎钳 lǎohǔqián [M. WD 把 bǎ]

visibility N 能见度 néngjiàndù, 视程 shìchéng

visible ADJ 能看得见的 néng kàndejiàn de, 可见的 kějiàn de

vision N 1 视力 shìlì 2 幻想 huànxiǎng 3 远见 yuǎnjiàn

visionary ADJ 有远见的 yǒu yuǎnjiàn de, 有眼光的 yǒu yǎnguāng de

visit I v 1 看望 kànwàng 2 参观 cānguān,

访问 fǎngwèn II N 1 看望 kànwàng, 拜访 bàifǎng 2 访问 fǎngwèn, 参观 cānguān

visitation N 1 访问 fǎngwèn 2 探视（权）tànshì (quán)

visitor N 1 访问者 fǎngwènzhě, 访客 fǎngkè 2 参观者 cānguānzhě

visor N 1 帽舌 màoshé 2（汽车的）遮阳板 (qìchē de) zhēyángbǎn

visual ADJ 视觉的 shìjué de, 视力的 shìlì de

visual aid 直观教具 zhíguān jiàojù visual arts 视觉艺术 shìjué yìshù

visualize V 想象 xiǎngxiàng, 设想 shèxiǎng

vital ADJ 1 至关重要的 zhìguān zhòngyào de 2 生命的 shēngmìng de

vital signs 生命特征 shēngmìng tèzhēng

vital statistics 人口动态统计 rénkǒu dòngtài tǒngjì

vitality N 活力 huólì, 生命力 shēngmìnglì

vitamin N 维生素 wéishēngsù, 维他命 wéitāmíng

viticulture N 葡萄栽培术 pútao zāipéi shù, 葡萄园管理 pútaoyuán guǎnlǐ

vitriolic ADJ 刻毒的 kèdú de, 尖刻的 jiānkè de

vivacious ADJ 活泼的 huópo de, 快活的 kuàihuo de

vivid ADJ 1 生动的 [+描写] shēngdòng de [+miáoxiě], 逼真的 bīzhēn de 2 鲜艳明亮的 [+色彩] xiānyàn míngliàng de [+sècǎi]

vivid imagination 丰富的想象力 fēngfù de xiǎngxiànglì

VJ (= video jockey) ABBREV 电视音乐节目主持人 diànshì yīnyuè jiémù zhǔchírén

V-neck N 鸡心领 jīxīnlǐng

V-neck sweater 鸡心领羊毛衫 jīxīnlǐng yángmáoshān

VOA (= Voice of America) ABBREV 美国之音 Měiguó zhī yīn

vocabulary N 1 词汇 cíhuì 2 专业词汇 zhuānyè cíhuì, 术语 shùyǔ

business vocabulary 商业词汇 shāngyè cíhuì

vocal I ADJ 1 嗓音的 sǎngyīn de vocal cords 声带 shēngdài

vocal music 声乐 shēngyuè
2 直言不讳的 zhíyán búhuì de
a vocal critic 直言不讳的批评者 zhíyán búhuì de pīpíngzhě
II N 歌唱 gēchàng, 歌咏 gēyǒng
vocation N **1** 职业 zhíyè, 工作 gōngzuò
sense of vocation 敬业精神 jìngyè jīngshén
2 神召 shén zhào,（宗教）使命感 (zōngjiào) shǐmìnggǎn
vocational ADJ 职业训练的 zhíyè xùnliàn de
vocational school 职业学校 zhíyè xuéxiào
vociferous ADJ 大声的 dàshēng de, 强烈表达的 qiángliè biǎodá de
vogue N 时尚 shíshàng, 风行 fēngxíng
a vogue word 流行语 liúxíngyǔ
voice N **1** 说话声 shuōhuàshēng, 声音 shēngyīn **2** 嗓子 sǎngzi, 嗓音 sǎngyīn
to raise one's voice 提高嗓音 tígāo sǎngyīn
voice mail 语音信箱 yǔyīn xìnxiāng
3 发言权 fāyánquán
to give voice to sth 对某事发表意见 duì mǒushì fābiǎo yìjiàn
void **I** ADJ 无效的 wúxiào de
null and void（法律上）无效的 (fǎlǜshàng) wúxiào de
be void of 毫无 háowú
II N 空虚感 kōngxūgǎn, 空白 kòngbái
to fill the void 填补空虚感 tiánbǔ kōngxūgǎn
III V 使 [+协议] 无效 shǐ [+xiéyì] wúxiào, 使…作废 shǐ...zuòfèi
volatile ADJ 不确定的 bú quèdìng de, 动荡不定的 dòngdàng búdìng de
volcano N 火山 huǒshān [M. WD 座 zuò]
active/dormant volcano 活／死火山 huó／sǐ huǒshān
volition N 意志（力）yìzhì (lì)
of one's own volition 自愿地 zìyuàn de
volley N **1** [炮弹／子弹+] 齐射 [pàodàn/zǐdàn+] qíshè **2** 一连串 [+质问／批评] yīliánchuàn (zhìwèn/pīpíng) **3**（球类比赛中的）拦击 (qiúlèi bǐsài zhòng de) lánjí, 截踢 jiétī

volleyball N 排球（运动）páiqiú (yùndòng)
volt N 伏特 fútè
voltage N 电压 diànyā
voluble ADJ 健谈的 jiàntán de, 滔滔不绝的 tāotāo bù jué de
volume N **1** 音量 yīnliàng **2** 容量 róngliàng **3**（书籍）册 (shūjí) cè
voluminous ADJ **1** 篇幅很长的 piānfu hěn cháng de **2** 容量大的 róngliàng dà de
voluntary ADJ 自愿的 zìyuàn de, 志愿的 zhìyuàn de
volunteer **I** N 志愿人员 zhìyuàn rényuán, 义工 yìgōng
Red Cross volunteer 红十字会义工 Hóngshízìhuì yìgōng
II V 自愿 zìyuàn, 自告奋勇 zìgào fènyǒng
voluptuous ADJ 丰满的 fēngmǎn de, 丰乳肥臀的 fēng rǔ féi tún de
vomit **I** V 呕吐 ǒutù, 吐出 tùchū **II** N 呕吐物 ǒutù wù
voodoo N 伏都教 fúdújiào
voodoo doll 巫毒娃娃 wūdú wáwa
voracious ADJ **1** 食量很大的 shíliàng hěn dà de, 贪吃的 tānchī de **2** 求知欲旺盛的 qiúzhīyù wàngshèng de
vortex N 漩涡 xuánwō, 旋风 xuànfēng
vote **I** N **1** 表决 biǎojué, 投票 tóupiào
the vote 得票总数 dépiào zǒngshù
vote of no confidence 不信任投票 bú xìnrèn tóupiào
II V **1** 投票 tóupiào
voting booth 投票站 tóupiàozhàn
2 评选 píngxuǎn
be voted the best program 被评选为最佳节目 bèi píngxuǎn wéi zuìjiā jiémù
to vote with one's feet 退席表示反对 tuìxí biǎoshì fǎnduì
voter N 选民 xuǎnmín, 投票人 tóupiàorén
vouch V (to vouch for) 为…担保 wéi...dānbǎo, 保证 bǎozhèng
voucher N 代金券 dàijīnquàn, 凭证 píngzhèng
gift voucher 礼券 lǐquàn
2 收据 shōujù, 收条 shōutiáo
vow **I** N 誓言 shìyán
marriage vows 结婚誓言 jiéhūn shìyán, 婚誓 hūnshì

ll v 发誓 fāshì, 起誓 qǐshì

vowel N 元音 yuányīn

voyage N 航行 hángxíng
Bon Voyage! 旅途愉快! Lǚtú yúkuài!
ll v 航海 hánghǎi, 航行 hángxíng

voyeur N 1 窥淫狂 kuīyínkuáng 2 特别喜欢窥视他人隐私的人 tèbié xǐhuan kuīshì tārén yǐnsī de rén

vulgar ADJ 低俗的 dīsú de, 粗俗的 cūsú de

vulnerable ADJ 1 脆弱的 cuìruò de, 敏感的 mǐngǎn de 2 易受攻击的 yìshòu gōngjī de
be vulnerable to terrorist attacks 很容易受到恐怖活动攻击的 hěn róngyì shòudào kǒngbù huódòng gōngjī de

vulture N 秃鹫 tūjiù [M. WD 只 zhī]

W

wacko N 怪人 guàirén, 疯子 fēngzi

wacky ADJ 疯疯癫癫的 fēngfeng diāndiān de, 古怪的 gǔguài de

wad N 一叠 yì dié
a wad of money 一叠钱 yì dié qián

waddle v (像鸭子一样) 摇摇摆摆地走 (xiàng yāzi yíyàng) yáoyáo bǎibǎi de zǒu

wade v 涉 (水) shè (shuǐ), 蹚 (水) tāng (shuǐ)

wafer N 1 华夫饼干 huáfū bǐnggān, 威化饼干 wēihuà bǐnggān [M. WD 块 kuài] 2 (宗教) 圣饼 (zōngjiào) shèngbǐng

waffle N 蛋奶烘饼 dànnǎi hōngbǐng

waft v [气味／音乐声+] 飘荡 [qìwèi/yīnyuè shēng+] piāodàng

wag v 1 [狗+] 摇尾巴 [gǒu+] yáo wěibā 2 [人+] 摇手指 [rén+] yáo shǒuzhǐ

wage¹ N 工资 gōngzī
wage freeze 工资冻结 gōngzī dòngjié
minimum wage (法定) 最低工资 (fǎdìng) zuì dī gōngzī

wage² v 发动 fādòng

wager I v 打赌 dǎ dǔ, 下赌注 xià dǔzhù
ll N 打赌 dǎ dǔ, 赌注 dǔzhù

wagon N 1 客货两用车 kèhuò liǎngyòng-chē [M. WD 辆 liàng] 2 (老式) 马拉货车 (lǎoshì) mǎlā huòchē

wail I v 1 [人+] 大声哭叫 [rén+] dàshēng kūjiào, 嚎啕大哭 háotáo dàkū 2 [警报器+] 呼啸 [jǐngbàoqì+] hūxiào **ll** N 1 大哭声 dàkūshēng 2 呼啸声 hūxiàoshēng

waist N 腰 yāo
waistline 腰围 yāowéi

wait I v 1 等 děng, 等候 děnghou
to wait up 不睡觉等候 bú shuìjiào děnghou
2 (to wait on) 服侍 fúshi, 伺候 cìhou
ll N 等候 děnghou

waiter N (饭店) 服务员 [fàndiàn+] fúwùyuán

waitress N (饭店) 女服务员 (fàndiàn) nǚ fúwùyuán

waive v 放弃 [+权利] fàngqì [+quánlì], 取消 [+规定] qǔxiāo [+guīdìng]

waiver N 弃权声明书 qìquán shēngmíng shū

wake¹ v (PT woke; PP woken) 1 醒 xǐng 2 叫醒 jiàoxǐng **ll** v 守灵 shǒulíng

wake² N 1 船的尾波 chuán de wěi bō, 航迹 hángjì 2 (in the wake of) 紧接着 jǐnjiēzhe, 在…以后 zài...yǐhòu

wakeful ADJ 不能入眠的 bùnéng rùmián de, 醒着的 xǐngzhe de

waken v 1 醒 (来) xǐng (lái) 2 叫醒 jiàoxǐng, 唤醒 huànxǐng
to waken at the baby's cry 听到婴儿哭而醒来 tīngdào yīng'ér kū ér xǐnglái

wake-up call N 1 叫醒电话 jiàoxǐng diàn-huà 2 警钟 jǐngzhōng, 警示 jǐngshì

waking ADJ 醒着的 xǐngzhe de
waking hours 醒着的时间 xǐngzhe de shíjiān

walk I v 走 zǒu, 步行 bùxíng
to walk the dog 溜狗 liùgǒu
to walk away 不负责任地离开 bú fù zérèn de líkāi
ll N 1 走 zǒu, 行走 xíngzǒu 2 步行路径 bùxíng lùjìng
to go for/take a walk 散步 sànbù

walkie-talkie N 步话机 bùhuàjī, 无线电对讲机 wúxiàndiàn duìjiǎngjī

walking papers N 辞退书 cítuìshū [M. WD 份 fèn], 解雇通知单 jiěgù tōngzhīdān [M. WD 份 fèn/张 zhāng]

walking stick N 拐杖 guǎizhàng [M. WD 根 gēn], 手杖 shǒuzhàng [M. WD 根 gēn]

walk-on N 未获体育奖学金的大学体育队队员 wèi huò tǐyù jiǎngxuéjīn de dàxué tǐyù duì duìyuán
walk-on part 跑龙套的角色 pǎo lóngtào de juésè

walkover N 轻而易举的胜利 qīng ér yìjǔ de shènglì

walk-up N 无电梯的大楼 wú diàntī de dàlóu

walkway N 人行通道 rénxíng tōngdào, 有遮走道 yǒu zhē zǒudào

wall I N 墙 qiáng
the Great Wall (of China) (中国) 长城 (Zhōngguó) Chángchéng
II v 1 (to wall … in) 用墙围起来 yòng qiáng wéi qǐlái 2 (to wall … up) 用砖堵上 yòng zhuān dǔ shàng

wallaby N 澳洲沙袋鼠 Àozhōu shādàishǔ

wallet N 皮夹 pídiā, 钱包 qiánbāo
a fat wallet (钱装得) 鼓鼓的皮夹 (qián zhuāng dé) gǔgǔ de pídiā

wallow v 1 [动物+] 快乐地打滚 (dòngwù+] kuàilè de dǎgǔn 2 (to wallow in self-pity) 沉溺于自怜 chénnì yú zìlián

wallpaper N 墙纸 qiángzhǐ, 壁纸 bìzhǐ

walnut N 核桃 hétáo [M. WD 颗 kē], 胡桃 hútáo [M. WD 颗 kē]

walrus N 海象 hǎixiàng [M. WD 头 tóu]

waltz N 华尔兹舞 (曲) huá'ěrzīwǔ (qū), 圆舞 (曲) yuánwǔ (qū) II v 跳华尔兹舞 tiào huá'ěrzīwǔ

wan ADJ 苍白的 [+脸色] cāngbái de [+liǎnsè], 憔悴的 qiáocuì de

wand N 魔杖 mózhàng [M. WD 根 gēn]

wander v 1 游荡 yóudàng, 漫游 mànyóu
to wander off 走开 zǒukāi, 走散 zǒusàn 2 偏离话题 piānlí huàtí, 离题 lítí 3 思想不集中 sīxiǎng bù jízhōng, 走神 zǒushén

wanderlust N 旅游癖 lǚyóupǐ, 游山玩水的强烈欲望 yóushān wánshuǐ de qiángliè yùwàng

wane v 1 衰败 shuāibài, 没落 mòluò 2 [月亮+] 缺 / 亏 [yuèliang+] quē/kuī II N 衰败 shuāibài, 没落 mòluò

on the wane 正在衰落 zhèngzài shuāiluò

wangle v 哄骗 hǒngpiàn
to wangle sth out of sb 从某人那里用巧计得到某物 cóng mǒurén nàli yòng qiǎojì dédào mǒuwù
to wangle one's way out of 设法脱身 shèfǎ tuōshēn

want I v 1 要 yào, 想 xiǎng, 想要 xiǎngyào 2 缺乏 quēfá II N 需要但缺乏的事物 xūyào dàn quēfá de shìwù
for want of sth 由于缺乏某事物 yóuyú quēfá mǒushíwù
for want of a better word 因为没有更好的词语 yīnwèi méiyǒu gèng hǎo de cíyǔ

want ad N (报纸上) 分类广告 (bàozhǐ shàng) fēnlèi guǎnggào

wanted ADJ 被警方追捕的 bèi jǐngfāng zhuībǔ de

wanton ADJ 肆意的 sìyì de, 胡乱的 húluàn de
a wanton killing 滥杀 lànshā

war N 1 战争 zhànzhēng 2 斗争 dòuzhēng, 竞争 jìngzhēng
war bride 战时新娘 zhànshí xīnniáng
war crime 战争罪行 zhànzhēng zuìxíng
to declare war on 向…宣战 xiàng… xuānzhàn
to wage war on 与…作战 yǔ…zuòzhàn

warble v [鸟+] 啭鸣 [niǎo+] zhuànmíng, 象鸟一样歌唱 xiàng niǎo yíyàng gēchàng

ward I N 1 病房 bìngfáng
maternity/surgical ward (妇) 产科 / 外科病房 (fù) chǎnkē/wàikēbìngfáng 2 被监护人 bèi jiānhùrén 3 (城市中的) 选区 (chéngshì zhòngde) xuǎnqū II v (to ward off) 防止 fángzhǐ

warden N 1 监护人 jiānhùrén, 管理员 guǎnlǐyuán
warden of an old people's home 养老院管理员 yǎnglǎoyuàn guǎnlǐyuán 2 监督人员 jiāndū rényuán
traffic warden 交通执勤人员 jiāotōng zhíqín rényuán 3 监狱长 jiānyùzhǎng

wardrobe N **1** 大衣柜 dàyīguì, 衣橱 yīchú **2**（个人所有的）衣服（gèrén suǒyǒu de）yīfu **3**（剧团）戏装管理部（jùtuán）xìzhuāng guǎnlǐ bù

warehouse N 货栈 huòzhàn, 仓库 cāngkù

wares N（不在商店出售的）货物（búzài shāngdiàn chūshòu de）huòwù, 商品 shāngpǐn

warfare N 战争 zhànzhēng
guerrila warfare 游击战 yóujīzhàn
nuclear warfare 核战争 hézhànzhēng

warhead N（导弹）弹头（dǎodàn）dàntóu

warlike ADJ 好战的 hàozhàn de, 善战的 shànzhàn de

warm I ADJ **1** 温暖的 wēnnuǎn de **2** 热情友好的 rèqíng yǒuhǎo de II V 使…温暖 shǐ...wēnnuǎn, 使…暖和 shǐ...nuǎnhuo
to warm up to sb 对某人产生好感 duì mǒurén chǎnshēng hǎogǎn, 喜欢上某人 xǐhuan shàng mǒurén

warm-blooded ADJ 温血的 [+动物] wēnxuè de [+dòngwù], 恒温的 héngwēn de

warm-hearted ADJ 热心（肠）的 rèxīn (cháng) de, 热情的 rèqíng de

warmth N **1** 温暖 wēnnuǎn, 暖和 nuǎnhuo **2** 热情友好 rèqíng yǒuhǎo

warn V 警告 jǐnggào, 提醒 tíxǐng
To be warned is to be prepared. 受到警告，就是让你做好准备。Shòudao jǐnggào, jiùshì ràng nǐ zuòhǎo zhǔnbèi.

warning N 警告 jǐnggào, 提醒 tíxǐng

warp I N 弯曲 wānqū, 变形 biànxíng II V **1**（使…）变形（shǐ...）biànxíng **2**（使…）反常（shǐ...）fǎncháng, 扭曲 niǔqū

warrant I N **1** 令 lìng, 证 zhèng
arrest warrant 逮捕证 dàibǔzhèng
search warrant 搜查证 sōucházhèng
2 充分理由 chōngfèn lǐyóu II V 提供充分理由 tígōng chōngfèn lǐyóu, 成为…的理由 chéngwéi...de lǐyóu

warranty N 保修单 bǎoxiūdān, 产品质量保证书 chǎnpǐn zhìliàng bǎozhèngshū

warren N 野兔窝 yětùwō

warrior N 战士 zhànshì, 斗士 dòushì

warship N 军舰 jūnjiàn, 战舰 zhànjiàn

wartime N 战争时期 zhànzhēng shíqī, 战时 zhànshí

wary ADJ 小心翼翼的 xiǎoxīn yìyì de, 戒备的 jièbèi de

was See be

wash I V **1** 洗xǐ
to wash one's hands of 与…脱离关系 yǔ...tuōlí guānxi, 不再参与 búzài cānyù **2** 站得住脚 zhàn dé zhù jiǎo II N **1** 洗 xǐ, 洗涤 xǐdí **2** 正在洗的衣服 zhèngzài xǐ de yīfu
to do the wash 洗衣服 xǐyī fú **3** 洗涤剂 xǐdíjì
face wash 洗面乳 xǐmiànrǔ
mouth wash 漱口（药）水 shùkǒu (yào) shuǐ

washable ADJ 可洗的 kě xǐ de, 耐洗的 nàixǐ de

washcloth N（洗脸）毛巾（xǐliǎn）máojīn

washed-out ADJ 褪色的 tuìsè de, 变白的 biànbái de

washed up ADJ 没有前途的 méiyǒu qiántú de, 彻底失败的 chèdǐ shībài de

washer, washing machine N 洗衣机 xǐyījī

washing N 洗好的衣服 xǐ hǎode yīfu
to hang the washing out to dry 把洗好的衣服挂出去晒干 bǎ xǐhǎo de yīfu guàchūqu shàigān

washroom N 洗手间 xǐshǒujiān, 厕所 cèsuǒ

wasp N 黄蜂 huángfēng

wastage N 耗费（量）hào fèi (liáng), 浪费 làngfèi

waste I V 浪费 làngfèi
Waste not, want not. 不浪费，就不会缺乏。Bú làngfèi, jiù bú huì quēfá.
II N **1** 浪费 làngfèi **2** 废料 fèiliào, 垃圾 lājī
waste water 废水 fèishuǐ
3 荒地 huāngdì, 不毛之地 bùmáo zhī dì III ADJ 废弃的 fèiqì de, 废物的 fèiwù de
waste tank 大垃圾箱 dà lājīxiāng

wasteful ADJ 浪费的 làngfèi de, 糟蹋的 zāota de

waste(paper) basket N 废纸篓 fèizhǐlǒu

watch I V **1** 看 kàn, 注视 zhùshì **2** 观看

guānkàn **3** 注意 zhùyì **II** N **1** 表 biǎo, 手表 shǒubiǎo

to watch out 留意 liúyì, 小心 xiǎoxīn

2 关注 guānzhù, 注意 zhùyì

to keep a close watch on sb/sth 密切注意某人／某事 mìqiè zhùyì mǒurén/mǒushì

3 留意 liúyì

be on the watch for sth 留意某事 liúyì mǒushì

watchdog N **1** 监督者 jiāndūzhě **2** 看门狗 kānméngǒu

watchful ADJ 提防的 dīfang de, 警戒的 jǐngjiè de

watchman N 守卫 shǒuwèi, 守门人 shǒuménrén

watchword N 口号 kǒuhào, 标语 biāoyǔ

water I N 水 shuǐ

water bottle 水瓶 shuǐpíng, 水壶 shuǐhú

water polo 水球（运动）shuǐqiú (yùndòng)

water shed 分水岭 fēnshuǐlǐng

drinking water 饮用水 yǐnyòngshuǐ

fresh water 淡水 dànshuǐ

running water 自来水 zìláishuǐ

II v **1** 浇水 jiāoshuǐ **2** 流口水 liú kǒushuǐ **3** [眼睛+] 流泪 [yǎnjing+] liú lèi **4** 给 [动物+] 饮水 gěi [dòngwù+] yǐn shuǐ

watercolor N **1** 水彩画 shuǐcǎihuà [M. WD 幅 fú] **2** 水彩颜料 shuǐcǎi yánliào

waterfall N 瀑布 pùbù

waterfront N 河／湖／海滨 hé/hú/hǎibīn

waterhole N **1**（动物饮水的）水坑 (dòngwù yǐn shuǐ de) shuǐkēng **2**（常去的）酒巴 (cháng qù de) jiǔbā

watering can N 酒水壶 sǎshuǐhú

watermark N **1**（纸上的）水印 (zhǐ shàng de) shuǐyìn **2** 水位标志 shuǐwèi biāozhì

watermelon N 西瓜 xīguā

watertight ADJ **1** 不透水的 bútòushuǐ de

a watertight compartment 水密舱 shuǐmìcāng

2 周密的 zhōumì de, 毫无破绽的 háowú pòzhàn de

a watertight argument 无懈可击的论点 wúxiè kějī de lùndiǎn

waterway N 水路 shuǐlù, 航道 hángdào

waterworks N 供水系统 gōngshuǐ xìtǒng

to turn on the waterworks（为了别人的同情）哭起来(wèile biéren de tóngqíng) kūqǐlái

watery ADJ 含水过多的 hánshuǐ guòduō de, 味淡的 wèidàn de

watt N 瓦（特）wǎ (tè)

wave I v **1** 挥手 huī shǒu, 招手 zhāo shǒu

to wave goodbye to 向…告别 xiàng… gàobié

to wave … off 挥手示意要…走开 huī shǒu shìyì yào…zǒukāi

2 挥动 huīdòng **II** N **1** 浪 làng, 波浪 bōlàng **2** 光波 guāngbō, 声波 shēngbō, 无线电波 wúxiàn diànbō

long/medium/short waves（无线电）长／中／短波 (wúxiàndiàn) cháng/zhōng/duǎnbō

3 高潮 gāocháo, 骤增 zhòuzēng

crime wave 犯罪高峰 fànzuì gāofēng, 犯罪浪潮 fànzuì làngcháo

4 攻击 gōngjībō

waves of soldiers 一波一波的士兵 yì bō yì bō de shìbīng

waveband N（无线电）波段 (wúxiàndiàn) bōduàn

wavelength N（无线电）波长 (wúxiàndiàn) bōcháng

waver v **1** 动摇 dòngyáo, 犹豫 yóuyù **2** 摇摆 yáobǎi

wavy ADJ 波浪形的 bōlàngxíng de **2** 卷曲的 [+头发] juǎnqū de [+tóufa]

wax¹ I N **1** 蜡 là **2** 耳垢 ěrgòu **II** v **1** 给 [+地板] 上蜡 gěi [+dìbǎn] shàng là **2** 以 wax eloquent/poetic) 滔滔不绝地说／诗情十足地说 tāotāo bùjué de shuō/shīqíng shízú de shuō

wax² v [月亮+] 渐渐变圆 [yuèliang+] jiànjiàn biàn yuán

waxworks N 蜡像 làxiàng

way N **1** 路 lù, 道路 dàolù **2** 边 biān, 面面 miàn **3** 办法 bànfǎ, 方法 fāngfǎ **4** 作风 zuòfēng, 态度 tàidu

way of life 生活方式 shēnghuó fāngshì

to go out of one's way 特地 tèdi

to make way 让路 rànglù

waylay (PT & PP **waylaid**) v **1**（为了讲

话）路上拦住 [+人] (wèile jiǎnghuà) lùshang lánzhù [+rén] 2 拦路抢劫 lánlù qiǎngjié

way-out ADJ 新奇古怪的 xīnqí gǔguài de, 时髦的 shímáo de

wayside N 路边 lùbiān

wayward ADJ 走入歧路的 zǒurù qílù de, 行为不良的 xíngwéi bùliáng de

WC (= water closet) ABBREV 厕所 cèsuǒ

we PRON 我们 wǒmen

weak ADJ 1 虚弱的 xūruò de 2 软弱的 ruǎnruò de
to be weak in 在…方面很弱 zài… fāngmiàn hěn ruò

weaken V （使…）变弱 (shǐ…) biàn ruò, 弱化 ruòhuà
to weaken sb's determination 动摇某人的决心 dòngyáo mǒurén de juéxīn

weakling N 身体虚弱的人 shēntǐ xūruò de rén, 没有力气的人 méiyǒu lìqi de rén

weakness N 1 虚弱 xūruò, 软弱 ruǎnruò
physical weakness 身体虚弱 shēntǐ xūruò
2 弱点 ruòdiǎn, 缺点 quēdiǎn
strengths and weaknesses 强项和弱点 qiángxiàng hé ruòdiǎn, 长处和缺点 chángchu hé quēdiǎn
3 偏爱的人／东西 piān'ài de rén/dōngxi
to have a weakness for chocolate 偏爱巧克力 piān'ài qiǎokèlì, 嗜好吃巧克力 shìhào chī qiǎokèlì

wealth N 1 财富 cáifù 2 大量 dàliàng
a wealth of information 大量信息 dàliàng xìnxī

wealthy ADJ 富有的 fùyǒu de
the wealthy 富人 fùrén

wean V 1 使 [+婴儿] 断奶 shǐ [+yīng'ér] duànnǎi 2 使 [+人] 戒瘾 [+坏习惯] shǐ [+rén] jièdiào [+huài xíguàn]
to gradually wean him off the drugs 使他逐步戒掉毒品 shǐ tā zhúbù jièdiào dúpǐn

weapon N 1 武器 wǔqì
weapons of mass destruction (WMD) 大规模杀伤性武器 dà guīmó shāshāng wǔqì
2 手段 shǒuduàn

secret weapon 秘密武器 mìmì wǔqì, 秘而不宣的手段 mì'érbùxuān de shǒuduàn

wear I V (PT **wore**; PP **worn**) 1 穿 chuān 2 戴 dài
to wear one's heart on one's sleeve 公开表露真实感情 gōngkāi biǎolù zhēnshí gǎnqíng
3 磨损 mósǔn
to wear sth out 把某事物用坏 bǎ mǒushìwù yòng huài
II N 1 服装 fúzhuāng
casual/men's/women's/children's wear 便装／男子服装／女子服装／儿童服装 biànzhuāng/nánzǐ fúzhuāng/nǚzǐ fúzhuāng/értóng fúzhuāng
2 磨损 mósǔn
wear and tear （长期使用引起的）磨损 (chángqī shǐyòng yǐnqǐ de) mósǔn

wearing ADJ 1 消耗性的 xiāohàoxìng de, 损耗的 sǔnhào de 2 让人疲倦／厌烦的 ràng rén píjuàn/yànfán de

wearisome ADJ 让人疲倦／厌烦的 ràng rén píjuàn/yànfán de

weary I ADJ 精疲力尽的 jīngpí lìjìn de
II V 使 [+人] 厌倦 shǐ [+rén] yànjuàn

weasel I N 1 黄鼠狼 huángshǔláng, 鼬 yòu 2 滑头骗子 huátóu piànzi
weasel word 滑头话 huátóuhuà
II V 狡猾地逃避责任 jiǎohuá de táobì zérèn

weather I N 天气 tiānqì
weather bureau 气象局 qìxiàngjú
weather forecast 天气预报 tiānqì yùbào
under the weather 身体不舒服 shēntǐ bù shūfú
II V 经受住 [+风暴] jīngshòu zhù [+fēngbào]

weather-beaten ADJ 饱经风霜的 bǎojīng fēngshuāng de, 经受日晒雨淋的 jīngshòu rìshàiyǔlín de

weatherman N 气象预报员 qìxiàng yùbàoyuán

weave I V 1 (PT **wove**; PP **woven**) 1 织 [+布] zhī [+bù] 2 编造 biānzào, 编织 biānzhī 3 (PT & PP **weaved**) 穿插行

进 chuānchā xíngjìn **II** N 编织（法）biānzhī (fǎ)

web N 1 网 wǎng

web of deceit 错综复杂的骗局 cuòzōng fùzá de piànjú

2 (= World Wide Web) 互联网 hùliánwǎng

web browser 互联网浏览器 hùliánwǎng liúlǎnqì

web page 网页 wǎngyè

3 （鸭子的）蹼 (yāzi de) pǔ

webbed ADJ （趾间）有蹼的 (zhǐ jiān) yǒu pǔ de

web-footed ADJ 有蹼足的 yǒu pǔzú de

website N 网址 wǎngzhǐ

wed V 1 结婚 jiéhūn **2** (be wedded to) 拘泥于 jūnì yú

wedding N 婚礼 hūnlǐ

wedding anniversary 结婚周年纪念日 jiéhūn zhōunián jìniànrì

wedding ring 结婚戒指 jiéhūn jièzhǐ

church wedding 在教堂里举行的婚礼 zài jiàotáng lǐ jǔxíng de hūnlǐ

wedge I N 1 楔子 xiēzi, 楔形物 xiēxíngwù

to drive a wedge between … and … 在…和…之间挑拨离间 zài…hé…zhījiān tiǎobō líjiàn

II V 把…挤入 bǎ…jǐrù

to wedge a door open 在门下塞东西使它开着 zài ménxià sāi dōngxi shǐ tā kāizhe

wedlock N 已婚状态 yǐhūn zhuàngtài, 婚姻 hūnyīn

Wedesday N 星期三 xīngqīsān, 周三 zhōusān

wee ADJ 一丁点儿 yìdīngdiǎnr

the wee hours 凌晨 língchén, 半夜一两点钟 bànyè yī liǎng diǎnzhōng

weed I N 1 野草 yěcǎo, 杂草 zácǎo **2** 大麻烟 dàmáyān **II** V 除草 chú cǎo

to weed out 排除 páichú, 淘汰 táotài

weedy ADJ 1 杂草丛生的 [+园子] zácǎo cóngshēng de [+yuánzi] **2** 身高而瘦弱的 shēn gāo ér shòuruò de

week N 周 zhōu, 星期 xīngqī

weekday N 工作日（星期一到星期五）gōngzuòrì (xīngqīyī dào xīngqīwǔ)

weekend N 周末 zhōumò

weekend retreat 周末休养地 zhōumò xiūyǎngdì

long weekend 长周末 cháng zhōumò

weekly I ADJ 每周的 měi zhōu de, 每星期的 měi xīngqī de **II** N 周报 zhōubào [M. WD 期/本 qī/běn], 周刊 zhōukān [M. WD 期/本 qī/běn]

weeknight N 工作日夜晚 gōngzuòrì yèwǎn

weep (PT & PP wept) V 流泪 liú lèi, 哭 kū

to weep and wail 嚎啕大哭 háotáo dàkū

weigh V 1 称重量 chēng zhòngliàng **2** 仔细考虑 zǐxì kǎolǜ

to weigh sth against sb 权衡比较 quánhéng bǐjiào

to weigh one's words 推敲用词 tuīqiāo yòng cí

to weigh anchor 起锚 qǐ máo, 启程 qǐ chéng

weight I N 1 重量 zhòngliàng **2** 体重 tǐzhòng

to gain weight 增加体重 zēngjiā tǐzhòng

3 负担 fùdān, 重担 zhòngdàn **4** 重要性 zhòngyàoxìng, 影响 yǐngxiǎng

to throw one's weight behind sth 利用某人的影响支持做某事 liyòng mǒurén de yǐngxiǎng zhīchí zuò mǒushì

5 （锻炼用的）杠铃 (duànliàn yòng de) gànglíng [M. WD 副/tào] **II** V 加重量 jiā zhòngliáng

weightless ADJ 失重的 shīzhòng de

weighty ADJ 重要的 zhòngyào de, 重大的 zhòngdà de

weird ADJ 怪异的 guàiyì de, 古怪的 gǔguài de

welcome I ADJ 受欢迎的 shòu huānyíng de **II** V 欢迎 huānyíng **III** N 欢迎 huānyíng **IV** INTERJ 欢迎 huānyíng

Welcome to Boston! 欢迎您来波士顿! Huānyíng nín lái Bōshìdùn!

weld V 1 焊接 hànjiē, 熔接 róngjiē **2** 团结 tuánjié, 拧成一股绳 níngchéng yì gǔ shéng **II** N 焊接点 hànjiēdiǎn

welfare N 1 福利 fúlì, 福祉 fúzhǐ **2** 福利救济金 fúlì jiùjìjīn

welfare state 福利国家 fúlì guójiā, 福利制度 fúlì zhìdù

well¹ I ADV 1 好 hǎo
Well done! 干得好! Gàn de hǎo! 好样的! Hǎo yàng de!
2 相当地 xiāngdāng de, 很 hěn 3 彻底地 chèdǐ de, 完全地 wánquán de II ADJ 身体好 shēntǐ hǎo, 健康 jiànkāng III INTERJ 1 好吧 hǎo ba 2 唉 ài 3 嗯 ng
as well as 也 yě
might as well 不妨 bùfāng

well² I N 井 jǐng II V (to well up) 流出 liúchū

well-advised ADJ (确实) 应该 (quèshí) yīnggāi

well-balanced ADJ 1 均衡的 jūnhéng de
well-balanced diet 营养成份均衡的饮食 yíngyǎng chéngfèn jūnhéng de yǐnshí
2 (头脑) 清醒的 [+人] (tóunǎo) qīngxǐng de [+rén], 高度理智的 gāodù lǐzhì de

well-being N 感觉良好 gǎnjué liánghǎo, 健康 jiànkāng, 幸福 xìngfú

well-bred ADJ 有教养的 yǒu jiàoyǎng de, 修养好的 xiūyǎng hǎo de

well-done ADJ 煮得熟透 zhǔde shútòu

well-earned ADJ 依靠辛勤工作挣来的 yīkào xīnqín gōngzuò zhènglái de, 理应得到的 lǐyīng dédào de

well-groomed ADJ 衣着整齐 / 讲究的 yīzhuó zhěngqí/jiǎngjiu de

well-grounded ADJ 有确凿证据的 [+想法] yǒu quèzáo zhèngjù de [+xiǎngfǎ] 2 训练有素的 [+人] xùnliàn yǒusù de [+rén]

well-informed ADJ 消息灵通的 xiāoxi língtōng de, 对…知识渊博的 duì...zhīshi yuānbó de

well-intentioned ADJ 出于好意的 chūyú hǎoyì de, 好心的 hǎoxīn de

well-known ADJ 著名的 zhùmíng de

well-meaning ADJ 本意良好的 běnyì liánghǎo de

well-off ADJ 富有的 fùyǒu de

well-read ADJ 熟读得很多的 shū dú de hěn duō de, 知识面很广的 zhīshímiàn hěn guǎng de

well-spoken ADJ 善于辞令的 shànyú cílìng de

well-thought-of ADJ 受到好评的 shòudào hǎopíng de, 受欢迎的 shòu huānyíng de

well-timed ADJ 时机合适的 shíjī héshì de, 及时的 jíshí de

well-to-do ADJ 富有的 fùyǒu de, 有相当地位的 yǒu xiāngdāng dìwèi de

well-wisher N 表示良好祝愿的人 biǎoshì liánghǎo zhùyuàn de rén, 祝福者 zhùfúzhě

well-worn ADJ 穿旧的 chuān jiùde, 用得过多的 yòng de guòduō de
a well-worn excuse 用得太多的借口 yòng de tài duō de jièkǒu

Welsh ADJ, N 威尔士语 Wēi'ěrshìyǔ, 威尔士人 Wēi'ěrshìrén

welt N 1 (被虫咬后的) 肿块 (bèi chóng yǎo hòu de) zhǒngkuài 2 (被打后的) 伤痕 (bèi dǎ hòu de) shānghén

welter N (a welter of sth) 一大堆乱七八糟的东西 / 事情 yídàduī luànqī bāzāo de dōngxi/shìqing

wench N 姑娘 gūniang, 少妇 shàofù

went See **go**

wept See **weep**

were See **be**

werewolf N 会变成狼的人 huì biànchéng láng de rén, 狼人 lángrén

west I N 1 西 (面) xī (miàn) II ADJ 1 西 xī, 西面的 xīmiàn
the West 西方 Xīfāng
2 来自西面的 láizì xīmiàn de III ADV 朝西 cháo xī, 向西 xiàng xī

westbound ADJ 向西行驶的 xiàng xī xíngshǐ de, 往西的 wǎng xī de

westerly ADV, ADJ 在西方 (地 / 的) zài xīfāng (de), 向西方 (的) xiàng xīfāng (de)
westerly wind 西风 xīfēng

western I ADJ 1 西面的 xīmiàn de, 西部的 xībù de 2 西方的 xīfāng de II N 西部电影 xībù diànyǐng
western United States 美国西部 Měiguó xībù

Westerner N 西方人 Xīfāngrén

westward ADJ, ADV 朝西方地 / 的 cháo xīfāng de

635

wet I ADJ 1 湿的 shī de, 潮湿的 cháoshī de 2 下雨的 xiàyǔ de
Wet paint. 油漆未干。Yóuqī wèi gān.
II v 1 把…弄湿 bǎ…nòngshī 2 (to wet oneself) 尿裤 niào kù, 小便失禁 xiǎobiàn shījìn

whack I v 猛击 měngjī, 重创 zhòngchuāng II N 重击声 zhòngjī shēng
out of whack [机器+] 不正常运转 [jī-qì+] bú zhèngcháng yùnzhuǎn, 坏了 huàile

whale N 鲸（鱼）jīng (yú)

whaling N 捕鲸（业）bǔjīng (yè)

wharf N 码头 mǎtou, 停泊处 tíngbóchù

what PRON 1 什么 shénme 2 多么 duōme

whatever I PRON 1 任何…的事物 rènhé…de shìwù, 随便什么 suíbiàn shénme 2 无论如何 wúlùn rúhé, 不管什么 bùguǎn shénme II ADV 任何的 rènhé de

wheat N 小麦 xiǎomài, 麦子 màizi
wheat flour 面粉 miànfěn
whole wheat (bread) 全麦面包 quán-mài miànbāo

wheedle v 哄骗 hǒngpiàn, 甜言蜜语地骗取 tiányán mìyǔ de piànqǔ

wheel I N 1 轮子 lúnzi, 车轮 chēlún 2 方向盘 fāngxiàng pán II v 1 用 [+轮椅] yòng [+lúnyǐ] 运送 yùnsòng 2 突然转过身来 tūrán zhuǎn guò shēn lái
to wheel and deal 玩弄花招 wánnòng huāzhāo, 投机取巧 tóujī qǔqiǎo

wheelchair N 轮椅 lúnyǐ

wheeze I v 发出呼哧呼哧的声音 fāchū hūchīhūchī de shēngyīn, 气喘吁吁 qìchuǎn xūxū II N 呼哧呼哧的声音 hūchīhūchī de shēngyīn

wheezy ADJ 气喘吁吁的 qìchuǎn xūxū de

when I ADV 1 什么时候 shénme shíhou 2 那时候 nàshíhou II CONJ 当…的时候 dāng…de shíhou, …的时候 …de shíhou

whence ADV 从那里 cóng nàlǐ

whenever I CONJ 1 每当 měidāng 2 无论什么时候 wúlùn shénme shíhòu II ADV 无论什么时候 wúlùn shénme shíhòu

where N I ADV 1 什么地方 shénme dìfang, 哪里 nǎlǐ 2 在那里 zài nàlǐ II CONJ 但是 dànshì, 而 ér

whereabouts I N 去向 qùxiàng, 下落 xiàluò
the whereabouts of the missing girl 失踪女孩的下落 shīzōng nǚhái de xiàluò II ADV 哪个地方 nǎge dìfang

whereas CONJ 而 ér, 然而 rán'ér

whereby ADV 由此 yóucǐ, 借以 jièyǐ

wherein ADV 在那里 zài nàlǐ, 在那方面 zài nà fāngmiàn

whereof ADV 关于那个 guānyú nàge

whereupon CONJ 即刻 jíkè, 马上 mǎshàng

wherever ADV 无论在哪里 wúlùn zài nǎli, 不论何处 búlùn héchù
wherever possible 要是有可能 yàoshi yǒu kěnéng, 只要有可能 zhǐyào yǒu kěnéng

wherewithal N (the wherewithal to do sth) 做某事的钱 zuò mǒushì de qián

whet v (to whet one's appetite) 激起某人的兴趣 jīqǐ mǒurén de xìngqù, 吊起某人的胃口 diàoqǐ mǒurén de wèikǒu

whether CONJ …还是 …háishì, …是不是 …shìbushì

whew INTERJ 哎呀 āiyā

which I PRON, ADJ 哪（个）nǎ (ge) II CONJ …的那个…的 de nàge/nàxiē

whichever ADJ, PRON 不论哪个 búlùn nǎge, 不论哪里 búlùn nǎli

whiff N 1 气味 qìwèi, 味儿 wèir 2 有一点儿 yǒu yìdiǎnr, 极少的 jí shǎo de
whiff of danger 有一点儿危险 yǒu yìdiǎnr wēixiǎn

while I CONJ 1 同时 tóngshí 2 虽然 suīrán 3 但是 dànshì, 而 ér II N 一会儿 yíhuìr
all the while 一直 yìzhí, 始终 shǐzhōng
for a while 曾经 céngjīng, 有一段时间 yǒu yí duàn shíjiān
III v (to while away the hours) 消磨时间 xiāomó shíjiān

whim N 一时的兴致 yìshí de xìngzhì, 一时的想法 yìshí de xiǎngfǎ
on a whim 一时兴起 yìshí xīngqǐ

whimper I v 呜咽 wūyè, 抽泣 chōuqì II N 呜咽声 wūyèshēng, 抽泣声 chuòqìshēng
with hardly a whimper 一声不响地 yì shēng bù xiǎng de

whimsical ADJ 离奇古怪的 líqí gǔguài de, 异想天开的 yìxiǎng tiānkāi de

whimsy N 离奇古怪 líqí gǔguài, 稀奇 xīqí

whine I v 1 哀叫 āijiào, 哭哭啼啼 kūkū títí 2 机器的隆隆声 jīqì de lónglóng shēng II N 1 哀叫声 āijiàoshēng 2 隆隆声 lónglóngshēng

whip I N 1 鞭子 biānzi [M. WD 条 tiáo] 2 政党的纪律督导员 zhèngdǎng de jìlǜ dūdǎoyuán II v 1 鞭打 biāndǎ 2 搅打 [+奶油] 使变稠 jiǎodǎ [+nǎiyóu] shǐ biàn chóu 3 迅速行进 xùnsù xíngjìn
to whip up 煽动起 shāndòngqǐ, 激起 jīqǐ

whipping N 鞭刑 biānxíng, 鞭笞 biānchī
whipping cream 搅奶油 guànnǎiyóu

whirl v 1 （使…）迅速旋转 (shǐ….) xùnsù xuánzhuǎn 2 [头+] 眩晕 [tóu+] xuànyūn

whirlpool N 漩涡 xuánwō 2 漩涡式浴缸 xuánwōshì yùgāng

whisk I v 搅拌 jiǎobàn
to whisk away 将 [+人] 迅速带走 jiāng [+rén] xùnsù dàizǒu II N 搅拌器 jiǎobànqì

whisker N 1 （男人的）连鬓胡子 (nánren de) liánbìn húzi, 髯 rán 2 （猫／老虎的）须 (māo/lǎohǔ de) xū [M. WD 根 gēn]

whisky N 威士忌（酒）wēishìjì (jiǔ)

whisper I v 耳语 ěryǔ, 说悄悄话 shuō qiāoqiāohuà II N 耳语 ěryǔ, 悄悄话 qiāoqiāohuà

whistle I v 1 吹口哨 chuī kǒushào 2 吹哨子 chuī shàozi II N 哨子 shàozi

whistle-blower N （内部）告发者 (nèibù) gàofāzhě, 揭露（公司／机构）内部非法行为的人 jiēlù (gōngsī/jīgòu) nèibù fēifǎ xíngwéi de rén

whistle-stop N （火车）小站 (huǒchē) xiǎo zhàn, 小镇 xiǎo zhèn
whistle-stop tour 沿途逗留很多地方的旅行 yántú dòuliú hěn duō dìfang de lǚxíng

white I ADJ 1 白色的 báisè de
white blood cell 白血球 báixuèqiú
white bread 白面包 bái miànbāo
white Christmas 下雪的圣诞节 xiàxuě de Shèngdànjié

white elephant 贵重而无用的东西 guìzhòng ér wúyòng de dōngxi

white paper 白皮书 báipíshū

white pollution 噪音污染 zàoyīn wūrǎn

white slavery 拐卖妇女到异国卖淫 guǎimài fùnǚ dào yìguó màiyín

white trash 白人垃圾 báirén lājī, 贫穷无知的白人 pínqióng wúzhī de báirén 2 白种人的 báizhǒngrén de

white supremacy 白种人优越感 báizhǒngrén yōuyuègǎn
II N 1 白（颜）色 bái (yán) sè
White House（美国）白宫 (Měiguó) Báigōng
white lie 善意的谎言 shànyì de huǎngyán
2 白人 báirén, 白种人 báizhǒngrén 3 眼白 yǎnbái 4 蛋白 dànbái 5 白（葡萄）酒 bái (pútao) jiǔ

whiteboard N 白板 báibǎn

white-collar ADJ 白领阶层的 báilǐng jiēcéng de
white-collar crime 白领罪行 báilǐng zuìxíng

whiten v （使…）变白 (shǐ…) biànbái

whitepepper N 白胡椒粉 bái hújiāofěn

whitewash I v 1 用石灰水刷刷 [+墙壁] yòng shíhuǐshuǐ fěnshuā [+qiángbì] 2 掩饰 [+真相] yǎnshì [+zhēnxiàng], 粉饰 fěnshì II N 1 石灰水 shíhuǐshuǐ 2 掩饰真相 yǎnshì zhēnxiàng, 遮掩丑闻 zhēyǎn chǒuwén

whither CONJ, ADV 向何处去 xiàng héchù qù

whittle v （使…）逐渐减少 (shǐ…) zhújiàn jiǎnshǎo
to whittle away 削弱 xuēruò, 减弱 jiǎnruò

whiz¹ v 飕飕飞驰 sōusōu fēichí

whiz² N 1 奇才 qícái, 高手 gāoshǒu
whiz kid 神童 shéntóng
2 (to take a whiz) 撒尿 sāniào

WHO (= World Health Organization) ABBREV 世界卫生组织 Shìjiè Wèishēng Zǔzhī

who I PRON 谁 shéi
who's who of sth 某一方面的名人大全

637

mǒu yì fāngmiàn de míngrén dàquán, 某一方面所有的名人 mǒu yì fāngmiàn suǒyǒu de míngrén
II CONJ …的那个／那些人 …de nàge／nàxiē rén

whoever PRON 无论谁 wúlùn shéi, 不管什么人 bùguǎn shénmérén

whole ADJ **1** 整个的 zhěng ge de, 全部的 quánbù de
in the whole wide world 全世界 quán shìjiè, 这个世界上 zhège shìjièshang **2** 完整的 wánzhěng de
whole mushroom 完整的蘑菇 wánzhěng de mógu, 整个蘑菇 zhěnggè mógu **II** N 整体 zhěngtǐ, 全部 quánbù
on the whole 总的来说 zǒng de lái shuō, 整体上 zhěngtǐ shàng

whole-hearted ADJ 全心全意的 quánxīn quányì de, 全力以赴的 quánlì yǐfù de

wholesale I N 批发 pīfā II ADJ 批发的 pīfā de
wholesale price 批发价 pīfājià

wholesaler N 批发商 pīfāshāng, 批发公司 pīfā gōngsī

wholesome ADJ **1** 有利于健康的 yǒulì yú jiànkāng de **2** 有益于道德的 yǒuyì yú dàodé de

wholly ADV 完全（地）wánquán (de), 彻底（地）chèdǐ (de)

whom PRON 谁 shéi

whore N 妓女 jìnǚ, 婊子 biǎozi

whose ADJ, PRON 谁的 shéi de

why I ADV 为什么 wèishénme II N (the whys and wherefores) 原因 yuányīn, 理由 lǐyóu

wick N 蜡烛芯 làzhúxīn [M. WD 根 gēn]

wicked ADJ **1** 不讲道德的 bù jiǎng dàodé de, 有坏心思的 yǒu huài xīnsī de **2** 淘气的 táoqì de, 调皮的 tiáopí de

wicker I N 干枝条 gān zhītiáo, 藤条 téngtiáo [M. WD 根 gēn] II ADJ 干枝条编的 gān zhītiáo biān de, 藤条编的 téngtiáo biān de
wicker chair 枝编椅子 zhī biān yǐzi

wide ADJ **1** 宽的 kuān de, 宽阔的 kuānkuò de **2** 广泛的 guǎngfàn de, 范围很大的 fànwéi hěn dà de

a wide variety 品种多样 pǐnzhǒng duōyàng **3** 远离的 yuǎnlí de
wide off the mark 远离目标 yuǎnlí mùbiāo, 离目标很远 lí mùbiāo hěn yuǎn

widely ADV 广泛地 guǎngfàn de, 普遍地 pǔbiàn de

widen V **1** (使…) 变宽 (shǐ…) biàn kuān, [眼睛+] 睁大 [yǎnjing+] zhēngdà **2** (使…) 增大 (shǐ…) zēngdà

widespread ADJ 广泛的 guǎngfàn de, 分布很广的 fēnbù hěn guǎng de
the widespread use of the cellphone 手机的广泛使用 shǒujī de guǎngfàn shǐyòng

widow N 寡妇 guǎfu, 遗孀 yíshuāng

widower N 鳏夫 guānfū

width N 宽度 kuāndù

wield V **1** 挥动 huīdòng [+工具 +gōngjù], 挥舞 huīwǔ **2** 施展 shīzhǎn [+影响／权力 +yǐngxiǎng/quánlì]

wife N 妻子 qīzi, 太太 tàitai

wig N 假（头）发 jiǎ (tóu) fà

wiggle V 扭动 niǔdòng, 摆动 bǎidòng

wild I ADJ **1** 野的 yě de, 野生的 yěshēng de **2** 感情奔放的 gǎnqíng bēnfàng de, 不受拘束的 bú shòu jūshù de
to be wild about 对…狂热 duì… kuángrè **3** 不同寻常的 bù tóng xúncháng de
wild card 不定因素 búdìng yīnsù, 捉摸不定的人／事 zhuōmo bú dìng de rén／shì
wild guess 乱猜 luàncāi, 瞎猜 xiācāi **4** 荒野的 huāngyě de, 荒芜的 huāngwú de II N (the wilds) 荒无人烟的地方 huāngwú rényān de dìfang, 荒原 huāngyuán

wildcat I N 野猫 yěmāo II ADJ 冒险的 màoxiǎn de, 靠不住的 kàobuzhù de
wildcat strike（未经工会批准的）自发罢工 (wèijīng gōnghuì pīzhǔn de) zìfā bàgōng

wilderness N 荒无人烟的地方 huāngwú rényān de dìfang, 荒原 huāngyuán

wildfire N 野火 yěhuǒ, 凶猛的（森林）大火 xiōngměng de (sēnlín) dàhuǒ

wildfowl N 野禽 yěqín

wild-goose chase N 白费力气的努力 báifèi lìqì de nǔlì

wildlife N 野生动物 yěshēng dòngwù

wildly ADV 疯狂地 fēngkuáng de

wiles N 花言巧语 huāyánqiǎoyǔ, 巧计 qiǎojì

will I MODAL V (PT would) [NEG will not ABBREV won't] 1 会 huì, 将要 jiāngyào 2 愿 yuàn, 愿意 yuànyì II N 1 意志 yìzhì Where there is a will, there is a way. 有志者事竟成。Yǒuzhìzhě shì jìng chéng. 2 遗嘱 yízhǔ

willful ADJ 任性的 rènxìng de, 一意孤行的 yíyì gūxíng de

willing ADJ 愿意 yuànyì

willow N 柳（树）liǔ (shù) [M. WD 棵 kē]

willpower N 意志力 yìzhìlì, 克制力 kèzhìlì

wily ADJ 狡猾的 jiǎohuá de, 会玩花招的 huì wán huāzhāo de

wimp N 1 懦弱的人 nuòruò de rén, 无用的人 wúyòng de rén 2 瘦弱的人 shòuruò de rén

win I V (PT & PP won) 赢（得）yíng (dé) 2 获得 huòdé, 取得 qǔdé to win sb's heart 获得某人的爱情 huòdé mǒurén de àiqíng II N（体育比赛）获胜 (tǐyù bǐsài) huòshèng, 赢 yíng

wince V, N 皱眉头 zhòu méitou, 倒吸一口气 dǎo xī yì kǒu qì to wince at 感到不自在 gǎndào bú zìzài

winch I N 绞车 jiǎochē, 吊车 diàochē II V（用吊车）提起来 (yòng diàochē) tíqǐ lái

wind[1] N 风 fēng The wind of change 变革的趋势 biàngé de qūshì wind chime 风铃 fēnglíng wind turbine 风力发电机 fēnglì fādiànjī to get wind of 听到…的风声 tīngdào... de fēngshēng to take the wind out of sb's sails 使某人丧失信心 shǐ mǒurén sàngshī xìnxīn

wind[2] (PT & PP wound) V 1 缠绕 chánrǎo 2 给 [+钟表] 上发条 gěi [+zhōngbiǎo] shàng fātiáo

to wind down（使…）平静下来 (shǐ...) píngjìng xiàlai to wind up（以…）告终 (yǐ...) gàozhōng, 结束 jiéshù 3 曲折 qūzhé, 迤逦 wēiyí

windbag N 喋喋不休的人 diédié bùxiū de rén

windbreaker N 风衣 fēngyī [M. WD 件 jiàn]

windfall N 意外之财 yìwàizhīcái, 意外收益 yìwài shōuyì

wind instrument N 管乐器 guǎnyuèqì

windmill N 风车 fēngchē [M. WD 座 zuò]

window N 1 窗子 chuāngzi, 窗户 chuānghu 2 橱窗 chúchuāng window dressing ①（商店）橱窗布置 (shāngdiàn) chūchuāng bùzhì ②装饰门面 zhuāngshì ménmian, 弄虚作假 nòngxū zuòjiǎ window shopping 浏览商店橱窗 liúlǎn shāngdiàn chúchuāng, 逛街 guàngjiē 3（计算机）窗口 (jìsuànjī) chuāngkǒu

windowpane N 窗玻璃 chuāng bōli

windpipe N 气管 qìguǎn

windshield N（汽车／摩托车）挡风玻璃 (qìchē/mótuōchē) dǎngfēng bōli, 挡风窗 dǎngfēngchuāng windshield wiper 雨刷 yǔshuā

windsock N 风向标 fēngxiàngbiāo, 风向袋 fēngxiàngdài

windswept ADJ 1 强风席卷的 [+平原] qiángfēng xíjuǎn de [+píngyuán] 2 被风吹乱的 [+头发] bèi fēng chuī luàn de [+tóufa]

windy ADJ 风大的 fēng dà de, 多风的 duō fēng de

wine N 酒 jiǔ, 葡萄酒 pútaojiǔ wine bar 酒巴 jiǔbā wine cellar 酒窖 jiǔjiào wine tasting 品酒 pǐn jiǔ wine vinegar 酒醋 jiǔ cù

wing I N 1 翅膀 chìbǎng 2（飞机）机翼 (fēijī) jīyì 3（大楼）侧翼 (dàlóu) cèyì, 侧厅 cè tīng 4（政党中的）派系 (zhèngdǎng zhòngde) pàixì left/right wing 左／右翼 zuǒ/yòuyì to take sb under one's wing 保护某人 bǎohù mǒurén

to take wings 开始起飞 kāishǐ qǐfēi, 很快发展壮大 hěn kuài fāzhǎn zhuàngdà
II v 1 飞行 fēixíng, 飞翔 fēixiáng **2** (to wing it) 临时凑成 línshí còuchéng
wings N (舞台的) 侧面 (wǔtái de) cèmiàn

wingspan N 翼幅 yìfú

wink V, N 1 眨眼 (示意) zhǎyǎn (shìyì)
to wink at 睁一眼闭一眼 zhēng yì yǎn bì yì yǎn, 假装没有看到 jiǎzhuāng méiyǒu kàndào
not to sleep a wink 一点都没有睡着 yìdiǎn dōu méiyǒu shuìzháo
2 [灯光+] 闪烁 [dēngguāng+] shǎnshuò

winner N 1 获胜者 huòshèngzhě **2** 获奖者 huòjiǎngzhě

winning ADJ 1 获胜的 huòshèng de
winning score 获胜的得分 huòshèng de défēn
winning team 获胜的 (球) 队 huòshèng de (qiú) duì
2 赢得好感的 yíngdé hǎo gǎn de, 迷人的 mírén de
a winning smile 迷人的微笑 mírén de wēixiào

winnings N 赢得的钱 yíngdé de qián [M. WD 笔 bǐ]

winnow V 筛选 shāixuǎn
to winnow out 剔去 tiqù, 去掉 qùdiào

winsome ADJ 赢得人心的 yíngdé rénxīn de, 令人喜欢的 lìngrénxǐhuan de

winter I N 冬天 dōngtiān, 冬季 dōngjì
Winter Olympics 冬季奥林匹克运动会 Dōngjì Àolínpǐkè Yùndònghuì
winter solstice 冬至 dōngzhì
II v 过冬 (天) guòdōng (tiān)

wintergreen N 冬青树 dōngqīngshù

wintertime N 冬天 dōngtiān, 冬季 dōngjì

wintry ADJ 寒冬似的 hándōng shìde, 冬天的 dōngtiān de

wipe I v 擦 cā, 揩 kāi
to wipe the floor with sb 彻底打败某人 chèdǐ dǎbài mǒurén
to wipe the slate clean 把以往一笔勾销 bǎ yǐwǎng yì bǐ gōuxiāo, 忘掉过去 (的不愉快) wàngdiào guòqù (de bù yúkuài)

II N 1 擦 cā, 揩 kāi 2 (一次性) 抹布 (yícìxìng) mābù

wiper N See windshield

wire I N 1 金属线 jīnshǔxiàn, 铅丝 qiānsī **2** 电线 diànxiàn
wire transfer 电子转账 diànzǐ zhuǎnzhàng
II v 1 接电线 jiē diànxiàn, 接通电源 jiētōng diànyuán **2** 电汇 (钱) diànhuì (qián)
to get wired up 极其兴奋 jíqí xīngfèn

wiretap V (在电话线上) 搭线窃听 (zài diànhuàxiàn shàng) dāxiàn qiètīng

wiring N (供电) 线路 (gōngdiàn) xiànlù

wiry ADJ 1 瘦而结实的 (人) shòu ér jiēshí de (rén) 2 硬而卷曲的 (头发) yìng ér juǎnqū (de tóufa)

wisdom N 智慧 zhìhuì
wit and wisdom 风趣的智慧 fēngqù de zhìhui
with the wisdom of hindsight 以事后之明 yǐ shìhòu zhī míng, 当事后诸葛亮 dāng shìhòu Zhūgě Liàng (→ to be as wise as the legendary Zhuge Liang)

wise I ADJ 明智的 míngzhì de, 智慧的 zhìhuì de
wise guy 自作聪明的讨厌家伙 zì zuò cōngmíng de tǎoyàn jiāhuo
II v (to wise up) 明白过来 míngbai guòlai, 醒悟 xǐngwù

wisecrack N 俏皮话 qiàopíhuà, 风凉话 fēngliánghuà

wish I v 1 想要 xiǎngyào **2** 但愿 dànyuàn **3** 祝愿 zhùyuàn, 祝愿 zhùyuàn II N 愿望 yuànwàng

wishywashy ADJ 1 优柔寡断的 yōuróuguǎduàn de **2** 淡的 [+颜色] dàn de [+yánsè]

wisp N 一小把 yì xiǎo bǎ, 一缕 yì lǚ
a wisp of hair 一缕头发 yì lǚ tóufa
a wisp of smoke 一缕轻烟 yì lǚ qīngyān

wistful ADJ 渴望的 kěwàng de, 忧愁的 yōuchóu de

wit N 1 风趣 fēngqù
quick wit 急智 jízhì, 风趣迅速应对的能力 fēngqù xùnsù yìngduì de nénglì
2 说话风趣的人 shuōhuà fēngqù de rén
3 机智 jīzhì

to be at one's wit's end 束手无策 shùshǒu wú cè, 一点办法都没有了 yìdiǎn bànfǎ dōu méiyǒu le

to gather one's wits 镇定下来 zhèndìng xiàlai, 别慌张 bié huāngzhāng

witch N 巫婆 wūpó, 妖婆 yāopó

witchcraft N 巫术 wūshù, 妖法 yāofǎ

witchdoctor N 巫医 wūyī

witch-hunt N 迫害 pòhài

with PREP **1** 和…在一起 hé…zài yìqǐ **2** 有 yǒu, 具有 jùyǒu **3** 带 dài, 带有 dàiyǒu **4** 在…一边 zài…yì biān

withdraw v **1** 撤回 chèhuí, 收回 shōuhuí **2** 提取（钱）tíqǔ (qián) **3** 撤退 chètuì **4** 退出 [+比赛] tuìchū [+bǐsài]

withdrawal N **1** 提款（额）tíkuǎn (é) **2**（军队）撤退 (jūnduì) chètuì **3** 退出 tuìchū **4** 戒毒 jiè dú, 脱瘾 tuō yǐn

withdrawn ADJ 不与人交往的 bù yǔ rén jiāowǎng de, 沉默寡言的 chénmò guǎyán de

wither v 枯萎 kūwěi, 干枯 gānkū

to wither and die 渐渐衰弱直至死亡 jiànjiàn shuāiruò zhízhì sǐwáng

withering ADJ 咄咄逼人的 duōduō bīrén de, 尖刻的 jiānkè de

withhold v 拒绝给予 jùjué jǐyǔ

to withhold evidence from the police 对警方隐瞒证据 duì jǐngfāng yǐnmán zhèngjù

within PREP, ADV 在…之内 zài…zhīnèi

from within 在内部 zài nèibù

without PREP 没有 méiyǒu

without a doubt 毫无疑问 háo wú yíwèn

without fail 一定 yídìng

withstand v 经受（住）jīngshòu (zhù), 忍耐 rěnnài

to withstand the test of time 经受了时间的考验 jīngshòule shíjiān de kǎoyàn

witness I N 证人 zhèngrén, 见证人 jiànzhèngrén

witness stand 证人席 zhèngrénxí

to bear witness to 证明 zhèngmíng

II v（亲眼）目睹 (qīnyǎn) mùdǔ, 亲历 qīnlì

witty ADJ 风趣的 fēngqù de, 妙趣横生的 miàoqù héngshēng de

wizard N 奇才 qícái, 怪才 guài cái

computer wizard 电脑奇才 diànnǎo qícái

wizened ADJ 干瘪的 gānbiě de, 干瘦的 gānshòu de

wobbly ADJ 摇摆的 yáobǎi de, 颤动的 chàndòng de

woe N 灾难 zāinàn, 痛苦 tòngkǔ

woebegone ADJ 愁苦的 chóukǔ de, 愁眉苦脸的 chóuméi kǔliǎn de

woeful ADJ 糟透的 zāotòu de, 极坏的 jí huài de

wok N（中国式的）炒菜锅 (Zhōngguó shì de) chǎocàiguō

woke See wake¹

woken See wake¹

wolf N 狼 láng [M. WD 条 tiáo/只 zhī] II v (to wolf down) 狼吞虎咽地吃 lángtūn hǔyàn de chī

woman (PL **women**) N 女人 nǚrén, 妇女 fùnǚ

womanizer N 玩弄女性的人 wánnòng nǚxìng de rén, 好色鬼 hàosèguǐ

womanly ADJ 有女性特征的 yǒu nǚxìng tèzhēng de, 有女人气质的 yǒu nǚrén qìzhì de

womb N 子宫 zǐgōng

won See win

wonder I v **1** 想知道 xiǎng zhīdào, 疑惑 yíhuò **2** 怀疑 huáiyí, 不相信 bù xiāngxìn **3** 询问 qīngwèn II N **1** 惊奇 jīngqí **2** 奇迹 qíjì

the Seven Wonders of the World 世界七大奇迹 shìjiè qī dà qíjī

seven days/nineteen days wonder 不能维持的好事 bùnéng wéichí de hǎoshì, 昙花一现 tánhuā yíxiàn

III ADJ 奇异的 qíyì de, 效果特好的 xiàoguǒ tè hǎo de

wonderful ADJ **1** 极好的 jí hǎo de, 极妙的 jí miào de **2** 精彩的 jīngcǎi de

won't See will

woo v 追求 zhuīqiú, 讨好 tǎohǎo

wood N 木（头）mù (tou)

woodcutter N 伐木工人 fámù gōngrén, 伐木者 fámùzhě

wooded ADJ 长满树木的 zhǎngmǎn

shùmù de, 树木茂盛的 shùmù màoshèng de

wooden ADJ **1** 木头的 mùtou de, 木制
的 mùzhì de **2** 呆板的 [+人] dāibǎn de
[+人], 木纳的 [+人] mù nà de [+人]

woodpecker N 啄木鸟 zhuómùniǎo

woods N 树林 shùlín, 林地 líndì
not out of the woods 还没有脱离困境
hái méiyǒu tuōlí kùnjìng

woodwork N 木建部份 mùjiàn bùfen

woody ADJ 木质的 mùzhì de, 木头的
mùtou de

woof INTERJ 狗汪汪叫 gǒu wāngwāng jiào

wool N 羊毛 yángmáo
wool carpet 羊毛地毯 yángmáodìtǎn
to pull the wool over sb's eyes 蒙骗某
人 mēngpiàn mǒurén

woolens N 针织毛衣 zhēnzhī máoyī, 毛料
衣服 máoliào yīfu

woolly ADJ 象羊毛一样的 xiàng yángmáo
yíyàng de

woozy ADJ 虚弱的 xūruò de, 眩晕的
xuànyūn de

word I N **1** 词 cí, 词语 cíyǔ, 字 zì
word processor（计算机）文字处理软
件 (jìsuànjī) wénzì chǔlǐ ruǎnjiàn
2 话 huà, 话语 huàyǔ
swear/dirty word 脏话 zānghuà, 骂人
话 màrénhuà
to have the final word 最后决定 zuìhòu
juédìng, 拍板 pāibǎn
to put in a good word for 为…说好话
wèi...shuō hǎohuà
3 谈话 tánhuà **4** 消息 xiāoxi **5** 承诺
chéngnuò, 保证 bǎozhèng
a man of his word 讲信用的人 jiǎng
xìnyòng de rén
on my word 以名誉担保 yǐ míngyù
dānbǎo
II v 斟词酌句地表达 zhēn cí zhuó jù de
biǎodá

wording N 措词用语 cuòcí yòngyǔ

wordy ADJ 话太多的 huà tài duō de, 唠叨
的 láodao de

wore See **wear**

work I v **1** 工作 gōngzuò **2** 运转 yùnzhuǎn
to work out 算出来 suànchūlái

3 行得通 xíngdetōng II N **1** 工作
gōngzuò, 职业 zhíyè
work clothes 工作服 gōngzuòfú
2 著作 zhùzuò, 作品 zuòpǐn

workaholic N 工作狂 gōngzuòkuáng

workday N 工作日 gōngzuòrì

worker N 工人 gōngrén, 工作者
gōngzuòzhě

workforce N 劳动人口 láodòng rénkǒu,
劳动力 láodònglì

working ADJ **1** 劳动的 láodòng de, 工作的
gōngzuò de
working class 工人阶级 gōngrén jiējí
working girl 年轻职业妇女 niánqīng
zhíyè fùnǚ, 妓女 jìnǚ
2 为了工作的 wèile gōngzuò de
working breakfast/lunch 工作早餐／午
餐 gōngzuò zǎocān/wǔcān
a working definition 可以使用的定义
kěyǐ shǐyòng de dìngyì
a working knowledge of 能对付工作的
néng duìfu gōngzuò de, 足够的 zúgòu
de

workings N（组织／系统的）运行方式
(zǔzhī/xìtǒng de) yùnxíng fāngshì

workload N 工作量 gōngzuòliàng

workman N 工匠 gōngjiàng, 工人
gōngrén

workmanship N 工艺 gōngyì, 手艺 shǒuyì

workout N 锻炼（时间）duànliàn (shíjiān),（赛前）训练 (sài qián) xùnliàn

workplace N 工作场所 gōngzuò
chǎngsuǒ

workroom N 工作室 gōngzuòshì, 工作坊
gōngzuò fāng

works N 工厂 gōngchǎng

worksheet N 活页练习题 huóyè liànxítí,
工作单 gōngzuòdān

workshop N 车间 chējiān, 工场
gōngchǎng

workstation N 工作区 gōngzuòqū

world I N **1** 世界 shìjiè
the Third World 第三世界 Dìsān Shìjiè
in the world ① 世界上 shìjièshang
② 到底 dàodǐ
2 领域 lǐngyù, 界 jiè
financial world 金融界 jīnróngjiè

3 人类（社会）rénlèi (shèhuì)

way of the world 世故人情 shìgù rénqíng

world-class ADJ 世界一流水平的 shìjiè yīliú shuǐpíng de, 世界级的 shìjièjí de

world-class artist 世界级艺术家 shìjièjí yìshùjiā

worldly ADJ **1** 老于世故的 lǎoyú shìgùde, 社会经验丰富的 shèhuì jīngyàn fēngfù de **2** 世俗的 shìsú de, 尘世间的 chénshì jiān de

all the worldly possessions 某人的全部家当 mǒurén de quánbù jiādang

World Series N 世界职业棒球竞标赛 Shìjiè Zhíyè Bàngqiú Jìngbiāosài

worldwide ADJ 世界范围的 shìjiè fànwéi-de, 全世界的 quánshìjiè de

World Wide Web (ABBREV **WWW**) N 互联网 hùliánwǎng

worm I N **1** 蠕虫 rúchóng [M. WD 条 tiáo] **2** 寄生虫 jìshēngchóng [M. WD 条 tiáo] II v 象虫子一样蠕动 xiàng chóngzi yíyàng rúdòng

to worm one's way into sb's confidence 渐渐骗取某人的信任 jiànjiàn piànqǔ mǒurén de xìnrèn

worn[1] See **wear**

worn[2] ADJ **1** 用得很破旧的 yòng de hěn pòjiù de, 破损的 pòsǔn de **2** 疲倦的 píjuàn de

worn-out ADJ **1** 穿破了的 [+衣服] chuān-pò le de [+yīfu] **2** 精疲力竭的 [+人] jīngpí lìjié de [+rén]

worried ADJ 担心的 dānxīn de, 担忧的 dānyōu de

worry I v 担忧 dānyōu, 担心 dānxīn II N **1** 担忧 dānyōu, 忧愁 yōuchóu **2** 让人担忧的事 ràng rén dānyōu de shì

worrywart N （总是）忧心忡忡的人 (zǒngshì) yōuxīn chōngchōng de rén

worse I ADJ, ADV 比较坏 bǐjiào huài, 更坏 gèng huài

to go from bad to worse 越来越坏 yuèláiyuè huài, 越来越糟 yuèláiyuè zāo II N 更坏的事 gèng huài de shì

to take a turn for the worse 变得更坏 biàn de gèng huài, 恶化 èhuà

worsen v 更坏 gèng huài, 恶化 èhuà

worship I N **1** 敬奉上帝／神 jìngfèng Shàngdì/shén

house of worship 敬奉上帝／神的场所 jìngfèng Shàngdì/shén de chǎngsuǒ, （佛教）庙宇 (Fójiào) miàoyǔ, （基督教）教堂 (Jīdūjiào) jiàotáng, （穆斯林）清真寺 (Mùsīlín) qīngzhēnsì **2** 崇拜 chóngbài II v **1** 敬奉 [+上帝] jìng-fèng [+Shàngdì], 拜 [+神] bài [+shén] **2** 崇拜 [+人] chóngbài [+rén], 敬仰 jìngyǎng

worst I ADJ, ADV 最坏 zuì huài

at worst 最坏 zuì huài, 最坏的情况 zuì huài de qíngkuàng

II N 最坏的人／事 zuì huài de rén/shì

when/if worst comes to worst 万一发生最坏的情况 wànyī fāshēng zuì huài de qíngkuàng

worth I ADJ 值得 zhídé

An ounce of prevention is worth a pound of cure. 一两预防值得一磅治疗。（→ 预防为主。）Yì liǎng yùfáng zhídé yí bàng zhìliáo. (→ Yùfáng wéi zhǔ.)

II N 价值 jiàzhí

worthless ADJ 没有价值的 méiyǒu jiàzhí de, 没用的 méi yòng de

worthwhile ADJ 值得花时间／金钱／精力 zhídé huā shíjiān/jīnqián/jīnglì, 合算的 hésuàn de

worthy ADJ 值得尊敬的 zhídé zūnjìng de

be worthy of consideration 值得考虑的 zhídé kǎolǜ de

would MODEL V (PT of **will**) [NEG **would not** ABBREV **wouldn't**]

wound[1] I N 伤 shāng, 伤口 shāngkǒu II v **1** 使…受伤 shǐ...shòushāng **2** 伤害 shānghài

wound[2] v See **wind**[2]

wove See **weave**

woven See **weave**

wow INTERJ 哇 wā, 呀 yā

wrangle v, N 争吵 zhēngchǎo, 吵架 chǎojià

wrap I v 裹 bāo, 包裹 bāoguǒ

to wrap up 结束 jiéshù

II N 1 塑料保鲜膜 sùliào bǎoxiān mó 2 披肩 pījiān 3 三明治卷 sānmíngzhì juàn

wrath N 愤怒 fènnù, 震怒 zhènnù

wrathful ADJ 愤怒的 fènnù de, 大怒的 dà nù de

wreak V (to wreak havoc) 造成巨大破坏 zàochéng jùdà pòhuài

to wreak vengeance on sb 对某人狠狠报复 duì mǒurén hěnhěn bàofu

wreath N 花环 huāhuán, 花圈 huāquān

wreck I V 毁坏 huǐhuài, 毁掉 huǐdiào

II N 1 毁坏 huǐhuài, 破灭 pòmiè 2 失事船只／飞机的残骸 shīshì chuánzhī/fēijī de cánhái 3 快要精神崩溃的人 kuàiyào jīngshén bēngkuì de rén

wreckage N 1 毁坏 huǐhuài, 破坏 pòhuài 2 飞机／船只／建筑物被毁后的残骸 fēijī/chuánzhī/jiànzhùwù bèi huǐ hòu de cánhái

wrench I V 1 挣脱 zhèngtuō 2 扭伤 niǔshāng **II** N 1 扳手 bānshǒu [M. WD 把 bǎ]

to throw a wrench in sth 对某事捣乱 duì mǒushì dǎoluàn, 破坏某事 pòhuài mǒushì

2 悲痛 bēitòng, 悲伤 bēishāng 3 扭伤 niǔshāng

wrest V 1 抢夺 qiǎngduó, 猛拧 měng nǐng 2 夺取 duóqǔ, 夺得 duódé

wrestle V 摔跤 shuāijiāo, 扭打 niǔdǎ

to wrestle with ① 与…扭打 yǔ…niǔdǎ ② 费劲得搬 fèijìn dé bān

wrestling N 摔跤（运动）shuāijiāo (yùndòng)

wretch N 讨厌鬼 tǎoyànguǐ, 淘气鬼 táoqìguǐ

poor wretch 可怜的人 kělián de rén

wriggle V 蠕动 rúdòng, 扭动 niǔdòng

to wriggle out of sth 找借口逃避 zhǎo jièkǒu táobì, 找借口脱身 zhǎo jièkǒu tuōshēn

wring (PT & PP wrung) V 把…拧干 bǎ…nínggàn

to wring one's hands 搓着手（表示焦虑）cuōzhe shǒu (biǎoshì jiāolǜ)

to wring sb's neck 对某人发烦恼 duì mǒurén fā fánnǎo

wrinkle I N 1 （皮肤的）皱纹 (pífū de)

zhòuwén 2 （衣服）皱褶 (yīfu) zhòu zhě

to iron out the wrinkles 解决一些小问题 jiějué yìxiē xiǎo wèntí

II V 起皱纹 qǐ zhòuwén

to wrinkle one's nose 皱起鼻子 zhòu qǐ bízi

wrist N 手腕 shǒuwàn

wristband N 护腕 hùwàn, 腕带 wàndài

wristwatch N 手表 shǒubiǎo [M. WD 块 kuài/只 zhī]

writ N （法院的）令状 (fǎyuàn de) lìngzhuàng

write V (PT wrote; PP written) 1 写 xiě 2 写信 xiě xìn

to write off 注销 [+坏账] zhùxiāo [+huài zhàng], 一笔勾销 yì bǐ gòuxiāo 3 开 [+支票] kāi [+zhīpiào]

to write out 详细写出 [+清单] xiángxì xiěchū [+qīngdān]

write-off N 注销 zhùxiāo, 勾销 gōuxiāo

writer N 1 作家 zuòjiā 2 会写作的人 huì xiězuò de rén

write-up N （报纸的）评论文章 (bàozhǐ de) pínglùn wénzhāng

writhe V 扭动 niǔdòng

to writhe in pain 痛得打滚 tòng de dǎgǔn

writing N 1 书写 shūxiě, 写作 xiězuò 2 笔迹 bǐjì 3 著作 zhùzuò

written I See write **II** ADJ 书面（的）shūmiàn (de)

wrong I ADJ 1 错的 cuò de, 错误的 cuòwù de 2 不合适的 bùhéshì de

to be on the wrong track 思路不对 sīlù bú duì, 路子不对 lùzi bú duì

to get on the wrong side of sb 冒犯某人 màofàn mǒurén

II ADV 错 cuò

to go wrong 出错 chūcuò, 弄错 nòngcuò

III N 1 错误 cuòwù

to be in the wrong 犯错误 fàn cuòwù 2 冤屈 yuānqū **IV** V 不公正地对待 bù gōngzhèng de duìdài, 冤枉 yuānwang

wrongdoing N 违法的事 wéifǎ de shì, 错事 cuò shì

wrongful ADJ 不公正的 bù gōngzhèng de, 非法的 fēifǎ de

644

a wrongful death 由他人非法造成的死亡 yóu tārén fēifǎ zàochéng de sǐwáng

wrote See **write**

wrung See **wring**

wry ADJ 嘲笑的 cháoxiào de, 露出怪相的 lòuchu guàixiàng de
a wry smile 嘲弄的微笑 cháonòng de wēixiào, 苦笑 kǔxiào

WTO (= World Trade Organization) AB-BREV 世界贸易组织 Shìjiè Màoyì Zǔzhī

www see **World Wide Web**

X

X-chromosome N 染色体 X rǎnsètǐ

xenophobia N 排外情绪 páiwài qíngxù, 恐外症 kǒng wàizhèng

xerox I N（静电）复印（件）(jìngdiàn) fùyìn (jiàn) II V（用复印机）复印 (yòng fùyìnjī) fùyìn

X-mas N See **Christmas**

X-ray I N X射线 X shèxiàn, X光 X guāng, X光检查 X guāng jiǎnchá II V 用X射线检查 yòng X shèxiàn jiǎnchá

Y

yacht N 游艇 yóutǐng [M. WD 艘 sōu], 大型帆船 dàxíng fānchuán [M. WD 艘 sōu]

yachting N 驾驶游艇 jiàshǐ yóutǐng, 帆船比赛 fānchuán bǐsài

yahoo I N 粗鄙的人 cūbǐ de rén II INTERJ 好哇 hǎo wā

yam N 山药 shānyao

yank V 使劲拉 shǐjìn lā, 猛扯 měng chě

Yankee N 1 美国佬 Měiguólǎo 2（美国）北方佬 (Měiguó) běifānglǎo

yap V 1 [小狗+] 乱叫 [xiǎogǒu+] luànjiào, 狂吠 kuángfèi 2 哇啦哇啦地乱叫 wālā wālā de luànjiào

yard N 1 院子 yuànzi 2 码 mǎ (= 3 feet)
yard sale（在家院子里）旧货贱卖 (zài jiā yuànzi lǐ) jiùhuò jiànmài
yard stick 衡量标准 héngliáng biāozhǔn, 评判尺度 píngpàn chǐdù

yarn N 1 奇闻轶事 qíwén yìshì, 夸张的冒险故事 kuāzhāng de màoxiǎn gùshi 2 纱线 shāxiàn

yawn I N 哈欠 hāqian II V 1 打哈欠 dǎ hāqian 2 产生差距 chǎnshēng chājù
a yawning gap 巨大差距 jùdà chājù

Y-chromosome N Y染色体 Y rǎnsètǐ

year N 1 年 nián 2 岁 suì
academic/school year 学年 xuénián
all year round 一年到头 yì nián dào tóu, 终年 zhōngnián
never in a million years 绝不可能 juébù kěnéng, 肯定不会 kěndìng bú huì

yearbook N 年鉴 niánjiàn [M. WD 本 běn]

yearling N（一两岁的）小动物 (yì liǎng suì de) xiǎo dòngwù, 幼马 yòumǎ

yearly ADJ 每年的 měi nián de, 年度的 niándù de

yeast N 酵母 jiàomǔ, 发酵物 fājiàowù

yell V 叫嚷 jiàorǎng, 喊叫 hǎnjiào II N 啦啦队的喊叫声 lālāduì de hǎnjiàoshēng
a yell of protest 抗议声 kàngyìshēng

yellow I ADJ 黄色的 huángsè de II N 黄色 huángsè
Yellow Pages 黄页 huángyè, 商业电话簿 shāngyè diànhuàbù
III V 变黄 biàn huáng

yelp V 尖叫 jiānjiào, 喊叫 hǎnjiào

yen[1] N 日元 Rìyuán

yen[2] N 渴望 kěwàng, 热望 rèwàng

yes INTERJ 是 shì, 是的 shì de

yesterday ADV N 昨天 zuótiān

yet I ADV 还 hái, 仍然 réngrán II CONJ 可是 kěshì, 然而 rán'ér

yield V 1 产生 [+结果] chǎnshēng [+jiéguǒ] 2 出产 [+农产品] chūchǎn [+nóngchǎnpǐn] 3（被迫）交出 [+权利] (bèipò) jiāochū [+quánlì] 4 屈从 [+压力] qūcóng [+yālì], 服从 fúcóng
to yield to traffic on the right 给右边的车辆让道 gěi yòubian de chēliàng ràngdào
II N 收益 shōuyì, 产量 chǎnliáng

yippee INTERJ 好哇 hǎo wā, 太好了！Tài hǎo le!

yodel N 岳得尔唱法 yuèdéěr chàngfǎ, 岳得尔曲调 yuèdéěr qǔdiào

yoga N 瑜伽（法）yújiā (fǎ)

yogurt N 酸奶 suānnǎi

yoke N 1 牛轭 niú'è 2 束缚 shùfù
  yoke of tradition 传统的束缚 chuántŏng de shùfù

yokel N 土包子 tǔbāozi, 乡巴佬 xiāngbālǎo

yolk N 蛋黄 dànhuáng

yonder ADV 那边 nàbian, 远方 yuǎnfāng

you PRON 你 nǐ, 您 nín, 你们 nǐmen

young I ADJ 1 幼年的 yòunián de 2 年轻的 niánqīng de
  young at heart 人老心不老 rén lǎo xīn bù lǎo
  II N 1 年轻人 niánqīngrén 2 仔崽, 雏 chú

youngster N 孩子 háizi, 年轻人 niánqīngrén

your ADJ 你的 nǐ de, 您的 nín de, 你们的 nǐmen de

yours PRON 你的 nǐde, 您的 nín de, 你们的 nǐmen de

yourself PRON (PL **yourselves**) 你自己 nǐ zìjǐ, 您自己 nín zìjǐ

youth N 1 青年时代 qīngnián shídài 2 青春 qīngchūn 3 青年 qīngnián

youthful ADJ 1 年轻人的 niánqīngrén de 2 富有青春活力的 fùyǒu qīngchūn huólì de

yowl V N 大声惨叫 dàshēng cǎnjiào

yuck INTERJ 呸 pēi, 恶心 èxīn

Yule N 圣诞节 Shèngdànjié

yum INTERJ 好味道 hǎo wèidao, 好吃 hǎochī

yummy ADJ 好吃的 hǎochī de, 好味道的 hǎo wèidao de

yuppie N 雅皮士 yāpíshì

Z, z

zany ADJ 滑稽可笑的 huájī kěxiào de

zap V 1 用电波攻击 yòng diànbō gōngjī, 摧毁 cuīhuǐ 2（计算机）速combust信息 (jìsuànjī) sùde xìnxī 3 用遥控器转换电视频道 yòng yáokòngqì zhuǎnhuàn diànshì píndào

zeal N 热情 rèqíng, 热忱 rèchén

zebra N 斑马 bānmǎ [M. WD 匹 pǐ]

Zen N 禅宗 chánzōng

zenith N 顶点 dǐngdiǎn, 顶峰 dǐngfēng

zephyr N 微风 wēifēng, 和风 héfēng

zero I NUM 零 líng
  zero growth 零增长 líng zēngzhǎng
  zero hour 开始时刻 kāishǐ shíkè
  II V (to zero in on sb/sth) 把注意力集中在某人／某事 bǎ zhùyìlì jízhōng zài mǒurén/mǒushì

zest N 热情 rèqíng, 热心 rèxīn

zigzag N 1 之字形 zhīzìxíng, Z字形 Z zìxíng II V 曲折行进 qūzhé xíngjìn

zillion N 极大的数目 jídà de shùmù

zinc (Zn) N 锌 xīn

zip N 拉（拉链）lā (lāliàn)
  to zip sth open/close 把某物的拉链拉开／拉上 bǎ mǒuwù de lāliàn lā kāi/lā shàng
  Zip your lip! 闭嘴! Bì zuǐ! 别作声! Bié zuòshēng!

zip code N 邮政编号 yóuzhèng biānhào

zip file N（计算机）压缩文件 (jìsuànjī) yāsuō wénjiàn

zip gun N 自制手枪 zìzhì shǒuqiāng

zipper N 拉链 lāliàn [M. WD 条 tiáo]

zodiac N 黄道带 huángdàodài, 黄道十二宫图 huángdào shí'èr gōngtú
  Chinese Zodiac 属相 shǔxiang, 生肖 shēngxiào

zombie N 1 还魂尸 huánhúnshī 2 行动缓慢思维迟钝的人 xíngdòng huǎnmàn sīwéi chídùn de rén

zone N 区域 qūyù, 地带 dìdài

zoning N 划分区域 huàfēn qūyù, 分区布局 fēnqū bùjú

zoo N 动物园 dòngwùyuán

zoology N 动物学 dòngwùxué

zoom V 1 [汽车+] 飞速行进 [qìchē+] fēisù xíngjìn, 疾驶 jíshǐ 2 [股票+] 陡升 [gǔpiào+] dǒushēng, 猛增 měngzēng
  to zoom in/out 把镜头拉近／推远 bǎ jìngtóu lājìn/tuī yuǎn

zucchini N 小胡瓜 xiǎohúguā

zygote N 受精卵 shòujīngluǎn

zzz N 呼呼（的鼾声）hūhū (de hānshēng)